PEARSON CRIMINAL JUSTICE

Central New Mexico Community College
CJ 1001 Custom Text

Pearson Custom Publishing

New York Boston San Francisco
London Toronto Sydney Tokyo Singapore Madrid
Mexico City Munich Paris Cape Town Hong Kong Montreal

Senior Vice President, Editorial and Marketing: Patrick F. Boles
Sponsoring Editor: Debbie Coniglio
Marketing Specialist: Kelly Forsberg
Development Editor: Kelly Harris
Operations Manager: Eric M. Kenney
Database Product Manager: Jennifer Berry

Cover Art: Police Car: Courtesy of Veer/Alloy Photography. Gavel: Courtesy of iStockphoto/Christine Balderas. Behind the Bars: Courtesy of iStockphoto/Simon Podgorsek.

Printed in the United States of America.

Please visit our website at *www.pearsoncustom.com.*

Attention bookstores: For permission to return any unsold stock, contact us at *pe-uscustomreturns@pearson.com.*

Pearson Custom Publishing is a division of

PEARSON

www.pearsonhighered.com

ISBN 10: 0558449166
ISBN 13: 9780558449162

Contents

What Is Criminal Justice? 1

Chapter Outline

- Introduction
- A Brief History of Crime in America
- The Theme of This Book
- Social Justice
- American Criminal Justice: System and Functions
- American Criminal Justice: The Process
- Due Process and Individual Rights
- The Role of Research in Criminal Justice
- Multiculturalism and Diversity in Criminal Justice

Learning Objectives

After reading this chapter, you should be able to

- Provide a brief history of crime in America.
- Identify the theme on which this textbook builds, and highlight the differences between the individual-rights and public-order perspectives.
- Explain the relationship of criminal justice to social justice and to other wider notions of equity and fairness.
- Explain the structure of the American criminal justice system in terms of its major components and the functions they serve.
- Describe the process of American criminal justice, including the stages of criminal case processing.
- Explain the meaning of due process of law, and identify where due process guarantees can be found in the American legal system.
- Describe the role of research in contemporary criminal justice.
- Explain how multiculturalism and diversity present special challenges to, and opportunities for, the American system of criminal justice.

"The rights guaranteed to criminal suspects, defendants, offenders, and prisoners were not included in the Bill of Rights for the benefit of criminals. They are fundamental political rights that protect all Americans from governmental abuse of power. These rights are found in the Fourth, Fifth, Sixth, Eighth, and Fourteenth Amendments. They include the guarantee against unreasonable search and seizure, the right to reasonable bail, the right to due process of law, and the right to be free from cruel and unusual treatment. This "bundle of rights" is indispensable to a free society."

—American Civil Liberties Union[1]

"The Constitution is not a suicide pact."

—Former Secretary of State Warren Christopher, after terrorists destroyed the World Trade Center in New York City in 2001[2]

Introduction

▸▸▸ Hear the author discuss this chapter at mycrimekit.com.

Five days after Hurricane Katrina made landfall near New Orleans in 2005, the *Washington Post* described the devastated metropolitan area as "a city of despair and lawlessness."[3] The *Wall Street Journal* ran headlines proclaiming that the city had "plunged into anarchy."[4] As the winds relented, looters ravaged stores, gunshots rang out, and armed gangs could be seen roaming the streets that hadn't been flooded. Some looters used forklifts and construction equipment to bust through storm shutters and steel doors protecting gun shops, liquor stores, and pharmacies.[5] The New Orleans Police Department, hamstrung by the absence of one-third of its 1,600 officers and the loss of critical communications channels and emergency equipment, struggled to keep control over its facilities. In one unflooded precinct, officers used an armored personnel carrier to survey the chaos.[6] Officers from another precinct were forced to barricade themselves in their three-story administrative center, renaming it Fort Apache after a film in which a police station is attacked. "You have to understand," said Juan Lopez, one of the officers who took refuge in the precinct house, "New Orleans was a violent place before the hurricane. After the hurricane, the city just let loose."[7]

You're looking now not only at a rescue operation but a gigantic crime scene.

—Newscaster, ABC Nightly News, commenting on the World Trade Center site a few days after the September 11, 2001, attacks[ii]

The storm set into motion a number of events that are still sending shock waves throughout American society. The physical damage done by the hurricane, estimated at billions of dollars, was made worse by the massive social disorder that followed. Thousands of displaced people left their homes—with many never expected to return. Law enforcement and assistance agencies throughout the region suffered serious disruptions in their ability to provide services. Some officers walked off the job, and citizens were left to fend for themselves until thousands of National Guard troops armed with automatic weapons arrived to restore order in the wind- and flood-ravaged area.

▲ New Orleans business owner Bob Rue standing in front of his rug store in the aftermath of Hurricane Katrina. His hastily created sign warns potential looters to stay away. Some say that the central purpose of the criminal justice system is the maintenance of social order. Others say that the justice system must respect the rights of those whom it processes. Are the two perspectives mutually exclusive?
Charlie Riedel/AP Wide World Photos

The Katrina disaster, which created opportunities for those bent on criminal activity, illustrated the tenuous nature of social order. The social disorganization that followed Katrina continued long after the storm and involved a myriad of criminal offenses—including thousands of people arrested for defrauding the Federal Emergency Management Agency (FEMA), the government agency responsible for helping out after a disaster. FEMA fraud was so widespread that reports showed the number of households receiving FEMA emergency checks in four Louisiana parishes exceeded the number of households that existed there before the storm hit.[8] Almost 360,000 households applied for FEMA's Expedited Assistance payments in Orleans Parish alone—although the area had only 182,000 homes before Katrina. In one case that drew the attention of federal prosecutors, 33-year-old Kenneth McClain was charged with 14 counts of fraud in an elaborate conspiracy that allegedly scammed more than $10,000 in federal relief checks. McClain, who had 27 aliases and a number of open arrest warrants when caught, lived in Texas, far from the storm's wrath. He is accused of using stolen identities, some belonging to dead people, to file for assistance and then waiting in a Texas motel room for the aid checks to arrive.[9]

A very different kind of criminal event thrust itself on American society and our justice system with the September 11, 2001, terrorist attacks that targeted New York City's World Trade Center and the Pentagon. Those attacks, including one on an airliner that crashed in the Pennsylvania countryside, left nearly 3,000 people dead and caused billions of dollars in property damage. They have since been classified as the most destructive criminal activity ever to have been perpetrated on U.S. soil. The resulting "war on terrorism" changed the face of world politics and ushered in a new era in American society. Before the attacks, most Americans lived

An artist's rendition of the New York City skyline as it will look once buildings envisioned by renowned architect Daniel Libeskind are constructed on the 16-acre World Trade Center site. The plan includes a soaring Freedom Tower that will stand 1,776 feet tall, several other towers, and a memorial to the nearly 3,000 people who were killed in the terrorist attacks that demolished the twin towers in 2001. How did those attacks change the American justice system?
Skidmore, Owings, & Merrill LLP/Getty Images—GINS/Entertainment News & Sports

relatively secure lives, largely unfettered by fear of random personal attack. Following September 11, however, a heated debate has taken place between those wanting to enforce powerful crime-prevention and security measures and others seeking to preserve the individual rights and freedoms that have long been characteristic of American life. This issue, which has continued to feed TV talk shows and newspaper editorials nationwide, asks Americans to determine which rights, freedoms, and conveniences (if any) they are willing to sacrifice to increase personal and public safety. It also anticipates a theme that is discussed at length later in this chapter.

Regardless of your personal position in the ongoing debate between freedom and safety, it is important to recognize that terrorism is a potentially horrendous **crime**. Many states and the federal government have statutes outlawing terrorism, although terrorism itself can involve many other kinds of crimes. In the case of the World Trade Center and Pentagon attacks, for example, the crimes committed included murder, kidnapping, hijacking, grand theft, felonious assault, battery, conspiracy, and arson.

crime
Conduct in violation of the criminal laws of a state, the federal government, or a local jurisdiction, for which there is no legally acceptable justification or excuse.[iii]

A Brief History of Crime in America

Crime does more than expose the weakness in social relationships; it undermines the social order itself, by destroying the assumptions on which it is based.
—*James Q. Wilson, UCLA*[iv]

What we call *criminal activity* has undoubtedly been with us since the dawn of history, and crime control has long been a primary concern of politicians and government leaders worldwide. Still, the American experience with crime during the last half century has been especially influential in shaping the criminal justice system of today. In this country, crime waves, including an 1850–1880 crime epidemic which was apparently related to social upheaval caused by large-scale immigration and the Civil War, have come and gone.[10] A spurt of widespread organized criminal activity was associated with the Prohibition years of the early twentieth century. Following World War II, however, American crime rates remained relatively stable until the 1960s.

The 1960s and 1970s saw a burgeoning concern for the rights of ethnic and racial minorities, women, people with physical and mental challenges, and many other groups. The civil rights movement of the period emphasized equality of opportunity and respect for individuals, regardless of race, color, creed, gender, or personal attributes. As new laws were passed and suits filed, court involvement in the movement grew. Soon a plethora of hard-won individual rights and prerogatives, based on the U.S. Constitution, the Bill of Rights, and new federal and state legislation, were recognized and guaranteed. By the 1980s, the civil rights movement had profoundly affected all areas of social life—from education and employment to the activities of the criminal justice system.

individual rights
The rights guaranteed to all members of American society by the U.S. Constitution (especially those found in the first ten amendments to the Constitution, known as the *Bill of Rights*). These rights are particularly important to criminal defendants facing formal processing by the criminal justice system.

This emphasis on **individual rights** was accompanied by a dramatic increase in reported criminal activity. While some researchers doubted the accuracy of official accounts, reports by the Federal Bureau of Investigation (FBI) of "traditional" crimes like murder, rape, and assault increased considerably during the 1970s and into the 1980s. Many theories were advanced to explain this leap in observed criminality. Some analysts of American culture, for example, suggested that the combination of newfound freedoms and long-pent-up hostilities of the socially and economically deprived worked to produce social disorganization, which in turn increased criminality.

By the mid-1980s, the dramatic increase in the sale and use of illicit drugs threatened the foundation of American society. Cocaine, and later laboratory-processed "crack," spread to every corner of America. The country's borders were inundated with smugglers intent on reaping quick fortunes. Large cities became havens for drug gangs, and many inner-city areas were all but abandoned to highly armed and well-financed drug racketeers. Cities experienced dramatic declines in property values, and residents wrestled with an eroding quality of life.

By the close of the 1980s, neighborhoods and towns were fighting for their communal lives. Huge rents had been torn in the national social fabric, and the American way of life, long taken for granted, was under the gun. Traditional values appeared in danger of going up in smoke along with the crack being consumed openly in some parks and resorts. Looking for a way to stem the tide of increased criminality, many took up the call for "law and order." In response, President Ronald Reagan created a cabinet-level "drug czar" position to coordinate the "war on drugs." Careful thought was given at the highest levels to using the military to patrol the sea-lanes and air corridors through which many of the illegal drugs entered the country. President George H. W. Bush, who followed Reagan into office, quickly embraced and expanded the government's antidrug efforts.

In 1992, the videotaped beating of Rodney King, an African-American motorist, at the hands of Los Angeles–area police officers splashed across TV screens throughout the country and shifted the public's focus onto issues of police brutality and the effective management of law enforcement personnel. As the King incident seemed to show, when racial minorities came face-to-face with agents of the American criminal justice system, justice didn't always result. Although initially acquitted by a California jury—which contained no African-American members—two of the officers who beat King were convicted in a 1993 federal courtroom of violating his civil rights.[11]

Then the very next year, law enforcement agencies were again criticized when agents of the Bureau of Alcohol, Tobacco, Firearms and Explosives (ATF) and the FBI faced off with David Koresh and members of his Branch Davidian cult in Waco, Texas. The conflict began when ATF agents assaulted Koresh's fortress-like compound, leaving four agents and six cult members dead. It ended 51 days later with the fiery deaths of Koresh and 71 of his followers, many of whom were children. The event led to a congressional investigation and charges that the ATF and the FBI had been ill prepared to deal successfully with large-scale domestic resistance and had reacted more out of alarm and frustration than wisdom. Attorney General Janet Reno refused to blame agents for misjudging Koresh's intentions, although 11 Davidians were later acquitted of charges that they had murdered the federal agents.

People expect both safety and justice and do not want to sacrifice one for the other.
—*Christopher Stone, President and Director, Vera Institute of Justice*

Soon afterward, a few spectacular crimes that received widespread coverage in the news media fostered a sense among the American public that crime in the United States was out of hand and that strict new measures were needed to combat it. One such crime was the 1995 bombing of the Alfred P. Murrah Federal Building in Oklahoma City by antigovernment extremists. Another was the 1999 Columbine High School massacre in Colorado that left 12 students and one teacher dead.[12]

The public's perception that crime rates were growing, coupled with a belief that offenders frequently went unpunished or received only a judicial slap on the wrist, led to a burgeoning emphasis on responsibility and punishment. By the late 1990s, a strong shift away from the claimed misdeeds of the criminal justice system was well under way, and a newfound emphasis on individual accountability began to blossom among an American public fed up with crime and fearful of its own victimization. Growing calls for enhanced responsibility quickly began to replace the previous emphasis on individual rights. As a juggernaut of conservative opinion made itself felt on the political scene, Senator Phil Gramm of Texas observed that the public wants to "grab violent criminals by the throat, put them in prison [and] stop building prisons like Holiday Inns."[13]

Then, in an event that changed the course of our society, public tragedy became forever joined with private victimization in our collective consciousness after a series of highly destructive and well-coordinated terrorist attacks on New York City and Washington, D.C., on September 11, 2001. Those attacks resulted in the collapse and total destruction of the twin 110-story towers of the World Trade Center and a devastating explosion at the Pentagon. Thousands of people perished, and many were injured. Although law enforcement and security agencies were unable to prevent the September 11 attacks, many have since moved from a reactive to a proactive posture in the fight against terrorism.

The September 11 attacks also made clear that adequate law enforcement involves a global effort at controlling crime and reducing the risk of injury and loss to law-abiding people both at home and abroad. The attacks showed that criminal incidents that take place on the other side of the globe can impact those of us living in the United States, and they illustrated how the acquisition of skills needed to understand diverse cultures can help in the fight against crime and terrorism.

An especially important new tool in the law enforcement arsenal is the federal **USA PATRIOT Act**,[14] enacted in 2001 as a legislative response to terrorism. The law, whose provisions were reauthorized by Congress with minor revisions in 2006, is officially known as the Uniting and Strengthening America by Providing Appropriate Tools Required to Intercept and Obstruct Terrorism Act of 2001 (from which the acronym *USA PATRIOT* is derived). The law dramatically increases the investigatory authority of federal, state, and local police agencies, although sometimes only temporarily. The expanded police powers created under the legislation are not limited to investigations of terrorist activity but apply to many different criminal offenses. Terrorism is a criminal act, and preventing terrorism and investigating terrorist incidents after they occur are highly important roles for local, state, and federal law enforcement agencies.

USA PATRIOT Act
A federal law (Public Law 107-56) enacted in response to terrorist attacks on the World Trade Center and the Pentagon on September 11, 2001. The law, officially titled the Uniting and Strengthening America by Providing Appropriate Tools Required to Intercept and Obstruct Terrorism Act, substantially broadened the investigative authority of law enforcement agencies throughout America and is applicable to many crimes other than terrorism. The law was slightly revised and reauthorized by Congress in 2006.

A different kind of offending, corporate and white-collar crime, took center stage in 2002 and 2003 as President George W. Bush called on Congress to stiffen penalties for unscrupulous business executives who knowingly falsify their company's financial reports.[15] The president's request came amidst declining stock market values, shaken investor confidence, and threats to the viability of employee pension plans in the wake of a corporate crime wave involving criminal activities that had been planned and undertaken by executives at a number of leading corporations. In an effort to restore order to American financial markets, President Bush signed the Sarbanes-Oxley Act on July 30, 2002.[16] The law, which has been called "the single most important piece of legislation affecting corporate governance, financial disclosure and the practice of public accounting since the US securities laws of the early 1930s,"[17] is intended to deter corporate fraud and to hold business executives accountable for their actions.

White-collar crime continues to be a focus of federal prosecutors, and in 2006 former Enron executives Kenneth Lay and Jeff Skilling were convicted of conspiracy to commit securities and wire fraud in what some called "the biggest business scandal in U.S. history"—the collapse of energy-trading giant Enron Corporation.[18] The company's troubles resulted in the loss of billions of dollars of investors' money.

For a detailed look at crimes that have shaped the past hundred years, see Web Extra 1–1 at mycrimekit.com. Library Extra 1–1 at mycrimekit.com also describes the changing nature of crime in America.

Web EXTRA

Library EXTRA

▲ Prosecutors in the Enron Corporation case speaking to reporters in Houston in 2006 after a jury found two former chief executives guilty of fraud. Corporate and white-collar crime came under federal scrutiny after the "technology bubble" burst on Wall Street in 2000–2001. Should corporate criminals be treated differently from other offenders?
Michael Stravato/The New York Times

Individual Rights Versus Public Order

This text examines the American system of criminal justice and the agencies and processes that constitute it. It builds on a theme that is especially valuable for studying criminal justice today: *individual rights versus public order.* This theme draws on historical developments that have shaped our legal system and our understandings of crime and justice. It is one of the primary determinants of the nature of contemporary criminal justice—including criminal law, police practice, sentencing, and corrections.

A strong emphasis on individual rights rose to the forefront of American social thought during the 1960s and 1970s, a period known as the *civil rights era.* The civil rights era led to the recognition of fundamental personal rights that had previously been denied illegally to many people on the basis of race, ethnicity, gender, sexual preference, or disability. The civil rights movement soon expanded to include the rights of many other groups, including criminal suspects, parolees and probationers, trial participants, prison and jail inmates, and victims. As the emphasis on civil rights grew, new laws and court decisions broadened the rights available to many.

The treatment of criminal suspects was afforded special attention by those who argued that the purpose of any civilized society should be to secure rights and freedoms for each of its citizens—including those suspected and convicted of crimes. Rights advocates feared unnecessarily restrictive government action and viewed it as an assault on basic human dignity and individual liberty. They believed that at times it was necessary to sacrifice some degree of public safety and predictability to guarantee basic freedoms. Hence criminal rights activists demanded a justice system that limits police powers and that holds justice agencies accountable to the highest procedural standards.

I would rather be exposed to the inconveniences attending too much liberty than to those attending too small a degree of it.
—Thomas Jefferson

During the 1960s and 1970s, the dominant philosophy in American criminal justice focused on guaranteeing the rights of criminal defendants while seeking to understand the root causes of crime and violence. The past 25 years, however, have witnessed increased interest in an ordered society, in public safety, and in the rights of crime victims. This change in attitudes was likely brought about by national frustration with the perceived inability of our society and its justice system to prevent crimes and to consistently hold offenders to heartfelt standards of

Freedom or Safety? You Decide.

Giuliani Says: "Freedom Is about Authority"

As we move through the early years of the twenty-first century, the challenge for the criminal justice system, it seems, is to balance individual rights and personal freedoms with social control and respect for legitimate authority. Years ago, during the height of what was then a powerful movement to win back control of our nation's cities and to rein in skyrocketing crime rates, the *New York Post* sponsored a conference on crime and civil rights. The keynote speaker at that conference was New York City's Mayor Rudolph W. Giuliani. In his speech, Giuliani, who sought the Republican nomination as a presidential candidate in 2008, identified the tension between personal freedoms and individual responsibilities as the crux of the crime problem then facing his city and the nation. We mistakenly look to government and elected officials, Giuliani said, to assume responsibility for solving the problem of crime when, instead, each individual citizen must become accountable for fixing what is wrong with our society. "We only see the oppressive side of authority. . . . What we don't see is that freedom is not a concept in which people can do anything they want, be anything they can be. Freedom is about authority. Freedom is about the willingness of every single human being to cede to lawful authority a great deal of discretion about what you do."

YOU DECIDE

What did Giuliani mean when he said, "What we don't see is that freedom is not a concept in which people can do anything they want, be anything they can be"? How can we, as a society, best balance individual rights and personal freedoms with social control and respect for legitimate authority?

Reference: Philip Taylor, "Civil Libertarians: Giuliani's Efforts Threaten First Amendment," Freedom Forum Online, http://www.freedomforum.org.

right and wrong. Increased conservatism in the public-policy arena was given new life by the September 11, 2001, terrorist attacks and by widely publicized instances of sexual offenses targeting children. It continues to be sustained by the many stories of violent victimization that seem to be the current mainstay of the American media.

We must not defeat our liberties in trying to defend them.
—Former National Security Adviser Anthony Lake[v]

Today, public perspectives have largely shifted away from seeing the criminal as an unfortunate victim of poor social and personal circumstances who is inherently protected by fundamental human and constitutional rights to seeing him or her as a dangerous social predator who usurps the rights and privileges of law-abiding citizens. Reflecting the "get tough on crime" attitudes of today, many Americans demand to know how offenders can better be held accountable for violations of the criminal law. In 2006, for example, at least 14 governors signed laws designed to extend prison sentences for sex offenders, restrict where released sex offenders can live, and improve public notification of their whereabouts. More bills are pending as this book goes to press, including one in Louisiana that would require convicted offenders to carry bright orange driver's licenses stamped with the words "sex offender," and another in South Carolina that would make some molesters eligible for the death penalty.[19]

Even so, the tension between individual rights and social responsibility still forms the basis for most policy-making activity in the criminal justice arena. Those who fight for individual rights continue to carry the banner of civil and criminal rights for the accused and the convicted, while public-order activists loudly proclaim the rights of the victimized and call for an increased emphasis on social responsibility and criminal punishment for convicted criminals. In keeping with these realizations, our theme can be stated as follows:

> There is widespread recognition in contemporary society of the need to balance (1) the freedoms and privileges of our nation's citizens and the respect accorded the rights of individuals faced with criminal prosecution against (2) the valid interests that society has in preventing future crimes, in maintaining public safety, and in reducing the harm caused by criminal activity. While the personal freedoms guaranteed to law-abiding citizens as well as to criminal suspects by the Constitution, as interpreted by the U.S. Supreme Court, must be closely guarded, the urgent social needs of communities for controlling unacceptable behavior and protecting law-abiding citizens from harm must be recognized. Still to be adequately addressed are the needs and interests of victims and the fear of crime and personal victimization often prevalent in the minds of many law-abiding citizens.

The arc of the moral universe is long, but it bends towards justice.
—Barack Obama, quoting Martin Luther King, Jr.

Figure 1 represents our theme and shows that most people today who intelligently consider the criminal justice system assume one of two viewpoints. We will refer to those who seek to protect personal freedoms and civil rights within society, and especially within the criminal

FIGURE 1
Individual Rights Versus Public Order.
Balancing the concern for individual rights with the need for public order through the administration of criminal justice is the theme of this book.

individual-rights advocate
One who seeks to protect personal freedoms within the process of criminal justice.

public-order advocate
One who believes that under certain circumstances involving a criminal threat to public safety, the interests of society should take precedence over individual rights.

justice process, as **individual-rights advocates**. Those who suggest that under certain circumstances involving criminal threats to public safety, the interests of society (especially crime control and social order) should take precedence over individual rights will be called **public-order advocates**. Recently, retired U.S. Supreme Court Justice Sandra Day O'Connor summed up the differences between these two perspectives by asking, "At what point does the cost to civil liberties from legislation designed to prevent terrorism [and crime] outweigh the added security that that legislation provides?"[20]

Social Justice

On September 20, 2001, in the immediate aftermath of the terrorist attacks on the World Trade Center and the Pentagon, President Bush delivered a televised address to the American people. In his rallying cry to a nation about to embark on a war against world terrorism, Bush said, "We

▶ A crowd reacting outside the San Mateo County (California) courthouse as guilty verdicts are returned in the 2005 California murder trial of Scott Peterson. Criminal justice and social justice are concepts that are closely tied in most people's minds. What does the word *justice* mean to you?
Justin Sullivan/AP Wide World Photos

will bring our enemies to justice, or we will bring justice to our enemies."[21] The word *justice* is powerful, and—at the time—the president's choice of words spoke to all Americans.

The reality, however, is that *justice* is an elusive term. As the war on terrorism began, for example, no one who heard the president's speech knew exactly what justice might mean and what form it might eventually take. Even to those living within the same society, justice means different things. And just as *justice* can be an ambiguous term for politicians, even in times of war, it is not always clear how justice can be achieved in the criminal justice system. For example, is "justice for all" a reasonable expectation of today's—or tomorrow's—system of criminal justice? The answer is unclear because individual interests and social needs often diverge. From the perspective of a society or an entire nation, justice can look very different than it does from the perspective of an individual or a small group of people. Because of this dilemma, we now turn our attention to the nature of justice.

When you know both the accuser and the accused, as we so often do, the conflict between civil rights and victims' rights is seldom completely black or white. And it is the gray areas in between that make the debate so difficult.

—*Columnist Vicki Williams, writing on crime in a small American town*

British philosopher and statesman Benjamin Disraeli (1804–1881) defined **justice** as "truth in action." A popular dictionary defines it as "the principle of moral rightness, or conformity to truth."[22] **Social justice** is a concept that embraces all aspects of civilized life. It is linked to notions of fairness and to cultural beliefs about right and wrong. Questions of social justice can arise about relationships between individuals, between parties (such as corporations and agencies of government), between the rich and the poor, between the sexes, between ethnic groups and minorities—between social connections of all sorts. In the abstract, the concept of social justice embodies the highest personal and cultural ideals.

justice
The principle of fairness; the ideal of moral equity.

social justice
An ideal that embraces all aspects of civilized life and that is linked to fundamental notions of fairness and to cultural beliefs about right and wrong.

Civil justice, one component of social justice, concerns itself with fairness in relationships between citizens, government agencies, and businesses in private matters, such as those involving contractual obligations, business dealings, hiring, and equality of treatment. **Criminal justice**, on the other hand, refers to the aspects of social justice that concern violations of the criminal law. As mentioned earlier, community interests in the criminal justice sphere demand the apprehension and punishment of law violators. At the same time, criminal justice ideals extend to the protection of the innocent, the fair treatment of offenders, and fair play by the agencies of law enforcement, including courts and correctional institutions.

civil justice
The civil law, the law of civil procedure, and the array of procedures and activities having to do with private rights and remedies sought by civil action. Civil justice cannot be separated from social justice because the justice enacted in our nation's civil courts reflects basic American understandings of right and wrong.

Criminal justice, ideally speaking, is "truth in action" within the process that we call the **administration of justice**. It is therefore vital to remember that justice, in the truest and most satisfying sense of the word, is the ultimate goal of criminal justice—and of the day-to-day practices and challenges that characterize the American criminal justice system. Reality, unfortunately, typically falls short of the ideal and is severely complicated by the fact that justice seems to wear different guises when viewed from diverse vantage points. To some people, the criminal justice system and criminal justice agencies often seem biased in favor of the powerful. The laws they enforce seem to emanate more from well-financed, organized, and vocal interest groups than they do from any idealized sense of social justice. As a consequence, disenfranchised groups, those who do not feel as though they share in the political and economic power of society, are often wary of the agencies of justice, seeing them more as enemies than as benefactors.

criminal justice
In the strictest sense, the criminal (penal) law, the law of criminal procedure, and the array of procedures and activities having to do with the enforcement of this body of law. Criminal justice cannot be separated from social justice because the justice enacted in our nation's criminal courts reflects basic American understandings of right and wrong.

On the other hand, justice practitioners, including police officers, prosecutors, judges, and corrections officials, frequently complain that their efforts to uphold the law garner unfair public criticism. The realities of law enforcement and of "doing justice," they say, are often overlooked by critics of the system who have little experience in dealing with offenders and victims. We must recognize, practitioners often tell us, that those accused of violating the criminal law face an elaborate process built around numerous legislative, administrative, and organizational concerns. Viewed realistically, although the criminal justice process can be fine-tuned to take into consideration the interests of ever-larger numbers of people, it rarely pleases everyone. The outcome of the criminal justice process in any particular case is a social product, and like any product that is the result of group effort, it must inevitably be a patchwork quilt of human emotions, reasoning, and concerns.

administration of justice
The performance of any of the following activities: detection, apprehension, detention, pretrial release, post-trial release, prosecution, adjudication, correctional supervision, or rehabilitation of accused persons or criminal offenders.[vi]

Whichever side we choose in the ongoing debate over the nature and quality of criminal justice in America, it is vital that we recognize the plethora of pragmatic issues involved in the administration of justice while also keeping a clear focus on the justice ideal.[23] Was justice done, for example, in the 2005 criminal trial of pop music superstar Michael Jackson on charges of child molestation or in the 1995 murder trial of former football great O. J. Simpson? What about the trials of the Los Angeles police officers accused of beating Rodney King? Similarly, we might ask, was justice done in the arrest and lengthy detention of hundreds of Muslims after September 11, 2001—even though most were later released when no evidence could be found linking them to any crime?[24] While answers to such questions may reveal a great deal about the

CJ News

Who Watches the Watchers?

In some cities in Europe and the United States, a person can be videotaped by surveillance cameras hundreds of times a day, and it's safe to say that most of the time no one is actually watching.

But the advent of "intelligent video"—software that raises the alarm if something on camera appears amiss—means Big Brother will soon be able to keep a more constant watch, a prospect that is sure to heighten privacy concerns.

Combining motion detection technology with the learning capabilities of video game software, these new systems can detect people loitering, walking in circles, or leaving a package. New microphone technology can isolate the sound of a gunshot and direct the attached camera to swivel and zoom in on the source. Sensitivity may reach the point where microphones could pick out the word "explosives" spoken in a crowd.

"There's just not enough personnel to watch every single camera," said Chicago emergency operations chief Andrew Velasquez. "We are piloting analytic software right now . . . where you can set that particular camera to watch for erratic behavior, or someone leaving a suitcase on the sidewalk."

Since the attacks on the United States of September 11, 2001, sections of New York, Washington, Los Angeles, Chicago, and even a few smaller U.S. towns have been blanketed with closed-circuit cameras. Privately owned cameras are also proliferating.

The encroachment on privacy in what civil libertarians call a "surveillance society" may be a price willingly paid by citizens who fear terrorism and crime.

But ever-alert software capable of maintaining a continuous "watch" on security cameras multiplies the risks of harassing innocent people, privacy experts say.

"I don't buy it. The number of false positives are going to be astronomical," said David Holtzman, author of *Privacy Lost*. "It's extremely dangerous to abrogate legitimate law enforcement authority . . . to a camera."

In Chicago's darkened, windowless surveillance center, Velasquez looks forward to using new technology, which has had some success elsewhere.

The port of Jacksonville, Florida, has dispensed with human monitoring of cameras altogether by sending alerts and live video to the personal digital assistant of the nearest officer on patrol, according to a spokesman for ObjectVideo Inc.

ObjectVideo is one of two dozen companies seeking to perfect so-called intelligent video—an industry whose sales will grow from $60 million to $400 million within five years, according to global consulting group Frost & Sullivan.

Meanwhile, Texas is evaluating a pilot program in which it allowed Internet access to video of unmanned sections of its border with Mexico and urged viewers to send an e-mail if they spotted something.

"The cameras don't replace police officers. They are in essence a force multiplier. They serve as an extra set of eyes," Velasquez said.

The Chicago center is manned 24 hours a day by veteran police officers. A dozen screens depict a few street corners and a stadium, while others are tuned to cable news or websites.

▲ A Chicago police department surveillance camera system and microphone unit positioned high above the street. This surveillance system includes a camera, high-bandwidth wireless communication, a strobe light, and a gunshot-recognition system, all in a bulletproof enclosure. The city is installing the surveillance system to spot crimes or terrorist activity. Do such units infringe on the personal freedoms of Chicago residents?
Safety Dynamics

They can retrieve video from thousands of cameras and their universe is expanded by private cameras owned by cooperating buildings and stores, but they can monitor only a few at a time.

Velasquez said his officers receive training on privacy and constitutional rights—for example it is illegal to look into private homes and offices—and digital recordings hold his officers accountable and prevent abuses that have occurred elsewhere.

In Britain, which has 4.2 million government security cameras, 2 million in London alone, a study showed that male surveillance workers sometimes ogled women on their screens, while others focused on minorities excessively.

But privacy experts also note another British study, from 2002, which said surveillance cameras did not lower overall crime rates and merely pushes crime elsewhere.

"Cameras are great tools for solving crime. They're not really that helpful in preventing crime," said Ed Yohnka of the American Civil Liberties Union.

Velasquez disputed the conclusion that cameras don't prevent crime, saying he constantly fields requests from residents asking for a camera to make their neighborhood safer.

He said cameras contributed to a drop in violent crime in the city of Chicago in recent years, a drop that is widely attributed to improved police work in countering gangs and street-corner drug dealing. At the same time, gang activity has surged in some Chicago suburbs.

The city's prosecutors said they rarely use video evidence in court from the cameras, which are encased in bulletproof boxes topped by blue flashing lights and are a common sight in crime-ridden neighborhoods.

Downtown, the cameras are less obtrusive, though a pair mounted on a park fountain was removed after an outcry that they defiled the art.

Holtzman, the privacy expert, wondered where the line will be drawn if authorities opt to use the cameras to spy on suspects or to sniff out low-level crimes.

There are no legal barriers to video being subpoenaed by, for instance, a divorce lawyer seeking evidence of infidelity, he said.

"I think there's a certain amount of freedom you want to give people that live in the city to kind of screw up a little bit," he said.

For the latest in crime and justice news, visit the Talk Justice news feed at http://www.crimenews.info.

Source: Copyright 2007 Reuters. Reprinted with permission.

American criminal justice system, they also have much to say about the perspectives of those who provide them.

American Criminal Justice: System and Functions

The Consensus Model

So far, we have described a **criminal justice system**[25] consisting of the component agencies of police, courts, and corrections. Each of these components can, in turn, be described in terms of its functions and purpose (Figure 2).

The systems perspective on criminal justice is characterized primarily by its assumption that the various parts of the justice system work together by design to achieve the wider purpose we have been calling *justice*. Hence the systems perspective on criminal justice generally encompasses a point of view called the **consensus model**. The consensus model assumes that each of the component parts of the criminal justice system strives toward a common goal and that the movement of cases and people through the system is smooth due to cooperation between the various components of the system.

The systems model of criminal justice is more an analytic tool than a reality, however. An analytic model, whether in the hard sciences or in the social sciences, is simply a convention chosen for its explanatory power. By explaining the actions of criminal justice officials—such as arrest, prosecution, and sentencing—as though they were systematically related, we are able to envision a fairly smooth and predictable process (which is described in more detail later in this chapter).

The systems model has been criticized for implying a greater level of organization and cooperation among the various agencies of justice than actually exists. The word *system* calls to mind a near-perfect form of social organization. The modern mind associates the idea of a system with machine-like precision in which the problems of wasted effort, redundancy, and conflicting actions are quickly corrected. In practice, the justice system has nowhere near this level of perfection, and the systems model is admittedly an oversimplification. Conflicts among and within agencies are rife; individual actors within the system often do not share immediate goals; and the system may move in different directions depending on political currents, informal arrangements, and personal discretion.

criminal justice system
The aggregate of all operating and administrative or technical support agencies that perform criminal justice functions. The basic divisions of the operational aspects of criminal justice are law enforcement, courts, and corrections.

consensus model
A criminal justice perspective that assumes that the system's components work together harmoniously to achieve the social product we call *justice*.

If we do not maintain Justice, Justice will not maintain us.
—*Francis Bacon*

The Conflict Model

The **conflict model** provides another approach to the study of American criminal justice. The conflict model says that the interests of criminal justice agencies tend to make actors within the system self-serving. According to this model, the goals of individual agencies often conflict, and pressures for success, promotion, pay increases, and general accountability fragment the efforts of the system as a whole, leading to a criminal justice *non*system.[26]

conflict model
A criminal justice perspective that assumes that the system's components function primarily to serve their own interests. According to this theoretical framework, justice is more a product of conflicts among agencies within the system than it is the result of cooperation among component agencies.

FIGURE 2
The Core Components of the American Criminal Justice System and Their Functions.

The Police

- Enforce the law
- Investigate crimes
- Apprehend offenders
- Reduce and prevent crime
- Maintain public order
- Ensure community safety
- Provide emergency and related community services
- Protect the fundamental rights and freedoms of individuals

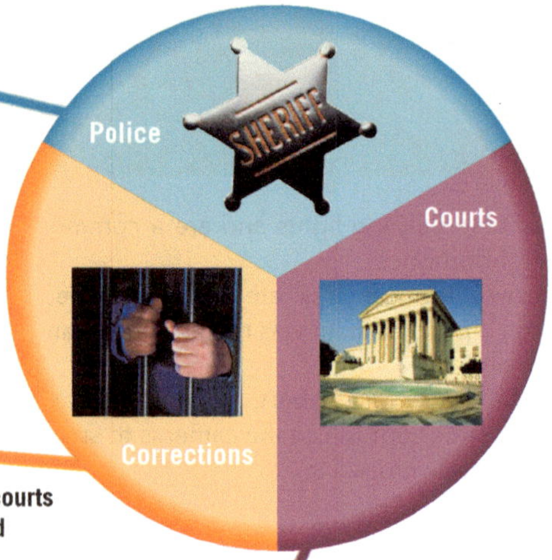

Correctional Agencies

- Carry out sentences imposed by the courts
- Provide safe and humane custody and supervision of offenders
- Protect the community
- Rehabilitate, reform, and reintegrate convicted offenders back into the community
- Respect the legal and human rights of the convicted

Criminal Courts

- Conduct fair and impartial trials
- Decide criminal cases
- Ensure due process
- Determine guilt or innocence
- Impose sentences on the guilty
- Uphold the law
- Require fairness throughout the justice process
- Protect the rights and freedoms of anyone facing processing by the justice system
- Provide a check on the exercise of power by other justice system agencies*

*Fairness, professionalism, integrity, and impartiality are expected of all criminal justice personnel at every stage of criminal case processing, and it is a special duty of the courts to ensure that these expectations are met.

It is commonly assumed that these three components—law enforcement (police, sheriffs, marshals), the judicial process (judges, prosecutors, defense lawyers), and corrections (prison officials, probation [officers], and parole officers)—add up to a "system" of criminal justice. A system implies some unity of purpose and organized interrelationship among component parts. In the typical American city and state, and under federal jurisdiction as well, no such relationship exists. There is, instead, a reasonably well-defined criminal process, a continuum through which each accused offender may pass: from the hands of the police, to the jurisdiction of the courts, behind the walls of a prison, then back onto the street.

—*National Commission on the Causes and Prevention of Violence*

Everywhere across the nation, we are more concerned with ensuring that criminal activity does not repeat itself, rather than keeping criminal activity from occurring in the first place.

—*Tony Fabelo, Executive Director, Texas Criminal Justice Policy Council*

A classic study of clearance rates by criminologist Jerome H. Skolnick provides support for the idea of a criminal justice nonsystem.[27] Clearance rates are a measure of crimes solved by the police. The more crimes the police can show they have solved, the better they look to the public they serve. Skolnick discovered an instance in which a burglar was caught red-handed during the commission of a burglary. After his arrest, the police suggested that he confess to many unsolved burglaries that they knew he had not committed. In effect they said, "Help us out, and we will try to help you out!" The burglar did confess—to more than 400 other burglaries. Following the confession, the police were satisfied because they could say they had "solved" many burglaries, and the suspect was pleased as well because the police and the prosecutor agreed to speak on his behalf before the judge.

Both models have something to tell us. Agencies of justice with a diversity of functions (police, courts, and corrections) and at all levels (federal, state, and local) are linked closely enough for the term *system* to be meaningfully applied to them. On the other hand, the very size of the criminal justice undertaking makes effective cooperation between component agencies difficult. The police, for example, have an interest in seeing offenders put behind bars. Prison officials, on the other hand, are often working with extremely overcrowded facilities. They may favor early-release programs for certain categories of offenders, such as those judged to be nonviolent. Who wins out in the long run might just be a matter of internal politics and quasi-official wrangling. Everyone should be concerned, however, when the goal of justice is affected, and sometimes even sacrificed, because of conflicts within the system.

American Criminal Justice: The Process

Whether part of a system or a nonsystem, the agencies of criminal justice must process the cases that come before them. An analysis of criminal justice case processing provides a "road map" to the criminal justice system itself. The process in most state systems is similar. See **Web Extra 1–2** at mycrimekit.com for more information about the process shown in the figure.

Justice cannot be for one side alone, but must be for both.
—*Eleanor Roosevelt*

Web EXTRA

Investigation and Arrest

The modern justice process begins with investigation. After a crime has been discovered, evidence is gathered at the scene when possible, and a follow-up investigation attempts to reconstruct the sequence of activities. Although a few offenders are arrested at the scene of the crime, most are apprehended later. In such cases, an arrest **warrant** issued by a judge provides the legal basis for an apprehension by police.

warrant
In criminal proceedings, a writ issued by a judicial officer directing a law enforcement officer to perform a specified act and affording the officer protection from damages if he or she performs it.

An arrest, in which a person is taken into custody, limits the arrestee's freedom. Arrest is a serious step in the process of justice and involves a discretionary decision made by the police seeking to bring criminal sanctions to bear. Most arrests are made peacefully, but if a suspect tries to resist, a police officer may need to use force. Only about half of all people arrested are eventually convicted, and of those, only about a quarter are sentenced to a year or more in prison.

During arrest and before questioning, defendants are usually advised of their constitutional rights, as enumerated in the famous U.S. Supreme Court decision of *Miranda* v. *Arizona*.[28] Defendants are told:

> (1) "You have the right to remain silent." (2) "Anything you say can and will be used against you in court." (3) "You have the right to talk to a lawyer for advice before we ask you any questions, and to have him with you during questioning." (4) "If you cannot afford a lawyer, one will be appointed for you before any questioning if you wish." (5) "If you decide to answer questions now without a lawyer present, you will still have the right to stop answering at any time. You also have the right to stop answering at any time and may talk with a lawyer before deciding to speak again." (6) "Do you wish to talk or not?" and (7) "Do you want a lawyer?"[29]

While the federal government occasionally may make a great advance in the direction of civil liberties, they can also make a very disastrous reversal.
—*Supreme Court Justice Robert H. Jackson*[vii]

Although popular television programs about the criminal justice system almost always show an offender being given a rights advisement at the time of arrest, the *Miranda* decision requires only that police advise a person of his or her rights prior to questioning. An arrest without questioning does not require a warning. When an officer interrupts a crime in progress, public-safety considerations may make it reasonable for the officer to ask a few questions prior to a rights advisement. Many officers, however, feel they are on sound legal ground only by advising suspects of their rights immediately after arrest.

Booking

Following arrest, suspects are booked. During **booking**, which is an administrative procedure, pictures are taken, fingerprints are made, and personal information such as address, date of birth, weight, and height is gathered. Details of the charges are recorded, and an administrative record of the arrest is created. At this time, suspects are often advised of their rights again and are asked to sign a form on which each right is written. The written form generally contains a statement acknowledging the advisement of rights and attesting to the fact that the suspect understands them.

booking
A law enforcement or correctional administrative process officially recording an entry into detention after arrest and identifying the person, the place, the time, the reason for the arrest, and the arresting authority.

Pretrial Activities

First Appearance

Within hours of arrest, suspects must be brought before a magistrate (a judicial officer) for an initial appearance. The judge will tell them of the charges against them, will again advise them of their rights, and may sometimes provide the opportunity for **bail**.

bail
The money or property pledged to the court or actually deposited with the court to effect the release of a person from legal custody.

Most defendants are released on recognizance into their own care or the care of another or are given the chance to post a bond during their first appearance. A bond may take the form

The current crisis in criminal and juvenile justice is fueled by the public's conviction that the system no longer represents an effective response to the problem of crime.

—Reinventing Probation Council

of a cash deposit or a property bond in which a house or other property serves as collateral against flight. Those who flee may be ordered to forfeit the posted cash or property. Suspects who are not afforded the opportunity for bail because their crimes are very serious or who do not have the needed financial resources are taken to jail to await the next stage in the justice process.

If a defendant doesn't have a lawyer, one will be appointed at the first appearance. To retain a court-appointed lawyer, the defendant may have to demonstrate financial hardship. The names of assigned lawyers are usually drawn off the roster of practicing defense attorneys in the county. Some jurisdictions use public defenders to represent indigent defendants.

preliminary hearing
A proceeding before a judicial officer in which three matters must be decided: (1) whether a crime was committed, (2) whether the crime occurred within the territorial jurisdiction of the court, and (3) whether there are reasonable grounds to believe that the defendant committed the crime.

probable cause
A set of facts and circumstances that would induce a reasonably intelligent and prudent person to believe that a specified person has committed a specified crime. Also, reasonable grounds to make or believe an accusation. Probable cause refers to the necessary level of belief that would allow for police seizures (arrests) of individuals and full searches of dwellings, vehicles, and possessions.

information
A formal written accusation submitted to a court by a prosecutor, alleging that a specified person has committed a specified offense.

indictment
A formal written accusation submitted to the court by a grand jury, alleging that a specified person has committed a specified offense, usually a felony.

grand jury
A group of jurors who have been selected according to law and have been sworn to hear the evidence and to determine whether there is sufficient evidence to bring the accused person to trial, to investigate criminal activity generally, or to investigate the conduct of a public agency or official.

arraignment
Strictly, the hearing before a court having jurisdiction in a criminal case in which the identity of the defendant is established, the defendant is informed of the charge and of his or her rights, and the defendant is required to enter a plea. Also, in some usages, any appearance in criminal court before trial.

Preliminary Hearing

The primary purpose of a **preliminary hearing**, also sometimes called a *preliminary examination*, is to establish whether sufficient evidence exists against a person to continue the justice process. At the preliminary hearing, the hearing judge will seek to determine whether there is **probable cause** to believe that (1) a crime has been committed and (2) the defendant committed it. The decision is a judicial one, but the process provides the prosecutor with an opportunity to test the strength of the evidence at his or her disposal.

The preliminary hearing also allows defense counsel the chance to assess the strength of the prosecution's case. As the prosecution presents evidence, the defense is said to "discover" what it is. Hence the preliminary hearing serves as a discovery function for the defense. If the defense attorney thinks the evidence is strong, he or she may suggest that a plea bargain be arranged. All defendants, including those who are indigent, have a right to be represented by counsel at the preliminary hearing.

Information or Indictment

In some states, the prosecutor may seek to continue the case against a defendant by filing an **information** with the court. An information, which is a formal written accusation, is filed on the basis of the outcome of the preliminary hearing.

Other states require that an **indictment** be returned by a **grand jury** before prosecution can proceed. The grand jury hears evidence from the prosecutor and decides whether the case should go to trial. In effect, the grand jury is the formal indicting authority. It determines whether probable cause exists to charge the defendant formally with the crime. Grand juries can return an indictment on less than a unanimous vote.

The grand jury system has been criticized because it is one-sided. The defense has no opportunity to present evidence; the grand jury is led only by the prosecutor, often through an appeal to emotions or in ways not permitted in a trial. At the same time, the grand jury is less bound by specific rules than a trial jury. For example, a grand jury member once told the author that a rape case had been dismissed because the man had taken the woman to dinner first. Personal ignorance and subcultural biases are far more likely to play a role in grand jury hearings than in criminal trials. In defense of the grand jury system, however, defendants who are clearly innocent will likely not be indicted. A grand jury's refusal to indict can save the system considerable time and money by preventing cases lacking in evidence from further processing by the criminal justice system.

Arraignment

The **arraignment** is "the first appearance of the defendant before the court that has the authority to conduct a trial."[30] At arraignment, the accused stands before a judge and hears the information, or indictment, against him as it is read. Defendants are again notified of their rights and are asked to enter a plea. Acceptable pleas generally include (1) not guilty, (2) guilty, and (3) no contest (*nolo contendere*), which may result in conviction but can't be used later as an admission of guilt in civil proceedings. Civil proceedings (or private lawsuits), while not covered in detail in this book, provide an additional avenue of relief for victims or their survivors. Convicted offenders increasingly face suits brought against them by victims seeking to collect monetary damages.

The Federal Rules of Criminal Procedure specify that "arraignment shall be conducted in open court and shall consist of reading the indictment or information to the defendant or stating to him the substance of the charge and calling on him to plead thereto. He shall be given a copy of the indictment or information before he is called upon to plead."[31]

Guilty pleas are not always accepted by the judge. If the judge believes a guilty plea is made under duress or is due to a lack of knowledge on the part of the defendant, the plea will be rejected and a plea of "not guilty" will be substituted for it. Sometimes defendants "stand mute," that is, they refuse to speak or to enter a plea of any kind. In that case, the judge will enter a plea of "not guilty" on their behalf.

If you break the law, we're going to hold you accountable, and there will be tough consequences for your actions.
—*North Carolina Governor Jim Hunt*[viii]

Adjudication

Under the Sixth Amendment to the U.S. Constitution, every criminal defendant has a right to a **trial** by jury. The U.S. Supreme Court, however, has held that petty offenses are not covered by the Sixth Amendment guarantee and that the seriousness of a case is determined by the way in which "society regards the offense." For the most part, "offenses for which the maximum period of incarceration is six months or less are presumptively petty."[32] In *Blanton* v. *City of North Las Vegas* (1989), the Court held that "a defendant can overcome this presumption and become entitled to a jury trial, only by showing that . . . additional penalties [such as fines and community service] viewed together with the maximum prison term, are so severe that the legislature clearly determined that the offense is a serious one."[33] The *Blanton* decision was further reinforced in the case of *U.S.* v. *Nachtigal* (1993).[34]

trial
In criminal proceedings, the examination in court of the issues of fact and relevant law in a case for the purpose of convicting or acquitting the defendant.

In most jurisdictions, many criminal cases never come to trial. The majority are "pleaded out," that is, they are dispensed of as the result of a bargained plea, or they are dismissed for one of a variety of reasons. Studies have found that as many as 82% of all sentences are imposed in criminal cases because of guilty pleas rather than trials.[35]

In cases that do come to trial, the procedures governing the submission of evidence are tightly controlled by procedural law and precedent. *Procedural law* specifies the type of evidence that may be submitted, the credentials of those allowed to represent the state or the defendant, and what a jury is allowed to hear.

Precedent refers to understandings built up through common usage and also to decisions rendered by courts in previous cases. Precedent in the courtroom, for example, requires that lawyers request permission from the judge before approaching a witness. It also can mean that excessively gruesome items of evidence may not be used or must be altered in some way so that their factual value is not lost in the strong emotional reactions they may create.

Some states allow trials for less serious offenses to occur before a judge if defendants waive their right to a trial by jury. This is called a *bench trial.* Other states require a jury trial for all serious criminal offenses.

Trials are expensive and time-consuming. They pit defense attorneys against prosecutors. Regulated conflict is the rule, and jurors are required to decide the facts and apply the law as the judge explains it to them. In some cases, however, a jury may be unable to decide. Such a jury is said to be *deadlocked*, and the judge declares a mistrial. The defendant may be tried again when a new jury is impaneled.

Sentencing

Once a person has been convicted, it becomes the responsibility of the judge to impose some form of punishment. The sentence may take the form of supervised probation in the community, a fine, a prison term, or some combination of these. Defendants will often be ordered to pay the costs of court or of their own defense if they are able.

Prior to sentencing, a sentencing hearing may be held in which lawyers on both sides present information concerning the defendant. The judge may also ask a probation or parole officer to compile a presentence report, which contains information on the defendant's family and business situation, emotional state, social background, and criminal history. This report helps the judge make an appropriate sentencing decision.

The criminal justice system is composed of a sprawling bureaucracy with many separate agencies that are largely autonomous and independent.
—*Gary LaFree, Ph.D., University of New Mexico*

Judges traditionally have had considerable discretion in sentencing, although new state and federal laws now place limits on judicial discretion in some cases, requiring that a sentence "presumed" by law be imposed. Judges still retain enormous discretion, however, in specifying whether sentences on multiple charges are to run consecutively or concurrently. Offenders found guilty of more than one charge may be ordered to serve one sentence after another is completed, which is called a **consecutive sentence**, or may be told that their sentences will run at the same time, which is called a **concurrent sentence**.

consecutive sentence
One of two or more sentences imposed at the same time, after conviction for more than one offense, and served in sequence with the other sentence. Also, a new sentence for a new conviction, imposed upon a person already under sentence for a previous offense, which is added to the previous sentence, thus increasing the maximum time the offender may be confined or under supervision.

concurrent sentence
One of two or more sentences imposed at the same time, after conviction for more than one offense, and served at the same time. Also, a new sentence for a new conviction, imposed upon a person already under sentence for a previous offense, which is served at the same time as the previous sentence.

Many convictions are appealed. The appeals process can be complex and can involve both state and federal judiciaries. An appeal is based on the defendant's claim that rules of procedure were not followed properly at some earlier stage in the justice process or that the defendant was denied the rights guaranteed by the U.S. Constitution.

Corrections

Once an offender has been sentenced, the corrections stage begins. Some offenders are sentenced to prison, where they "do time" for their crimes. Once in the correctional system, they are classified according to local procedures and are assigned to confinement facilities and treatment programs. Newer prisons today bear little resemblance to the massive bastions of the past, which isolated offenders from society behind huge stone walls. Many modern prisons, however, still suffer from a "lock psychosis" (a preoccupation with security) among top- and mid-level administrators as well as a lack of significant rehabilitation programs.

Probation and Parole

Not everyone who is convicted of a crime and sentenced ends up in prison. Some offenders are ordered to prison only to have their sentences suspended and a probationary term imposed. They may also be ordered to perform community service as a condition of their probation. During the term of probation, these offenders are required to submit to supervision by a probation officer and to meet other conditions set by the court. Failure to do so results in revocation of probation and imposition of the original prison sentence.

Offenders who have served a portion of their prison sentences may be freed on parole. They are supervised by a parole officer and assisted in their readjustment to society. As in the case of probation, failure to meet the conditions of parole may result in revocation of parole and a return to prison.

Library EXTRA

Web EXTRA

Learn more about the criminal justice process at Library Extra 1–2 at mycrimekit.com. For a critical look at the justice system, visit Web Extra 1–3 at mycrimekit.com.

Due Process and Individual Rights

due process
A right guaranteed by the Fifth, Sixth, and Fourteenth Amendments of the U.S. Constitution and generally understood, in legal contexts, to mean the due course of legal proceedings according to the rules and forms established for the protection of individual rights. In criminal proceedings, due process of law is generally understood to include the following basic elements: a law creating and defining the offense, an impartial tribunal having jurisdictional authority over the case, accusation in proper form, notice and opportunity to defend, trial according to established procedure, and discharge from all restraints or obligations unless convicted.

The U.S. Constitution requires that criminal justice case processing be conducted with fairness and equity; this requirement is referred to as **due process**, which, simply put, means procedural fairness.[36] It recognizes the individual rights of criminal defendants facing prosecution by a state or the federal government. Under the due process standard, rights violations may become the basis for the dismissal of evidence or of criminal charges, especially at the appellate level. Table 1 outlines the basic rights to which defendants in criminal proceedings are generally entitled.

Due process underlies the first ten amendments to the Constitution, which are collectively known as the *Bill of Rights.* It is specifically guaranteed by the Fifth, Sixth, and Fourteenth Amendments and is succinctly stated in the Fifth, which reads, "No person shall be . . . deprived of life, liberty, or property, without due process of law." The Fourteenth Amendment makes due process binding on the states, that is, it requires individual states to respect the due process rights of U.S. citizens who come under their jurisdiction.

The courts, and specifically the U.S. Supreme Court, have interpreted and clarified the guarantees of the Bill of Rights. The due process standard was set in the 1960s by the Warren Court (1953–1969), following a number of far-reaching Supreme Court decisions that affected criminal procedure. Led by Chief Justice Earl Warren, the Warren Court is remembered for its concern with protecting the innocent against the massive power of the state in criminal proceedings.[37] As a result of its tireless efforts to institutionalize the Bill of Rights, the daily practice of modern American criminal justice is now set squarely upon the due process standard.

CJ News

Police Recruits in Heavy Demand

Police departments, desperate to beef up their ranks, are using unprecedented recruiting tactics that include luring officer candidates from other cities and offering dramatically increased pay, housing allowances, and other perks.

The aggressive recruiting efforts have become particularly common in cities such as Phoenix and Lexington, Ky., where local governments are emerging from budget slumps and hiring more officers to keep up with the public safety needs of rapidly growing areas.

To expand its pool of candidates for 500 jobs over the next two years, Phoenix's 2,969-officer department is recruiting on the Los Angeles Police Department's turf in Southern California. The $300,000 campaign includes TV and newspaper ads that tout Phoenix's lower cost of living.

▲ Los Angeles Police Department rookie officers applauding during their graduation ceremony at the police academy in the city's picturesque Elysian Park. Would you consider a job in policing?
J. Emilio Flores/LaOpinion/NewsCom

Los Angeles' 9,000-member department, which is seeking 720 officers, has responded by hiring its own recruiting strategist. "Southern California is a big market," Los Angeles Police Cmdr. Kenneth Garner says. "It's open season out here."

Honolulu's police department, which has struggled to find applicants on the Hawaiian Islands, is following a strategy similar to Phoenix's. The 1,800-officer department, trying to fill 200 openings, recently sent recruiters to San Diego and Portland, Ore., and got commitments from dozens of prospects.

Lexington raised starting salaries from $26,000 to $34,000 to help boost its 540-member force by 200 officers over four years. The city offers officers up to $7,400 for down payments on houses.

Other police agencies are dangling perks such as bonuses for recruits who speak foreign languages, says Elaine Deck, who tracks recruiting for the International Association of Chiefs of Police. Such perks have become more prevalent as departments have faced stiff competition for recruits in an economy that has created many higher-paying alternatives to police work.

"There are so many [departments] looking for officers," Deck says. The market is so competitive, she says, that departments for the first time are "recruiting whole families. . . . Everything is on the table: bilingual bonuses, housing allowances, you name it."

Some police departments have sent recruiters to other cities to sign up experienced officers from other agencies. Paul Schultz, police chief in Lafayette, Colo., says his 40-officer unit has been raided by larger agencies. "We've had officers go out on assignments where they have been recruited on the job."

For the latest in crime and justice news, visit the Talk Justice news feed at http://www.crimenews.info.

Source: Kevin Johnson, "Police Recruits in Heavy Demand," *USA Today*, November 11, 2005, p. 1A.

The Role of the Courts in Defining Rights

Although the Constitution deals with many issues, what we have been calling *rights* are open to interpretation. Many modern rights, although written into the Constitution, would not exist in practice were it not for the fact that the U.S. Supreme Court decided, at some point in history, to recognize them in cases brought before it. In the well-known case of *Gideon* v. *Wainwright* (1963),[38] for example, the Supreme Court embraced the Sixth Amendment guarantee of a right to a lawyer for all criminal defendants and mandated that states provide lawyers for defendants who are unable to pay for them. Before *Gideon*, court-appointed attorneys for defendants unable to afford their own counsel were practically unknown, except in capital cases and in some federal courts. After the *Gideon* decision, court-appointed counsel became commonplace, and measures were instituted in jurisdictions across the nation to select attorneys fairly for indigent defendants. It is important to note, however, that while the Sixth Amendment specifically says, among other things, that "in all criminal prosecutions, the accused shall enjoy the right . . . to have the Assistance of Counsel for his defence," it does not say, in so many words, that the state is *required* to provide counsel. It is the U.S. Supreme Court interpreting the Constitution that has said that.

African-American men comprise less than 6% of the U.S. population and almost one-half of its criminal prisoners.
—*Bureau of Justice Statistics*

TABLE 1 Individual Rights Guaranteed by the Bill of Rights[1]

A right to be assumed innocent until proven guilty
A right against unreasonable searches of person and place of residence
A right against arrest without probable cause
A right against unreasonable seizure of personal property
A right against self-incrimination
A right to fair questioning by the police
A right to protection from physical harm throughout the justice process
A right to an attorney
A right to trial by jury
A right to know the charges
A right to cross-examine prosecution witnesses
A right to speak and present witnesses
A right not to be tried twice for the same crime
A right against cruel or unusual punishment
A right to due process
A right to a speedy trial
A right against excessive bail
A right against excessive fines
A right to be treated the same as others, regardless of race, sex, religious preference, and other personal attributes

[1]As interpreted by the U.S. Supreme Court.

Criminal justice cannot be achieved in the absence of social justice.
—*American Friends' Service Committee*[ix]

The U.S. Supreme Court is very powerful, and its decisions often have far-reaching consequences. The decisions rendered by the justices in cases like *Gideon* become, in effect, the law of the land. For all practical purposes, such decisions often carry as much weight as legislative action. For this reason, we speak of "judge-made law" (rather than legislated law) in describing judicial precedents that affect the process of justice.

▶ A criminal defendant at a preliminary hearing. Everyone facing criminal prosecution in the United States is guaranteed a constitutional right to due process, meaning that defendants must be afforded a fair opportunity to participate in every stage of criminal proceedings. Should due process rights extend to all offenders—even accused terrorists?
AP Wide World Photos

CJ Careers

Why Study Criminal Justice?

As this chapter points out, criminal justice, as an academic area, is one of the fastest-growing disciplines in the United States. While the discipline has been expanding for more than a decade, much job growth is still to come, as the table in this box shows.

The events of September 11, 2001, have made the study of criminal justice more relevant than ever, and many of today's students use their criminal justice major as a path to a fulfilling job serving the nation and helping protect local communities. A criminal justice career offers students a way of contributing to society, and it permits them to give something back to the country and to the community that nurtured them. For many, a criminal justice career reaffirms the American way of life by supporting the values on which it is based.

Other students are attracted to the study of criminal justice because it facilitates exploration of the tension that exists within American society between individual rights and freedoms, on the one hand, and the need for public safety and security, on the other. That tension—between individual rights and public order—forms the theme upon which this textbook is built, and it is discussed in detail elsewhere in this chapter.

For more information on rapidly expanding criminal justice careers, read *Where the Jobs Are: Mission Critical Opportunities for America*, available on the Web at http://www.justicestudies.com.jobs.htm.

Projected Occupation Growth, 2006–2016

OCCUPATION	WORKFORCE GROWTH (%)
Criminal investigators	17
Court reporters	25
Correctional officers	16
Gaming surveillance officers	34
Police officers	11
Probation officers	11
Private security officers	18
Social workers	22
Paralegal workers	22
Lawyers	11
Computer programmers	–4
Computer hardware engineers	5
Production managers	–6
Office clerks	–8
Sales	–22

Source: Bureau of Labor Statistics, *Occupational Outlook Handbook Online* (January 31, 2008). Web available at http://www.bls.gov/oco/ocoic.htm#C. Accessed September 30, 2008.

Rights that have been recognized by court decisions are subject to continual refinement, and although the process of change is usually very slow, new interpretations may broaden or narrow the scope of applicability accorded to constitutional guarantees.

The Ultimate Goal: Crime Control through Due Process

Two primary goals were identified in our discussion of our theme: (1) the need to enforce the law and to maintain public order and (2) the need to protect individuals from injustice, especially at the hands of the criminal justice system. The first of these principles values the efficient arrest and conviction of criminal offenders. It is often referred to as the **crime-control model** of justice. The crime-control model was first brought to the attention of the academic community in Stanford University law professor Herbert Packer's cogent analysis of the state of criminal justice in the late 1960s.[39] For that reason, it is sometimes referred to as *Packer's crime-control model*.

crime-control model
A criminal justice perspective that emphasizes the efficient arrest and conviction of criminal offenders.

The second principle is called the **due process model** because of its emphasis on individual rights. Due process is intended to ensure that innocent people are not convicted of crimes; it is a fundamental part of American criminal justice. It requires a careful and informed consideration of the facts of each individual case. Under the due process model, police are required to recognize the rights of suspects during arrest, questioning, and handling. Similarly, prosecutors and judges must recognize constitutional and other guarantees during trial and the presentation of evidence.

due process model
A criminal justice perspective that emphasizes individual rights at all stages of justice system processing.

The dual goals of crime control and due process are often assumed to be opposing goals. Indeed, some critics of American criminal justice argue that the practice of justice is too often concerned with crime control at the expense of due process. Other analysts of the American scene maintain that our type of justice coddles offenders and does too little to protect the innocent. While it is impossible to avoid ideological conflicts like these, it is also realistic to think

Liberty is the perfection of civil society, but still authority must be acknowledged essential to its very existence.

—David Hume

CJ Careers

U.S. Federal Government 2008 General Schedule Pay

Basic pay under the federal General Schedule (GS) pay plan is shown in the following table. Annual salaries for federal law enforcement officers, which are higher than for most other federal employees in the same grade, are also indicated.

For additional federal employment information, visit http://www.opm.gov, the official U.S. government website for job and employment information.

SALARY GRADE	MOST FEDERAL EMPLOYEES	FEDERAL LAW ENFORCEMENT PERSONNEL	SALARY GRADE	MOST FEDERAL EMPLOYEES	FEDERAL LAW ENFORCEMENT PERSONNEL	SALARY GRADE	MOST FEDERAL EMPLOYEES*
GS-1	$17,064	NA	GS-6	$29,276	$34,156	GS-11	$48,148
GS-2	19,165	NA	GS-7	32,534	36,870	GS-12	57,709
GS-3	20,911	$25,093	GS-8	36,030	38,432	GS-13	68,625
GS-4	23,475	28,173	GS-9	39,795	41,122	GS-14	81,093
GS-5	26,264	32,389	GS-10	43,824	45,285	GS-15	95,390

*Includes law enforcement.

Note: GS pay is adjusted geographically, and most federal jobs pay a higher salary than that shown in the table. Locality payments in the continental United States range from 8.6% to 19%. Pay rates outside the continental United States are 10% to 25% higher. Also, certain hard-to-fill jobs, usually in the scientific, technical, and medical fields, may have higher starting salaries. Exact pay information can be found in federal position vacancy announcements. To view the most recent general federal pay scale and locality pay charts, go to http://www.opm.gov/oca.

of the American system of justice as representative of *crime control through due process*—that is, as a system of **social control** that is fair to those whom it processes. This model of *law enforcement infused with the recognition of individual rights* provides a workable conceptual framework for understanding the American system of criminal justice.

social control
The use of sanctions and rewards within a group to influence and shape the behavior of individual members of that group. Social control is a primary concern of social groups and communities, and it is their interest in the exercise of social control that leads to the creation of both criminal and civil statutes.

The Role of Research in Criminal Justice

The study of criminal justice as an academic discipline began in this country in the late 1920s, when August Vollmer (1876–1955), the former police chief of the Los Angeles Police Department (LAPD), persuaded the University of California to offer courses on the subject.[40] Vollmer was joined by his former student Orlando W. Wilson (1900–1972) and by William H. Parker (who later served as chief of the LAPD from 1950 to 1966) in calling for increased professionalism in police work through better training.[41] Largely as a result of Vollmer's influence, early criminal justice education was practice oriented; it was a kind of extension of on-the-job training for working practitioners. Hence, in the early days of the discipline, criminal justice students were primarily focused on the application of general management principles to the administration of police agencies. Criminal justice came to be seen as a practical field of study concerned largely with issues of organizational effectiveness.

By the 1960s, however, police training came to be augmented by criminal justice education[42] as students of criminal justice began to apply the techniques of social scientific research—many of them borrowed from sister disciplines like **criminology**, sociology, psychology, and political science—to the study of all aspects of the justice system. Scientific research into the operation of the criminal justice system was encouraged by the 1967 President's Commission on Law Enforcement and Administration of Justice, which influenced passage of the Safe Streets and Crime Control Act of 1968. The Safe Streets Act led to the creation of the National Institute of Law Enforcement and Criminal Justice, which later became the National Institute of Justice (NIJ). As a central part of its mission, NIJ continues to support research in the criminal justice field through substantial funding for scientific explorations into all aspects of the discipline, and it funnels much of the $3 billion spent annually by the U.S. Department of Justice to local communities to help fight crime.

criminology
The scientific study of the causes and prevention of crime and the rehabilitation and punishment of offenders.

While much of today's criminal justice research is grounded in the social sciences, a major source of research information about the practical impact of technology on the criminal justice system is the National Law Enforcement and Corrections Technology Center (NLECTC). This network of regional centers and specialty offices located across the country offers no-cost assistance to help law enforcement and corrections agencies implement current and emerging technologies. NLECTC provides a wealth of online information for anyone interested in technology assessment as applied to criminal justice. The agency's free newsletter, *TechBeat*, is published four times each year, both on paper and in electronic format. To request a subscription, e-mail asknlectc@nlectc.org. You can visit NLECTC on the Web via **Web Extra 1–4** at mycrimekit.com. Once there, you will be able to search the site's Virtual Library, which offers hundreds of publications on topics ranging from Biological, Chemical and Radiological Defense to Transportation Infrastructure Security.

Web EXTRA

Scientific research has become a major element in the increasing professionalization of criminal justice, both as a career field and as a field of study. There is a strong call today within criminal justice policy-making circles for the application of evidence-based practices in the justice field. As the word is used here, *evidence* does not refer to evidence of a crime but means, instead, *findings* that are supported by studies. Hence, **evidence-based practice** refers to crime-fighting strategies that have been scientifically tested and are based on social science research. Evidence-based practices can be expected to play an expanded role in policy making and in the administration of criminal justice for years to come.

evidence-based practice
Crime-fighting strategies that have been scientifically tested and are based on social science research.

Multiculturalism and Diversity in Criminal Justice

In late 2007, 58-year-old Tom Green, a Mormon sentenced in 2001 to a lengthy term in a Utah prison after being convicted of four counts of bigamy, was paroled.[43] Green, who had five wives, another five former wives, and 32 known children when he entered prison in 2001,[44] was also convicted of child rape arising from his marriage to a 13-year-old girl in 1986.

The Church of Jesus Christ of Latter-day Saints brought plural marriage to Utah in the early nineteenth century, but the state legislature banned the practice more than 100 years ago. Today, the church officially excommunicates polygamists, although the Fundamentalist Church of Jesus Christ of Latter Day Saints (FLDS), an offshoot of the mainstream church, practices polygamy in arranged marriages that often pair underage girls with older men.

Green was the first polygamist prosecuted in Utah in almost 50 years. Green's supporters claimed that it was because of the 2002 Winter Olympics held in Salt Lake City that polygamists, including Green, were targeted. In 2007, however, in a continuing crackdown on polygamists, Warren Steed Jeffs, a leader of the FLDS, was convicted of conspiring to rape a child and of being an accessory to child rape for performing a marriage involving a 14-year-old girl and her 19-year-old cousin. Jeffs, who was on the FBI's Ten Most Wanted list, is awaiting sentencing as this book goes to press. Finally, in 2008, Texas authorities armed with search warrants entered the Yearning for Zion ranch in Eldorado, Texas, an FLDS community compound, after receiving a call from a young woman who said she had been forced into an underage marriage with an older man inside the compound and had become pregnant. The 1,700-acre fenced ranch, a former game preserve, was bought by the FLDS in 2003. A number of large dormitory-style homes were then quickly built, along with a small medical center, a cheese factory, a rock quarry, a water treatment plant, and a large, white limestone temple.[45]

Without security, government cannot deliver, nor can the people enjoy, the prosperity and opportunities that flow from freedom and democracy.
—Former U.S. Attorney General Alberto Gonzales[x]

Some estimate the number of polygamists living in Utah and Arizona today at over 30,000,[46] and the existence of such alternative family lifestyles is just one indicator that the United States is a multicultural and diverse society.

Multiculturalism describes a society that is home to a multitude of different cultures, each with its own set of norms, values, and routine behaviors. While American society today is truly a multicultural society, composed of a wide variety of racial and ethnic heritages, diverse religions, incongruous values, disparate traditions, and distinct languages, multiculturalism in America is not new. For thousands of years before Europeans arrived in the Western Hemisphere, tribal nations of Native Americans each spoke their own language, were bound to customs that differed significantly from one another, and practiced a wide range of religions. European immigration, which began in earnest in the seventeenth century, led to greater

multiculturalism
The existence within one society of diverse groups that maintain unique cultural identities while frequently accepting and participating in the larger society's legal and political systems.[xi] *Multiculturalism* is often used in conjunction with the term *diversity* to identify many distinctions of social significance.

America, known the world over as the land of the free, was founded on the principle of liberty and justice for all. . . . Yet, at the same time, some 2 million of our citizens are denied their freedom. . . . At some point we must ask ourselves: What is the moral price we pay as a nation for locking up our youth rather than lifting them up?
—*Reverend Jesse L. Jackson, Sr.*[xii]

Library EXTRA

diversity still. Successive waves of immigrants, along with the slave trade of the early and mid-nineteenth century,[47] brought a diversity of values, beliefs, and patterns of behavior to American shores that frequently conflicted with prevailing cultures. Differences in languages and traditions fed the American melting pot of the late nineteenth and early twentieth centuries and made effective communication between groups difficult.

The face of multiculturalism in America today is quite different than it was in the past, due largely to relatively high birthrates among some minority populations and the huge but relatively recent immigration of Spanish-speaking people from Mexico, Cuba, Central America, and South America. Part of that influx consists of substantial numbers of undocumented immigrants who have entered the country illegally and who, because of experiences in their home countries, may have a special fear of police authority and a general distrust for the law. Such fears make members of this group hesitant to report being victimized, and their undocumented status makes them easy prey for illegal scams like extortion, blackmail, and documentation crimes. Learn more about immigration and crime via **Library Extra 1–3** at mycrimekit.com.

Diversity characterizes both immigrant and U.S.-born individuals. Census Bureau statistics show that people identifying themselves as white account for 71% of the U.S. population—a percentage that has been dropping steadily for at least the past 40 years. People of Hispanic origin constitute approximately 12% of the population and are the fastest-growing group in the country. Individuals identifying themselves as African-American make up another 12% of the population, and people of Asian and Pacific Island origin make up almost 4% of the total. Native Americans, including American Indians, Eskimos, and Aleuts, account for slightly less than 1% of all Americans.[48] Statistics like these, however, are only estimates, and their interpretation is complicated by the fact that surveyed individuals may be of mixed race. Nonetheless, it is clear that American society today is ethnically and racially quite diverse.

Race and *ethnicity* are only buzzwords that people use when they talk about multiculturalism. After all, neither race nor ethnicity determines a person's values, attitudes, or behavior.

▲ A migrant worker in California holding a Spanish-English dictionary. American society is multicultural, composed of a wide variety of racial and ethnic heritages, diverse religions, incongruous values, disparate traditions, and distinct languages. What impact does the multicultural nature of our society have on the justice system?
Jae C. Hong/AP Wide World Photos

Just as there is no uniquely identifiable "white culture" in American society, it is a mistake to think that all African-Americans share the same values or that everyone of Hispanic descent honors the same traditions or even speaks Spanish.

E Pluribus Unum (Out of Many, One)

Multiculturalism, as the term is used today, is but one form of diversity. Taken together, these two concepts—multiculturalism and diversity—encompass many distinctions of social significance. The broad brush of contemporary multiculturalism and social diversity draws attention to variety along racial, ethnic, subcultural, generational, faith, economic, and gender lines. Lifestyle diversity is also important. The fact that influential elements of the wider society are less accepting of some lifestyles than others doesn't mean that such lifestyles aren't recognized from the viewpoint of multiculturalism. It simply means that at least for now, some lifestyles are accorded less official acceptability than others. As a result, certain lifestyle choices, even within a multicultural society that generally respects and encourages diversity, may still be criminalized, as in the case of polygamy.

For now, it is sufficient to recognize that the diverse values, perspectives, and behaviors characteristic of various groups within our society have a significant impact on the justice system. Whether it is the confusion that arises from a police officer's commands to a non-English-speaking suspect, the need for interpreters in the courtroom, a deep-seated distrust of the police in some minority communities, a lack of willingness among some immigrants to report crime, the underrepresentation of women in criminal justice agencies, or some people's irrational suspicions of Arab-Americans following the September 11 terrorist attacks, diversity and multiculturalism present special challenges to the everyday practice of criminal justice in America. Finally, as we shall see, the demands and expectations placed on justice agencies in multicultural societies involve a dilemma that is closely associated with our theme: how to protect the rights of individuals to self-expression while ensuring social control and the safety and security of the public.

Summary

- The American experience with crime during the last half century has been especially influential in shaping the criminal justice system of today. Although crime waves have come and gone, some events during the past century stand out as especially significant, including a spurt of widespread organized criminal activity associated with the Prohibition years of the early twentieth century, the substantial increase in "traditional" crimes during the 1960s and 1970s, the threat to the American way of life represented by illicit drugs around the same time, and the terrorist attacks of September 11, 2001.
- Our theme is one of individual rights versus public order. As this chapter points out, the personal freedoms guaranteed to law-abiding citizens as well as to criminal suspects by the Constitution must be closely guarded. At the same time, the urgent social needs of communities for controlling unacceptable behavior and protecting law-abiding citizens from harm must be recognized. This theme is represented by two opposing groups: individual-rights advocates and public-order advocates. The fundamental challenge facing the practice of American criminal justice is in achieving efficient enforcement of the laws while simultaneously recognizing and supporting the legal rights of suspects and the legitimate personal differences and prerogatives of individuals.
- Although justice may be an elusive concept, it is important to recognize that criminal justice is tied closely to notions of social justice, including personal and cultural beliefs about equity and fairness. As a goal to be achieved, criminal justice refers to those aspects of social justice that concern violations of the criminal law. While community interests in the administration of criminal justice demand the apprehension and punishment of law violators, criminal justice ideals extend to the protection of the innocent, the fair treatment of offenders, and fair play by justice administration agencies.
- In this chapter, we described the process of American criminal justice as a system with three major components—police, courts, and corrections—all of which can be described as working together toward a common goal. We warned, however, that a systems viewpoint is useful

primarily for the simplification that it provides. A more realistic approach to understanding criminal justice may be the nonsystem approach. As a nonsystem, the criminal justice process is depicted as a fragmented activity in which individuals and agencies within the process have interests and goals that at times coincide but often conflict.

- The stages of criminal case processing include investigation and arrest, booking, first appearance in court, defendant's preliminary hearing, return of an indictment by the grand jury or filing of an information by the prosecutor, arraignment of the defendant before the court, adjudication or trial, sentencing, and corrections. As a field of study, corrections includes jails, probation, imprisonment, and parole.
- The principle of due process, which underlies the first ten amendments to the U.S. Constitution, is central to American criminal justice. Due process (also called *due process of law*) means procedural fairness and requires that criminal case processing be conducted with fairness and equity. The ultimate goal of the criminal justice system in America is achieving crime control through due process.
- The study of criminal justice as an academic discipline began in this country in the late 1920s and is well established today. Scientific research has become a major element in the increasing professionalization of criminal justice, and there is an increasingly strong call for the application of evidence-based practices in the justice field. Evidence-based practices are crime-fighting strategies that have been scientifically tested and that are based on social science research.
- American society today is a multicultural society, composed of a wide variety of racial and ethnic heritages, diverse religions, incongruous values, disparate traditions, and distinct languages. Multiculturalism complicates the practice of American criminal justice since there is rarely universal agreement in our society about what is right or wrong or about what constitutes justice. As such, multiculturalism represents both challenges and opportunities for today's justice practitioners.

Key Concepts

Terms

administration of justice
arraignment
bail
booking
civil justice
concurrent sentence
conflict model
consecutive sentence
consensus model
crime
crime-control model
criminal justice
criminal justice system
criminology
due process
due process model
evidence-based practice
grand jury
indictment
individual rights
individual-rights advocate
information
justice
multiculturalism
preliminary hearing
probable cause
public-order advocate
social control
social justice
trial
USA PATRIOT Act
warrant

Questions for Review

1. Describe the American experience with crime during the last half century. What noteworthy criminal incidents or activities can you identify during that time, and what social and economic conditions might have produced them?
2. What are the differences between the individual-rights perspective and the public-order perspective?
3. What is justice? What aspects of justice does this chapter discuss? How does criminal justice relate to social justice and to other wider notions of equity and fairness?
4. What are the main components of the criminal justice system? How do they interrelate? How might they conflict?
5. List the stages of case processing that characterize the American system of criminal justice, and describe each stage.
6. What is meant by the term *due process of law*? Where in the American legal system are guarantees of due process found?
7. What is the role of research in criminal justice? What is meant by the term *evidence-based practice*? How can research influence crime-control policy?
8. What is multiculturalism? What is social diversity? What impact do multiculturalism and diversity have on the practice of criminal justice in contemporary American society?

To participate in an online discussion of these topics and others, join the CJ Brief e-mail discussion list at mycrimekit.com.

Web Quest

Familiarize yourself with the *Criminal Justice: A Brief Introduction* Companion Website and with its many features. To get there, point your browser to http://www.mycrimekit.com. Once you've opened the site, you'll be able to read the latest crime and justice news, join the *Criminal Justice: A Brief Introduction* e-mail discussion list, and research a wide variety of criminal justice topics. You can learn about your textbook's chapter objectives, practice with online review questions, preview chapter summaries, submit electronic homework to your instructor, and enjoy many Web-based criminal justice projects. (If your instructor decides to use the electronic homework feature of the site, it's always a good idea to keep a copy of any materials that you submit.) The site also allows you to listen to the author introduce each chapter.

Unique Web Extras and book-specific Library Extras substantially enhance the learning opportunities your text offers. Web Extras bring the justice system to life by providing a wealth of links to relevant and informative sites. Library Extras help you learn more about important topics in the justice field via the textbook's electronic library. Library Extras include the latest reports and bulletins from the Bureau of Justice Statistics, the National Institute of Justice, the Bureau of Justice Assistance, the FBI, the Department of Homeland Security, and other agencies. The author has selected each report to complement the textbook and to enhance your learning experience.

One Web resource of special importance is the Prentice Hall Criminal Justice Cybrary (*Cybrary* means "cyber-library"). Known to justice professionals as "the world's crime and justice directory," the Cybrary contains annotated links to more than 12,000 crime and justice sites throughout the nation and around the world. Because it is continually updated and fully searchable, the Cybrary can be an invaluable tool as you write term papers or do Web-based research on crime and justice. You can reach the Cybrary directly by going to http://www.cybrary.info.

To complete this Web Quest online, go to the Web Quest module in Chapter 1 of the *Criminal Justice: A Brief Introduction* Companion Website at mycrimekit.com.

Notes

i. Quoted in Charles E. Silberman, *Criminal Violence, Criminal Justice* (New York: Random House, 1978), p. 12.
ii. ABC News, September 16, 2001.
iii. All boldfaced terms are explained whenever possible using definitions provided by the Bureau of Justice Statistics under a mandate of the Justice System Improvement Act of 1979. That mandate found its most complete expression in the *Dictionary of Criminal Justice Data Terminology* (Washington, DC: Bureau of Justice Statistics, 1982), the second edition of which provides the wording for many definitions in this text.
iv. Quoted in Silberman, *Criminal Violence, Criminal Justice,* p. 12.
v. ABC News, September 11, 2001.
vi. Adapted from U.S. Code, Title 28, Section 20.3 (2[d]). Title 28 of the U.S. Code defines the term *administration of criminal justice.*
vii. Philip B. Kurland, "Robert H. Jackson," in Leon Friedman and Fred L. Israel, eds., *The Justices of the United States Supreme Court, 1789–1969: Their Lives and Major Opinions,* Vol. 4 (New York: Chelsea House, 1969), p. 2565.
viii. Quoted in *Criminal Justice Newsletter,* September 16, 1997, p. 1.
ix. American Friends' Service Committee, *Struggle for Justice: A Report on Crime and Punishment in America* (New York: Farrar, Straus & Giroux, 1971).
x. Prepared remarks of U.S. Attorney General Alberto Gonzales, Address to the National Association of Counties Legislative Conference, Washington, DC, March 7, 2005.
xi. Adapted from Robert M. Shusta et al., *Multicultural Law Enforcement,* 2nd ed. (Upper Saddle River, NJ: Prentice Hall, 2002), p. 443.
xii. Reverend Jesse L. Jackson, Sr., "Liberty and Justice for Some: Mass Incarceration Comes at a Moral Cost to Every American," July 10, 2001, http://www.motherjones.com/prisons/print_liberty.html (accessed January 2, 2007).

---

1. American Civil Liberties Union website, http://www.aclu.org/issues/criminal/iscj.html (accessed January 22, 2009).
2. ABC News, September 11, 2001. Christopher was repeating a phrase generally attributed to former U.S. Supreme Court Justice Arthur Goldberg.
3. Sam Coates and Dan Eggen, "A City of Despair and Lawlessness," *Washington Post,* September 2, 2005, p. A1.
4. Mark Gongloff, "Anarchy in New Orleans," *Wall Street Journal,* September 1, 2005.
5. "Looters Ransack Stores in Downtown New Orleans," *Wall Street Journal,* August 31, 2005.
6. Ibid.
7. Kevin Johnson, "Officers at 'Fort Apache' Finally Get Breather," *USA Today,* September 7, 2005, p. 3A.
8. Kevin McCoy, "Fraud Mounts in Katrina Aid Program," *USA Today,* February 13, 2006, p. 1A.
9. Ibid.
10. For a thorough discussion of immigration as it relates to crime, see Ramiro Martinez, Jr., and Matthew T. Lee, "On Immigration and Crime," in National Institute of Justice, *Criminal Justice 2000, Vol. 1: The Nature of Crime—Continuity and Change* (Washington, DC: U.S. Department of Justice, Office of Justice Programs, 2000).
11. "Cries of Relief," *Time,* April 26, 1993, p. 18; and "King II: What Made the Difference?" *Newsweek,* April 26, 1993, p. 26.

12. "Inside Columbine," *Rocky Mountain News,* http://www.rockymountainnews.com/drmn/columbine (accessed July 4, 2008).
13. "Cries of Relief."
14. Public Law 107-56.
15. Laurence McQuillan, "Bush to Urge Jail for Execs Who Lie," *USA Today,* July 9, 2002, http://www.usatoday.com/news/washdc/2002/07/09/bush-business.htm (accessed July 9, 2006).
16. Sarbanes-Oxley Act of 2002 (officially known as the Public Company Accounting Reform and Investor Protection Act), Public Law 107-204, 116 Stat. 745 (July 30, 2002).
17. PricewaterhouseCoopers, "The Sarbanes-Oxley Act," http:// www.pwcglobal.com/Extweb/NewCoAtWork.nsf/docid/D0D7F79003C6D64485256CF30074D66C (accessed July 8, 2007).
18. "Enron's Lay, Skilling Convicted," Associated Press, May 25, 2006.
19. Wendy Koch, "States Get Tougher with Sex Offenders," *USA Today,* May 24, 2006, p. 1A.
20. Ibid.
21. George W. Bush, "Presidential Address to the Nation," September 20, 2001.
22. *The American Heritage Dictionary on CD-ROM* (Boston: Houghton Mifflin, 1991).
23. For a good overview of the issues involved, see Judge Harold J. Rothwax, *Guilty: The Collapse of Criminal Justice* (New York: Random House, 1996).
24. For one perspective on the detention of Muslims following September 11, 2001, see the plaintiff's motion to stay proceedings on defendant's summary judgment motion pending discovery, in *Center for National Security Studies* v. *U.S. Department of Justice,* U.S. District Court for the District of Columbia (Civil Action No. 01–2500; January 2002), http://www.aclu.org/court/cnssjan22.pdf (accessed September 24, 2007).
25. The systems model of criminal justice is often attributed to the frequent use of the term *system* by the 1967 Presidential Commission in its report *The Challenge of Crime in a Free Society* (Washington, DC: U.S. Government Printing Office, 1967).
26. One of the first published works to use the nonsystem approach to criminal justice was the American Bar Association's *New Perspective on Urban Crime* (Washington, DC: ABA Special Committee on Crime Prevention and Control, 1972).
27. Jerome H. Skolnick, *Justice without Trial* (New York: John Wiley, 1966), p. 179.
28. *Miranda* v. *Arizona,* 384 U.S. 436, 16 L.Ed.2d 694, 86 S.Ct. 1602 (1966).
29. North Carolina Justice Academy, *Miranda Warning Card* (Salemburg, NC: North Carolina Justice Academy, n.d.).
30. John M. Scheb and John M. Scheb II, *American Criminal Law* (St. Paul, MN: West, 1996), p. 32.
31. Federal Rules of Criminal Procedure, 10.
32. *Blanton* v. *City of North Las Vegas,* 489 U.S. 538, 103 L.Ed.2d 550, 109 S.Ct. 1289 (1989).
33. Ibid.
34. *U.S.* v. *Nachtigal,* 122 L.Ed.2d 374, 113 S.Ct. 1072, 1073 (1993), *per curiam.*
35. Barbara Borland and Ronald Sones, *Prosecution of Felony Arrests* (Washington, DC: Bureau of Justice Statistics, 1991).
36. "The Defendants' Rights at a Criminal Trial," http://www.mycounsel.com/content/arrests/court/rights.html (accessed February 10, 2008).
37. For a complete and now-classic analysis of the impact of decisions made by the Warren Court, see Fred P. Graham, *The Due Process Revolution: The Warren Court's Impact on Criminal Law* (New York: Hayden Press, 1970).
38. *Gideon* v. *Wainwright,* 372 U.S. 353 (1963).
39. Herbert Packer, *The Limits of the Criminal Sanction* (Stanford, CA: Stanford University Press, 1968).
40. For an excellent history of policing in the United States, see Edward A. Farris, "Five Decades of American Policing, 1932–1982," *Police Chief* (November 1982), pp. 30–36.
41. Gene Edward Carte, "August Vollmer and the Origins of Police Professionalism," *Journal of Police Science and Administration,* Vol. 1, No. 1 (1973), pp. 274–281.
42. Chris Eskridge distinguishes between police *training,* which is "job-specific" and is intended to teach trainees *how* to do something (like fire a weapon), and *justice education,* whose purpose is to "develop a general spirit of inquiry." See C. W. Eskridge, "Criminal Justice Education and Its Potential Impact on the Sociopolitical-Economic Climate of Central European Nations," *Journal of Criminal Justice Education,* Vol. 14, No. 1 (spring 2003), pp. 105–118; and James O. Finckenauer, "The Quest for Quality in Criminal Justice Education," *Justice Quarterly,* Vol. 22, No. 4 (December 2005), pp. 413–426.
43. "Polygamist Wins Parole from Utah State Prison," Associated Press, August 27, 2007.
44. See Patrick O'Driscoll, "Utah Steps Up Prosecutions of Polygamists," *USA Today,* May 14, 2001, p. 5A.
45. Information for this story comes from Associated Press, "Sect Investigation Moving to Courtroom," April 14, 2008. Web posted at http://www.usatoday.com/news/nation/2008-04-14-sect-governor_N.htm (accessed April 14, 2008).
46. "Polygamist Wins Parole from Utah State Prison."
47. On March 22, 1794, the U.S. Congress barred American citizens from transporting slaves from the United States to another nation or between foreign nations. On January 1, 1808, the importation of slaves into the United States became illegal, and Congress charged the U.S. Revenue Cutter Service (now known as the U.S. Coast Guard) with enforcing the law on the high seas. Although some slave ships were seized, the importation of Africans for sale as slaves apparently continued in some southern states until the early 1860s. See U.S. Coast Guard, "U.S. Coast Guard in Illegal Immigration (1794–1971)," http://www.uscg.mil/hq/g-o/g-opl/mle/amiohist.htm (accessed October 13, 2007).
48. U.S. Census Bureau website, http://www.census.gov (accessed March 22, 2006). Population statistics are estimates because race is a difficult concept to define and Census Bureau interviewers allow individuals to choose more than one race when completing census forms.

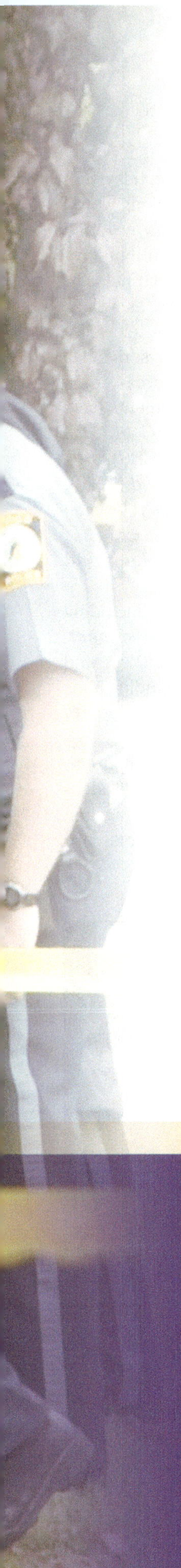

The Crime Picture

2

Chapter Outline

- Introduction
- The UCR/NIBRS Program
- The National Crime Victimization Survey
- Comparisons of the UCR and the NCVS
- Special Categories of Crime

Learning Objectives

After reading this chapter, you should be able to

- Describe the history and nature of the FBI's UCR/NIBRS Program, and explain what it can tell us about crime in the United States today.
- Describe the history and nature of the National Crime Victimization Survey Program, and explain what it can tell us about crime in the United States today.
- Identify the special categories of crime discussed in this chapter, and explain why they are of contemporary significance.

"It may turn out that a free society cannot really prevent crime. Perhaps its causes are locked so deeply into the human personality, the intimate processes of family life, and the subtlest aspects of the popular culture that coping is the best that we can hope for."

—James Q. Wilson, University of California, Los Angeles[1]

"No one way of describing crime describes it well enough."

—President's Commission on Law Enforcement and Administration of Justice

From Chapter 2 of *Criminal Justice: A Brief Introduction*, Eighth Edition. Frank Schmalleger.

Introduction

▶▶▶ Hear the author discuss this chapter at mycrimekit.com.

According to broadcast ratings guru *MediaWeek*, the most popular scripted show on television today is the CBS crime drama *CSI: Crime Scene Investigation.*[2] The series' top ranking would seem to be no small feat for a cop show that has to compete with the likes of widely watched offerings like *American Idol, Desperate Housewives, ER, Survivor*, and *Lost*—until one realizes that the American public is fascinated with hard-hitting crime dramas. And that helps to explain the success of shows like the *CSI* spin-offs, *CSI: Miami* and *CSI: New York*, as well as to explain why the NBC-TV show *Law and Order* is the longest-running drama on television today and the second-longest running drama ever.[3] Like *CSI*, the *Law and Order* series has generated its own spin-offs, including *Law and Order: Criminal Intent* and *Law and Order: Special Victims' Unit.* Taken together, more than 600 original *Law and Order* segments have aired. Other crime and justice shows on TV today include *Blind Justice* (ABC), *Cold Case* (CBS), *Criminal Minds* (CBS), *The District* (CBS), *The Evidence* (ABC), *Hack* (CBS), *JAG* (CBS), *NCIS* (CBS), *Numb3rs* (CBS), *Prison Break* (Fox), *The Shield* (FX), *Wanted* (TNT), *The Wire* (HBO), and *Without a Trace* (CBS). Like this textbook, many of today's television shows deliver content across a variety of media. View the online CSI crime labs at **Web Extra 2–1** at mycrimekit.com, and see some real-life crime-prevention links sponsored by *Law and Order: SVU* at **Web Extra 2–2**. Visit a real cold case squad at **Web Extra 2–3**.

Web EXTRA

The public's interest in crime has also given birth to reality TV crime shows, including *America's Most Wanted* (which premiered on Fox in 1988), *COPS, Crime and Punishment*, and *Wildest Police Videos.* Similarly, video magazine shows like *60 Minutes*, *20/20*, and *Nightline* frequently focus on justice issues, and any number of recent movies—including films like *SWAT, Training Day, 2 Fast 2 Furious, The Green Mile, Runaway Jury*, and *Minority Report*—play off the public's fascination with crime and the personal drama it fosters.

This chapter has a dual purpose. First, it provides a statistical overview of crime in contemporary America by examining information on reported and discovered crimes. Second, it identifies special categories of crime that are of particular interest today, including crime against women, crime against the elderly, hate crime, corporate and white-collar crime, organized crime, gun crime, drug crime, cybercrime, and terrorism.

▶ The cast of the CBS-TV show *CSI.* The American public has long been enthralled with crime shows, and since the terrorist attacks of 2001, the public's concern with personal safety has surged. Why do so many people like to watch TV crime shows?
CBS/Landov Media

Although we will look at many crime statistics in this chapter, it is important to remember that statistical aggregates of reported crime, whatever their source, do not reveal the lost lives, human suffering, lessened productivity, and reduced quality of life that crime causes. Unlike the fictional characters on TV crime shows, real-life crime victims as well as real-life offenders lead intricate lives—they have families, hold jobs, and dream dreams. As we examine the crime statistics, we must not lose sight of the people behind the numbers.

We can have as much or as little crime as we please; depending on what we choose to count as criminal.
—Herbert L. Packer

Crime Data and Social Policy

Crime statistics provide an overview of criminal activity. If used properly, a statistical picture of crime can serve as a powerful tool for creating social policy. Decision makers at all levels, including legislators, other elected officials, and administrators throughout the criminal justice system, rely on crime data to analyze and evaluate existing programs, to fashion and design new crime-control initiatives, to develop funding requests, and to plan new laws and crime-control legislation. Many "get tough" policies, such as the three-strikes movement that swept the country during the 1990s, have been based in large part on the measured ineffectiveness of existing programs to reduce the incidence of repeat offending.

However, some people question just how objective—and therefore how useful—crime statistics are. Social events, including crime, are complex and difficult to quantify. Even the decision of which crimes should be included and which excluded in statistical reports is itself a judgment reflecting the interests and biases of policy makers. Moreover, public opinion about crime is not always realistic. As well-known criminologist Norval Morris points out, the news media do more to influence public perceptions of crime than any official data do.[4] During the four-year period (in the mid-1990s) covered by Morris's study, for example, the frequency of crime stories reported in the national media increased fourfold. During the same time period, crime was at the top of the list in subject matter covered in news stories at both the local and national levels. The irony, says Morris, is that "the grossly increasing preoccupation with crime stories came at a time of steadily declining crime and violence." However, as Morris adds, "aided and abetted by this flood of misinformation, the politicians, federal and state and local, fostered the view that the public demands our present 'get tough' policies."[5]

The Collection of Crime Data

Nationally, crime statistics come from two major sources: (1) the FBI's **Uniform Crime Reporting (UCR) Program** (also known today as the UCR/NIBRS Program), which produces an annual overview of major crime titled *Crime in the United States*; and (2) the **National Crime Victimization Survey (NCVS)** of the **Bureau of Justice Statistics (BJS)**. The most widely quoted numbers purporting to describe crime in America today probably come from the UCR/NIBRS Program, although the statistics it produces are based largely on *reports* to the police by victims of crime.

Uniform Crime Reporting (UCR) Program
A statistical reporting program run by the FBI's Criminal Justice Information Services (CJIS) division. The UCR Program publishes *Crime in the United States,* which provides an annual summation of the incidence and rate of reported crimes throughout the United States.

National Crime Victimization Survey (NCVS)
An annual survey of selected American households conducted by the Bureau of Justice Statistics to determine the extent of criminal victimization—especially unreported victimization—in the United States.

Bureau of Justice Statistics (BJS)
A U.S. Department of Justice agency responsible for the collection of criminal justice data, including the annual National Crime Victimization Survey.

Recently, some professional organizations, most notably the Washington-based Police Executive Research Forum (PERF), have undertaken their own efforts to gather crime data. For example, PERF polled police departments across the country for data related to violent crime.[6] PERF surveys also ask police chiefs to provide subjective impressions of crime trends in their cities and towns.

The statistics gathered by PERF, similar to those in the UCR/NIBRS Program, are based on law enforcement agencies' reports of crimes. PERF notes, however, that because its "members are police chiefs, sheriffs, and other law enforcement executives, PERF is able to obtain official crime statistics from many of the nation's largest jurisdictions and to release those figures several months before the nationwide tallies are released by the FBI."[7]

A fourth source of crime data is offender self-reports based on surveys that ask respondents to reveal any illegal activity in which they have been involved. Offender self-reports are not discussed in detail in this chapter because surveys utilizing them are not national in scope and are not undertaken regularly. Moreover, offenders are often reluctant to accurately report ongoing or recent criminal involvement, making information derived from these surveys somewhat unreliable and less than current. However, the available information from offender self-reports reveals that serious criminal activity is considerably more widespread than most "official" surveys show (Figure 1).

FIGURE 1
The Criminal Justice Funnel.
Source: Derived from Tracey Kyckelhahn and Thomas H. Cohen, *Felony Defendants in Large Urban Countries, 2004* (Washington, DC: Bureau of Justice Statistics, 2008).

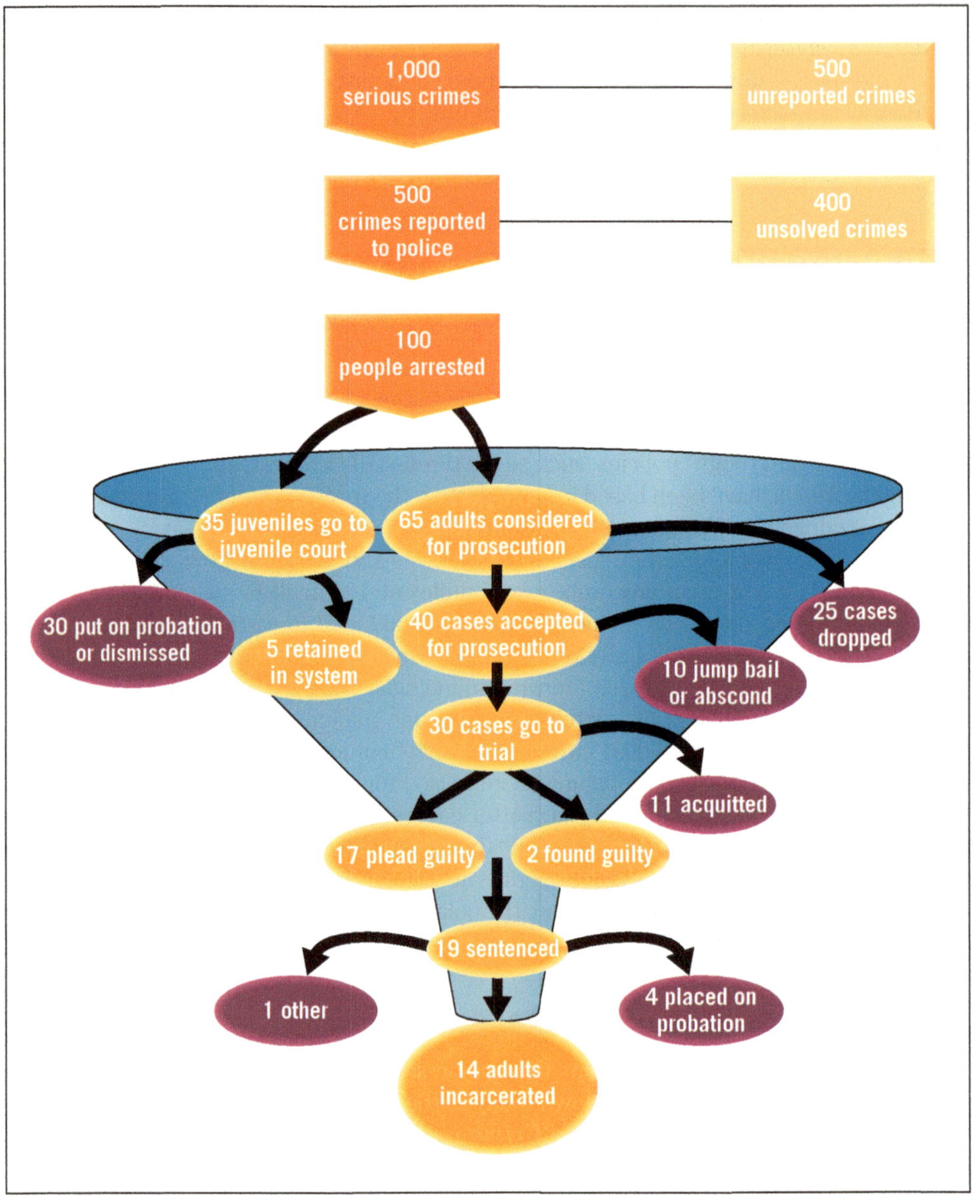

The typical mass murderer is extraordinarily ordinary.
—*James Alan Fox, Northeastern University*

Other regular publications also contribute to our knowledge of crime patterns throughout the nation. One such publication is the *Sourcebook of Criminal Justice Statistics*—an annual compilation of national information on crime and on the criminal justice system. The *Sourcebook* is produced by the BJS, and a Web-based version of the *Sourcebook* is continually updated as data become available. The National Institute of Justice (NIJ; the primary research arm of the U.S. Department of Justice), the Office of Juvenile Justice and Delinquency Prevention (OJJDP), the Federal Justice Statistics Resource Center, and the National Victim's Resource Center provide still more information on crime patterns. Visit **Web Extra 2–4** at mycrimekit.com for an overview of the many sources of crime data. The *Sourcebook* is available directly at **Library Extra 2–1** at mycrimekit.com.

Web EXTRA

Library EXTRA

The UCR/NIBRS Program

Development of the UCR Program

In 1930, Congress authorized the U.S. attorney general to survey crime in America, and the Federal Bureau of Investigation (FBI) was designated to implement the program. In short order, the bureau built on earlier efforts by the International Association of Chiefs of Police

(IACP) to create a national system of uniform crime statistics. As a practical measure, IACP had recommended the use of readily available information, and so it was that citizens' crime reports to the police became the basis of the FBI's plan.[8]

During its first year of operation, the FBI's UCR Program received reports from 400 cities in 43 states; 20 million people were covered by that first comprehensive survey. Today, approximately 16,000 law enforcement agencies provide crime information for the program, with data coming from city, county, and state departments. To ensure uniformity in reporting, the FBI has developed standardized definitions of offenses and terminologies used in the program. A number of publications, including the *Uniform Crime Reporting Handbook* and the *Manual of Law Enforcement Records*, are supplied to participating agencies, and training for effective reporting is available through FBI-sponsored seminars and instructional literature.

Following IACP recommendations, the original UCR Program was designed to permit comparisons over time through construction of a **Crime Index**. The index summed the occurrences of seven major offenses—murder, forcible rape, robbery, aggravated assault, burglary, larceny-theft, and motor vehicle theft—and expressed the result as a crime rate based on population. In 1979, by congressional mandate, an eighth offense—arson—was added to the index. The Crime Index, first published in *Crime in the United States* in 1960, was the title used for a simple aggregation of the seven main offense classifications (called Part I offenses). A Modified Crime Index later referred to the original Crime Index offenses plus arson.

Crime Index
A now-defunct but once-inclusive measure of the UCR Program's violent and property crime categories, or what are called *Part I offenses*. The Crime Index, long featured in the FBI's publication *Crime in the United States*, was discontinued in 2004. The index had been intended as a tool for geographic (state-to-state) and historical (year-to-year) comparisons via the use of crime rates (the number of crimes per unit of population). However, criticism that the index was misleading arose after researchers found that the largest of the index's crime categories, larceny-theft, carried undue weight and led to an underappreciation of changes in the rates of more violent and serious crimes.

Over the years, however, concern grew that the Crime Index did not provide a clear picture of criminality because it was skewed by the offense with the highest number of reports—typically larceny-theft. The sheer volume of larceny-theft offenses overshadowed more serious but less frequently committed offenses, skewing perceptions of crime rates for jurisdictions with high numbers of larceny-thefts but low numbers of serious crimes like murder and forcible rape. In June 2006, the FBI's Criminal Justice Information Services (CJIS) Advisory Policy Board officially discontinued the use of the Crime Index in the UCR/NIBRS Program and in its publications and directed the FBI to instead publish simple violent crime totals and property crime totals until a more viable index could be developed.[9]

Although work to develop such an index is still ongoing, UCR/NIBRS Program crime categories continue to provide useful comparisons of specific reported crimes over time and between jurisdictions. It is important to recognize, as you read through the next few pages, that today's UCR/NIBRS Program categories tend to parallel statutory definitions of criminal behavior, but they are not legal classifications—only conveniences created for statistical-reporting purposes. Because many of the definitions of crime are derived from official UCR/NIBRS Program terminology, you should remember that UCR/NIBRS terminology may differ from statutory definitions of crime.

The National Incident-Based Reporting System

Beginning in 1988, the FBI's UCR Program initiated development of a new national crime-collection effort called the **National Incident-Based Reporting System (NIBRS)**. NIBRS represents a significant redesign of the original UCR Program. Whereas the original UCR system was "summary based," the newly enhanced NIBRS is incident driven (Table 1). Under NIBRS, city, county, state, and federal law enforcement agencies throughout the country furnish detailed data on crime and arrest activities at the incident level either to the individual state incident-based reporting programs or directly to the federal NIBRS Program.

National Incident-Based Reporting System (NIBRS)
An incident-based reporting system that collects detailed data on every single crime occurrence. NIBRS data are replacing the kinds of summary data that have traditionally been provided by the FBI's Uniform Crime Reporting Program.

NIBRS is not a separate report; rather it is the new methodology underlying the contemporary UCR system—hence our use of the term *UCR/NIBRS* in describing today's Uniform Crime Reporting Program. Whereas the old UCR system depended on statistical tabulations of crime data, which were often little more than frequency counts, the new UCR/NIBRS system gathers many details about each criminal incident. Included among them is information on place of occurrence, weapon used, type and value of property damaged or stolen, personal characteristics of the offender and the victim, nature of any relationship between the two, and disposition of the complaint.

Those who insist that crime never pays have never met an identity thief. Identity theft not only pays, it pays extremely well.

—*Jonathan Turley*[i]

Under UCR/NIBRS, the traditional distinctions between Part I and Part II offenses are being replaced with 22 general offenses: arson, assault, bribery, burglary, counterfeiting, embezzlement, extortion, forcible sex offenses, fraud, gambling, homicide, kidnapping, larceny, motor vehicle theft, narcotics offenses, nonforcible sex offenses, pornography, prostitution, receiving

TABLE 1 Differences between the Traditional UCR and Enhanced UCR/NIBRS Reporting

Traditional UCR	Enhanced UCR/NIBRS
Consists of monthly aggregate crime counts	Consists of individual incident records for the eight major crimes and 38 other offenses, with details on offense, victim, offender, and property involved
Records one offense per incident, as determined by the hierarchy rule, which suppresses counts of lesser offenses in multiple-offense incidents	Records each offense occurring in an incident
Does not distinguish between attempted and completed crimes	Distinguishes between attempted and completed crimes
Records rape of females only	Records rape of males and females
Collects assault information in five categories	Restructures definition of assault
Collects weapon information for murder, robbery, and aggravated assault	Collects weapon information for all violent offenses
Provides counts on arrests for the eight major crimes and 21 other offenses	Provides details on arrests for the eight major crimes and 49 other offenses

Source: Adapted from *Effects of NIBRS on Crime Statistics*, BJS Special Report (Washington, DC: Bureau of Justice Statistics, 2000), p. 1.

stolen property, robbery, vandalism, and weapons violations. Other offenses on which UCR/NIBRS data are being gathered include bad checks, vagrancy, disorderly conduct, driving under the influence, drunkenness, nonviolent family offenses, liquor-law violations, Peeping Tom activity, runaways, trespassing, and a general category of all "other" criminal law violations. UCR/NIBRS also collects data on an expanded array of attributes involved in the commission of offenses, including whether the offender is suspected of using alcohol, drugs or narcotics, or a computer in the commission of the offense.

The FBI began accepting crime data in NIBRS format in January 1989. Although the bureau intended to have NIBRS fully in place by 1999, delays have been routine, and the NIBRS format has not yet been fully adopted. Because it is a flexible system, changes continue to be made in the data gathered under UCR/NIBRS. In 2003, for example, three new data elements were added to the survey to collect information on law enforcement officers killed and assaulted. Another new data element has been added to indicate the involvement of gang members in reported offenses.

The goals of the innovations introduced under NIBRS are to enhance the quantity, quality, and timeliness of crime-data collection by law enforcement agencies and to improve the methodology used for compiling, analyzing, auditing, and publishing the collected data. A major advantage of UCR/NIBRS, beyond the sheer increase in the volume of data collected, is the ability that NIBRS provides to break down and combine crime offense data into specific information.[10]

Library EXTRA

Web EXTRA

In keeping with the FBI's interest in technological improvements and in order to make reports of crime data more widely available, in 2006 the FBI moved all UCR/NIBRS data reporting to the Internet and stopped paper production of its annual publication, *Crime in the United States*. Efforts to make the electronic versions more useful and searchable continue. The latest edition of *Crime in the United States* can be viewed at **Library Extra 2–2** at mycrimekit.com. To learn more about the effects of NIBRS innovations on crime statistics, including comparisons of traditional UCR summary data with the newer, more detailed UCR/NIBRS data, see **Web Extra 2–5** at mycrimekit.com. Finally, the BJS provides an NIBRS information website, which can be accessed via **Web Extra 2–6**.

Other changes in crime reporting were brought about by the 1990 Crime Awareness and Campus Security Act, which requires colleges to publish annual security reports.[11] Most campuses share crime data with the FBI, increasing the reported national incidence of a variety of offenses. The U.S. Department of Education reported that 48 murders and 3,680 forcible sex offenses occurred on and around college campuses in 2004. Also reported were 5,915 robberies, 7,076 aggravated assaults, 39,740 burglaries, and 13,874 motor vehicle thefts.[12] Although these numbers may seem high, it is important to realize that except for the crimes of rape and sexual assault, college students experience violence at average annual rates that are lower than those for nonstudents in the same age group.[13] Rates of rape and sexual assault do not differ statistically between students and nonstudents. For the latest campus crime statistics, see Web Extra 2–7 at mycrimekit.com. Library Extra 2–3 provides statistical information on the sexual victimization of college women.

Web EXTRA

Library EXTRA

Historical Trends

Most UCR/NIBRS information is reported as a rate of crime. Rates are computed as the number of crimes per some unit of population. National reports generally make use of large units of population, such as 100,000 people. Hence, the rate of rape reported by the UCR/NIBRS Program for 2007 was 29.6 forcible rapes per every 100,000 inhabitants of the United States.[14] Rates allow for a meaningful comparison over areas and across time. The rate of reported rape for 1960, for example, was only about 10 per 100,000. We expect the number of crimes to increase as population grows, but rate increases are cause for concern because they indicate that reports of crime are increasing faster than the population is growing. Rates, however, require interpretation. Since the definition of rape that the FBI uses in reporting statistics on that crime includes only female victims, the rate of victimization might be more meaningfully expressed in terms of every 100,000 female inhabitants. Similarly, although there is a tendency to judge an individual's risk of victimization based on rates, such judgments tend to be inaccurate since they are based purely on averages and do not take into consideration individual life circumstances, such as place of residence, wealth, and educational level. While rates may tell us about aggregate conditions and trends, we must be very careful when applying them to individual cases.

Since the FBI's UCR Program began, there have been three major shifts in crime rates—and we now seem to be witnessing the beginning of a fourth. The first occurred during the early 1940s, when crime decreased sharply due to the large number of young men who entered military service during World War II. Young males make up the most crime-prone segment of the population, and their deployment overseas did much to lower crime rates at home. From 1933 to 1941, the Crime Index declined from 770 to 508 offenses per every 100,000 members of the American population.[15]

The second noteworthy shift in offense statistics was a dramatic increase in most forms of crime between 1960 and the early 1990s. Several factors contributed to the increase in reported crime during this period. One was also linked to World War II. With the end of the war and the return of millions of young men to civilian life, birthrates skyrocketed between 1945 and 1955, creating a postwar baby boom. By 1960, the first baby boomers were teenagers—and had entered a crime-prone age. This disproportionate number of young people produced a dramatic increase in most major crimes.

Other factors contributed to the increase in reported crime during the same period. Modified reporting requirements made it less stressful for victims to file police reports, and the publicity associated with the rise in crime sensitized victims to the importance of reporting. Crimes that might have gone undetected in the past began to figure more prominently in official statistics. Similarly, the growing professionalization of some police departments resulted in greater and more accurate data collection, making some of the most progressive departments appear to be associated with the largest crime increases.[16]

The 1960s were tumultuous years. The Vietnam War, a vibrant civil rights struggle, the heady growth of secularism, a dramatic increase in the divorce rate, diverse forms of "liberation," and the influx of psychedelic and other drugs all combined to fragment existing institutions. Social norms were blurred, and group control over individual behavior declined substantially. The "normless" quality of American society in the 1960s contributed greatly to the rise in crime.

From 1960 to 1980, crime rates rose from 1,887 to 5,950 offenses per every 100,000 U.S. residents. In the early 1980s, when postwar boomers began to age out of the crime-prone years and American society emerged from the cultural drift that had characterized the previous 20 years, crime rates leveled out briefly. Soon, however, an increase in drug-related criminal activity led crime rates—especially violent crime rates—to soar once again. Crime rates peaked during the early 1990s.

Crime is like cutting grass. Just because you cut it down doesn't mean it's going to stay there.
—Senator Joseph R. Biden, Jr.[ii]

A third major shift came with a significant decline in the rates of most major crimes being reported between 1991 and 2007. During these years, the crime rate dropped from 5,897 to

3,730 offenses per every 100,000 residents—sending it down to levels not seen since 1975. The U.S. Department of Justice suggests various reasons for the decline[17]:

- A coordinated, collaborative, and well-funded national effort to combat crime, beginning with the Safe Streets Act of 1968 and continuing through the USA PATRIOT Act of 2001
- Stronger, better-prepared criminal justice agencies, resulting from increased spending by federal and state governments on crime-control programs
- The growth in popularity of innovative police programs, such as community policing
- An aggressive approach to gun control, including the Brady Handgun Violence Prevention Act (discussed later in this chapter)
- A strong victims' movement and enactment of the 1984 federal Victims of Crime Act and the 1994 Violence against Women Act (discussed later in this chapter), which established the Office for Victims of Crime in the U.S. Department of Justice
- Sentencing reform, including various "get tough on crime" initiatives
- A substantial growth in the use of incarceration due to changes in sentencing law practice
- The "war on drugs," begun in the 1970s,[18] which resulted in stiff penalties for drug dealers and repeat drug offenders
- The increased use of the death penalty
- Advances in forensic science and enforcement technology, including the increased use of real-time communications, the growth of the Internet, and the advent of DNA evidence

More important than new strict laws, an expanded justice system and police funding, or changes in crime-fighting technologies, however, may have been influential economic and demographic factors that were largely beyond the control of policy makers but that combined to produce substantial decreases in rates of crime—including economic expansion and a significant shift in demographics caused by aging of the population. During the 1990s, unemployment decreased by 36% in the United States while the number of people ages 20 to 34 declined by 18%. Hence, it may have been the ready availability of jobs combined with demographic shifts in the population—not the official efforts of policy makers—that produced a noteworthy decrease in crime during the 1990s. Read noted criminologist Alfred Blumstein's analysis of crime's decline in Library Extra 2–4 at mycrimekit.com to learn more about why crime rates fell during the 1990s.

Library EXTRA

A fourth shift in crime trends seems to be starting now. Some think that recent economic uncertainty, an increased jobless rate among unskilled workers, the growing number of ex-convicts who are back on the streets, the recent growth in the teenage population in this country, the increasing influence of gangs, copycat crimes, and the lingering social disorganization brought on by natural disasters like Hurricane Katrina in 2005 may lead to sustained increases in crime.[19] "We're probably done seeing declines in crime rates for some time to come," says Jack Riley, director of the Public Safety and Justice Program at RAND Corporation in Santa Monica, California. "The question," says Riley, "is how strong and how fast will those rates [rise], and what tools do we have at our disposal to get ahead of the curve."[20]

In 2006, in an effort to draw attention to spiking rates of violent crime in a number of major cities, PERF released a report titled *A Gathering Storm: Violence in America*. PERF was concerned that official FBI data would take too long to gather and might be released too late to effectively combat the growing trend in violence that it felt it had identified. The information used as the basis for the 2006 PERF report had been compiled from law enforcement executives at a "violent crime summit" held at the Mayflower Hotel in Washington, D.C. PERF said that its data show that there are a number of cities across the country reporting large changes in the extent and nature of violent crime.

The great 1990s crime drop ended with the 1990s. The new millennium brings a different picture.
—James Alan Fox, Northeastern University[iii]

A second PERF report, this one titled *Violent Crime in America: 24 Months of Alarming Trends*, was released in 2007 and found even more reason for concern.[21] The report noted that urban violent crime increased significantly in 2006 and that "many cities experienced double-digit or even triple-digit percentage increases in homicides and other violence."

PERF authors said that the most recent crime statistics showed a worsening of a trend first identified by PERF in mid-2005, "when PERF began to hear rumblings from its members that 'violent crime is making a comeback.'"[22]

Finally, in 2008, the Third Way Culture Program, a Washington, D.C.–based nonpartisan strategy center, released a report with conclusions similar to those reached by PERF. Titled *The Impending Crime Wave*,[23] the Third Way report identified what it called "four dangerous new trends" that it sees leading to heightened rates of serious crime in the near future. Those four trends are described as follows: (1) "the reentry explosion" (seen as "a massive and unprecedented population of prisoners reentering society and returning to their often troubled neighborhoods"); (2) "the lengthening shadow of illegal immigration" (said to attract a new kind of opportunistic criminal who serves members of a shadow economy); (3) "the sprawling parentless neighborhood of the Internet" (that puts children at risk of sexual predation and other crimes); and (4) "the surging youth population" (seen as "a demographic surge that is responsible for a million new teenagers and young adults, who are statistically far more prone to commit crimes than the general population"). The entire Third Way report is available online as Library Extra 2–5 at mycrimekit.com.

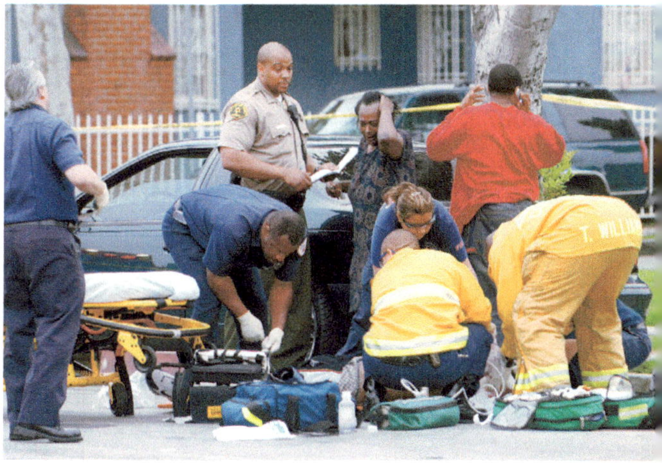

▲ Los Angeles Sheriff's Department deputies and Compton Fire Department personnel working at the scene of a shooting in Compton, California, in 2006. Some experts fear that violent crime may be starting to rise in big cities after two decades of decline. What would be the consequences for American cities if crime were to increase?
Photo by Bob Riha, Jr./ USA Today

UCR/NIBRS in Transition

Reports of crime data available through the UCR/NIBRS Program are now going through a transitional phase as the FBI integrates more NIBRS-based data into its official summaries. The transition to NIBRS reporting is complicated by the fact that not only does NIBRS gather more kinds of data than the older summary UCR Program did, but the definitions used for certain kinds of criminal activity under NIBRS are different than they were under the traditional UCR Program. The standard reference publication that the FBI designates for use by police departments in scoring and reporting crimes that occur within their jurisdiction is the *Uniform Crime Reporting Handbook*, and it is the most recent edition of that handbook that guides and informs the discussion of crime statistics that you will find in the next few pages. You can access the entire 164-page *Uniform Crime Reporting Handbook* at Library Extra 2–6 at mycrimekit.com. A thorough review of that document shows that much of the traditional UCR summary data-reporting terminology and structure remains in place. Learn more about the kinds of information recorded under NIBRS at Library Extra 2–7.

Library EXTRA

Library EXTRA

Freedom or Safety? You Decide.

A Dress Code for Bank Customers?

Dark glasses, a hooded sweatshirt, and a hat have been called the "uniform of choice" for bank robbers. In July 2002, in an effort to thwart a dramatic increase in robberies, some Massachusetts banks began posting requests for customers to remove hats, hoods, and sunglasses before entering financial establishments.

Not all banks, however, posted the signs. "I think what you have to weigh is convenience to customers versus the added benefits in terms of identifying suspects with a measure like this," said Melodie Jackson, spokeswoman for Citizens Bank of Massachusetts. "We're taking a very close look at things."

Banks in other parts of the country soon followed suit. By October 2002, 26 banks and credit unions with 141 locations in and around Springfield, Missouri, had posted signs asking visitors to remove sunglasses, hats, and anything that might hide their faces.

Today, such signs are commonplace at banks throughout the country, and it is likely that this request will soon become the *de facto* standard at banking and other financial venues.

YOU DECIDE

Are bank "dress codes" asking too much of customers? How would you feel about doing business with a bank that posts requests like those described here?

References: Michael S. Rosenwald and Emily Ramshaw, "Banks Post Dress Code to Deter Robbers," *Boston Globe*, July 13, 2002; and "Missouri Banks Attempt Unmasking Robbers," *Police Magazine* online, http://www.policemag.com/t_newspick.cfm?rank571952 (accessed October 25, 2002).

FIGURE 2
The FBI Crime Clock, Which Shows the Frequency of Commission of Major Crimes in 2007.
Source: Adapted from Federal Bureau of Investigation, *Crime in the United States, 2007*.

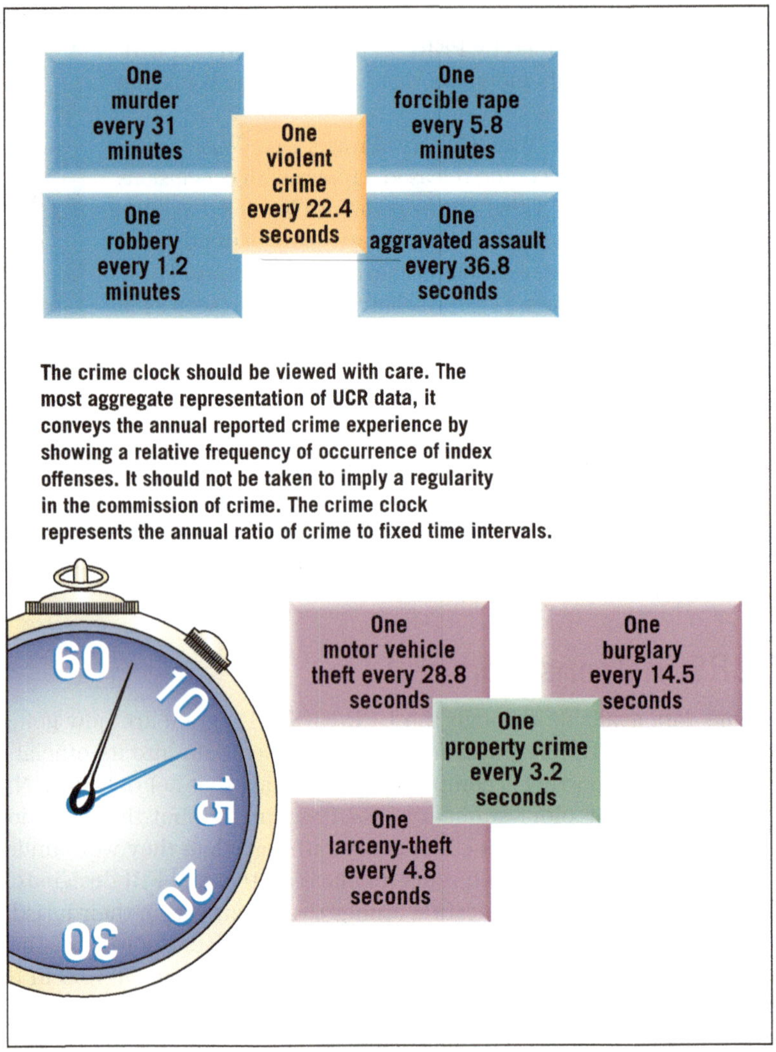

Figure 2 shows the FBI crime clock, which has long been calculated annually as a shorthand way of diagramming crime frequency in the United States. Note that crime clock data imply a regularity to crime that, in reality, does not exist.[24] Also, although the crime clock is a useful diagrammatic tool, it is not a rate-based measure of criminal activity and does not allow easy comparisons over time. Seven major crimes are included in the figure: murder, forcible rape, robbery, aggravated assault, burglary, larceny-theft, and motor vehicle theft.

The crime clock distinguishes between two categories of offenses: violent crimes and property crimes. The **violent crimes** (or personal crimes) are murder, forcible rape, robbery, and aggravated assault. The **property crimes** (as Figure 2 shows) are burglary, larceny-theft, and motor vehicle theft. Other than the use of this simple dichotomy, UCR/NIBRS data do not provide a clear measure of the severity of the crimes they cover.

violent crime
A UCR/NIBRS summary offense category that includes murder, rape, robbery, and aggravated assault.

property crime
A UCR/NIBRS summary offense category that includes burglary, larceny-theft, motor vehicle theft, and arson.

Like most UCR/NIBRS statistics, crime clock data are based on crimes reported to (or discovered by) the police. For a few offenses, the numbers reported are probably close to the numbers that actually occur. Murder, for example, is a crime that is difficult to conceal because of its seriousness. Even where the crime is not immediately discovered, the victim is often quickly missed by family members, friends, and associates, and someone files a "missing persons" report with the police. Auto theft is another crime that is reported in numbers similar to its actual rate of occurrence, probably because insurance companies require that the victim file a police report before they will pay the claim.

clearance rate
A traditional measure of investigative effectiveness that compares the number of crimes reported or discovered to the number of crimes solved through arrest or other means (such as the death of the suspect).

A commonly used term in today's UCR/NIBRS reports is **clearance rate**, which refers to the proportion of reported crimes that have been "solved." Clearances are judged primarily on the basis of arrests and do not involve judicial disposition. Once an arrest has been made, a crime is regarded as having been "cleared" for reporting purposes. Exceptional clearances (sometimes

TABLE 2 Major Crimes Known to the Police, 2007 (UCR/NIBRS Part I Offenses)

Offense	Number	Rate per 100,000	Clearance Rate
Personal/Violent Crimes			
Murder	16,929	5.6	61.2%
Forcible rape	90,427	30.0	40.0
Robbery	445,125	147.6	25.9
Aggravated assault	855,856	283.8	54.1
Property Crimes			
Burglary	2,179,140	722.5	12.4
Larceny–theft	6,568,572	2,177.8	18.6
Motor vehicle theft	1,095,769	363.3	12.6
Arson[1]	64,332	24.7	18.7
U.S. Total	**11,316,150**	**3,755.3**	

[1]Arson can be classified as either a property crime or a violent crime, depending on whether personal injury or loss of life results from its commission. It is generally classified as a property crime, however. Arson statistics are incomplete for 2007.

Source: Adapted from Federal Bureau of Investigation, *Crime in the United States, 2007* (Washington, DC: U.S. Department of Justice, 2008).

called *clearances by exceptional means*) can result when law enforcement authorities believe they know who committed a crime but cannot make an arrest. The perpetrator may, for example, have fled the country or died. Table 2 summarizes UCR/NIBRS program statistics for 2007.

Part I Offenses

Murder

Murder is the unlawful killing of one human being by another.[25] UCR/NIBRS statistics on murder describe the yearly incidence of all willful and unlawful homicides within the United States. Included in the count are all cases of nonnegligent manslaughter that have been reported to or discovered by the police. Not included in the count are suicides, justifiable homicides (that is, those committed in self-defense), deaths caused by negligence or accident, and murder attempts. In 2007, some 16,929 murders came to the attention of police departments across the United States. First-degree murder is a criminal homicide that is planned; second-degree murder is an intentional and unlawful killing but one that is generally unplanned and that happens "in the heat of the moment."

murder
The unlawful killing of a human being. *Murder* is a generic term that in common usage may include first- and second-degree murder, manslaughter, involuntary manslaughter, and other similar offenses.

Murder is the smallest numerical category in the **Part I offenses**. The 2007 murder rate was 5.6 homicides for every 100,000 residents of the United States. Generally, murder rates peak in the warmest months; in 2007, the greatest number of murders occurred in August. Geographically, murder is most common in the southern states. However, because those states are also the most populous, a meaningful comparison across regions of the country is difficult.

Part I offenses
A UCR/NIBRS offense group used to report murder, rape, robbery, aggravated assault, burglary, larceny-theft, motor vehicle theft, and arson, as defined under the FBI's UCR/NIBRS Program.

Age is no barrier to murder. Statistics for 2007 reveal that 210 infants (children under the age of one) were victims of homicide, as were 261 people age 75 and over.[26] Young adults between ages 20 and 24 were the most likely to be murdered. Murder perpetrators were also most common in this age group.

Firearms are the weapon used most often to commit murder. In 2007, guns were used in 68% of all killings. Handguns outnumbered shotguns almost 15 to one in the murder statistics, with rifles used almost as often as shotguns. Knives were used in approximately 12% of all murders. Other weapons included explosives, poison, narcotics overdose, blunt objects like clubs, and hands, feet, and fists.

The public is properly obsessed with safety. Of industrialized countries, the U.S. has the highest rate of violent crime.
—*Bob Moffitt, Heritage Foundation*

Only 12.9% of all murders in 2007 were perpetrated by offenders classified as "strangers." In 46% of all killings, the relationship between the parties had not yet been determined. The largest category of killers was officially listed as "acquaintances," which probably includes a large number of former friends. Arguments cause most murders (40.6%), but murders also occur during the

▲ Self-confessed serial killer Gary L. Ridgway. The 54-year-old Ridgway, known as the Green River Strangler, is said to be the nation's worst captured serial killer. In 2003, Ridgway admitted to killing 48 women over a 20-year period in the Pacific Northwest. He is now serving life in prison without possibility of parole. What's the difference between serial killers and mass murderers?
Elaine Thompson/Reuters/Landov Media

commission of other crimes, such as robbery, rape, and burglary. Homicides that follow from other crimes are more likely to be impulsive rather than planned.

Murders may occur in sprees, which "involve killings at two or more locations with almost no time break between murders."[27] One spree killer, John Allen Muhammad, 41, part of the "sniper team" that terrorized the Washington, D.C., area in 2002, was arrested along with 17-year-old Jamaican immigrant Lee Boyd Malvo in the random shootings of 13 people in Maryland, Virginia, and Washington, D.C., over a three-week period. Ten of the victims died.[28] In 2003, Muhammad and Malvo were convicted of capital murder; Muhammad was sentenced to die, and Malvo was given a second sentence of life without the possibility of parole in 2006 after he struck a deal with prosecutors in an effort to avoid the death penalty.[29]

In contrast to spree killing, mass murder entails "the killing of four or more victims at one location, within one event."[30] Recent mass murderers have included Seung-Hui Cho, who killed 33 people and wounded 20 on the campus of Virginia Polytechnic Institute and State University in Blacksburg, Virginia, in 2007; Timothy McVeigh, who was the antigovernment Oklahoma City bomber; Mohammed Atta and the terrorists he led, who carried out the September 11, 2001, attacks against American targets; and George Hennard, who killed 24 and wounded 20 at a Luby's Cafeteria in Killeen, Texas, in 1991.

Yet another kind of murder, serial murder, happens over time and officially "involves the killing of several victims in three or more separate events."[31] In cases of serial murder, days, months, or even years may elapse between killings.[32] Some of the more infamous serial killers of recent years are the confessed Wichita BTK murderer, Dennis Rader[33]; Jeffrey Dahmer, who received 936 years in prison for the murders of 15 young men (and who was himself later murdered in prison); Ted Bundy, who killed many college-age women; Henry Lee Lucas, now in a Texas prison, who confessed to 600 murders but later recanted (yet was convicted of 11 murders and linked to at least 140 others)[34]; Ottis Toole, who was Lucas's partner in crime; cult leader Charles Manson, who is still serving time for ordering followers to kill seven Californians, including famed actress Sharon Tate; Andrei Chikatilo, the Russian "Hannibal Lecter," who killed 52 people, mostly schoolchildren[35]; David Berkowitz, also known as the "Son of Sam," who killed six people on lovers' lanes around New York City; Theodore Kaczynski, the Unabomber, who perpetrated a series of bomb attacks on "establishment" figures; Seattle's Green River killer, Gary Leon Ridgway, a 54-year-old painter who in 2003 confessed to killing 48 women in the 1980s; and the infamous "railroad killer" Angel Maturino Resendiz, who was convicted of only one murder—that of Dr. Claudia Benton, which occurred in 1998—although he is suspected of many more.[36]

Library EXTRA

rape
Unlawful sexual intercourse achieved through force and without consent. Broadly speaking, the term *rape* has been applied to a wide variety of sexual attacks and may include same-sex rape and the rape of a male by a female. Some jurisdictions refer to same-sex rape as *sexual battery.*

forcible rape (UCR/NIBRS)
The carnal knowledge of a female, forcibly and against her will. For statistical-reporting purposes, the FBI defines *forcible rape* as "unlawful sexual intercourse with a female, by force and against her will, or without legal or factual consent." Statutory rape differs from forcible rape in that it generally involves nonforcible sexual intercourse with a minor.

Federal homicide laws changed in 2004 when President George Bush signed the Unborn Victims of Violence Act.[37] The act, which passed the Senate by only one vote, made it a separate federal crime to "kill or attempt to kill" a fetus "at any stage of development" during an assault on a pregnant woman. The fetal homicide statute, better known as Laci and Conner's Law, after homicide victims Laci Peterson and her unborn son (whom she had planned to name Conner), specifically prohibits the prosecution of "any person for conduct relating to an abortion for which the consent of the pregnant woman, or a person authorized by law to act on her behalf, has been obtained."

Because murder is such a serious crime, it consumes substantial police resources. Consequently, over the years the offense has shown the highest clearance rate of any major crime. Over 61% of all homicides were cleared in 2007. Figure 3 shows clearance rates for all Part I offenses except arson. Learn more about homicide trends in the United States at Library Extra 2–8 at mycrimekit.com.

Forcible Rape

The term **rape** is often applied to a wide variety of sexual attacks, including same-sex rape and the rape of a male by a female. For statistical-reporting purposes, however, the term **forcible rape** has a specific and somewhat different meaning. The UCR/NIBRS Program defines *forcible rape* as "the carnal knowledge of a female forcibly and against her will."[38] By definition, rapes

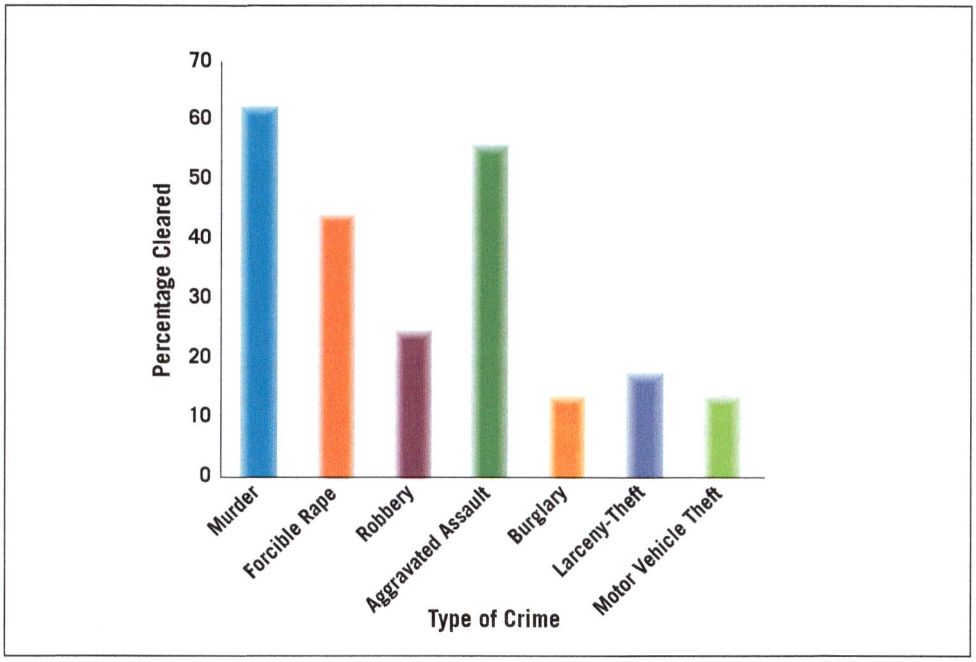

FIGURE 3
Crimes Cleared by Arrest, 2007.
Source: Federal Bureau of Investigation, *Crime in the United States, 2007.*

reported under the summary UCR Program are always of females. Although today our society acknowledges that males can be the victims of sexual assault, the *Uniform Crime Reporting Handbook*, which serves as a statistical-reporting guide for law enforcement agencies, says, "Sexual attacks on males are excluded from the rape category and should be classified as assaults or other sex offenses depending on the nature of the crime and the extent of the injury."[39] While it was not part of original UCR terminology, some jurisdictions refer to same-sex rape as **sexual battery**. Incidents of sexual battery are reportable under today's UCR/NIBRS Program as sexual offenses but do not enter the statistics on rape. Statutory rape, where no force is involved but the victim is younger than the age of consent, is not included in rape statistics, but attempts to commit the rape of a female by force or the threat of force are.

sexual battery
The intentional and wrongful physical contact with a person, without his or her consent, that entails a sexual component or purpose.

Forcible rape is the least reported of all violent crimes. Estimates are that only one out of every four forcible rapes is reported to the police. An even lower figure was reported by a 1992 government-sponsored study, which found that only 16% of rapes were reported.[40] The victim's fear of embarrassment was the most commonly cited reason for nonreports. In the past, reports of rapes were often handled in ways that made victims feel further victimized. Information was usually taken by desk sergeants or male detectives who were typically insensitive to victims' needs, and the physical examination victims had to endure was often a traumatizing experience in itself. Also, many states routinely permitted the woman's past sexual history to be revealed in detail in the courtroom if a trial ensued. But the past few decades have seen many changes designed to facilitate accurate reporting of rape and other sex offenses. Trained female detectives often interview the victims, physicians have become better educated in handling the psychological needs of victims, and sexual histories are no longer regarded as relevant in most trials.

UCR/NIBRS statistics show 90,427 reported forcible rapes for 2007, a slight decrease over the number of offenses reported for the previous year. Rape reports have generally increased, even in years when reports of other violent crimes have been on the decline. The offense of rape follows homicide in its seasonal variation. The greatest numbers of forcible rapes in 2007 were reported in the hot summer months, while the lowest numbers were recorded in January, February, November, and December.

Rape is frequently committed by a man known to the victim, as in the case of **date rape**. Victims may be held captive and subjected to repeated assaults.[41] In the crime of heterosexual rape, any female—regardless of age, appearance, or occupation—is a potential victim. Through personal violation, humiliation, and physical battering, rapists seek a sense of personal aggrandizement and dominance. Victims of rape often experience a lessened sense of personal worth; feelings of despair, helplessness, and vulnerability; a misplaced sense of guilt; and a lack of control over their personal lives.

date rape
The unlawful forced sexual intercourse with a female against her will that occurs within the context of a dating relationship. Date rape, or acquaintance rape, is a subcategory of rape that is of special concern today.

Contemporary wisdom holds that forcible rape is often a planned violent crime that serves the offender's need for power rather than sexual gratification.[42] The "power thesis" has its origins in the writings of Susan Brownmiller, who argued in 1975 that the primary motivation leading to rape is the male desire to "keep women in their place" and to preserve gender inequality through violence.[43] Although many writers on the subject of forcible rape have generally accepted the power thesis, at least one study has caused some to rethink it. In a 1995 survey of imprisoned serial rapists, for example, Dennis Stevens found that "lust" was reported most often (41%) as "the primary motive for predatory rape."[44]

Statistically speaking, most rapes are committed by acquaintances of the victims and often betray a trust or friendship. Date rape, which falls into this category, appears to be far more common than previously believed. Recently, the growing number of rapes perpetrated with the use of the "date rape drug" Rohypnol have alarmed law enforcement personnel. Rohypnol is an illegal pharmaceutical substance that is virtually tasteless. Available on the black market, it dissolves easily in drinks and can leave anyone who consumes it unconscious for hours, making them vulnerable to sexual assault.

Rape within marriage, which has not always been recognized as a crime, is a growing area of concern in American criminal justice, and many laws have been enacted during the past few decades to deter it. Similarly, even though UCR/NIBRS Program statistics officially report only the rape or attempted rape of females, some state statutes criminalize the rape of a male by a female. When it occurs, this offense is typically statutory rape. In 2007, for example, sixth-grade Wilmington, Delaware, science teacher Rachel L. Holt, a 34-year-old divorcee, was sentenced to ten years in prison after pleading guilty to second-degree rape. She had initially been charged with 28 counts of first-degree rape—which prosecutors said was based on the number of times she had had sex with a 13-year-old male student whom she had plied with alcohol and let drive her car. The intense affair took place over a one-week period.

Web EXTRA

Library EXTRA

Learn more about the crime of rape and what people can do to protect themselves at **Web Extra 2–8** at mycrimekit.com. Read about statistical measures relating to the sexual victimization of women at **Library Extra 2–9** at mycrimekit.com.

Robbery

robbery (UCR/NIBRS)
The unlawful taking or attempted taking of property that is in the immediate possession of another by force or violence and/or by putting the victim in fear. Armed robbery differs from unarmed, or strong-arm, robbery in that it involves a weapon. Contrary to popular conceptions, highway robbery does not necessarily occur on a street—and rarely in a vehicle. The term *highway robbery* applies to any form of robbery that occurs outdoors in a public place.

Robbery is a personal crime involving a face-to-face confrontation between victim and perpetrator. It is often confused with burglary, which is primarily a property crime. (We'll examine burglary later.) Weapons may be used in robbery, or strong-arm robbery may occur through intimidation. Purse snatching and pocket picking are not classified as robbery by the UCR/NIBRS Program but are included under the category of larceny-theft.

In 2007, individuals were the most common target of robbers. Banks, gas stations, convenience stores, and other businesses were the second most common target, with residential robberies accounting for only 15.2% of the total. In 2007, 445,125 robberies were reported to the police. Of that number, 44% were highway robberies, meaning that the crime occurred outdoors, most commonly as the victim was walking. Strong-arm robberies, in which the victim was intimidated but no weapon was used, accounted for 39% of the total robberies reported. Guns were used in 43% of all robberies, and knives were used in 8%. Armed robbers are dangerous; guns are actually discharged in 20% of all robberies.[45]

When a robbery occurs, the UCR/NIBRS Program scores the event as one robbery, even when a number of victims were robbed during the event. With the move toward incident-driven reporting, however, the revised UCR/NIBRS Program will soon make data available on the number of individuals robbed in each incident. Because statistics on crime follow what's known as the *hierarchy rule*, they show only the most serious offense that occurred during a particular episode. Hence, robberies are often hidden when they occur in conjunction with more serious crimes. For example, 3% of robbery victims are also raped, and a large number of homicide victims are robbed.[46]

Robbery is primarily an urban offense, and most arrestees are young male minorities. The robbery rate in cities in 2007 was 170 per every 100,000 inhabitants, whereas it was only 16.3 in rural areas. Eighty-eight percent of those arrested for robbery in 2007 were male, 65% were under the age of 25, and 58% were minorities.[47]

If people here were not getting killed on the job in homicides, we would have quite a low rate of fatalities.

—Samuel Ehrenhalt, former Labor Department official, commenting on findings that show murder to be the top cause of on-the-job deaths in New York City

Aggravated Assault

In April 2006, Arthur J. McClure, 22, of Fort Myers, Florida, was arrested when he allegedly took the head off of an Easter Bunny costume that he was wearing and punched Erin Johansson of

Cape Coral, Florida, after the young mother apparently became upset that a mall photo set was closing ten minutes early.[48] The incident was witnessed by dozens of people, including many children who had gathered to have their pictures taken with the rabbit. McClure, who denied he struck Johansson, was fired after the incident.

Assaults are of two types: simple (misdemeanor) and aggravated (felonious). For statistical-reporting purposes, simple assaults typically involve pushing and shoving. While simple assault may also at times include fistfights, the correct legal term to describe such incidents is *battery*. **Aggravated assaults** are distinguished from simple assaults in that either a weapon is used or the assault victim requires medical assistance. When a deadly weapon is employed, an aggravated assault may be charged as attempted murder even if no injury results.[49] In some cases, the UCR/NIBRS Program scores these attempted assaults as aggravated assault because of the potential for serious consequences.

In 2007, 855,856 cases of aggravated assault were reported to law enforcement agencies in the United States. Assault reports were most frequent in summer months and least frequent in February, November, December, and January. Most aggravated assaults were committed with blunt objects or objects near at hand (34%), while hands, feet, and fists were also commonly used (26%). Less frequently used were knives (19%) and firearms (21%). Because those who commit assaults are often known to their victims, aggravated assaults are relatively easy to solve. About 54% of all aggravated assaults reported to the police in 2007 were cleared by arrest.

assault (UCR/NIBRS)
An unlawful attack by one person upon another. Historically, *assault* meant only the attempt to inflict injury on another person; a completed act constituted the separate offense of battery. Under modern statistical usage, however, attempted and completed acts are grouped together under the generic term *assault*.

aggravated assault
The unlawful, intentional inflicting, or attempted or threatened inflicting, of serious injury upon the person of another. While *aggravated assault* and *simple assault* are standard terms for reporting purposes, most state penal codes use labels like *first-degree* and *second-degree* to make such distinctions.

Burglary

Although it may involve personal and even violent confrontation, **burglary** is primarily a property crime. Burglars are interested in financial gain and usually fence (that is, illegally sell) stolen items, recovering a fraction of their cash value. About 2.2 million burglaries were reported to the police in 2007. Dollar losses to burglary victims totaled $4.3 billion, with an average loss per offense of $1,991.

The UCR/NIBRS Program employs three classifications of burglary: (1) forcible entry, (2) unlawful entry where no force is used, and (3) attempted forcible entry. In most jurisdictions, force need not be employed for a crime to be classified as burglary. Unlocked doors and open windows are invitations to burglars, and the legal essence of burglary consists not so much of a forcible entry as it does of the intent to trespass and steal. In 2007, 61.1% of all burglaries were forcible entries, 32.4% were unlawful entries, and 6.5% were attempted forcible entries.[50] The most dangerous burglaries were those in which a household member was home (about 10% of all burglaries).[51] Residents who were home during a burglary suffered a greater than 30% chance of becoming the victim of a violent crime.[52] However, while burglary may evoke images of dark-clothed strangers breaking into houses in which families lie sleeping, burglaries more often are of unoccupied homes and take place during daylight hours.

burglary (UCR/NIBRS)
The unlawful entry of a structure to commit a felony or a theft (excludes tents, trailers, and other mobile units used for recreational purposes). Under the UCR/NIBRS Program, the crime of burglary can be reported if (1) an unlawful entry of an unlocked structure has occurred, (2) a breaking and entering (of a secured structure) has taken place, or (3) a burglary has been attempted.

The clearance rate for burglary, as for other property crimes that we'll look at later, is generally low. In 2007, the clearance rate for burglary was only 12.4%. Burglars usually do not know

A man threatening a police officer with a beer bottle in Sydney, Australia, in December 2005, after ethnic tensions erupted into running battles between police and a mob of thousands of youths. An assault is an unlawful attack upon one person by another. What is the difference between assault and aggravated assault?
Rob Griffith/AP Wide World Photos

Multiculturalism and Diversity

Race and the Criminal Justice System

Several years ago, Professor Lani Guinier of the University of Pennsylvania School of Law was interviewed on *Think Tank*, a public television show. Guinier was asked by Ben Wattenberg, the program's moderator, "When we talk about crime, crime, crime, are we really using a code for black, black, black?" Guinier responded this way: "To a great extent, yes, and I think that's a problem, not because we shouldn't deal with the disproportionate number of crimes that young black men may be committing, but because if we can't talk about race, then when we talk about crime, we're really talking about other things, and it means that we're not being honest in terms of acknowledging what the problem is and then trying to deal with it."[1]

Crimes, of course, are committed by individuals of all races. The link between crimes—especially violent, street, and predatory crimes—and race, however, shows a striking pattern. In most crime categories, arrests of black offenders equal or exceed arrests of whites. In any given year, arrests of blacks account for more than 50% of all arrests for violent crimes. Blacks, however, comprise only 12% of the U.S. population. When *rates* (which are based upon the relative proportion of racial groups) are examined, the statistics are even more striking. The murder rate among blacks, for example, is ten times that of whites. Similar rate comparisons, when calculated for other violent crimes, show that far more blacks than whites are involved in other street crimes, such as assault, burglary, and robbery. Related studies show that 30% of all young black men in America are under correctional supervision on any given *day*—a far greater percentage than for members of any other race in the country.[2]

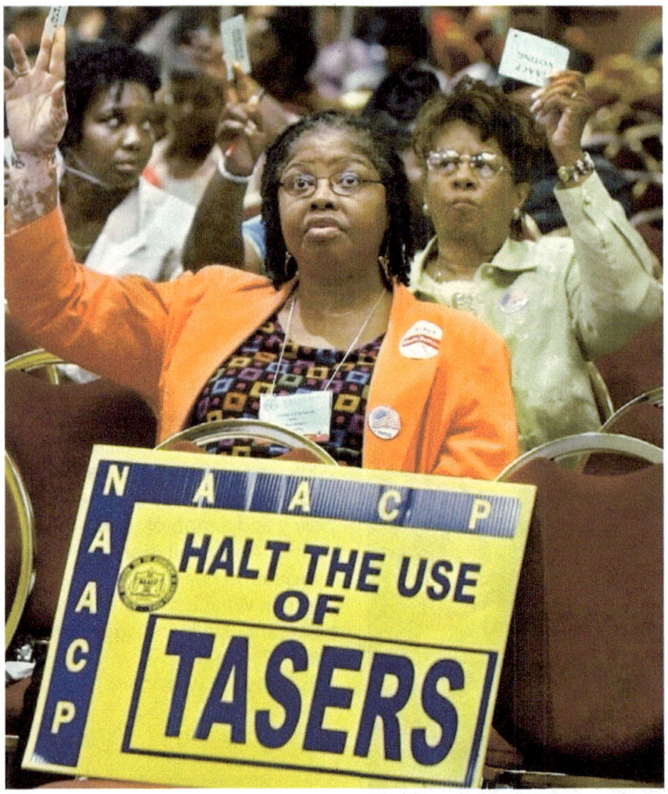

▲ NAACP members protesting the police use of Tasers. Some claim that the justice system puts members of underrepresented groups at risk for unfair treatment. Others say the system is equitable. What do you think?
Rick Wood/Milwaukee Journal Sentinel/*NewsCom*

The real question for anyone interested in the justice system is how to explain such huge race-based disparities. Some authors maintain that racial differences in arrests and in rates of imprisonment are due to the differential treatment of African-Americans at the hands of a discriminatory criminal justice system. Marvin D. Free, Jr., for example, says that the fact that African-Americans are underrepresented as criminal justice professionals results in their being overrepresented in arrest and confinement statistics.[3] Some police officers, says Free, are more prone to arrest blacks than whites, frequently arrest blacks without sufficient evidence to support criminal charges, and overcharge in criminal cases involving black defendants—resulting in misleading statistical tabulations that depict blacks as being responsible for a greater proportion of crime than is, in fact, the case.

Other writers disagree. In *The Myth of a Racist Criminal Justice System*, for example, William Wilbanks claims that while the practice of American criminal justice may have been significantly racist in the past and while some vestiges of racism may indeed remain, the system today is by and large objective in its processing of criminal defendants.[4] Using statistical data, Wilbanks shows that "at every point from arrest to parole there is little or no evidence of an overall racial effect, in that the percentage outcomes for blacks and whites are not very different."[5] Wilbanks claims to have reviewed "all the available studies that have examined the possible existence of racial discrimination from arrest to parole." In essence, he says, "this examination of the available evidence indicates that support for the 'discrimination thesis' is sparse, inconsistent, and frequently contradictory." Even studies published after Wilbanks' analysis appeared continue to support his findings. In 2008, for example, a review of the impact of race on parole decision making found that "race did not have a significant impact on decisions at the preliminary screening stage or the parole release stage."[6]

Wilbanks, however, is careful to counter arguments advanced by those who continue to suggest that the system is racist. He writes, for example, "Perhaps the black/white gap at arrest is a product of racial bias by the police in that the police are more likely to select and arrest black than white offenders. The best evidence on this question comes from the National Crime Survey [that] interviews 130,000 Americans each year about crime victimization. . . . The percent of offenders described by victims as being black is generally consistent with the percent of offenders who are black according to arrest figures."

Contemporary research appears to discount claims that today's American justice system is racist. In 2006, for example, Pauline K. Brennan, a criminologist at the University of Nebraska at Omaha, examined the effects of race and ethnicity on the sentencing of female misdemeanants and found that "race/ethnicity did not directly affect sentencing."[7] Brennan discovered, however, that black and Hispanic females "were more likely to receive jail sentences than their White counterparts due to differences in things like prior record and charge severity."

A fundamental critique of Wilbanks' thesis comes from Coramae Richey Mann, who says that his overreliance on quantitative or statistical data fails to capture the reality of racial discrimination within the justice system.[8] White victims, says Mann, tend to overreport being victimized by black offenders because they often misperceive Hispanic and other minority offenders as black. Similarly, she says, black victims are sometimes reluctant to report victimization—especially at the hands of whites.

Mann's arguments are discounted by those who point out that the statistics appear to be overwhelming. *If* they are accurate, then another question emerges: Why do blacks commit more crimes? Wilbanks says, "The assertion that the criminal justice system is not racist does not address the reasons why blacks appear to offend at higher rates than whites before coming into contact with the criminal justice system.... It may be that racial discrimination in American society has been responsible for conditions (for example, discrimination in employment, housing, and education) that lead to higher rates of offending by blacks."

Marvin Free, Jr., suggests that African-Americans are still systematically denied equal access to societal resources that would allow for full participation in American society—resulting in a higher rate of law violation. In a work that considers such issues in great detail, John Hagan and Ruth D. Peterson acknowledge the reality of higher crime rates among ethnic minorities and attribute them to (1) concentrated poverty, (2) joblessness, (3) family disruption, and (4) racial segregation.[9]

The question of *actual* fairness of the justice system can be quite different from one of *perceived* fairness. As University of Maryland Professor Katheryn K. Russell points out, "Study after study has shown that blacks and whites hold contrary views on the fairness of the criminal justice system's operation; blacks tend to be more cautious in their praise and frequently view the system as unfair and racially biased; by contrast whites have a favorable impression of the justice system. . . . The point is not that whites are completely satisfied with the justice system, but rather that, relative to blacks, they have faith in the system."[10] One reason for such differences may be that blacks are more likely to be victims of police harassment and brutality or may know someone who has been.

Even if blacks do engage in more criminal activity than whites, says noted criminologist Thomas J. Bernard, higher rates of offending may be due, at least in part, to their perception that members of their group have historically been treated unfairly by agents of social control—resulting in anger and defiance, which express themselves in criminal activity.[11] Hence, says Bernard, crime—at least crime committed by minority group members—becomes a kind of protest against a system that is perceived as fundamentally unfair.

According to Russell, inequities in the existing system may propel African-Americans into crime and combine with stereotypical images in the popular media to perpetuate what she calls the *criminalblackman myth*. The criminalblackman myth, says Russell, is a stereotypical portrayal of black men as *inherently* more sinister, evil, and dangerous than their white counterparts. The myth of the criminalblackman, adds Russell, is self-perpetuating, resulting in continued frustration, more crime, and growing alienation among African-Americans.

---

1 Quoted in "For the Record," *Washington Post* wire service, March 3, 1994.
2 Marvin D. Free, Jr., *African-Americans and the Criminal Justice System* (New York: Garland, 1996).
3 Ibid.
4 William Wilbanks, *The Myth of a Racist Criminal Justice System* (Monterey, CA: Brooks/Cole, 1987).
5 William Wilbanks, "The Myth of a Racist Criminal Justice System," *Criminal Justice Research Bulletin*, Vol. 3, No. 5 (Huntsville, TX: Sam Houston State University, 1987), p. 2.
6 Kathryn D. Morgan and Brent Smith, "The Impact of Race on Parole Decision-Making," *Justice Quarterly*, Vol. 25, No. 2 (June 2008), pp. 411–412.
7 Pauline K. Brennan, "Sentencing Female Misdemeanants: An Examination of the Direct and Indirect Effects of Race/Ethnicity," *Justice Quarterly*, Vol. 23, No. 1 (March 2006), pp. 60–95.
8 Coramae Richey Mann, "The Reality of a Racist Criminal Justice System," in Barry W. Hancock and Paul M. Sharp, eds., *Criminal Justice in America: Theory, Practice, and Policy* (Upper Saddle River, NJ: Prentice Hall, 1996), pp. 51–59.
9 John Hagan and Ruth D. Peterson, *Crime and Inequality* (Stanford, CA: Stanford University Press, 1995).
10 Katheryn K. Russell, "The Racial Hoax as Crime: The Law as Affirmation," *Indiana Law Journal*, Vol. 71 (1996), pp. 593–621.
11 Thomas J. Bernard, "Angry Aggression among the 'Truly Disadvantaged,'" *Criminology*, Vol. 28, No. 1 (1990), pp. 73–96.

their victims, and in cases where they do, burglars conceal their identity by committing their crime when the victim is not present.

Larceny-Theft

In 2002, 25-year-old Thad Roberts and 22-year-old Tiffany Fowler were arrested in Orlando, Florida, and charged with stealing moon rocks from the Johnson Space Center in Houston, Texas. Roberts had been working as a student intern at the center, and Fowler was a Space Center employee.[53] Officials realized that the lunar samples, along with a number of meteorites, were missing when they discovered that a 600-pound safe had disappeared from the Houston facility. They had been alerted to the loss by messages placed on a website run by a mineralogy club in Antwerp, Belgium, offering "priceless moon rocks collected by Apollo astronauts" for sale for up to $5,000 per gram. Roberts and Fowler were arrested by federal agents pretending to be potential purchasers.

Identity theft is a newer type of crime. See Exhibit 1 for more information on identity theft.

identity theft
A crime in which an imposter obtains key pieces of information, such as Social Security and driver's license numbers, to obtain credit, merchandise, and services in the name of the victim. The victim is often left with a ruined credit history and the time-consuming and complicated task of repairing the financial damage.[iv]

CJ Exhibit 1

Identity Theft: A New Kind of Larceny

In 2005, ChoicePoint, a personal-information clearinghouse with huge stores of private data on millions of Americans, announced that it had been the victim of a fraud perpetrated by thieves posing as legitimate business customers.[1] The firm quickly notified more than 145,000 people nationwide that critical personal information, including credit scores, Social Security numbers, street addresses, and more, had been stolen in what looked like a massive identity theft scheme. Later that year, more than 100,000 Bank of America and Wachovia customers were notified that their financial records might have been stolen.[2] MasterCard reported that 40 million credit card accounts had been compromised by a security breach at a payment-processing center.[3]

Identity theft, which involves obtaining credit, merchandise, or services by fraudulent personal representation, is a special kind of larceny. According to a recent federal survey, 9.9 million Americans were victims of identity theft in 2007, although most did not report the crime.[4] The latest statistics available from the Bureau of Justice Statistics show that 6.4 million households representing 5.5% of all households in the United States "discovered that at least one member experienced one or more types of identity theft" in 2005.[5] Only a year earlier, BJS reported that 3.6 million households (3% of the nation's total) had been similarly victimized—meaning that the incidence of identity theft almost doubled in a 12-month span.[6] If the statistics are accurate, identity theft is the fastest-growing type of crime in America.

▲ World-renowned professional golfer Tiger Woods. In 2000, Woods became the victim of identity theft when 29-year-old Anthony Lemar Taylor of Sacramento, California, used Woods' identity to charge $17,000 on the golfer's charge cards. Why is identity theft so prevalent today? How can it be stopped?
Amy Sacnetta/ AP Wide World Photos

Identity theft became a federal crime in 1998 with the passage of the Identity Theft and Assumption Deterrence Act.[7] The law makes it a crime whenever anyone "knowingly transfers or uses, without lawful authority, a means of identification of another person with the intent to commit, or to aid or abet, any unlawful activity that constitutes a violation of federal law, or that constitutes a felony under any applicable state or local law."

The 2004 Identity Theft Penalty Enhancement Act[8] added two years to federal prison sentences for criminals convicted of using stolen credit card numbers and other personal data to commit crimes. It also prescribed prison sentences for those who use identity theft to commit other crimes, including terrorism, and it increased penalties for defendants who exceed or abuse the authority of their position in unlawfully obtaining or misusing means of personal identification.

Anyone can fall prey to identity theft—even celebrities. In 2000, for example, golfer Tiger Woods learned that his identity had been stolen and that credit cards taken out in his name had been used to steal $17,000 worth of merchandise, including a 70-inch TV, stereos, and a used luxury car. In 2001, the thief, 30-year-old Anthony Lemar Taylor, who looks nothing like Woods, was convicted of falsely obtaining a driver's license using the name of Eldrick T. Woods (Tiger's given name), Woods' Social Security number, and his birth date. Because Taylor already had 20 previous convictions of all kinds on his record, he was sentenced to 200 years in prison under California's three-strikes law.[9] Like Woods, most victims of identity theft do not even know that their identities have been stolen until they receive bills for merchandise they haven't purchased.

According to the National White Collar Crime Center, identity thieves use several common techniques. Some engage in "Dumpster diving," going through trash bags, cans, or Dumpsters to get copies of checks, credit card and bank statements, credit card applications, or other records that typically bear identifying information. Others use a technique called "shoulder surfing." It involves simply looking over the victim's shoulder as he or she enters personal information into a computer or on a written form. Eavesdropping is another simple, yet effective, technique that identity thieves often use. Eavesdropping can occur when the victim is using an ATM machine, giving credit card or other personal information over the phone, or dialing the number for their telephone calling card. Criminals can also obtain personal identifying information from potential victims through the Internet. Some Internet users, for example, reply to "spam" (unsolicited e-mail) that promises them all sorts of attractive benefits while requesting identifying data, such as checking account or credit card numbers and expiration dates, along with their name and address.[10] Identity theft perpetrated through the use of high technology depends on the fact that a person's legal and economic identity in contemporary society is largely "virtual" and supported by technology.

Learn more about identity theft via Library Extra 2–10, and read the National Strategy to Combat Identity Theft at Library Extra 2–11 at mycrimekit.com. You can take a personal ID Theft Safety Quiz online at Library Extra 2–12 at mycrimekit.com.

Library EXTRA

[1]John Waggoner, "ID Theft Scam Spreads across USA," *USA Today*, February 22, 2005, p. 1A.
[2]Paul Nowell, "Info on 100,000 Bank Users Possibly Stolen," *USA Today*, May 24, 2005, p. B6.
[3]Eric Dash and Tom Zeller, "MasterCard Says 40 Million Files Put at Risk," *New York Times*, June 18, 2005, p. A1.
[4]United States Postal Service, Postal Inspectors, "Identity Theft Is America's Fastest-Growing Crime," http://www.usps.com/postalinspectors/idthft_ncpw.htm (accessed May 21, 2008).
[5]Katrina Baum, *Identity Theft, 2005* (Washington, DC: Bureau of Justice Statistics, 2007).
[6]Katrina Baum, *Identity Theft, 2004* (Washington, DC: Bureau of Justice Statistics, 2006).
[7]U.S. Code, Title 18, Section 1028.
[8]HR 1731 (2004).
[9]"Three Strikes, He's Out: Woods' Identity Thief Gets 200 Years-to-Life," Associated Press, April 28, 2001.
[10]Much of the information in this paragraph is adapted from National White Collar Crime Center, "WCC Issue: Identity Theft," http://www.nw3c.org/papers/Identity_Theft.pdf (accessed May 18, 2008).

Larceny is another name for theft, and the UCR/NIBRS Program uses the term **larceny-theft** to describe theft offenses. Some states distinguish between simple larceny and grand larceny, categorizing the crime based on the dollar value of what is stolen. Larceny-theft, as defined by the UCR/NIBRS Program, includes the theft of valuables of any dollar amount. The reports specifically list the following offenses as types of larceny (listed here in order of declining frequency):

larceny-theft (UCR/NIBRS)
The unlawful taking or attempted taking, carrying, leading, or riding away of property, from the possession or constructive possession of another. Motor vehicles are excluded. Larceny is the most common of the eight major offenses, although probably only a small percentage of all larcenies is actually reported to the police because of the small dollar amounts involved.

- Thefts from motor vehicles
- Shoplifting
- Thefts from buildings
- Thefts of motor vehicle parts and accessories
- Bicycle thefts
- Thefts from coin-operated machines
- Purse snatching
- Pocket picking

Thefts of farm animals (known as *rustling*) and thefts of most types of farm machinery also fall into the larceny category. In fact, larceny is such a broad category that it serves as a kind of catchall in the UCR/NIBRS Program. In 1995, for example, Yale University officials filed larceny charges against 25-year-old student Lon Grammer, claiming that he had fraudulently obtained university funds.[54] The university maintained that Grammer had stolen his education by forging college and high school transcripts and concocting letters of recommendation prior to admission. Grammer's alleged misdeeds, which Yale University officials said misled them into thinking that Grammer, a poor student before attending Yale, had an exceptional scholastic record, permitted him to receive $61,475 in grants and loans during the time he attended the school. Grammer was expelled.

Reported thefts vary widely, in terms of both the objects stolen and their value. Stolen items range from pocket change to a $100 million aircraft. For reporting purposes, crimes entailing embezzlement, con games, forgery, and worthless checks are specifically excluded from the count of larceny. Because larceny has traditionally been considered a crime that requires physical possession of the item appropriated, some computer crimes, including thefts engineered through online access or thefts of software and information, have not been scored as larcenies unless computer equipment, electronic circuitry, or computer media were actually stolen. In 2004, however, the FBI confirmed that it was working with Cisco Systems, Inc., to investigate the possible theft of some of the company's intellectual property.[55] The theft involved approximately 800 megabytes of proprietary software code used to control the company's Internet routers. Since hardware manufactured by Cisco Systems accounts for more than 60% of all routers used on the Internet,[56] officials feared that the lost software could represent a major security threat for the entire Internet.

In a field like criminal justice, where sensitive issues abound, none is more sensitive than the issue of race and gender bias.
—*Gary LaFree, University of New Mexico*

From a statistical standpoint, the most common form of larceny in recent years has been theft of motor vehicle parts, accessories, and contents. Tires, wheels, hubcaps, radar detectors, stereos, satellite radios, CD players, compact discs, and cellular phones account for many of the items reported stolen.

Reports to the police in 2007 showed 6,568,572 larcenies nationwide, with the total value of property stolen placed at $5.8 billion. Larceny-theft is the most frequently reported major crime, according to the UCR/NIBRS Program. It may also be the program's most underreported crime category because small thefts rarely come to the attention of the police. The average value of items reported stolen in 2007 was about $885.

Motor Vehicle Theft

For record-keeping purposes, the UCR/NIBRS Program defines *motor vehicles* as self-propelled vehicles that run on the ground and not on rails. Included in the definition are automobiles, motorcycles, motor scooters, trucks, buses, and snowmobiles. Excluded are trains, airplanes, bulldozers, most farm and construction machinery, ships, boats, and spacecraft; the theft of these would be scored as larceny-theft.[57] Vehicles that are temporarily taken by individuals who have lawful access to them are not thefts. Hence, spouses who jointly own all property may drive the family car, even though one spouse may think of the vehicle as his or her exclusive personal property.

motor vehicle theft (UCR/NIBRS)
The theft or attempted theft of a motor vehicle. *Motor vehicle* is defined as a self-propelled road vehicle that runs on land surface and not on rails. The stealing of trains, planes, boats, construction equipment, and most farm machinery is classified as larceny under the UCR/NIBRS Program, not as motor vehicle theft.

As we said earlier, because most insurance companies require police reports before they will reimburse car owners for their losses, most occurrences of **motor vehicle theft** are reported to law enforcement agencies. Some reports of motor vehicle thefts, however, may be false. People who have damaged their own vehicles in solitary crashes or who have been unable to sell them may try to force insurance companies to "buy" them through reports of theft.

In 2007, 1,095,769 motor vehicles were reported stolen. The average value per stolen vehicle was $6,755, making motor vehicle theft a $7.4 billion crime. The clearance rate for motor vehicle theft was only 12.6% in 2007. Large city agencies reported the lowest rates of clearance (9.4%), while rural counties had the highest rate (26%). Many stolen vehicles are quickly disassembled and the parts resold, since auto parts are much more difficult to identify and trace than are intact vehicles. In some parts of the country, chop shops—which take stolen vehicles apart and sell their components—operate like big businesses, and one shop may strip a dozen or more cars per day.

Motor vehicle theft can turn violent, as in cases of carjacking—a crime in which offenders usually force the car's occupants onto the street before stealing the vehicle. For example, in February 2000, Christy Robel watched helplessly as her six-year-old son Jake was dragged to his death after a man jumped behind the wheel of her car and sped off.[58] Robel had left the car running with the boy inside as she made a brief stop at a Kansas City sandwich shop. The carjacker, 35-year-old Kim L. Davis, tried to push Jake from the car as he made his escape, but the boy became entangled in his seat belt and was dragged for five miles at speeds of more than 80 mph. In October 2001, Davis was convicted of murder and was sentenced to spend the rest of his life in prison without possibility of parole.[59] The BJS estimates that around 34,000 carjackings occur annually and account for slightly more than 1% of all motor vehicle thefts.[60] Arrest reports for motor vehicle theft show that the typical offender is a young male: 57% percent of all arrestees in 2007 were under the age of 25, and 82.3% were male.

Arson

arson (UCR/NIBRS)
Any willful or malicious burning or attempt to burn, with or without intent to defraud, a dwelling house, public building, motor vehicle or aircraft, personal property of another, and so on. Some instances of arson result from malicious mischief, some involve attempts to claim insurance money, and some are committed in an effort to disguise other crimes, such as murder, burglary, or larceny.

The UCR/NIBRS Program received crime reports from more than 16,000 law enforcement agencies in 2007.[61] Of these, only 14,197 submitted data on **arson** (the intentional burning of property). Even fewer agencies provided complete data as to the type of arson (the nature of the property burned), the estimated monetary value of the property, the ownership, and so on. Arson data include only the fires that are determined through investigation to have been willfully or maliciously set. Fires of unknown or suspicious origin are excluded from arson statistics.[62]

The intentional and unlawful burning of structures (houses, storage buildings, manufacturing facilities, and so on) was the type of arson reported most often in 2007 (24,542 instances). The arson of vehicles was the second most common category, with 17,259 such burnings reported. The average dollar loss per instance of arson in 2007 was $17,289, and total nationwide property damage was placed at close to $1 billion.[63] As with most property crimes, the clearance rate for arson was low—only 18.7% nationally. The crime of arson exists in a kind of statistical limbo. In 1979, Congress ordered that it be added as an eighth Part I offense. Today, however, many law enforcement agencies still have not begun making regular reports to the FBI on arson offenses in their jurisdictions.

TABLE 3 UCR/NIBRS Part II Offenses, 2007

Offense Category	Number of Arrests
Simple assaults	1,305,693
Forgery and counterfeiting	103,448
Fraud	252,873
Embezzlement	22,381
Stolen property (e.g., receiving)	122,061
Vandalism	291,575
Weapons (e.g., carrying)	188,891
Prostitution and related offenses	77,607
Sex offenses (e.g., statutory rape)	83,979
Drug-law violations	1,841,182
Gambling	12,161
Offenses against the family (e.g., nonsupport)	122,812
Driving under the influence	1,427,494
Liquor-law violations	633,654
Public drunkenness	589,402
Disorderly conduct	709,105
Vagrancy	33,666
Curfew violations/loitering	143,002
Runaways	108,879

Source: Adapted from Federal Bureau of Investigation, *Crime in the United States, 2007* (Washington, DC: U.S. Department of Justice, 2008).

Some of these difficulties have been resolved through the Special Arson Program, authorized by Congress in 1982. In conjunction with the National Fire Data Center, the FBI now operates a Special Arson Reporting System, which focuses on fire departments across the nation. The reporting system is designed to provide data to supplement yearly UCR arson tabulations.[64]

Part II Offenses

The UCR Program also includes information on what the FBI calls **Part II offenses**. Part II offenses, which are generally less serious than those that make up the Part I offenses category, include a number of social-order, or so-called victimless, crimes. The statistics on Part II offenses are for recorded arrests, not for crimes reported to the police. The logic inherent in this form of scoring is that most Part II offenses would never come to the attention of the police were it not for arrests. Part II offenses are shown in Table 3, with the number of estimated arrests made in each category for 2007.

Part II offenses
A UCR/NIBRS offense group used to report arrests for less serious offenses. Agencies are limited to reporting only arrest information for Part II offenses, with the exception of simple assault.

A Part II offense arrest is counted each time a person is taken into custody. As a result, the statistics in Table 3 do not report the number of suspects arrested but rather the number of arrests made. Some suspects were arrested more than once.

The National Crime Victimization Survey

A second major source of statistical data about crime in the United States is the NCVS, which is based on victim self-reports rather than on police reports. The NCVS is designed to estimate the occurrence of all crimes, whether reported or not.[65] The NCVS was first conducted in 1972. It built on efforts in the late 1960s by both the National Opinion Research Center and the President's Commission on Law Enforcement and the Administration of Justice to uncover what some had been calling the **dark figure of crime**. This term refers to those crimes that are not reported to the police and that remain unknown to officials. Before the development of the NCVS, little was known about such unreported and undiscovered offenses.

dark figure of crime
Crime that is not reported to the police and that remains unknown to officials.

Early data from the NCVS changed the way criminologists thought about crime in the United States. The use of victim self-reports led to the discovery that crimes of all types were more prevalent than UCR statistics indicated. Many cities were shown to have victimization rates that were more than twice the rate of reported offenses. Others, like Saint Louis, Missouri, and Newark, New Jersey, were found to have rates of victimization that very nearly approximated reported crime. New York, often thought of as a high-crime city, was discovered to have one of the lowest rates of self-reported victimization.

NCVS data are gathered by the BJS through a cooperative arrangement with the U.S. Census Bureau.[66] Twice each year, Census Bureau personnel interview household members in a nationally representative sample of approximately 43,000 households (about 76,000 people). Approximately 150,000 interviews of individuals age 12 or older are conducted annually. Households stay in the sample for three years, and new households rotate into the sample regularly.

The NCVS collects information on crimes suffered by individuals and households, whether or not those crimes were reported to law enforcement. It estimates the proportion of each crime type reported to law enforcement, and it summarizes the reasons that victims give for reporting or not reporting. BJS statistics are published in annual reports titled *Criminal Victimization* and *Crime and the Nation's Households.*

Using definitions similar to those employed by the UCR/NIBRS Program, the NCVS includes data on the national incidence of rape, sexual assault, robbery, assault, burglary, personal and household larceny, and motor vehicle theft. Not included are murder, kidnapping, and victimless crimes (crimes that, by their nature, tend to involve willing participants). Commercial robbery and the burglary of businesses were dropped from NCVS reports in 1977. The NCVS employs a hierarchical counting system similar to that of the pre-NIBRS system: It counts only the most "serious" incident in any series of criminal events perpetrated against the same individual. Both completed and attempted offenses are counted, although only people 12 years of age and older are included in household surveys.

NCVS statistics for recent years reveal the following:

- Approximately 15% of American households are touched by crime every year.
- About 16 million victimizations occur each year.
- City residents are almost twice as likely as rural residents to be victims of crime.
- About half of all violent crimes, and slightly more than one-third of all property crimes, are reported to police.[67]
- Victims of crime are more often men than women.
- Younger people are more likely than the elderly to be victims of crime.
- Blacks are more likely than whites or members of other racial groups to be victims of violent crimes.
- Violent victimization rates are highest among people in lower-income families.

A report by the BJS found that in 2006, NCVS crime rates had reached their lowest level since the survey began.[68] Declines began in the mid-1990s, with violent crime rates dropping 57% between 1993 and 2006.[69] While these statistics indicate that in recent years crime rates have declined, UCR statistics, which go back almost another 40 years, show that today's crime rate is still many times what it was in the early and middle years of the twentieth century.[70] A comparison of UCR/NIBRS and NCVS data can be found in Table 4. Explore the latest NCVS data at Web Extra 2–9 at mycrimekit.com.

Web EXTRA

Many researchers trust NCVS data more than UCR/NIBRS data because they believe that self-reports provide a more accurate gauge of criminal incidents than do police reports. Learn more about the use of self-report surveys in the measurement of crime and delinquency via Library Extras 2–13 and 2–14 at mycrimekit.com.

Library EXTRA

Comparisons of the UCR and the NCVS

As mentioned earlier in this chapter, crime statistics from the UCR/NIBRS and the NCVS reveal crime patterns that are often the bases for social policies created to deter or reduce crime. These policies also build on explanations for criminal behavior found in more elaborate interpretations of the statistical information. Unfortunately, however, researchers too often forget that statistics, which are merely descriptive, can be weak in explanatory power. For example,

TABLE 4 Comparison of UCR/NIBRS and NCVS Data

Offense	UCR/NIBRS, 2007	NCVS, 2006[1]
Personal/Violent Crimes		
Homicide	16,929	—
Forcible rape[2]	90,427	272,350
Robbery	445,125	711,570
Aggravated assault	855,856	1,354,750
Property Crimes		
Burglary[3]	2,179,140	3,539,760
Larceny	6,568,572	14,275,150
Motor vehicle theft	1,095,769	993,910
Arson[4]	64,332	—
Total of All Crimes Recorded	**11,316,150**	**21,147,490**

[1]NCVS data cover "households touched by crime," not absolute numbers of crime occurrences. More than one victimization may occur per household, but only the number of households in which victimizations occur enters the tabulations.

[2]NCVS statistics include both rape and sexual assault.

[3]NCVS statistics include only household burglary and attempts.

[4]Arson data are incomplete in the UCR/NIBRS and are not reported by the NCVS.

Source: Compiled from U.S. Department of Justice, *Criminal Victimization, 2007* (Washington, DC: Bureau of Justice Statistics, 2007); and Federal Bureau of Investigation, *Crime in the United States, 2007* (Washington, DC: U.S. Department of Justice, 2008).

NCVS data show that "household crime rates" are highest for households (1) headed by blacks, (2) headed by younger people, (3) with six or more members, (4) headed by renters, and (5) located in central cities.[71] Such findings, combined with statistics that show that most crime occurs among members of the same race, have led some researchers to conclude that values among certain black subcultural group members both propel them into crime and make them targets of criminal victimization. The truth may be, however, that crime is more a function of inner-city location than of culture. From simple descriptive statistics, it is difficult to know which is the case. Learn more about the UCR/NIBRS Program and the NCVS, and see how they compare, by viewing **Web Extra 2–10** at mycrimekit.com.

Web EXTRA

Like most statistical data–gathering programs in the social sciences, the UCR/NIBRS and the NCVS programs are not without problems. Because UCR/NIBRS data are based primarily on citizens' crime reports to the police, there are several inherent difficulties. First, not all people report when they are victimized. Some victims are afraid to contact the police, while others may not believe that the police can do anything about the offense. Second, certain kinds of crimes are reported rarely, if at all. These include victimless crimes, also known as *social-order offenses*, such as drug use, prostitution, and gambling. Similarly, white-collar and high-technology offenses, such as embezzlement and computer crime—because they often go undiscovered—probably enter the official statistics only rarely. Third, victims' reports may not be entirely accurate. Victims' memories may be faulty, victims may feel the need to impress or please the police, or they may be under pressure from others to misrepresent the facts. Finally, all reports are filtered through a number of bureaucratic levels, which increases the likelihood that inaccuracies will enter the data. As noted methodologist Frank Hagan points out, "The government is very keen on amassing statistics. They collect them, add to them, raise them to the nth power, take the cube root, and prepare wonderful diagrams. But what you must never forget is that every one of these figures comes in the first instance from the *chowty dar* [village watchman], who puts down what he damn pleases."[72]

In contrast to the UCR/NIBRS dependence on crimes reported by victims who seek out the police, the NCVS relies on door-to-door surveys and personal interviews for its data. Survey results, however, may be skewed for several reasons. First, no matter how objective survey questions may appear to be, survey respondents inevitably provide their personal interpretations and descriptions of what may or may not have been a criminal event. Second, by its very nature, the survey includes information from those people who are most willing to talk to surveyors;

more reclusive people are less likely to respond regardless of the level of victimization they may have suffered. Also, some victims are afraid to report crimes even to nonpolice interviewers, while others may invent victimizations for an interviewer's sake. As the first page of the NCVS report admits, "Details about the crimes come directly from the victims, and no attempt is made to validate the information against police records or any other source."[73]

Finally, because both the UCR/NIBRS and the NCVS are human artifacts, they contain only data that their creators think appropriate. UCR/NIBRS statistics for 2001, for example, do not include a tally of those who perished in the September 11, 2001, terrorist attacks because FBI officials concluded that the events were too "unusual" to count. Although the FBI's 2001 *Crime in the United States* acknowledges "the 2,830 homicides reported as a result of the events of September 11, 2001," it goes on to say that "these figures have been removed" from the reported data.[74] Crimes that result from an anomalous event but excluded from reported data highlight the arbitrary nature of the data-collection process itself.

Special Categories of Crime

crime typology
A classification of crimes along a particular dimension, such as legal category, offender motivation, victim behavior, or characteristics of individual offenders.

A **crime typology** is a classification scheme used in the study and description of criminal behavior. There are many typologies, all of which have an underlying logic. The system of classification that derives from any particular typology may be based on legal criteria, offender motivation, victim behavior, characteristics of individual offenders, or the like. Criminologists Terance D. Miethe and Richard C. McCorkle note that crime typologies "are designed primarily to simplify social reality by identifying homogeneous groups of crime behaviors that are different from other clusters of crime behaviors."[75] Hence, one common but simple typology contains only two categories of crime: violent and property. In fact, many crime typologies contain overlapping or nonexclusive categories—just as violent crimes may involve property offenses, and property offenses may lead to violent crimes. Thus no one typology is likely to capture all of the nuances of criminal offending.

Social relevance is a central distinguishing feature of any meaningful typology, and it is with that in mind that the remaining sections of this chapter briefly highlight crimes of special importance today. They are crime against women, crime against the elderly, hate crime, corporate and white-collar crime, organized crime, gun crime, drug crime, cybercrime, and terrorism.

Crime against Women

The victimization of women is a special area of concern, and both the UCR/NIBRS and the NCVS contain data on gender as it relates to victimization. Statistics show that women are victimized less frequently than men in every major personal crime category other than rape.[76] The overall U.S. rate of violent victimization is about 25 per 1,000 males age 12 or older, and 18 per 1,000 females.[77] When women become victims of violent crime, however, they are more likely than men to be injured (29% versus 22%, respectively).[78] Moreover, a larger proportion of women than men make modifications in the way they live because of the threat of crime.[79] Women, especially those living in cities, have become increasingly careful about where they travel and the time of day they leave their homes—particularly if they are unaccompanied—and in many settings are often wary of unfamiliar males.

stalking
Repeated harassing and threatening behavior by one individual against another, aspects of which may be planned or carried out in secret. Stalking might involve following a person, appearing at a person's home or place of business, making harassing phone calls, leaving written messages or objects, or vandalizing a person's property. Most stalking laws require that the perpetrator make a credible threat of violence against the victim or members of the victim's immediate family.

Date rape, familial incest, spousal abuse, **stalking**, and the exploitation of women through social-order offenses like prostitution and pornography are major issues facing American society today. Testimony before Congress tagged domestic violence as the largest cause of injury to American women.[80] Former Surgeon General C. Everett Koop once identified violence against women by their partners as the number one health problem facing women in America.[81] Findings from the National Violence against Women Survey (NVAWS) reveal the following[82]:

- Physical assault is widespread among American women. Fifty-two percent of surveyed women said that they had been physically assaulted as a child or as an adult.
- Approximately 1.9 million women are physically assaulted in the United States each year.
- Eighteen percent of women experienced a completed or attempted rape at some time in their lives.

- Of those reporting rape, 22% were under 12 years old, and 32% were between 12 and 17 years old, when they were first raped.
- Native American and Alaska Native women were most likely to report rape and physical assault, while Asian/Pacific Islander women were least likely to report such victimization. Hispanic women were less likely to report rape than non-Hispanic women.
- Women report significantly more partner violence than men. Twenty-five percent of surveyed women and only 8% of surveyed men said they had been raped or physically assaulted by a current or former spouse, cohabiting partner, or date.
- Violence against women is primarily partner violence. Seventy-six percent of the women who had been raped or physically assaulted since age 18 were assaulted by a current or former husband, cohabiting partner, or date, compared with 18% of the men.
- Women are significantly more likely than men to be injured during an assault. Thirty-two percent of the women and 16% of the men who had been raped since age 18 were injured during their most recent rape; 39% of the women and 25% of the men who were physically assaulted since age 18 were injured during their most recent physical assault.
- Eight percent of surveyed women and 2% of surveyed men said they had been stalked at some time in their lives. According to survey estimates, approximately 1 million women and 371,000 men are stalked annually in the United States.

Cyberspace has become a fertile field for illegal activity. With the use of new technology and equipment which cannot be policed by traditional methods, cyberstalking has replaced traditional methods of stalking and harassment. In addition, cyberstalking has led to offline incidents of violent crime. Police and prosecutors need to be aware of the escalating numbers of these events and devise strategies to resolve these problems through the criminal justice system.

—Linda Fairstein, Chief, Sex Crimes Prosecution Unit, Manhattan District Attorney's Office[v]

A detailed BJS analysis found that women who are victims of violent crime are twice as likely to be victimized by strangers as by people whom they know.[83] However, they are far more likely than men to be victimized by a current or former intimate partner. When the perpetrators are known to them, women are most likely to be violently victimized by ex-husbands, boyfriends, and spouses (in descending order of incidence). The BJS study also found that separated or divorced women are six times more likely to be victims of violent crime than widows, four and a half times more likely than married women, and three times more likely than widowers and married men. Other findings indicate that (1) women living in central-city areas are considerably more likely to be victimized than women residing in the suburbs; (2) suburban women, in turn, are more likely to be victimized than women living in rural areas; (3) women from low-income families experience the highest amount of violent crime; (4) the victimization of women falls as family income rises; (5) unemployed women, female students, and those in the armed forces are the most likely of all women to experience violent victimization; (6) black women are victims of violent crime more frequently than are women of any other race; (7) Hispanic women are victimized more frequently than white women; and (8) women in the age range of 20 to 24 are most at risk for violent victimization, while those age 16 to 19 make up the second most likely group of victims. Learn more about violence against women via Library Extra 2–15 at mycrimekit.com.

Library EXTRA

Survey findings like these show that more must be done to alleviate the social conditions that result in the victimization of women. Suggestions already under consideration call for expansion in the number of federal and state laws designed to control domestic violence, broadening of the federal Family Violence Prevention and Services Act, federal help in setting up state advocacy offices for battered women, increased funding for battered women's shelters, and additional funds for prosecutors and courts to develop spousal abuse units. The federal Violent Crime Control and Law Enforcement Act of 1994 was designed to meet many of these needs through a subsection titled the Violence against Women Act (VAWA). That act signified a major shift in our national response to domestic violence, stalking (which is often part of the domestic violence continuum), and sexual assault crimes. For the first time in our nation's history, violent crimes against women were addressed in relation to the more general problem of gender inequality.

The VAWA seeks to eradicate violence against women at all levels, and the act allocated $1.6 billion to fight violence against women. Included are funds to (1) educate police, prosecutors, and judges about the special needs of female victims; (2) encourage pro-arrest policies in cases of domestic abuse; (3) provide specialized services for female victims of crime; (4) fund battered women's shelters across the country; and (5) support rape education in a variety of settings nationwide. The law also extends "rape shield law" protections to civil cases and to all criminal cases in order to bar irrelevant inquiries into a victim's sexual history. VAWA was reauthorized by Congress in 2000. Read the text of the original VAWA legislation at Web Extra 2–11 at mycrimekit.com.

Web EXTRA

Multiculturalism and Diversity

Gender Issues in Criminal Justice

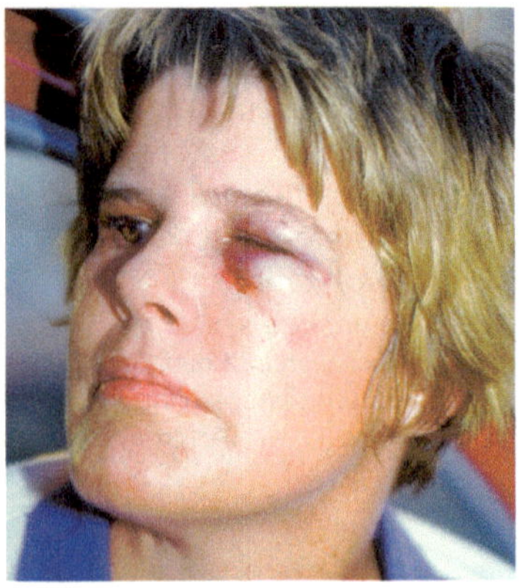

A battered woman posing for police photographers who are documenting her injuries. Intimate partner violence is a problem of special concern to the criminal justice system, and violence against women is an area that is receiving legislative attention, as evidenced by the federal Violence against Women Act. How might laws designed to protect women be improved?
Michael Newman/PhotoEdit Inc.

The Violent Crime Control and Law Enforcement Act of 1994 included significant provisions intended to enhance gender equality throughout the criminal justice system. Title IV of the Violent Crime Control and Law Enforcement Act, known as the Violence against Women Act (VAWA) of 1994, contains the Safe Streets for Women Act. This act increased federal penalties for repeat sex offenders and requires mandatory restitution for sex crimes, including costs related to medical services (including physical, psychiatric, and psychological care); physical and occupational therapy or rehabilitation; necessary transportation, temporary housing, and child-care expenses; lost income; attorneys' fees, including any costs incurred in obtaining a civil protection order; and any other losses suffered by the victim as a result of the offense. The act also requires that compliance with a restitution order be made a condition of probation or supervised release (if such a sentence is imposed by the court) and provides that violation of the order will result in the offender's imprisonment.

Chapter 2 of VAWA provided funds for grants to combat violent crimes against women. The purpose of funding was to assist states and local governments to "develop and strengthen effective law enforcement and prosecution strategies to combat violent crimes against women, and to develop and strengthen victim services in cases involving violent crimes against women." The law also provided funds for the "training of law enforcement officers and prosecutors to more effectively identify and respond to violent crimes against women, including the crimes of sexual assault and domestic violence"; for "developing, installing, or expanding data collection and communication systems, including computerized systems, linking police, prosecutors, and courts or for the purpose of identifying and tracking arrests, protection orders, violations of protection orders, prosecutions, and convictions for violent crimes against women, including the crimes of sexual assault and domestic violence"; and for developing and strengthening "victim services programs, including sexual assault and domestic violence programs."

The act also created the crime of crossing state lines in violation of a protection order and the crime of crossing state lines to commit assault on a domestic partner. It established federal penalties for the latter offense of up to life in prison in cases where death results.

Chapter 3 of the act provided funds to increase the "safety for women in public transit and public parks." It authorized up to $10 million in grants through the Department of Transportation to enhance lighting, camera surveillance, and security telephones in public transportation systems used by women.

Chapter 5 of VAWA funded the creation of hot lines, educational seminars, informational materials, and training programs for professionals who provide assistance to victims of sexual assault. Another portion of the law, titled the Safe Homes for Women Act, increased grants for battered women's shelters, encouraged arrest in cases of domestic violence, and provided for the creation of a national domestic violence hot line to provide counseling, information, and assistance to victims of domestic violence. The act also mandates that any protection order issued by a state court must be recognized by the other states and by the federal government and must be enforced "as if it were the order of the enforcing state."

VAWA was reauthorized by Congress in 2000 and again in 2005.[1] The 2000 reauthorization provided $3.3 billion in continuation funding and earmarked a portion of the money for programs that coordinate the work of victims' advocates, police, and prosecutors in the fight against domestic violence. The second reauthorization provided continuation monies for critical programs and funded the development of new services to respond to evolving community needs. In recognition of the fact that domestic violence sometimes leaves victims without homes, the 2006 legislation made funds available to expand services to the homeless, including the development of transitional housing options.

[1]VAWA 2005 was signed into law by President George W. Bush on January 5, 2006. It is officially known as the Violence against Women and Department of Justice Reauthorization Act of 2005 (Public Law 109-162).

cyberstalking
The use of the Internet, e-mail, and other electronic communication technologies to stalk another person.[vi]

Library EXTRA

Finally, the passage of antistalking legislation by all 50 states and the District of Columbia provides some measure of additional protection to women (since women comprise 80% of all stalking victims[84]). On the federal level, the seriousness of stalking was addressed when Congress passed the interstate stalking law in 1996.[85] The law[86] also addresses **cyberstalking**, or the use of the Internet by perpetrators seeking to exercise power and control over their victims by threatening them directly or by posting misleading and harassing information about them. Cyberstalking can be especially insidious because it does not require that the perpetrator and the victim be in the same geographic area. Similarly, electronic communication technologies lower the barriers to harassment and threats; a cyberstalker does not need to confront the victim physically.[87] Learn more about stalking and cyberstalking at Library Extra 2–16 at mycrimekit.com.

Crime against the Elderly

Relative to other age groups, older victims rarely appear in the crime statistics. Criminal victimization seems to decline with age, suggesting that older people are only infrequently targeted by violent and property criminals. Moreover, older people are more likely than younger individuals to live in secure areas and to have the financial means to provide for their own personal security.

Victimization data pertaining to older people come mostly from the NCVS, which, for such purposes, looks at people age 65 and older. The elderly generally experience the lowest rate of victimization of any age group in both violent and property crime categories.[88] Some aspects of crime against older people are worth noting. In general, elderly crime victims are more likely than younger victims to

- Be victims of property crime (nine out of ten crimes committed against the elderly are property crimes, compared to fewer than four in ten crimes against people between ages 12 and 24)
- Face offenders who are armed with guns
- Be victimized by strangers
- Be victimized in or near their homes during daylight hours
- Report their victimization to the police, especially when they fall victim to violent crime
- Be physically injured

With each arrest, indictment and prosecution, we sent this clear, unmistakable message: corrupt corporate executives are no better than common thieves.

—U.S. Attorney General John Ashcroft, commenting on the arrests of former WorldCom executives[vii]

In addition, elderly people are less likely to attempt to protect themselves when they are victims of violent crime. Only 49% of elderly victims attempt to protect themselves versus 70% of younger victims. Certain categories of elderly people are victimized disproportionately. Relative to their numbers, black men are more often victims, and separated or divorced people and urban residents have higher rates of victimization than do other elderly people. Even though their risk of victimization is considerably less, older people fear crime more than younger people; however, they are less likely to take crime-prevention measures than any other age group. Only 6% of households headed by people older than age 65 have an alarm, and only 16% of such households report engraving their valuables (versus a 25% national average).

The elderly face special kinds of victimization that only rarely affect younger adults, such as physical abuse at the hands of caregivers. Criminal physical abuse of the elderly falls into two categories: domestic and institutional. Domestic abuse often occurs at the hands of caregivers who are related to their victims; institutional abuse occurs in residential settings like retirement centers, nursing homes, and hospitals. Both forms of elder abuse may also involve criminal sexual victimization. To learn more about domestic and institutional elder abuse, visit the National Center on Elder Abuse (NCEA) via **Web Extra 2–12** at mycrimekit.com.

Web EXTRA

The elderly are also more often targeted by con artists. Confidence schemes center on commercial and financial fraud (including telemarketing fraud), charitable donation fraud, funeral and cemetery fraud, real estate fraud, caretaker fraud, automobile and home repair fraud, living trust fraud, health care fraud (e.g., promises of "miracle cures"), and health care provider fraud (overbilling and unjustified repeat billing by otherwise legitimate health care providers). False "friends" may intentionally isolate elderly targets from others in the hopes of misappropriating money through short-term secret loans or outright theft. Similarly, a younger person may feign romantic involvement with an elderly victim or pretend to be devoted to the senior in order to solicit money or receive an inappropriate gift or inheritance. The U.S. Senate's Special Committee on Aging provides additional information on such crimes at its Elder Justice Center website, which can be accessed via **Web Extra 2–13** at mycrimekit.com.

Web EXTRA

Finally, crime against the elderly will likely undergo a significant increase as baby boomers enter their retirement years. Not only will the elderly comprise an increasingly larger segment of the population as boomers age, but it is anticipated that they will be wealthier than any preceding generation of retirees, making them attractive targets for scam artists and property criminals.[89]

Hate Crime

hate crime (UCR/NIBRS)
A criminal offense committed against a person, property, or society that is motivated, in whole or in part, by the offender's bias against a race, religion, disability, sexual orientation, or ethnicity/national origin.

A significant change in crime-reporting practices resulted from the Hate Crime Statistics Act,[90] signed into law by President George H. W. Bush in 1990. The act mandates a statistical tally of **hate crimes**; data collection under the law began in 1991. Congress defined *hate crime* as an

FIGURE 4
Motivation of Hate-Crime Offenders, 2007.

Note: Total may be more than 100% due to rounding.
Source: Federal Bureau of Investigation, *Crime in the United States, 2007*.

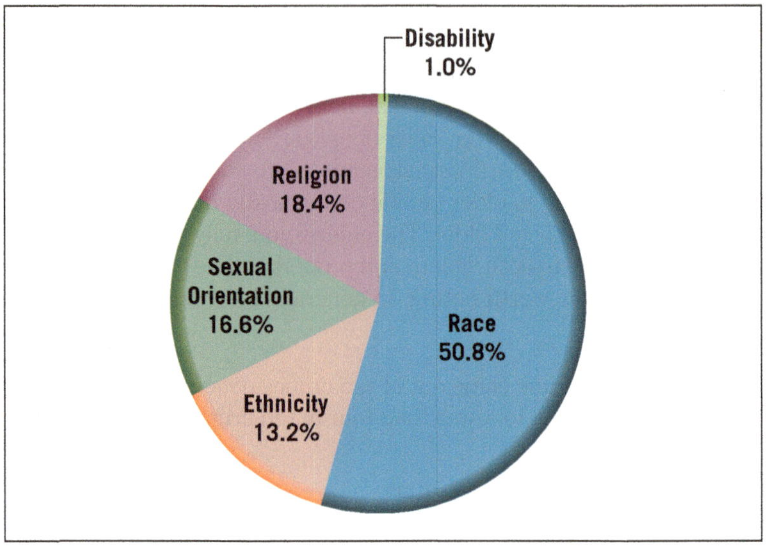

offense "in which the defendant's conduct was motivated by hatred, bias, or prejudice, based on the actual or perceived race, color, religion, national origin, ethnicity, gender, or sexual orientation of another individual or group of individuals."[91] In 2007, police agencies reported a total of 7,624 hate-crime incidents, including three murders, across the country. As Figure 4 shows, 18.4% of the incidents were motivated by religious bias, 50.8% were caused by racial hatred, and 13.2% were driven by prejudice against ethnicity or national origin. Another 16.6% of all hate crimes were based on sexual orientation, most committed against males believed by their victimizers to be homosexuals.[92] A relatively small number of hate crimes targeted people with physical or mental disabilities.

Following the terrorist attacks of September 11, 2001, authorities in some jurisdictions reported a dramatic shift in the nature of hate crime, with race-motivated crimes declining and crimes motivated by religion or ethnicity increasing sharply.[93] Islamic individuals, in particular, became the target of many such crimes.

Most hate crimes consist of intimidation, although vandalism, simple assault, and aggravated assault also account for a number of hate-crime offenses. A few robberies and rapes were also classified as hate crimes in 2007.

One particularly heinous and widely publicized hate crime culminated in death sentences for John William King, 24, and Lawrence Russell Brewer, 32, two white residents of Jasper

▶ Evidence of a hate crime: Nazi symbols spray-painted on Arab graves. Why are hate crimes given special attention under the law?
Reuters/Vincent Kessler/Landov Media

County, Texas.[94] In separate trials in 1999, King and Brewer were found guilty of first-degree murder in the death of James Byrd, Jr., a 49-year-old black man. Using a chain, King and Brewer lashed Byrd to a pickup truck and dragged him over three miles of rural Texas asphalt to his death. If executed, King or Brewer will become only the second white person ever put to death in Texas for killing a black person. A third white supremacist, 24-year-old Shawn Allen Berry, was found guilty of participating in the crime and was sentenced to life in prison. On June 3, 2008, Byrd's surviving family members gathered in Houston, Texas, for a tribute to mark the tenth anniversary of Byrd's death.[95] Some attendees swore not to let the memory of what happened to him fade.

Although hate crimes are popularly conceived of as crimes motivated by racial enmity, the Violent Crime Control and Law Enforcement Act of 1994 created a new category of "crimes of violence motivated by gender." Congress defined this crime as "a crime of violence committed because of gender or on the basis of gender, and due, at least in part, to an animus based on the victim's gender." The 1994 act did not establish separate penalties for gender-motivated crimes, anticipating that they would be prosecuted as felonies under existing laws. The 1994 act also mandated that crimes motivated by biases against people with disabilities be considered hate crimes.

Hate crimes are sometimes called *bias crimes.* One form of bias crime that bears special mention is *homophobic homicide*, a term that refers to the murder of a homosexual by those opposed to that lifestyle. Learn more about hate crime and what can be done to address it at Library Extras 2–17 and 2–18 at mycrimekit.com.

Library EXTRA

Corporate and White-Collar Crime

In 2008, U.S. District Judge Colleen McMahon sentenced Samuel Israel III, age 48, to 20 years in prison, saying that Israel was the mastermind behind the collapsed hedge fund Bayou Group.[96] The fund's demise, which cost investors more than $400 million, shocked Wall Street and threatened the health of the entire $1.8 trillion hedge fund industry. "Financial fraud [and] white-collar crimes are every bit as heinous as every other type of crime and they will be punished severely," McMahon told Israel. In addition to prison time, Israel was ordered to pay $300 million in restitution to shareholders and to forfeit a bank account that held more than $100 million.

Israel is but one of a number of people recently prosecuted for financial crimes. Between 2001 and 2003, accounting fraud and the ensuing bankruptcies of energy broker Enron Corporation and telecommunications giant WorldCom reduced the holdings of investment and retirement accounts across the country and around the world, wiping out hundreds of billions of dollars' worth of investor equity and taking a significant toll on the wealth of many Americans. Other publicly traded companies that have recently faced investigation include cable services provider Adelphia Communications Corporation (now part of Comcast Communications); French-based media conglomerate Vivendi Universal; national discount retailer Kmart; fiber optics giant Global Crossing; multinational conglomerate Tyco International; accounting firm Arthur Andersen (whose employees served as auditors and accountants for bankrupt Enron); Metabolife, a leading seller of products containing the herbal stimulant ephedrine, which faced a criminal investigation by the U.S. Justice Department into whether the company had lied about drug safety[97]; and London-based auction house Sotheby's. In 2004, Adelphia founder John Rigas and his son, former Adelphia chief financial officer Timothy Rigas, were found guilty of 18 counts of securities and bank fraud, of conspiring to loot the cable company of millions of dollars, and of misleading its investors.[98] John Rigas, age 80, was sentenced to 15 years in prison, while his son received a 20-year sentence.[99] In 2005, in a case that came to epitomize corporate greed, former Tyco CEO L. Dennis Kozlowski and former Tyco finance chief Mark H. Swartz were convicted of looting their former company of nearly $600 million.[100] About the same time, Bernard J. Ebbers, the 63-year-old former chief executive of WorldCom, was sentenced to serve 25 years behind bars for his role in the nation's largest account fraud. Finally, in 2006 former Enron executives Jeff Skilling and Kenneth Lay were convicted of conspiracy to commit securities and wire fraud in the collapse of energy-trading giant Enron Corporation.[101] The 52-year-old Skilling, Enron's former chief executive officer, received a 24-year sentence. Lay, 64, the company's founder, died from heart failure while awaiting sentencing.

Under the American system of criminal justice, corporations can be treated as separate legal entities and can be convicted of violations of the criminal law under a legal principle known as the *identification doctrine.* In 2002, for example, a federal jury convicted global account-

I'm signing a good bill.... It says loud and clear to corporate America, we expect you to be responsible, we expect you to be responsible with the people's money. We expect you to be responsible for the shareholders and your employees and if you're not, we're going to investigate you, arrest you and prosecute you.

—*President George W. Bush, at the signing of the Sarbanes-Oxley Act of 2002*[viii] ing firm Arthur Andersen of obstruction of justice after its employees shredded documents related to Enron's bankruptcy in an effort to impede an investigation by securities regulators. The conviction, which was overturned by a unanimous U.S. Supreme Court in 2005,[102] capped the firm's demise, and it ended U.S. operations in August 2002.[103]

corporate crime
A violation of a criminal statute by a corporate entity or by its executives, employees, or agents acting on behalf of and for the benefit of the corporation, partnership, or other form of business entity.[ix]

white-collar crime
Violations of the criminal law committed by a person of respectability and high social status in the course of his or her occupation. Also, nonviolent crime for financial gain utilizing deception and committed by anyone who has special technical or professional knowledge of business or government, irrespective of the person's occupation.

Although corporations may be convicted of a crime, the human perpetrators of **corporate crime** are business executives known as *white-collar criminals.* **White-collar crime** was first defined in 1939 by Edwin H. Sutherland in his presidential address to the American Sociological Society.[104] Sutherland proposed that "crime in the suites" (a reference to corporate offices) rivaled the importance of street crime in its potential impact on American society.

In July 2002, President George W. Bush unveiled plans to create a new Corporate Fraud Task Force within the federal government and proposed a new law providing criminal penalties for corporate fraud. He told corporate leaders on Wall Street, "At this moment, America's greatest economic need is higher ethical standards—standards enforced by strict laws and upheld by responsible business leaders."[105] A few months later, the president signed into law the Sarbanes-Oxley Act.[106] The new law created tough provisions designed to deter and punish corporate and accounting fraud and corruption and to protect the interests of workers and shareholders. Under the Sarbanes-Oxley Act, corporate officials (chief executive officers and chief financial officers) must personally vouch for the truth and accuracy of their companies' financial statements, and federal penalties for obstructing justice and, specifically, for shredding or destroying documents that might aid in a criminal investigation of business practices are substantially increased. Learn more about corporate and white-collar crime at the National White Collar Crime Center (NW3C) via **Web Extra 2–14** at mycrimekit.com. Established in 1992, the NW3C provides a national support system for the prevention, investigation, and prosecution of multijurisdictional economic crimes. Learn more about how corporations can be held accountable from CorpWatch via **Web Extra 2–15**.

Web EXTRA

Organized Crime

organized crime
The unlawful activities of the members of a highly organized, disciplined association engaged in supplying illegal goods or services, including gambling, prostitution, loan-sharking, narcotics, and labor racketeering, and in other unlawful activities.[x]

For many people, the term **organized crime** conjures up images of the Mafia (also called the *Cosa Nostra*) or the hit HBO TV series *The Sopranos.* Although organized criminal activity is decidedly a group phenomenon, the groups involved in such activity in the United States today display a great deal of variation. During the past few decades in the United States, the preeminence of traditional Sicilian American criminal organizations has fallen to such diverse criminal associations as the Black Mafia, the Cuban Mafia, the Haitian Mafia, the Colombian cartels, and Asian criminal groups like the Chinese Tongs and street gangs, Japanese yakuza, and Vietnamese gangs. Included here as well might be inner-city gangs, the best known of which are probably the Los Angeles Crips and Bloods and the Chicago Vice Lords, international drug rings, outlaw motorcycle gangs like the Hell's Angels and the Pagans, and other looser associations of small-time thugs, prison gangs, and drug dealers. Noteworthy among these groups—especially for their involvement in the lucrative drug trade—are the Latino organized bands, including the Dominican, Colombian, Mexican, and Cuban importers of cocaine, heroin, marijuana, and other controlled substances.

▲ Actor James Gandolfini (Tony Soprano) from HBO's hit series *The Sopranos* is shown on the right. The popular show explored the life of fictionalized organized crime figures in New Jersey. Why was the show such a hit with viewers?
Globe Photos, Inc.

The unlawful activities of organized groups that operate across national boundaries are especially significant. Such activity is referred to as **transnational organized crime.** Transnational criminal associations worthy of special mention are the Hong Kong–based Triads, the South American cocaine cartels, the Italian Mafia, the Japanese yakuza, the Russian *Mafiya,* and the West African crime groups—each of which extends its reach well beyond its home country. In some parts of the world, close links between organized crime and terrorist groups involve money laundering, which provides cash to finance the activities of terrorist cells and to finance paramilitary efforts to overthrow established governments.

Former CIA Director R. James Woolsey points out that "while organized crime is not a new phenomenon today, some governments find their authority besieged at home and their foreign policy interests imperiled abroad. Drug trafficking, links between drug traffickers and terrorists, smuggling of illegal aliens, massive financial and bank fraud, arms smuggling, potential involvement in the theft and sale of nuclear material, political intimidation, and corruption all constitute a poisonous brew—a mixture potentially as deadly as what we faced during the cold war."[107] The challenge for today's criminal justice student is to recognize that crime does not respect national boundaries. Crime is global, and what happens in one part of the world could affect us all.[108]

transnational organized crime
Unlawful activity undertaken and supported by organized criminal groups operating across national boundaries.

Gun Crime

Guns and gun crime seem to pervade American culture. On October 13, 2007, for example, well-known Rapper T.I. (Clifford Harris) was arrested just hours before he was to take the stage at the BET Hip-Hop Awards. T.I. had been nominated in nine different award categories and had been expected to perform that evening. The 27-year-old self-proclaimed King of the South was charged with attempting to buy several machine guns and silencers from undercover agents, and he was unable to take the stage after his arrest by agents of the federal Bureau of Alcohol, Tobacco, Firearms and Explosives (ATF). The rapper, already a convicted drug felon, was said to have previously purchased firearms on at least four different occasions. In 2006, T.I.'s best friend, Philant Johnson, was killed in a postperformance gun battle in Cincinnati.

Months earlier, a 2007 shooting spree at the Virginia Polytechnic Institute and State University in Blacksburg, Virginia, in which 33 people (including the gunman) died and 20 were wounded, led to one of the most intense debates over gun control in this country in decades. CJ Exhibit 2 provides additional information on the issue of gun control.

Constitutional guarantees of the right to bear arms have combined with historical circumstances to make ours a well-armed society. Guns are used in many types of crimes. Each year, approximately 1 million serious crimes—including homicide, rape, robbery, and assault—involve the use of a handgun. In a typical year, approximately 10,000 murders are committed in the United States with firearms. A recent report by the BJS found that 18% of state prison inmates and 15% of federal inmates were armed at the time they committed the crime for which they were imprisoned,[109] and 9% of those in state prisons said they fired a gun while committing the offense for which they were serving time.[110]

Both federal and state governments have responded to the public concern over the ready availability of handguns. In 1994, Congress passed the Brady Handgun Violence Prevention Act, which President Bill Clinton signed into law. The law was named for former Press Secretary James Brady, who was shot and severely wounded in an attempt on President Ronald Reagan's life on March 30, 1981. The law mandated a five-day waiting period before the purchase of a handgun, and it established a national instant criminal background check system that firearms dealers must use before selling a handgun. Under the system, licensed importers, manufacturers, and dealers are required to verify the identity of a firearm purchaser using a valid photo ID (such as a driver's license); must submit the purchaser's application to ensure that the applicant's receipt or possession of a handgun would not violate federal, state, or local law[111]; and must contact the system to receive a unique identification number authorizing the purchase before they transfer the handgun.

While the Brady law may limit retail purchases of handguns by felons, a BJS study found that most offenders obtain weapons from friends or family members or "on the street" rather than attempt to purchase them at retail establishments.[112] In 2001, undercover congressional investigators were able to show that applicants using fake forms of identification, such as counterfeit driver's licenses with fictitious names, could easily circumvent Brady law provisions.[113] Moreover, according to these studies, an ever-growing number of violent criminals are now carrying handguns. A 2006 study found no evidence that stringent gun-control laws have an impact on crime.[114] The study, which used data from all 50 states, found that gun-control laws do not have an impact on the crime rate or on the occurrence of any specific type of serious crime. Such laws are ineffective

▲ Rapper T.I. (Clifford Harris), shown here attending the 2007 MTV Video Music Awards, was arrested on a number of firearms charges just hours before he was to take the stage at the 2007 BET Hip-Hop Awards.
Robyn Beck/Agence France Presse/Getty Images

CJ Exhibit 2

Gun Control

The Second Amendment to the U.S. Constitution reads, "A well regulated Militia, being necessary to the security of a free State, the right of the people to keep and bear Arms, shall not be infringed." For many years, the official position of the U.S. Justice Department had been that the Second Amendment merely gives states the collective right to organize and arm militias in order to protect the public interest and that it does not mean that individual citizens have a constitutional right to own firearms. On May 7, 2002, however, in two briefs filed with the U.S. Supreme Court by U.S. Solicitor General Theodore B. Olson, the Justice Department officially reversed course, declaring, "The current position of the United States . . . is that the Second Amendment more broadly protects the rights of individuals, including persons who are not members of any militia or engaged in active military service or training, to possess and bear their own firearms, subject to reasonable restrictions designed to prevent possession ... of types of firearms that are particularly suited to criminal misuse."[1] Although the government's briefs did not ask the justices to take any action, they were seen by many as representing a significant victory for advocates of private gun ownership, such as the NRA. Nonetheless, few imagine that the apparent change in policy will lead to significant modifications in existing gun-control legislation, much of which was passed in the 1990s.

One of those laws, the Violent Crime Control and Law Enforcement Act of 1994,[2] regulated the sale of firearms within the United States and originally banned the manufacture of 19 military-style assault weapons, including those with specific combat features such as high-capacity ammunition clips capable of holding more than ten rounds. The ban on assault weapons ended in 2004, however, when it was not renewed by Congress. The 1994 law also prohibited the sale or transfer of a gun to a juvenile, as well as the possession of a gun by a juvenile, and it prohibited gun sales to, and possession by, people subject to family violence restraining orders.

The 1996 Domestic Violence Offender Gun Ban[3] prohibits individuals convicted of misdemeanor domestic-violence offenses from owning or using firearms. Soon after the law was passed, however, it became embroiled in controversy when hundreds of police officers across the country who had been convicted of domestic-violence offenses were found to be in violation of the ban. A number of officers lost their jobs, while others were placed in positions that did not require them to carry firearms. While some legislators pushed to exempt police officers and military personnel from the ban's provisions, others argued that they should be included. Feminist Majority President Eleanor Smeal was angered. "Rather than trying to seek an exemption for police officers and military personnel who are abusers, we should be concerned with why we are recruiting so many abusers for these positions," she said.[4]

Following the 1999 Columbine High School shooting, a number of states moved to tighten controls over handguns and assault weapons. The California legislature, for example, restricted gun purchases to one per month and tightened a ten-year-old ban on assault weapons. Similarly, Illinois passed a law requiring that gun owners lock their weapons away from anyone under age 14.

In 2004, at the urging of major police organizations, the U.S. Senate scuttled plans for a gun-industry protection bill. However, the bill was revived in 2005 and passed both houses of Congress before being signed into law by President George W. Bush on October 31 of that year. Known as the Protection of Lawful Commerce in Firearms Act, the law grants gunmakers and most gun dealers immunity from lawsuits brought by victims of gun crimes and their survivors. The law removes negligence as viable grounds for a civil suit against a gun dealer who carelessly sells a gun to someone who is at risk for using it in a crime; the law states that the dealer can be sued only if he or she knew of the gun buyer's criminal intent before the purchase. Gunmakers were made immune from suits alleging product liability for having manufactured potentially lethal items.

In 2008, in the case of District of *Columbia* v. *Heller*,[5] the U.S. Supreme Court came down firmly in support of private gun ownership when it ruled that the constitution's Second Amendment protects an individual's right to possess a firearm, and to use that firearm for traditionally lawful purposes, such as self-defense within the home. The *Heller* case addressed three strict gun control ordinances that the District of Columbia City Council had enacted in 1976, and which entirely banned anyone from carrying a handgun or other deadly or dangerous weapon without a license within the District. The ordinances also required that any firearms, such as rifles and shotguns, be kept either disassembled or with a trigger lock in place. Prior to *Heller*, the Supreme Court has not squarely addressed a Second Amendment case since 1939, and had never previously decided whether the Second Amendment confers a right to bear arms upon individuals or only upon the militias it refers to in its opening clause. In the intervening 69 years, however, many federal and state governments had passed laws regulating and restricting

Assault Weapons: A Primer

Legal Definition

A weapon that can accept a magazine, or bullet chamber, that can easily be removed. It has at least two "assault" features, such as a flash suppressor (which suppresses the light when the weapon is fired) or a protruding pistol grip (which allows it to be held like a pistol).

Intratec TEC-9/DC-9
Made in the USA. Semiautomatic version of the automatic pistol. Can handle magazines with up to 50 rounds.

Well-Known Types

Colt AR-15
Made in the USA. Semiautomatic version of the M-16 military rifle. Holds 9 rounds standard, more with "high-capacity" magazines. Has a pistol grip and flash suppressor.

Streetsweeper
U.S.-made version of the Striker-12 shotgun that is made in South Africa. Police often have cited its use among gangs. Holds 12 rounds in a rotating chamber.

Beretta AR-70
Made in Italy. Assault rifle that initially was used by Italian special forces. Can fire 650 rounds per minute; its magazine can hold 30 rounds. Comes with pistol grips.

Norinco MAK-90
Made in China. Semiautomatic version of the AK-47. Has a 30-round magazine but can handle larger magazines.

***Note:* Firearms not to scale.**

From USA TODAY, a division of Garnett Co., Inc. Reprinted with Permission. www.usatoday.com.

the ownership and use of guns, making the *Heller* decision especially significant.

In the area of advancing technology, scientific progress may soon offer new possibilities in the field of ballistics. Nanotechnological solutions, for example, are now available that can stamp a handgun's serial number on each shell casing fired by that gun. The method uses invisibly engraved firing pins that leave a clear microimpression on each shell casing that they strike.[6]

No doubt, the debate over handgun ownership and acceptable forms of legal regulation will be with us for years to come, and tragic incidents involving handguns and other weapons will continue to make the news. Read, for example, the 2007 *Report to the President on Issues Raised by the Virginia Tech Tragedy* at Library Extra 2–20 at mycrimekit.com.

Library EXTRA

[1]"Justice Department Reverses Second-Amendment Interpretation," http://www.jointogether.org/gv/news/summaries/reader/0,2061,550836,00.html (accessed August 17, 2006).
[2]PL 103-322, 108 Stat. 1796 (codified as amended in scattered sections of 18, 21, 28, 42, etc., U.S.).
[3]PL 104-208, an amendment to U.S. Code, Title 18, Section 921(a). Also known as the Lautenberg Amendment.
[4]Jacob R. Clark, "Police Careers May Take a Beating from Fed Domestic-Violence Law," *Law Enforcement News*, Vol. 23, No. 461 (February 14, 1997), p. 1.
[5]*District of Columbia* v. *Heller*, U.S. Supreme Court, No. 07–290 (decided June 26, 2008).
[6]Nicola Senin, Roberto Groppetti, Luciano Garofano, Paolo Fratini, and Michele Pierni, "Three-Dimensional Surface Topography Acquisition and Analysis for Firearm Identification," *Journal of Forensic Sciences*, Vol. 51, No. 2 (2006), pp. 282–295.

in reducing crime, the study authors said, because they do not substantially reduce the availability of firearms to criminal offenders.

In Congress, debate continues about whether to require gun manufacturers to create and retain "ballistic fingerprints" (the marks left on a bullet by the barrel of the gun from which it was fired) of each weapon they produce. Although a national ballistics fingerprinting requirement may still be years away, two states—Maryland and New York—already require that a record be kept of the "fingerprint" characteristics of each new handgun sold.[115]

In 2007, California Governor Arnold Schwarzenegger signed legislation requiring that microstamping technology be employed in all new semiautomatic pistols sold in the state after January 1, 2010.[116] Microstamping uses laser engraving to encode a weapon's serial number on each cartridge that it fires up, and California authorities believe that the technology will allow handguns to be traced to their manufacturer and then the first purchaser using only spent cartridges left at crime scenes.

Learn more about promising strategies to reduce gun violence at Library Extra 2–19 at mycrimekit.com. For the latest information on gun violence and gun laws, visit the Brady Center to Prevent Gun Violence via Web Extra 2–16 at mycrimekit.com. The National Rifle Association (NRA) site at Web Extra 2–17 provides support for responsible access to firearms.

Library EXTRA

Web EXTRA

Drug Crime

In 2008, 96 young men—including 75 San Diego State University (SDSU) students—were arrested on a variety of drug and weapons charges as a result of a joint Drug Enforcement Agency (DEA)/local police operation called Sudden Fall. During the operation, undercover officers infiltrated seven of the university's fraternity houses and seized four pounds of cocaine, 50 pounds of marijuana, 48 hydroponic marijuana plants, 350 Ecstasy pills, 30 vials of hash oil, methamphetamine, psilocybin (mushrooms), various illicit prescription drugs, a shotgun, three semiautomatic pistols, various sets of brass knuckles, and $60,000 in cash. The agents said that they also found evidence of widespread drug dealing at SDSU's fraternity houses. The investigation had begun a year earlier after a cocaine overdose caused the death of a 19-year-old female student on the SDSU campus. "This operation shows how accessible and pervasive illegal drugs continue to be on our college campuses and how common it is for students to be selling to other students," said San Diego County District Attorney Bonnie Dumanis.[117]

The White House Office of National Drug Control Policy (ONDCP) estimates annual illicit drug sales in the United States of around $65 billion, while the United Nations says that illegal drug revenue in the United States, Canada, and Mexico totals around $142 billion yearly.[118] Unlike most major crimes, drug-law violations continue to increase, lending support to those who

▶ San Diego County Deputy District Attorney Damon Mosler (at podium) points to drugs and firearms seized during the arrest of 96 people, including 75 students at San Diego State University, in 2008 after an extensive undercover investigation called Operation Sudden Fall. How common are illegal drugs on the nation's university campuses?
Dennis Poroy/AP Wide World Photos

feel that this country is experiencing more overall crime than traditional tabulations show. The relentless increase in drug violations largely accounts for the fact that America's prison populations have continued to grow, even when official crime rates are declining. Figure 5 shows the number of suspects arrested for drug-law violations in the United States between 1975 and 2007.

Alone, drug-law violations are themselves criminal, but more and more studies are linking drug abuse to other serious crimes. An early study by the RAND Corporation found that most of the "violent predators" among prisoners had extensive histories of heroin abuse, often in combination with alcohol and other drugs.[119] Some cities reported that a large percentage of their homicides were drug related.[120] More recent studies also link drug abuse to other serious crimes. Community leaders perceive, and data analyses confirm, that crack cocaine profoundly impacts violent

FIGURE 5
Drug Arrests in the United States, 1975–2007.
Source: Federal Bureau of Investigation, *Crime in the United States*, various years.

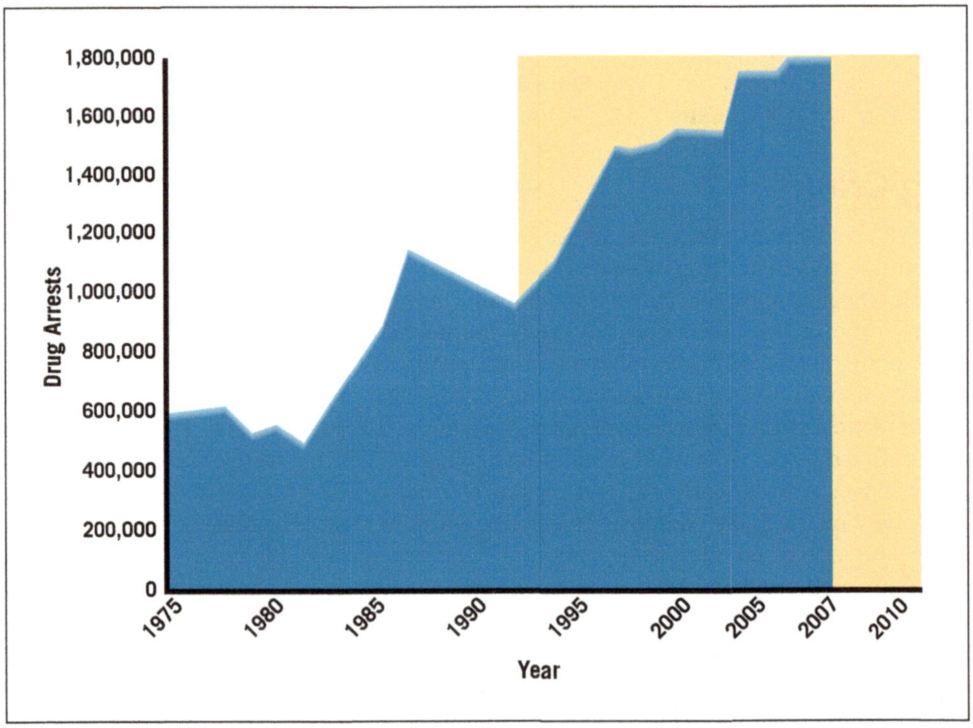

CJ Careers

Drug Enforcement Administration

Name: James L. Capra
Position: Chief of Domestic Operations
City: Arlington, Virginia
Colleges Attended: Marist College and Seton Hall University
Year Hired: 1987

"Although I was influenced by my father, a retired New York City police officer, I didn't choose this career; it chose me. I truly believe that individuals who seek out careers as law enforcement professionals are answering a calling in their lives. They have a desire to serve others, and they embody the finest attributes of what it means to be a public servant . . . . One of the greatest challenges I have is ensuring that DEA uses every resource available to disrupt and dismantle those drug-trafficking organizations that impact the United States. What raises the stakes on this challenge is that there are now terrorist organizations that rely on drug proceeds to finance their terrorist activity against our nation and its citizens . . . . DEA is a single-mission agency; it takes drugs off the street and puts bad guys in jail, and we do this very creatively, with great distinction and honor. One of the greatest rewards is witnessing the incredible impact we have in making our towns, cities, states, and, for that matter, our nation a safer place to live, work, and play."

TYPICAL POSITIONS

Special agent, criminal investigator, chemist, diversion investigator, and intelligence research specialist. Special agents conduct clandestine surveillance, infiltrate drug-trafficking organizations, conduct investigations, arrest violators, confiscate controlled substances, collect and prepare evidence, and testify in criminal court cases.

EMPLOYMENT REQUIREMENTS

Applicants for the GS-5 level must (1) be a U.S. citizen, (2) be between the ages of 21 and 36 at time of hiring, (3) hold a four-year college degree, (4) be in good health, (5) pass a comprehensive background investigation, (6) hold a valid driver's license, (7) possess effective oral and written communications skills, and (8) have three years of general job experience. Applicants for the GS-7 level must also demonstrate *one* of the following: (1) a 2.95 overall college grade point average, (2) a 3.5 grade point average in the applicant's major field of study, (3) a standing in the upper one-third of the applicant's graduating class, (4) membership in a national honorary scholastic society, (5) one year of successful graduate study, or (6) one year of specialized experience (defined as "progressively responsible investigative experience").

OTHER REQUIREMENTS

Applicants must (1) be willing to travel frequently, (2) submit to a urinalysis test designed to detect the presence of controlled substances, and (3) successfully complete a two-month formal training program at the FBI's Training Center in Quantico, Virginia. Special-agent applicants must be in excellent physical condition, possess sharp hearing, and have uncorrected vision of at least 20/200 and corrected vision of 20/20 in one eye and at least 20/40 in the other. (Radial keratotomy is disqualifying.) They must also possess normal color vision and be capable of heavy lifting (including carrying 45 pounds or more).

SALARY

Entry-level positions for individuals with four-year college degrees begin at GS-7. Appointments are made at higher pay grades for individuals possessing additional education and experience.

BENEFITS

Benefits include (1) 13 days of sick leave annually, (2) two and a half to five weeks of paid vacation and ten paid federal holidays each year, (3) federal health and life insurance, and (4) a comprehensive retirement program.

DIRECT INQUIRIES TO:

Drug Enforcement Administration
Special Agent Recruitment Unit
Office of Personnel
700 Army Navy Dr.
Alexandria, VA 22202
Phone: 800-DEA-4288
Website: http://www.dea.gov

For more information on the rapidly expanding criminal justice careers area, read *Where the Jobs Are: Mission Critical Opportunities for America*, available on the Web at http://www.justicestudies.com/jobs.htm.

Source: Drug Enforcement Administration.

crime, with homicide rates closely tracking cocaine use levels among adult male arrestees.[121] Prisoner survey data show that 19% of state inmates and 16% of federal prisoners reported committing their most recent offense to obtain money for drugs.[122] A 2000 study found that 13.3% of convicted jail inmates said that they had committed their offense to get money for drugs.[123]

Criminal justice system costs associated with the handling of drug offenders have increased substantially in recent years. Between 1984 and 2002, for example, the annual number of defendants charged with a drug offense in federal courts increased from 11,854 to more than 30,000.[124] Similarly, between 1984 and 2002, drug offenses accounted for an increased proportion of the federal criminal caseload, even when charges weren't brought. During 1984, 18% of referrals to U.S. attorneys were drug related, compared to 31% during 2002.[125] Some of the

Library EXTRA

increase stems from changes in federal drug laws. Whatever the cause, the drug–crime link is costly to society and shows few signs of abating. Learn more about drug crime and efforts being made to combat it at Library Extra 2–21 at mycrimekit.com.

High-Technology and Computer Crime

malware
Malicious computer programs such as viruses, worms, and Trojan horses.

In March 2006, the Ziff Davis digital publication *eWeek* reported the release on the Internet of a **malware** software program that encrypts files on an infected computer and then demands a $300 ransom for e-mail delivery of a decryption password.[126] The malware, identified as Cryzip, makes data files on infected computers unavailable to legitimate users and displays step-by-step instructions on how to pay a ransom with a credit card for file retrieval. Cryzip is a type of software known as *ransomware,* and its release points to an increasing level of sophistication among online thieves practicing computer crime.

computer crime
Any crime perpetrated through the use of computer technology. Also, any violation of a federal or state computer-crime statute. Also called *cybercrime.*

Computer crimes, also called *cybercrimes* or *information technology crimes,* use computers and computer technology as tools in crime commission. Thefts of computer equipment, although sometimes spectacular, are not computer crimes but are instead classified as larcenies. "True" computer criminals go beyond the theft of hardware, focusing instead on the information stored in computer systems and manipulating it in a way that violates the law.

While a generally accepted typology of computer-based crime has yet to be developed,[127] Peter Grabosky of the Australian Institute of Criminology suggests that most such crimes fall into one of the following broad categories[128]: (1) theft of services, such as telephone or long-distance access; (2) communications in furtherance of criminal conspiracies—for example, the e-mail communications said to have taken place between members of Osama bin Laden's al-Qaeda terrorist network[129]; (3) information piracy and forgery—that is, the stealing of trade secrets or copyrighted information; (4) dissemination of offensive materials, such as child pornography, and extortion threats, such as those made against financial institutions by hackers claiming the ability to destroy the institutions' electronic records; (5) electronic money laundering and tax evasion through electronic funds transfers that conceal the origin of financial proceeds; (6) electronic vandalism and terrorism, including computer viruses, worms, Trojan horses, and cyberterrorism—that is, cyberattacks on critical components of a nation's infrastructure, such as its banking system; (7) telemarketing fraud, including investment frauds and illegitimate electronic auctions; (8) illegal interception of telecommunications—that is, illegal eavesdropping; and (9) electronic funds transfer fraud—specifically, the illegal interception and diversion of legitimate transactions.

Many of the crimes committed via the Internet—like prostitution, drug sales, theft, and fraud—are not new forms of offending. They are, rather, traditional forms of offending that use new technology in their commission. In 2003, for example, Jill Ellen McGrath, age 35, and her husband, Christopher Thomas Davis, age 34, were arrested by police in Redondo Beach, California, and charged with pimping, pandering, drug possession, and child endangerment. Police said that the couple had run a call-girl service out of their house for years and had advertised the services of about 30 prostitutes on the Internet. "Some of these girls remind you of soccer moms," said Sergeant Jeff Hinks.[130] "Some of them were married. Some had kids. Their husbands had no idea what they were doing." Police said that a number of the women earned as much as $600 per hour, with the operators taking a 30% cut.

U.S. Customs and Border Protection Senior Special Agent Donald Daufenbach, an international expert in child pornography and the Internet, points out that "the Internet is like anything else: It can be bent or perverted for nefarious purposes. . . . The Internet has absolutely changed the way people communicate with each other, changed the way people conduct commerce, changed the way people do research, changed the way people entertain themselves and changed the way people break the law."[131] Daufenbach added, "It's just a new version of what the mails or what the telephones used to be. . . . People are catching on pretty quick, but law enforcement is lagging behind miserably in this whole endeavor."

computer virus
A computer program designed to secretly invade systems and either modify the way in which they operate or alter the information they store. Viruses are destructive software programs that may effectively vandalize computers of all types and sizes.

Computer viruses have become a special concern of the general computer user during the past several years, especially as more people have connected to the Internet. Computer viruses were brought to public attention in 1988 when the Pakistani virus (or Pakistani brain virus) became widespread in personal and office computers across the United States.[132] The Pakistani virus was created by Amjad Farooq Alvi and his brother Basit Farooq Alvi, two cut-rate computer software dealers in Lahore, Pakistan. The Alvi brothers made copies of costly software products and sold them at low prices to mostly Western shoppers looking for a bargain. Motivated by convoluted logic, the brothers hid a virus on each disk they sold to punish buyers for seeking to evade copyright laws. Since then, many other virus attacks have made headlines, including the infamous Michelangelo virus in 1992; the intentional distribution of infected software on an AIDS-related research CD-ROM distributed about the same time; the Kournikova virus in 2000; and the Sircam, Nimda, W32, NastyBrew, Berbew, Mydoom, and Code Red worms, all of which made their appearance or were substantially modified by their creators between 2001 and 2006.

Another form of cybercrime called **software piracy**, the unauthorized copying of software programs, also appears to be rampant. According to the Software & Information Industry Association (SIIA), global losses from software piracy total nearly $12.2 billion annually.[133] The SIIA says that 38% of all software in use in the world today has been copied illegally. Some countries have especially high rates of illegal use. Of all the computer software in use in Vietnam, for example, SIIA estimates that 97% has been illegally copied, while 95% of the software used in China and 92% of the software used in Russia are thought to be pirated—resulting in a substantial loss in manufacturers' revenue.

software piracy
The unauthorized duplication of software or the illegal transfer of data from one storage medium to another. Software piracy is one of the most prevalent computer crimes in the world.

In 2003, federal legislators acted to criminalize the sending of unsolicited commercial e-mail, or **spam**. The federal CAN-SPAM Act (Controlling the Assault of Non-Solicited Pornography and Marketing), which took effect on January 1, 2004, regulates the sending of "commercial electronic mail messages."[134] The law, which applies equally to mass mailings and to individual e-mail messages, defines commercial electronic mail messages as electronic mail whose *primary purpose* is the "commercial advertisement or promotion of a commercial product or service." The CAN-SPAM law requires that a commercial e-mail message include the following three features: (1) a clear and conspicuous identification that the message is an advertisement or solicitation, (2) an opt-out feature, allowing recipients to opt out of future mailings, and (3) a valid physical address identifying the sender. Some experts estimate that 80% of all e-mail today is spam,[135] and a number of states have enacted their own antispam laws.

spam
Unsolicited commercial bulk e-mail (UCBE), whose primary purpose is the commercial advertisement or promotion of a commercial product or service.

In 2005, the U.S. Supreme Court agreed to hear an appeal from the music industry, and in the landmark case of *MGM* v. *Grokster*,[136] the Court found that online file-sharing services may be held liable for copyright infringement if they promote their services explicitly as a way for users to download copyrighted music and other content. Attempts to legislatively criminalize the downloading of digitized music and movies began on Capitol Hill in 2003. If the proposed legislation is enacted, illegal downloaders could face prison terms of up to five years.[137]

One form of cybercrime that relies primarily on social engineering to succeed is *phishing* (pronounced *fishing*). Phishing is a relatively new form of high-technology fraud that uses official-looking e-mail messages to elicit responses from victims, directing them to phony websites. Microsoft Corporation says that phishing is "the fastest-growing form of online fraud in the world today."[138] Phishing e-mails typically instruct recipients to validate or update account information before their accounts are canceled. Phishing schemes, which have targeted most major banks, the Federal Deposit Insurance Corporation, IBM, eBay, PayPal, and some major health care providers, are designed to steal valuable information such as credit card numbers, Social Security numbers, user IDs, and passwords. In 2004, Gartner Inc., a leading provider of research and analysis on the global information technology industry, released a report estimating that some 57 million adult Americans received phishing e-mails during the spring of 2004 and that 11 million recipients clicked on the link contained in the messages.[139] Gartner estimated that 1.78 million recipients actually provided personal information to the thieves behind the phishing schemes.

The 2005 Computer Crime and Security Survey, conducted annually by the Computer Security Institute (CSI) and the FBI, found that 53% of the large businesses, medical institutions, universities, and government agencies participating in the survey reported detecting security-related breaches of their computer networks in 2004.[140] The survey also found that only about half of all reported breaches originated outside the organization. Other researchers have determined that some of the most serious corporate computer security threats come from employees, including 70% of all unauthorized access to information systems incidents and 95% of all network intrusions that result in significant financial loss.[141] The CSI/FBI report found that the highest average annual computer security expenditure per employee ($497) in 2004 was reported by state governments. The federal government reported spending only $30 per federal employee to secure its computers in 2004, while the telecommunications industry reported annual computer security expenditures averaging $132 per employee.[142]

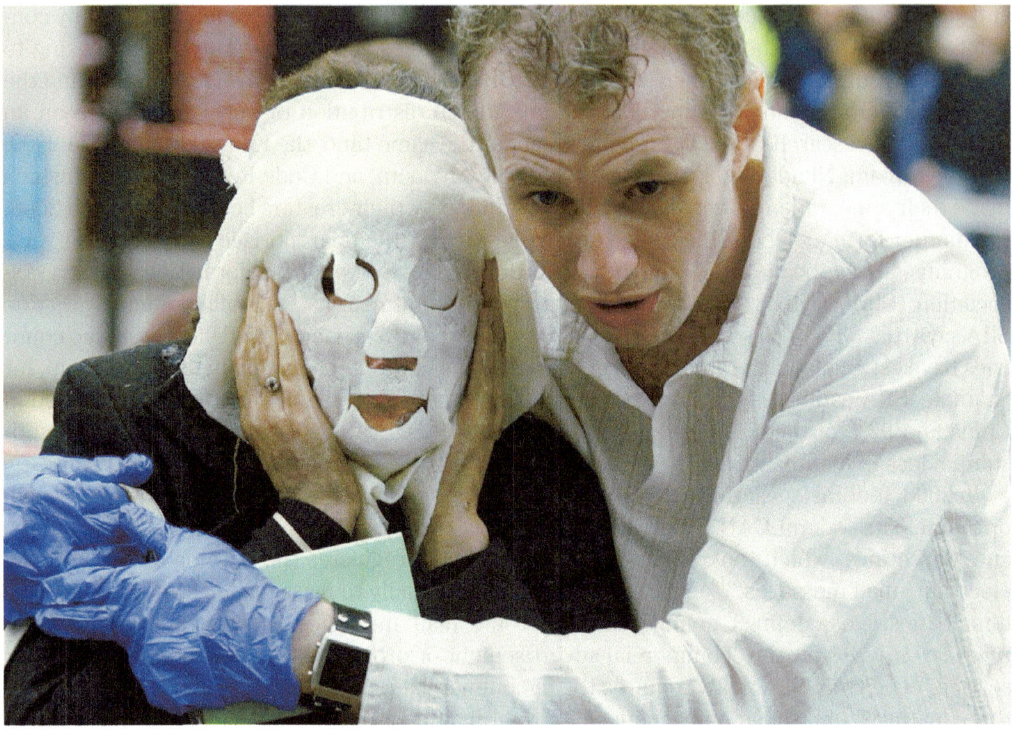

A commuter being helped away from the Edgware Road Underground Station following terrorist bombings in London's subway system in 2005. How might future acts of terrorism be prevented?
Jane Mingay/AP Wide World Photos

In 2004, the BJS released initial results from its 2001 National Computer Security Survey (NCSS), which had been conducted in collaboration with the U.S. Census Bureau.[143] The 2004 report summarized findings from a pilot survey of 500 companies nationwide. Nearly three-fourths of businesses surveyed reported detecting at least one computer security incident during the previous 12-month period. Computer viruses were the most common type of incident reported (65%), followed by denial-of-service attacks (25%) and vandalism or sabotage of computer equipment or computer networks (19%). Other crimes, such as fraud, theft of proprietary information, and embezzlement, were also reported. Not surprisingly, the largest companies experienced the greatest number of incidents. When fully implemented, the NCSS will provide the first official national statistics on the extent and consequences of cybercrime against the nation's 5.3 million businesses. You may access BJS's NCSS as Library Extra 2–22 at mycrimekit.com. The CSI/FBI Computer Crime and Security Survey can be found online as Library Extra 2–23.

Library EXTRA

Terrorism

Background

Terrorism as a criminal activity and the prevention of further acts of terrorism became primary concerns of American justice system officials following the September 11, 2001, attacks on the World Trade Center and the Pentagon. Long before the September 11 attacks, however, terrorism was a concern of law enforcement and other government officials. In 2001, for example, international terrorist attacks totaled 864 worldwide—down from the 1,106 reported a year earlier.[144]

There is no single definition of terrorism that is applicable to all places and all circumstances. Some definitions are statutory in nature, while others were created for such practical purposes as gauging success in the fight against terrorism. The FBI, for example, defines **terrorism** as "a violent act or an act dangerous to human life in violation of the criminal laws of the United States or of any state to intimidate or coerce a government, the civilian population, or any segment thereof, in furtherance of political or social objectives."[145] One of the most comprehensive and widely used definitions of terrorist activity can be found in the federal Immigration and Nationality Act, an excerpt of which appears in CJ Exhibit 3.

terrorism
A violent act or an act dangerous to human life in violation of the criminal laws of the United States or of any state committed to intimidate or coerce a government, the civilian population, or any segment thereof in furtherance of political or social objectives.[xi]

Types of Terrorism

It is important to distinguish between two major forms of terrorism: domestic and international. Such distinctions are generally made in terms of the origin, base of operations, and objectives

CJ Exhibit 3

What Is Terrorist Activity?

Federal law enforcement efforts directed against agents of foreign terrorist organizations derive their primary authority from the Immigration and Nationality Act, found in Chapter 12 of the U.S. Code. The act defines *terrorist activity* as follows.

(ii) "Terrorist activity" defined

As used in this chapter, the term "terrorist activity" means any activity which is unlawful under the laws of the place where it is committed (or which, if committed in the United States, would be unlawful under the laws of the United States or any State) and which involves any of the following:

I. The hijacking or sabotage of any conveyance (including an aircraft, vessel, or vehicle).
II. The seizing or detaining, and threatening to kill, injure, or continue to detain, another individual in order to compel a third person (including a governmental organization) to do or abstain from doing any act as an explicit or implicit condition for the release of the individual seized or detained.
III. A violent attack upon an internationally protected person (as defined in section 1116(b)(4) of title 18) or upon the liberty of such a person.
IV. An assassination.
V. The use of any—
   a. biological agent, chemical agent, or nuclear weapon or device, or
   b. explosive or firearm (other than for mere personal monetary gain), with intent to endanger, directly or indirectly, the safety of one or more individuals or to cause substantial damage to property.
VI. A threat, attempt, or conspiracy to do any of the foregoing.

(iii) "Engage in terrorist activity" defined

As used in this chapter, the term "engage in terrorist activity" means to commit, in an individual capacity or as a member of an organization, an act of terrorist activity or an act which the actor knows, or reasonably should know, affords material support to any individual, organization, or government in conducting a terrorist activity at any time, including any of the following acts:

I. The preparation or planning of a terrorist activity.
II. The gathering of information on potential targets for terrorist activity.
III. The providing of any type of material support, including a safe house, transportation, communications, funds, false documentation or identification, weapons, explosives, or training, to any individual the actor knows or has reason to believe has committed or plans to commit a terrorist activity.
IV. The soliciting of funds or other things of value for terrorist activity or for any terrorist organization.
V. The solicitation of any individual for membership in a terrorist organization, terrorist government, or to engage in a terrorist activity.

of a terrorist organization. **Domestic terrorism** refers to the unlawful use of force or violence by a group or an individual who is based and operates entirely within the United States and its territories without foreign direction and whose acts are directed at elements of the U.S. government or population.[146] **International terrorism**, in contrast, is the unlawful use of force or violence by a group or an individual who has some connection to a foreign power or whose activities transcend national boundaries against people or property to intimidate or coerce a government, the civilian population, or any segment thereof in furtherance of political or social objectives.[147] International terrorism is sometimes mistakenly called *foreign terrorism*, a term that, strictly speaking, refers only to acts of terrorism that occur outside the United States.

Another new kind of terrorism, called **cyberterrorism**, is lurking on the horizon. Cyberterrorism makes use of high technology, especially computers and the Internet, in the planning and carrying out of terrorist attacks. The term was coined in the 1980s by Barry Collin, a senior research fellow at the Institute for Security and Intelligence in California, who used it to refer to the convergence of cyberspace and terrorism.[148] It was later popularized by a 1996 RAND report that warned of an emerging "new terrorism" distinguished by how terrorist groups organize and by how they use technology. The report warned of a coming "netwar" or "infowar" consisting of coordinated cyberattacks on our nation's economic, business, and military infrastructure.[149] A year later, FBI Agent Mark M. Pollitt offered a working definition of *cyberterrorism*, saying that it is "the premeditated, politically motivated attack against information, computer systems, computer programs, and data which results in violence against noncombatant targets by subnational groups or clandestine agents."[150]

Scenarios describing cyberterrorism possibilities are imaginative and diverse. Some have suggested that a successful cyberterrorist attack on the nation's air traffic control system might

domestic terrorism
The unlawful use of force or violence by a group or an individual who is based and operates entirely within the United States and its territories without foreign direction and whose acts are directed at elements of the U.S. government or population.[xii]

international terrorism
The unlawful use of force or violence by a group or an individual who has some connection to a foreign power or whose activities transcend national boundaries against people or property in order to intimidate or coerce a government, the civilian population, or any segment thereof in furtherance of political or social objectives.[xiii]

cyberterrorism
A form of terrorism that makes use of high technology, especially computers and the Internet, in the planning and carrying out of terrorist attacks.

cause airplanes to collide in midair or that an attack on food- and cereal-processing plants that drastically altered the levels of certain nutritional supplements might sicken or kill a large number of our nation's young children. Other such attacks might cause the country's power grid to collapse or might muddle the records and transactions of banks and stock exchanges. Possible targets in such attacks are almost endless. A 2005 national survey of computer security experts (Figure 6) found that almost half were expecting a "digital Pearl Harbor," in which American society would be plunged into chaos by malicious hackers, to occur within the next few years.[151]

In 2008, FBI Director Robert S. Mueller III identified three organizational levels that characterize violent extremists seeking to damage the United States and its interests.[152] The top tier, Muller said, "is the core al-Qaeda organization, which has established new sanctuaries in the ungoverned spaces, tribal areas, and frontier provinces of Pakistan." The middle tier Mueller called the most complex. "We are finding," he said "small groups who have some ties to an established terrorist organization, but are largely self-directed. Think of them as al-Qaeda franchises—hybrids of homegrown radicals and more sophisticated operatives." The bottom tier, Mueller noted, "is made up of homegrown extremists. They are self-radicalizing, self-financing, and self-executing. They meet up on the Internet instead of in foreign training camps. They have no formal affiliation with al-Qaeda, but they are inspired by its message of violence."

Terrorist groups are active throughout the world, and the United States is not their only target. Terrorist organizations operate in South America, Africa, the Middle East, Latin America, the Philippines, Japan, India, Ireland, England, Nepal, and some of the now independent states of the former Soviet Union. The Central Intelligence Agency (CIA) reports that "between now and 2015 terrorist tactics will become increasingly sophisticated and designed to achieve mass casualties."[153] The CIA also notes that nations "with poor governance; ethnic, cultural, or religious tensions; weak economies; and porous borders will be prime breeding grounds for terrorism."[154] Read the entire CIA report on global trends that may increase the risk of terrorism at Library Extra 2–24 at mycrimekit.com. The U.S. Department of State's annual report, *Patterns of Global Terrorism,* can be found at Library Extra 2–25, and the 2004 final report of the National Commission on Terrorist Attacks upon the United States (the 911 Commission) can be read at Library Extra 2–26.

Library EXTRA

The current situation leads many observers to conclude that the American justice system is not fully prepared to deal with the threat represented by domestic and international terrorism. Prior intelligence-gathering efforts that focused on such groups have largely failed, leading to military intervention in places like Afghanistan and Iraq. Such failures are at least partially understandable, given that many terrorist organizations are tight-knit and very difficult for intelligence operatives to penetrate. In December 2005, members of the 911 Commission held a final news conference in which they lambasted the lack of progress made by federal officials charged with implementing safeguards to prevent future terrorist attacks within the United States. Former commission chairman Thomas Kean called it "shocking" that the nation remains so vulnerable. "We shouldn't need another wake-up call," said Kean. "We believe that the terrorists will strike again."[155]

FIGURE 6
Anticipated Cyberterrorism Attack Time Frame.
Source: Figure by Jae Yang and Suzy Parker, "USA Today Snapshots," *USA Today*, October 6, 2005, p. B1; citing 2005 *CSO Magazine* national survey of 389 chief security officers and security executives. From USA TODAY, a division of Garnett Co., Inc. Reprinted with Permission. www.usatoday.com.

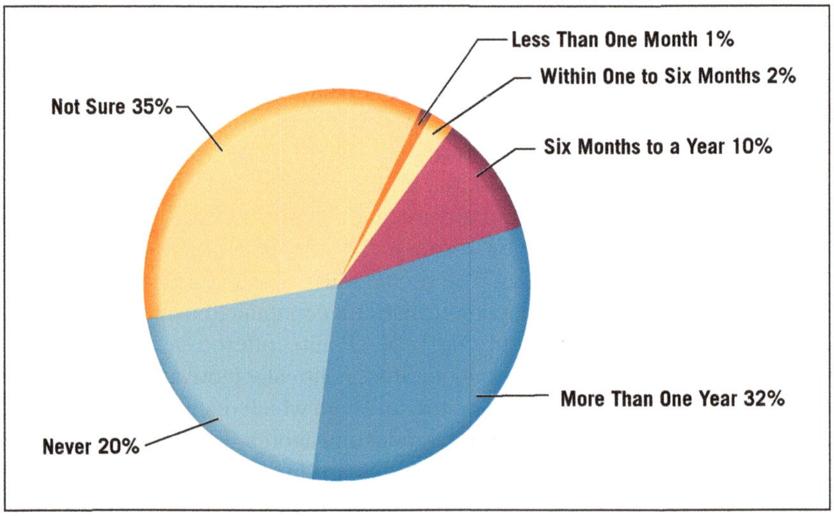

CJ News

FBI Warns of Growing Threat from Islamic Extremists "Next Door"

Plots by American-based Islamic terrorists with no direct ties to international terror networks form a large and growing threat to the American homeland, FBI and other security officials say.

"The trend we're seeing is that we are uncovering more instances of people here who have been radicalized . . . where there is not a direct thumbprint of al-Qaeda," says John Miller, the FBI's assistant director for public affairs.

Justice Department records show that the FBI and other federal and local agencies have led prosecutions of a dozen such alleged plots since the Sept. 11 attacks on New York City and Washington. One such prosecution began in May 2007, when five New Jersey Muslim men were charged with plotting to kill soldiers at the Army's Fort Dix, N.J., compound. A sixth man was charged with helping the group obtain illegal firearms.

The government has won terrorism convictions in seven cases. Others are ongoing.

The focus on American-based terror cells is a shift from post 9/11 thinking, when intelligence and security officials expected attacks to come from "sleeper cells" of al-Qaeda agents who, like the Washington and New York City attackers, had filtered into the USA from abroad.

"That was my intuition at the time," says George Tenet in an interview. Tenet was CIA director from 1997 to 2004 and just released a book, *At the Center of the Storm*, about his tenure. Tenet says the lesson is "don't get fixed on a particular face [because] there may be multiple kinds of faces."

Pasquale D'Amuro, the FBI's counterterrorism chief in 2002 and 2003, says the alleged New Jersey plot appears to be such a case. The six men arrested, he notes, were born in the former Yugoslavia, Jordan and Turkey and had lived in the USA without incident. One was a citizen, two were legal residents and three were here illegally. They had lived here at least six years, neighbors told the Associated Press.

"If they look like the neighbors next door, it's because that's what they are," says D'Amuro, CEO of Giuliani Security and Safety in New York.

"That they would come here, be welcomed and then want to attack us—that's what people have a hard time understanding."

In some cases, such as that of six Yemeni-Americans in Lackawanna, N.Y., the accused plotters had undergone training at terrorist camps overseas but had not focused on an American target. In others, such as the New Jersey plot, the government alleges that plotters had identified targets and were trying to purchase arms.

In six cases, accused plotters sought out undercover agents or informers posing as al-Qaeda representatives. In two cases, alleged plotters are accused of swearing allegiance to al-Qaeda in ceremonies staged by the phony Islamists. In eight cases, the accused plotters were native-born Americans, including about a dozen who were converts to Islam.

Intelligence analysts say the lack of an al-Qaeda-led terror strike here may signal that the group is waiting until it can mount an attack that will equal the 9/11 strikes in casualties and publicity value.

For the latest in crime and justice news, visit the Talk Justice news feed at http://www.crimenews.info.

Source: Richard Willing, "FBI, security officials warn of growing threat from Islamic extremists 'next door,'" *USA Today*, http://www.usatoday.com/news/nation/2007-05-13-homegrown-bottomstrip_N.htm (accessed May 13, 2007). From USA TODAY, a division of Garnett Co., Inc. Reprinted with Permission. www.usatoday.com.

A mosque in Dearborn, Michigan. The greater Detroit area is thought to have about 200,000 Arab-Americans—said to be the densest Arab population of any community outside of the Middle East. While most American Muslims are peaceful, law-abiding citizens, the FBI has warned about a threat from homegrown radical Islamic fundamentalists. Do you think that such a threat should be taken seriously?
Andy Larsen

Library EXTRA

Web EXTRA

Initial efforts to develop a comprehensive plan of protection for the nation's critical infrastructure began in 2001 when President George W. Bush created the Office of Homeland Security, making its director a cabinet member. It became a department of the federal government in 2002. Similarly, in an effort to protect vital interests from future acts of terrorism, the U.S. government is building a whole new Internet of its own. Dubbed GOVNET, the service will provide secure voice and data communications for critical government functions by remaining physically and electronically separate from existing Internet routers and gateways.[156] Visit the Department of Homeland Security via Web Extra 2–18 at mycrimekit.com, and view Library Extra 2–27 to learn more about ways of protecting the nation's critical information infrastructure from attacks by terrorists, criminals, and vandals. You can track national and international terror incidents as they occur through the National Counterterrorism Center's Worldwide Incidents Tracking Center, which is available at mycrimekit.com as Web Extra 2–19.

Summary

- The FBI's Uniform Crime Reporting (UCR) Program began in the 1930s when Congress authorized the U.S. attorney general to survey crime in America. Today's UCR/NIBRS Program provides annual data on the number of reported Part I offenses, or major crimes, as well as information about arrests that have been made for less serious, Part II offenses. The Part I offenses are murder, forcible rape, robbery, aggravated assault, burglary, larceny-theft, motor vehicle theft, and arson. The Part II offenses category covers many more crimes, including drug offenses, driving under the influence, and simple assault. Modifications to the UCR Program, which has traditionally provided only summary crime data, are occurring with the implementation of the new National Incident-Based Reporting System (NIBRS). It represents a significant redesign of the original UCR Program and gathers many details about each criminal incident, such as place of occurrence, weapon used, type and value of property damaged or stolen, personal characteristics of the offender and the victim, nature of any relationship between the two, and disposition of the complaint.
- The National Crime Victimization Survey (NCVS) is the second major source of statistical data about crime in the United States. The NCVS, which was first conducted in 1972, is based on victim self-reports rather than on police reports. The NCVS originally built on efforts by both the National Opinion Research Center and the 1967 President's Commission on Law Enforcement and the Administration of Justice to uncover what some had been calling the *dark figure of crime*—that is, those crimes that are not reported to the police and that are relatively hidden from justice system officials. An analysis of victim self-report data led to the realization that crimes of all types were more prevalent than UCR statistics had previously indicated.
- This chapter discusses a number of special categories of crime, including crime against women, crime against the elderly, hate crime, corporate and white-collar crime, organized crime, gun crime, drug crime, cybercrime, and terrorism. Each of these categories is of special concern in contemporary society.

Key Concepts

Terms

aggravated assault
arson
assault
Bureau of Justice Statistics (BJS)
burglary
clearance rate
computer crime
computer virus
corporate crime
Crime Index
crime typology
cyberstalking
cyberterrorism
dark figure of crime
date rape
domestic terrorism
forcible rape
hate crime
identity theft
international terrorism
larceny-theft
malware
motor vehicle theft
murder
National Crime Victimization Survey (NCVS)

National Incident-Based Reporting System (NIBRS)
organized crime
Part I offenses
Part II offenses
property crime
rape
robbery
sexual battery
software piracy
spam
stalking
terrorism
transnational organized crime
Uniform Crime Reporting (UCR) Program
violent crime
white-collar crime

Questions for Review

1. Describe the historical development of the FBI's Uniform Crime Reporting Program, and list the crimes on which it reports. How is the ongoing implementation of the National Incident-Based Reporting System changing the UCR Program? How will data reported under the new UCR/NIBRS differ from the crime statistics reported under the traditional UCR Program?
2. Describe the history of the National Crime Victimization Survey. What do data from the NCVS tell us about crime in the United States today?
3. What are the special categories of crime discussed in this chapter? Why are they important?

To participate in an online discussion of these topics and others, join the CJ Brief e-mail discussion list at mycrimekit.com.

Web Quest

Visit the Prentice Hall Cybrary of Criminal Justice Links on the Web at http://www.cybrary.info, and familiarize yourself with the Cybrary's features. Note that a number of general categories are listed on the home page. (Click "Show All Categories" at the bottom of the page to see more.) The power of the Cybrary lies in its advanced search capabilities.

Practice using the Cybrary's search feature. Once you have become familiar with how the search feature works, use it to find links to the FBI's Uniform Crime Reporting Program (look for the FBI's home page), the *Sourcebook of Criminal Justice Statistics*, and data from the BJS National Crime Victimization Survey.

Visit all three sites to gather information on the crime of rape. Compare the availability of information on rape at these three sites. Compare the sites in other ways. Which do you find most useful? Why? Submit your answers to your instructor if asked to do so.

To complete this Web Quest online, go to the Web Quest module in Chapter 2 of the *Criminal Justice: A Brief Introduction* Companion Website at mycrimekit.com.

Notes

i. Jonathan Turley, "Arrest Me . . . Before I Strike Again," *USA Today,* February 22, 2005, p. 13A.
ii. Dan Eggen, "Major Crimes in U.S. Increase: 2001 Rise Follows Nine Years of Decline," *Washington Post,* June 23, 2002, p. A1.
iii. Ibid.
iv. Identity Theft Resource Center website, http:// www.idtheftcenter.org (accessed April 24, 2008).
v. Violence against Women Office, *Stalking and Domestic Violence: Report to Congress* (Washington, DC: U.S. Department of Justice, 2001), p. 5.
vi. Ibid.
vii. Andrew Backover, "Two Former WorldCom Execs Charged," *USA Today* Online, August 1, 2002, http://www.usatoday.com/money/industries/telecom/2002-08-01-worldcom-execs-surrender_x.htm (accessed August 2, 2006).
viii. Michael Suzanne Malveaux, "Bush to CEO's: No More Fudging the Books," CNN.com, July 3, 2002. Web posted at http://www.cnn.com/2002/ALLPOLITICS/07/03/bush.corporate.reform (accessed July 30, 2002).
ix. Michael L. Benson, Francis T. Cullen, and William J. Maakestad, *Local Prosecutors and Corporate Crime* (Washington, DC: National Institute of Justice, 1992), p. 1.
x. The Organized Crime Control Act of 1970.
xi. Federal Bureau of Investigation Counterterrorism Section, *Terrorism in the United States, 1987* (Washington, DC: FBI, December 1987).
xii. Federal Bureau of Investigation, *FBI Policy and Guidelines: Counterterrorism.* Web posted at http://www.fbi.gov/contact/fo/jackson/cntrterr.htm (accessed August 26, 2002).
xiii. Ibid.

1. James Q. Wilson, "Point of View," *Chronicle of Higher Education,* June 10, 1992, p. A40.
2. "The Programming Insider," *MediaWeek,* February 22, 2005. See also Bill Keveney, "Crime Pays for 'CSI' Franchise," *USA Today,* September 16, 2004, p. D1.
3. NBC-TV, "Law and Order: About the Show," http://www.nbc.com/Law_&_Order/about (accessed March 7, 2006).

4. Norval Morris, "Crime, the Media, and Our Public Discourse," National Institute of Justice, Perspectives on Crime and Justice video series, recorded May 13, 1997.
5. Ibid.
6. See, for example, *A Gathering Storm: Violent Crime in America* (Washington, DC: Police Executive Research Forum, 2006).
7. Police Executive Research Forum, *Violent Crime in America: 24 Months of Alarming Trends* (Washington, DC: PERF, 2007).
8. Federal Bureau of Investigation, *Crime in the United States, 1987* (Washington, DC: U.S. Department of Justice, 1988), p. 1.
9. Federal Bureau of Investigation, "About the UCR Program," no date, http://www.fbi.gov/ucr/05cius/about/about_ucr.html (accessed May 29, 2007). The term "crime index" was originally recommended for reevaluation in 2004, but it wasn't until 2006 that use of the term was officially discontinued.
10. See the FBI's UCR/NIBRS website at http://www.fbi.gov/hq/ cjisd/ ucr.htm (accessed August 27, 2005).
11. The 1990 Crime Awareness and Campus Security Act (Public Law 101-542) required college campuses to commence publishing annual security reports beginning in September 1992.
12. U.S. Department of Education, *Summary Campus Crime and Security Statistics, 2002–2004* (Washington, DC: U.S. Department of Education, 2007).
13. Katrina Baum and Patsy Klaus, *Violent Victimization of College Students, 1995–2002* (Washington, DC: Bureau of Justice Statistics, 2005).
14. Federal Bureau of Investigation, *Crime in the United States, 2006* (Washington, DC: U.S. Department of Justice, 2007).
15. President's Commission on Law Enforcement and Administration of Justice, *The Challenge of Crime in a Free Society* (Washington, DC: U.S. Government Printing Office, 1967). The commission relied on Uniform Crime Reports data. The other crime statistics reported in this section come from Uniform Crime Reports for various years.
16. Frank Hagan, *Research Methods in Criminal Justice and Criminology* (New York: Macmillan, 1982).
17. U.S. Department of Justice, *Fiscal Years 2000–2005 Strategic Plan* (Washington, DC: U.S. Government Printing Office, 2000).
18. The war on drugs, and the use of that term, can be traced back to the Nixon administration. See Dan Baum, *Smoke and Mirrors: The War on Drugs and the Politics of Failure,* reprint ed. (Boston: Little, Brown, 1997).
19. John J. DiIulio, Jr., "The Question of Black Crime," *Public Interest* (fall 1994), pp. 3–12.
20. Quoted in Dan Eggen, "Major Crimes in U.S. Increase: 2001 Rise Follows Nine Years of Decline," *Washington Post,* June 23, 2002, p. A1.
21. Police Executive Research Forum, *Violent Crime in America: 24 Months of Alarming Trends*, http://www.policeforum.org/upload/Violent%20Crime%20Report%203707_140194792_392007143035.pdf (accessed August 18, 2008).
22. Ibid., p. i.
23. Jim Kessler, Rachel Laser, Michael Earls, and Nikki Yamashiro, *The Impending Crime Wave: Four Dangerous New Trends and How to Stop Them* (Washington, DC: The Third Way Foundation, February 2008).
24. That is, while crime clock data may imply that one murder occurs every half hour or so, most murders actually occur during the evening, and only a very few take place around sunrise.
25. Most offense definitions in this chapter are derived from those used by the UCR/NIBRS Program and are taken from the FBI's *Crime in the United States, 2006* or from the Bureau of Justice Statistics, *Criminal Justice Data Terminology,* 2nd ed. (Washington, DC: BJS, 1981).
26. These and other statistics in this chapter are derived primarily from the FBI's *Crime in the United States, 2006.*
27. Bureau of Justice Statistics, *Report to the Nation on Crime and Justice,* 2nd ed. (Washington, DC: U.S. Government Printing Office, 1988), p. 4.
28. "Feds Deny Thwarting Sniper Suspect's Confession," CNN.com, October 31, 2002, http://www.cnn.com/2002/US/10/30/snipers.interrogation/index.html (accessed October 31, 2002).
29. "Sniper Malvo Given Second Life Sentence," *USA Today,* October 27, 2004, p. 3A.
30. BJS, *Report to the Nation on Crime and Justice,* p. 4.
31. Ibid.
32. For excellent coverage of serial killers, see Steven Egger, *The Killers among Us: An Examination of Serial Murder and Its Investigation* (Upper Saddle River, NJ: Prentice Hall, 1998); Steven A. Egger, *Serial Murder: An Elusive Phenomenon* (Westport, CT: Praeger, 1990); and Stephen J. Giannangelo, *The Psychopathology of Serial Murder: A Theory of Violence* (New York: Praeger, 1996).
33. "BTK" stands for "Bind, Torture, and Kill," an acronym that Rader applied to himself in letters he sent to the media during the 1970s.
34. Several years ago, Lucas recanted all of his confessions, saying that he had never killed anyone—except possibly his mother, a killing he said he didn't remember. See "Condemned Killer Admits Lying, Denies Slayings," *Washington Post,* October 1, 1995.
35. Chikatilo was executed in 1994.
36. See Mark Babineck, "Railroad Killer Gets Death Penalty," Associated Press, May 22, 2000, http://cnews.tribune.com/news/tribune/story/0,1235,tribune-nation-37649,00.html (accessed March 3, 2002).
37. Public Law 108-212.
38. FBI, *Crime in the United States, 2007.*
39. Federal Bureau of Investigation, *Uniform Crime Reporting Handbook, 2004* (Washington, DC: FBI, 2005), p. 19.
40. "Study: Rape Vastly Underreported," Associated Press, April 26, 1992.
41. Ronald Barri Flowers, *Women and Criminality: The Woman as Victim, Offender, and Practitioner* (Westport, CT: Greenwood Press, 1987), p. 36.
42. A. Nichols Groth, *Men Who Rape: The Psychology of the Offender* (New York: Plenum Press, 1979).
43. Susan Brownmiller, *Against Our Will: Men, Women, and Rape* (New York: Simon and Schuster, 1975).
44. Dennis J. Stevens, "Motives of Social Rapists," *Free Inquiry in Creative Sociology,* Vol. 23, No. 2 (November 1995), pp. 117–126.
45. BJS, *Report to the Nation on Crime and Justice,* p. 5.
46. Ibid.
47. FBI, *Crime in the United States, 2007.* For UCR program reporting purposes, *minorities* are defined as African-Americans, Native Americans, Asians, Pacific Islanders, and Alaskan Natives.
48. "Easter Bunny Charged with Battery for Mall Attack," Associated Press, April 18, 2006.
49. This offense is sometimes called *assault with a deadly weapon with intent to kill* (AWDWWITK).
50. FBI, *Crime in the United States, 2007.*
51. BJS, *Report to the Nation on Crime and Justice,* p. 6.
52. Ibid.
53. "Four Arrested for Stealing Moon Rocks," Associated Press, July 23, 2002; and Sheena McFarland, "U. Student Arrested for Moon Rock Theft," *Daily Utah Chronicle* online, http://www.dailyutahchronicle.com/main.cfm/include/detail/storyid/259076.html (accessed August 22, 2005).
54. "Yale Says Student Stole His Education," *USA Today,* April 12, 1995, p. 3A.
55. Steven J. Vaughan-Nichols, "Cisco Source Code Reportedly Stolen," *eWeek,* May 18, 2004, http://www.eweek.com/article2/0,1759,1593862,00.asp (accessed May 17, 2007).
56. Ibid.
57. FBI, *Uniform Crime Reporting Handbook, 2004,* p. 28.
58. Matt Stearns and Donald Bradley, "Boy's Last Moments of Life Are Frozen in Mother's Memory," *Kansas City Star,* February 23, 2000.
59. "Jury Recommends Life Term in Dragging Death Wednesday," Associated Press, October 3, 2001.

60. Patsy Klaus, *Carjacking, 1993–2002* (Washington, DC: Bureau of Justice Statistics, July 2004).
61. FBI, *Crime in the United States, 2007*.
62. As indicated in the UCR definition of *arson*. See Federal Bureau of Investigation, *Crime in the United States, 1998* (Washington, DC: U.S. Department of Justice, 1999).
63. FBI, *Crime in the United States, 2007*.
64. Ibid.
65. "Trends in Crime and Victimization," *Criminal Justice Research Reports*, Vol. 2, No. 6 (July/August 2001), p. 83.
66. For additional information, see Michael Rand and Shannan M. Catalano, *Criminal Victimization, 2006* (Washington, DC: Bureau of Justice Statistics, 2007); and Patsy A. Klaus, *Crime and the Nation's Households, 2006* (Washington, DC: Bureau of Justice Statistics, 2007).
67. Klaus, *Crime and the Nation's Households, 2006*.
68. Rand and Catalano, *Criminal Victimization, 2006*.
69. Ibid., p. 1.
70. See, for example, President's Commission on Law Enforcement and Administration of Justice, *The Challenge of Crime in a Free Society*, pp. 22–23.
71. BJS, *Report to the Nation on Crime and Justice*, p. 27.
72. Hagan, *Research Methods in Criminal Justice and Criminology*, p. 89.
73. Bureau of Justice Statistics, *Criminal Victimization in the United States, 1985* (Washington, DC: U.S. Government Printing Office, 1987), p. 1.
74. FBI, *Crime in the United States, 2001*, preliminary data, http://www.fbi.gov./ucr/01prelim.pdf (accessed August 27, 2002).
75. Terance D. Miethe and Richard C. McCorkle, *Crime Profiles: The Anatomy of Dangerous Persons, Places, and Situations* (Los Angeles: Roxbury, 1998), p. 19.
76. The definition of *rape* employed by the UCR/NIBRS Program, however, automatically excludes crimes of homosexual rape such as might occur in prisons and jails. As a consequence, the rape of males is excluded from the official count for crimes of rape.
77. Rand and Catalano, *Criminal Victimization, 2006*, p. 4.
78. Thomas Simon et al., *Injuries from Violent Crime, 1992–98* (Washington, DC: Bureau of Justice Statistics, 2001), p. 5.
79. See, for example, Elizabeth Stanko, "When Precaution Is Normal: A Feminist Critique of Crime Prevention," in Loraine Gelsthorpe and Allison Morris, eds., *Feminist Perspectives in Criminology* (Philadelphia: Open University Press, 1990).
80. For more information, see Eve S. Buzawa and Carl G. Buzawa, *Domestic Violence: The Criminal Justice Response* (Thousand Oaks, CA: Sage, 1996).
81. "Battered Women Tell Their Stories to the Senate," *Charlotte (NC) Observer*, July 10, 1991, p. 3A.
82. Patricia Tjaden and Nancy Thoennes, *Full Report of the Prevalence, Incidence, and Consequences of Violence against Women: Findings from the National Violence against Women Survey* (Washington, DC: National Institute of Justice, 2000).
83. Caroline Wolf Harlow, *Female Victims of Violent Crime* (Washington, DC: Bureau of Justice Statistics, 1991).
84. Violence against Women Office, *Stalking and Domestic Violence: Report to Congress* (Washington, DC: U.S. Department of Justice, 2001).
85. U.S. Code, Title 18, Section 2261A.
86. As modified through VAWA 2000.
87. Violence against Women Office, *Stalking and Domestic Violence*.
88. Many of the data in this section come from Bureau of Justice Statistics, *Crimes against Persons Age 65 or Older, 1993–2002* (Rockville, MD: BJS, 2005).
89. Lamar Jordan, "Law Enforcement and the Elderly: A Concern for the Twenty-First Century," *FBI Law Enforcement Bulletin*, May 2002, pp. 20–23.
90. Public Law 101-275.
91. H.R. 4797, 102d Cong. 2d Sess. (1992).
92. FBI, *Crime in the United States, 2007*.
93. "Sept. 11 Attacks Cited in Nearly 25 Percent Increase in Florida Hate Crimes," Associated Press, August 30, 2002.
94. "Dragging Death Still Haunts Family," APB News, June 7, 1999, http://www.apbnews.com/newscenter/breakingnews/1999/06/07/byrd060701.html (accessed January 2, 2000).
95. "Nationline," *USA Today*, June 2, 2008, p. 3A.
96. Leslie Gevirtz and Martha Graybow, "Bayou's Boss Sentenced to 20 Years in Prison," Reuters, April 14, 2008.
97. Rita Rubin, "Justice Investigates Metabolife," *USA Today*, August 16–18, 2002, p. 1A.
98. Brooke A. Masters and Ben White, "Adelphia Founder, Son Convicted of Fraud," *Washington Post*, July 9, 2004, p. E1.
99. Dionne Searcey and Li Yuan, "Adelphia's John Rigas Gets 15 Years," *Wall Street Journal*, June 21, 2005, p. A3.
100. Samuel Maull, "Ex-Tyco Execs Convicted in Second Trial," WashingtonPost.com, June 18, 2005, http://www.washingtonpost.com/wp-dyn/content/article/2005/06/17/AR2005061700863.html (accessed May 17, 2007).
101. "Enron's Lay, Skilling Convicted," Associated Press, May 25, 2006.
102. *Andersen* v. *U.S.*, 544 U.S. 696 (2005).
103. Public Broadcasting System, "Enron: After the Collapse," http://www.pbs.org/newshour/bb/business/enron/player6.html (accessed August 27, 2005).
104. Edwin H. Sutherland, "White-Collar Criminality," *American Sociological Review* (February 1940), p. 12.
105. Scott Lindlaw, "Bush to Propose Crackdown on Corporate Abuses: President's Own Business Dealings Come under Scrutiny," Associated Press, July 9, 2002, http://www.washingtonpost.com/wp-dyn/articles/A43384-2002Jul9.html (accessed May 17, 2005).
106. Public Law 107-204.
107. R. James Woolsey, as quoted on the Transnational Threats Initiative home page of the Center for Strategic and International Studies (CSIS), http://www.csis.org/tnt/index.htm (accessed August 22, 2007).
108. These ideas were originally expressed by Assistant U.S. Attorney General Laurie Robinson in an address given at the Twelfth International Congress on Criminology, Seoul, Korea, August 28, 1998.
109. Caroline Wolf Harlow, *Firearm Use by Offenders* (Washington, DC: Bureau of Justice Statistics, 2001).
110. Ibid., p. 1.
111. U.S. Code, Title 18, Section 922(q)(1)(A).
112. Harlow, *Firearm Use by Offenders*.
113. *Firearms Purchased from Federal Firearm Licensees Using Bogus Identification* (Washington, DC: General Accounting Office, 2001).
114. John C. Moorhouse and Brent Wanner, "Does Gun Control Reduce Crime or Does Crime Increase Gun Control?" *CATO Journal*, Vol. 103 (2006), pp. 103–124.
115. Sarah Brady, "Statement on the Sniper Shootings," October 8, 2002, http://www.bradycampaign.org/press/release.asp?Record 5429 (accessed October 16, 2005).
116. "Microstamping of Firearms Required by California Law," *Criminal Justice Newsletter*, October 2, 2007, p. 1.
117. Tony Perry, "96 Arrested in San Diego State Drug Bust," *Los Angeles Times*, May 7, 2008. Web posted at http://www.latimes.com/news/local/la-me-drugbust7-2008may07,0,3741335.story?page=1 (accessed May 7, 2008).
118. As cited in Donna Leinwand, "Drug, Terror Rings Find New Ways to Launder Money," *USA Today*, January 12, 2006, p. 5A.
119. J. M. Chaiken and M. R. Chaiken, *Varieties of Criminal Behavior* (Santa Monica, CA: RAND Corporation, 1982).
120. D. McBride, "Trends in Drugs and Death," paper presented at the annual meeting of the American Society of Criminology, Denver, CO, 1983.

121. National Criminal Justice Reference Service, *The Micro Domain: Behavior and Homicide,* http://www.ncjrs.org/pdffiles/167262-3.pdf (accessed February 23, 2002).
122. Bureau of Justice Statistics, *Substance Abuse and Treatment: State and Federal Prisoners* (Washington, DC: U.S. Department of Justice, January 1999).
123. Bureau of Justice Statistics, *Drug Use, Testing, and Treatment in Jails* (Washington, DC: U.S. Department of Justice, May 2000).
124. Information in this paragraph comes from John Scalia, *Federal Drug Offenders, 1999, with Trends, 1984–99* (Washington, DC: Bureau of Justice Statistics, 2001); and Bureau of Justice Statistics, *Federal Criminal Case Processing, 2002—With Trends 1982–2002* (Washington, DC: BJS, 2005).
125. Ibid.
126. Ryan Naraine, "Cryzip Trojan Encrypts Files, Demands Ransom," eWeek.com, March 13, 2006. Web posted at http://www.eweek.com/article2/0,1895,1937408,00.asp?kc=ewnws031406dtx1k0000599 (accessed January 5, 2007).
127. For suggested computer-crime categories, see Peter Grabosky, "Computer Crime: A Criminological Overview," paper presented at the Workshop on Crimes Related to the Computer Network, Tenth United Nations Congress on the Prevention of Crime and the Treatment of Offenders, Vienna, Austria, April 15, 2000. Web posted at http://www.aic.gov.au/conferences/other/compcrime/computercrime.pdf (accessed January 12, 2002). Also see David L. Carter, "Computer Crime Categories: How Techno-Criminals Operate," *FBI Law Enforcement Journal* (July 1995), pp. 21–26.
128. Grabosky, "Computer Crime."
129. Kevin Johnson, "Hijackers' E-Mails Sifted for Clues," *USA Today,* October 11, 2001.
130. "Husband, Wife Charged with Running Prostitution Ring from Home," Associated Press wire service, December 18, 2003.
131. Richard Zitrin, "Woman Charged with Online Prostitution," APB Online, June 10, 1999. Web posted at http://www.apbonline.com/911/1999/06/10/hooker0610_01.html (accessed June 19, 1999).
132. "Invasion of the Data Snatchers!" *Time,* September 26, 1988, pp. 62–67.
133. Software Information & Industry Association, *Report on Global Software Piracy, 2000.* Web posted at http://www.siia.net/piracy/pubs/piracy2000.pdf (accessed August 1, 2005).
134. Public Law 108-187.
135. Peter Firstbrook, "META Trend Update: The Changing Threat Landscape," The Meta Group, March 24, 2005. Web posted at http://www.metagroup.com/us/displayArticle.do?oid551768 (accessed July 5, 2005).
136. *MGM* v. *Grokster,* U.S. Supreme Court, No. 04-480 (decided June 27, 2005).
137. Pending federal legislation, known as the Conyers-Berman bill, would allow felony charges to be brought against users of illegal peer-to-peer services and would provide for a maximum prison term of five years.
138. Gregg Keizer, "Microsoft Says Phishing Bad, Offers Little New for Defense," *TechWeb News,* March 15, 2005. Web posted at http://www.techweb.com/wire/159900391 (accessed July 7, 2005).
139. Avivah Litan, "Phishing Victims Likely Will Suffer Identity Theft Fraud," Gartner, Inc., May 14, 2004. Web posted at http://www.gartner.com/DisplayDocument?ref5g_search&id544811 (accessed July 6, 2005).
140. Computer Security Institute, *2005 CSI/FBI Computer Crime and Security Survey* (Southampton, PA: Computer Security Institute, 2005), pp. 8–9. Web posted at http://i.cmpnet.com/gocsi/db_area/pdfs/fbi/FBI2004.pdf (accessed January 2, 2007).
141. "Focus on Physical Security, Too," *eWeek,* January 27, 2003, p. 6a.
142. Ibid., p. 5.
143. Ramona R. Rantala, *Cybercrime against Businesses: Pilot Test Results, 2001 Computer Security Survey* (Washington, DC: Bureau of Justice Statistics, 2004).
144. Emergency Response and Research Institute, *Summary of Emergency Response and Research Institute Terrorism Statistics: 2000 and 2001.* Web posted at http://www.emergency.com/2002/terroris00-01.pdf (accessed August 22, 2002).
145. Federal Bureau of Investigation, Counterterrorism Section, *Terrorism in the United States, 1987* (Washington, DC: FBI, 1987), in which the full version of the definition offered here can be found. See also *FBI Policy and Guidelines: Counterterrorism,* which offers a somewhat less formal definition of the term. Web posted at http://www.fbi.gov/contact/fo/jackson/cntrterr.htm (accessed January 15, 2002).
146. Adapted from *FBI Policy and Guidelines: Counterterrorism.*
147. Ibid.
148. See Barry Collin, "The Future of Cyberterrorism," *Crime and Justice International* (March 1997), pp. 15–18.
149. John Arquilla and David Ronfeldt, *The Advent of Netwar* (Santa Monica, CA: RAND Corporation, 1996).
150. Mark M. Pollitt, "Cyberterrorism: Fact or Fancy?" in *Proceedings of the Twentieth National Information Systems Security Conference*, October 1997, pp. 285–289.
151. "Chief Security Officers Remind Citizens of the Dangers of Cyberattacks and Recommend Tips," *CSO Magazine* online. Web posted at http://www2.csoonline.html/info/release.html?CID=9065 (accessed August 28, 2006).
152. Robert S. Mueller III, executive speech at Chatham House (London, England), April 7, 2008. Web available at http://www.fbi.gov/pressrel/speeches/mueller040708.htm (accessed May 20, 2008).
153. Central Intelligence Agency, National Foreign Intelligence Council, *Global Trends, 2015: A Dialogue about the Future with Nongovernment Experts* (Washington, DC: U.S. Government Printing Office, 2000).
154. Ibid.
155. Mimi Hall, "Report: USA Left Open to Attack," *USA Today,* December 6, 2005, p. 1A.
156. "U.S. Plans New Secure Government Internet," Associated Press wire service, October 11, 2001.

The Search for Causes

3

The Search for Causes

LEARNING OBJECTIVES

After reading this chapter, you should be able to

- Explain the nature of criminological theory and discuss the role that social research plays in the development of such theory.
- Describe the Classical School of criminology, and show how it continues to influence criminological theorizing today.
- Describe the basic features of biological theories of crime causation, and know their shortcomings.
- Explain how the mapping of human DNA has enhanced contemporary psychobiological understandings of criminal behavior.
- Describe the fundamental assumptions of psychological explanations for crime, and know the shortcomings of such explanations.
- Describe the basic features of sociological theories of crime causation.
- Describe social process theories of criminology, and identify the kinds of crime-control policies that might be based on them.
- Describe conflict theories of criminality, and identify the kinds of crime-control policies that might be based on them.
- Identify three emergent theories of crime causation.

OUTLINE

During the last several years, violent crime in America has been decreasing. And all Americans are grateful. . . . But, unfortunately, American society is still far too violent. The violent crime rate in the United States remains among the highest in the industrialized world.

—President George W. Bush[1]

I could kill everyone without blinking an eye!

—Charlie Manson[2]

Hear the author discuss this chapter at cjtoday.com

Introduction

In August 2006, well-known rapper Busta Rhymes was arrested by New York City police after he performed at the AmsterJam Music Festival. He was charged with assault for allegedly attacking a man who spit on his car.[3] A few months later, Rhymes—whose legal name is Trevor Smith—was accused of beating his former driver, Edward Hatchett, and of kicking him in the ribs during a dispute over back pay. The alleged attack, which was said to have taken place outside of Rhymes's Lower Manhattan office, left Hatchett with cuts, bruises, and substantial pain, according to a court complaint.[4]

Brushes with the law are nothing new to Rhymes. In February 2006, his bodyguard, 29-year-old Israel Ramirez, was shot to death outside a Brooklyn studio where Rhymes was recording a music video. About the same time, the performer and another of his bodyguards were sued by a fan who said the two men beat him after he asked for an autograph. Rhymes's arrest record extends back at least as far as 1998, when he and his manager were apprehended and charged with third-degree criminal possession of a concealed weapon. Police reportedly found an unregistered but loaded .45-caliber semiautomatic handgun in the singer's Mercedes after they stopped him for erratic driving.[5] Rhymes's most recent arrest came shortly before dawn on February 21, 2007, when he was stopped and taken into custody in Lower Manhattan for driving with a suspended license. According to police, Rhymes was pulled over for running a red light at 5:30 A.M.[6]

Rapper Busta Rhymes arriving at the 2006 BET Awards in Los Angeles. Rhymes has been arrested numerous times, leading some to claim that rap and some forms of hip-hop music lead to crime. What do you think?

Getty Images, Inc.

Rhymes is certainly not the only rapper to become acquainted with the criminal justice system. In April 2000, hip-hop artist Curtis "50 Cent" Jackson, a rising star in the world of hard-core rap music, was shot nine times in front of his grandmother's home in New York City.[7] One of the bullets hit him in the face. "50," as the singer is known to his fans, survived the shooting but spent months recovering. Two years later, 50 was back on the music scene, having recorded a top-selling album, *Get Rich or Die Tryin'*, propelled by his hit song "In Da Club." In 2002, he made headlines when he was arrested on New Year's Eve for illegal possession of a handgun.[8] 50 told fans that he'd had a bulletproof jacket made for his six-year-old son. In 2005, 50 released the album *The Massacre*, which quickly went Platinum, and his songs "Disco Inferno," "Candy Shop," and "P.I.M.P." topped the hip-hop charts.

As these stories illustrate, violent crime is no stranger to the world of hard-core rap music. Murdered rap stars include Tupac Shakur, Notorious B.I.G., Big L., and the Lost Boyz's hip-hop hype man Raymond "Freaky Tah" Rogers. Whether rap music merely reflects the social conditions under which its artists come of age or whether it is a direct cause of the violence that surrounds them is a question to which we will return shortly.

No discussion of crime and of the criminal justice system would be complete without considering the *causes* of crime and **deviance**. Criminologists search for answers to the fundamental questions about what causes crime: Why do people commit crime? What are the root causes of violence and aggression? Are people basically good, or are they motivated only by self-interest? More precisely, we might ask, "Why does a particular person commit a particular crime on a given occasion and under specific circumstances?"

deviance

A violation of social norms defining appropriate or proper behavior under a particular set of circumstances. Deviance often includes criminal acts.

In this chapter, we will look at the causes of crime. Before we begin, however, some brief definitions are in order. *Crime* is a violation of the criminal law without acceptable legal justification,[9] while *deviant behavior* is a violation of social norms that specify appropriate or proper behavior under a particular set of circumstances. Deviant behavior is a broad category that often includes crime.

Many theories have been advanced to explain all sorts of rule-violating behavior. Some observers of the contemporary scene, for example, blame much of today's crime on commonplace episodes of violence in the American media—especially on television, in music, and on film. Experts who study the media estimate that the average American child watches 8,000 murders and 100,000 acts of violence while growing up.[10] At an international conference, Suzanne Stutman, president of the Institute for Mental Health Initiatives, a nonprofit organization in Washington, D.C., reported that studies consistently show that the extent of exposure to television violence in childhood is a good predictor of future criminal behavior.[11] One particular study, released in 2002, found that watching just one hour of television a day can make a person more violent toward others.[12] The study, which was conducted over a 25-year period at New York's Columbia University, used police records to confirm that 45% of young men who had watched three or more hours of television a day went on to commit at least one aggressive act against another person, compared to 9% of young men who had watched for less than one hour per day.

Robert Brown, executive director of the Washington, D.C., Children's Trust Neighborhood Initiative, lays much of the blame for contemporary violence on rap music, especially "gangsta rap" and some forms of hip-hop. "So many of our young men," says Brown, "have accepted false icons of manhood for themselves . . . because the popular culture of videos and rap—Snoop Doggy Dogg and the rest—reinforces that this is the correct way to be. Guys . . . try to exude an aura that says, 'I am so bad that I am not afraid to take your life or to offer mine up in the process.' "[13]

An African American critic of gangsta rap puts it this way: "The key element is aggression—in rappers' body language, tone, and witty rhymes—that often leaves listeners hyped, on edge, angry about . . . something. Perhaps the most important element in gangsta rap is its messages, which center largely around these ideas: that women are no more than 'bitches and hos,' disposable playthings who exist merely for men's abusive delight; that it's cool to use any means necessary to get the material things you want; and most importantly, it's admirable to be cold-blooded and hard."[14] The Reverend Arthur L. Cribbs, Jr., an African American social critic, agrees. Cribbs calls gangsta rap "nothing but modern-day violence and vulgarity wrapped and packaged in blackface."[15]

Most people agree that media violence harms society. According to one survey, "57% of the public thinks violence in the media is a major factor in real-life violence" of all kinds.[16] But it is less than clear whether violence in the media and aggressive themes in popular music are indeed a cause of crime, as many believe, or merely a reflection of the social conditions that exist in many American communities today. Findings from studies on the effect of television viewing, for example, may be inadvertently spotlighting existing criminal tendencies among lower-class undereducated teenagers with enough time on their hands for extensive TV viewing. Hence, getting legislators to address the issue of violence in the media is difficult. For example,

The political right believes that the root cause of violent crime is bad genes or bad morals. Not so, says the left. The root cause of violent crime is bad housing or dead-end jobs. And I tell you that while doing something about the causes of violence surely requires a political ideology, the only way we can determine what those causes are in the first place is to check our ideologies at the door and to try to keep our minds open as wide, and for as long, as we can bear.

—John Monahan, speaking at the U.S. Sentencing Commission's Inaugural Symposium on Crime and Punishment

a proposed labeling system for video games and other forms of entertainment was advanced several years ago by Representatives Zach Wamp (R-Tenn.) and Bart Stupak (D-Mich.). They argued that the government requires warning labels on food, alcohol, and tobacco and should do likewise on sources of violence, but the proposal was voted down 266-161.[17]

Criminological Theory

It is easy to understand why the entertainment industry and the media are often targeted as the cause of crime and criminal violence. However, many other types of explanations for crime are also viable, such as genetic abnormalities, individual psychological differences, and variations in patterns of early socialization that may predispose some people to crime and violence. Likewise, it is prudent to examine social institutions such as the family, schools, and churches for their role in reducing or enhancing the likelihood of criminality among people.

One thing is certain: There is no single cause of crime; it is rooted in a diversity of causal factors and takes a variety of forms, depending on the situation in which it occurs. Nonetheless, some theories of human behavior help us understand why certain people engage in acts that society defines as criminal or deviant, while others do not. A **theory** is a kind of model. Theories posit relationships, often of a causal sort, between events and things under study. Formally, a complete theory consists of a series of interrelated propositions that attempt to describe, explain, predict, and ultimately control some class of events. A theory's explanatory power derives primarily from its inherent logical consistency, and theories are tested by how well they describe and predict reality. In other words, a good theory provides a relatively complete understanding of the phenomenon under study, and carefully made observations support predictions based on the theory. A good theory fits the facts, and it stands up to continued scrutiny. Figure 1 uses the association between poverty and crime as an example to diagram the important aspects of theory creation in the social sciences.

theory

A set of interrelated propositions that attempt to describe, explain, predict, and ultimately control some class of events. A theory is strengthened by its logical consistency and is "tested" by how well it describes and predicts reality.

History is rife with theories purporting to explain rule-violating behavior. For example, an old Roman theory, based on ancient observations that more crime and deviance occur on nights with a full moon, proposed that the moon causes a kind of temporary insanity, or *lunacy.* According to this theory, deviant behavior isn't random; it waxes and wanes in cadence with the lunar cycle. Although modern statisticians have noted an association between phases of the moon and crime rates, the precise mechanism by which the moon influences behavior—if it does—has never been adequately explained.

As mentioned, a complete theory attempts to flesh out all of the causal links between phenomena that are associated or "correlated." For example, some comprehensive theories of lunacy suggest that light from the full moon stimulates the reticular-activating system (RAS) in the limbic portion of the human brain, which makes people more excitable and hyperactive—and thus more likely to behave in deviant ways and to commit crime. Others have suggested, quite simply, that people commit more crimes when the moon is full because it is easier to see.

Theories, once created, must be tested to determine whether they are valid, and modern criminology has become increasingly scientific.[18] Theory testing usually involves the development of **hypotheses** based on what the theory under scrutiny would predict. A theory of lunacy, for example, might be tested in a variety of ways, including (1) observing rates of crime and deviance on nights when the light of the full moon is obscured by clouds (we would expect no rise in crime rates if the RAS or visibility explanations are correct); and (2) examining city crime rates on full-moon nights—especially in well-lit city areas where the light of the moon hardly increases visibility. If the predictions made by a theory are validated by careful observation, the theory gains greater acceptability.

hypothesis

An explanation that accounts for a set of facts and that can be tested by further investigation. Also, something that is taken to be true for the purpose of argument or investigation.[i]

Generally accepted research designs—coupled with careful data-gathering strategies and statistical techniques for data analysis—have yielded considerable confidence in certain explanations for crime, while at the same time disproving others. Theories of crime causation that have met rigorous scientific tests for acceptability give policymakers the intellectual basis they need to create informed crime-control strategies. The ultimate goal of **research** and theory building in criminology is to provide models that permit a better understanding of criminal behavior and that enhance the development of strategies intended to address the problem of crime.

research

The use of standardized, systematic procedures in the search for knowledge.

While we will use the word *theory* in describing various explanations for crime throughout this chapter, it should be recognized that the word is only loosely applicable to some of the perspectives we will discuss. As noted, many social scientists insist that to be considered "theories," explanations must consist of sets of clearly stated, logically interrelated, and measurable propositions. The fact that few of the "theories" that follow rise above the level of organized conjecture, and that many others are not readily amenable to objective scrutiny through scientific testing, is one of the greatest failures of social science today.

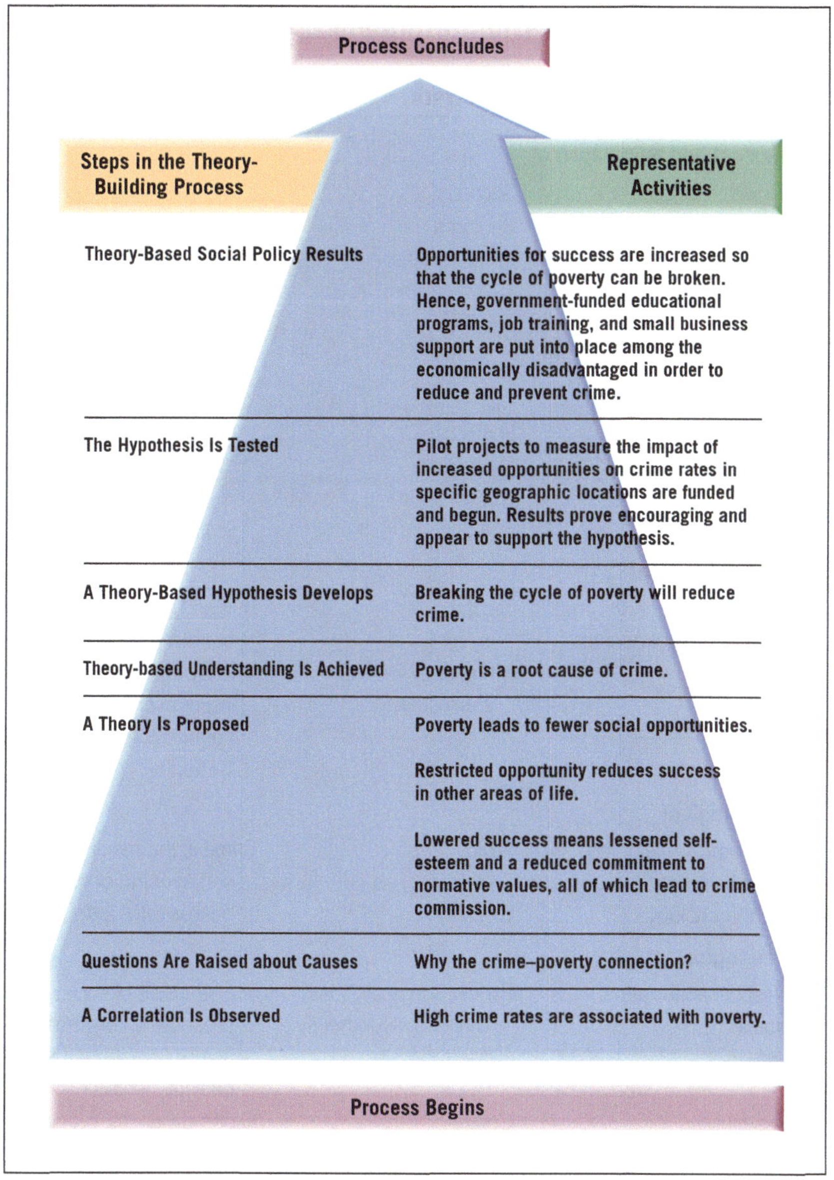

FIGURE 1

Steps in criminological theory building and social policy creation.

Also, many contemporary theories of deviant and criminal behavior are far from complete, offering only limited ideas rather than complete explanations for the behavior in question. Moreover, when we consider the wide range of behaviors regarded as criminal—from murder to drug use to white-collar crime—it is difficult to imagine a theory that can explain them all.

For our purposes, explanations of criminal behavior fall into eight general categories:

- Classical
- Biological
- Psychobiological
- Psychological
- Sociological
- Social process
- Conflict
- Emergent

The differences among these approaches are summarized in Table 1. A ninth category could be **interdisciplinary theories**. These approaches integrate a variety of theoretical viewpoints in an attempt to explain crime and violence. Harvard University's Project on Human Development in

interdisciplinary theory

An approach that integrates a variety of theoretical viewpoints in an attempt to explain something, such as crime and violence.

TABLE 1 Types of Criminological Theory

Type	Theorists	Characteristics
Classical and Neoclassical		
Free will theories	Beccaria	Crime is caused by the individual exercise of free will.
Hedonistic calculus	Bentham	Prevention is possible through swift and certain punishment that offsets any gains to be had through criminal behavior.
Rational choice theory	Cohen & Felson	
Routine activities theory		
Biological		
Phrenology	Gall	"Criminal genes" cause deviant behavior. Criminals are identifiable through physical characteristics or genetic makeup. Treatment is generally ineffective, but aggression may be usefully redirected.
Atavism	Lombroso	
Criminal families	Dugdale; Goddard	
Somatotypes	Sheldon	
Psychobiological		
Chromosome theory	Jacobs	Human DNA, environmental contaminants, nutrition, hormones, physical trauma, and body chemistry play important and interwoven roles in producing human cognition, feeling, and behavior—including crime.
Biochemical approaches		
Heredity	Mednick; Wilson & Herrnstein	
Psychological		
Behavioral conditioning	Pavlov	Crime is the result of inappropriate behavioral conditioning or a diseased mind. Treatment necessitates extensive behavioral therapy.
Psychoanalysis	Freud	
Psychopathology	Cleckley	
Sociological		
Social disorganization	Park & Burgess; Shaw & McKay Durkheim; Merton	The structure of society and its relative degree of organization or disorganization are important actors contributing to the prevalence of criminal behavior.
Anomie		
Subcultures	Cohen	Group dynamics, group organization, and subgroup relationships form the causal nexus out of which crime develops. Effective social policy may require basic changes in patterns of socialization and an increase in accepted opportunities for success.
Focal concerns	Miller	
Subculture of violence	Wolfgang & Ferracuti	
Social Process		
Differential association	Sutherland	Crime results from the failure of self-direction, inadequate social roles, or association with defective others. Social policy places responsibility for change on the offender.
Social learning	Burgess & Akers	
Containment	Reckless	
Social control	Hirschi	
Neutralization	Sykes & Matza	
Labeling	Becker	The source of criminal behavior is unknown, but an understanding of crime requires recognition that the definition of crime is imposed on behavior by the wider society. Individuals defined as "criminal" may be excluded by society from "normal" opportunities. Therapy requires a total reorientation of the offender.

TABLE 1 Types of Criminological Theory *(continued)*

Type	Theorists	Characteristics
Social development theory Life course perspective	Sampson & Laub	Human development occurs simultaneously on many levels, including psychological, biological, familial, interpersonal, cultural, societal, and ecological. The life course perspective notes that criminal behavior tends to follow an identifiable pattern throughout a person's life cycle.
Conflict		
Radical criminology	Turk; Vold; Chambliss	Conflict is fundamental to social life. Crime is a natural consequence of social, political, and economic inequities.
Peacemaking criminology	Pepinsky; Quinney	Fundamental changes to the structure of society are needed to eliminate crime.
Emergent		
Feminist criminology	Adler; Simon; Daly & Chesney-Lind	Feminist criminology emphasizes the need for gender awareness in the criminological enterprise.
Constitutive criminology	Henry & Milovanovic	Crime is a social phenomenon and, as such, is socially constructed.
Postmodern criminology	Henry & Milovanovic	Deconstructionist approaches challenge existing theories in order to replace them with perspectives more relevant to the modern era.

Chicago Neighborhoods is one example of an ongoing interdisciplinary study of the causes of crime. Described in more detail later in this chapter, the Harvard project is examining the roles of personality, school, and community as they contribute to juvenile delinquency and criminal behavior. See Web Extra 3–1 at cjtoday.com for more information on the project. Web Extra 3–2 leads to more information on the general categories of criminological theory mentioned here, and Library Extra 3–1 at cjtoday.com discusses recent theoretical developments in the field of criminological theory.

WEB Extra

LIBRARY Extra

The Classical School

Theories of the **Classical School** of crime causation dominated criminological thought for much of the late eighteenth and early nineteenth centuries. These theories represented a noteworthy advance over previous thinking about crime because they moved beyond superstition and mysticism as explanations for deviance. As noted criminologist Stephen Schafer puts it, "In the eighteenth-century individualistic orientation of criminal law, the act was judged and the man made responsible."[19] A product of the Enlightenment then sweeping through Europe, the Classical School demanded recognition of rationality and the ability to exercise informed choice in human social life.

Classical School

An eighteenth-century approach to crime causation and criminal responsibility that grew out of the Enlightenment and that emphasized the role of free will and reasonable punishments. Classical thinkers believed that punishment, if it is to be an effective deterrent, has to outweigh the potential pleasure derived from criminal behavior.

Most classical theories of crime causation, both old and new, make certain basic assumptions. Among them are these:

- Crime is caused by the individual exercise of free will. Human beings are fundamentally rational, and most human behavior is the result of free will coupled with rational choice.
- Pain and pleasure are the two central determinants of human behavior.
- Crime erodes the bond that exists between individuals and society and is therefore an immoral form of behavior.

- Punishment, a necessary evil, is sometimes required to deter law violators from repeating their crime and to serve as an example to others who would also violate the law.
- Crime prevention is possible through swift and certain punishment that offsets any gains to be had through criminal behavior.

Cesare Beccaria: Crime and Punishment

In 1764, Cesare Beccaria (1738–1794) published his *Essays on Crimes and Punishment.* The book was an immediate success and stirred a hornet's nest of controversy over the treatment of criminal offenders. Beccaria proposed basic changes in the criminal laws of his day to make them more "humanitarian." He called for the abolition of physical punishment and an end to the death penalty. Beccaria is best remembered for his suggestion that punishment should be just sufficient to deter criminal behavior but should never be excessive. Because Beccaria's writings stimulated many other thinkers throughout the eighteenth and early nineteenth centuries, he is referred to today as the founder of the Classical School of criminology.

Jeremy Bentham: Hedonistic Calculus

WEB Extra

Among those influenced by Beccaria was the Englishman Jeremy Bentham (1748–1832). Bentham devised a "hedonistic calculus," which essentially said that the exercise of free will would cause an individual to avoid committing a crime as long as the punishment for committing that crime outweighed the benefits to be derived from committing it. Bentham termed this philosophy of social control *utilitarianism*. Both Bentham and Beccaria agreed that punishment had to be "swift and certain"—as well as just—to be effective. Learn more about Jeremy Bentham at **Web Extra 3–3** at cjtoday.com.

The Neoclassical Perspective

neoclassical criminology

A contemporary version of classical criminology that emphasizes deterrence and retribution and that holds that human beings are essentially free to make choices in favor of crime and deviance or conformity to the law.

rational choice theory

A perspective on crime causation that holds that criminality is the result of conscious choice. Rational choice theory predicts that individuals will choose to commit crime when the benefits of doing so outweigh the costs of disobeying the law.

routine activities theory

A neoclassical perspective that suggests that lifestyles contribute significantly to both the amount and the type of crime found in any society.

A contemporary theory with roots in the Classical School, **neoclassical criminology** is a perspective that owes much to the early classical thinkers. Although classical criminology focuses primarily on pleasure and pain as motivators of human behavior, neoclassical criminology places greater emphasis on rationality and cognition. Central to such perspectives is **rational choice theory**, which holds that criminality is largely the result of conscious choices that people make. According to the theory, offenders choose to violate the law when they believe that the benefits of doing so outweigh the costs.

Rational choice theory is represented by a somewhat narrower perspective called **routine activities theory**. Routine activities theory was first proposed by Lawrence Cohen and Marcus Felson in 1979.[20] Cohen and Felson argued that lifestyles significantly affect both the amount and type of crime found in any society, and they noted that "the risk of criminal victimization varies dramatically among the circumstances and locations in which people place themselves and their property."[21] Lifestyles that contribute to criminal opportunities are likely to result in crime because they increase the risk of potential victimization.[22] For example, a person who routinely uses an ATM late at night in an isolated location is far more likely to be preyed on by robbers than is someone who stays home after dark. Rational choice theorists concentrate on "the decision-making process of offenders confronted with specific contexts" and have shifted "the focus of the effort to prevent crime . . . from broad social programs to target hardening, environmental design or any impediment that would [dissuade] a motivated offender from offending."[23]

Central to the routine activities approach is the claim that crime is likely to occur when a motivated offender and a suitable target come together in the absence of a *capable guardian*. Capable guardians are those who effectively discourage crime and prevent it from occurring. Members of neighborhood watch groups, for example, might be capable guardians. Capable guardians do not necessarily have to confront would-be offenders directly but might be people who have completed classes in crime prevention and who have taken steps to reduce their chances of victimization.

[Television] poisons the minds of our young people . . . with destructive messages of casual violence and even more casual sex.

—Bob Dole, former Senator and Republican presidential candidate

Social Policy and Classical Theories

Much of the practice of criminal justice in America today is built on concepts provided by Classical School theorists. Many contemporary programs designed to prevent crime, for example, have their philosophical roots in the classical axioms of deterrence and punishment. Modern heirs of the Classical School see punishment as central to criminal justice policy, use evidence of high crime rates to argue that punishment is a necessary crime preventive, and believe punishment is a natural and deserved consequence of criminal activity. Such thinkers call for greater prison capacity and new prison construction. The term *public-order advocate* can be applied to modern-day proponents of classical theory who frequently seek stiffer criminal laws and greater penalties for criminal activity. The emphasis on punishment as an appropriate response to crime, however, whether founded on principles of deterrence or revenge, and the resulting packed courtrooms and overcrowded prisons, has left many contemporary criminal justice policy initiatives foundering.

Biological explanations shaped criminology at its inception, and today they are reemerging with fresh vigor and increased potential.

—Nicole Rafter, Northeastern University[ii]

Biological Theories

Biological theories of crime causation, which had fallen into disrepute during the past few decades, are beginning to experience something of a contemporary resurgence. Most early theories of the **Biological School** of crime causation, which built on inherited or bodily characteristics and features, made certain fundamental assumptions. Among them are these:

Biological School

A perspective on criminological thought that holds that criminal behavior has a physiological basis.

- Basic determinants of human behavior, including criminal tendencies, are constitutionally or genetically based.
- The basic determinants of human behavior, including criminality, may be passed on from generation to generation. In other words, a penchant for crime may be inherited.
- At least some human behavior is the result of biological propensities inherited from more primitive developmental stages in the evolutionary process. Some human beings may be further along the evolutionary ladder than others, and their behavior may reflect it.

Franz Joseph Gall: Phrenology

The idea that the quality of a person can be judged by a study of the person's face is as old as antiquity. Even today, we often judge people on their looks, saying, "He has an honest face" or "She has tender eyes." Horror movies play on unspoken cultural themes to shape the way a "maniac" might look. Jack Nicholson's portrayal of a crazed killer in *The Shining* and Anthony Hopkins's role as a serial killer in *The Silence of the Lambs* turned that look into fortunes at the box office.

Franz Joseph Gall (1758–1828) was one of the first thinkers to theorize about the idea that bodily constitution might reflect personality. Gall was writing at a time when it was thought that organs throughout the body determined one's mental state and behavior. People were said to be "hard-hearted" or to have a "bad spleen" that filled them with bile. Gall focused on the head and the brain and called his approach *cranioscopy*. It can be summarized in four propositions:

- The brain is the organ of the mind.
- The brain consists of localized faculties or functions.
- The shape of the skull reveals the underlying development (or lack of development) of areas within the brain.
- The personality can be revealed by a study of the skull.

Gall never systematically tested his theory in a way that would meet contemporary scientific standards. Even so, his approach to predicting behavior, which came to be known as **phrenology**, quickly spread throughout Europe. Gall's student, Johann Gaspar Spurzheim (1776–1853), brought phrenology to America in a series of lectures and publications on the subject. By 1825, 29 phrenological journals were being produced in the United States and Britain.[24] Until the turn of the twentieth century, phrenology remained popular in some American circles, where it was used in diagnostic schemes to classify new prisoners.

phrenology

The study of the shape of the head to determine anatomical correlates of human behavior.

Cesare Lombroso: Atavism

Gall's theory was "deterministic" in the sense that it left little room for choice. What a person did depended more on the shape of the skull than on the exercise of free will. Other biological theories would soon build on that premise. One of the best known is that created by the Italian psychologist Cesare Lombroso (1835–1909).

Cesare Lombroso (left), who has been dubbed "the father of modern criminology," posing with friend Louis Lombard in a rare photograph from 1909. What concepts developed by Lombroso might still be applicable today?
Culver Pictures, Inc.

Lombroso began his criminal anthropology with a postmortem evaluation of famous criminals, including one by the name of Vilella. Before Vilella died, Lombroso had the opportunity to interview him on a number of occasions. After Vilella's death, Lombroso correlated earlier observations of personality traits with measurable physical abnormalities. As a result of this and other studies, Lombroso concluded that criminals were atavistic human beings—throwbacks to earlier stages of evolution who were not sufficiently mentally advanced for successful life in the modern world. **Atavism** was identifiable in suspicious individuals, Lombroso suggested, through measures designed to reveal "primitive" physical characteristics.

atavism

A condition characterized by the existence of features thought to be common in earlier stages of human evolution.

In the late nineteenth century, Charles Darwin's theory of evolution was rapidly being applied to a wide range of fields. It was not surprising, therefore, that Lombroso linked evolution and criminality. What separated Lombroso from his predecessors, however, was that he continually refined his theory through ongoing observation. Based on studies of known offenders, whom he compared to conformists, Lombroso identified a large number of atavistic traits, which, he claimed, characterized criminals. Among them were long arms, large lips, crooked noses, an abnormally large amount of body hair, prominent cheekbones, two eyes of different colors, and ears that lacked clearly defined lobes.

Atavism implies that certain people are born criminals. Throughout his life, Lombroso grappled with the task of determining what proportion of the total population of offenders were born criminals. His estimates ranged at different times between 70% and 90%. Career criminals and those who committed crimes of opportunity without atavistic features he termed *criminaloids*, and he recognized the potential causative roles of greed, passion, and circumstance in their behavior.

Today, Lombroso is known as the founder of the **Positivist School** of criminology because of the role observation played in the formulation of his theories. Stephen Schafer calls Lombroso "the father of modern criminology"[25] because most contemporary criminologists follow in the tradition that Lombroso began—scientific observation and a comparison of theory with fact.

Positivist School

An approach to criminal justice theory that stresses the application of scientific techniques to the study of crime and criminals.

THE EVIDENCE FOR AND AGAINST ATAVISM

After Lombroso died, two English physicians, Charles Goring and Karl Pearson, conducted a test of atavism, studying more than 3,000 prisoners and comparing them along physiological criteria to an army detachment known as the Royal Engineers. No significant differences were found between the two groups, and Lombroso's ideas rapidly began to fall into disrepute.

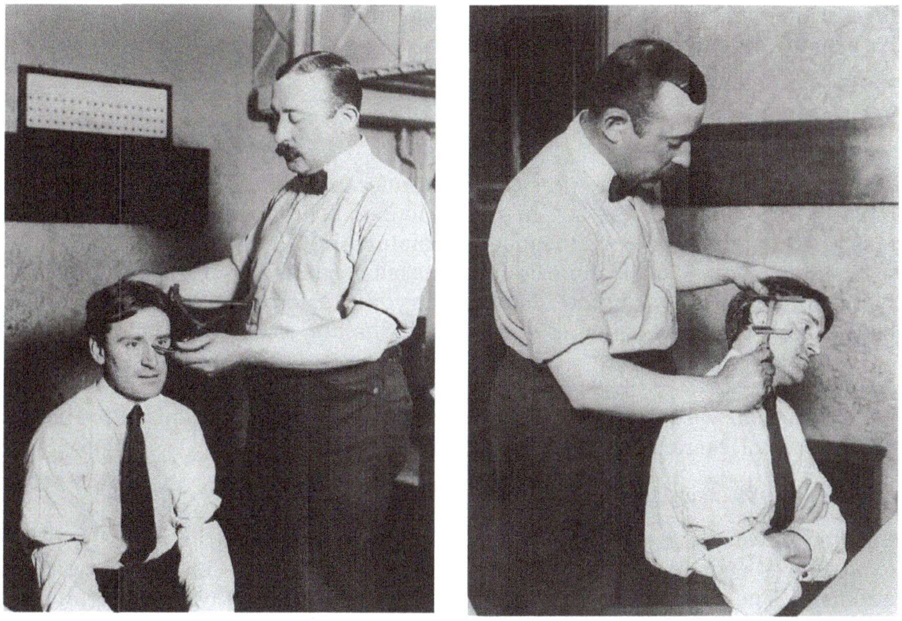

The Bertillion system of identification being applied to a subject in the years prior to the development of fingerprinting. The theory of atavism, based on the ideas of Charles Darwin, supported the use of physical anthropology in the identification of offenders. Why have sociological theories largely replaced simple biological approaches to explaining crime?
Courtesy of the Library of Congress

A further study of atavism was published in 1939 by Earnest A. Hooton, a distinguished Harvard University anthropologist. Hooton spent 12 years constructing anthropometric profiles—profiles based on human body measurements—of 13,873 male convicts in ten different American states. He measured each inmate in 107 different ways and compared them to 3,203 volunteers from National Guard units, firehouses, beaches, and hospitals. Surprisingly, Hooton did find some basis for Lombroso's beliefs, and he concluded that the inmate population in his study demonstrated a decided physical "inferiority."

However, Hooton never recognized that the prisoners he studied were only a subgroup of the population of all offenders throughout the country. They were, in fact, the least successful offenders—the ones who had been caught and imprisoned. Hooton may have unknowingly measured other criminals—the ones who had avoided capture—among his "conformist" population. Hence the "inferiority" Hooton observed may have been an artificial product of a process of selection (arrest) by the justice system.

Criminal Families

The concept of biological inheritance has been applied to "criminal families" as well as to individuals. The idea of mental degeneration as an inherited contributor to crime was first explored by Richard Dugdale.[26] Dugdale used the family tree method to study a family he called the Jukes, publishing his findings in 1877. The Juke lineage had its beginning in America with "Max" (whose last name is unknown), a descendant of Dutch immigrants to New Amsterdam in the early eighteenth century. Two of Max's sons married into the notorious "Juke family of girls," six sisters, all of whom were illegitimate. Male Jukes were reputed to have been "vicious," while Ada, one of the sisters, had an especially bad reputation and eventually came to be known as "the mother of criminals."

Dugdale found that, during the next 75 years, Ada's heirs included 1,200 people, most of whom were "social degenerates." Only a handful of socially productive progeny could be identified. In 1915, Dugdale's study of the Jukes was continued by Arthur A. Estabrook, who extended the line to include 2,094 descendants and found just as few conformists.

A similar study was published by Henry Goddard in 1912.[27] Goddard examined the Kallikak family, which contained two clear lines of descent. One emanated from an affair that Revolutionary War soldier Martin Kallikak had with a "feebleminded" barmaid. She bore a son, and the line eventually produced 480 identifiable descendants. After the war, Kallikak returned home and married a "virtuous" Quaker woman in Philadelphia. This legitimate line produced 496 offspring by 1912, of whom only three were abnormal; not one was criminal. The illegitimate group, however, contained over half "feebleminded" or deviant progeny.

The underlying suppositions of these studies are that degenerate and feebleminded people are produced and propagated through bad genetic material and that crime is an outlet for degenerate urges. However, these studies fail to recognize any effect that socialization and life circumstances have on the development of criminal behavior.

William Sheldon: Somatotypes

somatotyping

The classification of human beings into types according to body build and other physical characteristics.

"Constitutional" theories of crime causation refer to the *physical constitution*, or bodily characteristics, of offenders. The last of the famous constitutional theorists was William Sheldon (1893–1977), who developed the idea of **somatotyping**.

Sheldon studied 200 juvenile delinquents between the ages of 15 and 21 at the Hayden Goodwill Institute in Boston and decided that the young men possessed one of three somatotypes (or body types). The types of bodies described by Sheldon were (in his words):

- *Mesomorphs* with a relative predominance of muscle, bone, and connective tissue
- *Endomorphs* with a soft roundness throughout the various regions of the body; short tapering limbs; small bones; and soft, smooth, velvety skin
- *Ectomorphs* characterized by thinness, fragility, and delicacy of body

Sheldon developed a system of measurements by which an individual's physique could be expressed as a combination of three numbers, such as 4.0–4.0–3.5 (the representation of an average male). The numbers represented the degree of mesomorphy, endomorphy, and ectomorphy present in the individual on a scale of 0 to 7, where 0 indicates a complete lack of features of one category. American females were said to average 5.0–3.0–3.5 on the scale. Sheldon wrote that each somatotype was possessed of a characteristic personality, and he believed that predominantly mesomorphic individuals were most prone to aggression, violence, and delinquency.[28]

Social Policy and Biological Theories

WEB Extra

Because traditional biological theories of crime causation attribute the cause of crime to fundamental physical characteristics that are not easily modified, they suggest the need for extreme social policies. During the 1920s and early 1930s, for example, biological theories of crime causation, especially those focusing on inherited mental degeneration, led to the eugenics movement, under which mentally handicapped women were sometimes sterilized to prevent them from bearing offspring. The eugenics movement was institutionalized by the 1927 U.S. Supreme Court case of *Buck* v. *Bell*, in which Justice Oliver Wendell Holmes, Jr., writing in support of a Virginia statute permitting sterilization, said, "It is better for all the world, if instead of waiting to execute degenerate offspring for crime, or to let them starve for their imbecility, society can prevent those persons who are manifestly unfit from continuing their kind."[29] Visit **Web Extra 3–4** at cjtoday.com to learn more about biological theories of crime and violence.

Psychobiological Theories

During the past few decades, researchers have taken a sophisticated approach to biological theorizing about the causes of crime. Contemporary biochemical and physiological perspectives are sometimes termed *psychobiology*. The psychobiology of crime highlights the role of human DNA, environmental contaminants, nutrition, hormones, physical trauma (especially to the brain), and body chemistry in human cognition, feeling, and behavior.

Chromosome Theory

The detailed mapping of human DNA and other recent advances in the field of recombinant DNA have rekindled interest in genetic correlates of deviant behavior. More sophisticated than their historical counterparts, the biological theories of today often draw on the latest medical advances or build on popular health concerns.

The links between chromosome patterns and crime were first explored in the 1960s. A normal female has a chromosome structure often diagrammed as "XX" because of how the sex-determining gene pair looks in an electron microscope. A male has a Y chromosome in place of the second X, for a typical male XY pattern. Although it had been known for some time that a few people have abnormal patterns that include "extra" chromosomes (such as XXX females, XXY males with Klinefelter's syndrome, and XXYY "double males"), it wasn't until 1965 that the respected English journal *Nature* reported on the work of Patricia Jacobs, who identified **supermales**—men with an extra Y chromosome whose chromosome structure is diagrammed XYY. Jacobs found that supermales were more common in prisons than in the general population.[30]

supermale

A human male displaying the XYY chromosome structure.

Other early studies claimed that the XYY male was more aggressive than other males and that he possessed a number of specific physical and psychological traits, such as height (taller than 6 feet, 1 inch), thinness, acne, a tendency toward homosexuality, a somewhat low IQ, and "a marked tendency to commit a succession of apparently motiveless property crimes."[31] Later studies disputed many of these findings, and the significance of the XYY pattern for behavioral prediction is in doubt today.

Biochemical Factors and Imbalances

Research in the area of nutrition has produced some limited evidence that the old maxim "You are what you eat!" may contain more than a grain of truth. *Biocriminology* is a field of study that links violent or disruptive behavior to eating habits, vitamin deficiencies, genetics, and other conditions that affect body tissues.

One of the first studies to focus on chemical imbalances in the body as a cause of crime was reported in the British medical journal *Lancet* in 1943.[32] Authors of the study linked murder to hypoglycemia (low blood sugar), which is caused by too much insulin in the blood or by near starvation diets. Some researchers believe that hypoglycemia reduces the mind's capacity to reason effectively or to judge the long-term consequences of behavior.

Allergic reactions to common foods have been reported as the cause of violence and homicide in a number of studies.[33] Foods said to produce allergic reactions in sensitive individuals, leading to a swelling of the brain and brain stem, include milk, citrus fruit, chocolate, corn, wheat, and eggs. Involvement of the central nervous system in such allergies, it has been suggested, reduces the amount of learning that occurs during childhood and may contribute to delinquency as well as to adult criminal behavior. Some studies have implicated food additives, such as monosodium glutamate, dyes, and artificial flavorings, in producing criminal behavior.[34]

Other research has found that the amount of coffee and sugar consumed by inmates is considerably greater than in the outside population.[35] Theorists have suggested that high blood levels of caffeine and sugar produce antisocial behavior.[36] It is unclear whether inmates consume more coffee due to boredom or whether those with "excitable" personalities need the kind of stimulation coffee drinking produces. On the other hand, habitual coffee drinkers in nonprison populations have not been linked to crime, and other studies, such as that conducted by Mortimer Gross of the University of Illinois, show no link between the amount of sugar consumed and hyperactivity.[37] Similarly, studies "have not yielded evidence that a change in diet will result in [a] significant reduction in aggressive or antisocial behavior" among inmate populations.[38] Nonetheless, some prison programs have limited the intake of dietary stimulants through nutritional management and the substitution of artificial sweeteners for refined sugar.

Vitamins have also been examined for their impact on delinquency. Abram Hoffer found that disruptive children consumed far less than the optimum levels of vitamins B_3 and B_6 than did nonproblem youths.[39] He claimed that the addition of these vitamins to the diets of children who were deficient in them could control unruly behavior and improve school performance.

Overall, the role of food and diet in producing criminal behavior has not been well established. The American Dietetic Association and the National Council against Health Fraud have concluded that no convincing scientific relationship between crime and diet has yet been demonstrated.[40] Both groups are concerned that poor nutrition may result from programs that reduce or modify diets in an effort to affect behavior.

Hormones have also come under scrutiny as potential behavioral determinants. The male sex hormone, testosterone, has been linked to aggressiveness in males. Some studies of blood-serum levels of testosterone have shown a direct relationship[41] between the amount of hormone present and the degree of violence used by sex offenders,[42] and steroid abuse among bodybuilders has been linked to destructive urges and psychosis.[43] One 1998 study found that high levels of testosterone, especially when combined with low socioeconomic status, produced antisocial personalities, resulting in deviance and criminality.[44] In 2007, researchers at the University of Michigan at Ann Arbor found that the higher the blood levels of testosterone in young men, the more they enjoyed provoking anger in others.[45]

Some studies of brain chemistry have led researchers to conclude that low levels of certain neurotransmitters, especially serotonin, are directly related to a person's inability to control aggressive

The word needs to go out on the street. We have had it with violence. We have had it with violent people. We're tired of being told to try to understand their childhood or understand their past.

—Newt Gingrich, former Speaker of the House[iii]

impulses.[46] The presence of adequate serotonin levels in the human brain buffers irritating experiences that might otherwise result in anger and aggression. Low serotonin levels may result from the ingestion of toxic pollutants, such as the metals lead and manganese, according to one study.[47] Reduced serotonin levels, say other researchers, is sometimes found in men with an extra Y chromosome.[48]

Researchers have also implicated a malfunctioning endocrine system as a cause of physical abuse, antisocial behavior, and psychopathology. One Swedish study that focused on variations in blood-serum levels of two thyroid hormones, triiodothyronine (T_3) and thyroxine (FT_4), found that elevated T_3 levels were related to alcoholism and criminality.[49] Serum levels of FT_4 were found to be negatively correlated to such behavior.

Heredity and Other Physical Factors

Other physical factors have been shown to play a role in an individual's inclination toward criminality. Sarnoff Mednick, for example, found some basis for the claim that the autonomic nervous system (ANS) predisposes certain individuals toward criminality by limiting their ability to learn quickly.[50] He claims that those with a slow ANS are unable to inhibit antisocial behavior quickly enough to avoid punishment and stigmatization.[51] Physical trauma, especially brain injury, has also been shown to at times induce severe personality changes, including aggression and violent behavior in people with a previous behavioral history of neither.[52] Similarly, people born with certain abnormalities of the brain, especially frontal lobe dysfunction, may display a penchant for violence.[53] Frontal lobe dysfunction is sometimes caused by reduced cerebral blood flow.

Studies have shown that the behavior of biological children of criminals who are adopted at birth tends to reflect the criminality of biological parents, independent of the environment in which the children were raised.[54] Also, identical twins exhibit a greater similarity in behavior than do nonidentical (or "fraternal") twins, and a number of studies have shown that identical twins are more alike in patterns and degree of criminal involvement than are fraternal twins.[55]

Perhaps the best known of modern-day biological perspectives on crime was proposed by James Q. Wilson and Richard Herrnstein in their book *Crime and Human Nature*, published in 1985.[56] Wilson and Herrnstein argue that inherited traits, such as maleness, aggressiveness, mesomorphic body type, and low intelligence, combine with environmental influences, including poor schools and strained family life, to produce crime. Although the authors reject a firm determinism, asserting that it is the interaction between genetics and environment that determines behavior, they do claim that children who will eventually grow up to be criminals can sometimes be identified early in their lives. The most important factor in the diversion of potential offenders from lives of crime, according to Wilson and Herrnstein, is a healthy family life in which affection for others and conscience can develop.[57] Wilson and Herrnstein also use cross-cultural data from Japan, where crime rates are very low, to suggest that tendencies toward introversion among the Japanese result in fewer serious crimes than in the United States. The Wilson-Herrnstein thesis has been criticized for failing to explain crime that extends beyond "traditional lower-class street crime" and for failing to recognize the political nature of criminal definitions.[58]

Social Policy and Psychobiological Theories

Psychobiological theories often suggest modifying body chemistry to produce desirable behavioral changes. Hence, just as cancer researchers look for a "magic bullet" that might target defective chromosomes in the human immune system that allow for the growth of cancerous tissue, psychobiologists concerned with crime and its causes envision the day when similar techniques can be applied to the prevention and control of crime. If a gene for crime can be found, such researchers suggest, it might be turned off. In the meantime, psychobiologists have to be content with medicinal approaches to the treatment of crime and violence, such as employing tranquilizers, antipsychotic medications, mood-altering substances, and other drugs.

Studies show that drug treatments fashioned after psychobiological perspectives control aggressive and criminal behavior temporarily, but there is little evidence to suggest that they produce lasting results. In 1993, all biologically based theories of crime and violence were called into question by the National Academy of Sciences, whose review of hundreds of studies on the relationship among biology, violence, and crime concluded that "no patterns precise enough to be considered reliable biological markers for violent behavior have yet been identified."[59] The study did, however, find what it called "promising leads for future research."

Psychological Theories

Theories of the **Psychological School** of crime causation have an increasingly significant place in the criminological literature. Most psychological theories of crime make certain fundamental assumptions. Among them are these:

- The individual is the primary unit of analysis.
- Personality is the major motivational element within individuals, since it is the source of drives and motives.
- Crimes result from inappropriately conditioned behavior or from abnormal, dysfunctional, or inappropriate mental processes within the personality.
- Defective or abnormal mental processes may have a variety of causes, including a diseased mind and inappropriate learning or improper conditioning—often occurring in early childhood.

Psychological School

A perspective on criminological thought that views offensive and deviant behavior as the product of dysfunctional personality. Psychological thinkers identify the conscious, and especially the subconscious, contents of the human psyche as major determinants of behavior.

Behavioral Conditioning

Two threads were woven through early psychological theories. One emphasized **behavioral conditioning**, while the other focused mostly on personality disturbances and diseases of the mind. Taken together, these two foci constituted the early field of psychological criminology. Conditioning is a psychological principle that holds that the frequency of any behavior, including criminal or deviant behavior, can be increased or decreased through reward, punishment, and association with other stimuli. The concept of conditioned behavior was popularized through the work of the Russian physiologist Ivan Pavlov (1849–1936), whose work with dogs won him the Nobel Prize in physiology and medicine in 1904. Similarly, behavioral psychologists suggest that criminal behavior, which may be inherently rewarding under many circumstances, tends to be more common in those who are able to avoid punishment when involved in rule-breaking behavior.

behavioral conditioning

A psychological principle that holds that the frequency of any behavior can be increased or decreased through reward, punishment, and association with other stimuli.

Freudian Psychoanalysis

The name most widely associated with the field of psychology is that of Sigmund Freud (1856–1939). Freudian theory posits the existence of an id, an ego, and a superego within the personality.[60] The id is the source of drives, which are seen as primarily sexual. The ego is a rational mental entity, which outlines paths through which the desires of the id can be fulfilled. The ego is often called the *reality principle* because of the belief that it relates desires to practical behavioral alternatives. The superego is a guiding principle, often compared to conscience, that judges the quality of the alternatives presented by the ego according to the standards of right and wrong acquired by the personality of which it is a part. Freud wrote very little about crime, but his followers, who developed the school of Freudian **psychoanalysis**, believe that crime can result from at least three conditions.

psychoanalysis

A theory of human behavior, based on the writings of Sigmund Freud, that sees personality as a complex composite of interacting mental entities.

The first possible source of criminal behavior is a weak superego, which cannot responsibly control the drives that emanate from the id. Sex crimes, crimes of passion, murder, and other violent crimes are thought to follow inadequate superego development. People who lack fully developed superegos are often called *psychopaths* or *sociopaths* to indicate that they cannot see beyond their own interests. Canadian criminologist Gwynn Nettler observes that "civilization is paid for through development of a sense of guilt."[61]

Freud also created the concept of sublimation to explain the process by which one thing is symbolically substituted for another. He believed that sublimation was necessary when the direct pursuit of one's desires was not possible. Freud suggested, for example, that many children learned to sublimate negative feelings about their mothers. In the society in which Freud developed his theories, mothers closely controlled the lives of their children, and Freud saw the developing child as continually frustrated in seeking freedom to act on his or her own. The strain produced by this conflict could not be directly expressed by the child because the mother also controlled rewards and punishments. Hence, dislike for one's mother (which Freud thought was especially strong in boys) might show itself symbolically later in life. Crimes against women could then be explained as being committed by men expressing a symbolic hatred.

A final Freudian explanation for criminality is based on the death instinct, or Thanatos, which Freud believed each of us carries. Thanatos is the often-unrecognized desire of animate matter to return to the inanimate. Potentially self-destructive activities, including smoking, speeding, skydiving,

A battered woman turning away from her husband. When a woman is victimized, it is often at the hands of an "intimate other," such as a spouse or a boyfriend. Sigmund Freud suggested that a male batterer acts out a deep-seated resentment toward women that resulted from his childhood relationship with his mother. Why is this kind of theoretical perspective rarely given credence by criminologists today?

Francisco Cruz/SuperStock, Inc.

bad diets, "picking fights," and so on, can be explained by Thanatos. The self-destructive wish may also motivate offenders to commit crimes that are themselves dangerous or self-destructive—such as burglary, assault, murder, prostitution, and drug use—or it may result in unconscious efforts to be caught. Criminals who leave evidence behind may be responding to some basic need for apprehension and punishment.

Psychopathology and Crime

psychopathology

The study of pathological mental conditions—that is, mental illness.

From a psychiatric point of view, crime might also occur because of a diseased mind or a disordered personality—conditions that may collectively be referred to as *psychopathy.* The study of psychopathic mental conditions is called **psychopathology**. The role of a disordered personality in crime causation was central to early psychiatric theorizing. In 1944, for example, the well-known psychiatrist David Abrahamsen wrote, "When we seek to explain the riddle of human conduct in general and of antisocial behavior in particular, the solution must be sought in the personality."[62] Later, some psychiatrists went so far as to claim that criminal behavior itself is only a symptom of a more fundamental psychiatric disorder.[63]

psychopath

A person with a personality disorder, especially one manifested in aggressively antisocial behavior, which is often said to be the result of a poorly developed superego.

By the 1930s, psychiatrists had begun to develop the concept of a psychopathic personality. This personality type, which by its very definition is asocial, was fully developed by Hervey Cleckley in his 1941 book, *The Mask of Sanity.*[64] Cleckley described the **psychopath**, also called a *sociopath*, as a "moral idiot" whose central defining characteristic is the inability to accurately imagine how others think and feel. Hence, it becomes possible for a psychopath to inflict pain and engage in cruelty without appreciation for the victim's suffering. Charles Manson, for example, whom some have called a psychopath, once told a television reporter, "I could take this book and beat you to death with it, and I wouldn't feel a thing. It'd be just like walking to the drugstore." According to Cleckley, psychopathic indicators appear early in life, often in the teenage years. They include lying, fighting, stealing, and vandalism. Even earlier signs may be found, according to some authors, in bed-wetting, cruelty to animals, sleepwalking, and fire setting.[65]

While the terms *psychopath* and *criminal* are not synonymous, individuals manifesting characteristics of a psychopathic personality are likely, sooner or later, to run afoul of the law. As one writer says, "The impulsivity and aggression, the selfishness in achieving one's own immediate needs, and the disregard for society's rules and laws bring these people to the attention of the criminal justice system."[66]

I really truly tried to stop—but I couldn't.

—Henry Louis Wallace, convicted killer of nine women, in a tape-recorded interview with police

Although much studied, the causes of psychopathy are unclear. Somatogenic causes, or those that are based on physiological aspects of the human organism, include (1) a malfunctioning central nervous system characterized by a low state of arousal, which drives the sufferer to seek excitement, and (2) brain abnormalities, which may be present in most psychopaths from birth.

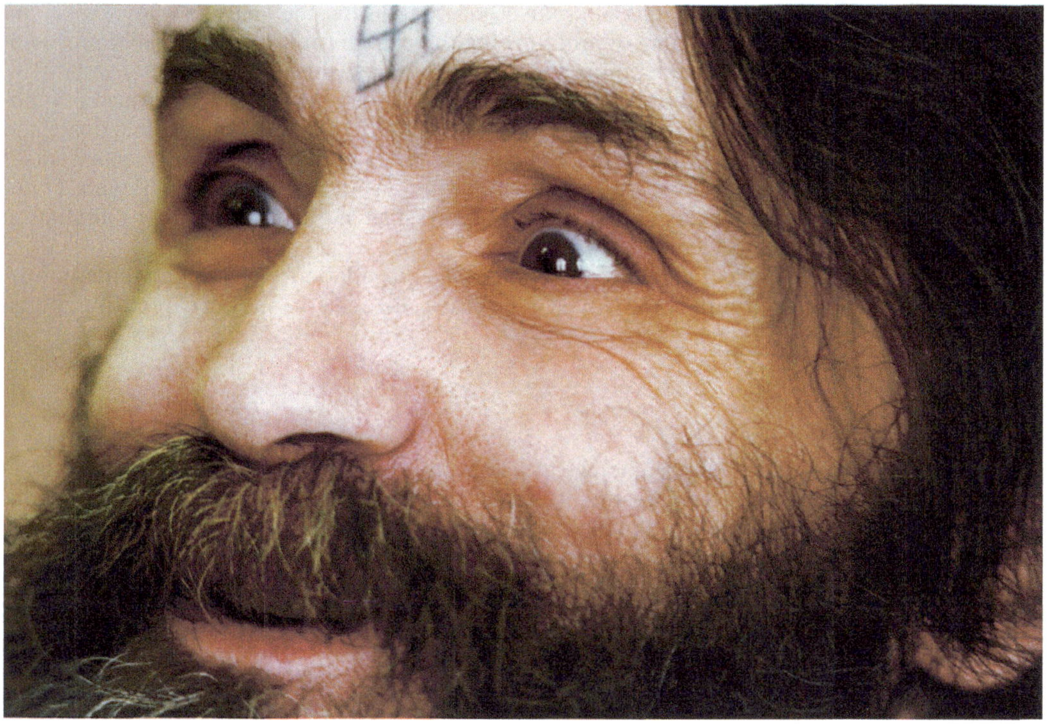

Charles Manson, one of the most photographed criminal offenders of all time, 20 years after he and his "family" shocked the world with their gruesome crimes. What do you think motivated Manson?
Grey Villet

Psychogenic causes, or those rooted in early interpersonal experiences, include the inability to form attachments to parents or other caregivers early in life, sudden separation from the mother during the first six months of life, and other forms of insecurity during the first few years of life. In short, a lack of love or the sensed inability to unconditionally depend on one central loving figure (typically the mother in most psychological literature) immediately following birth is often posited as a major psychogenic factor contributing to psychopathic development. Learn more about psychopathology and crime at Library Extra 3–2 at cjtoday.com. Read more about the Manson murders at Web Extra 3–5 at cjtoday.com.

LIBRARY Extra   WEB Extra

The Psychotic Offender

Another form of mental disorder is called **psychosis**. Psychotic people, according to psychiatric definitions, are out of touch with reality in some fundamental way. They may suffer from hallucinations, delusions, or other breaks with reality. For example, a psychotic may believe that he or she is a famous historical figure or may see spiders crawling on a bare wall. Psychoses may be either organic (that is, caused by physical damage to, or abnormalities in, the brain) or functional (that is, with no known physical cause). Psychotic people have also been classified as schizophrenic or paranoid schizophrenic. **Schizophrenics** are characterized by disordered or disjointed thinking, in which the types of logical associations they make are atypical of other people. Paranoid schizophrenics suffer from delusions and hallucinations.

Psychoses may lead to crime in a number of ways. Following the Vietnam War, for example, a number of former American soldiers suffering from a kind of battlefield psychosis killed friends and family members, thinking they were enemy soldiers. These men, who had been traumatized by battlefield experiences in Southeast Asia, relived their past on American streets.

psychosis
A form of mental illness in which sufferers are said to be out of touch with reality.

schizophrenic
A mentally ill individual who suffers from disjointed thinking and possibly from delusions and hallucinations.

Psychological Profiling

Psychological profiling is the attempt to derive a composite picture of an offender's social and psychological characteristics from the crime he or she committed and from the manner in which it was committed. Psychological profiling began during World War II as an effort by William Langer (1896–1977), a government psychiatrist hired by the Office of Strategic Services, to predict Adolf Hitler's actions.[67] Profiling in criminal investigations is based on the belief that criminality, because it is a form of behavior, can be viewed as symptomatic of the offender's

psychological profiling
The attempt to categorize, understand, and predict the behavior of certain types of offenders based on behavioral clues they provide.

personality. Psychological evaluations of crime scenes, including the analysis of evidence, are used to re-create the offender's frame of mind during the commission of the crime. A profile of the offender is then constructed to help in the investigation of suspects.

During the 1980s, the Federal Bureau of Investigation (FBI) led the movement toward psychological profiling[68] through its focus on violent sex offenses[69] and arson.[70] FBI profilers described "lust murderers" and serial arsonists. Often depicted as loners with an aversion to casual social contact, lust murderers were shown to rarely arouse suspicions in neighbors or employers. Other personality types became the focus of police efforts to arrest such offenders through a prediction of what they might do next.

New areas for psychological profiling include hostage negotiation[71] and international terrorism.[72] Right-wing terrorist groups in the United States have also been the subject of profiling efforts.

Social Policy and Psychological Theories

Crime-control policies based on psychological perspectives are primarily individualistic. They are oriented toward individualized treatment, characteristically exposing the individual offender to various forms of therapy intended to overcome the person's propensity for criminality.

dangerousness

The likelihood that a given individual will later harm society or others. Dangerousness is often measured in terms of recidivism, or the likelihood that an individual will commit an additional crime within five years following arrest or release from confinement.

Most crime-control strategies based on psychological theories emphasize assessing personal **dangerousness**, through psychological testing and other efforts to identify personality-based characteristics that predict interpersonal aggression. Although the ability to accurately predict future dangerousness is of great concern to today's policymakers, definitions of *dangerousness* are fraught with difficulty. As some authors have pointed out, "Dangerousness is not an objective quality like obesity or brown eyes; rather it is an ascribed quality like trustworthiness."[73] Hence, dangerousness is not necessarily a personality trait that is stable or easily identifiable. Even if it were, some studies of criminal careers show that involvement in crime decreases with age.[74] As one author puts it, if "criminality declines more or less uniformly with age, then many offenders will be 'over the hill' by the time they are old enough to be plausible candidates for preventive incarceration."[75]

Before crime-control policies can be based on present understandings of dangerousness, research must answer several questions: Can past behavior predict future behavior? Do former instances of criminality foretell additional ones? Are there other identifiable characteristics that violent offenders might manifest that could serve as warning signs to criminal justice decision makers faced with the dilemma of whether to release convicted felons?

Sociological Theories

Chicago School

A sociological approach that emphasizes demographics (the characteristics of population groups) and geographics (the mapped location of such groups relative to one another) and that sees the social disorganization that characterizes delinquency areas as a major cause of criminality and victimization.

social disorganization

A condition said to exist when a group is faced with social change, uneven development of culture, maladaptiveness, disharmony, conflict, and lack of consensus.

Sociological theories are largely an American contribution to the study of crime causation. In the 1920s and 1930s, the famous **Chicago School** of sociology explained criminality as a product of society's impact on the individual. The structure of prevailing social arrangements, the interaction between individuals and groups, and the social environment were all seen as major determinants of criminal behavior.

Sociological perspectives on crime causation are quite diverse. Most, however, build on certain fundamental assumptions. Among them are these:

- Social groups, social institutions, the arrangements of society, and social roles all provide the proper focus for criminological study.
- Group dynamics, group organization, and subgroup relationships form the causal nexus out of which crime develops.
- The structure of society and the relative degree of social organization or **social disorganization** are important factors contributing to the prevalence of criminal behavior.

All sociological perspectives on crime share the foregoing characteristics, but particular theories may give greater or lesser weight to the following aspects of social life:

- The clash of norms and values among variously socialized groups
- Socialization and the process of association between individuals
- The existence of subcultures and varying types of opportunities

CJ News

Was Eric Clark Insane or Just Troubled?

The phone roused Terry Clark from sleep. She eyed the clock: 5 A.M. Who could be calling at this hour?

"Flagstaff Police Department," a voice announced, abruptly. The next minutes and hours would pass like a slow-moving horror film where the evil emerges bit by bit.

At first, investigators told her only that a policeman had been shot. She heard a name, Officer Jeff Moritz. He was called to the neighborhood after residents reported a pickup circling round and round, blaring loud music.

Her son Gentry's pickup sat abandoned—driver's-side door flung open, keys in the ignition, a Dr. Dre CD in the player—next to the sidewalk where the police officer had died.

Her son was the prime suspect. Not Gentry, though, who had been at home in bed, safe. Her other son. Eric. The one who had been a star football player and a good student with dreams.

The one who just two months earlier had called his mother and father aliens.

SLAYING SHOCKED TOWN

What happened in those early morning hours of June 21, 2000, left an entire town in shock. The victim was the only police officer ever killed in the line of duty in this mountain community north of Phoenix.

He was a caring cop who cut firewood for the handicapped and bought burgers for hungry transients he arrested. He was a husband and father with one young son and a second on the way.

The accused was a 17-year-old high school senior who had a history of marijuana use and had been arrested two months earlier for drunken driving and drug possession. Police had found two dozen hits of LSD in his car.

A portrait quickly emerged of a drug-crazed teen with no regard for life. But as the facts slowly surfaced so did a different picture of Eric Michael Clark—that of a decent boy from a stable family who had descended into schizophrenia.

With this revelation came a question: How do you measure justice when a killer is a mentally ill kid?

It took three years for Eric Clark to be found competent to stand trial. His lawyers pushed for a verdict of "guilty except insane," meaning incarceration in a psychiatric facility. Instead, a judge found him guilty of first-degree, intentional murder and sentenced him to life in prison, where treatment isn't assured.

On Wednesday, the U.S. Supreme Court is scheduled to take up the case of *Clark* v. *Arizona* and the issue of just how difficult states can make it for criminal defendants to prove insanity.

It's the first time the court has dealt with a direct constitutional challenge to the insanity defense since lawmakers around the country imposed new restrictions following John Hinckley's acquittal by reason of insanity in the 1981 shooting of President Reagan.

"When is it just to punish, or not?" says Richard Bonnie, director of the Institute of Law, Psychiatry and Public Policy at the University of Virginia. "There are some cases where a person was so mentally disturbed at the time of the offense that it would be inhumane and morally objectionable to convict and punish them."

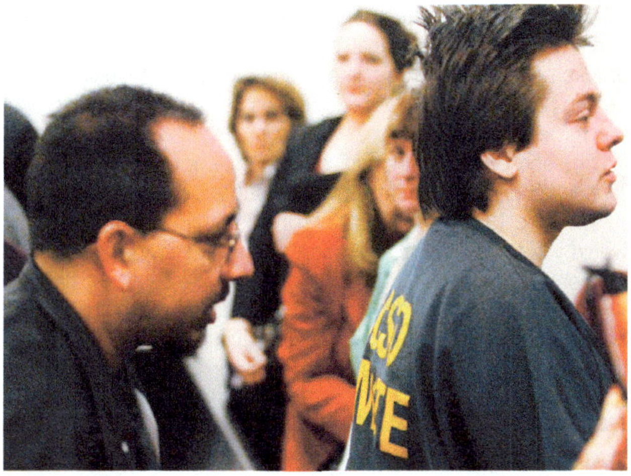

Eric Clark leaving the Coconino County Courthouse in Arizona prior to sentencing. Clark was convicted of killing Flagstaff police officer Jeff Moritz but claimed that he saw the officer as an alien from outer space. At the time of the killing, Clark was just 17 years old. Should Clark be imprisoned, treated for his mental illness, or both?

*Courtesy Josh Biggs/*Arizona Daily Sun

SIGNPOSTS OF MENTAL ILLNESS

Looking back now, Terry Clark remembers things, little things, and wonders when it all started.

Eric was a gifted athlete who played soccer, baseball, basketball, football. As a running back at Flagstaff High, he was one of the young stars selected to play varsity and dreamed of becoming a professional athlete. Then he lost interest in sports.

He had been popular—a homecoming court nominee—but his friends quit calling. His grades, usually As and Bs, took a dive.

On June 21, 1999, Terry and her husband, Dave, had their son admitted to Aspen Hill, a local mental health facility. He'd abandoned his car on a road.

At Aspen Hill, Eric tested positive for marijuana, and Terry wondered whether drugs had triggered his behavior. But doctors alluded to something else—the possibility of schizophrenia. With no mental illness on either side of the family, Terry pushed that idea aside.

Eric seemed to improve and she had him discharged after only three days. "He's getting better," Terry convinced herself. He got worse.

That fall, Eric quit school. He became obsessed with Y2K, took his dad's debit card and charged $1,700 worth of survival gear. He wore layers upon layers of clothing and carried his possessions in a garbage bag.

When January 1, 2000, came and went, Eric's mood improved. He went back to high school. "He's getting better," Terry thought again—until Eric started mentioning "them."

That April, Eric suddenly referred to her as an alien. Eric called his father an alien, too. "If you'd go get some tools," he told them matter-of-factly, "I'd show you."

(continued)

CJ News (continued)

Terry now believed the doctors were right about schizophrenia. She was relieved when, that same month, Eric was arrested on drunken driving and drug charges; she thought that would lead to getting help. But authorities decided to postpone prosecution until Eric turned 18 later in the year.

She and Dave searched for counselors, but Eric refused to go. Terry left messages at treatment facilities that were never returned.

On June 19, 2000, Eric called his mother an alien again. "How would you like to be me," he said, "and never know who your real mother is?"

Terry contacted her lawyer and begged him to convince the county to pursue the drug charges. Prosecutors still wanted to wait until Eric was an adult, so he'd face longer prison time if convicted.

INTENT OR INSANITY?

Investigators surmise that sometime after 1:30 A.M. on June 21, 2000, Eric made his way home, sneaked into his brother Gentry's bedroom, took his keys and left in Gentry's truck.

What happened after that, and why, no one can know for certain; Eric never talked about the events of that morning.

At the 2003 trial, prosecutors and defense attorneys agreed that Eric suffered from paranoid schizophrenia and was mentally ill. But legal insanity is another matter; Arizona law spells out its limited use as a defense.

"A person may be found guilty except insane if, at the time of the commission of the criminal act, the person was afflicted with a mental disease or defect of such severity that the person did not know the criminal act was wrong," the law states.

The prosecutor, Assistant Attorney General David Powell, argued Eric did know. "Officer Moritz walked into . . . an ice-cold ambush," he said at trial.

Defense lawyers insisted Eric's psychosis was so severe he was incapable of hatching such a plan.

They noted that two months after the shooting, Eric called his parents from jail and told them Flagstaff was a "platinum city" inhabited by 50,000 aliens. Before hanging up, he added: "The only thing that will stop aliens are bullets."

In his appeal to the U.S. Supreme Court, lawyer David Goldberg asserts that Arizona law is so restrictive that it violates a mentally ill defendant's right to a fair trial.

For one, he says, Arizona law prohibited the trial court from considering Eric's mental illness in weighing whether he intentionally killed the police officer. Testimony about his mental illness was not permitted until the second phase of the two-part trial.

Goldberg also argues that Arizona's right-wrong test is too narrow in determining legal insanity. Eric might have known that killing was wrong in the abstract, Goldberg says, but if he believed Moritz was an alien, "he didn't understand the nature of what he was doing."

The Supreme Court's decision, expected later this year, could also mean a retrial for Eric Clark, something the Moritz family would see as unjust.

"An angry young man who sets out to kill a cop, or anybody else, ought to be locked up for the rest of his life," says the victim's father, Dan Moritz, a psychologist who questions whether Clark actually is a paranoid schizophrenic.

For the Clarks, a new trial would mean a chance for their son to receive psychiatric care.

"Lock him up for his crime," Terry Clark says, "but treat him for his mental illness, please. Eric didn't choose to be mentally ill. It chose him."

For the latest in crime and justice news, visit the Talk Justice news feed at http://www.crimenews.info.

Author's note: Eric Clark's conviction was upheld by the U.S. Supreme Court.

Source: "Was Eric Clark Insane or Just Troubled?" © April 15, 2006 by the Associated Press. Reprinted by permission.

Social Ecology Theory

In the 1920s, during the early days of sociological theorizing, the University of Chicago brought together such thinkers as Robert Park, Ernest Burgess,[76] Clifford Shaw, and Henry McKay.[77] Park and Burgess recognized that Chicago, like most cities, could be mapped according to its social characteristics. Their map resembled a target with a bull's-eye in the center. Shaw and McKay adapted these concentric zones to the study of crime when they realized that the zones nearest the center of the city had the highest crime rates. In particular, zone 2 (one removed from the center) consistently showed the highest crime rate over time, regardless of the groups or nationalities inhabiting it. This "zone of transition"—so called because new immigrant groups moved into it as earlier ones became integrated into American culture and moved out—demonstrated that crime was dependent to a considerable extent on aspects of the social structure of the city itself. Structural elements identified by Shaw and McKay included poverty, illiteracy, lack of schooling, unemployment, and illegitimacy. In combination, these elements were seen to lead to social disorganization, which in turn produced crime.

Anomie Theory

The French word **anomie** has been loosely translated as a condition of "normlessness." Anomie entered the literature as a sociological concept with the writings of Émile Durkheim (1858–1917) in the late nineteenth century.[78] Robert Merton (1910–2003) applied anomie to criminology in 1938 when he used the term to describe a disjunction between socially acceptable goals and means in American society.[79]

anomie

A socially pervasive condition of normlessness. Also, a disjunction between approved goals and means.

Merton believed that while the same goals and means are held out by society as desirable for everyone, they are not equally available to all. Socially approved goals in American society, for example, include wealth, status, and political power. The acceptable means to achieve these goals are education, wise investment, and hard work. Unfortunately, however, opportunities are not equally distributed throughout society, and some people turn to illegitimate means to achieve the goals they are pressured to reach. Still others reject both acceptable goals and legitimate means of reaching them.

Merton represented his theory with a chart, shown in Table 2. *Conformists* accept both the goals and means that society holds out as legitimate, while *innovators* accept the goals but reject the means, instead using illegal means to gain money, power, and success. It is the innovators whom Merton identified as criminal. The inherent logic of the model led Merton to posit other social types. *Ritualists* are those who reject success goals but still perform their daily tasks in conformity with social expectations. They might hold regular jobs but lack the desire to advance in life. *Retreatists* reject both the goals and the means and usually drop out of society by becoming derelicts, drug users, hermits, or the like. *Rebels* constitute a special category. Their desire to replace the existing system of socially approved goals and means with some other system more to their liking makes them the revolutionaries of the theory.

Merton believed that categories are not intentionally selected by the individuals who occupy them but rather are imposed on people by structural aspects of society. Where people live, how wealthy their family is, and what ethnic background they come from are all significant determinants of the "box" into which people are placed.

Modern writers on anomie recognize that normlessness is not likely to be expressed as criminality unless people who experience it also feel that they are capable of doing something to change their lives. As Catherine Ross and John Mirowsky put it, "A person who has high levels of normlessness and powerlessness is less likely to get in trouble with the law than a person who has a high level of normlessness and a high level of instrumentalism."[80]

Merton's anomie theory drew attention to the lack of equal opportunity that existed in society at the time he was writing. While considerable efforts have been made to eradicate it, much of that inequality continues today.

If we are ever to reduce the tragic toll of crime in society, we must compare the measured benefits of incarceration to less costly and more productive crime prevention strategies—especially those programs aimed at helping high-risk families and young people escape the hopelessness that surrounds their lives.

—Barry Krisberg, President, National Council on Crime and Delinquency

Subcultural Theory

Another sociological contribution to criminological theory is the idea of a subculture. A subculture is a group of people who participate in a shared system of values and norms that are at variance with those of the larger culture. Subcultural explanations of crime posit the existence of group values that support criminal behavior. Subcultures were first recognized in the enclaves formed by immigrants who came to America during the early part of the twentieth century. Statistics have shown that certain immigrant groups had low crime rates.[81] Among them were the

TABLE 2 Merton's Anomie Theory and Implied Types of Criminality

Category	Goals	Means	Examples
Conformist	+	+	Law-abiding behavior
Innovator	+	–	Property offenses, white-collar crimes
Retreatist	–	–	Drug use/addiction, vagrancy, some "victimless" crimes
Ritualist	–	+	A repetitive and mundane lifestyle
Rebel	±	±	Political crime (for example, environmental activists who violate the law, violence-prone antiabortionists)

Source: Adapted with the permission of the Free Press, a division of Simon & Schuster Adult Publishing Group, from *Social Theory and Social Structure*, Revised and Enlarged Edition by Robert K. Merton.

CJ Futures

The Physical Environment and Crime

Social ecology theory—an outgrowth of the Chicago School of sociological thought, which flourished during the 1920s and 1930s—posited a link between physical location and crime. A modern perspective, called *crime prevention through environmental design* (CPTED), bears a strong resemblance to earlier ecological theories. CPTED, which was first formulated in the 1960s and 1970s, focuses on the settings in which crimes occur and on techniques for reducing vulnerability within those settings. Because defensible space concepts are being increasingly applied to the design of physical facilities, including housing, parking garages, public buildings, and even entire neighborhoods, it is highly likely that applications of CPTED will accelerate throughout the twenty-first century.

Second-generation **defensible space theory**, upon which contemporary CPTED is built, developed around 1980 and considered more carefully how the impact of physical features on fear and victimization depends on other social and cultural features in the setting. Second-generation defensible space theory employed the **broken windows thesis**, which holds that physical deterioration and an increase in unrepaired buildings lead to increased concerns for personal safety among area residents. Heightened concerns, in turn, lead to further decreases in maintenance and repair and to increased delinquency, vandalism, and crime among local residents, which spawn even further deterioration both in a sense of safety and in the physical environment. Offenders from other neighborhoods are then increasingly attracted by the area's perceived vulnerability.

Research on CPTED has shown environmental design to be effective in lowering crime and crime-related public-order problems. Effective use of CPTED to alter features of the physical environment can affect potential offenders' perceptions about a possible crime site, their evaluations of the opportunities associated with that site, and the availability and visibility of one or more natural guardians at or near the site. CPTED is based on the belief that offenders decide whether to commit a crime in a particular location after they evaluate the area's features, including (1) the ease of entry to the area, (2) the visibility of the target to others—that is, the chance of being seen, (3) the attractiveness or vulnerability of the target, (4) the likelihood that criminal behavior will be challenged or thwarted if discovered, and (5) the ease of egress—that is, the ability to quickly and easily leave the area once the crime has been committed.

According to the National Institute of Justice, CPTED suggests four approaches to making a location more resistant to crime and to crime-related public-order problems:

- *Housing design or block layout*—making it more difficult to commit crimes by (1) reducing the availability of crime targets, (2) removing barriers that prevent easy detection of potential offenders or of an offense in progress, and (3) increasing physical obstacles to committing a crime.
- *Land use and circulation patterns*—creating safer use of neighborhood space by reducing routine exposure of potential offenders to crime targets. This can be accomplished through careful attention to walkways, paths, streets, traffic patterns, and locations and hours of operation of public spaces and facilities. Street closings or revised traffic patterns that decrease vehicular volume may, under some conditions, encourage residents to better maintain the sidewalks and streets in front of their houses.
- *Territorial features*—encouraging the use of territorial markers or fostering conditions that will lead to more extensive marking to indicate that the block or site is occupied by vigilant residents. Sponsoring cleanup and beautification contests and creating controllable, semiprivate outdoor locations may encourage such activities. This strategy focuses on small-scale, private, and semipublic sites, usually within predominantly residential locales. It is most relevant at the street-block level and below. It enhances the chances that residents themselves will generate semifixed features that demonstrate their involvement in and watchfulness over a particular delimited location.
- *Physical maintenance*—controlling physical deterioration to reduce offenders' perceptions that areas are vulnerable to crime and that residents are so fearful they would do nothing to stop a crime. Physical improvements may reduce the signals of vulnerability and increase commitment to joint protective activities. Physical deterioration, in all probability, not only influences the cognition and behavior of potential offenders but also shapes how residents behave and what they think about other residents.

A run-down city street. To explain crime, criminologists sometimes use the "broken windows" approach, which says that neighborhood deterioration leads to rising crime rates. Similarly, poverty, unemployment, a relative lack of formal education, and low skill levels, which often characterize inner-city populations, seem to be linked to criminality. Why?

Peter Byron/PhotoEdit Inc.

For additional information on CPTED via the Crime Mapping Research Center, see **Web Extra 3–6** at cjtoday.com. **WEB Extra**

References: Derek J. Paulsen and Matthew B. Robinson, *Spatial Aspects of Crime: Theory and Practice* (Boston: Allyn and Bacon, 2004); Oscar Newman, *Defensible Space* (New York: Macmillan, 1972); Oscar Newman, *Creating Defensible Space* (Washington, DC: HUD 1996); James Q. Wilson and George Kelling, "Broken Windows," *Atlantic Monthly*, March 1982; Dan Fleissner and Fred Heinzelmann, *Crime Prevention through Environmental Design and Community Policing* (Washington, DC: NIJ, 1996); Ralph B. Taylor and Adele V. Harrell, *Physical Environment and Crime* (Washington, DC: NIJ, 1996); Mary S. Smith, *Crime Prevention through Environmental Design in Parking Facilities* (Washington, DC: NIJ, 1996); and Corey L. Gordon and William Brill, *The Expanding Role of Crime Prevention through Environmental Design in Premises Liability* (Washington, DC: NIJ, 1996).

Scandinavians, Chinese, Dutch, Germans, and Japanese. Other immigrant groups, including Italians, Mexicans, Puerto Ricans, and Africans, demonstrated a significantly greater propensity for involvement in crime.[82]

Albert Cohen (b. 1918) coined the term **reaction formation** to encompass the rejection of middle-class values by status-seeking lower-class youths who find they are not permitted access to approved opportunities for success.[83] In Cohen's eyes, reaction formation leads to the development of gangs and perpetuates the existence of subcultures. Walter Miller described the focal concerns of subcultural participants in terms of "trouble," "toughness," "excitement," "smartness," "fate," and "autonomy."[84] It is a focus on such concerns, Miller suggested, that leads members of criminal subcultures into violations of the law. Richard Cloward and Lloyd Ohlin proposed the existence of an illegitimate opportunity structure that permits delinquent youths to achieve in ways that are outside of legitimate avenues to success.[85]

During the 1950s, Marvin Wolfgang and Franco Ferracuti examined homicide rates in Philadelphia and found that murder was a way of life among certain groups.[86] They discovered a "wholesale" and a "retail" price for murder—which depended on who was killed and who did the killing. Killings that occurred within violent subgroups were more likely to be partially excused than those that happened elsewhere. The term **subculture of violence** has come to be associated with their work and has since been applied to other locations across the country.

Critiques of subcultural theory have been numerous. A major difficulty for these theories lies in the fact that studies involving self-reports of crime commission have shown that much violence and crime occur outside of "criminal" subcultures. Many middle- and upper-class lawbreakers are able to avoid the justice system and therefore do not enter the "official" crime statistics. Hence, criminal subcultures may be those in which crime is more visible rather than more prevalent.

defensible space theory

The belief that an area's physical features may be modified and structured so as to reduce crime rates in that area and to lower the fear of victimization that residents experience.

broken windows thesis

A perspective on crime causation that holds that the physical deterioration of an area leads to higher crime rates and an increased concern for personal safety among residents.

reaction formation

The process whereby a person openly rejects that which he or she wants or aspires to but cannot obtain or achieve.

subculture of violence

A cultural setting in which violence is a traditional and often accepted method of dispute resolution.

Social Policy and Sociological Theories

Theoretical approaches that fault the social environment as the root cause of crime point to social action as a panacea. A contemporary example of intervention efforts based on sociological theories can be found in Targeted Outreach,[87] a program operated by the Boys and Girls Clubs of America. The program's philosophy is based on studies undertaken at the University of Colorado that showed that at-risk youths could be effectively diverted from the juvenile justice system through the provision of positive alternatives. The program recruits at-risk youngsters—many as young as seven years old—and diverts them into activities that are intended to promote a sense of belonging, competence, usefulness, and power. Social programs like Targeted Outreach are intended to change the cultural conditions and societal arrangements that are thought to lead people into crime.

Social Process Theories

While psychological approaches to crime causation seek to uncover aspects of the personality hidden even from the mind in which they reside, and while sociological theories look to institutional arrangements in the social world to explain crime, social process approaches focus on the interaction between individuals and society. Most **social process theories** highlight the role of social learning. They build on the premise that behavior—both "good" and "bad"—is learned, and they suggest that "bad" behavior can be unlearned. Social process theories are often the most attractive to contemporary policymakers because they demand that responsibility be placed on the offender for actively participating in rehabilitation efforts and because they are consistent with popular cultural and religious values centered on teaching right from wrong.

social process theory

A perspective on criminological thought that highlights the process of interaction between individuals and society. Most social process theories highlight the role of social learning.

Differential Association Theory

In 1939, Edwin Sutherland (1883–1950) published the third edition of his *Principles of Criminology*. It contained, for the first time, a formalized statement of his theory of differential association, a perspective that Sutherland based on the "laws of imitation" described by Gabriel Tarde (1843–1904), a French sociologist.

The theory of differential association explains crime as a natural consequence of the interaction with criminal lifestyles. Sutherland suggested that children raised in crime-prone environments were often isolated and unable to experience the values that would otherwise lead to conformity. Differential association provides the basis for much research in modern criminology.[88] Even popular stories of young drug pushers, for instance, often refer to the fact that inner-city youths imitate what they see. Some residents of poverty-ridden ghettos learn quickly that fast money can be made in the illicit drug trade, and they tend to follow the examples of material "success" that they see around them.

Differential association views crime as the product of socialization and sees it as being acquired by criminals according to the same principles that guide the learning of law-abiding behavior in conformists. Differential association removes criminality from the framework of the abnormal and places it squarely within a general perspective applicable to all behavior. In the 1947 edition of his text, Sutherland wrote, "Criminal behavior is a part of human behavior, has much in common with non-criminal behavior, and must be explained within the same general framework as any other human behavior."[89] A study of the tenets of differential association (listed in Table 3) shows that Sutherland believed that even the sources of behavioral motivation are much the same for conformists and criminals, that is, both groups strive for money and success but choose different paths to the same goal.

However, differential association theory fails to explain why people have the associations they do and why some associations affect certain individuals more than others. Why, for example, are most prison guards unaffected by their constant association with offenders, while a few take advantage of their position to smuggle contraband? The theory has also been criticized for being so general and imprecise as to allow for little testing.[90] Complete testing of the theory would require that all of the associations a person has ever had be recorded and analyzed from the standpoint of the individual—a clearly impossible task.

Other theorists continue to build on Sutherland's early work. Robert Burgess and Ronald Akers, for example, have constructed a differential association–reinforcement theory that seeks to integrate Sutherland's original propositions with the work of American psychologist B. F. Skinner's work on conditioning.[91] Burgess and Akers suggest that although values and behavior patterns are learned in association with others, the primary mechanism through which such learning occurs is operant conditioning. Reinforcement is the key, they say, to understanding any social learning as it takes place. The name **social learning theory** has been widely applied to the work of Burgess and Akers. It is somewhat of a misnomer, however, since the term can easily encompass a wide range of approaches and should not be limited to one specific combination of the ideas found in differential association and reinforcement theory.

social learning theory

A psychological perspective that says that people learn how to behave by modeling themselves after others whom they have the opportunity to observe.

Restraint Theories

As we have seen throughout this chapter, most criminological theories posit a cause of crime.[92] Some theories, however, focus less on causes than on constraints—those forces that keep people from committing a crime. These theories are called *restraint theories*. However, since they focus primarily on why people do not break the law, restraint theories provide only half of the causal picture. They are especially weak in identifying the social-structural sources of motivations to commit crimes.[93] Also, the ways in which bonds with different institutions interact with one

TABLE 3 Sutherland's Principles of Differential Association

1. Criminal behavior is learned.
2. Criminal behavior is learned in interaction with others in a process of communication.
3. The principal part of the learning of criminal behavior occurs within intimate personal groups.
4. When criminal behavior is learned, the learning includes (a) techniques of committing the crime, which are sometimes very complicated, sometimes very simple, and (b) the specific direction of motives, drives, rationalizations, and attitudes.
5. The specific direction of motives and drives is learned from definitions of the legal codes as favorable or unfavorable.
6. A person becomes delinquent because of an excess of definitions favorable to violations of law over definitions unfavorable to violations of law.
7. Differential associations may vary in frequency, duration, priority, and intensity.
8. The process of learning criminal behavior by association with criminal and anticriminal patterns involves all the mechanisms that are involved in any other learning.
9. Although criminal behavior is an expression of general needs and values, it is not explained by those general needs and values since noncriminal behavior is an expression of the same needs and values.

Source: Edwin Sutherland, *Principles of Criminology*, 4th ed. (Chicago: J. B. Lippincott, 1947), pp. 6–7.

another and with personal attributes, as well as the variety of bonds that operate throughout the life cycle, have yet to be clarified.[94]

CONTAINMENT THEORY

Containment theory, a type of restraint theory offered by Walter Reckless (1899–1988), assumes that all of us are subject to inducements to crime.[95] Some of us resist these "pushes" toward criminal behavior, while others do not. The difference, according to Reckless, can be found in forces that contain, or control, behavior.

Reckless described two types of **containment:** outer and inner. Outer containment depends on social roles and the norms and expectations that apply to them. People who occupy significant roles in society find themselves insulated from deviant tendencies. A corporate executive, for example, is less apt to hold up a liquor store than is a drifter. The difference, according to Reckless, is not due solely to income, but also to the pressure the executive feels to conform.

containment

The aspects of the social bond and of the personality that act to prevent individuals from committing crimes and engaging in deviance.

Inner containment involves a number of factors, such as conscience, a positive self-image, a tolerance for frustration, and aspirations that are in line with reality. Reckless believed that inner containment is more powerful than outer containment; inner containment functions even in secret. For example, an inner-directed person who comes across a lost purse feels compelled to locate its rightful owner and return it. If theft or greed crosses the mind of an inner-directed person, he will say to himself, "I'm not that kind of person. That would be wrong."

Reckless studied small close-knit societies—including the Hutterites, Mennonites, and Amish—in developing his theory. He realized that the "containment of behavior . . . is . . . maximized under conditions of isolation and homogeneity of culture, class, and population."[96] Hence, its applicability to modern American society, with its considerable heterogeneity of values and perspectives, is questionable.

SOCIAL CONTROL THEORY

Travis Hirschi emphasized the bond between individuals and society as the primary operative mechanism in his *social control theory*.[97] Hirschi identified four components of that bond: (1) emotional attachments to significant others, (2) a commitment to appropriate lifestyles, (3) involvement or immersion in conventional values, and (4) a belief in the "correctness" of social obligations and the rules of the larger society. These components act as social controls on deviant and criminal behavior; as they weaken, social control suffers, and the likelihood of crime and deviance increases. Using self-reports of delinquency from high school students in California, Hirschi concluded that youngsters who were less attached to teachers and parents and who had few positive attitudes about their own accomplishments were more likely to engage in crime and deviance than were others.[98]

NEUTRALIZATION TECHNIQUES

Complementing restraint theory is the *neutralization approach* of Gresham Sykes and David Matza.[99] The neutralization approach centers on rationalizations that allow offenders to shed feelings of guilt and responsibility for their behavior. Sykes and Matza believed that most people drift into and out of criminal behavior but will not commit a crime unless they have available to them techniques of neutralization. Their study primarily concerned juveniles for whom, they suggested, neutralization techniques provided only a temporary respite from guilt. That respite, however, lasted long enough to avoid the twinges of conscience while a crime was being committed. Neutralization techniques include the following:

- Denial of responsibility ("I'm a product of my background.")
- Denial of injury ("No one was really hurt.")
- Denial of the victim ("They deserved it.")
- Condemnation of the condemners ("The cops are corrupt.")
- Appeal to higher loyalties ("I did it for my friends.")

Like containment theory, restraint theories tend to depend on a general agreement as to values, or they assume that offenders are simply conformists who suffer temporary lapses. Neutralization techniques, by definition, are only needed when the delinquent has been socialized into middle-class values or where conscience is well developed. Even so, neutralization techniques do not in themselves explain crime. Such techniques are available to us all, if we make only a slight effort to conjure them up. The real question is why some people readily allow proffered neutralizations to affect their behavior, while others effortlessly discount them.

Labeling Theory

labeling theory

A social process perspective that sees continued crime as a consequence of the limited opportunities for acceptable behavior that follow from the negative responses of society to those defined as offenders.

As we saw earlier in this chapter, the worth of any theory of behavior is proved by how well it reflects the reality of the social world. In practice, however, theoretical perspectives find acceptance in the academic environment via a number of considerations. **Labeling theory**, for example, became fashionable in the 1960s. Its popularity may have been due more to the cultural environment into which it was introduced rather than to any inherent quality of the theory itself.

Labeling theory was first introduced by Frank Tannenbaum (1893–1969) in 1938 under the rubric of *tagging*.[100] He wrote, "The young delinquent becomes bad because he is defined as bad and because he is not believed if he is good." He went on to say, "The process of making the criminal, therefore, is a process of tagging. . . . It becomes a way of stimulating . . . and evolving the very traits that are complained of. . . . The person becomes the thing he is described as being."[101] Tannenbaum focused on society's power to *define* an act or an individual as bad and drew attention to the group need for a scapegoat in explaining crime. The search for causes inherent in individuals was not yet exhausted, however, and Tannenbaum's theory fell mostly on deaf ears.

moral enterprise

The process undertaken by an advocacy group to have its values legitimated and embodied in law.

By the 1960s, the social and academic environments in America had changed, and the issue of responsibility was seen more in terms of the group than the individual. In his book *Outsiders*, published in 1963, Howard Becker pointed out that criminality is not a quality inherent in an act or in a person. Crime, said Becker, results from a social definition, through law, of unacceptable behavior. That definition arises through **moral enterprise**, by which groups on both sides of an issue debate and eventually legislate their notion of what is moral and what is not. Becker wrote, "The central fact about deviance [is that] it is created by society. . . . Social groups create deviance by making the rules whose infraction constitutes deviance."[102]

The criminal label, however, produces consequences for labeled individuals that may necessitate continued criminality. In describing the criminal career, Becker wrote, "To be labeled a criminal one need only commit a single criminal offense. . . . Yet the word carries a number of connotations specifying auxiliary traits characteristic of anyone bearing the label."[103] The first time a person commits a crime, the behavior is called *primary deviance* and may be a merely transitory form of behavior.

However, in the popular mind, a "known" criminal is not to be trusted, should not be hired because of the potential for crimes on the job, and would not be a good candidate for the military, marriage, or any position requiring responsibility. Society's tendency toward such thinking, Becker suggested, closes legitimate opportunities, ensuring that the only new behavioral alternatives available to the labeled criminal are deviant ones. Succeeding episodes of criminal behavior are seen as a form of secondary deviance that eventually becomes stabilized in the behavioral repertoire and self-concept of the labeled person.[104]

Labeling theory can be critiqued along a number of dimensions. First, it is not really a "theory" in that labeling does not uncover the genesis of criminal behavior. It is more useful in describing how such behavior continues than in explaining how it originates. Second, labeling theory does not recognize the possibility that the labeled individual may make successful attempts at reform and may shed the negative label. Finally, the theory does not provide an effective way of dealing with offenders. Should people who commit crimes not be arrested and tried so as to avoid the consequences of negative labels? It would be exceedingly naïve to suggest that all repeat criminal behavior would cease, as labeling theory might predict, if people who commit crimes are not officially "handled" by the system.

The Life Course Perspective

social development theory

An integrated view of human development that points to the process of interaction among and between individuals and society as the root cause of criminal behavior.

life course perspective

An approach to explaining crime and deviance that investigates developments and turning points in the course of a person's life.

Some of the most recent perspectives on crime causation belong to a subcategory of social process thought called **social development theory**. According to the social development perspective, human development occurs simultaneously on many levels, including the psychological, biological, familial, interpersonal, cultural, societal, and ecological levels. Hence, social development theories tend to be integrated theories—that is, theories that combine various points of view on the process of development. Theories that fall into this category, however, highlight the process of interaction between individuals and society as the root cause of criminal behavior. In particular, they emphasize that a critical period of transition occurs in a person's life as he or she moves from childhood to adulthood.

One social development perspective of special significance is the **life course perspective**. According to Robert Sampson and John Laub, who named the life course perspective in 1993, criminal behavior typically follows an identifiable pattern throughout a person's life cycle.[105] In the lives of those who eventually become criminal, crime-like or deviant behavior is relatively rare during early childhood, tends to begin as sporadic instances during early adolescence, becomes more common during the late-teen and early-adult years, and then gradually diminishes as the person gets older.

Sampson and Laub also use the idea of *transitions* in the life course, or turning points that identify significant events in a person's life and represent the opportunity for people to turn either away from or toward deviance and crime. An employer who gives an employee a second chance, for example, may provide a unique opportunity that helps determine the future course of that person's life. Similarly, the principle of *linked lives*, also common to life course theories, highlights the fact that no one lives in isolation. Events in the life course are constantly being influenced by family members, friends, acquaintances, employers, teachers, and so on. Not only might such influences determine the life course of any given individual, but they are active throughout the life course. Figure 2 diagrams some of the life course influences experienced by most adolescents. Also shown in the diagram are desired outcomes and positive and negative indicators of development.

In 1986, the federal Office of Juvenile Justice and Delinquency Prevention (OJJDP) began funding a study of life pathways as they lead to criminality. The Program of Research on the Causes and Correlates of Delinquency continues to produce results.[106] Researchers have been examining how delinquency, violence, and drug use develop within and are related to various social contexts, including the family, peer groups, schools, and the surrounding community. To date, the study has identified three distinct pathways to delinquency, which are shown in Figure 3. These pathways are not mutually exclusive and can sometimes converge:

- The *authority conflict pathway*, along which children begin to move during their early years (as early as three or four years old), involves stubborn behavior and resistance to parental authority. Defiance of authority begins around age 11, and authority avoidance (that is, truancy, running away) begins about the same time.
- The *covert pathway*, which starts around age ten with minor covert acts such as shoplifting and lying, quickly progresses to acts of vandalism involving property damage. Moderate to severe delinquency frequently begins a year or two later.
- The *overt pathway* is marked by minor aggression, such as bullying, that develops around age 11 or 12. The overt pathway leads to fighting and physical violence during the teenage years and tends to eventuate in serious violent criminality that may include rape, robbery, and assault.

A similar study is under way at the Project on Human Development in Chicago Neighborhoods (PHDCN), mentioned earlier in this chapter. PHDCN researchers are "tracing how criminal behavior develops from birth to age 32."[107] Participating researchers come from a variety of scientific backgrounds and include psychiatrists, developmental psychologists, sociologists, criminologists, physicians, educators, statisticians, and public health officials. The study focuses on the influence of communities, peers, families, and health-related, cognitive, and emotional factors to decipher the lines along which crime and delinquency are likely to develop. Learn more about the OJJDP's causes and correlates study at Web Extra 3–7 at cjtoday.com; find out more about the PHDCN project at Web Extra 3–8 and Library Extra 3–3; and read about the possible effects of childhood victimization on later criminality at Library Extra 3–4.

An honest and fully professional police community would acknowledge in its police education the root causes of crime—poverty, unemployment, underemployment, racism, poor health care, bad housing, weak schools, mental illness, alcoholism, addiction, single-parent families, teenage pregnancy, and a society of selfishness and greed.

—Patrick V. Murphy, former New York City Police Commissioner

WEB Extra LIBRARY Extra

Conflict Theories

Basic to the **conflict perspective** is the belief that conflict is a fundamental aspect of social life and can never be fully resolved. From the conflict point of view, formal agencies of social control at best merely coerce the unempowered or the disenfranchised to comply with the rules established by those in power. Laws become tools of the powerful, tools that are useful in keeping others from wresting control over important social institutions. Social order, rather than being the result of any consensus or process of dispute resolution, rests on the exercise of power through law. The conflict perspective can be described in terms of four key elements:[108]

- Society is composed of diverse social groups, and diversity is based on distinctions that people hold to be significant, such as gender, sexual orientation, and social class.
- Conflict among groups is unavoidable because of differing interests and differing values. Hence, conflict is inherent in social life.
- The fundamental nature of group conflict centers on the exercise of political power. Political power is the key to the accumulation of wealth and to other forms of power.
- Laws are the tools of power and further the interests of those powerful enough to make them. Laws allow those in control to gain what they define (through the law) as legitimate access to scarce resources and to deny (through the law) such access to the politically disenfranchised.

conflict perspective

A theoretical approach that holds that crime is the natural consequence of economic and other social inequities. Conflict theorists highlight the stresses that arise among and within social groups as they compete with one another for resources and for survival. The social forces that result are viewed as major determinants of group and individual behavior, including crime.

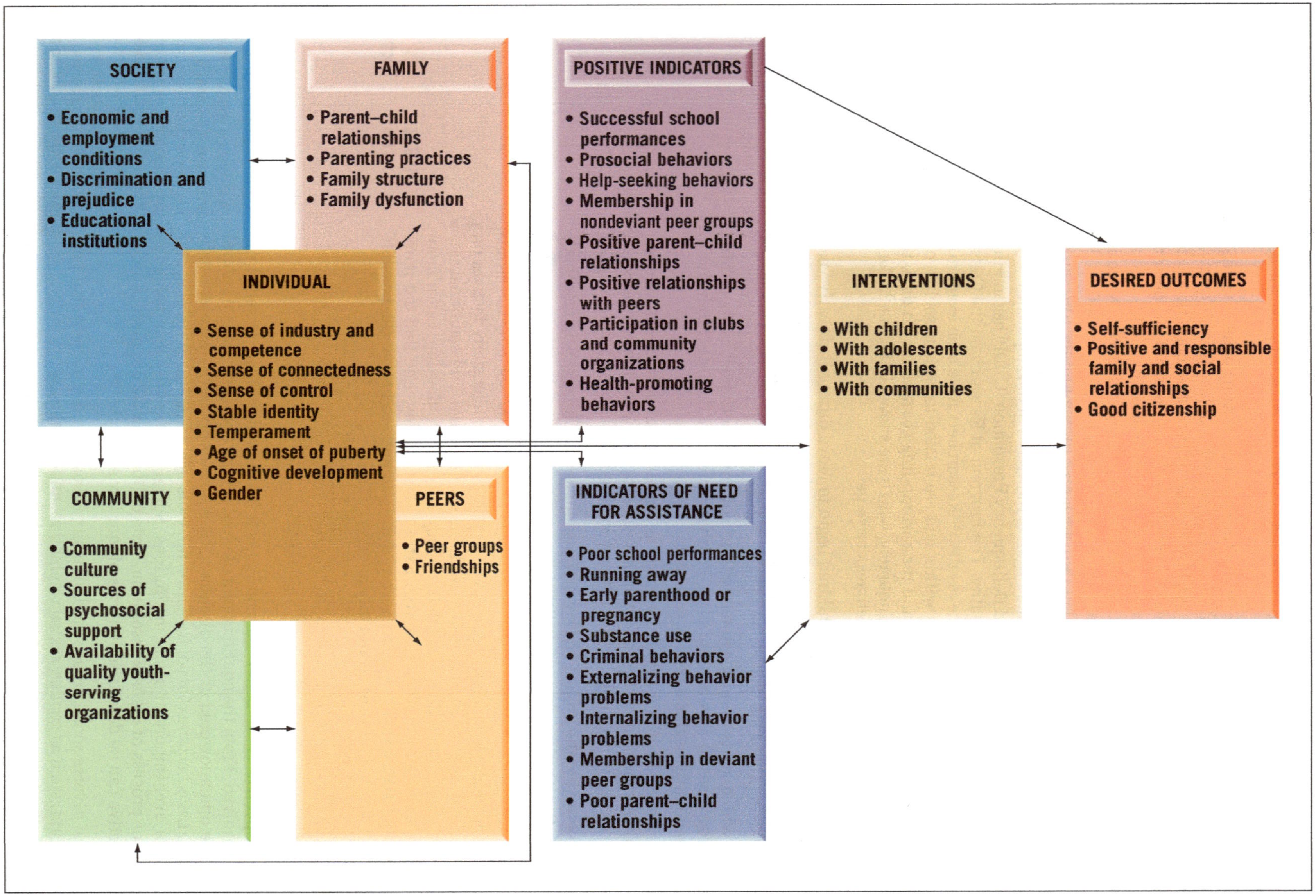

FIGURE 2

A conceptual model of adolescent development.

Source: Family and Youth Services Bureau, *Understanding Youth Development: Promoting Positive Pathways of Growth* (Washington, DC: U.S. Dept. of Health and Human Services, 2000).

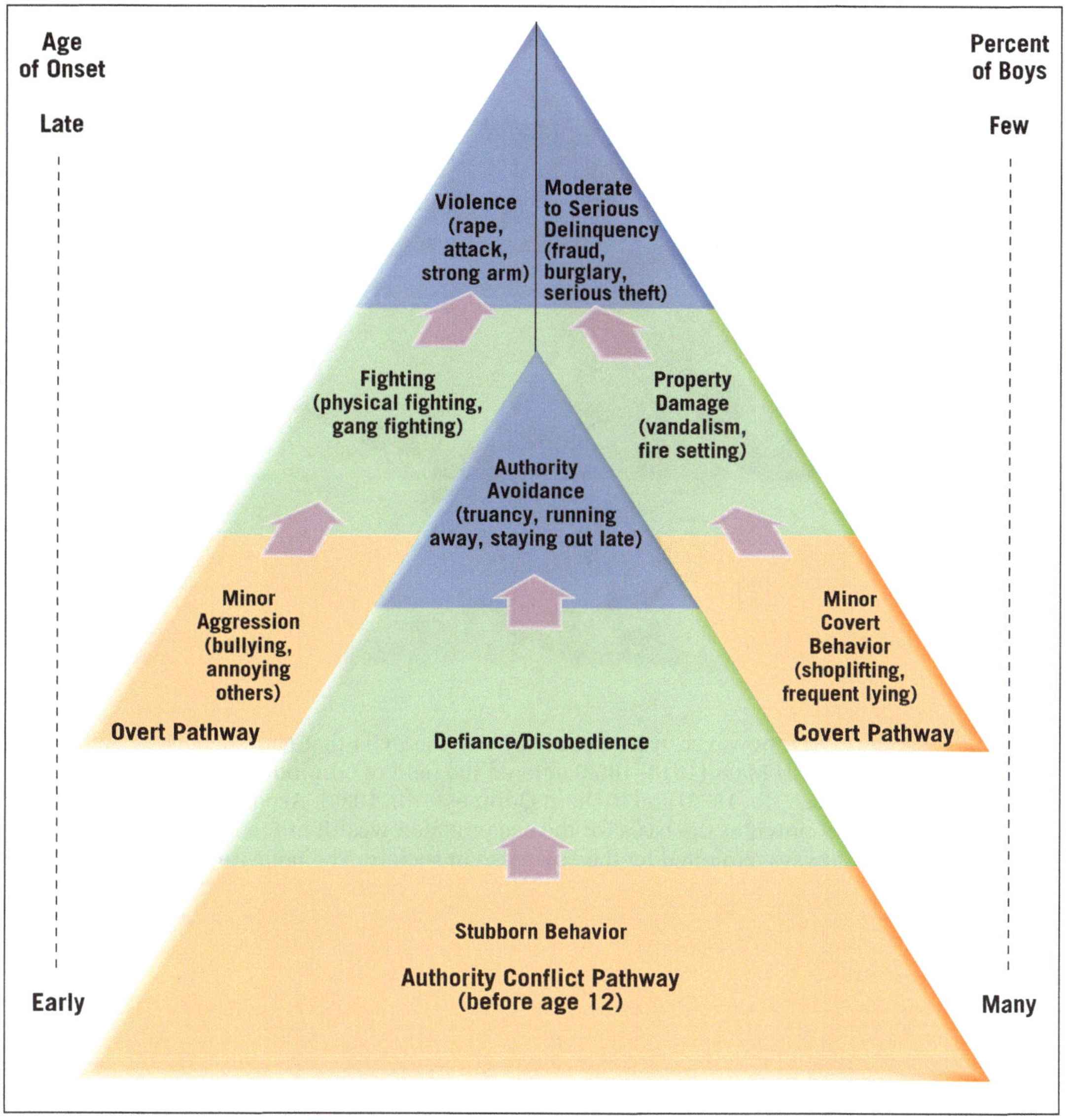

FIGURE 3

Three pathways to disruptive behavior and delinquency.

Source: Barbara Tatem Kelley et al., *Developmental Pathways in Boys' Disruptive and Delinquent Behavior* (Washington, DC: Office of Juvenile Justice and Delinquency Prevention, 1997).

Radical Criminology

Criminological theory took a new direction during the 1960s and 1970s, brought about in part by the turmoil that characterized American society during that period. **Radical criminology** placed the blame for criminality and deviant behavior squarely on officially sanctioned cultural and economic arrangements. The distribution of wealth and power in society was held to be the primary cause of criminal behavior, especially among those who were disenfranchised. Poverty and discrimination were seen to lead to frustration and pent-up hostilities that were expressed through murder, rape, theft, and other crimes.

radical criminology

A conflict perspective that sees crime as engendered by the unequal distribution of wealth, power, and other resources, which adherents believe is especially characteristic of capitalist societies.

Radical criminology had its roots in early conflict theories and in the thought of Dutch criminologist Willem Bonger. Some authors have distinguished between conflict theory and radical criminology by naming them "conservative conflict theory" and "radical conflict theory" respectively.[109] The difference between the two theories, however, is mostly in the rhetoric of the times. Conservative conflict theories held that conflict was a natural part of any society and that struggles for power and control would always occur. "Losers" of conflicts were defined as "criminal," and constraints on their behavior would be legislated. Characteristic of this perspective are the approaches of Austin Turk[110] (b. 1934) and George Vold (1896–1967). An even earlier conflict perspective can be found in the culture conflict notions of Thorsten Sellin, who was concerned with the clash of immigrant values and traditions with those of established American culture.[111]

Radical criminology went a step further. It recognized that the struggle to control resources is central to society, and it encompassed the notion that the law is a tool of the powerful. The focus

A homeless man walking by an expensive home. Radical criminologists claim that the inequitable distribution of wealth in society produces frustrations and pent-up hostilities that lead to criminality. In this view, the powerful use the criminal law as a tool to maintain their place in the social world. Do you agree? Why or why not?
Joel Stettenheim/Corbis/Bettmann

of radical criminology, however, was capitalism and the evils that capitalism was believed to entail. The ideas of Karl Marx (1818–1883) entered the field of criminology through the writings of William Chambliss[112] (b. 1933) and Richard Quinney[113] (b. 1934). According to Marx, the labor of the lower classes provides the basis for the accumulated wealth of the upper classes, and the lower classes are always exploited by the "owners" in society. The poor were trained to believe that capitalism was in their best interests and the working classes suffered under the consequences of a "false class consciousness" perpetrated by the powerful. Marx believed that only when the exploited workers realized their exploitation would they rebel and change society for the better.

American radical criminology built on the ideals of the 1960s and charged that the "establishment," controlled by the upper classes, perverted justice through the unequal application of judicial sanctions. As David Greenberg observes, "Many researchers attributed the overrepresentation of blacks and persons from impoverished family backgrounds in arrest and conviction statistics to the discriminatory practices of the enforcement agencies. It was not that the poor stole more, but rather that when they did, the police were more likely to arrest them."[114] Conflict theories of criminality face the difficulty of realistic implementation. Radical criminology, in particular, is flawed by its narrow emphasis on capitalist societies. It fails to recognize adequately the role of human nature in the creation of social classes and in the perpetuation of the struggle for control of resources. Radical criminology implies that a utopian social arrangement—perhaps communism—would eliminate most crime. Such a belief is contrary to historical experience: A close look at any contemporary communist society will reveal both social conflict and crime.

Peacemaking Criminology

peacemaking criminology

A perspective that holds that crime-control agencies and the citizens they serve should work together to alleviate social problems and human suffering and thus reduce crime.

Peacemaking criminology, which some theorists see as a mature expression of earlier conflict theories, holds that crime-control agencies and the citizens they serve should work together to alleviate social problems and human suffering and thus reduce crime.[115] Criminology as peacemaking has its roots in ancient Christian and Eastern philosophies, as well as in traditional conflict theory. Peacemaking criminology, which includes the notion of service and has also been called *compassionate criminology*, suggests that "compassion, wisdom, and love are essential for understanding the suffering of which we are all a part, and for practicing a criminology of nonviolence."[116] Peacemaking criminology also holds that official agents of social control need to work with both the victimized and the victimizers to achieve a new world order that is more just and fair to all who live in it. In a fundamental sense, peacemaking criminologists exhort their colleagues to transcend personal dichotomies to end the political and ideological divisiveness that separates people. "If we ourselves cannot know peace . . . how will our acts disarm hatred and violence?" they ask.[117]

Peacemaking criminology was popularized by the works of Harold Pepinsky[118] and Richard Quinney[119] beginning in 1986. Both Pepinsky and Quinney restate the problem of crime control from one of "how to stop crime" to one of "how to make peace" within society and among citizens and criminal justice agencies. Peacemaking criminology draws attention to many issues, among them the perpetuation of violence through the continuation of social policies based on dominant forms of criminological theory, the role of education in peacemaking, "commonsense theories of crime," crime control as human rights enforcement, and conflict resolution within community settings.[120]

When internal cultures conflict, it can be as destructive as a collision between an iceberg and an ocean liner. Misunderstanding between two cultural groups can lead to conflict and, taken to the extreme, physical confrontations.

—Sherman Block, Los Angeles County Sheriff

Social Policy and Conflict Theories

Because radical and conflict criminologists view social inequality as the cause of crime, many suggest that the only way to achieve real change in the rate of crime is through revolution. Revolution—because it holds the promise of greater equality for underrepresented groups and because it mandates a redistribution of wealth and power—is thought necessary for any lasting reduction in crime.

Some contemporary writers on radical criminology, however, have attempted to address the issue of what can be done under our current system, because they recognize that a sudden and total reversal of existing political arrangements within the United States is highly unlikely. Hence, they have begun to focus on promoting "middle-range policy alternatives" to the present system, including "equal justice in the bail system, the abolition of mandatory sentences, prosecution of corporate crimes, increased employment opportunities, and promoting community alternatives to imprisonment."[121] Likewise, programs to reduce prison overcrowding, efforts to highlight injustices within the current system, the elimination of racism and other forms of inequality in the handling of both victims and offenders, growing equality in criminal justice system employment, and the like are all frequently mentioned as mid-range strategies for bringing about a justice system that is fairer and closer to the radical ideal.

Raymond Michalowski summarizes the policy directions envisioned by today's radical criminologists when he says, "We cannot be free from the crimes of the poor until there are no more poor; we cannot be free from domination of the powerful until we reduce the inequalities that make domination possible; and we cannot live in harmony with others until we begin to limit the competition for material advantage over others that alienates us from one another."[122]

Emergent Perspectives

A number of new and developing criminological perspectives deserve special mention. They include feminist criminology, constitutive criminology, and postmodern criminology. We will briefly discuss each in the sections that follow.

Feminist Criminology

As some writers in the developing field of **feminist criminology** have observed, "Women have been virtually invisible in criminological analysis until recently and much theorizing has proceeded as though criminality is restricted to men."[123] Another puts it this way: "[Traditional] criminological theory assumes a woman is like a man."[124] Feminist criminologists are now working to change long-cherished notions of crime and of criminal justice so that the role of women in both crime causation and crime control might be better appreciated.[125]

feminist criminology

A developing intellectual approach that emphasizes gender issues in criminology.

One of the first writers to attempt a definitive explanation of the criminality of women was Otto Pollak. Pollak's book, *The Criminality of Women*,[126] written in 1950, suggested that women commit the same number of offenses as men but that most of their criminality is hidden. Pollak claimed that women's roles at the time, primarily those of homemaker and mother, served to disguise their criminal undertakings. He also proposed that chivalrous treatment by a male-dominated justice system acted to bias every stage of criminal justice processing in favor of women. Hence, according to Pollak, although women are just as criminal as men, they are rarely arrested, tried, or imprisoned. In fact, although the criminality of women may approach or exceed that of men in selected offense categories, today it is safe to say that Pollak was incorrect in his assessment of the degree of female criminality; overall women commit far fewer crimes than men.

Early works in the field of feminist criminology include Freda Adler's *Sisters in Crime*[127] and Rita Simon's *Women and Crime*.[128] Both books were published in 1975, and in them the authors claimed that the existing divergences in crime rates between men and women were due primarily to socialization rather than biology. Women, claimed these authors, were taught to believe in personal limitations, faced reduced socioeconomic opportunities, and, as a result, suffered from lowered aspirations. As gender equality increased, they said, it could be expected that male and female criminality would take on similar characteristics. More recent researchers, however, have not found this to be true; substantial differences between the criminality of men and women remain, even as gender equality grows.[129]

Contemporary feminist thinking in criminology is represented by the works of writers like Kathleen Daly and Meda Chesney-Lind.[130] Daly and Chesney-Lind emphasize the need for a "gender-aware" criminology and stress the usefulness of applying feminist thinking to criminological analysis. Gender, say these writers, is a central organizing principle of contemporary life. Feminist criminology suggests that theories of crime causation and prevention must include women and that more research on gender-related issues in the field is badly needed. Additionally, some authors say, "Criminologists should begin to appreciate that their discipline and its questions are a product of white, economically privileged men's experiences."[131] They suggest that rates of female criminality, which are lower than those of males, may show that criminal behavior is not as "normal" as once thought. Because modern-day criminological perspectives were mostly developed by white middle-class males, the propositions and theories they advance fail to take into consideration women's "ways of knowing."[132] Hence, the fundamental challenge posed by feminist criminology is this: Do existing theories of crime causation apply as well to women as they do to men? Or, as Daly and Chesney-Lind put it, given the current situation in theory development, "do theories of men's crime apply to women?"[133] Read some of Chesney-Lind's recent work via Library Extra 3–5 at cjtoday.com.

LIBRARY Extra

Recent perspectives on female criminality stress the fact "that a key to understanding and responding to women as offenders is understanding their status as crime victims."[134] Psychologist Cathy Spatz Widom, for example, examined the life cycle of female offenders, looking for links between childhood abuse and neglect and later criminality. Widom suggests that the successful socialization of girls can be "derailed" by early victimization through mechanisms such as "running away, deficits in cognitive ability and achievement, growing up without traditional social controls, engaging in relationships with deviant or delinquent individuals, and failing to learn the social and psychological skills necessary for successful adult development."[135]

Contemporary statistics tell us that although females make up 51% of the population of the United States, they are arrested for only 17.8% of all violent crimes and 31.6% of property crimes. The relatively limited involvement of women in the FBI's eight major crimes can be seen in Table 4. Data show that the number of female offenders is increasing faster than the number of male offenders, however. Between 1970 and 2000, the number of crimes committed by men grew by 46%, while crimes committed by women increased 144%. Violent crimes by men increased 82% during the period; by women, 260%. Property crimes perpetrated by men grew by 3%; by women, 85%.[136]

Relative increases in the FBI's Part II offenses tell a similar story. Arrests of women for embezzlement, for example, increased by more than 228% between 1970 and 2000, versus only 8.5% for men—reflecting women's increased entry into areas of financial responsibility. Arrests of women for drug abuse grew by 289%, and liquor-law violations by women increased 285% (versus 96% for men).[137] In two officially reported categories—prostitution and runaways—women outnumber men in the volume of offenses committed.[138] Other crimes in which significant numbers of women (relative to men) are involved include larceny-theft (where 38.5% of reported crimes are committed by women), forgery and counterfeiting (39.8%), fraud (44.9%), and embezzlement (50.4%).[139] Nonetheless, as Table 4 shows, female offenders still account for only a small proportion of all reported crimes. Statistics on female criminality are difficult to interpret since reports of increasing female criminality may reflect the greater equality of treatment accorded women in contemporary society more than they do actual increases in criminal activity. In the past, when women committed crimes, they were dealt with less formally than is likely to be the case today.

When women do commit serious crimes, they are more often followers than leaders. A study of women in correctional settings, for example, found that women are far more likely to assume "secondary follower roles during criminal events" than "dominant leadership roles."[140] Only 14% of women surveyed played primary roles, but those who did "felt that men had little influence in initiating or leading them into crime." African American women were found to be more likely to play "primary and equal crime roles" with men or with female accomplices than were white or Hispanic women. Statistics such as these dispel the myth that the female criminal in America has taken her place alongside the male offender—in terms of either leadership roles or the absolute number of crimes committed.

TABLE 4 Male and Female Involvement in Crime: Offense Patterns, 2006

UCR Index Crime	Percentage of All Arrests: Males	Percentage of All Arrests: Females
Murder and nonnegligent manslaughter	89.1	10.9
Rape	98.7	1.3
Robbery	88.7	11.3
Aggravated assault	79.3	20.7
Burglary	85.5	14.5
Larceny-theft	62.3	37.7
Motor vehicle theft	82.3	17.7
Arson	83.0	17.0

Gender Differences

- Men are more likely than women to be arrested for serious crimes, such as murder, rape, robbery, and burglary.
- Arrest, jail, and prison data all suggest that more women than men who commit crimes are involved in property crimes, such as larceny, forgery, fraud, and embezzlement, and in drug offenses.

Source: Federal Bureau of Investigation, *Crime in the United States, 2006* (Washington, DC: U.S. Dept. of Justice, 2007).

Constitutive Criminology

In the early 1900s, George Herbert Mead[141] (1863–1931) set forth a theory called *symbolic interaction*, in which he demonstrated how people give meaning to the things around them and to their lives. About the same time, William Thomas[142] (1863–1947) explained that the significance of any human behavior is relative to the intentions behind it and to the situation in which it is interpreted. Hence, behavior that in one place or at one time is seen as acceptable, in another place or time may be perceived as deviant or even criminal. From this viewpoint, crime, like any other social phenomenon, is more a definition imposed by society on a particular type of activity than it is a quality inherent in the behavior itself. As a consequence, crime may mean different things to different people and is, no doubt, variously interpreted by the offender, by the victim, and by agents of social control. Seen this way, the significance of criminal behavior depends on one's interests in the crime and one's point of view and is ultimately knowable only to those who participate in it. Central to this way of thinking are the following principles:

- The significance of any behavior depends on a social consensus about what that behavior "means."
- Crime is the product of an active process of interpretation and social definition.
- Continued criminal activity may be more a consequence of the limited opportunities for acceptable behavior that are imposed on individuals defined as "criminal" than it is a product of choice.

Contemporary criminologists Stuart Henry and Dragan Milovanovic use the term **constitutive criminology** to refer to the process by which human beings create "an ideology of crime that sustains it as a concrete reality."[143] A central feature of constitutive criminology is its assertion that individuals shape their world while also being shaped by it. Constitutive criminology claims that crime and crime control are not "object-like entities" but constructions produced through a social process in which offender, victim, and society are all involved.[144] "We are concerned with the ways in which human agents actively coproduce that which they take to be crime," write Henry and Milovanovic. For these theorists, the idea of crime itself is a social construction, and researchers, they say, should recognize that criminals and victims are also "emergent realities." In short, constitutive criminology focuses on the social process by which crime and criminology become cultural realities.[145] Read some of Milovanovic's work via Library Extra 3–6 at cjtoday.com.

constitutive criminology

The study of the process by which human beings create an ideology of crime that sustains the notion of crime as a concrete reality.

LIBRARY Extra

postmodern criminology

A branch of criminology that developed after World War II and that builds on the tenets of postmodern social thought.

deconstructionist theory

One of the emerging approaches that challenges existing criminological perspectives to debunk them and that works toward replacing them with concepts more applicable to the postmodern era.

Postmodern Criminology

Before concluding this chapter, it is important to note that **postmodern criminology** is a term applied to a wide variety of novel perspectives that have developed in recent decades. It encompasses evolving paradigms with such intriguing names as *chaos theory*, *discourse analysis*, *topology theory*, *critical theory*, *realist criminology*, *constitutive theory*, and *anarchic criminology*.[146] Postmodern criminology builds on the belief that past criminological approaches have failed to realistically assess the true causes of crime and have therefore failed to offer workable solutions for crime control—or if they have, that such theories and solutions may have been appropriate at one time but no longer apply to the postmodern era. Because postmodern criminology challenges and debunks existing perspectives, it is referred to as *deconstructionist*, and such theories are sometimes called **deconstructionist theories.**

SUMMARY

- A theory is a proposed model of causal relationships between events and things under study. This chapter defines *theory* as a series of interrelated propositions that attempt to describe, explain, predict, and ultimately control some class of events. A good theory fits the facts and stands up to continued scrutiny. The goal of social research in criminology is to assist in the development of theoretical models that permit a better understanding of criminal behavior and that enhance the development of strategies intended to address the problem of crime.
- The Classical School of criminology, which was in vogue throughout the late eighteenth and early nineteenth centuries, held that crime is caused by the individual exercise of free will and that it can be deterred through the promise of swift and certain punishment. Classical criminology continues to be influential through today's neoclassical thought, represented by rational choice and routine activities theories.
- Biological theories posit a genetic or a physiological basis for deviant and criminal behavior. The notion of a "weak" gene that might predispose some people toward criminal activity has been expanded to include the impact of environmental contaminants, poor nutrition, and food additives on behavior. Studies of fraternal twins and chromosome structure have helped bring biological theories into the modern day. Such theories, however, have their shortcomings, including a lack of recognition of other perspectives that might help better explain criminality. Similarly, strict biological theories attribute the cause of crime to fundamental physical characteristics that are not easily modified.
- Psychobiological perspectives on crime causation note the role that human DNA, environmental contaminants, nutrition, hormones, physical trauma, and body chemistry play in behavior that violates the law. The detailed mapping of human DNA and other recent advances in the field of recombinant DNA have rekindled interest in genetic correlates of criminal behavior.
- Psychological explanations of crime are individualistic. Some psychoanalytic theories see offenders as psychotic, psychopathic, or sociopathic. Other psychological theories claim that criminal behavior is a type of conditioned response. The stimulus-response model sees criminal behavior as the consequence of a conditioning process that extends over the entire life span of an individual. As with most other theories, psychological perspectives remain plagued by shortcomings. Among them are questions about whether past behavior can accurately predict future behavior and whether there are identifiable characteristics that violent offenders might manifest that could serve as warning signs of impending criminal activity.
- Sociological theories hold that the individual is a product of his or her social environment. They emphasize the role that social structure, inequality, and socialization play in criminality. Although they are today's perspective of choice, the danger of most sociological approaches is that they tend to deny the significance of any influences beyond those that are mediated through social interaction.
- Social process theories of criminology claim that crime results from the failure of self-direction, from inadequate social roles, or from associating with others who are already criminal. Social policies based on such theories place responsibility for change largely on the offender.

- Conflict perspectives attempt to explain crime by noting that conflict is fundamental to social life and by claiming that crime is a natural consequence of social, political, and economic inequity. Conflict criminologists believe that fundamental changes in the structure of society are needed if crime is to be eliminated or curtailed.
- Included among emergent approaches to explaining crime are feminist criminology, constitutive criminology, and postmodern criminology. Feminist criminology challenges some long-held notions of crime and criminal justice that have been based solely on understandings of male criminality. Constitutive criminology highlights the fact that crime is a socially created phenomenon and that without some cultural agreements about right and wrong as reflected in the criminal laws of a society, crime, as we think of it, would not exist. Postmodern criminology, the last of the approaches discussed in this chapter, is often more an effort to debunk previous perspectives than it is a theoretical perspective in its own right.

KEY TERMS

anomie
atavism
behavioral conditioning
Biological School
broken windows thesis
Chicago School
Classical School
conflict perspective
constitutive criminology
containment
dangerousness
deconstructionist theory
defensible space theory
deviance
feminist criminology
hypothesis
interdisciplinary theory
labeling theory
life course perspective
moral enterprise
neoclassical criminology
peacemaking criminology
phrenology
Positivist School
postmodern criminology
psychoanalysis
psychological profiling
Psychological School
psychopath
psychopathology
psychosis
radical criminology
rational choice theory
reaction formation
research
routine activities theory
schizophrenic
social development theory
social disorganization
social learning theory
social process theory
somatotyping
subculture of violence
supermale
theory

KEY NAMES

Freda Adler
Cesare Beccaria
Howard Becker
Jeremy Bentham
Ernest Burgess
Meda Chesney-Lind
Hervey Cleckley
Albert Cohen
Lawrence Cohen
Kathleen Daly
Marcus Felson
Sigmund Freud

Franz Joseph Gall
Stuart Henry
Richard Herrnstein
John H. Laub
Cesare Lombroso
Henry McKay
Sarnoff Mednick
Robert Merton
Walter Miller
Dragan Milovanovic
Robert Park
Harold Pepinsky
Richard Quinney
Walter Reckless
Robert J. Sampson
Clifford Shaw
William Sheldon
Rita Simon
Edwin Sutherland
James Q. Wilson
Marvin Wolfgang

QUESTIONS FOR REVIEW

1. What is a theory? Describe the steps in criminological theory building, and explain the role that social research plays in the development of theories about crime.
2. List the basic assumptions of classical theories of crime causation, and describe the neoclassical perspective.
3. Describe the basic features of biological theories of crime causation. What shortcomings of the biological perspective can you identify?
4. How has the mapping of human DNA enhanced contemporary psychobiological understandings of criminal behavior?
5. Describe the basic features of psychological explanations for crime. What are the shortcomings of this perspective?
6. Describe the basic features of sociological explanations for crime. What are the shortcomings of this perspective?
7. Describe social process theories of crime causation, including labeling theory and the life course perspective. What types of crime-control policies might be based on such theories?
8. Describe conflict theories of crime causation, including radical criminology and peacemaking criminology. What sorts of crime-control policies might be predicated on the basis of such theories?
9. What is meant by "emergent perspectives"? List and describe three emergent perspectives on crime causation.

QUESTIONS FOR REFLECTION

1. What evidence-based practices might be developed as a result of the studies discussed in this chapter?
2. What is the relationship between punishment and classical and neoclassical thought? With what types of offenders might punishment be the most effective in reducing recidivism?
3. Do you think that biological theories successfully explain the causes of crime? Why or why not?
4. What role, if any, might psychobiological theories play in the development of crime-reduction strategies?
5. Do you think that psychological theories of crime causation are sound? Why or why not?

6. Do you think that sociological theories are sound? Why or why not?

Discuss your answers to these questions and other issues on the CJ Today e-mail discussion list (join the list at cjtoday.com).

WEB QUEST

One of the most informative criminal justice–related sites on the Web is the National Criminal Justice Reference Service (NCJRS). Visit the NCJRS at ncjrs.org, or use the Cybrary to locate the NCJRS. Once you have found NCJRS, explore each of the major informational categories it provides: Corrections, Courts, Crime, Crime Prevention, Drugs, Justice System, Juvenile Justice, Law Enforcement, and Victims.

Visit each category, and make a note of the features available. View at least one document from each category. Write a summary of each document (you should have a total of nine), and submit the summaries to your instructor if asked to do so.

Reenter each NCJRS category, and make a note of the websites referenced there. Visit at least three sites under each category, and write a brief description of each site (you should have a total of 27). Submit the descriptions to your instructor if asked to do so.

To complete this Web Quest online, go to the Web Quest module of the *Criminal Justice Today* Companion Website at cjtoday.com.

NOTES

i. *The American Heritage Dictionary and Electronic Thesaurus on CD-ROM* (Boston: Houghton Mifflin, 1987).

ii. Nicole Rafter, "Earnest A. Hooton and the Biological Tradition in American Criminology," *Criminology*, Vol. 42, No. 3 (2004), p. 735.

iii. "Gingrich Says Felons Should Be Tracked by Satellite," Reuters, March 4, 1995.

---

1. George W. Bush, "Remarks by the President on Project Safe Neighborhoods," Pennsylvania Convention Center, Philadelphia, May 14, 2001, http://www.whitehouse.gov/news/releases/2001/05/20010514-1.html (accessed April 28, 2007).
2. Quoted in Gwynn Nettler, *Killing One Another* (Cincinnati, OH: Anderson, 1982), p. 194.
3. "Rapper Busta Rhymes Arrested, Charged with Assault," *USA Today*, August 21, 2006, http://www.usatoday.com/life/people/2006-08-20-busta-arrest_x.htm?csp=34 (accessed January 3, 2008).
4. "Busta Rhymes Arrested, Accused of Traffic Violation in New York," *International Herald Tribune*, February 22, 2007, http://www.iht.com/articles/ap/2007/02/23/arts/NA-A-E-MUS-US-People-Busta-Rhymes.php (accessed January 3, 2008).
5. "Busta Rhymes and Manager Arrested," MTV online, December 28, 1998, http://www.mtv.com/news/articles/1426787/19981228/rhymes_busta.jhtml (accessed January 3, 2008).
6. "Busta Rhymes Arrested, Accused of Traffic Violation in New York."
7. "50 Cent," http://www.who2.com/50cent.html (accessed August 28, 2007).
8. Jason Birchmeier, "50 Cent: Bio," *All Music Guide*, http://www.mtv.com/bands/az/50_cent/bio.jhtml (accessed August 30, 2007).
9. Behavior that violates the criminal law may not be "crime" if accompanied by an acceptable legal justification or excuse. Justifications and excuses that are recognized by the law may serve as defenses to a criminal charge.
10. This and many of the statistics in these opening paragraphs come from Jonathan Wright, "Media Are Mixed Blessing, Criminologists Say," Reuters, May 2, 1995.
11. See "Comments of James T. Hamilton before the Federal Communications Commission, in the Matter of Industry Proposal for Rating Video Programming," May 23, 1997, citing Suzanne Stutman, Joanne Cantor, and Victoria Duran, *What Parents Want in a Television Rating System: Results of a National Survey* (Madison: University of Wisconsin, 1996); Wes Shipley and Gary Cavender, "Murder and Mayhem at the Movies," *Journal of Criminal Justice and Popular Culture*, Vol. 9, No. 1 (2001), pp. 1–14; and Suzanne Stutman, Joanne Cantor, and Victoria Duran, "What Parents Want in a Television Rating System: Results of a National Survey (Washington, DC: National Parent Teacher Association, 2002), http://www.pta.org/ptacommunity/tvreport.asp (accessed August 21, 2007).
12. Jeffrey Johnson, "Television Viewing and Aggressive Behavior during Adolescence and Adulthood," *Science*, Vol. 295 (2002), pp. 2468–2471.
13. Wright, "Media Are Mixed Blessing, Criminologists Say."
14. Nathan McCall, "My Rap against Rap," *Washington Post* wire service, November 14, 1993.
15. Arthur L. Cribbs, Jr., "Gangsta Rappers Sing White Racists' Tune," *USA Today*, December 27, 1993, p. 9A.
16. U.S. News/UCLA Survey on the Media and Violence, reported in "Hollywood: Right Face," *U.S. News and World Report*, May 15, 1995, p. 71.
17. See "Congress Hopes Ten Commandments Curb Violence," APB Online, June 17, 1999, http://www.apbonline.com/911/1999/06/17/congress061701.html (accessed March 1, 2000).
18. The word *scientific* is used here to refer to the application of generally accepted research strategies designed to reject explanations that rival the one under study.
19. Stephen Schafer, *Theories in Criminology* (New York: Random House, 1969), p. 109.
20. L. E. Cohen and Marcus Felson, "Social Change and Crime Rate Trends: A Routine Activity Approach," *American*

Sociological Review, Vol. 44, No. 4 (August 1979), pp. 588–608. Also see Marcus Felson and L. E. Cohen, "Human Ecology and Crime: A Routine Activity Approach," *Human Ecology*, Vol. 8, No. 4 (1980), pp. 389–406; Marcus Felson, "Linking Criminal Choices, Routine Activities, Informal Control, and Criminal Outcomes," in Derek B. Cornish and Ronald V. Clarke, eds., *The Reasoning Criminal: Rational Choice Perspectives on Offending* (New York: Springer-Verlag, 1986), pp. 119–128; and Ronald V. Clarke and Marcus Felson, eds., *Advances in Criminological Theory: Routine Activity and Rational Choice* (New Brunswick, NJ: Transaction, 1993).

21. Cohen and Felson, "Social Change and Crime Rate Trends," p. 595.
22. For a test of routine activities theory as an explanation for victimization in the workplace, see John D. Wooldredge, Francis T. Cullen, and Edward J. Latessa, "Victimization in the Workplace: A Test of Routine Activities Theory," *Justice Quarterly*, Vol. 9, No. 2 (June 1992), pp. 325–335.
23. Werner Einstadter and Stuart Henry, *Criminological Theory: An Analysis of Its Underlying Assumptions* (Fort Worth, TX: Harcourt Brace, 1995), p. 70.
24. For a modern reprint of a widely read nineteenth-century work on phrenology, see Orson Squire Fowler and Lorenzo Niles Fowler, *Phrenology: A Practical Guide to Your Head* (New York: Chelsea House, 1980).
25. Schafer, *Theories in Criminology*, p. 123.
26. Richard Louis Dugdale, *The Jukes: A Study in Crime, Pauperism, Disease, and Heredity*, 3rd ed. (New York: G. P. Putnam's Sons, 1985).
27. Henry Herbert Goddard, *The Kallikak Family: A Study in the Heredity of Feeblemindedness* (New York: Macmillan, 1912).
28. For more information, see Richard Herrnstein, "Crime File: Biology and Crime," a study guide (Washington, DC: National Institute of Justice, n.d.).
29. *Buck* v. *Bell*, 274 U.S. 200, 207 (1927).
30. Patricia Jacobs et al., "Aggressive Behavior, Mental Subnormality, and the XYY Male," *Nature*, Vol. 208 (1965), pp. 1351–1352.
31. Schafer, *Theories in Criminology*, p. 193.
32. D. Hill and W. Sargent, "A Case of Matricide," *Lancet*, Vol. 244 (1943), pp. 526–527.
33. See, for example, A. R. Mawson and K. J. Jacobs, "Corn Consumption, Tryptophan, and Cross-National Homicide Rates," *Journal of Orthomolecular Psychiatry*, Vol. 7 (1978), pp. 227–230; and A. Hoffer, "The Relation of Crime to Nutrition," *Humanist in Canada*, Vol. 8 (1975), p. 8.
34. See, for example, C. Hawley and R. E. Buckley, "Food Dyes and Hyperkinetic Children," *Academy Therapy*, Vol. 10 (1974), pp. 27–32; and Alexander Schauss, *Diet, Crime, and Delinquency* (Berkeley, CA: Parker House, 1980).
35. "Special Report: Measuring Your Life with Coffee Spoons," *Tufts University Diet and Nutrition Letter*, Vol. 2, No. 2 (April 1984), pp. 3–6.
36. See, for example, "Special Report: Does What You Eat Affect Your Mood and Actions?" *Tufts University Diet and Nutrition Letter*, Vol. 2, No. 12 (February 1985), pp. 4–6.
37. See *Tufts University Diet and Nutrition Letter*, Vol. 2, No. 11 (January 1985), p. 2; and "Special Report: Why Sugar Continues to Concern Nutritionists," *Tufts University Diet and Nutrition Letter*, Vol. 3, No. 3 (May 1985), pp. 3–6.
38. Diana H. Fishbein and Susan E. Pease, "Diet, Nutrition, and Aggression," in Marc Hillbrand and Nathaniel J. Pallone, eds., *The Psychobiology of Aggression: Engines, Measurement, Control* (New York: Haworth Press, 1994), pp. 114–117.
39. A. Hoffer, "Children with Learning and Behavioral Disorders," *Journal of Orthomolecular Psychiatry*, Vol. 5 (1976), p. 229.
40. "Special Report: Does What You Eat Affect Your Mood and Actions?" p. 4.
41. See, for example, R. T. Rada, D. R. Laws, and R. Kellner, "Plasma Testosterone Levels in the Rapist," *Psychomatic Medicine*, Vol. 38 (1976), pp. 257–268.
42. Later studies, however, have been less than clear. See, for example, J. M. Dabbs, Jr., "Testosterone Measurements in Social and Clinical Psychology," *Journal of Social and Clinical Psychology*, Vol. 11 (1992), pp. 302–321.
43. "The Insanity of Steroid Abuse," *Newsweek*, May 23, 1988, p. 75.
44. E. G. Stalenheim et al., "Testosterone as a Biological Marker in Psychopathy and Alcoholism," *Psychiatry Research*, Vol. 77, No. 2 (February 1998), pp. 79–88.
45. Michelle M. Wirth and Oliver C. Schultheiss, "Basal Testosterone Moderates Responses to Anger Faces in Humans," *Physiology and Behavior*, Vol. 90 (2007), pp. 496–505.
46. For a summary of such studies, see Serena-Lynn Brown, Alexander Botsis, and Herman M. Van Praag, "Serotonin and Aggression," in Hillbrand and Pallone, eds., *The Psychobiology of Aggression*, pp. 28–39.
47. Roger D. Masters, Brian Hone, and Anil Doshi, "Environmental Pollution, Neurotoxicity, and Criminal Violence," in J. Rose, ed., *Environmental Toxicology* (London and New York: Gordon and Breach, 1997).
48. B. Bioulac et al., "Serotonergic Functions in the XYY Syndrome," *Biological Psychiatry*, Vol. 15 (1980), pp. 917–923.
49. E. G. Stalenheim, L. von Knorring, and L. Wide, "Serum Levels of Thyroid Hormones as Biological Markers in a Swedish Forensic Psychiatric Population," *Biological Psychiatry*, Vol. 43, No. 10 (May 15, 1998), pp. 755–761.
50. Sarnoff Mednick and Jan Volavka, "Biology and Crime," in Norval Morris and Michael Tonry, eds., *Crime and Justice* (Chicago: University of Chicago Press, 1980), pp. 85–159.
51. Sarnoff Mednick and S. Gloria Shaham, eds., *New Paths in Criminology* (Lexington, MA: D. C. Heath, 1979).
52. For a good survey of studies in this area, see Laurence Miller, "Traumatic Brain Injury and Aggression," in Hillbrand and Pallone, eds., *The Psychobiology of Aggression*, pp. 91–103.
53. For an excellent overview of such studies, see Shari Mills and Adrian Raine, "Neuroimaging and Aggression," in Hillbrand and Pallone, eds., *The Psychobiology of Aggression*, pp. 145–158.
54. R. B. Cattell, *The Inheritance of Personality and Ability: Research Methods and Findings* (New York: Academic Press, 1982).
55. Karl Christiansen, "A Preliminary Study of Criminality among Twins," in Sarnoff Mednick and Karl O. Christiansen, eds., *Biosocial Bases of Criminal Behavior* (New York: Gardner Press, 1977).
56. James Q. Wilson and Richard J. Herrnstein, *Crime and Human Nature* (New York: Simon and Schuster, 1985).
57. "Criminals Born and Bred," *Newsweek*, September 16, 1985, p. 69.
58. William J. Chambliss, *Exploring Criminology* (New York: Macmillan, 1988), p. 202.
59. A. Reiss and J. Roth, eds., *Understanding and Preventing Violence* (Washington, DC: National Academy Press, 1993).
60. Sigmund Freud, *A General Introduction to Psychoanalysis* (New York: Boni and Liveright, 1920).
61. Nettler, *Killing One Another*, p. 79.
62. David Abrahamsen, *Crime and the Human Mind* (reprint, Montclair, NJ: Patterson Smith, 1969), p. 23.

63. See Adrian Raine, *The Psychopathology of Crime: Criminal Behavior as a Clinical Disorder* (Orlando, FL: Academic Press, 1993).
64. Hervey M. Cleckley, *The Mask of Sanity: An Attempt to Reinterpret the So-Called Psychopathic Personality* (St. Louis, MO: Mosby, 1941).
65. Nettler, *Killing One Another*, p. 179.
66. Albert I. Rabin, "The Antisocial Personality—Psychopathy and Sociopathy," in Hans Toch, ed., *Psychology of Crime and Criminal Justice* (Prospect Heights, IL: Waveland Press, 1979), p. 330.
67. Richard L. Ault and James T. Reese, "A Psychological Assessment of Crime Profiling," *FBI Law Enforcement Bulletin* (March 1980), pp. 22–25.
68. John E. Douglas and Alan E. Burgess, "Criminal Profiling: A Viable Investigative Tool against Violent Crime," *FBI Law Enforcement Bulletin* (December 1986), pp. 9–13.
69. Robert R. Hazelwood and John E. Douglass, "The Lust Murderer," *FBI Law Enforcement Bulletin* (April 1980), pp. 18–22.
70. A. O. Rider, "The Firesetter—A Psychological Profile," *FBI Law Enforcement Bulletin* (June 1980), pp. 4–11.
71. M. Reiser, "Crime-Specific Psychological Consultation," *Police Chief* (March 1982), pp. 53–56.
72. Thomas Strentz, "A Terrorist Psychosocial Profile: Past and Present," *FBI Law Enforcement Bulletin* (April 1988), pp. 13–19.
73. Jill Peay, "Dangerousness—Ascription or Description," in M. P. Feldman, ed., *Violence*, Vol. 2 of *Developments in the Study of Criminal Behavior* (New York: John Wiley, 1982), p. 211, citing N. Walker, "Dangerous People," *International Journal of Law and Psychiatry*, Vol. 1 (1978), pp. 37–50.
74. See, for example, Michael Gottfredson and Travis Hirschi, *A General Theory of Crime* (Stanford, CA: Stanford University Press, 1990); and Travis Hirschi and Michael Gottfredson, "Age and the Explanation of Crime," *American Journal of Sociology*, Vol. 89 (1983), pp. 552–584.
75. David F. Greenberg, "Modeling Criminal Careers," *Criminology*, Vol. 29, No. 1 (1991), p. 39.
76. Robert E. Park and Ernest Burgess, *Introduction to the Science of Sociology*, 2nd ed. (Chicago: University of Chicago Press, 1924); and Robert E. Park, ed., *The City* (Chicago: University of Chicago Press, 1925).
77. Clifford R. Shaw and Henry D. McKay, "Social Factors in Juvenile Delinquency," in *Report on the Causes of Crime*, National Commission on Law Observance and Enforcement report no. 13, Vol. 2 (Washington, DC: U.S. Government Printing Office, 1931); and Clifford R. Shaw, *Juvenile Delinquency in Urban Areas* (Chicago: University of Chicago Press, 1942).
78. Émile Durkheim, *Suicide* (reprint, New York: Free Press, 1951).
79. Robert K. Merton, "Social Structure and Anomie," *American Sociological Review*, Vol. 3 (1938), pp. 672–682.
80. Catherine E. Ross and John Mirowsky, "Normlessness, Powerlessness, and Trouble with the Law," *Criminology*, Vol. 25, No. 2 (May 1987), p. 257.
81. See Nettler, *Killing One Another*, p. 58.
82. This is not to say that all members of these groups engaged in criminal behavior, but rather that statistics indicated higher average crime rates for these groups than for certain others immediately after immigration to the United States.
83. Albert K. Cohen, *Delinquent Boys: The Culture of the Gang* (Glencoe, IL: Free Press, 1958).
84. Walter B. Miller, "Lower Class Culture as a Generating Milieu of Gang Delinquency," *Journal of Social Issues*, Vol. 14 (1958), pp. 5–19.
85. Richard Cloward and Lloyd Ohlin, *Delinquency and Opportunity: A Theory of Delinquent Gangs* (New York: Free Press, 1960).
86. Marvin Wolfgang, *Patterns in Criminal Homicide* (Philadelphia: University of Pennsylvania Press, 1958). See also Marvin Wolfgang and Franco Ferracuti, *The Subculture of Violence: Toward an Integrated Theory in Criminology* (London: Tavistock, 1967).
87. "Gang Prevention through Targeted Outreach—Boys and Girls Clubs of America," http://ojjdp.ncjrs.org/pubs/gun_violence/sect08-k.html (accessed April 10, 2007).
88. See, for example, James D. Orcutt, "Differential Association and Marijuana Use: A Closer Look at Sutherland (with a Little Help from Becker)," *Criminology*, Vol. 25, No. 2 (1987), pp. 341–358.
89. Edwin Sutherland, *Principles of Criminology*, 4th ed. (Chicago: J. B. Lippincott, 1947), p. 4.
90. John E. Conklin, *Criminology*, 3rd ed. (New York: Macmillan, 1989), p. 278.
91. Robert L. Burgess and Ronald L. Akers, "A Differential Association-Reinforcement Theory of Criminal Behavior," *Social Problems*, Vol. 14 (fall 1996), pp. 128–147.
92. Some theories are multicausal and provide explanations for criminal behavior that include a diversity of "causes."
93. For a more elaborate criticism of this sort, see Conklin, *Criminology*, p. 260.
94. Ibid.
95. Walter C. Reckless, *The Crime Problem*, 4th ed. (New York: Appleton-Century-Crofts, 1961).
96. Ibid., p. 472.
97. Travis Hirschi, *Causes of Delinquency* (Berkeley: University of California Press, 1969).
98. Ibid., p. 472.
99. Gresham Sykes and David Matza, "Techniques of Neutralization: A Theory of Delinquency," *American Sociological Review*, Vol. 22 (1957), pp. 664–670.
100. Many of the concepts used by Howard Becker in explicating his theory of labeling were, in fact, used previously not only by Frank Tannenbaum but also by Edwin M. Lemert. Lemert wrote of "societal reaction" and "primary and secondary deviance" and even used the word *labeling* in his book *Social Pathology* (New York: McGraw-Hill, 1951).
101. Frank Tannenbaum, *Crime and the Community* (Boston: Ginn, 1938), pp. 19–20.
102. Howard Becker, *Outsiders: Studies in the Sociology of Deviance* (New York: Free Press, 1963), pp. 8–9.
103. Ibid.
104. Ibid., p. 33.
105. Robert J. Sampson and John H. Laub, *Crime in the Making: Pathways and Turning Points through the Life Course* (Cambridge, MA: Harvard University Press, 1993).
106. Katharine Browning et al., "Causes and Correlates of Delinquency Program," *OJJDP Fact Sheet* (Washington, DC: U.S. Dept. of Justice, April 1999).
107. MacArthur Foundation, "The Project on Human Development in Chicago Neighborhoods," http://www.macfound.org/research/hcd/hcd_5.htm (accessed January 5, 2007).
108. Adapted from Raymond Michalowski, "Perspectives and Paradigm: Structuring Criminological Thought," in Robert F. Meier, ed., *Theory in Criminology* (Beverly Hills, CA: Sage, 1977).
109. See George B. Vold, *Theoretical Criminology* (New York: Oxford University Press, 1986).

110. Austin T. Turk, *Criminality and the Legal Order* (Chicago: Rand McNally, 1969).

111. Thorsten Sellin, *Culture Conflict and Crime* (New York: Social Science Research Council, 1938).

112. William J. Chambliss and Robert B. Seidman, *Law, Order, and Power* (Reading, MA: Addison-Wesley, 1971).

113. Richard Quinney, *The Social Reality of Crime* (Boston: Little, Brown, 1970).

114. David F. Greenberg, *Crime and Capitalism* (Palo Alto, CA: Mayfield, 1981), p. 3.

115. For examples of how this might be accomplished, see F. H. Knopp, "Community Solutions to Sexual Violence: Feminist/Abolitionist Perspectives," in Harold E. Pepinsky and Richard Quinney, eds., *Criminology as Peacemaking* (Bloomington: Indiana University Press, 1991), pp. 181–193; and S. Caringella-MacDonald and D. Humphries, "Sexual Assault, Women, and the Community: Organizing to Prevent Sexual Violence," in Pepinsky and Quinney, eds., *Criminology as Peacemaking*, pp. 98–113.

116. Richard Quinney, "Life of Crime: Criminology and Public Policy as Peacemaking," *Journal of Crime and Justice*, Vol. 16, No. 2 (1993), pp. 3–9.

117. Ram Dass and P. Gorman, *How Can I Help? Stories and Reflections on Service* (New York: Alfred A. Knopf, 1985), p. 165, as cited in Richard Quinney and John Wildeman, *The Problem of Crime: A Peace and Social Justice Perspective*, 3rd ed. (Mayfield, CA: Mountain View Press, 1991), p. 116, originally published as *The Problem of Crime: A Critical Introduction to Criminology* (New York: Bantam, 1977).

118. See, for example, Harold E. Pepinsky, "This Can't Be Peace: A Pessimist Looks at Punishment," in W. B. Groves and G. Newman, eds., *Punishment and Privilege* (Albany, NY: Harrow and Heston, 1986); Harold E. Pepinsky, "Violence as Unresponsiveness: Toward a New Conception of Crime," *Justice Quarterly*, Vol. 5 (1988), pp. 539–563; and Pepinsky and Quinney, eds., *Criminology as Peacemaking*.

119. See, for example, Richard Quinney, "Crime, Suffering, Service: Toward a Criminology of Peacemaking," *Quest*, Vol. 1 (1988), pp. 66–75; Richard Quinney, "The Theory and Practice of Peacemaking in the Development of Radical Criminology," *Critical Criminologist*, Vol. 1, No. 5 (1989), p. 5; and Quinney and Wildeman, *The Problem of Crime*.

120. All of these themes are addressed, for example, in Pepinsky and Quinney, eds., *Criminology as Peacemaking*.

121. Michael J. Lynch and W. Byron Groves, *A Primer in Radical Criminology*, 2nd ed. (Albany, NY: Harrow and Heston, 1989), p. 128.

122. Raymond J. Michalowski, *Order, Law, and Crime: An Introduction to Criminology* (New York: Random House, 1985), p. 410.

123. Don C. Gibbons, *Talking about Crime and Criminals: Problems and Issues in Theory Development in Criminology* (Englewood Cliffs, NJ: Prentice Hall, 1994), p. 165, citing Loraine Gelsthorpe and Alison Morris, eds., *Feminist Perspectives in Criminology* (Bristol, England: Open University Press, 1990).

124. Sally S. Simpson, "Feminist Theory, Crime, and Justice," *Criminology*, Vol. 27, No. 4 (1989), p. 605.

125. For an excellent overview of feminist theory in criminology and for a comprehensive review of research regarding female offenders, see Joanne Belknap, *The Invisible Woman: Gender Crime and Justice* (Belmont, CA: Wadsworth, 1996).

126. Otto Pollak, *The Criminality of Women* (Philadelphia: University of Pennsylvania Press, 1950).

127. Freda Adler, *Sisters in Crime: The Rise of the New Female Criminal* (New York: McGraw-Hill, 1975).

128. Rita J. Simon, *Women and Crime* (Lexington, MA: Lexington Books, 1975).

129. See, for example, Darrell J. Steffensmeir, "Sex Differences in Patterns of Adult Crime, 1965–1977: A Review and Assessment," *Social Forces*, Vol. 58 (1980), pp. 1098–1099.

130. See, for example, Kathleen Daly and Meda Chesney-Lind, "Feminism and Criminology," *Justice Quarterly*, Vol. 5, No. 5 (December 1988), pp. 497–535.

131. Ibid., p. 506.

132. Ibid.

133. Ibid., p. 514.

134. Cathy Spatz Widom, "Childhood Victimization and the Derailment of Girls and Women to the Criminal Justice System," in Beth E. Richie et al., eds., *Research on Women and Girls in the Justice System* (Washington, DC: National Institute of Justice, 2000), p. iii.

135. Ibid., pp. 27–36.

136. Federal Bureau of Investigation, *Crime in the United States, 1970* (Washington, DC: U.S. Dept. of Justice, 1971); and Federal Bureau of Investigation, *Crime in the United States, 2000* (Washington, DC: U.S. Dept. of Justice, 2001).

137. Ibid.

138. Federal Bureau of Investigation, *Crime in the United States, 2000* (Washington, DC: U.S. Dept. of Justice, 2001).

139. Federal Bureau of Investigation, *Crime in the United States, 2006* (Washington, DC: U.S. Dept. of Justice, 2007).

140. Leanne Fiftal Alarid et al., "Women's Roles in Serious Offenses: A Study of Adult Felons," *Justice Quarterly*, Vol. 13, No. 3 (September 1996), pp. 432–454.

141. George Herbert Mead and Charles W. Morris, eds., *Mind, Self, and Society* (Chicago: University of Chicago Press, 1934).

142. William I. Thomas and Florian Znaneicki, *The Polish Peasant in Europe and America* (Chicago: University of Chicago Press, 1918).

143. Stuart Henry and Dragan Milovanovic, "Constitutive Criminology: The Maturation of Critical Theory," *Criminology*, Vol. 29, No. 2 (May 1991), p. 293.

144. Dragan Milovanovic, *Postmodern Criminology* (Hamden, CT: Garland, 1997).

145. See also Stuart Henry and Dragan Milovanovic, *Constitutive Criminology: Beyond Postmodernism* (London: Sage, 1996).

146. For an excellent and detailed discussion of many of these approaches, see Milovanovic, *Postmodern Criminology*.

Policing: Purpose and Organization

4

Chapter Outline

- Introduction
- The Police Mission
- American Policing Today: From the Federal to the Local Level
- Police Administration
- Policing Epochs and Styles
- Police–Community Relations
- Evidence-Based Policing
- Discretion and the Individual Officer

Learning Objectives

After reading this chapter, you should be able to

- Explain the police mission in democratic societies.
- List and describe the three major levels of public law enforcement in the United States today.
- Discuss the various components of police administration, including management, chain of command, organization, and department structure.
- Identify the various historical stages of development in American policing, and describe the characteristics of each stage.
- Describe community policing, and explain how it differs from traditional forms of policing.
- Explain evidence-based policing, and demonstrate the potential that it holds in the area of police management.
- Explain police discretion, and identify some of the factors that influence a police officer's use of discretion.

"The purpose of the police service is to uphold the law fairly and firmly; to prevent crime; to pursue and bring to justice those who break the law; to keep the . . . peace; to protect, help and reassure the community; and to be seen to do this with integrity, common sense and sound judgment."

—*United Kingdom Police Service, Statement of Common Purpose*

"The tragedies of September 11, 2001, have forever changed the roles of traditional law enforcement in this country."

—*Major Cities Chiefs Association*[1]

From Chapter 4 of *Criminal Justice: A Brief Introduction*, Eighth Edition. Frank Schmalleger.

Introduction

▶▶▶ Hear the author discuss this chapter at mycrimekit.com.

In mid-November 2003, thousands of demonstrators protesting the proposed creation of the Free Trade Area of the Americas (FTAA) clashed with hundreds of Miami police officers equipped with riot gear. The protesters were targeting a meeting by foreign trade ministers to express concern that the creation of the 34-nation FTAA would send thousands of U.S. jobs overseas, exploit cheap labor, and waste natural resources.[2]

Although most demonstrators paraded peacefully and avoided confrontations, some pulled down crowd-control barriers with grappling hooks and scuffled with officers who were trying to maintain order. Before the melee ended, officers had to use batons, plastic shields, concussion grenades, pepper spray, and stun guns to regain control over the unruly protesters. Armored personnel carriers stood ready to move into "hot spots." "We're basically trying to maintain the peace downtown," said police spokesperson Jorge Pino, as demonstrators advanced on police lines.[3] By the time the event ended, 74 people had been arrested and 42 protesters were injured, including ten who had to be hospitalized. Three police officers were also hurt. As the Miami riots demonstrate, the maintenance of social order is an important part of police work today.

The Police Mission

The basic purposes of policing in democratic societies are to (1) enforce the laws of the society of which the police are a part, (2) apprehend offenders who participate in crime, (3) prevent crime, (4) preserve domestic peace and tranquility, and (5) provide the community with needed enforcement-related services. Simply put, as Sir Robert Peel, founder of the British system of policing, explained in 1822, "The basic mission for which the police exist is to reduce crime and disorder."[4] In the paragraphs that follow, we turn our attention to these five basic elements of the police mission.

Enforcing the Law

The police operate under an official public mandate that requires them to enforce the law. Collectively speaking, police agencies are the primary enforcers of federal, state, and local criminal laws. Not surprisingly, police officers see themselves as crime fighters, a view shared by the public and promoted by the popular media.

▶ Miami riot police advancing through burning trash to control demonstrators protesting a meeting of foreign delegates who were attempting to negotiate an international free-trade agreement in 2003. Order maintenance is an important part of the police mission. What other aspects of the police mission can you identify?
David Adame/AP Wide World Photos

Although it is the job of the police to enforce the law, it is not their *only* job. Practically speaking, most officers spend the majority of their time answering nonemergency public service calls,[5] controlling traffic, or writing tickets. Most are not involved in intensive, ongoing crime-fighting activities. Research shows that only about 10% to 20% of all calls to the police involve situations that actually require a law enforcement response (that is, situations that might lead to arrest and eventual prosecution), a fact that is described in more detail later in this chapter.[6]

Even when the police are busy enforcing laws, they can't enforce them all. Police resources, including labor, vehicles, and investigative assets, are limited, causing officers to focus more on certain types of law violation than on others. Old laws prohibiting minor offenses that today hold little social significance, like spitting on the sidewalk or scaring horses with a noisy automobile, are typically relegated to the dustbin of statutory history. Even though they are still "on the books," few (if any) officers even think about enforcing such laws. A number of writers have observed that the police tend to tailor their enforcement efforts to meet the contemporary concerns of the populace they serve.[7] For example, if the local community is upset about "massage parlors" operating in certain neighborhoods, it is likely that the local police department will bring enforcement efforts to bear that might eventually lead to the relocation or closing of such businesses. Although the enforcement practices of police agencies are significantly influenced by community interests, individual officers take their cue on enforcement priorities from their departments, their peers, and their supervisors. Learn more about how police supervisory styles influence patrol officer behavior at Library Extra 4–1 at mycrimekit.com.

Library EXTRA

The police are expected not only to enforce the law but also to support it. This means that the personal actions of law enforcement personnel should be exemplary and should inspire others to respect and obey the law. Off-duty officers who are seen speeding down the highway or smoking marijuana at a party, for example, do a disservice to the police profession and engender disrespect for all agents of enforcement and for the law itself. Hence, in an important sense, we can say that respect for the law begins with the personal and public behavior of law enforcement officers.

Apprehending Offenders

Some offenders are apprehended during the investigation of a crime or even during its commission or immediately afterward. Fleeing Oklahoma City bomber Timothy McVeigh, for example, was stopped by an Oklahoma Highway Patrol officer on routine patrol only 90 minutes after the destruction of the Alfred P. Murrah Federal Building[8] for driving a car with no license plate. When the officer questioned McVeigh about a bulge in his jacket, McVeigh admitted that it was a gun. The officer then took McVeigh into custody for carrying a concealed weapon. Typically, McVeigh would then have made an immediate appearance before a judge and have been released on bail. As fate would have it, however, the judge assigned to see McVeigh was involved in a protracted divorce case. The longer jail stay proved to be McVeigh's undoing. As the investigation into the bombing progressed, profiler Clinton R. Van Zandt of the Federal Bureau of Investigation (FBI) Behavioral Science Unit concluded that the bomber was likely a native-born white male in his twenties who had been in the military and was probably a member of a fringe militia group—all of which were true of McVeigh.[9] Working together, the FBI and the Oklahoma State Police realized that McVeigh was a likely suspect and questioned him. While McVeigh's capture was the result of a bit of good luck, many offenders are only caught as the result of extensive police work involving a painstaking investigation.

Preventing Crime

Crime prevention is a proactive approach to the problem of crime; it is "the anticipation, recognition and appraisal of a crime risk and initiation of action to remove or reduce it."[10] In preventing crime, police agencies act before a crime happens, thus preventing victimization from occurring. Although the term *crime prevention* is relatively new, the idea is probably as old as human society. Securing valuables, limiting access to sensitive areas, and monitoring the activities of suspicious people are techniques that were in use long before the establishment of Western police forces in the 1800s.

crime prevention
The anticipation, recognition, and appraisal of a crime risk and the initiation of action to eliminate or reduce it.

▲ Chief Deputy Paula Townsend of the Watauga County (North Carolina) Sheriff's Department carrying 11-month-old Breanna Chambers to safety in 2005 after the capture of the child's parents. The parents, who were already wanted on charges related to methamphetamine manufacture, were charged with additional counts of child abduction, felonious restraint, and assault with a gun after they abducted Breanna and her two-year-old brother, James Paul Chambers, from a foster home. Today's police officers are expected to enforce the law while meeting the needs of the community. Do those goals conflict? If so, how?
Watauga Democrat/*Marie Freeman/AP Wide World Photos*

Techniques and Programs

Modern crime-prevention efforts aim not only to reduce crime and criminal opportunities and lower the potential rewards of criminal activity but also to lessen the public's fear of crime.[11] Law enforcement–led crime-prevention efforts include both techniques and programs. Crime-prevention *techniques* include access control (including barriers to entry and exit), surveillance (such as video surveillance), theft-deterrence devices (that is, locks, alarms, and tethers), lighting, and visibility landscaping. Crime prevention through environmental design (CPTED) is a tool that can be used by crime-prevention specialists, including architects and public-safety consultants.

In contrast to techniques, crime-prevention *programs* are organized efforts that focus resources on reducing a specific form of criminal threat. The Philadelphia Police Department's Operation Identification, for example, is designed to discourage theft and to help recover stolen property.[12] The program seeks to educate citizens on the importance of identifying, marking, and listing their valuables to deter theft (because marked items are more difficult to sell) and to aid in their recovery. Through Operation Identification, the police department provides engraving pens, suggests ways of photographing and engraving valuables, and provides window decals and car bumper stickers that identify citizens as participants in the program. Other crime-prevention programs typically target school-based crime, gang activity, drug abuse, violence, domestic abuse, identity theft, vehicle theft, or neighborhood crimes such as burglary.

Today's crime-prevention programs depend on community involvement, an open flow of information, and education for the public as to risks and possible preventive measures. For example, Neighborhood Watch programs build on active observation by homeowners and businesspeople on the lookout for anything unusual. Crime Stoppers International and Crime Stoppers USA are examples of privately sponsored programs that accept tips about criminal activity that they pass on to the appropriate law enforcement organization. Crime Stoppers International can be accessed at Web Extra 4–1, and the National Crime Prevention Council can be found at Web Extra 4–2 at mycrimekit.com.

Web EXTRA

CompStat

Law enforcement's ability to prevent crimes relies in part on the ability of police planners to predict when and where crimes will occur. Effective prediction means that limited police resources can be correctly assigned to the areas with the greatest need. One technique for predicting criminal activity is **CompStat**.[13] While CompStat may sound like a software program, it is actually a process of crime analysis and police management developed by the New York City Police Department in the mid-1990s[14] to help police managers better assess their performance and foresee the potential for crime. The CompStat process involves first collecting and analyzing the information received from 9-1-1 calls and officer reports.[15] This detailed and timely information is then mapped using special software developed for the purpose. The resulting map sequences, generated over time, reveal the time and place of crime patterns and identify hot spots of ongoing criminal activity. The maps also show the number of patrol officers active in an area, ongoing investigations, arrests made, and so on, thus helping commanders see which anticrime strategies are working.

CompStat
A crime-analysis and police-management process built on crime mapping that was developed by the New York City Police Department in the mid-1990s.

CrimeStat, a Windows-based spatial statistics analysis software program for analyzing crime-incident locations, is a second technique for predicting criminal activity and produces results similar to CompStat's.[16] Developed by Ned Levine and Associates with grants from the National Institute of Justice (NIJ), CrimeStat provides statistical tools for crime mapping and analysis—including identification of crime hot spots, spatial distribution of incidents, and distance analysis—that help crime analysts target offenses that might be related to one another. CrimeStat software is available online via Web Extra 4–3; Web Extra 4–4 provides a link to chicagocrime.org, which overlays crime statistics on maps of the city.

Web EXTRA

Preserving the Peace

Enforcing the law, investigating crime and apprehending offenders, and preventing crime are all daunting tasks requiring the full attention of police departments. There are, after all, many laws and numerous offenders. Still, crimes are clearly defined by statute and are therefore limited in number. Peacekeeping, however, is a virtually limitless police activity involving not only activities that violate the law (and hence the community's peace) but many other activities as well. Law enforcement officers who supervise parades, public demonstrations, and picketing strikers, for example, typically attempt to ensure that the behavior of everyone involved remains civil so that it does not disrupt community life.

Robert H. Langworthy, who has written extensively about the police, says that keeping the peace is often left up to individual officers.[17] Basically, he says, departments depend on patrol officers "to define the peace and decide how to support it," and an officer is doing a good job when his or her "beat is quiet, meaning there are no complaints about loiterers or traffic flow, and commerce is supported."

Many police departments focus on quality-of-life offenses as a crime-reduction and peacekeeping strategy. **Quality-of-life offenses** are minor law violations (sometimes called *petty crimes*) that demoralize residents and businesspeople by creating disorder (for example, excessive noise, graffiti, abandoned cars, and vandalism) or by reflecting social decay (panhandling and aggressive begging, public urination, prostitution, roaming youth gangs, public consumption of alcohol, and street-level substance abuse).[18] Homelessness, while not necessarily a violation of the law (unless it involves some form of trespass),[19] is also typically addressed under quality-of-life programs through police interviews with the homeless, many of whom are relocated to shelters or hospitals or are arrested for some other offense. Many claim that reducing the number of quality-of-life offenses in a community can restore a sense of order, reduce the fear of crime, and lessen the number of serious crimes that occur. However, quality-of-life programs have been criticized by those who say that the police should not be taking a law enforcement approach to social and economic problems.[20]

quality-of-life offense
A minor violation of the law (sometimes called a *petty crime*) that demoralizes community residents and businesspeople. Quality-of-life offenses involve acts that create physical disorder (for example, excessive noise and vandalism) or that reflect social decay (for example, panhandling and prostitution).

A similar approach to keeping the peace can be found in the broken windows model of policing.[21] This thesis is based on the notion that physical decay, such as litter and abandoned buildings, can breed disorder in a community and can lead to crime by signaling that laws are not being enforced.[22] Such decay, the theory postulates, pushes law-abiding citizens to withdraw from the streets, which sends a signal that lawbreakers can operate freely.[23] The broken windows thesis suggests that by encouraging the repair of rundown buildings and controlling disorderly behavior in public spaces, police agencies can create an environment in which serious crime cannot easily flourish.[24]

While desirable, public order has its own costs. Noted police author Charles R. Swanson says, "The degree to which any society achieves some amount of public order through police action

Fidelity, bravery, and integrity.
—Motto of the Federal Bureau of Investigation

depends in part upon the price that society is willing to pay to obtain it."[25] Swanson goes on to describe the price to be paid in terms of (1) police resources paid for by tax dollars and (2) "a reduction in the number, kinds, and extent of liberties" that are available to members of the public.

Providing Services

Writers for the NIJ observe that "any citizen from any city, suburb, or town across the United States can mobilize police resources by simply picking up the phone and placing a direct call to the police."[26] "Calling the cops" has been described as the cornerstone of policing in a democratic society. About 70% of the millions of daily calls to 9-1-1 systems across the country are directed to the police, although callers can also request emergency medical and fire services.

Calls received by 9-1-1 operators are prioritized and then relayed to patrol officers, specialized field units, or other emergency personnel. In 2001, for example, the Hastings (Minnesota) Police Department handled a total of 12,895 calls for service.[27] A breakdown of those calls shows that there were 1,837 calls related to serious crimes such as arson, assault, auto theft, burglary, larceny, rape, and robbery. The remaining 11,058 calls were nonemergency calls involving lost and found articles, minor motor vehicle accidents, barking dogs, suspicious persons, and parking and traffic violation reports. Numbers like these have led some cities to adopt nonemergency "Citizen Service System" call numbers in addition to 9-1-1. More than a dozen metropolitan areas, including Baltimore, Dallas, Detroit, Las Vegas, New York, and San Jose, now staff 3-1-1 nonemergency systems around the clock. Plans are afoot in some states to adopt the 3-1-1 system statewide.

American Policing Today: From the Federal to the Local Level

The organization of American law enforcement has been called the most complex in the world. Three major legislative and judicial jurisdictions exist in the United States—federal, state, and local—and each has created a variety of police agencies to enforce its laws. Unfortunately, little uniformity is seen among jurisdictions regarding the naming, function, or authority of enforcement agencies. The matter is complicated still more by the rapid growth of private security firms, which operate on a for-profit basis and provide services that have traditionally been regarded as law enforcement activities.

Federal Agencies

Dozens of federal law enforcement agencies are distributed among 14 U.S. government departments and 28 nondepartmental entities (Table 1). In addition to the enforcement agencies listed in the table, many other federal government offices are involved in enforcement through inspection, regulation, and control activities. At the beginning of 2007, the Government Accounting Office (GAO) reported that nonmilitary federal agencies employ a total of 139,929 law enforcement officers, which it defined as individuals authorized to perform any of four specific functions: (1) conduct criminal investigations, (2) execute search warrants, (3) make arrests, or (4) carry firearms.[28] The FBI, one of the best-known federal law enforcement agencies, is described in the paragraphs that follow.

Web EXTRA

Library EXTRA

Visit the home pages of many federal law enforcement agencies via **Web Extra 4–5** at mycrimekit.com. Learn more about staffing levels of federal criminal justice agencies at **Library Extra 4–2**.

Background of the FBI

The FBI may be the most famous law enforcement agency in the country and in the world. The FBI has traditionally been held in high regard by many Americans, who think of it as an example of what a law enforcement organization should be and who believe that FBI agents are exemplary police officers. William Webster, former director of the FBI, reflected this sentiment when he said, "Over the years the American people have come to expect the most professional law enforcement from the FBI. Although we use the most modern forms of management and technology in the fight against crime, our strength is in our people—in the character of the men

TABLE 1 American Policing: Federal Law Enforcement Agencies

Department of Agriculture
U.S. Forest Service

Department of Commerce
Bureau of Export Enforcement
National Marine Fisheries Administration

Department of Defense
Air Force Office of Special Investigations
Army Criminal Investigation Division
Defense Criminal Investigative Service
Naval Investigative Service

Department of Energy
National Nuclear Safety Administration
Office of Mission Operations
Office of Secure Transportation

Department of Health and Human Services
Food and Drug Administration (FDA), Office of Criminal Investigations

Department of Homeland Security (DHS)
Federal Law Enforcement Training Center (FLETC)
Federal Protective Service
Transportation Security Administration
U.S. Coast Guard
U.S. Customs and Border Protection (CBP), including U.S. Border Patrol
U.S. Immigration and Customs Enforcement (ICE)
U.S. Secret Service (SS)

Department of the Interior
Bureau of Indian Affairs
Bureau of Land Management
Fish and Wildlife Service
National Park Service
U.S. Park Police

Department of Justice
Bureau of Alcohol, Tobacco, Firearms, and Explosives (AFT)
Bureau of Prisons (BOP)
Drug Enforcement Administration (DEA)
Federal Bureau of Investigation (FBI)
U.S. Marshals Service

Department of Labor
Office of Labor Racketeering

Department of State
Diplomatic Security Service

Department of Transportation
Federal Air Marshals Program

Department of the Treasury
Internal Revenue Service (IRS), Criminal Investigation Division
Treasury Inspector General for Tax Enforcement

Department of Veterans Affairs (VA)
Office of Security and Law Enforcement

U.S. Postal Service
Postal Inspection Service

Other Offices with Enforcement Personnel
Administrative Office of the U.S. Courts
AMTRAK Police
Bureau of Engraving and Printing Police
Environmental Protection Agency (EPA), Criminal Investigations Division
Federal Reserve Board
Tennessee Valley Authority (TVA)
U.S. Capitol Police
U.S. Mint
U.S. Supreme Court Police
Washington, D.C., Metropolitan Police Department

Note: Virtually every cabinet-level federal agency has its own Office of Inspector General, which has enforcement authority.

and women of the FBI. For that reason we seek only those who have demonstrated that they can perform as professional people who can, and will, carry on our tradition of fidelity, bravery, and integrity."[29]

The history of the FBI spans 100 years. It began in 1908 as the Bureau of Investigation; it was designed to serve as the investigative arm of the U.S. Department of Justice. The creation of the bureau was motivated, at least in part, by the inability of other agencies to stem the rising tide of American political and business corruption.[30] Learn about the history of the FBI at Web Extra 4–6.

Web EXTRA

CJ News

FBI Retools "Most Wanted" List

Those grainy mug shots, once confined to post office lobbies, are coming to a billboard near you.

The FBI is retooling its Ten Most Wanted list into an increasingly multimedia international appeal for help as it tries to keep its signature program relevant in a crowded media landscape.

"We're trying to exploit every opportunity," FBI spokesman Chris Allen says. The strategy is "probably pretty surprising for a government agency."

Among the changes:

- Launching a billboard campaign. Earlier this month, the FBI began featuring top fugitives on billboards in 20 cities.
- Expanding the list's international reach. The FBI is building on its broadcast alliance with the popular *America's Most Wanted* TV show to solicit tips on similar programs in Hungary, Israel, the Netherlands, Great Britain, and Germany.
- Posting video. The FBI has video of the most recent sightings of some fugitives on its Top 10 website.

In the billboard deal with Clear Channel Outdoor Holdings Inc., which is donating the space, the FBI will get access to about 150 electronic billboards, Allen says.

In Los Angeles, images of Most Wanted suspect Emigdio Preciado, Jr., accused in the attempted murders of two sheriff's deputies, are on display throughout the city.

Marine Cpl. Cesar Laurean, a suspect in the murder of pregnant Lance Cpl. Maria Lauterbach, is not on the Top Ten list, but his image appears on some billboards.

As of December, 489 fugitives had appeared on the list since it began in 1950. Of those, 458 have been located, at least 150 with citizen help, the FBI says. Agents hunt for an estimated 12,000 fugitives at a time.

Rex Tomb, a former chief of the FBI's investigative publicity unit, says the list reflects the evolving nature of crime. The bureau added Osama bin Laden after the 1998 U.S. embassy bombings in Africa. "In the 1950s, it was bank robbery," Tomb says. "Now, you see bin Laden up there."

The bureau last year quietly removed accused cop killer Donald Eugene Webb from the Top 10, marking only the sixth time a fugitive was taken off before capture.

"That's pretty valuable real estate, and you have to make sure . . . there is going to be a benefit," Tomb says. "Sometimes it works. Sometimes it doesn't."

See the FBI's 10 most wanted fugitives at http://www.fbi.gov/wanted.htm.

For the latest in crime and justice news, visit the Talk Justice news feed at http://www.crimenews.info.

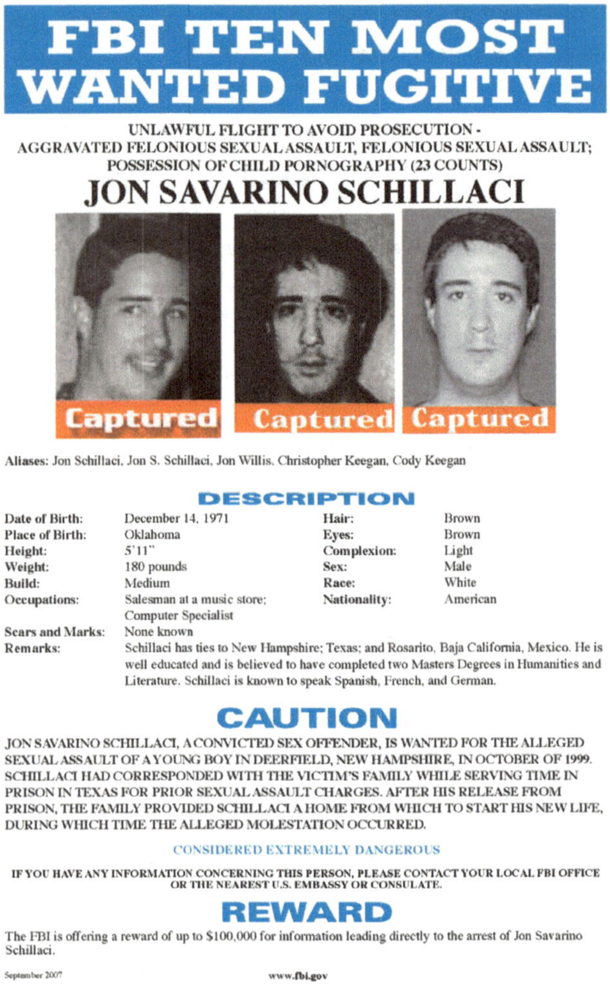

▲ One of the fugitives on the FBI's Ten Most Wanted list, Jon Savarino Schillaci, is a convicted sex offender wanted for the sexual assault of a young boy in Deerfield, New Hampshire. The crime occurred in 1999, and Schillaci has been on the FBI's Most Wanted List for years. How is the FBI changing the way it uses new media and other outlets to publicize information about fugitives who are on the list?
Federal Bureau of Investigation

Source: Kevin Johnson, "FBI Retools Most Wanted List," *USA Today*, January 16, 2008. Web available at http://www.usatoday.com/news/nation/2008-01-16-Top10_N.htm. From USA TODAY, a division of Garnett Co., Inc. Reprinted with permission.

The official purpose of today's FBI is succinctly stated in the agency's mission statement: "The Mission of the FBI is to protect and defend the United States against terrorist and foreign intelligence threats, to uphold and enforce the criminal laws of the United States, and to provide leadership and criminal justice services to federal, state, municipal, and international agencies and partners."[31]

FBI headquarters are located in the J. Edgar Hoover Building on Pennsylvania Avenue in Washington, D.C. Special agents and support personnel who work at the agency's headquarters organize and coordinate FBI activities throughout the country and around the world. Headquarters staffers determine investigative priorities, oversee major cases, and manage the organization's resources, technology, and personnel.

The daily work of the FBI is done through 56 field offices and 400 satellite offices (known as *resident agencies*). A special agent in charge oversees each field office, except for the three largest field offices in Washington, D.C., Los Angeles, and New York City, each of which is headed by an assistant director.

The FBI also operates legal attaché offices (called *Legats*) in a number of major cities around the world, including London and Paris. Such offices permit the international coordination of enforcement activities and facilitate the flow of law enforcement–related information between the FBI and police agencies in host countries. In 1995, a few years after the end of the cold war, the FBI opened a legal attaché office in Moscow. The Moscow office assists Russian police agencies in the growing battle against organized crime in that country and helps American officials track suspected Russian criminals operating in the United States. Also in 1995, an Eastern European version of the FBI Academy, known as the International Law Enforcement Academy (ILEA), opened in Budapest, Hungary. Its purpose is to train police administrators from all of Eastern Europe in the latest crime-fighting techniques.[32]

What we need to do better is be predictive. We have to be proactive. We have to develop the capability to anticipate attacks. We have to develop the capability of looking around corners. And that is the change. That is the shift in focus particularly at headquarters.

—Robert S. Mueller[i]

A little over a decade ago, the FBI formed the National Computer Crime Squad (NCCS) to investigate violations of the federal Counterfeit Access Device and Computer Fraud and Abuse Act of 1984, the Computer Fraud and Abuse Act of 1986 (CFAA),[33] and other federal computer-crime laws. The NCCS focuses on computer crimes such as (1) intrusions of public switched networks (telephone company networks), (2) major computer network intrusions, (3) network integrity violations, (4) privacy violations, (5) industrial espionage, (6) pirated computer software, and (7) other crimes in which a computer is centrally involved. In recent years, the FBI has created individual computer-crime investigation teams in each of its field offices within the United States.

The FBI also operates the Combined DNA Index System (CODIS), a computerized forensic database of DNA profiles of offenders convicted of serious crimes (such as rape, other sexual assaults, murder, and certain crimes against children), as well as DNA profiles from unknown offenders.[34] CODIS, now a part of the National DNA Index System (NDIS), was formally authorized by the federal DNA Identification Act of 1994.[35] It is being enhanced daily through the work of federal, state, and local law enforcement agencies that take DNA samples from biological evidence gathered at crime scenes and from offenders themselves. The computerized CODIS system can rapidly identify a perpetrator when it finds a match between an evidence sample and a stored profile. By 1998, every state had enacted legislation establishing a CODIS database and requiring that DNA from offenders convicted of certain serious crimes be entered into the system. As of January 2006, the CODIS database contained more than 3 million DNA profiles.[36] Learn more about CODIS at **Web Extra 4–7**.

Web EXTRA

As the FBI has grown, some of its functions have become geographically dispersed. Headquartered in Clarksburg, West Virginia, the Criminal Justice Information Services (CJIS) Division serves as the central repository for criminal justice information services in the FBI. The FBI describes the division as "a customer-driven organization providing state-of-the-art identification and information services to local, state, federal, and international criminal justice communities." In support of these activities, the CJIS Division has developed an advisory process that involves sharing management and policy-making decisions with local, state, and federal criminal justice agencies. The CJIS Division includes the Fingerprint Identification Program, the National Crime Information Center Program, the Uniform Crime Reporting Program, and the Integrated Automated Fingerprint Identification System (IAFIS). IAFIS is a computer-based system that can store, process, analyze, and retrieve millions of fingerprints in a relatively short period of time.

The FBI Laboratory Division, located in Quantico, Virginia, operates one of the largest and most comprehensive crime laboratories in the world. It provides services related to the scientific solution and prosecution of crimes throughout the country. It is also the only full-service federal forensic laboratory in the United States. Laboratory activities include crime-scene searches, special surveillance photography, latent-fingerprint examinations, forensic examinations of evidence (including DNA testing), court testimony by laboratory personnel, and other scientific and technical services. The FBI offers laboratory services, free of charge, to all law enforcement agencies in the United States. Learn more about the FBI's administrative divisions, including the activities of each, via **Web Extra 4–8** at mycrimekit.com.

Web EXTRA

▲ FBI Director Robert S. Mueller explaining his agency's shift in priorities following the 2001 terrorist attacks on the World Trade Center and the Pentagon. How did the agency's priorities change?
AP Wide World Photos

The FBI also runs a National Academy Program, which is part of its Training Division. The program offered its first class in 1935 and had 23 students. It was then known as the FBI National Police Training School. In 1940, the school moved from Washington, D.C., to the U.S. Marine Amphibious Base at Quantico, Virginia. In 1972, the facility expanded to 334 acres, and the FBI Academy, as we know it today, officially opened.[37] According to the most recent statistics available, the academy program has produced 37,990 graduates since it began operations. This includes 2,475 graduates from 151 foreign countries and 328 graduates from U.S. territories and possessions. More than 200 sessions have been offered since inception of the training program. Visit the FBI Academy on the Web via **Web Extra 4–9** at mycrimekit.com.

Web EXTRA

The FBI and Counterterrorism

The FBI's counterterrorism efforts became especially important following the September 11, 2001, attacks on the World Trade Center in New York City and the Pentagon. Two months after the attacks, then-U.S. Attorney General John Ashcroft announced a major "reorganization and mobilization" of the FBI and other federal agencies, such as the Immigration and Naturalization Service (now U.S. Citizenship and Immigration Services, an office of the Department of Homeland Security). Speaking at a press conference in Washington, D.C., Ashcroft said:

The attacks of September 11 [2001] have redefined the mission of the Department of Justice. Defending our nation and defending the citizens of America against terrorist attacks [are] now our first and overriding priority. To fulfill this mission, we are devoting all the resources necessary to eliminate terrorist networks, to prevent terrorist attacks, and to bring to justice those who kill Americans in the name of murderous ideologies. We are engaged in an aggressive arrest and detention campaign of lawbreakers with a single objective: to get terrorists off the street before they can harm more Americans.

—John Ashcroft
Former U.S. Attorney General

> Our strategic plan mandates fundamental change in several of the most critical components of American justice and law enforcement, starting with the organization that is at the center of our counterterrorism effort, the Federal Bureau of Investigation. In its history, the FBI has been many things: the protector of our institutions when they were under assault from organized crime; the keeper of our security when it was threatened by international espionage; and the defender of our civil rights when they were denied to some Americans on the basis of their race, color or creed. Today the American people call upon the Federal Bureau of Investigation to put prevention of terrorism at the center of its law enforcement and national security efforts.[38]

Since that time, the FBI has reshaped its priorities to focus on preventing future terrorist attacks. This effort is managed by the Counterterrorism Division at FBI headquarters and is emphasized at every field office, resident agency, and Legat. Headquarters administers a national threat warning system that allows the FBI to instantly distribute important terrorism-related bulletins to law enforcement agencies and public safety departments throughout the country. "Flying Squads" provide specialized counterterrorism knowledge and experience, language capabilities, and analytic support as needed to FBI field offices and Legats.

To combat terrorism, the FBI's Counterterrorism Division collects, analyzes, and shares information and critical intelligence with various federal agencies and departments—including the Central Intelligence Agency (CIA), the National Security Agency (NSA), and the Department of Homeland Security (DHS)—and with law enforcement agencies throughout the country. An essential weapon in the FBI's battle against terrorism is the Joint Terrorism Task Force (JTTF).

In testimony before Congress in 2005, FBI Director Robert S. Mueller III identified three areas of special concern relative to the bureau's ongoing antiterrorism efforts. First, said Mueller, "is the threat from covert operatives who may be inside the U.S. who have the intention to facilitate or conduct an attack."[39] The very nature of trained covert operatives, said the director, is that they are difficult to detect. "I remain very concerned about what we are *not* seeing," said Mueller. Second, Mueller identified a concern "with the growing body of sensitive reporting that continues to show al-Qaeda's clear intention to obtain and ultimately use some form of chemical, biological, radiological, nuclear, or high-energy explosives (CBRNE) material in its attacks against America." Finally, said Mueller, "We remain concerned about the potential for al-Qaeda to . . . exploit radical American converts and other indigenous extremists." Read more about Director Mueller's vision for the future of the FBI in the FBI's 132-page *Strategic Plan for 2004–2009* at Library Extra 4–3.

Library EXTRA

State Agencies

Most state police agencies were created in the late nineteenth or early twentieth century to meet specific needs. The Texas Rangers, created in 1835 before Texas attained statehood, functioned as a military organization responsible for patrolling the republic's borders. The apprehension of Mexican cattle rustlers was one of the main concerns.[40] Massachusetts, targeting vice control, was the second state to create a law enforcement agency. Today, a wide diversity of state policing agencies exists. Table 2 provides a list of typical state-sponsored law enforcement agencies.

State law enforcement agencies are usually organized after one of two models. In the first, a centralized model, the tasks of major criminal investigations are combined with the patrol of state highways. Centralized state police agencies generally do the following:

- Assist local law enforcement departments in criminal investigations when asked to do so
- Operate centralized identification bureau
- Maintain a centralized criminal records repository
- Patrol the state's highways
- Provide select training for municipal and county officers

The Pennsylvania Constabulary, known today as the Pennsylvania State Police, was the first modern force to combine these duties and has been called the "first modern state police agency."[41] Michigan, New Jersey, New York, Vermont, and Delaware are a few of the states that patterned their state-level enforcement activities after the Pennsylvania model.

The second state model, the decentralized model of police organization, characterizes operations in the southern United States but is found as well in the Midwest and in some western states. The model draws a clear distinction between traffic enforcement on state highways and other state-level law enforcement functions by creating at least two separate agencies. North Carolina, South Carolina, and Georgia are a few of the many states that employ both a highway patrol and a state bureau of investigation. The names of the respective agencies may vary, however, even though their functions are largely the same. In North Carolina, for example, the two major state-level law enforcement agencies are the North Carolina Highway Patrol and the State Bureau of Investigation. Georgia fields a highway patrol and the Georgia Bureau of Investigation, and South Carolina operates a highway patrol and the South Carolina Law Enforcement Division.

TABLE 2 American Policing: State Law Enforcement Agencies

Alcohol law enforcement agencies	Port authorities	State police
Fish and wildlife agencies	State bureaus of investigation	State university police
Highway patrol	State park services	Weigh station operations

CJ Careers

Federal Bureau of Investigation

Name: Kevin Kendrick
Position: Section Chief, Executive Development and Selection Program, Administrative Services Division
City: Washington, D.C.
College Attended: Wayne State University
Year Hired: 1981

"Seeing the good work that officers were doing when I was in school at Wayne State opened my eyes to the possibility of a career in law enforcement. I saw this as a wonderful opportunity to do something positive. Every day at the FBI is different. I can honestly say this is the greatest part of the job: the variety of assignments, the interaction with other agencies, and the community. It's an incredible way to get things done. We do something that means something. We are having an impact on people's lives."

TYPICAL POSITIONS

Special agent, crime laboratory technician, ballistics technician, computer operator, fingerprint specialist, explosives examiner, document expert, and other nonagent technical positions. FBI activities include investigations into organized crime, white-collar crime, public corruption, financial crime, fraud against the government, bribery, copyright matters, civil rights violations, bank robbery, extortion, kidnapping, air piracy, terrorism, foreign counterintelligence, interstate criminal activity, fugitive and drug-trafficking matters, and other violations of federal statutes. The FBI also works with other federal, state, and local law enforcement agencies in investigating matters of joint interest and in training law enforcement officers from around the world.

EMPLOYMENT REQUIREMENTS

General employment requirements include (1) an age between 23 and 37; (2) excellent physical health; (3) uncorrected vision of not less than 20/200, correctable to 20/20 in one eye and at least 20/40 in the other eye; (4) good hearing; (5) U.S. citizenship; (6) a valid driver's license; (7) successful completion of a comprehensive background investigation; (8) a law degree or a bachelor's degree from an accredited college or university; (9) successful completion of an initial written examination; (10) an intensive formal interview; and (11) urinalysis. A polygraph examination may also be required.

OTHER REQUIREMENTS

Special-agent entry programs exist in the areas of law, accounting, languages, engineering/science, and a general "diversified" area. They require a minimum of three years of full-time work experience, preferably with a law enforcement agency. Candidates who otherwise meet entry requirements and who possess one or more of the following critical skills are currently deemed essential to address the agency's increasingly complex responsibilities and will be given priority in the hiring process: (1) computer science and other information technology specialties; (2) engineering; (3) physical sciences (physics, chemistry, biology, and so on); (4) foreign language proficiency (Arabic, Farsi, Pashtu, Urdu, all dialects of Chinese, Japanese, Korean, Russian, Spanish, and Vietnamese); (5) foreign counterintelligence; (6) counterterrorism; and (7) military intelligence experience. The FBI emphasizes education and especially values degrees in law, graduate studies, and business and accounting. Most nonagent technical career paths also require bachelor's or advanced degrees and U.S. citizenship.

SALARY

In mid-2007, Special Agent trainees at the FBI Academy were paid at GS-10, step 1 ($43,441), plus the Quantico, Virginia, locality adjustment (17.50%) during their time at the FBI Academy. This equated to $51,043 on an annualized basis. Newly assigned special agents are paid at GS-10, step 1 ($43,441), plus locality pay and availability pay. Locality pay (which ranges from 12.5% to 28.7% of base salary depending upon office assignment) is additional compensation to account for differences in the labor market between different areas. Availability pay is a 25% increase in adjusted salary (base salary plus locality pay) for all special agents due to their requirement to average a 50-hour workweek over the course of the year. Thus, with the locality and availability pay adjustments, new special agents in their first Field Offices earned between $61,100 and $69,900 in 2007. New Special Agents assigned to certain designated high-cost offices (New York, San Francisco, Los Angeles, San Diego, Washington, D.C., Boston, and Newark) may also be paid a onetime relocation bonus of approximately $22,000 to help offset higher real estate and living costs. Special agents can advance to GS-13 in field assignments and to GS-15 or higher in supervisory and management positions.

BENEFITS

Benefits include (1) 13 days of sick leave annually, (2) two and a half to five weeks of paid vacation and ten paid federal holidays each year, (3) federal health and life insurance, and (4) a comprehensive retirement program.

DIRECT INQUIRIES TO:

Federal Bureau of Investigation
J. Edgar Hoover Building
935 Pennsylvania Avenue, N.W.
Washington, DC 20535–0001
Phone: 202-324-3000 (or check your local telephone book)
Website: http://www.fbi.gov, or visit http://fbijobs.com

For more information on the rapidly expanding criminal justice careers area, read *Where the Jobs Are: Mission Critical Opportunities for America*, available on the Web at http://www.justicestudies.com/jobs.htm.

States that use the decentralized model usually have a number of other adjunct state-level law enforcement agencies. North Carolina, for example, has created a State Wildlife Commission with enforcement powers, a Board of Alcohol Beverage Control with additional agents, and a separate Enforcement and Theft Bureau for enforcement of certain motor vehicle and theft laws. Learn more about state-level law enforcement agencies by visiting Web Extra 4–10 at mycrimekit.com.

Web EXTRA

Local Agencies

Local police agencies, including city and county agencies, represent a third level of law enforcement activity in the United States. The term *local police* encompasses a wide variety of agencies. Municipal departments, rural sheriffs' departments, and specialized groups like campus police and transit police can all be grouped under the "local" rubric. Large municipal departments are highly visible because of their vast size, huge budgets, and innovative programs. The nation's largest law enforcement agency, the New York City Police Department, for example, has about 45,000 full-time employees, including almost 38,000 full-time sworn officers.[42]

The most fundamental weakness in crime control is the failure of federal and state governments to create a framework for local policing. Much of what is wrong with the police is the result of the absurd, fragmented, unworkable nonsystem of more than 17,000 local departments.

—Patrick V. Murphy
Former New York City Police Commissioner

Far greater in number, however, are small-town and county sheriffs' departments. There are approximately 12,760 municipal police departments and 3,100 sheriffs' departments in the United States.[43] Every incorporated municipality in the country has the authority to create its own police force. Some very small communities hire only one officer, who fills the roles of chief, investigator, and night watch—as well as everything in between. The majority of local agencies employ fewer than ten full-time officers, and about three in eight agencies (more than 7,000 in all) employ fewer than five full-time officers. These smaller agencies include 2,245 (or 12%) with just one full-time officer and 1,164 (or 6%) with only part-time officers.[44] A few communities contract with private security firms for police services, and still others have no active police force at all, depending instead on local sheriffs' departments to deal with law violators.

City police chiefs are typically appointed by the mayor or selected by the city council. Their departments' jurisdictions are limited by convention to the geographic boundaries of their communities. **Sheriffs**, on the other hand, are elected public officials whose agencies are responsible for law enforcement throughout the counties in which they function. Sheriffs' deputies mostly patrol the unincorporated areas of the county, or those that lie between municipalities. They do, however, have jurisdiction throughout the county, and in some areas they routinely work alongside municipal police to enforce laws within towns and cities.

sheriff
The elected chief officer of a county law enforcement agency. The sheriff is usually responsible for law enforcement in unincorporated areas and for the operation of the county jail.

Sheriffs' departments are generally responsible for serving court papers, including civil summonses, and for maintaining security within state courtrooms. Sheriffs also run county jails and are responsible for more detainees awaiting trial than any other type of law enforcement department in the country. For example, the Los Angeles (L.A.) County Jail System, operated by the Custody Operations Division of the L.A. County Sheriff's Department (LASD), is the largest in the world.[45] In 2003, with eight separate facilities, the Custody Division of the LASD had an average daily population of 18,423 inmates—considerably larger than the number of inmates held in many state prison systems.[46] More than 2,200 uniformed officers and 1,265 civilian employees work in the Custody Division of the LASD, and that division alone operates with a yearly budget in excess of $200 million.[47]

Sheriffs' departments remain strong across most of the country, although in parts of New England, deputies mostly function as court agents with limited law enforcement duties. One report found that most sheriffs' departments are small, with more than half of them employing fewer than 25 sworn officers.[48] Only 12 departments employ more than 1,000 officers. Even so, southern and western sheriffs are still considered the chief law enforcement officers in their counties.

A list of conventional police agencies found at the local level is shown in Table 3. For information on selected local law enforcement agencies, view Web Extra 4–11 at mycrimekit.com. Visit Library Extras 4–4 and 4–5 to learn more about staffing levels at local and state police agencies.

Web EXTRA

Library EXTRA

TABLE 3 American Policing: Local Law Enforcement Agencies

Campus police	Housing authority agencies	Sheriffs' departments
City/county agencies	Marine patrol agencies	Transit police
Constables	Municipal police departments	Tribal police
Coroners or medical examiners		

A group of Texas Rangers providing additional security during a scheduled execution at Huntsville, Texas, in 2000. The Texas Rangers have long been held in high regard among state police agencies. What are the different kinds of policing in the United States today? How do they relate to one another?
Bob Daemmrich/Stock Boston

Information Sharing among Agencies

In March 2008, more than 900 federal, state, and local law enforcement and homeland security officials attended the National Fusion Center Conference in Washington, D.C.[49] Fusion centers, a new concept in policing, pool and analyze information from law enforcement agencies at all levels, looking for meaningful patterns and actionable intelligence. Fusion centers currently operate in 37 states and have received $380 million in federal funding over the last five years.[50] These centers are largely an outgrowth of one of the 9/11 Commission's criticisms that law enforcement agencies don't talk to each other as they should.

Fusion centers vary greatly in size and in the equipment and personnel available to them. Some are small, consisting of little more than limited conference facilities and only a few participants. Others are large high-technology offices that make use of the latest information and computer technologies and that house representatives from many different organizations. Some fusion centers are physically located within the offices of other agencies. The Kentucky Fusion Center, for example, is housed within the state's Department of Transportation building in the state's capitol. Others operate out of stand-alone facilities and are physically separated from parent agencies.

Similarly, although information sharing is their central purpose, the activities of fusion centers are not uniform. Some centers perform investigations, some make arrests, some exist only to share information. A number of fusion centers, like the National Counterterrorism Center and the National Gang Intelligence Center, focus on clearly defined issues. Most of today's fusion centers do more than target terrorists, however, and work to collect information on a wide variety of offenders, gangs, immigrant smuggling operations, and other threats. Recognizing that actionable intelligence can come from seemingly unrelated areas, Michael Mines, the FBI's deputy assistant director of intelligence, says that the nation's network of fusion centers is intended to "maximize the ability to detect, prevent, investigate, and respond to criminal and terrorist activity."[51]

Many fusion centers are still developing, and a number of problems remain. Obtaining security clearances for employees of local law enforcement agencies, for example, has sometimes been difficult or time-consuming. Even representatives of federal agencies like the DHS and the FBI sometimes refuse to accept each other's clearances. Nonetheless, a recent hearing before the House intelligence subcommittee shows that federal lawmakers are hopeful about the success of fusion centers and are willing to find the federal dollars needed to continue to support them. As Jane Harman (D–Calif.), chairwoman of the House intelligence subcommittee, said recently that "everyone recognizes that fusion centers hold tremendous promise."[52]

◄ Commander Jeffrey L. Wobbleton (right) speaks with an intelligence analyst in Maryland's fusion center. The three-year-old fusion center, located near Baltimore, houses members of 23 local, state, and federal agencies. The center is hidden behind a bolted door with no nameplate in a quiet office park. Fusion centers represent an attempt to generate actionable intelligence through the integrated information-sharing efforts of law enforcement agencies at all levels.
Robert A. Reeder/The Washington Post/*Pictopia.com*

Police Administration

Police management entails administrative activities that control, direct, and coordinate police personnel, resources, and activities in the service of crime prevention, the apprehension of criminals, the recovery of stolen property, and the performance of a variety of regulatory and helping services.[53] Police managers include sworn law enforcement personnel with administrative authority, from the rank of sergeant to captain, chief, or sheriff, and civilian personnel, such as police commissioners, attorneys general, state secretaries of crime control, and public-safety directors.

police management
The administrative activities of controlling, directing, and coordinating police personnel, resources, and activities in the service of crime prevention, the apprehension of criminals, the recovery of stolen property, and the performance of a variety of regulatory and helping services.

Police Organization and Structure

Almost all American law enforcement organizations are formally structured among divisions and along lines of authority. Roles within police agencies generally fall into one of two categories: line and staff. **Line operations** are field or supervisory activities directly related to daily police work; **staff operations** include support roles such as administration. In organizations that have line operations only, authority flows from the top down in a clear, unbroken line,[54] and no supporting elements (media relations, training, fiscal management divisions, and so on) exist. All line operations are directly involved in providing field services. Because almost all police agencies need support, only the smallest departments have only line operations.

line operations
In police organizations, the field activities or supervisory activities directly related to day-to-day police work.

staff operations
In police organizations, activities (such as administration and training) that provide support for line operations.

Most police organizations include both line and staff operations. In such organizations, line managers are largely unencumbered with staff operations such as budgets, training, scientific analysis of evidence, legal advice, shift assignments, and personnel management. Support personnel handle these activities, freeing line personnel to focus on the day-to-day requirements of providing field services.

In a line and staff agency, divisions are likely to exist within both line operations and staff operations. For example, field services, a line operation, may be broken down into enforcement and investigation. Administrative services, a staff operation, may be divided into human resources management, training and education, materials supply, finance management, and facilities management. The line and staff structure easily accommodates functional areas of responsibility within line and staff divisions. The organizational chart detailing the line and staff structure of the Los Angeles Police Department is shown in Figure 1.

Crime is a community problem and stands today as one of the most serious challenges of our generation. Our citizens must . . . recognize their responsibilities in its suppression.
—*O. W. Wilson*

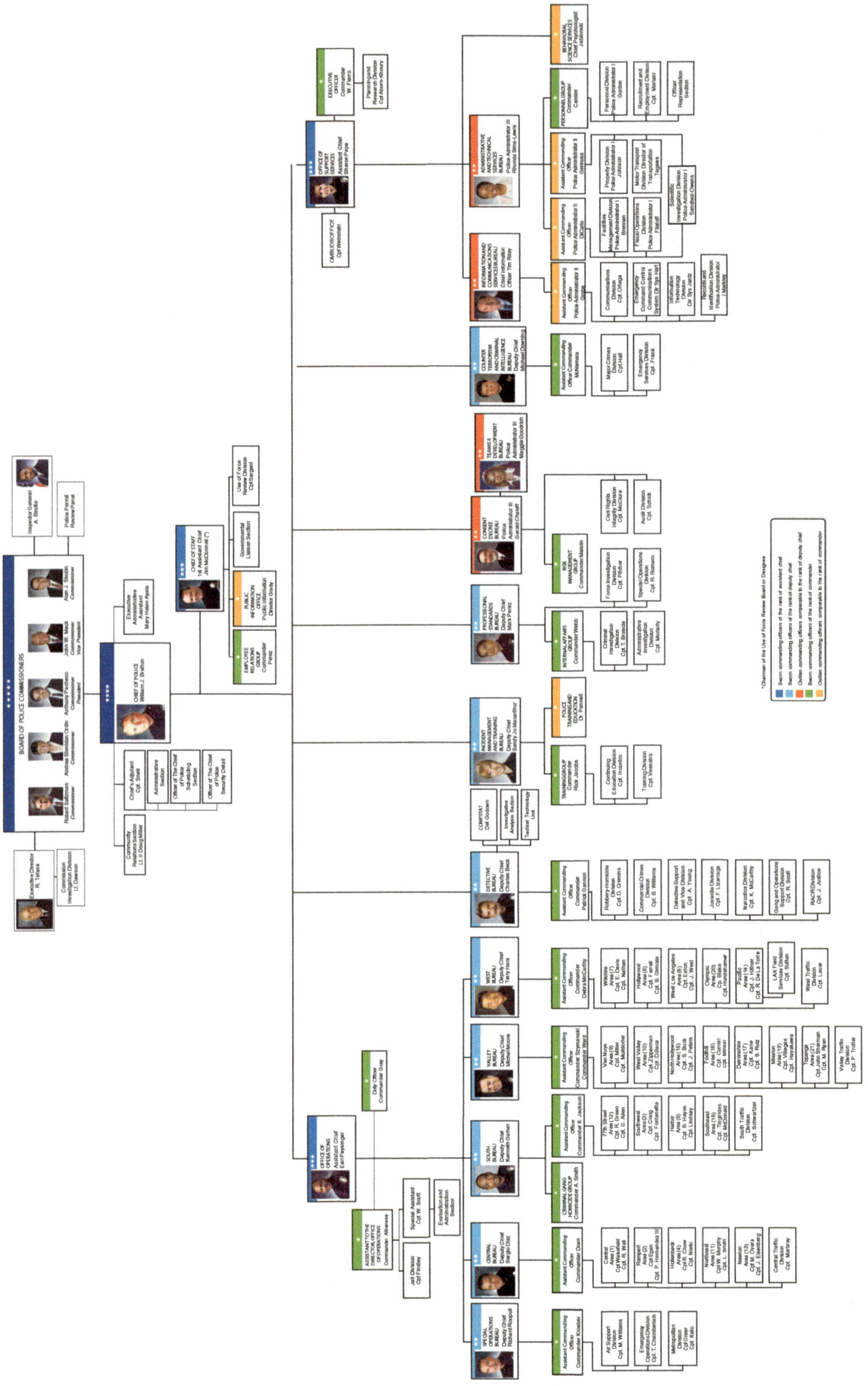

FIGURE 1

Organizational Chart of the Los Angeles Police Department.

Source: Los Angeles Police Department, "LAPD Organization Chart," July 1, 2008, http://lapdonline.org/inside_the_lapd/pdf_view/5056. Reprinted with permission.

Chain of Command

The organizational chart of any police agency shows a hierarchical **chain of command**, or the order of authority within the department. The chain of command clarifies who reports to whom. Usually, the chief of police or sheriff is at the top of the command chain (although his or her boss may be a police commissioner, city council, or mayor), followed by the subordinate leaders of each division. Because police departments employ a quasi-military chain-of-command structure, the titles assigned to personnel (captain, lieutenant, sergeant) are similar to those used by the military. It is important for individual personnel to know who is in charge; hence, unity of command is an important principle that must be firmly established within the department. When unity of command exists, every individual has only one supervisor to whom he or she answers and from whom, under normal circumstances, he or she takes orders. **Span of control** refers to the number of police personnel or the number of units supervised by a particular commander. For example, one sergeant may be in charge of five or six officers; they represent the sergeant's span of control.

chain of command
The unbroken line of authority that extends through all levels of an organization, from the highest to the lowest.

span of control
The number of police personnel or the number of units supervised by a particular officer.

Policing Epochs and Styles

Policing Epochs

The history of American policing can be divided into four epochs,[55] each distinguishable by the relative dominance of a particular approach to police operations (Figure 2). The first period, the political era, was characterized by close ties between police and public officials. It began in the 1840s and ended around 1930. Throughout the period, American police agencies tended to serve the interests of powerful politicians and their cronies, providing public-order and order-maintenance services almost as an afterthought. The second period, the reform era, began in the 1930s and lasted until the 1970s. It was characterized by pride in professional crime fighting. Police departments during this period focused most of their resources on solving "traditional" crimes, such as murder, rape, and burglary, and on capturing offenders. The third period, and the one that continues to characterize much of contemporary policing in America today, is the community policing era—an approach to policing that stresses the service role of police officers and envisions a partnership between police agencies and their communities.

The fourth period, policing to secure the homeland, is quite new and continues to evolve.[56] The homeland security era grew out of national concerns with terrorism prevention born of the terrorist attacks of September 11, 2001. As police scholar Gene Stephens explains it, "The twenty-first century has put policing into a whole new milieu—one in which the causes of crime and disorder often lie outside the immediate community, demanding new and innovative approaches."[57] A decline in street crime, says Stephens, has been replaced by concern with new and more insidious types of offending, including terrorism and Internet-assisted crimes. These new kinds of crimes, says Stephens, while they threaten the integrity of local communities, often involve offenders thousands of miles away. Nonetheless, as we shall see later in this chapter, the homeland security era builds substantially upon the community policing philosophy with which it coexists.

The influence of each of the first three historical phases survives today in what noted social commentator and Presidential Medal of Freedom recipient James Q. Wilson[58] calls "policing styles."[59] A style of policing describes how a particular agency sees its purpose and chooses the methods it uses to fulfill that purpose. Wilson's three policing styles—which he does not link to any particular historical era—are (1) the watchman (which is characteristic of the political era), (2) the legalistic (which is professional crime fighting of the reform era), and (3) the service (which is becoming more common today). These three styles characterize nearly all municipal law enforcement agencies now operating in the United States, although some departments are a mixture of two or more styles.

The Watchman Style of Policing

Police departments marked by the **watchman style** of policing are primarily concerned with achieving a goal that Wilson called "order maintenance." They see their job as controlling illegal and disruptive behaviors. The watchman style makes considerable use of discretion compared

watchman style
A style of policing marked by a concern for order maintenance. Watchman policing is characteristic of lower-class communities where informal police intervention into the lives of residents is employed in the service of keeping the peace.

Era	Political Era	Reform Era	Community Era	Homeland Security Era
Time Period	1840s–1930	1930–1970s	1970s–Today	2001–Today
Characteristics	Close ties between the police and public officials. Uniformed officers in paramilitary-style organizations serving the interests of the politically powerful.	Pride in professional crime fighting. An emphasis on solving "traditional" crimes and capturing offenders.	Police departments work to identify and serve the needs of their communities. Envisions a partnership between local police agencies and their communities.	Policing to secure the homeland; emphasis on terrorism prevention. Builds on partnerships with the community to gather actionable intelligence to circumvent threats of terrorism.
Catalyst	The need for social order and security in a dynamic and rapidly changing society.	Citizen calls for reform and the development of police professionalism. The removal of politics from policing.	The realization that effective community partnerships can help prevent and solve crimes.	The terrorist attacks of September 11, 2001, and ongoing threats to the safety and security of all Americans.
Example	Police departments and officers were closely tied to their city's political system. Local "ward politicians" hired officers for their own purposes.	"G-men" and the crackdown on organized crime. Progressive policing, led by men like August Vollmer and O. W. Wilson.	A focus on quality-of-life offenses as a crime-reduction and peacekeeping strategy. The broken windows model of policing.	Creation of counterterrorism divisions and offices within departments. Collaboration between police agencies and the sharing of information needed to identify threats.

FIGURE 2
Historical Eras in American Policing.

Freedom or Safety? You Decide.

Liberty Is a Double-Edged Sword

This chapter builds on the following theme: For police action to be "just," it must recognize the rights of individuals while holding them accountable to the social obligations defined by law. It is important to realize that many democratically inspired legal restraints on the police stem from the Bill of Rights, which comprises the first ten amendments to the U.S. Constitution. Such restraints help ensure individual freedoms in our society and prevent the development of a "police state" in America.

In police work and elsewhere, the principles of individual liberty and social justice are cornerstones on which the American way of life rests. Ideally, the work of police agencies, as well as the American system of criminal justice, is to ensure justice while guarding liberty. The liberty–justice issue is the dual thread that holds together the tapestry of the justice system, from the simplest daily activities of police officers on the beat to the often complex and lengthy renderings of the U.S. Supreme Court.

For the criminal justice system as a whole, the question becomes this: How can individual liberties be maintained in the face of the need for official action, including arrest, interrogation, incarceration, and the like? The answer is far from simple, but it begins with the recognition that liberty is a double-edged sword, entailing obligations as well as rights.

YOU DECIDE

What does it mean to say "For police action to be 'just' it must recognize the rights of individuals while holding them accountable to the social obligations defined by law"? How can police agencies accomplish this? What can individual officers do to help their agencies in this regard?

to the legalistic style. Order in watchman-style communities may be arrived at by using informal police intervention, including persuasion and threats, or even by "roughing up" a few disruptive people from time to time. Some authors have condemned this style of policing, suggesting that it is unfairly found in lower-class or lower-middle-class communities, especially where interpersonal relations include a fair amount of violence or physical abuse.

The watchman style of policing appears to have been in use in Los Angeles, California, at the time of the infamous Rodney King beating. Following the riots that ensued, the Independent Commission on the Los Angeles Police Department (the Christopher Commission) determined that the Los Angeles police "placed greater emphasis on crime control over crime prevention, a policy that distanced cops from the people they serve."[60]

The Legalistic Style of Policing

Departments operating under the **legalistic style** of policing enforce the letter of the law. For example, an officer who tickets a person going 71 mph in a 70-mph speed zone is likely a member of a department that adheres to the legalistic style of policing. Conversely, legalistic departments routinely avoid community disputes arising from violations of social norms that do not break the law. Police expert Gary Sykes calls this enforcement style "laissez-faire policing" in recognition of its hands-off approach to behaviors that are simply bothersome or inconsiderate of community principles.[61]

legalistic style
A style of policing marked by a strict concern with enforcing the precise letter of the law. Legalistic departments may take a hands-off approach to disruptive or problematic behavior that does not violate the criminal law.

The Service Style of Policing

In police departments using the **service style**, which strives to meet the needs of a community and serve its members, the police see themselves more as helpers than as soldiers in a war on crime, and they work with social services and other agencies to provide counseling for minor offenders and to assist community groups in preventing crimes and solving problems. Prosecutors may support the service style of policing by agreeing not to prosecute law violators who seek psychiatric help or who voluntarily participate in programs like Alcoholics Anonymous, family counseling, or drug treatment. The service style is supported in part by citizens who seek to avoid the embarrassment that might result from a public airing of personal problems, thereby reducing the number of criminal complaints filed, especially in minor disputes. While the service style of policing may seem more appropriate to wealthy communities or small towns, it can also exist in cities whose police departments actively seek citizen involvement in identifying issues that the police can help address.

service style
A style of policing marked by a concern with helping rather than strict enforcement. Service-oriented police agencies are more likely to take advantage of community resources, such as drug-treatment programs, than are other types of agencies.

Police–Community Relations

The 1960s were fraught with riots, unrest, and student activism as the war in Vietnam, civil rights concerns, and other social movements produced large demonstrations and marches. The police, generally inexperienced in crowd control, were all too often embroiled in tumultuous encounters—even pitched battles—with citizen groups that viewed the police as agents of "the establishment." To manage these new challenges, the legalistic style of policing, so common in America until then, began to yield to the newer service-oriented style of policing.

police–community relations (PCR)
An area of police activity that recognizes the need for the community and the police to work together effectively and that is based on the notion that the police derive their legitimacy from the community they serve. Many police agencies began to explore PCR in the 1960s and 1970s.

As social disorganization increased, police departments across the nation, seeking to understand and better cope with the problems they faced, created **police–community relations (PCR)** programs. PCR programs represented a movement away from an exclusive police emphasis on the apprehension of law violators and meant increasing the level of positive police–citizen interaction. At the height of the PCR movement, city police departments across the country opened storefront centers where citizens could air complaints and interact easily with police representatives. As police scholar Egon Bittner recognized in 1976, PCR programs need to reach to "the grassroots of discontent," where citizen dissatisfaction with the police exists,[62] if they are to be truly effective.

In many contemporary PCR programs, public-relations officers are appointed to provide an array of services, such as Neighborhood Watch programs, drug-awareness workshops, identification projects (using police equipment and expertise to mark valuables for identification in the event of theft), and victims' assistance programs. Modern PCR programs, however, often fail to achieve their goal of increased community satisfaction with police services because they focus on servicing groups already well satisfied with the police. PCR initiatives that do reach disaffected community groups are difficult to manage and may even alienate participating officers from the communities they are assigned to serve. Thus, as Bittner noted, "while the first approach fails because it leaves out those groups to which the program is primarily directed, the second fails because it leaves out the police department."

Team Policing

team policing
The reorganization of conventional patrol strategies into "an integrated and versatile police team assigned to a fixed district."[ii]

During the 1960s and 1970s, a number of communities experimented with the concept of **team policing**, which rapidly became an extension of the PCR movement. With team policing, officers were assigned semipermanently to particular neighborhoods, where they were expected to become familiar with the inhabitants and with their problems and concerns. Patrol officers were given considerable authority in processing complaints, from receipt through resolution. Crimes were investigated and solved at the local level, with specialists called in only if the re-

▶ Los Angeles police bike patrol officers conferring with a supervisor. The community policing concept requires that officers become an integral part of the communities they serve. How can community policing help to both prevent and solve crimes?
Michael Newman/PhotoEdit Inc.

sources needed to continue an investigation were not available locally. Some authors called team policing a "technique to deliver total police services to a neighborhood."[63] Others, however, dismissed it as "little more than an attempt to return to the style of policing that was prevalent in the United States over a century ago."[64]

Every society gets the kind of criminal it deserves. What is equally true is that every community gets the kind of law enforcement it insists on.

—Robert Kennedy
Former U.S. Attorney General[iii]

Community Policing

During the past 20 years, the role of the police in police–community relations has changed considerably. Originally, the PCR model was based on the fact that many police administrators saw police officers as enforcers of the law who were isolated from, and often in opposition to, the communities they policed. As a result, PCR programs were often a shallowly disguised effort to overcome public suspicion and community hostility.

Today, increasing numbers of law enforcement administrators embrace the role of service provider. Modern departments frequently help citizens solve a vast array of personal problems, many of which involve no law-breaking activity. For example, officers regularly aid sick or distraught people, organize community crime-prevention efforts, resolve minor domestic disputes, regulate traffic, and educate children and teens about drug abuse. Because service calls far exceed calls directly related to law violations, most officers more often make referrals for interpersonal problems to agencies such as Alcoholics Anonymous, domestic-violence centers, and drug-rehabilitation programs rather than make arrests.

In contemporary America, some say, police departments function a lot like business corporations. According to Harvard University's Executive Session on Policing, three generic kinds of "corporate strategies" guide American policing: (1) strategic policing, (2) problem-solving policing, and (3) community policing.[65]

Strategic policing, something of a holdover from the reform era, "emphasizes an increased capacity to deal with crimes that are not well controlled by traditional methods."[66] Strategic policing retains the traditional police goal of professional crime fighting but enlarges the enforcement target to include nontraditional kinds of criminals, such as serial offenders, gangs and criminal associations, drug-distribution networks, and sophisticated white-collar and computer criminals. To meet its goals, strategic policing generally makes use of innovative enforcement techniques, including intelligence operations, undercover sting operations, electronic surveillance, and sophisticated forensic methods.

strategic policing
A type of policing that retains the traditional police goal of professional crime fighting but enlarges the enforcement target to include nontraditional kinds of criminals, such as serial offenders, gangs and criminal associations, drug-distribution networks, and sophisticated white-collar and computer criminals. Strategic policing generally makes use of innovative enforcement techniques, including intelligence operations, undercover stings, electronic surveillance, and sophisticated forensic methods.

The other two strategies give greater recognition to Wilson's service style. **Problem-solving policing** (or problem-oriented policing) takes the view that many crimes are caused by existing social conditions in the communities. To control crime, problem-oriented police managers attempt to uncover and effectively address these underlying social problems. Problem-solving policing makes thorough use of community resources, such as counseling centers, welfare programs, and job-training facilities. It also attempts to involve citizens in crime prevention through education, negotiation, and conflict management. For example, police may ask residents of poorly maintained housing areas to clean up litter, install better lighting, and provide security devices for their houses and apartments in the belief that clean, well-lighted, secure areas are a deterrent to criminal activity.

problem-solving policing
A type of policing that assumes that many crimes are caused by existing social conditions within the community and that crimes can be controlled by uncovering and effectively addressing underlying social problems. Problem-solving policing makes use of community resources, such as counseling centers, welfare programs, and job-training facilities. It also attempts to involve citizens in crime prevention through education, negotiation, and conflict management.

The third and newest strategy, **community policing** (sometimes called community-oriented policing), goes a step beyond the other two. It has been described as "a philosophy based on forging a partnership between the police and the community, so that they can work together on solving problems of crime, [and] fear of crime and disorder, thereby enhancing the overall quality of life in their neighborhoods."[67] This approach addresses the causes of crime to reduce the fear of crime and social disorder through problem-solving strategies and police–community partnerships.

The community policing concept evolved from the early works of police researchers George Kelling and Robert Trojanowicz. Their studies of foot-patrol programs in Newark, New Jersey,[68] and Flint, Michigan,[69] showed that "police could develop more positive attitudes toward community members and could promote positive attitudes toward police if they spent time on foot in their neighborhoods."[70] Trojanowicz's *Community Policing,* published in 1990,[71] may be the definitive work on this topic.

community policing
"A collaborative effort between the police and the community that identifies problems of crime and disorder and involves all elements of the community in the search for solutions to these problems."[iv]

Community policing seeks to actively involve the community in the task of crime control by creating an effective working partnership between the community and the police.[72] Under the community policing ideal, community members and the police are expected to share responsibility for establishing and maintaining peaceful neighborhoods.[73] As a result, community policing permits members of the community to participate more fully than ever before in defining the police role. Police expert Jerome H. Skolnick says community policing is "grounded on the notion that, together, police and public are more effective and more humane coproducers of safety and public order than are the police alone."[74] According to Skolnick, community policing involves at least one of four elements: (1) community-based crime prevention, (2) reorientation of patrol activities to emphasize the importance of nonemergency services, (3) increased police accountability to the public, and (4) decentralization of command, including a greater use of civilians at all levels of police decision making.[75] As one writer explains it, "Community policing seeks to integrate what was traditionally seen as the different law enforcement, order maintenance and social service roles of the police. Central to the integration of these roles is a working partnership with the community in determining what neighborhood problems are to be addressed, and how."[76] Table 4 highlights the differences between traditional and community policing.

Community policing, or variations of it, has become the national mantra of the American police.

—Jack R. Greene
Northeastern University[v]

TABLE 4 Traditional versus Community Policing

Question	Traditional Policing	Community Policing
Who are the police?	The police are a government agency principally responsible for law enforcement.	The police are the public, and the public are the police. Police officers are paid to give full-time attention to the duties of every citizen.
What is the relationship of the police force to other public-service departments?	Priorities often conflict.	The police are one department among many responsible for improving the quality of life.
What is the role of the police?	To solve crimes.	To solve problems.
How is police efficiency measured?	By detection and arrest rates.	By the absence of crime and disorder.
What are the highest priorities?	Crimes that are high value (for example, bank robberies) and crimes with violence.	Whatever problems disturb the community most.
What do police deal with?	Incidents.	Citizens' problems and concerns.
What determines the effectiveness of police?	Response times.	Public cooperation.
What view do police take of service calls?	They deal with them only if there is no real police work to do.	They view them as a vital function and a great opportunity.
What is police professionalism?	Providing a swift, effective response to serious crime.	Keeping close to the community.
What kind of intelligence is most important?	Crime intelligence (study of particular crimes or series of crimes).	Criminal intelligence (information about the activities of individuals or groups).
What is the essential nature of police accountability?	Highly centralized; governed by rules, regulations, and policy directives; accountable to the law.	Local accountability to community needs.
What is the role of headquarters?	To provide the necessary rules and policy directives.	To foster organizational values.
What is the role of the press liaison department?	To keep the "heat" off operational officers so they can get on with the job.	To coordinate an essential channel of communication with the community.
How do the police regard prosecutions?	As an important goal.	As one tool among many.

Source: William R. Parks II, "Community Policing: A Foundation for Restorative Justice," Web posted at http://www.realjustice.org/Pages/t2000papers/t2000_wparks.html (accessed March 5, 2008). Originally printed in Malcolm K. Sparrow, *Implementing Community Policing* (Washington, DC: National Institute of Justice, 1988), pp. 8–9.

Community policing is a two-way street. It requires not only police awareness of community needs but also both involvement and crime-fighting action on the part of citizens themselves. As Detective Tracie Harrison of the Denver Police Department explains, "When the neighborhood takes stock in their community and they're serious they don't want crime, then you start to see crime go down. . . . They're basically fed up and know the police can't do it alone."[77]

A successful community policing program . . . requires officers to be well versed in cultural diversity and competent to perform tasks needed to accomplish their duties. This, obviously, requires considerable training for officers at all levels of the department.

—Samuel D. Pratcher
Chief of Police, Wilmington, Delaware

Police departments throughout the country continue to join the community policing bandwagon. A 2001 report by the Bureau of Justice Statistics (BJS) showed that state and local law enforcement agencies across the United States had nearly 113,000 full-time sworn personnel regularly engaged in community policing activities.[78] BJS noted that only about 21,000 officers would have been so categorized in 1997. At the time of the report, 64% of local police departments serving 86% of all residents had full-time officers engaged in some form of community policing activity, compared to 34% of departments serving 62% of all residents in 1997.

The Chicago Police Department launched its comprehensive community policing program, called Chicago's Alternative Policing Strategy (CAPS), in 1993. The development of a strategic plan for "reinventing the Chicago Police Department," from which CAPS evolved, included significant contributions by Mayor Richard M. Daley, who noted that community policing "means doing more than responding to calls for service and solving crimes. It means transforming the Department to support a new, proactive approach to preventing crimes before they occur. It means forging new partnerships among residents, business owners, community leaders, the police, and City services to solve long-range community problems."[79] Read the mayor's original report, written in conjunction with the Chicago Police Department, at Library Extra 4–6 at mycrimekit.com. Today, CAPS functions on a department-wide basis throughout the city. Learn more about CAPS via Web Extra 4–12 at mycrimekit.com. A review of Chicago's experience with community policing is available at Library Extra 4–7.

Web EXTRA

Library EXTRA

Although community policing efforts began in metropolitan areas, the community engagement and problem-solving spirit of these programs have spread to rural regions. Sheriffs' departments operating community policing programs sometimes refer to them as "neighborhood-oriented policing" in recognition of the decentralized nature of rural communities. A Bureau of Justice Assistance (BJA) report on neighborhood-oriented policing notes that "the stereotypical view is that police officers in rural areas naturally work more closely with the public than do officers in metropolitan areas."[80] This view, warns the BJA, may not be entirely accurate, and rural departments would do well "to recognize that considerable diversity exists among rural communities and rural law enforcement agencies." Hence, as in metropolitan areas, effective community policing requires the involvement of all members of the community in identifying and solving problems.

The emphasis on community policing continues to grow. Title I of the Violent Crime Control and Law Enforcement Act of 1994, known as the Public Safety Partnership and Community Policing Act of 1994, highlighted community policing's role in combating crime and funded (among other things) "increas[ing] the number of law enforcement officers involved in activities that are focused on interaction with members of the community on proactive crime control and prevention by redeploying officers to such activities." The avowed purposes of the Community Policing Act were to (1) substantially increase the number of law enforcement officers interacting directly with the public (through a program known as Cops on the Beat); (2) provide additional and more effective training to law enforcement officers to enhance their problem solving, service, and other skills needed in interacting with community members; (3) encourage development and implementation of innovative programs to permit community members to assist local law enforcement agencies in the prevention of crime; and (4) encourage development of new technologies to assist local law enforcement agencies in reorienting their emphasis from reacting to crime to preventing crime.

In response to the 1994 law, the U.S. Department of Justice created the Office of Community Oriented Policing Services (COPS). The COPS Office administered the funds necessary to add 100,000 community policing officers to our nation's streets—the number originally targeted by law. In 1999, the U.S. Department of Justice and COPS reached an important milestone by funding the last of the 100,000 officers ahead of schedule and under budget. Although the Community Policing Act originally provided COPS funding only through 2000, Congress has continued to fund COPS, making another $500 million available for the hiring of an additional 50,000 officers.[81] In 2002, the COPS Office adopted the theme "Homeland Security through Community Policing," which emphasizes the local police officer's crucial role in gathering

Web EXTRA

information on terrorist suspects—a topic that is discussed later in this chapter. The federal COPS Office can be found at Web Extra 4–13.

About the same time that the Violent Crime Control and Law Enforcement Act was passed, the Community Policing Consortium, based in Washington, D.C., began operations. Administered and funded by the U.S. Department of Justice's BJA, the consortium provides a forum for training and information exchange in the area of community policing. Members of the consortium include the International Association of Chiefs of Police, the National Sheriff's Association, the Police Executive Research Forum, the Police Foundation, and the National Organization of Black Law Enforcement Executives. Visit the Community Policing Consortium via Web Extra 4–14 at mycrimekit.com.

Web EXTRA

Community Policing and Antiterrorism

Noted police scholar David L. Carter says that "a common concern expressed by police executives is that the shift toward increased counterterrorism responsibilities may require a shift of resources away from community policing."[82] That concern, he says, is misdirected because community policing provides a natural conduit for information gathering and the development of counterterrorism intelligence. Information gathered by state and local police departments can be funneled to federal agencies, especially the FBI, that have been charged with developing national security intelligence. Carter notes that the "increased social tension" resulting from the current concern with terrorism has led to a greater need "to maintain a close, interactive dialogue between law enforcement and the community."

The importance of community policing in the fight against terrorism was reflected in comments made by FBI Director Robert Mueller during the summer of 2004. While pointing to photographs of seven terrorist suspects believed to be in the United States, Mueller said: "We need the support of the American people . . . to cooperate when called upon, as agents will be reaching out to many across the nation to help gather information and intelligence . . . to be aware of your surroundings and report anything suspicious . . . to 'BOLO' [Be On the LookOut] for those pictured above. . . . Have you seen them in your communities? Have you heard that someone might be helping them to hide? Do you have any idea where they might be? If so, we need you to come forward."[83]

Members of the U.S. Department of Justice's Global Intelligence Working Group (GIWG) also recognized the importance of community-oriented policing efforts when developing the national intelligence sharing plan. "Over the past decade," members noted, "thousands of community policing officers have been building close and productive relationships with the citizens they serve."[84] Community policing officers, they observed, "have immediate and unfettered access to local, neighborhood information as it develops. Citizens are aware of and seek out [community policing] officers to provide them with new information that may be useful to criminal interdiction or long-term problem solving. The positive nature of police/citizen relationships promotes a continuous and reliable transfer of information from one to the other. It is time to maximize the potential for community policing efforts to serve as a gateway of locally based information to prevent terrorism, and all other crimes."[85]

The Office for Domestic Preparedness (ODP) of the DHS describes the roles community policing can play in the intelligence process as including the following[86]:

If the grants for community policing begin to fade away . . . we may very well see the end of the community policing era.
—*Willard M. Oliver*
Sam Houston State University

- Provide materials to community policing contacts that may aid in the recognition of terrorism-related activities in order to make members of the community aware of suspicious actions, behaviors, and events
- Organize community meetings to emphasize prevention strategies, vigilance, and public awareness
- Ensure that members of the community are aware of the means of and processes for relaying information to police officers and police organizations
- Encourage crime prevention, proactive policing, and close working relationships between the police and the community

In any successful police–community interaction, information flows both ways. Consequently, while community policing efforts seek information from the public about offenders, police departments can also communicate critical information to the public in order to aid in crime prevention and fear reduction.

Critique of Community Policing

As some authors have noted, "Community policing has become the dominant theme of contemporary police reform in America."[87] Yet problems have plagued the movement since its inception.[88] For one thing, the range, complexity, and evolving nature of community policing programs make their effectiveness difficult to measure.[89] Moreover, citizen satisfaction with police performance can be difficult to conceptualize and quantify. Most early studies examined citizens' attitudes developed through face-to-face interaction with individual police officers. They generally found a far higher level of dissatisfaction with the police among African-Americans than among most other groups. Recent findings continue to show that the attitudes of African-Americans toward the police remain poor. The wider reach of these studies, however, led evaluators to discover that this dissatisfaction may be rooted in overall quality of life and type of neighborhood.[90] Since, on average, African-Americans continue to experience a lower quality of life than most other U.S. citizens and because they often live in neighborhoods characterized by economic problems, drug trafficking, and street crime, recent studies conclude that it is these conditions of life, rather than race, that are most predictive of citizen dissatisfaction with the police.

Pressures—from the community, from peers, from the circumstances in which police find themselves—are intense.

—James Q. Wilson
Former Chairman of the Board, the Police Foundation

Those who study community policing have often been stymied by ambiguity surrounding the concept of community.[91] Sociologists, who sometimes define the word *community* as "any area in which members of a common culture share common interests,"[92] tend to deny that a community needs to be limited geographically. Police departments, on the other hand, tend to define communities "within jurisdictional, district or precinct lines, or within the confines of public or private housing developments."[93] Robert Trojanowicz cautioned police planners that "the impact of mass transit, mass communications and mass media [has] widened the rift between a sense of community based on geography and one [based] on interest."[94]

Researchers who follow the police definition of the term *community* recognize that there may be little consensus within and between members of a local community about community problems and appropriate solutions. Robert Bohm and colleagues at the University of Central Florida have found, for example, that while there may be some "consensus about social problems and their solutions . . . the consensus may not be community-wide." It may, in fact, exist only among "a relatively small group of 'active' stakeholders who differ significantly about the seriousness of most of the problems and the utility of some solutions."[95]

Finally, there is continuing evidence that not all police officers or managers are willing to accept nontraditional images of police work. One reason is that the goals of community policing often conflict with standard police performance criteria (such as arrests), leading to a perception among officers that community policing is inefficient at best and, at worst, a waste of time.[96] Similarly, many officers are loathe to take on new responsibilities as service providers whose role is more defined by community needs and less by strict interpretation of the law.

Some authors have warned that **police subculture** is so committed to a traditional view of police work, which is focused almost exclusively on crime fighting, that efforts to promote community policing can demoralize an entire department, rendering it ineffective at its basic tasks.[97] As the Christopher Commission found following the 1992 Rodney King riots, "Too many . . . patrol officers view citizens with resentment and hostility; too many treat the public with rudeness and disrespect."[98] Some analysts warn that only when the formal values espoused by today's innovative police administrators begin to match those of rank-and-file officers can any police agency begin to perform well in terms of the goals espoused by community policing reformers.[99]

police subculture
A particular set of values, beliefs, and acceptable forms of behavior characteristic of American police with which the police profession strives to imbue new recruits. Socialization into the police subculture commences with recruit training and continues thereafter.

Some public officials, too, are unwilling to accept community policing. Ten years ago, for example, New York City Mayor Rudolph W. Giuliani criticized the police department's Community Police Officer Program (CPOP), saying that it "has resulted in officers doing too much social work and making too few arrests."[100] Similarly, many citizens are not ready to accept a greater involvement of the police in their personal lives. Although the turbulent, protest-prone years of the 1960s and early 1970s are long gone, some groups remain suspicious of the police. No matter how inclusive community policing programs become, it is doubtful that the gap between the police and the public will ever be entirely bridged. The police role of restraining behavior that violates the law will always produce friction between police departments and some segments of the community. Learn more about measures of police effectiveness, including those related to community policing, at Library Extra 4–8 at mycrimekit.com.

Library EXTRA

CJ News

Border Patrol Tries to Lure Retired Troops

The Border Patrol, scrambling to hire thousands of agents by the end of the year, is taking its recruiting efforts overseas to try to enlist military veterans as they leave their tours of duty.

Two teams of agency officers just returned from visiting six U.S. military bases in Germany where they persuaded nearly 100 veterans to apply to join the Homeland Security Department as border agents.

"This is a premier law enforcement agency, and we offer an opportunity for service on the front lines of the country," said Joe Arata, a recruiter for Homeland Security's Customs and Border Protection (CBP) division, which includes the Border Patrol.

CBP spokeswoman Tara Dunlop said the department plans to do more recruiting overseas.

The Homeland Security Department has been trying to drastically increase the number of agents along the nation's open borders.

The recruiting drive also comes at a time when law enforcement agencies nationwide, from city and state police departments to the FBI, are competing for hires.

In 2001, the Border Patrol had fewer than 10,000 agents covering the northern and southern borders with Canada and Mexico. A buildup in recent years has brought the ranks to 15,500.

President Bush has said he wanted the size of the agency doubled, to 20,000 agents, by the time he left office in January 2009.

The government has done some unconventional recruiting, plastering the Border Patrol's name on the side of a NASCAR racer and sending CBP's honor guard to professional football games in Texas and Michigan.

On April 19, Dunlop said, recruiters plan to blanket Ohio in a massive "Buckeye Blitz" recruiting effort that will cover the state's seven biggest cities. The agency routinely recruits at U.S. military bases and at job fairs within the USA.

In Germany, Arata said, recruiters went after military veterans looking for their next career and promoted the Border Patrol as an agency that pays up to $70,000 a year after three years. An average Army sergeant with four years' service would earn $26,964 base pay, plus housing and other benefits.

Union chief T. J. Bonner, president of the National Border Patrol Council, criticized the Bush administration for not hiring more agents sooner.

He said the push to hire thousands of agents so quickly inevitably will result in the same problems other major law enforcement agencies and police departments have run into when they hired too many officers too fast: poor training and inexperience.

"This will cause headaches down the road," Bonner said. "This is serious business. It takes a great deal of training and experience to mature. They should slow it down."

Before they are sent to the border to work, new agents go through 55 days of training at the Border Patrol's academy in Artesia, N.M.

If they don't speak Spanish, they take another 40 days of intensive language training, Dunlop said.

▲ U.S. Border Patrol agents setting out on patrol along the border with Mexico. The Border Patrol, which has been scrambling to hire thousands of agents, has started recruiting military veterans as they leave their tours of duty. Would you want to be a Border Patrol agent?
U.S. Department of Homeland Security

She said the academy averages 50 trainees per class and graduates an average of two classes per week.

For the latest in crime and justice news, visit the Talk Justice news feed at http://www.crimenews.info.

Source: Mimi Hall, "Border Patrol Tries to Lure Retired Troops," *USA Today*, April 13, 2008. Web available at http://www.usatoday.com/news/military/2008-04-13-Borderrecruit_N.htm. From USA TODAY, a division of Garnett Co., Inc. Reprinted by permission.

Evidence-Based Policing

The Law Enforcement Assistance Administration

In 1969, with the passage of the Omnibus Crime Control and Safe Streets Act, the U.S. Congress created the **Law Enforcement Assistance Administration (LEAA)**. LEAA was charged with combating crime through the expenditure of huge amounts of money in support of crime-prevention and crime-reduction programs. Some have compared the philosophy establishing LEAA to that which supported the American space program's goal of landing people on the moon: Put enough money into any problem, and it will be solved! Unfortunately, the crime problem was more difficult to address than the challenge of a moon landing; even after the expenditure of nearly $8 billion, LEAA had not come close to its goal. In 1982, LEAA expired when Congress refused it further funding.

Law Enforcement Assistance Administration (LEAA)
A now-defunct federal agency established under Title I of the Omnibus Crime Control and Safe Streets Act of 1968 to funnel federal funding to state and local law enforcement agencies.

The legacy of LEAA is an important one for police managers, however. The research-rich years of 1969 to 1982, supported largely through LEAA funding, have left a plethora of scientific findings relevant to police administration and, more importantly, have established a tradition of program evaluation within police management circles. This tradition, which is known as **scientific police management**, is a natural outgrowth of LEAA's insistence that every funded program contain a plan for its evaluation. *Scientific police management* refers to the application of social science techniques to the study of police administration for the purpose of increasing effectiveness, reducing the frequency of citizen complaints, and enhancing the efficient use of available resources. The heyday of scientific police management occurred in the 1970s, when federal monies were far more readily available to support such studies than they are today.

scientific police management
The application of social sciences techniques to the study of police administration for the purpose of increasing effectiveness, reducing the frequency of citizen complaints, and enhancing the efficient use of available resources.

LEAA was not alone in funding police research during the 1970s. On July 1, 1970, the Ford Foundation announced the establishment of a Police Development Fund totaling $30 million, to be spent over the next five years to support major crime-fighting strategies of police departments. This funding led to the establishment of the Police Foundation, which continues to exist today with the mission of "foster[ing] improvement and innovation in American policing."[101] Police Foundation–sponsored studies during the past 20 years have added to the growing body of scientific knowledge about policing.

Today, federal support for criminal justice research and evaluation continues under the NIJ and the BJS, both part of the Office of Justice Programs (OJP). OJP, created by Congress in 1984, provides federal leadership in developing the nation's capacity to prevent and control crime. The National Criminal Justice Reference Service (NCJRS), a part of NIJ, assists researchers nationwide in locating information applicable to their research projects. "Custom searches" of the NCJRS computer database can be done online and can yield abundant information in most criminal justice subject areas. NIJ also publishes a series of informative periodic reports, such as the *NIJ Journal* and *NIJ Research in Review*, which serve to keep criminal justice practitioners and researchers informed about recent findings. View the NIJ online publication list at Web Extra 4–15 at mycrimekit.com.

Web EXTRA

The Kansas City Experiment

History

By far the most famous application of social research principles to police management was the **Kansas City experiment** regarding preventive patrol.[102] The results of the year-long experiment were published in 1974. The study, sponsored by the Police Foundation, divided the southern part of Kansas City into 15 areas. Five of these "beats" were patrolled in the usual fashion. In another group of five beats, patrol activities were doubled. The final third of the beats received a novel treatment indeed: No patrols were assigned to them, and no uniformed officers entered that part of the city unless they were called. The program was kept secret, and citizens were unaware of the difference between the patrolled and unpatrolled parts of the city.

Kansas City experiment
The first large-scale scientific study of law enforcement practices. Sponsored by the Police Foundation, it focused on the practice of preventive patrol.

The results of the Kansas City experiment were surprising. Records of "preventable crimes" (those toward which the activities of patrol were oriented), such as burglary, robbery, auto theft, larceny, and vandalism, showed no significant differences in rate of occurrence among the three experimental beats. Similarly, citizens didn't seem to notice the change in patrol patterns in the two areas where patrol frequency was changed. Surveys conducted at the conclusion of the experiment showed no difference in citizens' fear of crime before and after the study. The 1974

Effective police work in the emerging society will depend less on the holster and more on the head.

—*Alvin Toffler*

You can't measure what a patrolman standing on a corner has prevented. There is no product at the end of a policeman's day.

—*Charles McCarthy*[vi]

study can be summed up in the words of the author of the final report: "The whole idea of riding around in cars to create a feeling of omnipresence just hasn't worked. . . . Good people with good intentions tried something that logically should have worked, but didn't."[103] This study has been credited with beginning the now-established tradition of scientific studies of policing.

A second Kansas City study focused on "response time."[104] It found that even consistently fast police response to citizen reports of crime had little effect either on citizen satisfaction with the police or on the arrest of suspects. The study uncovered the fact that most reports made to the police came only after a considerable amount of time had passed. Hence the police were initially handicapped by the timing of the report, and even the fastest police response was not especially effective.

Effects

The Kansas City studies greatly affected managerial assumptions about the role of preventive patrol and traditional strategies for responding to citizen calls for assistance. As Joseph Lewis, then director of evaluation at the Police Foundation, said, "I think that now almost everyone would agree that almost anything you do is better than random patrol."[105]

directed patrol
A police-management strategy designed to increase the productivity of patrol officers through the scientific analysis and evaluation of patrol techniques.

While the Kansas City studies called into question some basic assumptions about patrol, it remains the backbone of police work. New patrol strategies for the effective utilization of human resources have led to various activities of **directed patrol**. One form of directed patrol varies the number of officers involved in patrolling according to the time of day or the frequency of reported crimes within an area. The idea is to put the most officers on the street where and when crime is most prevalent. Wilmington, Delaware, was one of the first cities to make use of split-force patrol, in which only a part of the patrol force performs routine patrol.[106] The remaining officers respond to calls for service, take reports, and conduct investigations.

In response to the Kansas City study on response time, some cities have prioritized calls for service,[107] ordering a quick police response only when crimes are in progress or when serious crimes have occurred. Less significant offenses, such as minor larcenies and certain citizen complaints, are handled by using the mail or by having citizens come to the police station to make a report.

Early policing studies, such as the Kansas City patrol experiment, were designed to identify and probe some of the basic assumptions that guided police work. The initial response to many such studies was "Why should we study that? Everybody knows the answer already!" As in the case of the Kansas City experiment, however, it soon became obvious that conventional wisdom was not always correct. Scientific studies of special significance to law enforcement are summarized in Table 5.

Law enforcement is a tool of power.

—*Alvin Toffler*

Evidence-Based Policing Today

At the close of the twentieth century, noted police researcher Lawrence W. Sherman addressed an audience of criminal justice policy makers, scholars, and practitioners at the Police Founda-

▶ Members of the Kansas City (Missouri) Police Department being briefed on security measures for a planned city tour by President George W. Bush. Scientific police management was given early credence by studies of preventive patrol undertaken in Kansas City in 1974. What have scientific studies of the police since that time demonstrated?
Courtesy of the Media Office of the Kansas City Missouri Police Department

TABLE 5 Selected Scientific Studies in Law Enforcement

Year	Study Name	Focus
2007	Tactical Intelligence-Driven Enforcement, Operation TIDE (Detroit)	Successful effort to reduce violent crime in targeted areas by identifying, arresting, and prosecuting the most violent gun-using offenders
2005	Effectiveness of Designated Driver Programs	Designated driver campaigns to reduce highway accidents
2002	Reducing Gun Violence (Indianapolis)	Targeted police patrols to reduce gun crime and violence
2001	Boston's Operation Ceasefire Evaluation	Citywide effort to reduce gun violence, especially gang-related homicides
1999	National Evaluation of Weed-and-Seed Programs	Weed-and-seed programs in eight states
1998	Community Policing in Action (Indianapolis)	Police and citizen cooperation and neighborhood security
1994	Kansas City Gun Experiment	Supplemental police patrol to reduce gun crime
1992	New York City Police Department's Cadet Corps Study	Level of education among officers, and hiring of minority officers
1992	Metro-Dade Spouse Abuse Experiment Replication (Florida)	Replication of a 1984 Minneapolis study
1991	Quality Policing in Madison, Wisconsin	Community policing and participatory police management
1990	Minneapolis "Hot Spot" Patrolling	Intensive patrol of problem areas
1987	Newport News (Virginia) Problem-Oriented Policing	Police solutions to community crime Problems
1986	Crime Stoppers: A National Evaluation	Media crime-reduction programs
1986	Reducing Fear of Crime in Houston and Newark	Strategies for fear reduction among urban populations
1984	Minneapolis Domestic Violence Experiment	Effective police action in domestic-violence situations
1981	Newark Foot Patrol Experiment	Costs versus benefits of foot patrol
1977	Cincinnati Team Policing Experiment	Team versus traditional policing
1977	Patrol Staffing in San Diego	One- versus two-officer units
1976	Police Response Time (Kansas City)	Citizen satisfaction with police response
1976	Police and Interpersonal Conflict	Police intervention in domestic and other disputes
1976	Managing Investigations	Detective–patrol officer teams
1976	Kansas City Peer Review Panel	Improvement in police behavior
1974	Kansas City Preventive Patrol Experiment	Effectiveness of police patrol

tion in Washington, D.C., and called for a new approach to American policing that would use research to guide and evaluate practice. "Police practices should be based on scientific evidence about what works best," Sherman told his audience. Sherman's lecture, titled "Evidence-Based Policing: Policing Based on Science, Not Anecdote,"[108] popularized the term **evidence-based policing (EBP)**. EBP, says Sherman, "is the use of best available research on the outcomes of police work to implement guidelines and evaluate agencies, units, and officers."[109] In other words, EBP uses research into everyday police procedures to evaluate current practices and to guide officers and police executives in future decision making. In any discussion of EBP, it is important to remember that the word *evidence* refers to scientific evidence, not criminal evidence.

evidence-based policing (EBP)
The use of best available research on the outcomes of police work to implement guidelines and evaluate agencies, units, and officers.[vii]

"The basic premise of evidence-based practice," says Sherman, "is that we are all entitled to our own opinions, but not to our own facts."[110] Our own facts, or our beliefs about the way things should be done, says Sherman, often turn out to be wrong. During the civil rights movement of the 1960s and 1970s, for example, police executives in many areas took a heavy-handed approach in their attempts to control demonstrators. Images of tear gas filling the streets, high-pressure fire hoses being aimed at marchers, and police dogs biting fleeing demonstrators symbolize that era for many people. This heavy-handed approach had unintended consequences and served to inflame protesters. Situations that might have otherwise been contained with simple crowd-control tactics and the use of physical barriers became largely uncontrollable. Sherman reminds us that "the mythic power of subjective and unstructured wisdom holds back every field and keeps it from systematically discovering and implementing what works best in repeated tasks." In 2008, the EBP movement gained additional traction when Sherman taught a course on the topic to police leaders from a number of countries at Cambridge University's Institute of Criminology. "There is a need for much more scientific guidance behind the way police are used," Sherman told representatives at Cambridge. "In Britain, the government has invested heavily in police resources, but we have not established how to obtain best value for money in deploying those resources. This is an opportunity for us to do that, working in a collaborative way with the police and tying together the education of police officers and the research base of criminology."[111]

Today's EBP model has been called the single "most powerful force for change" in policing today.[112] Leading the movement toward EBP are organizations like the FBI's Futures Working Group and the Campbell Crime and Justice Group. FBI Supervisory Special Agent Carl J. Jensen III, a member of the Futures Working Group, notes that in the future "successful law enforcement executives will have to be consumers and appliers of research." They won't need to be researchers themselves, Jensen notes, "but they must use research in their everyday work."[113] The Campbell Crime and Justice Group, which emphasizes the use of experimental studies in crime and justice policy making, can be accessed via **Web Extra 4–16** at mycrimekit.com.

Web EXTRA

Discretion and the Individual Officer

police discretion
The opportunity of law enforcement officers to exercise choice in their daily activities.

Even as law enforcement agencies struggle to adapt to the threats posed by international terrorism, individual officers continue to retain considerable discretion in terms of their actions. **Police discretion** refers to the exercise of choice by law enforcement officers in the decision to investigate or apprehend, the disposition of suspects, the carrying out of official duties, and the application of sanctions. As one author has observed, "Police authority can be, at once, highly specific and exceedingly vague."[114] Decisions to stop and question someone, arrest a suspect, and perform many other police tasks are made solely by individual officers and must often be made quickly and in the absence of any close supervision. Kenneth Culp Davis, who pioneered the study of police discretion, says, "The police make policy about what law to enforce, how much to enforce it, against whom, and on what occasions."[115] To those who have contact with the police, the discretionary authority exercised by individual officers is of greater significance than all the department manuals and official policy statements combined.

Patrolling officers often decide against a strict enforcement of the law, preferring instead to handle situations informally. Infractions where minor law violations are committed, crimes committed out of the officer's presence where the victim refuses to file a complaint, and certain violations of the criminal law where the officer suspects that sufficient evidence to guarantee a conviction is lacking may all lead to discretionary action short of arrest. Although the widest exercise of discretion is more likely in routine situations involving relatively less serious violations of the law, serious and clear-cut criminal behavior may occasionally result in discretionary decisions not to make an arrest. Drunk driving, possession of controlled substances, and assault are but a few examples of crimes in which on-the-scene officers may decide warnings or referrals are more appropriate than arrest.

Studies of police discretion have found that a number of factors influence the discretionary decisions of individual officers:

Every day [as a police officer] you get to be a different person. In that regard it is the best job in the world. You get to play many roles: rabbi, lawyer, social worker, psychiatrist.
—*Salvatore Maniscalco*
New York Police Officer

- *Background of the officer.* Law enforcement officers bring to the job all of their previous life experiences. Values shaped through early socialization in the family, as well as attitudes acquired from ongoing socialization, influence the decisions an officer will make. If the officer has learned prejudice against certain ethnic groups, it is likely that this prejudice will manifest itself in enforcement decisions. Officers who place a high value on the nuclear family may handle spousal abuse, child abuse, and domestic disputes in predetermined ways.

- *Characteristics of the suspect.* Some officers treat men and women differently. A police friend of the author has voiced the belief that women "are not generally bad . . . but when they do go bad, they go very bad." His official treatment of women has been tempered by this belief. Very rarely will this officer arrest a woman, but when he does, he spares no effort to see her incarcerated. Other characteristics of the suspect that may influence police decisions include demeanor, style of dress, and grooming.[116] Belligerent suspects are often seen as "asking for it" and as challenging police authority. Well-dressed suspects are likely to be treated with deference, but poorly groomed suspects can expect less respectful treatment. Suspects sporting personal styles with a message—biker's attire, unkempt beards, outlandish haircuts, and other nonconformist styles—are more likely to be arrested than are others.
- *Department policy.* Discretion, while not entirely subject to control by official policy, can be influenced by it. If a department has targeted certain kinds of offenses or if supervisors adhere to strict enforcement guidelines and closely monitor dispatches and other communications, the discretionary release of suspects will be quite rare.
- *Community interest.* Public attitudes toward certain crimes will increase the likelihood of arrest for suspected offenders. Contemporary attitudes toward crimes involving children—including child sex abuse, sale of drugs to minors, domestic violence involving children, and child pornography—have all led to increased and strict enforcement of laws governing such offenses across the nation. Communities may identify particular problems affecting them and ask law enforcement to respond. For example, the city of Fayetteville, North Carolina, which is adjacent to a major military base, was plagued some years ago by a downtown area notorious for prostitution and massage parlors. Once the community voiced its concern over the problem and clarified its economic impact on the city, the police responded with a series of highly effective arrests, which eliminated massage parlors within city limits. Departments that require officers to live in the areas they police recognize that community interests affect citizens and officers alike.
- *Pressure from victims.* Victims who refuse to file a complaint are commonly associated with certain crimes, such as spousal abuse, the "robbery" of drug merchants, and assaults on customers of prostitutes. When victims refuse to cooperate with the police, there is often little that can be done. On the other hand, some victims are very vocal in insisting that their victimization be recognized and dealt with. Victim-assistance groups, such as People Assisting Victims and the Victim's Assistance Network, have sought to keep pressure on police departments and individual investigators to ensure the arrest and prosecution of suspects.
- *Disagreement with the law.* Some laws lack a popular consensus. Among them are laws relating to many "victimless" offenses, such as gambling, homosexuality, lesbianism, prostitution, drug use, pornography, and some crimes involving alcohol. Not all of these behaviors are even crimes in certain jurisdictions. Gambling is legal in Atlantic City, New Jersey; aboard cruise ships; on some Native American reservations; and in parts of Nevada. Many states have now legalized homosexuality, lesbianism, and most forms of sexual behavior between consenting adults. Prostitution is officially sanctioned in portions of Nevada, and some drug offenses have been "decriminalized," with offenders being ticketed rather than arrested. Unpopular laws are not likely to bring much attention from law enforcement officers. Sometimes such crimes are regarded as just "part of the landscape" or as the consequence of laws that have not kept pace with a changing society. When arrests do occur, it may be because individuals investigated for more serious offenses were caught in the act of violating an unpopular statute. For example, drug offenders arrested in the middle of the night may be "caught in the act" of an illegal sexual activity when the police break in. Charges may then include "crime against nature" as well as possession or sale of drugs.

▲ An officer writing a traffic ticket. Police officers wield a wide degree of discretion, and an individual officer's decision to enforce a particular law or to effect an arrest varies not just with the law's applicability to a particular set of circumstances but with the officer's subjective judgments about the nature of appropriate enforcement activity. What other factors influence police discretion?
David Young-Wolff/PhotoEdit Inc.

The foundations of a successful community policing strategy are the close, mutually beneficial ties between police and community members.
—Bureau of Justice Statistics

Citizens are coproducers of justice.

—*Bureau of Justice Statistics, Princeton Project*

On the other hand, certain behaviors that are not law violations and that may even be protected by guarantees of free speech may be annoying, offensive, or disruptive according to the normative standards of a community or the personal standards of an officer. Where the law has been violated and the guilty party is known to the officer, the evidence necessary for a conviction in court may be "tainted" or in other ways not usable. Gary Sykes, in recognizing these possibilities, says, "One of the major ambiguities of the police task is that officers are caught between two profoundly compelling moral systems: justice as due process . . . and conversely, justice as righting a wrong as part of defining and maintaining community norms."[117] In such cases, discretionary police activity may take the form of "street justice" and may approach vigilantism.

- *Available alternatives.* Police discretion can be influenced by the officer's awareness of alternatives to arrest. Community treatment programs, including outpatient drug and alcohol counseling, psychiatric or psychological services, and domestic dispute–resolution centers, may be considered by officers looking for a way out of official action.
- *Personal practices of the officer.* Some officers view the violation of particular laws less seriously than do other officers. The police officer who has an occasional marijuana cigarette with friends at a party may be inclined to deal less harshly with minor drug offenders than nonuser officers. The officer who routinely exceeds speed limits while driving the family car may be lenient with speeders encountered while on duty.

Summary

- The fundamental police mission in democratic societies includes five components: (1) enforcing the law (especially the criminal law), (2) apprehending offenders, (3) preventing crime, (4) preserving domestic peace, and (5) providing the community with needed enforcement-related services.
- Contemporary American policing presents a complex picture that is structured along federal, state, and local lines. Each federal agency empowered by Congress to enforce specific statutes has its own enforcement arm. In addition, tasks deemed especially significant by state legislatures, such as patrol of the highways, have resulted in the creation of specialized law enforcement agencies under state jurisdiction. For many of today's local law enforcement agencies, created under county and municipal authority, patrol retains a central role—with investigation, interrogation, and numerous support roles rounding out an increasingly specialized profession.
- Police administration involves the activities of managing, controlling, directing, and coordinating police personnel, resources, and activities in the service of preventing crime, apprehending criminals, recovering stolen property, and performing regulatory and helping services. Virtually all American law enforcement organizations are formally structured among divisions and along lines of authority. Roles within police agencies usually fall into one of two categories: line and staff. Line operations are field or supervisory activities directly related to daily police work; staff operations include support roles such as administration.
- Three historical policing epochs are identified in this chapter: (1) the political era, (2) the reform era, and (3) the community policing era. The contemporary emphasis on terrorism prevention, alongside the need for a rapid response to threats of terrorism, has led to what some see as a new era: policing to secure the homeland. Homeland security policing relies upon the established framework of community policing for the purpose of gathering intelligence to prevent terrorism.
- Community policing is built on the principle that police departments and the communities they serve should work together as partners in the fight against crime. Police–community relations programs represent a movement away from an exclusive police emphasis on the apprehension of law violators and signify an increasing level of positive police–citizen interaction.
- Evidence-based policing consists of the use of best available research on the outcomes of police work to implement guidelines and evaluate agencies, units, and officers. EBP uses research into everyday police procedures to evaluate current practices and to guide officers

and police executives in future decision making. When discussing EBP, it is important to remember that the word *evidence* refers to scientific evidence, not criminal evidence. Today's EBP model has been called the single "most powerful force for change" in policing today.

- Police discretion refers to the opportunity for police officers to exercise choice in their enforcement activities. Put another way, discretion refers to the exercise of choice by law enforcement officers in the decision to investigate or apprehend, the disposition of suspects, the carrying out of official duties, and the application of sanctions. The widest exercise of discretion can be found in routine situations involving relatively less serious violations of the law, but serious criminal behavior may also result in discretionary decisions not to make an arrest.

Key Concepts

Terms

chain of command
community policing
CompStat
crime prevention
directed patrol
evidence-based policing (EBP)
Kansas City experiment
Law Enforcement Assistance Administration (LEAA)
legalistic style
line operations
police–community relations (PCR)
police discretion
police management
police subculture
problem-solving policing
quality-of-life offense
scientific police management
service style
sheriff
span of control
staff operations
strategic policing
team policing
watchman style

Questions for Review

1. What are the basic purposes of policing in democratic societies? How are they consistent with one another? In what ways might they be inconsistent?
2. What are the three major levels of public law enforcement described in this chapter? Why do we have so many different types of enforcement agencies in the United States? What problems, if any, do you think are created by such a diversity of agencies?
3. What are the various features of police administration described in this chapter? What is meant by chain of command?
4. What stages of historical development did American police agencies experience? How did policing styles differ by historical era?
5. What is community policing? How does it differ from traditional policing? Does community policing offer a real opportunity to improve policing services in the United States? Why or why not?
6. What is meant by police discretion? How does the practice of discretion by today's officers affect their departments and the policing profession as a whole?

To participate in an online discussion of these topics and others, join the CJ Brief e-mail discussion list at mycrimekit.com.

Web Quest

Visit at least four of the federal law enforcement agencies listed under Web Extra 4–5 at mycrimekit.com. Use the online information that each site provides to describe each agency in terms of its history, organization, and mission. Do the same with at least four of the state-level law enforcement agencies listed under Web Extra 4–10 and with at least four of the local law enforcement agencies listed under Web Extra 4–11. If you would like to use federal, state, or local agencies other than those listed at mycrimekit.com, you can find many such sites in the Cybrary at http://www.cybrary.info.

Assemble a notebook (or disk) containing the information you have gathered, organized by level and by agency. Submit the material to your instructor if asked to do so.

To complete this Web Quest online, go to the Web Quest module in Chapter 4 of the *Criminal Justice: A Brief Introduction* Companion Website at mycrimekit.com.

Notes

i. Quote of the Day, *New York Times*, May 30, 2002.
ii. Sam S. Souryal, *Police Administration and Management* (St. Paul, MN: West, 1977), p. 261.
iii. Robert Kennedy, *The Pursuit of Justice*, part 3, "Eradicating Free Enterprise in Organized Crime" (New York: Harper and Row, 1964).
iv. Community Policing Consortium, *What Is Community Policing?* (Washington, DC: Community Policing Consortium, 1995).
v. Jack R. Greene, "Community Policing in America: Changing the Nature, Structure, and Function of the Police," in Julie Horney, ed., *Criminal Justice 2000*, Vol. 3 (Washington, DC: Department of Justice, 2000), p. 301.
vi. Cited in Anderson's Police Pages at http://www.spiritwindsstudio.com/app/quotatio.htm.
vii. Lawrence W. Sherman, *Evidence-Based Policing* (Washington, DC: Police Foundation, 1998), p. 3.

---

1. Major Cities Chiefs Association, *Terrorism: The Impact on State and Local Law Enforcement* (Intelligence Commanders Conference Report), June 2002. Web posted at http://www.neiassociates.org/mccintelligencereport.pdf (accessed September 30, 2005).
2. "Police, Protestors Clash Near Miami Trade Talks," CNN.com, November 20, 2003. Web posted at http://www.cnn.com/2003/US/South/11/20/miami.protests (accessed June 3, 2006).
3. "Demonstrators, Police Clash during Free Trade Talks," *USA Today*, November 20, 2003. Web posted at http://www.usatoday.com/news/nation/2003-11-20-miami-protests_x.htm (accessed June 3, 2007).
4. Andrew P. Sutor, *Police Operations: Tactical Approaches to Crimes in Progress* (St. Paul, MN: West, 1976), p. 68, citing Peel.
5. C. D. Hale, *Police Patrol: Operations and Management* (Englewood Cliffs, NJ: Prentice Hall, 1994).
6. Victor Kappeler et al., *The Mythology of Crime and Criminal Justice* (Prospect Heights, IL: Waveland Press, 1996).
7. Darl H. Champion and Michael K. Hooper, *Introduction to American Policing* (New York: McGraw-Hill, 2003), p. 133.
8. Details for this story come from Ted Ottley, "Bad Day Dawning," Court TV's Crime Library. Web posted at http://www.crimelibrary.com/serial_killers/notorious/mcveigh/dawning_1.html (accessed June 22, 2003).
9. Ibid.
10. This definition has been attributed to the National Crime Prevention Institute (see http://www.lvmpd.com/community/crmtip25.htm).
11. See Steven P. Lab, *Crime Prevention at a Crossroads* (Cincinnati, OH: Anderson, 1997).
12. See the Philadelphia Police Department's Operation Identification website at http://www.ppdonline.org/ppd4_home_opid.htm.
13. The term *CompStat* is sometimes interpreted to mean computer statistics, comparative statistics, or computer comparative statistics, although it is generally accorded no specific meaning.
14. Learn more about CompStat from Vincent E. Henry, *The COMPSTAT Paradigm: Management Accountability in Policing, Business, and the Public Sector* (Flushing, NY: Looseleaf Law Publications, 2002).
15. Much of the information in this section comes from the Philadelphia Police Department, "The COMPSTAT Process." Web posted at http://www.ppdonline.org/ppd_compstat.htm (accessed May 28, 2007).
16. See Ned Levine, *CrimeStat: A Spatial Statistics Program for the Analysis of Crime Incident Locations,* version 2.0 (Houston, TX: Ned Levine and Associates; Washington, DC: National Institute of Justice, May 2002).
17. Robert H. Langworthy and Lawrence P. Travis III, *Policing in America: A Balance of Forces,* 2nd ed. (Upper Saddle River, NJ: Prentice Hall, 1999), p. 194.
18. Adapted from Bronx County (New York) District Attorney's Office, "Quality of Life Offenses," December 24, 2002. Web posted at http://www.bronxda.net/fighting_crime/quality_of_life_offenses.html (accessed June 20, 2003).
19. Other violations may be involved as well. On December 29, 2000, for example, Judge John S. Martin, Jr., of the Federal District Court in Manhattan, ruled that homeless people in New York City could be arrested for sleeping in cardboard boxes in public. Judge Martin held that a city Sanitation Department regulation barring people from abandoning cars or boxes on city streets could be applied to the homeless who were sleeping in boxes.
20. Norman Siegel, executive director of the New York Civil Liberties Union, as reported in "Quality of Life Offenses Targeted," *Western Queens Gazette*, November 22, 2000. Web posted at http://www.qgazette.com/News/2000/1122/Editorial_pages/e01.html (accessed June 12, 2007).
21. The broken windows thesis was first suggested by George L. Kelling and James Q. Wilson in "Broken Windows: The Police and Neighborhood Safety," *Atlantic Monthly*, March 1982. The article is available online at http://www.theatlantic.com/politics/crime/windows.htm.
22. For a critique of the broken windows thesis, see Bernard E. Harcourt, *Illusion of Order: The False Promise of Broken Windows Policing* (Cambridge, MA: Harvard University Press, 2001).
23. Peter Schuler, "Law Professor Harcourt Challenges Popular Policing Method, Gun Violence Interventions," *Chicago Chronicle*, Vol. 22, No. 12 (March 20, 2003), http://chronicle.uchicago.edu/030320/harcourt.shtml (accessed August 28, 2008).
24. George L. Kelling, Catherine M. Coles, and James Q. Wilson, *Fixing Broken Windows: Restoring Order and Reducing Crime in Our Communities,* reprint (New York: Touchstone, 1998).
25. Charles R. Swanson, Leonard Territo, and Robert W. Taylor, *Police Administration: Structures. Processes, and Behavior,* 4th ed. (Upper Saddle River, NJ: Prentice Hall, 1998), p. 1.
26. Lorraine Mazerolle et al., *Managing Citizen Calls to the Police: An Assessment of Nonemergency Call Systems* (Washington, DC: National Institute of Justice, 2001), p. 1-1.
27. The Hastings (Minnesota) Police Department website at http://www.ci.hastings.mn.us/Police/deptnews.htm (accessed May 24, 2006).
28. Government Accounting Office, "Federal Law Enforcement: Survey of Federal Civilian Law Enforcement Functions and Authorities," December 2006 (highlights of GAO-07-121).
29. U.S. Department of Justice, *A Proud History, a Bright Future: Careers with the FBI,* pamphlet (Washington, DC: DOJ, October 1986), p. 1.
30. Much of the information in this section comes from U.S. Department of Justice, *The FBI: The First Seventy-Five Years* (Washington, DC: U.S. Government Printing Office, 1986).
31. Some of the information in this section is adapted from Federal Bureau of Investigation, "Facts and Figures 2003." Web posted at http://www.fbi.gov/priorities/priorities.htm (accessed March 25, 2006).
32. Telephone conversation with FBI officials, April 21, 1995.
33. Public Laws 98-473 and 99-474.
34. Information in this section comes from Christopher H. Asplen, "National Commission Explores Its Future," *NIJ Journal* (January 1999), pp. 17–24.
35. The DNA Identification Act is Section 210301 of the Violent Crime Control and Law Enforcement Act of 1994.
36. Federal Bureau of Investigation, "NDIS Statistics." Web posted at http://www.fbi.gov/hq/lab/codis/clickmap.htm (accessed January 4, 2007).

37. Much of the information in this paragraph comes from the FBI Academy website at http://www.fbi.gov/hq/td/academy/academy.htm (accessed March 3, 2002).
38. "Attorney General Ashcroft and Deputy Attorney General Thompson Announce Reorganization and Mobilization of the Nation's Justice and Law Enforcement Resources," U.S. Department of Justice press release, November 8, 2001.
39. Testimony of Robert S. Mueller III, director of the Federal Bureau of Investigation, before the Senate Committee on Intelligence of the U.S. Senate, February 16, 2005.
40. Henry M. Wrobleski and Karen M. Hess, *Introduction to Law Enforcement and Criminal Justice,* 4th ed. (St. Paul, MN: West, 1993), p. 34.
41. Ibid., p. 35.
42. New York City Police Department website at http://nyc.gov/html/nypd/html/faq/faq_police.shtml#1 (accessed August 28, 2008).
43. Brian A. Reaves, *Census of State and Local Law Enforcement Agencies, 2004* (Washington, DC: Bureau of Justice Statistics, 2007).
44. Ibid. See also Matthew J. Hickman and Brian A. Reaves, *Local Police Departments, 2003* (Washington, DC: Bureau of Justice Statistics, 2006).
45. Note, however, that New York City jails may have daily populations that, on a given day, exceed those of Los Angeles County.
46. Los Angeles County Sheriff's Department, "About LASD." Web posted at http://www.lasd.org/aboutlasd/about.html (accessed June 25, 2006).
47. The Police Assessment Resource Center, *The Los Angeles County Sheriff's Department—19th Semiannual Report* (Los Angeles: PARC, February 2005); and telephone communication with Deputy Ethan Marquez, L.A. County Sheriff's Department, Custodial Division, January 24, 2002.
48. Brian A. Reaves, *Census of State and Local Law Enforcement Agencies, 2004* (Washington, DC: Bureau of Justice Statistics, 2007).
49. Office of the Director of National Intelligence (ODNI), "Second National Fusion Center Conference Held to Foster Greater Collaboration," news release, March 20, 2008.
50. Estimates of the number of centers vary, and classifying a work group as a "fusion center" depends largely on the perspective assumed. A March 2008 press release by the federal Office of the Director of National Intelligence (see previous note) put the number of operational fusion centers at more than 50 in 46 states.
51. Michael C. Mines, "Statement before the House Committee on Homeland Security, Subcommittee on Intelligence, Information Sharing, and Terrorism Risk Assessment," September 27, 2007.
52. "State and Local Fusion Centers Face Challenges as They Grow," *Criminal Justice Newsletter*, September 18, 2007, p.1.
53. The elements of this definition draw on the now-classic work by O. W. Wilson, *Police Administration* (New York: McGraw-Hill, 1950), pp. 2–3.
54. Charles R. Swanson, Leonard Territo, and Robert W. Taylor, *Police Administration: Structures, Processes, and Behavior* (Upper Saddle River, NJ: Prentice Hall, 1998), p. 167.
55. For more information on the first three categories, see Francis X. Hartmann, "Debating the Evolution of American Policing," *Perspectives on Policing,* No. 5 (Washington, DC: National Institute of Justice, 1988).
56. Willard M. Oliver, "The Homeland Security Juggernaut: The End of the Community Policing Era," *Crime and Justice International*, Vol. 20, No. 79 (2004), pp. 4–10. See also Willard M. Oliver, "The Era of Homeland Security: September 11, 2001 to . . .," *Crime and Justice International*, Vol. 21, No. 85 (2005), pp. 9–17.
57. Gene Stephens, "Policing the Future: Law Enforcement's New Challenges," *The Futurist*, March/April 2005, pp. 51–57.
58. To learn more about Wilson, see "Presidential Medal of Freedom Recipient James Q. Wilson." Web posted at http://www.medaloffreedom.com/JamesQWilson.htm (accessed January 5, 2006).
59. James Q. Wilson, *Varieties of Police Behavior: The Management of Law and Order in Eight Communities* (Cambridge, MA: Harvard University Press, 1968).
60. Independent Commission on the Los Angeles Police Department, *Report of the Independent Commission on the Los Angeles Police Department* (Los Angeles: The Commission, 1991).
61. Gary W. Sykes, "Street Justice: A Moral Defense of Order Maintenance Policing," *Justice Quarterly*, Vol. 3, No. 4 (December 1986), p. 505.
62. Egon Bittner, "Community Relations," in Alvin W. Cohn and Emilio C. Viano, eds., *Police Community Relations: Images, Roles, Realities* (Philadelphia: J. B. Lippincott, 1976), pp. 77–82.
63. Paul B. Weston, *Police Organization and Management* (Pacific Palisades, CA: Goodyear, 1976), p. 159.
64. Hale, *Police Patrol.*
65. Mark H. Moore and Robert C. Trojanowicz, "Corporate Strategies for Policing," *Perspectives on Policing,* No. 6 (Washington, DC: National Institute of Justice, 1998).
66. Ibid., p. 6.
67. Community Policing Consortium, *Community Policing Is Alive and Well* (Washington, DC: Community Policing Consortium, 1995), p. 1.
68. George L. Kelling, *The Newark Foot Patrol Experiment* (Washington, DC: Police Foundation, 1981).
69. Robert C. Trojanowicz, "An Evaluation of a Neighborhood Foot Patrol Program," *Journal of Police Science and Administration*, Vol. 11 (1983), pp. 410–419.
70. Bureau of Justice Assistance, *Understanding Community Policing: A Framework for Action* (Washington, DC: Bureau of Justice Statistics, 1994), p. 10.
71. Robert C. Trojanowicz and Bonnie Bucqueroux, *Community Policing* (Cincinnati, OH: Anderson, 1990).
72. Moore and Trojanowicz, "Corporate Strategies for Policing," p. 8.
73. S. M. Hartnett and W. G. Skogan, "Community Policing: Chicago's Experience," *National Institute of Justice Journal* (April 1999), pp. 2–11.
74. Jerome H. Skolnick and David H. Bayley, *Community Policing: Issues and Practices around the World* (Washington, DC: National Institute of Justice, 1988).
75. Ibid.
76. William L. Goodbody, "What Do We Expect New-Age Cops to Do?" *Law Enforcement News* (April 30, 1995), pp. 14, 18.
77. Sam Vincent Meddis and Desda Moss, "Many 'Fed-Up' Communities Cornering Crime," *USA Today*, May 22, 1995, p. 8A.
78. Matthew J. Hickman and Brian A. Reaves, *Community Policing in Local Police Departments, 1997 and 1999*, Bureau of Justice Statistics Special Report (Washington, DC: U.S. Department of Justice, 2001).
79. Richard M. Daley and Matt L. Rodriguez, *Together We Can: A Strategic Plan for Reinventing the Chicago Police Department* (Chicago: Chicago Police Department, 1993). Web posted at http://www.ci.chi.il.us/CommunityPolicing/Statistics/Reports/TWC.pdf (accessed March 5, 2007).
80. Bureau of Justice Assistance, *Neighborhood-Oriented Policing in Rural Communities: A Program Planning Guide* (Washington, DC: Bureau of Justice Statistics, 1994), p. 4.
81. See the COPS Office website at http://www.usdoj.gov/cops (accessed January 22, 2008).
82. David L. Carter, *Law Enforcement Intelligence: A Guide for State, Local, and Tribal Law Enforcement Agencies* (Washington, DC: U.S. Department of Justice, 2004), p. 39.
83. FBI, "Protecting America from Terrorist Attacks," Press BOLO for US, May 26, 2004. Web posted at http://www.fbi.gov/page2/may04/bolo052604.htm (accessed August 28, 2007).
84. Office of Justice Programs, *The National Criminal Intelligence Sharing Plan* (Washington, DC: U.S. Department of Justice, 2005), p. 4.
85. International Association of Chiefs of Police, *Recommendations from the IACP Intelligence Summit, Criminal Intelligence*

Sharing: A National Plan for Intelligence-Led Policing at the Local, State and Federal Levels (Alexandria, VA: IACP, 2002), p. 2.

86. Office for Domestic Preparedness, *Guidelines for Homeland Security* (Washington, DC: U.S. Department of Homeland Security, 2003).
87. Jihong Zhao, Nicholas P. Lovrich, and Quint Thurman, "The Status of Community Policing in American Cities: Facilitators and Impediments Revisited," *Policing*, Vol. 22, No. 1 (1999), p. 74.
88. For a good critique and overview of community policing, see Geoffrey P. Alpert et al., *Community Policing: Contemporary Readings* (Prospect Heights, IL: Waveland Press, 1998).
89. Jack R. Greene, "Community Policing in America: Changing the Nature, Structure, and Function of the Police," in U.S. Department of Justice, *Criminal Justice 2000,* Vol. 3 (Washington, DC: DOJ, 2000), pp. 299–370.
90. Michael D. Reisig and Roger B. Parks, "Experience, Quality of Life, and Neighborhood Context: A Hierarchical Analysis of Satisfaction with Police," *Justice Quarterly*, Vol. 17, No. 3 (2000), p. 607.
91. Mark E. Correla, "The Conceptual Ambiguity of Community in Community Policing: Filtering the Muddy Waters," *Policing*, Vol. 23, No. 2 (2000), pp. 218–233.
92. Adapted from Donald R. Fessler, *Facilitating Community Change: A Basic Guide* (San Diego: San Diego State University, 1976), p. 7.
93. Daniel W. Flynn, *Defining the "Community" in Community Policing* (Washington, DC: Police Executive Research Forum, 1998).
94. Robert C. Trojanowicz and Mark H. Moore, *The Meaning of Community in Community Policing* (East Lansing: Michigan State University's National Neighborhood Foot Patrol Center, 1988).
95. Robert M. Bohm, K. Michael Reynolds, and Stephen T. Holms, "Perceptions of Neighborhood Problems and Their Solutions: Implications for Community Policing," *Policing*, Vol. 23, No. 4 (2000), p. 439.
96. Ibid., p. 442.
97. Malcolm K. Sparrow, "Implementing Community Policing," *Perspectives on Policing*, No. 9 (Washington, DC: National Institute of Justice, 1988).
98. "L. A. Police Chief: Treat People Like Customers," *USA Today*, March 29, 1993, p. 13A.
99. Robert Wasserman and Mark H. Moore, "Values in Policing," *Perspectives in Policing*, No. 8 (Washington, DC: National Institute of Justice, 1988), p. 7.
100. "New York City Mayor Sparks Debate on Community Policing," *Criminal Justice Newsletter*, Vol. 25, No. 2 (January 18, 1994), p. 1.
101. Thomas J. Deakin, "The Police Foundation: A Special Report," *FBI Law Enforcement Bulletin* (November 1986), p. 2.
102. George L. Kelling et al., *The Kansas City Patrol Experiment* (Washington, DC: Police Foundation, 1974).
103. Kevin Krajick, "Does Patrol Prevent Crime?" *Police* (September 1978), pp. 11–13 (quoting George Kelling).
104. William Bieck and David Kessler, *Response Time Analysis* (Kansas City, MO: Board of Police Commissioners, 1977). See also J. Thomas McEwen et al., *Evaluation of the Differential Police Response Field Test: Executive Summary* (Alexandria, VA: Research Management Associates, 1984); and Lawrence Sherman, "Policing Communities: What Works?" in Michael Tonry and Norval Morris, eds., *Crime and Justice: An Annual Review of Research,* Vol. 8 (Chicago: University of Chicago Press, 1986), pp. 343–386.
105. Krajick, "Does Patrol Prevent Crime?"
106. Ibid.
107. Ibid.
108. "Evidence-Based Policing," Police Foundation press release, March 17, 1998. Web posted at www.policefoundation.org/docs/evidence.html (accessed January 5, 2006).
109. Lawrence W. Sherman, *Evidence-Based Policing* (Washington, DC: Police Foundation, 1998), p. 3.
110. Much of the information in this section comes from Sherman, *Evidence-Based Policing.*
111. "World's Top Police Officers to Study at Cambridge University," University of Cambridge, News and Events, December 3, 2007. Web available at http://www.admin.cam.ac.uk/news/dp/2007120301 (accessed July 5, 2008).
112. Carl J. Jensen III, "Consuming and Applying Research: Evidence-Based Policing," *Police Chief*, Vol. 73, No. 2 (February 2006). Web posted at http://policechiefmagazine.org/magazine/index.cfm?fuseaction=display_arch&article_id=815&issue_id=22006 (accessed May 17, 2007).
113. Ibid.
114. Howard Cohen, "Overstepping Police Authority," *Criminal Justice Ethics* (summer/fall 1987), pp. 52–60.
115. Kenneth Culp Davis, *Police Discretion* (St. Paul, MN: West, 1975).
116. See, for example, Robert Shepard Engel, James J. Sobol, and Robert E. Worden, "Further Exploration of the Demeanor Hypothesis: The Interaction of Effects of Suspects' Characteristics and Demeanor on Police Behavior," *Justice Quarterly*, Vol. 17, No. 2 (2000), p. 235.
117. Sykes, "Street Justice," p. 505.

Policing: Legal Aspects

5

Chapter Outline

- Introduction
- The Abuse of Police Power
- Individual Rights
- Search and Seizure
- Arrest
- The Intelligence Function

Learning Objectives

After reading this chapter, you should be able to

- Identify legal restraints on police action, and list instances of the abuse of police power.
- Explain how the Bill of Rights and democratically inspired legal restraints help to protect personal freedoms in our society.
- Describe the circumstances under which police officers may properly conduct searches or seize property.
- Define *arrest*, and describe how popular depictions of the arrest process may not be consistent with legal understandings of the term.
- Describe the intelligence function, including police interrogations, and explain the role of *Miranda* warnings.

" "Yeah," the detective mumbled. "Fifteen guys. You might want to think about that. Only two of us ..." He shook his head. "Sneaking a bunch of cops into a neighborhood like this is going to be like trying to sneak the sun past a rooster...." As he started up the stairs, Angelo reached not for his gun but for his wallet. He took out a Chase Manhattan calendar printed on a supple but firm slip of plastic. He flicked the card at Rand. "I'll open the door with this. You step in and freeze them." "Jesus Christ, Angelo," the agent almost gasped. "We can't do that. We haven't got a warrant." "Don't worry about it, kid," Angelo said, drawing up to the second door on the right on the second floor. "It ain't a perfect world." "

—Larry Collins and Dominique Lapierre[1]

Introduction

▶▶▶ Hear the author discuss this chapter at mycrimekit.com.

Early on a cold November morning in 2006, 23-year-old Sean Bell left a bachelor party at New York City's Kalua Cabaret strip club with two of his friends and climbed into his gray Nissan Altima. Although Bell, who was to be married later that day, didn't know it, undercover New York City Police Department (NYPD) officers had been staking out the club in an investigation into suspected drug and gun dealing there. What happened next remains unclear, but after a chaotic confrontation between Bell's group and the police, followed by a crash involving a van carrying some of the NYPD officers and Bell's car, officers opened fire on the vehicle, firing 50 rounds before the shooting ended. Bell died at the scene, and his friends were seriously injured. The officers later said that they thought Bell and his companions were armed and that they might have been drug dealers. It was not clear if Bell ever knew that the men, dressed in plain clothes, were police officers; he may have thought that he was being robbed or carjacked. On March 17, 2007, a Queens, New York, grand jury indicted three of the detectives involved in the case, charging two with first- and second-degree manslaughter and a third with reckless endangerment.

Shortly after the indictments were handed down, demonstrators paraded through Queens demanding justice for Bell, who was African-American, as were two of the three officers indicted in the shooting. New York City Mayor Michael R. Bloomberg urged residents to "respect the result of our justice system." He added, "It also needs to be said that being a police officer ... is a very dangerous job. And although a trial will decide whether crimes were committed in this case, day in and day out the N.Y.P.D. does an incredible job under very difficult circumstances."[2] The mayor's words seemed prophetic when, on April 25, 2008, Judge Arthur J. Cooperman found the defendants not guilty of any crime. Describing the evidence, Judge Cooperman said that it was reasonable for the detectives to fear that someone in the crowd had been

▲ Protesters at a rally in Queens, New York, demanding answers for the fatal police shooting of Sean Bell as he left a bachelor's party on the night before his wedding in 2006. Bell, who was unarmed, was killed by NYPD officers who fired 50 rounds at him and two friends after they drove Bell's car into a minivan carrying plainclothes officers who were investigating the club where the party took place. The officers were found "not guilty" in a 2008 trial. Might "contagious shooting" explain what happened that night?
Reuters/Mike Segar/Landov Media

carrying a gun on the night that the shooting took place. He added that many of the prosecution's witnesses, including Bell's friends and the two wounded victims, were simply not believable.[3]

The Bell shooting was reminiscent of the death of West African immigrant Amadou Diallo, who was killed in a hail of 41 bullets in 1999 as he stood in a New York City doorway and apparently reached for his identification after being told to raise his hands. Diallo reportedly had a poor command of the English language and may not have understood police commands to stay still. Officers had apparently mistaken him for a suspect they were pursuing. Although the officers who shot Diallo were charged with second-degree murder, they were later acquitted.[4] Law enforcement experts said that what happened in both the Bell and Diallo cases might be explained by "contagious shooting"—gunfire that spreads among officers "in the adrenaline-pumping, split-second heat of the moment"[5] who believe that they, or their colleagues, are facing a deadly threat.[6]

Not all questionable cases of police use of force involve shootings. Two months after Hurricane Katrina devastated New Orleans, members of the city's overworked police department became embroiled in a public relations nightmare when an Associated Press Television News (APTN) crew working in the French Quarter filmed two white officers beating an apparently dazed and unresisting 64-year-old African-American retired elementary school teacher named Robert Davis. A third officer could be seen grabbing and shoving an APTN producer working with the news team. As the incident ended, Davis, whose family had property in the city, was arrested and charged with public intoxication, resisting arrest, battery on a police officer, and public intimidation. He later told reporters that he hadn't had an alcoholic drink in 25 years but that trouble began when he asked a mounted officer for directions.[7] New Orleans Police Superintendent Warren Riley was quick to condemn the officers' behavior. "The actions that were observed on this video are certainly unacceptable [to] this department," Riley said as he announced the firings of officers Lance Schilling and Robert Evangelist, as well as the suspension without pay of another officer, S. M. Smith. Soon afterward, the U.S. Department of Justice announced that it was opening a civil rights investigation into the incident.[8]

The Abuse of Police Power

The Rodney King Incident

National publicity surrounding the Davis beating was considerably less intense than that which centered on the 1991 videotaped beating of motorist Rodney King by Los Angeles Police Department (LAPD) officers. King, an unemployed 25-year-old African-American, was stopped by LAPD officers for an alleged violation of motor vehicle laws. Police said King had been speeding and had refused to stop for a pursuing patrol car. Officers claimed to have clocked his 1988 Hyundai at 115 mph on the suburban Los Angeles Foothill Freeway—even though the car's manufacturer later said the vehicle was not capable of speeds over 100 mph.

Eventually King did stop, but then officers of the LAPD appeared to attack him, shocking him twice with electronic stun guns and striking him with nightsticks and fists. Kicked in the stomach, face, and back, he was left with 11 skull fractures, missing teeth, a crushed cheekbone, and a broken ankle. A witness told reporters that she heard King begging officers to stop the beating but that they "were all laughing, like they just had a party."[9] King eventually underwent surgery for brain injuries. Officers involved in the beating claimed that King, at 6 feet 3 inches and 225 pounds, appeared strung out on phencyclidine (PCP) and that he and his two companions made the officers feel threatened.[10]

The entire incident was captured on videotape by an amateur photographer with a night-sensitive video camera. The two-minute videotape was repeatedly broadcast over national television and was picked up by hundreds of local TV stations. The furor that erupted over the tape led to the ouster of LAPD Chief Daryl Gates and initiated a Justice Department review of law enforcement practices across the country.[11]

In 1992, a California jury found four police defendants not guilty—a verdict that resulted in days of rioting across Los Angeles. A year later, however, in the spring of 1993, two of the officers, Sergeant Stacey Koon and Officer Laurence Powell, were found guilty in federal court of denying King his constitutional right "not to be deprived of liberty without due process of law, including the right to be ... free from the intentional use of unreasonable force."[12] Later that year, both were sentenced to two and a half years in prison, far less than might have been expected under federal sentencing guidelines. They were released from prison in December 1995, and a three-year court battle over whether federal sentencing guidelines were violated was resolved in the officers' favor in 1996. Officers Theodore Briseno and Timothy Wind were exonerated at the federal level.

In 1994, King settled a civil suit against the city of Los Angeles for a reported $3.8 million. Observers later concluded that King himself was not a model citizen. At the time of the beating, he was on parole after having served time in prison for robbery. Since then he has been arrested on a variety of other charges, including battery, assault, drug use, and indecent exposure.[13] Regardless, King's 1991 beating continues to serve as a rallying point for individual-rights activists concerned with ensuring that citizens remain protected from the abuse of police power in an increasingly conservative society. Learn more about the Rodney King incident and its ramifications at Web Extra 5–1 at mycrimekit.com.

Web EXTRA

This chapter shows how no one is above the law—even the police. It describes the legal environment surrounding police activities, from search and seizure through arrest and the interrogation of suspects. As we shall see throughout, democratically inspired legal restraints on the police help ensure individual freedoms in our society and prevent the development of a police state in America. Like anything else, however, the rules by which the police are expected to operate are in constant flux, and their continuing development forms the meat of this chapter. For a police perspective on these issues, visit Web Extra 5–2 at mycrimekit.com.

Web EXTRA

A Changing Legal Climate

Bill of Rights
The popular name given to the first ten amendments to the U.S. Constitution, which are considered especially important in the processing of criminal defendants.

The Constitution of the United States is designed—especially in the **Bill of Rights**—to protect citizens against abuses of police power (Table 1). However, the legal environment surrounding the police in modern America is much more complex than it was just 45 years ago. Up until that time, the Bill of Rights was largely given only lip service in criminal justice proceedings around the country. In practice, law enforcement, especially on the state and local levels, revolved around tried-and-true methods of search, arrest, and interrogation that sometimes left little room for recognition of individual rights. Police operations during that period were often far more informal than they are today, and investigating officers frequently assumed that they could come and go as they pleased, even to the extent of invading someone's home without a search warrant. Interrogations could quickly turn violent, and the infamous "rubber hose," which was reputed to leave few marks on the body, was probably more widely used during the questioning of suspects than many would like to believe. Similarly, "doing things by the book" could mean the use of thick telephone books for beating suspects, since the books spread out

There is more law at the end of the policeman's nightstick than in all the decisions of the Supreme Court.

—Alexander "Clubber" Williams
Late-nineteenth-century New York police officer

TABLE 1 Constitutional Amendments of Special Significance to the American System of Justice

This Right is Guaranteed	By this Amendment
The right against unreasonable searches and seizures	Fourth
The right against arrest without probable cause	Fourth
The right against self-incrimination	Fifth
The right against "double jeopardy"	Fifth
The right to due process of law	Fifth, Sixth, Fourteenth
The right to a speedy trial	Sixth
The right to a jury trial	Sixth
The right to know the charges	Sixth
The right to cross-examine witnesses	Sixth
The right to a lawyer	Sixth
The right to compel witnesses on one's behalf	Sixth
The right to reasonable bail	Eighth
The right against excessive fines	Eighth
The right against cruel and unusual punishments	Eighth
The applicability of constitutional rights to all citizens, regardless of state law or procedure	Fourteenth

the force of blows and left few visible bruises. Although such abuses were not necessarily day-to-day practices in all police agencies and although they probably did not characterize more than a relatively small proportion of all officers, such conduct pointed to the need for greater control over police activities so that even the potential for abuse might be curtailed.

In the 1960s the U.S. Supreme Court, under the direction of Chief Justice Earl Warren (1891–1974), accelerated the process of guaranteeing individual rights in the face of criminal prosecution. Warren Court rulings bound the police to strict procedural requirements in the areas of investigation, arrest, and interrogation. Later rulings scrutinized trial court procedures and enforced humanitarian standards in sentencing and punishment. The Warren Court also seized on the Fourteenth Amendment and made it a basis for judicial mandates requiring that both state and federal criminal justice agencies adhere to the Court's interpretation of the Constitution. The apex of the individual-rights emphasis in Supreme Court decisions was reached in the 1966 case of ***Miranda* v. *Arizona***,[14] which established the famous requirement of a police "rights advisement" of suspects. In wielding its brand of idealism, the Warren Court (which held sway from 1953 until 1969) accepted the fact that a few guilty people would go free so that the rights of the majority of Americans would be protected.

In the decades since the Warren Court, a new conservative Court philosophy has resulted in Supreme Court decisions that have brought about what some call a "reversal" of Warren-era advances in the area of individual rights. By creating exceptions to some of the Warren Court's rules and restraints and by allowing for the emergency questioning of suspects before they are read their rights, a changed Supreme Court has recognized the realities attending day-to-day police work and the need of ensuring public safety.

Individual Rights

Checks and Balances

The Constitution of the United States provides for a system of checks and balances among the legislative, judicial, and executive (presidential) branches of government. One branch of government is always held accountable to the other branches. The system is designed to ensure that no one individual or agency can become powerful enough to usurp the rights and freedoms guaranteed under the Constitution. Without accountability, it is possible to imagine a police state in which the power of law enforcement is absolute and is related more to political considerations and personal vendettas than to objective considerations of guilt or innocence.

Under our system of government, courts become the arena for dispute resolution, not just between individuals but between citizens and the agencies of government. After handling by the justice system, people who feel they have not received the respect and dignity due them under the law can appeal to the courts for redress. Such appeals are usually based on procedural issues and are independent of more narrow considerations of guilt or innocence.

In this chapter, we focus on cases that are important for having clarified constitutional guarantees concerning individual liberties within the criminal justice arena. They involve issues that most of us have come to call *rights*. Rights are concerned with procedure, that is, with how police and other actors in the criminal justice system handle each part of the process of dealing with suspects. Rights violations have often become the basis for the dismissal of charges, the acquittal of defendants, or the release of convicted offenders after an appeal to a higher court.

Due Process Requirements

As you may recall, due process is a requirement of the Fifth, Sixth, and Fourteenth Amendments to the U.S. Constitution, which mandates that justice system officials respect the rights of accused individuals throughout the criminal justice process. Most due process requirements of relevance to the police pertain to three major areas: (1) evidence and investigation (often called *search* and *seizure*), (2) arrest, and (3) interrogation. Each of these areas has been addressed by a plethora of landmark U.S. Supreme Court decisions. **Landmark cases** produce substantial changes both in the understanding of the requirements of due process and in the practical day-to-day operations of the justice system. Another way to think of landmark cases is that they help significantly in clarifying the "rules of the game"—the procedural guidelines by which the police and the rest of the justice system must abide.

landmark case
A precedent-setting court decision that produces substantial changes both in the understanding of the requirements of due process and in the practical day-to-day operations of the justice system.

[The police] are not perfect; we don't sign them up on some far-off planet and bring them into police service. They are products of society, and let me tell you, the human product today often is pretty weak.
—*Daryl Gates*
Former Los Angeles Police Chief

The three areas we will discuss have been well defined by decades of court precedent. Keep in mind, however, that judicial interpretations of the constitutional requirement of due process are constantly evolving. As new decisions are rendered and as the composition of the Court itself changes, major changes and additional refinements may occur.

Search and Seizure

The Fourth Amendment to the U.S. Constitution declares that people must be secure in their homes and in their persons against unreasonable searches and seizures. This amendment reads, "The right of the people to be secure in their persons, houses, papers, and effects, against unreasonable searches and seizures, shall not be violated, and no Warrants shall issue, but upon probable cause, supported by Oath or affirmation, and particularly describing the place to be searched, and the persons or things to be seized." The Fourth Amendment, a part of the Bill of Rights, was adopted by Congress and became effective on December 15, 1791.

The language of the Fourth Amendment is familiar to all of us. "Warrants," "probable cause," and other phrases from the amendment are frequently cited in editorials, TV news shows, and daily conversations about **illegally seized evidence**. It is the interpretation of these phrases over time by the U.S. Supreme Court, however, that has given them the impact they have on the justice system today.

illegally seized evidence
Any evidence seized without regard to the principles of due process as described by the Bill of Rights. Most illegally seized evidence is the result of police searches conducted without a proper warrant or of improperly conducted interrogations.

The Exclusionary Rule

The first landmark case concerning search and seizure was that of ***Weeks* v. *U.S*.** (1914).[15] Freemont Weeks was suspected of using the U.S. mail to sell lottery tickets, a federal crime. Weeks was arrested, and federal agents went to his home to conduct a search. They had no search warrant, because at the time investigators did not routinely use warrants. They confiscated many incriminating items of evidence, as well as some of the suspect's personal possessions, including clothes, papers, books, and even candy.

Prior to trial, Weeks's attorney asked that the personal items be returned, claiming that they had been illegally seized under Fourth Amendment guarantees. A judge agreed and ordered the materials returned. On the basis of the evidence that was retained, however, Weeks was convicted in federal court and was sentenced to prison. He appealed his conviction through other courts, and his case eventually reached the U.S. Supreme Court. There, his lawyer reasoned that if some of his client's belongings had been illegally seized, then the remainder of them were also taken improperly. The Court agreed and overturned Weeks's earlier conviction.

The *Weeks* case forms the basis of what is now called the **exclusionary rule**, which holds that evidence illegally seized by the police cannot be used in a trial. The rule acts as a control over police behavior and specifically focuses on the failure of officers to obtain warrants authorizing them either to conduct searches or to effect arrests (especially where arrest may lead to the acquisition of incriminating statements or to the seizure of physical evidence).

exclusionary rule
The understanding, based on U.S. Supreme Court precedent, that incriminating information must be seized according to constitutional specifications of due process or it will not be allowed as evidence in a criminal trial.

It is important to note, incidentally, that Freemont Weeks could have been retried on the original charges following the Supreme Court decision in his case. He would not have faced double jeopardy because he was in fact not *finally* convicted on the earlier charges. His conviction was nullified on appeal, resulting in neither a conviction nor an acquittal. Double jeopardy becomes an issue only when a defendant faces retrial on the same charges following acquittal at his or her original trial or when the defendant is retried after having been convicted.

The decision of the Supreme Court in the *Weeks* case was binding, at the time, only on federal officers because only federal agents were involved in the illegal seizure. Learn more about *Weeks* v. *U.S*. at Library Extra 5–1 at mycrimekit.com.

Library EXTRA

Problems with Precedent

The *Weeks* case demonstrates the Supreme Court's power in enforcing what we have called the "rules of the game." It also lays bare the much more significant role that the Court plays in rule creation. Until the *Weeks* case was decided, federal law enforcement officers had little reason to think they were acting in violation of due process. Common practice had not required that they obtain a warrant before conducting searches. The rule that resulted from *Weeks* was new, and it would forever alter the enforcement activities of federal officers.

The *Weeks* case reveals that the present appeals system, focusing as it does on the "rules of the game," presents a ready-made channel for the guilty to go free. There is little doubt that Freemont Weeks had violated federal law; a jury had convicted him. Yet he escaped punishment because of the illegal behavior of the police—behavior that, until the Court ruled, had been widely regarded as legitimate. Even if the police knowingly violate the principles of due process, which they sometimes do, our sense of justice is compromised when the guilty go free. Famed Supreme Court Justice Benjamin Cardozo (1870–1938) once complained, "The criminal is to go free because the constable has blundered."

Analysts of the criminal justice system have long considered three possible solutions to this problem. The first suggests that rules of due process, especially when newly articulated by the courts, should be applied only to future cases, not to the initial case in which they are stated. The justices in the *Weeks* case, for example, might have said, "We are creating the 'exclusionary rule' based on our realization in this case. Law enforcement officers are obligated to use it as a guide in all future searches. However, insofar as the guilt of Mr. Weeks was decided by a jury under rules of evidence existing at the time, we will let that decision stand."

▲ An officer patting down a suspect. The legal environment surrounding the police helps ensure proper official conduct. In a stop like this, inappropriate behavior on the part of the officer can later become the basis for civil or criminal action against the officer and the police department. What might constitute "inappropriate behavior"?
John Boykin/PhotoEdit Inc.

A second solution would punish police officers or other actors in the criminal justice system who act illegally but would not allow the guilty defendant to escape punishment. This solution would be useful in applying established precedent where officers and officials had the benefit of clearly articulated rules and should have known better. Under this arrangement, any officer today who intentionally violates due process guarantees might be suspended, be reduced in rank, lose pay, or be fired. Some authors have suggested that decertification might serve as "an alternative to traditional remedies for police misconduct."[16] Departments that employed the decertification process would punish violators by removing their certification as police officers. Because officers in every state except Hawaii[17] must meet the certification requirements of state boards in order to hold employment, some authors argue that decertification would have a much more personal (and therefore more effective) impact on individual officers than the exclusionary rule ever could.[18]

A third possibility would allow the Supreme Court to address theoretical questions involving issues of due process. Concerned supervisors and officials could ask how the Court would rule "if ...". As things now work, the Court can only address real cases and does so on a **writ of *certiorari***, in which the Court orders the record of a lower court case to be prepared for review.

writ of *certiorari*
A writ issued from an appellate court for the purpose of obtaining from a lower court the record of its proceedings in a particular case. In some states, this writ is the mechanism for discretionary review. A request for review is made by petitioning for a writ of *certiorari*, and the granting of review is indicated by the issuance of the writ.

The difficulty with these solutions, however, is that they would substantially reduce the potential benefits available to defendants through the appeals process. Hence they would effectively eliminate the process itself.

The Fruit of the Poisonous Tree Doctrine

The Court continued to build on the rules concerning evidence with its ruling in ***Silverthorne Lumber Co. v. U.S.*** (1920).[19] In 1918, Frederick Silverthorne and his sons operated a lumber company and were accused of avoiding payment of federal taxes. When asked to turn over the company's books to federal investigators, the Silverthornes refused, citing their Fifth Amendment privilege against self-incrimination.

Shortly thereafter, federal agents descended on the lumber company and, without a search warrant, seized the company's books. The Silverthornes' lawyer appeared in court and asked that the materials be returned, citing the need for a search warrant, as had been established in the *Weeks* case. The prosecutor agreed, and the books were returned to the Silverthornes.

The Silverthornes came to trial thinking they would be acquitted because the evidence against them was no longer in the hands of prosecutors. In a surprise move, however, the prosecution introduced photographic copies that they had made from the returned books. The Silverthornes were convicted in federal court. Their appeal eventually reached the U.S. Supreme Court. The Court ruled that just as illegally seized evidence cannot be used in a trial,

Freedom or Safety? You Decide.

The Conch Republic

The citizens of the tiny island town of Key West, Florida, have always prided themselves on being different. Hence, it should have come as no surprise when, on April 23, 1982, the island's mayor issued a proclamation seceding from the United States and declaring Key West a new nation named the "Conch Republic." The decision to withdraw from the Union came in reaction to a 19-mile-long traffic jam created when authorities from the Task Force on South Florida Crime set up a checkpoint on U.S. 1—the only highway traversing the Florida Keys. Law enforcement officers used the checkpoint to examine the driver's licenses of travelers leaving the Keys and meticulously searched vehicles looking for contraband and illegal immigrants. At the time of the roadblock, at least one law enforcement official estimated that up to 80% of all marijuana and cocaine entering the nation was coming through southern Florida, and Key West was said to be the "drug-smuggling capital of America."

In 1982, as today, the primary legal industry in Key West was tourism, and island officials feared that long delays at police roadblocks would keep visitors away. Protests about the roadblock were lodged with the White House, the Florida governor's office, and U.S. congressional offices—all to no avail. Then-Vice President George H. W. Bush's press secretary issued a statement saying, "You have illegal immigrants and crime on the streets.... There's going to be some inconvenience. I think most people would want a little inconvenience compared to having grocery stores held up and senior citizens mugged in the streets."

Island officials, however, didn't agree and hired an attorney to seek an injunction against the roadblock, arguing that it violated the Fourth Amendment's restriction against unreasonable search and seizure. "Unless they see the hand of a Haitian sticking out of the trunk or marijuana wafting out of the car, they don't have probable cause," said David Horan, the town's attorney. When the roadblock remained in place, island leaders issued a secession proclamation and promptly applied to the U.S. government for foreign aid.

For its part, the U.S. government ignored the secession movement, but the roadblock was quietly removed two months after it was put in place. Island residents, however, still celebrate April 23 as the day when, as one former Key West mayor put it, "the brave men and women of the Conch Republic gave up their lunch hour to secede from the United States."

YOU DECIDE

Although Key West's secession was never taken very seriously by the people involved in it in 1982, it illustrates an undeniable tension between freedom and security that continues to characterize American society today. How would you describe that tension in your own words? Are Americans today more or less willing to sacrifice some of their personal rights and freedoms in the interest of safety than they were 25 years ago?

Reference: Cynthia Crossen, "To Fight Car Searches, a Florida City Declared Itself a Foreign Nation," *Wall Street Journal* online, January 19, 2005. Web posted at http://online.wsj.com/article_print/0,SB110609219909929528,00.html.

neither can evidence be used that *derives* from an illegal seizure.[20] The conviction of the Silverthornes was overturned, and they were set free.

fruit of the poisonous tree doctrine
A legal principle that excludes from introduction at trial any evidence later developed as a result of an illegal search or seizure.

The *Silverthorne* case articulated a new principle of due process that today we call the **fruit of the poisonous tree doctrine**. This doctrine is potentially far reaching. Complex cases developed after years of police investigative effort may be ruined if defense attorneys are able to demonstrate that the prosecution's case was originally based on a search or seizure that violated due process. In such cases, it is likely that all evidence will be declared "tainted" and will become useless.

The Warren Court (1953–1969)

Before the 1960s, the U.S. Supreme Court intruded only infrequently on the overall operation of the criminal justice system at the state and local levels. As one author has observed, however, the 1960s were a time of youthful idealism, and "without the distraction of a depression or world war, individual liberties were examined at all levels of society."[21] Hence, while the exclusionary rule became an overriding consideration in federal law enforcement from the time that it was first defined by the Supreme Court in the *Weeks* case in 1914, it was not until 1961 that the Court, under Chief Justice Earl Warren, decided a case that was to change the face of American law enforcement forever. That case, ***Mapp* v. *Ohio*** (1961),[22] made the exclusionary rule applicable to criminal prosecutions at the state level. Beginning with the now-famous *Mapp* case, the Warren Court charted a course that would guarantee nationwide recognition of individual rights, as it understood them, by agencies at all levels of the criminal justice system.

The public safety exception [to the exclusionary rule] was intended to protect the police, as well as the public, from danger.
—U.S. v. Brady *819 F.2d 884 (1987)*

Police officers examining suspected controlled substances after a raid. The exclusionary rule means that illegally gathered evidence cannot be used later in court, requiring that police officers pay close attention to how they gather and handle evidence. How did the exclusionary rule come into being?
Chris O'Meara/AP Wide World Photos

Application of the Exclusionary Rule to the States

Mapp v. *Ohio* (1961) made the exclusionary rule applicable to criminal prosecutions at the state level. Dolree Mapp was suspected of harboring a fugitive wanted in a bombing. When Ohio police officers arrived at her house, she refused to admit them. Eventually, they forced their way in. During the search that ensued, pornographic materials were uncovered. Mapp was arrested and eventually convicted under a state law that made possession of such materials illegal.

Because of prior decisions by the U.S. Supreme Court, including *Wolf* v. *Colorado* (1949),[23] officers believed that the exclusionary rule did not apply to agents of state and local law enforcement. However, in a wide-reaching and precedent-setting decision, Mapp's conviction was overturned on appeal by a majority of Warren Court justices who decided that the U.S. Constitution, under the Fourteenth Amendment's due process guarantee, mandates that state and local law enforcement officers be held to the same standards of accountability as federal officers. The justices said that since the evidence against Mapp had been illegally obtained, it could not be used against her in any court of law in the United States. The precedent established in *Mapp* v. *Ohio* firmly applied the principles developed in *Weeks* and *Silverthorne* to trials in state courts, making police officers at all levels accountable to the rule of law, which, as embodied in the words of the Fourteenth Amendment, reads, "No State shall ... deprive any person of life, liberty, or property, without due process of law; nor deny to any person within its jurisdiction the equal protection of the laws." Learn more about the case of *Mapp* v. *Ohio* at Library Extra 5–2 at mycrimekit.com.

Library EXTRA

Searches Incident to Arrest

Another important Warren-era case, that of ***Chimel* v. *California*** (1969),[24] involved both arrest and search activities by local law enforcement officers. Ted Chimel was convicted of the burglary of a coin shop based on evidence gathered at his home, where he was arrested. Officers, armed with an arrest warrant but not a search warrant, had taken Chimel into custody when they arrived at his residence and had proceeded with a search of his entire three-bedroom house, including the attic, a small workshop, and the garage. Although officers realized that the search might be challenged in court, they justified it by claiming that it was conducted not so much to uncover evidence but as part of the arrest process. Searches that are conducted incident to arrest, they argued, are necessary for the officers' protection and should not require a search warrant. Coins taken from the burglarized coin shop were found in various places in Chimel's residence, including the garage, and were presented as evidence against him at trial.

Chimel's appeal eventually reached the U.S. Supreme Court, which ruled that the search of Chimel's residence, although incident to arrest, became invalid when it went beyond the person arrested and the area subject to that person's "immediate control." The thrust of the Court's decision was that searches during arrest can be made to protect arresting officers but that with-

TABLE 2 Implications of *Chimel* v. *California* (1969)

What Arresting Officers May Search
The defendant
The physical area within easy reach of the defendant
Valid Reasons for Conducting a Search
To protect the arresting officers
To prevent evidence from being destroyed
To keep the defendant from escaping
When a Search Becomes Illegal
When it goes beyond the defendant and the area within the defendant's immediate control
When it is conducted for other than a valid reason

out a search warrant, their scope must be strongly circumscribed. The legal implications of *Chimel* v. *California* are summarized in Table 2.

The decision in the *Chimel* case built on the 1950 U.S. Supreme Court case of *U.S.* v. *Rabinowitz* (1950).[25] Rabinowitz, a stamp collector, had been arrested and charged by federal agents with selling altered postage stamps to defraud other collectors. Employing a valid arrest warrant, officers arrested Rabinowitz at his place of employment and then proceeded to search his desk, file cabinets, and safe. They did not have a search warrant, but his office was small—only one room—and the officers conducted the search with a specific object in mind, the illegal stamps. Eventually, 573 altered postage stamps were seized in the search, and Rabinowitz was convicted in federal court of charges related to selling altered stamps.

Rabinowitz's appeal to the U.S. Supreme Court, based on the claim that the warrantless search of his business was illegal, was denied. The Court ruled that the Fourth Amendment provides protection against *unreasonable* searches but that the search in this case followed legally from the arrest of the suspect. In the language used by the Court, "It is not disputed that there may be reasonable searches, incident to arrest, without a search warrant. Upon acceptance of this established rule that some authority to search follows from lawfully taking the person into custody, it becomes apparent that such searches turn upon the reasonableness under all the circumstances and not upon the practicability of procuring a search warrant, for the warrant is not required."

Since the early days of the exclusionary rule, other court decisions have highlighted the fact that "the Fourth Amendment protects people, not places."[26] In other words, although the commonly heard claim that "a person's home is his or her castle" has a great deal of validity within the context of constitutional law, people can have a reasonable expectation to privacy in "homes" of many descriptions. Apartments, duplex dwellings, motel rooms—even the cardboard boxes or makeshift tents of the homeless—can all become protected places under the Fourth Amendment. In *Minnesota* v. *Olson* (1990),[27] for example, the U.S. Supreme Court extended the protection against warrantless searches to overnight guests residing in the home of another. The capacity to claim the protection of the Fourth Amendment, said the Court, depends on whether the *person* who makes that claim has a legitimate expectation of privacy in the place searched.

In 1998, in the case of *Minnesota* v. *Carter*,[28] the Court held that for a defendant to be entitled to Fourth Amendment protection, "he must demonstrate that he personally has an expectation of privacy in the place searched, and that his expectation is reasonable." The Court noted that "the extent to which the Amendment protects people may depend upon where those people are. While an overnight guest may have a legitimate expectation of privacy in someone else's home ... one who is merely present with the consent of the householder may not." Hence, an appliance repair person visiting a residence is unlikely to be accorded privacy protection while on the job.

In 2006, in the case of *Georgia* v. *Randolph*,[29] the Court ruled that police officers may not enter a home to conduct a warrrantless search if one resident gives permission but the other says no. The *Randolph* case invalidated the use as evidence of a cocaine-coated straw that had been seized inside a home during a police search in which Scott Fitz Randolph's wife had given permission for the couple's home to be searched. At the time the search was conducted, Randolph and his wife were involved in a domestic dispute and he was physically present as police searched the couple's residence. Randolph had already refused a police request for a search before his wife told officers that they could come inside and then led them to a bedroom and pointed out the straw. The *Randolph* ruling was a narrow one and centered on the stated refusal by a physically present co-occupant to permit warrantless entry in the absence of evidence of abuse or other circumstances that might otherwise justify an immediate police entry.[30]

The Burger Court (1969–1986) and Rehnquist Court (1986–2005)

During the 1980s and 1990s, the United States experienced a swing toward conservatism, giving rise to a renewed concern with protecting the interests—financial and otherwise—of those who live within the law. The Reagan–Bush years, and the popularity of the two presidents who many thought embodied "old-fashioned" values, reflected the tenor of a nation seeking a return to "simpler," less volatile times.

Throughout the late 1980s, the U.S. Supreme Court mirrored the nation's conservative tenor by distancing itself from some earlier decisions of the Warren Court. While the Warren Court embodied the individual-rights heyday in Court jurisprudence, Court decisions beginning in the 1970s were generally supportive of a "greater good era"—one in which the justices increasingly acknowledged the importance of social order and communal safety. Under Chief Justice Warren E. Burger, the new Court adhered to the principle that criminal defendants who claimed violations of their due process rights needed to bear most of the responsibility of showing that police went beyond the law in the performance of their duties. This tenet is still held by the Court today.

Good-Faith Exceptions to the Exclusionary Rule

The Burger Court, which held sway from 1969 until 1986, "chipped away" at the strict application of the exclusionary rule originally set forth in the *Weeks* and *Silverthorne* cases. In the 1984 case of *U.S.* v. *Leon*,[31] the Court recognized what has come to be called the **good-faith exception** to the exclusionary rule. In this case, the Court modified the exclusionary rule to allow evidence that officers had seized in "reasonable good faith" to be used in court, even though the search was later ruled illegal. The suspect, Alberto Leon, was placed under surveillance for drug trafficking following a tip from a confidential informant. Burbank (California) Police Department investigators applied for a search warrant based on information gleaned from the surveillance, believing they were in compliance with the Fourth Amendment requirement that "no Warrants shall issue, but upon probable cause."

good-faith exception
An exception to the exclusionary rule. Law enforcement officers who conduct a search or who seize evidence on the basis of good faith (that is, when they believe they are operating according to the dictates of the law) and who later discover that a mistake was made (perhaps in the format of the application for a search warrant) may still use the seized evidence in court.

Probable cause is a tricky but important concept. Its legal criteria are based on facts and circumstances that would cause a reasonable person to believe that a particular other person has committed a specific crime. Before a warrant can be issued, police officers must satisfactorily demonstrate probable cause in a written affidavit to a magistrate[32]—a low-level judge who ensures that the police establish the probable cause needed for warrants to be obtained. Upon a demonstration of probable cause, the magistrate will issue a warrant authorizing law enforcement officers to effect an arrest or conduct a search.

probable cause
A set of facts and circumstances that would induce a reasonably intelligent and prudent person to believe that a particular other person has committed a specific crime. Also, reasonable grounds to make or believe an accusation. Probable cause refers to the necessary level of belief that would allow for police seizures (arrests) of individuals and full searches of dwellings, vehicles, and possessions.

In *U.S.* v. *Leon*, a warrant was issued, and a search of Leon's three residences yielded a large amount of drugs and other evidence. Although Leon was convicted of drug trafficking, a later ruling in a federal district court resulted in the suppression of evidence against him on the basis that the original affidavit prepared by the police had not, in the opinion of the reviewing court, been sufficient to establish probable cause.

The federal government petitioned the U.S. Supreme Court to consider whether evidence gathered by officers acting in good faith as to the validity of a warrant should fairly be excluded at trial. The impending modification of the exclusionary rule was presaged in the first sentences of the Court's written decision: "This case presents the question whether the Fourth Amendment exclusionary rule should be modified so as not to bar the use in the prosecution's case-in-chief of evidence obtained by officers acting in reasonable reliance on a search warrant issued by a detached and neutral magistrate but ultimately found to be unsupported by probable cause." The Court continued, "When law enforcement officers have acted in objective good faith or their transgressions have been minor, the magnitude of the benefit conferred on such guilty defendants offends basic concepts of the criminal justice system." Reflecting the renewed conservatism of the Burger Court, the justices found for the government and reinstated Leon's conviction.

In that same year, the Supreme Court case of *Massachusetts* v. *Sheppard* (1984)[33] further reinforced the concept of good faith. In the *Sheppard* case, officers executed a search warrant that failed to describe accurately the property to be seized. Although they were aware of the error, a magistrate had assured them that the warrant was valid. After the seizure was complete and a conviction had been obtained, the Massachusetts Supreme Judicial Court reversed the finding of the trial court. Upon appeal, the U.S. Supreme Court reiterated the good-faith exception and reinstated the original conviction.

The cases of *Leon* and *Sheppard* represented a clear reversal of the Warren Court's philosophy, and the trend continued with the 1987 case of *Illinois* v. *Krull*. In *Krull*,[34] the Court, now under the leadership of Chief Justice William H. Rehnquist, held that the good-faith exception applied to a warrantless search supported by state law even though the state statute was later found to violate the Fourth Amendment. Similarly, another 1987 Supreme Court case, *Maryland* v. *Garrison*,[35] supported the use of evidence obtained with a search warrant that was inaccurate in its specifics. In *Garrison*, officers had procured a warrant to search an apartment, believing it was the only dwelling on the building's third floor. After searching the entire floor, they discovered that it housed more than one apartment. Even so, evidence acquired in the search was held to be admissible based on the reasonable mistake of the officers.

The 1990 case of *Illinois* v. *Rodriguez*[36] further diminished the scope of the exclusionary rule. In *Rodriguez*, a badly beaten woman named Gail Fischer complained to police that she had been assaulted in a Chicago apartment. Fischer led police to the apartment—which she indicated she shared with the defendant—produced a key, and opened the door to the dwelling. Inside, investigators found the defendant, Edward Rodriguez, asleep on a bed, with drug paraphernalia and cocaine spread around him. Rodriguez was arrested and charged with assault and possession of a controlled substance.

Upon appeal, Rodriguez demonstrated that Fischer had not lived with him for at least a month and argued that she could no longer be said to have legal control over the apartment. Hence, the defense claimed, Fischer had no authority to provide investigators with access to the dwelling. According to arguments made by the defense, the evidence, which had been obtained without a warrant, had not been properly seized. The Supreme Court disagreed, ruling that "even if Fischer did not possess common authority over the premises, there was no Fourth Amendment violation if the police *reasonably believed* at the time of their entry that Fischer possessed the authority to consent."

In 1995, in the case of *Arizona* v. *Evans*,[37] the U.S. Supreme Court created a "computer errors exception" to the exclusionary rule, holding that a traffic stop that led to the seizure of marijuana was legal even though officers conducted the stop based on an arrest warrant that should have been deleted from the computer database to which they had access. The arrest warrant reported to the officers by their computer had actually been quashed a few weeks earlier but, through the oversight of a court employee, had never been removed from the database.

In reaching its decision, the high court reasoned that police officers could not be held responsible for a clerical error made by a court worker and concluded that the arresting officers had acted in good faith based on the information available to them at the time of the arrest. In addition, the majority opinion said that "the rule excluding evidence obtained without a warrant was intended to deter police misconduct, not mistakes by court employees."

Legal scholars have suggested that the exclusionary rule may undergo even further modification in the near future. Some analysts of the contemporary scene point to the fact that "the Court's majority is [now] clearly committed to the idea that the exclusionary rule is not directly part of the Fourth Amendment (and Fourteenth Amendment due process), but instead is an evidentiary device instituted by the Court to effectuate it."[38] In other words, if the Court should be persuaded that the rule is no longer effective or that some other strategy would better achieve the aim of protecting individual rights, the rule could be abandoned entirely. A general listing of established exceptions to the exclusionary rule, along with other investigative powers created by court precedent, is provided in Table 3.

During Rehnquist's tenure as chief justice, the Court invoked a characteristically conservative approach to many important criminal justice issues—from limiting the exclusionary rule[39] and generally broadening police powers to sharply limiting the opportunities for state prisoners to bring appeals in federal courts.[40] Preventive detention, "no-knock" police searches,[41] the

TABLE 3 Selected Investigative Activities Supported by Court Precedent

This Police Power	Is Supported By
Arrest based on computer error made by clerk	*Arizona* v. *Evans* (1995)
Authority to enter and/or search an "open field" without a warrant	*U.S.* v. *Dunn* (1987) *Oliver* v. *U.S.* (1984) *Hester* v. *U.S.* (1924)
Authority to search incident to arrest and/or to conduct a protective sweep in conjunction with an in-home arrest	*Maryland* v. *Buie* (1990) *U.S.* v. *Edwards* (1974) *Chimel* v. *California* (1969)
Gathering of incriminating evidence during interrogation in noncustodial circumstances	*Yarborough* v. *Alvarado* (2004) *Thompson* v. *Keohane* (1996) *Stansbury* v. *California* (1994) *U.S.* v. *Mendenhall* (1980) *Beckwith* v. *U.S.* (1976)
Gathering of incriminating evidence during *Miranda*-less custodial interrogation	*U.S.* v. *Patane* (2004)
Inevitable discovery of evidence	*Nix* v. *Williams* (1984)
"No-knock" searches or quick entry	*Brigham City* v. *Stuart* (2006) *Hudson* v. *Michigan* (2006) *U.S.* v. *Barnes* (2003) *Richards* v. *Wisconsin* (1997) *Wilson* v. *Arkansas* (1995)
Prompt action in the face of threat to public or personal safety or destruction of evidence	*U.S.* v. *Banks* (2003) *Borchardt* v. *U.S.* (1987) *New York* v. *Quarles* (1984) *Warden* v. *Hayden* (1967)
Seizure of evidence in good faith, even in the face of some exclusionary rule violations	*Illinois* v. *Krull* (1987) *U.S.* v. *Leon* (1984)
Seizure of evidence in plain view	*Horton* v. *California* (1990) *Coolidge* v. *New Hampshire* (1971) *Harris* v. *U.S.* (1968)
Stop and frisk/request personal identification	*Hiibel* v. *Sixth Judicial District Court of Nevada* (2004) *Terry* v. *Ohio* (1968)
Use of police informants in jail cells	*Arizona* v. *Fulminante* (1991) *Illinois* v. *Perkins* (1990) *Kuhlmann* v. *Wilson* (1986)
Warrantless naked-eye aerial observation of open areas and/or greenhouses	*Florida* v. *Riley* (1989) *California* v. *Ciraolo* (1986)
Warrantless search incident to a lawful arrest	*U.S.* v. *Rabinowitz* (1950)
Warrantless seizure of abandoned materials and refuse	*California* v. *Greenwood* (1988)
Warrantless vehicle search where probable cause exists to believe that the vehicle contains contraband and/or that the occupants have been lawfully arrested	*Thornton* v. *U.S.* (2004) *Ornelas* v. *U.S.* (1996) *California* v. *Acevedo* (1991) *California* v. *Carney* (1985) *U.S.* v. *Ross* (1982) *New York* v. *Belton* (1981) *Carroll* v. *U.S.* (1925)

death penalty,[42] and habitual offender statutes[43] (often known as *three-strikes laws*) all found decisive support under Chief Justice Rehnquist.[44]

Following Rehnquist's death in 2005, John G. Roberts, Jr., became the nation's seventeenth Chief Justice. Roberts had previously served as a judge on the U.S. Court of Appeals for the District of Columbia Circuit. Court watchers predict that the Court under Roberts is likely to continue the Rehnquist Court's conservative ways.

The Plain-View Doctrine

plain view
A legal term describing the ready visibility of objects that might be seized as evidence during a search by police in the absence of a search warrant specifying the seizure of those objects. To lawfully seize evidence in plain view, officers must have a legal right to be in the viewing area and must have cause to believe that the evidence is somehow associated with criminal activity.

Police officers have the opportunity to begin investigations or to confiscate evidence, without a warrant, based on what they find in **plain view** and open to public inspection. The plain-view doctrine was succinctly stated in the U.S. Supreme Court case of *Harris* v. *U.S.* (1968),[45] in which a police officer inventorying an impounded vehicle discovered evidence of a robbery.[46] In the *Harris* case, the Court ruled that "objects falling in the plain view of an officer who has a right to be in the position to have that view are subject to seizure and may be introduced in evidence."[47]

The plain-view doctrine is applicable in common situations such as crimes in progress, fires, accidents, and other emergencies. A police officer responding to a call for assistance, for example, might enter a residence intending to provide aid to an injured person and find drugs or other contraband in plain view. If so, the officer would be within his or her legitimate authority to confiscate the materials and to effect an arrest if the owner can be identified.

The plain-view doctrine applies only to sightings by the police under legal circumstances—that is, in places where the police have a legitimate right to be and, typically, only if the sighting was coincidental. Similarly, the incriminating nature of the evidence seized must have been "immediately apparent" to the officers making the seizure.[48] If officers conspired to avoid the necessity for a search warrant by helping to create a plain-view situation through surveillance, duplicity, or other means, the doctrine likely would not apply.

The plain-view doctrine was restricted by later federal court decisions. In the 1982 case of *U.S.* v. *Irizarry*,[49] the First Circuit Court of Appeals held that officers could not move objects to gain a view of evidence otherwise hidden from view. In the Supreme Court case of *Arizona* v. *Hicks* (1987),[50] the requirement that evidence be in plain view, without requiring officers to move or dislodge objects, was reiterated. In the *Hicks* case, officers responded to a shooting in an apartment. A bullet had been fired in a second-floor apartment and had gone through the floor, injuring a man in the apartment below. The quarters of James Hicks were found to be in considerable disarray when investigating officers entered. As officers looked for the person who might have fired the weapon, they discovered and confiscated a number of guns and a stocking mask, such as might be used in robberies. In one corner, officers noticed two expensive stereo sets. One of the officers, suspecting that the stereos were stolen, went over to the equipment and was able to read the serial numbers of one of the components from where it rested. Some of the serial numbers, however, were not clearly visible, and the investigating officer moved some of the equipment in order to read the numbers. When he called the numbers in to headquarters, he was told that the stereos indeed had been stolen. They were seized, and James Hicks was arrested. Hicks was eventually convicted on a charge of armed robbery, based on the evidence seized.

Upon appeal, the *Hicks* case reached the U.S. Supreme Court, which ruled that the officer's behavior had become illegal when he moved the stereo equipment to record the serial numbers. The Court held that people have a "reasonable expectation to privacy,"[51] which means that officers lacking a search warrant, even when invited into a residence, must act more like guests than inquisitors.

Most evidence seized under the plain-view doctrine is discovered "inadvertently"—that is, by accident.[52] However, in 1990, the U.S. Supreme Court ruled in the case of ***Horton* v. *California***[53] that "even though inadvertence *is* a characteristic of most legitimate 'plain view' seizures, it is not a necessary condition."[54] In the *Horton* case, a warrant was issued authorizing the search of Terry Brice Horton's home for stolen jewelry. The affidavit, completed by the officer who requested the warrant, alluded to an Uzi submachine gun and a stun gun—weapons purportedly used in the jewelry robbery. It did not request that those weapons be listed on the search warrant. Officers searched the defendant's home but did not find the stolen jewelry. They did, however, seize a number of weapons, among them an Uzi, two stun guns, and a .38-caliber revolver. Horton was convicted of robbery in a trial in which the seized weapons were introduced into evidence. He appealed his conviction, claiming that officers had reason to

The touchstone of the Fourth Amendment is reasonableness. The Fourth Amendment does not proscribe all state-initiated searches and seizures. It merely proscribes those which are unreasonable.

—Florida v. Jimeno
500 U.S. 248 (1991)

believe that the weapons were in his home at the time of the search, so they were not seized inadvertently. His appeal was rejected by the Court. As a result of the *Horton* case, inadvertence is no longer considered a condition necessary to ensure the legitimacy of a seizure that results when evidence other than that listed in a search warrant is discovered. See CJ Exhibit 1 for more on evidence and the plain-view doctrine.

Emergency Searches of Property and Emergency Entry

Certain emergencies may justify a police officer's decision to search or enter premises without a warrant. In 2006, for example, in the case of *Brigham City* v. *Stuart*,[55] the Court recognized the need for emergency warrantless entries under certain circumstances when it ruled that police officers "may enter a home without a warrant when they have an objectively reasonable basis for believing that an occupant is seriously injured or imminently threatened with such injury." The case involved police entry into a private home to break up a fight.

According to the Legal Counsel Division of the Federal Bureau of Investigation (FBI), there are three threats that "provide justification for emergency warrantless action."[56] They are clear dangers (1) to life, (2) of escape, and (3) of the removal or destruction of evidence. Any one of these situations may create an exception to the Fourth Amendment's requirement of a search warrant.

Emergency searches, or those conducted without a warrant when special needs arise, are legally termed *exigent circumstances searches*. When emergencies necessitate a quick search of premises, however, law enforcement officers are responsible for demonstrating that a dire situation existed that justified their actions. Failure to do so successfully in court will, of course, taint any seized evidence and make it unusable.

emergency search
A search conducted by the police without a warrant, which is justified on the basis of some immediate and overriding need, such as public safety, the likely escape of a dangerous suspect, or the removal or destruction of evidence.

The U.S. Supreme Court first recognized the need for emergency searches in 1967 in the case of *Warden* v. *Hayden*.[57] In that case, the Court approved the warrantless search of a residence following reports that an armed robber had fled into the building. In *Mincey* v. *Arizona* (1978),[58] the Supreme Court held that "the Fourth Amendment does not require police officers to delay in the course of an investigation if to do so would gravely endanger their lives or the lives of others."[59]

A 1990 decision, rendered in the case of *Maryland* v. *Buie*,[60] extended the authority of police to search locations in a house where a potentially dangerous person could hide while an arrest warrant is being served. The *Buie* decision was meant primarily to protect investigators from potential danger and can apply even when officers lack a warrant, probable cause, or even reasonable suspicion.

In 1995, in the case of ***Wilson* v. *Arkansas***,[61] the U.S. Supreme Court ruled that police officers generally must knock and announce their identity before entering a dwelling or other premises, even when armed with a search warrant. Under certain emergency circumstances, however, exceptions may be made, and officers may not need to knock or to identify themselves before entering.[62] In *Wilson*, the Court added that the Fourth Amendment requirement that searches be reasonable "should not be read to mandate a rigid rule of announcement that ignores countervailing law enforcement interests." Hence officers need not announce themselves, the Court said, when suspects may be in the process of destroying evidence, officers are pursuing a recently escaped arrestee, or officers' lives may be endangered by such an announcement. Because the *Wilson* case involved an appeal from a drug dealer who was apprehended by police officers who entered her unlocked house while she was flushing marijuana down a toilet, some said that it establishes a "drug-law exception" to the knock-and-announce requirement.

In 1997, in ***Richards* v. *Wisconsin***,[63] the Supreme Court clarified its position on "no-knock" exceptions, saying that individual courts have the duty in each case to "determine whether the facts and circumstances of the particular entry justified dispensing with the requirement." The Court went on to say that "[a] 'no knock' entry is justified when the police have a reasonable suspicion that knocking and announcing their presence, under the particular circumstances, would be dangerous or futile, or that it would inhibit the effective investigation of the crime. This standard strikes the appropriate balance," said the Court, "between the legitimate law enforcement concerns at issue in the execution of search warrants and the individual privacy interests affected by no knock entries."

In this case, we hold that this common-law "knock and announce" principle forms a part of the reasonableness inquiry under the Fourth Amendment.
—Wilson v. Arkansas
514 U.S. 927 (1995)

In 2001, in the case of *Illinois* v. *McArthur*,[64] the U.S. Supreme Court ruled that police officers with probable cause to believe that a home contains contraband or evidence of criminal

CJ Exhibit 1
Plain-View Requirements

Following the opinion of the U.S. Supreme Court in the case of *Horton* v. *California* (1990), items seized under the plain-view doctrine may be admissible as evidence in a court of law if *both* of the following conditions are met:

1. The officer who seized the evidence was in the viewing area lawfully.
2. The officer had probable cause to believe that the evidence was somehow associated with criminal activity.

▲ Latasha Smith (shown here sitting on a curb), who was arrested for failing to appear in court for a previous misdemeanor violation. Although the concept of plain view is difficult to define, Smith provides a personal example of the concept. After Dallas narcotics officers searched the house behind her for crack cocaine, they turned their attention to Smith and discovered the outstanding charges. How would you explain the concept of plain view?
AP Wide World Photos

activity may reasonably prevent a suspect found outside the home from reentering it while they apply for a search warrant. In 2003, in a case involving drug possession, the Court held that a 15- to 20-second wait after officers knocked, announced themselves, and requested entry was sufficient to satisfy Fourth Amendment requirements.[65]

In the 2006 case of *Hudson* v. *Michigan*,[66] the Court surprised many when it ruled that evidence found by police officers who enter a home to execute a warrant without first following the knock-and-announce requirement can be used at trial despite that constitutional violation. In the words of the Court, "The interests protected by the knock-and-announce rule include human life and limb (because an unannounced entry may provoke violence from a surprised resident), property (because citizens presumably would open the door upon an announcement, whereas a forcible entry may destroy it), and privacy and dignity of the sort that can be offended by a sudden entrance." But, said the Court, "the rule has never protected one's interest in preventing the government from seeing or taking evidence described in a warrant." The justices reasoned that the social costs of strictly adhering to the knock-and-announce rule are considerable and may include "the grave adverse consequence that excluding relevant incriminating evidence always entails—the risk of releasing dangerous criminals." In a ruling that some said signaled a new era of lessened restraints on the police, the Court's majority opinion said that since the interests violated by ignoring the knock-and-announce rule "have nothing to do with the seizure of the evidence, the exclusionary rule is inapplicable."

Anticipatory Warrants

Anticipatory warrants are search warrants issued on the basis of probable cause to believe that evidence of a crime, while not currently at the place described, will likely be there when the warrant is executed. Such warrants anticipate the presence of contraband or other evidence of criminal culpability but do not claim that the evidence is present at the time that the warrant is requested or issued.

anticipatory warrant
A search warrant issued on the basis of probable cause to believe that evidence of a crime, while not currently at the place described, will likely be there when the warrant is executed.

Anticipatory warrants are no different in principle from ordinary search warrants. They require an issuing magistrate to determine that it is probable that contraband, evidence of a crime, or a fugitive will be on the described premises when the warrant is executed.

The constitutionality of anticipatory warrants was affirmed in 2006, in the U.S. Supreme Court case of *U.S.* v. *Grubbs*. In *Grubbs*,[67] an anticipatory search warrant had been issued for Grubbs's house based on a federal officer's affidavit stating that the warrant would not be executed until a parcel containing a videotape of child pornography—which Grubbs had ordered from an undercover postal inspector—was received at and physically taken into Grubbs's residence. After the package was delivered, the anticipatory search warrant was executed, the videotape seized, and Grubbs arrested.

Arrest

Officers seize not only property but people as well, a process referred to as arrest. Most people think of arrest in terms of what they see on popular TV crime shows: The suspect is chased, subdued, and "cuffed" after committing some loathsome act in view of the camera. Some arrests do occur that way. In reality, however, most arrests are far more mundane.

In technical terms, an **arrest** occurs whenever a law enforcement officer restricts a person's freedom to leave. There may be no yelling of "You're under arrest!"; no *Miranda* warnings may be offered; and, in fact, the suspect may not even consider himself or herself to be in custody. Arrests, and the decisions to enforce them, evolve as the situations between officers and suspects develop. A situation usually begins with polite conversation and a request by the officer for information. Only when the suspect tries to leave and tests the limits of the police response may the suspect discover that he or she is really in custody. In the 1980 case of *U.S.* v. *Mendenhall*,[68] Justice Potter Stewart set forth the "free to leave" test for determining whether a person has been arrested. Stewart wrote, "A person has been 'seized' within the meaning of the Fourth Amendment only if in view of all the circumstances surrounding the incident, a reasonable person would have believed that he was not free to leave." The "free to leave" test has been repeatedly adopted by the Court as the test for a seizure. In 1994, in the case of *Stansbury* v. *California*,[69] the Court once again used such a test in determining the point at which an arrest had been made. In *Stansbury*, where the focus was on the interrogation of a suspected child molester and murderer, the Court ruled, "In determining whether an individual was in custody, a court must examine all of the circumstances surrounding the interrogation, but the ultimate inquiry is simply whether there [was] a formal arrest or restraint on freedom of movement of the degree associated with a formal arrest."

arrest
The act of taking an adult or juvenile into physical custody by authority of law for the purpose of charging the person with a criminal offense, a delinquent act, or a status offense, terminating with the recording of a specific offense. Technically, an arrest occurs whenever a law enforcement officer curtails a person's freedom to leave.

Youth and inexperience do not automatically undermine a reasonable person's ability to assess when someone is free to leave. Hence, in the 2004 case of *Yarborough* v. *Alvarado*,[70] the U.S. Supreme Court found that a 17-year-old boy's two-hour interrogation in a police station without a *Miranda* advisement was not custodial, even though the boy confessed to his involvement in a murder and consequently was later arrested. The boy, said the Court, had not actually been in police custody even though he was in a building used by the police for questioning, because actions taken by the interviewing officer indicated that the juvenile had been free to leave. Whether a person is actually free to leave, said the Court, can only be determined by examining the totality of the circumstances surrounding the interrogation.[71]

The 2005 U.S. Supreme Court case of *Muehler* v. *Mena*[72] made clear that an officer's authority to detain occupants of a dwelling incident to the execution of a valid search warrant is absolute and unqualified and does not require any justification beyond the warrant itself—even when the occupants are not suspected of any wrongdoing. In other words, officers who are conducting a lawful search under the authority of a warrant may detain persons found occupying the premises being searched in order to prevent flights in the event incriminating evidence is found, to minimize the risk of harm to the officers, and simply to facilitate the search itself.[73]

You can only protect your liberties in this world by protecting the other man's freedom.
—*Clarence Darrow*

Arrests that follow the questioning of a suspect are probably the most common type of arrest. When the decision to arrest is reached, the officer has come to the conclusion that a crime has been committed and that the suspect is probably the one who committed it. The presence of these elements constitutes the probable cause needed for an arrest. Probable cause is the basic minimum necessary for an arrest under any circumstances.

Arrests may also occur when the officer comes upon a crime in progress. Such situations often require apprehension of the offender to ensure the safety of the public. Most arrests made during crimes in progress, however, are for misdemeanors rather than felonies. In fact, many states do not allow arrest for a misdemeanor unless it is committed in the presence of an officer, since visible crimes in progress clearly provide the probable cause necessary for an arrest. In 2001, in a case that made headlines nationwide,[74] the U.S. Supreme Court upheld a warrantless arrest made by Lago Vista (Texas) Patrolman Bart Turek for a seat belt violation. In what many saw as an unfair exercise of discretion, Turek stopped and then arrested Gail Atwater, a young local woman whom he observed driving a pickup truck in which she and her two small children (ages three and five) were unbelted. Facts in the case showed that Turek verbally berated the woman after stopping her vehicle and that he handcuffed her, placed her in his squad car, and drove her to the local police station, where she was made to remove her

CJ News

Legal Issues Being Raised in Subway Searches

Even more than security experts and intelligence analysts, one group of employees has become central to the new program of bag searches in the transit networks of the New York region: lawyers.

The decision in July 2005 to have police officers inspect the belongings of thousands of subway riders has opened a thicket of legal and constitutional issues, involving criminal procedure, transit security and concerns about potential misuse of the new tactic.

Donna Lieberman, the executive director of the New York Civil Liberties Union, said the organization had begun work on a federal lawsuit, which could be filed soon. Such a challenge will most likely claim that the policy violates the Fourth Amendment's prohibition against "unreasonable searches and seizures."

And at a news conference in Brooklyn, Capt. Eric Adams, the president of a group of black police officers, said its members were worried that riders of Middle Eastern, African, or Asian descent would be disproportionately targeted in the searches, despite official assurances to the contrary.

New Jersey Transit and the Port Authority of New York and New Jersey started random searches on their trains and in their buses and stations, joining the city police and the Metropolitan Transportation Authority in conducting searches.

The four agencies have tried to sidestep a potential legal minefield by carefully specifying the limits and objectives of the policies, but the legality of the searches could well rest on subtle distinctions in the way they are carried out.

"It is by no means a foregone conclusion that these searches will be found reasonable under the Fourth Amendment," said Tracey Maclin, a law professor at Boston University. "The number of people involved, the nature and severity of the intrusions, and the uncertain duration of the searches all make this fundamentally very different from anything we have seen before."

At least three United States Supreme Court cases will probably influence any judge assessing the searches.

In 1979, in *Delaware* v. *Prouse*, the court held that random traffic stops, left to the discretion of police officers, were unconstitutional. In 1990, in *Michigan* v. *Sitz*, the court upheld the legality of sobriety checkpoints in which a consistent proportion of drivers was stopped. The court ruled that such roadblocks were permitted as a way to prevent drunken driving.

The court has set limits on those roadblocks, however. In 2000, in ***Indianapolis* v. *Edmond***, it struck down the use of traffic checkpoints to stop drivers so that trained dogs could sniff the vehicles for narcotics. Unlike checkpoints to make sure that drivers were sober or had valid licenses and registrations, the court said, roadblocks for general law enforcement were unconstitutional.

David D. Cole, a law professor at Georgetown University, said the government was likely to succeed in demonstrating a special need for the current searches in New York.

A judge evaluating a legal challenge, he said, would probably look at three factors: whether the searches are truly random or use standardized criteria; whether riders were given advance notice or provided their consent to the searches; and the degree of intrusiveness. "It's very hard to predict how these cases will turn out, because it's such an open-ended balancing test," he said.

▲ A police officer checks the bag of a subway rider at New York City's 42nd Street/Bryant Park station. Should random bag checks be permitted, or do they unfairly impinge on the rights of people wanting to ride the subway?
John Marshall Mantel/AP Wide World Photos

According to a two-page directive sent to all police commanders following the July 2005 subway bombings in London, the searches were begun "to increase deterrence and detection of potential terrorist activity and to give greater protection to the mass transit-riding public." The directive authorized the police to inspect "backpacks, containers, and other carry-on items which are capable of containing explosive devices."

The policy includes several provisions that could help in defending the new searches from court challenges.

First, although Mayor Michael R. Bloomberg and Police Commissioner Raymond W. Kelly have described the searches as "random," they should rely on a precise frequency that is not subject to officers' discretion, according to the directive.

A supervisor at each checkpoint is supposed to determine the frequency of searches—1 in every 5, 12, or 20 passengers, for example—based on the volume of passengers, the number of officers available and the "flow of commuter traffic."

Second, extensive steps were taken to notify the public about the searches. At subway stations and train terminals, megaphone and public-address systems were used. Notices were handwritten on dry-erase boards in the booths in most subway stations. At many checkpoints, the police have set up signs on easels near the turnstiles.

The directive states that individuals who refuse to be searched can leave the subway system, and that such a refusal "shall not constitute probable cause for an arrest or reasonable suspicion for a forcible stop."

The degree of intrusiveness could become a thorny issue. The directive provides that officers may open a package and "physically inspect and manipulate the contents to ensure it does not contain an explosive device." Leaving aside the issue of illegal drugs or weapons, some riders have already voiced misgivings about having the police examine sensitive possessions, like medications and personal hygiene products.

Lawyers have been used extensively in writing the search policies. The deputy police commissioner for legal matters, S. Andrew Schaffer, formerly the general counsel for New York University, joined Mr. Kelly and top police commanders in completing their plans for the searches.

Similarly, Catherine A. Rinaldi, the general counsel for the Metropolitan Transportation Authority, was "intimately involved" in plans for searches on the Long Island Rail Road and Metro-North Commuter Railroad, according to Tom Kelly, a spokesman for the authority.

Ronald Susswein, an assistant attorney general in New Jersey, said that the New Jersey Transit searches would not be conducted arbitrarily. "This is not a criminal enforcement procedure," he said. "We're not trying to catch anyone. We're trying to deter terrorism."

While the majority of riders interviewed since the searches began said they supported the searches, a few have expressed concerns.

"For a split second, I thought that because of my skin complexion, they picked me," said James Hamilton, 38, whose attaché case was searched at Herald Square. "I'm not sure if I had brown hair and blue eyes, that that would have happened." He has black hair, dark brown eyes, and a dark complexion.

Charles Wilson, 35, a schoolteacher whose bag was searched at Fulton Street in Lower Manhattan, said, "This is not going to make things better between the police and people of color." Mr. Wilson is black.

Captain Adams, whose organization, 100 Blacks in Law Enforcement Who Care, held a news conference immediately after the searches began, said he believed that discrimination was likely in practice, if not intent. "You can say 'no profiling,' but when you have a police department that has a history of profiling, it is going to practice what it knows," he said.

A police spokesman, Paul J. Browne, said he strongly disagreed. "These inspections are being conducted in a constitutional manner and have been met with enthusiastic cooperation by the overwhelming majority of riders we've come into contact with," he said.

For the latest in crime and justice news, visit the Talk Justice news feed at http://www.crimenews.info.

Source: Sewell Chan and Kareem Fahim, "Legal Issues Being Raised on Searches in Subways," *The New York Times*, July 24, 2005.

shoes, jewelry, and eyeglasses and empty her pockets. Officers took her "mug shot" and placed her alone in a jail cell for about an hour, after which she was taken before a magistrate and released on $310 bond. Atwater was charged with a misdemeanor violation of Texas seat belt law. She later pleaded no contest and paid a $50 fine. Soon afterward, she and her husband filed a Section 1983 lawsuit against the officer, his department, and the police chief, alleging that the actions of the officer violated Atwater's Fourth Amendment right to be free from unreasonable seizures. The Court, however, concluded that "the Fourth Amendment does not forbid a warrantless arrest for a minor criminal offense, such as a misdemeanor seatbelt violation punishable only by a fine."

Most jurisdictions allow arrest for a felony without a warrant when a crime is not in progress, as long as probable cause can be established; some, however, require a warrant. In those jurisdictions, arrest warrants are issued by magistrates when police officers can demonstrate probable cause. Magistrates will usually require that the officers seeking an arrest warrant submit a written affidavit outlining their reason for the arrest. In the case of *Payton* v. *New York* (1980),[75] the U.S. Supreme Court ruled that unless the suspect gives consent or an emergency exists, an arrest warrant is necessary if an arrest requires entry into a suspect's private residence.[76] In *Payton*, the justices held that "[a]bsent exigent circumstances," the "firm line at the entrance to the house ... may not reasonably be crossed without a warrant." The Court reiterated its *Payton* holding in the 2002 case of *Kirk* v. *Louisiana*.[77] In *Kirk*, which involved an anonymous complaint about drug sales said to be taking place in the apartment of Kennedy Kirk, the justices reaffirmed their belief that "[t]he Fourth Amendment to the United States Constitution has drawn a firm line at the entrance to the home, and thus, the police need both probable cause to either arrest or search, and exigent circumstances to justify a nonconsensual warrantless intrusion into private premises."

Searches Incident to Arrest

The U.S. Supreme Court has established a clear rule that police officers have the right to conduct a search of a person being arrested and to search the area under the arrestee's immediate control to protect themselves from attack. This is true even if the officer and the arrestee are of different sexes.

search incident to an arrest
A warrantless search of an arrested individual conducted to ensure the safety of the arresting officer. Because individuals placed under arrest may be in possession of weapons, courts have recognized the need for arresting officers to protect themselves by conducting an immediate search of arrestees without obtaining a warrant.

reasonable suspicion
The level of suspicion that would justify an officer in making further inquiry or in conducting further investigation. Reasonable suspicion may permit stopping a person for questioning or for a simple pat-down search. Also, a belief, based on a consideration of the facts at hand and on reasonable inferences drawn from those facts, that would induce an ordinarily prudent and cautious person under the same circumstances to conclude that criminal activity is taking place or that criminal activity has recently occurred. Reasonable suspicion is a *general* and reasonable belief that a crime is in progress or has occurred, whereas probable cause is a reasonable belief that a *particular* person has committed a *specific* crime.

This "rule of the game" regarding **search incident to an arrest** was created in the *Rabinowitz* and *Chimel* cases discussed earlier. It became firmly established in other cases involving personal searches, such as the 1973 case of ***U.S.* v. *Robinson*.**[78] After Robinson had been stopped for a traffic violation, it was learned that his driver's license had expired. He was arrested for operating a vehicle without a valid license. Officers subsequently searched the defendant to be sure he wasn't carrying a weapon and discovered a substance that later proved to be heroin. He was convicted of drug possession but appealed. When Robinson's appeal reached the U.S. Supreme Court, the Court upheld an officer's right to conduct a search without a warrant for purposes of personal protection and to use the fruits of the search when it turns up contraband. In the words of the Court, "A custodial arrest of a suspect based upon probable cause is a reasonable intrusion under the Fourth Amendment; that intrusion being lawful, a search incident to the arrest requires no additional jurisdiction."[79]

The Court's decision in *Robinson* reinforced an earlier ruling in ***Terry* v. *Ohio*** (1968)[80] involving a seasoned officer who conducted a pat-down search of two men whom he suspected were casing a store, about to commit a robbery. The arresting officer was a 39-year veteran of police work who testified that the men "did not look right." When he approached them, he suspected they might be armed. Fearing for his life, he quickly spun the men around, put them up against a wall, patted down their clothing, and found a gun on one of the men. The man, Terry, was later convicted in Ohio courts of carrying a concealed weapon.

Terry's appeal was based on the argument that the suspicious officer had no probable cause to arrest him and therefore no cause to search him. The search, he argued, was illegal, and the evidence obtained should not have been used against him. The Supreme Court disagreed, saying, "In view of these facts, we cannot blind ourselves to the need for law enforcement officers to protect themselves and other prospective victims of violence in situations where they may lack probable cause for an arrest."

The *Terry* case set the standard for a brief stop and frisk based on reasonable suspicion. Attorneys refer to such brief encounters as *Terry-type stops*. **Reasonable suspicion** can be defined as a belief, based on a consideration of the facts at hand and on reasonable inferences drawn from those facts, that would induce an ordinarily prudent and cautious person under the same circumstances to conclude that criminal activity is taking place or that criminal activity has recently occurred. It is the level of suspicion needed to justify an officer in making further inquiry or in conducting further investigation. Reasonable suspicion, which is a *general* and reasonable belief that a crime is in progress or has occurred, should be differentiated from probable cause. Probable cause, as noted earlier, is a reasonable belief that a *particular* person has committed a *specific* crime. It is important to note that the *Terry* case, for all the authority it conferred on officers, also made it clear that officers must have reasonable grounds for any stop and frisk that they conduct. Read more about the case of *Terry* v. *Ohio* at Library Extra 5–3 at mycrimekit.com.

Library EXTRA

In 1989, in the case of *U.S.* v. *Sokolow*,[81] the Supreme Court clarified the basis on which law enforcement officers, lacking probable cause to believe that a crime has occurred, may stop and briefly detain a person for investigative purposes. In *Sokolow*, the Court ruled that the legitimacy of such a stop must be evaluated according to a "totality of circumstances" criterion in which all aspects of the defendant's behavior, taken in concert, may provide the basis for a legitimate stop based on reasonable suspicion. In this case, the defendant, Andrew Sokolow, appeared suspicious to police because while traveling under an alias from Honolulu, he had paid $2,100 in $20 bills (from a large roll of money) for two airplane tickets after spending a surprisingly small amount of time in Miami. In addition, the defendant was obviously nervous and checked no luggage. A warrantless airport investigation by Drug Enforcement Administration (DEA) agents uncovered more than 1,000 grams of cocaine in the defendant's belongings. In upholding Sokolow's conviction, the Court ruled that although no single type of behavior was proof of illegal activity, all his actions together created circumstances under which suspicion of illegal activity was justified.

In 2002, the Court reinforced the *Sokolow* decision in *U.S.* v. *Arvizu* when it ruled that the "balance between the public interest and the individual's right to personal security"[82] "tilts in favor of a standard less than probable cause in brief investigatory stops of persons or vehicles ... if the officer's action is supported by reasonable suspicion to believe that criminal activity may be afoot."[83] In the words of the Court, "This process allows officers to draw on their own experiences and specialized training to make inferences from and deductions about the cumulative information available."[84]

In 1993, in the case of *Minnesota* v. *Dickerson*,[85] the U.S. Supreme Court placed new limits on an officer's ability to seize evidence discovered during a pat-down search conducted for protective reasons when the search itself was based merely on suspicion and failed to immediately reveal the presence of a weapon. In this case, Timothy Dickerson, who was observed leaving a building known for cocaine trafficking, was stopped by Minneapolis police officers after they noticed him acting suspiciously. The officers decided to investigate further and ordered Dickerson to submit to a pat-down search. The search revealed no weapons, but the officer conducting it testified that he felt a small lump in Dickerson's jacket pocket, believed it to be a lump of crack cocaine after examining it with his fingers, and then reached into Dickerson's pocket and retrieved a small bag of cocaine. Dickerson was arrested, tried, and convicted of possession of a controlled substance. His appeal, which claimed that the pat-down search had been illegal, eventually made its way to the U.S. Supreme Court. The high court ruled that "if an officer lawfully pats down a suspect's outer clothing and feels an object whose contour or mass makes its identity immediately apparent, there has been no invasion of the suspect's privacy beyond that already authorized by the officer's search for weapons." However, in *Dickerson*, the justices ruled that "the officer never thought that the lump was a weapon, but did not immediately recognize it as cocaine." The lump was determined to be cocaine only after the officer "squeezed, slid, and otherwise manipulated the pocket's contents." Hence, the Court held, the officer's actions in this case did not qualify under what might be called a "plain feel" exception. In any case, said the Court, the search in *Dickerson* went far beyond what is permissible under *Terry*, where officer safety was the crucial issue. The Court summed up its ruling in *Dickerson* this way: "While *Terry* entitled [the officer] to place his hands on respondent's jacket and to feel the lump in the pocket, his continued exploration of the pocket after he concluded that it contained no weapon was unrelated to the sole justification for the search under *Terry*" and was therefore illegal.

▲ Arresting officers patting down a drug suspect. The courts have generally held that to protect themselves and the public, officers have the authority to search suspects being arrested. What are the limits of such searches?
Craig Filipacchi/Getty Images—GINS/Entertainment News & Sports

Just as arrest must be based on probable cause, officers may not stop and question an unwilling citizen whom they have no reason to suspect of a crime. In the case of *Brown* v. *Texas* (1979),[86] two Texas law enforcement officers stopped the defendant and asked for identification. Ed Brown, they later testified, had not been acting suspiciously, nor did they think he might have a weapon. The stop was made simply because officers wanted to know who he was. Brown was arrested under a Texas statute that required a person to identify himself properly and accurately when asked to do so by peace officers. Eventually, his appeal reached the U.S. Supreme Court, which ruled that under the circumstances of the *Brown* case, a person "may not be punished for refusing to identify himself."

In the 2004 case of *Hiibel* v. *Sixth Judicial District Court of Nevada*,[87] however, the Court upheld Nevada's "stop and identify" law that requires a person to identify himself or herself to police if they encounter the person under circumstances that reasonably indicate that he or she "has committed, is committing or is about to commit a crime." The *Hiibel* case was an extension of the reasonable suspicion doctrine set forth earlier in *Terry*.

In ***Smith* v. *Ohio*** (1990),[88] the Court held that an individual has the right to protect his or her belongings from unwarranted police inspection. In *Smith*, the defendant was approached by two officers in plain clothes who observed that he was carrying a brown paper bag. The officers asked him to "come here a minute" and, when he kept walking, identified themselves as police officers. The defendant threw the bag onto the hood of his car and attempted to protect it from the officers' intrusion. Marijuana was found inside the bag, and the defendant was arrested. Since there was little reason to stop the suspect in this case and because control over the bag was not thought necessary for the officers' protection, the Court found that the Fourth Amendment protects both "the traveler who carries a toothbrush and a few articles of clothing in a paper bag" and "the sophisticated executive with the locked attaché case."

The following year, however, in what some Court observers saw as a turnabout, the Court ruled in ***California* v. *Hodari D.*** (1991)[89] that suspects who flee from the police and throw away evidence as they retreat may later be arrested based on the incriminating nature of the abandoned evidence. The significance of *Hodari* for future police action was highlighted by California prosecutors who pointed out that cases like *Hodari* occur "almost every day in this nation's urban areas."[90]

Police work is the only profession that gives you the test first, then the lesson.
—*Anonymous*

In 2000, the Court decided the case of William Wardlow.[91] Wardlow had fled upon seeing a caravan of police vehicles converge on an area of Chicago known for narcotics trafficking. Officers caught him, however, and conducted a pat-down search of his clothing for weapons, revealing a handgun. The officers arrested Wardlow on weapons charges, but his lawyer argued that police had acted illegally in stopping him since they did not have reasonable suspicion that he had committed an offense. The Illinois Supreme Court agreed with Wardlow's attorney, holding that "sudden flight in a high crime area does not create a reasonable suspicion justifying a *Terry* stop because flight may simply be an exercise of the right to 'go on one's way.' "[92] The case eventually reached the U.S. Supreme Court, which overturned the Illinois court, finding instead that the officers' actions did not violate the Fourth Amendment. In the words of the Court, "This case, involving a brief encounter between a citizen and a police officer on a public street, is governed by *Terry*, under which an officer who has a reasonable, articulable suspicion that criminal activity is afoot may conduct a brief, investigatory stop. While 'reasonable suspicion' is a less demanding standard than probable cause, there must be at least a minimal level of objective justification for the stop. An individual's presence in a 'high crime area,' standing alone, is not enough to support a reasonable, particularized suspicion of criminal activity, but a location's characteristics are relevant in determining whether the circumstances are sufficiently suspicious to warrant further investigation.... In this case, moreover, it was also Wardlow's unprovoked flight that aroused the officers' suspicions. Nervous, evasive behavior is another pertinent factor in determining reasonable suspicion ... and headlong flight is the consummate act of evasion."[93]

Emergency Searches of Persons

It is easy to imagine emergency situations in which officers may have to search people based on quick decisions: a person who matches the description of an armed robber, a woman who is found unconscious on the floor, a man who has what appears to be blood on his shoes. Such searches can save lives by disarming fleeing felons or by uncovering a medical reason for an emergency situation. They may also prevent criminals from escaping or destroying evidence.

Emergency searches of persons, like those of premises, fall under the exigent circumstances exception to the warrant requirement of the Fourth Amendment. In the 1979 case of *Arkansas* v. *Sanders*,[94] the Supreme Court recognized the need for such searches "where the societal costs of obtaining a warrant, such as danger to law officers or the risk of loss or destruction of evidence, outweigh the reasons for prior recourse to a neutral magistrate."[95]

The 1987 case of *U.S.* v. *Borchardt*,[96] decided by the Fifth Circuit Court of Appeals, held that Ira Eugene Borchardt could be prosecuted for heroin uncovered during medical treatment, even though the defendant had objected to the treatment. Borchardt was a federal inmate when he was found unconscious in his cell. He was taken to a hospital, where tests revealed heroin in his blood. His heart stopped, and he was revived using cardiopulmonary resuscitation (CPR). Borchardt was given three doses of Narcan, a drug used to counteract the effects of heroin, and he improved, regaining consciousness. The patient refused requests to pump his stomach but began to become lethargic, indicating the need for additional Narcan. Eventually, he vomited nine plastic bags full of heroin, along with two bags which had burst. The heroin was turned over to federal officers, and Borchardt was eventually convicted of heroin possession. Attempts to exclude the heroin from evidence were unsuccessful, and the appeals court ruled that the necessity of the emergency situation overruled the defendant's objections to the search of his person.

The Legal Counsel Division of the FBI provides the following guidelines for conducting emergency warrantless searches of individuals where the possible destruction of evidence is at issue.[97] (Keep in mind that there may be no probable cause to *arrest* the individual being searched.) All four conditions must apply:

1. There was probable cause at the time of the search to believe that there was evidence concealed on the person searched.
2. There was probable cause to believe an emergency threat of destruction of evidence existed at the time of the search.
3. The officer had no prior opportunity to obtain a warrant authorizing the search.
4. The action was no greater than necessary to eliminate the threat of destruction of evidence.

CJ Careers

Bureau of Immigration and Customs Enforcement (ICE)

Name: Tamara N. Johnson
Position: Immigration Enforcement Agent
City: Dallas
College Attended: Northwestern State University
Year Hired: 2000

"I pursued a career in criminal justice because I believed that the criminal justice system lacked an effective form of rehabilitation. I wanted to make a difference and have an impact on repeat offenders in minority neighborhoods by establishing a form of rehabilitation that would not perpetuate criminal behavior. Recruiters [from the Immigration and Naturalization Service] came to my university and did a presentation. I applied and took the test.

The greatest challenge of my job is being impartial, offering unbiased information and treating each detainee equally, regardless of their ethnicity, age, sex, or offense. It is also challenging working in a male-dominated career. Although I'm a female, I'm expected to respond to situations and provide backup for my male counterpart.

The greatest reward of my job has been the opportunity to travel throughout the world. I've been exposed to many different cultures and customs. I've ridden a camel over the Sahara Desert and walked along the Nile River. I've learned survival skills and to always be prepared. The experiences and opportunities I have gained as an immigration enforcement officer have been priceless."

TYPICAL POSITIONS

Criminal investigator (special agent), immigration enforcement agent, detention enforcement agent, and deportation officer. The Bureau of Immigration and Customs Enforcement (ICE), a part of the Department of Homeland Security, focuses on the enforcement of immigration and customs laws within the United States, the protection of specified federal buildings, and air and marine enforcement.

EMPLOYMENT REQUIREMENTS

The applicant must be a U.S. citizen between 21 and 36 years of age, must be in good medical condition, and must possess a valid driver's license. General employment requirements include (1) a comprehensive written exam, (2) a structured employment interview, and (3) a background investigation. Appointment at the GS-5 level requires (1) a bachelor's degree from an accredited college or university; (2) three years of progressively responsible experience that demonstrates the ability to (a) analyze problems to identify significant factors, gather pertinent data, and recognize solutions; (b) plan and organize work; and (c) communicate effectively orally and in writing; or (3) an equivalent combination of education and experience.

OTHER REQUIREMENTS

Applicants are required to submit to urinalysis to screen for illegal drug use prior to appointment and will be subject to random testing after being hired. Selected candidates will attend basic training at the Immigration Officer Academy in Glynco, Georgia.

SALARY

Successful candidates are typically hired at the GS-5 or GS-7 level, depending on education and work experience.

BENEFITS

Benefits include (1) 13 days of sick leave annually, (2) two and a half to five weeks of paid vacation and ten paid federal holidays each year, (3) federal health and life insurance, and (4) a comprehensive retirement program.

DIRECT INQUIRIES TO:

Department of Homeland Security
Twin Cities Hiring Center, Recruitment Unit
One Federal Dr.
Fort Snelling, MN 55111-4055
Phone: 612-725-3496
Website: http://www.bice.gov

For more information on the rapidly expanding criminal justice careers area, read *Where the Jobs Are: Mission Critical Opportunities for America*, available on the Web at http://www.justicestudies.com/jobs.htm.

Note: The views expressed in this profile do not necessarily represent the views of the U.S. Department of Justice, the federal Bureau of Immigration and Customs Enforcement, or the United States.

Vehicle Searches

Vehicles present a special law enforcement problem. They are highly mobile, and when a driver or an occupant is arrested, the need to search the vehicle may be immediate.

The first significant Supreme Court case involving an automobile was that of ***Carroll* v. *U.S.***[98] in 1925. In the *Carroll* case, a divided Court ruled that a warrantless search of an automobile or other vehicle is valid if it is based on a reasonable belief that contraband is present. In 1964, however, in the case of *Preston* v. *U.S.*,[99] the limits of warrantless vehicle searches were defined. Preston was arrested for vagrancy and taken to jail. His vehicle was impounded, towed to the police garage, and later searched. Two revolvers were uncovered in the glove compartment, and more incriminating evidence was found in the trunk. Preston was convicted on weapons possession and other charges and eventually appealed to the U.S. Supreme Court. The Court held that the warrantless search of Preston's vehicle had occurred while the automobile was in secure custody and had therefore been illegal. Time and circumstances would have permitted acquisition of a warrant to conduct the search, the Court reasoned.

When the search of a vehicle occurs after it has been impounded, however, that search may be legitimate if it is undertaken for routine and reasonable purposes. In the case of *South Dakota* v. *Opperman* (1976),[100] for example, the Court held that a warrantless search undertaken for purposes of inventorying and safekeeping the personal possessions of the car's owner was not illegal. The intent of the search, which had turned up marijuana, had not been to discover contraband but to secure the owner's belongings from possible theft. Again, in *Colorado* v. *Bertine* (1987),[101] the Court reinforced the idea that officers may open closed containers found in a vehicle while conducting a routine search for inventorying purposes. In the words of the Court, such searches are "now a well-defined exception in the warrant requirement." In 1990, however, in the precedent-setting case of *Florida* v. *Wells*,[102] the Court agreed with a lower court's suppression of marijuana evidence discovered in a locked suitcase in the trunk of a defendant's impounded vehicle. In *Wells*, the Court held that standardized criteria authorizing the search of a vehicle for inventorying purposes were necessary before such a discovery could be legitimate. Standardized criteria, said the Court, might take the form of department policies, written general orders, or established routines.

Generally speaking, where vehicles are concerned, an investigatory stop is permissible under the Fourth Amendment if supported by reasonable suspicion,[103] and a warrantless search of a stopped car is valid if it is based on probable cause.[104] Reasonable suspicion can expand into probable cause when the facts in a given situation so warrant. In the 1996 case of *Ornelas* v. *U.S.*,[105] for example, two experienced Milwaukee police officers stopped a car with California license plates that had been spotted in a motel parking lot known for drug trafficking after the Narcotics and Dangerous Drugs Information System (NADDIS) identified the car's owner as a known or suspected drug trafficker. One of the officers noticed a loose panel above an armrest in the vehicle's backseat and then searched the car. A package of cocaine was found beneath the panel, and the driver and a passenger were arrested. Following conviction, the defendants appealed to the U.S. Supreme Court, claiming that no probable cause to search the car existed at the time of the stop. The majority opinion, however, noted that in the view of the court that originally heard the case, "the model, age, and source-State origin of the car, and the fact that two men traveling together checked into a motel at 4 o'clock in the morning without reservations, formed a drug-courier profile and ... this profile together with the [computer] reports gave rise to a reasonable suspicion of drug-trafficking activity.... [I]n the court's view, reasonable suspicion became probable cause when [the deputy] found the loose panel."[106] Probable cause permits a warrantless search of a vehicle because it is able to quickly leave a jurisdiction. This exception to the exclusionary rule is called the **fleeting-targets exception**.[107]

fleeting-targets exception
An exception to the exclusionary rule that permits law enforcement officers to search a motor vehicle based on probable cause but without a warrant. The fleeting-targets exception is predicated on the fact that vehicles can quickly leave the jurisdiction of a law enforcement agency.

Warrantless vehicle searches can extend to any area of the vehicle and may include sealed containers, the trunk, and the glove compartment if officers have probable cause to conduct a purposeful search or if officers have been given permission to search the vehicle. In the 1991 case of *Florida* v. *Jimeno*,[108] arresting officers stopped a motorist, who gave them permission to search his car. The defendant was later convicted on a drug charge when a bag on the floor of the car was found to contain cocaine. Upon appeal to the U.S. Supreme Court, however, he argued that the permission given to search his car did not extend to bags and other items within the car. In a decision that may have implications beyond vehicle searches, the Court held that "[a] criminal suspect's Fourth Amendment right to be free from unreasonable searches is not violated when, after he gives police permission to search his car, they open a closed container found within the car that might reasonably hold the object of the search. The amendment is satisfied when, under the circumstances, it is objectively reasonable for the police to believe that the scope of the suspect's consent permitted them to open the particular container."[109]

In *U.S.* v. *Ross* (1982),[110] the Court found that officers had not exceeded their authority in opening a bag in the defendant's trunk that was found to contain heroin. The search was held to be justifiable on the basis of information developed from a search of the passenger compartment. The Court said, "If probable cause justifies the search of a lawfully stopped vehicle, it justifies the search of every part of the vehicle and its contents that may conceal the object of the search."[111] Moreover, according to the 1996 U.S. Supreme Court decision in *Whren* v. *U.S.*,[112] officers may stop a vehicle being driven suspiciously and then search it once probable cause has developed, even if their primary assignment centers on duties other than traffic enforcement

Freedom or Safety? You Decide.

Religion and Public Safety

In 2003, Florida Judge Janet Thorpe ruled that a Muslim woman could not wear a veil while being photographed for a state driver's license. The woman, Sultaana Freeman, claimed that her religious rights were violated when the state department of motor vehicles required that she reveal her face for the photograph. She offered to show her eyes, but not the rest of her face, to the camera.

Judge Thorpe said, however, that a "compelling interest in protecting the public from criminal activities and security threats" did not place an undue burden on Freeman's ability to practice her religion.

After the hearing, Freeman's husband, Abdul-Maalik Freeman, told reporters, "This is a religious principle; this is a principle that's imbedded in us as believers. So, she's not going to do that. We'll take the next step, and this is what we call the American way." Howard Marks, the Freemans' attorney, said that he would file an appeal in a higher court.

YOU DECIDE

Do the demands of public safety justify the kind of restriction on religious practice described here? Should photo IDs, such as driver's licenses, be replaced with other forms of identification (such as an individual's stored DNA profile) in order to accommodate the beliefs of individuals like the Freemans?

Reference: "Judge: No Veil in Driver's License Photo," Associated Press wire services, June 6, 2003.

or "if a reasonable officer would not have stopped the motorist absent some additional law enforcement objective" (which in the case of *Whren* was drug enforcement).

Motorists[113] and their passengers may be ordered out of stopped vehicles in the interest of officer safety, and any evidence developed as a result of such a procedure may be used in court. In 1997, for example, in the case of *Maryland* v. *Wilson*,[114] the U.S. Supreme Court overturned a decision by a Maryland court that held that crack cocaine found during a traffic stop was seized illegally when it fell from the lap of a passenger ordered out of a stopped vehicle by a Maryland state trooper. The Maryland court reasoned that the police should not have authority to order seemingly innocent passengers out of vehicles—even vehicles that have been stopped for legitimate reasons. The Supreme Court cited concerns for officer safety in overturning the Maryland court's ruling and held that the activities of passengers are subject to police control. Similarly, in 2007, in the case of *Brendlin* v. *California*, the Court ruled that passengers in stopped vehicles are necessarily detained as a result of the stop and that they should expect that, for safety reasons, officers will exercise "unquestioned police command" over them for the duration of the stop.[115] Consequently, however, any passenger in a stopped automobile may use his or her Fourth Amendment rights to challenge the stop's legality.

In 1998, however, the U.S. Supreme Court placed clear limits on warrantless vehicle searches. In the case of *Knowles* v. *Iowa*,[116] an Iowa policeman stopped Patrick Knowles for speeding, issued him a citation, but did not make a custodial arrest. The officer then conducted a full search of his car without Knowles's consent and without probable cause. Marijuana was found, and Knowles was arrested. At the time, Iowa state law gave officers authority to conduct full-blown automobile searches when issuing only a citation. The Supreme Court found, however, that while concern for officer safety during a routine traffic stop may justify the minimal intrusion of ordering a driver and passengers out of a car, it does not by itself justify what it called "the considerably greater intrusion attending a full field-type search." Hence while a search incident to arrest may be justifiable in the eyes of the Court, a search incident to citation clearly is not.

In the 1999 case of *Wyoming* v. *Houghton*,[117] the Court ruled that police officers with probable cause to search a car may inspect passengers' belongings found in the car that are capable of concealing the object of the search. *Thornton* v. *U.S.* (2004) established the authority of arresting officers to search a car without a warrant even if the driver had previously exited the vehicle.[118]

In 2005, in the case of *Illinois* v. *Caballes*,[119] the Court held that the use of a drug-sniffing dog during a routine and lawful traffic stop is permissible and may not even be a search within the meaning of the Fourth Amendment. In writing for the majority, Justice John Paul Stevens said that "the use of a well-trained narcotics-detection dog—one that does not expose non-

Library EXTRA

contraband items that otherwise would remain hidden from public view—during a lawful traffic stop generally does not implicate legitimate privacy interests." Learn more about motor vehicle searches at Library Extra 5–4.

Roadblocks and Motor Vehicle Checkpoints

The Fourth and Fourteenth Amendments to the U.S. Constitution guarantee liberty and personal security to all people residing within the United States. Courts have generally held that police officers have no legitimate authority to detain or arrest people who are going about their business in a peaceful manner, in the absence of probable cause to believe that a crime has been committed. In a number of instances, however, the U.S. Supreme Court has decided that community interests may necessitate a temporary suspension of personal liberty, even when probable cause is lacking. One such case is that of *Michigan Dept. of State Police* v. *Sitz* (1990),[120] which involved the legality of highway sobriety checkpoints, including those at which nonsuspicious drivers are subjected to scrutiny. In *Sitz*, the Court ruled that such stops are reasonable insofar as they are essential to the welfare of the community as a whole. That the Court reached its conclusion based on pragmatic social interests is clear from the words used by Chief Justice Rehnquist:

> No one can seriously dispute the magnitude of the drunken driving problem or the States' interest in eradicating it. Media reports of alcohol-related death and mutilation on the Nation's roads are legion. Drunk drivers cause an annual death toll of over 25,000 and in the same time span cause nearly one million personal injuries and more than five billion dollars in property damage.... [T]he balance of the State's interest in preventing drunken driving, the extent to which this system can reasonably be said to advance that interest, and the degree of intrusion upon individual motorists who are briefly stopped weigh in favor of the state program.

In a second case, *U.S.* v. *Martinez-Fuerte* (1976),[121] the Court upheld brief suspicionless seizures at a fixed international checkpoint designed to intercept illegal aliens. The Court noted that "to require that such stops always be based on reasonable suspicion would be impractical because the flow of traffic tends to be too heavy to allow the particularized study of a given car necessary to identify it as a possible carrier of illegal aliens. Such a requirement also would

▸ A police officer searching a vehicle in San Diego, California. Warrantless vehicle searches, where the driver is suspected of a crime, have generally been justified by the fact that vehicles are highly mobile and can quickly leave police jurisdiction. Can passengers in the vehicle also be searched?
Mike Karlsson/Arresting Images

largely eliminate any deterrent to the conduct of well-disguised smuggling operations, even though smugglers are known to use these highways regularly."[122]

In 2000, however, in what some people saw as a change in direction, the Court struck down a narcotics checkpoint program established by the Indianapolis Police Department in 1998. Under the program, stopped drivers were told that they were at a drug checkpoint, and officers examined each driver's license and registration while visually assessing the driver for signs of impairment. Drug-sniffing dogs were then walked around the vehicle's exterior. On average, motorists were stopped for three minutes. In ruling the program illegal, the justices held that the Fourth Amendment prohibits even a brief "seizure" of a motorist "under a program whose primary purpose is ultimately indistinguishable from the general interest in crime control." The Court's written opinion in *Indianapolis* v. *Edmond*[123] indicated that similar programs with the purpose of verifying driver's licenses and vehicle registrations would continue to be permissible because they were not intended to "detect evidence of ordinary criminal wrongdoing."

In fact, in 2004, in the case of *Illinois* v. *Lidster*,[124] the Court held that information-seeking highway roadblocks are permissible. In distinguishing this kind of stop from that in *Edmond*, the Court said that *Edmond*-type stops targeted motorists themselves and were intended to determine whether a vehicle's occupants were committing a crime when stopped. The stop in *Lidster*, said the Court, was different because its intent was merely to solicit motorists' help in solving a crime. "The law," said the Court, "ordinarily permits police to seek the public's voluntary cooperation in a criminal investigation."

Watercraft and Motor Homes

The 1983 case of *U.S.* v. *Villamonte-Marquez*[125] widened the *Carroll* decision (discussed earlier) to include watercraft. The case involved an anchored sailboat occupied by Villamonte-Marquez, which was searched by a U.S. Customs officer after one of the crew members appeared unresponsive to being hailed. The officer thought he smelled burning marijuana after boarding the vessel and, through an open hatch, saw burlap bales that he suspected might be contraband. A search proved him correct, and the ship's occupants were arrested. Their conviction was overturned upon appeal, but the U.S. Supreme Court reversed the appellate court. The Court reasoned that a vehicle on the water can easily leave the jurisdiction of enforcement officials, just as a car or truck can.

In *California* v. *Carney* (1985),[126] the Court extended police authority to conduct warrantless searches of vehicles to include motor homes. Earlier arguments had been advanced that a motor home, because it is more like a permanent residence, should not be considered a vehicle for purposes of search and seizure. In a 6–3 decision, the Court rejected those arguments, reasoning that a vehicle's appointments and size do not alter its basic function of providing transportation.

Houseboats were brought under the automobile exception to the Fourth Amendment warrant requirement in the 1988 Tenth Circuit Court case of *U.S.* v. *Hill*.[127] In the *Hill* case, DEA agents developed evidence that led them to believe that methamphetamine was being manufactured aboard a houseboat traversing Lake Texoma in Oklahoma. Because a storm warning had been issued for the area, agents decided to board and to search the boat before obtaining a warrant. During the search, an operating amphetamine laboratory was discovered, and the boat was seized. In an appeal, the defendants argued that the houseboat search had been illegal because agents lacked a warrant to search their home. The appellate court, however, in rejecting the claims of the defendants, ruled that a houseboat, because it is readily mobile, may be searched without a warrant when probable cause exists to believe that a crime has been or is being committed.

Suspicionless Searches

In two 1989 decisions, the U.S. Supreme Court ruled for the first time in its history that there may be instances when the need to ensure public safety provides a **compelling interest** that negates the rights of any individual to privacy, permitting **suspicionless searches**—those that occur when a person is not suspected of a crime. In the case of *National Treasury Employees Union* v. *Von Raab* (1989),[128] the Court, by a 5–4 vote, upheld a program of the U.S. Customs Service that required mandatory drug testing for all workers seeking promotions or job transfers involving drug interdiction and the carrying of firearms. The Court's majority opinion read, "We think the government's need to conduct the suspicionless searches required by the

compelling interest
A legal concept that provides a basis for suspicionless searches when public safety is at issue. (Urinalysis tests of train engineers are an example.) It is the concept on which the U.S. Supreme Court cases of *Skinner* v. *Railway Labor Executives' Association* (1989) and *National Treasury Employees Union* v. *Von Raab* (1989) turned. In those cases, the Court held that public safety may sometimes provide a sufficiently compelling interest to justify limiting an individual's right to privacy.

suspicionless search
A search conducted by law enforcement personnel without a warrant and without suspicion. Suspicionless searches are permissible only if based on an overriding concern for public safety.

Customs program outweighs the privacy interest of employees engaged directly in drug interdiction, and of those who otherwise are required to carry firearms."

The second case, *Skinner* v. *Railway Labor Executives' Association* (1989),[129] was decided on the same day. In *Skinner*, the justices voted 7 to 2 to permit the mandatory testing of railway crews for the presence of drugs or alcohol following serious train accidents. The *Skinner* case involved evidence of drugs in a 1987 train wreck outside of Baltimore, Maryland, in which 16 people were killed and hundreds were injured.

The 1991 Supreme Court case of ***Florida* v. *Bostick***,[130] which permitted warrantless "sweeps" of intercity buses, moved the Court deeply into conservative territory. The *Bostick* case came to the attention of the Court as a result of the Broward County (Florida) Sheriff's Department's routine practice of boarding buses at scheduled stops and asking passengers for permission to search their bags. Terrance Bostick, a passenger on one of the buses, gave police permission to search his luggage, which was found to contain cocaine. Bostick was arrested and eventually pleaded guilty to charges of drug trafficking. The Florida Supreme Court, however, found merit in Bostick's appeal, which was based on a Fourth Amendment claim that the search of his luggage had been unreasonable. The Florida court held that "a reasonable passenger in [Bostick's] situation would not have felt free to leave the bus to avoid questioning by the police," and it overturned the conviction.

In terms that apply equally to seizures of property and to seizures of persons, the Fourth Amendment has drawn a firm line at the entrance to the house. Absent exigent circumstances, that threshold may not reasonably be crossed without a warrant.

—Payton v. New York *445 U.S. 573, 590 (1980)*

The state appealed to the U.S. Supreme Court, which held that the Florida Supreme Court had erred in interpreting Bostick's *feelings* that he was not free to leave the bus. In the words of the Court, "Bostick was a passenger on a bus that was scheduled to depart. He would not have felt free to leave the bus even if the police had not been present. Bostick's movements were 'confined' in a sense, but this was the natural result of his decision to take the bus." In other words, Bostick was constrained not so much by police action as by his own feelings that he might miss the bus were he to get off. Following this line of reasoning, the Court concluded that warrantless, suspicionless "sweeps" of buses, "trains, planes, and city streets" are permissible as long as officers (1) ask individual passengers for permission before searching their possessions, (2) do not coerce passengers to consent to a search, and (3) do not convey the message that citizen compliance with the search request is mandatory. Passenger compliance with police searches must be voluntary for the searches to be legal.

In contrast to the tone of Court decisions more than two decades earlier, the justices did not require officers to inform passengers that they were free to leave or that they had the right to deny officers the opportunity to search (although Bostick himself was so advised by Florida officers). Any reasonable person, the Court ruled, should feel free to deny the police request. In the words of the Court, "The appropriate test is whether, taking into account all of the circumstances surrounding the encounter, a reasonable passenger would feel free to decline the officers' requests or otherwise terminate the encounter." The Court continued, "Rejected, however, is Bostick's argument that he must have been seized because no reasonable person would freely consent to a search of luggage containing drugs, since the 'reasonable person' test presumes an innocent person."

Critics of the decision saw it as creating new "gestapo-like" police powers in the face of which citizens on public transportation will feel compelled to comply with police requests for search authority. Dissenting Justices Harry Blackmun, John Paul Stevens, and Thurgood Marshall held that "the bus sweep at issue in this case violates the core values of the Fourth Amendment." The Court's majority, however, defended its ruling by writing, "[T]he Fourth Amendment proscribes unreasonable searches and seizures; it does not proscribe voluntary cooperation." In mid-2000, however, in the case of *Bond* v. *U.S.*,[131] the Court ruled that physical manipulation of a carry-on bag in the possession of a bus passenger without the owner's consent does violate the Fourth Amendment's proscription against unreasonable searches.

In the case of ***U.S.* v. *Drayton*** (2002),[132] the U.S. Supreme Court reiterated its position that police officers are not required to advise bus passengers of their right to refuse to cooperate with officers conducting searches or to refuse to be searched. In *Drayton*, the driver of a bus allowed three police officers to board the bus as part of a routine drug and weapons interdiction effort. One officer knelt on the driver's seat, facing the rear of the bus, while another officer stayed in the rear, facing forward. A third officer, named Lang, worked his way from back to front, speaking with individual passengers as he went. To avoid blocking the aisle, Lang stood next to or just behind each passenger with whom he spoke. He later testified that passengers who declined to cooperate or who chose to exit the bus at any time would have been allowed to do so without argument; that most people were willing to cooperate; that in his experience, passengers often leave buses for a cigarette or a snack while officers are on board; and that although he sometimes informed passengers of their right to refuse to cooperate, he did not do so on the day in question. As Lang approached Christopher Drayton and Clifton Brown, Jr., who were seated together, he held up his badge long enough for them to identify him as an officer. Speaking just loudly enough for the two to hear, he declared that the police were looking for drugs and weapons and asked if they had any bags. When both of them pointed to a bag overhead, Lang asked if they minded if he checked it. Brown agreed, and a search of the bag revealed no contraband. Lang then asked Brown whether he minded if the officer checked his person. Brown agreed, and a pat-down search revealed hard objects similar to drug packages in both of Brown's thigh areas, resulting in his arrest. Lang then asked Drayton, "Mind if I check you?" When Drayton agreed, a pat down revealed objects similar to those found on Brown, and Drayton was also arrested. A further search of the two men revealed that Drayton and Brown had taped cocaine between their legs. Both were charged with federal drug crimes. In court, their attorneys moved to suppress the cocaine as evidence, arguing that their consent to the pat-down searches was invalid. In denying the motions, the federal district court determined that the police conduct was not coercive and that the defendants' consent to the search had been voluntary. The Eleventh Circuit Court, however, reversed that finding based on the belief that bus passengers do not feel free to disregard officers' requests to search in the absence of some positive indication that consent may be refused.

In 2004, the U.S. Supreme Court made it clear that suspicionless searches of vehicles at our nation's borders are permitted, even when the searches are extensive. In the case of *U.S.* v. *Flores-Montano*,[133] customs officials disassembled the gas tank of a car belonging to a man entering the country from Mexico and found that it contained 37 kilograms of marijuana. Although the officers admitted that their actions were not motivated by any particular belief that the search would reveal contraband, the Court held that Congress has always granted "plenary authority to conduct routine searches and seizures at the border without probable cause or a warrant." The Court stated that "the Government's authority to conduct suspicionless inspections at the border includes the authority to remove, disassemble, and reassemble a vehicle's fuel tank."

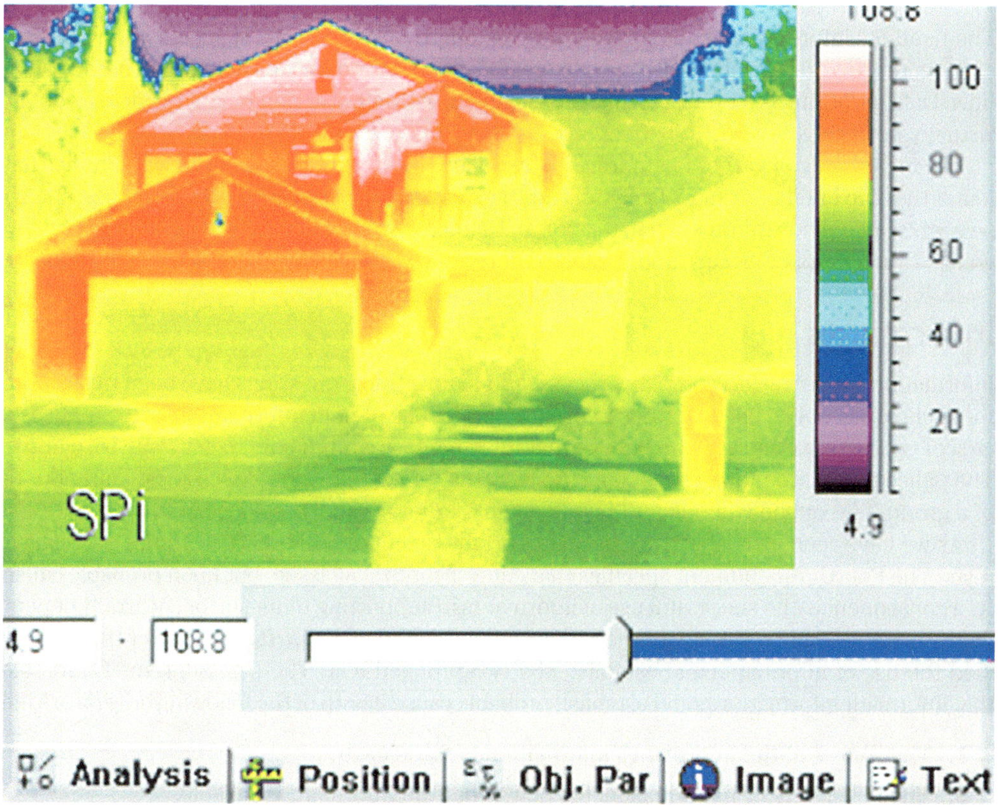

A photo created by a thermal-imaging device. The photo shows "hot spots" in a suspected marijuana grower's home that might be produced by lights used to grow the plants indoors. In *Kyllo* v. *U.S.* (2001), the U.S. Supreme Court held that the police may not use such devices without a search warrant. What was the Court's rationale?

Image compliments of Sierra Pacific Innovations Corporation (SPI), www.x20.org

High-Technology Searches

The burgeoning use of high technology to investigate crime and to uncover violations of the criminal law is forcing courts throughout the nation to evaluate the applicability of constitutional guarantees in light of high-tech searches and seizures. In 1996, the California appellate court decision in *People* v. *Deutsch*[134] presaged the kinds of issues that are likely to be encountered as American law enforcement expands its use of cutting-edge technology. In *Deutsch*, judges faced the question of whether a warrantless scan of a private dwelling with a thermal-imaging device constitutes an unreasonable search within the meaning of the Fourth Amendment. Such devices (also called *forward-looking infrared [FLIR] systems*) measure radiant energy in the radiant heat portion of the electromagnetic spectrum[135] and display their readings as thermographs. The "heat picture" that a thermal imager produces can be used, as it was in the case of Dorian Deutsch, to reveal unusually warm areas or rooms that might be associated with the cultivation of drug-bearing plants, such as marijuana. Two hundred cannabis plants, which were being grown hydroponically under high-wattage lights in two walled-off portions of Deutsch's home, were seized following an exterior thermal scan of her home by a police officer who drove by at 1:30 in the morning. Because no entry of the house was anticipated during the search, the officer had acted without a search warrant. The California court ruled that the scan was an illegal search because "society accepts a reasonable expectation of privacy" surrounding "nondisclosed activities within the home."[136]

In the similar case of ***Kyllo* v. *U.S.*** (2001),[137] the U.S. Supreme Court reached much the same conclusion. Based on the results of a warrantless search conducted by officers using a thermal-imaging device, investigators applied for a search warrant of Kyllo's home. The subsequent search uncovered more than 100 marijuana plants that were being grown under bright lights. In overturning Kyllo's conviction on drug-manufacturing charges, the Court held (with regard to the original warrantless search with the thermal-imaging device), "Where, as here, the Government uses a device that is not in general public use, to explore details of a private home that would previously have been unknowable without physical intrusion, the surveillance is a Fourth Amendment 'search,' and is presumptively unreasonable without a warrant."[138] Learn more about the issues surrounding search and seizure at **Web Extra 5–3** at mycrimekit.com.

Web EXTRA

The Intelligence Function

The need for information leads police investigators to question both suspects and informants and, even more often, potentially knowledgeable citizens who may have been witnesses or victims. Data gathering is a crucial form of intelligence; without it, enforcement agencies would be virtually powerless to plan and effect arrests.

The importance of gathering information in police work cannot be overstressed. Studies have found that the one factor most likely to lead to arrest in serious crimes is the presence of a witness who can provide information to the police. Undercover operations, Neighborhood Watch programs, Crime Stopper groups, and organized detective work all contribute this vital information.

Informants

Information gathering is a complex process, and many ethical questions have been raised about the techniques police use to gather information. The use of paid informants, for example, is an area of concern to ethicists who believe that informants are often paid to get away with crimes. The police practice (endorsed by some prosecutors) of agreeing not to charge one offender out of a group if he or she will talk and testify against others is another concern.

As we have seen, probable cause is an important aspect of both police searches and legal arrests. The Fourth Amendment specifies that "no Warrants shall issue, but upon probable cause." As a consequence, the successful use of informants in supporting requests for a warrant depends on the demonstrable reliability of their information. The case of *Aguilar* v. *Texas* (1964)[139] clarified the use of informants and established a two-pronged test. The U.S. Supreme Court ruled that informant information could establish probable cause if both of the following criteria are met:

1. The source of the informant's information is made clear.
2. The police officer has a reasonable belief that the informant is reliable.

The two-pronged test of *Aguilar* v. *Texas* was intended to prevent the issuance of warrants on the basis of false or fabricated information. The case of *U.S.* v. *Harris* (1971)[140] provided an exception to the two-pronged *Aguilar* test. The *Harris* Court recognized the fact that when an informant provides information that is damaging to him or her, it is probably true. In *Harris*, an informant told police that he had purchased non-tax-paid whiskey from another person. Since the information also implicated the informant in a crime, it was held to be accurate, even though it could not meet the second prong of the *Aguilar* test. "Admissions of crime," said the Court, "carry their own indicia of credibility—sufficient at least to support a finding of probable cause to search."[141]

The right of the people to be secure in their persons, houses, papers, and effects, against unreasonable searches and seizures, shall not be violated, and no Warrants shall issue, but upon probable cause, supported by Oath or affirmation, and particularly describing the place to be searched, and the persons or things to be seized.
—*Fourth Amendment to the U.S. Constitution*

In 1983, in the case of *Illinois* v. *Gates*,[142] the Court adopted a totality-of-circumstances approach, which held that sufficient probable cause for issuing a warrant exists where an informant can be reasonably believed on the basis of everything that the police know. The *Gates* case involved an anonymous informant who provided incriminating information about another person through a letter to the police. Although the source of the information was not stated and the police were unable to say whether the informant was reliable, the overall sense of things, given what was already known to police, was that the information supplied was probably valid. In *Gates*, the Court held that probable cause exists when "there is a fair probability that contraband or evidence of a crime will be found in a particular place."

In the 1990 case of ***Alabama* v. *White***,[143] the Supreme Court ruled that an anonymous tip, even in the absence of other corroborating information about a suspect, could form the basis for an investigatory stop if the informant accurately predicted the *future* behavior of the suspect. The Court reasoned that the ability to predict a suspect's behavior demonstrates a significant degree of familiarity with the suspect's affairs. In the words of the Court, "Because only a small number of people are generally privy to an individual's itinerary, it is reasonable for the police to believe that a person with access to such information is likely to also have access to reliable information about that individual's illegal activities."[144]

In 2000, in the case of *Florida* v. *J.L.*, the Court held that an anonymous tip that a person is carrying a gun does not, without more, justify a police officer's stop and frisk of that person. Ruling that such a search is invalid under the Fourth Amendment, the Court rejected the suggestion of a firearm exception to the general stop-and-frisk rule.[145]

The identity of informants may be kept secret only if sources have been explicitly assured of confidentiality by investigating officers or if a reasonably implied assurance of confidentiality has been made. In ***U.S. Dept. of Justice* v. *Landano*** (1993),[146] the U.S. Supreme Court required that an informant's identity be revealed through a request made under the federal Freedom of Information Act. In that case, the FBI had not specifically assured the informant of confidentiality, and the Court ruled that "the government is not entitled to a presumption that all sources supplying information to the FBI in the course of a criminal investigation are confidential sources."

Police Interrogation

In 2003, Illinois became the first state in the nation to require the electronic recording of police interrogations and confessions in homicide cases.[147] State lawmakers hoped that the use of recordings would reduce the incidence of false confessions as well as the likelihood of convictions based on such confessions. Under the law, police interrogators must create video- or audiotape recordings of any questioning involving suspects. The law prohibits the introduction in court of statements and confessions that have not been taped. Proponents of the law say that it will prevent police intimidation of murder suspects and will put an end to coerced confessions.

interrogation
The information-gathering activity of police officers that involves the direct questioning of suspects.

The U.S. Supreme Court has defined **interrogation** as any behaviors by the police "that the police should know are reasonably likely to elicit an incriminating response from the suspect."[148] Hence interrogation may involve activities that go well beyond mere verbal questioning, and the Court has held that interrogation may include "staged lineups, reverse lineups, positing guilt, minimizing the moral seriousness of crime, and casting blame on the victim or society." It is noteworthy that the Court has also held that "police words or actions normally attendant to arrest and custody do not constitute interrogation" unless they involve pointed or directed questions. Hence an arresting officer may instruct a suspect on what to do and may chitchat with him or her without engaging in interrogation within the meaning of the law. Once police officers make inquiries intended to elicit information about the crime in question, however, interrogation has begun. The interrogation of suspects, like other areas of police activity, is subject to constitutional limits as interpreted by the courts, and a series of landmark decisions by the U.S. Supreme Court has focused on police interrogation.

Physical Abuse

The first in a series of significant cases was that of ***Brown* v. *Mississippi***,[149] decided in 1936. The *Brown* case began with the robbery of a white store owner in Mississippi in 1934. During the robbery, the victim was killed. A posse formed and went to the home of a local African-American man rumored to have been one of the perpetrators. They dragged the suspect from his home, put a rope around his neck, and hoisted him into a tree. They repeated this process a number of times, hoping to get a confession from the man but failing to do so. The posse was headed by a deputy sheriff who then arrested other suspects in the case and laid them over chairs in the local jail and whipped them with belts and buckles until they "confessed." These confessions were used in the trial that followed, and all three defendants were convicted of murder. Their convictions were upheld by the Mississippi Supreme Court. In 1936, however, the case was reviewed by the U.S. Supreme Court, which overturned all of the convictions, saying that it was difficult to imagine techniques of interrogation more "revolting" to the sense of justice than those used in this case.

Inherent Coercion

inherent coercion
The tactics used by police interviewers that fall short of physical abuse but that nonetheless pressure suspects to divulge information.

Interrogation need not involve physical abuse for it to be contrary to constitutional principles. In the case of *Ashcraft* v. *Tennessee* (1944),[150] the U.S. Supreme Court found that interrogation involving **inherent coercion** was not acceptable. Ashcraft had been charged with the murder of his wife, Zelma. He was arrested on a Saturday night and interrogated by relays of skilled interrogators until Monday morning, when he purportedly made a statement implicating himself in the murder. During questioning, he had faced a blinding light but was not physically mistreated. Investigators later testified that when the suspect requested cigarettes, food, or water, they "kindly" provided them. The Court's ruling, which reversed Ashcraft's conviction, made it plain that the Fifth Amendment guarantee against self-incrimination prohibits any form of official coercion or pressure during interrogation.

A similar case, *Chambers* v. *Florida*, was decided in 1940.[151] In that case, four black men were arrested without warrants as suspects in the robbery and murder of an aged white man. After several days of questioning in a hostile atmosphere, the men confessed to the murder. The confessions were used as the primary evidence against them at their trial, and all four were sentenced to die. Upon appeal, the U.S. Supreme Court held that "the very circumstances surrounding their confinement and their questioning, without any formal charges having been brought, were such as to fill petitioners with terror and frightful misgivings."[152] Learn more about the case of *Chambers* v. *Florida* at Library Extra 5–5 at mycrimekit.com.

Library EXTRA

Psychological Manipulation

psychological manipulation
The manipulative actions by police interviewers, designed to pressure suspects to divulge information, that are based on subtle forms of intimidation and control.

Not only must interrogation be free of coercion and hostility, but it also cannot involve sophisticated trickery designed to ferret out a confession. Interrogators do not necessarily have to be scrupulously honest in confronting suspects, and the expert opinions of medical and psychiatric practitioners may be sought in investigations. However, the use of professionals skilled in **psychological manipulation** to gain confessions was banned by the Court in the case of *Leyra* v. *Denno*[153] in 1954, during the heyday of psychiatric perspectives on criminal behavior.

In the *Leyra* case, detectives employed a psychiatrist to question Camilo Leyra, who had been charged with the hammer slayings of his parents. Leyra had been led to believe that the medical doctor to whom he was introduced in an interrogation room had actually been sent to help him with a sinus problem. Following a period of questioning, including subtle suggestions by the psychiatrist that he would feel better if he confessed to the murders, Leyra did indeed confess.

The Supreme Court, on appeal, ruled that the defendant had been effectively and improperly duped by the police. In the words of the Court, "Instead of giving petitioner the medical advice and treatment he expected, the psychiatrist by subtle and suggestive questions simply continued the police effort of the past days and nights to induce petitioner to admit his guilt. For an hour and a half or more the techniques of a highly trained psychiatrist were used to break petitioner's will in order to get him to say he had murdered his parents."[154]

In 1991, in the case of ***Arizona* v. *Fulminante***,[155] the U.S. Supreme Court threw an even more dampening blanket of uncertainty over the use of sophisticated techniques to gain a confession.

Oreste Fulminante was an inmate in a federal prison when he was approached secretly by a fellow inmate who was an FBI informant. The informant told Fulminante that other inmates were plotting to kill him because of a rumor that he had killed a child. He offered to protect Fulminante if he was told the details of the crime. Fulminante then described his role in the murder of his 11-year-old stepdaughter. Fulminante was arrested for that murder, tried, and convicted.

On appeal to the U.S. Supreme Court, Fulminante's lawyers argued that his confession had been coerced because of the threat of violence communicated by the informant. The Court agreed that the confession had been coerced and ordered a new trial at which the confession could not be admitted into evidence. Simultaneously, however, the Court found that the admission of a coerced confession should be considered a harmless "trial error" that need not necessarily result in reversal of a conviction if other evidence still proves guilt. The decision was especially significant because it partially reversed the Court's earlier ruling, in *Chapman* v. *California* (1967),[156] where it was held that forced confessions were such a basic form of constitutional error that they automatically invalidated any conviction to which they related. Fulminante was again convicted at his second trial where his confession was not entered into evidence, and he was sentenced to die. The Arizona Supreme Court, however, overturned his conviction, ruling that testimony describing statements the victim had made about fearing for her life prior to her murder, and which had been entered into evidence, were hearsay and had prejudiced the jury.[157]

The Right to a Lawyer at Interrogation

In 1964, in the case of ***Escobedo* v. *Illinois***,[158] the right to have legal counsel present during police interrogation was recognized. Danny Escobedo was arrested without a warrant for the murder of his brother-in-law, made no statement during his interrogation, and was released the same day. A few weeks later, another person identified Escobedo as the killer. Escobedo was rearrested and taken back to the police station. During the interrogation that followed, officers told him that they "had him cold" and that he should confess. Escobedo asked to see his lawyer but was told that an interrogation was in progress and that he couldn't just go out and see his lawyer. Soon the lawyer arrived and asked to see Escobedo. Police told him that his client was being questioned and could be seen after questioning concluded. Escobedo later claimed that while he repeatedly asked for his lawyer, he was told, "Your lawyer doesn't want to see you." Eventually, Escobedo confessed and was convicted at trial on the basis of his confession. Upon appeal, the U.S. Supreme Court overturned Escobedo's conviction, ruling that counsel is necessary at police interrogations to protect the rights of the defendant and should be provided when the defendant desires.

▲ Ernesto Miranda, shown here after a jury convicted him for a second time. Miranda's conviction on rape and kidnapping charges after arresting officers failed to advise him of his rights led to the now-famous *Miranda* warnings. How do the *Miranda* warnings read?
AP Wide World Photos

In 1981, the case of *Edwards* v. *Arizona*[159] established a "bright-line rule" (that is, specified a criterion that cannot be violated) for investigators to use in interpreting a suspect's right to counsel. In *Edwards*, the U.S. Supreme Court reiterated its *Miranda* concern that once a suspect who is in custody and is being questioned has requested the assistance of counsel, all questioning must cease until an attorney is present. In 1990, the Court refined the rule in ***Minnick* v. *Mississippi***,[160] when it held that after the suspect has had an opportunity to consult his or her lawyer, interrogation may *not* resume unless the lawyer is present. Similarly, according to *Arizona* v. *Roberson* (1988),[161] the police may not avoid the suspect's request for a lawyer by beginning a new line of questioning, even if it is about an unrelated offense. In 1994, however, in the case of *Davis* v. *U.S.*,[162] the Court "put the burden on custodial suspects to make unequivocal invocations of the right to counsel." In the *Davis* case, a man being interrogated in the death of a sailor waived his *Miranda* rights but later said, "Maybe I should talk to a lawyer." Investigators asked the suspect clarifying questions, and he responded, "No, I don't want a lawyer." Upon conviction he appealed, claiming that interrogation should have ceased when he mentioned a lawyer. The Court, in affirming the conviction, stated that "it will often be good police practice for the interviewing officers to clarify whether or not [the suspect] actually wants an attorney."

Suspect Rights: The *Miranda* Decision

***Miranda* warnings**
The advisement of rights due criminal suspects by the police before questioning begins. *Miranda* warnings were first set forth by the U.S. Supreme Court in the 1966 case of *Miranda* v. *Arizona*.

In the area of suspect rights, no case is as famous as that of *Miranda* v. *Arizona* (1966),[163] which established the well-known **Miranda warnings**. Many people regard *Miranda* as the centerpiece of the Warren Court due process rulings.

The case involved Ernesto Miranda, who was arrested in Phoenix, Arizona, and was accused of having kidnapped and raped a young woman. At police headquarters, he was identified by the victim. After being interrogated for two hours, Miranda signed a confession that formed the basis of his later conviction on the charges.

On appeal, the U.S. Supreme Court rendered what some regard as the most far-reaching opinion to have affected criminal justice in the last half century. The Court ruled that Miranda's conviction was unconstitutional because "[t]he entire aura and atmosphere of police interrogation without notification of rights and an offer of assistance of counsel [tend] to subjugate the individual to the will of his examiner."

The Court continued, saying that the suspect "must be warned prior to any questioning that he has the right to remain silent, that anything he says can be used against him in a court of law, that he has the right to the presence of an attorney, and that if he cannot afford an attorney one will be appointed for him prior to any questioning if he so desires. Opportunity to exercise these rights must be afforded to him throughout the interrogation. After such warnings have been given, and such opportunity afforded him, the individual may knowingly and intelligently waive these rights and agree to answer the questions or make a statement. But unless and until such warnings and waiver are demonstrated by the prosecution at the trial, no evidence obtained as a result of interrogation can be used against him."

To ensure that proper advice is given to suspects at the time of their arrest, the now-famous *Miranda* rights are read before any questioning begins. These rights, as they appear on a *Miranda* warning card commonly used by police agencies, appear in CJ Exhibit 2.

Once suspects have been advised of their *Miranda* rights, they are commonly asked to sign a paper that lists each right in order to confirm that they were advised of their rights and that they understand each right. Questioning may then begin, but only if suspects waive the right not to talk or to have a lawyer present during interrogation.

In 1992, *Miranda* rights were effectively extended to illegal immigrants living in the United States. In a settlement of a class-action lawsuit reached in Los Angeles with the Immigration and Naturalization Service, U.S. District Court Judge William Byrne, Jr., approved the printing of millions of notices in several languages to be given to arrestees. The approximately 1.5 million illegal aliens arrested each year must be told they may (1) talk with a lawyer, (2) make a phone call, (3) request a list of available legal services, (4) seek a hearing before an immigration judge, (5) possibly obtain release on bond, and (6) contact a diplomatic officer representing their country. This kind of thing was "long overdue," said Roberto Martinez of the American Friends Service Committee's Mexico-U.S. border program. "Up to now, we've had total mistreatment of civil rights of undocumented people."[164]

When the *Miranda* decision was originally handed down, some hailed it as ensuring the protection of individual rights guaranteed under the Constitution. To guarantee those rights, they suggested, no better agency is available than the police themselves, since the police are present at the initial stages of the criminal justice process. Critics of *Miranda*, however, argued that the decision put police agencies in the uncomfortable and contradictory position not only of enforcing the law but also of having to offer defendants advice on how they might circumvent conviction and punishment. Under *Miranda*, the police partially assume the role of legal adviser to the accused.

In 1999, however, in the case of *U.S.* v. *Dickerson*,[165] the Fourth Circuit U.S. Court of Appeals upheld an almost-forgotten law that Congress had passed in 1968 with the intention of overturning *Miranda*. That law, Section 3501 of Chapter 223, Part II of Title 18 of the U.S. Code, says that "a confession ... shall be admissible in evidence if it is voluntarily given." Upon appeal in 2000, the U.S. Supreme Court upheld its original *Miranda* ruling by a 7 to 2 vote and found that *Miranda* is a constitutional rule (that is, a fundamental right inherent in the U.S. Constitution) that cannot be dismissed by an act of Congress. "*Miranda* and its progeny," the majority wrote in ***Dickerson* v. *U.S.***, will continue to "govern the admissibility of statements made during custodial interrogation in both state and federal courts."[166]

On June 28, 2004, in the case of ***U.S.* v. *Patane***,[167] the U.S. Supreme Court continued refinement of its original 1966 *Miranda* ruling. *Patane* surprised some Court watchers because

CJ Exhibit 2

The *Miranda* Warnings

ADULT RIGHTS WARNING

Suspects 18 years old or older who are in custody must be advised of the following rights before any questioning begins:

1. You have the right to remain silent.
2. Anything you say can be used against you in a court of law.
3. You have the right to talk to a lawyer and to have a lawyer present while you are being questioned.
4. If you want a lawyer before or during questioning but cannot afford to hire a lawyer, one will be appointed to represent you at no cost before any questioning.
5. If you answer questions now without a lawyer here, you still have the right to stop answering questions at any time.

WAIVER OF RIGHTS

After reading and explaining the rights of a person in custody, an officer must also ask for a waiver of those rights before any questioning.

The following waiver questions must be answered affirmatively, either by express answer or by clear implication. Silence alone is not a waiver.

1. Do you understand each of these rights I have explained to you? (Answer must be YES.)
2. Having these rights in mind, do you now wish to answer questions? (Answer must be YES.)
3. Do you now wish to answer questions without a lawyer present? (Answer must be YES.)

The following question must be asked of juveniles ages 14, 15, 16, and 17:

1. Do you now wish to answer questions without your parents, guardians, or custodians present? (Answer must be YES.)

Source: North Carolina Justice Academy. Reprinted with permission.

in it the Court held that "a mere failure to give *Miranda* warnings does not, by itself, violate a suspect's constitutional rights or even the *Miranda* rule."

The *Patane* case began with the arrest of a convicted felon after a federal agent told officers that the man owned a handgun illegally. At the time of arrest, the officers tried to advise the defendant of his rights, but he interrupted them, saying that he already knew his rights. The officers then asked him about the pistol, and he told them where it was. After the weapon was recovered, the defendant was charged with illegal possession of a firearm by a convicted felon.

At first glance, *Patane* appears to contradict the fruit of the poisonous tree doctrine that the Court established in the 1920 case of *Silverthorne Lumber Co.* v. *U.S.*[168] and that *Wong Sun* v. *U.S.* (1963)[169] made applicable to verbal evidence derived immediately from an illegal search and seizure. An understanding of *Patane*, however, requires recognition of the fact that the *Miranda* rule is based on the self-incrimination clause of the Fifth Amendment to the U.S. Constitution. According to the Court in *Patane*, "that Clause's core protection is a prohibition on compelling a criminal defendant to testify against himself at trial." It cannot be violated, the Court said, "by the introduction of nontestimonial evidence obtained as a result of voluntary statements." In other words, according to the Court, only (1) coerced statements and (2) those voluntary statements made by a defendant that might directly incriminate him or her at a later trial are precluded by a failure to read a suspect his or her *Miranda* rights. Such voluntary statements would, of course, include such things as an outright confession.

Significantly, however, oral statements must be distinguished, the Court said, from the "physical fruits of the suspect's unwarned but voluntary statements." In other words, if an unwarned suspect is questioned by police officers and tells the officers where they can find an illegal weapon or a weapon that has been used in a crime, the weapon can be recovered and later introduced as evidence at the suspect's trial. If the same unwarned suspect, however, tells police that he committed a murder, then his confession will not be allowed into evidence at trial. The line drawn by the Court is against the admissibility of *oral statements* made by an unwarned defendant, not the *nontestimonial physical evidence* resulting from continued police investigation of such statements. Under *Patane*, the oral statements themselves cannot be admitted, but the physical evidence derived from them can be. "Thus," wrote the justices in *Patane*, "admission of nontestimonial physical fruits (the pistol here) does not run the risk of admitting into trial an accused's coerced incriminating statements against himself."

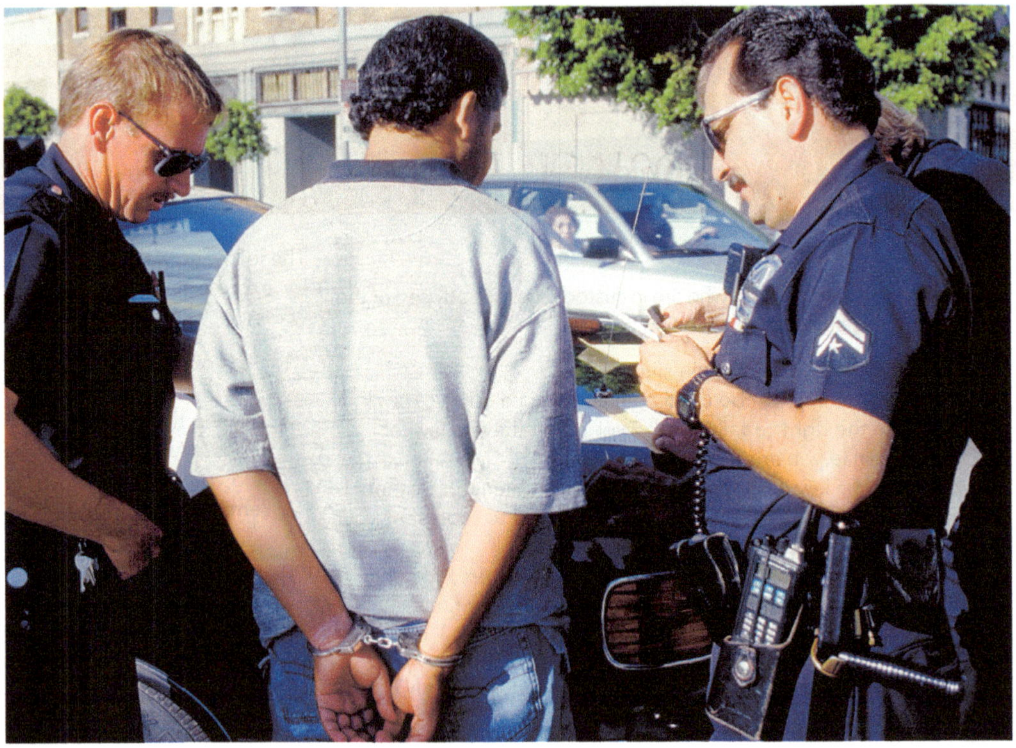

▶ A suspect being read his *Miranda* rights immediately after arrest. Officers often read *Miranda* rights from a card to preclude the possibility of mistake. What might be the consequences of a mistake?
Michael Newman/PhotoEdit Inc.

Waiver of *Miranda* Rights by Suspects

While every person is entitled to stand silent, it is more virtuous for the wrongdoer to admit his offense and accept the punishment he deserves.... It is wrong, and subtly corrosive of our criminal justice system, to regard an honest confession as a mistake.
—*Justice Antonin Scalia Dissenting in* Minnick v. Mississippi, *498 U.S. 146 (1990)*

Suspects in police custody may legally waive their *Miranda* rights through a voluntary "knowing and intelligent" waiver. A knowing waiver can only be made if a suspect has been advised of his or her rights and was in a condition to understand the advisement. A rights advisement made in English to a Spanish-speaking suspect, for example, cannot produce a knowing waiver. Likewise, an intelligent waiver of rights requires that the defendant be able to understand the consequences of not invoking the *Miranda* rights. In the case of *Moran* v. *Burbine* (1986),[170] the U.S. Supreme Court defined an intelligent and knowing waiver as one "made with a full awareness both of the nature of the right being abandoned and the consequences of the decision to abandon it." Similarly, in *Colorado* v. *Spring* (1987),[171] the Court held that an intelligent and knowing waiver can be made even though a suspect has not been informed of all the alleged offenses about which he or she is about to be questioned.

Inevitable-Discovery Exception to *Miranda*

The case of Robert Anthony Williams provides a good example of the change in the U.S. Supreme Court philosophy, alluded to earlier in this chapter, from an individual-rights perspective toward a public-order perspective. The case epitomizes what some have called a "nibbling away" at the advances in defendant rights, which reached their apex in *Miranda*. The case began in 1969, at the close of the Warren Court era, when Williams was convicted of murdering a ten-year-old girl, Pamela Powers, around Christmas-time. Although Williams had been advised of his rights, detectives searching for the girl's body were riding in a car with the defendant when one of them made what has since come to be known as the "Christian burial speech." The detective told Williams that since Christmas was almost upon them, it would be "the Christian thing to do" to see to it that Pamela could have a decent burial rather than having to lay in a field somewhere. Williams relented and led detectives to the body. However, because Williams had not been reminded of his right to have a lawyer present during his conversation with the detective, the Supreme Court in *Brewer* v. *Williams* (1977)[172] overturned Williams's conviction, saying that the detective's remarks were "a deliberate eliciting of incriminating evidence from an accused in the absence of his lawyer."

In 1977, Williams was retried for the murder, but his remarks in leading detectives to the body were not entered into evidence. The discovery of the body was itself used, however, prompting another appeal to the Supreme Court based on the argument that the body should not have been used as evidence since it was discovered due to the illegally gathered statements. This time, in ***Nix v. Williams*** (1984),[173] the Supreme Court affirmed Williams's second conviction, holding that the body would have been found anyway, since detectives were searching in the direction where it lay when Williams revealed its location. That ruling came during the heyday of the Burger Court and clearly demonstrates a tilt by the Court away from suspects' rights and an accommodation with the imperfect world of police procedure. The *Williams* case, as it was finally resolved, is said to have created the *inevitable-discovery exception* to the *Miranda* requirements. The inevitable-discovery exception means that evidence, even if it was otherwise gathered inappropriately, can be used in a court of law if it would have invariably turned up in the normal course of events.

Public-Safety Exception to *Miranda*

Also in 1984, the U.S. Supreme Court established what has come to be known as the *public-safety exception* to the *Miranda* rule. The case of *New York* v. *Quarles*[174] centered on a rape in which the victim told police her assailant had fled, with a gun, into a nearby A & P supermarket. Two police officers entered the store and apprehended the suspect. One officer immediately noticed that the man was wearing an empty shoulder holster and, apparently fearing that a child might find the discarded weapon, quickly asked, "Where's the gun?" Quarles was convicted of rape but appealed his conviction, requesting that the weapon be suppressed as evidence because officers had not advised him of his *Miranda* rights before asking him about it. The Supreme Court disagreed, stating that considerations of public safety were overriding and negated the need for rights advisement before limited questioning that focused on the need to prevent further harm.

The U.S. Supreme Court has also held that in cases when the police issue *Miranda* warnings, a later demonstration that a person may have been suffering from mental problems does not necessarily negate a confession. *Colorado* v. *Connelly* (1986)[175] involved a man who approached a Denver police officer and said he wanted to confess to the murder of a young girl. The officer immediately informed him of his *Miranda* rights, but the man waived them and continued to talk. When a detective arrived, the man was again advised of his rights and again waived them. After being taken to the local jail, the man began to hear "voices" and later claimed that it was these voices that had made him confess. At the trial, the defense moved to have the earlier confession negated on the basis that it was not voluntarily or freely given because of the defendant's mental condition. Upon appeal, the U.S. Supreme Court disagreed, saying that "no coercive government conduct occurred in this case." Hence "self-coercion," be it through the agency of a guilty conscience or faulty thought processes, does not appear to bar prosecution based on information revealed willingly by a suspect.

In another refinement of *Miranda*, the lawful ability of a police informant placed in a jail cell along with a defendant to gather information for later use at trial was upheld in the 1986 case of *Kuhlmann* v. *Wilson*.[176] The passive gathering of information was judged to be acceptable, provided that the informant did not make attempts to elicit information.

In the case of ***Illinois v. Perkins*** (1990),[177] the Court expanded its position to say that under appropriate circumstances, even the active questioning of a suspect by an undercover officer posing as a fellow inmate does not require *Miranda* warnings. In *Perkins*, the Court found that, lacking other forms of coercion, the fact that the suspect was not aware of the questioner's identity as a law enforcement officer ensured that his statements were freely given. In the words of the Court, "The essential ingredients of a 'police-dominated atmosphere' and compulsion are not present when an incarcerated person speaks freely to someone that he believes to be a fellow inmate."

Miranda and the Meaning of Interrogation

Modern interpretations of the applicability of *Miranda* warnings turn on an understanding of interrogation. The *Miranda* decision, as originally rendered, specifically recognized the need for police investigators to make inquiries at crime scenes to determine facts or to establish identities. As long as the individual questioned is not yet in custody and as long as probable cause is lacking in the investigator's mind, such questioning can proceed without *Miranda* warnings. In such cases, interrogation, within the meaning of *Miranda*, has not yet begun.

The case of *Rock* v. *Zimmerman* (1982)[178] provides a different sort of example—one in which a suspect willingly made statements to the police before interrogation began. The suspect had burned his own house and shot and killed a neighbor. When the fire department arrived, he began shooting again and killed the fire chief. Cornered later in a field, the defendant, gun in hand, spontaneously shouted at police, "How many people did I kill? How many people are dead?"[179] These spontaneous questions were held to be admissible evidence at the suspect's trial.

It is also important to recognize that the Supreme Court, in the *Miranda* decision, required that officers provide warnings only in those situations involving *both* arrest and custodial interrogation—what some call the ***Miranda* triggers**. In other words, it is generally permissible for officers to take a suspect into custody and listen without asking questions while he or she tells a story. Similarly, they may ask questions without providing a *Miranda* warning, even within the confines of a police station house, as long as the person questioned is not a suspect and is not under arrest.[180] Warnings are required only when officers begin to actively and deliberately elicit responses from a suspect whom they know has been indicted or who is in custody.

***Miranda* triggers**
The dual principles of custody and interrogation, both of which are necessary before an advisement of rights is required.

Officers were found to have acted properly in the case of *South Dakota* v. *Neville* (1983)[181] in informing a man suspected of driving while intoxicated (DWI), without reading him his rights, that he would stand to lose his driver's license if he did not submit to a Breathalyzer test. When the driver responded, "I'm too drunk. I won't pass the test," his answer became evidence of his condition and was permitted at trial.

A third-party conversation recorded by the police after a suspect has invoked the *Miranda* right to remain silent may be used as evidence, according to a 1987 ruling in *Arizona* v. *Mauro*.[182] In *Mauro*, a man who willingly conversed with his wife in the presence of a police tape recorder, even after invoking his right to keep silent, was held to have effectively abandoned that right.

When a waiver is not made, however, in-court references to a defendant's silence following the issuing of *Miranda* warnings are unconstitutional. In the 1976 case of *Doyle* v. *Ohio*,[183] the U.S. Supreme Court definitively ruled that "a suspect's [post-*Miranda*] silence will not be used against him." Even so, according to the Court in ***Brecht* v. *Abrahamson*** (1993),[184] prosecution efforts to use such silence against a defendant may not invalidate a finding of guilt by a jury unless the "error had substantial and injurious effect or influence in determining the jury's verdict."[185]

Finally, the 2004 case of *Missouri* v. *Seibert*[186] addressed the legality of a two-step police interrogation technique in which suspects were questioned and—if they made incriminating statements—were then advised of their *Miranda* rights and questioned again. The justices found that such a technique could not meet constitutional muster, writing, "When the [*Miranda*] warnings are inserted in the midst of coordinated and continuing interrogation, they are likely to mislead and deprive a defendant of knowledge essential to his ability to understand the nature of his rights and the consequences of abandoning them.... And it would be unrealistic to treat two spates of integrated and proximately conducted questioning as independent interrogations ... simply because *Miranda* warnings formally punctuate them in the middle."

Gathering of Special Kinds of Nontestimonial Evidence

The role of law enforcement is complicated by the fact that suspects are often privy to special evidence of a nontestimonial sort. Nontestimonial evidence is generally physical evidence, and most physical evidence is subject to normal procedures of search and seizure. A special category of nontestimonial evidence, however, includes very personal items that may be within or part of a person's body, such as ingested drugs, blood cells, foreign objects, medical implants, and human DNA. Also included in this category might be fingerprints and other kinds of biological residue. The gathering of such special kinds of nontestimonial evidence is a complex area rich in precedent. The Fourth Amendment guarantee that people be secure in their homes and in their persons has generally been interpreted by the courts to mean that the improper seizure of physical evidence of any kind is illegal and will result in exclusion of that evidence at trial. When very personal kinds of nontestimonial evidence are considered, however, the issue becomes more complicated.

The Right to Privacy

Two 1985 cases, *Hayes* v. *Florida*[187] and *Winston* v. *Lee*,[188] are examples of limits the courts have placed on the seizure of very personal forms of nontestimonial evidence. The *Hayes* case established the right of suspects to refuse to be fingerprinted when probable cause necessary to effect an arrest does not exist. *Winston* demonstrated the inviolability of the body against surgical and other substantially invasive techniques that might be ordered by authorities against a suspect's will.

In the *Winston* case, Rudolph Lee, Jr., was found a few blocks from the scene of a robbery with a gunshot wound in his chest. The robbery had involved an exchange of gunshots by a store owner and the robber, with the owner noting that the robber had apparently been hit by a bullet. At the hospital, the store owner identified Lee as the robber. The prosecution sought to have Lee submit to surgery to remove the bullet in his chest, arguing that the bullet would provide physical evidence linking him to the crime. Lee refused the surgery, and in *Winston* v. *Lee*, the U.S. Supreme Court ruled that Lee could not be ordered to undergo surgery because such a magnitude of intrusion into his body was unacceptable under the right to privacy guaranteed by the Fourth Amendment. The *Winston* case was based on precedent established in *Schmerber* v. *California* (1966).[189] The *Schmerber* case turned on the extraction against the defendant's will of a blood sample to be measured for alcohol content. In *Schmerber*, the Court ruled that warrants must be obtained for bodily intrusions unless fast action is necessary to prevent the destruction of evidence by natural physiological processes.

Body-Cavity Searches

In early 2005, officers of the Suffolk County (New York) Police Department arrested 36-year-old Terrance Haynes and charged him with marijuana possession.[190] After placing him in the back of a patrol car, Haynes appeared to choke and had difficulty breathing. Soon his breathing stopped, prompting officers to use the Heimlich maneuver, which dislodged a plastic bag from Haynes's windpipe. The bag contained 11 packets of cocaine. Although Haynes survived the ordeal, he now faces up to 25 years in prison.

While some suspects might literally "cough up" evidence, some are more successful at hiding it *in* their bodies. Body-cavity searches are among the most problematic types of searches for police today. "Strip" searches of convicts in prison, including the search of body cavities, have generally been held to be permissible.

The 1985 Supreme Court case of *U.S.* v. *Montoya de Hernandez*[191] focused on the issue of "alimentary canal smuggling," in which the offender typically swallows condoms filled with cocaine or heroin and waits for nature to take its course to recover the substance. In the *Montoya* case, a woman known to be a "balloon swallower" arrived in the United States on a flight from Colombia. She was detained by customs officials and given a pat-down search by a female agent. The agent reported that the woman's abdomen was firm and suggested that X rays be taken. The suspect refused and was given the choice of submitting to further tests or taking the next flight back to Colombia. No flight was immediately available, however, and the suspect was placed in a room for 16 hours, where she refused all food and drink. Finally, a court order for an X ray was obtained. The procedure revealed "balloons," and the woman was detained another four days, during which time she passed numerous cocaine-filled plastic condoms. The Court ruled that the woman's confinement was not unreasonable, based as it was on the supportable suspicion that she was "body-packing" cocaine. Any discomfort she experienced, the Court ruled, "resulted solely from the method that she chose to smuggle illicit drugs."[192]

Electronic Eavesdropping

Modern technology makes possible increasingly complex forms of communication. One of the first and best known of the U.S. Supreme Court decisions involving electronic communications was the 1928 case of *Olmstead* v. *U.S.*[193] In *Olmstead*, bootleggers used their home telephones to discuss and transact business. Agents tapped the lines and based their investigation and ensuing arrests on conversations they overheard. The defendants were convicted and eventually appealed to the high court, arguing that the agents had in effect seized information illegally without a search warrant in violation of the defendants' Fourth Amendment right to be secure in their homes. The Court ruled, however, that telephone lines were not an extension of the defendants' home and therefore were not protected by the constitutional guarantee of security. Subsequent federal statutes (discussed shortly) have substantially modified the significance of *Olmstead*.

Recording devices carried on the body of an undercover agent or an informant were ruled to produce admissible evidence in *On Lee* v. *U.S.* (1952)[194] and *Lopez* v. *U.S.* (1963).[195] The 1967 case of *Berger* v. *New York*[196] permitted wiretaps and "bugs" in instances where state law provided for the use of such devices and where officers obtained a warrant based on probable cause.

The Court appeared to undertake a significant change of direction in the area of electronic eavesdropping when it decided the case of *Katz* v. *U.S.* in 1967.[197] Federal agents had monitored a number of Katz's telephone calls from a public phone using a device separate from the phone lines and attached to the glass of the phone booth. The Court, in this case, stated that what a person makes an effort to keep private, even in a public place, requires a judicial decision, in the form of a warrant issued upon probable cause, to unveil. In the words of the Court, "The government's activities in electronically listening to and recording the petitioner's words violated the privacy upon which he justifiably relied while using the telephone booth and thus constituted a 'search and seizure' within the meaning of the Fourth Amendment."

In 1968, with the case of *Lee* v. *Florida*,[198] the Court applied the Federal Communications Act[199] to telephone conversations that may be the object of police investigation and held that evidence obtained without a warrant could not be used in state proceedings if it resulted from a wiretap. The only person who has the authority to permit eavesdropping, according to that act, is the sender of the message.

The Federal Communications Act, originally passed in 1934, does not specifically mention the potential interest of law enforcement agencies in monitoring communications. Title III of the Omnibus Crime Control and Safe Streets Act of 1968, however, mostly prohibits wiretaps but does allow officers to listen to electronic communications when (1) an officer is one of the parties involved in the communication, (2) one of the parties is not the officer but willingly decides to share the communication with the officer, or (3) officers obtain a warrant based on probable cause. In the 1971 case of *U.S.* v. *White*,[200] the Court held that law enforcement officers may intercept electronic information when one of the parties involved in the communication gives his or her consent, even without a warrant.

In 1984, the Supreme Court decided the case of *U.S.* v. *Karo*,[201] in which DEA agents had arrested James Karo for cocaine importation. Officers had placed a radio transmitter inside a 50-gallon drum of ether purchased by Karo for use in processing the cocaine. The transmitter was placed inside the drum with the consent of the seller of the ether but without a search warrant. The shipment of ether was followed to the Karo house, and Karo was arrested and convicted of cocaine-trafficking charges. Karo appealed to the U.S. Supreme Court, claiming that the radio beeper had violated his reasonable expectation of privacy inside his premises and that, without a warrant, the evidence it produced was tainted. The Court agreed and overturned his conviction.

Minimization Requirement for Electronic Surveillance

The Supreme Court established a minimization requirement pertinent to electronic surveillance in the 1978 case of *U.S.* v. *Scott*.[202] *Minimization* means that officers must make every reasonable effort to monitor only those conversations, through the use of phone taps, body bugs, and the like, that are specifically related to the criminal activity under investigation. As soon as it becomes obvious that a conversation is innocent, then the monitoring personnel are required to cease their invasion of privacy. Problems arise if the conversation occurs in a foreign language, if it is "coded," or if it is ambiguous. It has been suggested that investigators involved in electronic surveillance maintain logbooks of their activities that specifically show monitored conversations, as well as efforts made at minimization.[203]

The Electronic Communications Privacy Act of 1986

Electronic Communications Privacy Act (ECPA)
A law passed by Congress in 1986 establishing the due process requirements that law enforcement officers must meet in order to legally intercept wire communications.

Passed by Congress in 1986, the **Electronic Communications Privacy Act (ECPA)**[204] brought major changes in the requirements law enforcement officers must meet to intercept wire communications (those involving the human voice). The ECPA deals specifically with three areas of communication: (1) wiretaps and bugs, (2) pen registers that record the numbers dialed from a telephone, and (3) tracing devices that determine the number from which a call emanates. The act also addresses the procedures to be followed by officers in obtaining records relating to communications services, and it establishes requirements for gaining access to stored electronic communications and records of those communications. The ECPA basically requires that investigating officers must obtain wiretap-type court orders to eavesdrop on *ongoing communications*. The use of pen registers and recording devices, however, is specifically excluded by the law from court order requirements.[205]

A related measure, the Communications Assistance for Law Enforcement Act of 1994,[206] appropriated $500 million to modify the U.S. phone system to allow for continued wiretapping by law enforcement agencies. The law also specifies a standard-setting process for the redesign of existing equipment that would permit effective wiretapping in the face of coming technological advances. In the words of the FBI's Telecommunications Industry Liaison Unit, "This law requires telecommunications carriers, as defined in the Act, to ensure law enforcement's ability, pursuant to court order or other lawful authorization, to intercept communications notwithstanding advanced telecommunications technologies."[207] In 2006, 1,839 wiretap requests were approved by federal and state judges, and approximately 4.6 million conversations were intercepted by law enforcement agencies throughout the country.[208]

The Telecommunications Act of 1996

Title V of the Telecommunications Act of 1996[209] made it a federal offense for anyone engaged in interstate or international communications to knowingly use a telecommunications device "to create, solicit, or initiate the transmission of any comment, request, suggestion, proposal, image, or other communication which is obscene, lewd, lascivious, filthy, or indecent, with intent to annoy, abuse, threaten, or harass another person." The law also provided special penalties for anyone who "makes a telephone call ... without disclosing his identity and with intent to annoy, abuse, threaten, or harass any person at the called number or who receives the communication" or who "makes or causes the telephone of another repeatedly or continuously to ring, with intent to harass any person at the called number; or makes repeated telephone calls" for the purpose of harassing a person at the called number.

A section of the law, known as the Communications Decency Act (CDA),[210] criminalized the transmission to minors of "patently offensive" obscene materials over the Internet or other computer telecommunications services. Portions of the CDA, however, were invalidated by the U.S. Supreme Court in the case of *Reno* v. *ACLU* (1997).[211]

The USA PATRIOT Act of 2001

The USA PATRIOT Act of 2001, which is also discussed in CJ Exhibit 3, made it easier for police investigators to intercept many forms of electronic communications. Under previous federal law, for example, investigators could not obtain a wiretap order to intercept *wire* communications for violations of the Computer Fraud and Abuse Act.[212] In several well-known investigations, however, hackers had stolen teleconferencing services from telephone companies and then used those services to plan and execute hacking attacks.

The PATRIOT Act has not diminished our liberty. It has defended our liberty and made America more secure.
—President George W. Bush
Columbus, Ohio, June 9, 2005

The act[213] added felony violations of the Computer Fraud and Abuse Act to Section 2516(1) of Title 18 of the U.S. Code—the portion of federal law that lists specific types of crimes for which investigators may obtain a wiretap order for wire communications.

The USA PATRIOT Act of 2001 also modified that portion of the ECPA that governs law enforcement access to stored electronic communications (such as e-mail) to include stored wire communications (such as voice mail). Before the modification, law enforcement officers needed to obtain a wiretap order (rather than a search warrant) to obtain unopened voice communications. Because today's e-mail messages may contain digitized voice "attachments," investigators were sometimes required to obtain both a search warrant and a wiretap order to learn the contents of a specific message. Under the act, the same rules now apply to both stored wire communications and stored electronic communications. Wiretap orders, which are often much more difficult to obtain than search warrants, are now only required to intercept real-time telephone conversations.

Before passage of the USA PATRIOT Act, federal law allowed investigators to use an administrative subpoena (that is, a subpoena authorized by a federal or state statute or by a federal or state grand jury or trial court) to compel Internet service providers to provide a limited class of information, such as a customer's name, address, length of service, and means of payment. Also under previous law, investigators could not subpoena certain records, including credit card numbers or details about other forms of payment for Internet service. Such information,

CJ Exhibit 3

The USA PATRIOT Act of 2001 and the USA PATRIOT Improvement and Reauthorization Act of 2005

On October 26, 2001, President George W. Bush signed into law the USA PATRIOT Act, also known as the Uniting and Strengthening America by Providing Appropriate Tools Required to Intercept and Obstruct Terrorism Act. The law, which was drafted in response to the September 11, 2001, terrorist attacks on the World Trade Center and the Pentagon, substantially increased the investigatory authority of federal, state, and local police agencies. The act permits longer jail terms for certain suspects arrested without a warrant, broadens authority for **"sneak and peek" searches** (searches conducted without prior notice and in the absence of the suspect), and enhances the power of prosecutors. The law also increases the ability of federal authorities to tap phones (including wireless devices), share intelligence information, track Internet usage, crack down on money laundering, and protect U.S. borders. Many of the crime-fighting powers created under the legislation are not limited to acts of terrorism but apply to many different kinds of criminal offenses. The 2001 law led individual-rights advocates to question whether the government unfairly expanded police powers at the expense of civil liberties. Major provisions of the law relevant to law enforcement investigations in general are shown in this box.

One Hundred Seventh Congress
of the
United States of America

AT THE FIRST SESSION

Begun and held at the City of Washington on Wednesday,
the third day of January, two thousand and one

An Act

To deter and punish terrorist acts in the United States and around the world, to enhance law enforcement investigatory tools, and for other purposes.

Be it enacted by the Senate and House of Representatives of the United States of America in Congress assembled,

SECTION 1. SHORT TITLE AND TABLE OF CONTENTS.

(a) SHORT TITLE—This Act may be cited as the "Uniting and Strengthening America by Providing Appropriate Tools Required to Intercept and Obstruct Terrorism (USA PATRIOT Act) Act of 2001."

TITLE II—ENHANCED SURVEILLANCE PROCEDURES SEC. 203. AUTHORITY TO SHARE CRIMINAL INVESTIGATIVE INFORMATION.

(b) AUTHORITY TO SHARE ELECTRONIC, WIRE, AND ORAL INTERCEPTION INFORMATION.—

1. LAW ENFORCEMENT.—Section 2517 of title 18, United States Code, is amended by inserting at the end the following:
   "(6) Any investigative or law enforcement officer, or attorney for the Government, who by any means authorized by this chapter, has obtained knowledge of the contents of any wire, oral, or electronic communication, or evidence derived therefrom, may disclose such contents to any other Federal law enforcement, intelligence, protective, immigration, national defense, or national security official to the extent that such contents include foreign intelligence or counterintelligence (as defined in section 3 of the National Security Act of 1947 (50 U.S.C. 401a)), or foreign intelligence information (as defined in subsection 19 of section 2510 of this title), to assist the official who is to receive that information in the performance of his official duties. Any Federal official who receives information pursuant to this provision may use that information only as necessary in the conduct of that person's official duties subject to any limitations on the unauthorized disclosure of such information."

SEC. 213. AUTHORITY FOR DELAYING NOTICE OF THE EXECUTION OF A WARRANT.

Section 3103a of title 18, United States Code, is amended—

1. by inserting "(a) IN GENERAL.—" before "In addition"; and
2. by adding at the end the following:
   "(b) DELAY.—With respect to the issuance of any warrant or court order under this section, or any other rule of law, to search for and seize any property or material that constitutes evidence of a criminal offense in violation of the laws of the United States, any notice required, or that may be required, to be given may be delayed if—

   "(1) the court finds reasonable cause to believe that providing immediate notification of the execution of the warrant may have an adverse result (as defined in section 2705);

   "(2) the warrant prohibits the seizure of any tangible property, any wire or electronic communication (as defined in section 2510), or, except as expressly provided in chapter 121, any stored wire or electronic information, except where the court finds reasonable necessity for the seizure; and

   "(3) the warrant provides for the giving of such notice within a reasonable period of its execution, which period may thereafter be extended by the court for good cause shown."

What This Means

The USA PATRIOT Act amends Title 18, Section 3103, of the U.S. Code to create a uniform standard authorizing courts to delay notification of lawful searches if the court finds "reasonable cause" to believe that providing immediate notification of the execution of the warrant may have an "adverse result" (such as endangering the life or physical safety of an individual, flight from prosecution, evidence tampering, or witness intimidation) or might otherwise seriously jeopardize an investigation or unduly delay a trial. This section of the USA PATRIOT Act is primarily designed to authorize delayed notice of *searches* rather than delayed notice of *seizures*. The USA PATRIOT Improvement and Reauthorization Act of 2005, which became law in 2006, clarified *delayed notification* to mean 30 days after the search has been conducted, with the possibility of a delay of up to 90 days under special circumstances.

SEC. 216. MODIFICATION OF AUTHORITIES RELATING TO USE OF PEN REGISTERS AND TRAP AND TRACE DEVICES.

(b) ISSUANCE OF ORDERS.—

1. IN GENERAL.—Section 3123(a) of title 18, United States Code, is amended to read as follows:

"(a) IN GENERAL.—

"(1) ATTORNEY FOR THE GOVERNMENT.—Upon an application made under section 3122(a)(1), the court shall enter an *ex parte* order authorizing the installation and use of a pen register or trap and trace device anywhere within the United States, if the court finds that the attorney for the Government has certified to the court that the information likely to be obtained by such installation and use is relevant to an ongoing criminal investigation."

What This Means

Although Congress enacted a pen/trap statute in 1986 (which made possible the collection of noncontent traffic information associated with communications, such as the phone number dialed from a particular telephone), it could not anticipate the dramatic expansion in electronic communications that would occur in the next 15 years, including communications over computer networks.

Section 216 of the USA PATRIOT Act updates the pen/trap statute in three important ways: (1) The amendments clarify that law enforcement may use pen/trap orders to trace communications on the Internet and other computer networks; (2) pen/trap orders issued by federal courts now have nationwide effect; and (3) law enforcement authorities must file a special report with the court whenever they use a pen/trap order to install their own monitoring device on computers belonging to a public provider.

SEC. 219. SINGLE-JURISDICTION SEARCH WARRANTS FOR TERRORISM.

Rule 41(a) of the Federal Rules of Criminal Procedure is amended by inserting after "executed" the following: "and (3) in an investigation of domestic terrorism or international terrorism (as defined in section 2331 of title 18, United States Code), by a Federal magistrate judge in any district in which activities related to the terrorism may have occurred, for a search of property or for a person within or outside the district."

What This Means

Under prior law, Rule 41(a) of the Federal Rules of Criminal Procedure required that a search warrant be obtained within a district for searches within that district. The only exception was for cases in which property or a person within the district might leave the district before the warrant could be executed. The rule created what some saw as unnecessary delays and burdens in the investigation of terrorist activities and networks that spanned a number of districts, because warrants had to be obtained separately in each district. Section 219 purports to solve that problem by providing that in domestic or international terrorism cases, a search warrant may be issued by a magistrate judge in any district in which activities related to the terrorism have occurred for a search of property or persons located within or outside of the district.

CIVIL RIGHTS IMPLICATIONS

While many aspects of the USA PATRIOT Act have been criticized as potentially unconstitutional, Section 213, which authorizes delayed notice of the execution of a warrant, may be most vulnerable to challenge. The American Civil Liberties Union (ACLU) maintains that under this section, law enforcement agents could enter a house, apartment, or office with a search warrant while the occupant is away, search through his or her property, and take photographs without having to tell the suspect about the search until later.[1] The ACLU also believes that this provision is illegal because the Fourth Amendment to the Constitution protects against unreasonable searches and seizures and requires the government to obtain a warrant and to give notice to the person whose property will be searched before conducting the search. The notice requirement enables the suspect to assert his or her Fourth Amendment rights.

Read the entire USA PATRIOT Act of 2001 via Library Extra 5–6 at mycrimekit.com. Title 18 of the U.S. Code is available at Library Extra 5–7. The USA PATRIOT Improvement and Reauthorization Act of 2005 is available at Library Extra 5–8.

[1] Much of the information in this paragraph is taken from American Civil Liberties Union, "How the Anti-Terrorism Bill Expands Law Enforcement 'Sneak and Peek' Warrants." Web posted at http://www.aclu.org/congress/1102301b.html (accessed February 12, 2005).

References: USA PATRIOT Improvement and Reauthorization Act of 2005 (Public Law 109-177); U.S. Department of Justice, Field Guidance on Authorities (Redacted) Enacted in the 2001 Anti-Terrorism Legislation (Washington, DC: DOJ, no date). Web posted at http://www.epic.org/terrorism/DOJguidance.pdf; USA PATRIOT Act, 2001 (Public Law 107-56); American Civil Liberties Union, "How the Anti-Terrorism Bill Expands Law Enforcement 'Sneak and Peek' Warrants." Web posted at http://www.aclu.org/congress/1102301b.html; and American Civil Liberties Union, "How the Anti-Terrorism Bill Limits Judicial Oversight of Telephone and Internet Surveillance." Web posted at http://www.aclu.org/congress/1102301g.html.

however, can be highly relevant in determining a suspect's true identity because, in many cases, users register with Internet service providers using false names.

Previous federal law[214] was also technology specific, relating primarily to telephone communications. Local and long-distance telephone billing records, for example, could be subpoenaed but not billing information for Internet communications or records of Internet session times and durations. Similarly, previous law allowed the government to use a subpoena to

"sneak and peek" search
A search that occurs in the suspect's absence and without his or her prior knowledge. Also known as a *delayed notification search*.

obtain the customer's "telephone number or other subscriber number or identity" but did not define what that phrase meant in the context of Internet communications.

The USA PATRIOT Act amended portions of this federal law[215] to update and expand the types of records that law enforcement authorities may obtain with a subpoena. "Records of session times and durations," as well as "any temporarily assigned network address," may now be gathered. Such changes should make the process of identifying computer criminals and tracing their Internet communications faster and easier.

Finally, the USA PATRIOT Act facilitates the use of roving, or multipoint, wiretaps. Roving wiretaps, issued with court approval, target a specific individual and not a particular telephone number or communications device. Hence, law enforcement agents armed with an order for a multipoint wiretap can follow the flow of communications engaged in by a person as he or she switches from one cellular phone to another or to a wired telephone.

In 2006, President George W. Bush signed the USA PATRIOT Improvement and Reauthorization Act of 2005[216] into law. Also referred to as PATRIOT II, the act made permanent 14 provisions of the original 2001 legislation that had been slated to expire and extended others for another four years (including the roving wiretap provision and a provision that allows authorities to seize business records). It also addressed some of the concerns of civil libertarians who had criticized the earlier law as too restrictive. Finally, the new law provided additional protections for mass transportation systems and seaports, closed some legal loopholes in laws aimed at preventing terrorist financing, and included a subsection called the Combat Methamphetamine Enforcement Act (CMEA). The CMEA contains significant provisions intended to strengthen federal, state, and local efforts designed at curtailing the spread of methamphetamine use. Learn more about electronic surveillance and wiretapping in criminal cases via Web Extra 5–4 at mycrimekit.com, and read the complete 2006 USA PATRIOT Act reauthorization legislation at Library Extra 5–9.

Web EXTRA

Library EXTRA

Electronic and Latent Evidence

The Internet, computer networks, and automated data systems present many new opportunities for committing criminal activity.[217] Computers and other electronic devices are increasingly being used to commit, enable, or support crimes perpetrated against people, organizations, and property. Whether the crime involves attacks against computer systems or the information they contain or more traditional offenses such as murder, money laundering, trafficking, or fraud, the proper seizure of **electronic evidence** that is specifically described in a valid search warrant has become increasingly important.

Electronic evidence is "information and data of investigative value that are stored in or transmitted by an electronic device."[218] Such evidence is often acquired when physical items, such as computers, removable disks, CDs, DVDs, magnetic tape, flash memory chips, cellular telephones, personal digital assistants, and other electronic devices, are collected from a crime scene or are obtained from a suspect.

electronic evidence
Information and data of investigative value that are stored in or transmitted by an electronic device.[i]

latent evidence
Evidence of relevance to a criminal investigation that is not readily seen by the unaided eye.

digital criminal forensics
The lawful seizure, acquisition, analysis, reporting, and safeguarding of data from digital devices that may contain information of evidentiary value to the trier of fact in criminal events.[ii]

Electronic evidence has special characteristics: (1) It is latent; (2) it can transcend national and state borders quickly and easily; (3) it is fragile and can easily be altered, damaged, compromised, or destroyed by improper handling or improper examination; (4) it may be time sensitive. Like DNA or fingerprints, electronic evidence is **latent evidence** because it is not readily visible to the human eye under normal conditions. Special equipment and software are required to "see" and evaluate electronic evidence. In the courtroom, expert testimony may be needed to explain the acquisition of electronic evidence and the examination process used to interpret it.

In 2002, in recognition of the special challenges posed by electronic evidence, the Computer Crime and Intellectual Property Section (CCIPS) of the Criminal Division of the U.S. Department of Justice released a how-to manual for law enforcement officers called *Searching and Seizing Computers and Obtaining Electronic Evidence in Criminal Investigations.*[219] The manual, which is a how-to in **digital criminal forensics**, can be accessed via Library Extra 5–10 at mycrimekit.com.

Library EXTRA

About the same time, the Technical Working Group for Electronic Crime Scene Investigation (TWGECSI) released a much more detailed guide for law enforcement officers to use in gathering electronic evidence. The manual, *Electronic Crime Scene Investigation: A Guide for First Responders*,[220] grew out of a partnership formed in 1998 between the National Cybercrime Training Partnership, the Office of Law Enforcement Standards, and the National Institute of Justice. The working group was asked to identify, define, and establish basic criteria to assist federal and state agencies in handling electronic investigations and related prosecutions.

TWGECSI guidelines say that law enforcement must take special precautions when documenting, collecting, and preserving electronic evidence to maintain its integrity. The guidelines also note that the first law enforcement officer on the scene (commonly called the *first responder*) should take steps to ensure the safety of everyone at the scene and to protect the integrity of all evidence, both traditional and electronic. The entire TWGECSI guide, which includes many practical instructions for investigators working with electronic evidence, is available at Library Extra 5–11 at mycrimekit.com.

Library EXTRA

Once digital evidence has been gathered, it must be analyzed. Consequently, in 2004, the government-sponsored Technical Working Group for the Examination of Digital Evidence (TWGEDE) published *Forensic Examination of Digital Evidence: A Guide for Law Enforcement*.[221] Among the guide's recommendations are that digital evidence should be acquired in a manner that protects and preserves the integrity of the original evidence and that examination should only be conducted on a *copy* of the original evidence. The entire guide, which is nearly 100 pages long, can be accessed via Library Extra 5–12 at mycrimekit.com.

Library EXTRA

Warrantless searches bear special mention in any discussion of electronic evidence. In the 1999 case of *U.S.* v. *Carey*,[222] a federal appellate court held that the consent a defendant had given to police for his apartment to be searched did not extend to the search of his computer once it was taken to a police station. Similarly, in *U.S.* v. *Turner*,[223] the First Circuit Court of Appeals held that the warrantless police search of a defendant's personal computer while in his apartment exceeded the scope of the defendant's consent.

Summary

- Legal restraints on police action stem primarily from the U.S. Constitution's Bill of Rights, especially the Fourth, Fifth, and Sixth Amendments, which (along with the Fourteenth Amendment) require due process of law. Most due process requirements of relevance to police work concern three major areas: (1) evidence and investigation (often called *search* and *seizure*), (2) arrest, and (3) interrogation. Each of these areas has been addressed by a number of important U.S. Supreme Court decisions, and it is the discussion of those decisions and their significance for police work that makes up the bulk of this chapter's content.
- The Bill of Rights was designed to protect citizens against abuses of police power. It does so by guaranteeing due process of law for everyone suspected of having committed a crime and by ensuring the availability of constitutional rights to all citizens, regardless of state or local law or procedure. Within the context of criminal case processing, due process requirements mandate that all justice system officials, not only the police, respect the rights of accused individuals throughout the criminal justice process.
- The Fourth Amendment to the Constitution declares that people must be secure in their homes and in their persons against unreasonable searches and seizures. Consequently, law enforcement officers are generally required to demonstrate probable cause in order to obtain a search warrant if they are to legally conduct searches and seize the property of criminal suspects. The Supreme Court has established that police officers, in order to protect themselves from attack, have the right to search a person being arrested and to search the area under the arrestee's immediate control.
- An arrest takes place whenever a law enforcement officer restricts a person's freedom to leave. Arrests may occur when an officer comes upon a crime in progress, but most jurisdictions also allow warrantless arrests for felonies when a crime is not in progress, as long as probable cause can later be demonstrated.

- Information that is useful for law enforcement purposes is called *intelligence*, and as this chapter has shown, intelligence gathering is vital to police work. The need for useful information often leads police investigators to question suspects, informants, and potentially knowledgeable citizens. When suspects who are in custody become subject to interrogation, they must be advised of their *Miranda* rights before questioning begins. The *Miranda* warnings, which were mandated by the Supreme Court in the 1966 case of *Miranda* v. *Arizona*, are listed in this chapter. They ensure that suspects know their rights—including the right to remain silent—in the face of police interrogation.

Key Concepts

Terms

anticipatory warrant
arrest
Bill of Rights
compelling interest
digital criminal forensics
Electronic Communications Privacy Act (ECPA)
electronic evidence
emergency search
exclusionary rule
fleeting-targets exception
fruit of the poisonous tree doctrine
good-faith exception
illegally seized evidence
inherent coercion
interrogation
landmark case
latent evidence
Miranda triggers
Miranda warnings
plain view
probable cause
psychological manipulation
reasonable suspicion
search incident to an arrest
"sneak and peek" search
suspicionless search
writ of *certiorari*

Cases

Alabama v. *White*
Arizona v. *Fulminante*
Brecht v. *Abrahamson*
Brown v. *Mississippi*
California v. *Hodari D.*
Carroll v. *U.S.*
Chimel v. *California*
Dickerson v. *U.S.*
Escobedo v. *Illinois*
Florida v. *Bostick*
Horton v. *California*
Illinois v. *Perkins*
Indianapolis v. *Edmond*
Kyllo v. *U.S.*
Mapp v. *Ohio*
Minnick v. *Mississippi*
Miranda v. *Arizona*
Nix v. *Williams*
Richards v. *Wisconsin*
Silverthorne Lumber Co. v. *U.S.*
Smith v. *Ohio*
Terry v. *Ohio*
U.S. Dept. of Justice v. *Landano*
U.S. v. *Drayton*
U.S. v. *Patane*
U.S. v. *Robinson*
Weeks v. *U.S.*
Wilson v. Arkansas

Questions for Review

1. Name some of the legal restraints on police action, and list some types of behavior that might be considered abuse of police authority.
2. How do the Bill of Rights and democratically inspired legal restraints on the police help ensure personal freedoms in our society?
3. Describe the legal standards for assessing searches and seizures conducted by law enforcement agents.
4. What is arrest, and when does it occur? How do legal understandings of the term differ from popular depictions of the arrest process?
5. What is the role of interrogation in intelligence gathering? List each of the *Miranda* warnings. Which recent U.S. Supreme Court cases have affected *Miranda* warning requirements?

To participate in an online discussion of these topics and others, join the CJ Brief e-mail discussion list at mycrimekit.com.

Web Quest

Create a list of every U.S. Supreme Court decision discussed in this chapter. Group the cases by subject (that is, vehicle searches, searches following arrest, interrogation, and so on), and list them in order by year of decision. Use the Web to collect full-text opinions from the Court for as many of these cases as you can find. (*Hint*: Visit the Legal Information Institute at Cornell University at http://www.law.cornell.edu for some of the best Supreme Court information available anywhere.) Submit the materials you find to your instructor if asked to do so.

Note: This is a large project, and your instructor may ask that you work with just one area (such as vehicle searches) or may assign the entire project to your class, asking individual students or groups of students to be responsible for separate subjects.

To complete this Web Quest online, go to the Web Quest module in Chapter 5 of the *Criminal Justice: A Brief Introduction* Companion Website at mycrimekit.com.

Notes

i. Adapted from Technical Working Group for Electronic Crime Scene Investigation, *Electronic Crime Scene Investigation: A Guide for First Responders* (Washington, DC: National Institute of Justice, 2001), p. 2.

ii. Adapted from Larry R. Leibrock, "Overview and Impact on 21st Century Legal Practice: Digital Forensics and Electronic Discovery," no date. Web posted at http://www.courtroom21.net/FDIC.pps (accessed July 5, 2008).

1. Larry Collins and Dominique Lapierre, *The Fifth Horseman* (New York: Simon and Schuster, 1980).
2. Ellen Barry and Colin Moynihan, "Three Detectives Plead Not Guilty in 50-Shot Killing," *New York Times*, March 20, 2007, http://www.nytimes.com/2007/03/20/nyregion/20cops.html, (accessed August 28, 2008).
3. Michael Wilson, "3 Detectives Acquitted in Bell Shooting," *New York Times*, April 26, 2008, www.nytimes.com/2008/04/26/nyregion/26BELL.html?ref=nyregion (accessed August 28, 2008).
4. Cara Buckley, "Diallo Verdict May Have Made Prosecutors Cautious," *New York Times*, March 20, 2007, http://www.nytimes.com/2007/03/20/nyregion/20charges.html?fta=y (accessed August 28, 2008).
5. Marcus Baram, "How Common Is Contagious Shooting?" ABC News, November 17, 2006. Web posted at http://abcnews.go.com/Politics/story?id=2681947&page=1 (accessed May 21, 2007).
6. Michael Wilson, "50 Shots Fired, and the Experts Offer a Theory," *New York Times*, November 27, 2006, http://www.nytimes.com/2006/11/27/nyregion/27fire.html (accessed August 28, 2008).
7. "Victim of Police Beating Says He Was Sober," Associated Press, October 10, 2005. Web posted at http://www.msnbc.msn.com/id/9645260 (accessed July 10, 2007).
8. "New Investigation May Postpone Police Trial in Video-Tape," KATC-TV. Web posted at http://www.katc.com/Global/story.asp?S=4345819&nav=EyAz (accessed March 19, 2008).
9. "Police Brutality!" *Time*, March 25, 1991, p. 18.
10. "Police Charged in Beating Case Say They Feared for Their Lives," *Boston Globe*, May 22, 1991, p. 22.
11. "Police Brutality!" pp.16–19.
12. "Cries of Relief," *Time*, April 26, 1993, p. 18.
13. "Rodney King Slams SUV into House, Breaks Pelvis," CNN.com, April 16, 2003. Web posted at http://www.cnn.com/2003/US/West/04/15/rodney.king.ap/index.html (accessed April 18, 2006).
14. *Miranda* v. *Arizona*, 384 U.S. 436 (1966).
15. *Weeks* v. *U.S.*, 232 U.S. 383 (1914).
16. Roger Goldman and Steven Puro, "Decertification of Police: An Alternative to Traditional Remedies for Police Misconduct," *Hastings Constitutional Law Quarterly*, Vol. 15 (1988), pp. 45–80.
17. Hawaii's police departments set their own training requirements. The Honolulu Police Department, for example, requires six and a half months of student officer training and another 14 weeks of postgraduation field training. See the Honolulu Police Department's website at http://www.honolulupd.org/main/training.htm (accessed March 27, 2008).
18. Goldman and Puro, "Decertification of Police."
19. *Silverthorne Lumber Co.* v. *U.S.*, 251 U.S. 385 (1920).
20. Ibid.
21. Clemmens Bartollas, *American Criminal Justice* (New York: Macmillan, 1988), p. 186.
22. *Mapp* v. *Ohio*, 367 U.S. 643 (1961).
23. *Wolf* v. *Colorado*, 338 U.S. 25 (1949).
24. *Chimel* v. *California*, 395 U.S. 752 (1969).
25. *U.S.* v. *Rabinowitz*, 339 U.S. 56 (1950).
26. *Katz* v. *U.S.*, 389 U.S. 347, 88 S.Ct. 507 (1967).
27. *Minnesota* v. *Olson*, 110 S.Ct. 1684 (1990).
28. *Minnesota* v. *Carter*, 525 U.S. 83 (1998).
29. *Georgia* v. *Randolph*, U.S. Supreme Court, No. 04-1067 (decided March 22, 2006).
30. The ruling left open the possibility that any evidence relating to criminal activity undertaken by the consenting party might be admissible in court. In the words of the Court, refusal by a co-occupant "renders entry and search unreasonable and invalid as to him."
31. *U.S.* v. *Leon*, 468 U.S. 897, 104 S.Ct. 3405, 82 L.Ed.2d 677, 52 U.S.L.W. 5155 (1984).
32. Judicial titles vary among jurisdictions. Many lower-level state judicial officers are called *magistrates.* Federal magistrates, however, generally have a significantly higher level of judicial authority.
33. *Massachusetts* v. *Sheppard*, 104 S.Ct. 3424 (1984).
34. *Illinois* v. *Krull*, 107 S.Ct. 1160 (1987).
35. *Maryland* v. *Garrison*, 107 S.Ct. 1013 (1987).
36. *Illinois* v. *Rodriguez*, 110 S.Ct. 2793 (1990).
37. *Arizona* v. *Evans*, 115 S.Ct. 1185, 131 L.Ed.2d 34 (1995).
38. William H. Erickson, William D. Neighbors, and B. J. George, Jr., *United States Supreme Court Cases and Comments* (New York: Matthew Bender, 1987), Section 1.13[7].
39. See *California* v. *Acevedo*, 500 U.S. 565 (1991); *Ornelas* v. *U.S.*, 517 U.S. 690 (1996); and others.

40. See *Edwards* v. *Balisok*, 520 U.S. 641 (1997); *Booth* v. *Churner*, 532 U.S. 731 (2001); and *Porter* v. *Nussle*, 534 U.S. 516 (2002).
41. See *Wilson* v. *Arkansas*, 115 S.Ct. 1914 (1995); and *Richards* v. *Wisconsin*, 117 S.Ct. 1416 (1997).
42. See *McCleskey* v. *Kemp*, 481 U.S. 279, 107 S.Ct. 1756, 95 L.Ed.2d 262 (1987); *McCleskey* v. *Zant*, 499 U.S. 467, 493–494 (1991); *Coleman* v. *Thompson*, 501 U.S. 722 (1991); *Schlup* v. *Delo*, 115 S.Ct. 851, 130 L.Ed.2d 808 (1995); *Felker* v. *Turpin, Warden*, 117 S.Ct. 30, 135 L.Ed.2d 1123 (1996); *Boyde* v. *California*, 494 U.S. 370 (1990); and others.
43. See *Ewing* v. *California*, 538 U.S. 11 (2003); and *Lockyer* v. *Andrade*, 538 U.S. 63 (2003).
44. Richard Lacayo and Viveca Novak, "How Rehnquist Changed America," *Time*, June 30, 2003, pp. 20–25.
45. *Harris* v. *U.S.*, 390 U.S. 234 (1968).
46. The legality of plain-view seizures was also confirmed in earlier cases, including *Ker* v. *California*, 374 U.S. 23, 42–43 (1963); *U.S.* v. *Lee*, 274 U.S. 559 (1927); *U.S.* v. *Lefkowitz*, 285 U.S. 452, 465 (1932); and *Hester* v. *U.S.*, 265 U.S. 57 (1924).
47. As cited in Kimberly A. Kingston, "Look But Don't Touch: The Plain View Doctrine," *FBI Law Enforcement Bulletin* (December 1987), p. 18.
48. *Horton* v. *California*, 110 S.Ct. 2301, 47 CrL. 2135 (1990).
49. *U.S.* v. *Irizarry*, 673 F.2d 554, 556–67 (1st Cir. 1982).
50. *Arizona* v. *Hicks*, 107 S.Ct. 1149 (1987).
51. See *Criminal Justice Today*, North Carolina Justice Academy (fall 1987), p. 24.
52. Inadvertence, as a requirement of legitimate plain-view seizures, was first cited in the U.S. Supreme Court case of *Coolidge* v. *New Hampshire*, 403 U.S. 443, 91 S.Ct. 2022 (1971).
53. *Horton* v. *California*, 110 S.Ct. 2301, 47 CrL. 2135 (1990).
54. Ibid.
55. *Brigham City* v. *Stuart*, U.S. Supreme Court, No. 05-502 (decided May 22, 2006).
56. John Gales Sauls, "Emergency Searches of Premises," Part 1, *FBI Law Enforcement Bulletin* (March 1987), p. 23.
57. *Warden* v. *Hayden*, 387 U.S. 294 (1967).
58. *Mincey* v. *Arizona*, 437 U.S. 385, 392 (1978).
59. Sauls, "Emergency Searches of Premises," p. 25.
60. *Maryland* v. *Buie*, 110 S.Ct. 1093 (1990).
61. *Wilson* v. *Arkansas*, 115 S.Ct. 1914 (1995).
62. For additional information, see Michael J. Bulzomi, "Knock and Announce: A Fourth Amendment Standard," *FBI Law Enforcement Bulletin* (May 1997), pp. 27–31.
63. *Richards* v. *Wisconsin*, 117 S.Ct. 1416 (1997), syllabus.
64. *Illinois* v. *McArthur*, 531 U.S. 326 (2001).
65. *U.S.* v. *Banks*, 124 S.Ct. 521 (December 2, 2003).
66. *Hudson* v. *Michigan*, U.S. Supreme Court, No. 04-1360 (decided June 15, 2006).
67. *U.S.* v. *Grubbs*, U.S. Supreme Court, No. 04-1414 (decided March 21, 2006).
68. *U.S.* v. *Mendenhall*, 446 U.S. 544 (1980).
69. *Stansbury* v. *California*, 114 S.Ct. 1526, 1529, 128 L.Ed.2d 293 (1994).
70. *Yarborough* v. *Alvarado*, 541 U.S. 652 (2004).
71. *Thompson* v. *Keohane*, 516 U.S. 99, 112 (1996).
72. *Muehler* v. *Mena*, 125 S.Ct. 1465 (2005).
73. See *Michigan* v. *Summers,* 452 U.S. 692 (1981).
74. *Atwater* v. *Lago Vista*, 532 U.S. 318 (2001).
75. *Payton* v. *New York*, 445 U.S. 573 (1980).
76. In 1981, in the case of *U.S.* v. *Steagald* (451 U.S. 204), the Court ruled that a search warrant is also necessary when the planned arrest involves entry into a third party's premises.
77. *Kirk* v. *Louisiana*, 536 U.S. 635 (2002).
78. *U.S.* v. *Robinson*, 414 U.S. 218 (1973).
79. Ibid.
80. *Terry* v. *Ohio*, 392 U.S. 1 (1968).
81. *U.S.* v. *Sokolow*, 109 S.Ct. 1581 (1989).
82. The Court was quoting from *U.S.* v. *Brignoni-Ponce*, 422 U.S. 873, 878 (1975).
83. *U.S.* v. *Arvizu*, 534 U.S. 266 (2002).
84. Ibid.
85. *Minnesota* v. *Dickerson*, 113 S.Ct. 2130, 124 L.Ed.2d 334 (1993).
86. *Brown* v. *Texas*, 443 U.S. 47 (1979).
87. *Hiibel* v. *Sixth Judicial District Court of Nevada*, 542 U.S. 177 (2004).
88. *Smith* v. *Ohio*, 110 S.Ct. 1288 (1990).
89. *California* v. *Hodari D.*, 111 S.Ct. 1547 (1991).
90. *Criminal Justice Newsletter*, May 1, 1991, p. 2.
91. *Illinois* v. *Wardlow*, 528 U.S. 119 (2000).
92. Ibid., syllabus. Web posted at http://supct.law.cornell.edu/supct/html/98-1036.ZS.html (accessed April 1, 2008).
93. Ibid.
94. *Arkansas* v. *Sanders*, 442 U.S. 753 (1979).
95. Ibid.
96. *U.S.* v. *Borchardt*, 809 F.2d 1115 (5th Cir. 1987).
97. *FBI Law Enforcement Bulletin* (January 1988), p. 28.
98. *Carroll* v. *U.S.*, 267 U.S. 132 (1925).
99. *Preston* v. *U.S.*, 376 U.S. 364 (1964).
100. *South Dakota* v. *Opperman*, 428 U.S. 364 (1976).
101. *Colorado* v. *Bertine*, 479 U.S. 367, 107 S.Ct. 741 (1987).
102. *Florida* v. *Wells*, 110 S.Ct. 1632 (1990).
103. *Terry* v. *Ohio*, 392 U.S. 1 (1968).
104. *California* v. *Acevedo*, 500 U.S. 565 (1991).
105. *Ornelas* v. *U.S.*, 517 U.S. 690, 696 (1996).
106. Ibid.
107. The phrase is usually attributed to the 1991 U.S. Supreme Court case of *California* v. *Acevedo* (500 U.S. 565 [1991]). See Devallis Rutledge, "Taking an Inventory," *Police*, November 1995, pp. 8–9.
108. *Florida* v. *Jimeno*, 111 S.Ct. 1801 (1991).
109. Ibid., syllabus. Web posted at http://laws.findlaw.com/us/500/248.html (accessed March 2, 2008).
110. *U.S.* v. *Ross*, 456 U.S. 798 (1982).
111. Ibid.
112. *Whren* v. *U.S.*, 517 U.S. 806 (1996).
113. See *Pennsylvania* v. *Mimms*, 434 U.S. 106 (1977).
114. *Maryland* v. *Wilson*, 117 S.Ct. 882 (1997).
115. *Brendlin* v. *California*, 551 U.S. (2007).
116. *Knowles* v. *Iowa*, 525 U.S. 113 (1998).
117. *Wyoming* v. *Houghton*, 526 U.S. 295 (1999).
118. *Thornton* v. *United States*, 541 U.S. 615 (2004).
119. *Illinois* v. *Caballes*, 543 U.S. 405 (2005).
120. *Michigan Dept. of State Police* v. *Sitz*, 110 S.Ct. 2481 (1990).
121. *U.S.* v. *Martinez-Fuerte*, 428 U.S. 543 (1976).
122. Ibid., syllabus.
123. *Indianapolis* v. *Edmond*, 531 U.S. 32 (2000).
124. *Illinois* v. *Lidster*, 540 U.S. 419 (2004).
125. *U.S.* v. *Villamonte-Marquez*, 462 U.S. 579 (1983).
126. *California* v. *Carney*, 471 U.S. 386, 105 S.Ct. 2066, 85 L.Ed.2d 406, 53 U.S.L.W. 4521 (1985).
127. *U.S.* v. *Hill*, 855 F.2d 664 (10th Cir. 1988).
128. *National Treasury Employees Union* v. *Von Raab*, 489 U.S. 656 (1989).
129. *Skinner* v. *Railway Labor Executives' Association*, 489 U.S. 602 (1989).
130. *Florida* v. *Bostick*, 111 S.Ct. 2382 (1991).
131. *Bond* v. *U.S.*, 529 U.S. 334 (2000).
132. *U.S.* v. *Drayton*, 122 S.Ct. 2105 (2002).
133. *U.S.* v. *Flores-Montano*, 541 U.S. 149 (2004).
134. *People* v. *Deutsch*, 96 C.D.O.S. 2827 (1996).
135. The thermal imager differs from infrared devices (such as night-vision goggles) in that infrared devices amplify the infrared spectrum of light, whereas thermal imagers register solely the portion of the infrared spectrum that we call *heat.*
136. *People* v. *Deutsch,* 96 C.D.O.S. 2827 (1996).
137. *Kyllo* v. *U.S.*, 533 U.S. 27 (2001).

138. Ibid.
139. *Aguilar* v. *Texas*, 378 U.S. 108 (1964).
140. *U.S.* v. *Harris*, 403 U.S. 573 (1971).
141. Ibid., at 584.
142. *Illinois* v. *Gates*, 426 U.S. 213 (1983).
143. *Alabama* v. *White*, 110 S.Ct. 2412 (1990).
144. Ibid., at 2417.
145. *Florida* v. *J.L.*, 529 U.S. 266 (2000).
146. *U.S Dept. of Justice* v. *Landano*, 113 S.Ct. 2014, 124 L.Ed.2d 84 (1993).
147. Richard Willing, "Third Law First to Order Taping Murder Confessions," *USA Today*, July 18, 2003, p. 3A.
148. *South Dakota* v. *Neville*, 103 S.Ct. 916 (1983).
149. *Brown* v. *Mississippi*, 297 U.S. 278 (1936).
150. *Ashcraft* v. *Tennessee*, 322 U.S. 143 (1944).
151. *Chambers* v. *Florida*, 309 U.S. 227 (1940).
152. Ibid.
153. *Leyra* v. *Denno*, 347 U.S. 556 (1954).
154. Ibid.
155. *Arizona* v. *Fulminante*, 111 S.Ct. 1246 (1991).
156. *Chapman* v. *California*, 386 U.S. 18 (1967).
157. *State* v. *Fulminante*, No. CR-95-0160.
158. *Escobedo* v. *Illinois*, 378 U.S. 478 (1964).
159. *Edwards* v. *Arizona*, 451 U.S. 477, 101 S.Ct. 1880, 68 L.Ed.2d 378 (1981).
160. *Minnick* v. *Mississippi*, 498 U.S. 146 (1990).
161. *Arizona* v. *Roberson*, 486 U.S. 675, 108 S.Ct. 2093 (1988).
162. *Davis* v. *U.S.*, 114 S.Ct. 2350 (1994).
163. *Miranda* v. *Arizona*, 384 U.S. 436 (1966).
164. "Immigrants Get Civil Rights," *USA Today*, June 11, 1992, p. 1A.
165. *U.S.* v. *Dickerson*, 166 F.3d 667 (1999).
166. *Dickerson* v. *U.S.*, 530 U.S. 428 (2000).
167. *U.S.* v. *Patane*, 542 U.S. 630 (2004).
168. *Silverthorne Lumber Co.* v. *U.S.*, 251 U.S. 385 (1920).
169. *Wong Sun* v. *U.S.*, 371 U.S. 471 (1963).
170. *Moran* v. *Burbine*, 475 U.S. 412, 421 (1986).
171. *Colorado* v. *Spring*, 479 U.S. 564, 107 S.Ct. 851 (1987).
172. *Brewer* v. *Williams*, 430 U.S. 387 (1977).
173. *Nix* v. *Williams*, 104 S.Ct. 2501 (1984).
174. *New York* v. *Quarles*, 104 S.Ct. 2626, 81 L.Ed.2d 550 (1984).
175. *Colorado* v. *Connelly*, 107 S.Ct. 515, 93 L.Ed.2d 473 (1986).
176. *Kuhlmann* v. *Wilson*, 477 U.S. 436 (1986).
177. *Illinois* v. *Perkins*, 495 U.S. 292 (1990).
178. *Rock* v. *Zimmerman*, 543 F.Supp. 179 (M.D. Pa. 1982).
179. Ibid.
180. See *Oregon* v. *Mathiason*, 429 U.S. 492, 97 S.Ct. 711 (1977).
181. *South Dakota* v. *Neville*, 103 S.Ct. 916 (1983).
182. *Arizona* v. *Mauro*, 107 S.Ct. 1931, 95 L.Ed.2d 458 (1987).
183. *Doyle* v. *Ohio*, 426 U.S. 610 (1976).
184. *Brecht* v. *Abrahamson*, 113 S.Ct. 1710, 123 L.Ed.2d 353 (1993).
185. Citing *Kotteakos* v. *U.S.*, 328 U.S. 750 (1946).
186. *Missouri* v. *Seibert*, 542 U.S. 600 (2004).
187. *Hayes* v. *Florida*, 470 U.S. 811, 105 S.Ct. 1643 (1985).
188. *Winston* v. *Lee*, 470 U.S. 753, 105 S.Ct. 1611 (1985).
189. *Schmerber* v. *California*, 384 U.S. 757 (1966).
190. "Man Coughs Up Cocaine While in Custody," *Police Magazine* online, March 4, 2005. Web posted at http://www.policemag.com/t_newspick.cfm?rank574703 (accessed January 4, 2007).
191. *U.S.* v. *Montoya de Hernandez*, 473 U.S. 531, 105 S.Ct. 3304 (1985).
192. Ibid.
193. *Olmstead* v. *U.S.*, 277 U.S. 438 (1928).
194. *On Lee* v. *U.S.*, 343 U.S. 747 (1952).
195. *Lopez* v. *U.S.*, 373 U.S. 427 (1963).
196. *Berger* v. *New York*, 388 U.S. 41 (1967).
197. *Katz* v. *U.S.*, 389 U.S. 347 (1967).
198. *Lee* v. *Florida*, 392 U.S. 378 (1968).
199. Federal Communications Act of 1934, 47 U.S.C. Section 151.
200. *U.S.* v. *White*, 401 U.S. 745 (1971).
201. *U.S.* v. *Karo*, 468 U.S. 705 (1984).
202. *U.S.* v. *Scott*, 436 U.S. 128 (1978).
203. For more information, see *FBI Law Enforcement Bulletin* (June 1987), p. 25.
204. Electronic Communications Privacy Act of 1986, Public Law 99-508.
205. For more information on the ECPA, see Robert A. Fiatal, "The Electronic Communications Privacy Act: Addressing Today's Technology," *FBI Law Enforcement Bulletin* (April 1988), pp. 24–30.
206. Communications Assistance for Law Enforcement Act of 1994, Public Law 103-414.
207. Federal Bureau of Investigation, "Notice: Implementation of the Communications Assistance for Law Enforcement Act," February 23, 1995.
208. Administrative Office of the United States Courts, *2006 Wiretap Report.* Web posted at http://www.uscourts.gov/wiretap06/contents.html (accessed July 20, 2008).
209. Telecommunications Act of 1996, Public Law 104, 110 Statute 56.
210. Title 47, U.S.C.A., Section 223(a)(1)(B)(ii) (Supp. 1997).
211. *Reno* v. *ACLU*, 117 S.Ct. 2329 (1997).
212. 18 U.S.C. Section 1030.
213. Section 202.
214. 18 U.S.C. Section 2703(c).
215. Ibid.
216. Public Law 109-177.
217. Adapted from Technical Working Group for Electronic Crime Scene Investigation, *Electronic Crime Scene Investigation: A Guide for First Responders* (Washington, DC: National Institute of Justice, 2001), from which much of the information in this section is taken.
218. Ibid., p. 2.
219. Computer Crime and Intellectual Property Section, U.S. Department of Justice, *Searching and Seizing Computers and Obtaining Electronic Evidence in Criminal Investigations* (Washington, DC: U.S. Department of Justice, 2002). Web posted at http://www.usdoj.gov/criminal/cybercrime/s&smanual2002.htm (accessed August 4, 2007).
220. Technical Working Group, *Electronic Crime Scene Investigation*, p. 2.
221. Technical Working Group for the Examination of Digital Evidence, *Forensic Examination of Digital Evidence: A Guide for Law Enforcement* (Washington, DC: National Institute of Justice, 2004).
222. *U.S.* v. *Carey*, 172 F.3d 1268 (10th Cir. 1999).
223. *U.S.* v. *Turner*, 169 F.3d 84 (1st Cir. 1999).

Policing: Issues and Challenges

6

Chapter Outline

- Introduction
- Police Personality and Culture
- Corruption and Integrity
- The Dangers of Police Work
- Terrorism's Impact on Policing
- Police Civil Liability
- Racial Profiling and Biased Policing
- Police Use of Force
- Professionalism and Ethics
- Ethnic and Gender Diversity in Policing
- Private Protective Services

Learning Objectives

After reading this chapter, you should be able to

- Describe the police working personality, relating it to police culture.
- List and describe different types of police corruption, and discuss possible methods for building police integrity.
- Explain the dangers of police work, and discuss what can be done to reduce those dangers.
- Describe the changed role of American police in the post-9/11 environment.
- Describe the civil liability issues associated with policing, and identify common sources of civil suits against the police.
- Describe racial profiling and biased policing, and explain why they have become significant issues in policing today.
- Describe the situations in which police officers are most likely to use force, and provide some guidelines for determining when too much force has been used.
- Demonstrate why professionalism and ethics are important in policing today.
- Identify some of the issues related to ethnic and gender diversity in policing, and suggest ways of addressing them.
- Describe the nature and extent of private protective services in the United States today, and discuss what role you think they will play in the future.

"The continuous threat of terrorism has thrust domestic preparedness obligations to the very top of the law enforcement agenda."

—Colonel Joel Leson, Director, IACP Center for Police Leadership[1]

From Chapter 6 of *Criminal Justice: A Brief Introduction*, Eighth Edition. Frank Schmalleger.

Introduction

▶▶▶ Hear the author discuss this chapter at mycrimekit.com.

Today's police officers and administrators face many complex issues. Some concerns, such as corruption, on-the-job dangers, and the use of deadly force, derive from the very nature of police work. Others, like racial profiling and exposure to civil liability, have arisen due to common practices, characteristic police values, public expectations, legislative action, and ongoing societal change. Certainly one of the most significant challenges facing American law enforcement today is policing a multicultural society. All of these issues are discussed in the pages that follow. We begin, however, with the police recruit socialization process. It is vital to understand this process because the values and expectations learned through it not only contribute to the nature of many important police issues but also determine how the police view and respond to those issues.

Police Personality and Culture

police subculture
The set of informal values that characterize the police force as a distinct community with a common identity.[i]

New police officers learn what is considered appropriate police behavior by working with seasoned veterans. Through conversations with other officers in the locker room, in a squad car, or over a cup of coffee, a new recruit is introduced to the value-laden subculture of police work. **Police subculture** can be understood as "the set of informal values which characterize the police force as a distinct community with a common identity."[2] This process of informal socialization plays a much bigger role than formal police academy training in determining how rookies come to see police work. Through it, new officers gain a shared view of the world that can best be described as "streetwise." Streetwise cops know what official department policy is, but they also know the most efficient way to get a job done. By the time rookie officers become streetwise, they know which of the various informal means of accomplishing the job are acceptable to other officers. The police subculture creates few real mavericks, but it also produces few officers who view their jobs exclusively in terms of public mandates and official dictums.

police working personality
All aspects of the traditional values and patterns of behavior evidenced by police officers who have been effectively socialized into the police subculture. Characteristics of the police personality often extend to the personal lives of law enforcement personnel.

In the 1960s, renowned criminologist Jerome Skolnick described what he called the **police working personality**.[3] Skolnick's description of the police personality was consistent with William Westley's classic study of the Gary (Indiana) Police Department, in which he found a police culture with its own "customs, laws, and morality,"[4] and with Arthur Niederhoffer's observation that cynicism was pervasive among officers in New York City.[5] More recent authors have claimed that the "big curtain of secrecy" surrounding much of police work shields knowledge of the nature of the police personality from outsiders.[6] Taken in concert, these writers offer a picture of the police working personality shown in Table 1.

Some characteristics of the police working personality are essential for survival and effectiveness. For example, because officers are often exposed to highly emotional and potentially

▶ New York City police officers celebrate after the completion of a training ceremony. The police working personality has been characterized as authoritarian, suspicious, and conservative. How does the police working personality develop?
Gregory Bull/AP Wide World Photos

TABLE 1 The Police Personality

Authoritarian	Cynical	Secret	Efficient
Suspicious	Hostile	Conservative	Prejudiced
Insecure	Loyal	Individualistic	Dogmatic
Honorable			

threatening confrontations with belligerent people, they must develop efficient authoritarian strategies for gaining control over others. Similarly, a suspicious nature makes for a good police officer, especially during interrogations and investigations.

However, other characteristics of the police working personality are not so advantageous. For example, many officers are cynical and some can be hostile toward members of the public who do not share their conservative values. These traits result from regular interaction with suspects, most of whom deny any wrongdoing even when they are clearly guilty in the eyes of the police. Eventually, personal traits that result from typical police work become firmly ingrained, setting the cornerstone of the police working personality.

There are at least two sources of the police personality. On the one hand, it may be that components of the police personality already exist in some individuals and draw them toward police work.[7] Supporting this view are studies that indicate that police officers who come from conservative backgrounds view themselves as defenders of middle-class morality.[8] On the other hand, some aspects of the police personality can be attributed to the socialization into the police subculture that rookie officers experience when they are inducted into police ranks.

Researchers have reported similar elements in police subculture throughout the United States.[9] They have concluded that like all cultures, police subculture is a relatively stable collection of beliefs and values that is unlikely to change from within. Police subculture may, however, be changed through external pressures, such as new hiring practices, investigations into police corruption or misuse of authority, and commission reports that create pressures for police reform.[10] Learn more about police subculture and police behavior at Web Extra 6–1 at mycrimekit.com.

Web EXTRA

Corruption and Integrity

Although most law enforcement officers perform their duties responsibly and with honor, some do not. In 2006, for example, Border Patrol Agent Oscar Antonio Ortiz pleaded guilty to charges of conspiracy to smuggle aliens into the United States, making a false claim to U.S. citizenship, making a false statement in the acquisition of a firearm, and being an illegal alien in possession of a firearm.[11] Ortiz, a Mexican citizen who was born in Tijuana, secured a job with the Border Patrol in 2001 by using a fake birth certificate that listed Chicago as his place of birth. Court documents show that he conspired with at least one other Border Patrol agent to smuggle more than 100 Mexican nationals into the United States. Officials revealed that intercepted phone calls between Ortiz and another agent spoke of payments of up to $2,000 per person smuggled into the United States. The recorded calls also discussed rates that human traffickers working with the agents should be charged to secure the agents' cooperation.[12] On July 28, 2006, a federal district court judge sentenced Ortiz to serve 60 months in prison. He will likely be deported after his sentence is complete.

Good cops always seem to be able to identify causes of problems and to come up with the least troublesome ways of solving them.
—Jerome Skolnick

The kind of corruption seen in Ortiz's case pales alongside that of two retired New York City police detectives who were convicted in 2006 of giving confidential information to mob leaders and of misusing their authority as law enforcement officers to kidnap and kill rival gangsters.[13] Federal prosecutors successfully portrayed retired police investigator Louis Eppolito, 56, and his former partner, Stephen Caracappa, 63, as assassins working for the Luchese crime family. The two are suspected of killing at least eight men in one of the city's most spectacular police corruption scandals ever. Their convictions, on 70 counts of racketeering, came 20 years after their first victim was gunned down in a New York City parking garage. Caracappa, who may have been the trigger man in most of the killings, was known for helping to create the New York Police Department (NYPD) Organized Crime Homicide Unit and was described as "a gatekeeper

Multiculturalism and Diversity

Policing a Multicultural Society

Members of some social groups have backgrounds, values, and perspectives that, while not directly supportive of law-breaking, contrast sharply with those of many police officials. Robert M. Shusta, a well-known writer on multicultural law enforcement, says that police officers "need to recognize the fact of poor police–minority relations historically, including *unequal* treatment under the law."[1] Moreover, says Shusta, "many officers and citizens are defensive with each other because their contact is tinged with negative historical 'baggage.'"

In other words, even though discrimination in the enforcement of the criminal law may not be commonplace today, it *was* in the past—and perceptions built on past experience are often difficult to change. Moreover, if the function of law enforcement is to "protect and serve" law-abiding citizens from all backgrounds, then it becomes vital for officers to understand and respect differences in habits, customs, beliefs, patterns of thought, and traditions.[2] Hence, as Shusta says, "the acts of approaching, communicating, questioning, assisting, and establishing trust with members of different groups require special knowledge and skills that have nothing to do with the fact that 'the law is the law' and must be enforced equally. Acquiring sensitivity, knowledge, and skills leads to [an increased appreciation for the position of others] that will contribute to improved communications with members of all groups."[3]

How can police officers acquire greater sensitivity to the issues involved in policing a diverse multicultural society? Some researchers suggest that law enforcement officers of *all* backgrounds begin by exploring their own prejudices. Prejudices, which are judgments or opinions formed before facts are known and which usually involve negative or unfavorable thoughts about groups of people, can lead to discrimination. Most people, including police officers, are able to reduce their tendency to discriminate against those who are different by exploring and uprooting their own personal prejudices.

One technique for identifying prejudices is cultural awareness training. As practiced in some police departments today, cultural awareness training explores the impact of culture on human behavior—and especially law-breaking behavior. Cultural awareness training generally involves four stages[4]:

- *Clarifying the relationship between cultural awareness and police professionalism.* As Shusta explains it, "The more professional a police officer is, the more sophisticated he or she is in responding to people of all backgrounds and the more successful he or she is in cross-cultural contact."[5]
- *Recognizing personal prejudices.* In the second stage of cultural awareness training, participating officers are asked to recognize and identify their own personal prejudices and biases. Once prejudices have been identified, trainers strive to show how they can affect daily behavior.
- *Acquiring sensitivity to police–community relations.* In this stage of training, participating officers learn about historical and existing community perceptions of the police. Training can often be enhanced through the use of carefully chosen and well-qualified guest speakers or participants from minority communities.
- *Developing interpersonal relations skills.* The goal of this last stage of training is to assist with the development of the positive verbal and nonverbal communications skills necessary for successful interaction with community members. Many trainers believe that basic skills training will result in the continuing development of such skills because officers will quickly begin to see the benefits (in terms of lessened interpersonal conflict) of effective interpersonal skills.

[1]Robert M. Shusta et al., *Multicultural Law Enforcement: Strategies for Peacekeeping in a Diverse Society*, 2nd ed. (Upper Saddle River, NJ: Prentice Hall, 2002), p. 4.
[2]Ibid., p. 16.
[3]Ibid., p. 4.
[4]Ibid., pp. 104–106.
[5]Ibid., p. 4.

of information about Mafia killings investigated by police." Although the jurors remained anonymous throughout the trial for protection from possible retaliation, one of them, a building safety official from Long Island, told reporters after the trial that he was shocked at the detectives for having broken their oath to uphold the law. "When you're given an oath, and an oath as precious as being a police officer, and a duty to protect and serve people, that is the highest oath ever," said the juror. "It's like, 'How dare you violate that oath?' . . . [W]hen you violate [that] oath, you lose the respect of the people you're sworn to protect."[14]

police corruption
The abuse of police authority for personal or organizational gain.[ii]

Police corruption has been a problem in American society since the early days of policing. It is probably an ancient and natural tendency of human beings to attempt to placate or win over those in positions of authority over them. This tendency is complicated in today's materialistic society by greed and by the personal and financial benefits to be derived from evading the law. The temptations toward illegality offered to police range from a free cup of coffee given by a small restaurant owner in the thought that one day it may be necessary to call on the officer's goodwill, perhaps for something as simple as a traffic ticket, to huge monetary bribes arranged by drug dealers to guarantee that the police will look the other way as an important shipment of contraband arrives. As noted criminologist Carl B. Klockars says, policing, by its very nature, "is an occupation that is rife with opportunities for misconduct. Policing is a highly discretionary, coercive activity that routinely takes place in private settings, out of the sight of supervisors, and in the presence of witnesses who are often regarded as unreliable."[15]

The effects of police corruption can be far-reaching. As Michael Palmiotto of Wichita State University notes, "Not only does misconduct committed by an officer personally affect that officer, it also affects the community, the police department that employs the officer and every police department and police officer in America. Frequently, negative police actions caused by inappropriate police behavior reach every corner of the nation, and at times, the world."[16]

Exactly what constitutes corruption is not always clear. Ethicists say that police corruption ranges from minor offenses to serious violations of the law. In recognition of what some have called corruption's "slippery slope,"[17] most police departments now explicitly prohibit even the acceptance of minor gratuities. The slippery slope perspective holds that even a small thank-you accepted from a member of the public can lead to a more ready acceptance of larger bribes. An officer who begins to accept, and then expect, gratuities may soon find that his or her practice of policing becomes influenced by such gifts and that larger ones soon follow. At that point, the officer may easily slide to the bottom of the moral slope, which was made slippery by previous small concessions.

Thomas Barker and David Carter, who have studied police corruption in depth, make the distinction between "occupational deviance," which is motivated by the desire for personal benefit, and "abuse of authority, which occurs most often to further the organizational goals of law enforcement, including arrest, ticketing, and the successful conviction of suspects."[18]

FBI Special Agent Frank Perry, former chief of the bureau's ethics unit, distinguishes between police deviance and police corruption. Police deviance, according to Perry, consists of "unprofessional on- and off-duty misconduct, isolated instances of misuse of position, improper relationships with informants or criminals, sexual harassment, disparaging racial or sexual comments, embellished/falsified reporting, time and attendance abuse, insubordination, nepotism, cronyism, and noncriminal unauthorized disclosure of information."[19] Deviance, says Perry, is a precursor to individual and organizational corruption. It may eventually lead to outright corruption unless police supervisors and internal affairs units are alert to the warning signs and actively intervene to prevent corruption from developing.

Figure 1 sorts examples of police corruption into levels of seriousness, though not everyone would agree with this ranking. In fact, a survey of 6,982 New York City police officers found that 65% did not classify excessive force, which we define later in this chapter, as a corrupt behavior.[20] Likewise, 71% of responding officers said that accepting a free meal is not a corrupt practice; another 15% said that personal use of illegal drugs by law enforcement officers should not be considered corruption.

Nearly all men can stand adversity, but if you want to test a man's character, give him power.

—Abraham Lincoln[iii]

In the early 1970s, Frank Serpico made headlines as he testified before the **Knapp Commission** on police corruption in New York City.[21] Serpico, an undercover operative within the police department, revealed a complex web of corruption in which money and services routinely changed hands in "protection rackets" created by unethical officers. The authors of the Knapp Commission report distinguished between two types of corrupt officers, which they termed "grass eaters" and "meat eaters."[22] "Grass eating," the most common form of police corruption, was described as illegitimate activity that occurs from time to time in the normal course of police work. It involves mostly small bribes or relatively minor services offered by citizens seeking to avoid arrest and prosecution. "Meat eating" is a much more serious form of corruption, involving as it does the active seeking of illicit money-making opportunities by officers. Meat eaters solicit bribes through threat or intimidation, whereas grass eaters make the simpler mistake of not refusing bribes that are offered.

Knapp Commission
A committee that investigated police corruption in New York City in the early 1970s.

In 1993, during 11 days of corruption hearings reminiscent of the Knapp Commission era, a parade of crooked New York police officers testified before a commission headed by former Judge and Deputy Mayor Milton Mollen. Among the many revelations, officers spoke of dealing drugs, stealing confiscated drug funds, stifling investigations, and beating innocent people. Officer Michael Dowd, for example, told the commission that he had run a cocaine ring out of his station house in Brooklyn and had bought three homes on Long Island and a Corvette with the money he made. Most shocking of all, however, were allegations that high-level police officials attempted to hide embarrassing incidents in a "phantom file" and that many officials may have condoned unprofessional and even criminal practices by the officers under their command.

FIGURE 1
Types and Examples of Police Corruption.

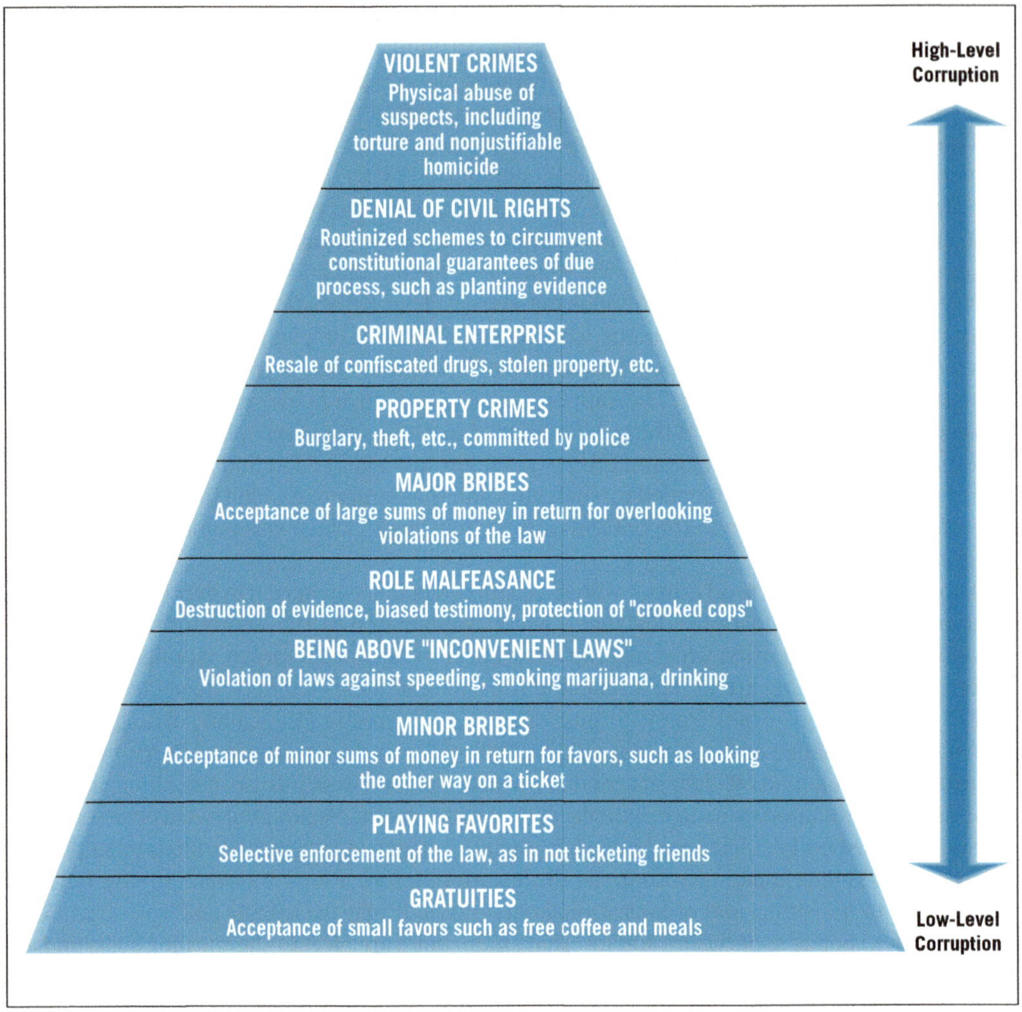

If you ever get lost, you can go find a policeman. The policeman will help you because he is your friend.
—*A second-grade teacher*

Honest officers, including internal affairs investigators, described how their efforts to end corruption among their fellows had been defused and resisted by higher authorities.

Repercussions from the Mollen Commission hearings continue to be felt. In 2004, for example, a New York State judge ruled that the city of New York must pay special disability benefits to former police officer Jeffrey W. Baird, who served as an informer for the commission. Baird helped uncover corruption while working as an internal affairs officer but suffered from post-traumatic stress disorder after fellow officers threatened him, vandalized his work area, and sent obscene materials to his home.[23]

Corruption in the Los Angeles Police Department's (LAPD) Rampart Division was slated to be fictionalized in a planned Franchise Pictures 2008 movie, *Notorious.*[24] The movie, in which Sylvester Stallone was to star as an LAPD detective, suggests that rappers Biggie Smalls (aka Notorious B.I.G.) and Tupac Shakur were killed as part of a conspiracy involving the police, gang members, and officials from the music industry. The true Rampart scandal, although it involved widespread and significant police corruption, was a somewhat more mundane affair.

The scandal began in mid-2000 when the LAPD became embroiled in accusations of corruption that centered on the Rampart Division's antigang unit, known as CRASH (Community Resources Against Street Hoodlums).[25] Many of the unit's officers were accused of operating like a criminal organization to frame hundreds of people through using threats and beatings, by planting evidence, and by committing perjury. They and other officers were alleged to be running a drug ring while eliminating competition from civilian dealers by framing them and seeing them sent to prison.[26] Seven shootings and at least two killings, said to be perpetrated by police officers, were among the illegal activities allegedly committed by officers. The scandal came to light after LAPD Officer Rafael Perez was caught stealing $1 million worth of cocaine from an evidence room. In exchange for an offer of leniency, Perez turned informant and cooperated with prosecutors. Perez, who was also accused of murder by a former girlfriend, provided investigators with details about ongoing corruption in the Rampart area.[27] As events unfolded, LAPD Chief Bernard Parks was accused by prosecutors of withholding critical information needed to build a case against the accused officers. According to prosecutors, the LAPD, under the direction of Chief Parks, "failed to provide arrest reports, witness statements and background information." The prosecutors claimed that "on several occasions, the LAPD . . . actually hindered the progress of the investigation."[28] Parks was replaced as chief by William J. Bratton in 2002.

By 2005, more than 100 falsely obtained convictions had been thrown out, and 20 LAPD officers had left active duty.[29] Another seven officers were convicted of conspiring to frame innocent people, but a judge overturned three of the convictions on procedural grounds. The remaining four officers received sentences of up to five years in prison.[30] The Los Angeles City Attorney agreed to pay a total of $70.2 million to settle approximately 214 lawsuits stemming from the corruption scandal. At the time of the settlement, the *Los Angeles Times* complained that much of the money, averaging $400,000 per settlement, went to "drug dealers, gang members and other criminals who said they had been framed, shot, beaten or otherwise mistreated by police."[31] The largest settlement, $15 million, went to former gang member Javier Francisco Ovando, who had been paralyzed by a police shooting. In responding to critics, Cindy Miscikowski, chairwoman of the Los Angeles City Council's Public Safety Committee, pointed out that "regardless of who the plaintiffs were, there was evidence of wrongdoing. That's what we had to recognize. . . . Civil rights are civil rights, and they apply to everyone across the board."[32]

The LAPD is now operating under a consent decree, a legally binding agreement with the U.S. Department of Justice (DOJ) that calls for major reforms. The decree requires the department to install a computer system to track complaints and disciplinary actions against LAPD officers; to collect data on the racial makeup of citizens stopped for traffic violations; and to create a special unit within the department to investigate shootings and beatings by police officers to determine whether excessive force was used.[33] Rafael Perez, sentenced to five years

▲ The Los Angeles Police Department's Rampart station office, where a corruption scandal occurred in 2000 and 2001. A number of officers assigned to the Rampart Division were investigated on charges ranging from falsifying evidence to the theft and sale of illegal drugs. In what some have called "the biggest police scandal case in Los Angeles history," many criminal cases had to be dismissed. What other forms can police corruption take?
David McNew/Liaison/Getty Images, Inc.

Web EXTRA

in prison, warned young officers as he was sentenced that "whoever chases monsters must see that he not become a monster himself."[34] Learn more about the Rampart scandal at **Web Extra 6–2** at mycrimekit.com.

Money—The Root of Police Evil?

Years ago, Edwin Sutherland applied the concept of *differential association* to the study of deviant behavior.[35] Sutherland suggested that frequent, continued association of one person with another makes the associates similar. Of course, Sutherland was talking about criminals, not police officers. Consider, however, the dilemma of average officers: Their job entails issuing traffic citations to citizens who try to talk their way out of a ticket, dealing with prostitutes who feel hassled by police, and arresting drug users who think it should be their right to do what they want as long as "it doesn't hurt anyone"; they regularly encounter personal hostility and experience consistent and often quite vocal rejection of society's formalized norms; and they receive relatively low pay, which indicates to them that their work is not really valued. By looking at the combination of these factors, it is easy to understand how officers often develop a jaded attitude toward the society they are sworn to protect.

Police officers' low pay may be a critical ingredient of the corruption mix. Salaries paid to police officers in this country have been notoriously low when compared to those of other professions involving personal dedication, extensive training, high stress, and risk of bodily harm. As police professionalism increases, many police administrators hope that salaries will rise. No matter how much police pay grows, however, it will never be able to compete with the staggering amounts of money to be made through dealing in contraband.

Working hand in hand with monetary pressures toward corruption is the moral dilemma produced by unenforceable laws that provide the basis for criminal profit. During the Prohibition era, the Wickersham Commission warned of the potential for official corruption inherent in the legislative taboos on alcohol. The immense demand for drink called into question the wisdom of the law while simultaneously providing vast resources designed to circumvent it. Today's drug scene bears some similarities to the Prohibition era. As long as many people are willing to make large financial and other sacrifices to feed the drug trade, the pressures on the police to embrace corruption will remain substantial.

Building of Police Integrity

The difficulties of controlling corruption can be traced to several factors, including the reluctance of police officers to report corrupt activities by their fellow officers, the reluctance of police administrators to acknowledge the existence of corruption in their agencies, the benefits of corrupt transactions to the parties involved, and the lack of victims willing to report corruption. High moral standards, however, embedded in the principles of the police profession and effectively communicated to individual officers through formal training and peer-group socialization can raise the level of integrity in any department. There are, of course, many officers of great personal integrity who hold to the highest of professional ideals. There is evidence that law enforcement training programs are becoming increasingly concerned with instruction designed to reinforce the high ideals many recruits bring to police work. As one Federal Bureau of Investigation (FBI) article explains it, "Ethics training must become an integral part of academy and in-service training for new and experienced officers alike."[36]

Ethics training is part of a "reframing" strategy that emphasizes integrity to target police corruption. In 1997, for example, the National Institute of Justice (NIJ) released a report titled *Police Integrity: Public Service with Honor*.[37] The report, based on recommendations made by participants in a national symposium on police integrity, suggested (1) integrating ethics training into the programs offered by newly funded Regional Community Policing Institutes throughout the country, (2) broadening research activities in the area of ethics through NIJ-awarded grants for research on police integrity, and (3) conducting case studies of departments that have an excellent track record in the area of police integrity.

The NIJ report was followed in 2001 by a DOJ document titled *Principles for Promoting Police Integrity*.[38] The foreword to that document states, "For community policing to be successful, and crime reduction efforts to be effective, citizens must have trust in the police. All of

Ethics and Professionalism

The Law Enforcement Oath of Honor

On my honor, I will never
Betray my badge, my integrity,
My character or the public trust.
I will always have the courage to hold
Myself and others accountable
for our actions.
I will always uphold the Constitution,
My community, and the agency I serve.

Honor means that one's word is given as a guarantee.

Betray is defined as breaking faith with the public trust.

Badge is the symbol of your office.

Integrity is being the same person in both private and public life.

Character means the qualities that distinguish an individual.

Public trust is a charge of duty imposed in faith toward those you serve.

Courage is having the strength to withstand unethical pressure, fear or danger.

Accountability means that you are answerable and responsible to your oath of office.

Community is the jurisdiction and citizens served.

THINKING ABOUT ETHICS

1. How is the Law Enforcement Oath of Honor similar to the Law Enforcement Code of Ethics, which is also found in this chapter? How does it differ? How do the two support one another?

Source: Adopted at the 107th International Association of Chiefs of Police Annual Conference, November 15, 2000. Reprinted with permission.

us must work together to address the problems of excessive use of force and racial profiling, and—equally important—the perceptions of many minority residents that law enforcement treats them unfairly, if we are to build the confidence in law enforcement necessary for continued progress. Our goal must be professional law enforcement that gives all citizens of our country the feeling that they are being treated fairly, equally and with respect." The report covered such topics as the use of force; complaints and misconduct investigations; accountability and effective management; training; nondiscriminatory policing; and recruitment, hiring, and retention. Read the full report, which provides examples of promising police practices and policies in support of increased integrity, at Library Extra 6–1 at mycrimekit.com.

Library EXTRA

In 2000, the International Association of Chiefs of Police (IACP), in an effort to reinforce the importance of ethical standards in policing, adopted the Law Enforcement Oath of Honor, shown in an Ethics and Professionalism box in this chapter. The IACP suggests that the Law Enforcement Oath of Honor should be seen by individual officers as a statement of commitment to ethical behavior. It is meant to reinforce the principles embodied in the Law Enforcement Code of Ethics, which is printed in an Ethics and Professionalism box later in this chapter.

To introduce and implement new police ideas is not easy, but it is possible. More than that, it is essential if we are to achieve elementary public safety in American cities and confidence in the police by those who are being policed.

—*Jerome H. Skolnick and David H. Bayley*[iv]

In December 2005, the DOJ weighed in on the issue of police integrity with a Research for Practice report titled *Enhancing Police Integrity*.[39] The 2005 report noted that "an agency's culture of integrity, as defined by clearly understood and implemented policies and rules, may be more important in shaping the ethics of police officers than hiring the 'right' people."[40] Report authors also noted that officers tend to evaluate the seriousness of various types of misconduct by observing and assessing their department's response in detecting and disciplining it. If unwritten policies conflict with written policies, the authors observed, then the resulting confusion undermines an agency's overall integrity-enhancing efforts. *Enhancing Police Integrity* is available online at Library Extra 6–2 at mycrimekit.com.

Library EXTRA

Most large law enforcement agencies have their own division of **internal affairs**, which is empowered to investigate charges of wrongdoing made against officers. Where necessary, state police agencies may be called on to examine reported incidents. Federal agencies, including the FBI and the Drug Enforcement Administration (DEA), involve themselves when corruption goes far enough to violate federal statutes. The DOJ, through various investigative offices, has the authority to examine possible violations of civil rights that may result from the misuse of

internal affairs
The branch of a police organization tasked with investigating charges of wrongdoing involving members of the department.

police authority. The DOJ is often supported in these endeavors by the American Civil Liberties Union (ACLU), the National Association for the Advancement of Colored People (NAACP), and other watchdog groups.

Drug Testing of Police Employees

On November 17, 2000, the U.S. Court of Appeals for the Fourth Circuit found that the chief of police in Westminster, Maryland, had acted properly in asking a doctor to test an officer's urine for the presence of heroin without the officer's knowledge.[41] Westminster Police Officer Eric Carroll had gone to the local hospital complaining of tightness in his chest and fatigue. The doctor who examined Carroll diagnosed him as suffering from high blood pressure. Carroll was placed on disability leave for three days. While Carroll was gone, the police chief received a call from someone who said that Carroll was using heroin. The chief verified the caller's identity and then called the department doctor and asked him to test Carroll for drugs—but directed that the officer not be informed of the test. When Carroll returned to the physician for a follow-up visit, the doctor took a urine sample, saying that it was to test for the presence of blood. Although no blood was found in Carroll's urine, it did test positive for heroin. As a consequence, Officer Carroll's employment with the department was terminated. He then sued in federal court, alleging conspiracy, defamation, and violations of his constitutional rights. The Fourth Circuit Court of Appeals, however, determined that the chief's actions were reasonable because, among other things, Carroll had signed a preemployment waiver that permitted the department to conduct drug tests at any time, with or without cause.[42]

There is more to being a professional than just looking like one.

—Rob Edwards

The widespread potential for police corruption created by illicit drugs has led to focused efforts to combat drug use by officers. Drug-testing programs in local police departments are an example of such efforts. The IACP has developed a Model Drug Testing Policy for police managers. The policy, designed to meet the needs of local departments, suggests the following[43]:

- Testing all who are applicants and recruits for drug or narcotics use
- Testing current employees when performance difficulties or documentation indicates a potential drug problem
- Testing current employees when they are involved in the use of excessive force or when they suffer or cause on-duty injury
- Routinely testing all employees who are assigned to special "high-risk" areas, such as narcotics and vice

Today, many police departments require their officers to submit to routine drug testing, and in 2008, the NYPD began randomly testing its officers for anabolic steroid abuse. The department began the testing after several police officers were linked to the investigation of a Brooklyn pharmacy suspected of illegally selling millions of dollars of steroids and human growth hormone.[44]

The courts have supported drug testing based on a reasonable suspicion that drug abuse has been or is occurring (***Maurice Turner* v. *Fraternal Order of Police***, 1985),[45] although random testing of officers was banned by the New York State Supreme Court in the case of *Philip Caruso, President of P.B.A.* v. *Benjamin Ward, Police Commissioner* (1986).[46] Citing overriding public interests, a 1989 decision by the U.S. Supreme Court upheld the testing of U.S. Customs personnel applying for transfer into positions involving drug-law enforcement or requiring a firearm.[47] Many legal issues surrounding employee drug testing remain to be resolved in court, however.

Complicating this issue is the fact that drug and alcohol addictions are "handicaps" protected by the Federal Rehabilitation Act of 1973. As such, federal law enforcement employees, as well as those working for agencies with federal contracts, are entitled to counseling and treatment before action can be taken toward termination.

Employee drug testing in police departments, as in many other agencies, is a sensitive subject. Some claim that existing tests for drug use are inaccurate, yielding a significant number of "false positives." Repeated testing and high threshold levels for narcotic substances in the blood may eliminate many of these concerns. Less easy to address, however, is the belief that drug testing intrudes on the personal rights and professional dignity of individual employees. Learn more about employee drug-testing policies in police departments at **Web Extra 6–3** at mycrimekit.com, and discover more about corruption and the continuing drive toward police integrity with Library Extras 6–3 and 6–4.

Web EXTRA

Library EXTRA

The Dangers of Police Work

On October 15, 1991, the National Law Enforcement Officers' Memorial was unveiled in Washington, D.C. The memorial contained the names of 12,561 law enforcement officers killed in the line of duty, including U.S. Marshals Service Officer Robert Forsyth, who in 1794 became the nation's first law enforcement officer to be killed. More than 5,000 names have been added since opening day.[48] At the memorial, an interactive video system provides visitors with brief biographies and photographs of officers who have died. Tour the memorial by visiting Web Extra 6–4 at mycrimekit.com.

Web EXTRA

As the memorial proves, police work is, by its very nature, dangerous. Although many officers never once fire their weapons in the line of duty, we also know that some officers meet death while performing their jobs. On-the-job police deaths occur from stress, training accidents, and auto crashes; however, it is violent death at the hands of criminal offenders that police officers and their families fear most.

Violence in the Line of Duty

At one o'clock on the morning of April 17, 2005, 50-year-old Providence (Rhode Island) Police Department Detective Sergeant James L. Allen was shot and killed with his own service weapon inside the Providence Public Safety Complex. Allen was in the process of questioning 26-year-old Esteban Carpio about the stabbing and robbery of an 86-year-old woman that had taken place the day before.[49] Carpio, who was not under arrest and whose handcuffs had been removed, apparently grabbed Allen's weapon during a brief struggle and shot the officer. After the killing, Carpio shot out a third-story window, jumped to the ground, and attempted to escape. Injured in the fall, he was apprehended a few blocks away. Detective Allen, whose father is a retired police captain, had served with the Providence Police Department for 27 years and is survived by a wife and two daughters.[50]

Unlike the soldier fighting a war on foreign soil, police officers, who provide for our safety at home, have never been given the honor that was their due.

—Hubert Williams
President, the Police Foundation[v]

▲ The flag-draped casket of slain Providence (Rhode Island) Police Department Detective Sgt. James L. Allen is carried out of Providence's Saint Thomas Church following funeral services in 2005. Allen, 50, was shot with his own service weapon inside the Providence Police Department headquarters while questioning a suspect about the stabbing and robbery of an elderly woman. How might the dangers associated with police work be reduced?
Chitose Suzuki/AP Wide World Photos

FIGURE 2
U.S. Law Enforcement Officers Killed in the Line of Duty, 2007.
Source: Based on data from the Officer Down Memorial Page website, http://www.odmp.org.

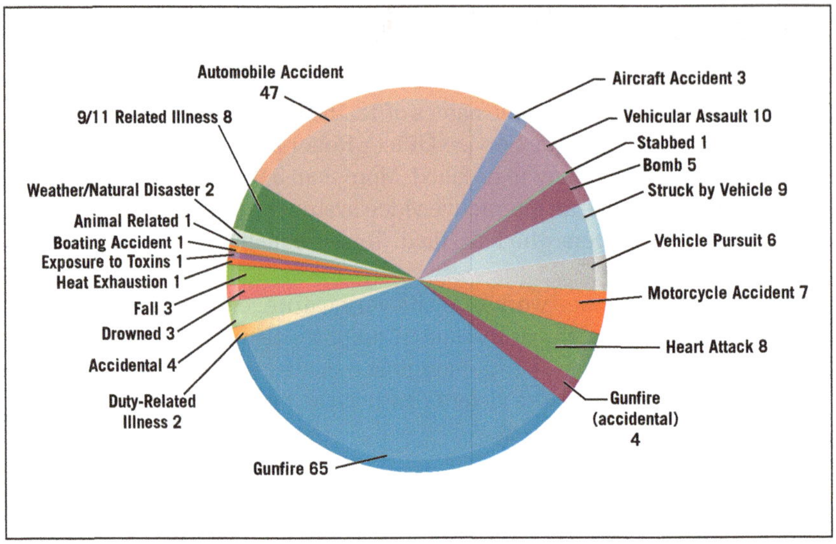

Most officers who are shot are killed by lone suspects armed with a single weapon. In 2007, 188 American law enforcement officers were killed in the line of duty.[51] Figure 2 shows the number of officers killed in different types of incidents. In 2001, the attacks on the World Trade Center resulted in the greatest ever single-incident loss of life of on-duty law enforcement officers when 72 police officers perished.[52]

A study by the FBI found that slain officers appeared to be good-natured and conservative in the use of physical force, "as compared to other law enforcement officers in similar situations. They were also perceived as being well-liked by the community and the department, friendly to everyone, laid back, and easy going."[53] Finally, the study, which was published before the September 11, 2001, terrorist attacks, also found that most officers who were killed failed to wear protective vests.

For statistics on police killings to have meaning beyond the personal tragedy they entail, it is necessary to place them within a larger framework. There are approximately 730,000 state and local police employees in this country[54] and another 88,000 federal agents.[55] Such numbers demonstrate that the rate of violent death among law enforcement officers in the line of duty is small indeed—and it appears to be declining.

A significant decline in police deaths from all causes in 2008 prompted Craig Floyd, Chairman of the National Law Enforcement Officers Memorial Fund, to attribute the drop to an enhanced focus on officer safety by police departments and officers' unions. "Clearly, there is a heightened awareness [of the need for safety] among officers, trainers, union leaders and chiefs," Floyd said.[56] Others attribute the decline in law enforcement deaths to a renewed push for the use of body armor; an increased availability of less-lethal weapons; a broader use of mandatory handcuffing, even at traffic stops; widespread and better analysis of police dashboard videos to critique officer behavior; and better arming of police officers.

Risk of Disease and Infected Evidence

biological weapons
A biological agent used to threaten human life (for example, anthrax, smallpox, or any infectious disease).[vi]

Dangers other than violence also threaten enforcement officers. The increase in serious diseases that can be transmitted by blood and other body fluids, the possible planned release of active **biological weapons** such as anthrax or smallpox, and the fact that crime and accident scenes are inherently dangerous combine to make *caution* a necessary watchword among investigators and first responders. Routine criminal and accident investigations hold the potential for infection through minor cuts and abrasions resulting from contact with the broken glass and torn metal of a wrecked vehicle, the sharp edges of knives found at the scene of an assault or murder, or drug implements such as razor blades and hypodermic needles secreted in vehicles, homes, and pockets. Such minor injuries, previously shrugged off by many police personnel, have become a focal point for warnings about the dangers of AIDS, hepatitis B, tuberculosis, and other diseases spread through contact with infected blood.

In 1988, in Sonoma County, California, Sheriff Dick Michaelson became the first law enforcement supervisor to announce a clear-cut case of AIDS infection in an officer caused by interaction with a suspect. A deputy in Michaelson's department apparently contracted AIDS a few years earlier when he was pricked by a hypodermic needle during a pat-down search.[57]

Infection can also occur from the use of breath alcohol instruments on infected persons, the handling of evidence of all types, seemingly innocuous implements such as staples, the emergency delivery of babies in squad cars, and the attack (especially bites) by infected individuals who are being questioned or who are in custody. Understandably, officers are concerned about how to handle the threat of AIDS and other bloodborne diseases. However, as a publication of the NYPD reminds its officers, "Police officers have a professional responsibility to render assistance to those who are in need of our services. We cannot refuse to help. Persons with infectious diseases must be treated with the care and dignity we show all citizens."[58]

Of equal concern is the threat of biological agents. Although crime scenes and sites known to harbor (or that are suspected of harboring) dangerous active biological agents require a response by teams equipped with special protective equipment, all law enforcement officers should take reasonable precautions against exposure to the wide variety of infectious agents known to exist at even routine crime scenes. Emergency management agencies generally recommend a number of precautions to defend against exposure to infectious substances, as shown in Table 2.

TABLE 2 Biological Incident Law Enforcement Concerns

Concern	Precaution and Response
Suspicious material	Responding officers should not handle or come in close physical contact with suspicious material. If it is necessary to handle the material to evaluate it, officers should wear surgical gloves and masks and wash their hands thoroughly with soap and water after handling it.
Human bites	The biter usually receives the victim's blood. Viral transmission through saliva is highly unlikely. If bitten by anyone, milk the wound to make it bleed, wash the area thoroughly, and seek medical attention.
Spitting	Viral transmission through saliva is highly unlikely.
Urine/feces	Virus has been isolated in only very low concentrations in urine and not at all in feces. No cases of AIDS or AIDS virus infection associated with either urine or feces have been reported.
Cuts/puncture wounds	Use caution when handling sharp objects and searching areas hidden from view. Needle-stick studies show risk of infection is very low.
CPR/first aid	To eliminate the already minimal risk associated with CPR, use masks/airways. Avoid blood-to-blood contact by keeping open wounds covered and wearing gloves when in contact with bleeding wounds.
Body removal	Observe crime-scene rules; do not touch anything. Those who must come in contact with blood or other body fluids should wear gloves.
Casual contact	No cases of AIDS or AIDS virus infection have been attributed to casual contact.
Any contact with blood or body fluids	Wear gloves if contact with blood or body fluids is considered likely. If contact occurs, wash thoroughly with soap and water; clean up spills with one part water to nine parts household bleach.
Contact with dried blood	No cases of infection have been traced to exposure to dried blood. The drying process itself appears to inactivate the virus. Despite low risk, however, caution dictates wearing gloves, a mask, and protective shoe coverings if exposure to dried blood particles is likely (for example, crime-scene investigation).

References: Michigan Department of Community Health, *Anthrax (Bacillus anthracis) Information for Health Care Providers.* Web posted at http://www.michigan. gov/documents/Healthcare_provider_FAQ-anthrax_08-2004_104327_7.pdf (accessed June 12, 2008); Massachusetts Administrative Office of the Trial Court, *Personnel Policies and Procedures Manual,* Section 24.000 ("Statement of Policy and Procedures on AIDS"). Web posted at http://www.state.ma.us/courts/admin/hr/section24.html (accessed January 25, 2006); and "Collecting and Handling Evidence Infected with Human Disease-Causing Organisms," *FBI Law Enforcement Bulletin,* July 1987.

To better combat the threat of infectious diseases among public-safety employees and health care professionals, the federal Bloodborne Pathogens Act of 1991[59] requires that police officers receive proper training in how to prevent contamination by bloodborne infectious agents; the act also requires that police officers undergo an annual refresher course on the topic.

Police departments will face an increasing number of legal challenges in the years to come in cases involving infectious diseases such as AIDS and in cases involving the release of biological agents. Predictable areas of concern include (1) the need to educate officers and other police employees about AIDS, anthrax, and other serious infectious diseases; (2) the responsibility of police departments to prevent the spread of AIDS and other infectious diseases in police lockups; and (3) the necessity of effective and nondiscriminatory enforcement activities and lifesaving measures by police officers in environments contaminated with active biological agents. With regard to nondiscriminatory activities, the NIJ has suggested that legal claims in support of an officer's refusal to render assistance to people with AIDS would probably not be effective in court.[60] The reason is twofold: The officer has a basic duty to render assistance to individuals in need of it, and the possibility of AIDS transmission by casual contact has been scientifically established as extremely remote.

A final issue of growing concern involves activities by police officers infected with the AIDS virus. Few statistics are currently available on the number of officers with AIDS, but public reaction to those officers may be a developing problem that police managers will soon need to address.

Stress and Fatigue among Police Officers

In the week after Hurricane Katrina, two New Orleans police officers used their service weapons to take their own lives. One was Sgt. Paul Accardo, the department's spokesperson; the other was patrolman Lawrence Celestine, an officer described by Deputy Police Chief W. J. Riley as "an outstanding cop."[61] Feelings of powerlessness, personal loss, and an inability to help those in need all seriously heightened the level of stress felt by officers in New Orleans following the 2005 hurricane. "The most stressing part is seeing the citizens we serve every day being treated like refugees," said Riley. "There were cops walking through the crowd at the convention center and people were coming up to beg for food. Not being able to help is a difficult thing. People were calling our names because we knew them and to not be able to help, man, that's stressful."[62]

Traumatic events, like hurricanes, terrorist attacks, and violent confrontations, are instantly stressful, but long-term stress, whose debilitating effects accumulate over years, may be the most insidious and least visible of all threats facing law enforcement personnel today. While some degree of stress can be a positive motivator, serious stress over long periods of time is generally regarded as destructive, even life-threatening.

Stress is a natural component of police work.[63] The American Institute of Stress, based in Yonkers, New York, ranks policing among the top ten stress-producing jobs in the country.[64] Danger, frustration, paperwork, the daily demands of the job, and a lack of understanding from family members and friends contribute to the negative stress that officers experience. The Bureau of Justice Statistics points out the following:

> [E]xposure to violence, suffering, and death is inherent to the profession of the law enforcement officer. There are other sources of stress as well. Officers who deal with offenders on a daily basis may perceive the public's opinion of police performance to be unfavorable; they often are required to work mandatory, rotating shifts; and they may not have enough time to spend with their families. Police officers also face unusual, often highly disturbing, situations, such as dealing with a child homicide victim or the survivors of vehicle crashes.[65]

Some stressors in police work are particularly destructive. One is frustration brought on by the inability to be effective, regardless of the amount of personal effort expended. The crux of police work involves making arrests based on thorough investigations that lead to convictions and the removal of individuals who are damaging to the social fabric of the community—all under the umbrella of criminal law. Unfortunately, reality is often far from the ideal: Arrests may not lead to convictions, evidence available to the officer may not be allowed in court, the sentences imposed may seem too light to the arresting officer. The feelings of powerlessness and frustration that come from seeing repeat offenders back on the streets and from witnessing numerous injustices worked on seemingly innocent victims may greatly stress police officers and cause them to question the purpose of their professional lives. It may also lead to desperate attempts to find relief. As one researcher observes, "The suicide rate of police officers is more than twice that of the general population."[66]

Another source of stress—that of living with constant danger—is incomprehensible to most of us and to the family members of many officers. As one officer says, "I kick in a door and I've gotta talk some guy into putting a gun down. . . . And I go home, and my wife's upset because the lawn isn't cut and the kids have been bad. Now, to her that's a real problem."[67] Yet the support of family and friends is crucial for handling stress.

Stress is not unique to the police profession, but because of the "macho" attitude that has traditionally been associated with police work, denial of the stress may be found more often among police officers than in other occupational groups. Certain types of individuals are probably more susceptible to the negative effects of stress than are others. The type A personality, popularized 30 years ago, is more likely to perceive life in terms of pressure and performance, whereas type B people are more laid back and less likely to suffer from the negative effects of stress. Police ranks, drawn as they are from the general population, are filled with both stress-sensitive and stress-resistant personalities.

Stress Reduction

It is natural to want to reduce stress.[68] Humor helps, even if it's somewhat cynical. Health care professionals, for example, are noted for their ability to joke even though they are caring for patients who are seriously ill or even dying. At times, police officers use humor similarly to defuse their reactions to dark or threatening situations. Keeping an emotional distance from stressful events is another way of coping with them, although such distance is not always easy to maintain. Police officers who have had to deal with serious cases of child abuse often report that they experience emotional turmoil as a consequence.

Exercise, meditation, deep breathing, biofeedback, self-hypnosis, guided imaging, induced relaxation, subliminal conditioning, music, prayer, and diet have all been cited as useful techniques for stress reduction. Devices to measure stress levels are available in the form of handheld heart-rate monitors, blood pressure devices, "biodots" (which change color according to the amount of blood flow in the extremities), and psychological inventories.

A new approach to managing stress among police officers holds that the amount of stress an officer experiences is directly related to his or her reactions to potentially stressful situations.[69] Officers who can filter out extraneous stimuli and who can distinguish between truly threatening situations and those that are benign are much less likely to report job-related stressors than those lacking these abilities. Because stress-filtering abilities are often closely linked to innate personality characteristics, some researchers suggest careful psychological screening of police applicants to better identify those who have a natural ability to cope with situations that others might perceive as stressful.[70]

Foremost among the demands that confront police in the post-September 11 environment is the ability to effectively and efficiently collect, assess, disseminate, and act on intelligence information regarding threats posed by transnational and domestic terrorists.

—Colonel Joel Leson, Director, IACP Center for Police Leadership[vii]

A police officer's family members often report feelings of stress that are directly related to the officer's work. As a result, some departments have developed innovative programs to allay family stress. The Collier County (Florida) Spousal Academy, for example, is a family support program that offers training to spouses and other domestic partners of deputies and recruits who are enrolled in the department's training academy. The ten-hour program deals directly with issues that are likely to produce stress and informs participants of department and community resources that are available to help them. Peer-support programs for spouses and life partners and for the adolescent children of officers are also beginning to operate nationwide. Library Extra 6–5 at mycrimekit.com provides a comprehensive overview of issues related to police officer stress.

Library EXTRA

Officer Fatigue

Like stress, fatigue can affect a police officer's performance. As criminologist Bryan Vila points out, "Tired, urban street cops are a national icon. Weary from overtime assignments, shift work, night school, endless hours spent waiting to testify, and the emotional and physical demands of the job, not to mention trying to patch together a family and social life during irregular islands of off-duty time, they fend off fatigue with coffee and hard-bitten humor."[71] Vila found levels of police officer fatigue to be six times as high as those of shift workers in industrial and mining jobs.[72] As Vila notes, few departments set work-hour standards, and fatigue associated with the pattern and length of work hours may be expected to contribute to police accidents, injuries, and misconduct.

To address the problem, Vila recommends that police departments "review the policies, procedures, and practices that affect shift scheduling and rotation, overtime moonlighting, the number of consecutive work hours allowed, and the way in which the department deals with overly tired employees."[73] Vila also suggests controlling the work hours of police officers, "just as we control the working hours of many other occupational groups."[74]

Terrorism's Impact on Policing

In April 2005, three British nationals were charged with plotting to bomb five financial buildings in New York City, New Jersey, and Washington, D.C. The men—Dhiren Barot, age 32; Nadeem Tarmohamed, age 26; and Qaisar Shaffi, age 25—allegedly served as al-Qaeda scouts and performed reconnaissance on the buildings.[75] The three had been arrested by British authorities in August 2004, and information gathered during the arrest led homeland security officials to convene a press conference at the Citigroup tower in Midtown Manhattan. The nation was told that known al-Qaeda operatives had conducted surveillance at several large New York financial centers, including the New York Stock Exchange.[76] Officials said that the terrorists may have been planning to use truck bombs targeting Wall Street in an effort to disrupt world financial markets. Outgoing Homeland Security Secretary Tom Ridge stressed the seriousness of the threat when he told reporters who had gathered for the briefing, "This is the most significant, detailed piece of information about any particular region that we have come across in a long, long time, perhaps ever."[77] In response to the announcement, the NYPD set up barricades and vehicle checkpoints and mobilized heavily armed officers specially trained in antiterrorism tactics to patrol the financial district. Downtown city streets took on the embattled look of a city at war.

The incident made clear the changed role of American police agencies in a new era of international terrorism that began with the September 11, 2001, attacks on American targets. While the core mission of American police departments has not changed, law enforcement agencies

▲ A Washington, D.C., Metro Transit police officer searches a train after subway bombings in London prompted increased security in 2005. How has the threat of terrorism altered the police role in America?
Reuters/Larry Downing/Landov Media

at all levels now devote an increased amount of time and other resources to preparing for possible terrorist attacks and to gathering the intelligence necessary to thwart them.

In today's post-9/11 world, local police departments play an especially important role in responding to the challenges of terrorism. They must help prevent attacks and respond when attacks occur—offering critical evacuation, emergency medical, and security functions to help stabilize communities following an incident. A recent survey of 250 police chiefs by the Police Executive Research Forum (PERF) found that the chiefs strongly believe that their departments can make valuable contributions to terrorism prevention by using community policing networks to exchange information with citizens and to gather intelligence.[78] Read the results of the PERF survey online at Library Extra 6–6 at mycrimekit.com.

Library EXTRA

The Council on Foreign Relations, headquartered in New York City and Washington, D.C., agrees with PERF that American police departments can no longer assume that federal counterterrorism efforts alone will be sufficient to protect the communities they serve. Consequently, says the council, many police departments have responded by doing the following[79]:

- Strengthening liaisons with federal, state, and local agencies, including fire departments and other police departments
- Refining their training and emergency response plans to address terrorist threats, including attacks with weapons of mass destruction
- Increasing patrols and shoring up barriers around landmarks, places of worship, ports of entry, transit systems, nuclear power plants, and so on
- More heavily guarding public speeches, parades, and other public events
- Creating new counterterrorism divisions and reassigning officers to counterterrorism from other divisions, such as drug enforcement
- Employing new technologies, such as X-ray-like devices, to scan containers at ports of entry and sophisticated sensors to detect a chemical, biological, or radiological attack

The extent of local departments' engagement in such preventive activities depends substantially on budgetary considerations and is strongly influenced by the assessed likelihood of attack. For example, the NYPD, which has firsthand experience in responding to terrorist attacks (23 of its officers were killed when the World Trade Center towers collapsed), has created a special bureau headed by a deputy police commissioner responsible for counterterrorism training, prevention, and investigation.[80] About 1,000 officers have been reassigned to antiterrorism duties, and the department is training its entire 38,000-member force in how to respond to biological, radiological, and chemical attacks.[81] The NYPD has assigned detectives to work abroad with law enforcement agencies in Canada, Israel, Southeast Asia, and the Middle East to track terrorists who might target New York City,[82] and it now employs officers with a command of the Pashtun, Farsi, and Urdu languages of the Middle East to monitor foreign television, radio, and Internet communications. The department has also invested heavily in new hazardous materials protective suits, gas masks, and portable radiation detectors.

It is very important that our first line of defense against terrorism—the seven hundred thousand officers on the street—be given adequate training and background information on terrorism, the methods and techniques of the terrorists, and the likelihood of an imminent attack.

—Major Cities Chiefs Association[viii]

In November 2004, in an effort to provide the law enforcement community and policy makers with guidance on critical issues related to antiterrorism planning and critical incident response, the IACP announced its "Taking Command Initiative." The IACP described the initiative as "an aggressive project to assess the current state of homeland security efforts in the United States and to develop and implement the actions necessary to protect our communities from the specter of both crime and terrorism."[83] Initial deliberations under the initiative led the IACP to conclude that "the current homeland security strategy is handicapped by a fundamental flaw: It was developed without sufficiently seeking or incorporating the advice, expertise, or consent of public safety organizations at the state, tribal, or local level."[84] Building on that premise, the IACP identified five key principles that it says must form the basis of any effective national homeland security strategy[85]:

1. Homeland security proposals must be developed in a local context, acknowledging that local (not federal) authorities have the primary responsibility for preventing, responding to, and recovering from terrorist attacks.
2. Prevention, not just response and recovery, must be paramount in any national, state, or local security strategy. For too long, federal strategies have minimized the importance of prevention, focusing instead on response and recovery.

3. Because of their daily efforts to combat crime and violence in their communities, state and local law enforcement officers are uniquely situated to identify, investigate, and apprehend suspected terrorists.
4. Homeland security strategies must be coordinated nationally, not federally.
5. A truly successful national strategy must recognize, embrace, and value the vast diversity among state and local law enforcement and public-safety agencies. A "one size fits all" approach will fail to secure our homeland.

Web EXTRA

Library EXTRA

Finally, in 2005, the IACP coordinated publication of a Post-9/11 Policing Project resource titled *Assessing and Managing the Terrorism Threat.* The Post-9/11 Policing Project is a collaborative effort of the IACP, the National Sheriffs' Association (NSA), the National Organization of Black Law Enforcement Executives (NOBLE), the Major Cities Chiefs Association (MCCA), and the Police Foundation. Learn more about the ongoing Taking Command Initiative as its leaders work to "transform the concept of a locally designed, nationally coordinated homeland security strategy into a reality" at Web Extra 6–5, and download the publication *Assessing and Managing the Terrorism Threat* at Library Extra 6–7.

As the IACP recognizes, workable antiterrorism programs at the local level require effective sharing of critical information between agencies. FBI-sponsored Joint Terrorism Task Forces (JTTFs) facilitate this by bringing together federal and local law enforcement personnel to focus on specific threats. The FBI currently has established or authorized JTTFs in each of its 56 field offices. In addition to the JTTFs, the FBI has created Regional Terrorism Task Forces (RTTFs) to share information with local enforcement agencies. Through the RTTFs, FBI special agents assigned to terrorism prevention and investigation meet twice a year with their federal, state, and local counterparts for common training, discussion of investigations, and intelligence sharing. The FBI says that "the design of this non-traditional terrorism task force provides the necessary mechanism and structure to direct counterterrorism resources toward localized terrorism problems within the United States."[86] Six RTTFs are currently in operation: Inland Northwest, South Central, Southeastern, Northeast Border, Deep South, and Southwest.

Law enforcement administrators can no longer afford to respond to contemporary and future problems with the "solutions" of yesterday.
—Justin J. Dintino and Frederick T. Martens[ix]

Another FBI counterterrorism component, Field Intelligence Groups (FIGs), was developed following recommendations contained in the final report of the 9/11 Commission. That report said that the FBI should build a reciprocal relationship with state and local agencies, maximizing the sharing of information. FIGs, which now exist in all 56 FBI field offices, work closely with JTTFs to provide valuable services to law enforcement personnel at the state and local levels. According to the FBI, FIGs "generate intelligence products and disseminate them to the intelligence and law enforcement communities to help guide investigative, program, and policy decisions."[87]

Given the changes that have taken place in American law enforcement since the terrorist attacks of September 11, 2001, some say that traditional distinctions between crime, terrorism, and war are fading and that, at least in some instances, military action and civil law enforcement are becoming integrated. The critical question for law enforcement administrators in the near future may be one of discerning the role that law enforcement is to play in the emerging global context.

Intelligence-Led Policing and Antiterrorism

intelligence-led policing
The collection and analysis of information to produce an intelligence end product designed to inform police decision making at both the tactical and strategic levels.[x]

criminal intelligence
The information compiled, analyzed, and/or disseminated in an effort to anticipate, prevent, or monitor criminal activity.[xi]

In 2005, the DOJ embraced the concept of **intelligence-led policing** (ILP) as an important technique to be employed by American law enforcement agencies in the battle against terrorism.[88] Intelligence is information that has been analyzed and integrated into a useful perspective. The information used in the development of effective intelligence is typically gathered from many sources, such as newspapers, surveillance, covert operations, financial records, electronic eavesdropping, interviews, the Internet, and interrogations. Law enforcement intelligence, or **criminal intelligence**, is the result of a "process that evaluates information collected from diverse sources, integrates the relevant information into a cohesive package, and produces a conclusion or estimate about a criminal phenomenon by using the scientific approach to problem solving."[89] Although criminal investigation is typically part of the intelligence-gathering process, the intelligence function of a police department is more exploratory and more broadly focused than a single criminal investigation.[90]

ILP (also known as *intelligence-driven policing*) is the use of criminal intelligence to guide policing. A detailed description of ILP and its applicability to American law enforcement agencies is provided in the FBI publication *The Law Enforcement Intelligence Function* by David L. Carter of Michigan State University's school of criminal justice. The document is available at mycrimekit.com as Library Extra 6–8.

Library EXTRA

According to Carter, criminal intelligence "is a synergistic product intended to provide meaningful and trustworthy direction to law enforcement decision makers about complex criminality, criminal enterprises, criminal extremists, and terrorists."[91] Carter goes on to point out that law enforcement intelligence consists of two types: tactical and strategic. Tactical intelligence "includes gaining or developing information related to threats of terrorism or crime and using this information to apprehend offenders, harden targets, and use strategies that will eliminate or mitigate the threat." Strategic intelligence, in contrast, provides information to decision makers about the changing nature of threats for the purpose of "developing response strategies and reallocating resources" to accomplish effective prevention.

Not every agency (especially small ones) has the staff or resources needed to create a dedicated intelligence unit. Even without an intelligence unit, however, a law enforcement organization should have the ability to effectively utilize the information and intelligence products that are developed and disseminated by organizations at all levels of government. In other words, even though a police agency may not have the resources necessary to analyze all of the information it acquires, it should still be able to mount an effective response to credible threat information that it receives. Learn more about the law enforcement intelligence function and ILP at Library Extra 6–9 at mycrimekit.com.

Library EXTRA

Information Sharing and Antiterrorism

The need to effectively share criminal intelligence across jurisdictions and between law enforcement agencies nationwide became apparent with the tragic events of September 11, 2001. Consequently, governments at all levels are today working toward the creation of a fully integrated criminal justice information system. According to a recent task force report, a fully integrated criminal justice information system is "a network of public safety, justice and homeland security computer systems which provides to each agency the information it needs, at the time it is needed, in the form that it is needed, regardless of the source and regardless of the physical location at which it is stored."[92] The information that is provided should be complete, accurate, and formatted in whatever way is most useful for the agency's tasks. In a fully integrated criminal justice information system, information would be made available at the practitioner's workstation, whether that workstation is a patrol car, desk, laptop, or judge's bench. Within such a system, each agency shares information not only with other agencies in its own jurisdiction but with multiple justice agencies on the federal, state, and local levels. In such an idealized justice information system, accurate information is also available to nonjustice agencies with statutory authority and a legal obligation to check criminal histories before licensing, employment, weapons purchase, and so on.

One widely used information-sharing system is Law Enforcement Online (LEO). LEO, an intranet intended exclusively for use by the law enforcement community, is a national interactive computer communications system and information service. A user-friendly system, it can be accessed by any approved employee of a duly constituted local, state, or federal law enforcement agency or by an approved member of an authorized law enforcement special-interest group. LEO provides a state-of-the-art communications mechanism to link all levels of law enforcement throughout the United States. The system includes password-accessed e-mail, Internet chat rooms, an electronic library, an online calendar, special-interest topical focus areas, and self-paced distance-learning modules.[93]

The need for improving homeland security requires a joint effort of all levels of law enforcement, including local, state and federal agencies.
—*Major Cities Chiefs Association*[xii]

Another important law enforcement information-sharing resource is the International Justice and Public Safety Information Sharing Network, which uses the acronym **NLETS**. NLETS members include all 50 states, most federal agencies and territories, and the Royal Canadian Mounted Police (RCMP). NLETS, which has been in operation for nearly 40 years, was formerly called the National Law Enforcement Telecommunications System. It has recently been enhanced to facilitate a variety of encrypted digital communications, it now links 30,000 agencies and more than half a million access devices in the United States and Canada, and it facilitates nearly 41 million transmissions each month. Information available through NLETS includes state criminal histories, homeland alert messages, immigration databases, driver records and vehicle registrations, aircraft registrations, AMBER alerts, weather advisories,

NLETS
An acronym referring to the International Justice and Public Safety Information Sharing Network.

Web EXTRA

and hazardous materials (HAZMAT) notifications and regulations. You can reach NLETS on the Web at Web Extra 6–6.

Although NLETS and LEO continue to evolve, most experts agree that a fully integrated nationwide criminal justice information system does not yet exist.[94] Efforts to create one, however, found their beginning in the 2003 National Criminal Intelligence Sharing Plan (NCISP). The NCISP was developed under the auspices of the DOJ's Global Justice Information Sharing Initiative and authored by its Global Intelligence Working Group (GIWG).[95] Federal, local, state, and tribal law enforcement representatives all had a voice in the development of the plan. The NCISP provides specific steps that can be taken by law enforcement agencies to participate in the sharing of critical law enforcement and terrorism prevention information.

Plan authors note that not every agency has the staff or resources needed to create a formal intelligence unit. Even without a dedicated intelligence unit, however, the plan says that every law enforcement organization needs to have the ability to effectively consume the intelligence available from a wide range of organizations at all levels of government.[96]

In 2006, U.S. Representative Bennie Thompson (D–MS), chairman of the House Committee on Homeland Security, proposed establishing a National Center for Intelligence-Led Policing.[97] The center, which is intended to solve many of the intelligence-gathering and -sharing problems identified in this chapter, would have four primary functions:

1. Promoting the law enforcement intelligence process and ILP in order to promote a common understanding of these concepts among police officers and sheriffs' officers nationwide
2. Identifying best practices in these areas and sharing them with all law enforcement agencies
3. Providing training resources to educate officers about ILP and to make it relevant to their daily work
4. Establishing a technology and research development capability to assess existing technologies relevant to ILP and to identify needs currently lacking a technology solution

The center, according to documents prepared by Thompson's office, would help develop and coordinate the education, training, and professional services necessary to establish a common foundation for ILP across the country:

> [T]he Center should provide police and sheriffs' officers with a common and consistent understanding of the importance of contributing credible and relevant law enforcement information as part of the intelligence cycle at both the federal and non-federal levels; the process by which that information becomes useful and actionable intelligence; and a set of clear and consistent procedures to facilitate uniform sharing policies across the nation, including policies for protecting privacy and civil liberties.[98]

Library EXTRA

The NCISP is available in its entirety at mycrimekit.com as Library Extra 6–10. A congressional document proposing the creation of a National Center for Intelligence-Led Policing can be read at Library Extra 6–11.

Police Civil Liability

In 1996, 51-year-old Richard Kelley filed suit in federal court against the Massachusetts State Police and the Weymouth (Massachusetts) Police Department.[99] The suit resulted from an incident during which, Kelley alleged, state troopers and Weymouth police officers treated him as a drunk rather than recognizing that he had just suffered a stroke while driving. According to Kelley, following a minor traffic accident caused by the stroke, officers pulled him from his car, handcuffed him, dragged him along the ground, and ignored his pleas for help—forcing him to stay at a state police barracks for seven hours before taking him for medical treatment. Drunk-driving charges against Kelley were dropped after medical tests failed to reveal the presence of any intoxicating substances in his body.

civil liability
The potential responsibility for payment of damages or other court-ordered enforcement as a result of a ruling in a lawsuit. Civil liability is not the same as criminal liability, which means "open to punishment for a crime."[xiii]

Suits of **civil liability** brought against law enforcement personnel are of two types: state and federal. Suits brought in state courts have generally been the more common form of civil litigation involving police officers. In recent years, however, an increasing number of suits have been brought in federal courts on the claim that the civil rights of the plaintiff, as guaranteed by federal law, were denied.

Common Sources of Civil Suits

Police officers may become involved in a variety of situations that could result in civil suits against the officers, their superiors, and their departments. Major sources of police civil liability are listed in Table 3. Charles R. Swanson, an expert in police procedure, says that the most common sources of lawsuits against the police are "assault, battery, false imprisonment, and malicious prosecution."[100]

Of all complaints brought against the police, assault charges are the best known, being subject to high media visibility. Less visible (but not uncommon) are civil suits charging the police with false arrest or false imprisonment. In the 1986 case of ***Malley v. Briggs***,[101] the U.S. Supreme Court held that a police officer who effects an arrest or conducts a search on the basis of an improperly issued warrant may be liable for monetary damages when a reasonably well-trained officer, under the same circumstances, "would have known that his affidavit failed to establish probable cause and that he should not have applied for the warrant." Significantly, the Court ruled that an officer "cannot excuse his own default by pointing to the greater incompetence of the magistrate."[102] The officer, rather than the judge who issued the warrant, is ultimately responsible for establishing the basis for pursuing the arrest or search.

When an officer makes an arrest without just cause or simply impedes an individual's right to leave the scene without good reason, he or she may be liable for the charge of false arrest. Officers who "throw their weight around" are especially subject to this type of suit, grounded as it is in the abuse of police authority. Because employers may be sued for the negligent or malicious actions of their employees, many police departments are being named as codefendants in lawsuits today.

Civil suits are also brought against officers whose actions are deemed negligent. High-speed vehicle pursuits are especially dangerous because of the potential for injury to innocent bystanders. In the case of ***Biscoe v. Arlington County*** (1984),[103] for example, Alvin Biscoe was awarded $5 million after he lost both legs as a consequence of a high-speed chase while he was waiting to cross the street. Biscoe, an innocent bystander, was struck by a police car that went out of control. The officer driving the car had violated department policies prohibiting high-speed chases, and the court found that he had not been properly trained.

Departments may protect themselves to some degree through training combined with regulations limiting the authority of their personnel. One year after the *Biscoe* case was decided, for example, a Louisiana police officer, who had an accident while driving 75 mph in a 40-mph zone, was found to be negligent and was held liable for damages.[104] However, the department was not held liable because it had a policy limiting emergency driving to no more than 20 mph over the posted speed limit and because officers were trained in that policy.

TABLE 3 Major Sources of Police Civil Liability
Failure to protect property in police custody
Negligence in the care of suspects in police custody
Failure to render proper emergency medical assistance
Failure to prevent a foreseeable crime
Failure to aid private citizens
Lack of due regard for the safety of others
False arrest
False imprisonment
Inappropriate use of deadly force
Unnecessary assault or battery
Malicious prosecution
Violation of constitutional rights
Pattern of unfair and inequitable treatment
Racial profiling

The FBI states that "a traffic accident constitutes the most common terminating event in an urban pursuit."[105] Hence, some cities are actively replacing high-speed vehicle pursuits with surveillance technologies employing unmanned aerial vehicles (UAVs). Although helicopters have long been used in this capacity, the advent of UAV technology promises to make the tracking of fleeing suspects much quicker and far safer for all involved.

Law enforcement supervisors may be the object of lawsuits by virtue of the fact that they are responsible for the actions of their officers. If it can be shown that supervisors were negligent in hiring (as when someone with a history of alcoholism, mental problems, sexual deviance, or drug abuse is employed) or if supervisors failed in their responsibility to properly train officers before arming and deploying them, they may be found liable for damages.

In the 1989 case of the ***City of Canton, Ohio* v. *Harris***,[106] the U.S. Supreme Court ruled that a "failure to train" can become the basis for legal liability on the part of a municipality where the "failure to train amounts to deliberate indifference to the rights of persons with whom the police come in contact."[107] In that case, Geraldine Harris was arrested and taken to the Canton, Ohio, police station. While at the station, she slumped to the floor several times. Officers left her on the floor and did not call for medical assistance. Upon release, Harris's family took her to a local hospital, where she was found to be suffering from several emotional ailments. Harris was hospitalized for a week and received follow-up outpatient treatment for the next year.

In the 1997 case of *Board of the County Commissioners of Bryan County, Oklahoma* v. *Brown*, however, the Supreme Court ruled that to establish liability, plaintiffs must show that "the municipal action in question was not simply negligent, but was taken with 'deliberate indifference' as to its known or obvious consequences."[108] In *Brown*, a deputy named Burns was hired by the sheriff of Bryan County, Oklahoma. Burns later used excessive force in arresting a woman, and the woman sued the county for damages, claiming that Deputy Burns had been hired despite his criminal record. In fact, some years earlier, Burns had pleaded guilty to various driving infractions and other misdemeanors, including assault and battery—a charge resulting from a college fight. At trial, a spokesperson for the sheriff's department admitted to receiving Burns's driving and criminal records but said he had not reviewed either in detail before the department decided to hire Burns. Nonetheless, the Supreme Court held that deliberate indifference on the part of the county had not been established because the plaintiff had not demonstrated that "Burns's background made his use of excessive force in making an arrest a plainly obvious consequence of the hiring decision." According to this decision, a municipality (in this case, a county) may not be held liable solely because it employs a person with an arrest record.

Federal Lawsuits

1983 lawsuit
A civil suit brought under Title 42, Section 1983, of the U.S. Code against anyone who denies others their constitutional right to life, liberty, or property without due process of law.

Civil suits alleging police misconduct that are filed in federal courts are often called **1983 lawsuits** because they are based on Section 1983 of Title 42 of the U.S. Code—an act passed by Congress in 1871 to ensure the civil rights of men and women of all races. That act requires due process of law before any person can be deprived of life, liberty, or property and specifically provides redress for the denial of these constitutional rights by officials acting under color of state law. It reads as follows:

> Every person who, under color of any statute, ordinance, regulation, custom, or usage, of any State or Territory, subjects, or causes to be subjected, any citizen of the United States or other person within the jurisdiction thereof to the deprivation of any rights, privileges, or immunities secured by the Constitution and laws, shall be liable to the party injured in an action at law, suit in equity, or other proper proceeding for redress.[109]

A 1983 suit may be brought, for example, against officers who shoot suspects under questionable circumstances, thereby denying them their right to life without due process. Similarly, an officer who makes an arrest based on accusations that he or she knows to be untrue may be subject to a 1983 lawsuit.

***Bivens* action**
A civil suit, based on the case of *Bivens* v. *Six Unknown Federal Agents*, brought against federal government officials for denying the constitutional rights of others.

Another type of liability action, this one directed specifically at federal officials or enforcement agents, is called a ***Bivens* action**. The case of ***Bivens* v. *Six Unknown Federal Agents*** (1971)[110] established a path for legal action against agents enforcing federal laws, which is similar to that found in a 1983 suit. *Bivens* actions may be addressed against individuals but not against the United States or its agencies.[111] Federal officers have generally been granted a

CJ News

Police Brutality Cases on the Rise

Federal prosecutors are targeting a rising number of law enforcement officers for alleged brutality, Justice Department statistics show. The heightened prosecutions come as the nation's largest police union fears that agencies are dropping standards to fill thousands of vacancies and "scrimping" on training.

Cases in which police, prison guards and other law enforcement authorities have used excessive force or other tactics to violate victims' civil rights have increased 25% (281 vs. 224) from fiscal years 2001 to 2007 over the previous seven years, the department says.

During the same period, the department says it won 53% more convictions (391 vs. 256). Some cases result in multiple convictions.

Federal records show the vast majority of police brutality cases referred by investigators are not prosecuted.

University of Toledo law professor David Harris, who analyzes police conduct issues, says it will take time to determine whether the cases represent a sustained period of more aggressive prosecutions or the beginnings of a surge in misconduct.

The cases involve only a fraction of the estimated 800,000 police in the USA, says James Pasco, executive director of the National Fraternal Order of Police (FOP), the nation's largest police union.

Even so, he says, the FOP is concerned that reduced standards, [less] training and promotion of less experienced officers into the higher police ranks could undermine more rigid supervision. "These are things we are worried about," Pasco says.

For the past few years, dozens of police departments across the country have scrambled to fill vacancies. The recruiting effort, which often features cash bonuses, has intensified since 9/11, because many police recruits have been drawn to military service.

In its post-Sept. 11 reorganization, the FBI listed police misconduct as one of its highest civil rights priorities to keep pace with an anticipated increase in police hiring through 2009.

The increasing Justice numbers generally correspond to a USA TODAY analysis of federal law enforcement prosecutions using data compiled by the Transactional Records Access Clearinghouse at Syracuse University.

Those data show 42 law enforcement prosecutions during the first 10 months of fiscal year 2007, a 66% increase from all of fiscal 2002 and a 61% rise from a decade ago. David Burnham, the co-founder of the TRAC database, says prosecutions appear to be increasing, but "more important" are the numbers of cases prosecutors decline.

Last year, 96% of cases referred for prosecution by investigative agencies were declined. In 2005, 98% were declined, a rate that has remained "extremely high" under every administration dating to President Carter, according to a TRAC report.

The high refusal rates, say Burnham and law enforcement analysts, result in part from the extraordinary difficulty in prosecuting abuse cases. Juries are conditioned to believe cops, and victims' credibility is often challenged.

"When police are accused of wrongdoing, the world is turned upside down," Harris says. "In some cases, it may be impossible for (juries) to make the adjustment."

For the latest in crime and justice news, visit the Talk Justice news feed at http://www.crimenews.info.

Source: Kevin Johnson, "Police Brutality Cases on Rise since 9/11," *USA Today*, December 17, 2007. http://www.usatoday.com/news/nation/2007-12-17-Copmisconduct_N.htm. From USA TODAY, a division of Garnett Co., Inc. Reprinted with permission.

Canadian police officers participate in martial arts training. Rigorous police training, high professional standards, and effective supervision can reduce the likelihood of civil lawsuits against police departments. Why?
CIPS Inc./TDPE combined police training projects, Mojacar, Spain

Everyone is a prisoner of his own experiences. No one can eliminate prejudices—just recognize them.

—Edward R. Murrow

court-created qualified immunity and have been protected from suits where they were found to have acted in the belief that their action was consistent with federal law.[112]

In the past, the doctrine of sovereign immunity barred legal actions against state and local governments. Sovereign immunity was a legal theory that held that a governing body could not be sued because it made the law and therefore could not be bound by it. Immunity is a much more complex issue today. Some states have officially abandoned any pretext of immunity through legislative action. New York State, for example, has declared that public agencies are equally as liable as private agencies for violations of constitutional rights. Other states, like California, have enacted statutory provisions that define and limit governmental liability.[113] A number of state immunity statutes have been struck down by court decisions. In general, states are moving in the direction of setting dollar limits on liability and adopting federal immunity principles to protect individual officers, including "good-faith" and "reasonable belief" rules.

At the federal level, the concept of sovereign immunity is embodied in the Federal Tort Claims Act (FTCA),[114] which grants broad immunity to federal government agencies engaged in discretionary activities. When a federal employee is sued for a wrongful or negligent act, the Federal Employees Liability Reform and Tort Compensation Act of 1988, commonly known as the Westfall Act, empowers the attorney general to certify that the employee was acting within the scope of his or her office or employment at the time of the incident. Upon certification, the employee is dismissed from the action, and the United States is substituted as defendant; the case then falls under the governance of the FTCA.

The U.S. Supreme Court has supported a type of "qualified immunity" for individual officers (as opposed to the agencies for which they work) that "shields law enforcement officers from constitutional lawsuits if reasonable officers believe their actions to be lawful in light of clearly established law and the information the officers possess." The Supreme Court has also described qualified immunity as a defense "which shields public officials from actions for damages unless their conduct was unreasonable in light of clearly established law."[115] The Court states that "the qualified immunity doctrine's central objective is to protect public officials from undue interference with their duties and from potentially disabling threats of liability."[116] In the context of a warrantless arrest, the Court said in ***Hunter v. Bryant*** (1991),[117] "even law enforcement officials who reasonably but mistakenly conclude that probable cause is present are entitled to immunity."[118]

The doctrine of qualified immunity, as it exists today, rests largely on the 2001 U.S. Supreme Court decision of *Saucier* v. *Katz*,[119] in which the Court established a two-pronged test for assessing constitutional violations by government agents.[120] First, the court hearing the case must decide whether the facts, taken in the light most favorable to the party asserting the injury, show that the defendant's conduct violated a constitutional right. Second, the court must then decide whether that right was clearly established. For a right to be clearly established, the Court ruled, "it would be clear to a reasonable [defendant] that his conduct was unlawful in the situation he confronted." In summary, qualified immunity protects law enforcement agents from being sued for damages unless they violate clearly established law that a reasonable official in the agents' position would have known.

In 2007, in the case of *Scott* v. *Harris*, the Supreme Court sided with an officer who had rammed a speeding car driven by a teenager, sending it down an embankment and leaving the driver a quadriplegic.[121] The justices reasoned that the driver "intentionally placed himself and the public in danger by unlawfully engaging in reckless, high-speed flight" and noted that those who might have been harmed had the officer not forced him off the road "were entirely innocent." The Court concluded that it was reasonable for the officer, Deputy Timothy Scott, to take the action that he did and rejected the "argument that safety could have been assured if the police simply ceased their pursuit." In essence, the Court found that "a police officer's attempt to terminate a dangerous high-speed car chase that threatens the lives of innocent bystanders does not violate the Fourth Amendment, even when it places the fleeing motorist at risk of serious injury or death."

Criminal charges can be brought against officers who overstep legal boundaries or who act in violation of set standards. In 2001, for example, in the case of ***Idaho* v. *Horiuchi***,[122] the Ninth U.S. Circuit Court of Appeals ruled that federal law enforcement officers are not immune from state prosecution where their actions violate state law "either through malice or excessive zeal." The case involved FBI sharpshooter Lon Horiuchi, who was charged with negligent manslaughter by prosecutors in Boundary County, Idaho, following a 1992 incident at Ruby Ridge. Learn more about the Ruby Ridge incident at Library Extra 6–12 at mycrimekit.com.

Library EXTRA

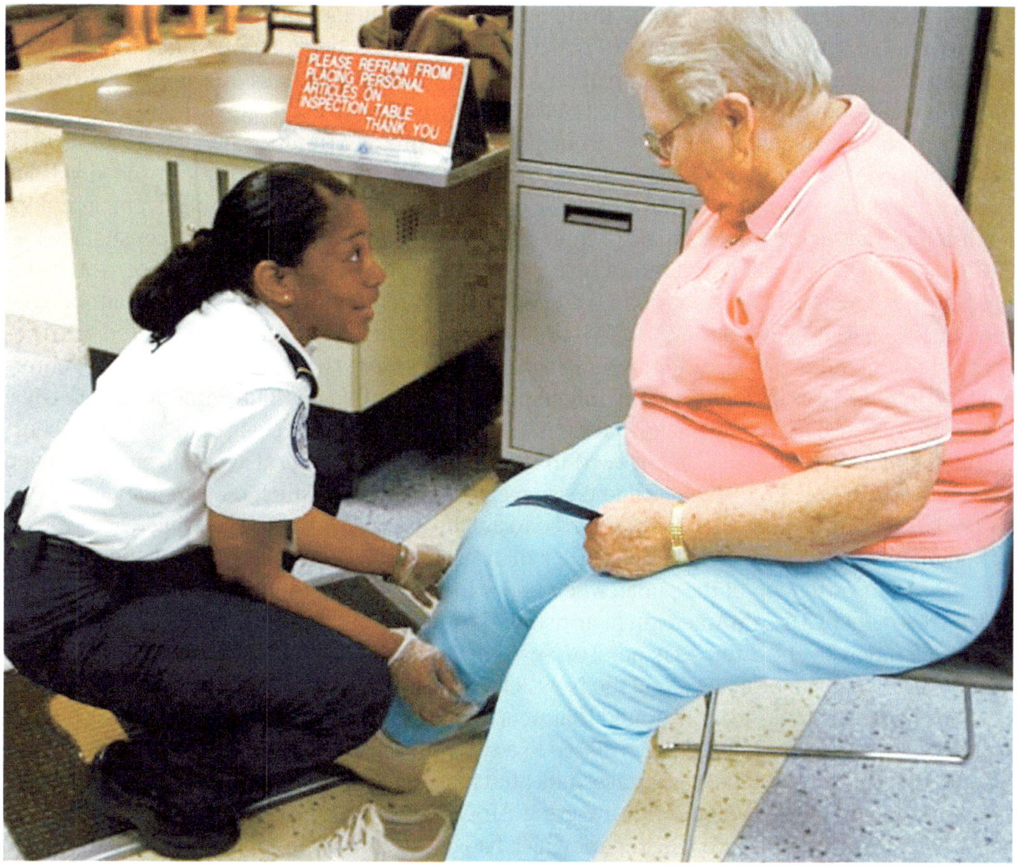

▲ A female passenger is subjected to heightened security screening at Dallas–Forth Worth International Airport. Some people fear that the use of profiling techniques holds the potential to unfairly discriminate against members of certain racial and ethnic groups. Others suggest that the careful use of profiling can provide an important advantage in an age of scarce resources. Which perspective appeals to you?
Mark Williams

Today, most police departments at both state and federal levels carry liability insurance to protect themselves against the severe financial damage that can result from the loss of a large civil suit. Some officers also acquire private policies that provide coverage in the event they are named as individuals in a civil suit. Both types of insurance policies generally cover legal fees up to a certain amount, regardless of the outcome of the case. Police departments that face civil prosecution because of the actions of an officer may find that legal and financial liability extends to supervisors, city managers, and the community itself. Where insurance coverage does not exist or is inadequate, city coffers may be nearly drained to meet the damages awarded.[123]

A 2001 study of a large sample of police chiefs throughout Texas found that most believed that lawsuits or the threat of civil litigation against the police makes it harder for individual officers to do their jobs. Most of the chiefs espoused the idea that adequate training, better screening of applicants, close supervision of officers, and "treating people fairly" all reduced the likelihood of lawsuits.[124]

Racial Profiling and Biased Policing

Racial Profiling

Racial profiling first received national attention in the late 1990s. **Racial profiling** can be defined as any police action initiated on the basis of the race, ethnicity, or national origin of a suspect rather than on the behavior of that individual or on information that leads the police to a particular individual who has been identified as being, or having been, engaged in criminal activity.[125]

racial profiling
"Any police-initiated action that relies on the race, ethnicity, or national origin rather than [1] the behavior of an individual, or [2] on information that leads the police to a particular individual who has been identified as being, or having been, engaged in criminal activity."[xiv]

The alleged use by police of racial profiling may take a number of forms. Minority accounts of disparate treatment at the hands of police officers include being stopped for being "in the wrong car" (for example, a police stop of an African-American youth driving an expensive late-model BMW); being stopped and questioned for being in the wrong neighborhood (that is, police stops of members of minority groups driving through traditionally white residential neighborhoods); and being harassed at the hands of police officers for petty traffic violations (such as underinflated tires, failure to signal properly before switching lanes, vehicle equipment failure, act of driving less than 10 mph above the speed limit, or illegible license plate).[126]

Profiling was originally intended to help catch drug couriers attempting to enter the country. The U.S. Customs Service and the DEA developed a number of "personal indicators" that seemed, from the agency's day-to-day enforcement experiences, to be associated with increased likelihood of law violation. Among the indicators were these: speaking Spanish, entering the United States on flights originating in particular Central and South American countries, being an 18- to 32-year-old male, having purchased tickets with cash, and having a short planned stay (often of only a day or two) in the United States. Federal agents frequently used these criteria in deciding which airline passengers to search and which bags to inspect.

Racial profiling has been derisively referred to as "driving while black" or "driving while brown," although it may also apply to situations other than those involving traffic violations. Racial profiling came to the attention of the public when police in New Jersey and Maryland were accused of unfair treatment of African-American motorists and admitted that race was a factor in traffic stops.

A 1999 report by the attorney general of New Jersey concluded that New Jersey state troopers *had* engaged in racial profiling along the New Jersey Turnpike.[127] The report, which tracked traffic stops between 1997 and 1998, found that people of color constituted 40.6% of the stops made on the turnpike. Although few stops resulted in a search, 77.2% of individuals searched were people of color. An analysis of these searches indicated that 10.5% of the searches that involved white motorists and 13.5% of the searches involving African-American motorists resulted in arrest or seizure.[128] An earlier racial profiling report, which had been compiled in support of a lawsuit against the state of New Jersey, showed that African-Americans comprised 13.5% of New Jersey Turnpike users and 15% of drivers who were speeding.[129] At the same time, blacks represented 35% of those stopped and 73.2% of those arrested. The lawsuit resulted in the suppression of evidence in many criminal cases involving black motorists who had been arrested on the turnpike.

It is practically an article of faith among young, black males that they are more likely than whites to be stopped, frisked, spread-eagled, and arrested by the police, often on the flimsiest of charges.
—Hutchinson Report, July 2001

In 2003, in response to widespread public outcry over the use of racial profiling, the DOJ banned its practice in all federal law enforcement agencies except in cases that involve the possible identification of terrorist suspects.[130] According to the DOJ, "The guidance provides that in making routine law enforcement decisions—such as deciding which motorists to stop for traffic infractions—consideration of the driver's race or ethnicity is absolutely forbidden."[131]

Those who defend the use of racial profiling by the police argue that it is not a bigoted practice when based on facts (such as when a police department decides to increase patrols in a particular area because of exceptionally high crime rates) or when significant criminal potential exists among even a few members of a group. An example of the latter is the widespread public suspicions that focused on Arab-Americans (and other Arabs living in the United States or traveling through the country) following the terrorist attacks of September 11, 2001. As soon as it was publicly announced that the hijackers had been of Middle Eastern origin, some flight crews demanded that Arab-looking passengers be removed from their airplanes before takeoff, and passengers refused to fly with people who looked like Arabs.[132]

None of this is to say, of course, that race or ethnicity somehow inherently causes crime (or that it somehow causes poverty or increases the risk of victimization). If anything, race and ethnicity may simply display a significant correlation with certain types of crime, as they do with certain kinds of victimization. Hence, although the *real* causes of criminality may be socialization into criminal subcultures, economically deprived neighborhoods, lack of salable job skills, and intergenerational poverty, and not race per se, to some law enforcement agencies race provides one more indicator of the likelihood of criminality. David Cole, a professor at Georgetown University's Law Center, for example, notes that in the minds of many police officials, "racial and ethnic disparities reflect not discrimination [or bigotry] but higher rates of offenses among minorities."[133] "Nationwide," says Cole, "blacks are 13 times more likely to be sent to state prisons for drug convictions than are whites, so it would seem rational for police to assume that all other things being equal, a black driver is more likely than a white driver to be carrying drugs." Statistics like this, of course, may further enhance police focus on minorities and may result in even

Freedom or Safety? You Decide.

Was the LAPD's Community Mapping Project a Form of Religious Profiling?

In 2007, the Los Angeles Police Department announced that it would terminate plans to have its counterterrorism unit identify isolated social enclaves within the city. Weeks earlier Deputy Chief Michael P. Downing, who heads the department's counterterrorism bureau, issued a press release detailing how the LAPD intended to work with the University of Southern California's Center for Risk and Economic Analysis of Terrorism Events to determine which areas of the city were socially isolated and susceptible to "violent, ideologically based extremism."

The plan had been originally touted as a mapping project "intended to study the language, culture, history, socioeconomic conditions, and country of origin of various communities and neighborhoods" and as an effort to "help groups integrate into broader society by offering access to government and social services."

Although the plan did not specifically target Muslim neighborhoods, Islamic leaders felt that it was a thinly disguised form of racial and religious profiling and that it was aimed squarely at them and at members of their communities. Islamic leaders protested the plan, saying that any mapping based on faith and ethnicity is inappropriate for police departments, which should be concerned instead with crime mapping. "Police should not be in the business of analyzing political views, and religious views," said Hussam Ayloush, a member of the Los Angeles chapter of the Council on American-Islamic Relations.

Estimates hold that about half a million Muslims live in California's Los Angeles, Riverside, and Orange counties.

YOU DECIDE

1. Is Hussam Ayloush right in saying that police departments should concern themselves with crime mapping and not with other forms of mapping in the cities they serve? Why or why not?
2. Was the LAPD's proposed community mapping project really a form of religious and ethnic profiling? If so, should such profiling be permitted? Why or why not?

References: Peter Prengaman, "LAPD Shelves Muslim Mapping Plan," the Associated Press, November 15, 2007; Mimi Hall, "LAPD Plan Draws Ire from Muslims," *USA Today*, November 9–11, 2007, p. 1A; and Andrea Stone, "Federal Panel Wants to Shut Islamic School in Virginia," *USA Today*, October 19, 2007, p. 20A.

more arrests, thereby reinforcing the beliefs on which racial profiling by enforcement agents is based. Such observations led esteemed sociologist Amitai Etzioni to declare in 2001 that racial profiling is not necessarily racist.[134] Moreover, warned Etzioni, an end to racial profiling "would penalize those African-American communities with high incidences of violent crime" because they would lose the levels of policing that they need to remain relatively secure.

Regardless of arguments offered in support of racial profiling as an enforcement tool, the practice has been widely condemned as being contrary to basic ethical principles. National public opinion polls conducted by the Gallup Poll Organization seem to show that most Americans believe that racial discrimination of any kind is inherently unethical and not permissible in a free society.[135] Moreover, as Christopher Stone, known for his writings on racial justice, explains, "Most people of all races and ethnic groups are never convicted of a crime, but stereotypes can work to brand all members of some groups with suspicion . . . putting an undue burden on innocent members of these groups."[136]

From a more pragmatic viewpoint, however, racial profiling is unacceptable because it weakens the public's confidence in the police, thereby decreasing police–citizen trust and cooperation. As some authors explain, "Truly effective policing will only be achieved when police both protect their neighborhoods from crime and respect the civil liberties of all residents. When law enforcement practices are perceived to be biased, unfair, or disrespectful, communities of color are less willing to trust and confide in police officers, report crimes, participate in problem-solving activities, be witnesses at trials, or serve on juries."[137] These authors summarize the current situation with regard to racial profiling this way: "The challenge that confronts American police organizations is how to sustain the historic decline in rates of criminal activity while enhancing police legitimacy in the eyes of the communities they serve. Appropriately addressing allegations of racial profiling is central to this new mission."[138] Learn more about racial profiling and police management via Library Extra 6–13 at mycrimekit.com.

Library EXTRA

Racially Biased Policing

In 2001, PERF released a detailed report titled *Racially Biased Policing: A Principled Response*.[139] PERF researchers surveyed more than 1,000 police executives, analyzed material from over 250 law enforcement agencies, and sought input from law enforcement agency

We must strive to eliminate any racial, ethnic, or cultural bias that may exist among our ranks.

—Sherman Block
Los Angeles County Sheriff

personnel, community activists, and civil rights leaders about racial bias in policing. Researchers concluded that "the vast majority of law enforcement officers—of all ranks, nationwide—are dedicated men and women committed to serving all citizens with fairness and dignity."[140] Most police officers, said the report, share an intolerance for racially biased policing. The report's authors noted that some police behaviors may be misinterpreted as biased when, in fact, the officers are just doing their job. "The good officer continually scans the environment for anomalies to normalcy—for conditions, people and behavior that are unusual for that environment," they said. "In learning and practicing their craft, officers quickly develop a sense for what is normal and expected, and conversely, for what is not."[141] Hence for officers of any race to take special notice of unknown young white males who unexpectedly appear in a traditionally African-American neighborhood, for example, might be nothing other than routine police procedure. Such an observation, however, is not in itself sufficient for an investigatory stop but might be used in conjunction with other trustworthy and relevant information already in the officers' possession—such as the officers' prior knowledge that young white men have been routinely visiting a particular apartment complex in the neighborhood to purchase drugs—to justify such a stop.

Library EXTRA

The PERF report provides many specific recommendations to help police departments be free of bias. One recommendation, for example, says that "supervisors should monitor activity reports for evidence of improper practices and patterns. They should conduct spot-checks and regular sampling of in-car videotapes, radio transmissions, and in-car computer and central communications records to determine if both formal and informal communications are professional and free from racial bias and other disrespect."[142] Read the entire PERF report at Library Extra 6–14 at mycrimekit.com.

Police Use of Force

police use of force
The use of physical restraint by a police officer when dealing with a member of the public.[xv]

Police use of force is defined as the use of physical restraint by a police officer when dealing with a member of the public.[143] Law enforcement officers are authorized to use the amount of force that is reasonable and necessary given the circumstances. Most officers are trained in the use of force and typically encounter numerous situations during their careers when the use of force is appropriate—for example, when making some arrests, restraining unruly combatants, or controlling a disruptive demonstration. Force may involve hitting; holding or restraining; pushing; choking; threatening with a flashlight, baton, or chemical or pepper spray; restraining with a police dog; or threatening with a gun; some definitions of police use of force also include handcuffing.

The NIJ estimates that over 45 million people nationwide have face-to-face contact with the police over a typical 12-month period and that approximately 1.5%, or about 500,000 of these people, become subject to the use of force or the threat of force.[144] When handcuffing is included in the definition of force, the number of people subjected to force increases to 1.2 million, or slightly more than 2.5% of those having contact with the police. Other studies show that police use weaponless tactics in approximately 80% of use-of-force incidents and that half of all use-of-force incidents involve merely grabbing or holding the suspect.[145]

Studies show that police use force in fewer than 20% of adult custodial arrests. Even in instances where force is used, the police primarily use weaponless tactics (Figure 3). Female officers are less likely to use physical force and firearms and are more likely to use chemical weapons (mostly pepper spray) than their male counterparts. Figure 4 shows the types of encounters in which the use of force is most likely to be employed.

excessive force
The application of an amount or frequency of force greater than that required to compel compliance from a willing or unwilling subject.[xvi]

A more complex issue is the use of excessive force. The IACP defines **excessive force** as "the application of an amount and/or frequency of force greater than that required to compel compliance from a willing or unwilling subject."[146] When excessive force is employed, the activities of the police often come under public scrutiny and receive attention from the media and legislators. Police officers' use of excessive force can also result in lawsuits by members of the public who feel that they have been treated unfairly. Whether the use of excessive force is aberrant behavior on the part of an individual officer or is a practice of an entire law enforcement agency, both the law and public opinion generally condemn it.

Kenneth Adams, an associate dean at the University of Central Florida and an expert in the use of force by police, notes that there is an important difference between the terms *excessive force*, such as shoving or pushing when simply grabbing a suspect would be adequate, and the

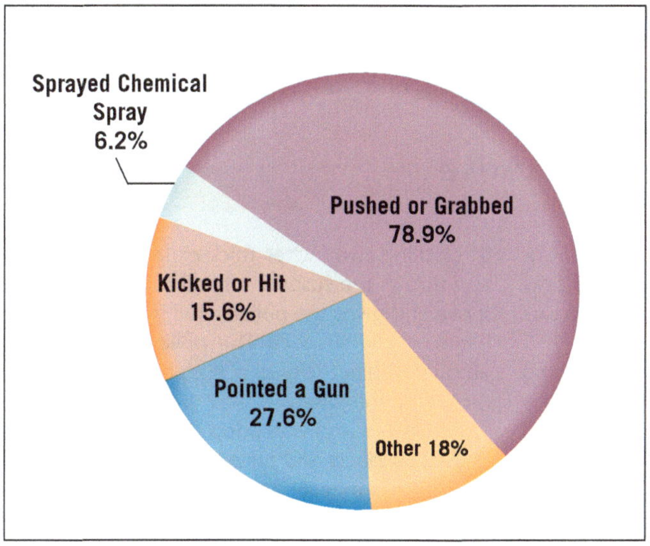

FIGURE 3
Citizen Reports of Types of Force Used by Police Officers during Adult Custodial Arrests Involving Force.
Note: Percents total more than 100 because some respondents reported more than one type of force.
Source: Matthew R. Durose et al., *Contacts between Police and Public* (Washington, DC: Bureau of Justice Statistics, February 2005), p. 17.

excessive use of force, which refers to the phenomenon of force being used unacceptably, often on a department-wide basis. The term, says Adams, "deals with relative comparisons among police agencies, and there are no established criteria for judgment."[147] *Use of excessive force* and the *excessive use of force* may be distinguished from the *illegal use of force*, which refers to situations in which the use of force by police violates a law or statute.[148]

Nothing's so sacred as honor.
—Inscription on Wyatt Earp's headstone

In a study reported in 2001, Geoffrey Alpert and Roger Dunham found that the "force factor"—the level of force used by the police relative to the suspect's level of resistance—is a key element to consider in attempting to reduce injuries to both the police and suspects.[149] The force factor is calculated by measuring both the suspect's level of resistance and the officer's level of force on an equivalent scale and by then subtracting the level of resistance from the level of police force used. Results from the study indicate that, on average, the level of force that officers use is closely related to the type of training that their departments emphasize.

Excessive force can also be symptomatic of **problem police officers**. Problem police officers are those who exhibit problem behavior, as indicated by high rates of citizen complaints and use-of-force incidents and by other evidence.[150] The Christopher Commission, which studied the structure and operation of the LAPD in the wake of the Rodney King beating, found a number of repeat offenders on the LAPD force.[151] According to the commission, approximately 1,800 LAPD officers were alleged to have used excessive force or improper tactics between 1986 and 1990. Of these officers, more than 1,400 had only one or two allegations against them, another 183 officers had four or more allegations, 44 had six or more, 16 had eight or more, and one had 16 such allegations. The commission also found that, generally speaking, the 44 officers

problem police officer
A law enforcement officer who exhibits problem behavior, as indicated by high rates of citizen complaints and use-of-force incidents and by other evidence.[xvii]

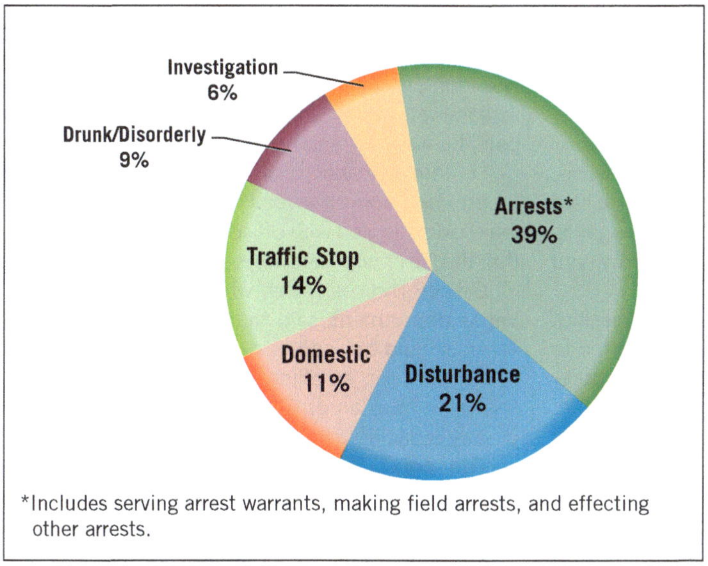

FIGURE 4
Police Use of Force by Type of Encounter.
Source: International Association of Chiefs of Police, *Police Use of Force in America, 2001* (Alexandria, VA: IACP, 2001), p. iii.

CJ News

As Shocks Replace Bullets, Questions Arise

The police in Seattle have had their share of high-profile violent or deadly run-ins with protesters, mentally ill suspects and other lawbreakers. But in 2003, for the first time in 15 years, no one here was shot and killed by the police.

Miami, a city with a long history of police shootings and ensuing civil unrest, had no police shootings [in 2003], fatal or otherwise, for the first time in 14 years. In Phoenix, where such shootings reached a level over the last several years that far outpaced the rate of much larger cities, deadly police shootings fell sharply in 2003, to their lowest rate in 14 years.

In these cities and in a fast-growing number of the nation's police departments, officers are carrying a slick new weapon, the Taser gun, which looks a lot like a pistol but does not shoot to kill.

Though officials say the Taser gun, which fires a stunning jolt of electricity, is not solely responsible for a decline in police killings, many departments say it has made a huge difference. Its supporters say the Taser is saving lives, protecting officers and suspects in standoffs that might otherwise have left someone dead or seriously injured.

"This is 100 percent more humane," said Officer Tom Burns, who has carried a Taser gun for the past two and a half years on bicycle patrol in Seattle.

But as the Taser spreads rapidly, it is raising questions about whether the weapon, which can also be applied directly to the skin as a stun gun, could be abused by the police. The Taser zaps suspects with 50,000 volts of electricity, disabling them for five seconds at a time. Critics say the weapon is ripe for abuse because the shock leaves no obvious mark, other than what looks like a small bee sting. Human rights groups in the United States and abroad have called Tasers potential instruments of torture.

They are now being used by more than 4,000 police departments. Roughly 170 new departments are buying the high-tech electro-shock guns every month, and the Army has begun using them in Iraq, according to Taser International, the Arizona company that makes them. More than one-third of Seattle's 600 patrol officers carry Tasers. In Miami, Phoenix and a growing number of cities, every officer has one.

Tasers have often been introduced in the wake of public outcry over deadly police shootings. That was the case in Seattle, Denver, Austin, Tex., and Portland, Ore., as part of an effort to reduce killings through the use of training programs and "less lethal" weapons.

"You have to think about the alternatives," said Officer Burns, who also carries pepper spray and a .40-caliber Glock pistol. He said he had used the Taser five times on suspects who seemed eager to attack or were difficult to control. "And without this technology you might have to break it down to very brutal methods."

Officer Burns was on the scene in 1999 when Seattle police shot and killed a mentally ill man, a widely publicized incident that led to soul-searching in the department and a plan that among other things involved the purchase of Tasers.

The newest Tasers are an advanced version of technology that was developed in the 1970's but was not considered by the police to be effective until recently. The electrical pulses travel from the gun through two 21-foot-long wires that look like a stretched-out Slinky tipped with barbed probes. If the probes pierce skin or a layer of clothing two inches thick or less, the jolt contracts the muscles and throws the suspect off balance. It makes the suspect unable to move and gives the police a full five seconds with every "tasing" to handcuff the suspect. The police say that 50,000 volts is a safe amount of electricity to absorb and that suspects shot with a Taser recover immediately.

But critics and watchdog groups say the Taser could be used to torture suspects and prison inmates to extract confessions or taunt them, and Amnesty International has called for a ban on their use pending studies on their long-term effects. Human rights and civil liberties groups are also questioning whether the electro-shocks that Tasers deliver are potentially deadly.

"Surely it's better than being killed," said Dan Handelman, a founder of Portland Copwatch, a group that has been critical of that city's growing use of Tasers over the last year. "But it's not necessarily an acceptable replacement because it's not being used—at least in Portland—in place of lethal force; it's being used for compliance."

Across the country in recent months, several suspects who were shot with Tasers, sometimes repeatedly, have died. But officials said other health problems, like heart conditions and drug overdoses, were the cause.

The American Civil Liberties Union of Colorado urged the Denver Police Department two weeks ago to limit its use of Tasers. The group cited a rising number of deaths nationally, saying 16 suspects in custody had died after being subdued with Tasers or stun guns in 2003, up from 10 in 2002 and 3 in 2001. But none of the deaths were officially attributed to the effect of the weapons.

In Las Vegas, William Lomax, 26, died last month after being arrested and, according to witnesses and the police, shot with a Taser four or five times, which critics of the Police Department said was an excessive use of force. Investigators said that Mr. Lomax had been under the influence of drugs, but that the cause of death was still under investigation.

Marsha Bell, 22, said she saw Mr. Lomax, her cousin, arrested on February 21 at her apartment complex, where he often visited his family. After he had a run-in with security guards, the police were called.

"He was on the ground," Ms. Bell said in a telephone interview. "He had two pairs of handcuffs on him, and I didn't know the Taser was being used until I heard him screaming. He kept screaming and screaming, saying, 'Oh God, Jesus, please no.' He was screaming in pain; he was hurt and he didn't resist."

Lt. Tom Monahan of the Las Vegas Metropolitan Police Department, which bought several hundred Tasers last year, said that Mr. Lomax had struggled with officers, security guards and paramedics, and that the Taser was used while officers were trying to handcuff him.

Officer Thomas Miller, who conducts Taser training for the Las Vegas department, said that there were clear guidelines on when Tasers should be used.

"In the past, an officer would have to fight," Officer Miller said. "Now we have an option to stop that before it gets to that point, greatly reducing the risk to the officer and the suspect."

The police do say that a Taser would never replace lethal weapons if an officer felt his life was in imminent danger, like when a suspect is wielding a knife or a gun at close proximity, or when no other officer is available to provide "lethal cover" for an officer using the Taser. Most departments allow officers on the scene to make that judgment call.

In the New York City Police Department, supervisors and members of the large Emergency Service Unit, which helps patrol officers in violent situations, carry Tasers, but patrol officers do not, the police said.

The newest models cost $799 each, according to Taser International, the leading producer of the weapons. But company officials, who have seen their stock skyrocket over the last year, say the savings to police departments that might otherwise be sued over violent confrontations or shootings are potentially huge.

The police and other supporters of the new technology also say there are built-in safeguards to prevent abuse of the guns. Each Taser, which is powered by batteries, has a data port that records each shock and is used by police departments when they prepare incident reports, allowing supervisors to count how many times a Taser was fired.

Steve Tuttle, a spokesman for Taser International, which is based in Scottsdale, Ariz., said the company continually reviewed data and had found few instances among about 70,000 episodes so far of abuse or inappropriate use.

"If there's a bad apple out there, the technology we made will catch that bad apple," Mr. Tuttle said. "We've won the lottery in terms of great success, stock market-wise, but with that comes much more scrutiny."

Officer Burns of the Seattle department said the police could not deny that a misguided officer could abuse any weapon. But he said that there had been numerous instances in Seattle where officers had used the Taser instead of fists, nightsticks, guns or pepper spray, which can have much longer effects than Taser shocks, and that suspects had recovered immediately.

"Shooting someone is not a badge of honor," Officer Burns said. "It's something no one wants to do. No police officer in the world is paid to die; no police officer in the world is paid to get hurt."

For the latest in crime and justice news, visit the Talk Justice news feed at http://www.crimenews.info.

Author's Update: Amid continuing controversy over the safety of stun weapons, the two largest law enforcement divisions of the Department of Homeland Security—the Bureau of Immigration and Customs Enforcement (ICE) and the Bureau of Customs and Border Protection (CBP)—recently rejected the use of stun guns for about 20,000 agents and officers.

Source: Sarah Kershaw, "As Shocks Replace Police Bullets, Deaths Fall But Questions Arise," *New York Times*, March 7, 2004.

with six complaints or more had received positive performance evaluations that failed to record "sustained" complaints or to discuss their significance.

Recent studies have found that problem police officers do not differ significantly in race or ethnicity from nonproblem officers, although they tend to be male and have disciplinary records that are more serious than those of other officers. Some departments are developing early-warning systems to allow police managers to identify potentially problematic officers and to reduce problem police officer behavior. Learn more about police use of force, as well as force used against the police, from Library Extras 6–15 and 6–16 at mycrimekit.com.

Library EXTRA

Deadly Force

Generally speaking, **deadly force** is likely to cause death or great bodily harm. The FBI defines *deadly force* as "the intentional use of a firearm or other instrument resulting in a high probability of death."[152] According to a report released by the Bureau of Justice Statistics in 2001, the number of justifiable homicides by police averages "nearly 400 felons each year."[153]

deadly force
The force likely to cause death or great bodily harm. Also, "the intentional use of a firearm or other instrument resulting in a high probability of death."[xviii]

The use of deadly force by law enforcement officers, especially when it is *not* considered justifiable (as in the *Horiuchi* case mentioned earlier in this chapter), is one area of potential civil liability that has received considerable attention in recent years. Historically, the "fleeing felon rule" applied to most U.S. jurisdictions. It held that officers could use deadly force to prevent the escape of a suspected felon even when that person represented no immediate threat to the officer or to the public.

The 1985 U.S. Supreme Court case of ***Tennessee v. Garner***[154] specified the conditions under which deadly force could be used in the apprehension of suspected felons. Edward Garner, a 15-year-old suspected burglar, was shot to death by Memphis police after he refused their order to halt and attempted to climb over a chain-link fence. In an action initiated by Garner's father, who claimed that his son's constitutional rights had been violated, the Court held that the use of deadly force by the police to prevent the escape of a fleeing felon could be justified only where the suspect could reasonably be thought to represent a significant threat of serious injury or death to the public or to the officer and where deadly force is necessary to effect the arrest. In reaching its decision, the Court declared that "[t]he use of deadly

▲ Cincinnati Police Officer Princess Davis talking with community member Gil Steinberger following a police-sponsored showing of a movie for senior citizens. The event was part of police efforts to improve police–community relations in the city following the November 30, 2003, beating death of 41-year-old Nathaniel Jones. Jones, a 350-pound black man who had ingested PCP and cocaine, lunged at two white officers and knocked one of them down before other officers beat him in an effort to subdue him. His family, charging that excessive force had been used, filed a wrongful death lawsuit against the city in federal court. How can police agencies win the support of the communities they serve?
Al Behrman/AP Wide World Photos

force to prevent the escape of *all* felony suspects, whatever the circumstances, is constitutionally unreasonable."

In 1989, in the case of ***Graham v. Connor***,[155] the Court established the standard of "objective reasonableness" under which an officer's use of deadly force could be assessed in terms of "reasonableness at the moment." In other words, whether deadly force has been used appropriately should be judged, the Court said, from the perspective of a reasonable officer on the scene and not with the benefit of "20/20 hindsight." The justices wrote, "The calculus of reasonableness must embody allowance for the fact that police officers are often forced to make split-second judgments—in circumstances that are tense, uncertain, and rapidly evolving—about the amount of force that is necessary in a particular situation."

The calculus of reasonableness must embody allowance for the fact that police officers are often forced to make split-second judgments—in circumstances that are tense, uncertain, and rapidly evolving—about the amount of force that is necessary in a particular situation.
—Graham v. Connor, *490 U.S. 386, 396–397 (1989)*

In 1995, following investigations into the actions of federal agents at the deadly siege of the Branch Davidian compound at Waco, Texas, and the tragic deaths associated with a 1992 FBI assault on antigovernment separatists in Ruby Ridge, Idaho, the federal government announced that it was adopting an "imminent danger" standard for the use of deadly force by federal agents. The imminent danger standard restricts the use of deadly force to those situations in which the lives of agents or others are in danger. As the new standard was announced, federal agencies were criticized for taking so long to adopt it. The federal deadly force policy, as adopted by the FBI, contains the following elements[156]:

- *Defense of life.* Agents may use deadly force only when necessary, that is, only when they have probable cause to believe that the subject poses an imminent danger of serious physical injury or death to the agents or to others.
- *Fleeing subject.* Deadly force may be used to prevent the escape of a fleeing subject if there is probable cause to believe that the subject has committed a felony involving the infliction or threatened infliction of serious physical injury or death and that the subject's escape would pose an imminent danger of serious physical injury or death to the agents or to others.
- *Verbal warning.* If feasible, and if doing so would not increase the danger to the agents or to others, a verbal warning to submit to the authority of the agents should be given before the use of deadly force.

- *Warning shot.* Agents may not fire warning shots.
- *Vehicle.* Agents may not fire weapons solely to disable moving vehicles. Weapons may be fired at the driver or other occupant of a moving motor vehicle only when the agents have probable cause to believe that the subject poses an imminent danger of serious physical injury or death to the agents or to others and when the use of deadly force does not create a danger to the public that outweighs the likely benefits of its use.

Studies of killings by the police have often focused on claims of discrimination—that black and minority suspects are more likely to be shot than whites—but research has not provided solid support for such claims. While individuals shot by police are more likely to be minorities, an early study by James Fyfe found that police officers will generally respond with deadly force when mortally threatened and that minorities are considerably more likely to use weapons in assaults on officers than are whites.[157] Complicating the picture further, Fyfe's study showed that minority officers are involved in the shootings of suspects more often than other officers, a finding that may be due to the assignment of minority officers to inner-city and ghetto areas. However, a later study by Fyfe, which analyzed police shootings in Memphis, Tennessee, found that black property offenders were twice as likely as whites to be shot by police.[158]

Although relatively few police officers ever fire their weapons at suspects during the course of their careers, those who do may find themselves embroiled in a web of social, legal, and personal complications. It is estimated that in an average year, 600 suspects are killed by public police in America, while another 1,200 are shot and wounded, and 1,800 are shot at and missed.[159] The personal side of police shootings is well summarized in the title of an article that appeared in *Police Magazine*. The article, "I've Killed That Man Ten Thousand Times," demonstrates how police officers who have to use their weapons may be haunted by years of depression and despair.[160] Not long ago, according to author Anne Cohen, all departments did to help officers who had shot someone was to "give him enough bullets to reload his gun." The stress and trauma that result from police shootings are only now being realized, and many departments have yet to develop mechanisms for adequately dealing with them.[161]

▲ Demonstrators in Harris County, Texas, protest the police use of Tasers. This less-lethal weapon, manufactured by Taser International, incapacitates potential attackers by delivering an electrical shock to the person's nervous system. The technology is intended to reduce injury rates to both suspects and officers. Why do some people oppose its use?
Copyright 2005 Houston Chronicle Publishing Company. Reprinted with permission. All rights reserved.

Police officers have particular difficulty dealing with instances of "suicide by cop," in which individuals bent on dying engage in behavior that causes responding officers to resort to deadly force. On March 10, 2005, for example, John T. Garczynski, Jr., a father of two preteen boys, died in a hail of 26 police bullets fired by officers who had surrounded his vehicle in a Boca Raton, Florida, condominium parking lot.[162] Garczynski, a Florida Power and Light Company employee, had been separated from his wife months earlier and appeared to have been despondent over financial problems and the breakup of his marriage. The night before his death, Garczynski met his wife at a bowling alley and handed her a packet containing a suicide note, a typed obituary, and a eulogy to be read at his funeral. After he left, Garczynski's wife called police, and officers used the help of a cell phone company to locate Garczynski. As deputies surrounded Garczynski's 2003 Ford Explorer, he attempted to start the vehicle. One of the officers yelled "Freeze!" and then shouted "Let me see your hands!" It was at that point, deputies said, that Garczynski pointed a gun at them and they fired.

Rebecca Stincelli, author of the book *Suicide by Cop: Victims from Both Sides of the Badge*,[163] says an incident like that involving Garczynski can be devastating for police officers. "In the past, people have used rope, a gun, gas, jumped off a building. A police officer is just another method," said Stincelli. "They say it's nothing personal. [But] they are wrong. It's very personal" for the officers involved.[164] The FBI says, "Suicide-by-cop incidents are painful and damaging experiences for the surviving families, the communities, and all law enforcement professionals."[165]

A study of fatal shootings by Los Angeles police officers found that an astonishingly large number—over 10%—could be classified as "suicide by cop."[166] Recently, researchers have identified three main "suicide by cop" categories: direct confrontations, in which suicidal subjects instigate attacks on police officers for the purpose of dying; disturbed interventions, in which potentially suicidal subjects take advantage of police intervention in their suicide attempt in order to die; and criminal interventions, in which criminal suspects prefer death to capture and arrest.[167]

Less-Lethal Weapons

Recent media reports tell of weapons being developed for the military that incapacitate rather than kill. Among them are flash guns (more formally known as optical systems incapacitaters), which use powerful strobe lights to trigger "flicker illness"; sonic weapons, which employ intense inaudible sounds to cause pain; and focused microwave beams, which can produce extreme physical pain at close range. Such weapons, which employ less-lethal technologies, are being contemplated for use by military planners seeking to separate enemy fighters from civilian populations.[168] They might also be used by civilian law enforcement agencies in border enforcement or during riots or in other crowd-control situations where physical force is needed but where permanent injury is to be avoided.

Less-lethal weapons also offer what may be a problem-specific solution to potential incidents of "suicide by cop," as well as a generic solution to at least some charges of use of excessive force. **Less-lethal weapons** are those that are designed to disable, capture, or immobilize a suspect rather than kill him or her. Efforts to provide law enforcement officers with less-lethal weapons began in 1987.[169] Stun guns, Tasers, rubber bullets, beanbag projectiles, and pepper spray are examples of such weapons that are currently in use. More exotic types of less-lethal weapons, however, are on the horizon. These include snare nets that are fired from shotguns, disabling sticky foam that can be sprayed from a distance, microwave beams that heat the tissue of people exposed to them until they desist in their illegal or threatening behavior or lose consciousness, and high-tech guns that fire bolts of electromagnetic energy at a target, causing painful sensory overload and violent muscle spasms. The NIJ states, "The goal is to give line officers effective and safe alternatives to lethal force."[170]

less-lethal weapon
A weapon that is designed to disable, capture, or immobilize—but not kill—a suspect. Occasional deaths do result from the use of such weapons, however.

As their name implies, however, less-lethal weapons are not always safe. On October 21, 2004, for example, 21-year-old Emerson College student Victoria Snelgrove died hours after being hit in the eye with a plastic pepper-spray-filled projectile that police officers fired at a rowdy crowd celebrating the Red Sox victory over the New York Yankees in the final game of the American League Championship Series in 2004. Witnesses said that officers fired the projectile into the crowd after a reveler near Fenway Park threw a bottle at a mounted Boston police officer.[171]

Professionalism and Ethics

Police administrators have responded in a variety of ways to issues of corruption, danger, and liability. Among the most significant responses have been calls for increased **police professionalism** at all levels of policing. A profession is an organized undertaking characterized by a body of specialized knowledge acquired through extensive education[172] and by a well-considered set of internal standards and ethical guidelines that hold members of the profession accountable to one another and to society. Associations of like-minded practitioners generally serve to create and disseminate standards for the profession as a whole.

police professionalism
The increasing formalization of police work and the accompanying rise in public acceptance of the police.

Contemporary policing has many of the attributes of a profession. Specialized knowledge in policing includes a close familiarity with criminal law, laws of procedure, constitutional guarantees, and relevant Supreme Court decisions; a working knowledge of weapons and hand-to-hand tactics, driving skills, and vehicle maintenance; a knowledge of radio communications; report-writing abilities; interviewing and interrogation techniques; and media and human relations skills. Other specialized knowledge may include equipment operation (such as vehicular radar, the Breathalyzer, and the polygraph), special weapons skills, conflict resolution, and hostage negotiation. Supervisory personnel require an even wider range of skills, including gen-

The ability of the police to fulfill their sacred trust will improve as a lucid sense of ethical standards is developed.
—Patrick V. Murphy
Former Commissioner, New York City Police Department

CJ Careers

Bureau of Alcohol, Tobacco, Firearms and Explosives (ATF)

Name: Robert M. Young, Jr.
Position: Special Agent/Criminal Investigator
City: Lexington, Kentucky
College Attended: Rider University
Year Hired: 1998

"I pursued a career in criminal justice because I am not the type of person who enjoys working a nine-to-five office job. I like having a career where each day presents its own unique challenges. For instance, there are days when I may be in court testifying, days investigating an arson or explosive incident, or days in the field participating in an undercover operation. I believe it is this ever-changing work environment that attracts such a diverse and unique group of individuals to careers in law enforcement. . . .

I believe the greatest challenge I have encountered in my job is the difficulty in trying to adequately balance the demands of the job with the demands of my personal life. . . . There is no greater reward for a law enforcement officer than that of seeing the look of appreciation on the face of a crime victim after the defendant has been convicted and sentenced for the crime that was investigated."

TYPICAL POSITIONS

Special agent, explosives expert, criminal investigator, firearms specialist, bomb-scene investigator, liquor-law violations investigator, fingerprint identification specialist, intelligence research specialist, and forensic chemist. The Bureau of Alcohol, Tobacco, Firearms and Explosives (ATF) has primary investigative jurisdiction among federal agencies for the investigation of international arms trafficking, illegal arms movement, and illegal use of explosives.

EMPLOYMENT REQUIREMENTS

GS-5 ATF special agent applicants must meet the same employment requirements as most other federal agents, including (1) successful completion of the Treasury Enforcement Agent Examination, (2) a field interview, (3) a full field background investigation leading to successful certification for a top-secret clearance, and (4) a bachelor's degree from an accredited college or university or three years of general experience, one of which must be equivalent to at least the GS-4 level.

OTHER REQUIREMENTS

Other general requirements for employment as a federal officer apply. An applicant must (1) be a U.S. citizen, (2) be between 21 and 37 years old, (3) be in good physical health, (4) hold a current, valid U.S. driver's license, (5) pass a polygraph examination, and (6) have eyesight of no less than 20/100 uncorrected, and corrected vision of at least 20/30 in one eye and 20/20 in the other. New agents undergo eight weeks of specialized training at the Federal Law Enforcement Training Center in Glynco, Georgia.

SALARY

A bachelor's degree qualifies applicants for appointment at the GS-5 level, although appointments may be made at the GS-7 level for college graduates who are able to demonstrate superior academic achievement (that is, class standing in the upper third of their graduating class, a cumulative undergraduate grade point average of 2.95 or better, or membership in a national honor society recognized by the Association of College Honor Societies). GS-9 appointments require a master's degree, two full academic years of progressively higher-level graduate education, or one year of specialized experience equivalent to the next lower grade in the federal service. Depending on geographic area of assignment, this salary can be raised from 16% to 30% above the established base level.

BENEFITS

Benefits include (1) 13 days of sick leave annually, (2) two and a half to five weeks of paid vacation and ten paid federal holidays each year, (3) federal health and life insurance, and (4) a comprehensive retirement program.

DIRECT INQUIRIES TO:

Bureau of Alcohol, Tobacco, Firearms and Explosives
Personnel Division
Room 4100
650 Massachusetts Ave., N.W.
Washington, DC 20226
Phone: 202-927-5690
Website: http://atf.treas.gov

For more information on the rapidly expanding criminal justice careers area, read *Where the Jobs Are: Mission Critical Opportunities for America*, available on the Web at http://www.justicestudies.com/jobs.htm.

Note: The views expressed in this profile do not necessarily represent the views of the U.S. Department of Justice; the Bureau of Alcohol, Tobacco, Firearms, and Explosives; or the United States.

eral and personnel administrative skills, management techniques, and strategies for optimum utilization of human and physical resources.

Police work is guided by an ethical code that was originally developed in 1956 by the Peace Officer's Research Association of California (PORAC) in conjunction with Dr. Douglas M. Kelley of Berkeley's School of Criminology.[173] The current version of the Law Enforcement Code of Ethics is reproduced in an Ethics and Professionalism box above. Ethics training has been

Ethics and Professionalism

The Law Enforcement Code of Ethics

As a Law Enforcement Officer, my fundamental duty is to serve mankind; to safeguard lives and property; to protect the innocent against deception, the weak against oppression or intimidation, and the peaceful against violence or disorder; and to respect the Constitutional rights of all men to liberty, equality, and justice.

I will keep my private life unsullied as an example to all; maintain courageous calm in the face of danger, scorn, or ridicule; develop self-restraint; and be constantly mindful of the welfare of others. Honest in thought and deed in both my personal and official life, I will be exemplary in obeying the laws of the land and the regulations of my department. Whatever I see or hear of a confidential nature or that is confided to me in my official capacity will be kept secret unless revelation is necessary in the performance of my duty.

I will never act officiously or permit personal feelings, prejudices, animosities, or friendships to influence my decisions. With no compromise for crime and with relentless prosecution of criminals, I will enforce the law courteously and appropriately without fear or favor, malice or ill will, never employing unnecessary force or violence, and never accepting gratuities.

I recognize the badge of my office as a symbol of public faith, and I accept it as a public trust to be held so long as I am true to the ethics of the police service. I will constantly strive to achieve these objectives and ideals, dedicating myself before God to my chosen profession . . . law enforcement.

THINKING ABOUT ETHICS

1. Why does the Law Enforcement Code of Ethics ask law enforcement officers "to respect the Constitutional rights of all men to liberty, equality, and justice"? Does such respect further the goals of law enforcement? Why or why not?
2. Why is it important for a law enforcement officer to "keep my private life unsullied as an example to all"? What are the potential consequences of *not* doing so?

Source: International Association of Chiefs of Police. Reprinted with permission.

integrated into most basic law enforcement training programs, and calls for expanded training in **police ethics** are being heard from many corners. A comprehensive resource for enhancing awareness of law enforcement ethics, called the "Ethics Toolkit," is available from the IACP and the federal office of Community Oriented Policing Services (COPS) via Web Extra 6–7.

Web EXTRA

police ethics
The special responsibility to adhere to moral duty and obligation that is inherent in police work.

Many professional associations are associated with police work. One such organization, the Arlington, Virginia–based IACP, has done much to raise professional standards in policing and continually strives for improvements in law enforcement nationwide. In like manner, the Fraternal Order of Police (FOP) is one of the best-known organizations of public-service workers in the United States. The FOP is the world's largest organization of sworn law enforcement officers, with more than 318,000 members in more than 2,100 lodges.

Accreditation is another avenue toward police professionalism. The Commission on Accreditation for Law Enforcement Agencies (CALEA) was formed in 1979. Police departments seeking accreditation through the commission must meet hundreds of standards in areas as diverse as day-to-day operations, administration, review of incidents involving the use of a weapon by officers, and evaluation and promotion of personnel. As of March 15, 2005, nearly 580 (3.3%) of the nation's 17,784 law enforcement agencies were accredited,[174] while a number of others were undergoing the accreditation process. However, many accredited agencies are among the nation's largest; as a result, 25% of full-time law enforcement officers in the United States at the state and local levels are members of CALEA-accredited programs.[175] Although accreditation makes possible the identification of high-quality police departments, it is often not valued by agency leaders because it offers few incentives. Accreditation does not guarantee a department any rewards beyond that of peer recognition. Visit CALEA online via Web Extra 6–8 at mycrimekit.com.

Peace Officer Standards and Training (POST) program
The official program of a state or legislative jurisdiction that sets standards for the training of law enforcement officers. All states set such standards, although not all use the term *POST*.

Web EXTRA

Education and Training

Basic law enforcement training requirements were begun in the 1950s by the state of New York and through a voluntary **Peace Officer Standards and Training (POST) program** in California. (Additional information on California's POST standards can be accessed via Web Extra 6–9 at mycrimekit.com.) Today, every jurisdiction mandates POST-like requirements,

Web EXTRA

although they vary considerably from region to region. Modern police education generally involves training in subject areas as diverse as human relations, firearms and weapons, communications, legal aspects of policing, patrol, criminal investigations, administration, report writing, and criminal justice systems. According to a 1999 Bureau of Justice Statistics report, the median number of hours of classroom training required of new officers is highest in state police agencies (823) and lowest in sheriffs' departments (448)[176]; the requirements for county and municipal police are 760 and 640 hours, respectively. Standards continue to be modified. In 2002, for example, the California Commission on POST responded to statewide concerns over racial profiling by adding material to the police training curriculum to ensure that all California law enforcement officers receive training "that reinforces the fact that racial profiling has a profound negative impact on communities and cannot be tolerated."[177]

A good cop stays a rookie at heart, excited by every shift.
—A Nashville, Tennessee, policeman

Federal law enforcement agents receive schooling at the Federal Law Enforcement Training Center (FLETC) in Glynco, Georgia. The center provides training for about 60 federal law enforcement agencies, excluding the FBI and the DEA, which have their own training academies in Quantico, Virginia. The center also offers advanced training to state and local police organizations through the National Center for State and Local Law Enforcement Training, located on the FLETC campus. Specialized schools, such as Northwestern University's Traffic Institute, have also been credited with raising the level of police practice from purely operational concerns to a more professional level.

In 1987, in a move to further professionalize police training, the American Society for Law Enforcement Trainers was formed at the Ohio Peace Officer Training Academy. Today, the organization is known as the American Society for Law Enforcement Training (ASLET). Based in Frederick, Maryland, ASLET works to ensure quality in peace officer training and confers the title Certified Law Enforcement Trainer (CLET) on police training professionals who meet its high standards. ASLET also works with the Police Training Network (on the Web at http://www.policetraining.net) to provide an ongoing and comprehensive calendar of law enforcement training activities nationwide.

A more recent innovation in law enforcement training is the Police Training Officer (PTO) program, whose development was funded by the COPS office starting in 1999.[178] The PTO program was designed by the Reno (Nevada) Police Department, in conjunction with PERF, as an alternative model for police field training. In fact, it represents the first new postacademy field training program for law enforcement agencies in more than 30 years. PTO uses contemporary methods of adult education and a version of problem-based learning specifically adapted to the police environment. It incorporates community policing and problem-solving principles and, according to the COPS office, fosters "the foundation for life-long learning that prepares new officers for the complexities of policing today and in the future."[179] Learn more about PTO at Library Extra 6–17 at mycrimekit.com.

Library EXTRA

As the concern for quality policing builds, increasing emphasis is also being placed on the formal education of police officers. As early as 1931, the National Commission on Law Observance and Enforcement (the Wickersham Commission) highlighted the importance of a well-educated police force by calling for "educationally sound" officers.[180] In 1967, the President's Commission on Law Enforcement and Administration of Justice voiced the belief that "the ultimate aim of all police departments should be that all personnel with general enforcement powers have baccalaureate degrees."[181] At the time, the average educational level of police officers in the United States was 12.4 years—slightly beyond a high school degree. In 1973, the National Advisory Commission on Criminal Justice Standards and Goals made the following specific recommendation: "Every police agency should, no later than 1982, require as a condition of initial employment the completion of at least four years of education . . . at an accredited college or university."[182]

However, recommendations do not always translate into practice. A report found that 16% of state police agencies require a two-year college degree and 4% require a four-year degree. County police are the next most likely to require either a two-year (13%) or four-year (3%) degree.[183] Among sheriffs' departments, 6% require a degree, including 1% with a four-year degree requirement.[184] A 2002 report on police departments in large cities found that the percentage of departments requiring new officers to have at least some college rose from 19% in 1990 to 37% in 2000, and the percentage requiring a two-year or four-year degree grew from

6% to 14% over the same period.[185] A Dallas Police Department[186] policy requiring a minimum of 45 semester hours of successful college-level study for new recruits was upheld in 1985 by the Fifth U.S. Circuit Court of Appeals in the case of *Davis* v. *Dallas*.[187]

An early survey of police departments by PERF stressed the need for educated police officers, citing the following benefits that accrue to police agencies from the hiring of educated officers[188]: (1) better written reports, (2) enhanced communications with the public, (3) more effective job performance, (4) fewer citizen complaints, (5) greater initiative, (6) wiser use of discretion, (7) heightened sensitivity to racial and ethnic issues, and (8) fewer disciplinary problems. However, there are drawbacks to having more educated police forces: Educated officers are more likely to leave police work and to question orders, and they request reassignment more frequently than noneducated officers.

Most federal agencies require college degrees for entry-level positions. Among them are the FBI, the DEA, the Bureau of Alcohol, Tobacco, Firearms and Explosives, the Secret Service, the Bureau of Customs and Border Protection, and the Bureau of Immigration and Customs Enforcement (ICE).

Recruitment and Selection

All professions need informed, dedicated, and competent personnel. When the National Advisory Commission on Criminal Justice Standards and Goals issued its 1973 report on the police, it bemoaned the fact that "many college students are unaware of the varied, interesting, and challenging assignments and career opportunities that exist within the police service."[189] Today, police organizations actively recruit new officers from two- and four-year colleges and universities, technical institutions, and professional organizations. The national commission report stressed the setting of high standards for police recruits and recommended a strong emphasis on minority recruitment, an elimination of residence requirements (which required officers to live in the area they were hired to serve) for new officers, a decentralized application and testing procedure, and various recruiting incentives.

A Bureau of Justice Statistics study published in 2006 found that local police departments use a variety of applicant-screening methods.[190] Nearly all use personal interviews, and a large majority use basic skills tests, physical agility measurements, medical exams, drug tests, psychological evaluations, and background investigations into the personal character of applicants. Among departments serving 25,000 or more residents, about eight in ten use physical agility tests and written aptitude tests, more than half check credit records, and about half use personality inventories and polygraph exams. After training, successful applicants are typically placed on probation for one year. The probationary period in police work has been called the "first true job-related test . . . in the selection procedure,"[191] providing the opportunity for supervisors to gauge the new officer's response to real-life situations.

Effective policing, however, may depend more on innate personal qualities than on educational attainment or credit history. One of the first people to attempt to describe the personal attributes necessary in a successful police officer, famed 1930s police administrator August Vollmer, said that the public expects police officers to have "the wisdom of Solomon, the courage of David, the strength of Samson, the patience of Job, the leadership of Moses, the kindness of the Good Samaritan, the strategic training of Alexander, the faith of Daniel, the diplomacy of Lincoln, the tolerance of the Carpenter of Nazareth, and finally, an intimate knowledge of every branch of the natural, biological, and social sciences."[192] More practically, O. W. Wilson, the well-known police administrator of the 1940s and 1950s, once enumerated some "desirable personal qualities of patrol officers"[193]: (1) initiative; (2) responsibility; (3) the ability to deal alone with emergencies; (4) the capacity to communicate effectively with people from diverse social, cultural, and ethnic backgrounds; (5) the ability to learn a variety of tasks quickly; (6) the attitude and ability necessary to adapt to technological changes; (7) the desire to help people in need; (8) an understanding of others; (9) emotional maturity; and (10) sufficient physical strength and endurance.

High-quality police recruits, an emphasis on training with an eye toward ethical aspects of police performance, and higher levels of education are beginning to raise police pay, which has traditionally been low. The acceptance of police work as a true profession should contribute to significantly higher rates of pay in coming years.

Multiculturalism and Diversity

Investigating Crime in a Multicultural Setting

In the mid-1990s, the Washington, D.C.–based National Crime Prevention Council (NCPC) published an important guide for American law enforcement officers who work with multicultural groups. The principles it contains can be applied equally to most foreign-born individuals living in the United States and are especially important to patrol officers and criminal investigators.

The NCPC guide points out that it is important for well-intentioned newcomers to this country to learn that the law enforcement system in the United States is not a national police force but a series of local, state, and federal agencies that take seriously their obligation to "serve and protect" law-abiding residents. Newcomers need to know that police officers can teach them how to protect themselves and their families from crime. Many immigrants, especially political refugees, come from countries in which the criminal justice system is based on tyranny, repression, and fear.

The NCPC suggests that law enforcement officers and other members of the criminal justice system can help ease this transition by working not only to communicate with immigrants but also to understand them and the complexities of their native cultures. The mere absence of conflict in a neighborhood does not mean that residents of different cultures have found harmony and a cooperative working relationship, says the NCPC. True multicultural integration occurs when various cultures reach a comfortable day-to-day interaction marked by respect, interest, and caring.

▲ NYPD officers respond to a call for service in New York City's Chinatown. American society is a multicultural society, composed of a wide variety of racial and ethnic heritages, diverse religions, incongruous values, disparate traditions, and distinct languages. How does multiculturalism impact American policing?
Ting-Li Wang/The New York Times

Communities in which immigrants and law enforcement have established close positive ties benefit considerably, according to the NCPC. Immigrants gain greater access to police and other services, such as youth programs, victim assistance, parenting classes, medical assistance programs, business networking, and neighborhood groups. Crime decreases in communities where law enforcement officers help immigrants learn to protect themselves against crime.

For police officers working in communities in which "language is a serious barrier between cultures," the NCPC suggests the following pointers for communicating more effectively:

- Be patient when speaking with someone who does not clearly understand your language. Speak slowly and distinctly. Be willing to repeat words or phrases if necessary. Remember that shouting never helps a nonnative speaker understand better.
- Be careful with your choice of words, selecting those that are clear, straightforward, and simple to understand. Avoid colloquialisms and slang.
- Allow extra time for investigation when the people involved have not mastered English.
- Be sure that anyone who serves as an interpreter is fully qualified and has had experience. Interpreting under pressure is a difficult task; lack of training can lead to mistakes.
- Be candid about your ability to speak or understand a language. Trying to "fake it" just leads to confusion, misunderstanding, and misspent time.
- Never assume that someone is less intelligent just because he or she doesn't speak English well.

Web EXTRA

Visit the NCPC via Web Extra 6–10 at mycrimekit.com.

Reference: Adapted from National Crime Prevention Council, *Building and Crossing Bridges: Refugees and Law Enforcement Working Together* (Washington, DC: NCPC, 1994).

Ethnic and Gender Diversity in Policing

In 2003, Annetta W. Nunn took the reins of the Birmingham (Alabama) Police Department. For many, Nunn, a 44-year-old African-American mother and Baptist choir singer, symbolizes the changes in American policing during the past few decades. The new chief sits in a chair once occupied by Eugene "Bull" Connor, an arch segregationist and a national symbol of the South's fight against integration who jailed thousands of civil rights demonstrators during the 1960s. A 23-year veteran of the department, Nunn heads a force of 838 men and women.

A 1968 survey of police supervisors by the National Advisory Commission on Civil Disorders[194] found a marked disparity between the number of black and white officers in leadership positions. One of every 26 black police officers had been promoted to the rank of sergeant, while the ratio among whites was 1 in 12. Only one of every 114 black officers had become a lieutenant, while among whites the ratio was one in 26. At the level of captain, the disparity was even greater: One out of every 235 black officers had achieved the rank of captain, while one of every 53 whites had climbed to that rank.

▲ Birmingham (Alabama) Chief of Police Annetta Nunn. Nunn's appointment in 2003 is indicative of expanded opportunities in policing for women and minorities. Nunn, an African-American who holds a bachelor's degree in criminal justice from the University of Alabama, was four years old in 1963, when thousands of civil rights demonstrators in Birmingham were beaten and arrested on orders of Police Chief Eugene "Bull" Connor. How do communities benefit from police agencies that are socially and culturally diverse?
Birmingham Police Department

Today, many departments, through dedicated recruitment efforts, have dramatically increased their complement of officers from underrepresented groups. The Metropolitan Detroit Police Department, for example, now has a force that is more than 30% black. Nationwide, racial and ethnic minorities comprised 23.6% of full-time sworn police personnel in 2003—up from 17.0% in 1990[195]—and getting closer to the percentage of racial and ethnic minorities in our nation's population, which the U.S. Census Bureau reports is approximately 32%.[196] From 1990 to 2003, the number of African-American local police officers increased by 14,800 (or 37%), and the number of Hispanic officers increased by 22,300 (or 98%). Moreover, a 2006 study of 123 African-American police executives in the United States found that they were generally well accepted by their peers, well integrated into their leadership roles, and socially well adjusted.[197]

Although ethnic minorities are now employed in policing in significant numbers, women are still significantly underrepresented. The 2001 Status of Women in Policing Survey, conducted by the National Center for Women and Policing (NCWP), found that women fill only 12.7% of all sworn law enforcement positions nationwide.[198] On the other hand, the NCWP notes that women account for 46.5% of employed people over the age of 16 nationwide, meaning that they are "strikingly under-represented within the field of sworn law enforcement."[199] Key findings from the survey show the following[200]:

- Women currently fill 12.7% of all sworn law enforcement positions among municipal, county, and state agencies in the United States with 100 or more sworn officers. Women of color hold 4.8% of these positions.
- Between 1990 and 2001, the representation of women in sworn law enforcement ranks has increased from 9% to 12.7%—a gain of less than 4%, or less than 0.5% each year.
- If the slow growth rate of women in policing holds, women will not achieve equal representation within the police profession for another 70 years, and many experts caution that time alone may not be sufficient to substantially increase the number of female officers.
- Women hold 7.3% of sworn top command law enforcement positions, 9.6% of supervisory positions, and 13.5% of line operation positions. Women of color hold 1.6% of sworn top command law enforcement positions, 3.1% of supervisory positions, and 5.3% of line operation positions.
- Fifty-six percent of the agencies surveyed reported no women in top command positions, and 88% of the agencies reported no women of color in their highest ranks.
- State agencies trail municipal and county agencies by a wide margin in hiring and promoting women. Specifically, 5.9% of the sworn law enforcement officers in state agencies are women, which is significantly lower than the percentage reported by municipal agencies (14.2%) and county agencies (13.9%).

- Consent decrees mandating the hiring and promotion of women and minorities are a significant factor in the gains women have made in law enforcement. Of the 25 agencies with the highest percentage of sworn women, ten are subject to this type of consent decree. In sharp contrast, only four of the 25 agencies with the lowest percentage of sworn women operate under a consent decree.
- On average, in agencies without a consent decree mandating the hiring and promotion of women and minorities, women comprise 9.7% of sworn personnel, whereas those agencies with a consent decree in force average 14.0% women in their ranks. The percentage of women of color is 6.3% in agencies without a consent decree and 11.7% in agencies operating under one.[201]

▲ Lieutenant Gail Marsh of the Redmond (Washington) Police Department. Women in uniform are a common sight throughout our nation's cities and towns. What special benefits can women bring to policing?
Therese Frare/Black Star

It is unclear just how many women actually *want* to work in policing. Nonetheless, many police departments continue to make substantial efforts to recruit and retain women because they understand the benefits of having more women among the ranks of sworn officers. Benefits stem from the fact that female police officers tend to use less physical force than male officers and are less likely to be accused of using excessive force; female officers are better at defusing and de-escalating potentially violent confrontations with citizens; female officers often possess better communication skills than their male counterparts; and they are better able to facilitate the cooperation and trust required to implement a community policing model. Moreover, the NCWP says that "female officers often respond more effectively to incidents of violence against women—crimes that represent one of the largest categories of calls to police departments. Increasing the representation of women on the force is also likely to address another costly problem for police administrators—the pervasive problem of sex discrimination and sexual harassment—by changing the climate of modern law enforcement agencies."[202] Finally, "because women frequently have different life experiences than men, they approach policing with a different perspective, and the very presence of women in the field will often bring about changes in policies and procedures that benefit both male and female officers."[203] For additional information on how police departments can recruit and retain female officers, see Library Extra 6–18 at mycrimekit.com.

Library EXTRA

Women as Effective Police Officers

A 2007 review of the status of women in policing found that "women police officers are no longer viewed as a unique presence in law enforcement and their ability to perform the job is less likely to be measured against traditional standards, though indoctrination in law enforcement continues to stress masculinity over ability."[204] One research report on female police officers in Massachusetts found that female officers (1) are "extremely devoted to their work," (2) "see themselves as women first, and then police officers," and (3) are more satisfied when working in nonuniformed capacities.[205] The researcher identified two groups of female officers: (1) those who felt themselves to be well integrated into their departments and were confident in their jobs and (2) those who experienced strain and on-the-job isolation. The officers' children were cited as a significant influence on what their self-perceptions were and on the way in which they viewed their jobs. The demands that attend child rearing in contemporary society were found to be a major factor contributing to the resignation of female officers. The study also found that the longer female officers stayed on the job, the greater the stress and frustration they tended to experience, primarily as a consequence of the uncooperative attitudes of male officers. Some of the female officers interviewed identified networking as a potential solution to the stresses encountered by female officers but also said that when women get together to solve problems, they are seen as

Respect and appreciation for diversity relating to gender, race, victims, and people with special needs are central to recognizing human rights. Police agencies that understand and value diverse communities create structures and systems that reach outward, enjoining and empowering police officers and citizens to collaborate in problem solving on issues of crime and disorder.
—*Police Executive Research Forum*[xix]

"crybabies" rather than professionals. Said one of the women in the study, "We've lost a lot of good women who never should have left the job. If we had helped each other, maybe they wouldn't have left."[206]

Some studies have found that female officers are often underutilized and that many departments are hesitant to assign women to patrol and to other potentially dangerous field activities.[207] As a consequence, some women in police work experience frustration and a lack of satisfaction with their jobs. An analysis of the genderization of the criminal justice workplace by Susan Ehrlich Martin and Nancy C. Jurik, for example, points out that gender inequality is part of a historical pattern of entrenched forms of gender interaction relating to the division of labor, power, and culture.[208] According to Martin and Jurik, women working in the justice system are viewed in terms of such historically developed filters, causing them to be judged and treated according to normative standards developed for men rather than for women. As a consequence, formal and informal social controls continue to disenfranchise women who wish to work in the system and make it difficult to recognize the specific contributions that they make as women.

Methods to Increase the Number of Minorities and Women in Police Work

The contemporary restructuring of policing separates both the authorization of security and the activity of policing from what is recognized as formal government. In doing so, the distinction between "public" and "private" itself becomes problematic.

—David H. Bayley and Clifford D. Shearing[xx]

To increase the representation of ethnic minorities and women in police work, the Police Foundation recommends (1) involving underrepresented groups in affirmative action and long-term planning programs undertaken by police departments, (2) encouraging the development of an open system of promotion whereby women can feel free to apply for promotion and in which qualified individuals of any race or gender will face equity in the promotion process, and (3) using periodic audits to ensure that female officers are not being underutilized by being ineffectively tracked into clerical and support positions.[209]

Networking has taken root among the nation's female police officers, as attested to by the growth of organizations like the International Association of Women Police, based in New York City. Networks offer support to female officers and help them deal with the dilemmas of their job. Mentoring is another method for introducing women to police work.[210] Mentoring creates semiformal relationships between experienced female officers and rookies. Through this relationship, problems can be addressed as they arise, and the experienced officer can guide her junior partner through the maze of formal and informal expectations that surround the job of policing.

Women have entered the ranks of police administration. The 2,000-member International Association of Women Police estimates, for example, that there are more than 100 female chiefs of police throughout the country. Another growing organization, the Women's Police Chief Association, offers networking opportunities to women seeking and holding high rank within police departments nationwide.[211] The National Center for Women and Policing, which is a project of the Feminist Majority Foundation, provides a nationwide resource for law enforcement agencies, community leaders, and public officials seeking to increase the numbers of female police officers in their communities.

Barriers to diversity continue to fall. In 1979, for example, San Francisco became the first city in the world to actively recruit homosexuals for its police force. That action reduced the fear of reporting crimes among many homosexuals, who for years had been victims of organized assaults by bikers and street gangs. During the Clinton administration, Attorney General Janet Reno ordered all Justice Department agencies to end hiring discrimination based on sexual orientation.

Private Protective Services

Growth of Private Protective Services

Public police are employed by the government and enforce public laws. Private security personnel work for corporate employers and secure private interests. Private security has been defined as "those self-employed individuals and privately funded business entities and

Freedom or Safety? You Decide.

Do Sex Offender Websites Spur Vigilantism?

In 2006, officials in Maine decided to temporarily shut down the state's sex offender website after two convicted sex offenders whose identifying information was listed in the online registry were shot and killed. The site provides names, addresses, ages, and offender histories for more than 2,200 nonincarcerated registered sex offenders residing in Maine.

One of the offenders who died, 57-year-old Joseph Gray, was shot five times through a window after being awakened by barking dogs at three o'clock in the morning while sleeping on his living room couch. Gray had been convicted in Massachusetts in 1992 of indecent assault and battery on a child and child rape and had been sentenced to four to six years in prison. Five hours later, William Elliott, age 24, a registered sex offender living in Corinth, Maine, was shot and killed as he answered the door to his ramshackle trailer. In 2002, Elliott had pleaded guilty to two misdemeanor counts of sexual abuse of a minor. The charges stemmed from an intimate relationship he had with a girl two weeks shy of her 16th birthday when he was 19 years old.

On the night of the killings, Canadian Stephen Marshall, a 20-year-old dishwasher from Nova Scotia and the only suspect in the killings, died when he shot himself in the head with a .45-caliber handgun as police stopped and boarded a bus he was riding to Boston. Marshall had been visiting his father in Houlton, Maine, a town near the Canadian border, where the two had planned to go target shooting. Maine Department of Public Safety officials had quickly zeroed in on Marshall after they determined that he had logged on to the state's sex offender registry and obtained information on the victims and 32 other men shortly before the killings. Investigators found a small-caliber pistol and a laptop computer in his backpack.

Charles Onley, a research associate at the Center for Sex Offender Management, a U.S. Department of Justice project, told reporters following the Maine killings that critics had previously warned that online offender registries could be used to facilitate vigilante-type killings. The only other known case of vigilantism linked to a sex offender website occurred in August 2005, when Washington State resident Michael Mullen killed two sex offenders in Bellingham, Washington, after locating them through the city's online sex offender registry. At the time, Don Pierce, executive director of the Washington Association of Sheriffs and Police Chiefs, said that "the value [of sex offender registries] to the community far outweighs the risks."

YOU DECIDE

1. Should society's interest in knowing the identities and residential locations of released sex offenders supersede the concerns for personal safety that those offenders may have?
2. Do you agree with Don Pierce that the value of sex offender registries far outweighs their risks? Why or why not?

References: Lisa Wangsness and Kathleen Burge, "Police Investigate Alleged Gunman's Motives in Killings," *Boston Globe*, April 18, 2006; and Emily Bazar, "Suspected Shooter Found Sex Offenders' Homes on Website," *USA Today*, April 18, 2006.

organizations providing security-related services to specific clientele for a fee, for the individual or entity that retains or employs them, or for themselves, in order to protect their persons, private property, or interests from various hazards."[212] The growth in the size of private security in recent years has been phenomenal. In 2002, for example, $212.7 million was spent for security arrangements at the Olympic winter games in Salt Lake City, Utah—leading to the employment of more than 40,000 private security personnel in association with the event.[213]

Law enforcement can ill afford to continue its traditional policy of isolating and even ignoring the activities of private security.

—*Crime and Protection in America, National Institute of Justice*

A report released by the NIJ in 2001, titled *The New Structure of Policing*,[214] found that "policing is being transformed and restructured in the modern world" in ways that were unanticipated only a few decades ago. Much of the change is due to the development of **private protective services** as an important adjunct to public law enforcement activities in the United States and throughout much of the rest of the world. The NIJ report says that "the key to [understanding] the transformation is that policing, meaning the activity of making societies safe, is no longer carried out exclusively by governments" and that the distinction between private and public police has begun to blur. According to NIJ, "[G]radually, almost imperceptibly, policing has been 'multilateralized,'" meaning that "a host of nongovernmental agencies have undertaken to provide security services." As a result, the NIJ report says that "policing has entered a new era, an era characterized by a transformation in the governance of security." The report concludes:

private protective services
The independent or proprietary commercial organizations that provide protective services to employers on a contractual basis.

- In most countries, certainly in the democratic world, private police outnumber public police.
- In these same countries, people spend more time in their daily lives in places where visible crime prevention and control are provided by nongovernmental groups than by governmental police agencies.

- The reconstruction of policing is occurring worldwide despite differences in wealth and economic systems.

Library EXTRA

View the NIJ report in its entirety via Library Extra 6–19 at mycrimekit.com.

According to the *Hallcrest Report II*, another widely disseminated document describing the private security industry, more people are employed in private security than in all local, state, and federal police agencies combined.[215] Nearly 2 million people are estimated to be working in private security today, whereas slightly less than half that number are engaged in public law enforcement activities.[216] According to the *Hallcrest Report II*, employment in the field of private security is anticipated to continue to expand by around 4% per year, while public police agencies are expected to grow by only 2.8% per year for the foreseeable future. Still faster growth is predicted in private security industry revenues, which are expected to increase about 7% per year, a growth rate almost three times greater than that projected for the gross national product (GNP). Table 4 lists the ten largest private security agencies in business today and some of the services they offer.

Private agencies provide tailored policing funded by the guarded organization rather than through the expenditure of public monies. Experts estimate that the money spent on private security in this country exceeds the combined budgets of all law enforcement agencies—local, state, and federal.[217] Contributing to this vast expenditure is the federal government, which is itself a major employer of private security personnel, contracting for services that range from guards to highly specialized electronic snooping and computerized countermeasures at military installations and embassies throughout the world.

Major reasons for the quick growth of the American proprietary security sector include (1) an increase in crimes in the workplace; (2) an increase in fear (real or perceived) of crime and terrorism; (3) the fiscal crises of the states, which have limited public protection; and (4) an increased public and business awareness and use of more cost-effective private security products and services.[218]

Without close scrutiny, it has become difficult to tell whether policing is being done by a government using sworn personnel, by a government using a private security company, by a private security company using civilian employees, by a private company using public police, or by a government employing civilians.

—David H. Bayley and Clifford D. Shearing[xxi]

Integration of Public and Private Security

As the private security field grows, its relationship to public law enforcement continues to evolve. Some people feel that "today, a distinction between public and private policing is increasingly meaningless."[219] As a result, the focus has largely shifted from an analysis of competition between the sectors to the recognition that each form of policing can help the other. One

TABLE 4 American Policing: Private Security Agencies

Largest Private Security Agencies in the United States		
Advance Security, Inc.	Globe Security	Security Bureau, Inc.
Allied Security, Inc.	Guardsmark, Inc.	Wackenhut Corp.
American Protective Services	Pinkerton's, Inc.	Wells Fargo Guard Services
Burns International Security Services		
Private Security Services		
Airline security	Computer/information security	
Automated teller machine (ATM) services	Executive protection	Railroad detectives
	Hospital security	School security
Bank guards	Loss-prevention specialists	
Company guards	Nuclear facility security	Store/mall security

Source: Adapted from William C. Cunningham, John J. Strauchs, and Clifford W. Van Meter, *The Hallcrest Report II: Private Security Trends, 1970–2000* (McLean, VA: Hallcrest Systems, 1990).

government-sponsored report makes the following policy recommendations, which are designed to maximize the cooperative crime-fighting potential of existing private and public security resources[220]:

▲ A private security officer conferring with a sworn public law enforcement officer. How can cooperation among private security companies and public law enforcement agencies help solve and prevent crimes?
Michael Newman/PhotoEdit Inc.

1. The resources of proprietary and contract security should be brought to bear in cooperative, community-based crime prevention and security awareness programs.
2. An assessment should be made of (1) the basic police services the public is willing to support financially, (2) the types of police services most acceptable to police administrators and the public for transfer to the private sector, and (3) which services might be performed for a lower unit cost by the private sector with the same level of community satisfaction.
3. With special police powers, security personnel could resolve many or most minor criminal incidents prior to police involvement. State statutes providing such powers could also provide for standardized training and certification requirements, thus assuring uniformity and precluding abuses. . . . Ideally, licensing and regulatory requirements would be the same for all states, with reciprocity for firms licensed elsewhere.
4. Law enforcement agencies should be included in the crisis-management planning of private organizations. . . . Similarly, private security should be consulted when law enforcement agencies are developing SWAT [special weapons and tactics] and hostage-negotiation teams. The federal government should provide channels of communication with private security with respect to terrorist activities and threats.
5. States should enact legislation permitting private security firms access to criminal history records in order to improve the selection process for security personnel and also to enable businesses to assess the integrity of key employees.
6. Research should . . . attempt to delineate the characteristics of the private justice system; identify the crimes most frequently resolved; assess the types and amount of unreported crime in organizations; quantify the redirection of [the] public criminal justice workload . . . and examine [the] . . . relationships between private security and . . . components of the criminal justice system.
7. A federal tax credit for security expenditures, similar to the energy tax credit, might be a cost-effective way to reduce police workloads.

Summary

- The police personality is created through informal pressures on officers by a powerful police subculture that communicates values that support law enforcement interests. This chapter described the police personality as (among other things) authoritarian, conservative, honorable, loyal, cynical, dogmatic, hostile, prejudiced, secret, and suspicious.
- Various types of police corruption were described in this chapter, including "grass eating," which includes officers accepting small bribes and free services by those wishing to avoid legal problems, and "meat eating," which includes much more serious forms of corruption such as an officer actively seeking illegal moneymaking opportunities through the exercise of his or her law enforcement duties. Ethics training was mentioned as part of a reframing strategy that emphasizes integrity in an effort to target police corruption. Also discussed was a recent U.S. Department of Justice report that focused on enhancing policing integrity and that cited a police department's culture of integrity as more important in shaping the ethics of police officers than hiring the "right" people.

- The dangers of police work are many and varied. They consist of violent victimization, disease, exposure to biological or chemical toxins, stressful encounters with suspects and victims, and on-the-job fatigue. Stress-management programs, combined with department policies designed to reduce exposure to dangerous situations and agency practices that support officers' needs, can help combat the dangers and difficulties that police officers face in their day-to-day work.
- Policing in America was forever changed by the events of September 11, 2001. Local law enforcement agencies, many of which previously saw community protection and peacekeeping as their primary roles, are being called upon to protect against potential terrorist threats with international roots. The contemporary emphasis on terrorism prevention, alongside the need for a rapid response to threats of terrorism, has led to what some see as a new era of policing to secure the homeland. Homeland security policing builds upon the established framework of community policing for the purpose of gathering intelligence to prevent terrorism. Consequently, the notion of intelligence-led policing (ILP) has become significant and provides a glimpse at one of the features that may characterize American policing in the future.
- Civil liability issues are very important in policing. They arise because officers and their agencies sometimes inappropriately use power to curtail the civil and due process rights of criminal suspects. Both police departments and individual police officers can be targeted by civil lawsuits. Federal suits based on claims that officers acted with disregard for an individual's right to due process are called 1983 lawsuits because they are based on Section 1983 of Title 42 of the U.S. Code. Another type of civil suit that can be brought specifically against federal agents is a *Bivens* action. Although the doctrine of sovereign immunity barred legal action against state and local governments in the past, recent court cases and legislative activity have restricted the opportunity for law enforcement agencies and their officers to exercise claims of immunity.
- Racial profiling, or racially biased policing, is any police action initiated on the basis of the race, ethnicity, or national origin of a suspect rather than on the behavior of that individual or on information that leads the police to a particular individual who has been identified as being or having been engaged in criminal activity. Racial profiling is a bigoted practice unworthy of the law enforcement professional. It has been widely condemned as contrary to basic ethical principles; further, it weakens the public's confidence in the police, thereby decreasing police–citizen trust and cooperation. This chapter pointed out, however, that racial or ethnic indicators associated with particular suspects or suspect groups may have a place in legitimate law enforcement strategies if they accurately relate to suspects who are being sought for criminal law violations.
- Law enforcement officers are authorized to use the amount of force that is reasonable and necessary in a particular situation. Many officers have encounters where the use of force is appropriate. Nonetheless, studies show that the police use force in fewer than 20% of adult custodial arrests. Even in instances where force is used, police officers primarily use weaponless tactics. Excessive force is the application of an amount and/or frequency of force greater than that required to compel compliance from a willing or unwilling subject.
- Police professionalism requires that today's law enforcement officers adhere to ethical codes and standards established by the profession. Police professionalism places important limits on the discretionary activities of individual enforcement personnel and helps officers and the departments they work for gain the respect and regard of the public they police.
- This chapter points out that ethnic minorities are now employed in policing in numbers that approach their representation in the general population. Women, however, are still significantly underrepresented. Questions can be raised about the degree of minority participation in the command structure of law enforcement agencies, about the desire of significant numbers of women to work in policing, and the respect accorded to women and members of other underrepresented groups who work in law enforcement by their fellow officers.
- Private policing, represented by the recent tremendous growth of for-hire security agencies, adds another important dimension to American policing. While public police are employed by the government and enforce public laws, private security personnel work for corporate or private employers and secure private interests. Private security personnel outnumber

public law enforcement officers in the United States by nearly three to one, and private agencies provide tailored protective services funded by the guarded organization rather than by taxpayers. Recognizing the important services that private security personnel provide, many municipal police departments have begun concerted efforts to involve security organizations in their crime-detection and crime-prevention efforts.

Key Concepts

Terms

1983 lawsuit
biological weapons
Bivens action
civil liability
criminal intelligence
deadly force
excessive force
intelligence-led policing
internal affairs
Knapp Commission
less-lethal weapon
NLETS
Peace Officer Standards and Training (POST) program
police corruption
police ethics
police professionalism
police subculture
police use of force
police working personality
private protective services
problem police officer
racial profiling

Cases

Biscoe v. *Arlington County*
Bivens v. *Six Unknown Federal Agents*
City of Canton, Ohio v. *Harris*
Graham v. *Connor*
Hunter v. *Bryant*
Idaho v. *Horiuchi*
Malley v. *Briggs*
Maurice Turner v. *Fraternal Order of Police*
Tennessee v. *Garner*

Questions for Review

1. What is the police working personality? What are its central features? How does it develop? How does it relate to police culture?
2. What are the different types of police corruption? What themes run through the findings of the Knapp Commission and the Wickersham Commission? What innovative steps might police departments take to reduce or eliminate corruption among their officers?
3. What are the dangers of police work? What can be done to reduce those dangers?
4. How has the threat of terrorist attacks affected American policing today? Are American police agencies prepared to prevent and respond to terrorism? Explain.
5. What are some of the civil liability issues associated with policing? How can civil liability be reduced?
6. What is racial profiling? Why has it become a significant issue in policing today?
7. In what kinds of situations are police officers most likely to use force? When has too much force been used?
8. Is police work a profession? Explain. What are the advantages of viewing policing as a profession? How can police professionalism be enhanced?
9. What ethnic and gender differences characterize policing today? What is the social significance of this diversity?
10. What are the nature and extent of private protective services in the United States today? What role do you think private protective services will play in the future? How can the quality of these services be ensured?

To participate in an online discussion of these topics and others, join the CJ Brief e-mail discussion list at mycrimekit.com.

Web Quest

Visit the National Criminal Justice Reference Service (NCJRS) at http://www.ncjrs.gov. Click on the "Advanced Search" option and then on "Hints on Searching the NCJRS Web Site" to view tips on performing effective searches, modifying search queries, and interpreting search results. Write a description of the search techniques available under "Advanced Search," including wild-card, proximity, concept, Boolean, and pattern searching. What does the help text suggest you do if you find too much in your search? If you find too little? For additional information, you might want to visit http://www.ncjrs.gov/tutorial/search.html.

Revisit the NCJRS advanced search page, and click on the "Library/Abstracts" tab. What is the NCJRS Abstracts Database? How does it differ from the NCJRS full-text collection?

After you have familiarized yourself with searching techniques, put your skills to use by conducting a search of the NCJRS site to identify documents on homeland security and policing. (*Note:* You may have to develop your own search strategy using other keywords in combination with "security" or "police" to narrow down the results of your search.) What kinds of documents did you find? What conclusions, if any, did you come to about the police role in homeland security after reading these documents?

To complete this Web Quest online, go to the Web Quest module in Chapter 6 of the *Criminal Justice: A Brief Introduction* Companion Website at mycrimekit.com.

Notes

i. Janine Rauch and Etienne Marais, "Contextualizing the Waddington Report." Web posted at http://www.wits.ac.za/csvr/papers/papwadd.html (accessed January 5, 2008).
ii. Carl B. Klockars et al., *The Measurement of Police Integrity*, National Institute of Justice Research in Brief (Washington, DC: NIJ, 2000), p. 1.
iii. Karyn S. Hunttings, *Quotation World*. Web posted at http://s-2000.com/quoteworld/character.html (accessed March 20, 2007).
iv. Jerome H. Skolnick and David H. Bayley, *The New Blue Line: Police Innovation in Six American Cities* (New York: Free Press, 1986), p. 229.
v. Police Foundation, *Annual Report 1991* (Washington, DC: Police Foundation, 1992).
vi. Technical Working Group on Crime Scene Investigation, *Crime Scene Investigation: A Guide for Law Enforcement* (Washington, DC: National Institute of Justice, 2000), p. 12.
vii. Joel Leson, *Assessing and Managing the Terrorism Threat* (Washington, DC: U.S. Department of Justice, 2005).
viii. Major Cities Chiefs Association, *Terrorism: The Impact on State and Local Law Enforcement*. Intelligence Commanders Conference Report (June 2002). Web posted at http://www.neiassociates.org/mccintelligencereport.pdf (accessed September 30, 2008).
ix. Justin J. Dintino and Frederick T. Martens, *Police Intelligence Systems in Crime Control* (Springfield, IL: Charles C. Thomas, 1983), p. 58.
x. Angus Smith, ed., *Intelligence-Led Policing* (Richmond, VA: International Association of Law Enforcement Intelligence Analysts, 1997), p. 1.
xi. Office of Justice Programs, *The National Criminal Intelligence Sharing Plan* (Washington, DC: U.S. Department of Justice, 2005), p. 27.
xii. Major Cities Chiefs Association, *Terrorism*.
xiii. Adapted from Gerald Hill and Kathleen Hill, *The Real Life Dictionary of the Law*. Web posted at http://www.law.com (accessed June 11, 2008).
xiv. Deborah Ramirez, Jack McDevitt, and Amy Farrell, *A Resource Guide on Racial Profiling Data Collection Systems: Promising Practices and Lessons Learned* (Washington, DC: U.S. Department of Justice, 2000), p. 3.
xv. National Institute of Justice, *Use of Force by Police: Overview of National and Local Data* (Washington, DC: NIJ, 1999).
xvi. International Association of Chiefs of Police, *Police Use of Force in America 2001* (Alexandria, VA: IACP, 2001), p. 1.
xvii. Samuel Walker, Geoffrey P. Albert, and Dennis J. Kenney, *Responding to the Problem Police Officer: A National Study of Early Warning Systems* (Washington, DC: National Institute of Justice, 2000).
xviii. Sam W. Lathrop, "Reviewing Use of Force: A Systematic Approach," *FBI Law Enforcement Bulletin* (October 2000), p. 18.
xix. Lorie Fridell et al., *Racially Biased Policing: A Principled Response* (Washington, DC: Police Executive Research Forum, 2001), p. 41.
xx. David H. Bayley and Clifford D. Shearing, *The New Structure of Policing: Description, Conceptualization, and Research Agenda* (Washington, DC: National Institute of Justice, 2001), p. 5.
xxi. Bayley and Shearing, *The New Structure of Policing*.

1. Joel Leson, *Assessing and Managing the Terrorism Threat* (Washington, DC: U.S. Department of Justice, 2005).
2. Janine Rauch and Etienne Marasis, "Contextualizing the Waddington Report." Web posted at http://www.wits.ac.za/csvr/papers/papwadd.html (accessed January 5, 2008).
3. Jerome H. Skolnick, *Justice without Trial: Law Enforcement in a Democratic Society* (New York: John Wiley, 1966).
4. William A. Westley, *Violence and the Police: A Sociological Study of Law, Custom, and Morality* (Cambridge, MA: MIT Press, 1970); and William A. Westley, "Violence and the Police," *American Journal of Sociology*, Vol. 49 (1953), pp. 34–41.
5. Arthur Niederhoffer, *Behind the Shield: The Police in Urban Society* (Garden City, NY: Anchor, 1967).
6. Thomas Barker and David L. Carter, *Police Deviance* (Cincinnati, OH: Anderson, 1986). See also Christopher P. Wilson, *Cop Knowledge: Police Power and Cultural Narrative in Twentieth-Century America* (Chicago, IL: University of Chicago Press, 2000).
7. Richard Bennett and Theodore Greenstein, "The Police Personality: A Test of the Predispositional Model," *Journal of Police Science and Administration*, Vol. 3 (1975), pp. 439–445.
8. James Teevan and Bernard Dolnick, "The Values of the Police: A Reconsideration and Interpretation," *Journal of Police Science and Administration* (1973), pp. 366–369.
9. Bennett and Greenstein, "The Police Personality," pp. 439–445.
10. Ibid.
11. Office of the U.S. Attorney for the Southern District of California press release, July 28, 2006.
12. NBC News San Diego, "Border Patrol Agent Faces Immigrant-Smuggling Charges," August 5, 2005. http://www.nbcsandiego.com/news/4816916/detail.html (accessed July 4, 2007).
13. Alan Feuer, "2 Ex-Detectives Guilty in Killings," *New York Times*, April 7, 2006. Web posted at http://www.nytimes.com/2006/04/07/nyregion/07cops.html (accessed April 7, 2006).
14. Andy Newman, "A Juror's Question That Went Unanswered: 'How Dare You Violate That Oath?'" *New York Times*, April 7, 2006. Web posted at http://www.nytimes.com/2006/04/07/nyregion/07scene.html (accessed April 7, 2006).
15. Carl B. Klockars et al., "The Measurement of Police Integrity," *National Institute of Justice Research in Brief* (Washington, DC: NIJ, 2000), p. 1.
16. Michael J. Palmiotto, ed., *Police Misconduct: A Reader for the Twenty-First Century* (Upper Saddle River, NJ: Prentice Hall, 2001), preface.
17. Tim Prenzler and Peta Mackay, "Police Gratuities: What the Public Thinks," *Criminal Justice Ethics* (winter/spring 1995), pp. 15–25.
18. Thomas Barker and David L. Carter, *Police Deviance* (Cincinnati, OH: Anderson, 1986). For a detailed overview of the issues involved in police corruption, see Victor E. Kappeler, Richard D. Sluder, and

Geoffrey P. Alpert, *Forces of Deviance: Understanding the Dark Side of Policing*, 2nd ed. (Prospect Heights, IL: Waveland Press, 1998); Dean J. Champion, *Police Misconduct in America: A Reference Handbook* (Santa Barbara, CA: Abo-Clio, 2002); and Kim Michelle Lersch, ed., *Policing and Misconduct* (Upper Saddle River, NJ: Prentice Hall, 2002).

19. Frank L. Perry, "Repairing Broken Windows: Preventing Corruption within Our Ranks," *FBI Law Enforcement Bulletin* (February 2001), pp. 23–26.
20. "Nationline: NYC Cops—Excess Force Not Corruption," *USA Today*, June 16, 1995, p. 3A.
21. *Knapp Commission Report on Police Corruption* (New York: George Braziller, 1973).
22. Ibid.
23. Sabrina Tavernise, "Victory for Officer Who Aided Corruption Inquiry," *New York Times*, April 3, 2004.
24. See IMDb.com, "Notorious (2008)." http://www.imdb.com/title/tt0371115/. The movie, which was delayed, is said to be in production as this book goes to press.
25. See Erwin Chemerinsky, *An Independent Analysis of the Los Angeles Police Department's Board of Inquiry Report on the Rampart Scandal*, September 11, 2000. Web posted at http://www.usc.edu/dept/law/faculty/chemerinsky/rampartfinalrep.html (accessed January 10, 2002).
26. Linda Deutsch, "Appeals Court Intercedes in LAPD Corruption Trial," Associated Press wire service, October 12, 2000. Web posted at http://www.newstimes.com/archive2000/oct12/nah.htm (accessed January 20, 2002).
27. "Three LAPD Officers Convicted," *USA Today* online, November 15, 2000 (accessed July 16, 2001).
28. "Prosecutors: LAPD Hindering Police Corruption Trial," Associated Press wire service, October 6, 2000. Web posted at http://www. newstimes.com/archive2000/oct06/nac.htm (accessed February 2, 2002).
29. Scott Glover and Matt Lait, "LAPD Settling Abuse Scandal," *Los Angeles Times*, March 31, 2005.
30. "Three LAPD Officers Convicted" and "This Week's Corrupt Cop Story." Web posted at http://www.stopthedrugwar.org/chronicle/266/copcorruption.shtml (accessed October 2, 2003).
31. Glover and Lait, "LAPD Settling Abuse Scandal."
32. Ibid.
33. Tina Daunt and Jim Newton, "Council OKs Police Reform Pact with Justice Department," *Los Angeles Times* online, November 3, 2000 (accessed May 20, 2006).
34. Scott Glover and Matt Lait, "A Tearful Perez Gets Five Years," *Los Angeles Times* online, February 26, 2000 (accessed August 28, 2001).
35. Edwin H. Sutherland and Donald Cressey, *Principles of Criminology*, 8th ed. (Philadelphia: J. B. Lippincott, 1970).
36. Tim R. Jones, Compton Owens, and Melissa A. Smith, "Police Ethics Training: A Three-Tiered Approach," *FBI Law Enforcement Bulletin* (June 1995), pp. 22–26.
37. Stephen J. Gaffigan and Phyllis P. McDonald, *Police Integrity: Public Service with Honor* (Washington, DC: National Institute of Justice, 1997).
38. U.S. Department of Justice, *Principles for Promoting Police Integrity: Examples of Promising Police Practices* (Washington, DC: DOJ, 2001).
39. National Institute of Justice, *Enhancing Police Integrity* (Washington, DC: U.S. Department of Justice, 2005).
40. Ibid., p ii.
41. *Carroll* v. *City of Westminster*, 233 F.3d 208, 210–11 (4th Cir. 2000).
42. The material in this paragraph is adapted from Sharon Burrell, "Random Drug Testing of Police Officers Upheld," *Legal Views* (Office of the County Attorney, Montgomery County, Maryland), Vol. 6, No. 2 (February 2001), p. 4.
43. International Association of Chiefs of Police, *Employee Drug Testing* (St. Paul, MN: IACP, 1999).
44. Tom Hays, "NYPD to Start Random Steroid Testing," Associated Press, April 9, 2008. Web posted at http://www.wtopnews.com/?sid=1383781&nid=104 (accessed July 24, 2008).
45. *Maurice Turner* v. *Fraternal Order of Police*, 500 A.2d 1005 (D.C. 1985).
46. *Philip Caruso, President of P.B.A.* v. *Benjamin Ward, Police Commissioner*, New York State Supreme Court, Pat. 37, Index no. 12632-86, 1986.
47. *National Treasury Employees Union* v. *Von Raab*, 489 U.S. 656, 659 (1989).
48. National Law Enforcement Officers' Memorial Fund website. http://www.nleomf.org/TheMemorial/memorial.htm (accessed July 1, 2008).
49. Officer Down Memorial Page, "James Loyd Allen." Web posted at http://www.odmp.org/officer.php?oid=17737 (accessed August 28, 2006).
50. Providence Police Department, "James L. Allen Memorial Page." Web posted at http://www.providencepolice.com/jimmyallen.html (accessed August 28, 2006).
51. National Law Enforcement Memorial Fund, http://www.nleomf.org/TheMemorial/Facts/causes.htm (accessed June 15, 2008).
52. Officer Down Memorial Page, http://www.odmp.org/yeardisp.php?year52001 (accessed January 16, 2001).
53. Anthony J. Pinizzotto and Edward F. Davis, "Cop Killers and Their Victims," *FBI Law Enforcement Bulletin* (December 1992), p. 10.
54. Bureau of Labor Statistics, *Occupational Outlook Handbook, 2000–01 Edition* (Washington, DC: BLS, 2000); and Brian A. Reaves and Timothy C. Hart, *Law Enforcement Management and Administrative Statistics, 1999: Data for Individual State and Local Agencies with 100 or More Officers* (Washington, DC: Bureau of Justice Statistics, 2000). Note that LEMAS only includes data from approximately 700 state and local law enforcement agencies that employ 100 or more full-time sworn personnel and that assign 50 or more of these officers to respond to calls for service. LEMAS reports finding 402,000 full-time sworn personnel among those departments in its 1999 survey. BLS data are more comprehensive and include part-time personnel.
55. Brian A. Reaves and Timothy C. Hart, *Federal Law Enforcement Officers, 2000* (Washington, DC: Bureau of Justice Statistics, 2001).
56. Kevin Johnson, "Better Defense Tactics Helping to Curb Police Deaths," *USA Today*, April 22, 2008, p. 3A.
57. As reported by the Headline News Network, April 26, 1988.
58. *AIDS and Our Workplace*, New York City Police Department pamphlet, November 1987.
59. See Occupational Safety and Health Administration, OSHA Bloodborne Pathogens Act of 1991 (29 CFR 1910.1030).
60. *National Institute of Justice Reports*, No. 206 (November/December 1987).
61. "Suicides, Resignations Hit New Orleans' Thin Blue Line," *USA Today*, September 4, 2005. Web posted at http://www.usatoday.com/news/nation/2005-09-04-neworleanspolicesuicides_x.htm (accessed April 2, 2006).
62. Ibid.
63. See "On-the-Job Stress in Policing: Reducing It, Preventing It," *National Institute of Justice Journal* (January 2000), pp. 18–24.
64. "Stress on the Job," *Newsweek*, April 25, 1988, p. 43.
65. "On-the-Job Stress in Policing," p. 19.
66. Kevin Barrett, "Police Suicide: Is Anyone Listening?" *Journal of Safe Management of Disruptive and Assaultive Behavior* (spring 1997), pp. 6–9.
67. Ibid.
68. For an excellent review of coping strategies among police officers, see Robin N. Haarr and Merry Morash, "Gender, Race, and Strategies of Coping with Occupational Stress in Policing," *Justice Quarterly*, Vol. 16, No. 2 (June 1999), pp. 303–336.
69. Mark H. Anshel, "A Conceptual Model and Implications for Coping with Stressful Events in Police Work," *Criminal Justice and Behavior*, Vol. 27, No. 3 (2000), p. 375.

70. Ibid.
71. Bryan Vila, "Tired Cops: Probable Connections between Fatigue and the Performance, Health, and Safety of Patrol Officers," *American Journal of Police,* Vol. 15, No. 2 (1996), pp. 51–92.
72. Bryan Vila et al., *Evaluating the Effects of Fatigue on Police Patrol Officers: Final Report* (Washington, DC: National Institute of Justice, 2000).
73. Bryan Vila and Dennis Jay Kenney, "Tired Cops: The Prevalence and Potential Consequences of Police Fatigue," *National Institute of Justice Journal,* No. 248 (2002), p. 19.
74. Bryan Vila and Erik Y. Taiji, "Fatigue and Police Officer Performance," paper presented at the annual meeting of the American Society of Criminology, Chicago, 1996.
75. Toni Locy, "Three Men Indicted on Terror Charges," *USA Today,* April 13, 2005, p. 1A.
76. Details for this story are taken from Thor Valdmanis, "Wall Street Stays on Guard against Terror Attacks," *USA Today,* August 23, 2004. Web posted at http://www.usatoday.com/money/markets/us/2004-08-03-wall-street_x.htm (accessed January 10, 2006).
77. Ibid.
78. Police Executive Research Forum, *Local Law Enforcement's Role in Preventing and Responding to Terrorism* (Washington, DC: PERF, October 2, 2001). Web posted at http://www.policeforum.org/terrorismfinal.doc (accessed June 1, 2003).
79. Council on Foreign Relations, "Terrorism Questions and Answers: Police Departments." Web posted at http://www.terrorismanswers.com/security/police.html (accessed April 19, 2005).
80. Ibid.
81. Michael Weissenstein, "NYPD Shifts Focus to Terrorism, Long Considered the Turf of Federal Agents," Associated Press, March 21, 2003. Web posted at http://www.nj.com/newsflash/national/index.ssf?/cgi-free/getstory_ ssf.cgi?a0801_BC_NYPD-Counterterror&&news&newsflash-national (accessed May 25, 2003).
82. Ibid.
83. International Association of Chiefs of Police, *From Hometown Security to Homeland Security: IACP's Principles for a Locally Designed and Nationally Coordinated Homeland Security Strategy* (Alexandria, VA: IACP, 2005).
84. Ibid.
85. Joseph G. Estey, "President's Message: Taking Command Initiative—An Update" (Washington, DC: International Association of Chiefs of Police, 2005). Web posted at http://www.theiacp.org/documents/index.cfm?fuseaction5document&document_id5697 (accessed July 25, 2005).
86. Robert J. Jordan (FBI), Congressional Statement on Information Sharing before the U.S. Senate Committee on the Judiciary, Subcommittee on Administrative Oversight and the Courts, Washington, DC, April 17, 2002. Web posted at http://www.fbi.gov/congress/congress02/jordan041702.htm (accessed April 19, 2006).
87. Suzel Spiller, "The FBI's Field Intelligence Groups and Police: Joining Forces," *FBI Law Enforcement Bulletin* (May 2006), pp. 2–6.
88. The concept of intelligence-led policing appears to have been first fully articulated in Angus Smith, ed., *Intelligence-Led Policing* (Richmond, VA: International Association of Law Enforcement Intelligence Analysts, 1997).
89. David L. Carter, *Law Enforcement Intelligence: A Guide for State, Local, and Tribal Law Enforcement Agencies* (Washington, DC: U.S. Department of Justice, 2004), p. 7.
90. Much of the information and some of the wording in this section are taken from Carter, *Law Enforcement Intelligence*.
91. David L. Carter,"The Law Enforcement Intelligence Function," *FBI Law Enforcement Bulletin,* Vol. 74, No. 6 (June 2005), pp. 1–10.
92. Governor's Commission on Criminal Justice Innovation, *Final Report* (Boston: The Commission, 2004), p. 57, from which much of the wording in the rest of this paragraph is taken.
93. Federal Bureau of Investigation, Law Enforcement online. Web posted at http://www.fbi.gov/hq/cjisd/leo.htm (accessed September 1, 2006).
94. Bernard H. Levin, "Sharing Information: Some Open Secrets and a Glimpse at the Future," *Police Futurist,* Vol. 14, No. 1 (winter 2006), pp. 8–9.
95. The plan was an outgrowth of the IACP Criminal Intelligence Sharing Summit held in Alexandria, Virginia, in March 2002. Results of the summit are documented in International Association of Chiefs of Police, *Recommendations from the IACP Intelligence Summit, Criminal Intelligence Sharing*.
96. Office of Justice Programs, *The National Criminal Intelligence Sharing Plan* (Washington, DC: U.S. Department of Justice, 2003).
97. "Incoming Homeland Security Chairman Introduces Strategy Aimed at Improving Information Sharing," *IACP Capitol Report,* December 14, 2006, p. 2.
98. *LEAP: A Law Enforcement Assistance and Partnership Strategy—Improving Information Sharing between the Intelligence Community and State, Local, and Tribal Enforcement* (Washington, DC: U.S. House of Representatives, 2006), p. 8.
99. "Stroke Victim Sues State over Arrest," Associated Press wire service, April 24, 1996.
100. Charles R. Swanson, Leonard Territo, and Robert W. Taylor, *Police Administration: Structures, Processes, and Behavior,* 2nd ed. (New York: Macmillan, 1988).
101. *Malley* v. *Briggs,* 475 U.S. 335, 106 S.Ct. 1092 (1986).
102. Ibid., at 4246.
103. *Biscoe* v. *Arlington County,* 238 U.S. App. D.C. 206, 738 F.2d 1352, 1362 (1984). See also 738 F.2d 1352 (D.C. Cir. 1984), *cert. denied;* 469 U.S. 1159; and 105 S.Ct. 909, 83 L.E.2d 923 (1985).
104. *Kaplan* v. *Lloyd's Insurance Co.,* 479 So.2d 961 (La. App. 1985).
105. John Hill, "High-Speed Police Pursuits: Dangers, Dynamics, and Risk Reduction," *FBI Law Enforcement Bulletin* (July 2002), pp. 14–18.
106. *City of Canton, Ohio* v. *Harris,* 489 U.S. 378 (1989).
107. Ibid., at 1204.
108. *Board of the County Commissioners of Bryan County, Oklahoma* v. *Brown,* 520 U.S. 397 (1997).
109. Title 42, U.S. Code, Section 1983.
110. *Bivens* v. *Six Unknown Federal Agents,* 403 U.S. 388 (1971).
111. See *F.D.I.C.* v. *Meyer,* 510 U.S. 471 (1994), in which the U.S. Supreme Court reiterated its ruling under *Bivens,* stating that only government employees and not government agencies can be sued.
112. *Wyler* v. *U.S.,* 725 F.2d 157 (2d Cir. 1983).
113. California Government Code, Section 818.
114. Federal Tort Claims Act, 28 U.S.C. 1346(b), 2671–2680.
115. *Elder* v. *Holloway,* 114 S.Ct. 1019, 127 L.Ed.2d 344 (1994).
116. Ibid.
117. *Hunter* v. *Bryant,* 112 S.Ct. 534 (1991).
118. William U. McCormack, "Supreme Court Cases: 1991–1992 Term," *FBI Law Enforcement Bulletin* (November 1992), p. 30.
119. *Saucier* v. *Katz,* 533 U.S. 194 (2001).
120. See also *Brosseau* v. *Haugen,* 543 U.S. 194 (2004).
121. *Scott* v. *Harris,* U.S. Supreme Court, No. 05-1631 (decided April 30, 2007).
122. *Idaho* v. *Horiuchi,* 253 F.3d 359 (9th Cir. 06/05/2001).
123. For more information on police liability, see Daniel L. Schofield, "Legal Issues of Pursuit Driving," *FBI Law Enforcement Bulletin* (May 1988), pp. 23–29.
124. Michael S. Vaughn, Tab W. Cooper, and Rolando V. del Carmen, "Assessing Legal Liabilities in Law Enforcement: Police Chiefs' Views," *Crime and Delinquency,* Vol. 47, No. 1 (2001), p. 3.
125. Adapted from Deborah Ramirez, Jack McDevitt, and Amy Farrell, *A Resource Guide on Racial Profiling Data Collection Systems: Promising Practices and Lessons Learned* (Washington, DC: U.S. Department of Justice, 2000), p. 3.

126. David Harris, *Driving While Black: Racial Profiling on Our Nation's Highways* (Washington, DC: American Civil Liberties Union, 1999).
127. Peter Verniero and Paul Zoubek, *New Jersey Attorney General's Interim Report of the State Police Review Team Regarding Allegations of Racial Profiling* (Trenton: Office of the New Jersey Attorney General, 1999).
128. This paragraph is adapted from Ramirez, McDevitt, and Farrell, *A Resource Guide on Racial Profiling Data Collection Systems,* pp. 7–8.
129. *State of New Jersey* v. *Pedro Soto et al.,* Superior Court of New Jersey, 734 A.2d 350, 1996.
130. "Justice Department Bars Race Profiling, with Exception for Terrorism," *Criminal Justice Newsletter* (July 15, 2003), pp. 6–7.
131. "Justice Department Issues Policy Guidance to Ban Racial Profiling," U.S. Department of Justice press release (No. 355), June 17, 2003.
132. Blaine Harden and Somini Sengupta, "Some Passengers Singled Out for Exclusion by Flight Crew," *New York Times,* September 22, 2001.
133. David Cole and John Lambreth, "The Fallacy of Racial Profiling," *New York Times* online, May 13, 2001. Web posted at http://college1.nytimes.com/buests/articles/2001/05/13/846196.xml (accessed August 28, 2004).
134. Amitai Etzioni, "Another Side of Racial Profiling," *USA Today,* May 21, 2001, p. 15A.
135. Gallup Poll Organization, *Racial Profiling Is Seen as Widespread, Particularly among Young Black Men* (Princeton, NJ: Gallup Poll Organization, December 9, 1999), p. 1.
136. Christopher Stone, "Race, Crime, and the Administration of Justice," *National Institute of Justice Journal* (April 1999), p. 28.
137. Ramirez, McDevitt, and Farrell, *A Resource Guide on Racial Profiling Data Collection Systems,* p. 3.
138. Ibid., p. 55.
139. Police Executive Research Forum, *Racially Biased Policing: A Principled Response* (Washington, DC: PERF, 2001).
140. Ibid., foreword.
141. Ibid., p. 39.
142. Ibid., p. 47.
143. Some of the material in this section is adapted or derived from National Institute of Justice, *Use of Force by Police: Overview of National and Local Data* (Washington, DC: NIJ, 1999).
144. Matthew R. Durose, Erica L. Schmitt, and Patrick A. Langan, *Contacts between Police and the Public* (Washington, DC: Bureau of Justice Statistics, 2005).
145. Joel H. Garner and Christopher D. Maxwell, "Measuring the Amount of Force Used by and against the Police in Six Jurisdictions," in National Institute of Justice, *Use of Force by Police,* p. 41.
146. International Association of Chiefs of Police, *Police Use of Force in America 2001* (Alexandria, VA: IACP, 2001), p. 1.
147. Kenneth Adams, "What We Know about Police Use of Force," in National Institute of Justice, *Use of Force by Police: Overview of National and Local Data* (Washington, DC: NIJ, 1999), p. 4.
148. International Association of Chiefs of Police, *Police Use of Force in America 2001.*
149. Geoffrey P. Alpert and Roger G. Dunham, *The Force Factor: Measuring Police Use of Force Relative to Suspect Resistance—A Final Report* (Washington, DC: National Institute of Justice, 2001).
150. Samuel Walker, Geoffrey P. Alpert, and Dennis J. Kenney, *Responding to the Problem Police Officer: A National Study of Early Warning Systems* (Washington, DC: National Institute of Justice, 2000).
151. See Human Rights Watch, "The Christopher Commission Report," from which some of the wording in the paragraph is adapted. Web posted at http://www.hrw.org/reports98/police/uspo73.htm (accessed March 30, 2002).
152. Sam W. Lathrop, "Reviewing Use of Force: A Systematic Approach," *FBI Law Enforcement Bulletin* (October 2000), p. 18.
153. Jodi M. Brown and Patrick A. Langan, *Policing and Homicide, 1976–98: Justifiable Homicide by Police, Police Officers Murdered by Felons* (Washington, DC: Bureau of Justice Statistics, 2001), p. iii.
154. *Tennessee* v. *Garner,* 471 U.S. 1 (1985).
155. *Graham* v. *Connor,* 490 U.S. 386, 396–397 (1989).
156. John C. Hall, "FBI Training on the New Federal Deadly Force Policy," *FBI Law Enforcement Bulletin* (April 1996), pp. 25–32.
157. James Fyfe, *Shots Fired: An Examination of New York City Police Firearms Discharges* (Ann Arbor, MI: University Microfilms, 1978).
158. James Fyfe, "Blind Justice? Police Shootings in Memphis," paper presented at the annual meeting of the Academy of Criminal Justice Sciences, Philadelphia, March 1981.
159. It is estimated that American police shoot at approximately 3,600 people every year. See William Geller, *Deadly Force* study guide, Crime File Series (Washington, DC: National Institute of Justice, no date).
160. Anne Cohen, "I've Killed That Man Ten Thousand Times," *Police Magazine* (July 1980).
161. For more information, see Joe Auten, "When Police Shoot," *North Carolina Criminal Justice Today,* Vol. 4, No. 4 (summer 1986), pp. 9–14.
162. Details for this story come from Stephanie Slater, "Suicidal Man Killed by Police Fusillade," *Palm Beach Post,* March 11, 2005, p. 1A.
163. Rebecca Stincelli, *Suicide by Cop: Victims from Both Sides of the Badge* (Folsom, CA: Interviews & Interrogations Institute, 2004).
164. Slater, "Suicidal Man Killed by Police Fusillade."
165. Anthony J. Pinizzotto, Edward F. Davis, and Charles E. Miller III, "Suicide by Cop: Defining a Devastating Dilemma," *FBI Law Enforcement Bulletin,* Vol. 74, No. 2 (February 2005), p. 15.
166. "Ten Percent of Police Shootings Found to Be 'Suicide by Cop,'" *Criminal Justice Newsletter* (September 1, 1998), pp. 1–2.
167. Robert J. Homant and Daniel B. Kennedy, "Suicide by Police: A Proposed Typology of Law Enforcement Officer–Assisted Suicide," *Policing: An International Journal of Police Strategies and Management,* Vol. 23, No. 3 (2000), pp. 339–355.
168. David Hambling, "Flash Gun," *Science News,* May 10–16, 2008, pp. 38–40.
169. David W. Hayeslip and Alan Preszler, "NIJ Initiative on Less-Than-Lethal Weapons." *NIJ Research in Brief* (Washington, DC: National Institute of Justice, 1993).
170. Ibid.
171. Thomas Farragher and David Abel, "Postgame Police Projectile Kills an Emerson Student," *Boston Globe,* October 22, 2004. Web posted at http://www.boston.com/sports/baseball/redsox/articles/2004/10/22/postgame_police_projectile_kills_an_emerson_student (accessed July 25, 2005).
172. Michael Siegfried, "Notes on the Professionalization of Private Security," *Justice Professional* (spring 1989).
173. See Edward A. Farris, "Five Decades of American Policing, 1932–1982: The Path to Professionalism," *Police Chief* (November 1982), p. 34.
174. E-mail correspondence with Janice Dixon at the Commission on Accreditation for Law Enforcement Agencies, March 16, 2005. Agency estimates are from Brian A. Reaves and Matthew J. Hickman, *Census of State and Local Law Enforcement Agencies, 2000* (Washington, DC: Bureau of Justice Statistics, 2002).
175. *CALEA Update,* No. 81 (February 2003). Web posted at http:// www.calea.org/newweb/newsletter/No81/81index.htm (accessed May 21, 2003).
176. Brian A. Reaves and Andrew L. Goldberg, *Law Enforcement Management and Administrative Statistics, 1997: Data for Individual State and Local Law Enforcement Agencies with 100 or More Officers* (Washington, DC: Bureau of Justice Statistics, 1999).
177. California Commission on POST, "California Responds to Racial Profiling." Web posted at http://www.post.ca.gov/surveys/racialprofile.htm (accessed March 3, 2006).

178. Information in this paragraph comes from "PTO Program," COPS Office, U.S. Department of Justice (no date). Web posted at http://www.cops.usdoj.gov/print.asp?Item=461 (accessed June 3, 2007).
179. Ibid.
180. National Commission on Law Observance and Enforcement, *Report on Police* (Washington, DC: U.S. Government Printing Office, 1931).
181. President's Commission on Law Enforcement and Administration of Justice, *The Challenge of Crime in a Free Society* (Washington, DC: U.S. Government Printing Office, 1967).
182. National Advisory Commission on Criminal Justice Standards and Goals, *Report on the Police* (Washington, DC: U.S. Government Printing Office, 1973).
183. Reaves and Goldberg, *Law Enforcement Management and Administrative Statistics, 1997.*
184. Ibid.
185. Brian A. Reaves and Matthew J. Hickman, *Police Departments in Large Cities, 1990–2000* (Washington, DC: Bureau of Justice Statistics, 2002), p. 1.
186. "Dallas PD College Rule Gets Final OK," *Law Enforcement News* (July 7, 1986), pp. 1, 13.
187. *Davis* v. *Dallas,* 777 F.2d 205 (5th Cir. 1985).
188. David L. Carter, Allen D. Sapp, and Darrel W. Stephens, *The State of Police Education: Policy Direction for the Twenty-First Century* (Washington, DC: Police Executive Research Forum, 1989), pp. xxii–xxiii.
189. National Advisory Commission on Criminal Justice Standards and Goals, *Report on the Police,* p. 238.
190. Matthew J. Hickman and Brian A. Reaves, *Local Police Departments 2003* (Washington, DC: Bureau of Justice Statistics, 2006), p. 5.
191. Matthew J. Hickman and Brian A. Reaves, *Local Police Departments 2000* (Washington, DC: Bureau of Justice Statistics, 2003), p. 270.
192. August Vollmer, *The Police and Modern Society* (Berkeley: University of California Press, 1936), p. 222.
193. O. W. Wilson and Roy Clinton McLaren, *Police Administration,* 4th ed. (New York: McGraw-Hill, 1977), p. 259.
194. *Report of the National Advisory Commission on Civil Disorders* (New York: E. P. Dutton, 1968), p. 332.
195. Hickman and Reaves, *Local Police Departments, 2003.*
196. U.S. Census Bureau, *National Population Estimates: Characteristics.* Web posted at http://www.census.gov/popest/national/asrh/NC-EST2005-srh.html.
197. R. Alan Thompson, "Black Skin—Brass Shields: Assessing the Presumed Marginalization of Black Law Enforcement Executives," *American Journal of Criminal Justice,* Vol. 30, No. 2 (2006), pp. 163–175.
198. National Center for Women and Policing, *Equality Denied: The Status of Women in Policing, 2001* (Los Angeles: NCWP, 2002), p. 1.
199. Ibid.
200. Ibid., pp. 4–5, from which some of the wording in the list is taken.
201. National Center for Women and Policing, *Equality Denied: The Status of Women in Policing, 2000* (Los Angeles: NCWP, 2001).
202. National Center for Women and Policing, *Recruiting and Retaining Women: A Self-Assessment Guide for Law Enforcement* (Los Angeles: NCWP, 2001), p. 22.
203. Ibid.
204. Mary Dodge, "Women in Policing: Time to Forget the Differences and Focus on the Future," *Criminal Justice Research Reports,* July/August 2007, p. 82.
205. C. Lee Bennett, "Interviews with Female Police Officers in Western Massachusetts," paper presented at the annual meeting of the Academy of Criminal Justice Sciences, Nashville, TN, March 1991.
206. Ibid., p. 9.
207. Carole G. Garrison, Nancy K. Grant, and Kenneth L. J. McCormick, "Utilization of Police Women," unpublished manuscript.
208. Susan Ehrlich Martin and Nancy C. Jurik, *Doing Justice, Doing Gender: Women in Law and Criminal Justice Occupations* (Thousand Oaks, CA: Sage, 1996).
209. Police Foundation, *On the Move: The Status of Women in Policing* (Washington, DC: Police Foundation, 1990).
210. See, for example, Pearl Jacobs, "Suggestions for the Greater Integration of Women into Policing," paper presented at the annual meeting of the Academy of Criminal Justice Sciences, Nashville, TN, March 1991; and Cynthia Fuchs Epstein, *Deceptive Distinctions: Sex, Gender, and the Social Order* (New Haven, CT: Yale University Press, 1988).
211. See Sara Roen, "The Longest Climb," *Police* (October 1996), pp. 44–46, 66.
212. *Private Security: Report of the Task Force on Private Security* (Washington, DC: U.S. Government Printing Office, 1976), p. 4.
213. "Olympic Committee to Review Salt Lake Security in Wake of Terror Attacks," Associated Press, September 17, 2001.
214. David H. Bayley and Clifford D. Shearing, *The New Structure of Policing: Description, Conceptualization, and Research Agenda* (Washington, DC: National Institute of Justice, 2001).
215. William C. Cunningham, John J. Strauchs, and Clifford W. Van Meter, *The Hallcrest Report II: Private Security Trends, 1970–2000* (McLean, VA: Hallcrest Systems, 1990).
216. Includes full-time employees working for local police, sheriffs' departments, special police, and state police. See Brian A. Reaves and Andrew L. Goldberg, *Census of State and Local Law Enforcement Agencies, 1996* (Washington, DC: Bureau of Justice Statistics, 1998); Reaves and Hart, *Law Enforcement Management and Administrative Statistics, 1999;* and Bureau of Labor Statistics, *Occupational Outlook Handbook, 2000–01 Edition.*
217. See http://www.spyandsecuritystore.com.conex.html (accessed June 5, 2008).
218. Cunningham, Strauchs, and Van Meter, *The Hallcrest Report II,* p. 236.
219. Bayley and Shearing, *The New Structure of Policing,* p. 15.
220. National Institute of Justice, *Crime and Protection in America: A Study of Private Security and Law Enforcement Resources and Relationships—Executive Summary* (Washington, DC: U.S. Department of Justice, 1985), pp. 59–72.

The Courts

7

Chapter Outline

- Introduction
- History and Structure of the American Court System
- The State Court System
- The Federal Court System
- Pretrial Activities

Learning Objectives

After reading this chapter, you should be able to

- Describe the development of the American court system.
- Outline the structure of a typical state court system, and describe the jurisdiction of various types of state and local courts.
- Identify the three levels of the federal judiciary, and enumerate some of the differences between the state and federal court systems.
- Explain the typical steps taken during pretrial activities, and list the key factors considered by judicial officers in assessing the risks associated with pretrial release.

"Courts are one of the few institutions of American government that have outperformed our expectations. We've come to look at them as the ultimate safeguard of our rights."

—New York University law professor Burt Neuborn[1]

"No person shall be held to answer for a capital, or otherwise infamous crime, unless on a presentment or indictment of a Grand Jury . . . ; nor shall any person be subject for the same offence to be twice put in jeopardy of life or limb; nor shall be compelled in any criminal case to be a witness against himself, nor be deprived of life, liberty, or property without due process of law."

—Fifth Amendment to the U.S. Constitution

Introduction

▶▶▶ Hear the author discuss this chapter at mycrimekit.com.

On March 11, 2005, rape suspect Brian Nichols grabbed a deputy's gun and shot her in the face as he was being prepared for transfer from a jail holding cell to an Atlanta courtroom.[2] Nichols, age 33, then took the gun and crossed a pedestrian bridge into the courthouse area where he entered the eighth-floor courtroom in which his trial was scheduled to be held. Once inside, he shot and killed Superior Court Judge Rowland Barnes and court reporter Julie Ann Brandau. Both were in the midst of a civil hearing, with no police officers present. Nichols then fled down a stairwell, shooting and killing Fulton County Deputy Sheriff Hoyt Teasley whom he encountered along the way. Following several carjackings, Nichols came upon U.S. Customs Agent David Wilhelm as the agent worked on his house in Atlanta's Buckhead section. Nichols killed Wilhelm and took his truck, fleeing to the Atlanta suburb of Duluth. He became the focus of the largest manhunt in Georgia history before his capture a day later at a Gwinnett County condominium where he had been holding 26-year-old Ashley Smith captive.

Nichols's courthouse rampage came only a week after the husband and elderly mother of a federal judge, Joan Humphrey Lefkow, were found shot to death in the basement of the family's Chicago home.[3] A few days later the case seemed solved when 57-year-old Bart Ross shot himself to death during a Wisconsin traffic stop. Ross, stopped for having a burned-out taillight, left a suicide note saying that he had killed the judge's family. DNA from a cigarette butt found in the Lefkow house after the killings confirmed Ross's presence at the murder scene.[4] A medical

▲ A deputy is wheeled into a waiting ambulance (top left) in the aftermath of shootings at the Fulton County Courthouse in Atlanta, Georgia, in 2005; the deputy later died. Also killed in the shootings were Superior Court Judge Rowland Barnes (bottom left) and court reporter Julie Ann Brandau (bottom right). The shooter, rape suspect Brian Nichols (top right), grabbed a deputy's gun as he was being transferred from a holding cell. He escaped after the shootings, only to be captured the next day at a nearby condominium. How can courtrooms be made more secure?

*Photo by Ben Gray/*Atlanta Journal–Constitution; *John Bazemore/AP Wide World Photos; and Photo by Brent Sanderlin/*Atlanta Journal–Constitution malpractice case in which Ross had been the plaintiff, and which had earlier been dismissed by Judge Lefkow, apparently served as a motive in the killings.

Incidents like those in Atlanta and Chicago highlight the critical role that our nation's courts and the personnel who staff them play in the American system of justice. Breaches of courtroom security endanger courtroom participants and threaten the effective administration of justice. Without courts to decide guilt or innocence and to impose sentence on those convicted of crimes, the activities of law enforcement agencies would become meaningless.

There are many different kinds of courts in the United States, but courts at all levels dispense justice daily and work to ensure that all official actors in the justice system carry out their duties in recognition of the rule of law. Court precedents have defined the legality of enforcement efforts and correctional action. To provide a picture of how courts work, this chapter will describe the American court system at both the state and federal levels.

History and Structure of the American Court System

Two types of courts function within the American criminal justice system: state courts and federal courts. Figure 1 outlines the structure of today's **federal court system**, and Figure 2 diagrams a typical **state court system**. This dual-court system is the result of general agreement among the nation's founders about the need for individual states to retain significant legislative authority and judicial autonomy separate from federal control. Under this concept, the United States developed as a relatively loose federation of semi-independent provinces. New states joining the union were assured of limited federal intervention into local affairs. State legislatures were free to create laws, and state court systems were needed to hear cases in which violations of those laws occurred.

federal court system
The three-tiered structure of federal courts, comprising U.S. district courts, U.S. courts of appeals, and the U.S. Supreme Court.

state court system
A state judicial structure. Most states generally have at least three court levels: trial courts, appellate courts, and a state supreme court.

In the last 200 years, states' rights have gradually waned relative to the power of the federal government, but the dual-court system still exists. Even today, state courts do not hear cases involving alleged violations of federal law, nor do federal courts get involved in deciding issues of state law unless there is a conflict between local or state statutes and federal constitutional guarantees. When such conflicts arise, claimed violations of federal due process guarantees—especially those found in the Bill of Rights—can provide the basis for appeals made to federal courts by offenders convicted in state court systems. Learn more about the dual-court system in America at Library Extra 7–1 at mycrimekit.com.

Library EXTRA

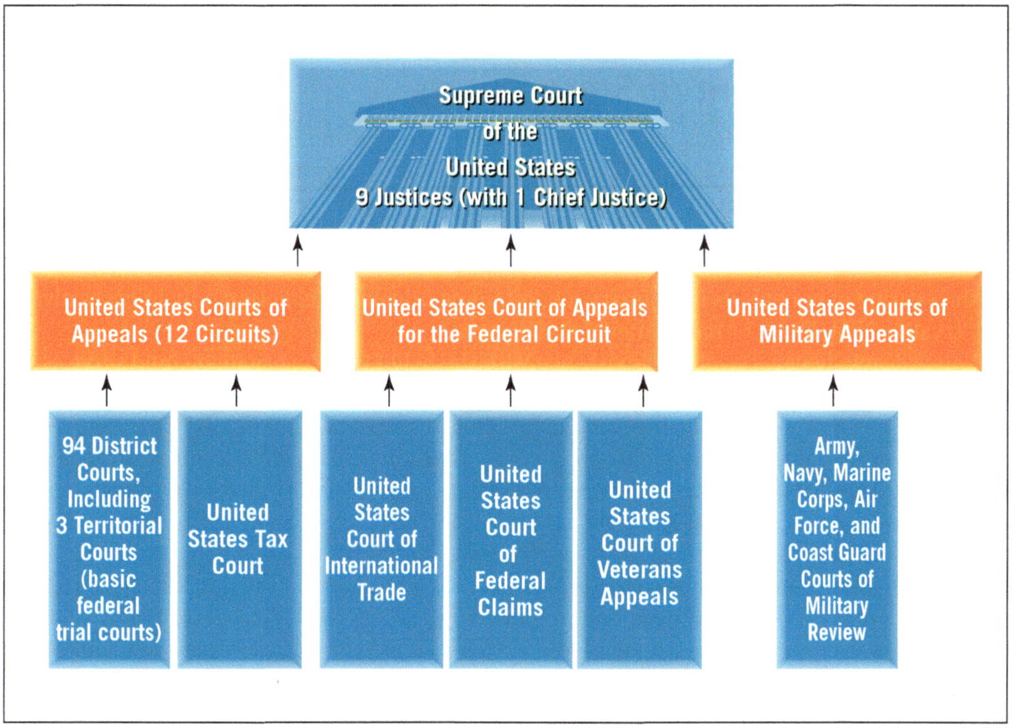

FIGURE 1
The Structure of the Federal Courts.

FIGURE 2
A Typical State Court System.

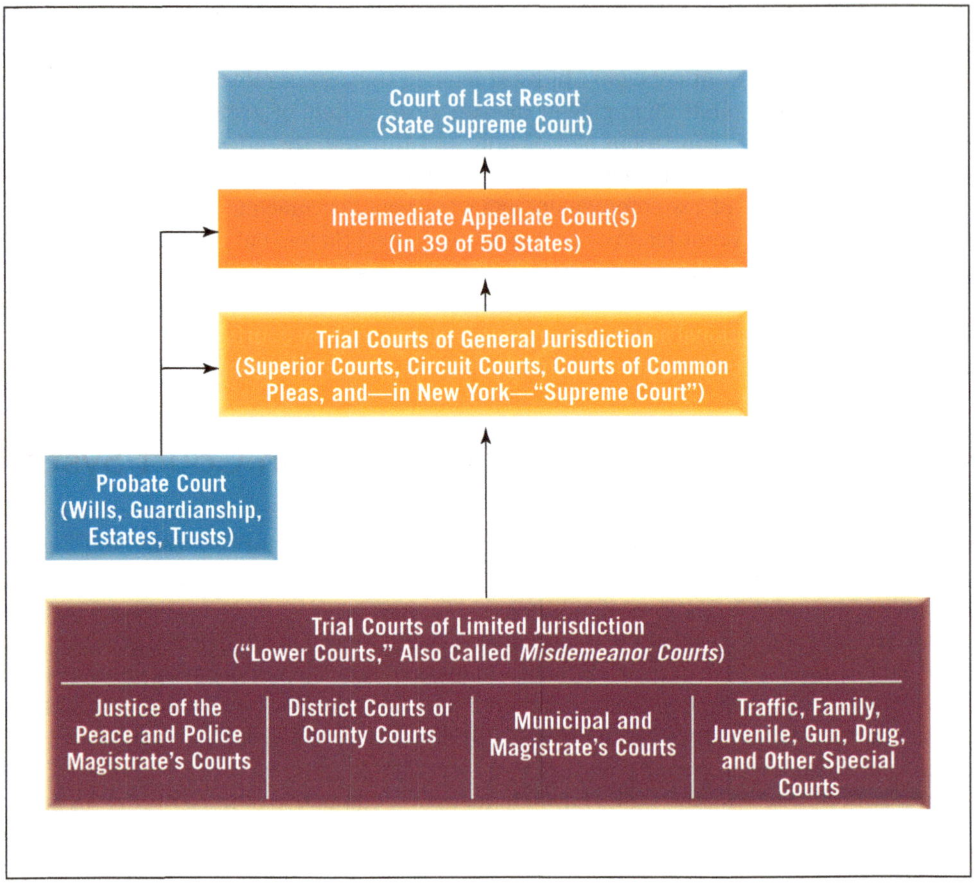

jurisdiction
The territory, subject matter, or people over which a court or other justice agency may exercise lawful authority, as determined by statute or constitution.

This chapter describes both state and federal court systems in terms of their historical development, **jurisdiction**, and current structure. Because it is within state courts that the majority of criminal cases originate, we turn our attention first to them.

The State Court System

The Development of State Courts

Each of the original American colonies had its own court system for resolving disputes, both civil and criminal. As early as 1629, the Massachusetts Bay Colony had created a General Court, composed of the governor, his deputy, 18 assistants, and 118 elected officials. The General Court was a combined legislature and court that made laws, held trials, and imposed sentences.[5] By 1639, as the colony grew, county courts were created, and the General Court took on the hearing of appeals as its primary job, retaining original jurisdiction only in cases involving "tryalls of life, limm, or banishment" and divorce.[6]

Pennsylvania began its colonial existence with the belief that "every man could serve as his own lawyer."[7] The Pennsylvania system utilized "common peacemakers" who served as referees in disputes. Parties to a dispute, including criminal suspects, could plead their case before a common peacemaker they had chosen, and the decision of the peacemaker was binding on the parties. Although the Pennsylvania referee system ended in 1766, lower-level judges, called *magistrates* in many other jurisdictions, are still referred to as *justices of the peace* in Pennsylvania and a few other states.

By 1776, all of the American colonies had established fully functioning court systems. The practice of law, however, was substantially inhibited by a lack of trained lawyers. A number of the early colonies even displayed a strong reluctance to recognize the practice of law as a profession. A Virginia statute enacted in 1645, for example, provided for the removal of "mercenary attorneys" from office and prohibited the practice of law for a fee. Most other colonies retained strict control over the number of authorized barristers (another name for lawyers) by requiring formal training in English law schools and appointment by the governor. New York, which provided for the appointment of "counselors at law," permitted a total of only 41 lawyers to practice law between 1695 and 1769[8]—in large part due to a widespread distrust of formally trained attorneys.

The tenuous status of lawyers in the colonies was highlighted by the 1735 trial of John Zenger in New York. Zenger was the editor of the *New York Journal*, a newspaper, and was accused of slandering Governor William Cosby. When Cosby threatened to disbar any lawyer who defended Zenger, the editor hired Pennsylvania lawyer Andrew Hamilton, who was immune to the governor's threats because he was from out of state.[9]

Following the American Revolution, colonial courts provided the organizational basis for the growth of fledgling state court systems. Because there had been considerable diversity in the structure of colonial courts, state courts were anything but uniform. Initially, most states made no distinction between **original jurisdiction** (the lawful authority of a court to hear cases that arise within a specified geographic area or that involve particular kinds of law violations) and **appellate jurisdiction** (the lawful authority of a court to review a decision made by a lower court). Many, in fact, had no provisions for appeal; Delaware, for example, did not allow appeals in criminal cases until 1897. States that did permit appeals often lacked any established appellate courts and sometimes used state legislatures for that purpose.

original jurisdiction
The lawful authority of a court to hear or to act on a case from its beginning and to pass judgment on the law and the facts. The authority may be over a specific geographic area or over particular types of cases.

appellate jurisdiction
The lawful authority of a court to review a decision made by a lower court.

By the late nineteenth century, a dramatic increase in population, growing urbanization, the settlement of the West, and other far-reaching changes in the American way of life led to a tremendous increase in civil litigation and criminal arrests. Legislatures tried to keep pace with the rising tide of cases. They created a multiplicity of courts at the trial, appellate, and supreme court levels, calling them by a diversity of names and assigning them functions that sometimes bore little resemblance to those of similarly named courts in neighboring states. City courts, which were limited in their jurisdiction by community boundaries, arose to handle the special problems of urban life, such as disorderly conduct, property disputes, and enforcement of restrictive and regulatory ordinances. Other tribunals, such as juvenile courts, developed to handle special kinds of problems or special clients. Some, like magistrate's or small-claims courts, handled only minor law violations and petty disputes; still others, like traffic courts, were very narrow in focus. The result was a patchwork quilt of hearing bodies, some only vaguely resembling modern notions of a trial court.

State court systems developed by following one of several models. One was the New York State Field Code of 1848, which was eventually copied by most other states. The Field Code clarified jurisdictional claims and specified matters of court procedure, but it was later

◄ Junior high school children posing in the pillory in Williamsburg, Virginia. Just as criminal punishments have changed throughout the centuries, so too have criminal courts, which today provide a civilized forum for exploring conflicting claims about guilt and innocence. How might our courts continue to evolve?
Jeff Greenberg/PhotoEdit Inc.

amended so extensively that its usefulness as a model dissolved. Another court system model was provided by the federal Judiciary Act of 1789 and later by the federal Reorganization Act of 1801. States that followed the federal model developed a three-tiered structure of (1) trial courts of limited jurisdiction, (2) trial courts of general jurisdiction, and (3) appellate courts.

State Court Systems Today

The three-tiered federal model was far from perfect, however. Within the structure it provided, many local and specialized courts proliferated; traffic courts, magistrate's courts, municipal courts, recorder's courts, probate courts, and courts held by justices of the peace were but a few that functioned at the lower levels. A movement toward simplification of state court structures, led primarily by the American Bar Association and the American Judicature Society, began in the early twentieth century. Proponents of state court reform sought to unify redundant courts that held overlapping jurisdictions. Most reformers suggested a uniform model for states everywhere that would build on (1) a centralized court structure composed of a clear hierarchy of trial and appellate courts, (2) the consolidation of numerous lower-level courts with overlapping jurisdictions, and (3) a centralized state court authority that would be responsible for budgeting, financing, and managing all courts within a state.

The court reform movement continues today. Although reformers have made substantial progress in many states, there are still many differences between and among state court systems. Reform states, which early on embraced the reform movement, are now characterized by streamlined judicial systems consisting of precisely conceived trial courts of limited and general jurisdiction, supplemented by one or two appellate court levels. Nonreform, or traditional, states retain judicial systems that are a conglomeration of multilevel and sometimes redundant courts with poorly defined jurisdictions. Even in nonreform states, however, most criminal courts can be classified within the three-tiered structure of two trial court echelons and an appellate tier.

State Trial Courts

Trial courts are where criminal cases begin. The trial court conducts arraignments, sets bail, takes pleas, and conducts trials. (We will discuss these separate functions in more depth later in this chapter.) If the defendant is found guilty (or pleads guilty), the trial court imposes sentence. Trial courts of limited (or special) jurisdiction are also called *lower courts*. Lower courts are authorized to hear only less serious criminal cases, usually involving misdemeanors, or to hear special types of cases such as traffic violations, family disputes, and small claims. Courts of limited jurisdiction, which are depicted in TV shows like *Judge Judy* and *Joe Brown*, rarely hold jury trials, depending instead on the hearing judge to make determinations of both fact and law. At the lower-court level, a detailed record of the proceedings is not maintained, and case files only include information on the charge, the plea, the finding of the court, and the sentence. All but six of the states make use of trial courts of limited jurisdiction.[10]

These lower courts are much less formal than courts of general jurisdiction. In an intriguing analysis of court characteristics, Thomas A. Henderson, director of the National Center for State Courts, found that misdemeanor courts process cases according to a "decisional model."[11] The decisional model, said Henderson, is informal, personal, and decisive, and it depends on the quick resolution of relatively uncomplicated issues of law and fact.

Trial courts of general jurisdiction—variously called *high courts, circuit courts*, or *superior courts*—are authorized to hear any criminal case. In many states, they also provide the first appellate level for courts of limited jurisdiction. In most cases, superior courts offer defendants whose cases originated in lower courts the chance for a new trial instead of a review of the record of the earlier hearing. When a new trial is held, it is referred to as a **trial *de novo***.

trial *de novo*
Literally, "new trial." The term is applied to cases that are retried on appeal, as opposed to those that are simply reviewed on the record.

Henderson describes courts of general jurisdiction according to a "procedural model."[12] Such courts, he says, make full use of juries, prosecutors, defense attorneys, witnesses, and all of the other actors we usually associate with American courtrooms. The procedural model, which is far more formal than the decisional model, involves numerous court appearances to ensure that all of a defendant's due process rights are protected. The procedural model makes for a long, expensive, relatively impersonal, and highly formal series of legal maneuvers with many

▲ A criminal trial in progress. Why are courts sometimes called "the fulcrum of the criminal justice system"?
Ron Chapple/Taxi/Getty Images, Inc.–Taxi

professional participants—a fact clearly seen in the widely televised 1995 double-murder trial of famed athlete and television personality O. J. Simpson.

Trial courts of general jurisdiction operate within a fact-finding framework called the *adversarial process.* That process pits the interests of the state, represented by prosecutors, against the professional skills and abilities of defense attorneys. The adversarial process is not a free-for-all; rather, it is constrained by procedural rules specified in law and sustained through tradition. Take a virtual tour of California trial courts via Web Extra 7–1 at mycrimekit.com.

Web EXTRA

State Appellate Courts

Most states today have an appellate division, consisting of an intermediate appellate court (often called the *court of appeals*) and a high-level appellate court (generally termed the *state supreme court*). High-level appellate courts are referred to as **courts of last resort**, indicating that no other appellate route remains to a defendant within the state court system once the high court rules on a case. All states have supreme courts, although only 39 have intermediate appellate courts.[13]

court of last resort
The court authorized by law to hear the final appeal on a matter.

An **appeal** by a convicted defendant asks that a higher court review the actions of a lower court. Once they accept an appeal, courts within the appellate division do not conduct a new trial; instead, they review the case on the record. In other words, appellate courts examine the written transcript of lower-court hearings to ensure that those proceedings were carried out in a fair manner and in accordance with proper procedure and state law. They may also allow attorneys for both sides to make brief oral arguments and will generally consider other briefs or information filed by the appellant (the party initiating the appeal) or the appellee (the side opposed to the appeal). State statutes generally require that sentences of life imprisonment or death be automatically reviewed by the state supreme court.

appeal
The request that a court with appellate jurisdiction review the judgment, decision, or order of a lower court and set it aside (reverse it) or modify it.

Most convictions are affirmed on appeal. Occasionally, however, an appellate court will determine that the trial court erred in allowing certain kinds of evidence to be heard, that it failed to interpret properly the significance of a relevant statute, or that some other impropriety occurred. When that happens, the verdict of the trial court will be reversed, and the case may be sent back for a new trial, or *remanded.* When a conviction is overturned by an appellate court because of constitutional issues or when a statute is determined to be invalid, the state usually has recourse to the state supreme court; when an issue of federal law is involved, as when a state court has ruled a federal law unconstitutional, it goes to the U.S. Supreme Court.

Defendants who are not satisfied with the resolution of their case within the state court system may attempt an appeal to the U.S. Supreme Court. For such an appeal to have any chance of being heard, it must be based on claimed violations of the defendant's rights, as guaranteed under federal law or the U.S. Constitution. Under certain circumstances, federal district courts may also provide a path of relief for state defendants who can show that their federal constitutional rights were violated. However, in the 1992 case of ***Keeney* v. *Tamayo-Reyes***,[14] the U.S. Supreme Court ruled that a "respondent is entitled to a federal evidentiary hearing [only] if he can show cause for his failure to develop the facts in the state-court proceedings and actual prejudice resulting from that failure, or if he can show that a fundamental miscarriage of justice would result from failure to hold such a hearing." Justice Byron White, writing for the Court, said, "It is hardly a good use of scarce judicial resources to duplicate fact-finding in federal court merely because a petitioner has negligently failed to take advantage of opportunities in state court proceedings."

Likewise, in ***Herrera* v. *Collins*** (1993),[15] the Court ruled that new evidence of innocence is no reason for a federal court to order a new state trial if constitutional grounds are lacking. In *Herrera*, where the defendant was under a Texas death sentence for the murder of two police officers, the Court stated:

> Where a defendant has been afforded a fair trial and convicted of the offense for which he was charged, the constitutional presumption of innocence disappears. . . . Thus, claims of actual innocence based on newly discovered evidence have never been held [to be] grounds for relief, absent an independent constitutional violation occurring in the course of the underlying state criminal proceedings. To allow a federal court to grant relief . . . would in effect require a new trial 10 years after the first trial, not because of any constitutional violation at the first trial, but simply because of a belief that in light of his new found evidence a jury might find him not guilty at a second trial.

Library EXTRA

The *Keeney* and *Herrera* decisions have severely limited access by state defendants to federal courts. See Library Extra 7–2 at mycrimekit.com for additional information on challenging state court criminal convictions within the federal court system.

State Court Administration

state court administrator
A coordinator who assists with case-flow management, operating funds budgeting, and court docket administration.

To function efficiently, courts require uninterrupted funding, adequate staffing, trained support personnel, well-managed case flow, and coordination between levels and among jurisdictions. To oversee these and other aspects of judicial management, every state today has its own mechanism for court administration. Most make use of **state court administrators** who manage these operational functions. The following tasks are typical of state court administrators[16]:

- The preparation, presentation, and monitoring of a budget for the state court system
- The analysis of case flows and backlogs to determine where additional personnel, such as judges, prosecutors, and others, are needed
- The collection and publication of statistics describing the operation of state courts
- The effort to streamline the flow of cases through individual courts and the system as a whole
- The liaison between state legislatures and the court system
- The development or coordination of requests for federal and other outside funding
- The management of state court personnel, including promotions for support staff and the handling of retirement and other benefit packages for court employees
- The creation and coordination of plans for the training of judges and other court personnel (in conjunction with local chief judges and supreme court justices)
- The assignment of judges to judicial districts (especially in states that use rotating judgeships)
- The administrative review of payments to legal counsel for indigent defendants

State court administrators can receive assistance from the National Center for State Courts (NCSC) in Williamsburg, Virginia. The NCSC, founded in 1971 at the behest of Chief Justice Warren E. Burger, is an independent nonprofit organization dedicated to the improvement of the American court system. The NCSC provides the following services to state courts:

- Developing policies to enhance state courts
- Advancing state courts' interests within the federal government
- Securing sufficient resources for state courts

- Strengthening state court leadership
- Facilitating state court collaboration
- Providing a model for organizational administration

You can visit the NCSC via **Web Extra 7–2** at mycrimekit.com.

Web EXTRA

At the federal level, the court system is administered by the Administrative Office of the United States Courts (AOUSC), located in Washington, D.C. The AOUSC, created by Congress in 1939, prepares the budget and legislative agenda for federal courts and also performs audits of court accounts, manages funds for the operation of federal courts, compiles and publishes statistics on the volume and type of business conducted by the courts, and recommends plans and strategies to efficiently manage court business. You can visit the AOUSC via **Web Extra 7–3** at mycrimekit.com.

Web EXTRA

Dispute-Resolution Centers and Community Courts

Often, it is possible to resolve minor disputes (in which minor criminal offenses might otherwise be charged) without a formal court hearing. Some communities have **dispute-resolution centers**, which hear victims' claims of minor wrongs they have suffered, such as being subject to the passing of bad checks, trespassing, shoplifting, or petty theft. Such centers function today in more than 200 locations throughout the country.[17] Frequently staffed by volunteer mediators, such programs work to resolve disagreements without stressing blame. Dispute-resolution programs began in the early 1970s, with the earliest being the Community Assistance Project in Chester, Pennsylvania; the Columbus, Ohio, Night Prosecutor Program; and the Arbitration as an Alternative Program in Rochester, New York. Following the lead of these programs, the U.S. Department of Justice helped promote the development of three experimental Neighborhood Justice Centers in Los Angeles, Kansas City, and Atlanta. Each center accepted both minor civil and criminal cases.

dispute-resolution center
An informal hearing place designed to mediate interpersonal disputes without resorting to the more formal arrangements of a criminal trial court.

Mediation centers are often closely integrated with the formal criminal justice process and may substantially reduce the caseload of lower-level courts. Some centers are, in fact, run by the courts and work only with court-ordered referrals; others are semiautonomous but may be dependent on courts for endorsement of their decisions; and still others function with complete autonomy. Rarely, however, do dispute-resolution programs entirely supplant the formal criminal justice mechanism, and defendants who appear before a community mediator may later be charged with a crime. Community mediation programs have become a central feature of today's restorative-justice movement.

Recently, the community justice movement has led to the creation of innovative low-level courts in certain parts of the country. Unlike dispute-resolution centers, **community courts**

community court
A low-level court that focuses on quality-of-life crimes that erode a neighborhood's morale, that emphasizes problem solving rather than punishment, and that builds on restorative principles such as community service and restitution.

◄ Graduates of the Oakland County (Michigan) Community Dispute Resolution training program. Staffed largely by volunteers, dispute-resolution programs facilitate cooperative solutions to relatively low-level disputes in which minor criminal offenses might otherwise be charged. How do dispute-resolution programs and centers help relieve some of the pressures facing our criminal courts?
Photo courtesy of Oakland Mediation Center, Bloomfield Hills, MI

are always *official* components of the formal justice system and can hand down sentences, including fines and jail time, without the need for further judicial review. Community courts typically begin as grassroots movements undertaken by community residents and local organizations seeking to build confidence in the way offenders are handled for less serious offenses. Community courts generally sentence convicted offenders to work within the community, "where neighbors can see what they are doing."[18] Like dispute-resolution centers, community courts, which are sometimes called *problem-solving courts*, focus on quality-of-life crimes that erode a neighborhood's morale, emphasize problem solving rather than punishment, and build on restorative principles like community service and restitution.

Library EXTRA

Web EXTRA

Both mediation centers and community courts have been criticized because they typically work only with minor offenders, thereby denying the opportunity for mediation to victims and offenders in more serious cases. They have also come under criticism because defendants may see them as just another form of criminal sanction rather than as a true alternative to processing by the criminal justice system.[19] Dispute-resolution centers, in particular, have been criticized for doing little more than providing a forum for shouting matches between the parties involved. Learn more about dispute-resolution centers and community courts via **Library Extra 7–3** and **Web Extras 7–4** and **7–5** at mycrimekit.com.

The Federal Court System

Whereas state courts evolved from early colonial arrangements, federal courts were created by the U.S. Constitution. Article III, Section 1, of the Constitution provides for the establishment of "one supreme Court, and . . . such inferior Courts as the Congress may from time to time ordain and establish." Article III, Section 2, specifies that such courts are to have jurisdiction over cases arising under the Constitution, federal laws, and treaties. Federal courts are also to settle disputes between states and to have jurisdiction in cases where one of the parties is a state.

Today's federal court system represents the culmination of a series of congressional mandates that have expanded the federal judicial infrastructure so that it can continue to carry out the duties envisioned by the Constitution. Notable federal statutes that have contributed to the present structure of the federal court system include the Judiciary Act of 1789, the Judiciary Act of 1925, and the Magistrate's Act of 1968.

As a result of constitutional mandates, congressional action, and other historical developments, today's federal judiciary consists of three levels: (1) U.S. district courts, (2) U.S. courts of appeal, and (3) the U.S. Supreme Court. Each is described in turn in the following sections.

U.S. District Courts

The U.S. district courts are the trial courts of the federal court system.[20] Within limits set by Congress and the Constitution, the district courts have jurisdiction to hear nearly all categories of federal cases, including both civil and criminal matters. There are 94 federal judicial districts, including at least one district in each state (some states, like New York and California, have as many as four), the District of Columbia, and Puerto Rico. Each district includes a U.S. bankruptcy court as a unit of the district court. Three territories of the United States—the Virgin Islands, Guam, and the Northern Mariana Islands—have district courts that hear federal cases, including bankruptcy cases. There are two special trial courts that have nationwide jurisdiction over certain types of cases: The Court of International Trade addresses cases involving international trade and customs issues; the U.S. Court of Federal Claims has jurisdiction over most claims for money damages against the United States, disputes over federal contracts, unlawful "takings" of private property by the federal government, and a variety of other claims against the United States.

The judicial Power of the United States shall be vested in one supreme Court, and in such inferior Courts as the Congress may from time to time ordain and establish.
—*Article III of the U.S. Constitution*

Federal district courts have original jurisdiction over all cases involving alleged violations of federal statutes. A district may itself be divided into divisions and may have several places where the court hears cases. District courts were first authorized by Congress through the Judiciary Act of 1789, which allocated one federal court to each state. Because of population increases over the years, new courts have been added in a number of states.

Nearly 650 district court judges staff federal district courts. Because some courts are much busier than others, the number of district court judges varies from a low of two in some

CJ Careers

U.S. Marshals Service

PERSONAL PROFILE

Name: Larry Harper
Position: Deputy U.S. Marshal, Operations Division
City: Albuquerque, New Mexico
College Attended: University of New Mexico
Year Hired: 2003

"I went into law enforcement because I wanted to do my part in making my community safe. Even when I was a child, I knew I wanted to go into law enforcement. When I saw the Marshals Service while doing an internship in college, I knew this was where I wanted to be. I enjoy the flexibility of the job. . . . It's not the same every day."

TYPICAL POSITIONS

Deputy U.S. marshal. The mission of the U.S. Marshals Service is to protect the federal courts and to ensure the effective operation of the judicial system. Deputy U.S. marshals are involved in court security, fugitive investigations, witness security, transportation and custody of federal prisoners, management of seized assets, and special operations.

EMPLOYMENT REQUIREMENTS

The applicant must be a U.S. citizen between 21 and 36 years of age, must be in excellent physical condition, and must possess a valid driver's license and a good driving record. General employment requirements include (1) a comprehensive written exam, (2) a structured employment interview, and (3) a background investigation. Appointment at the GS-5 level requires (1) a bachelor's degree from an accredited college or university or (2) three years of "responsible volunteer or paid experience" or (3) an equivalent combination of education and experience.

OTHER REQUIREMENTS

Successful applicants must complete ten weeks of rigorous training at the U.S. Marshals Service Training Academy in Glynco, Georgia.

SALARY

Deputy U.S. marshals are typically hired at GS-5 or GS-7, depending on education and work experience.

BENEFITS

Benefits include (1) 13 days of sick leave annually, (2) two and a half to five weeks of paid vacation and ten paid federal holidays each year, (3) federal health and life insurance, and (4) a comprehensive retirement program.

DIRECT INQUIRIES TO:

U.S. Marshals Service
Human Resources Division—Law Enforcement Recruiting
Washington, DC 20530-1000
Phone: (202) 307-9400
Website: http://www.usdoj.gov/marshals

For more information on the rapidly expanding criminal justice careers area, read *Where the Jobs Are: Mission Critical Opportunities for America*, available on the Web at http://www.justicestudies.com/jobs.htm.

Note: The views expressed in this profile do not necessarily represent the views of the U.S. Department of Justice, the federal U.S. Marshals Service, or the United States.

jurisdictions to a high of 27 in others. District court judges are appointed by the president and confirmed by the Senate, and they serve for life. An additional 369 full-time and 110 part-time magistrate judges (referred to as *U.S. magistrates* before 1990) serve the district court system and assist the federal judges. Magistrate judges have the power to conduct arraignments and may set bail, issue warrants, and try minor offenders.

U.S. district courts handle tens of thousands of cases per year. During 2007, for example, 68,413 criminal cases[21] and 257,507 civil cases[22] were filed in U.S. district courts. Drug prosecutions, especially in courts located close to the U.S.–Mexico border, have led to considerable growth in the number of cases filed. Federal drug prosecutions in states abutting the Mexican border—California, Arizona, New Mexico, and Texas—more than doubled (from 2,864 to 6,116) between 1994 and 2000, and immigration prosecutions increased more than sevenfold (from 1,056 to 7,613).[23] During the last 20 years, the number of cases handled by the entire federal district court system has grown exponentially. The hiring of new judges and the creation of new courtroom facilities have not kept pace with the increase in caseload, and questions persist as to the quality of justice that overworked judges can deliver.

One of the most pressing issues facing district court judges is the fact that their pay, which at $154,700 in mid-2006[24] placed them in the top 1% of income-earning Americans, is small compared to what most could earn in private practice. Since 1993, the salaries of federal judges have remained relatively stagnant,[25] leading many judges to leave the bench.[26] In 2006, Chief

Library EXTRA

Justice John Roberts called Congress's failure to raise judges' pay "a direct threat to judicial independence"[27]; because of low pay, said Roberts, "judges effectively serve for a term dictated by their financial position rather than for life." Learn more about the federal courts via Library Extra 7–4 at mycrimekit.com.

U.S. Courts of Appeal

The 94 judicial districts are organized into 12 regional circuits, each of which has a U.S. court of appeals.[28] A court of appeals hears appeals from the district courts located within its circuit, as well as appeals from decisions of federal administrative agencies.

The U.S. Court of Appeals for the Federal Circuit and the 12 regional courts of appeal are often referred to as *circuit courts.* Early in the nation's history, the judges of the first courts of appeal visited each of the courts in one region in a particular sequence, traveling by horseback and riding the "circuit." Today, the regional courts of appeal review matters from the district courts of their geographic regions, from the U.S. Tax Court, and from certain federal administrative agencies. A disappointed party in a district court often has the opportunity to have the case reviewed in the court of appeals for the circuit. Each of the First through Eleventh Circuits includes three or more states, as illustrated in Figure 3.

Each court of appeals consists of six or more judges, depending on the caseload of the court. Circuit court judges are appointed for life by the president (with the advice and consent of the Senate). The judge who has served on the court the longest and who is under 65 years of age is designated as the chief judge, performs administrative duties in addition to hearing cases, and serves for a maximum term of seven years. There are 167 judges on the 12 regional courts of appeal.

Oyez, oyez, oyez! All persons having business before the honorable, the Supreme Court of the United States, are admonished to draw near and give their attention, for the court is now sitting. God save the United States and this honorable Court.

—Marshal's cry at the opening of public sessions of the U.S. Supreme Court

The U.S. Court of Appeals for the District of Columbia, which is often called the Twelfth Circuit, hears cases arising in the District of Columbia and has appellate jurisdiction assigned by Congress in legislation concerning many departments of the federal government. The U.S. Court of Appeals for the Federal Circuit (in effect, the Thirteenth Circuit) was created in 1982 by the merging of the U.S. Court of Claims and the U.S. Court of Customs and Patent Appeals. The court hears appeals in cases from the U.S. Court of Federal Claims, the U.S. Court of International Trade, the U.S. Court of Veterans Appeals, the International Trade Commission, the Board of Contract Appeals, the Patent and Trademark Office, and the Merit Systems Protection Board. The court also hears appeals from certain decisions involving the secretaries of the Department of Agriculture and the Department of Commerce and cases from district courts involving patents and minor claims against the federal government.

FIGURE 3
Geographic Boundaries of the U.S. Courts of Appeal and U.S. District Courts.

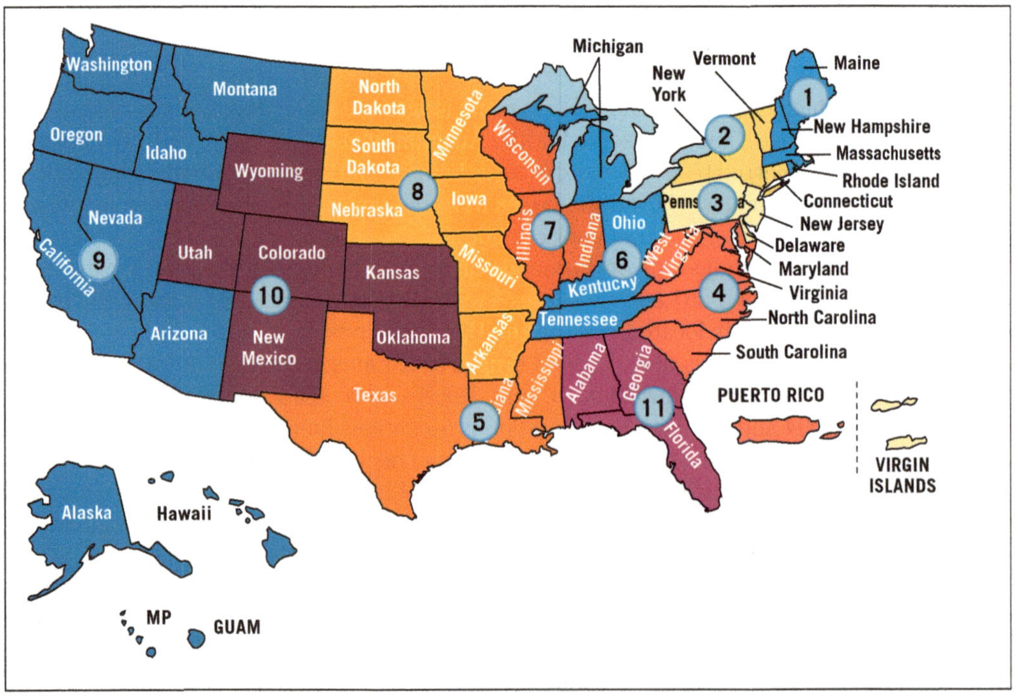

Almost all appeals from federal district courts go to the court of appeals serving the circuit in which the case was first heard. Federal appellate courts have appellate jurisdiction over the decisions of district courts within their circuits. Criminal appeals from federal district courts are usually heard by panels of three judges sitting on a court of appeals rather than by all the judges of each circuit. A defendant's request for appeal, when granted, has been interpreted to mean the opportunity for one appeal; hence, the U.S. Supreme Court need not necessarily hear the appeals of defendants who are dissatisfied with the decision of a federal appeals court.

Federal appellate courts operate under the Federal Rules of Appellate Procedure, although each has also created its own separate Local Rules. Local Rules may mean that one circuit, such as the Second, will depend heavily on oral arguments, while others may prefer written summary depositions. Appeals generally fall into one of three categories: (1) frivolous appeals, which have little substance, raise no significant new issues, and are generally disposed of quickly; (2) ritualistic appeals, which are brought primarily because of the demands of litigants, even though the probability of reversal is negligible; and (3) nonconsensual appeals, which entail major questions of law and policy and on which there is considerable professional disagreement among the courts and within the legal profession.[29] The probability of reversal is, of course, highest in the case of nonconsensual appeals.

Federal circuit courts face an ever-increasing workload. Between 2004 and 2005, the number of federal criminal appeals rose 28%, reaching record highs and marking a tenth consecutive record-breaking year.[30] Much of the growth in criminal appeals can be attributed to the U.S. Supreme Court decisions of *Blakely* v. *Washington* (2004)[31] and *U.S.* v. *Booker* (2005),[32] which brought into question the validity of many previously imposed federal criminal sentences.[33]

While the numbers of cases filed in both appellate courts and district courts continue to swell, the number of federal judges available to hear them has remained virtually unchanged, leading to huge increases in judicial workloads. Consequently, in 2007, the Judicial Conference of the United States, the primary policy-making arm of the federal courts, urged Congress to create 67 new federal judgeships in appellate and district courts.[34] The conference cited a need for nine permanent and three temporary court of appeals judgeships as well as 44 permanent and 11 temporary district judgeships. Congress has yet to act on the recommendation. Learn more about criminal appeals in federal courts via Library Extra 7–5 at mycrimekit.com.

Library EXTRA

The U.S. Supreme Court

At the apex of the federal court system stands the U.S. Supreme Court. The Supreme Court is located in Washington, D.C., across the street from the U.S. Capitol. The Court consists of nine justices, eight of whom are associate justices; the ninth presides over the Court as the chief justice of the United States (Table 1). Supreme Court justices are nominated by the president, are confirmed by the Senate, and serve for life. Lengthy terms of service are a tradition among

I left [the Supreme Court] . . . perfectly convinced that . . . a system so defective . . . would not obtain the energy, weight, and dignity which are essential to its affording due support to the national government, nor acquire the public confidence and respect which, as the last resort of the justice of the nation, it should possess.

—John Jay
First Chief Justice of the United States, in a letter to John Adams, 1801

TABLE 1 Justices of the U.S. Supreme Court (as of January 2009)

Justice	Start of Duty	Views
Chief Justice		
John G. Roberts, Jr.	September 2005	Conservative
Associate Justices		
John Paul Stevens	December 1975	Moderate to liberal
Antonin Scalia	September 1986	Very conservative
Anthony Kennedy	February 1988	Conservative
David H. Souter	October 1990	Conservative
Clarence Thomas	October 1991	Conservative
Ruth Bader Ginsburg	August 1993	Moderate to liberal
Stephen G. Breyer	August 1994	Moderate
Samuel A. Alito, Jr.	January 2006	Conservative

justices. One of the earliest chief justices, John Marshall, served the Court for 34 years, from 1801 to 1835. The same was true of Justice Stephen J. Field, who sat on the bench between 1863 and 1897. Justice Hugo Black passed the 34-year milestone, serving an additional month before retiring in 1971. Justice William O. Douglas set a record for longevity on the bench, retiring in 1975 after 36 years and six months of service. You can view the biographies of today's Supreme Court justices via Web Extra 7–6 at mycrimekit.com.

Web EXTRA

judicial review
The power of a court to review actions and decisions made by other agencies of government.

The Supreme Court of the United States wields immense power. The Court's greatest authority lies in its capacity for **judicial review** of lower-court decisions and state and federal statutes. By exercising its power of judicial review, the Court decides what laws and lower-court decisions are in keeping with the intent of the U.S. Constitution. The power of judicial review is not explicit in the Constitution but was anticipated by its framers. In the *Federalist Papers*, which urged adoption of the Constitution, Alexander Hamilton wrote that through the practice of judicial review, the Court would ensure that "the will of the whole people," as grounded in the Constitution, would be supreme over the "will of the legislature," which might be subject to temporary whims.[35] It was not until 1803, however, that the Court forcefully asserted its power of judicial review. In an opinion written for the case of ***Marbury* v. *Madison*** (1803),[36] Chief Justice John Marshall established the Court's authority as final interpreter of the U.S. Constitution, declaring, "It is emphatically the province of the judicial department to say what the law is."

Increasing Complexity of the Supreme Court

The evolution of the U.S. Supreme Court provides one of the most dramatic examples of institutional development in American history. Sparsely described in the Constitution, the Court has grown from a handful of circuit-riding justices into a modern organization that wields tremendous legal power over all aspects of American life. Much of the Court's growth has been due to its increasing willingness to mediate fundamental issues of law and to act as a buffer against arbitrary and capricious processing by the justice systems of the states and the national government.

The *Marbury* decision established the Court as a mighty force in federal government by virtue of the power of judicial review. The Court began to apply that power during the 1960s to issues of crime and justice at the state and local levels. You may recall that the Court signaled its change in orientation in 1961 with the case of *Mapp* v. *Ohio*,[37] which extended the exclusionary rule to the states. Such extension, combined with the near-simultaneous end of the hands-off doctrine that had previously exempted state prison systems from Court scrutiny, placed the authority of the Court squarely over the activities of state criminal justice systems. From that time forward, the Court's workload became increasingly heavy and today shows few signs of abatement.

▶ Protesters in front of the U.S. Supreme Court in 2004. Highlighting its importance as our nation's premier legal institution, the Court became the backdrop for a rally against the USA PATRIOT Act. Protesters claimed that the act unfairly denies foreign terror suspects the right to a quick and impartial hearing. How does the Court serve to balance individual rights and freedoms with the need for public safety and social order?
© William Philpott/Reuters/Corbis

The Supreme Court Today

The Supreme Court reviews the decisions of lower courts and may accept cases both from U.S. courts of appeal and from state supreme courts. It has limited original jurisdiction and does not conduct trials except for disputes between states and for some cases of attorney disbarment. For a case to be heard, at least four justices must vote in favor of a hearing. When the Court agrees to hear a case, it will issue a writ of *certiorari* to a lower court, ordering it to send the records of the case forward for review. Once having granted *certiorari*, the justices can revoke the decision; in such cases, a writ is dismissed by ruling it improvidently granted.

The U.S. Supreme Court may review any decision appealed to it that it decides is worthy of review. In fact, however, the Court elects to review only cases that involve a substantial federal question. Of approximately 5,000 requests for review received by the Court yearly, only about 200 are actually heard.

A term of the Supreme Court begins, by statute, on the first Monday in October and lasts until early July. The term is divided among sittings, when cases will be heard, and periods of time for the writing and delivering of opinions. Between 22 and 24 cases are heard at each sitting, with each side allotted 30 minutes for arguments before the justices. Intervening recesses allow justices time to study arguments and supporting documentation and to work on their opinions.

Decisions rendered by the Supreme Court are rarely unanimous. Instead, the opinion that a majority of the Court's justices agree on becomes the judgment of the Court. Justices who agree with the Court's judgment write concurring opinions if they agree for a different reason than the majority opinion or if they feel that they have some new light to shed on a legal issue involved in the case. Justices who do not agree with the decision of the Court write dissenting opinions, and those dissenting opinions may offer new possibilities for successful appeals made at a later date. Visit the U.S. Supreme Court via **Web Extra 7–7** at mycrimekit.com, and learn more about the federal judiciary via **Library Extra 7–6**.

▲ U.S. Supreme Court Chief Justice John G. Roberts, Jr., walking past an official portrait of his predecessor, former Chief Justice William H. Rehnquist, who died in office in 2005. Roberts, who served on the U.S. Court of Appeals for the District of Columbia Circuit prior to joining the nation's highest court, was nominated in 2005 by President George W. Bush to succeed Rehnquist. It is anticipated that Justice Roberts will play a key role in shaping the national debate on important issues for years to come. Do you think that a justice's personal values and beliefs might influence his or her decisions on important matters that come before the Court, or are such decisions merely a matter of impersonal application of relevant law?
Charles Dharapak/Getty Images, Inc.

Pretrial Activities

The next chapter discusses the steps in a criminal trial and describes the many roles assumed by courtroom participants, including judges, prosecutors, defense attorneys, victims, and defendants. A number of court-related activities, however, routinely take place *before* trial can begin. Although these activities (as well as the names given to them) vary among jurisdictions, they are described generally in the pages that follow.

The First Appearance

Following arrest, most defendants do not come into contact with an officer of the court until their **first appearance** before a magistrate or a lower-court judge.[38] A first appearance, sometimes called an *initial appearance* or *magistrate's review*, occurs when defendants are brought before a judge (1) to be given formal notice of the charges against them, (2) to be advised of their rights, (3) to be given the opportunity to retain a lawyer or to have one appointed to represent them, and (4) to possibly be afforded the opportunity for bail.

According to the procedural rules of all jurisdictions, defendants who have been taken into custody must be offered an in-court appearance before a magistrate "without unnecessary delay." The 1943 U.S. Supreme Court case of ***McNabb* v. *U.S.***[39] established that any unreasonable delay in an initial court appearance would make confessions inadmissible if interrogating officers obtained them during the delay. Based on the *McNabb* decision, 48 hours following arrest became the standard maximum time by which a first appearance should be held.

The first appearance may also involve a probable cause hearing, although such hearings may be held separately (or in some jurisdictions, they may be combined with the preliminary hearing) because they do not require the defendant's presence. Probable cause hearings are necessary when arrests are made without a warrant because such arrests do not require a prior judicial determination of probable cause. During a probable cause hearing, also called a *probable cause determination*, a judicial officer will review police documents and reports to ensure that probable

Web EXTRA

Library EXTRA

first appearance
An appearance before a magistrate during which the legality of the defendant's arrest is initially assessed and the defendant is informed of the charges on which he or she is being held. At this stage in the criminal justice process, bail may be set or pretrial release arranged. Also called *initial appearance*.

Multiculturalism and Diversity

The International Criminal Court

On April 12, 2000, the International Criminal Court (ICC) was created under the auspices of the United Nations. The ICC is a permanent criminal court for trying individuals (not countries) who commit the most serious crimes of concern to the international community, such as genocide, war crimes, and crimes against humanity (including the wholesale murder of civilians, torture, and mass rape). The ICC intends to be a global judicial institution with international jurisdiction complementing national legal systems around the world. Support for the ICC was developed through the United Nations, where more than 70 countries approved the court's creation by ratifying what is known as the Rome Statute of the International Criminal Court. The ICC's first prosecutor, Luis Moreno Ocampo of Argentina, was elected in April 2003.[1]

The ICC initiative began after World War II with unsuccessful efforts to establish an international tribunal to try individuals accused of war crimes.[2] In lieu of such a court, military tribunals were held in Nuremberg, Germany, and Tokyo, Japan, to try defendants accused of war crimes. Although the 1948 Genocide Convention called for an international criminal court, efforts to establish a permanent court were delayed for decades by the cold war and by the refusal of some national governments to accept the court's proposed international legal jurisdiction.

In December 1948, the UN General Assembly adopted the Universal Declaration of Human Rights and the Convention on the Prevention and Punishment of the Crime of Genocide. It also called for criminals to be tried "by such international penal tribunals as may have jurisdiction." A number of member states soon asked the United Nations International Law Commission (ILC) to study the possibility of establishing an international criminal court.

Development of the ICC was delayed by the cold war that took place between the world's superpowers, which were not willing to subject their military personnel or commanders to international criminal jurisdiction in the event of a "hot" war. In 1981, however, the UN General Assembly asked the ILC to consider creating an international Code of Crimes.

▲ UN Secretary-General Kofi Annan speaking at opening ceremonies that marked the signing of the Treaty on Establishment of the International Criminal Court in Rome, Italy, in 1998. What is the jurisdiction of the ICC?
UN/DPI/E. Schneider

The 1992 war in Bosnia-Herzegovina, which involved clear violations of the Genocide and Geneva Conventions, heightened world interest in the establishment of a permanent ICC. A few years later, 160 countries participated in a UN conference, held in Rome, to establish a criminal court.[3] At the end of that conference, member states voted overwhelmingly in favor of the Rome Statute, calling for the establishment of the ICC.

A few years ago, in what became a stumbling block on the road to the court's creation, the United States expressed concern about the ICC, saying that members of the American military could become subject to ICC jurisdiction. That concern led to U.S. efforts to delay the court's creation. The issue was resolved in 2002, when the UN Security Council voted to exempt members of the American military from prosecution by the court's War Crimes Tribunal.[4] The Security Council resolution, however, must be renewed annually if it is to remain in force.[5] In 2006, the U.S. Supreme Court seemed to further limit American recognition of international agreements in the area of criminal law when, in the case of *Sanchez-Llamas* v. *Oregon*,[6] the justices denied relief to two noncitizens arrested in the United States and not informed of their rights as foreigners under the Vienna Convention on Consular Relations to notify their local consulates of their arrest. Similarly, in 2008, the Court held that a ruling by the International Court of Justice (ICJ) did not require a new trial for a Mexican national convicted in Texas of murder. The man, Jose Ernesto Medellin, had been sentenced to die for participating in the gang rapes and murders of two young Texas girls. But the ICJ, an international court based in The Hague, Netherlands, which works to resolve treaty disputes between nations, found that Medellin's rights had been violated when Texas officials did not inform him of his right under an agreement signed decades ago by the United States and Mexico to contact Mexican consular officials when he was arrested. Chief Justice John Roberts, writing for the majority, found that the ICJ ruling "is not domestic law" and therefore is not applicable to the states.[7]

In 2005, in one of the ICC's first official actions, a panel of judges decided to allow independent Dutch investigators to carry out forensic tests in the Democratic Republic of Congo (DRC) as part of an ongoing investigation into the deaths of thousands of people in genocidal violence throughout central Africa.[8] Learn more about these efforts and other activities of the ICC by visiting the Coalition for an International Criminal Court via Web Extra 7–8 at mycrimekit.com. You can watch video streams of court hearings when the court is in session via Web Extra 7–9 (some archived streams are also available).

Web EXTRA

[1]See the Coalition for an International Criminal Court, "Building the Court." Web posted at http://www.iccnow.org/buildingthecourt.html (accessed July 10, 2006).
[2]Much of the information and some of the wording in this box are adapted from "The International Criminal Court Home Page." Web posted at http://www.iccnow.org/index.html; and the ICC "Timeline." Web posted at http://www.iccnow.org/html/timeline.htm (accessed April 12, 2006).
[3]The conference was officially known as the Conference of Plenipotentiaries on the Establishment of an International Criminal Court. *Plenipotentiary* is another word for "diplomat."

[4]Jan M. Olsen, "EU Welcomes U.S. Compromise on War Crimes Tribunal," Associated Press, July 13, 2002.

[5]United Nations Security Council Resolution No. 1422 (July 1, 2002).

[6]*Sanchez-Llamas* v. *Oregon*, U.S. Supreme Court, Nos. 04-10566 and 05-51 (decided June 28, 2006).

[7]"Supreme Court Overrules Bush, OKs Texas Execution," CNN.com/crime. Web posted at http://www.cnn.com/2008/CRIME/03/25/scotus.texas (accessed May 23, 2008).

[8]"Decision of Pre-Trial Chamber I on the Prosecutor's Request under Article 56 of the Rome Statute," ICC press release, April 26, 2005. Web posted at http://www.icc-cpi.int/press/pressreleases/105.html (accessed May 20, 2006).

cause supported the arrest. The review of the arrest proceeds in a relatively informal fashion, with the judge seeking to decide whether, at the time of apprehension, the arresting officer had reason to believe both (1) that a crime had been or was being committed and (2) that the defendant was the person who committed it. Most of the evidence presented to the judge comes either from the arresting officer or from the victim. If probable cause is not found to exist, the suspect is released. As with a first appearance, a probable cause hearing should take place within 48 hours.

When we have examined in detail the organization of the Supreme Court, and the entire prerogatives which it exercises, we shall readily admit that a more imposing judicial power was never constituted by any people.

—*Alexis de Tocqueville*
Democracy in America *(1835)*

In 1991, the U.S. Supreme Court, in a class-action suit entitled ***County of Riverside* v. *McLaughlin*,**[40] imposed a promptness requirement on probable cause determinations for in-custody arrestees. The Court held that "a jurisdiction that provides judicial determinations of probable cause within 48 hours of arrest will, as a general matter, comply with the promptness requirement." The Court specified, however, that weekends and holidays could not be excluded from the 48-hour requirement (as they had been in Riverside County, California) and that, depending on the specifics of the case, delays of fewer than two days may still be unreasonable.

During a first appearance, the suspect is not given an opportunity to present evidence, although the U.S. Supreme Court has held that defendants are entitled to representation by counsel at their first appearance.[41] Following a reading of the charges and an advisement of rights, counsel may be appointed to represent indigent defendants and proceedings may be adjourned until counsel can be obtained. In cases where a suspect is unruly, intoxicated, or uncooperative, a judicial review may occur without the suspect being present.

Some states waive a first appearance and proceed directly to arraignment (discussed later), especially when the defendant has been arrested on a warrant. In states that move directly to arraignment, the procedures undertaken to obtain a warrant are regarded as sufficient to demonstrate a basis for detention before arraignment.

Pretrial Release

A significant aspect of the first appearance hearing is the consideration of **pretrial release**. Defendants charged with very serious crimes, as well as those thought likely to escape or to injure others, are usually held in jail until trial. Such a practice is called *pretrial detention*. The majority of defendants, however, are afforded the opportunity for release. Many jurisdictions make use of pretrial services programs, which may also be called *early intervention programs*.[42] Such programs, which are typically funded by the states or by individual counties, perform two critical functions: (1) They gather and present information about newly arrested defendants and about available release options for use by judicial officers in deciding what (if any) conditions are to be set for defendants' release before trial, and (2) they supervise defendants released from custody during the pretrial period by monitoring their compliance with release conditions and by helping to ensure that they appear for scheduled court events. Learn more about pretrial services via Library Extra 7–7 at mycrimekit.com.

pretrial release
The release of an accused person from custody, for all or part of the time before or during prosecution, upon his or her promise to appear in court when required.

Library EXTRA

The initial pretrial release/detention decision is usually made by a judicial officer or by a specially appointed hearing officer after considering the background information provided by the pretrial services program, along with the representations made by the prosecutor and the defense attorney. In making this decision, judicial officers are concerned about two types of risk: (1) the risk of flight or nonappearance for scheduled court appearances and (2) the risk to public safety. In assessing these risks, judicial officers tend to focus on four key factors:

1. Seriousness of the current charge, as set forth in the complaint and the representations of the prosecutor
2. Defendant's prior criminal record, which is widely viewed as relevant when assessing the risk to public safety that would be posed by a decision to release or to set a relatively low bail bond
3. Information about the defendant, including community and family ties; employment status; housing; existence and nature of any substance-abuse problems; and (if the defendant has been arrested before) record of compliance with conditions of release set on previous occasions, including any failures to appear
4. Information about available supervisory options if the defendant is released

Bail

Bail is the most common release/detention decision-making mechanism in American courts. Bail serves two purposes: (1) It helps ensure reappearance of the accused, and (2) it prevents unconvicted persons from suffering imprisonment unnecessarily.

bail bond
A document guaranteeing the appearance of a defendant in court as required and recording the pledge of money or property to be paid to the court if he or she does not appear, which is signed by the person to be released and anyone else acting in his or her behalf.

Bail involves the posting of a bond as a pledge that the accused will return for further hearings. **Bail bonds** usually involve cash deposits but may be based on property or other valuables. A fully secured bond requires the defendant to post the full amount of bail set by the court. The usual practice, however, is for a defendant to seek privately secured bail through the services of a professional bail bondsman. The bondsman will assess a percentage (usually 10% to 15%) of the required bond as a fee, which the defendant will have to pay up front. Those who "skip bail" by hiding or fleeing will sometimes find that the court has ordered them to forfeit their bail. Forfeiture hearings must be held before a bond can be taken, and most courts will not order bail forfeited unless it appears that the defendant intends to avoid prosecution permanently. Bail forfeiture will often be reversed if the defendant later appears willingly to stand trial.

In many states, bondsmen are empowered to hunt down and bring back defendants who have fled. In some jurisdictions, bondsmen hold virtually unlimited powers and have been permitted by courts to pursue, arrest, and forcibly extradite their charges from foreign jurisdictions without

▸ Bounty hunter Duane "Dog" Chapman, owner of Bounty Hunter International and self-proclaimed "greatest bounty hunter in the world." Bounty hunters collect fees from bail bondsmen, who otherwise stand to forfeit money they have posted for clients who do not appear in court. Chapman, an ex-con born-again Christian, makes a living pursuing felons who fail to appear for their court dates after posting bail through a bondsman. He has over 6,000 captures to his credit. Read more about him at http://www.dogthebountyhunter.com. Would you consider work as a bounty hunter?
Jim Ruymen/REUTERS/Corbis/Bettmann

concern for the due process considerations or statutory limitations that apply to law enforcement officers.[43] Recently, however, a number of states have enacted laws that eliminate for-profit bail bond businesses, replacing them instead with state-operated pretrial services agencies. Visit the Professional Bail Agents of the United States via Web Extra 7–10 at mycrimekit.com to learn more about the job of bail bondsmen and to view the group's code of ethics.

Web EXTRA

Alternatives to Bail

The Eighth Amendment to the U.S. Constitution does not guarantee the opportunity for bail but does state that "[e]xcessive bail shall not be required." Some studies, however, have found that many defendants who are offered the opportunity for bail are unable to raise the money. Years ago, a report by the National Advisory Commission on Criminal Justice Standards and Goals found that as many as 93% of felony defendants in some jurisdictions were unable to make bail.[44]

To extend the opportunity for pretrial release to a greater proportion of nondangerous arrestees, a number of states and the federal government now make available various alternatives to the cash bond system. Alternatives include (1) release on recognizance, (2) property bond, (3) deposit bail, (4) conditional release, (5) third-party custody, (6) unsecured bond, and (7) signature bond.

Release on Recognizance (ROR) **Release on recognizance (ROR)** involves no cash bond, requiring as a guarantee only that the defendant agree in writing to return for further hearings as specified by the court. As an alternative to a cash bond, ROR was tested during the 1960s in a social experiment called the Manhattan Bail Project.[45] In the experiment, not all defendants were eligible for release on their own recognizance; those arrested for serious crimes, including murder, rape, and robbery, and defendants with extensive prior criminal records were excluded from participating in the project. The rest of the defendants were scored and categorized according to a number of "ideal" criteria used as indicators of both dangerousness and likelihood of pretrial flight. Criteria included (1) no previous convictions, (2) residential stability, and (3) good employment record. Those likely to flee were not released.

release on recognizance (ROR)
The pretrial release of a criminal defendant on his or her written promise to appear in court as required. No cash or property bond is required.

Studies of the bail project revealed that it released four times as many defendants before trial as had been freed under the traditional cash bond system.[46] Even more surprising was the finding that only 1% of those released fled from prosecution—the same percentage as for those set free on cash bonds.[47] Later studies, however, were unclear as to the effectiveness of ROR, with some finding a no-show rate as high as 12%.[48]

Property Bonds **Property bonds** substitute other items of value in place of cash. Land, houses, automobiles, stocks, and so on may be consigned to the court as collateral against pretrial flight.

property bond
The setting of bail in the form of land, houses, stocks, or other tangible property. In the event that the defendant absconds before trial, the bond becomes the property of the court.

Deposit Bail Deposit bail, an alternative form of cash bond available in some jurisdictions, places the court in the role of the bondsman, allowing the defendant to post a percentage of the full bail with the court. Unlike private bail bondsmen, court-run deposit bail programs usually return the amount of the deposit except for a small administrative fee (perhaps 1%). If the defendant fails to appear for court, the entire amount of court-ordered bail is forfeited.

Conditional Release Conditional release imposes a set of requirements on the defendant that might include participation in a drug-treatment program; staying away from specified others, such as potential witnesses; and attendance at a regular job. *Release under supervision* is similar to conditional release but adds the stipulation that defendants report to an officer of the court or to a police officer at designated times.

See CJ Exhibit 1 for a discussion of the different people and systems involved in making pretrial release decisions.

Third-Party Custody Third-party custody is a bail bond alternative that assigns custody of the defendant to an individual or agency that promises to ensure his or her later appearance in court.[49] Some pretrial release programs allow attorneys to assume responsibility for their clients in this fashion. If a defendant fails to appear, the attorney's privilege to participate in the program may be ended.

We are under a Constitution, but the Constitution is what the judges say it is, and the judiciary is the safeguard of our liberty and of our property under the Constitution.

—Charles Evans Hughes, Eleventh Chief Justice of the United States, in a speech before the Elmira (New York) Chamber of Commerce, 1907

Unsecured Bonds Unsecured bonds are based on a court-determined dollar amount of bail. Like a credit contract, this bail alternative requires no monetary deposit with the court. The defendant agrees in writing that failure to appear will result in forfeiture of the entire amount of the bond, which might then be taken in seizures of land, personal property, bank accounts, and so on.

CJ Exhibit 1

Nonjudicial Pretrial Release Decisions

In most American jurisdictions, judicial officers decide whether an arrested person will be detained or released. Some jurisdictions, however, allow others to make that decision. Some observers argue that the critical issue is not whether the decision maker is a judge but whether there are clear and appropriate criteria for making the decision, whether the decision maker has adequate information, and whether he or she has been well trained in pretrial release/detention decision making. Nonjudicial decision makers and release/detention mechanisms include the following:

- *Police officers and desk appearance tickets.* Desk appearance tickets, or citations, are summonses given to defendants at the police station, usually for petty offenses or misdemeanor charges. The tickets can greatly reduce the use of pretrial detention and can save the court system a great deal of time by avoiding initial pretrial release or bail hearings in minor cases. However, because they are typically based only on the current charge (and sometimes on a computer search to check for outstanding warrants), high-risk defendants could be released without supervision or monitoring. As computerized access to criminal history information becomes more available, enabling rapid identification of individuals with prior records who pose a risk to the community, desk appearance tickets may become more widely used.
- *Jail administrators.* In many jurisdictions, jail officials have the authority to release (or to refuse to book into jail) arrestees who meet certain criteria. In some localities, jail officials exercise this authority pursuant to a court order that specifies priorities with respect to the categories of defendants who can be admitted to the jail and those who are to be released when the jail population exceeds a court-imposed ceiling. The "automatic release" approach helps minimize jail crowding, but it does so at the risk of releasing some defendants who pose a high risk of becoming fugitives or committing criminal acts. To help minimize these risks, some sheriffs and jail administrators have developed their own pretrial services or "release on recognizance" units with staff who conduct risk assessments based on interviews with arrestees, information from references, and criminal history checks.
- *Bail schedules.* These predetermined schedules set levels of bail (from release on recognizance to amounts of surety bond) based solely on the offense charged. Depending on local practices, release pursuant to a bail schedule may take place at a police station, at the local jail, or at court. This practice saves time for judicial officers and allows rapid release of defendants who can afford to post the bail amount. However, release determinations based solely on the current charge are of dubious value because there is no proven relationship between a particular charge and risk of flight or subsequent crime. Release pursuant to a bail schedule depends simply on the defendant's ability to post the amount of the bond; moreover, when a defendant is released by posting bond, there is generally no procedure for supervision to minimize the risks of nonappearance and subsequent crime.
- *Bail bondsmen.* When a judicial officer sets the amount of bond that a defendant must produce to be released or when bond is set mechanically on the basis of a bail schedule, the real decision makers are often the surety bail bondsmen. If no bondsman will offer bond, the defendant without other sources of money remains in jail. The defendant's ability to pay a bondsman the 10% fee (and sometimes to post collateral) bears no relationship to his or her risk of flight or danger to the community.
- *Pretrial services agencies.* In some jurisdictions, pretrial services agencies have authority to release certain categories of defendants. The authority is usually limited to relatively minor cases, although agencies in a few jurisdictions can release some categories of felony defendants. Because the pretrial services agency can obtain information about the defendant's prior record, community ties, and other pending charges, its decision to release or detain is based on more extensive information and criteria than when the decision is based on a bail schedule. However, because these programs lack the independence of judicial officers, they can be targets of political and public pressure.

Source: Adapted from Barry Mahoney et al., *Pretrial Services Programs: Responsibilities and Potential* (Washington, DC: National Institute of Justice, 2001).

Signature Bonds Signature bonds allow release based on the defendant's written promise to appear. Signature bonds involve no particular assessment of the defendant's dangerousness or likelihood of later appearance in court. They are used only in cases of minor offenses such as traffic-law violations and some petty drug-law violations. Signature bonds may be issued by the arresting officer acting on behalf of the court.

Pretrial Release and Public Safety

Pretrial release is common practice. Approximately 57% of all state-level felony defendants[50] and 66% of all federal felony defendants[51] are released before trial (Figure 4). A growing movement, arguing that defendants released before trial may be dangerous to themselves or to others, seeks to reduce the number of defendants released under any conditions. Advocates of this conservative policy cite a number of studies documenting crimes committed by defendants released on bond. One study found that 16% of defendants released before trial were rearrested, and of those, 30% were arrested more than once.[52] Another study determined that as many as

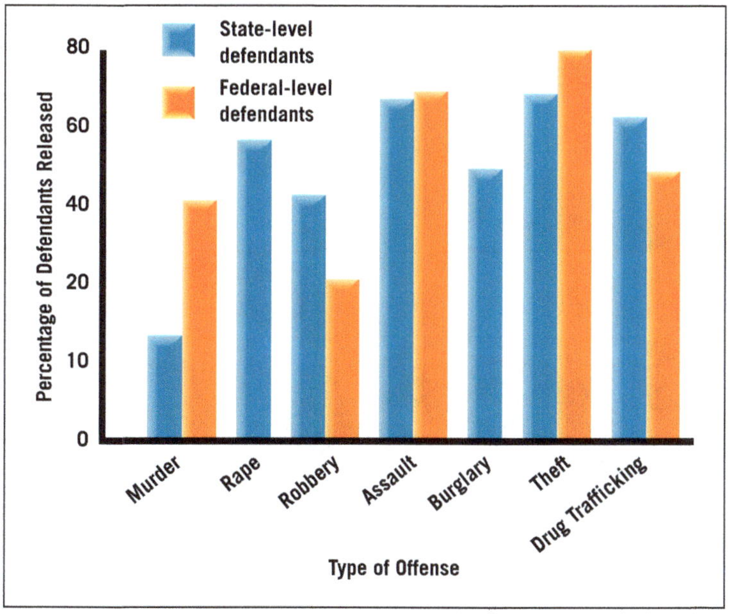

FIGURE 4
Proportion of State and Federal Felony Defendants Released before Trial.
Note: Federal pretrial release statistics are not available for the crimes of rape and burglary.
Sources: Tracey Kyckelhahn and Thomas H. Cohen, *Felony Defendants in Large Urban Counties, 2004* (Washington, DC: Bureau of Justice Statistics, 2008); and Thomas H. Cohen and Brian A. Reaves, *Pretrial Release of Felony Defendants in State Courts* (Washington, DC: Bureau of Justice Statistics, 2007).

41% of those released before trial for serious crimes, such as rape and robbery, were rearrested before their trial date.[53] Not surprisingly, such studies generally find that the longer the time spent out on bail before trial, the greater is the likelihood of misconduct.

In response to findings like these, some states have enacted **danger laws**, which limit the right to bail to certain kinds of offenders.[54] Other states, including Arizona, California, Colorado, Florida, and Illinois, have approved constitutional amendments restricting the use of bail.[55] Most such provisions exclude defendants charged with certain crimes from being eligible for bail and demand that other defendants being considered for bail meet stringent conditions. Some states combine these strictures with tough release conditions designed to keep close control over defendants before trial.

danger law
A law intended to prevent the pretrial release of criminal defendants judged to represent a danger to others in the community.

The 1984 federal Bail Reform Act allows federal judges to assess the danger of an accused to the community and to deny bail to defendants who are thought to be dangerous. In the words of the act, a suspect held in pretrial custody on federal criminal charges must be detained if "after a hearing . . . he is found to pose a risk of flight and a danger to others or the community and if no condition of release can give reasonable assurances against these contingencies."[56] Defendants seeking bail must demonstrate a high likelihood of later court appearance. The act also requires that a defendant have a speedy first appearance and that a detention hearing be held in conjunction with the initial appearance if he or she is to be detained.

In the 1990 case of ***U.S.* v. *Montalvo-Murillo***,[57] however, a defendant who was not provided with a detention hearing at the time of his first appearance and was subsequently released by an appeals court was found to have no "right" to freedom because of this "minor" statutory violation. The Supreme Court held that "unless it has a substantial influence on the outcome of the proceedings . . . failure to comply with the Act's prompt hearing provision does not require release of a person who should otherwise be detained" because "[a]utomatic release contravenes the statutory purpose of providing fair bail procedures while protecting the public's safety and assuring a defendant's appearance at trial."[58]

Court challenges to the constitutionality of pretrial detention legislation have not met with much success. The U.S. Supreme Court case of *U.S.* v. *Hazzard* (1984),[59] decided only a few months after enactment of federal bail reform, held that Congress was justified in providing for denial of bail to offenders who represent a danger to the community. Later cases have supported the presumption of flight, which federal law presupposes for certain types of defendants.[60]

The Grand Jury

The federal government and about half of the states use grand juries as part of the pretrial process. Grand juries comprise private citizens (often 23 in number) who hear evidence presented by the prosecution. Grand juries serve primarily as filters to eliminate from further processing any cases for which there is not sufficient evidence.

I have tried to minimize what I feel is one of the less desirable aspects of the job . . . that judges can become isolated from the people whose lives their decisions affect.
—Stephen Breyer
U.S. Supreme Court Justice

A grand jury in action. Grand jury proceedings are generally very informal, as this picture shows. What is the grand jury's job?
David Young-Wolff/Getty Images, Inc./Riser

In early times, grand juries served a far different purpose. The grand jury system began in England in 1166 as a way of identifying law violators. Lacking a law enforcement agency with investigative authority, the government looked to the grand jury as a source of information on criminal activity in the community. Even today, grand juries in most jurisdictions may initiate prosecution independently of the prosecutor, although they rarely do.

Grand jury hearings are held in secret, and the defendant is generally not afforded the opportunity to appear before the grand jury.[61] Similarly, the defense has no opportunity to cross-examine prosecution witnesses. Grand juries have the power to subpoena witnesses and to mandate a review of books, records, and other documents crucial to their investigation.

After hearing the evidence, the grand jury votes on the indictment (a formal listing of proposed charges) presented to it by the prosecution. If the majority of grand jury members agree to forward the indictment to the trial court, it becomes a "true bill" on which further prosecution will turn.

The Preliminary Hearing

States that do not use grand juries rely instead on a preliminary hearing "for charging defendants in a fashion that is less cumbersome and arguably more protective of the innocent."[62] In these jurisdictions, the prosecutor files an accusatory document called an *information*, or complaint, against the accused. A preliminary hearing is then held to determine whether there is probable cause to hold the defendant for trial. A few states, notably Georgia and Tennessee, use both the grand jury mechanism and a preliminary hearing as a "double check against the possibility of unwarranted prosecution."[63]

Although the preliminary hearing is not nearly as elaborate as a criminal trial, it has many of the same characteristics. The defendant is taken before a lower-court judge, who summarizes the charges and reviews the rights to which all criminal defendants are entitled. The prosecution may present witnesses and offers evidence in support of the complaint. The defendant is afforded the right to testify and may also call witnesses.

competent to stand trial
A finding by a court, when the defendant's sanity at the time of trial is at issue, that the defendant has sufficient present ability to consult with his or her attorney with a reasonable degree of rational understanding and that the defendant has a rational as well as factual understanding of the proceedings against him or her.

The primary purpose of the preliminary hearing is to give the defendant an opportunity to challenge the legal basis for his or her detention. At this point, defendants who appear to be or claim to be mentally incompetent may be ordered to undergo further evaluation to determine whether they are competent to stand trial. Being **competent to stand trial** may become an issue when a defendant appears to be incapable of understanding the proceedings or is unable to assist in his or her own defense due to mental disease or defect.

In 2003, the U.S. Supreme Court placed strict limits on the government's power to forcibly medicate some mentally ill defendants to make them competent to stand trial.[64] In the case of *Sell* v. *U.S.*,[65] the Court ruled that the use of antipsychotic drugs on a nonviolent offender who does not represent a danger while institutionalized must be in the defendant's best medical interest and be "substantially unlikely" to cause side effects that might compromise the fairness of the trial.

Barring a finding of mental incompetence, all that is required for the wheels of justice to grind forward is a demonstration "sufficient to justify a prudent man's belief that the suspect has committed or was committing an offense" within the jurisdiction of the court.[66] If the magistrate finds enough evidence to justify a trial, the defendant is bound over to the grand jury. In states that do not require grand jury review, the defendant is sent directly to the trial court. If the complaint against the defendant cannot be substantiated during the preliminary hearing, he or she is released. A release is not a bar to further prosecution, however, and the defendant may be rearrested if further evidence comes to light.

Arraignment and the Plea

Arraignment

Once an indictment has been returned or an information has been filed, the accused will be formally arraigned. Arraignment is "the first appearance of the defendant before the court that has the authority to conduct a trial."[67] Arraignment is generally a brief process with two purposes: (1) to once again inform the defendant of the specific charges against him or her and (2) to allow the defendant to enter a **plea**. The Federal Rules of Criminal Procedure allow for one of three types of pleas to be entered: guilty, not guilty, and *nolo contendere*. A ***nolo contendere*** (no-contest) plea is much the same as a guilty plea. A defendant who pleads "no contest" is immediately convicted and may be sentenced just as though he or she had pleaded guilty. A no-contest plea, however, is not an admission of guilt and provides one major advantage to defendants: It may not be used later as a basis for civil proceedings that seek monetary or other damages against the defendant.

Some defendants refuse to enter any plea and are said to "stand mute." Standing mute is a defense strategy that is rarely employed. Defendants who choose this alternative simply do not answer the request for a plea; however, for procedural purposes, a defendant who stands mute is considered to have entered a plea of not guilty.

plea
In criminal proceedings, the defendant's formal answer in court to the charge contained in a complaint, information, or indictment that he or she is guilty of the offense charged, is not guilty of the offense charged, or does not contest the charge.

nolo contendere
A plea of "no contest." A no-contest plea is used when the defendant does not wish to contest conviction. Because the plea does not admit guilt, however, it cannot provide the basis for later civil suits that might follow a criminal conviction.

Plea Bargaining

Guilty pleas often are not as straightforward as they might seem and are typically arrived at only after complex negotiations. **Plea bargaining** is this process of negotiations that usually involves the defendant, the prosecutor, and the defense counsel and is founded on the mutual interests of all involved. Defense attorneys and their clients will agree to a plea of guilty when they are unsure of their ability to win acquittal at trial. Prosecutors may be willing to bargain because the evidence they have against the defendant is weaker than they would like it to be. Plea bargaining offers prosecutors the additional advantage of a quick conviction without the need to commit the time and resources necessary for trial. Benefits to the accused include the possibility of reduced or combined charges, reduced defense costs, and a shorter sentence than might otherwise be anticipated.

plea bargaining
The process of negotiating an agreement among the defendant, the prosecutor, and the court as to an appropriate plea and associated sentence in a given case. Plea bargaining circumvents the trial process and dramatically reduces the time required for the resolution of a criminal case.

The U.S. Supreme Court has held that a guilty plea constitutes conviction.[68] To validate the conviction, negotiated pleas require judicial consent. Judges often accept pleas that are the result of a bargaining process because such pleas reduce the court's workload. Although few judges are willing to guarantee a sentence before a plea is entered, most prosecutors and criminal trial lawyers know what sentences to expect from typical pleas.

Bargained pleas are commonplace. Some surveys have found that 90% of all criminal cases prepared for trial are eventually resolved through a negotiated plea.[69] In a study of 37 big-city prosecutors, the Bureau of Justice Statistics found that for every 100 adults arrested on a felony charge, half were eventually convicted of either a felony or a misdemeanor.[70] Of all convictions, fully 94% were the result of a plea; only 6% of convictions were the result of a criminal trial.

After a guilty plea has been entered, it may be withdrawn with the consent of the court. In the case of *Henderson* v. *Morgan* (1976),[71] for example, the U.S. Supreme Court permitted a defendant to withdraw a plea of guilty nine years after it had been given. In that case, the defendant had originally entered a plea of guilty to second-degree murder but had attempted to withdraw it before trial. Reasons for wanting to withdraw the plea included the defendant's belief that he had not been completely advised as to the nature of the charge or the sentence he might receive as a result of the plea.

Some Supreme Court decisions, however, have enhanced the prosecutor's authority in the bargaining process by declaring that defendants cannot capriciously withdraw negotiated pleas.[72] Other rulings have supported discretionary actions by prosecutors in which sentencing recommendations were retracted even after bargains had been struck.[73] Some lower-court cases have upheld the government's authority to withdraw from a negotiated plea when the defendant fails to live up to certain conditions.[74] Conditions may include requiring the defendant to provide information on other criminals, on criminal cartels, or on activities of smugglers.

Although it is generally agreed that bargained pleas should relate in some way to the original charges, they do not always do so. Entered pleas may be chosen for the punishments likely to be associated with them rather than for their accuracy in describing the criminal offenses in which the defendants were involved.[75] This is especially true when the defendant wants to minimize the socially stigmatizing impact of the offense. For example, a charge of indecent liberties, in which the defendant is accused of sexual misconduct, may be pleaded out as assault, and such a plea, which takes advantage of the fact that indecent liberties can be considered a form of sexual assault, would effectively disguise the true nature of the offense.

Even though the Supreme Court has endorsed plea bargaining, the public sometimes views it suspiciously. Law-and-order advocates, who generally favor harsh punishments and long jail terms, claim that plea bargaining results in unjustifiably light sentences. As a consequence, prosecutors who regularly engage in the practice rarely advertise it. Plea bargaining can be a powerful prosecutorial tool, but this power carries with it the potential for misuse. Because they circumvent the trial process, plea bargains can be abused by prosecutors and defense attorneys who are more interested in the speedy resolution of cases than they are in seeing justice done. Carried to the extreme, plea bargaining may result in defendants being convicted of crimes they did not commit. Although it is rare, innocent defendants (especially those with prior criminal records) who think a jury will convict them—for whatever reason—may plead guilty to reduced charges to avoid a trial. In an effort to protect defendants against hastily arranged pleas, the Federal Rules of Criminal Procedure require judges to (1) inform the defendant of the various rights he or she is surrendering by pleading guilty, (2) determine that the plea is voluntary, (3) disclose any plea agreements, and (4) make sufficient inquiry to ensure there is a factual basis for the plea.[76]

There is no such thing as justice—in or out of court.
—*Clarence Darrow (1857–1938)*

Bargained pleas can take many forms and can be quite inventive. The case of Jeffrey Morse illustrates an unusual attempt at a bargained plea. In 1998, Morse, a convicted sex offender, petitioned courts in Illinois for permission to leave jail before sentencing for sexual assaults on two young girls so that he could undergo surgical castration. A judge agreed, and he was surgically castrated in a 45-minute outpatient procedure. Morse's mother noted that the surgery was done in an effort to avoid a long prison sentence. "He will cut whatever bodily part he has to [to] be able to reduce his sentence," she said.[77] Two months later, however, Kane County Judge Donald C. Hudson refused to show leniency for Morse; instead, Judge Hudson sentenced Morse to 26 years in prison, saying that he wouldn't "place a seal of approval on trading body parts for a lesser sentence."[78]

Summary

- Throughout the United States, there are two judicial systems. One consists of state and local courts established under the authority of state and local governments. The other is the federal court system, created by Congress under the authority of the Constitution of the United States. This dual-court system historically results from general agreement among the nation's founders about the need for individual states to retain significant legislative authority and judicial autonomy separate from federal control.
- In most states, criminal courts can be classified within a three-tiered structure of two trial court echelons and an appellate level. There are many differences between and among state court systems, however. So-called reform states are characterized by relatively streamlined judicial systems consisting of trial courts of limited and general jurisdiction, supplemented by one or two appellate court levels. Nonreform, or traditional, states tend to retain judicial systems that are a conglomeration of multilevel and sometimes redundant courts with poorly defined jurisdictions. Regardless of their organizational style, state courts have virtually unlimited power to decide nearly every type of case, subject only to limitations imposed by the U.S. Constitution, their own state constitutions, and state law.

- Today's federal judiciary consists of three levels: (1) U.S. district courts, (2) U.S. courts of appeal, and (3) the U.S. Supreme Court. Federal courts, located principally in larger cities, decide only those cases over which the Constitution gives them authority. The highest federal court, the U.S. Supreme Court, is located in Washington, D.C., and hears cases only on appeal from lower courts.
- Pretrial activities involve the first appearance, the grand jury hearing (in some states), the preliminary hearing, the arraignment, and the plea, all of which are described in this chapter. Before trial, one of the most important decisions facing the courts is that of pretrial release. In considering whether a criminal defendant should be released prior to trial, courts must balance the rights of the unconvicted defendant against the potential for future harm that person may represent. Judicial officers may assess the risks associated with pretrial release by considering (1) seriousness of the current charge, (2) defendant's prior criminal record, (3) personal information about the defendant, and (4) information about available supervisory options if the defendant is released.

Key Concepts

Terms

appeal
appellate jurisdiction
bail bond
community court
competent to stand trial
court of last resort
danger law
dispute-resolution center
federal court system
first appearance
judicial review
jurisdiction
nolo contendere
original jurisdiction
plea
plea bargaining
pretrial release
property bond
release on recognizance (ROR)
state court administrator
state court system
trial *de novo*

Cases

County of Riverside v. *McLaughlin*
Herrera v. *Collins*
Keeney v. *Tamayo-Reyes*
Marbury v. *Madison*
McNabb v. *U.S.*
U.S. v. *Montalvo-Murillo*

Questions for Review

1. How did the American court system develop? What are some of the unique features of American court history? What is the dual-court system? Why do we have a dual-court system in America?
2. How is a typical state court system structured? What different types of courts might exist at the state level, and what kinds of jurisdiction might they have?
3. What are the three levels characteristic of the federal judiciary? What are some of the differences between the state and federal court systems in America?
4. What steps are typically taken during pretrial activities (that is, before the start of a criminal trial)? What key factors are likely to be considered by judges attempting to assess the risks associated with the possible pretrial release of a criminal defendant?

To participate in an online discussion of these topics and others, join the CJ Brief e-mail discussion list at mycrimekit.com.

Web Quest

Visit the Federal Judiciary website run by the Administrative Office of the United States Courts at http://www.uscourts.gov. Using the materials available there, describe the purpose and history of the Administrative Office, the courts it serves, and the nature of the services it provides.

Also visit the National Center for State Courts at http://www.ncsconline.org. What is the mission of the NCSC? What are the divisions of the NCSC? What does each division do? What "affiliated associations" are listed on the NCSC home page? What is the purpose of each of these associations? Write down what you have learned, and submit it to your instructor if asked to do so.

To complete this Web Quest online, go to the Web Quest module in Chapter 7 of the *Criminal Justice: A Brief Introduction* Companion Website at mycrimekit.com.

Notes

1. Quoted in Joan Biskupic, "Courts Can't Unravel All Election Snags," *USA Today*, September 17, 2000.
2. Details for this story come from "Nichols to Make Court Appearance Today," CNN.com, March 15, 2005. Web posted at http://www.cnn.com/2005/LAW/03/14/atlanta.shooting (accessed April 5, 2008).
3. Don Babwin, "Man Claims to Have Slain Judge's Family," ABC News, March 10, 2005. Web posted at http://abcnews.go.com/US/wireStory?id5568738 (accessed April 5, 2006).
4. "Police Match DNA from Lefkow Killings to Suicide Victim," WISCTV.com, March 10, 2005. Web posted at http://www.channel3000.com/news/4270937/detail.html (accessed July 5, 2008).
5. Law Enforcement Assistance Administration, *Two Hundred Years of American Criminal Justice* (Washington, DC: U.S. Government Printing Office, 1976), p. 31.
6. Ibid.
7. Ibid.
8. Ibid., p. 32.
9. Ibid.
10. David B. Rottman, Carol R. Flango, and R. Shedine Lockley, *State Court Organization, 1993* (Washington, DC: Bureau of Justice Statistics, 1995), p. 11.
11. Thomas A. Henderson et al., *The Significance of Judicial Structure: The Effects of Unification on Trial Court Operations* (Washington, DC: National Institute of Justice, 1984).
12. Ibid.
13. In 1957, only 13 states had permanent intermediate appellate courts. Now, all but 12 states have these courts, and North Dakota is operating one on a temporary basis to assist in handling the rising appellate caseload in that state. See Rottman, Flango, and Lockley, *State Court Organization, 1993*, p. 5.
14. *Keeney* v. *Tamayo-Reyes*, 504 U.S. 1 (1992).
15. *Herrera* v. *Collins*, 113 S.Ct. 853, 122 L.Ed.2d 203 (1993).
16. H. Ted Rubin, *The Courts: Fulcrum of the Justice System* (Pacific Palisades, CA: Goodyear, 1976), p. 198.
17. Martin Wright, *Justice for Victims and Offenders* (Bristol, PA: Open University Press, 1991), p. 56.
18. "Bridging the Gap between Communities and Courts." Web posted at http://www.communityjustice.org (accessed November 22, 2008).
19. Wright, *Justice for Victims and Offenders,* pp. 104 and 106.
20. Most of the information and some of the wording in this section come from Administrative Office of the U.S. Courts, "Understanding the Federal Courts." Web posted at http://www.uscourts.gov/UFC99.pdf (accessed April 2, 2008).
21. Administrative Office of the U.S. Courts, "U.S. District Courts: Criminal Cases and Defendants Filed, Terminated, Pending." Web posted at http://www.uscourts.gov/judicialfactsfigures/2007/Table501.pdf (accessed September 4, 2008).
22. Administrative Office of the U.S. Courts, "U.S. District Courts: Civil Cases Filed, Terminated, Pending." Web posted at http://www.uscourts.gov/judicialfactsfigures/2007/Table401.pdf (accessed September 4, 2008).
23. Administrative Office of the U.S. Courts, op. cit.
24. Administrative Office of the U.S. Courts, "Comparison of Average Salaries of Deans and Senior Professors of Top Law Schools with U.S. District Court Judges." Web posted at http://www.uscourts.gov/judicialcompensation/payfactsheet.html, no date (accessed July 30, 2008).
25. See American Bar Association, *Federal Judicial Pay Erosion: A Report on the Need for Reform* (Chicago: ABA, 2001).
26. Although the Ethics Reform Act of 1989 was supposed to allow for a cost-of-living increase in federal judicial salaries, Congress blocked the automatic increases from 1995 to 1999 because they also applied to the salaries of members of Congress and were seen as politically unpalatable.
27. Justice John Roberts, "2005 Year-End Report on the Federal Judiciary," *The Third Branch*, Vol. 38, No. 1 (January 2006). Web posted at http://www.uscourts.gov/ttb/jan06ttb/yearend/index.html (accessed March 30, 2006).
28. Much of the information and some of the wording in this section come from Administrative Office of the U.S. Courts, "About the Federal Courts." Web posted at www.uscourts.gov/about.html (accessed October 4, 2008).
29. Stephen L. Wasby, *The Supreme Court in the Federal Judicial System*, 3rd ed. (Chicago: Nelson-Hall, 1988), p. 58.
30. "Workload of the Courts: The Federal Courts' Caseload," *The Third Branch*, Vol. 38, No. 1 (January 2006), appendix. Web posted at http://www.uscourts.gov/ttb/jan06ttb/appendix/index.html (accessed August 28, 2006).
31. *Blakely* v. *Washington*, 542 U.S. 296 (2004).
32. *U.S.* v. *Booker*, 543 U.S. 220 (2005).
33. "Workload of the Courts: The Federal Courts' Caseload."
34. Administrative Office of the U.S. Courts, "Federal Judiciary Says New Judgeships Needed," March 13, 2007. Web posted at http://www.uscourts.gov/Press_Releases/judconf031307.html (accessed September 5, 2008).
35. *The Supreme Court of the United States* (Washington, DC: U.S. Government Printing Office, no date), p. 4.
36. *Marbury* v. *Madison*, 1 Cranch 137 (1803).
37. *Mapp* v. *Ohio*, 367 U.S. 643 (1961).
38. *Arraignment* is also a term used to describe an initial appearance, although we will reserve use of that word to describe a later court appearance following the defendant's indictment by a grand jury or the filing of an information by the prosecutor.
39. *McNabb* v. *U.S.*, 318 U.S. 332 (1943).
40. *County of Riverside* v. *McLaughlin*, 111 S.Ct. 1661 (1991).
41. *White* v. *Maryland*, 373 U.S. 59 (1963).
42. Much of the information in this section comes from Barry Mahoney et al., *Pretrial Services Programs: Responsibilities and Potential* (Washington, DC: National Institute of Justice, 2001).
43. *Taylor* v. *Taintor*, 83 U.S. 66 (1873).
44. National Advisory Commission on Criminal Justice Standards and Goals, *The Courts* (Washington, DC: U.S. Government Printing Office, 1973), p. 37.
45. C. Ares, A. Rankin, and H. Sturz, "The Manhattan Bail Project: An Interim Report on the Use of Pretrial Parole," *New York University Law Review*, Vol. 38 (January 1963), pp. 68–95.
46. H. Zeisel, "Bail Revisited," *American Bar Foundation Research Journal*, Vol. 4 (1979), pp. 769–789.
47. Ibid.
48. "Twelve Percent of Those Freed on Low Bail Fail to Appear," *New York Times*, December 2, 1983, p. 1.
49. Bureau of Justice Statistics, *Report to the Nation on Crime and Justice*, 2nd ed. (Washington, DC: U.S. Department of Justice, 1988), p. 76.
50. Tracey Kyckelhahn and Thomas H. Cohen, *Felony Defendants in Large Urban Counties, 2004* (Washington, DC: Bureau of Justice Statistics, 2008), p. 2. Web posted at http://www.ojp.gov/bjs/pub/pdf/fdluc04.pdf (accessed June 4, 2006). See also Thomas H. Cohen and Brian A. Reaves, *Pretrial Release of Felony Defendants in State Courts* (Washington, DC: Bureau of Justice Statistics, 2007).
51. John Scalia, *Federal Pretrial Release and Detention, 1996* (Washington, DC: Bureau of Justice Statistics, 1999), p. 1. Web posted at http://www.ojp.usdoj.gov/bjs/pub/pdf/fprd96.pdf (accessed January 25, 2004).
52. Donald E. Pryor and Walter F. Smith, "Significant Research Findings Concerning Pretrial Release," *Pretrial Issues*, Vol. 4, No. 1 (Washington, DC: Pretrial Services Resource Center, February 1982). See also the Pretrial Services Resource Center on the Web at http://www.pretrial.org/mainpage.htm.
53. BJS, *Report to the Nation on Crime and Justice*, p. 77.
54. According to Joseph B. Vaughn and Victor E. Kappeler, the first such legislation was the 1970 District of Columbia Court Reform and Criminal Procedure Act. See Vaughn and Kappeler, "The Denial of

Bail: Pre-Trial Preventive Detention," *Criminal Justice Research Bulletin*, Vol. 3, No. 6 (Huntsville, TX: Sam Houston State University, 1987), p. 1.
55. Ibid.
56. Bail Reform Act of 1984, 18 U.S.C. 3142(e).
57. *U.S.* v. *Montalvo-Murillo*, 495 U.S. 711 (1990).
58. Ibid., syllabus.
59. *U.S.* v. *Hazzard*, 35 CrL. 2217 (1984).
60. See, for example, *U.S.* v. *Motamedi*, 37 CrL. 2394, CA 9 (1985).
61. A few states now have laws that permit the defendant to appear before the grand jury.
62. John M. Scheb and John M. Scheb II, *American Criminal Law* (St. Paul, MN: West, 1996), p. 31.
63. Ibid.
64. The information in this paragraph is adapted from Linda Greenhouse, "Supreme Court Limits Forced Medication of Some for Trial," *New York Times*, June 16, 2003. Web posted at http://www.nytimes.com/2003/06/17/politics/17DRUG.html (accessed June 17, 2003).
65. *Sell* v. *U.S.*, 123 S.Ct. 2174 (2003).
66. Federal Rules of Criminal Procedure, 5.1(a).
67. Scheb and Scheb, *American Criminal Law*, p. 32.
68. *Kercheval* v. *U.S.*, 274 U.S. 220, 223, 47 S.Ct. 582, 583 (1927); *Boykin* v. *Alabama*, 395 U.S. 238 (1969); and *Dickerson* v. *New Banner Institute, Inc.*, 460 U.S. 103 (1983).
69. Bureau of Justice Statistics, *The Prosecution of Felony Arrests* (Washington, DC: U.S. Government Printing Office, 1983).
70. Barbara Boland et al., *The Prosecution of Felony Arrests, 1987* (Washington, DC: U.S. Government Printing Office, May 1990).
71. *Henderson* v. *Morgan*, 426 U.S. 637 (1976).
72. *Santobello* v. *New York*, 404 U.S. 257 (1971).
73. *Mabry* v. *Johnson*, 467 U.S. 504 (1984).
74. *U.S.* v. *Baldacchino*, 762 F.2d 170 (1st Cir. 1985); *U.S.* v. *Reardon*, 787 F.2d 512 (10th Cir. 1986); and *U.S.* v. *Donahey*, 529 F.2d 831 (11th Cir. 1976).
75. For a classic discussion of such considerations, see David Sudnow, "Normal Crimes: Sociological Features of the Penal Code in a Public Defender Office," *Social Problems*, Vol. 123, No. 3 (winter 1965), p. 255.
76. Federal Rules of Criminal Procedure, No. 11.
77. "A Desperate Act," *Prime Time Live*, ABCNews.com, January 28, 1998. Web posted at http://archive.abcnews.go.com/onair/PTL/html-files/transcripts/ptl0128c.html (accessed July 21, 1999).
78. Dan Rozek, "Castration Doesn't Gain Leniency for Pedophile," *Chicago Sun-Times*, March 4, 1998.

The Courtroom Work Group and the Criminal Trial 8

Chapter Outline

- Introduction
- The Courtroom Work Group: Professional Courtroom Actors
- Outsiders: Nonprofessional Courtroom Participants
- The Criminal Trial
- Stages in a Criminal Trial
- Improvement of the Adjudication Process

Learning Objectives

After reading this chapter, you should be able to

- Identify and explain the roles of professional members of the courtroom work group.
- Identify and explain the roles of nonprofessional or nonjudicial courtroom participants.
- Describe the nature and purpose of the criminal trial.
- Identify the various stages of a criminal trial.
- Describe methods that have been suggested for improving the adjudication process.

> *"Lives are lost and won in the courts, lost and won in the law—every day, everywhere. Most of us seldom really think about this. But in the jury room, the thought cannot be avoided, since there you learn that justice doesn't merely happen (neatly, reliably, like a crystal taking shape in a distant vacuum); justice is, rather, done, made, manufactured. Made by imperfect, wrangling, venal and virtuous human beings, using whatever means are at their disposal. In the jury room, you discover that the whole edifice of social order stands, finally, on handicraft—there is no magic, no mathematics, no science, no angelic fixer who checks our juridical homework. This is a frightening thing, not least because any one of us could be accused of a crime."*
>
> *—D. Graham Burnett, jury foreman*[1]

From Chapter 8 of *Criminal Justice: A Brief Introduction*, Eighth Edition. Frank Schmalleger.

Introduction

▶▶▶ Hear the author discuss this chapter at mycrimekit.com.

On April 1, 2006, in what some may have thought was a cruel April Fool's joke, the *San Francisco Chronicle* announced that tenacious supporters of Scott Peterson—the young Modesto, California, man sentenced to die in 2005 for the Christmas Eve murders of his wife, Laci, and the couple's unborn son who was to be named Conner[2]—were offering a $250,000 reward for information that could exonerate Peterson.[3] The award was offered through the Peterson Family Fund website.

The American criminal justice system is theater to the world.
—Alan Dershowitz
Harvard University law professor

About the same time, Scott Peterson's mother, Jackie Peterson, filed papers at Stanislaus County Superior Court seeking $35,000 in reimbursement from the estate of Laci Peterson for almost two years of mortgage payments and other costs that she said she had paid to maintain the couple's home after her son's arrest in 2003.[4] The house was sold in July 2005.

Laci Peterson was 27 years old and eight months' pregnant when she disappeared on Christmas Eve of 2002. Her decomposed body was found four months later, washed up on a beach near the town of Richmond, California. The remains of Laci's unborn son were found nearby. Although the evidence against Peterson seemed strong, experts agree that it was mostly circumstantial and centered on an affair that he had been having with a woman named Amber Frey. Peterson, who is on death row at California's San Quentin State Prison, has always maintained his innocence and is appealing his conviction and sentence as the book that is the source

▲ Scott Peterson (top left) with defense attorney Mark Geragos; Scott's wife, Laci; and Judge Alfred A. Delucchi, who presided over Peterson's 2004 California murder trial. Peterson, age 30, was convicted of killing his 27-year-old wife and their unborn son. Their bodies, which were dumped into San Francisco Bay on Christmas Eve of 2002, washed ashore four months later near the spot where Peterson said he had been fishing when Laci disappeared. What was the evidence against Peterson?
Modesto Bee/Bart Ah You/*AP Wide World Photos; Modesto Police Department Handout/AP Wide World Photos;* Tribune News/Nick Lammers/*AP Wide World Photos*

of this chapter goes to press. "All of us remain deeply committed to Scott's innocence and to finding Laci's real killer," Lee Peterson, Scott Peterson's father, said in a recent statement.[5]

Not everyone in the Peterson family believes in Scott's innocence, however. In her book, *Blood Brother: 33 Reasons My Brother Scott Peterson Is Guilty,* Peterson's sister, Anne Bird, outlines the case against Scott and provides intimate details about the relationship between Scott and Laci, including what she believes led up to the killings.[6] The Peterson case captivated the country and made headlines worldwide. See a copy of the criminal indictment against Scott Peterson at Library Extra 8–1 at mycrimekit.com, and hear the verdicts against him being read at Web Extra 8–1 at mycrimekit.com.

Library EXTRA

Web EXTRA

The Courtroom Work Group: Professional Courtroom Actors

To the public eye, criminal trials frequently appear to be well-managed events even though they may entail quite a bit of drama. Like plays on a stage, trials involve many participants, each of whom has a different role to fill. Unlike such plays, however, they are real-life events, and the impact that a trial's outcome has on people's lives can be far-reaching.

Participants in a criminal trial can be divided into two categories: professionals and outsiders. The professionals are the official courtroom actors, who are well versed in criminal trial practice and who set the stage for and conduct the business of the court. Judges, prosecuting attorneys, defense attorneys, public defenders, and others who earn a living serving the court fall into this category. Professional courtroom actors are also called the **courtroom work group**. Some writers have pointed out that aside from statutory requirements and ethical considerations, courtroom interaction among professionals involves an implicit recognition of informal rules of civility, cooperation, and shared goals.[7] Hence even within the adversarial framework of a criminal trial, the courtroom work group is dedicated to bringing the procedure to a successful close.[8]

courtroom work group
The professional courtroom actors, including judges, prosecuting attorneys, defense attorneys, public defenders, and others who earn a living serving the court.

In contrast, outsiders—those trial participants who are only temporarily involved with the court—are generally unfamiliar with courtroom organization and trial procedure. Jurors and witnesses are outsiders; defendants and victims are also outsiders, even though they may have a greater personal investment in the outcome of the trial than anyone else.

This chapter examines trial court activities, building on the pretrial process. To place the trial process within its human context, however, the various roles of the many participants in a criminal trial are discussed first. Learn more about professional and nonprofessional courtroom participants at Web Extra 8–2 at mycrimekit.com.

Web EXTRA

The Judge

The Role of the Judge

The trial **judge** has the primary duty of ensuring justice. The American Bar Association (ABA) *Standards for Criminal Justice* describes the duties of the trial judge as follows: "The trial judge has the responsibility for safeguarding both the rights of the accused and the interests of the public in the administration of criminal justice. . . . The purpose of a criminal trial is to determine whether the prosecution has established the guilt of the accused as required by law, and the trial judge should not allow the proceedings to be used for any other purpose."[9]

judge
An elected or appointed public official who presides over a court of law and who is authorized to hear and sometimes to decide cases and to conduct trials.

In the courtroom, the judge holds ultimate authority, ruling on matters of law, weighing objections from both sides, deciding on the admissibility of evidence, and disciplining anyone who challenges the order of the court. In most jurisdictions, judges also sentence offenders after a verdict has been returned; in some states, judges decide guilt or innocence for defendants who waive a jury trial.

Most state jurisdictions have a chief judge who, besides serving on the bench as a trial judge, must also manage the court system. Management includes hiring staff, scheduling sessions of court, ensuring the adequate training of subordinate judges, and coordinating activities with other courtroom actors. Chief judges usually assume their position by virtue of seniority and rarely have any formal training in management. Hence the managerial effectiveness of a chief judge is often a matter of personality and dedication more than anything else.

Judicial Selection

Judges at the federal level are nominated by the president of the United States and take their place on the bench only after confirmation by the Senate. At the state level, things work somewhat differently. Depending on the jurisdiction, state judgeships are won through either popular election or political (usually gubernatorial) appointment. The processes involved in judicial selection at the state level are set by law.

Both judicial election and appointment have been criticized because each system allows politics to enter the judicial arena—although in somewhat different ways. Under the election system, judicial candidates must receive the endorsement of their parties, generate contributions, and manage an effective campaign. Under the appointment system, judicial hopefuls must be in favor with incumbent politicians to receive appointments. Because partisan politics plays a role in both systems, critics have claimed that sitting judges can rarely be as neutral as they should be. They carry to the bench with them campaign promises, personal indebtedness, and possible political agendas.

To hear patiently, to weigh deliberately and dispassionately, and to decide impartially; these are the chief duties of a judge.
—Albert Pike (1809–1891)

To counter some of these problems, a number of states have adopted the Missouri Plan (or the Missouri Bar Plan) for judicial selection,[10] which combines elements of both election and appointment. It requires candidates for judicial vacancies to undergo screening by a nonpartisan state judicial nominating committee. Candidates selected by the committee are reviewed by an arm of the governor's office, which selects a final list of names for appointment. Incumbent judges must face the electorate after a specified term in office. They then run unopposed in nonpartisan elections in which only their records may be considered. Voters have the choice of allowing a judge to continue in office or asking that another be appointed to take his or her place. Because the Missouri Plan provides for periodic public review of judicial performance, it is also called the *merit plan of judicial selection.*

Judicial Qualifications

A few decades ago, many states did not require any special training, education, or other qualifications for judges. Anyone (even someone without a law degree) who won election or was appointed could assume a judgeship. Today, however, almost all states require that judges in general jurisdiction and appellate courts hold a law degree, be a licensed attorney, and be a member of their state bar association. Many states also require newly elected judges to attend state-sponsored training sessions dealing with such subjects as courtroom procedure, evidence, dispute resolution, judicial writing, administrative record keeping, and ethics.

While most states provide instruction to meet the needs of trial judges, other organizations also provide specialized training. The National Judicial College (NJC), located on the campus of the University of Nevada at Reno, is one such institution. NJC was established in 1963 by the Joint Committee for the Effective Administration of Justice, chaired by Justice Tom C. Clark of the U.S. Supreme Court.[11] More than 3,000 judges enroll annually in courses offered by NJC, and many courses are offered online. NJC, in collaboration with the National Council of Juvenile and Family Court Judges and the University of Nevada at Reno, offers the nation's only advanced judicial degree programs, leading to a master's degree and Ph.D. in judicial studies.[12] Visit the NJC via **Web Extra 8–3** at mycrimekit.com.

Web EXTRA

In some parts of the United States, lower-court judges, such as justices of the peace, local magistrates, and "district" court judges, may still be elected without educational and other professional requirements. Today, in 43 states, some 1,300 nonlawyer judges are serving in mostly rural courts of limited jurisdiction.[13] In New York, for example, of the 3,300 judges in the state's unified court system, approximately 65% are part-time town or village justices, and approximately 80% of town and village justices are not lawyers.[14] The majority of cases that come before New York lay judges involve alleged traffic violations, although the cases may also include misdemeanors, small-claims actions, and some civil cases (of up to $3,000).

Even though some have defended lay judges as being closer to the citizenry in their understanding of justice,[15] in most jurisdictions the number of lay judges is declining. States that continue to use lay judges in lower courts do require that candidates for judgeships not have criminal records, and most states require that they attend special training sessions if elected.

The Prosecuting Attorney

prosecutor
An attorney whose official duty is to conduct criminal proceedings on behalf of the state or the people against those accused of having committed criminal offenses.

The **prosecutor**—called variously the *solicitor, district attorney, state's attorney, county attorney,* or *commonwealth attorney*—is responsible for presenting the state's case against the defendant. Technically speaking, the prosecuting attorney is the primary representative of the people by virtue of the belief that violations of the criminal law are an affront to the public. Except for federal prosecutors (called *U.S. attorneys*) and solicitors in five states, prosecutors are elected and generally serve four-year terms, with the possibility of continuing reelection.[16] Widespread criminal conspiracies, whether they involve government officials or private citizens, may require the services of a special prosecutor whose office can spend the time and resources needed for efficient prosecution.[17]

In many jurisdictions, because the job of prosecutor entails too many duties for one person to handle, most prosecutors supervise a staff of assistant district attorneys who do most in-court work. Assistants are trained attorneys, usually hired directly by the chief prosecutor and licensed to practice law in the state where they work. Approximately 2,300 chief prosecutors, assisted by 24,000 deputy attorneys, serve the nation's counties and cities.[18]

Another prosecutorial role has traditionally been that of quasi-legal adviser to local police departments. Because prosecutors are sensitive to the kinds of information needed for conviction, they may help guide police investigations and will exhort detectives to identify credible witnesses, uncover additional evidence, and the like. This role is limited, however. Police departments are independent of the administrative authority of the prosecutor, and cooperation between them, although based on the common goal of conviction, is purely voluntary. Moreover, close cooperation between prosecutors and police may not always be legal. A 1998 federal law known as the McDade-Murtha Law,[19] for example, requires that federal prosecutors abide by all state bar ethics rules. In late 2000, in a reflection of the federal sentiment, the Oregon Supreme Court temporarily ended police–prosecutor collaboration in that state in instances involving potential deception by law enforcement officers.[20] The court, ruling in the Oregon State Bar disciplinary case of *In re Gatti,*[21] held that all lawyers within the state, including government prosecutors overseeing organized crime, child pornography, and narcotics cases, must abide by the Oregon State Bar's strictures against dishonesty, fraud, deceit, and misrepresentation.[22] Under the court's ruling, a prosecutor in Oregon who encourages an undercover officer or an informant to misrepresent himself or herself could be disbarred and prohibited from practicing law. As a result of the highly controversial ruling, the Federal Bureau of Investigation (FBI) and the Drug Enforcement Administration (DEA) ended all big undercover operations in Oregon, and local police departments canceled many ongoing investigations. In 2002, the Oregon Supreme Court accepted an amendment to the state bar association's disciplinary rules to allow a lawyer to advise and to supervise otherwise lawful undercover investigations of violations of civil law, criminal law, or constitutional rights as long as the lawyer "in good faith believes there is a reasonable possibility that unlawful activity has taken place, is taking place or will take place in the foreseeable future."[23]

Once a trial begins, the job of the prosecutor is to vigorously present the state's case against the defendant. Prosecutors introduce evidence against the accused, steer the testimony of witnesses "for the people," and argue in favor of conviction. Because defendants are presumed innocent until proven guilty, the burden of demonstrating guilt beyond a reasonable doubt rests with the prosecutor.

Prosecutorial Discretion

In May 2007, North Carolina Attorney General Roy A. Cooper dismissed rape charges that had been brought against three former members of the Duke University lacrosse team, saying that the players were innocent of all charges. Those charges had been brought by Durham County Prosecutor Michael B. Nifong after an exotic dancer who had performed at a house party in 2006 told police that she had been raped, sodomized, strangled, and beaten by the partygoers. Contradictions in the accuser's statements, however, along with a lack of DNA and other evidence, convinced Cooper that the attack had never occurred. Cooper told CBS's *60 Minutes* that Nifong should have seen the contradictions himself. Calling Nifong "a rogue prosecutor," Cooper said that "when you have a prosecutor who takes advantage of his enormous power and overreaches like this, then yes, it's offensive."[24] Cooper added that other prosecutors "were offended by a prosecutor who didn't take the time to make sure that he had all of the facts straight

▲ Reporters shouting questions at Durham County (North Carolina) District Attorney Mike Nifong (right) after a community forum to discuss rape allegations that had been made against three members of the Duke University lacrosse team in 2006. Nifong, who would not abandon his quest to prosecute the men even when the accuser was discredited and DNA evidence seemed to definitively show that the men were innocent, was disbarred following a 2007 ethics hearing by the North Carolina State Bar Association. How did Nifong's actions (rightly or wrongly) demonstrate the power wielded by local prosecutors throughout the United States?
Gerry Broome/AP Wide World Photos

before leveling charges." A day later, Nifong apologized to the students, saying "to the extent that I made judgments that ultimately proved to be incorrect, I apologize to the three students that were wrongly accused." He added, "I also understand that when someone has been wrongly accused, the harm caused by the accusations might not be immediately undone merely by dismissing them. It is my sincere desire that the actions of Attorney General Cooper will serve to remedy any remaining injury that has resulted from these cases."[25] Calls for further action against Nifong led to his being disbarred in 2007 following an ethics hearing by the North Carolina Bar Association. He was later found guilty of criminal contempt of court and spent one day in jail.

The "Duke rape case," as it came to be known in the media, highlights the fact that American prosecutors occupy a unique position in the nation's criminal justice system by virtue of the considerable **prosecutorial discretion** they exercise. As U.S. Supreme Court Justice Robert H. Jackson noted in 1940, "The prosecutor has more control over life, liberty, and reputation than any other person in America."[26] Before a case comes to trial, the prosecutor may decide to accept a plea bargain, divert the suspect to a public or private social services agency, ask the suspect to seek counseling, or dismiss the case entirely for lack of evidence or for a variety of other reasons. Studies have found that the prosecution dismisses from one-third to one-half of all felony cases before trial or before a plea bargain is made.[27] Prosecutors also play a significant role before grand juries because states that use the grand jury system depend on prosecutors to bring evidence before the grand jury and to be effective in seeing indictments returned against suspects.

prosecutorial discretion
The decision-making power of prosecutors, based on the wide range of choices available to them, in the handling of criminal defendants, the scheduling of cases for trial, the acceptance of negotiated pleas, and so on. The most important form of prosecutorial discretion lies in the power to charge, or not to charge, a person with an offense.

In preparation for trial, the prosecutor decides what charges are to be brought against the defendant, examines the strength of the incriminating evidence, and decides which witnesses to call. Two important U.S. Supreme Court decisions have held that it is the duty of prosecutors to, in effect, assist the defense in building its case by making available any evidence in their possession. In the first case, *Brady* v. *Maryland* (1963),[28] the Court held that the prosecution is required to disclose to the defense evidence that directly relates to claims of either guilt or innocence. The second and more recent case is that of *U.S.* v. *Bagley,*[29] decided in 1985. In *Bagley,* the Court ruled that the prosecution must disclose any evidence that the defense requests. The Court reasoned that to withhold evidence, even when it does not relate directly to issues of guilt or innocence, may mislead the defense into thinking that such evidence does not exist.

In 2004, in a decision predicated upon *Brady,* the U.S. Supreme Court intervened to stop the execution of 45-year-old Texan Delma Banks ten minutes before it was scheduled to begin. In finding that prosecutors had withheld vital **exculpatory evidence**, or information that might have cleared Banks of blame, during his trial for the 1980 shooting death of a 16-year-old boy, the Court said that "a rule declaring 'prosecutor may hide, defendant must seek,' is not tenable in a system constitutionally bound to accord defendants due process."[30] Banks had spent 24 years on death row.

exculpatory evidence
Any information having a tendency to clear a person of guilt or blame.

One special decision that the prosecutor makes concerns the filing of separate or multiple charges. The decision to try a defendant simultaneously on multiple charges allows for the presentation of a considerable amount of evidence and permits an in-court demonstration of a complete sequence of criminal events. This strategy has an additional practical advantage: It saves time and money by substituting one trial for what might otherwise be a number of trials if each charge were to be brought separately before the court. From the prosecutor's point of view, however, trying the charges one at a time carries the advantage of allowing for another trial on a new charge if a "not guilty" verdict is returned.

The activities of the prosecutor do not end with a finding of guilt or innocence. Following conviction, prosecutors are usually allowed to make sentencing recommendations to the judge. They can be expected to argue that aggravating factors, prior criminal record, or especially heinous qualities of the offense in question call for strict punishment. When a convicted defendant appeals, prosecutors may need to defend their own actions and to argue, in briefs filed with appellate courts, that the conviction was properly obtained. Most jurisdictions also allow prosecutors to make recommendations when defendants they have convicted are being considered for parole or for early release from prison.

Until relatively recently, it had generally been held that prosecutors enjoyed much the same kind of immunity against liability in the exercise of their official duties that judges do. The 1976 U.S. Supreme Court case of ***Imbler* v. *Pachtman***[31] provided the basis for such thinking with its ruling that "state prosecutors are absolutely immune from liability . . . for their conduct in initiating a prosecution and in presenting the State's case." However, in the 1991 case of ***Burns* v. *Reed***,[32] the Court held that "[a] state prosecuting attorney is absolutely immune from liability for damages . . . for participating in a probable cause hearing, but not for giving legal advice to the police." The *Burns* case involved Cathy Burns of Muncie, Indiana, who allegedly shot her sleeping sons while laboring under a multiple personality disorder. To explore the possibility of multiple personality further, the police asked the prosecuting attorney if it would be appropriate for them to hypnotize the defendant. The prosecutor agreed that hypnosis would be a permissible avenue for investigation, and the suspect confessed to the murders while hypnotized. She later alleged in her complaint to the Supreme Court "that [the prosecuting attorney] knew or should have known that hypnotically induced testimony was inadmissible" at trial.[33]

From the moment you walk into the courtroom, you are the defendant's only friend.
—Michael E. Tigar
Austin defense attorney

The Abuse of Discretion

Because prosecutors have so much discretion in their decision making, there is considerable potential for abuse. Many types of discretionary decisions are always inappropriate: acceptance of guilty pleas to drastically reduced charges for personal considerations, decisions not to prosecute friends or political cronies, and overzealous prosecution by district attorneys seeking heightened visibility to support political ambitions.

Administrative decisions such as case scheduling, which can wreak havoc with the personal lives of defendants and the professional lives of defense attorneys, can also be used by prosecutors to harass defendants into pleading guilty. Some forms of abuse may be unconscious. At least one study suggests that some prosecutors have an inherent tendency toward leniency where female defendants are concerned and tend to discriminate against minorities when deciding whether to prosecute.[34]

Although the electorate is the final authority to which prosecutors must answer, gross misconduct by prosecutors may be addressed by the state supreme court or by the state attorney general's office. Short of addressing *criminal* misconduct, however, most of the options available to the court and to the attorney general are limited.

The Prosecutor's Professional Responsibility

As members of the legal profession, prosecutors are expected to abide by various standards of professional responsibility, such as those found in the ABA *Model Rules of Professional Conduct*. Most state bar associations have adopted their own versions of the ABA rules and expect their members to respect those standards. Consequently, serious violations of the rules may result in a prosecutor being disbarred from the practice of law. Official ABA commentary on Rule 3.8, Special Responsibilities of the Prosecutor, says that "a prosecutor has the responsibility of a minister of justice and not simply that of an advocate; the prosecutor's duty is to seek justice, not merely to convict. This responsibility carries with it specific obligations to see that the defendant is accorded procedural justice and that guilt is decided upon the basis of sufficient evidence."[35] Hence prosecutors are barred by the standards of the legal profession from advocating any fact or position that they know is untrue. Prosecutors have a voice in influencing public policy affecting the safety of America's communities through the National District Attorneys Association (NDAA). Visit the NDAA via Web Extra 8–4 at mycrimekit.com.

Web EXTRA

The Defense Counsel

defense counsel
A licensed trial lawyer, hired or appointed to conduct the legal defense of a person accused of a crime and to represent him or her before a court of law.

The **defense counsel** is a trained lawyer who may specialize in the practice of criminal law whose task is to represent the accused as soon as possible after arrest and to ensure that the defendant's civil rights are not violated during processing by the criminal justice system. Other duties of the defense counsel include testing the strength of the prosecution's case, taking part in plea negotiations, and preparing an adequate defense to be used at trial. In the preparation of a defense, criminal lawyers may enlist private detectives, experts, witnesses to the crime, and character witnesses. Some lawyers perform aspects of the role of private detective or of investigator themselves. Defense attorneys also review relevant court precedents to identify the best defense strategy.

Defense preparation often entails conversations between lawyer and defendant. Such discussions are recognized as privileged communications protected under the umbrella of attorney–client confidentiality; in other words, lawyers cannot be compelled to reveal information that their clients have confided to them.[36]

If the defendant is found guilty, the defense attorney will be involved in arguments at sentencing, may be asked to file an appeal, and will probably counsel the defendant and the defendant's family about any civil matters (payment of debts, release from contractual obligations, and so on) that must be arranged after sentence is imposed. Hence the work of the defense attorney encompasses many roles, including attorney, negotiator, investigator, confidant, family and personal counselor, social worker, and (as we shall see later) bill collector.

Three major categories of defense attorneys assist criminal defendants in the United States: (1) private attorneys, usually referred to as criminal lawyers or retained counsel; (2) court-appointed counsel; and (3) public defenders.

Private Attorneys

Private attorneys either have their own legal practices or work for law firms in which they are partners or employees. As those who have had to hire a defense attorney know, the fees of private attorneys can be high. Most privately retained criminal lawyers charge in the range of $100 to $200 per hour, and included in their bill is the time it takes to prepare for a case as well as time spent in the courtroom. High-powered criminal defense attorneys who have a reputation for successfully defending their clients can be far more expensive: Fees charged by famous criminal defense attorneys can run into the hundreds of thousands of dollars—and sometimes exceed $1 million—for handling just one case!

Few law students actually choose to specialize in criminal law, even though the job of a criminal lawyer may appear glamorous. Those who do specialize often begin their careers immediately following law school, while others seek to gain experience working as assistant district attorneys or assistant public defenders for a number of years before going into private practice. Visit the National Association of Criminal Defense Lawyers (NACDL) via Web Extra 8–5 and the Association of Federal Defense Attorneys (AFDA) via Web Extra 8–6 at mycrimekit.com to learn more about the practice of criminal law.

Web EXTRA

CJ Exhibit 1

Gideon v. *Wainwright* and Indigent Defense

Today, about three-fourths of state-level criminal defendants and one-half of federal defendants are represented in court by publicly funded counsel.[1] As recently as 40 years ago, however, the practice of publicly funded indigent defense was uncommon. That changed in 1963 when, in the case of *Gideon* v. *Wainwright*,[2] the U.S. Supreme Court extended the right to legal counsel to indigent defendants charged with a criminal offense. The reasoning of the Court is well summarized in this excerpt from the majority opinion written by Justice Hugo Black:

> Governments, both state and federal, quite properly spend vast sums of money to establish machinery to try defendants accused of crime. Lawyers to prosecute are everywhere deemed essential to protect the public's interest in an orderly society. Similarly, there are few defendants charged with crime, few indeed, who fail to hire the best lawyers they can get to prepare and present their defenses. That government hires lawyers to prosecute and defendants who have the money hire lawyers to defend are the strongest indications of the widespread belief that lawyers in criminal courts are necessities, not luxuries. The right of one charged with crime to counsel may not be deemed fundamental and essential to fair trials in some countries, but it is in ours. From the very beginning, our state and national constitutions and laws have laid great emphasis on procedural and substantive safeguards designed to assure fair trials before impartial tribunals in which every defendant stands equal before the law. This noble ideal cannot be realized if the poor man charged with crime has to face his accusers without a lawyer to assist him.

[1]Steven K. Smith and Carol J. DeFrances, *Indigent Defense* (Washington, DC: Bureau of Justice Statistics, 1996).
[2]*Gideon* v. *Wainwright*, 372 U.S. 335 (1963).

Court-Appointed Counsel

The Sixth Amendment to the U.S. Constitution guarantees criminal defendants the effective assistance of counsel. A series of U.S. Supreme Court decisions has established that defendants who are unable to pay for private criminal defense attorneys will receive adequate representation at all stages of criminal justice processing. In *Powell* v. *Alabama* (1932),[37] the Court held that the Fourteenth Amendment requires state courts to appoint counsel for defendants in capital cases who are unable to afford their own. In 1938, in *Johnson* v. *Zerbst*,[38] the Court overturned the conviction of an indigent federal inmate, holding that his Sixth Amendment due process right to counsel had been violated. The Court declared, "If the accused . . . is not represented by counsel and has not competently and intelligently waived his constitutional right, the Sixth Amendment stands as a jurisdictional bar to a valid conviction and sentence depriving him of his life or his liberty." The decision established the right of indigent defendants to receive the assistance of appointed counsel in all criminal proceedings in federal courts. The 1963 case of ***Gideon* v. *Wainwright***[39] extended the right to appointed counsel to all indigent defendants charged with a felony in state courts (see CJ Exhibit 1). In ***Argersinger* v. *Hamlin*** (1972),[40] the Court required adequate legal representation for anyone facing a potential sentence of imprisonment. Juveniles charged with delinquent acts were granted the right to appointed counsel in the case of *In re Gault* (1967).[41]

In 2002, a closely divided U.S. Supreme Court expanded the Sixth Amendment right to counsel, ruling that defendants in state courts who are facing relatively minor charges must be provided with an attorney at government expense even when they face only the slightest chance of incarceration. The case, *Alabama* v. *Shelton*,[42] involved a defendant named LeReed Shelton who was convicted of third-degree assault after taking part in a fistfight with another motorist following a minor traffic accident. Shelton had been advised of his right to have an attorney represent him at trial, and the judge who heard his case repeatedly warned him of the dangers of serving as his own attorney. Apparently unable to afford an attorney, Shelton proceeded to represent himself and was convicted and sentenced to 30 days in the county jail. The sentence was suspended, and he was placed on two years of unsupervised probation, fined $500, and ordered to make restitution and to pay the costs of court. Shelton soon appealed, however, and the Alabama Supreme Court ruled in his favor, reasoning that a suspended sentence constitutes a "term of imprisonment" no matter how unlikely it may be that the term will ever be served. Upon appeal by the state of Alabama, the case made its way to the U.S. Supreme Court, which agreed that "[a] suspended sentence is a prison term" and requires appointed counsel when an indigent defendant desires legal representation.

States have responded to the federal mandate for indigent defense in a number of ways. Most now use one of three systems to deliver legal services to criminal defendants who are unable to afford their own: (1) assigned counsel, (2) public defenders, and (3) contractual arrangements. Most such systems are administered at the county level, although funding arrangements may involve state, county, and municipal monies, as well as federal grants and court fees.

Assigned Counsel Assigned counsel, also known as court-appointed defense attorneys, are usually drawn from a roster of all practicing criminal attorneys within the jurisdiction of the trial court. Their fees are paid at a rate set by the state or local government. These fees are typically low, however, and may affect the amount of effort an assigned attorney puts into a case. In 2001, for example, New York's court-appointed attorneys were paid only $25 per hour for out-of-court preparation time and $40 an hour for time spent in the courtroom—a rate of pay that is ten to 20 times less than what they normally earn.[43]

public defender
An attorney employed by a government agency or subagency, or by a private organization under contract to a government body, for the purpose of providing defense services to indigents, or an attorney who has volunteered such service.

Public Defenders A **public defender** is a state-employed lawyer defending indigent defendants. A public defender program relies on full-time salaried staff, including defense attorneys, defense investigators, and office personnel. Defense investigators gather information in support of the defense effort and may interview friends, family members, and employers of the accused, with an eye toward effective defense. Public defender programs have become popular in recent years, with approximately 64% of counties nationwide now funding them.[44] A 1996 Bureau of Justice Statistics (BJS) report found that a public defender system is the primary method used to provide indigent counsel for criminal defendants and that 28% of state jurisdictions nationwide use public defender programs exclusively to provide indigent defense.[45] Critics charge that public defenders, because they are government employees, are not sufficiently independent from prosecutors and judges. For the same reason, clients may be suspicious of public defenders, viewing them as state functionaries. Finally, the huge caseloads typical of public defenders' offices create pressure toward an excessive use of plea bargaining.

Contractual Arrangements Through a third type of indigent defense, contract attorney programs, county and state officials arrange with local criminal lawyers to provide for indigent defense on a contractual basis. Individual attorneys, local bar associations, and multipartner law firms may all be tapped to provide services. Contract defense programs are the least widely used form of indigent defense at present, although their popularity is growing.

Critics of the current system of indigent defense point out that the system is woefully underfunded. Findings from the most recent National Survey of Indigent Defense Systems were published in 2001.[46] The survey found that states spent a total of $662,590,139 on indigent criminal defense in 1999. More than half of the money ($337 million) went to fund public defender programs, while assigned counsel programs cost $191 million, and contract attorney fees totaled $53 million. New Jersey, the most populous of the states covered by the survey, spent the most money ($73 million) on indigent criminal defense. While these figures may seem quite large, they total only about one-third the amount that states spend every year to prosecute criminal defendants. As a result, the report of the National Symposium on Indigent Defense proclaimed in 2000, "Indigent defense today, in terms of funding, caseloads, and quality, is in a chronic state of crisis."[47] Some question the quality of services available through public defender systems due to the fact that entry-level public defenders are paid poorly in comparison to what new attorneys entering private law firms might earn. In 2004, entry-level assistant public defenders in Massachusetts earned $35,000,[48] those in Georgia made $44,000, and those in Kentucky were paid $33,425; attorneys entering private practice can make much more. Moreover, the cost to the states for representing an indigent defendant averages around $490, while private attorney fees are generally much higher.[49]

O Lord, look down upon these the multitudes, and spread strife and dissension, so that this, Thy servant, might prosper.
—*Anonymous*
"The Lawyer's Prayer"

As a consequence of such limited funding, many public defender offices employ what critics call a "plead 'em and speed 'em through" strategy, often involving a heavy use of plea bargaining and initial meetings with clients in courtrooms as trials are about to begin. Mary Broderick of the National Legal Aid and Defender Association says, "We aren't being given the same weapons. . . . It's like trying to deal with smart bombs when all you've got is a couple of cap pistols."[50] Proposed enhancements to indigent defense systems are offered by the National Legal

Aid and Defender Association (NLADA). You can visit the NLADA via Web Extra 8–7 at mycrimekit.com.

Web EXTRA

The entire 200-page report of the National Symposium on Indigent Defense is available as Library Extra 8–2 at mycrimekit.com; the BJS 2001 overview of the National Survey of Indigent Defense Systems can be found at Library Extra 8–3. Library Extra 8–4 provides an overview of state-funded indigent defense services.

Library EXTRA

Although state indigent defense services are sometimes woefully underfunded, the same is not true of the federal system. The defense of indigent Oklahoma City bomber Timothy McVeigh, for example, cost taxpayers an estimated $13.8 million—which doesn't include the cost of his appeal or execution. McVeigh's expenses included $6.7 million for attorneys, $2 million for investigators, $3 million for expert witnesses, and approximately $1.4 million for office rent and secretarial assistance.[51]

In 2000, the BJS reported data on publicly financed counsel nationwide in two research reports that appear to conflict with the conclusions reached by the National Survey of Indigent Defense Systems.[52] BJS statisticians found that court-appointed defense attorneys represent 66% of federal felony defendants, as well as 82% of felony defendants in the nation's 75 most populous counties. The study also found that conviction rates for indigent defendants and those with their own lawyers were about the same in both federal and state courts. About 90% of the federal defendants and 75% of defendants in the most populous counties were found guilty regardless of the type of attorney they had. However, the study showed that those found guilty and represented by publicly financed attorneys were incarcerated at a higher rate than those defendants who paid for their own legal representation—88% compared to 77% in federal courts and 71% compared to 54% in the most populous counties. On average, however, prison sentences for defendants with publicly financed attorneys were shorter than were those with hired counsel. In federal district court, convicted defendants who had publicly financed attorneys were sentenced to less than five years on average, and those with private attorneys to just over five years. In large counties, those with publicly financed attorneys were sentenced to an average of two and a half years, while those with private attorneys were sentenced to three years.

Of course, defendants need not accept any assigned counsel. Defendants may waive their right to an attorney and undertake their own defense—a right held to be inherent in the Sixth Amendment to the U.S. Constitution by the U.S. Supreme Court in the 1975 case of *Faretta* v. *California*.[53] Self-representation is uncommon, however, and only 1% of federal inmates and 3% of state inmates report having represented themselves.[54] Some famous and relatively recent instances of self-representation can be found in the 1995 trial of Long Island Rail Road commuter train shooter Colin Ferguson, the 1999 trial of Dr. Jack Kevorkian, and the 2002 federal competency hearings of Zacarias Moussaoui.

Defendants who are not pleased with the lawyer appointed to defend them are in a somewhat different situation. They may request, through the court, that a new lawyer be assigned to represent them, as Timothy McVeigh did following his conviction and death sentence in the Oklahoma City bombing case. However, unless there is clear reason for reassignment, such as an obvious personality conflict between defendant and attorney, few judges are likely to honor a request of this sort; short of obvious difficulties, most judges will trust in the professionalism of appointed counsel.

State-supported indigent defense systems may also be called on to provide representation for clients upon appeal. An attorney who is appointed to represent an indigent defendant on appeal, however, may conclude that an appeal would be frivolous. If so, he or she may request that the appellate court allow him or her to withdraw from the case or that the court dispose of the case without requiring the attorney to file a brief arguing the merits of the appeal. In 1967, in the case of *Anders* v. *California*,[55] the U.S. Supreme Court found that to protect a defendant's constitutional right to appellate counsel, appellate courts must safeguard against the risk of accepting an attorney's negative assessment of a case where an appeal is not actually frivolous. The Court also found California's existing procedure for evaluating such requests to be inadequate, and the justices set forth an acceptable procedure. In 1979, in the case of *People* v. *Wende*,[56] the state of California adopted a new standardized procedure that, although not the same as that put forth in *Anders*, was designed to protect the right of a criminal defendant to appeal.

I don't know if I ever want to try another case. I don't know if I ever want to practice law again.
—Christopher Darden
Los Angeles County Assistant Prosecutor, expressing frustration over the O. J. Simpson case

The *Wende* standard was put to the test in the 2000 case of *Smith* v. *Robbins*.[57] The case began when convicted California murderer Lee Robbins told his court-appointed counsel that

CJ News

"*CSI* Effect" Has Juries Wanting More Evidence

Like viewers across the nation, folks in Galveston, Texas, watch a lot of TV shows about crime-scene investigators. Jury consultant Robert Hirschhorn couldn't be happier about that.

Hirschhorn was hired last year to help defense attorneys pick jurors for the trial of Robert Durst, a millionaire real estate heir who was accused of murdering and dismembering a neighbor, Morris Black. It was a case in which investigators never found Black's head. The defense claimed that wounds to the head might have supported Durst's story that he had killed Black in self-defense.

Hirschhorn wanted jurors who were familiar with shows such as *CSI: Crime Scene Investigation* to spot the importance of such a gap in the evidence. That wasn't difficult: In a survey of the 500 people in the jury pool, the defense found that about 70% were viewers of CBS's *CSI* or similar shows such as Court TV's *Forensic Files* or NBC's *Law & Order*.

Durst was acquitted in November. To legal analysts, his case seemed an example of how shows such as *CSI* are affecting action in courthouses across the USA by, among other things, raising jurors' expectations of what prosecutors should produce at trial.

Prosecutors, defense lawyers, and judges call it "the *CSI* effect," after the crime-scene shows that are among the hottest attractions on television. The shows—*CSI* and *CSI: Miami*, in particular—feature high-tech labs and glib and gorgeous techies. By shining a glamorous light on a gory profession, the programs also have helped to draw more students into forensic studies.

But the programs also foster what analysts say is the mistaken notion that criminal science is fast and infallible and always gets its man. That's affecting the way lawyers prepare their cases, as well as the expectations that police and the public place on real crime labs. Real crime-scene investigators say that because of the programs, people often have unrealistic ideas of what criminal science can deliver.

Like Hirschhorn, many lawyers, judges, and legal consultants say they appreciate how *CSI*-type shows have increased interest in forensic evidence.

"Talking about science in the courtroom used to be like talking about geometry—a real jury turnoff," says Hirschhorn, of Lewisville, Texas. "Now that there's this almost obsession with the (TV) shows, you can talk to jurors about (scientific evidence) and just see from the looks on their faces that they find it fascinating."

But some defense lawyers say *CSI* and similar shows make jurors rely too heavily on scientific findings and unwilling to accept that those findings can be compromised by human or technical errors.

Prosecutors also have complaints: They say the shows can make it more difficult for them to win convictions in the large majority of cases in which scientific evidence is irrelevant or absent.

"The lesson that both sides can agree on is, what's on TV does seep into the minds of jurors," says Paul Walsh, chief prosecutor in New Bedford, Mass., and president of the National District Attorneys Association. "Jurors are going to have information, or what they think is information, in mind. That's the new state of affairs."

Lawyers and judges say the *CSI* effect has become a phenomenon in courthouses across the nation:

- In Phoenix last month, jurors in a murder trial noticed that a bloody coat introduced as evidence had not been tested for DNA. They alerted the judge. The tests hadn't been needed because the defendant had acknowledged being at the murder scene. The judge decided that TV had taught jurors about DNA tests, but not enough about when to use them.
- Three years ago in Richmond, Va., jurors in a murder trial asked the judge whether a cigarette butt found during the investigation could be tested for links to the defendant. Defense attorneys had ordered DNA tests but had not yet introduced them into evidence. The jury's hunch was correct—the tests exonerated the defendant, and the jury acquitted him.
- In Arizona, Illinois, and California, prosecutors now use "negative evidence witnesses" to try to assure jurors that it is not unusual for real crime-scene investigators to fail to find DNA, fingerprints, and other evidence at crime scenes.
- In Massachusetts, prosecutors have begun to ask judges for permission to question prospective jurors about their TV-watching habits. Several states already allow that.
- Last year in Wilmington, Del., federal researchers studying how juries evaluate scientific evidence staged dozens of simulated trials. At one point, a juror struggling with especially complicated DNA evidence lamented that such problems never come up "on *CSI*."

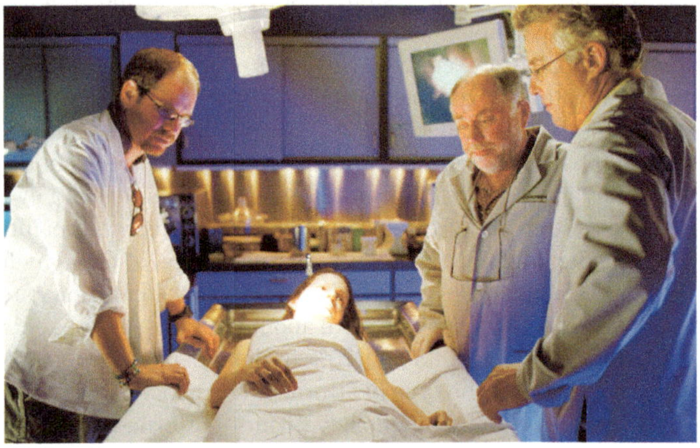

▲ Actors David Berman (as assistant coroner David Phillips), Robert David Hall (as coroner Al Robbins), and William Petersen (as Gil Grissom) examine a corpse in a scene from *CSI: Crime Scene Investigation*. Why might popular TV crime dramas like *CSI* lead to unrealistic expectations among today's criminal jurors?
© Neal Preston/CORBIS

The *CSI* effect also is being felt beyond the courtroom.

At West Virginia University, forensic science is the most popular undergraduate major for the second year in a row, attracting 13% of incoming freshmen this fall. In June, supporters of an Ohio library drew an overflow crowd of 200-plus to a luncheon speech on DNA by titling it "CSI: Dayton."

The Los Angeles County Sheriff's Department crime lab has seen another version of the *CSI* effect. Four technicians have left the lab for lucrative jobs as technical advisers to crime-scene programs. "They found a way to make science pay," lab director Barry Fisher says.

SHOWS' POPULARITY SOARS

CSI, which recently began its fifth season, was America's second-most-popular TV program during the 2004 season, after the Tuesday edition of *American Idol*.

CSI and a spinoff, *CSI: Miami* (which is about to begin its third season), have drawn an average of more than 40 million viewers a week during the past TV season. *Law & Order*, whose plots sometimes focus on forensic evidence, has been the 13th-most-watched show during the 2003–04 season, averaging about 15 million viewers. On cable, the Discovery Channel, A&E, and Court TV have programs that highlight DNA testing or the analysis of fingerprints, hair, and blood-spatter patterns.

CSI: NY, set in New York City, premiered in September 2005.

The *CSI* shows combine whiz-bang science with in-your-face interrogations to solve complex crimes. Some sample dialogue from actor David Caruso, the humorless monotone who plays investigator Horatio Caine on *CSI: Miami*: "He (the bad guy) doesn't know how evidence works, but you know what? He will."

The shows' popularity, TV historians say, is partly a result of their constant presence. Counting network and cable, at least one hour of crime–forensics programming airs in prime time six nights a week.

The stars of the shows often are the equipment—DNA sequencers, mass spectrometers, photometric fingerprint illuminators, scanning electron microscopes. But the technicians run a close second.

"It's 'geek chic,' the idea that kids who excel in science and math can grow up to be cool," says Robert Thompson, who teaches the history of TV programming at Syracuse University. "This is long overdue. . . . Cops and cowboys and doctors and lawyers have been done to death."

DEPARTING FROM REALITY

Some of the science on *CSI* is state-of-the-art. Real lab technicians can, for example, lift DNA profiles from cigarette butts, candy wrappers, and gobs of spit, just as their Hollywood counterparts do.

But some of what's on TV is far-fetched. Real technicians don't pour caulk into knife wounds to make a cast of the weapon. That wouldn't work in soft tissue. Machines that can identify cologne from scents on clothing are still in the experimental phase. A criminal charge based on "neuro-linguistic programming"—detecting lies by the way a person's eyes shift—likely would be dismissed by a judge.

But real scientists say *CSI*'s main fault is this: The science is always above reproach.

"You never see a case where the sample is degraded or the lab work is faulty or the test results don't solve the crime," says Dan Krane, president and DNA specialist at Forensic Bioinformatics in Fairborn, Ohio. "These things happen all the time in the real world."

Defense lawyers say the misconception that crime-scene evidence and testing are always accurate helps prosecutors. "Jurors expect the criminal justice system to work better than it does," says Betty Layne DesPortes, a criminal defense lawyer in Richmond, Va., who has a master's degree in forensic science.

She notes that during the past 15 years, human errors and corruption have skewed test results in crime labs in West Virginia, Pennsylvania, California, Texas, and Washington State.

But prosecutors say the shows help defense lawyers. Jurors who are regular viewers, they say, expect testable evidence to be present at all crime scenes.

In fact, they say, evidence such as DNA and fingerprints—the staple of *CSI* plots—is available in only a small minority of cases and can yield inconclusive results.

"Defense attorneys will get up there and bang the rail and say 'Where were the DNA tests?' to take advantage of the idea that's in the juror's mind," says Joshua Marquis, a prosecutor in Astoria, Ore. "You've got to do a lot of jury preparation to defeat that."

Some prosecutors have gone to great lengths to lower jurors' expectations about such evidence.

In Belleville, Ill., last spring, prosecutor Gary Duncan called on seven nationally recognized experts to testify about scientific evidence against a man accused of raping and murdering a 10-year-old girl. The witnesses included specialists in human and animal DNA, shoe-print evidence, population statistics, and human mitochondrial DNA, genetic material that is inherited only from one's mother and that seldom is used in criminal cases. Duncan won a conviction.

"I wanted to be certain the jury was clear on the evidence and its meaning," he says. "These days, juries demand that."

CSI producers acknowledge that they take some liberties with facts and the capabilities of science, but they say it's necessary to keep their story lines moving.

Elizabeth Devine, a former crime lab technician who writes and produces episodes of *CSI: Miami*, spoke at a training seminar for prosecutors last year in Columbia, S.C. She said that if the shows did not cut the time needed to perform DNA tests from weeks to minutes, a villain might not be caught before "episode five."

For all of *CSI*'s faults, some lab technicians say they have a soft spot for the TV version of their world. "It's great for getting people interested (in) careers" in forensic science, says Barbara Llewellyn, director of DNA analysis for the Illinois State Police.

Terry Melton, president of Mitotyping Technologies in State College, Pa., says the programs have made "jury duty something people now look forward to."

And Fisher says the shows have given "science types" like himself some unexpected cachet.

"When I tell someone what I do, I never have to explain it now," he says. "They know what a crime-scene (technician) does. At least, they think they do."

For the latest in crime and justice news, visit the Talk Justice news feed at http://www.crimenews.info.

Source: Richard Willing, "'*CSI* Effect' Has Juries Wanting More Evidence: People Expect Real Crime-Solving to Be Like the Hit TV Show," *USA Today*, August 5, 2004, p. 1A. From USA TODAY, a division of Garnett Co., Inc. Reprinted with permission.

he wanted to file an appeal. His attorney concluded that the appeal would be frivolous and filed a brief with the state court of appeals to that effect. The court agreed with the attorney's assessment, and the appeal was not heard. The California Supreme Court denied further review of the case. After exhausting his state postconviction remedies, Robbins appealed to the federal courts, arguing that he had been denied effective assistance of appellate counsel because his counsel's brief did not comply with one of the requirements in *Anders*—specifically, the requirement that the brief must mention "anything in the record that might arguably support the appeal." A federal district court agreed, concluding that there were at least two issues that might have supported Robbins's appeal. The court found that the failure to include them in the brief deviated from the *Anders* procedure and thus amounted to deficient performance by counsel. The Ninth Circuit Court agreed, concluding that *Anders* established a mandatory procedure as a standard against which the performance of appointed counsel could be assessed. When the case finally reached the U.S. Supreme Court, the justices held that the *Anders* procedure is only one method of satisfying the Constitution's requirements for indigent criminal appeals and that the states are free to adopt different procedures as long as those procedures adequately safeguard a defendant's right to appellate counsel.

Finally, in 2001, in the case of *Texas* v. *Cobb,*[58] the Supreme Court ruled that the Sixth Amendment right to counsel is "offense specific." It applies only to the offense with which a defendant is charged and not to other offenses, even if they are factually related to the charged offense.

The Ethics of Defense

The job of defense counsel, as we have already mentioned, is to prepare and offer a vigorous defense on behalf of the accused at trial and to appeal cases with merit. A proper defense at trial often involves the presentation of evidence and the examination of witnesses, both of which require careful thought and planning. Good attorneys may become emotionally committed to the outcomes of trials in which they are involved. Some lawyers, however, cross the line

▲ Defense attorney Lynne Stewart, age 65, who was sentenced to prison in 2006 for smuggling messages from her jailed client, the radical Egyptian sheik Omar Abdel-Rahman (aka the "blind sheik"), to his terrorist followers outside of prison. Our adversarial system requires that attorneys sometimes defend unpopular clients, but the defense role is carefully prescribed by ethical and procedural standards. How did Stewart's actions violate those standards?
Stephen Chernin/AP Wide World Photos

Ethics and Professionalism

The American Bar Association's *Model Rules of Professional Conduct*

To help attorneys understand what is expected of them, the ABA has provided significant guidance in the areas of legal ethics and professional responsibility. Specifically, the ABA has developed professional standards intended to serve as models for state bar associations and to guide legislative bodies focused on ensuring ethical behavior among attorneys.

The ABA's first major foray into the area of ethical guidelines resulted in the adoption of its original *Canons of Professional Ethics* on August 27, 1908. In 1913, in an effort to keep the association informed about state and local bar activities concerning professional ethics, the ABA established its Standing Committee on Professional Ethics. The name of the group was changed to the Committee on Ethics and Professional Responsibility in 1971, and the committee continues to function under that name today.

In 1969, the committee saw its *Model Code of Professional Responsibility* formally adopted by the ABA. Eventually, the majority of state and federal jurisdictions adopted their own versions of the Model Code.

In 1977, the ABA Commission on Evaluation of Professional Standards was created and charged with rethinking the ethical problems of the legal profession. During the next six years, the commission drafted the *Model Rules of Professional Conduct*, which was adopted by the ABA on August 2, 1983. The Model Rules effectively supplanted the *Model Code of Professional Responsibility*, and today most state and federal jurisdictions have adapted the Model Rules to their own particular circumstances.

The Model Rules have been periodically amended—most significantly in 2002—but continue to provide the touchstone ethical standards of the American legal profession today. Visit the ABA on the Internet at Web Extra 8–8 at mycrimekit.com, and learn about its Center for Professional Responsibility at Web Extra 8–9.

Web EXTRA

THINKING ABOUT ETHICS

1. Should a defense attorney represent a client whom he or she knows to be guilty?
2. Would it be unethical for an attorney to refuse to represent such a client? Why or why not?

Reference: American Bar Association, *Model Rules of Professional Conduct—Preface*. Web posted at http://www.abanet.org/cpr/mrpc/preface.html (accessed July 10, 2006).

when they lose their professional objectivity and embrace the wider cause of their clients. That's what happened to Lynne Stewart, age 65, who was convicted in 2005 of smuggling messages from her jailed client, the radical Egyptian sheik Omar Abdel-Rahman (aka the "blind sheik"), to his terrorist followers outside of prison.[59] Abdel-Rahman is serving life behind bars for his role in an unsuccessful 1993 plot to bomb New York City landmarks. Stewart, a 1960s-era radical, has often chosen to represent the most contemptible clients, believing that justice requires that everyone receive a vigorous defense. She was arrested, however, after she issued a public statement on behalf of the sheik expressing her client's withdrawal of support for a cease-fire involving his supporters in Egypt. Stewart had known in advance that making the statement violated an order to restrict the sheik's communications, but she later testified that she believed that violence is sometimes necessary to achieve justice. Other evidence showed that she had facilitated forbidden communications between Rahman and a translator by using prearranged cues such as tapping on a table, shaking a water bottle, and uttering key phrases like "chocolate" and "heart attack" during prison visits. In 2006 she was sentenced to serve 28 months in prison.

The nature of the adversarial process, fed by the emotions of the participants combined with the often privileged and extensive knowledge that defense attorneys have about their cases, is enough to tempt the professional ethics of some counselors. Because the defense counsel may often know more about the guilt or innocence of the defendant than anyone else prior to trial, the defense role is carefully prescribed by ethical and procedural considerations. Attorneys violate both law and the standards of their profession if they knowingly misrepresent themselves or their clients. As Michael Ratner, president of the Center for Constitutional Rights, put it when commenting on the Stewart case, "Lawyers need to be advocates, but they don't need to be accomplices."[60]

To help attorneys understand what is expected of them and what the appropriate limits of a vigorous defense might be, the ABA provides significant guidance in the areas of legal ethics and professional responsibility, as an Ethics and Professionalism box in this section explains. Even so, some attorney–client interactions remain especially tricky. Defense attorneys, for example, are under no obligation to reveal information obtained from a client without the client's

Society asks much of the criminal court. The court is expected to meet society's demand that serious offenders be convicted and punished, and at the same time it is expected to insure that the innocent and unfortunate are not oppressed.

—The President's Commission on Law Enforcement and Administration of Justice[i]

permission. However, as of 2004, all states permit defense lawyers to violate a client's confidentiality without fear of reprisal if they reasonably believe that doing so could prevent serious injury or death to another person. In 2004, with passage of a new evidence law broadening the state's evidence code, California joined the other 49 states in freeing attorneys to violate client confidentiality in such cases; California law makes disclosure discretionary, not mandatory. Kevin Mohr, a professor at Western State University College of Law in Fullerton, California, noted that the new law provides the first exception to the attorney–client privilege in California in more than 130 years. "A lawyer can now take action and intervene and prevent [a] criminal act from occurring," said Mohr.[61]

The California changes had been presaged by an action of the ABA, which eased its secrecy rules surrounding attorney–client relationships in 2001.[62] Prior to that time, ABA rules permitted criminal defense attorneys to disclose incriminating information about a client only to prevent substantial bodily harm or imminent death. The 2001 rule change dispensed with the word *imminent,* allowing attorneys to reveal clients' secrets in order to prevent substantial bodily harm or to stop future deaths.

Somewhat earlier, the 1986 U.S. Supreme Court case of *Nix* v. *Whiteside*[63] clarified the duty of lawyers to reveal known instances of client perjury. The *Nix* case came to the Court upon the complaint of the defendant, Whiteside, who claimed that he was deprived of the assistance of effective counsel during his murder trial because his lawyer would not allow him to testify untruthfully. Whiteside wanted to testify that he had seen a gun or something metallic in his victim's hand before killing him. Before trial, however, Whiteside admitted to his lawyer that he had actually seen no weapon, but he believed that to testify to the truth would result in his conviction. The lawyer told Whiteside that, as a professional counselor, he would be forced to challenge Whiteside's false testimony if it occurred and to explain to the court the facts as he knew them. On the stand, Whiteside said only that he *thought* the victim was reaching for a gun but did not claim to have seen one. He was found guilty of second-degree murder and appealed to the Supreme Court on the claim of inadequate representation. The Court, recounting the development of ethical codes in the legal profession, held that a lawyer's duty to a client "is limited to legitimate, lawful conduct compatible with the very nature of a trial as a search for truth. . . . Counsel is precluded from taking steps or in any way assisting the client in presenting false evidence or otherwise violating the law."[64]

The Bailiff

bailiff
The court officer whose duties are to keep order in the courtroom, to secure witnesses, and to maintain physical custody of the jury.

The **bailiff**, another member of the professional courtroom work group, is usually an armed law enforcement officer. The job of the bailiff, also called a *court officer,* is to ensure order in the courtroom, to announce the judge's entry into the courtroom, to call witnesses, and to prevent the escape of the accused (if the accused has not been released on bond). The bailiff also supervises the jury when it is sequestered and controls public and media access to jury members. Bailiffs in federal courtrooms are deputy U.S. marshals.

Courtrooms can be dangerous places, and bailiffs play a critical role in courtroom security. In an event that led to tightened courtroom security nationwide, George Lott opened fire in a courtroom in Tarrant County, Texas, in 1992, killing two lawyers and injuring three other people.[65] Lott, an attorney, was frustrated by the court's handling of his divorce and by child molestation charges that had been filed against him by his ex-wife. Lott was sentenced to die in 1993. Following the Lott incident and others like it, most courts began using metal detectors, and many now require visitors to leave packages, cellular phones, and objects that might conceal weapons in lockers or to check them with personnel before entering the courtroom.

A comprehensive courthouse security plan must, of course, extend beyond individual courtrooms. In 2005, around the time of the courthouse shootings in Atlanta, the National Center for State Courts (NCSC) released a comprehensive plan for improving security in state courthouses.[66] The plan contained a list of ten essential elements for court safety that include the need to (1) assess existing and potential threats, (2) identify physical strengths and weaknesses of existing courts, (3) develop a comprehensive emergency response plan, (4) be aware of the latest technologies in court security, and (5) build strong and effective partnerships among state courts, law enforcement agencies, and county commissioners. The complete list of NCSC recommendations is available at Library Extra 8–5.

Library EXTRA

Trial Court Administrators

Many states now employ trial court administrators whose job is to facilitate the smooth functioning of courts in particular judicial districts or areas. A major impetus toward the hiring of local trial court administrators came from the 1967 President's Commission on Law Enforcement and Administration of Justice. Examining state courts, the report found "a system that treats defendants who are charged with minor offenses with less dignity and consideration than it treats those who are charged with serious crimes."[67] A few years later, the National Advisory Commission on Criminal Justice Standards and Goals recommended that all courts with five or more judges create the position of trial court administrator.[68]

Court administrators provide uniform court management, assuming many of the duties previously performed by chief judges, prosecutors, and court clerks. Where trial court administrators operate, the ultimate authority for running the court still rests with the chief judge. Administrators, however, are able to relieve the judge of many routine and repetitive tasks, such as record keeping, scheduling, case-flow analysis, personnel administration, space utilization, facilities planning, and budget management; they may also take the minutes at meetings of judges and their committees.

Juror management is another area in which trial court administrators are becoming increasingly involved. Juror utilization studies can identify problems such as the overselection of citizens for the jury pool and the reasons for excessive requests to be excused from jury service. They can also suggest ways to reduce the time jurors waste waiting to be called or impaneled.

From what I see in my courtroom every day, many American juries might as well be using Ouija boards.
—*Judge Harold J. Rothwax*

Effective trial court administrators are able to track lengthy cases and identify bottlenecks in court processing. They then suggest strategies to make the administration of justice more efficient for courtroom professionals and more humane for lay participants.

The Court Reporter

The role of the court reporter (also called the *court stenographer* or *court recorder*) is to create a record of all that occurs during a trial. Accurate records are very important in criminal trial courts because appeals may be based entirely on what went on in the courtroom. Especially significant are all verbal comments made in the courtroom, including testimonies, objections, judge's rulings, judge's instructions to the jury, arguments made by lawyers, and results of conferences between the lawyers and the judge. Occasionally, the judge will rule that a statement should be "stricken from the record" because it is inappropriate or unfounded. The official trial record, often taken on a stenotype machine or an audio recorder, may later be transcribed in manuscript form and will become the basis for any appellate review of the trial.

Today's court stenographers often employ computer-aided transcription (CAT) software, which translates typed stenographic shorthand into complete and readable transcripts. Court reporters may be members of the National Court Reporters Association, the United States Court Reporters Association, or the Association of Legal Administrators—all of which support the activities of these professionals. You can visit the National Court Reporters Association via Web Extra 8–10 at mycrimekit.com.

Web EXTRA

The Clerk of Court

The duties of the clerk of court (also known as the *county clerk*) extend beyond the courtroom. The clerk maintains all records of criminal cases, including all pleas and motions made both before and after the actual trial. The clerk also prepares a jury pool, issues jury summonses, and subpoenas witnesses for both the prosecution and the defense. During the trial, the clerk (or an assistant) marks physical evidence for identification as instructed by the judge and maintains custody of that evidence; the clerk also swears in witnesses and performs other functions as the judge directs. Some states allow the clerk limited judicial duties, such as the power to issue warrants, to handle certain matters relating to individuals declared mentally incompetent,[69] and to serve as a judge of probate to oversee wills and the administration of estates.

▶ Expert witnesses may express opinions and draw conclusions in their area of expertise; they need not limit their testimony to facts alone. Why are expert witnesses permitted such leeway?
© Royalty-Free/CORBIS

Expert Witnesses

expert witness
A person who has special knowledge and skills recognized by the court as relevant to the determination of guilt or innocence. Unlike lay witnesses, expert witnesses may express opinions or draw conclusions in their testimony.

Most of the courtroom "insiders" we've talked about so far either are employees of the state or have ongoing professional relationships with the court (as in the case of defense counsel). Expert witnesses, however, may not have that kind of status, although some do. **Expert witnesses** are recognized as having specialized skills and knowledge in an established profession or technical area, and they must demonstrate their expertise through education, work experience, publications, and awards. Their testimony at trial provides an effective way of introducing scientific evidence in such areas as medicine, psychology, ballistics, crime-scene analysis, and photography. Unlike lay witnesses, they are allowed to express opinions and to draw conclusions, but only within their particular area of expertise. Expert witnesses, like the other courtroom actors described in this chapter, are generally paid professionals and (like all other witnesses) are subject to cross-examination.

One difficulty with expert testimony is that it can be confusing to the jury. Sometimes the trouble is due to the nature of the subject matter and sometimes to disagreements between the experts themselves. Often, however, it arises from the strict interpretation given to expert testimony by procedural requirements. The difference between medical and legal definitions of insanity, for example, points to a divergence in both history and purpose between the law and science. Courts that attempt to apply criteria like the M'Naghten rule in deciding claims of "insanity" are often faced with the testimony of psychiatric experts who refuse even to recognize the word; such experts may prefer, instead, to speak in terms of *psychosis* and *neurosis*, words that have no place in legal jargon. Because of the uncertainties they create, legal requirements may pit experts against one another and may confound the jury.

Even so, most authorities agree that expert testimony is usually viewed by jurors as more trustworthy than other forms of evidence. In a study of scientific evidence, one prosecutor commented that if he had to choose between presenting a fingerprint or an eyewitness at trial, he would always go with the fingerprint.[70] As a consequence of the effectiveness of scientific evidence, the National Institute of Justice recommends that "prosecutors consider the potential utility of such information in all cases where such evidence is available."[71]

Some expert witnesses traverse the country and earn very high fees by testifying at trials. DNA specialist John Gerdes, for example, was paid $100 per hour for his work in support of the defense in the 1995 O. J. Simpson criminal trial, and New York forensic pathologist Michael Baden charged $1,500 per day for time spent working for Simpson in Los Angeles. The laboratory for which Gerdes worked received more than $30,000 from Simpson's defense attorneys; Baden billed Simpson more than $100,000.[72] In 2008, Simpson was convicted by a Las Vegas jury on 12 felony counts stemming from a confrontation in a hotel room in 2007. The convictions came 13-years to the day after his 1995 acquittal.

Outsiders: Nonprofessional Courtroom Participants

Defendants, victims, jurors, and most witnesses are usually unwilling or inadvertent participants in criminal trials. Although they are outsiders who lack the status of paid professional participants, these are precisely the people who provide the grist for the judicial mill. The press, a willing player in many criminal trials, makes up another group of outsiders. Let's look now at each of these courtroom actors.

Lay Witnesses

Nonexpert witnesses, also known as **lay witnesses**, may be called to testify by either the prosecution or the defense. Lay witnesses may be eyewitnesses who saw the crime being committed or who came upon the crime scene shortly after the crime had occurred. Another type of lay witness is the character witness, who frequently provides information about the personality, family life, business acumen, and so on of the defendant in an effort to show that this is not the kind of person who would commit the crime with which he or she is charged. Of course, the victim may also be a witness, providing detailed and sometimes lengthy testimony about the defendant and the crime.

lay witness
An eyewitness, character witness, or other person called on to testify who is not considered an expert. Lay witnesses must testify to facts only and may not draw conclusions or express opinions.

A written document called a **subpoena** officially notifies witnesses that they are to appear in court to testify. Subpoenas are generally served by an officer of the court or by a police officer, though they are sometimes mailed. Both sides in a criminal case may subpoena witnesses and might ask that individuals called to testify bring with them books, papers, photographs, videotapes, or other forms of physical evidence. Witnesses who fail to appear when summoned may face contempt-of-court charges.

subpoena
A written order issued by a judicial officer or grand jury requiring an individual to appear in court and to give testimony or to bring material to be used as evidence. Some subpoenas mandate that books, papers, and other items be surrendered to the court.

The job of a witness is to provide accurate testimony concerning only those things of which he or she has direct knowledge. Normally, witnesses are not allowed to repeat things that others have told them unless they must do so to account for certain actions of their own. Since few witnesses are familiar with courtroom procedure, the task of testifying is fraught with uncertainty and can be traumatizing.

Everyone who testifies in a criminal trial must do so under oath, in which some reference to God is made, or after affirmation,[73] which is a pledge to tell the truth used by those who find either a reference or swearing to God objectionable.

All witnesses are subject to cross-examination. Lay witnesses may be surprised to find that cross-examination can force them to defend their personal and moral integrity. A cross-examiner may question a witness about past vicious, criminal, or immoral acts, even when such matters have never been the subject of a criminal proceeding.[74] As long as the intent of such questions is to demonstrate to the jury that the witness is not credible, the judge will normally permit them.

Witnesses have traditionally been shortchanged by the judicial process. Subpoenaed to attend court, they have often suffered from frequent and unannounced changes in trial dates. A witness who promptly responds to a summons to appear may find that legal maneuvering has resulted in unanticipated delays. Strategic changes by either side may make the testimony of some witnesses entirely unnecessary, and people who have prepared themselves for the psychological rigors of testifying often experience an emotional letdown.

To compensate witnesses for their time and to make up for lost income, many states pay witnesses for each day that they spend in court. Payments range from $5 to $30 per day,[75] although some states pay nothing at all. In a 2004 Chicago murder case in which Oprah Winfrey served as a juror, for example, all jurors, including Winfrey (a billionaire), were paid $17.20 a day for their services.[76] The 1991 U.S. Supreme Court case of ***Demarest* v. *Manspeaker et al.***[77] held that federal prisoners subpoenaed to testify are entitled to witness fees just as nonincarcerated witnesses would be.

The highest act of citizenship is jury service.
—Abraham Lincoln

CJ Careers

Criminalist

PERSONAL PROFILE

Name: J. Sippa Pardo-Hastings

Position: Senior Criminalist

City: Richmond, California

College Attended: University of California, Berkeley

Year Hired: 1994

"After studying ballet from childhood through my twenties, I felt the need to pursue my very early love of all things scientific. I returned to my early fictional role models, Nancy Drew and Sherlock Holmes, and realized that what interested me most was using science to solve mysteries—specifically, to solve crimes. After graduation, I assumed a criminalist position with the San Francisco City and County Crime Laboratory, a full-service forensic lab where I gained my initial professional experience. This included crime-scene processing (recognition and collection of potential evidence samples), serology (analysis of biological evidence), controlled substance analysis, as well as trial testimony in these same areas. Working with detectives and attorneys was especially compelling, as was learning about the "big picture" with respect to the criminal justice system and the role of the criminalist within this context. I then accepted a position as a criminalist with the California Department of Justice DNA lab, which was located in Berkeley. It was at this lab that I became immersed in forensic DNA analysis, a subsection of both serology and trace evidence. After several years of performing forensic DNA analyses, which often included court testimony throughout the state, I was promoted to the position of senior criminalist."

TYPICAL POSITIONS

Criminalist, forensic analyst, missing and unidentified persons (MUPS) specialist, and DNA databank/CODIS analyst. The criminalist is called on to render scientific opinions in written form as well as in court testimony. The criminalist may also visit violent crime scenes to collect potential evidence. Senior criminalists perform the most complex types of evidence examination and analyses of physical evidence associated with complex criminal investigations. The senior criminalist generally performs casework and/or research in areas of criminalistics such as crime-scene investigation, biological evidence, firearms and tool mark examinations, and trace evidence.

EMPLOYMENT REQUIREMENTS

Education equivalent to graduation from college with a major in one of the physical or biological sciences, including the equivalent of eight semester hours of general chemistry and three semester hours of quantitative analysis, or four years of professional experience in a physical or biological science laboratory performing independent research related to forensic science. (Possession of a master's degree in a physical or biological science may be substituted for one year of experience, and possession of a Ph.D. in a physical or biological science for two years of the required experience.) Successful completion of criminalist examination and completion of a successful interview are required. Senior criminalist positions require either two years of experience in the California state service performing the duties of a criminalist or four years of professional experience beyond the trainee level in a physical or biological science laboratory setting performing the duties of a chemist, biochemist, or a related position.

OTHER REQUIREMENTS

Personal qualities of successful applicants will include attention to detail, meticulous work habits, ability to focus, integrity, analytical ability, keenness of observation, patience, tact, ability to work independently, openness of mind, creative thinking, and good communication skills. The senior criminalist should be able to independently devise experiments and conduct research to address complex forensic science questions. Candidates must possess a state of health consistent with the ability to perform the assigned duties. A medical examination may be required. California Department of Justice regulations require preemployment investigations consisting of fingerprinting; inquiry to local, state, and national files to disclose criminal records; verification of minimum qualifications (i.e., college transcripts); financial status; previous employment background checks; and personal interviews to determine an applicant's suitability for employment.

SALARY (MONTHLY)

Range A: $2,674–$3,132; Range B: $3,499–$4,320; Range C: $4,215—$5,208; senior criminalist: $4,857–$6,012

BENEFITS

Benefits include (1) participation in the California Public Employee's Retirement System (CALPERS), (2) participation in the state health insurance and vision programs, (3) availability of dental insurance, and (4) earned vacation and sick leave.

DIRECT INQUIRIES TO:

California Department of Justice
Testing and Selection Unit
1300 "I" Street, 7th Floor
Sacramento, CA 95815
Attn: Criminalist Exam
Phone: (916) 324-5039

▲ A lay witness being sworn in before testifying in a criminal trial. Nonexpert witnesses must generally limit their testimony to facts about which they have direct knowledge. Why are such limits imposed?
© Royalty-Free/CORBIS

In an effort to make the job of witnesses less onerous, 39 states and the federal government have laws or guidelines requiring that witnesses be notified of scheduling changes and cancellations in criminal proceedings.[78] In 1982, Congress passed the Victim and Witness Protection Act, which required the U.S. attorney general to develop guidelines to assist victims and witnesses in meeting the demands placed on them by the justice system. A number of **victim assistance programs** (also called *victim/witness assistance programs*) have also taken up a call for the rights of witnesses and are working to make the courtroom experience more manageable.

victim assistance program
An organized program that offers services to victims of crime in the areas of crisis intervention and follow-up counseling and that helps victims secure their rights under the law.

Jurors

The Cook County (Chicago) jury on which television diva Oprah Winfrey served convicted a man of first-degree murder in 2004. "It was an eye-opener for all of us," Winfrey said after the three-day trial ended. "It was not an easy decision to make."[79]

Article III of the U.S. Constitution requires that "[t]he trial of all crimes . . . shall be by jury." **Jurors** are citizens selected for jury duty in a court of law. States have the authority to determine the number of jurors in criminal trial juries. Most states use juries composed of 12 people and one or two alternates designated to fill in for jurors who are unable to continue due to accident, illness, or personal emergency. Some states allow for juries smaller than 12 jurors, and juries with as few as six members have survived Supreme Court scrutiny.[80]

juror
A member of a trial or grand jury who has been selected for jury duty and is required to serve as an arbiter of the facts in a court of law. Jurors are expected to render verdicts of "guilty" or "not guilty" as to the charges brought against the accused, although they may sometimes fail to do so (as in the case of a hung jury).

Jury duty is regarded as a responsibility of citizenship. Other than juveniles and people in certain occupations, such as police personnel, physicians, members of the armed services on active duty, and emergency services workers, those who are called for jury duty must serve unless they can convince a judge that they should be excused for overriding reasons. Noncitizens, convicted felons, and citizens who have served on a jury within the past two years are excluded from jury service in most jurisdictions.

The names of prospective jurors are often gathered from the tax register, motor vehicle records, or voter registration rolls of a county or municipality. Minimum qualifications for jury service include adulthood, basic command of spoken English, citizenship, "ordinary intelligence," and local residency. Jurors are also expected to possess their "natural faculties," meaning that they should be able to hear, speak, see, move, and so forth. Some jurisdictions have recently allowed people with physical disabilities to serve as jurors, although the nature of the evidence to be presented in a case may preclude people with certain kinds of disabilities from serving.

Ideally, the jury should be a microcosm of society, reflecting the values, rationality, and common sense of the average person. The U.S. Supreme Court has held that criminal defendants have a right to have their cases heard before a jury of their peers.[81] Peer juries are those composed of a representative cross-section of the community in which the alleged crime occurred and where the trial is to be held. The idea of a peer jury stems from the Magna Carta's original guarantee of jury trials for "freemen." Freemen in England during the thirteenth century, however, were more likely to be of similar mind than is a cross-section of Americans today. Hence, although the duty of the jury is to deliberate on the evidence and, ultimately, to determine guilt or innocence, social dynamics may play just as great a role in jury verdicts as do the facts of a case.

In a 1945 case, *Thiel* v. *Southern Pacific Co.,*[82] the Supreme Court clarified the concept of a "jury of one's peers" by noting that while it is not necessary for every jury to contain representatives of every conceivable racial, ethnic, religious, gender, and economic group in the community, court officials may not systematically and intentionally exclude any juror solely because of his or her social characteristics.

In 2005, the ABA released a set of 19 principles intended to guide jury reform.[83] ABA President Robert J. Grey, Jr., said that the principles were aimed at improving the courts' treatment of jurors and to "move jury service into the 21st century." Some of the principles sound like a juror's bill of rights and include provisions to protect jurors' privacy and personal information, to inform jurors of trial schedules, and to "vigorously promote juror understanding of the facts and the law." Courts should instruct jurors "in plain and understandable language," the ABA report said. When trials conclude, the report continued, jurors should be advised by judges that they have the right to talk to anyone, including members of the press, and that they also have the right to refuse to talk to anyone about their jury service. Practical recommendations include allowing jurors to take notes, educating jurors regarding the essential aspects of a jury trial, and providing them with identical notebooks containing the court's preliminary instructions and selected exhibits that have been ruled admissible. Read the ABA's entire report, *Principles for Juries and Jury Trials,* at Library Extra 8–6, and learn more about what it's like to serve on a jury in a criminal trial at Web Extra 8–11.

Library EXTRA

Web EXTRA

The Victim

Not all crimes have clearly identifiable victims. Some, such as murder, do not have victims who survive. Where there is an identifiable surviving victim, however, he or she is often one of the most forgotten people in the courtroom. Although the victim may have been profoundly affected by the crime itself and is often emotionally committed to the proceedings and trial outcome, he or she may not even be permitted to participate directly in the trial process. Although a powerful movement to recognize the interests of victims is in full swing in this country, it is still not unusual for crime victims to be totally unaware of the final outcome of a case that intimately concerns them.[84]

Hundreds of years ago, the situation surrounding victims was far different. During the early Middle Ages in much of Europe, victims or their survivors routinely played a central role in trial proceedings and in sentencing decisions. They testified, examined witnesses, challenged defense contentions, and pleaded with the judge or jury for justice, honor, and often revenge. Sometimes they were even expected to carry out the sentence of the court, by flogging the offender or by releasing the trapdoor used for hangings. This "golden age" of the victim ended with the consolidation of power into the hands of monarchs, who declared that vengeance was theirs alone.

Today, victims (like witnesses) experience many of the following hardships as they participate in the criminal court process:

- Uncertainty as to their role in the criminal justice process
- General lack of knowledge about the criminal justice system, courtroom procedure, and legal issues
- Trial delays resulting in frequent travel, missed work, and wasted time

- Fear of the defendant or of retaliation from the defendant's associates
- Trauma of testifying and of cross-examination

The trial process itself can make for a bitter experience. If victims take the stand, defense attorneys may test their memory, challenge their veracity, or even suggest that they were somehow responsible for their own victimization. After enduring cross-examination, some victims report feeling as though they—and not the offender—were portrayed as the criminal to the jury. The difficulties encountered by victims have been compared to a second victimization at the hands of the criminal justice system.

The Defendant

Generally, defendants must be present at their trials. The Federal Rules of Criminal Procedure, like state rules, require that a defendant must be present at every stage of a trial, except that a defendant who is initially present may be voluntarily absent after the trial has commenced.[85] In ***Crosby* v. *U.S.*** (1993),[86] the U.S. Supreme Court held that a defendant may not be tried in absentia, even if he or she was present at the beginning of a trial, if his or her absence is due to escape or failure to appear. In a related issue in ***Zafiro* v. *U.S.*** (1993),[87] the justices held that, at least in federal courts, defendants charged with similar or related offenses may be tried together, even when their defenses differ substantially.

The majority of criminal defendants are poor, uneducated, and often alienated from the philosophy that undergirds the American justice system. Many are relatively powerless and are at the mercy of judicial mechanisms. However, experienced defendants, notably those who are career offenders, may be well versed in courtroom demeanor. As we discussed earlier, defendants in criminal trials may even choose to represent themselves, though such a choice may not be in their best interests.

Even without self-representation, every defendant who chooses to do so can substantially influence events in the courtroom. Defendants exercise choice in (1) selecting and retaining counsel, (2) planning a defense strategy in coordination with their attorney, (3) deciding what information to provide to (or withhold from) the defense team, (4) deciding what plea to enter, (5) deciding whether to testify personally, and (6) determining whether to file an appeal if convicted.

Nevertheless, even the most active defendants suffer from a number of disadvantages. One is the tendency of others to assume that anyone on trial must be guilty. Although a person is "innocent until proven guilty," the very fact that he or she is accused of an offense casts a shadow of suspicion that may foster biases in the minds of jurors and other courtroom actors. Another disadvantage lies in the often-substantial social and cultural differences that separate the offender from the professional courtroom staff. While lawyers and judges tend to identify with upper-middle-class values and lifestyles, few offenders do. The consequences of such a gap between defendant and courtroom staff may be insidious and far-reaching.

Spectators and the Press

Spectators and the press are often overlooked because they do not have an official role in courtroom proceedings. Both spectators and media representatives may be present in large numbers at any trial. Spectators include members of the families of both victim and defendant, friends of either side, and curious onlookers—some of whom are avocational court watchers. Journalists, TV reporters, and other members of the press are apt to be present at spectacular trials (those involving an especially gruesome crime or a famous personality) and at those involving a great deal of community interest. The right of reporters and spectators to be present at a criminal trial is supported by the Sixth Amendment's requirement of a public trial.

Press reports at all stages of a criminal investigation and trial often create problems for the justice system. Significant pretrial publicity about a case may make it difficult to find jurors who have not already formed an opinion as to the guilt or innocence of the defendant. News reports from the courtroom may influence or confuse nonsequestered jurors who hear them, especially when the reports contain information brought to the bench but not heard by the jury.

▶ Michael Jackson fans read copies of a special edition of the *Santa Maria Times* outside Jackson's Neverland Ranch on June 13, 2005, in Los Olivos, California. The 46-year-old singer was found not guilty of child molestation and other charges in a trial that lasted almost four months and involved testimony from 140 witnesses. What is the primary purpose of a criminal trial?
Ethan Miller/Getty Images–GINS/Entertainment News & Sports

In the 1976 case of *Nebraska Press Association* v. *Stuart,*[88] the U.S. Supreme Court ruled that trial court judges could not legitimately issue gag orders preventing the pretrial publication of information about a criminal case as long as the defendant's right to a fair trial and an impartial jury could be ensured by traditional means.[89] These means include (1) **change of venue**, whereby the trial is moved to another jurisdiction less likely to have been exposed to the publicity; (2) trial postponement, which would allow for memories to fade and emotions to cool; and (3) jury selection and screening to eliminate biased people from the jury pool. In 1986, the Court extended press access to preliminary hearings, which it said are "sufficiently like a trial to require public access."[90] In 1993, in the case of *Caribbean International News Corporation* v. *Puerto Rico,*[91] the Court effectively applied that requirement to territories under U.S. control.

change of venue
The movement of a trial or lawsuit from one jurisdiction to another or from one location to another within the same jurisdiction. A change of venue may be made in a criminal case to ensure that the defendant receives a fair trial.

Today, members of the press and their video, television, and still cameras are allowed into most state courtrooms. New York is one significant exception, and in 2004, a state court upheld the constitutionality of the 51-year-old law[92] prohibiting the use of cameras in that state's courts.[93] Forty-two states specifically allow cameras at most criminal trials,[94] although the majority require that permission be obtained from the judge before filming begins. Most states also impose restrictions on certain kinds of recording—of jurors or of juveniles, for example, or of conferences between an attorney and the defendant or between an attorney and the judge—although most states allow the filming of such proceedings without audio pickup. Only a few states ban television or video cameras outright. Indiana, Maryland, Mississippi, Nebraska, and Utah all prohibit audiovisual coverage of criminal trials; the District of Columbia prohibits cameras at trials and at appellate hearings.[95]

No citizen possessing all other qualifications which are or may be prescribed by law shall be disqualified for service as grand or petit juror in any court of the United States, or of any State, on account of race, color, or previous condition of servitude.

—18 U.S.C. 243

The U.S. Supreme Court has been far less favorably disposed to television coverage than have most state courts. In 1981, a Florida defendant appealed his burglary conviction to the Supreme Court,[96] arguing that the presence of television cameras at his trial had turned the court into a circus for attorneys and made the proceedings more a sideshow than a trial. The Supreme Court, recognizing that television cameras have an untoward effect on many people, found in favor of the defendant. In the words of the Court, "Trial courts must be especially vigilant to guard against any impairment of the defendant's right to a verdict based solely upon the evidence and the relevant law."

Cameras of all kinds have been prohibited in all federal district criminal proceedings since 1946 by Rule 53 of the Federal Rules of Criminal Procedure.[97] In 1972, the Judicial Conference of the United States adopted a policy opposing broadcast of civil proceedings in district courts, and that policy was incorporated into the Code of Conduct for United States Judges. Nonetheless, some district courts have local rules that allow photographs and filming during selected proceedings.

A three-year pilot project that allowed television cameras into six U.S. district courts and two appeals courts closed on December 31, 1994, when the Judicial Conference voted to end the project. Conference members expressed concerns that cameras were a distracting influence and were having a "negative impact on jurors [and] witnesses"[98] by exposing them to possible harm by revealing their identities. Still, some federal appellate courts have created their own policy on the use of cameras and broadcast equipment in the courtroom. The official policy of the U.S. Court of Appeals for the Ninth Circuit, for example, permits cameras and media broadcasts that meet certain rules. The policy stipulates, "Three business days advance notice is required from the media of a request to be present to broadcast, televise, record electronically, or take photographs at a particular session. Such requests must be submitted to the Clerk of Court." The policy adds, "The presiding judge of the panel may limit or terminate media coverage, or direct the removal of camera coverage personnel when necessary to protect the rights of the parties or to assure the orderly conduct of the proceedings."[99]

Today's new personal technologies, however, which include cellular telephones with digital camera capabilities, streaming Web-based video, and miniaturized recording devices, all threaten courtroom privacy. For more information on technology trends that might affect the use of cameras in courtrooms, see Library Extra 8–7 at mycrimekit.com.

Library EXTRA

The Criminal Trial

From arrest through sentencing, the criminal justice process is carefully choreographed. Arresting officers must follow proper procedure in the gathering of evidence and in the arrest and questioning of suspects. Magistrates, prosecutors, jailers, and prison officials are all subject to their own strictures. Nowhere, however, is the criminal justice process more closely circumscribed than it is at the criminal trial.

Procedure

The procedure in a modern courtroom is highly formalized. **Rules of evidence**, which govern the admissibility of evidence, and other procedural guidelines determine the course of a criminal hearing and trial. Rules of evidence are partially based on tradition, but all U.S. jurisdictions have formalized rules of evidence in written form. Criminal trials at the federal level generally adhere to the requirements of the Federal Rules of Evidence.

rules of evidence
The court rules that govern the admissibility of evidence at criminal hearings and trials.

Trials are also circumscribed by informal rules and professional expectations. An important component of law school education is the teaching of rules that structure and define appropriate courtroom demeanor. In addition to statutory rules, law students are thoroughly exposed to the ethical standards of their profession as found in ABA standards and other writings.

Nature and Purpose

In the remainder of this chapter, we will describe the chronology of a criminal trial and will comment on some of the widely accepted rules of criminal procedure. Before we begin the description, however, it is good to keep two points in mind. One is that the primary purpose of any criminal trial is the determination of the defendant's guilt or innocence. In this regard, it is important to recognize the crucial distinction that scholars make between factual guilt and legal guilt. The term *factual guilt* refers to the issue of whether the defendant is actually responsible for the crime of which he or she stands accused. If the defendant did it, then he or she is, in fact, guilty. *Legal guilt* is not as clear a term and is established only when the prosecutor presents evidence that is sufficient to convince the judge (when a jury trial has been waived and the judge determines the verdict) or the jury that the defendant is guilty as charged. The distinction between factual guilt and legal guilt is crucial because it points to the fact that the burden of proof rests with the prosecution, and it indicates the possibility that guilty defendants may, nonetheless, be found "not guilty."

The second point to remember is that criminal trials under our system of justice are built around an **adversarial system** (prosecution versus defense) and that central to this system is the advocacy model. Participating in the adversarial system are advocates for the state (the prosecution or the district attorney) and for the defendant (defense counsel, public defender, and so on). The philosophy behind the adversarial system is that the greatest number of just resolutions in criminal trials will occur when both sides are allowed to argue their cases effectively and vociferously before a fair and impartial jury. The system requires that advocates for both sides do their utmost, within the boundaries set by law and professional ethics, to protect and advance the interests of their clients (that is, the defendant and the state). The advocacy

adversarial system
The two-sided structure under which American criminal trial courts operate that pits the prosecution against the defense. In theory, justice is done when the more effective adversary is able to convince the judge or jury that his or her perspective on the case is the correct one.

model makes clear that it is not the job of the defense attorney or the prosecution to determine the guilt of any defendant. Hence even defense attorneys who are convinced that their client is guilty are still exhorted to offer the best possible defense and to counsel their client as effectively as possible.

The adversarial system has been criticized by some thinkers who point to fundamental differences between law and science in the way the search for truth is conducted.[100] While proponents of traditional legal procedure accept the belief that truth can best be uncovered through an adversarial process, scientists adhere to a painstaking process of research and replication to acquire knowledge. Most of us would agree that scientific advances in recent years may have made factual issues less difficult to ascertain. For example, some of the new scientific techniques in evidence analysis, such as DNA fingerprinting, can now unequivocally link suspects to criminal activity or even show that offenders once thought guilty are actually innocent. At least 328 convictions have been overturned using DNA evidence since Gary Dotson of Illinois became the first person exonerated through the use of such evidence in 1989. (Read about Dotson's case in "The Rape That Wasn't" via Library Extra 8–8 at mycrimekit.com.) According to Samuel R. Gross and colleagues at the University of Michigan Law School, who published a comprehensive study of exonerations in 2004, those 328 people "had spent more than 3,400 years in prison for crimes for which they should never have been convicted."[101] Exonerations tend to occur more frequently in cases where DNA evidence is relatively easy to acquire, such as rape and murder. False conviction rates for other crimes, like robbery, are much more difficult to assess using DNA. Hence, Gross states that "the clearest and most important lesson from the recent spike in rape exonerations is that false convictions that come to light are the tip of an iceberg."

Library EXTRA

The beauty of the jury is their morality. Tap into it.
—Tony Serra
San Francisco defense attorney

Whether scientific findings should continue to serve a subservient role to the adversarial process itself is a question now being raised. The ultimate answer will probably be determined by the results that the two processes are able to produce. If the adversarial model results in the acquittal of too many demonstrably guilty people because of legal "technicalities" or if the scientific approach identifies too many suspects inaccurately, either could be restricted.

Stages in a Criminal Trial

We turn now to a discussion of the steps in a criminal trial. As Figure 1 shows, trial chronology consists of eight stages:

1. Trial initiation
2. Jury selection

FIGURE 1
Stages in a Criminal Trial.

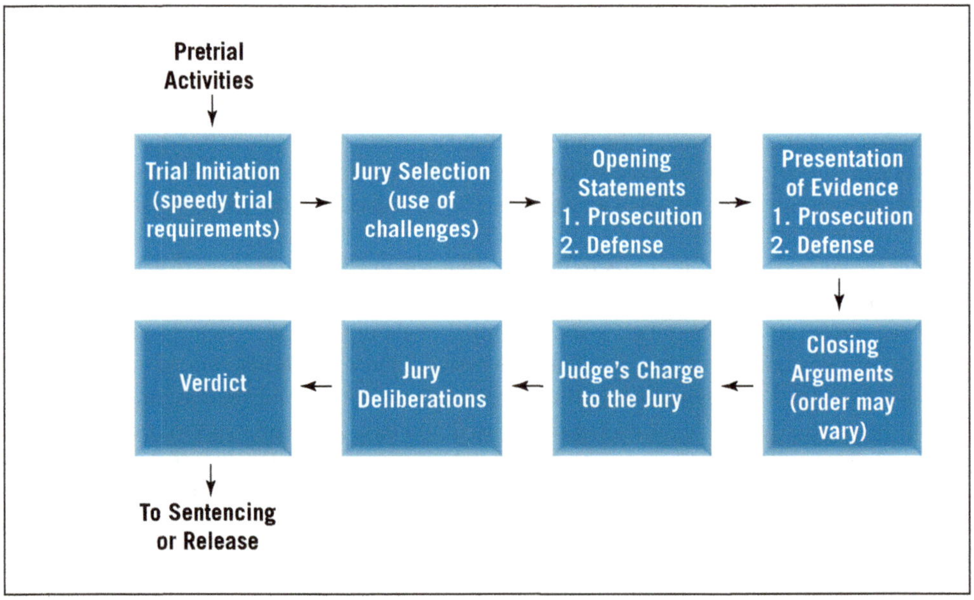

3. Opening statements
4. Presentation of evidence
5. Closing arguments
6. Judge's charge to the jury
7. Jury deliberations
8. Verdict

Jury deliberations and the verdict are discussed jointly. If the defendant is found guilty, a sentence is imposed by the judge at the conclusion of the trial.

Trial Initiation

In 2005, a Louisiana state appeals court threw out murder charges against James Thomas and ordered him released. Thomas, an impoverished day laborer, had been arrested in 1996 and spent eight and one-half years in jail waiting for a trial that never came. The ruling by the appeals court was widely seen as an indictment of Louisiana's understaffed and underfunded public defender system, members of which had simply been too busy to work on Thomas's case. A private attorney managed to get Thomas set free after his mother scraped together $500 to pay his fee.

The U.S. Constitution contains a speedy trial provision in its Sixth Amendment, which guarantees that "[i]n all criminal prosecutions, the accused shall enjoy the right to a speedy and public trial." Clogged court calendars, limited judicial resources, and general inefficiency, however, often combine to produce what appears to many to be unreasonable delays in trial initiation. The attention of the U.S. Supreme Court was brought to bear on trial delays in three precedent-setting cases: *Klopfer* v. *North Carolina* (1967),[102] *Barker* v. *Wingo* (1972),[103] and *Strunk* v. *U.S.* (1973).[104] The *Klopfer* case involved a Duke University professor and focused on civil disobedience in a protest against segregated facilities. In ruling on Klopfer's long-delayed trial, the Court asserted that the right to a speedy trial is a fundamental guarantee of the Constitution. In the *Barker* case, the Court held that Sixth Amendment guarantees to a quick trial could be illegally violated even in cases where the accused did not explicitly object to delays. In *Strunk*, it found that the denial of a speedy trial should result in the dismissal of all charges.

In 1974, against the advice of the Justice Department, the U.S. Congress passed the federal **Speedy Trial Act**.[105] The act allows for the dismissal of federal criminal charges in cases where the prosecution does not seek an indictment or information within 30 days of arrest (a 30-day extension is granted when the grand jury is not in session) or where a trial does not begin within

Speedy Trial Act
A 1974 federal law requiring that proceedings against a defendant in a criminal case begin within a specified period of time, such as 70 working days after indictment. Some states also have speedy trial requirements.

James Thomas, charged with murder in 1996 and freed in April 2005, after spending eight and a half years in a Louisiana jail waiting for his case to go to trial. A Louisiana state appeals court ruled that the state had taken too long to try him. Why are speedy trials required by our system of justice?
Bill Feig/AP Wide World Photos

In all criminal prosecutions, the accused shall enjoy the right to a speedy and public trial, by an impartial jury . . . and to be informed of the nature and cause of the accusation; to be confronted with the witnesses against him; to have compulsory process for obtaining witnesses in his favor, and to have the Assistance of Counsel for his defence.

—*Sixth Amendment to the U.S. Constitution*

Peremptory challenges betray the jury's democratic origins and undermine its representative function.

—*U.S. Supreme Court Justice Stephen Breyer*[ii]

70 working days after indictment or initial appearance for defendants who plead not guilty. If a defendant is not available for trial or if witnesses cannot be called within the 70-day limit, the period may be extended up to 180 days. Delays brought about by the defendant, through requests for a continuance or because of escape, are not counted in the specified time periods.

In an important 1988 decision, *U.S.* v. *Taylor,*[106] the U.S. Supreme Court applied the requirements of the Speedy Trial Act to the case of a drug defendant who had escaped following arrest. The Court made it clear that trial delays that derive from the willful actions of the defendant do not apply to the 70-day period. The Court also held that trial delays, even when they result from government action, do not necessarily provide grounds for dismissal if they occur "without prejudice." Delays without prejudice are those that are due to circumstances beyond the control of criminal justice agencies.

In 1993, an Indiana prisoner, William Fex, appealed a Michigan conviction on armed robbery and attempted murder charges, claiming that he had to wait 196 days after submitting a request to Indiana prison authorities for his Michigan trial to commence. In ***Fex* v. *Michigan*** (1993),[107] the U.S. Supreme Court ruled that "common sense compel[s] the conclusion that the 180-day period does not commence until the prisoner's disposition request has actually been delivered to the court and prosecutor of the jurisdiction that lodged the detainer against him." In Fex's case, Indiana authorities had taken 22 days to forward his request to Michigan.

However, in a 1992 case, ***Doggett* v. *U.S.***,[108] the Court held that a delay of eight and a half years violated speedy trial provisions because it resulted from government negligence. In *Doggett,* the defendant was indicted on a drug charge in 1980 but left the country for Panama, where he lived until 1982, when he reentered the United States. He lived openly in the United States until 1988, when a credit check revealed him to authorities. He was arrested, tried, and convicted of federal drug charges stemming from his 1980 indictment. In overturning his conviction, the U.S. Supreme Court ruled, "Even delay occasioned by the Government's negligence creates prejudice that compounds over time, and at some point, as here, becomes intolerable."[109]

In 2006, the Court refused to hear an appeal by suspected dirty bomb conspirator Jose Padilla, letting stand a lower court's decision that said the president could order a U.S. citizen who was arrested in this country for suspected ties to terrorism to be held indefinitely without charges and without going to trial.[110] Padilla, who was arrested in 2002, had been held for four years in a Navy brig without being charged with a crime. Shortly before Padilla's case was to come before the Court, however, he was transferred from military custody to the Federal Detention Facility in Miami, indicted on terrorism charges, and scheduled to go to trial—rendering his appeal moot. Although there was no official ruling in the case, Justice Kennedy, writing for himself, Justice Stevens, and Chief Justice Roberts observed that the federal district court in Miami, which was scheduled to hear the case, would now "be obliged to afford him the protection, including the right to a speedy trial, guaranteed to all federal criminal defendants."[111]

The federal Speedy Trial Act is applicable only to federal courts. However, the *Klopfer* case effectively made constitutional guarantees of a speedy trial applicable to state courts. In keeping with the trend toward reduced delays, many states have since enacted their own speedy trial legislation. Most state legislation sets a limit of 90 or 120 days as a reasonable period of time for a trial to commence.

Jury Selection

Challenges in Jury Selection

The Sixth Amendment guarantees the right to an impartial jury. An impartial jury is not necessarily an ignorant one. In other words, potential jurors will not always be excused from service on a jury if they have some knowledge of the case before them[112]; however, candidates who have already formed an opinion as to the guilt or innocence of a defendant are likely to be excused.

Some prospective jurors *try* to get excused, whereas others who would like to serve are excused because they are not judged to be suitable. Prosecution and defense attorneys use challenges to ensure the impartiality of the jury being impaneled. Three types of challenges are recognized in criminal courts: (1) challenges to the array, (2) challenges for cause, and (3) **peremptory challenges**.

peremptory challenge
The right to challenge a potential juror without disclosing the reason for the challenge. Prosecutors and defense attorneys routinely use peremptory challenges to eliminate from juries individuals who, although they express no obvious bias, are thought to be capable of swaying the jury in an undesirable direction.

Challenges to the array signify the belief, generally by the defense attorney, that the pool from which potential jurors are to be selected is not representative of the community or is biased in some significant way. A challenge to the array is argued before the hearing judge before jury selection begins.

During **jury selection**, both prosecution and defense attorneys question potential jurors in a process known as *voir dire* examination. Jurors are expected to be unbiased and free of preconceived notions of guilt or innocence; challenges for cause, which may arise during *voir dire* examination, make the claim that an individual juror cannot be fair or impartial. One special issue of juror objectivity has concerned the U.S. Supreme Court—whether jurors with philosophical opposition to the death penalty should be excluded from juries whose decisions might result in the imposition of capital punishment. In the case of *Witherspoon* v. *Illinois* (1968),[113] the Court ruled that a juror opposed to the death penalty could be excluded from such juries if it were shown that (1) the juror would automatically vote against conviction without regard to the evidence or (2) the juror's philosophical orientation would prevent an objective consideration of the evidence. The *Witherspoon* case left unresolved a number of issues, among them the concern that it is difficult to demonstrate how a juror would automatically vote, a fact that might not even be known to the juror before trial begins.

jury selection
The process whereby, according to law and precedent, members of a particular trial jury are chosen.

Another area of concern that the Supreme Court has addressed involves the possibility that jurors could be influenced by pretrial news stories. In 1991, for example, the Court decided the case of ***Mu'Min* v. *Virginia***.[114] Dawud Majud Mu'Min was a Virginia inmate who was serving time for first-degree murder. While accompanying a work detail outside the prison, he committed another murder. At the ensuing trial, eight of the 12 jurors who were seated admitted that they had heard or read something about the case, although none indicated that he or she had formed an opinion in advance as to Mu'Min's guilt or innocence. Following his conviction, Mu'Min appealed to the Supreme Court, claiming that his right to a fair trial had been denied due to pretrial publicity. The Court disagreed and upheld his conviction, citing the jurors' claims that they were not biased.

The third kind of challenge, the peremptory challenge, allows attorneys to remove potential jurors without having to give a reason. Peremptory challenges, used by both the prosecution and the defense, are limited in number: Federal courts allow each side up to 20 peremptory challenges in capital cases and as few as three in minor criminal cases[115]; states vary as to the number of peremptory challenges they permit.

A developing field that seeks to take advantage of peremptory challenges is **scientific jury selection**, which uses correlational techniques from the social sciences to gauge the likelihood that a potential juror will vote for conviction or acquittal. It makes predictions based on the economic, ethnic, and other personal and social characteristics of each member of the juror pool. Such techniques generally remove potential jurors who have any knowledge or opinions about the case to be tried; also removed are people who have been trained in the law or in criminal justice. Anyone working for a criminal justice agency or anyone who has a family member working for such an agency or for a defense attorney will likely be dismissed through peremptory challenges on the chance that they may be biased in favor of one side or the other. Additionally, scientific jury selection techniques may result in the dismissal of highly educated or professionally successful individuals to eliminate the possibility of such individuals exercising undue control over jury deliberations.

scientific jury selection
The use of correlational techniques from the social sciences to gauge the likelihood that potential jurors will vote for conviction or for acquittal.

Critics of the jury selection process charge that the end result is a jury composed of people who are uneducated, uninformed, and generally inexperienced at making any type of well-considered decision. Some jurors may not understand the charges against the defendant or comprehend what is required for a finding of guilt or innocence. Likewise, some may not even possess the attention span needed to hear all the testimony that will be offered in a case. As a consequence, critics say, decisions rendered by such a jury may be based more on emotion than on findings of fact.

Another emerging technique is the use of what is called a *shadow jury* to assess the impact of a defense attorney's arguments. Shadow jurors are hired court observers who sit in the courtroom and listen to what both sides in a criminal trial have to say. They hear evidence as it is presented and listen as witnesses are examined and cross-examined. Unlike professional legal experts, shadow jurors are laypeople who are expected to give defense attorneys a feel for what the "real" jurors are thinking and feeling as a case progresses, allowing for ongoing modifications in defense strategy.[116]

sequestered jury
A jury that is isolated from the public during the course of a trial and throughout the deliberation process.

After the wrangling over jury selection has run its course, the jury is sworn in and alternate jurors are selected (alternates may be called to replace jurors taken ill or dismissed from the jury because they don't conform to the requirements of jury service once trial has begun). At this point, the judge will decide whether the jury is to be sequestered during the trial. Members of **sequestered juries**, like those in the O. J. Simpson criminal trial, are not permitted to have contact with the public and are often housed in a motel or hotel until completion of the trial. Anyone who attempts to contact a sequestered jury or to influence members of a nonsequestered jury may be held accountable for jury tampering. Following jury selection, the stage is set for opening arguments[117] to begin.

Jury Selection and Race

Race alone cannot provide the basis for jury selection, and juries may not be intentionally selected for racial imbalance. As long ago as 1880, the U.S. Supreme Court held that "a statute barring blacks from service on grand or petit juries denied equal protection of the laws to a black man convicted of murder by an all-white jury."[118] Even so, peremptory challenges continued to tend toward racial imbalance. In 1965, for example, a black defendant in Alabama was convicted of rape by an all-white jury (the local prosecutor had used his peremptory challenges to exclude blacks from the jury). The case eventually reached the Supreme Court, where the conviction was upheld.[119] At that time, the Court refused to limit the practice of peremptory challenges, reasoning that to do so would place them under the same judicial scrutiny as challenges for cause.

However, in the 1986 case of *Batson* v. *Kentucky,*[120] following what many claimed was widespread abuse of peremptory challenges by prosecution and defense alike, the Supreme Court was forced to overrule its earlier decision. Batson, an African-American man, had been convicted of second-degree burglary and other offenses by an all-white jury. The prosecutor had used his peremptory challenges to remove all African-Americans from jury service at the trial. The Court agreed that the use of peremptory challenges for purposeful discrimination constitutes a violation of the defendant's right to an impartial jury.

The *Batson* decision laid out the requirements that defendants must prove when seeking to establish the discriminatory use of peremptory challenges. They include the need to prove that the defendant is a member of a recognized racial group that has been intentionally excluded from the jury and the need to raise a reasonable suspicion that the prosecutor used peremptory challenges in a discriminatory manner. Justice Thurgood Marshall, writing a concurring opinion in *Batson,* presaged what was to come: "The inherent potential of peremptory challenges to destroy the jury process," he wrote, "by permitting the exclusion of jurors on racial grounds should ideally lead the Court to ban them entirely from the criminal justice system."

A few years later, in *Ford* v. *Georgia* (1991),[121] the Court moved much closer to Justice Marshall's position when it remanded a case for a new trial because the prosecutor had misused peremptory challenges. The prosecutor had used nine of the ten peremptory challenges available under Georgia law to eliminate prospective black jurors. Following his conviction on charges of kidnapping, raping, and murdering a white woman, the black defendant, James Ford, argued that the prosecutor had demonstrated a systematic racial bias in other cases as well as his own. Specifically, Ford argued that his Sixth Amendment right to an impartial jury had been violated by the prosecutor's racially based method of jury selection. His appeal to the Supreme Court claimed that "the exclusion of members of the black race in the jury when a black accused is being tried is done in order that the accused will receive excessive punishment if found guilty, or to inject racial prejudice into the fact finding process of the jury."[122] While the Court did not find a basis for such a Sixth Amendment claim, it did determine that the civil rights of the jurors themselves had been violated under the Fourteenth Amendment due to a pattern of discrimination based on race.

In another 1991 case, ***Powers* v. *Ohio***,[123] the Court found in favor of a white defendant who claimed that his constitutional rights had been violated by the intentional exclusion of blacks from his jury through the use of peremptory challenges. In *Powers*, the Court held that "[a]lthough an individual juror does not have the right to sit on any particular petit jury, he or she does possess the right not to be excluded from one on account of race."

The jury is such a cornerstone of justice and the democratic process, [but] the jury process needs to be brought into the 21st century.

—Robert Grey, President of the American Bar Association[iii]

In ***Edmonson* v. *Leesville Concrete Co., Inc.*** (1991),[124] a civil case with significance for the criminal justice system, the Court held that peremptory challenges in *civil* suits were not acceptable if based on race: "The importance of [*Edmonson*] lies in the Court's significant expansion of the scope of state action—the traditionally held doctrine that private attorneys are immune to constitutional requirements because they do not represent the government." Justice Anthony Kennedy, writing for the majority, said that race-based juror exclusions are forbidden in civil lawsuits because jury selection is a "unique governmental function delegated to private litigants" in a public courtroom.

In the 1992 case of ***Georgia* v. *McCollum***,[125] the Court barred defendants and their attorneys from using peremptory challenges to exclude potential jurors on the basis of race (see CJ Exhibit 2). In *McCollum*, Justice Harry Blackmun, writing for the majority, said, "Be it at the hands of the state or defense, if a court allows jurors to be excluded because of group bias, it is a willing participant in a scheme that could only undermine the very foundation of our system of justice—our citizens' confidence in it."

Soon thereafter, peremptory challenges based on gender were similarly restricted (*J. E. B.* v. *Alabama*, 1994[126]), although at the time of this writing the Court has refused to ban peremptory challenges that exclude jurors because of religious or sexual orientation.[127] Also, in 1996, the Court refused to review "whether potential jurors can be stricken from a trial panel because they are too fat."[128] The case involved Luis Santiago-Martinez, a drug defendant whose lawyer objected to the prosecution's use of peremptory challenges "because the government," he said, "had used such strikes to discriminate against the handicapped, specifically the obese." The attorney, who was himself obese, claimed that thin jurors might have been unfairly biased against his arguments.

My experience was like being in prison.

—Tracy Hampton, who was excused from the Simpson criminal jury after four months of sequestration

In the 1998 case of *Campbell* v. *Louisiana*,[129] the Court held that a white criminal defendant can raise equal protection and due process objections to discrimination against blacks in the selection of grand jurors. Terry Campbell, who was white, objected to an apparent pattern of discrimination in the selection of grand jury forepeople. The foreperson of the Evangeline Parish, Louisiana, grand jury who heard second-degree murder charges against him (in the killing of another white man) was white, as had been all such forepeople for the last 16 years. The Supreme Court reasoned that "regardless of skin color, an accused suffers a significant 'injury in fact' when the grand jury's composition is tainted by racial discrimination." The Court also said, "The integrity of the body's decisions depends on the integrity of the process used to select the grand jurors."

Finally, in the 2003 case of *Miller-El* v. *Cockrell*,[130] the Court found that a convicted capital defendant's constitutional rights had been violated by Dallas County (Texas) prosecutors who engaged in intentional efforts to remove eligible African-Americans from the pool of potential jurors. Ten out of 11 eligible African-Americans were excluded through the use of peremptory strikes. A relevant portion of the Court's majority opinion reads as follows:

> In this case, debate as to whether the prosecution acted with a race-based reason when striking prospective jurors was raised by the statistical evidence demonstrating that 91% of the eligible African-Americans were excluded . . . ; and by the fact that three of the State's proffered race-neutral rationales for striking African Americans—ambivalence about the death penalty, hesitancy to vote to execute defendants capable of being rehabilitated, and the jurors' own family history of criminality—pertained just as well to some white jurors who were not challenged and who did serve on the jury.[131]

The decision was reaffirmed in the 2005 U.S. Supreme Court case of *Miller-El* v. *Dretke*.[132]

Opening Statements

The presentation of information to the jury begins with **opening statements** made by the prosecution and the defense. The purposes of opening statements are to advise the jury of what the attorneys intend to prove and to describe how such proof will be offered. Evidence is not offered during opening statements. Eventually, however, the jury will have to weigh the evidence presented during the trial and decide which side made the more effective arguments. When a defendant has little evidence to present, the main job of the defense attorney will be to dispute the veracity of the prosecution's version of the facts; under such circumstances, defense attorneys may choose not to present any evidence or testimony at all, focusing instead on the burden of proof requirement facing the prosecution. Such plans will generally be made clear during opening statements. At this time, the defense attorney is also likely to stress the human qualities of the defendant and to remind jurors of the awesome significance of their task.

opening statement
The initial statement of the prosecution or the defense, made in a court of law to a judge, or to a judge and jury, describing the facts that he or she intends to present during trial to prove the case.

CJ Exhibit 2

Peremptory Challenges and Race

A "peremptory challenge to a juror means that one side in a trial has been given the right to throw out a certain number of possible jurors before the trial without giving any reasons."[1]

As this definition—borrowed from a legal dictionary—indicates, attorneys were once able to remove unwanted potential jurors from a criminal case during jury selection procedures through the use of a limited number of peremptory challenges without having to provide any reason whatsoever for the choices they made. (Challenges for cause, on the other hand, although not limited in number, require an acceptable rationale for juror removal.) The understanding of peremptory challenges was changed by the 1991 landmark U.S. Supreme Court case of *Powers* v. *Ohio*.[2] The *Powers* case dealt with a white defendant's desire to ensure a racially balanced jury. In *Powers*, the Supreme Court identified three reasons why peremptory challenges may not be issued if based on race[3]:

> First, the discriminatory use of peremptory challenges causes the defendant cognizable injury, and he or she has a concrete interest in challenging the practice, because racial discrimination in jury selection casts doubt on the integrity of the judicial process and places the fairness of the criminal proceeding in doubt.
>
> Second, the relationship between the defendant and the excluded jurors is such that . . . both have a common interest in eliminating racial discrimination from the courtroom. . . . Third, it is unlikely that a juror dismissed because of race will possess sufficient incentive to set in motion the arduous process needed to vindicate his or her own rights.

The Court continued:

> The very fact that [members of a particular race] are singled out and expressly denied . . . all right to participate in the administration of the law, as jurors, because of their color, though they are citizens, and may be in other respects fully qualified, is practically a brand upon them, affixed by the law, an assertion of their inferiority, and a stimulant to that race prejudice which is an impediment to securing to individuals of that race equal justice which the law aims to secure to all others.

Near the end of its 1991 term, in a move that surprised many Court watchers, the Supreme Court extended to civil cases its ban on racially motivated peremptory challenges. In *Edmonson* v. *Leesville Concrete Co., Inc.*,[4] the Court ruled:

> The harms we recognized in *Powers* are not limited to the criminal sphere. A civil proceeding often implicates significant rights and interests. Civil juries, no less than their criminal counterparts, must follow the law and act as impartial fact-finders. And, as we have observed, their verdicts, no less than those of their criminal counterparts, become binding judgments of the Court. Racial discrimination has no place in the courtroom, whether the proceeding is civil or criminal.

Following *Powers* and *Edmonson*, it is clear that neither prosecuting nor civil attorneys in the future will be able to exclude minority jurors consistently unless they are able to articulate clearly credible race-neutral rationales for their actions.

Even so, recent dissenting opinions indicate that considerable sentiment may exist among the justices that could lead to the return of a broader use of peremptory challenges. In a dissenting opinion in *J. E. B.* v. *Alabama* (1994),[5] Justices Antonin Scalia, William H. Rehnquist, and Clarence Thomas wrote, "[T]he core of the Court's reasoning [banning peremptory challenges based on gender] is that peremptory challenges on the basis of any group characteristic subject to heightened scrutiny are inconsistent with the guarantee of the Equal Protection Clause. . . . Since all groups are subject to the peremptory challenge . . . it is hard to see how any group is denied equal protection."

Library EXTRA

Read Library Extra 8–9 at mycrimekit.com to learn more about the role of race in America's courtrooms today.

[1]Daniel Oran, *Oran's Dictionary of the Law* (St. Paul, MN: West, 1983), p. 312.
[2]*Powers* v. *Ohio*, 499 U.S. 400 (1991).
[3]Ibid.
[4]*Edmonson* v. *Leesville Concrete Co., Inc.*, 500 U.S. 614, 111 S.Ct. 2077, 114 L.Ed.2d 660 (1991).
[5]*J.E.B.* v. *Alabama*, 114 S.Ct. 1419, 128 L.Ed.2d 89 (1994).

Lawyers for both sides are bound by a good-faith ethical requirement in their opening statements. Attorneys may mention only the evidence that they believe actually can and will be presented as the trial progresses. Allusions to evidence that an attorney has no intention of offering are regarded as unprofessional and have been defined by the U.S. Supreme Court as "professional misconduct."[133] When material alluded to in an opening statement cannot, for whatever reason, later be presented in court, it offers opposing counsel an opportunity to discredit the other side.

Presentation of Evidence

The crux of the criminal trial is the presentation of evidence. First, the state is given the opportunity to present evidence intended to prove the defendant's guilt. After prosecutors have rested their case, the defense is afforded the opportunity to provide evidence favorable to the defendant.

Types of Evidence

Evidence can be either direct or circumstantial. **Direct evidence**, if believed, proves a fact without requiring the judge or jury to draw inferences. For example, direct evidence may consist of the information contained in a photograph or videotape. It might consist of testimonial evidence provided by a witness on the stand, and a straightforward statement by a witness, such as "I saw him do it!" is also a form of direct evidence.

Circumstantial evidence is indirect and requires the judge or jury to make inferences and to draw conclusions. At a murder trial, for example, a person who heard gunshots and moments later saw someone run by with a smoking gun in hand might testify to those facts. Even without an eyewitness to the actual homicide, the jury might later conclude that the person seen with the gun was the one who pulled the trigger and committed the crime. Contrary to popular belief, circumstantial evidence is sufficient to produce a verdict and conviction in a criminal trial. In fact, some prosecuting attorneys prefer to work entirely with circumstantial evidence, weaving a tapestry of the criminal act in their arguments to the jury.

Real evidence, which may be either direct or circumstantial, consists of physical material or traces of physical activity. Weapons, tire tracks, ransom notes, and fingerprints all fall into the category of real evidence. Real (or physical) evidence is introduced in the trial by means of *exhibits*, which are objects or displays that may be shown to members of the jury once they are formally accepted as evidence by the judge (see CJ Exhibit 3). Documentary evidence, which is one type of real evidence, includes writings such as business records, journals, written confessions, and letters; documentary evidence can extend beyond paper and ink to include data on magnetic and optical storage devices used in computer operations and video and voice recordings.

evidence
Anything useful to a judge or jury in deciding the facts of a case. Evidence may take the form of witness testimony, written documents, videotapes, magnetic media, photographs, physical objects, and so on.

direct evidence
The evidence that, if believed, directly proves a fact. Eyewitness testimony and videotaped documentation account for the majority of all direct evidence heard in the criminal courtroom.

circumstantial evidence
The evidence that requires interpretation or that requires a judge or jury to reach a conclusion based on what the evidence indicates. From the close proximity of the defendant to a smoking gun, for example, the jury might conclude that he or she pulled the trigger.

real evidence
Evidence that consists of physical material or traces of physical activity.

Evaluation of Evidence

One of the most significant decisions a trial court judge makes is deciding which evidence can be presented to the jury. In making that decision, judges will examine the relevance of the evidence to the case at hand (relevant evidence has a bearing on the facts at issue). For example, a decade or two ago, it was not unusual for a woman's sexual history to be brought out in rape trials. Under what are called rape shield statutes, most states today will not allow this practice, recognizing that these details often have no bearing on the case. Rape shield statutes have been strengthened by U.S. Supreme Court decisions, including the 1991 case of *Michigan* v. *Lucas*.[134]

Colorado's rape shield law played a prominent role in the 2004 case of Kobe Bryant. Bryant, a basketball superstar who was accused of sexually assaulting a 19-year-old Vail-area resort employee, claimed that the sexual encounter was consensual. Defense attorneys sought to have the Colorado law declared unconstitutional in an effort to show that injuries to the woman were the result of her having had sexual intercourse with multiple partners before and after her encounter with Bryant. The case against Bryant was dropped before going to trial.

In evaluating evidence, judges must also weigh the **probative value** of an item of evidence (its usefulness and relevance) against its potential inflammatory or prejudicial qualities. Even useful evidence may unduly bias a jury if it is exceptionally gruesome or is presented in such a way as to imply guilt. For example, gory photographs, especially color photographs, may be withheld from the jury's eyes. In one recent case, a new trial was ordered when photos of the crime scene were projected on a wall over the head of the defendant as he sat in the courtroom, and an appellate court found that presentation to have prejudiced the jury.

probative value
The degree to which a particular item of evidence is useful in, and relevant to, proving something important in a trial.

Sometimes evidence is found to have only limited admissibility, which means that the evidence can be used for a specific purpose but that it might not be accurate in other details. Photographs, for example, may be admitted as evidence for the narrow purpose of showing spatial relationships between objects under discussion, even if the photographs were taken under conditions that did not exist when the offense was committed (such as daylight).

When judges allow the use of evidence that may have been illegally or unconstitutionally gathered, grounds may be created for a later appeal if the trial concludes with a "guilty" verdict. Even when evidence is improperly introduced at trial, however, a number of Supreme Court decisions[135] have held that there may be no grounds for an effective appeal unless such introduction

CJ Exhibit 3

Pretrial and Post-Trial Motions

A *motion* is "an oral or written request made to a court at any time before, during, or after court proceedings, asking the court to make a specified finding, decision, or order."[1] Written motions are called *petitions*. This exhibit lists the most common motions made by both sides in a criminal case before and after trial.

MOTION FOR DISCOVERY

A motion for discovery, filed by the defense, asks the court to allow the defendant's lawyers to view the evidence that the prosecution intends to present at trial. Physical evidence, lists of witnesses, documents, photographs, and so on, which the prosecution plans to introduce in court, are usually made available to the defense as a result of a motion for discovery.

MOTION TO SUPPRESS EVIDENCE

The defense may file a motion to suppress evidence if it learns, in the preliminary hearing or through pretrial discovery, of evidence that it believes to have been unlawfully acquired.

MOTION TO DISMISS CHARGES

A variety of circumstances may result in the filing of a motion to dismiss charges. They include (1) an opinion, by defense counsel, that the indictment or information is not sound; (2) a violation of speedy trial legislation; (3) a plea bargain with the defendant, which may require testimony against codefendants; (4) the death of an important witness or the destruction or disappearance of necessary evidence; (5) the confession, by a supposed victim, that the facts in the case were fabricated; and (6) the success of a motion to suppress evidence that effectively eliminates the prosecution's case.

MOTION FOR CONTINUANCE

The motion for continuance seeks a delay in the start of the trial. Defense motions of this type are often based on an inability to locate important witnesses, the illness of the defendant, or a change in defense counsel immediately before trial.

MOTION FOR CHANGE OF VENUE

In well-known cases, pretrial publicity may lessen the opportunity for a case to be tried before an unbiased jury. A motion for change in venue asks that the trial be moved to some other area where prejudice against the defendant is less likely to exist.

MOTION FOR SEVERANCE OF OFFENSES

Defendants charged with a number of crimes may ask to be tried separately on all or some of the charges through use of a motion for severance of offenses. Although consolidating charges for trial saves time and money, some defendants believe that it is more likely to make them appear guilty.

MOTION FOR SEVERANCE OF DEFENDANTS

The motion for severance of defendants asks the court to try the accused separately from any codefendants. These motions are likely to be filed when the defendant believes that the jury may be prejudiced against him or her by evidence applicable only to other defendants.

MOTION TO DETERMINE PRESENT SANITY

A lack of "present sanity," even though it may be no defense against the criminal charge, can delay trial because a person cannot be tried, sentenced, or punished while insane. If a defendant is insane at the time a trial is to begin, a motion to determine present sanity may halt the proceedings until treatment can be arranged.

MOTION FOR A BILL OF PARTICULARS

The motion for a bill of particulars asks the court to order the prosecutor to provide detailed information about the charges that the defendant will be facing in court. Defendants charged with a number of offenses, or with a number of counts of the same offense, may make such a motion. They may, for example, seek to learn which alleged instances of an offense will become the basis for prosecution or which specific items of contraband allegedly found in their possession are held to violate the law.

MOTION FOR A MISTRIAL

A mistrial may be declared at any time, and a motion for a mistrial may be made by either side. Mistrials are likely to be declared in cases in which highly prejudicial comments are made by either attorney. Defense motions for a mistrial do not provide grounds for a later claim of double jeopardy.

MOTION FOR ARREST OF JUDGMENT

After the verdict of the jury has been announced but before the sentencing, the defendant may make a motion for arrest of judgment. With this motion, the defendant asserts that some legally acceptable reason exists as to why sentencing should not occur. Defendants who are seriously ill, who are hospitalized, or who have gone insane before judgment being imposed may file such a motion.

MOTION FOR A NEW TRIAL

After a jury has returned a guilty verdict, the court may entertain a motion for a new trial from the defense. Acceptance of such a motion is usually based on the discovery of new evidence that is of significant benefit to the defense and that will set aside the conviction.

[1]U.S. Department of Justice, *Dictionary of Criminal Justice Data Terminology*, 2nd ed. (Washington, DC: U.S. Government Printing Office, 1982).

"had substantial and injurious effect or influence in determining the jury's verdict."[136] Called the *harmless error rule*, this standard places the burden on the prosecution to show that the jury's decision would most likely have been the same even in the absence of the inappropriate evidence. The rule is not applicable when a defendant's constitutional guarantees are violated by "structural defects in the constitution of the trial mechanism" itself[137]—such as when a judge gives constitutionally improper instructions to a jury. (We'll discuss those instructions later in this chapter.)

Testimony of Witnesses

Testimony given by witnesses is generally the chief means by which evidence is introduced at trial. Witnesses may include victims, police officers, the defendant, specialists in recognized fields, and others with useful information to provide. Some of these witnesses may have been present during the commission of the offense, while most will have had only a later opportunity to investigate the situation or to analyze evidence.

testimony
The oral evidence offered by a sworn witness on the witness stand during a criminal trial.

Before a witness will be allowed to testify to any fact, the questioning attorney must establish the person's competence. Competence to testify requires that witnesses have personal knowledge of the information they will discuss and that they understand their duty to tell the truth.

One of the defense attorney's most critical decisions is whether to put the defendant on the stand. Defendants have a Fifth Amendment right to remain silent and to refuse to testify. In the precedent-setting case of *Griffin* v. *California* (1965),[138] the U.S. Supreme Court declared that if a defendant refuses to testify, prosecutors and judges are enjoined from even commenting on this fact, although a judge should instruct the jury that such a failure cannot be held to indicate guilt. In 2001, in the case of *Ohio* v. *Reiner*,[139] the U.S. Supreme Court extended Fifth Amendment protections to *witnesses* who deny any and all guilt in association with a crime for which another person is being prosecuted.

A jury consists of 12 persons chosen to decide who has the better lawyer.
—*Robert Frost (1874–1963)*

Direct examination of a witness takes place when a witness is first called to the stand. If the prosecutor calls the witness, the witness is referred to as a *witness for the prosecution*. Where the direct examiner is a defense attorney, the witness is called a *witness for the defense*.

The direct examiner may ask questions that require a "yes" or "no" answer or may ask narrative questions that allow the witness to tell a story in his or her own words. During direct examination, courts generally prohibit the use of leading questions, that is, those that suggest answers to the witness.[140]

Cross-examination refers to the examination of a witness by someone other than the direct examiner. Anyone who offers testimony in a criminal court has the duty to submit to cross-examination.[141] The purpose of cross-examination is to test the credibility and the memory of the witness.

Most states and the federal government restrict the scope of cross-examination to material covered during direct examination; questions about other matters, even though they may relate to the case before the court, are not allowed. A small number of states allow the cross-examiner to raise any issue as long as the court deems it relevant. Leading questions, generally disallowed in direct examination, are regarded as the mainstay of cross-examination. Such questions allow for a concise restatement of testimony that has already been offered and serve to focus efficiently on potential problems that the cross-examiner seeks to address.

Some witnesses commit **perjury**—that is, they make statements that they know to be untrue. Reasons for perjured testimony vary, but most witnesses who lie on the stand probably do so in an effort to help friends accused of crimes. Witnesses who perjure themselves are subject to impeachment, in which either the defense or the prosecution demonstrates that a witness has intentionally offered false testimony. For example, previous statements made by the witness may be shown to be at odds with more recent declarations. When it can be demonstrated that a witness has offered inaccurate or false testimony, the witness has been effectively impeached. Perjury is a serious offense in its own right, and dishonest witnesses may face fines or jail time.

perjury
The intentional making of a false statement as part of the testimony by a sworn witness in a judicial proceeding on a matter relevant to the case at hand.

At the conclusion of the cross-examination, the direct examiner may again question the witness. This procedure is called *redirect examination* and may be followed by a recross-examination and so on, until both sides are satisfied that they have exhausted fruitful lines of questioning.

Children as Witnesses

An area of special concern involves the use of children as witnesses in a criminal trial, especially when the children are also victims. Currently, in an effort to avoid what may be traumatizing direct confrontations between child witnesses and the accused, 37 states allow the use of videotaped testimony in criminal courtrooms, and 32 permit the use of closed-circuit television, which allows the child to testify out of the presence of the defendant. In 1988, however, in the case of ***Coy* v. *Iowa***,[142] the U.S. Supreme Court ruled that a courtroom screen, used to shield child witnesses from visual confrontation with a defendant in a child sex abuse case, had violated the confrontation clause of the Constitution (found in the Sixth Amendment).

On the other hand, in the 1990 case of ***Maryland* v. *Craig***,[143] the Court upheld the use of closed-circuit television to shield children who testify in criminal courts. The Court's decision was partially based on the realization that "a significant majority of States have enacted statutes to protect child witnesses from the trauma of giving testimony in child-abuse cases . . . [which] attests to the widespread belief in the importance of such a policy."

Although a face-to-face confrontation with a child victim may not be necessary in the courtroom, until 1992 the Supreme Court had been reluctant to allow into evidence descriptions of abuse and other statements made by children, even to child-care professionals, when those statements were made outside the courtroom. In ***Idaho* v. *Wright*** (1990),[144] the Court reasoned that such "statements [are] fraught with the dangers of unreliability which the Confrontation Clause is designed to highlight and obviate."

However, in ***White* v. *Illinois*** (1992),[145] the Court reversed its stance, ruling that in-court testimony provided by a medical provider and the child's babysitter, which repeated what the child had said to them concerning White's sexually abusive behavior, was permissible. The Court rejected White's claim that out-of-court statements should be admissible only when the witness is unavailable to testify at trial, saying instead, "A finding of unavailability of an out-of-court declarant is necessary only if the out-of-court statement was made at a prior judicial proceeding." Placing *White* within the context of generally established exceptions, the Court declared, "A statement that has been offered in a moment of excitement—without the opportunity to reflect on the consequences of one's exclamation—may justifiably carry more weight with a trier of fact than a similar statement offered in the relative calm of the courtroom. Similarly, a statement made in the course of procuring medical services, where the declarant knows that a false statement may cause misdiagnosis or mistreatment, carries special guarantees of credibility that a trier of fact may not think replicated by courtroom testimony."

The Hearsay Rule

hearsay
Something that is not based on the personal knowledge of a witness. Witnesses who testify about something they have heard, for example, are offering hearsay by repeating information about a matter of which they have no direct knowledge.

hearsay rule
The long-standing precedent that hearsay cannot be used in American courtrooms. Rather than accepting testimony based on hearsay, the court will ask that the person who was the original source of the hearsay information be brought in to be questioned and cross-examined. Exceptions to the hearsay rule may occur when the person with direct knowledge is dead or is otherwise unable to testify.

Hearsay is anything not based on the personal knowledge of a witness. A witness may say, for example, "John told me that Fred did it!" Such a witness becomes a hearsay declarant, and following a likely objection by counsel, the trial judge will have to decide whether the witness's statement will be allowed to stand as evidence. In most cases, the judge will instruct the jury to disregard the witness's comment, thereby enforcing the **hearsay rule**, which prohibits the use of "secondhand evidence." The hearsay rule is based on the Sixth Amendment's confrontation clause, which gives a criminal defendant the right to confront his or her accusers; in today's courts, that generally means the right to cross-examine witnesses against him or her.

Exceptions to the hearsay rule have been established by both precedent and tradition. One exception is the dying declaration, which is a statement made by a person who is about to die. When heard by a second party, it may usually be repeated in court, provided that certain conditions have been met. A dying declaration is generally a valid exception to the hearsay rule when it is made by someone who knows that he or she is about to die and when the statement made relates to the cause and circumstances of the impending death.

Spontaneous statements, also called excited utterances, provide another exception to the hearsay rule. A statement is considered spontaneous when it is made in the heat of excitement before the person has had time to make it up. For example, a defendant who is just regaining consciousness following a crime may make an utterance that could later be repeated in court by those who heard it.

Out-of-court statements, especially if they were recorded during a time when a person was experiencing great excitement or while a person was under considerable stress, may also become exceptions to the hearsay rule. Many states, for example, permit juries to hear 9-1-1 tape recordings or to read police transcripts of victim interviews without requiring that the people who made them appear in court. In two recent cases, however, the U.S. Supreme Court barred admission of tape-recorded 9-1-1 calls when the people making them were alive and in good health but not available for cross-examination. In *Crawford* v.

Washington,[146] a 2004 case, the Court disallowed a woman's tape-recorded eyewitness account of a fight in which her husband stabbed another man, holding that the Constitution bars admission of testimonal statements of a witness who did not appear at trial unless he or she was unable to testify, and the defendant had a prior opportunity for cross-examination. In *Davis* v. *Washington,*[147] decided in 2006, the Court held that a 9-1-1 call made by a woman who said that her former boyfriend was beating her had been improperly introduced as testimonal evidence. The woman had been subpoenaed but failed to appear in court. The key word in both cases is *testimonial*, and the Court indicated that "statements are non-testimonial when made in the course of police interrogation under circumstances objectively indicating that the primary purpose of interrogation is to enable police assistance to meet an ongoing emergency."[148]

The use of other out-of-court statements, such as writings or routine video or audio recordings, usually requires the witness to testify that the statements or depictions were accurate at the time they were made. Witnesses who so testify may be subject to cross-examination by the defendant's attorney. Nonetheless, this "past recollection recorded" exception to the hearsay rule is especially useful in drawn-out court proceedings that occur long after the crime. Under such circumstances, witnesses may no longer remember the details of an event; their earlier statements to authorities, however, can be introduced into evidence as past recollection recorded.

Closing Arguments

At the conclusion of a criminal trial, both sides have the opportunity for a final narrative presentation to the jury in the form of a **closing argument**. This summation provides a review and analysis of the evidence. Its purpose is to persuade the jury to draw a conclusion favorable to the presenter. Testimony can be quoted, exhibits referred to, and attention drawn to inconsistencies in the evidence presented by the other side.

closing argument
An oral summation of a case presented to a judge, or to a judge and jury, by the prosecution or by the defense in a criminal trial.

States vary as to the order of closing arguments. Nearly all allow the defense attorney to speak to the jury before the prosecution makes its final points. A few permit the prosecutor the first opportunity for summation. Some jurisdictions and the Federal Rules of Criminal Procedure[149] authorize a defense rebuttal (a rebuttal is a response to the closing argument of the other side).

◄ An attorney making a closing argument to the jury. What other features of the adversarial system can you identify?
© Royalty-Free/CORBIS

I do not know whether the jury is useful to those who are in litigation; but I am certain it is highly beneficial to those who decide the litigation; and I look upon it as one of the most efficacious means for the education of the people which society can employ.
—*Alexis de Tocqueville (1805–1859)*

Some specific issues may need to be addressed during summation. If, for example, the defendant has not taken the stand during the trial, the defense attorney's closing argument will inevitably stress that this failure to testify cannot be regarded as indicating guilt. Where the prosecution's case rests entirely on circumstantial evidence, the defense can be expected to stress the lack of any direct proof, and the prosecutor is likely to argue that circumstantial evidence can be stronger than direct evidence, since it is not as easily affected by human error or false testimony.

Judge's Charge to the Jury

After closing arguments, the judge charges the jury to "retire and select one of your number as a foreman . . . and deliberate upon the evidence which has been presented until you have reached a verdict." The words of the charge vary somewhat between jurisdictions and among judges, but all judges will remind members of the jury of their duty to consider objectively only the evidence that has been presented and of the need for impartiality. Most judges also remind jury members of the statutory elements of the alleged offense, of the burden of proof that rests on the prosecution, and of the need for the prosecution to have proved the defendant's guilt beyond a reasonable doubt before the jury can return a guilty verdict.

In their charge, many judges also provide a summary of the evidence presented, usually from notes they have taken during the trial, as a means of refreshing the jurors' memories of events. About half of all the states allow judges the freedom to express their own views as to the credibility of witnesses and the significance of evidence; the other states only permit judges to summarize the evidence in an objective and impartial manner.

Following the charge, the jury is removed from the courtroom and is permitted to begin its deliberations. In the absence of the jury, defense attorneys may choose to challenge portions of the judge's charge. If they feel that some oversight has occurred in the original charge, they may ask the judge to provide the jury with additional instructions or information. Such objections, if denied by the judge, often become the basis for an appeal when a conviction is returned.

Jury Deliberations and the Verdict

Deliberations Process

verdict
The decision of the jury in a jury trial or of a judicial officer in a nonjury trial.

In cases in which the evidence is either very clear or very weak, jury deliberations may be brief, lasting only a matter of hours or even minutes. Some juries, however, deliberate days or sometimes weeks, carefully weighing all the nuances of the evidence they have seen and heard. Many jurisdictions require that juries reach a unanimous **verdict** (decision), although the U.S. Supreme Court has ruled that unanimous verdicts are not required in noncapital cases.[150] Even so, some juries are unable to agree on any verdict. When a jury is deadlocked, it is said to be a *hung jury*. When a unanimous decision is required, juries may be deadlocked by the strong opposition of only one member to a verdict agreed on by all the others.

In some states, judges are allowed to add a boost to nearly hung juries by recharging them under a set of instructions that the Supreme Court put forth in the 1896 case of *Allen* v. *U.S.*[151] The Allen Charge, as it is known in those jurisdictions, urges the jury to vigorous deliberations and suggests to obstinate jurors that their objections may be ill-founded if they make no impression on the other jurors.

Problems with the Jury System

Judge Harold J. Rothwax, a well-known critic of today's jury system, tells the tale of a rather startling 1991 case over which he presided. The case involved a murder defendant, a handsome young man who had been fired by a New York company that serviced automated teller machines (ATMs). After being fired, the defendant intentionally caused a machine in a remote area to malfunction. When two former colleagues arrived to fix it, he robbed them, stole the money inside the ATM, and shot both men repeatedly. One of the men survived long enough to identify his former coworker as the shooter. The man was arrested, and a trial ensued; after three weeks of hearing the case, the jury deadlocked. Judge Rothwax later learned that the jury had voted

11 to one to convict the defendant, but the one holdout just couldn't believe that "someone so good-looking could . . . commit such a crime."[152]

Many routine cases as well as some highly publicized cases, like the murder trial of O. J. Simpson which the whole world watched, have called into question the ability of the American jury system to do its job—that is, to sort through the evidence and to accurately determine the defendant's guilt or innocence. In a televised 1995 trial, Simpson was acquitted of the charge that he murdered his ex-wife, Nicole Brown, and her friend Ronald Goldman outside Brown's home in 1994. Many people believed that strong evidence tied Simpson to the crimes, and the criminal trial left many people feeling unsatisfied with the criminal justice system and with the criminal trial process. Later, a civil jury ordered Simpson to pay $33.5 million to the Goldman family and to Nicole Brown's estate.

Because jurors are drawn from all walks of life, many cannot be expected to understand modern legal complexities and to appreciate all the nuances of trial court practice. It is likely that even the best-intentioned jurors cannot understand and rarely observe some jury instructions.[153] In highly charged cases, emotions are often difficult to separate from fact, and during deliberations, some juries are dominated by one or two members with forceful personalities. Jurors may also suffer from inattention or may be unable to understand fully the testimony of expert witnesses or the significance of technical evidence.

Jurors may be less than effective in cases where they fear personal retaliation. In the state-level trial of the police officers accused in the infamous Rodney King beating, for example, jurors reported being afraid for their lives due to the riots in Los Angeles that broke out after their "not guilty" verdict was announced. Some slept with weapons by their side, and others sent their children away to safe locations.[154] Because of the potential for harm that jurors faced in the 1993 federal trial of the same officers, U.S. District Judge John G. Davies ruled that the names of the jurors be forever kept secret. Members of the press called the secrecy order "an unprecedented infringement of the public's right of access to the justice system."[155] Similarly, in the 1993 trial of three black men charged with the beating of white truck driver Reginald Denny during the Los Angeles riots, Los Angeles Superior Court Judge John Ouderkirk ordered that the identities of the jurors not be released.

Opponents of the jury system have argued that it should be replaced by a panel of judges who would both render a verdict and impose sentence. Regardless of how well considered such a suggestion may be, such a change could not occur without modification of the Constitution's Sixth Amendment right to trial by jury.

An alternative suggestion for improving the process of trial by jury has been the call for professional jurors. Professional jurors would be paid by the government, as are judges, prosecutors, and public defenders, and would be expected to have the expertise to sit on any jury. Professional jurors would be trained to listen objectively and would be taught the kinds of decision-making skills necessary to function effectively within an adversarial context. They would hear one case after another, perhaps moving between jurisdictions in cases of highly publicized crimes.

A professional jury system offers these advantages:

1. *Dependability.* Professional jurors could be expected to report to the courtroom in a timely fashion and to be good listeners, since both would be required by the nature of the job.
2. *Knowledge.* Professional jurors would be trained in the law, would understand what a finding of guilt requires, and would know what to expect from other actors in the courtroom.
3. *Equity.* Professional jurors would understand the requirements of due process and would be less likely to be swayed by the emotional content of a case, having been schooled in the need to separate matters of fact from personal feelings.

In suits at common law . . . the right of trial by jury shall be preserved, and no fact tried by a jury, shall be otherwise reexamined in any Court of the United States, than according to the rules of the common law.
—Seventh Amendment to the U.S. Constitution

A professional jury system would not be without difficulties. Jurors under such a system might become jaded, deciding cases out of hand as routines lead to boredom. They might categorize defendants according to whether they "fit the type" for guilt or innocence based on the jurors' previous experiences. Job requirements for professional jurors would be difficult to establish without infringing on the jurors' freedom to decide cases as they understand them; for the same reason, any evaluation of the job performance of professional jurors would be a

Multiculturalism and Diversity

The Bilingual Courtroom

One of the central multicultural issues facing the criminal justice system today is the need for clear communication with recent immigrants and subcultural groups that have not been fully acculturated. Many such groups hold to traditions and values that differ from those held by the majority of Americans. Such differences influence the interpretation of things seen and heard. Even more basic, however, are language differences that might prevent effective communication with criminal justice system personnel.

This box focuses on the use of courtroom interpreters to facilitate effective and accurate communication. The role of the courtroom interpreter is to present neutral verbatim, or word-for-word, translations. Interpreters must provide true, accurate, and complete interpretations of the exact statements made by non-English-speaking defendants, victims, and witnesses—whether on the stand, in writing, or in court-related conferences. The Court Interpreters and Translators Association also requires, through its code of professional ethics, that translators remember their "absolute responsibility to keep all oral and written information gained completely confidential."

Although most court interpreters are actually present in the courtroom at the time of trial, telephone interpreting provides an alternative way for courts to reduce problems associated with the lack of access to qualified interpreters. Today, state court administrative offices in Florida, Idaho, New Jersey, and Washington State sponsor programs through which qualified interpreters in metropolitan counties are made available to courts in rural counties by telephone.

The federal Court Interpreters Act of 1978[1] specifically provides for the use of interpreters in federal courts. It applies to both criminal and civil trials and hearings. The act reads, in part, as follows[2]:

> The presiding judicial officers . . . shall utilize [an interpreter] . . . in judicial proceedings instituted by the United States, if the presiding judicial officer determines on such officer's own motion or on the motion of a party that such party (including the defendant in a criminal case), or a witness who may present testimony in such judicial proceedings—
>
> (A) speaks only or primarily a language other than English; or
>
> (B) suffers from a hearing impairment . . . so as to inhibit such party's comprehension of the proceedings or communication with counsel or the presiding officer, or so as to inhibit such witness's comprehension of questions and the presentation of such testimony.

As this extract from the statute shows, translators are also required for individuals with hearing impairments who communicate primarily through American Sign Language. The act does not require that an interpreter be appointed when a person has a speech impairment that is not accompanied by a hearing impairment. A court is not prohibited, however, from providing assistance to that person if it will aid in the efficient administration of justice.

Because it is a federal law, the Court Interpreters Act does not apply to state courts. Nonetheless, most states have enacted similar legislation. A few states are starting to introduce high-standard testing for court interpreters, although most states currently conduct little or no interpreter screening. The federal government and states with high standards for court interpreters generally require interpreter certification. To become certified, an interpreter must pass an oral examination, such as the federal court interpreter's examination or an examination administered by a state court or by a recognized international agency such as the United Nations.

There is growing recognition among professional court interpreters of the need for standardized interstate testing and certification programs. To meet that need, the National Center for State Courts created the Consortium for State Court Interpreter Certification. The consortium works to pool state resources for developing and administering court interpreter testing and training programs. The consortium's founding states were Minnesota, New Jersey, Oregon, and Washington, although many other states have since joined.

Because certified interpreters are not always available, even by telephone, most states have created a special category of "language-skilled interpreters." To qualify as a language-skilled interpreter, a person must demonstrate to the court's satisfaction his or her ability to interpret court proceedings from English to a designated language and from that language to English. Many states require sign language interpreters to hold a Legal Specialist Certificate, or its equivalent, from the Registry of Interpreters for the Deaf, showing that they are certified in American Sign Language. Learn more about language interpretation in the courts from the National Association of Judiciary Interpreters and Translators via Web Extra 8–12 at mycrimekit.com.

Web EXTRA

[1]28 U.S.C. section 1827.

[2]Ibid., at section 1827 (d) (1).

References: The National Association of Judiciary Interpreters and Translators website, http://www.najit.org; Madelynn Herman and Anne Endress Skove, "State Court Rules for Language Interpreters," memorandum number IS 99.1242, National Center for State Courts, Knowledge Management Office, September 8, 1999; Madelynn Herman and Dot Bryant, "Language Interpreting in the Courts," National Center for State Courts. Web posted at http://www.ncsc.dni.us/KMO/Projects/Trends/99-00/articles/CtInterpreters.htm; and National Crime Prevention Council, *Building and Crossing Bridges: Refugees and Law Enforcement Working Together* (Washington, DC: NCPC, 1994).

difficult call. Finally, professional jurors might not truly be peer jurors, since their social characteristics might be skewed by education, residence, and politics.

Improvement of the Adjudication Process

Courts today are coming under increasing scrutiny, and well-publicized trials, such as those of Michael Jackson, Andrea Yates, Martha Stewart, Scott Peterson, O. J. Simpson, and John Allen Muhammad, have heightened awareness of problems with the American court system. One of today's most important issues is reducing the number of jurisdictions by unifying courts. The current multiplicity of jurisdictions frequently leads to what many believe are avoidable conflicts and overlaps in the handling of criminal defendants. Problems are exacerbated by the lack of any centralized judicial authority in some states that might resolve jurisdictional and procedural disputes.[156] Proponents of unification suggest the elimination of overlapping jurisdictions, the creation of special-purpose courts, and the formulation of administrative offices in order to achieve economies of scale.[157]

The number of court-watch citizens' groups is also rapidly growing. Such organizations focus on the trial court level, but they are part of a general trend toward seeking greater openness in government decision making at all levels.[158] Court-watch groups regularly monitor court proceedings and attempt to document and often publicize inadequacies. They frequently focus on the handling of indigents, fairness in the scheduling of cases for trial, unnecessary court delays, reduction of waiting time, treatment of witnesses and jurors, and adequacy of rights advisements for defendants throughout judicial proceedings.

The statistical measurement of court performance is another area that is receiving increased attention. Research has looked at the efficiency with which prosecutors schedule cases for trial, the speed with which judges resolve issues, the amount of time judges spend on the bench, and the economic and other costs to defendants, witnesses, and communities involved in the judicial process.[159] Statistical studies of this type often attempt to measure elements of court performance as diverse as sentence variation, charging accuracy, fairness in plea bargaining, evenhandedness, delays, and attitudes toward the court by lay participants. Visit Library Extra 8–10 for more information on standards and measures in court performance.

Library EXTRA

Summary

- The courtroom work group is comprised of professional courtroom personnel, including the judge, the prosecuting attorney, the defense counsel, the bailiff, the local court administrator, the court reporter, the clerk of court, and expert witnesses. The courtroom work group is guided by statutory requirements and ethical considerations, and its members are generally dedicated to bringing the criminal trial and other courtroom procedures to a successful close.
- Also present in the courtroom during a criminal trial are "outsiders"—nonprofessional courtroom participants like witnesses and jurors. Nonprofessional courtroom participants include lay witnesses, jurors, the victim, the defendant, and spectators and members of the press. Nonprofessional or nonjudicial courtroom personnel may be unwilling or inadvertent participants in a criminal trial.
- The criminal trial involves an adversarial process that pits the prosecution against the defense. Trials are peer-based fact-finding processes intended to protect the rights of the accused while disputed issues of guilt or innocence are resolved. The primary purpose of a criminal trial is to determine whether a defendant, through his or her behavior, violated the criminal law of the jurisdiction in which the court has authority.

- A criminal trial has eight stages: trial initiation, jury selection, opening statements, presentation of evidence, closing arguments, judge's charge to the jury, jury deliberations, and verdict. Each is described in detail in this chapter. At least a few experts have suggested the training and use of a cadre of professional jurors, versed in the law and in trial practice, who could insulate themselves from media portrayals of famous defendants and who would resolve questions of guilt or innocence more on the basis of reason than emotion.
- The American court system has been called into question by some well-publicized trials of the last two decades, which have demonstrated apparent weaknesses in the trial process. Some people suggest that court unification might help address a number of today's problems by reducing the number of jurisdictions, resulting in more uniform procedures.

Key Concepts

Terms

adversarial system
bailiff
change of venue
circumstantial evidence
closing argument
courtroom work group
defense counsel
direct evidence
evidence
exculpatory evidence
expert witness
hearsay
hearsay rule
judge
juror
jury selection
lay witness
opening statement
peremptory challenge
perjury
probative value
prosecutor
prosecutorial discretion
public defender
real evidence
rules of evidence
scientific jury selection
sequestered jury
Speedy Trial Act
subpoena
testimony
verdict
victim assistance program

Cases

Argersinger v. *Hamlin*
Burns v. *Reed*
Coy v. *Iowa*
Crosby v. *U.S.*
Demarest v. *Manspeaker et al.*
Doggett v. *U.S.*
Edmonson v. *Leesville Concrete Co., Inc.*
Fex v. *Michigan*
Georgia v. *McCollum*
Gideon v. *Wainwright*
Idaho v. *Wright*
Imbler v. *Pachtman*
Maryland v. *Craig*
Mu'Min v. *Virginia*
Powers v. *Ohio*
White v. *Illinois*
Zafiro v. *U.S.*

Questions for Review

1. Who are the professional members of the courtroom work group, and what are their roles?
2. Who are the nonprofessional courtroom participants, and what are their roles?
3. What is the purpose of a criminal trial? What is the difference between factual guilt and legal guilt? What do we mean by the term *adversarial system*?
4. What are the various stages of a criminal trial? Describe each one.
5. How might the adjudication process be improved?

To participate in an online discussion of these topics and others, join the CJ Brief e-mail discussion list at mycrimekit.com.

Web Quest

Take a virtual tour of the U.S. Supreme Court Building via the multimedia Oyez Project, available on the Web at http://www.oyez.org/oyez/tour/. Once there, use the tour contents menu to help you navigate the site. Take a closer look at almost any area of the building, and get a 360-degree view of almost every room by clicking on the picture (hold the mouse button down and drag it). For this assignment, make use of all the navigational features available at the Oyez Project site to move through the Supreme Court Building. As you tour the building, write down what you see, and print out the images of each room you visit. Submit these descriptions and images to your instructor if asked to do so.

To complete this Web Quest online, go to the Web Quest module in Chapter 8 of the *Criminal Justice: A Brief Introduction* Companion Website at mycrimekit.com.

Notes

i. The President's Commission on Law Enforcement and Administration of Justice, *The Challenge of Crime in a Free Society* (Washington, DC: U.S. Government Printing Office, 1967), p. 125.
ii. *Miller-El* v. *Dretke,* 545 U.S. 231 (2005).
iii. Quoted in Richard Willing, "Courts Try to Make Jury Duty Less of a Choice," *USA Today,* March 17, 2005, p. 17A.

1. D. Graham Burnett, "Anatomy of a Verdict: The View from a Juror's Chair," *New York Times* magazine, August 26, 2001.
2. Details for this story come from "The Laci Peterson Case," Court TV online. Web posted at http://www.courttv.com/trials/peterson/index.html (accessed May 24, 2007).
3. Suzanne Herel, "Exoneration Effort for Scott Peterson," *San Francisco Chronicle,* April 1, 2006, p. B3.
4. "Scott Peterson's Mother Seeks Estate Cash," Salon.com, April 5, 2006. Web posted at http://www.salon.com/wire/ap/archive.html?wire=D8GQ0S6O0. html (accessed April 5, 2006).
5. "Update 2: Scott Peterson's Family Seeks 'Real Killer,'" Forbes.com, March 31, 2006. Web posted at http://www.forbes.com/business/manufacturing/feeds/ap/2006/03/31/ap2638842.html (accessed April 5, 2006).
6. Anne Bird, *Blood Brother: 33 Reasons My Brother Scott Peterson Is Guilty* (New York: HarperCollins, 2005).
7. See, for example, Jeffrey T. Ulmer, *Social Worlds of Sentencing: Courts Communities under Sentencing Guidelines* (Ithaca: State University of New York Press, 1997); and Roy B. Flemming, Peter F. Nardulli, and James Eisenstein, *The Craft of Justice: Politics and Work in Criminal Court Communities* (Philadelphia: University of Pennsylvania Press, 1993).
8. See, for example, Edward J. Clynch and David W. Neubauer, "Trial Courts as Organizations," *Law and Policy Quarterly,* Vol. 3 (1981), pp. 69–94.
9. American Bar Association, *ABA Standards for Criminal Justice: Special Functions of the Trial Judge*, 3rd ed. (Chicago: ABA, 2000).
10. In 1940, Missouri became the first state to adopt a plan for the "merit selection" of judges based on periodic public review.
11. National Judicial College, "About the NJC." Web posted at http://www.judges.org/about (accessed May 2, 2008).
12. See National Judicial College, *National Impact 2006*. Web posted at http://www.judges.org/downloads/general_information/national_impact06 (accessed May 22, 2006).
13. Doris Marie Provine, *Judging Credentials: Nonlawyer Judges and the Politics of Professionalism* (Chicago: University of Chicago Press, 1986).
14. Town and village justices in New York State serve part-time and may or may not be lawyers; judges of all other courts must be lawyers, whether or not they serve full-time. From New York State Commission on Judicial Conduct, *2001 Annual Report.* Web posted at http://www.scjc.state.ny.us/annual.html (accessed March 10, 2006).
15. Ibid.
16. Bureau of Justice Statistics, *Report to the Nation on Crime and Justice: The Data* (Washington, DC: U.S. Department of Justice, 1983).
17. For a discussion of the resource limitations that district attorneys face in combating corporate crime, see Michael L. Benson et al., "District Attorneys and Corporate Crime: Surveying the Prosecutorial Gatekeepers," *Criminology*, Vol. 26, No. 3 (August 1988), pp. 505–517.
18. Carol J. DeFrances and Greg W. Steadman, *Prosecutors in State Courts, 1996* (Washington, DC: Bureau of Justice Statistics, 1998).
19. 28 U.S.C. 530A.
20. Some of the wording in this paragraph is adapted from Kim Murphy, "Prosecutors in Oregon Find 'Truth' Ruling a Real Hindrance," *Los Angeles Times*, August 5, 2001.
21. S45801, Oregon Supreme Court, August 17, 2000.
22. The ruling was based on Disciplinary Rule 1-102 of the Oregon State Bar, which says, in part, that it is professional misconduct for a lawyer to "engage in conduct involving dishonesty, fraud, deceit or misrepresentation." The rule also prohibits a lawyer from violating this dishonesty provision through the acts of another. Also at issue was Disciplinary Rule 7-102, which prohibits a lawyer from "knowingly making a false statement of law or fact."
23. See *Oregon Code of Professional Responsibility*, R. 1-102(D) (2003).
24. "Duke Case DA's Apology Not Accepted," USA *Today,* May 13, 2007.
25. Duff Wilson, "Prosecutor Apologizes to Former Duke Players," *New York Times,* April 12, 2007.
26. Kenneth Culp Davis, *Discretionary Justice* (Baton Rouge: Louisiana State University Press, 1969), p. 190.
27. Barbara Borland, *The Prosecution of Felony Arrests* (Washington, DC: Bureau of Justice Statistics, 1983).
28. *Brady* v. *Maryland*, 373 U.S. 83 (1963).
29. *U.S.* v. *Bagley*, 473 U.S. 667 (1985).
30. *Banks* v. *Dretke*, 124 S.Ct. 1256, 1280 (2004).
31. *Imbler* v. *Pachtman*, 424 U.S. 409 (1976).
32. *Burns* v. *Reed*, 500 U.S. 478 (1991).
33. Ibid., complaint, p. 29.
34. Cassia Spohn, John Gruhl, and Susan Welch, "The Impact of the Ethnicity and Gender of Defendants on the Decision to Reject or Dismiss Felony Charges," *Criminology,* Vol. 25, No. 1 (1987), pp. 175–191.
35. American Bar Association Center for Professional Responsibility, *Model Rules of Professional Conduct* (Chicago: ABA, 2003), p. 87.
36. The same is true under federal law, and in almost all of the states, of communications between defendants and members of the clergy, psychiatrists and psychologists, medical doctors, and licensed social workers in the course of psychotherapy. See, for example, *Jaffee* v. *Redmond*, 116 S.Ct. 1923 (1996).
37. *Powell* v. *Alabama*, 287 U.S. 45 (1932).
38. *Johnson* v. *Zerbst*, 304 U.S. 458 (1938).

39. *Gideon* v. *Wainwright*, 372 U.S. 335 (1963).
40. *Argersinger* v. *Hamlin*, 407 U.S. 25 (1972).
41. *In re Gault*, 387 U.S. 1 (1967).
42. *Alabama* v. *Shelton*, 535 U.S. 654 (2002).
43. Jane Fritsch, "Pataki Rethinks Promise of a Pay Raise for Lawyers to the Indigent," *New York Times*, December 24, 2001.
44. Steven K. Smith and Carol J. DeFrances, *Indigent Defense* (Washington, DC: Bureau of Justice Statistics, 1996).
45. Ibid.
46. Carol J. DeFrances, *State-Funded Indigent Defense Services, 1999* (Washington, DC: National Institute of Justice, 2001), from which the information in this paragraph is derived.
47. National Symposium on Indigent Defense, *Improving Criminal Justice Systems through Expanded Strategies and Innovative Collaborations* (Washington, DC: Office of Justice Programs, 2000).
48. David Exum, "Big Demand, Small Paychecks: State Struggles to Retain Public Defenders," *Jobfind* print edition, April 11, 2004.
49. DeFrances, *State-Funded Indigent Defense Services, 1999.*
50. Ibid.
51. "Nationline: McVeigh's Defense Cost Taxpayers $13.8 Million," *USA Today*, July 3, 2001, p. 3A.
52. Caroline Wolf Harlow, *Defense Counsel in Criminal Cases* (Washington, DC: Bureau of Justice Statistics, 2000); and Carol J. DeFrances and Marika F. X. Litras, *Indigent Defense Service in Large Counties, 1999* (Washington, DC: Bureau of Justice Statistics, 2000).
53. *Faretta* v. *California*, 422 U.S. 806 (1975).
54. Smith and DeFrances, *Indigent Defense*, pp. 2–3.
55. *Anders* v. *California*, 386 U.S. 738 (1967).
56. *People* v. *Wende*, 25 Cal.3d 436, 600 P.2d 1071 (1979).
57. *Smith* v. *Robbins*, 528 U.S. 259 (2000).
58. *Texas* v. *Cobb*, 532 U.S. 162 (2001).
59. Details for this story come from Chisun Lee, "Punishing Mmes. Stewart: The Parallel Universes of Martha and Lynne," *The Village Voice*, February 15, 2005. Web posted at http://www.refuseandresist.org/article-print.php?aid51757 (accessed January 5, 2006).
60. "Lawyer Convicted of Terrorist Support," *USA Today,* February 11, 2005, p. 3A.
61. Mike McKee, "California State Bar to Allow Lawyers to Break Confidentiality," *The Recorder*, May 17, 2004. Web posted at http://www.law.com/jsp/article.jsp?id51084316038367 (accessed August 25, 2005).
62. "ABA Eases Secrecy Rules in Lawyer-Client Relationship," *USA Today*, August 7, 2001.
63. *Nix* v. *Whiteside*, 475 U.S. 157 (1986).
64. Ibid.
65. "Courtroom Killings Verdict," *USA Today*, February 15, 1993, p. 3A.
66. National Center for State Courts, *Improving Security in State Courthouses: Ten Essential Elements for Court Safety.* Web posted at http://www.ncsconline.org/what'sNew/TenPointPlan.htm (accessed October 20, 2005).
67. President's Commission on Law Enforcement and Administration of Justice, *The Challenge of Crime in a Free Society* (Washington, DC: U.S. Government Printing Office, 1967), p. 129.
68. National Advisory Commission on Criminal Justice Standards and Goals, *Courts* (Washington, DC: U.S. Government Printing Office, 1973), Standard 9.3.
69. See, for example, Joan G. Brannon, *The Judicial System in North Carolina* (Raleigh, NC: Administrative Office of the United States Courts, 1984), p. 14.
70. Joseph L. Peterson, "Use of Forensic Evidence by the Police and Courts," *Research in Brief* (Washington, DC: National Institute of Justice, 1987), p. 3.
71. Ibid., p. 6.
72. Jennifer Bowles, "Simpson-Paid Experts," Associated Press wire service, August 12, 1995.
73. *California* v. *Green*, 399 U.S. 149 (1970).
74. Patrick L. McCloskey and Ronald L. Schoenberg, *Criminal Law Deskbook* (New York: Matthew Bender, 1988), Section 17, p. 123.
75. Bureau of Justice Statistics, *Report to the Nation on Crime and Justice,* 2nd ed. (Washington, DC: BJS, 1988), p. 82.
76. Anna Johnson, "Jury with Oprah Winfrey Convicts Man of Murder," Associated Press, August 19, 2004.
77. *Demarest* v. *Manspeaker et al.,* 498 U.S. 184, 111 S.Ct. 599, 112 L.Ed.2d 608 (1991).
78. Bureau of Justice Statistics, *Report to the Nation on Crime and Justice.*
79. Johnson, "Jury with Oprah Winfrey Convicts Man of Murder."
80. *Williams* v. *Florida*, 399 U.S. 78, 90 S.Ct. 1893, 26 L.Ed.2d 446 (1970).
81. *Smith* v. *Texas*, 311 U.S. 128 (1940). That right does not apply when the defendants are facing the possibility of a prison sentence less than six months in length or even when the potential aggregate sentence for multiple petty offenses exceeds six months (see *Lewis* v. *U.S.*, 518 U.S. 322 [1996]).
82. *Thiel* v. *Southern Pacific Co.,* 328 U.S. 217 (1945).
83. American Bar Association, *Principles for Juries and Jury Trials* (Chicago: ABA, 2005).
84. The author was himself the victim of a felony some years ago. His car was stolen in Columbus, Ohio, and recovered a year later in Cleveland. He was informed that the person who had taken it was in custody, but he never heard what happened to him, nor could he learn where or whether a trial was to be held.
85. Federal Rules of Criminal Procedure, Rule 43.
86. *Crosby* v. *U.S.*, 113 S.Ct. 748, 122 L.Ed.2d 25 (1993).
87. *Zafiro* v. *U.S.*, 113 S.Ct. 933, 122 L.Ed.2d 317 (1993).
88. *Nebraska Press Association* v. *Stuart*, 427 U.S. 539 (1976).
89. However, it is generally accepted that trial judges may issue limited gag orders aimed at trial participants.
90. *Press Enterprise Company* v. *Superior Court of California, Riverside County,* 478 U.S. 1 (1986).
91. *Caribbean International News Corporation* v. *Puerto Rico,* 508 U.S. 147 (1993).
92. N.Y. Civil Rights Law, Section 52.
93. Tom Perrotta, "New York Law Banning Cameras in State Courts Found Constitutional," *New York Law Journal,* May 23, 2004.
94. Charles L. Babcock et al., "Fifty-State Survey of the Law Governing Audio-Visual Coverage of Court Proceedings." Web posted at http://www.jw.com/articles/details.cfm?articlenum5120 (accessed October 10, 2007).
95. See Radio-Television News Directors Association, "Cameras in the Court: A State-by-State Guide." Web posted at http://www.rtnda.org/foi/scc.shtml (accessed August 19, 2006).
96. *Chandler* v. *Florida,* 499 U.S. 560 (1981).
97. Rule 53 of the Federal Rules of Criminal Procedure reads, "The taking of photographs in the court room during the progress of judicial proceedings or radio broadcasting of judicial proceedings from the court room shall not be permitted by the court."
98. Harry F. Rosenthal, "Courts-TV," Associated Press wire service, September 21, 1994. See also "Judicial Conference Rejects Cameras in Federal Courts," *Criminal Justice Newsletter,* September 15, 1994, p. 6.
99. Web posted at http://www.ce9.uscourts.gov/web/OCELibra.nsf/504ca249c786e20f85256284006da7ab/ba060a3e537d2866882569760067ac8e?OpenDocument (accessed September 16, 2005).
100. Marc G. Gertz and Edmond J. True, "Social Scientists in the Courtroom: The Frustrations of Two Expert Witnesses," in Susette M. Talarico, ed., *Courts and Criminal Justice: Emerging Issues* (Beverly Hills, CA: Sage, 1985), pp. 81–91.
101. Samuel R. Gross et al., *Exonerations in the United States, 1989 through 2003*, April 4, 2004. Web posted at http://www.mindfully.org/Reform/2004/Prison-Exonerations-Gross19apr04.htm (accessed May 24, 2007).
102. *Klopfer* v. *North Carolina,* 386 U.S. 213 (1967).

103. *Barker* v. *Wingo*, 407 U.S. 514 (1972).
104. *Strunk* v. *U.S.*, 412 U.S. 434 (1973).
105. Speedy Trial Act, 18 U.S.C. 3161 (1974); Public Law 93-619.
106. *U.S.* v. *Taylor*, 487 U.S. 326, 108 S.Ct. 2413, 101 L.Ed.2d 297 (1988).
107. *Fex* v. *Michigan*, 113 S.Ct. 1085, 122 L.Ed.2d 406 (1993).
108. *Doggett* v. *U.S.*, 112 S.Ct. 2686 (1992).
109. William U. McCormack, "Supreme Court Cases: 1991–1992 Term," *FBI Law Enforcement Bulletin* (November 1992), pp. 28–29.
110. *Padilla* v. *Hanft*, No. 05-533, *cert. denied.*
111. Ibid.
112. See, for example, the U.S. Supreme Court's decision in the case of *Murphy* v. *Florida,* 410 U.S. 525 (1973).
113. *Witherspoon* v. *Illinois,* 391 U.S. 510 (1968).
114. *Mu'Min* v. *Virginia*, 500 U.S. 415 (1991).
115. Federal Rules of Criminal Procedure, Rule 24(6).
116. Learn more about shadow juries from Molly McDonough, "Me and My Shadow: Shadow Juries Are Helping Litigators Shape Their Cases during Trial," *National Law Journal* (May 17, 2001).
117. Although the words *argument* and *statement* are sometimes used interchangeably to refer to opening remarks, defense attorneys are enjoined from drawing conclusions or "arguing" to the jury at this stage in the trial. Their task, as described in the section that follows, is simply to explain to the jury how the defense will be conducted.
118. Supreme Court majority opinion in *Powers* v. *Ohio,* 499 U.S. 400 (1991), citing *Strauder* v. *West Virginia,* 100 U.S. 303 (1880).
119. *Swain* v. *Alabama,* 380 U.S. 202 (1965).
120. *Batson* v. *Kentucky,* 476 U.S. 79, 106 S.Ct. 1712 (1986).
121. *Ford* v. *Georgia*, 498 U.S. 411 (1991), footnote 2.
122. Ibid.
123. *Powers* v. *Ohio,* 499 U.S. 400 (1991).
124. *Edmonson* v. *Leesville Concrete Co., Inc.*, 500 U.S. 614, 111 S.Ct. 2077, 114 L.Ed.2d 660 (1991).
125. *Georgia* v. *McCollum*, 505 U.S. 42 (1992).
126. *J. E. B.* v. *Alabama,* 114 S.Ct. 1419 (1994).
127. See, for example, *Davis* v. *Minnesota,* 511 U.S. 1115 (1994).
128. Michael Kirkland, "Court Rejects Fat Jurors Case," United Press International wire service, January 8, 1996. The case was *Santiago-Martinez* v. *U.S.*, No. 95-567 (1996).
129. *Campbell* v. *Louisiana*, 523 U.S. 392 (1998).
130. *Miller-El* v. *Cockrell,* 537 U.S. 322 (2003).
131. Ibid., syllabus.
132. *Miller-El* v. *Dretke,* 545 U.S. 231 (2005).
133. *U.S.* v. *Dinitz*, 424 U.S. 600, 612 (1976).
134. *Michigan* v. *Lucas*, 500 U.S. 145 (1991).
135. *Kotteakos* v. *U.S.*, 328 U.S. 750 (1946); *Brecht* v. *Abrahamson,* 113 S.Ct. 1710, 123 L.Ed.2d 353 (1993); and *Arizona* v. *Fulminante*, 111 S.Ct. 1246 (1991).
136. The Court, citing *Kotteakos* v. *U.S.*, 328 U.S. 750 (1946), in *Brecht* v. *Abrahamson*, 113 S.Ct. 1710, 123 L.Ed.2d 353 (1993).
137. *Sullivan* v. *Louisiana,* 113 S.Ct. 2078, 124 L.Ed.2d 182 (1993).
138. *Griffin* v. *California*, 380 U.S. 609 (1965).
139. *Ohio* V. *Reiner,* 123 S.Ct. 1252, 532 U.S. 17 (2001).
140. Leading questions may, in fact, be permitted for certain purposes, including refreshing a witness's memory, impeaching a hostile witness, introducing undisputed material, and helping a witness with impaired faculties.
141. *In re Oliver,* 333 U.S. 257 (1948).
142. *Coy* v. *Iowa,* 487 U.S. 1012, 108 S.Ct. 2798 (1988).
143. *Maryland* v. *Craig,* 497 U.S. 836, 845–847 (1990).
144. *Idaho* v. *Wright,* 497 U.S. 805 (1990).
145. *White* v. *Illinois,* 112 S.Ct. 736 (1992).
146. *Crawford* v. *Washington,* 541 U.S. 36 (2004).
147. *Davis* v. *Washington*, 547 U.S. 813 (2006). See also *Hammon* v. *Indiana*, 547 U.S. 813 (2006).
148. *Davis* V. *Washington*, syllabus.
149. Federal Rules of Criminal Procedure, Rule 29.1.
150. See *Johnson* v. *Louisiana*, 406 U.S. 356 (1972); and *Apodaca* v. *Oregon*, 406 U.S. 404 (1972).
151. *Allen* v. *U.S.*, 164 U.S. 492 (1896).
152. Judge Harold J. Rothwax, *Guilty: The Collapse of Criminal Justice* (New York: Random House, 1996).
153. Amiram Elwork, Bruce D. Sales, and James Alfini, *Making Jury Instructions Understandable* (Charlottesville, VA: Michie, 1982).
154. "King Jury Lives in Fear from Unpopular Verdict," *Fayetteville (N.C.) Observer-Times*, May 10, 1992, p. 7A.
155. "Los Angeles Trials Spark Debate over Anonymous Juries," *Criminal Justice Newsletter* (February 16, 1993), pp. 3–4.
156. Some states have centralized offices called Administrative Offices of the Courts or something similar. Such offices, however, are often primarily data-gathering agencies with little or no authority over the day-to-day functioning of state or local courts.
157. See, for example, Larry Berkson and Susan Carbon, *Court Unification: Its History, Politics, and Implementation* (Washington, DC: U.S. Government Printing Office, 1978); and Thomas Henderson et al., *The Significance of Judicial Structure: The Effect of Unification on Trial Court Operators* (Alexandria, VA: Institute for Economic and Policy Studies, 1984).
158. See, for example, Thomas J. Cook et al., *Basic Issues in Court Performance* (Washington, DC: National Institute of Justice, 1982).
159. See, for example, Sorrel Wildhorn et al., *Indicators of Justice: Measuring the Performance of Prosecutors, Defense, and Court Agencies Involved in Felony Proceedings* (Lexington, MA: Lexington Books, 1977).

Sentencing

9

Chapter Outline

- Introduction
- The Philosophy and Goals of Criminal Sentencing
- Indeterminate Sentencing
- Structured Sentencing
- Innovations in Sentencing
- The Presentence Investigation
- The Victim—Forgotten No Longer
- Modern Sentencing Options
- Death: The Ultimate Sanction

Learning Objectives

After reading this chapter, you should be able to

- Describe the five goals of contemporary criminal sentencing.
- Describe the nature of indeterminate sentencing, and explain its purpose.
- Describe the nature of structured sentencing, and describe the different types of structured sentencing models in use today.
- Identify alternative sanctions, and assess recent sentencing innovations.
- Describe the nature and importance of the presentence investigation report.
- Describe the history of victims' rights and services, and discuss the growing role of the victim in criminal justice proceedings today.
- List four contemporary sentencing options.
- Outline the arguments for and against capital punishment.

"In sentencing, we have gone through determinate, indeterminate and back and forth in the last century. But in our time, life moves much faster. It took a hundred years from the peak of indeterminate sentencing, or the full realization of indeterminate sentencing values in the late 1870s to 1900 to wash away by the mid-1970s. . . . Is it possible that, with things happening so much faster, in just twenty or twenty-five years the cycle might once again be changing back in a different direction?"

—Michael Tonry, Director, Institute of Criminology, Cambridge University[1]

Introduction

▶▶▶ Hear the author discuss this chapter at mycrimekit.com.

On July 30, 2002, in what appeared to be an incident of vigilante justice, a small angry mob dragged two men from a crashed rental van and beat them to death with bricks and stones in a South Side Chicago neighborhood. The van had veered out of control and struck the front porch of a home, injuring three young women, one of them critically.[2] Witnesses said the vehicle appeared to accelerate wildly before hitting the women. "It all happened so fast, it seemed like he floored it or something," said witness Taquita Mixon, who saw the incident from her apartment window.[3] A bystander told reporters that one of the young men involved in the killings was the boyfriend of the critically injured woman.

While some in the neighborhood were ready to forgive the killers, others wanted them brought to trial. "It was an accident," one woman said of the beating. "I think emotions just got out of hand."[4] Another person disagreed, calling for those who participated in the killings to be arrested. "It's not going to bring them back, but it'll let them know you can't take the law in your own hands," she said.

sentencing
The imposition of a criminal sanction by a judicial authority.

In vigilante justice, a mob typically decides the fate of suspects before they can be fairly tried and formally sentenced. Under an organized system of criminal justice, **sentencing** is the imposition of a penalty on a person convicted of a crime. Sentencing follows an impartial judicial proceeding during which criminal responsibility is ascertained. Most sentencing decisions are made by judges, although in some cases, especially where a death sentence is possible, juries may be involved in a special sentencing phase of courtroom proceedings. The sentencing decision is one of the most difficult made by any judge or jury. Not only does it affect the future of the defendant—and at times it is a decision about his or her life or death—but society looks to sentencing to achieve a diversity of goals, some of which are not fully compatible with others.

This chapter examines sentencing in terms of both philosophy and practice. We will describe the goals of sentencing as well as the historical development of various sentencing models in the United States. This chapter also contains a detailed overview of victimization and victims' rights in general, especially as they relate to courtroom procedure and to sentencing practice. Federal sentencing guidelines and the significance of presentence investigations are also described. For an overview of sentencing issues, visit the Sentencing Project via Web Extra 9–1 at mycrimekit.com. Resources on sentencing and sentencing law are available at Web Extra 9–2.

Web EXTRA

The Philosophy and Goals of Criminal Sentencing

To make punishments efficacious, two things are necessary. They must never be disproportioned to the offense, and they must be certain.
—William Sims (1806–1870)

Traditional sentencing options have included imprisonment, fines, probation, and (for very serious offenses) death. Limits on the range of options available to sentencing authorities are generally specified by law. Historically, those limits have shifted as understanding of crime and the goals of sentencing have changed. Sentencing philosophies, or the justifications on which various sentencing strategies are based, are manifestly intertwined with issues of religion, morals, values, and emotions.[5] Philosophies that gained ascendancy at a particular point in history usually reflected more deeply held social values. Centuries ago, for example, it was thought that crime was due to sin and that suffering was the culprit's due, and judges were expected to be harsh. Capital punishment, torture, and painful physical penalties served this view of criminal behavior.

An emphasis on equitable punishments became prevalent around the time of the American and French Revolutions, brought about (in part) by Enlightenment philosophies. Offenders came to be seen as highly rational beings who intentionally and somewhat carefully chose their course of action. Sentencing philosophies of the period stressed the need for sanctions that outweighed the benefits to be derived from criminal activity. The severity of punishment became less important than quick and certain penalties.

Recent thinking has emphasized the need to limit offenders' potential for future harm by separating them from society. We also still believe that offenders deserve to be punished, and we have not entirely abandoned hope for their rehabilitation. Modern sentencing practices are influenced by five goals, which weave their way through widely disseminated professional and legal models, continuing public calls for sentencing reform, and everyday sentencing practices. Each goal represents a quasi-independent sentencing philosophy, since each makes distinctive assumptions about human nature and holds implications for sentencing practice. These are the five goals of contemporary sentencing:

1. Retribution
2. Incapacitation
3. Deterrence
4. Rehabilitation
5. Restoration

Retribution

Retribution, the earliest-known rationale for punishment, is a call for punishment based on a perceived need for vengeance. Most early societies punished all offenders who were caught. Early punishments were immediate—often without the benefit of a hearing—and they were often extreme, with little thought given to whether the punishment fit the crime. Exile and death, for example, were commonly imposed, even for relatively minor offenses. The Old Testament dictum of "an eye for an eye, a tooth for a tooth"—often cited as an ancient justification for retribution—was actually intended to reduce the severity of punishment for relatively minor crimes.

retribution
The act of taking revenge on a criminal perpetrator.

Today, retribution corresponds to the model of sentencing called **just deserts**, which holds that offenders are responsible for their crimes. When they are convicted and punished, they are said to have gotten their "just deserts." Retribution sees punishment as deserved, justified, and even required by the offender's behavior.[6] The primary sentencing tool of the just deserts model is imprisonment, but in extreme cases capital punishment (that is, death) becomes the ultimate retribution.

just deserts
A model of criminal sentencing that holds that criminal offenders deserve the punishment they receive at the hands of the law and that punishments should be appropriate to the type and severity of the crime committed.

▲ A courtroom drawing showing Rosemary Dillard, whose husband was killed on September 11, 2001, speaking to Zacarias Moussaoui, as family members of 9/11 victims listen in U.S. District Court in Alexandria, Virginia, during the sentencing hearing for the convicted al-Qaeda conspirator. On May 4, 2006, federal judge Leonie M. Brinkema sentenced the al-Qaeda plotter to life in prison with no possibility of release. Which of the sentencing goals discussed in this chapter likely played a role in the judge's sentencing decision?
Dana Verkouteren/AP Wide World Photos

Both in the public's view and in political policy making, retribution is still a primary goal of criminal sentencing. During the 1990s, as the public-order perspective with its emphasis on individual responsibility became dominant, public demands for retribution-based criminal punishments grew loud and clear. In the mid-1990s, for example, the Mississippi legislature, encouraged by then-Governor Kirk Fordice, voted to ban prison air conditioning, remove privately owned television sets from prison cells and dormitories, and prohibit weight lifting by inmates. Governor Fordice sent a "get tough" proposal to the legislature, which was quickly dubbed the "Clint Eastwood Hang 'Em High Bill"[7] and which required inmates to wear striped uniforms with the word *CONVICT* stamped on the back. State Representative Mac McInnis explained the state's retribution-inspired fervor this way: "We want a prisoner to look like a prisoner, to smell like a prisoner."[8] As critics note, however, none of these measures are likely to deter crime, but that is beside the point. The goal of retribution, after all, is not deterrence but satisfaction.[9]

Incapacitation

incapacitation
The use of imprisonment or other means to reduce the likelihood that an offender will commit future offenses.

Incapacitation, the second goal of criminal sentencing, seeks to protect innocent members of society from offenders who might harm them if not prevented from doing so. In ancient times, mutilation and amputation of the extremities were sometimes used to prevent offenders from repeating their crimes. Modern incapacitation strategies separate offenders from the community to reduce opportunities for further criminality. Incapacitation, sometimes called the *lock 'em up approach*, forms the basis for the modern movement toward prison "warehousing."

Unlike retribution, incapacitation requires only restraint, not punishment. Hence advocates of the incapacitation philosophy of sentencing are sometimes also active prison reformers, who want to humanize correctional institutions. Innovations in confinement offer new ways to achieve the goal of incapacitation without imprisonment. Remote location monitoring and biomedical intervention (such as chemical castration) may offer alternatives to imprisonment.

Deterrence

deterrence
A goal of criminal sentencing that seeks to inhibit criminal behavior through the fear of punishment.

specific deterrence
A goal of criminal sentencing that seeks to prevent a particular offender from engaging in repeat criminality.

general deterrence
A goal of criminal sentencing that seeks to prevent others from committing crimes similar to the one for which a particular offender is being sentenced by making an example of the person sentenced.

Deterrence uses the example or threat of punishment to convince people that criminal activity is not worthwhile; its overall goal is crime prevention. **Specific deterrence** seeks to reduce the likelihood of recidivism (repeat offenses) by convicted offenders, while **general deterrence** strives to influence the future behavior of people who have not yet been arrested and who may be tempted to turn to crime.

Deterrence is one of the more rational goals of sentencing because it is an easily articulated goal and because it is possible to investigate objectively the amount of punishment required to deter. It is generally agreed today that harsh punishments can virtually eliminate many minor forms of criminality.[10] Few traffic tickets would have to be written, for example, if minor driving offenses were punishable by death. A free society like our own, of course, is not willing to impose extreme punishments on petty offenders, and even harsh punishments are not demonstrably effective in reducing the incidence of serious crimes, such as murder and drug running.

Deterrence is compatible with the goal of incapacitation, since at least specific deterrence can be achieved through incapacitating offenders. Tufts University Professor Hugo Adam Bedau, however, points to significant differences between retribution and deterrence.[11] Retribution is oriented toward the past, says Bedau. It seeks to redress wrongs already committed. Deterrence, in contrast, is a strategy for the future and aims to prevent new crimes. But as legal philosopher H. L. A. Hart has observed, retribution can be the means through which deterrence is achieved.[12] By serving as an example of what might happen to others, punishment may have an inhibiting effect.

Rehabilitation

rehabilitation
The attempt to reform a criminal offender. Also, the state in which a reformed offender is said to be.

Rehabilitation seeks to bring about fundamental changes in offenders and their behavior. As in the case of deterrence, the ultimate goal of rehabilitation is a reduction in the number of criminal offenses. Whereas deterrence depends on a fear of the consequences of violating the law, rehabilitation generally works through education and psychological treatment to reduce the likelihood of future criminality.

The term *rehabilitation*, however, is a misnomer for the kinds of changes that its supporters seek. Rehabilitation literally means to return a person to his or her previous condition, just as medical rehabilitation programs seek to restore functioning to atrophied limbs, to rejuvenate injured organs, and to mend shattered minds. In the case of criminal offenders, however, it is likely that in most cases restoring criminals to their previous state will result in nothing but a more youthful type of criminality.

In the late 1970s, the rehabilitative goal in sentencing fell victim to the nothing-works doctrine, which was based on studies of recidivism rates that consistently showed that rehabilitation was more an ideal than a reality.[13] With as many as 90% of former convicted offenders returning to lives of crime following release from prison-based treatment programs, public sentiments in favor of incapacitation grew. Although the rehabilitation ideal has clearly suffered in the public arena, emerging evidence has begun to suggest that effective treatment programs do exist and may be growing in number.[14] See Library Extra 9–1 at mycrimekit.com to read more about treatment programs that work.

Library EXTRA

Restoration

Victims of crime and their families are frequently traumatized by their experiences. Some victims are killed, and others receive lasting physical or emotional injuries; for many, the world is never the same. The victimized may live in constant fear, be reduced in personal vigor, and be unable to form trusting relationships. **Restoration** is a sentencing goal that seeks to address this damage by making the victim and the community "whole again."

restoration
A goal of criminal sentencing that attempts to make the victim "whole again."

A U.S. Department of Justice report explains restoration this way:

> Crime was once defined as a "violation of the State." This remains the case today, but we now recognize that crime is far more. It is—among other things—a violation of one person by another. While retributive justice may address the first type of violation adequately, restorative justice is required to effectively address the latter. . . . Thus [through restorative justice] we seek to attain a balance between the legitimate needs of the community, the . . . offender, and the victim.[15]

The "healing" of all parties has many aspects, ranging from victim assistance initiatives to legislation supporting victims' compensation.

If you want a small prison population, make punishment certain. If you want a large prison population, make punishment uncertain.

—*Newt Gingrich, Former House Speaker*

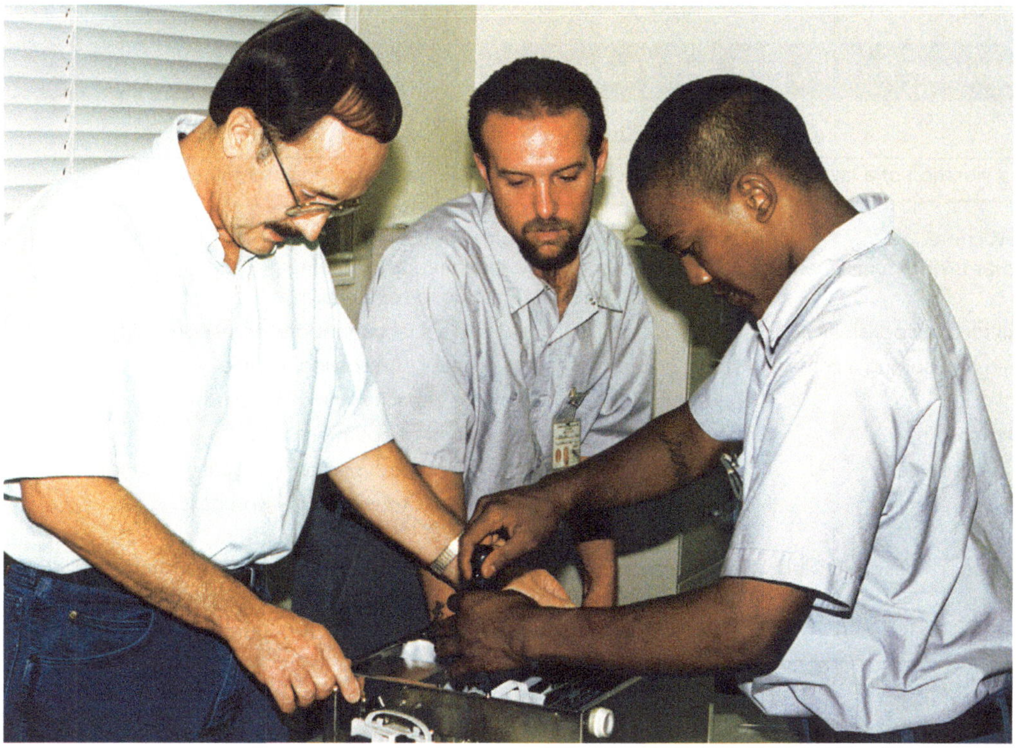

◄ Inmates in a California prison learning how to repair computer equipment. Skills acquired through such prison programs might translate into productive noncriminal careers. Rehabilitation is an important, but infrequently voiced, goal of modern sentencing practices. What are some other sentencing goals identified by the text?
Courtesy of Robert W. Winslow

restorative justice (RJ)
A sentencing model that builds on restitution and community participation in an attempt to make the victim "whole again."

Restorative justice (RJ) is also referred to as *balanced and restorative justice*. Conceptually, balance is achieved by giving equal consideration to community safety and offender accountability. Restorative justice focuses on "crime as harm, and justice as repairing the harm."[16] The community safety dimension of the RJ philosophy recognizes that the justice system has a responsibility to protect the public from crime and from offenders.[17] It also recognizes that the community can participate in ensuring its own safety. The accountability element defines criminal conduct in terms of obligations incurred by the offender, both to the victim and to the community.[18] RJ also has what some describe as a competency development element, which holds that offenders who enter the justice system should leave it more capable of participating successfully in the wider society than when they entered. In essence, RJ is community-focused; its primary goal is improving the quality of life for all members of the community. See Table 1 for a comparison of retributive justice and restorative justice.

Sentencing options that seek to restore the victim have focused primarily on restitution payments that offenders are ordered to make, either to their victims or to a general fund, which may then go to reimburse victims for suffering, lost wages, and medical expenses. In support of these goals, the 1984 Federal Comprehensive Crime Control Act specifically states: "If sentenced to probation, the defendant must also be ordered to pay a fine, make restitution, and/or work in community service."[19]

Vermont began a Sentencing Options Program in 1995 built around the concept of reparative probation. According to state officials, the Vermont reparative options program, which "requires the offender to make reparations to the victim and to the community, marks the first time in the United States that the Restorative Justice model has been embraced by a state department of corrections and implemented on a statewide scale."[20] Vermont's reparative program builds on "community reparative boards" consisting of five or six citizens from the community where the crime was committed and requires face-to-face public meetings between the offender and board representatives. Keeping in mind the program's avowed goals of "making the victim(s) whole again" and having the offender "make amends to the community," board members determine the specifics of the offender's sentence. Options are restitution, community service work, victim–offender mediation, victim empathy programs, driver-improvement courses, and the like.

Library EXTRA

Web EXTRA

Some advocates of the restoration philosophy of sentencing point out that restitution payments and work programs that benefit the victim can also have the added benefit of rehabilitating the offender. The hope is that such sentences may teach offenders personal responsibility through structured financial obligations, job requirements, and regularly scheduled payments. Learn more about restorative justice by visiting Library Extra 9–2 and Web Extra 9–3 at mycrimekit.com.

TABLE 1 Differences between Retributive and Restorative Justice

Retributive Justice	Restorative Justice
Crime is an act against the state, a violation of a law, an abstract idea.	Crime is an act against another person or the community.
The criminal justice system controls crime.	Crime control lies primarily with the community.
Offender accountability is defined as taking punishment.	Offender accountability is defined as assuming responsibility and taking action to repair harm.
Crime is an individual act with individual responsibility.	Crime has both individual and social dimensions of responsibility.
Victims are peripheral to the process of resolving a crime.	Victims are central to the process of resolving a crime.
The offender is defined by deficits.	The offender is defined by the capacity to make reparation.
The emphasis is on adversarial relationships.	The emphasis is on dialogue and negotiation.
Pain is imposed to punish, deter, and prevent.	Restitution is a means of restoring both parties; the goal is reconciliation.
The community is on the sidelines, represented abstractly by the state.	The community is the facilitator in the restorative process.
The response is focused on the offender's past behavior.	The response is focused on harmful consequences of the offender's behavior; the emphasis is on the future and on reparation.
There is dependence on proxy professionals.	There is direct involvement by both the offender and the victim.

Source: Adapted from Gordon Bazemore and Mark S. Umbreit, *Balanced and Restorative Justice: Program Summary* (Washington, DC: Office of Juvenile Justice and Delinquency Prevention, 1994), p. 7.

Indeterminate Sentencing

Explanation of Determinate Sentencing

While the *philosophy* of criminal sentencing is reflected in the goals of sentencing we have just discussed, different sentencing *practices* have been linked to each goal. During most of the twentieth century, for example, the rehabilitation goal was influential. Since rehabilitation requires that individual offenders' personal characteristics be closely considered in defining effective treatment strategies, judges were generally permitted wide discretion in choosing from among sentencing options. Although incapacitation is increasingly becoming the sentencing strategy of choice today, many state criminal codes still allow judges to impose fines, probation, or widely varying prison terms, all for the same offense. These sentencing practices, characterized primarily by vast judicial choice, constitute a model of **indeterminate sentencing**.

indeterminate sentencing
A model of criminal punishment that encourages rehabilitation through the use of general and relatively unspecific sentences (such as a term of imprisonment of from one to ten years).

Indeterminate sentencing has both a historical and a philosophical basis in the belief that convicted offenders are more likely to participate in their own rehabilitation if participation will reduce the amount of time they have to spend in prison. Inmates exhibiting good behavior will be released early, while recalcitrant inmates will remain in prison until the end of their terms. For that reason, parole generally plays a significant role in states that employ the indeterminate sentencing model.

Indeterminate sentencing relies heavily on judges' discretion to choose among types of sanctions and to set upper and lower limits on the length of prison stays. Indeterminate sentences are typically imposed with wording like this: "The defendant shall serve not less than five and not more than 25 years in the state's prison, under the supervision of the state department of correction." Judicial discretion under the indeterminate model also extends to the imposition of concurrent or consecutive sentences when the offender is convicted on more than one charge. Consecutive sentences are served one after the other, while concurrent sentences expire simultaneously.

The indeterminate model was also created to take into consideration detailed differences in degrees of guilt. Under this model, judges can weigh minute differences among cases, situations, and offenders. All of the following can be considered before sentence is passed: (1) whether the offender committed the crime out of a need for money, for the thrill of it, out of a desire for revenge, or "just for the hell of it"; (2) how much harm the offender intended; (3) how much the victim contributed to his or her own victimization; (4) what the extent of the damages inflicted was; (5) what the mental state of the offender was; (6) what the likelihood of successful rehabilitation is; and (7) to what degree the offender cooperated with authorities.

As a society we have at least in part created what we fear—a mass of convicts running loose through our society but unintegrated, hopeless, and hell-bent for reinstitutionalization, due in part to our focus on unrelenting lifelong punishment.
—Bernard H. Levin, Blue Ridge Community College[i]

Under the indeterminate sentencing model, the inmate's behavior (while incarcerated) is the primary determinant of the amount of time served. State parole boards wield great discretion under this model, acting as the final arbiters of the actual sentence served.

A few states employ a partially indeterminate sentencing model. They allow judges to specify only the maximum amount of time to be served; some minimum is generally implied by law but is not under the control of the sentencing authority. General practice is to set one year as a minimum for all felonies, although a few jurisdictions assume no minimum time at all, making offenders eligible for immediate parole.

Critiques of Indeterminate Sentencing

Indeterminate sentencing is still the rule in many jurisdictions, including Georgia, Hawaii, Iowa, Kentucky, Massachusetts, Michigan, Nevada, New York, North Dakota, Oklahoma, Rhode Island, South Carolina, South Dakota, Texas, Utah, Vermont, West Virginia, and Wyoming.[21] Since the 1970s, however, the model has come under fire for contributing to inequality in sentencing. Critics claim that the indeterminate model allows judges' personalities and personal philosophies to produce too wide a range of sentencing practices, from very lenient to very strict. The indeterminate model is also criticized for perpetuating a system under which offenders might be sentenced, at least by some judges, more on the basis of personal and social characteristics, such as race, gender, and social class, than on culpability.

Because of the personal nature of judicial decisions under the indeterminate model, offenders often depend on the advice and ploys of their attorneys to appear before a judge who is thought to be a good sentencing risk. Requests for delays are a common defense strategy in indeterminate sentencing states, where they are used to try to manipulate the selection of the judge involved in the sentencing decision.

gain time
The amount of time deducted from time to be served in prison on a given sentence as a consequence of participation in special projects or programs.

good time
The amount of time deducted from time to be served in prison on a given sentence as a consequence of good behavior.

Another charge leveled against indeterminate sentencing is that it tends to produce "dishonesty" in sentencing. Because of sentence cutbacks for good behavior and involvement in work and study programs, time served in prison is generally far less than sentences would seem to indicate. An inmate sentenced to five to ten years, for example, might actually be released in a couple of years after all **gain time** (amount of time deducted from a prison sentence based on project or program participation by the inmate), **good time** (amount of time deducted from a prison sentence based on good inmate behavior), and other special allowances have been calculated. (Some of the same charges can be leveled against determinate sentencing schemes under which corrections officials can administratively reduce the time served by an inmate.) A recent survey by the Bureau of Justice Statistics found that even violent offenders released from state prisons during the study period served, on average, only 51% of the sentences they originally received.[22] Nonviolent offenders served even smaller portions of their sentences. Table 2 shows the percentage of an imposed sentence that an offender sentenced to state prison in 1996 could expect to serve.

To ensure long prison terms in indeterminate jurisdictions, some court officials have gone to extremes. In 1994, for example, Oklahoma Judge Dan Owens sentenced convicted child molester Charles Scott Robinson to 30,000 years in prison.[23] Judge Owens, complying with the jury's efforts to ensure that Robinson would spend the rest of his life behind bars, sentenced him to serve six consecutive 5,000-year sentences (Robinson had 14 previous felony convictions).

▲ Singer Courtney Love being escorted into the Beverly Hills (California) courthouse by a Los Angeles County bailiff. In 2005 Love was sentenced to probation and ordered to undergo anger management counseling, pay fines, submit to random drug tests, and perform 100 hours of community service after she pleaded no contest to assault charges. The charges were related to an incident at the home of an ex-boyfriend. Love also pleaded guilty to a drug charge stemming from an earlier break-in at the same residence. Should Love have gone to prison?
Nick Ut/*AP Wide World Photos*

TABLE 2 Percentage of Sentence to Be Served, by New Court Commitments to State Prison

Offense Type	Percentage
Violent	51
Property	46
Drug	46
Public-order	49
Average for all felonies	**49**

Source: Paula M. Ditton and Doris James Wilson, *Truth in Sentencing in State Prisons* (Washington, DC: Bureau of Justice Statistics, 1999).

Structured Sentencing

Until the 1970s, all 50 states used some form of indeterminate (or partially indeterminate) sentencing. Eventually, however, calls for equity and proportionality in sentencing, heightened by claims of racial disparity in the sentencing practices of some judges,[24] led many states to move toward greater control over their sentencing systems.

Critics of the indeterminate model called for the recognition of three fundamental sentencing principles: proportionality, equity, and social debt. **Proportionality** refers to the belief that the severity of sanctions should bear a direct relationship to the seriousness of the crime committed. **Equity** means that similar crimes should be punished with the same degree of severity, regardless of the social or personal characteristics of offenders. According to the principle of equity, for example, two bank robbers in different parts of the country, who use the same techniques and weapons with the same degree of implied threat, should receive roughly the same sentence even though they are tried under separate circumstances and in different jurisdictions. The equity principle needs to be balanced, however, against the notion of **social debt**, meaning that an offender's criminal history should be considered in his or her sentencing. In the case of the bank robbers, the offender who has a prior criminal record can be said to have a higher level of social debt than the first-time robber, where all else is equal. Greater social debt, of course, suggests a more severe punishment or a greater need for treatment.

Beginning in the 1970s, a number of states addressed these concerns by developing a different model of sentencing, known as **structured sentencing**, which includes determinate, presumptive, and voluntary/advisory sentencing guidelines. One form of structured sentencing, called **determinate sentencing**, requires that a convicted offender be sentenced to a fixed term that may be reduced by good time (time off for good behavior) or gain time (time off in recognition of special efforts on the part of the inmate). Determinate sentencing states eliminated the use of parole and created explicit standards to specify the amount of punishment appropriate for a given offense; determinate sentencing practices also specify an anticipated release date for each sentenced offender.

In a 1996 report that traced the historical development of determinate sentencing, the National Council on Crime and Delinquency (NCCD) observed that "the term 'determinate sentencing' is generally used to refer to the sentencing reforms of the late 1970s. At that time, the legislatures of California, Illinois, Indiana, and Maine abolished the parole release decision and replaced indeterminate penalties with fixed (or flat) sentences that could be reduced by good-time provisions."[25]

In response to the then-growing determinate sentencing movement, a few states developed **voluntary/advisory sentencing guidelines** during the 1980s. These guidelines consist of recommended sentencing policies that are not required by law, are usually based on past sentencing practices, and serve as guides to judges; the guidelines may build on either determinate or indeterminate sentencing structures. Florida, Maryland, Massachusetts, Michigan, Rhode Island, Utah, and Wisconsin all experimented with voluntary/advisory guidelines during the 1980s. Voluntary/advisory guidelines constitute a second form of structured sentencing.

A third model of structured sentencing employs what NCCD calls "commission-based presumptive sentencing guidelines."[26] Presumptive sentencing became common in the 1980s as

proportionality
A sentencing principle that holds that the severity of sanctions should bear a direct relationship to the seriousness of the crime committed.

equity
A sentencing principle, based on concerns with social equality, that holds that similar crimes should be punished with the same degree of severity, regardless of the social or personal characteristics of the offenders.

social debt
A sentencing principle that holds that an offender's criminal history should objectively be taken into account in sentencing decisions.

structured sentencing
A model of criminal punishment that includes determinate and commission-created presumptive sentencing schemes, as well as voluntary/advisory sentencing guidelines.

determinate sentencing
A model of criminal punishment in which an offender is given a fixed term that may be reduced by good time or gain time. Under the model, for example, all offenders convicted of the same degree of burglary would be sentenced to the same length of time behind bars.

voluntary/advisory sentencing guidelines
The recommended sentencing policies that are not required by law.

presumptive sentencing
A model of criminal punishment that meets the following conditions: (1) The appropriate sentence for an offender convicted of a specific charge is presumed to fall within a range of sentences authorized by sentencing guidelines that are adopted by a legislatively created sentencing body, usually a sentencing commission; (2) sentencing judges are expected to sentence within the range or to provide written justification for departure; and (3) a mechanism is in place for review (usually appellate) of any departure from the guidelines.

Library EXTRA

aggravating circumstances
The circumstances relating to the commission of a crime that make it more grave than the average instance of that type of crime.

mitigating circumstances
The circumstances relating to the commission of a crime that may be considered to reduce the blameworthiness of the defendant.

truth in sentencing
A close correspondence between the sentence imposed on an offender and the time actually served before release from prison.[ii]

The root of revenge is in the weakness of the Soul; the most abject and timorous are the most addicted to it.
—*Akhenaton (circa 1375 B.C.)*

Web EXTRA

states began to experiment with sentencing guidelines developed by sentencing commissions. Guidelines for the model of **presumptive sentencing** differed from both determinate and voluntary/advisory guidelines in three respects: (1) They were not developed by the state legislature but by a sentencing commission that often represented a diverse array of criminal justice and sometimes private interests; (2) they were explicit and highly structured, typically relying on a quantitative scoring instrument to classify the offense for which a person was to be sentenced; (3) they were not voluntary/advisory in that judges had to adhere to the sentencing system or provide a written rationale for departing from it.

By 2006, the federal government and 16 states had established commission-created sentencing guidelines. Ten of the 16 states used presumptive sentencing guidelines; the remaining six relied on voluntary/advisory guidelines. As a consequence, with the advent of the twenty-first century, sentencing guidelines authored by legislatively created sentencing commissions had become the most popular form of structured sentencing. Learn more about the history of sentencing reform via Library Extras 9–3 and 9–4 at mycrimekit.com.

Guideline jurisdictions, which specified a presumptive sentence for a given offense, generally allowed for aggravating or mitigating circumstances—indicating a greater or lesser degree of culpability—which judges could take into consideration when imposing a sentence somewhat at variance from the presumptive term. **Aggravating circumstances** call for a tougher sentence and may include especially heinous behavior, cruelty, injury to more than one person, and so on.

Mitigating circumstances, which indicate that a lesser sentence is called for, are generally similar to legal defenses, although in this case they only reduce criminal responsibility, not eliminate it, and include such things as cooperation with the investigating authority, surrender, and good character. Common aggravating and mitigating circumstances are listed in CJ Exhibit 1.

Federal Sentencing Guidelines

In 1984, with the passage of the Comprehensive Crime Control Act, the federal government adopted presumptive sentencing for nearly all federal offenders.[27] The act also addressed the issue of **truth in sentencing**, meaning a close correspondence between the sentence imposed and actual time served. Under the old federal system, on average, good-time credits and parole reduced time served to about one-third of the actual sentence[28]; at the time, the sentencing practices of most states reflected the federal model. While sentence reductions may have benefited offenders, they often outraged victims, who felt betrayed by the sentencing process. The 1984 act nearly eliminated good-time credits[29] and began the process of both phasing out federal parole and eliminating the U.S. Parole Commission.[30] The emphasis on truth in sentencing created, in effect, a sentencing environment of "what you get is what you serve." Truth in sentencing, described as "a close correspondence between the sentence imposed upon those sent to prison and the time actually served prior to prison release,"[31] has become an important policy focus of many state legislatures and the U.S. Congress. The Violent Crime Control and Law Enforcement Act of 1994 set aside $4 billion in federal prison construction funds (called Truth in Sentencing Incentive Funds) for states that adopt truth-in-sentencing laws and are able to guarantee that certain violent offenders will serve 85% of their sentences.

Title II of the Comprehensive Crime Control Act, called the Sentencing Reform Act of 1984,[32] established the nine-member U.S. Sentencing Commission. The commission, which continues to function today, comprises presidential appointees, including three federal judges. The Sentencing Reform Act limited the discretion of federal judges by mandating the creation of federal sentencing guidelines, which federal judges were required to follow. The sentencing commission was given the task of developing structured sentencing guidelines to reduce disparity, promote consistency and uniformity, and increase fairness and equity in sentencing.

The guidelines established by the commission took effect in November 1987 but quickly became embroiled in a series of legal disputes, some of which challenged Congress's authority to form the U.S. Sentencing Commission. In January 1989, in the case of ***Mistretta* v. *U.S.***,[33] the U.S. Supreme Court held that Congress had acted appropriately in establishing the U.S. Sentencing Commission and that the guidelines developed by the commission could be applied in federal cases nationwide. The federal Sentencing Commission continues to meet at least once a year to review the effectiveness of the guidelines it created. Visit the U.S. Sentencing Commission via Web Extra 9–4 at mycrimekit.com.

CJ Exhibit 1

Aggravating and Mitigating Circumstances

Listed here are typical aggravating and mitigating circumstances that judges may consider in arriving at sentencing decisions in presumptive sentencing jurisdictions.

AGGRAVATING CIRCUMSTANCES

- The defendant induced others to participate in the commission of the offense.
- The offense was especially heinous, atrocious, or cruel.
- The defendant was armed with or used a deadly weapon during the crime.
- The defendant committed the offense to avoid or prevent a lawful arrest or to escape from custody.
- The offense was committed for hire.
- The offense was committed against a current or former law enforcement or correctional officer while that person was engaged in the performance of official duties or because of the past exercise of official duties.
- The defendant took advantage of a position of trust or confidence to commit the offense.

MITIGATING CIRCUMSTANCES

- The defendant has no record of criminal convictions punishable by more than 60 days of imprisonment.
- The defendant has made substantial or full restitution.
- The defendant has been a person of good character or has a good reputation in the community.
- The defendant aided in the apprehension of another felon or testified truthfully on behalf of the prosecution.
- The defendant acted under strong provocation, or the victim was a voluntary participant in the criminal activity or otherwise consented to it.
- The offense was committed under duress, coercion, threat, or compulsion that was insufficient to constitute a defense but that significantly reduced the defendant's culpability.
- At the time of the offense, the defendant was suffering from a mental or physical condition that was insufficient to constitute a defense but that significantly reduced the defendant's culpability.

Note: Recent U.S. Supreme Court rulings have held that facts influencing sentencing enhancements, other than prior record or admissions made by a defendant, must be determined by a jury, not by a judge.

Federal Guideline Provisions

As originally established, federal sentencing guidelines specified a sentencing range from which judges had to choose, but if a particular case had atypical features, judges were allowed to depart from the guidelines. Departures were generally expected only in the presence of aggravating or mitigating circumstances, a number of which are specified in the guidelines.[34] Aggravating circumstances may include the possession of a weapon during the commission of a crime, the degree of criminal involvement (whether the defendant was a leader or a follower in the criminal activity), and extreme psychological injury to the victim. Punishments also increase when a defendant violates a position of public or private trust, uses special skills to commit or conceal offenses, or has a criminal history. Defendants who express remorse, cooperate with authorities, or willingly make restitution may have their sentences reduced under the guidelines. Any departure from the guidelines may, however, become the basis for appellate review concerning the reasonableness of the sentence imposed, and judges who deviate from the guidelines were originally required to provide written reasons for doing so.

Putting people in prison is the single most important thing we've done [to decrease crime].

—*James Q. Wilson*
Professor Emeritus, University of California at Los Angeles[iii]

Federal sentencing guidelines are built around a table containing 43 rows, each corresponding to one offense level. The penalties associated with each level overlap those of the levels above and below to discourage unnecessary litigation. A person convicted of a crime involving $11,000, for example, and sentenced under the guidelines is unlikely to receive a penalty substantially greater than if the amount had been somewhat less than $10,000. A change of six levels roughly doubles the sentence imposed under the guidelines, regardless of the level at which one starts. Because of their matrix-like quality, federal sentencing provisions have been referred to as *structured*. The federal sentencing table is available at Web Extra 9–5 at mycrimekit.com.

Web EXTRA

The sentencing table also contains six rows corresponding to the criminal history category into which an offender falls, and these categories are determined on a point basis. Offenders earn points for previous convictions. For example, each prior sentence of imprisonment for more than one year and one month counts as three points, and two points are assigned for each prior prison sentence over six months or if the defendant committed the offense while on probation, parole, or work release. The system also assigns points for other types of previous convictions and for offenses committed less than two years after release from imprisonment. Points are added to determine the criminal history category into which an offender falls. Thirteen points or more are required for the highest category. At each offense level, sentences in the highest criminal history category are generally two to three times as severe as for the lowest category.

Defendants may also move into the highest criminal history category by virtue of being designated a career offender. Under the sentencing guidelines, a defendant is a career offender if "(1) the defendant was at least 18 years old at the time of the . . . offense, (2) the . . . offense is a crime of violence or trafficking in a controlled substance, and (3) the defendant has at least two prior felony convictions of either a crime of violence or a controlled substance offense."[35]

According to the U.S. Supreme Court, an offender may be adjudged a career offender in a single hearing, even when previous convictions are lacking. In ***Deal* v. *U.S.*** (1993),[36] the defendant, Thomas Lee Deal, was convicted in a single proceeding of six counts of carrying and using a firearm during a series of bank robberies in the Houston (Texas) area. A federal district court sentenced him to 105 years in prison as a career offender—five years for the first count and 20 years for each of the five other counts, with sentences to run consecutively. In the words of the Supreme Court, "We see no reason why [the defendant should not receive such a sentence], simply because he managed to evade detection, prosecution, and conviction for the first five offenses and was ultimately tried on all six in a single proceeding."

Plea Bargaining under the Guidelines

Plea bargaining plays a major role in the federal judicial system. Approximately 90% of all federal sentences are the result of guilty pleas,[37] and the large majority of those stem from plea negotiations. In the words of former Sentencing Commission Chairman William W. Wilkins, Jr., "With respect to plea bargaining, the Commission has proceeded cautiously. . . . The Commission did not believe it wise to stand the federal criminal justice system on its head by making too drastic and too sudden a change in these practices."[38]

Although the commission allowed plea bargaining to continue, it required that the agreement (1) be fully disclosed in the record of the court (unless there is an overriding and demonstrable reason why it should not be) and (2) detail the actual conduct of the offense. Under these requirements, defendants are unable to hide the actual nature of their offense behind a substitute plea, and information on the decision-making process itself is available to victims, the media, and the public.

In 1996, in the case of *Melendez* v. *U.S.*,[39] the U.S. Supreme Court held that a government motion requesting that a trial judge deviate from the federal sentencing guidelines as part of a cooperative plea agreement does not permit imposition of a sentence below a statutory minimum specified by law. In other words, under *Melendez*, while federal judges could depart from the guidelines, they could not accept plea bargains that would have resulted in sentences lower than the minimum required by law for a particular type of offense.

The Legal Environment of Structured Sentencing

A crucial critique of aggravating factors and their use in presumptive sentencing schemes was offered by the U.S. Supreme Court in 2000 in the case of ***Apprendi* v. *New Jersey***.[40] In *Apprendi*, the Court questioned the fact-finding authority of judges in making sentencing decisions, ruling that other than the fact of a prior conviction, any fact that increases the penalty for a crime beyond the prescribed statutory maximum is, in effect, an element of the crime, which must be submitted to a jury and proved beyond a reasonable doubt. The case involved Charles Apprendi, a New Jersey defendant who pleaded guilty to unlawfully possessing a firearm—an offense that carried a prison term of five to ten years under state law. Before sentence was imposed, however, the judge found that Apprendi had fired a number of shots into the home of an African-American family living in his neighborhood and concluded that he had done so to frighten the family and convince them to move. The judge held that statements made by Apprendi allowed the offense to be classified as a hate crime, which required a longer prison term under the sentencing enhancement provision of New Jersey's hate-crime statute than did the weapons offense to which Apprendi had confessed. The Supreme Court, in overturning the judge's finding and sentence, took issue with the fact that after Apprendi pleaded guilty, an

The Apprendi ruling has had a severely destabilizing effect on our criminal justice system.
—Sandra Day O'Connor U.S. Supreme Court Justice, dissenting in the case of Ring *v.* Arizona[iv]

enhanced sentence was imposed without the benefit of a jury-based fact-finding process. The high court ruled that "under the Due Process Clause of the Fifth Amendment and the notice and jury trial guarantees of the Sixth Amendment, any fact (other than prior conviction) that increases the maximum penalty for a crime must be charged in an indictment, submitted to a jury, and proven beyond a reasonable doubt."

The *Apprendi* case essentially says that requiring sentencing judges to consider facts not proven to a jury violates the federal Constitution. It raised the question of whether judges anywhere could legitimately deviate from established sentencing guidelines or apply sentence enhancements based solely on judicial determinations of aggravating factors—especially when such determinations involve findings of fact that might otherwise be made by a jury.[41]

In 2004, in the important case of ***Blakely* v. *Washington***,[42] the U.S. Supreme Court effectively invalidated any state sentencing schema that allow judges rather than juries to determine any factor that increases a criminal sentence, except for prior convictions. The Court found that because the facts supporting Blakely's increased sentence were neither admitted by the defendant himself nor found by a jury, the sentence violated the Sixth Amendment right to trial by jury. The *Blakely* decision required that the sentencing laws of eight states be rewritten.[43] Washington state legislators responded quickly and created a model law for other legislatures to emulate. The Washington law mandates that "the facts supporting aggravating circumstances shall be proved to a jury beyond a reasonable doubt," or "if a jury is waived, proof shall be to the court beyond a reasonable doubt." The Washington law can be read at Library Extra 9–5.

Library EXTRA

In 2007, in the case of *Cunningham* v. *California*,[44] the Supreme Court applied its reasoning in *Blakely* to California's determinate sentencing law, finding the law invalid because it placed sentence-elevating fact-finding within the judge's purview. As in *Blakely*, the California law was found to violate a defendant's Sixth Amendment right to trial by jury.

In 2005, in the combined cases of ***U.S.* v. *Booker***[45] and *U.S.* v. *Fanfan*,[46] attention turned to the constitutionality of *federal* sentencing practices that relied on extra-verdict determinations of fact in the application of sentencing enhancements. In *Booker*, the U.S. Supreme Court issued what some have called an "extraordinary opinion,"[47] which actually encompasses two separate decisions. The combined cases brought a dual issue before the Court: (1) whether fact-finding done by judges under federal sentencing guidelines violates the Sixth Amendment right to trial by jury; and (2) if so, whether the guidelines are themselves unconstitutional. As in the preceding cases discussed in this section, the Court found that on the first question, defendant Freddie Booker's drug-trafficking sentence had been improperly enhanced under the guidelines on the basis of facts found solely by a judge. In the view of the Court, the Sixth Amendment right to trial by jury is violated where, under a mandatory guidelines system, a sentence is increased because of an enhancement based on facts found by the judge that were not found by a jury nor admitted by the defendant.[48] Consequently, Booker's sentence was ruled unconstitutional and invalidated. On the second question, the Court reached a compromise and did not strike down the federal guidelines as many thought it would; instead, it held that the guidelines could be *considered* by federal judges during sentencing but that they were no longer mandatory.

In effect, the decisions in *Booker* and *Fanfan* turned the federal sentencing guidelines on their head, making them merely advisory and giving federal judges wide latitude in imposing punishments. While federal judges *must* still take the guidelines into consideration in reaching sentencing decisions, they do not have to follow them. In the words of the high court, "the federal sentencing statute, as modified by *Booker*, requires a court to give respectful consideration to the Guidelines, but permits the court to tailor the sentence in light of other concerns as well."[49] Deviations from the guidelines must still be explained, and in the words of the justices, "a district judge must consider the extent of any departure from the Guidelines and must explain the appropriateness of an unusually lenient or harsh sentence with sufficient justifications."[50]

In 2007, in a continued clarification of *Booker*, the Supreme Court ruled that federal appeals courts that hear challenges from defendants about prison time may presume that federal criminal sentences are reasonable if they fall within U.S. Sentencing Guidelines.[51] In that case, *Rita* v. *U.S.*, the Court held that "even if the presumption increases the likelihood that the judge, not the jury, will find 'sentencing facts,' it does not violate the Sixth Amendment." The justices reasoned that "a nonbinding appellate reasonableness presumption for Guidelines sentences does not *require* the sentencing judge to impose a Guidelines sentence." In another 2007 case, *Gall* v. *U.S.*,[52] the Court clarified its position on appelate review of sentencing decisions by lower

CJ Exhibit 2

Three Strikes and You're Out: A Brief History of the "Get Tough on Crime" Movement

In the spring of 1994, California legislators passed the state's now-famous "three strikes and you're out" bill. Amid much fanfare, Governor Pete Wilson signed the "three-strikes" measure into law, calling it "the toughest and most sweeping crime bill in California history."[1]

California's law, which is retroactive in that it counts offenses committed before the date the legislation was signed, requires a sentence of 25 years to life for three-time felons with convictions for two or more serious or violent prior offenses. Criminal offenders facing a "second strike" can receive up to double the normal sentence for their most recent offense. Parole consideration is not available until at least 80% of the sentence has been served.

Today, about half of the states have passed three-strikes legislation, and other states may be considering it. At the federal level, the Violent Crime Control and Law Enforcement Act of 1994 contains a three-strikes provision that mandates life imprisonment for federal criminals convicted of three violent felonies or drug offenses.

Questions remain, however, about the effectiveness of three-strikes legislation, and many people are concerned about its impact on the justice system. One year after it was signed into law, the California three-strikes initiative was evaluated by the RAND Corporation.[2] RAND researchers found that in the first year, more than 5,000 defendants were convicted and sentenced under the law's provisions. The large majority of those sentenced, however, had committed nonviolent crimes, causing critics of the law to argue that it is too broad; 84% of two-strikes convictions and nearly 77% of three-strikes convictions resulted from nonviolent drug or property crimes. A similar 1997 study of three-strikes laws in 22 states, conducted by the Campaign for an Effective Crime Policy (CECP), concluded that such legislation results in clogged court systems and crowded correctional facilities while encouraging two-time felons to take dramatic risks to avoid capture for a third offense.[3] A 1998 study found that only California and Georgia were making widespread use of three-strikes laws.[4] Other states, the study found, have narrowly written laws that are applicable to repeat offenders only in rare circumstances.

A 2001 study of the original California legislation and its consequences concluded that three-strikes laws are overrated.[5] According to the study, which was conducted by the Washington, D.C.–based Sentencing Project, "California's three-strikes law has increased the number and severity of sentences for nonviolent offenders—and contributed to the aging of the prison population—but has had no significant effect on the state's decline in crime." The study found that declines in California crime rates that are often attributed to the legislation are consistent with nationwide declines in the rate of crime and would mostly have occurred without the law. "Crime had been declining for several years prior to the enactment of the three-strikes law, and what's happening in California is very consistent with what's been happening nationally, including in states with no three-strikes law," said Marc Mauer, an author of the study.

Supporters of three-strikes laws argue that those convicted under them are career criminals who will be denied the opportunity to commit more violent crimes. "The real story here is the girl somewhere that did not get raped," said Mike Reynolds, a Fresno (California) photographer whose 18-year-old daughter was killed by a paroled felon. "The real story is the robbery that did not happen," he added.[6]

Practically speaking, California's three-strikes law has had a dramatic impact on the state's criminal justice system. By 1999, more than 40,000 people had been sentenced under the law. But the law has its critics. " 'Three strikes and you're out' sounds great to a lot of people," says Alan Schuman, president of the American Probation and Parole Association. "But no one will cop a plea when it gets to the third time around. We will have more trials, and this whole country works on plea bargaining and pleading guilty, not jury trials," Schuman said at a meeting of the association.[7] According to RAND, full enforcement of the law could cost as much as $5.5 billion annually—or $300 per California taxpayer.

Researchers at RAND conclude that while California's sweeping three-strikes legislation could cut serious adult crime by as much as one-third throughout the state, the high cost of enforcing the law may keep it from ever being fully implemented. In 1996, the California three-strikes controversy became even more complicated following a decision by the state supreme court (in *People* v. *Superior Court of San Diego–Romero*[8]) that California judges retain the discretion to reduce three-strikes sentences and to refuse to count previous convictions at sentencing "in furtherance of justice."

In 2003, however, in two separate cases, the U.S. Supreme Court upheld the three-strikes California convictions of Gary Ewing and Leandro Andrade in California.[9] Ewing, who had four prior felony convictions, had received a sentence of 25 years to life following his conviction for felony grand theft of three golf clubs. Andrade, who also had a long record, was sentenced to 50 years in prison for two petty theft convictions.[10] In writing for the Court in the *Ewing* case, Justice Sandra Day O'Connor noted that states should be able to decide when repeat offenders "must be isolated from society . . . to protect the public safety," even when nonserious crimes trigger the lengthy sentence. In deciding these two cases, both of which were based on Eighth Amendment claims, the Court found that it is *not* cruel and unusual punishment to impose a possible life term for a nonviolent felony when the defendant has a history of serious or violent convictions.

In 2004, Californians voted down Proposition 66, a ballot initiative that would have changed the state's three-strikes law so that only specified serious or violent crimes could be counted as third strikes. Passage of the proposition would also have meant that only previous convictions for violent or serious felonies, brought and tried separately, would have qualified for second- and third-strike sentence increases.

California's three-strikes law remains firmly in place. In its current form, it punishes anyone who commits a third felony, regardless of its severity, with a mandatory sentence of 25 years to life if the first two felonies were violent or serious.

[1]Michael Miller, "California Gets 'Three Strikes' Anti-Crime Bill," Reuters wire service, March 7, 1994.
[2]Dion Nissenbaum, "Three-Strikes First Year Debated," United Press International wire service, northern edition, March 6, 1995.
[3]Campaign for an Effective Crime Policy, *The Impact of Three Strikes and You're Out Laws: What Have We Learned?* (Washington, DC: CECP, 1997).
[4]Walter Dickey and Pam Stiebs Hollenhorst, "Three-Strikes Laws: Massive Impact in California and Georgia, Little Elsewhere," *Overcrowded Times*, Vol. 9, No. 6 (December 1998), pp. 2–8.
[5]Tamar Lewin, "Three-Strikes Law Is Overrated in California, Study Finds," *New York Times*, August 23, 2001, http://query.nytimes.com/gst/fullpage.html?res=9505E7DB1531F930A1575BC0A9679C8B63 (accessed September 2, 2008).
[6]Bruce Smith, "Crime Solutions," Associated Press wire service, January 11, 1995.
[7]Ryan S. King and Marc Mauer, *Aging behind Bars: "Three Strikes" Seven Years Later* (Washington, DC: Sentencing Project, August 2001).
[8]*People* v. *Superior Court of San Diego–Romero*, 13 Cal. 4th 497, 917 P.2d 628 (1996).
[9]*Ewing* v. *California*, 538 U.S. 11 (2003); and *Lockyer* v. *Andrade*, 538 U.S. 63 (2003).
[10]Under California law, a person who commits petty theft can be charged with a felony if he or she has prior felony convictions. The charge is known as "petty theft with prior convictions." Andrade's actual sentence was two 25-year prison terms to be served consecutively.

courts when it held that "because the Guidelines are now advisory, appellate review of sentencing decisions is limited to determining whether they are 'reasonable.' "

A recent survey by the U.S. Sentencing Commission found that 61.2% of all federal sentences handed down in the year following *Booker* and *Fanfan* were within ranges specified under federal sentencing guidelines[53]; in comparison, in the year prior to *Blakely*, 72.2% were within guideline ranges.[54] In light of the Court's decisions, it is now up to Congress to reconsider federal sentencing law in light of *Booker*—a process that is under way as this book goes to press.[55] In the meantime, some expect the federal courts to be flooded with inmates appealing their sentences.

Mandatory Sentencing

Mandatory sentencing, another form of structured sentencing, deserves special mention.[56] **Mandatory sentencing** is just what its name implies: a structured sentencing scheme that mandates clearly enumerated punishments for specific offenses or for habitual offenders convicted of a series of crimes. Mandatory sentencing, because it is truly *mandatory*, differs from presumptive sentencing, which allows at least a limited amount of judicial discretion within ranges established by published guidelines. Some mandatory sentencing laws require only modest mandatory prison terms (for example, three years for armed robbery), while others are much more far-reaching.

mandatory sentencing
A structured sentencing scheme that allows no leeway in the nature of the sentence required and under which clearly enumerated punishments are mandated for specific offenses or for habitual offenders convicted of a series of crimes.

Typical of far-reaching mandatory sentencing schemes are three-strikes laws, discussed in CJ Exhibit 2. Three-strikes laws (and in some jurisdictions, two-strikes laws) require mandatory sentences (sometimes life in prison without the possibility of parole) for offenders convicted of a third (or second) serious felony. Such mandatory sentencing enhancements are aimed at deterring known and potentially violent offenders and are intended to incapacitate convicted criminals through long-term incarceration.

Three-strikes laws impose longer prison terms than most earlier mandatory minimum sentencing laws. California's three-strikes law, for example, requires that offenders who are convicted of a violent crime and who have had two prior convictions serve a minimum of 25 years in prison; it also doubled prison terms for offenders convicted of a second violent felony.[57] Three-strikes laws also vary in breadth. The laws of some jurisdictions stipulate that both of the prior convictions and the current one be for violent felonies; others require only that the prior convictions be for violent felonies. Some three-strikes laws count only prior adult convictions, while others permit consideration of juvenile crimes.

By passing mandatory sentencing laws, legislators convey the message that certain crimes are deemed especially grave and that people who commit them deserve, and should expect, harsh sanctions. These laws are sometimes passed in response to public outcries following heinous or well-publicized crimes.

There is no single act that a legislature can do to return balance and fairness to sentencing than to repeal mandatory minimum provisions and return discretion to judges.
—*The Sentencing Project*[v]

diversion
The official suspension of criminal proceedings against an alleged offender at any point before the entering of a judgment and the referral of that person to a treatment or care program administered by a nonjustice or private agency.

Research findings on the impact of mandatory sentencing laws on the criminal justice system have been summarized by British criminologist Michael Tonry.[58] Tonry found that under mandatory sentencing, officials tend to make earlier and more selective decisions involving arrest, charging, and **diversion** (suspension of criminal proceedings before sentencing and referral to a private agency). They also tend to bargain less and to bring more cases to trial. Specifically, Tonry found the following:

1. Criminal justice officials and practitioners (police, lawyers, and judges) exercise discretion to avoid the application of laws they consider unduly harsh.
2. Arrest rates for target crimes tend to decline soon after mandatory sentencing laws take effect.
3. Dismissal and diversion rates increase during the early stages of case processing after mandatory sentencing laws become effective.
4. For defendants whose cases are not dismissed, plea bargain rates decline and trial rates increase.
5. For convicted defendants, sentencing delays increase.
6. When the effects of declining arrests, indictments, and convictions are taken into account, the enactment of mandatory sentencing laws has little impact on the probability that offenders will be imprisoned.
7. Sentences become longer and more severe. Mandatory sentencing laws may also occasionally result in unduly harsh punishments for marginal offenders who nonetheless meet the minimum requirements for sentencing under such laws.

Blakely suggests that the U.S. Constitution does not permit judges to find facts that increase applicable sentences, even though nearly all modern sentencing reforms have made judges central and essential sentencing fact finders.
—*Prof. Douglas A. Berman*
Ohio State University College of Law[vi]

In an analysis of federal sentencing guidelines, other researchers found that blacks receive longer sentences than whites, not because they received differential treatment by judges but because they constitute the large majority of those convicted of trafficking in crack cocaine (versus powdered cocaine)[59]—a crime Congress has singled out for especially harsh mandatory penalties. In 2006, for example, 82% of those sentenced under federal crack cocaine laws were black, and

▲ Sherelle Purnell, age 18, of Salisbury, Maryland, walking along the street in front of a Tiger Mart gas station wearing a sign declaring her offense. On July 30, 2004, Purnell drove away from the station without paying after pumping 2.78 gallons of fuel into her vehicle. This is an example of innovative judges sometimes making use of creative sentences in an attempt to deter offenders from future law violations. How effective a deterrent do you think Purnell's sentence will be?
Salisbury Daily Times/*Todd Dudek/AP Wide World Photos*

only 8.8% were white—even though more than two-thirds of people who use crack cocaine are white.[60] This pattern can be seen as constituting a "disparity in results," and partly for this reason, the U.S. Sentencing Commission has recommended to Congress that it eliminate the legal distinction between crack and regular cocaine for purposes of sentencing (a recommendation that Congress rejected). Recent indications, however, are that the heightened discretion available to federal judges in the wake of *Booker* and *Fanfan* is resulting in sentences that are similar for all types of cocaine trafficking and that vary more by the amount than the type of cocaine involved.[61]

Blakely is . . . so important and looms so large because it follows a social, political, and legal revolution through which sentencing has been transformed from a field once rightly accused of being "lawless" into a field now replete with law.

—Professor Douglas A. Berman Ohio State University College of Law[vii]

Innovations in Sentencing

Alternative Sentencing Options

In an ever-growing number of cases, innovative judges in certain jurisdictions have begun to use discretionary sentencing to impose truly unique punishments. In 2006, for example, Jennifer Wilbanks, the infamous "runaway bride," was sentenced to 120 hours of community service mowing the lawns of government buildings in Lawrenceville, Georgia.[62] Wilbanks made headlines months earlier when she disappeared four days before her scheduled Georgia wedding and turned up in Albuquerque, New Mexico, falsely claiming that she had been abducted and sexually assaulted. Wilbanks was punished by Gwinnett County Superior Court Judge Ronnie Batchelor following a plea agreement on charges of filing a false police report and lying to authorities. Similarly, in 2004, 18-year-old Sherelle Purnell was ordered by County Judge D. William Simpson to spend three hours walking along the grassy strip between a convenience store and a busy highway in Salisbury, Maryland, wearing a sign that read "I was caught stealing gas."[63] Purnell's actions had been recorded by a video surveillance device as she drove away without paying for 2.78 gallons of gas from a Tiger Mart. In Memphis, Tennessee, Judge Joe Brown escorted burglary victims to thieves' homes, inviting them to take whatever they wanted.[64] An Arkansas judge made shoplifters walk in front of the stores they stole from, carrying signs describing their crimes, and in California, a purse snatcher was ordered to wear noisy tap dancing shoes whenever he went out in public.[65]

Faced with prison overcrowding, high incarceration costs, and public calls for retribution, other judges have used shaming strategies to deter wrongdoers. At least one Florida court ordered those convicted of drunk driving to put a "Convicted DUI" sticker on their license plates. In 2001, Coshocton County (Ohio) Municipal Judge David Hostetler ordered two men to parade down the main street of their hometown dressed as women after the men, Jason Householder, age 23, and John Stockum, age 21, had been convicted of criminal damage for throwing beer bottles at a woman. The judge told the men that they could either comply with his order or go to jail for 60 days; he also fined them $250 each. Similarly, a few years ago Boston courts began ordering men convicted of sexual solicitation to spend time sweeping streets in Chinatown, an area known for prostitution, and the public was invited to watch men sentenced to the city's "John Sweep" program clean up streets and alleyways littered with used condoms and sexual paraphernalia.

There is considerable support in criminal justice literature for shaming as a crime-reduction strategy. Australian criminologist John Braithwaite, for example, found shaming to be a particularly effective strategy because, he said, it holds the potential to enhance moral awareness among offenders, thereby building conscience and increasing inner control.[66] Dan Kahan, a professor at the University of Chicago Law School, points out that "shame supplies the main motive why people obey the law, not so much because they're afraid of formal sanctions, but because they care what people think about them."[67]

Whether public shaming will continue to grow in popularity as an alternative sentencing strategy is unclear. What is clear, however, is that the American public and an ever-growing number of judicial officials are now looking for workable alternatives to traditional sentencing options.

Questions about Alternative Sanctions

Alternative sentencing includes the use of court-ordered community service, home detention, day reporting, drug treatment, psychological counseling, victim–offender programming, or intensive supervision in lieu of other, more traditional sanctions, such as imprisonment and fines.

alternative sentencing
The use of court-ordered community service, home detention, day reporting, drug treatment, psychological counseling, victim–offender programming, or intensive supervision in lieu of other, more traditional sanctions, such as imprisonment and fines.

Punishment, that is justice for the unjust.
—*Saint Augustine* (A.D. 354–430)

As prison populations continue to rise, alternative sentencing strategies are likely to become increasingly attractive. A number of questions must be answered, however, before most alternative sanctions can be employed with confidence. These questions were succinctly stated in a RAND Corporation study authored by Joan Petersilia.[68] Unfortunately, although the questions can be listed, few definitive answers are available yet. Here are some of the questions Petersilia poses:

- Do alternative sentencing programs threaten public safety?
- How should program participants be selected?
- What are the long-term effects of community sanctions on people assigned to these programs?
- Are alternative sanctions cost-effective?
- Who should pay the bill for alternative sanctions?
- Who should manage stringent community-based sanctions?
- How should program outcomes be judged?
- What kinds of offenders benefit most from alternative sentencing?

Library EXTRA

Learn more about sentencing in America today by reading the Sentencing Project's report, *The State of Sentencing 2007: Developments in Policy and Practice*, at Library Extra 9–6 at mycrimekit.com.

The Presentence Investigation

Before imposing sentence, a judge may request information on the background of a convicted defendant. This is especially true in indeterminate sentencing jurisdictions, where judges retain considerable discretion in selecting sanctions. Traditional wisdom has held that certain factors increase the likelihood of rehabilitation and reduce the need for lengthy prison terms. These factors include a good job record, satisfactory educational attainment, strong family ties, church attendance, no prior arrests for violent offenses, and psychological stability.

presentence investigation
The examination of a convicted offender's background before sentencing. Presentence investigations are generally conducted by probation or parole officers and are submitted to sentencing authorities.

Information about a defendant's background often comes to the judge in the form of a report of a **presentence investigation** (PSI). The task of preparing PSI reports usually falls to the probation or parole office, and the report takes one of three forms: (1) a detailed written report on the defendant's personal and criminal history, including an assessment of present conditions in the defendant's life (often called the *long form*); (2) an abbreviated written report summarizing the information most likely to be useful in a sentencing decision (the *short form*); and (3) a verbal report to the court made by the investigating officer based on field notes but structured according to established categories. A PSI report is much like a résumé, except that it focuses on what might be regarded as negative as well as positive life experiences.

The data on which a presentence report is based come from a variety of sources. The FBI National Crime Information Center (NCIC), begun in 1967, contains computerized information on people wanted for criminal offenses throughout the United States. Individual jurisdictions also maintain criminal records repositories that can provide comprehensive files on the criminal history of those who have been processed by the justice system.

Sometimes the defendant provides much of the information for the PSI. In this case, efforts must be made to corroborate the defendant's information; unconfirmed data are generally marked on the report as "defendant-supplied data" or simply "unconfirmed."

In a PSI report, most third-party data are subject to ethical and legal considerations. The official records of almost all agencies and organizations, though often an ideal source of information, are protected by state and federal privacy requirements; in particular, the federal Privacy Act of 1974[69] may limit access to these records. Investigators must first check on the legal availability of all records before requesting them and must receive in writing the defendant's permission to access the records. Other public laws, among them the federal Freedom of Information Act,[70] may make the presentence report available to the defendant, although courts and court officers have generally been held to be exempt from the provision of such statutes.

The final section of a PSI report is usually devoted to the investigating officer's recommendations. A recommendation may be made in favor of probation, split sentencing, a term of imprisonment, or any other sentencing option available in the jurisdiction. Participation in community service programs or in drug or substance abuse programs may be recommended for probationers. Most judges are willing to accept the report writer's recommendation because they recognize the professionalism of the presentence investigator and because they know that the investigator may be assigned to supervise the defendant if he or she is sentenced to a community alternative.

Jurisdictions vary in their use of the information in a PSI. Federal law mandates PSI reports in federal criminal courts and specifies 15 topical areas that each report must cover. The 1984 federal Determinate Sentencing Act directs report writers to include information on the classification of the offense and of the defendant under the offense-level and criminal history categories established by the statute. Some states require presentence reports only in felony cases, and some require them in cases where the defendant faces the possibility of incarceration for six months or more; other states have no requirement for PSI reports beyond those ordered by a judge.

Report writing, rarely anyone's favorite task, may seriously tax the limited resources of probation agencies. In September 2004, officers from the New York City Department of Probation wrote 2,414 reports for adult offenders and 461 reports for juvenile offenders, averaging about 10 reports per probation officer per month.[71] Learn more about the sentencing environment at Library Extra 9–7 at mycrimekit.com.

Library EXTRA

The Victim—Forgotten No Longer

Victims' Rights

Thanks to a grassroots resurgence of concern for the plight of victims that began in this country in the early 1970s, the sentencing process now frequently includes consideration of the needs of victims and their survivors.[72] In times past, although victims might testify at trial, the criminal justice system frequently downplayed victims' experiences, including the psychological trauma engendered both by having been victims and by having to endure the criminal proceedings that bring a criminal to justice. That changed in 1982 when the President's Task Force on Victims of Crime gave focus to a burgeoning victims' rights movement and urged the widespread expansion of victims' assistance programs during what was then their formative period.[73] Victims' assistance programs today offer services in the areas of crisis intervention and follow-up counseling and help victims secure their rights under the law.[74] Following successful prosecution, some victims' assistance programs also advise victims in the filing of civil suits to recoup financial losses directly from the offender. In the mid-1990s, the National Institute of Justice (NIJ) conducted a survey of 319 full-service victims' assistance programs based in law enforcement agencies and prosecutors' offices.[75] The survey found that "the majority of individuals seeking assistance were victims of domestic assault and the most common assistance they received was information about legal rights." Other common forms of assistance included help in applying for state victims' compensation aid and referrals to social services agencies.

About the same time, voters in California approved Proposition 8, a resolution which called for changes in the state's constitution to reflect concern for victims. A continuing goal of victims' advocacy groups is an amendment to the U.S. Constitution, which such groups say is needed to provide the same kind of fairness to victims that is routinely accorded to defendants. In the past, for example, the National Victims' Constitutional Amendment Project (NVCAP) has sought to add a phrase to the Sixth Amendment—"likewise, the victim, in every criminal prosecution, shall have the right to be present and to be heard at all critical stages of judicial proceedings." NVCAP now advocates the addition of a new amendment to the U.S. Constitution. Visit NVCAP via Web Extra 9–6 at mycrimekit.com.

Web EXTRA

In September 1996, a victims' rights constitutional amendment—Senate Joint Resolution 65—was proposed by a bipartisan committee in the U.S. Congress,[76] but problems of wording and terminology prevented its passage. A revised amendment was proposed in 1998,[77] but its wording was too restrictive for it to gain endorsement from victims' organizations.[78] In 1999, a new amendment was proposed by the Senate Judiciary Committee's Subcommittee on the Constitution, Federalism, and Property, but it did not make it to the Senate floor. The U.S. Department of Justice, which had previously supported the measure, reversed its position due

▶ Demonstrators in Washington, D.C., supporting a victims' rights amendment to the U.S. Constitution. What victims' rights would such an amendment be likely to contain?
MD Crime Victims' Resource Center, Inc.

to a provision in the proposed amendment that gives crime victims the right to be notified of any state or federal grant of clemency; the U.S. attorney general apparently believed that the provision would impede the power of the president. The legislation also lacked the support of President Bill Clinton and was officially withdrawn by its sponsors in 2000. The amendment may still have a future, however, as President George W. Bush expressed support for the measure[79] when he was in office, and 39 state attorneys general have publicly endorsed its adoption.[80] The text of the proposed amendment, known as Senate Joint Resolution 3, is reproduced in CJ Exhibit 3.

Although a victims' rights amendment to the federal Constitution may not yet be a reality, more than 30 states have passed their own victims' rights amendments,[81] and significant federal legislation has already been adopted. The 1982 Victim and Witness Protection Act (VWPA),[82] for example, requires judges to consider victim impact statements at federal sentencing hearings and places responsibility for their creation on federal probation officers. In 1984, the federal Victims of Crime Act (VOCA) was enacted with substantial bipartisan support. VOCA authorized federal funding to help states establish victims' assistance and victims' compensation programs. Under VOCA, the U.S. Department of Justice's Office for Victims of Crime provides a significant source of both funding and information for victims' assistance programs.

We will not punish a man because he hath offended, but that he may offend no more; nor does punishment ever look to the past, but to the future; for it is not the result of passion, but that the same thing be guarded against in time to come.
—Seneca (4 B.C.–A.D. 65)

The rights of victims were further strengthened under the Violent Crime Control and Law Enforcement Act of 1994, which created a federal right of allocution, or right to speak, for victims of violent and sex crimes. This gave victims the right to speak at the sentencing of their assailants. The 1994 law also requires sex offenders and child molesters convicted under federal law to pay restitution to their victims and prohibits the diversion of federal victims' funds to other programs. Other provisions of the 1994 law provide civil rights remedies for victims of felonies motivated by gender bias and extend rape shield law protections to civil cases and to all criminal cases, prohibiting inquiries into a victim's sexual history. A significant feature of the 1994 law can be found in a subsection titled the Violence against Women Act (VAWA). VAWA provides financial support for police, prosecutors, and victims' services in cases involving sexual violence or domestic abuse.

Much of the philosophical basis of today's victims' movement can be found in the restorative justice model, which was discussed briefly earlier in this chapter. Restorative justice emphasizes offender accountability and victim reparation, and it also provides the basis for victims' compensation programs, which are another means of recognizing the needs of crime victims. Today, all 50 states have passed legislation providing for monetary payments to victims of crime; such payments are primarily designed to compensate victims for medical expenses and lost wages. All existing programs require that applicants meet certain eligibility criteria, and most

CJ Exhibit 3

The Call for a Victims' Rights Amendment

In 2002, then-President George W. Bush announced his support for a constitutional amendment for victims of violent crime. Bush said, "In the year 2000, Americans were victims of millions of crimes. Behind each of these numbers is a terrible trauma, a story of suffering, and a story of lost security. Yet the needs of victims are often an afterthought in our criminal justice system. It's not just, it's not fair, and it must change. As we protect the rights of criminals, we must take equal care to protect the rights of the victims."

The president's remarks were made in support of a Senate Joint Resolution offered by Senators Jon Kyl of Arizona and Dianne Feinstein of California. The bill, which has been repeatedly introduced in the past, did not receive the support of President Bill Clinton during the eight years he was in office. The text of the Kyl–Feinstein resolution follows:

Proposing an amendment to the Constitution of the United States to protect the rights of crime victims:

> *Resolved by the Senate and the House of Representatives of the United States of America in Congress assembled (two-thirds of each House concurring therein),* That the following article is proposed as an amendment to the Constitution of the United States, which shall be valid for all intents and purposes as part of the Constitution when ratified by the legislatures of three-fourths of the several States within seven years from the date of its submission by the Congress:

ARTICLE—

Section 1. A victim of a crime of violence, as these terms may be defined by law, shall have the rights:

- to reasonable notice of, and not to be excluded from, any public proceedings relating to the crime;
- to be heard, if present, and to submit a statement at all such proceedings to determine a conditional release from custody, an acceptance of a negotiated plea, or a sentence;
- to the foregoing rights at a parole proceeding that is not public, to the extent those rights are afforded to the convicted offender;
- to reasonable notice of a release or escape from custody relating to the crime;
- to consideration of the interest of the victim that any trial be free from unreasonable delay;
- to an order of restitution from the convicted offender;
- to consideration for the safety of the victim in determining any conditional release from custody relating to the crime; and
- to reasonable notice of the rights established by this article.

Section 2. Only the victim or the victim's lawful representative shall have standing to assert the rights established by this article. Nothing in this article shall provide grounds to stay or continue any trial, reopen any proceeding or invalidate any ruling, except with respect to conditional release or restitution or to provide rights guaranteed by this article in future proceedings, without staying or continuing a trial. Nothing in this article shall give rise to or authorize the creation of a claim for damages against the United States, a State, a political subdivision, or a public officer or employee.

Section 3. The Congress shall have the power to enforce this article by appropriate legislation. Exceptions to the rights established by this article may be created only when necessary to achieve a compelling interest.

Section 4. This article shall take effect on the 180th day after the ratification of this article. The right to an order of restitution established by this article shall not apply to crimes committed before the effective date of this article.

Section 5. The rights and immunities established by this article shall apply in Federal and State proceedings, including military proceedings to the extent that the Congress may provide by law, juvenile justice proceedings, and proceedings in the District of Columbia and any commonwealth, territory, or possession of the United States.

Source: Senate Joint Resolution 3, 106th Congress.

set limits on the maximum amount of compensation that can be received. Generally disallowed are claims from victims who are significantly responsible for their own victimization, such as those who end up being the losers in fights they provoke. In 2002, California's victims' compensation program, the largest in the nation, provided $117 million to more than 50,000 victims for crime-related expenses. A comprehensive California proposal to improve victims' services, with applicability to victims' services programs throughout the nation, can be read at Library Extra 9–8 at mycrimekit.com.

Library EXTRA

In 2001, the USA PATRIOT Act amended the Victims of Crime Act of 1984 to make victims of terrorism and their families eligible for victims' compensation payments.[83] It also created an antiterrorism emergency reserve fund to help provide compensation to victims of terrorism. A year earlier, in November 2000, the federal Office for Victims of Crime (OVC) created the Terrorism and International Victims Unit (TIVU) to develop and manage programs and initiatives that help victims of domestic and international terrorism, mass violence, and crimes with transnational dimensions.[84]

When our criminal justice system treats victims as irrelevant bystanders, they are victimized for a second time. And because Americans are justifiably proud of our system and expect it to treat us fairly, the second violation of our rights can be traumatic.

—*George W. Bush*[viii]

On October 9, 2004, the U.S. Senate passed the Crime Victims' Rights Act,[85] as part of the Justice for All Act of 2004. Some saw the legislation as at least a partial statutory alternative to a constitutional crime victims' rights amendment. The Crime Victims' Rights Act establishes statutory rights for victims of federal crimes and gives them the necessary legal authority to assert those rights in federal court. The Crime Victims' Rights Act grants the following rights to victims of federal crimes[86]:

1. The right to be reasonably protected from the accused
2. The right to reasonable, accurate, and timely notice of any public proceeding involving the crime or of any release or escape of the accused
3. The right to be included in any such public proceeding
4. The right to be reasonably heard at any public proceeding involving release, plea, or sentencing
5. The right to confer with the federal prosecutor handling the case
6. The right to full and timely restitution as provided by law
7. The right to proceedings free from unreasonable delay
8. The right to be treated with fairness and with respect for the victim's dignity and privacy

Web EXTRA

In addition to establishing these rights, the legislation expressly requires federal courts to ensure that they are afforded to victims; in like manner, federal law enforcement officials are required to make their "best efforts to see that crime victims are notified of, and accorded," these rights. To teach citizens about the rights of victims of crime, the federal government created the e-resource crimevictims.gov, which you can access on the Internet via **Web Extra 9–7** at mycrimekit.com. The resource includes an online directory of crime victims' services, which can be searched locally, nationally, and internationally.

Victim Impact Statements

victim impact statement
The in-court use of victim- or survivor-supplied information by sentencing authorities seeking to make an informed sentencing decision.

Another consequence of the national victims' rights movement has been a call for the use of a **victim impact statement**—a written document describing the losses, suffering, and trauma experienced by the crime victim or by the victim's survivors—before sentencing. Judges are expected to consider such a statement in arriving at an appropriate sanction for the offender.

The drive to mandate inclusion of victim impact statements in sentencing decisions, already required in federal courts by the 1982 VWPA, was substantially enhanced by the "right of allocution" provision of the Violent Crime Control and Law Enforcement Act of 1994. Victim impact statements played a prominent role in the sentencing of Timothy McVeigh, who was convicted of the 1995 bombing of the Murrah Federal Building in Oklahoma City and was executed in 2001. Some states, however, have gone further than the federal government; in 1984 the state of California, for example, passed legislation giving victims a right to attend and participate in sentencing and parole hearings.[87] Approximately 20 states now have laws requiring citizen involvement in sentencing, and all 50 states and the District of Columbia "allow for some form of submission of a victim impact statement either at the time of sentencing or to be contained in the presentence investigation reports" made by court officers.[88] Where written victim impact statements are not available, courts may invite the victim to testify directly at sentencing. An alternative to written impact statements and to the appearance of victims at sentencing hearings is the victim impact video.

One study of the efficacy of victim impact statements found that sentencing decisions are rarely affected by them. In the words of the study, "These statements did not produce sentencing decisions that reflected more clearly the effects of crime on victims. Nor did we find much evidence that—with or without impact statements—sentencing decisions were influenced by our measures of the effects of crime on victims, once the charge and the defendant's prior record were taken into account."[89] The authors concluded that victim impact statements have little effect on courts because judges and other officials "have established ways of making decisions which do not call for explicit information about the impact of crime on victims." Learn more about the rights of crime victims and the history of the victims' movement at **Web Extra 9–8**.

Web EXTRA

Freedom or Safety? You Decide.

To What Degree Should the Personal Values of Workers in the Criminal Justice System Influence Job Performance?

In 2007 a 21-year-old college student who was visiting Tampa, Florida, for the annual Gasparilla festival, a pirate-themed parade, called police to say that she was attacked and raped while walking back to her car. Although the woman was not personally identified in news releases because of a policy restricting the release of the names of victims of sexual assault, her story took an interesting twist. Investigating officers first took her to a nearby rape crisis center where she was physically examined and given an initial emergency postcoital contraception pill, also known as a morning after pill, to prevent unwanted pregnancy.

Officers then drove the victim through the area where the attack was said to have taken place in an effort to find the rapist, and to pinpoint the scene of the crime. As they drove, officers entered the woman's identifying information into their car's computer system and discovered that a juvenile warrant that had been issued against her in 2003 for unpaid restitution in a theft case was still outstanding. Once they discovered the warrant, they promptly arrested the woman, booked, and jailed her. She remained behind bars for two days until her family was able to hire an attorney who arranged for her release.

During the time she was jailed, the victim said that a jail health care worker refused to administer a second—and required—dose of the morning after medication. The medicine's manufacturer specifies that two doses of the medication, administered 20 hours apart, are needed to prevent pregnancy. Some members of the local media, which accused the police department of insensitivity to the needs of crime victims, reported that the jail worker felt compelled to deny the woman the medication due to personal religious beliefs against use of the pill.

Vic Moore, the jailed woman's attorney, told reporters that he was "Shocked. Stunned. Outraged. I don't have words to describe it," he said. "She is not a victim of any one person. She is a victim of the system. There's just got to be some humanity involved when it's a victim of rape."

The Tampa Police Department, which was stung by media reports in the case, has since initiated a policy telling officers not to arrest a crime victim who has suffered injury or mental trauma whenever reasonably possible.

YOU DECIDE

1. To what extent (if at all) should the values of workers within the criminal justice system be allowed to influence their performance of job-related tasks?
2. Do you feel that the jail worker referenced in this story was within her "rights" by denying a second dose of the morning after pill to the victim of an alleged rape? Why or why not?

Reference: Phil Davis, "Rape Victim Is Jailed on Old Warrant," Associated Press, January 31, 2007.

Modern Sentencing Options

Sentencing Rationale

Sentencing is fundamentally a risk-management strategy designed to protect the public while serving the ends of retribution, incapacitation, deterrence, rehabilitation, and restoration. Because the goals of sentencing are difficult to agree on, so too are sanctions. Lengthy prison terms do little for rehabilitation, while community release programs can hardly protect the innocent from offenders bent on continuing criminality.

Assorted sentencing philosophies continue to permeate state-level judicial systems. Each state has its own sentencing laws, and frequent revisions of those statutes are not uncommon. Because of huge variations from one state to another in the laws and procedures that control the imposition of criminal sanctions, sentencing has been called "the most diversified part of the Nation's criminal justice process."[90]

There is at least one commonality, however. It can be found in the four traditional sanctions that continue to dominate the thinking of most legislators and judges: fines, probation, imprisonment, and death. Fines and the death penalty are discussed in this chapter.

In jurisdictions that employ indeterminate sentencing, fines, probation, and imprisonment are widely available to judges. The option selected generally depends on the severity of the offense and the judge's best guess as to the likelihood of the defendant's future criminal involvement. Sometimes two or more options are combined, such as when an offender is fined and sentenced to prison or placed on probation and fined in support of restitution payments.

[Unless the Constitution is amended] we will never correct the existing imbalance in this country between [a] defendant's irreducible constitutional rights and the current haphazard patchwork of victims' rights.

—*Janet Reno*
Former U.S. Attorney General

Jurisdictions that operate under presumptive sentencing guidelines generally limit the judge's choice to only one option and often specify the extent to which that option can be applied. Dollar amounts of fines, for example, are rigidly set, and prison terms are specified for each type of offense. The death penalty remains an option in a fair number of jurisdictions, but only for a highly select group of offenders.

A recent report by the Bureau of Justice Statistics on the sentencing practices of trial courts found that state courts convicted 1,079,000 felons in 2004.[91] Another 66,518 felony convictions occurred in federal courts. As shown in Figure 1, the report also found the following for offenders convicted of felonies in state courts:

- About 41% were sentenced to active prison terms.
- The average sentence length for those sent to state prisons has decreased since 1990 (from six years to four years and nine months).
- Felons sentenced in 2004 were likely to serve more of their sentence before release (50%) than those sentenced in 1990 (33%).
- Roughly 30% received jail sentences, usually involving less than a year's confinement.
- Those sent to jail received an average sentence of six months.
- Of the total, 28% percent were sentenced to probation with no jail or prison time to serve.
- The average probation sentence was 38 months.
- Fines were imposed on 33% of convicted felons, and restitution was ordered in 18% of cases.

Although the percentage of felons who receive active sentences may seem low, the number of criminal defendants receiving active prison time has increased dramatically. Figure 2 shows that the number of court-ordered prison commitments has increased nearly eightfold in the past 40 years.

Fines

While the fine is one of the oldest forms of punishment, the use of fines as criminal sanctions suffers from built-in inequities and a widespread failure to collect them. Inequities arise when offenders with vastly different financial resources are fined similar amounts; a fine of $100, for example, can place a painful economic burden on a poor defendant but is negligible when imposed on a wealthy offender.

Nonetheless, fines are once again receiving attention as a serious sentencing alternative. One reason for the renewed interest is the stress placed on state resources by burgeoning prison populations. The extensive imposition of fines not only results in less crowded prisons

FIGURE 1
The Sentencing of Convicted Felons in State Courts, by Type of Sentence.
Source: Data from Matthew R. Durose and Patrick A. Langan, *Felony Sentences in State Courts, 2004* (Washington, DC: Bureau of Justice Statistics, 2007).

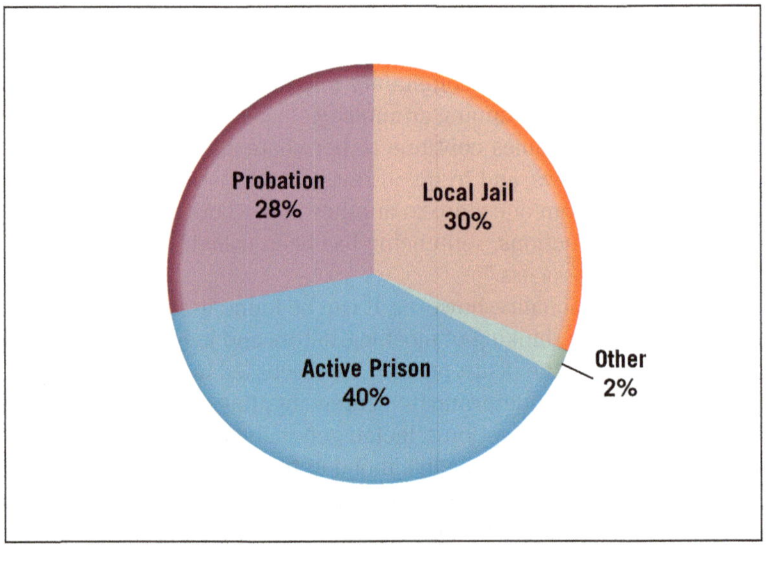

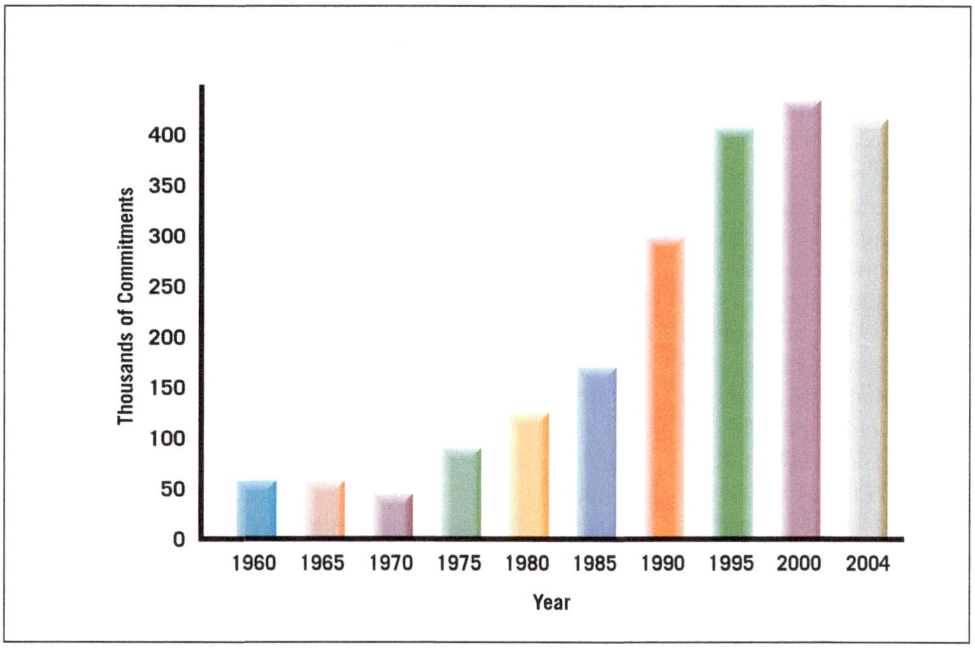

FIGURE 2
Court-Ordered Prison Commitments, 1960–2004.
Source: Data from Matthew R. Durose and Patrick A. Langan, *Felony Sentences in State Courts, 2004* (Washington, DC: Bureau of Justice Statistics, 2007), and other years.

but can contribute to state and local coffers and can lower the tax burden of law-abiding citizens. There are other advantages:

- Fines can deprive offenders of the proceeds of criminal activity.
- Fines can promote rehabilitation by enforcing economic responsibility.
- Fines can be collected by existing criminal justice agencies and are relatively inexpensive to administer.
- Fines can be made proportionate to both the severity of the offense and the ability of the offender to pay.

An NIJ survey found that an average of 86% of convicted defendants in courts of limited jurisdiction receive fines as sentences, some in combination with another penalty.[92] Fines are also widely used in courts of general jurisdiction, where the NIJ study found judges imposing fines in 42% of all cases that came before them for sentencing. Some studies estimate that more than $1 billion in fines are collected nationwide each year.[93]

Fines are often imposed for relatively minor law violations, such as driving while intoxicated, reckless driving, disturbing the peace, disorderly conduct, public drunkenness, and vandalism. Judges in many courts, however, report the use of fines for relatively serious violations of the law, including assault, auto theft, embezzlement, fraud, and sale and possession of various controlled substances. Fines are most likely to be imposed where the offender has both a clean record and the ability to pay.[94]

Opposition to the use of fines is based on the following four arguments:

1. Fines allow the release of convicted offenders into the community but do not impose stringent controls on their behavior.
2. Fines are a relatively mild form of punishment and are not consistent with the just deserts philosophy.
3. Fines discriminate against the poor and favor the wealthy (indigent offenders are especially subject to discrimination since they lack the financial resources with which to pay fines).
4. Fines are difficult to collect.

Of all the initiatives that this Congress could undertake, few will touch the heart of Americans as dearly as the measure seeking to ensure that the judicial process is just and fair for the victims of crime.
—*Orrin Hatch*
U.S. Senator (R–Utah)

A number of these objections can be answered by procedures that make available to judges complete financial information on defendants. Studies have found, however, that courts of limited jurisdiction, which are the most likely to impose fines, are also the least likely to have adequate information on offenders' financial status.[95] Perhaps as a consequence, judges are sometimes reluctant to impose fines. Two of the most widely cited objections by judges to the use of fines are that fines allow more affluent offenders to "buy their way out" and that poor offenders cannot pay fines.[96]

A solution to both objections can be found in the Scandinavian system of day fines. The day-fine system is based on the idea that fines should be proportionate to the severity of the offense but also need to take into account the financial resources of the offender. Day fines are computed by first assessing the seriousness of the offense, the defendant's degree of culpability, and his or her prior record as measured in "days." The use of days as a benchmark of seriousness is related to the fact that, without fines, the offender could be sentenced to a number of days (or months or years) in jail or prison. The number of days an offender is assessed is then multiplied by the daily wages that person earns. Hence, if two people are sentenced to a five-day fine but one earns only $20 per day and the other $200 per day, the first would pay a $100 fine and the second would pay $1,000.

In 2004, one of Finland's richest men, 27-year-old Jussi Salonoja, was fined a record 170,000 euros ($217,000) for speeding through the center of Helsinki.[97] Salonoja, heir to his family's international sausage business, was caught driving 80 kilometers per hour (kph) in a 40-kph zone. The fine was based on Salonoja's 2002 earnings, which were estimated at close to 7 million euros.

In the early 1990s, the NIJ reported on experimental day-fine programs conducted by the Richmond County Criminal Court in Staten Island, New York, and by the Milwaukee (Wisconsin) Municipal Court.[98] Both studies concluded that "the day fine can play a major . . . role as an intermediate sanction"[99] and that "the day-fine concept could be implemented in a typical American limited-jurisdiction court."[100] Those conclusions were supported by a 1996 RAND Corporation report that examined ongoing day-fine demonstration projects in Maricopa County, Arizona; Des Moines, Iowa; Bridgeport, Connecticut; and four counties in Oregon.[101]

Death: The Ultimate Sanction

Some crimes are especially heinous and seem to cry out for extreme punishment. In 2008, for example, in an especially atrocious murder, a 28-year-old grocery store stock clerk named Kevin Ray Underwood was sentenced to death in the murder of a ten-year-old girl in what authorities said was an elaborate plan to cannibalize the girl's flesh.[102] Underwood had been the girl's neighbor in Purcell, Oklahoma, and her mutilated body, covered with deep saw marks, was discovered in his apartment. Investigators told reporters that Underwood had sexually assaulted the little girl and

▶ Kevin Ray Underwood, who murdered his ten-year-old neighbor when he was 26. Underwood had planned to cannibalize the girl's body but was arrested before he could carry out his plans. He was sentenced to death in 2008. Was the sentence just?
The Oklahoman/*Steve Sisney/AP Wide World Photos*

planned to eat her corpse using the meat tenderizer and barbecue skewers that they confiscated from his kitchen. "In my 24 years as a prosecutor, this ranks as one of the most heinous and atrocious cases I've ever been involved with," said McClain County Prosecutor Tim Kuykendalls.

Many states today have statutory provisions that provide for a sentence of **capital punishment** (the death penalty) for especially repugnant crimes (known as **capital offenses**). Estimates are that more than 18,800 legal executions have been carried out in the United States since 1608, when records began to be kept on capital punishment.[103] Although capital punishment was widely used throughout the eighteenth and nineteenth centuries, the mid-twentieth century offered a brief respite in the number of offenders legally executed in this country. Between 1930 and 1967, the year in which the U.S. Supreme Court ordered a nationwide stay of pending executions, nearly 3,800 people were put to death; the peak years were 1935 and 1936, with nearly 200 legal killings each year. Executions declined substantially every year thereafter. Between 1967 and 1977, a *de facto* moratorium existed, with no executions carried out in any U.S. jurisdiction. Following the lifting of the moratorium, executions resumed (Figure 3). In 1983, only five offenders were put to death, while 65 were executed nationwide in 2003. A modern record for executions was set in 1999, with 98 executions—35 in Texas alone. Substantially fewer offenders (42) were executed in 2007.

capital punishment
The death penalty. Capital punishment is the most extreme of all sentencing options.

capital offense
A criminal offense punishable by death.

Today, the federal government and 37 of the 50 states[104] permit execution for first-degree murder, while treason, kidnapping, aggravated rape, murder of a police or correctional officer, and murder while under a life sentence are punishable by death in selected jurisdictions. New Jersey, which up until recently was among states with a death penalty, repealed its capital punishment statute in 2007, replacing it with a sentence of life in prison without possibility of parole.

The list of crimes punishable by death under federal jurisdiction increased dramatically with passage of the Violent Crime Control and Law Enforcement Act of 1994 and was expanded still further by the 2001 USA PATRIOT Act, a federal law that focuses on fighting terrorism. The list now includes a total of about 60 offenses. State legislators have also worked to expand the types of crimes for which a death sentence can be imposed. In 1997, for example, the Louisiana Supreme Court upheld the state's year-old child rape statute, which allows for the imposition of a capital sentence when the victim is younger than 12 years of age. The case involved an AIDS-infected father who raped his three daughters, ages five, eight, and nine. In upholding the father's death sentence, the Louisiana court ruled that child rape is "like no other crime."[105] In 2008, however, in the case of *Kennedy* v. *Louisiana*, the U.S. Supreme

We've never had a doubt about the guilt of Timothy McVeigh. But, we needed more than a guilty defendant. We needed an innocent system.
—John Ashcroft, Former U.S. Attorney General[ix]

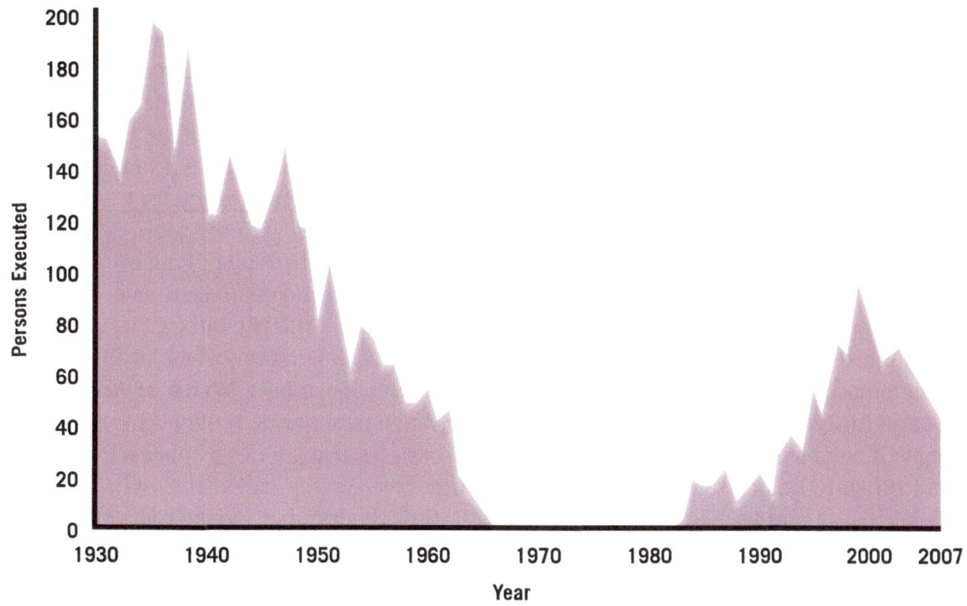

FIGURE 3
Court-Ordered Executions Carried Out in the United States, 1976–2007.
Source: Reprinted with permission from the Death Penalty Information Center.

Court ruled that the Eighth Amendment bars Louisiana (and other states) from imposing the death penalty for the rape of a child where the crime did not result, and was not intended to result, in the victim's death.[106]

A total of 3,228 offenders were under sentence of death throughout the United States on January 1, 2007.[107] The latest statistics show that 98.4% of those on death row are male, approximately 45.4% are white, 10.5% are Hispanic, 41.8% are African-American, and 2.3% are of other races (mostly Native American and Pacific Islander).[108]

Web EXTRA

Library EXTRA

Methods of imposing death vary by state. The majority of death penalty states authorize execution through lethal injection; electrocution is the second most common means of dispatch, while hanging, the gas chamber, and firing squads have survived, at least as options available to the condemned, in a few states.[109] For the most current statistical information on capital punishment, visit the Death Penalty Information Center (DPIC) at **Web Extra 9–9** at mycrimekit.com. Learn more about the history of capital punishment at **Library Extra 9–9** at mycrimekit.com.

Habeas Corpus Review

I think this country would be much better off if we did not have capital punishment. We cannot ignore the fact that in recent years a disturbing number of inmates on death row have been exonerated.

—John Paul Stevens
U.S. Supreme Court Justice[x]

The legal process through which a capital sentence is carried to conclusion is fraught with problems. One serious difficulty centers on the fact that automatic review of all death sentences by appellate courts and constant legal maneuvering by defense counsel often lead to a dramatic delay between the time the sentence is handed down and the time it is carried out. Today, an average of ten years and eight months passes between the imposition of a death penalty and execution.[110] Such lengthy delays, compounded by uncertainty over whether an execution will ever occur, directly contravene the generally accepted notion that punishment should be swift and certain.

Even death-row inmates can undergo life-altering changes. When that happens, long-delayed executions can become highly questionable events. The case of Stanley "Tookie" Williams, who was executed at California's San Quentin Prison in 2005 at age 51, is illustrative.[111] Williams, self-described cofounder of the infamous Crips street gang in the early 1970s, was sentenced to die for the brutal shotgun murders of four people during a robbery 26 years earlier. In 1993, however, he experienced what he called a "reawakening" and began working from prison as an antigang crusader. Williams found a sympathetic publisher and wrote a series of children's books titled *Tookie Speaks Out against Gang Violence.* The series was intended to help urban youth reject the lure of gang membership and embrace traditional values. He also wrote *Life in Prison,* an autobiography describing the isolation and despair experienced by death-row inmates. In his final years, Williams worked with his editor, Barbara Cottman Becnel, to create the Internet Project for Street Peace, a demonstration project linking teens from the rough-and-tumble streets of Richmond, California, to peers in Switzerland in an effort to help them avoid street violence. In 2001, Williams was nominated for the Nobel Peace Prize by a member of the Swiss Parliament and for the Nobel Prize in Literature by a number of college professors. Pleas to spare his life, which came from Jesse Jackson, anti–death penalty activist Sister Helen Prejean, the National Association for the Advancement of Colored People (NAACP), and others, were rejected by Governor Arnold Schwarzenegger, who said that "there is no reason to second-guess the jury's decision of guilt or raise significant doubts or serious reservations about Williams' convictions and death sentence."[112]

writ of *habeas corpus*
A writ that directs the person detaining a prisoner to bring him or her before a judicial officer to determine the lawfulness of the imprisonment.

In a speech before the American Bar Association (ABA) in 1989, then–Chief Justice William Rehnquist called for reforms of the federal *habeas corpus* system, which at the time allowed condemned prisoners virtually limitless opportunities for appeal. **Writs of *habeas corpus*** (Latin for "you have the body"), which require that a prisoner be brought into court to determine if he or she is being legally held, form the basis for many federal appeals made by prisoners on state death rows. In 1968, Chief Justice Earl Warren called the right to file *habeas* petitions, as guaranteed under the U.S. Constitution, the "symbol and guardian of individual liberty." Twenty years later, however, Rehnquist claimed that writs of *habeas corpus* were being used indiscriminately by death-row inmates seeking to delay executions even where grounds for delay did not exist. "The capital defendant does not need to prevail on the merits in order to accomplish his purpose," said Rehnquist. "He wins temporary victories by postponing a final adjudication."[113]

In a move to reduce delays in the conduct of executions, the U.S. Supreme Court, in the case of ***McCleskey* v. *Zant*** (1991),[114] limited the number of appeals a condemned person may lodge with the courts. Saying that repeated filing for the sole purpose of delay promotes "disrespect for the finality of convictions" and "disparages the entire criminal justice system," the Court established a two-pronged criterion for future appeals. According to *McCleskey,* in any petition beyond the first filed with the federal court, a capital defendant must (1) demonstrate good cause why the claim now being made was not included in the first filing and (2) explain how the absence of that claim may have harmed the petitioner's ability to mount an effective defense. Two months later, the Court reinforced *McCleskey* when it ruled, in ***Coleman* v. *Thompson*** (1991),[115] that state prisoners could not cite "procedural default," such as a defense attorney's failure to meet a state's filing deadline for appeals, as the basis for an appeal to federal court.

There can be no doubt that the taking of the life of the President creates much more societal harm than the taking of the life of a homeless person.

—*Charles Burson*
Tennessee Attorney General, arguing before the U.S. Supreme Court in Payne v.Tennessee[xi]

In 1995, in the case of ***Schlup* v. *Delo,***[116] the Court continued to define standards for further appeals from death-row inmates, ruling that before appeals based on claims of new evidence could be heard, "a petitioner must show that, in light of the new evidence, it is more likely than not that no reasonable juror would have found him guilty beyond a reasonable doubt." A "reasonable juror" was defined as one who "would consider fairly all of the evidence presented and would conscientiously obey the trial court's instructions requiring proof beyond a reasonable doubt."

Opportunities for federal appeals by death-row inmates were further limited by the Antiterrorism and Effective Death Penalty Act (AEDPA) of 1996,[117] which sets a one-year postconviction deadline for state inmates filing federal *habeas corpus* appeals. The deadline is six months for state death-row inmates who were provided a lawyer for *habeas* appeals at the state level. The act also requires federal courts to presume that the factual findings of state courts are correct; does not permit the claim of state court misinterpretations of the U.S. Constitution as a basis for *habeas* relief unless those misinterpretations are "unreasonable"; and requires that all petitioners must show, prior to obtaining a hearing, facts sufficient to establish by clear and convincing evidence that but for constitutional error, no reasonable fact finder would have found the petitioner guilty. The act also requires approval by a three-judge panel before an inmate can file a second federal appeal raising newly discovered evidence of innocence. In 1996, in the case of *Felker* v. *Turpin,*[118] the U.S. Supreme Court ruled that limitations on the authority of federal courts to consider successive *habeas corpus* petitions imposed by AEDPA are permissible since they do not deprive the U.S. Supreme Court of its original jurisdiction over such petitions.

Some recent statements by Supreme Court justices have indicated that long delays caused by the government in carrying out executions may render the punishment unconstitutionally cruel and unusual. One example comes from the 1998 case of *Elledge* v. *Florida,*[119] where the execution of William D. Elledge had been delayed for 23 years. Although the full Court refused to hear the case, Justice Stephen Breyer observed, "Twenty-three years under sentence of death is unusual—whether one takes as a measuring rod current practice or the practice in this country and in England at the time our Constitution was written." Moreover, wrote Breyer, execution after such a long delay could be considered cruel because Elledge "has experienced that delay because of the State's own faulty procedures and not because of frivolous appeals on his own part." Elledge still remains on death row at the Union Correctional Institution in Florida; he has been under sentence of death for 32 years.

Opposition to Capital Punishment

Thirty years ago, David Magris, who was celebrating his twenty-first birthday with a crime spree, shot Dennis Tapp in the back during a holdup, leaving Tapp a paraplegic. Tapp had been working a late-night shift, tending his father's quick-serve gas station. Magris went on to commit more robberies that night, killing 20-year-old Steven Tompkins in a similar crime. Although Margis was sentenced to death by a California court, the U.S. Supreme Court overturned the state's death penalty law in 1972, opening the door for Magris to be paroled in 1985. Long before Magris was freed from prison, however, Tapp had already forgiven him. A few minutes after the shooting happened, Tapp regained consciousness, dragged himself to a telephone, and called for help. The next thing he did was ask "God to forgive the man who did this to me."[120] Today, the men—both staunch death penalty opponents—are friends, and Magris is president of the Northern California Coalition to Abolish the Death Penalty. "Don't get me wrong," says Tapp. "What [David] did was wrong. . . . He did something stupid and he paid for it."[121]

Because the death penalty is such an emotional issue for many, attempts have been made to abolish capital punishment since the founding of the United States. The first recorded effort to

▶ Death penalty opponent Mark Bherand sits outside San Quentin Prison holding a sign as he awaits the execution of convicted killer Stanley "Tookie" Williams on December 13, 2005. Williams, reputed cofounder of the Crips street gang, had been convicted of four murders that occurred in 1979, and he was denied clemency by California Governor Arnold Schwarzenegger. How do you feel about capital punishment?
Justin Sullivan/Getty Images–GINS/ Entertainment News & Sports

Life is sacred. It's about the only sacred thing on earth—and no one has a right to do away with it.
—Aldona DeVetsco Mother of a murder victim, commenting on the execution of her son's killer

eliminate the death penalty occurred at the home of Benjamin Franklin in 1787.[122] At a meeting there on March 9 of that year, Dr. Benjamin Rush, a signer of the Declaration of Independence and a leading medical pioneer, read a paper against capital punishment to a small but influential audience. Although his immediate efforts came to naught, his arguments laid the groundwork for many debates that followed. Michigan, widely regarded as the first abolitionist state, joined the Union in 1837 without a death penalty; a number of other states, including Alaska, Hawaii, Massachusetts, Minnesota, West Virginia, and Wisconsin, have since spurned death as a possible sanction for criminal acts. As noted earlier, it remains a viable sentencing option in 38 of the states and in all federal jurisdictions, so arguments continue to rage over its value.

Today, six main rationales for abolishing capital punishment are heard:

1. The death penalty can be and has been inflicted on innocent people.
2. The death penalty is not an effective deterrent.
3. The imposition of the death penalty is, by the nature of our legal system, arbitrary.
4. The death penalty discriminates against certain ethnic and racial groups.
5. The death penalty is far too expensive to justify its use.
6. Human life is sacred, and killing at the hands of the state is not a righteous act but rather one that is on the same moral level as the crimes committed by the condemned.

The first five abolitionist claims are pragmatic, that is, they can be measured and verified or disproved by looking at the facts. The last claim is primarily philosophical and therefore not amenable to scientific investigation. Hence we shall briefly examine only the first five.

Death Penalty and Innocent People

The DPIC claims that 124 people in 25 states were freed from death row between 1973 and mid-2007 after it was determined that they were innocent of the capital crime of which they had been convicted.[123] One study of felony convictions that used analysis of DNA to provide post-conviction evidence of guilt or innocence found 28 cases in which defendants had been wrongly convicted and sentenced to lengthy prison terms. The study, *Convicted by Juries, Exonerated by Science*, effectively demonstrated that the judicial process can be flawed.[124] DNA testing can play a critical role in identifying wrongful convictions because, as Barry Scheck and Peter Neufeld (cofounders of the Innocence Project at the Benjamin N. Cardozo School of

Law), point out, "Unlike witnesses who disappear or whose recollections fade over time, DNA in biological samples can be reliably extracted decades after the commission of the crime. The results of such testing have invariably been found to have a scientific certainty that easily outweighs the eyewitness identification testimony or other direct or circumstantial proof that led to the original conviction."[125] They go on to say, "Very simply, . . . DNA testing has demonstrated that far more wrongful convictions occur than even the most cynical and jaded scholars had suspected."[126]

In 2006, for example, Floridian Alan Crotzer, age 45, was freed from prison after spending almost 24 years behind bars for two rapes that DNA tests later showed he didn't commit.[127] Crotzer had been convicted in 1982 of raping a 12-year-old girl and kidnapping, raping, and robbing a Tampa woman. Five eyewitnesses identified him as the shotgun-wielding leader of a gang of robbers who invaded a Tampa, Florida, home and assaulted the people inside. Crotzer was also convicted of aggravated assault, burglary, robbery, and attempted robbery and was sentenced to 130 years in prison. Although DNA testing was not readily available at the time he was tried, DNA tests performed in 2005 on rape kit evidence stored in a Florida Department of Law Enforcement locker since the crime proved Crotzer's innocence. The test's findings were supported by the admission of another man, Douglas James, one of the original suspects, that he had committed the crimes along with his brother and a childhood friend.[128] Shortly after learning of the test results, prosecutors asked Tampa Judge J. Rogers Padgett to set aside Crotzer's conviction and set him free. "The motion is granted. You are a free man," Padgett told Crotzer in a courtroom crowded with members of the press and Crotzer's family. Asked whether he would seek compensation from the state for the years he had spent behind bars, Crotzer told reporters, "There ain't no compensation for what they done to me; but I'm not bitter."[129]

A 2000 study by Columbia Law School professors James S. Liebman, Jeffrey Fagan, and Simon H. Rifkind examined 4,578 death penalty cases in state and federal courts from 1973 to 1995.[130] Liebman and Fagan found that appellate courts overturned the conviction or reduced the sentence in 68% of the cases examined; in 82% of the successful appeals, defendants were found to be deserving of a lesser sentence, while convictions were overturned in 7% of such appeals. According to the study's authors, "Our 23 years worth of findings reveal a capital punishment system collapsing under the weight of its own mistakes." You can read the Liebman–Fagan report in its entirety at Library Extra 9–10 at mycrimekit.com.

Library EXTRA

Claims of innocence are being partially addressed today by recently passed state laws that mandate DNA testing of all death-row inmates in situations where DNA testing might help establish guilt or innocence (that is, in cases where blood or semen from the perpetrator is available for testing).[131] In 2000, Illinois Governor George Ryan announced that he was suspending all executions in his state indefinitely, a proclamation that came after DNA testing showed that 13 Illinois death-row prisoners could not have committed the capital crimes of which they were convicted. (In a sad footnote to the Illinois proclamation,[132] former Governor Ryan, who drew international praise for his stance against the death penalty and who had been nominated for the Nobel Prize, was found guilty in 2006 of racketeering and fraud in a corruption scandal that ended his political career.[133]) In 2006, the New Jersey legislature voted to suspend use of the death penalty until a state task force made its report on whether capital punishment is fairly imposed.[134]

In 2004, in recognition of the potential of DNA testing to exonerate the innocent, President George W. Bush signed the Innocence Protection Act[135] into law. The act provides federal funds to eliminate the backlog of unanalyzed DNA samples in the nation's crime laboratories[136]; it also sets aside money to improve the capacity of federal, state, and local crime laboratories to conduct DNA analyses.[137] In addition, the act facilitates access to postconviction DNA testing for those serving time in state[138] or federal prisons or on death row, and it sets forth conditions under which a federal prisoner asserting innocence may obtain postconviction DNA testing of specific evidence. Similarly, the legislation requires the preservation of biological evidence by federal law enforcement agencies for any defendant under a sentence of imprisonment or death.

Not all claims of innocence are supported by DNA tests, however. In 2006, for example, DNA test results confirmed the guilt of Roger Keith Coleman, a Virginia coal miner who had steadfastly maintained his innocence until he was executed in 1992. Coleman, executed for the 1981 rape and murder of his sister-in-law, Wanda McCoy, in 1981, died declaring his innocence and proclaiming that he would one day be exonerated. His case became a cause célèbre for death penalty opponents, who convinced Virginia Governor Mark Warner to order DNA tests on surviving evidence. Coleman's supporters claimed that the tests would provide the first scientific

Developing a sentencing system that provides appropriate types and lengths of sentences for all offenders is a challenging task.

—National Conference of State Legislatures

CJ News

DNA Tests Fuel Urgency to Free the Innocent

After spending nearly 27 years buried in the vast Texas prison system for a crime he did not commit, Charles Chatman's first weeks of freedom have been overwhelming.

Each of the six rooms in his new apartment, including the bathroom, is larger than any of his previous cells. The gleaming entertainment system and sleek laptop from family, friends and attorneys might as well be hollow props on a movie set, because Chatman, 47, has little idea how to operate them—testimony to more than a generation lost behind bars.

Chatman was exonerated last month by DNA testing while serving a 99-year sentence for sexual assault. His release Jan. 3 marked the 15th such exoneration in Dallas County during the past five years, the most of any county in the nation. Aside from New York and Illinois, Dallas County also has produced more exonerations than any state.

As DNA technology and investigations identify a mounting number of wrongful convictions, the urgency to find others like Chatman is increasing. From Virginia to California, local prosecutors, law students and defense attorneys are combing through hundreds of thousands of old files in search of flawed convictions.

Last week, two men were cleared of separate murder convictions in Mississippi after new DNA testing led authorities to another man now charged in both slayings. It was the first time post-conviction DNA testing had led to an exoneration in Mississippi, one of eight states that does not have a law allowing for such testing. Lawyers with the Innocence Project pushed the state to move forward with the testing.

Since 1989, there have been 213 post-conviction DNA exonerations in the USA. Of those, 149 came in the past seven years, according to the Innocence Project, the parent organization of a far-flung network that helps prisoners obtain DNA testing or other evidence that could prove their innocence.

Among efforts to ferret out the wrongfully convicted:

- In Virginia, officials are conducting a sweeping examination of more than 534,000 files, the largest such review in U.S. history. Three years and five exonerations after the effort began, authorities have identified 2,215 more cases they say are worthy of scrutiny.

"If we identified (only) one guy who shouldn't be in prison, would it be worth it? I say yes," says Pete Marone, who as director of the state's Department of Forensic Science is helping to direct the review.

- A team of attorneys and law students at California Western Law School, part of the national Innocence Project network, fields up to 1,000 inmate requests for help each year.

Jeff Chinn, assistant director of the Southern California Innocence Project, says 5% to 10% of those requests are selected for further investigation. Since the program began in 2000, five have been exonerated, including Timothy Atkins, who was freed last year after serving 20 years in prison for a wrongful murder conviction.

- In Arizona, volunteer lawyers, law students and investigators have screened more than 2,500 cases in the past decade and secured one exoneration: Byron Lacy, freed in 2003 after serving six years for killing a security guard and wounding another man. About 20 other prisoners have won some kind of post-conviction relief, such as a shorter sentence.

▸ Texas prisoner Charles Chatman, age 46, hugging Dallas (Texas) Judge John Creuzot after DNA samples taken from a rape victim in 1981 failed to match Chatman. Chatman served nearly 27 years of a 99-year prison sentence before being exonerated. He became the fifteenth wrongfully convicted prisoner in Dallas County to be exonerated by DNA testing since 2001. Should wider use be made of DNA testing?
Tim Sharp/AP Wide World Photos

- In what may be the most aggressive move by a local prosecutor, Dallas County District Attorney Craig Watkins has turned over more than 400 files to law students working for the Innocence Project of Texas. The students are reviewing decisions by previous administrations to reject requests for DNA testing.

Watkins, Dallas County's first African-American district attorney, says opening the files may have been his easiest decision since being sworn in last year, even in a state where politicians have a reputation for supporting aggressive law-and-order policies.

"The reason I'm here is a result of what happened in the past," Watkins says. He cites a tradition of aggressive prosecution in Dallas and routine denials of prisoners' requests for post-conviction reviews, which he says shrouded past errors. Those errors have emerged, Watkins says, largely because the local forensics laboratory preserved the biological evidence at issue in many of the recent challenges by prisoners.

For many places, a review of convictions such as that in Dallas County is not possible because physical evidence has not been preserved. The lack of uniform preservation standards is a big concern among advocates for post-conviction challenges, says Peter Neufeld, co-founder of the Innocence Project.

But for Watkins, the available evidence offered "an opportunity to restore the credibility of this office."

JUDGE TAKES INTEREST IN CASE

In 17 years on the bench, Dallas Judge John Creuzot has heard countless defendants declare their innocence. But Chatman's 2001 application for post-conviction DNA testing was different.

"I noticed the guy had been inside for a long, long time," Creuzot says. At the time, Chatman had served 20 years of his 99-year sentence for rape.

It is rare for a prisoner to pursue a challenge after so long behind bars. Creuzot thought of boxer Rubin "Hurricane" Carter, freed after spending about 20 years in prison for the slayings of three men in New Jersey. Carter's case inspired the movie *Hurricane*.

"Maybe it was the movie," the judge says. "Something about (Chatman's case) caught me."

Chatman had lived in the same neighborhood as the rape victim. He was nearing the end of a four-year term of probation for a 1978 burglary conviction when she was attacked, and he was included in a police lineup of possible suspects. The victim identified him as her attacker, and he was convicted in 1981.

As Creuzot reviewed the file, the possible existence of untested DNA evidence and the identification of Chatman in the lineup—both among the most common reasons for a wrongful conviction—seemed to demand more scrutiny.

Months later, during Chatman's first appearance in Creuzot's courtroom, the judge says something else struck him and raised questions about Chatman's guilt. "I can just remember his face when he said: 'I didn't do this. I didn't do this,'" he says.

A first attempt at DNA testing of the assailant's biological sample by the Texas Department of Public Safety did not produce a result, according to a chronology of the case prepared by the district attorney's office.

Chatman feared that further testing also would prove inconclusive and consume the biological sample—and with it, any chance of exoneration. Chatman and Michelle Moore, his attorney from the Innocence Project of Texas, asked that additional analysis be suspended in 2004 until testing technology improved.

Moore says Chatman showed remarkable judgment—and patience—in seeking the delay. "How many people would have done that?" she asks.

The opportunity for more reliable testing came last December, when the judge ordered a new analysis using a method known as YSTR testing at Orchid Cellmark Inc., in nearby Farmers Branch, Texas. The new testing allows for better identification of male DNA profiles in samples in which female genetic material often is present, says Robert Giles, Orchid Cellmark's executive director of research and development.

Before ordering the test, Creuzot brought Chatman back to his office to see whether he wished to go forward, knowing that the new test—if inconclusive—likely would leave no more material to analyze.

"I asked him, 'Are you sure? This is it.'"

"Yes," Chatman responded. "I didn't do this."

At 8:30 A.M. on Jan. 2, weeks before results were due, the phone rang in Creuzot's office. Chatman's DNA was "not a match." Creuzot summoned an anxious Chatman from the county jail, where he was staying temporarily while awaiting the results.

"I knew what the test should say, but I still had that little doubt," Chatman says. "I had been a hard-luck guy for a long time."

When Chatman arrived, Creuzot stuck out his hand and said: "Man, Happy New Year!"

"He looked confused at first," the judge says. "I asked if he wanted to call somebody; I handed him my phone. He had never used a cell phone before, so I had to dial the number for him."

There was so much paperwork to process [that] Creuzot couldn't release Chatman immediately, so he ordered a celebratory lunch.

"I asked what kind of steak he wanted; he didn't know what to say, except to request that he wanted it 'cooked a lot,'" Creuzot says.

Chatman sat with the judge's 7-year-old son, Ethan, at a table in Creuzot's locked courtroom. (Ethan, on a holiday break from school, had accompanied his father to the office.) Chatman hadn't used a knife in years and began tearing the meat with his hands.

Lunch was one small measure of the seismic change in Chatman's world—a change Creuzot made official that day. He called the prison to inform the warden that Chatman was not coming back.

A "LOGISTICAL NIGHTMARE"

Creuzot was instrumental in securing Chatman's release, but not all of the wrongfully convicted have found similar advocates.

Lack of funding for post-conviction analysis, including DNA testing and expert testimony, has hamstrung prisoner-assistance campaigns. The percentage of overturned cases is small, and the challenges are daunting.

Virginia's Marone calls the historic effort there to review thousands of old cases a "logistical nightmare."

The broad review, ordered more than two years ago by then-governor Mark Warner, was triggered in part by the discovery of blood and other potential biological evidence attached to old case files, some dating to 1973. The evidence had never been disclosed. The state began reviewing all of the files from 1973 to 1988, the time period at issue.

(continued)

Because the files were not automated during that time, much of the project has required a hand-search of the documents in a labor-intensive and increasingly expensive examination. Marone says the analysis has cost about $1.4 million, and money is running out.

Virginia and the cash-strapped Arizona Justice Project had hoped to win some of the millions of dollars Congress set aside in 2006 to assist in DNA testing. Late last year, USA TODAY disclosed that the Justice Department had not distributed any of the money.

"That is wrong," Senate Judiciary Chairman Patrick Leahy said last month at a hearing to address the issue. "That is irresponsible."

The Justice Department, which pledges to resolve the problem, had said that rules imposed by Congress made it difficult for states to qualify.

For example, the law requires that states' attorneys general compel police departments to preserve biological evidence for testing. However, attorneys general don't always have authority over the operations of all police agencies.

In Dallas County, much of the work to identify the wrongfully convicted is falling to law students and volunteer lawyers. Crowded into a small jury room in the Frank Crowley Court Building, they leaf through thick case files, some more than three decades old.

Many of the students, drawn from local law schools, get no formal credit for the work. They work on all aspects of the cases, from re-interviewing witnesses to ensuring that those who are freed have new clothing when they leave prison.

Jessica Mines, 27, a second-year law student at Texas Wesleyan, says seeing the release of a prisoner like Chatman is "priceless."

CONSIDERING A LAWSUIT

Since Chatman's release, he has traveled to Washington, where he was welcomed at a Senate hearing and met briefly with Leahy, a vocal backer of legislation to help free the wrongfully convicted.

Chatman is eligible for up to $50,000 per year from the state for each of the 27 years of lost time. He is weighing a lawsuit over his incarceration and will get the state money only if he decides not to sue.

His family and attorneys provide much of what he has—the apartment, furniture and a new pickup. He earned a general educational development (GED) certificate in prison and is considering enrolling in college or pursuing a career as a welder or auto mechanic.

For now, the new truck mostly sits in a parking space because he fears he'll lose his way if he strays too far from his sprawling apartment complex. But there are plenty of other options for life outside his cell.

"I can just go take a bath," he says, "and lay in the tub any time I want."

For the latest in crime and justice news, visit the Talk Justice news feed at http://www.crimenews.info.

Source: Kevin Johnson, "DNA Tests Fuel Urgency to Free the Innocent," *USA Today*, February 19, 2008, p. 1A. From USA TODAY, a division of Garnett Co., Inc. Reprinted with permission. www.usatoday.com.

proof that an innocent man had been executed in the United States. Results from the tests, however, conclusively showed that blood and semen found at the crime scene had come from Coleman. After the test results were announced, James McCloskey, director of a New Jersey prison ministry and one of the leaders in the effort to clear Coleman's name told reporters, "We who seek the truth must live or die by the sword of DNA, [but] this particular truth feels like a kick in the stomach." Learn more about DNA testing and how it can help determine guilt or innocence from the President's DNA Initiative via **Web Extra 9–10** at mycrimekit.com.

Web EXTRA

Death Penalty and Deterrence

During the 1970s and 1980s, the deterrent effect of the death penalty became a favorite subject for debate in academic circles.[139] Studies of states that had eliminated the death penalty failed to show any increase in homicide rates.[140] Similar studies of neighboring states, in which jurisdictions retaining capital punishment were compared with those that had abandoned it, also failed to demonstrate any significant differences.[141] Although death penalty advocates remain numerous, few still argue for the penalty based on its deterrent effects. One study that has found support for use of the death penalty as a deterrent was reported in 2001 by Hashem Dezhbakhsh and his colleagues at Emory University.[142] According to the researchers, "Our results suggest that capital punishment has a strong deterrent effect. . . . In particular, each execution results, on average, in 18 fewer murders."[143] They note that most other studies in the area not only have been methodologically flawed but have failed to consider the fact that a number of states sentence select offenders to death but do not carry out executions. They write, "If criminals know that the justice system issues many death sentences but the executions are not carried out, then they may not be deterred by an increase in probability of a death sentence."[144]

There is no evidence of racial bias in the administration of the federal death penalty.

—John Ashcroft

Former U.S. Attorney General[xii]

Death Penalty and Arbitrariness

The third abolitionist claim, that the death penalty is arbitrary, is based on the belief that access to effective representation and to the courts themselves is differentially available to people with varying financial and other resources. The notion of arbitrariness also builds on beliefs that differences in jury composition, judges' personal dispositions and backgrounds, varying laws and procedures, and jurisdictional social characteristics may lead to varying sentences and could mean that a person who might be sentenced to die in one place might receive a lesser sentence elsewhere.

Access to the courts, which some see as more dependent on a changing legal environment than on fair standards of due process, is another area in which arbitrariness can play a role. In recent years, access to appellate courts has been restricted by a number of new state and federal laws. Such restrictions led the ABA House of Delegates in 1997 to cite what it called "an erosion of legal rights of death row inmates" and to urge an immediate halt to executions in the United States until the judicial process could be overhauled.[145] ABA delegates were expressing concerns that during the past decade, Congress and the states have unfairly limited death-row appeals through restrictive legislation. The ABA resolution also called for a halt to executions of people who are under 18 years of age or who are mentally retarded.

When I walked out of that execution chamber that night, I felt like I had been given my life back. It could not bring Cary back, but it gave us our life back.

—Charlotte Stout
Mother of an eight-year-old murder victim, after witnessing the killer's execution in 2000[xiii]

Death Penalty and Discrimination

The claim that the death penalty is discriminatory is harder to investigate. Although past evidence suggests that blacks and other minorities in the United States have been disproportionately sentenced to death,[146] more recent evidence is not as clear. At first glance, disproportionality seems apparent: 45 of the 98 prisoners executed between January 1977 and May 1988 were black or Hispanic, and 84 of the 98 had been convicted of killing whites.[147] A 1996 Kentucky study found that blacks accused of killing whites in that state between 1976 and 1991 had a higher-than-average probability of being charged with a capital crime and of being sentenced to die than did homicide offenders of other races.[148] For an accurate appraisal to be made, however, any claims of disproportionality must go beyond simple comparisons with racial representation in the larger population and must somehow measure both frequency and seriousness of capital crimes between and within racial groups. Following that line of reasoning, the Supreme Court, in the 1987 case of *McCleskey* v. *Kemp*,[149] held that a simple showing of racial discrepancies in the application of the death penalty does not constitute a constitutional violation. A 2001 study of racial and ethnic fairness in federal capital punishment sentences attempted to go beyond mere percentages in its analysis of the role played by race and ethnicity in capital punishment sentencing decisions.[150] Although the study, which closely reviewed 950 capital punishment cases, found that approximately 80% of federal death-row inmates are African-American, researchers found "no intentional racial or ethnic bias in how capital punishment was administered in federal cases."[151] Underrepresented groups were more likely to be sentenced to death, "but only because they are more likely to be arrested on facts that could support a capital charge, not because the justice system acts in a discriminatory fashion," the report said.[152] Read the entire report at Library Extra 9–11 at mycrimekit.com.

Library EXTRA

Another 2001 study, this one by New Jersey Supreme Court Special Master David Baime, found no evidence of bias against African-American defendants in capital cases in New Jersey during the period studied (August 1982 through May 2000). The study concluded, "Simply stated, we discern no sound basis from the statistical evidence to conclude that the race or ethnicity of the defendant is a factor in determining which cases advance to a penalty trial and which defendants are ultimately sentenced to death. The statistical evidence abounds the other way—it strongly suggests that there are no racial or ethnic disparities in capital murder prosecution and death sentencing rates."[153]

Evidence of socioeconomic discrimination in the imposition of the death penalty in Nebraska between 1973 and 1999 was found in a 2001 study of more than 700 homicide cases in that state. The study, which had been mandated by the state legislature, found that while race did not appear to influence death penalty decisions, killers of victims with high socioeconomic status received the death penalty four times as often as would otherwise be expected. According to the study, "The data document significant statewide disparities in charging and sentencing outcomes based on the socio-economic status of the victim."[154]

Death Penalty and Expense

The fifth claim, that the death penalty is too expensive, is difficult to explore. Although the "official" costs associated with capital punishment are high, many death penalty supporters argue that no cost is *too* high if it achieves justice. Death penalty opponents, on the other hand, point to the huge costs associated with judicial appeals and with the executions themselves. According

Retribution is the implementation of justice.
—Vincent Bugliosi
Prosecutor

to the Death Penalty Information Center, which maintains information on state-by-state estimates of such costs, "The death penalty costs North Carolina $2.16 million per execution *over* the costs of a non–death penalty murder case with a sentence of imprisonment for life."[155] The DPIC also says that some states spend far more on executions because of jurisdiction-specific litigation over such things as methods used. According to research cited by DPIC Director Richard C. Dieter, Florida spends $24 million for each execution that it carries out, and the death penalty costs California more than $100 million per event.[156] At those rates, a single execution costs many times what it would cost to imprison someone in a single cell at the highest security level for 40 years.[157] The death penalty can be expensive even in states where no executions have occurred. One 2005 New Jersey study, for example, found that the death penalty has cost state taxpayers more than $253 million in prosecution, appellate, and imprisonment costs since 1992, even though no one has been executed in New Jersey since 1963.[158] Learn more about the costs of capital punishment at Library Extra 9–12 at mycrimekit.com.

Library EXTRA

Justifications for Capital Punishment

On February 11, 2004, 47-year-old Edward Lewis Lagrone was executed by lethal injection in Huntsville, Texas, for the murder of three people in their home. Earlier, Lagrone had molested and impregnated one of the victims, a 10-year-old child, whom he shot in the head as she was trying to protect her 19-month-old sister.[159] Lagrone also killed two of the child's great-aunts who were in the house at the time of the attack. One of the women, 76-year-old Caola Lloyd, was deaf, blind, and bedridden with cancer. Prior to the killings, Lagrone had served seven years of a 20-year prison sentence for another murder and was on parole. "He's a poster child to justify the death penalty," said David Montague, the Tarrant County assistant district attorney who prosecuted Lagrone.

Like many others today, Prosecutor Montague feels that "cold-blooded murder" justifies a sentence of death. Justifications for the death penalty are collectively referred to as the *retentionist position.* The three retentionist arguments are (1) revenge, (2) just deserts, and (3) protection. Those who justify capital punishment as revenge attempt to appeal to the idea that survivors, victims, and the state are entitled to closure. Only after execution of the criminal perpetrator, they say, can the psychological and social wounds engendered by the offense begin to heal.

The just deserts argument makes the simple and straightforward claim that some people deserve to die for what they have done. Death is justly deserved; anything less cannot suffice as a sanction for the most heinous crimes. As U.S. Supreme Court Justice Potter Stewart once wrote, "The decision that capital punishment may be the appropriate sanction in extreme cases is an expression of the community's belief that certain crimes are themselves so grievous an affront to humanity that the only adequate response may be the penalty of death."[160]

The third retentionist claim, that of protection, asserts that offenders, once executed, can commit no further crimes. Clearly the least emotional of the retentionist claims, the protectionist argument may also be the weakest, since societal interests in protection can also be met in other ways, such as incarceration. In addition, various studies have shown that there is little likelihood of repeat offenses among people convicted of murder and later released, that is, the heinous Lagrone case is the exception, not the rule.[161] One reason for such results, however, may be that murderers generally serve lengthy prison sentences prior to release and may have lost whatever youthful propensity for criminality they previously possessed. For an intriguing dialogue between two U.S. Supreme Court justices over the constitutionality of the death penalty, see Web Extra 9–11 at mycrimekit.com.

Web EXTRA

The Courts and the Death Penalty

The U.S. Supreme Court has for some time served as a sounding board for issues surrounding the death penalty. One of the Court's earliest cases in this area was ***Wilkerson* v. *Utah*** (1878),[162] which questioned shooting as a method of execution and raised Eighth Amendment claims that firing squads constituted a form of cruel and unusual punishment. The Court disagreed, however, contrasting the relatively civilized nature of firing squads with the various forms of torture often associated with capital punishment around the time the Bill of Rights was written.

Excessive bail shall not be required, nor excessive fines imposed, nor cruel and unusual punishments inflicted.
—Eighth Amendment to the U.S. Constitution

CJ News

Wider Use of the Death Penalty Being Sought

At least a half-dozen states are considering broadening the death penalty, countering a national trend toward scaling back its use.

Lawmakers have proposed legislation that would increase the range of crimes eligible for execution. In Texas and Tennessee, for example, legislators want to include certain child molesters who did not murder their victims.

"The hope is that these monsters will see that Texas is serious about protecting children," says Rich Parsons, spokesman for Lt. Gov. David Dewhurst. Dewhurst, a Republican, is working with state senators to draft legislation that would make repeat offenders subject to capital punishment in some cases. "If they understand they could face the ultimate punishment, [they might] think twice," Parsons says.

▲ Texas Lt. Governor David Dewhurst (foreground) speaks during an Austin, Texas, news conference following a legislative session. The Texas Senate had just passed its version of "Jessica's Law," sponsored by Senator Bob Deuell (right). The law is a get-tough measure targeting sexual predators and includes a possible death sentence for those who are twice convicted of raping children under the age of 14. Should the death penalty apply only to those who kill?
Harry Cabluck/AP Wide World Photos

Virginia is considering bills that would make accomplices to murder, as well as killers of judges and court witnesses, eligible for the death penalty.

"I'm a believer in the deterrent effect of the death penalty," says Republican Delegate Todd Gilbert, a state prosecutor who sponsored two of the measures. "I know a number of states are reconsidering their position on the death penalty. . . . I feel confident Virginia's system is set up to work."

Lawmakers or courts have temporarily halted all executions in 11 states in the past year, most of them over concerns that lethal injection is cruel and unusual punishment, says Richard Dieter of the Death Penalty Information Center, which he says takes no position on the death penalty but has been critical of how it is applied.

In December, a convicted killer in Florida took 34 minutes to die and had chemical burns on his arms after a lethal injection procedure. After the execution, then-governor Jeb Bush created a commission to study possible improvements and halted executions until the commission releases its report.

Other states with proposals to expand the death penalty:

- *Missouri.* Gov. Matt Blunt said in his State of the State address [in January 2007] that he wants a mandatory death penalty for the murder of law enforcement officers. Blunt, a Republican, says the state must protect its public servants and the death penalty would be a deterrent. "This is the type of crime that calls for the death penalty," he says.

Robert Blecker, a law professor at New York Law School who specializes in the death penalty, says the Supreme Court has found mandatory death sentences unconstitutional because they don't allow defendants to present mitigating evidence. Blunt says his measure will take that into account.

- *Georgia.* GOP state Rep. Barry Fleming has introduced a bill to allow a judge to impose the death sentence if at least nine of 12 jurors—not all 12, as now—voted for it.
- *Utah.* The House passed a bill Tuesday making murder of a child under 14 subject to execution.

State Rep. Paul Ray, a Republican, introduced a bill to allow the death penalty for killing a child during abuse, sexual assault or kidnapping, even if prosecutors cannot prove intent to kill. He expects the House to vote [soon].

"We're going to send a message that if you kill our kids in Utah, we're going to kill you," he says. "In Utah, I don't think we use the death penalty enough."

For the latest in crime and justice news, visit the Talk Justice news feed at http://www.crimenews.info.

Source: Emily Bazar, "Wider Death Penalty Sought," *USA Today*, February 7, 2007, p. 1A. From USA TODAY, a division of Garnett Co., Inc. Reprinted by permission. www.usatoday.com.

Similarly, the Court supported electrocution as a permissible form of execution in ***In re Kemmler*** (1890).[163] In *Kemmler,* the Court defined cruel and unusual methods of execution as follows: "Punishments are cruel when they involve torture or a lingering death; but the punishment of death is not cruel, within the meaning of that word as used in the Constitution. It implies there is something inhuman and barbarous, something more than the mere extinguishing of life."[164] Almost 60 years later, the Court ruled that a second attempt at the electrocution of a convicted person, when the first did not work, did not violate the Eighth Amendment.[165] The Court reasoned that the initial failure was the consequence of accident or unforeseen circumstances and not the result of an effort on the part of executioners to be intentionally cruel.

It was not until 1972, however, in the landmark case of ***Furman* v. *Georgia***,[166] that the Court recognized "evolving standards of decency"[167] that might necessitate a reconsideration of Eighth Amendment guarantees. In a 5–4 ruling, the *Furman* decision invalidated Georgia's death penalty statute on the basis that it allowed a jury unguided discretion in the imposition of a capital sentence. The majority of justices concluded that the Georgia statute, which permitted a jury to decide issues of guilt or innocence while it weighed sentencing options, allowed for an arbitrary and capricious application of the death penalty.

Many other states with statutes similar to Georgia's were affected by the *Furman* ruling but moved quickly to modify their procedures. What evolved was the two-step procedure used today in capital cases. In the first stage, guilt or innocence is decided; if the defendant is convicted of a crime for which execution is possible or if he pleads guilty to such an offense, a second (or penalty) phase ensues. The penalty phase, a kind of mini-trial, generally permits the introduction of new evidence that may have been irrelevant to the question of guilt but that may be relevant to punishment, such as drug use or childhood abuse. In most death penalty jurisdictions, juries determine the punishment. However, in Arizona, Idaho, Montana, and Nebraska, the trial judge sets the sentence in the second phase of capital murder trials, and Alabama, Delaware, Florida, and Indiana allow juries only to recommend a sentence to the judge. One of the most widely followed penalty hearings took place in 2006, in the case of al-Qaeda conspirator Zacarias Moussaoui. After a six-week trial and seven days of deliberations, a federal jury of nine men and three women decided that Moussaoui should spend the rest of his life in prison rather than be executed for his part in the 9/11 attacks.[168]

There is only one basic human right, the right to do as you please unless it causes others harm. With it comes the only basic human duty, the duty to take the consequences.
—P. J. O'Rourke

The Supreme Court formally approved the two-step trial procedure in ***Gregg* v. *Georgia*** (1976).[169] In *Gregg*, the Court upheld the two-stage procedural requirements of Georgia's new capital punishment law as necessary for ensuring the separation of the highly personal information needed in a sentencing decision from the kinds of information reasonably permissible in a jury trial where issues of guilt or innocence alone are being decided. In the opinion written for the majority, the Court for the first time recognized the significance of public opinion in deciding on the legitimacy of questionable sanctions.[170] Its opinion cited the strong showing of public support for the death penalty following *Furman* to mean that death was still a socially and culturally acceptable penalty.

Post-*Gregg* decisions set limits on the use of death as a penalty for all but the most severe crimes. In 1977, in the case of ***Coker* v. *Georgia,***[171] the Court struck down a Georgia law imposing the death penalty for the rape of an adult woman; the Court concluded that capital punishment under such circumstances would be "grossly disproportionate" to the crime. A year earlier, in the 1976 case of ***Woodson* v. *North Carolina,***[172] a law requiring mandatory application of the death penalty for specific crimes was overturned.

In two 1990 rulings, *Blystone* v. *Pennsylvania*[173] and *Boyde* v. *California*,[174] the Court upheld state statutes dictating that death penalties must be imposed where juries find a lack of mitigating factors that could offset obvious aggravating circumstances. In the 1990 case of R. Gene Simmons, an Arkansas mass murderer convicted of killing 16 relatives during a 1987 shooting rampage, the Court granted inmates under sentence of death the right to waive appeals. Prior to the *Simmons* case,[175] any interested party could file a brief on behalf of the condemned—with or without their consent.

In 2005, in the case of *Deck* v. *Missouri*,[176] the Court forbade the use of visible shackles during the penalty phase of capital trials, unless special circumstances justify their use. Although the Court meant to maintain the dignity and decorum of trial proceedings by not forcing a person to plead for his or her life in shackles, the justices also recognized that judges may order the use of restraints when they are necessary to protect themselves and their courtrooms and to reduce the risk of escape for offenders who are especially likely to flee.

Recently, death-row inmates, and those who file cases on their behalf to test the boundaries of statutory acceptability, have been busy challenging state capital punishment laws. Most such challenges focus on the procedures involved in sentencing decisions. In 1994, for example, a challenge to the constitutionality of California's capital sentencing law, which requires the jury to consider details such as the circumstances of the offense, prior violent crimes by the defendant, and the defendant's age, was rejected in *Tuilaepa* v. *California*.[177]

Following *Apprendi* v. *New Jersey* (discussed earlier in this chapter), attorneys for an Arizona death-row inmate successfully challenged that state's practice of allowing judges, sitting without a jury, to make factual determinations necessary for imposition of the death penalty. In ***Ring* v. *Arizona*** (2002),[178] a jury had found Timothy Stuart Ring guilty of felony murder occurring in the course of an armed robbery for the killing of an armored car driver in 1994 but deadlocked on the charge of premeditated murder. Under Arizona law, Ring could not be sentenced to death, the statutory maximum penalty for first-degree murder, unless a judge made further findings in a separate sentencing hearing. The death penalty could be imposed only if the judge found the existence of at least one aggravating circumstance specified by law that was not offset by mitigating circumstances. During such a hearing, the judge listened to an accomplice who said that Ring planned the robbery and shot the guard. The judge then determined that Ring was the actual killer and found that the killing was committed for financial gain (an aggravating factor). Following the hearing, Ring was sentenced to death. His attorneys appealed, claiming that by the standards set forth in *Apprendi*, Arizona's sentencing scheme violated the Sixth Amendment's guarantee of a jury trial because it entrusted a judge with fact-finding powers that allowed Ring's sentence to be raised above what would otherwise have been the statutory maximum. The U.S. Supreme Court agreed and overturned Ring's sentence, finding that "Arizona's enumerated aggravating factors operate as the functional

At bottom, then, the Cruel and Unusual Punishments Clause prohibits the infliction of uncivilized and inhuman punishments. The State, even as it punishes, must treat its members with respect for their intrinsic worth as human beings. A punishment is "cruel and unusual," therefore, if it does not comport with human dignity.

—*William Brennan*

U.S. Supreme Court Justice concurring in Furman v. Georgia[xiv]

▲ Timothy Ring, the Arizona death-row inmate who won a 2002 U.S. Supreme Court case that might invalidate the death sentences of at least 150 other prisoners. In that case, *Ring* v. *Arizona*, the Court held that defendants have a Sixth Amendment right to have a jury, and not just a judge, determine the existence of aggravating factors justifying the death penalty. What other decisions, made by the Court since then, have further refined the *Ring* ruling?

Matt York/AP Wide World Photos

equivalent of an element of a greater offense." *Ring* established that juries—not judges—must decide the facts that lead to a death sentence. The *Ring* ruling called into question at least 150 judge-imposed death sentences[179] in at least five states (Arizona, Colorado, Idaho, Montana, and Nebraska).[180]

In 2003, in the case of *Summerlin* v. *Stewart*,[181] the U.S. Court of Appeals for the Ninth Circuit retroactively applied the *Ring* decision and vacated the death sentences of 100 prisoners in three states that fall within its jurisdiction. The court found that inmates in Arizona, Idaho, and Montana had been sent to death row by judges rather than juries in violation of *Ring* and ordered that their sentences be commuted to life in prison. Those sentences were reinstated, however, by the U.S. Supreme Court in the 2004 case of ***Schriro v. Summerlin***,[182] in which the retroactivity analysis of the Ninth Circuit Court was invalidated. The rule established in *Apprendi* and *Ring,* said the Court, could not be applied to sentences that had already been imposed because it was merely a new procedural rule and not a substantive change. Only substantive changes, said the Court, are watershed events retroactively applicable to sentences that have already been finalized. Soon after *Ring* was decided, however, the affected states began the process of amending their death penalty laws to bring them into line with the Court's new requirements.

Although questions may arise about sentencing practices, the majority of justices on today's high court seem largely convinced of the fundamental constitutionality of a sentence of death. Open to debate, however, is the constitutionality of *methods* for execution. In a 1993 hearing, *Poyner* v. *Murray*,[183] the U.S. Supreme Court hinted at the possibility of revisiting questions first raised in *Kemmler*. The case challenged Virginia's use of the electric chair, calling it a form of cruel and unusual punishment. Syvasky Lafayette Poyner, who originally brought the case before the Court, lost his bid for a stay of execution and was electrocuted in March 1993. Nonetheless, in *Poyner,* Justices David H. Souter, Harry A. Blackmun, and John Paul Stevens wrote, "The Court has not spoken squarely on the underlying issue since *In re Kemmler* . . . and the holding of that case does not constitute a dispositive response to litigation of the issue in light of modern knowledge about the method of execution in question."

In a still more recent ruling, members of the Court questioned the constitutionality of hanging, suggesting that it too may be a form of cruel and unusual punishment. In that case, *Campbell* v. *Wood* (1994),[184] the defendant, Charles Campbell, raped a woman, was released from prison at the completion of his sentence, and then went back and murdered her. His request for a stay of execution was denied since the law of Washington State, where the murder occurred, offered Campbell a choice of various methods of execution and, therefore, an alternative to hanging. Similarly, in 1996, the Court upheld California's death penalty statute, which provides for lethal injection as the primary method of capital punishment in that state.[185] The constitutionality of the statute had been challenged by two death-row inmates who claimed that a provision in the law that permitted condemned prisoners the choice of lethal gas in lieu of injection brought the statute within the realm of allowing cruel and unusual punishments.

Questions about the constitutionality of electrocution as a means of execution again came to the fore in 1997, when flames shot from the head and the leather mask covering the face of Pedro Medina during his Florida execution. Similarly, in 1999, blood poured from behind the mask covering Allen Lee "Tiny" Davis's face as he was put to death in Florida's electric chair. State officials claimed that the 344-pound Davis suffered a nosebleed brought on by hypertension and the blood-thinning medication that he had been taking. Photographs of Davis taken during and immediately after the execution showed him grimacing while bleeding profusely onto his chest and neck. In 2001, the Georgia Supreme Court declared electrocution to be unconstitutional, ending its use in that state.[186] The Georgia court cited testimony from lower court records showing that electrocution may not result in a quick death or in an immediate cessation of consciousness. By the time of the court's decision, however, the Georgia legislature had already passed a law establishing lethal injection as the state's sole method of punishment for capital crimes. Today, only one state, Nebraska, still uses electrocution as its sole method of execution.[187]

Nobody gets rehabilitated. Well, I shouldn't say no one; some of them die.

—Daryl Gates
Former Los Angeles Police Chief

In 2006, questions were raised about lethal injections constituting cruel and unusual punishment. Those questions originated with eyewitness accounts, postmortem blood testing, and execution logs that seemed to show that some of those executed remained conscious but paralyzed and experienced excruciating pain before dying.[188] Such claims focused on the composition of the chemical cocktail used in executions, which contains one drug (sodium thiopental, a short-acting barbiturate) to induce sleep, another (pancuronium bromide) to paralyze the muscles (but which does not cause unconsciousness), and a third (potassium chloride) to stop the heart. If the first chemical is improperly administered, the condemned person remains conscious, and the procedure can cause severe pain and discomfort. Complicating matters is the fact that the ethical codes of most professional medical organizations forbid medical practitioners to take life—meaning that although the codes are not legally binding, medical professionals are largely excluded from taking part in executions, other than to verify the fact that death has occurred. To counter fears that lethal injections cause pain, some states have begun using medical monitoring devices that show brain activity and can ensure that sleep is occurring.[189]

In 2008, the Court took up this issue in the case of *Baze* v. *Rees,* which had been brought by prisoners on Kentucky's death row.[190] The Court held that the capital punishment protocol used by Kentucky does not violate the Eighth Amendment because it does not create a substantial risk of wanton and unnecessary infliction of pain, torture, or lingering death. "Because some risk of pain is inherent in even the most humane execution method," wrote the justices, "the Constitution does not demand the avoidance of all risk of pain."

The U.S. Supreme Court has, however, ruled that certain personal characteristics of the perpetrator, such as mental inability and age, can be a bar to execution. In 2001, for example, in the case of *Penry* v. *Johnson,*[191] the U.S. Supreme Court found that a state trial court in Texas had failed to allow a jury to properly consider a murder defendant's low IQ and childhood abuse as mitigating factors when it found that his crime warranted the death penalty rather than life in prison. This was the second time that the Court had ordered a new sentencing hearing for Johnny Paul Penry, who was first convicted of brutally raping and murdering Pamela Carpenter on October 25, 1979, and had twice been sentenced to die.[192] In both cases, the Court found fault with Texas jury instructions and the system for their implementation, which restricted jurors from effectively weighing Penry's mental retardation as a mitigating circumstance in their sentencing decision. However, shortly after the Court's decision, Texas Governor Rick Perry vetoed legislation that would have banned the execution of mentally retarded death-row inmates throughout the state.[193]

Following *Penry,* the U.S. Supreme Court ruled in the case of ***Atkins* v. *Virginia*** (2002)[194] that executing mentally retarded people violates the Constitution's ban on cruel and unusual punishments.[195] The Court, following the lead of the federal government and the 18 states that had already banned such executions, noted that "a national consensus has developed against it." According to the Court, the standards by which the practice and imposition of capital punishment are to be judged today are not those that prevailed at the time the Bill of Rights was authored. They are, rather, "the evolving standards of decency that mark the progress of a maturing society."[196] Atkins, whose IQ was measured at 59 (100 is "average"), had been convicted of murdering a man during a robbery when he was 18 years old.

In what some thought an unusual turn of events, Johnny Paul Penry, whose case sparked national interest in the execution of the mentally retarded, was sentenced to death for a third time only 10 days after the *Atkins* ruling. The Texas jury that sentenced him rejected his claims of mental inadequacy.[197] Nonetheless, *Atkins* called into question the standing of a substantial number of death-row inmates across the country—many of whom are expected to appeal their convictions. The case also ushered in a national debate on how mental retardation should be measured. Finally, some people questioned the Court's wisdom in keeping mentally retarded offenders from facing the death penalty, saying that capital crimes involve moral judgments, not intellectual ones, and that even people of low intelligence should be expected to act morally.[198]

Evolving standards of human decency will finally lead to the abolition of the death penalty in this country.

—William Brennan
Former U.S. Supreme Court Justice

Although people with very low IQs may not be executed, serious mental illness is *not* a bar to execution unless it affects the condemned inmate's mind such that he or she doesn't know why he or she is on death row or doesn't understand the punishment he or she faces. In 2004, for example, Texas Governor Rick Perry rejected a recommendation by the Texas Board of Pardons and Paroles as well as a humanitarian request by the president of the European Union that he commute the sentence of mentally ill killer Kelsey Patterson to life imprisonment.[199]

Patterson, who apparently suffered from a particularly severe form of paranoid schizophrenia, frequently spoke of "remote control devices" and "implants" that controlled him and said that he committed acts involuntarily.[200] Patterson was executed shortly after the governor denied clemency. Patterson had been on death row since 1992 for the shooting death of a secretary and her boss at an oil company office in Palestine, Texas.

Finally, in 2007, a closely divided U.S. Supreme Court stayed the execution of Texas murderer Scott Panetti, who suffers from an especially severe form of schizophrenia. Panetti had killed his parents-in-law in 1992 by shooting them at close range inside their Texas home while his terrified wife and daughter watched. In preventing Panetti's execution, the Court held that "gross delusions stemming from a severe mental disorder may put an awareness of a link between a crime and its punishment in a context so far removed from reality that the punishment can serve no proper purpose."[201] Because the *Panetti* ruling focused narrowly on Panetti's particular form of mental illness, it is not expected to prevent the execution of other mentally ill death-row inmates.

Age *is* a bar to execution when the offender committed the crime when he or she was younger than 18, a standard announced in the 2005 U.S. Supreme Court case of *Roper* v. *Simmons*.[202] The majority opinion in the case, based on what the Court considered to be evolving standards of decency, was rendered after the justices heard evidence that juveniles are generally impetuous, immature, and vulnerable to negative peer pressure. The ruling invalidated the capital sentences of 72 death-row inmates in 12 states. Among the 962 people put to death between January 1976 and January 2004, 22 had committed their crimes as juveniles.[203]

[A] method of execution violates the Eighth Amendment only if it is deliberately designed to inflict pain.

—Concurring opinion of U.S. Supreme Court Justice Stephen Breyer in Baze v. Rees *(2008)*

Although there is as yet no *upper* age limit on executions, some have made the argument that a person may be too old and infirm to die at the hands of the state. Just such an argument was advanced in the case of San Quentin State Prison inmate Clarence Ray Allen before his January 17, 2006, execution. Allen's lawyers argued that the 76-year-old Allen, sentenced to die for a triple murder that he ordered from behind bars, was too old and too sick to be put to death. Executing someone like Allen—who had had two heart attacks and a stroke and who was legally blind, nearly deaf, diabetic, and confined to a wheelchair—"is beyond the borders of civilized behavior," said attorney Michael Satris.[204]

The Future of the Death Penalty

Support for the death penalty varies considerably from state to state and from one region of the country to another. Short of renewed Supreme Court intervention, the future of capital punishment may depend more on popular opinion than on arguments pro or con. A Gallup Poll taken in May 2003 found 79% of those polled in favor of the death penalty under certain circumstances. A similar poll by the same organization found that although most respondents voiced support for the death penalty, that support dropped to 53% when respondents were offered an alternative sentence of life without parole.[205] Pollsters also learned that the percentage of Americans supporting capital punishment appeared to increase substantially following the events of September 11, 2001.[206]

Ultimately, public opinion about the death penalty may turn on the issue of whether innocent people have been executed. According to a number of recent studies, Americans from all walks of life are less likely to support capital punishment if they believe that innocent people have been put to death at the hands of the justice system or that the death penalty is being applied unfairly.[207] A 2007 survey by the Death Penalty Information Center, for example, found that "a significant majority of 58% responding in this poll believed it was time for a moratorium on the death penalty while the process undergoes a careful review."[208] The study's authors note that support for the death penalty among Americans varies by race, with African-Americans less likely to support capital punishment than whites. They found that much of the difference, however, is explained by differing beliefs between the races about the number of executed innocents and the perceived fairness in application of capital sanctions. Consequently, execution of the innocent is at the center of today's debate concerning the legitimacy of capital punishment, and it is likely to determine the future of the death penalty in individual states as local legislatures move to mandate procedural enhancements meant to guarantee fairness.

Freedom or Safety? You Decide.

What Are the Limits of Genetic Privacy?

In 2005, police in Truro, Massachusetts, charged Christopher M. McCowen, a garbage man with a long rap sheet, with the murder of 46-year-old Christa Worthington, a fashion writer who had been raped and stabbed to death in the kitchen of her isolated home in 2002. The case, which had baffled authorities for three years, drew national interest when Truro authorities asked the town's 790 male residents to voluntarily submit saliva-swab DNA samples for analysis. Investigators were hoping to use genetic testing to match semen recovered from the murder scene with the killer. "We're trying to find the person who has something to hide . . . ," said Sgt. David Perry of the Truro Police Department. Although McCowen voluntarily submitted a DNA sample from a cheek swab in early 2004, it took the state crime lab more than a year to analyze it.

As the Massachusetts case shows, DNA profiling can be a powerful forensic tool, although its use in criminal investigations is barely 20 years old. The first well-known DNA forensic analysis occurred in 1986, when British police sought the help of Alec Jeffreys, a geneticist at the University of Leicester who is widely regarded as the father of "DNA fingerprinting." The police were trying to solve the vicious rape and murder of two young schoolgirls. At the center of their investigation was a young man who worked at a mental institution close to where the girls' bodies had been found. Soon after he was questioned, the man confessed to the crimes and was arrested, but police were uncertain of the suspect's state of mind and wanted to be sure that they had the right person.

Jeffreys compared the suspect's DNA to DNA taken from semen samples found on the victims. The samples did not match, leading to a wider police investigation. Lacking any clear leads, the authorities requested that all males living in the area of the killings voluntarily submit to DNA testing so that they might be excluded as suspects. By the fall of 1987 the number of men tested had exceeded 4,500, but the murderer still hadn't been found. Then, however, investigators received an unexpected tip. They learned that a local baker named Colin Pitchfork had convinced another man to provide a DNA sample in his place. Pitchfork was picked up and questioned. He soon confessed, providing details about the crime that only the perpetrator could know. Pitchfork became the 4,583rd man to undergo DNA testing, and his DNA proved a perfect match with that of the killer.

In the past 20 years, the use of DNA testing by police departments has come a long way. Today, the FBI's CODIS (Combined DNA Index System) database makes use of computerized records to match the DNA of individuals previously convicted of certain crimes with forensic samples gathered at crime scenes across the country.

Advocates of genetic privacy, however, question whether anyone—even those convicted of crimes—should be sampled against their wishes and have their genetic profiles added to government databases. The Truro case, in which the American Civil Liberties Union (ACLU) sent letters to the town's police chief and Cape Code prosecutor calling for an end to the "DNA dragnet," highlights what many fear—especially when local police announced that they would pay close attention to those who refused to cooperate. One commentator noted that it is "a very old trap" to say that "if you have nothing to hide, then why not cooperate?"

YOU DECIDE

What degree of "genetic privacy" should an individual be entitled to? Should the government require routine genetic testing of nonoffenders for identification purposes? How might such information be used in the event of a terrorist attack?

References: "Man Charged with 2002 Murder of Cape Cod Writer," *USA Today*, April 15, 2005. Web posted at http://www.usatoday.com/news/nation/2005-04-15-cape-cod-murder_x.htm; "ACLU Slams Mass DNA Collection," CBSNews.com, January 10, 2005. Web posted at http://www.cbsnews.com/stories/2005/01/10/national/main665938.shtml; and Howard C. Coleman and Eric D. Swenson, *DNA in the Courtroom: A Trial Watcher's Guide* (Seattle, WA: Genelex Corporation, web edition 2000). Web posted at http://www.genelex.com/paternitytesting/paternitybook.html.

In 2002, a special commission appointed by Illinois Governor George Ryan to examine the imposition of capital punishment in Illinois made its report, saying that the system through which capital sentences are imposed should be modified to encompass a number of procedural safeguards. Safeguards that were recommended included (1) tighter controls on how the police investigate cases, including a requirement that investigators "continue to pursue all reasonable lines of inquiry, whether these point toward or away from the suspect"; (2) controls on the potential fallibility of eyewitness testimony, including lineups where the person in charge is not aware of which person in the lineup is the suspect (to preclude him or her from unconsciously identifying the suspect); and (3) statutory reform so that the death penalty cannot be applied based solely on the testimony of any single accomplice or eyewitness without further corroboration.[209] In April 2003, incoming Illinois Governor Rod R. Blagojevich said that because of his concerns over executing innocent people, he would not lift his state's ban on executions even if the state's legislature passed a bill aimed at improving the system.[210]

In broad terms, the death penalty is about a search for justice and the safety of the community.

—Richard C. Dieter
Executive Director, Death Penalty Information Center[xv]

Summary

- The goals of criminal sentencing include retribution, incapacitation, deterrence, rehabilitation, and restoration. Retribution corresponds to the just deserts model of sentencing, which holds that offenders are responsible for their crimes. Incapacitation seeks to protect innocent members of society from offenders who might harm them if not prevented from doing so. The goal of deterrence is to prevent future criminal activity through the example or threat of punishment. Rehabilitation seeks to bring about fundamental changes in offenders and their behavior to reduce the likelihood of future criminality, and restoration seeks to address the damage done by crime by making the victim and the community "whole again."
- The indeterminate sentencing model is characterized primarily by vast judicial choice. It builds on the belief that convicted offenders are more likely to participate in their own rehabilitation if such participation will reduce the amount of time that they have to spend in prison.
- Structured sentencing is largely a child of the just deserts philosophy that grew out of concerns with proportionality, equity, and social debt—all of which this chapter discusses. A number of different types of structured sentencing models have been created, including determinate sentencing, which requires that a convicted offender be sentenced to a fixed term that may be reduced by good time or gain time, and a voluntary/advisory sentencing model, under which guidelines consist of recommended sentencing policies that are not required by law, are usually based on past sentencing practices, and are meant to serve as guides to judges. Mandatory sentencing, another form of structured sentencing, requires clearly enumerated punishments for specific offenses or for habitual offenders convicted of a series of crimes. The applicability of structured sentencing guidelines has been called into question by recent U.S. Supreme Court decisions.
- Alternative sanctions include the use of court-ordered community service, home detention, day reporting, drug treatment, psychological counseling, victim–offender mediation, and intensive supervision in lieu of other, more traditional, sanctions such as imprisonment and fines. A number of questions have been raised about alternative sentences, including questions about their impact on public safety, the cost-effectiveness of such sanctions, and the long-term effects of community sanctions on people assigned to alternative programs.
- Probation and parole officers routinely conduct presentence investigations to provide information that judges may use in deciding on the appropriate kind or length of sentence for convicted offenders.
- Historically, criminal courts have often allowed victims to testify at trial but have otherwise downplayed the experience of victimization and the suffering it causes. A new interest in the rights experience of victims, beginning in the 1970s in this country, has led to a greater legal recognition of victims' rights, including a right to allocution (the right to be heard during criminal proceedings). Many states have passed victims' rights amendments to their constitutions, although a federal victims' rights amendment has yet to be enacted. The Crime Victims' Rights Act of 2004 established statutory rights for victims of federal crimes and gives them the necessary legal authority to assert those rights in federal court.
- The four traditional sentencing options identified in this chapter are fines, probation, imprisonment, and—in cases of especially horrific offenses—death. The appropriateness of each sentencing option for various kinds of crimes was discussed, and the pros and cons of each were examined.
- Arguments for capital punishment identified in this chapter include revenge, just deserts, and protection of society. The revenge argument builds upon the need for personal and communal closure, while the just deserts argument makes the straightforward claim that some people deserve to die for what they have done. Societal protection is couched in terms of deterrence, since those who are executed cannot commit future crimes, and execution serves as an example to other would-be wrongdoers. Arguments against capital punishment are

based on findings that a death sentence has been imposed on innocent people, that the death penalty has not been found to be an effective deterrent, that it is often arbitrarily imposed, that it tends to discriminate against powerless groups and individuals, and that it is very expensive because of the numerous court appeals involved. Opponents also argue that the state should recognize the sanctity of human life.

Key Concepts

Terms

aggravating circumstances
alternative sentencing
capital offense
capital punishment
determinate sentencing
deterrence
diversion
equity
gain time
general deterrence
good time
incapacitation
indeterminate sentencing
just deserts
mandatory sentencing
mitigating circumstances
presentence investigation
presumptive sentencing
proportionality
rehabilitation
restoration
restorative justice (RJ)
retribution
sentencing
social debt
specific deterrence
structured sentencing
truth in sentencing
victim impact statement
voluntary/advisory sentencing guidelines
writ of *habeas corpus*

Cases

Apprendi v. *New Jersey*
Atkins v. *Virginia*
Blakely v. *Washington*
Coker v. *Georgia*
Coleman v. *Thompson*
Deal v. *U.S.*
Furman v. *Georgia*
Gregg v. *Georgia*
In re Kemmler
McCleskey v. *Zant*
Mistretta v. *U.S.*
Ring v. *Arizona*
Schlup v. *Delo*
Schriro v. *Summerlin*
U.S. v. *Booker*
Wilkerson v. *Utah*
Woodson v. *North Carolina*

Questions for Review

1. Describe the five goals of contemporary criminal sentencing discussed in this chapter. Which of these goals do you think ought to be the primary goal of sentencing? How might your choice vary with the type of offense? In what circumstances might your choice be less acceptable?
2. Illustrate the nature of indeterminate sentencing, and explain its positive aspects. What led some states to abandon indeterminate sentencing?
3. What is structured sentencing? What structured sentencing models are in use today? Which model holds the best promise for long-term crime reduction? Why?
4. What are alternative sanctions? Give some examples of alternative sanctions, and offer an assessment of how effective they might be.
5. What is a presentence investigation? How do PSIs contribute to the contents of presentence reports? How are presentence reports used?
6. Describe the history of victims' rights and services in this country. What role does the victim play in criminal justice proceedings today?
7. What are four modern sentencing options? Under what circumstances might each be appropriate?
8. Do you support or oppose the use of capital punishment? Outline the arguments on both sides of the issue.

To participate in an online discussion of these topics and others, join the CJ Brief e-mail discussion list at mycrimekit.com.

Web Quest

Visit the U.S. Sentencing Commission (USSC) on the Web at http://www.ussc.gov. Review the most recent publications and reports to Congress available at that site, and identify the current issues in federal sentencing. List and describe these issues. Also view the USSC employment opportunities listed at the site, and read the information about the Judicial Fellows Program.

Now visit the Sentencing Project at http://www.sentencingproject.org. (You can use the Cybrary to find sites that have moved since this book was published.) What is the mission of the Sentencing Project? How does that mission coincide with the interests of the National Association of Sentencing Advocates? (*Hint:* A link to this organization can be found on the Sentencing Project home page, or you can find it through the Cybrary.) Summarize what you have learned, and submit your findings to your instructor if asked to do so.

To complete this Web Quest online, go to the Web Quest module in Chapter 9 of the *Criminal Justice: A Brief Introduction* Companion Website at mycrimekit.com.

Notes

i. E-mail communication, Society of Police Futurists International, April 6, 2004.
ii. Lawrence A. Greenfeld, "Prison Sentences and Time Served for Violence," *Bureau of Justice Statistics Selected Findings,* No. 4 (April 1995).
iii. "The Crime Bust," *U.S. News & World Report,* May 25, 1998.
iv. *Ring* v. *Arizona,* 122 S.Ct. 2428, 153 L.Ed.2d 556 (2002); dissent.
v. Ryan S. King, *The State of Sentencing 2007: Developments in Policy and Practice* (Washington, DC: The Sentencing Project, 2008), p. 25.
vi. Douglas A. Berman, "The Roots and Realities of Blakely," *Criminal Justice,* Vol. 19, No. 4 (winter 2005), p. 5.
vii. Ibid.
viii. "President Calls for Crime Victims' Rights Amendment," White House press release, April 16, 2002. Web posted at http://www.whitehouse.gov/news/releases/2002/04/20020416-1.html (accessed September 13, 2002).
ix. "Judge Refuses to Delay McVeigh Execution," *New York Times,* June 6, 2001.
x. "Fireside Chat with U.S. Supreme Court Justices John Paul Stevens and Stephen Breyer," 53rd annual meeting of the Seventh Circuit Bar Association and Judicial Conference of the Seventh Circuit, Chicago, May 9, 2004.
xi. *Payne* v. *Tennessee,* 501 U.S. 808 (1991).
xii. *Criminal Justice Newsletter,* Vol. 31, No. 13 (2000), p. 1.
xiii. Laura Goodstein, "Death Penalty Falls from Favor as Some Lose Confidence in Its Fairness," *New York Times,* June 17, 2001.
xiv. *Furman* v. *Georgia,* 408 U.S. 238 (1972).
xv. Testimony of Richard C. Dieter before the New York State Assembly: Standing Committees on Codes, Judiciary, and Correction, January 25, 2005. Web posted at http://www.deathpenaltyinfo.org/NY-RCD-Test.pdf.

---

1. Michael Tonry, "Implementing, Changing, and Maintaining Sentencing Guidelines in the Political Climate of the 1990's." Web posted at http://students.washington.edu/ths123/state.htm (accessed January 3, 2006).
2. "Seven Charged in Chicago Beating Deaths," CNN.com, August 3, 2002 (accessed September 12, 2006).
3. " 'Brutal Beat-Down' Kills Chicago Men; Deaths Ruled Homicides," *USA Today,* July 31, 2002.
4. Quotations in this paragraph come from John W. Fountain, "Mob Kills Two after Truck Hits Women on a Stoop," *New York Times,* August 1, 2002.
5. For a thorough discussion of the philosophy of punishment and sentencing, see David Garland, *Punishment and Modern Society: A Study in Social Theory* (Chicago: University of Chicago Press, 1990). See also Ralph D. Ellis and Carol S. Ellis, *Theories of Criminal Justice: A Critical Reappraisal* (Wolfeboro, NH: Longwood Academic, 1989); and Colin Summer, *Censure, Politics, and Criminal Justice* (Bristol, PA: Open University Press, 1990).
6. Punishment is said to be required because social order (and the laws that represent it) could not exist for long if transgressions went unsanctioned.
7. "Back to the Chain Gang," *Newsweek,* October 17, 1994, p. 87.
8. Ibid.
9. For an excellent review of the "get tough" attitudes that influenced sentencing decisions during the 1990s, see Tamasak Wicharaya, *Simple Theory, Hard Reality: The Impact of Sentencing Reforms on Courts, Prisons, and Crime* (Albany: State University of New York Press, 1995).
10. For a thorough review of the literature on deterrence, see Raymond Paternoster, "The Deterrent Effect of the Perceived Certainty and Severity of Punishment: A Review of the Evidence and Issues," *Justice Quarterly,* Vol. 4, No. 2 (June 1987), pp. 174–217.
11. Hugo Adam Bedau, "Retributivism and the Theory of Punishment," *Journal of Philosophy,* Vol. 75 (November 1978), pp. 601–620.
12. H. L. A. Hart, *Punishment and Responsibility: Essays in the Philosophy of Law* (Oxford, England: Clarendon, 1968).
13. The definitive study during this period was Douglas Lipton, Robert Martinson, and J. Woks, *The Effectiveness of Correctional Treatment: A Survey of Treatment Valuation Studies* (New York: Praeger, 1975).
14. See, for example, Lawrence W. Sherman et al., *Preventing Crime: What Works, What Doesn't, What's Promising* (Washington, DC: National Institute of Justice, 1997).
15. Gordon Bazemore and Mark S. Umbreit, foreword to *Balanced and Restorative Justice: Program Summary* (Washington, DC: Office of Juvenile Justice and Delinquency Prevention, 1994).
16. Shay Bilchik, *Balanced and Restorative Justice for Juveniles: A Framework for Juvenile Justice in the 21st Century* (Washington, DC: Office of Juvenile Justice and Delinquency Prevention, 1997), p. ii.
17. Ibid., p.14.
18. Ibid.
19. 18 U.S.C. 3563 (a)(2).
20. E-mail communication with the Office of Reparative Programs, Department of Corrections, State of Vermont, July 3, 1995.
21. Donna Hunzeker, "State Sentencing Systems and 'Truth in Sentencing,'" *State Legislative Report,* Vol. 20, No. 3 (Denver: National Conference of State Legislatures, 1995).
22. Paula M. Ditton and Doris James Wilson, *Truth in Sentencing in State Prisons* (Washington, DC: Bureau of Justice Statistics, 1999).

23. "Oklahoma Rapist Gets 30,000 Years," United Press International wire service, southwest edition, December 23, 1994.
24. For a historical consideration of alleged disparities, see G. Kleck, "Racial Discrimination in Criminal Sentencing: A Critical Evaluation of the Evidence with Additional Evidence on the Death Penalty," *American Sociological Review,* No. 46 (1981), pp. 783–805; and G. Kleck, "Life Support for Ailing Hypotheses: Modes of Summarizing the Evidence for Racial Discrimination in Sentencing," *Law and Human Behavior,* No. 9 (1985), pp. 271–285.
25. National Council on Crime and Delinquency, *National Assessment of Structured Sentencing* (Washington, DC: Bureau of Justice Administration, 1996).
26. Ibid.
27. As discussed later in this chapter, federal sentencing guidelines did not become effective until 1987 and still had to meet many court challenges.
28. U.S. Sentencing Commission, *Federal Sentencing Guidelines Manual* (Washington, DC: U.S. Government Printing Office, 1987), p. 2.
29. Inmates can still earn a maximum of 54 days per year of good-time credit.
30. The Parole Commission Phaseout Act of 1996 requires the attorney general to report to Congress yearly as to whether it is cost-effective for the Parole Commission to remain a separate agency or whether its functions (and personnel) should be assigned elsewhere. Under the law, if the attorney general recommends assigning the Parole Commission's functions to another component of the Department of Justice, federal parole will continue as long as necessary.
31. Lawrence A. Greenfeld, *Prison Sentences and Time Served for Violence* (Washington, DC: Bureau of Justice Statistics, April 1995).
32. For an excellent review of the act and its implications, see Gregory D. Lee, "U.S. Sentencing Guidelines: Their Impact on Federal Drug Offenders," *FBI Law Enforcement Bulletin,* May 1995, pp. 17–21.
33. *Mistretta* v. *U.S.,* 488 U.S. 361, 371 (1989).
34. For an engaging overview of how mitigating factors might be applied under the guidelines, see *Koon* v. *U.S.,* 116 S.Ct. 2035, 135 L.Ed.2d 392 (1996).
35. U.S. Sentencing Commission, *Federal Sentencing Guidelines Manual,* p. 207.
36. *Deal* v. *U.S.,* 113 S.Ct. 1993, 124 L.Ed.2d 44 (1993).
37. U.S. Sentencing Commission, *Federal Sentencing Guidelines Manual,* p. 8.
38. National Institute of Justice, *Sentencing Commission Chairman Wilkins Answers Questions on the Guidelines,* NIJ Research in Action Series (Washington, DC: NIJ, 1987), p. 7.
39. *Melendez* v. *U.S.,* 117 S.Ct. 383, 136 L.Ed.2d 301 (1996).
40. *Apprendi* v. *New Jersey,* 120 S.Ct. 2348 (2000).
41. See, for example, Alexandra A. E. Shapiro and Jonathan P. Bach, "Applying 'Apprendi' to Federal Sentencing Rules," *New York Law Journal,* March 23, 2001. Web posted at http://www.lw.com/pubs/articles/pdf/applyingApprendi.pdf (accessed June 30, 2007); and Freya Russell, "Limiting the Use of Acquitted and Uncharged Conduct at Sentencing: *Apprendi* v. *New Jersey* and Its Effect on the Relevant Conduct Provision of the United States Sentencing Guidelines," *California Law Review,* Vol. 89 (July 2001), p. 1199.
42. *Blakely* v. *Washington,* 542 U.S. 296 (2004).
43. Blakely was convicted in 2005 of plotting to hire hit men to kill his ex-wife and daughter from his jail cell and sentenced to 35 years in prison.
44. *Cunningham* v. *California,* 549 U.S. 270 (2007).
45. *U.S.* v. *Booker,* 125 S.Ct. 738 (2005).
46. Combined with *U.S.* v. *Booker* (2005).
47. Stanley E. Adelman, "Supreme Court Invalidates Federal Sentencing Guidelines . . . to an Extent," *On the Line,* newsletter of the American Correctional Association (May 2005), p. 1.
48. See *United States* v. *Rodriguez,* 398 F.3d 1291, 1297 (11th Cir. 2005).
49. *Kimbrough* v. *United States,* U.S. Supreme Court, No. 06-6330 (decided December 10, 2007), syllabus.
50. *Gall* v. *United States,* U.S. Supreme Court, No. 06-7949 (decided December 10, 2007), syllabus.
51. *Rita* v. *U.S.,* U.S. Supreme Court, No. 06-5754 (decided June 21, 2007).
52. *Gall* v. *U.S.,* U.S. Supreme Court, No. 06-7949 (decided December 10, 2007).
53. "A Year after *Booker*: Most Sentences Still within Guidelines," *Third Branch,* newsletter of the Administrative Office of the U.S. Courts, Vol. 38, No. 2 (February 2006), p. 1.
54. Ibid.
55. Congress appears set to enact a guidelines system with mandatory minimum sentences and suggested maximum sentences. See "Congressional and Judicial Leaders at Odds over Sentencing Policy," *Criminal Justice Newsletter,* March 15, 2006, pp. 3–6.
56. Much of the material in this section is derived from Dale Parent et al., *Mandatory Sentencing,* NIJ Research in Action Series (Washington, DC: NIJ, 1997).
57. In mid-1996, the California Supreme Court ruled the state's three-strikes law an undue intrusion into judges' sentencing discretion, and California judges now use their own discretion in evaluating which offenses "fit" within the meaning of the law.
58. Michael Tonry, *Sentencing Reform Impacts* (Washington, DC: National Institute of Justice, 1987).
59. D. C. McDonald and K. E. Carlson, *Sentencing in the Courts: Does Race Matter? The Transition to Sentencing Guidelines, 1986–90* (Washington, DC: Bureau of Justice Statistics, 1993).
60. U.S. Sentencing Commission, *Special Report to Congress: Cocaine and Federal Sentencing Policy* (Washington, DC: U.S. Sentencing Commission, May 2007).
61. "Court Ruling Found to Reduce Crack Cocaine Prison Terms," *Corrections Journal* (February 7, 2006), p. 1.
62. " 'Runaway Bride' Pleads No Contest, Apologizes," CNN.com, June 3, 2005. Web posted at http://www.cnn.com/2005/LAW/06/02/wilbanks.case (accessed June 10, 2006).
63. "Public Humiliation," *Lawyer News,* July 31, 2004. Web posted at http://www.lawyernews.com/weblog/2004/08 (accessed July 5, 2005).
64. Much of the information in this section is taken from Haya El Nasser, "Paying for Crime with Shame: Judges Say 'Scarlet Letter' Angle Works," *USA Today,* June 26, 1996, p. 1A.
65. Richard Willing, "Thief Challenges Dose of Shame as Punishment," *USA Today,* August 18, 2004, p. 3A.
66. John Braithwaite, *Crime, Shame, and Reintegration* (Cambridge, England: Cambridge University Press, 1989).
67. Such evidence does, in fact, exist. See, for example, Harold G. Grasmick, Robert J. Bursik, Jr., and Bruce J. Arneklev, "Reduction in Drunk Driving as a Response to Increased Threats of Shame, Embarrassment, and Legal Sanctions," *Criminology,* Vol. 31, No. 1 (1993), pp. 41–67.
68. Joan Petersilia, *House Arrest,* National Institute of Justice Crime File Study Guide (Washington, DC: NIJ, 1988).
69. Privacy Act of 1974, 5 U.S.C.A. 522a, 88 Statute 1897, Public Law 93-579, December 31, 1974.
70. Freedom of Information Act, 5 U.S.C. 522, and amendments. The status of presentence investigative reports has not yet been clarified under this act to the satisfaction of all legal scholars, although state and federal courts are generally thought to be exempt from the provisions of the act.
71. City of New York, Citywide Accountability Program, S.T.A.R.S. (Statistical Tracking, Analysis, and Reporting System). Web posted at http://www.nyc.gov/html/prob/pdf/stars_92005.pdf (accessed May 12, 2006).
72. For a good review of the issues involved, see Robert C. Davis, Arthur J. Lurigio, and Wesley G. Skogan, *Victims of Crime,* 2nd ed. (Thousand Oaks, CA: Sage, 1997); and Leslie Sebba, *Third Parties: Victims and the Criminal Justice System* (Columbus: Ohio State University Press, 1996).

73. President's Task Force on Victims of Crime, *Final Report* (Washington, DC: U.S. Government Printing Office, 1982).
74. Peter Finn and Beverly N. W. Lee, *Establishing and Expanding Victim-Witness Assistance Programs* (Washington, DC: National Institute of Justice, 1988).
75. National Institute of Justice, *Victim Assistance Programs: Whom They Service, What They Offer* (Washington, DC: NIJ, 1995).
76. Senate Joint Resolution (SJR) 65 is a major revision of an initial proposal, SJR 52, which Senators Kyl and Feinstein introduced on April 22, 1996. Representative Henry Hyde introduced House Joint Resolution 174, a companion to SJR 52, and a similar proposal, House Joint Resolution 173, on April 22, 1996.
77. Senate Joint Resolution 44, 105th Congress.
78. See the National Center for Victims of Crime's critique of the 1998 amendment at http://www.ncvc.org/law/Ncvca.htm (accessed January 10, 2007).
79. "President Calls for Crime Victims' Rights Amendment," White House press release, April 16, 2002. Web posted at http://www.whitehouse.gov/news/releases/2002/04/20020416-1.html (accessed September 13, 2002).
80. "Attorneys General Strongly Support S.J. Res. 3," National Victims' Constitutional Amendment Network, April 21, 2000. Web posted at http://www.nvcan.org/news.htm (accessed January 22, 2007).
81. National Victims' Constitutional Amendment Passage, "States Victim Rights Amendments." Web posted at http://www.nvcap.org/stvras.htm (accessed August 28, 2006).
82. Public Law 97-291.
83. USA PATRIOT Act of 2001, Section 624.
84. Office for Victims of Crime, *Report to the Nation 2003* (Washington, DC: OVC, 2003).
85. S.2329.
86. U.S. Senate, Republican Policy Committee, Legislative Notice No. 63, April 22, 2004.
87. Proposition 8, California's Victim's Bill of Rights.
88. National Victim Center, Mothers against Drunk Driving, and American Prosecutors Research Institute, *Impact Statements: A Victim's Right to Speak; A Nation's Responsibility to Listen* (Washington, DC: Office for Victims of Crime, July 1994).
89. Robert C. Davis and Barbara E. Smith, "The Effects of Victim Impact Statements on Sentencing Decisions: A Test in an Urban Setting," *Justice Quarterly,* Vol. 11, No. 3 (September 1994), pp. 453–469.
90. Bureau of Justice Statistics, *Report to the Nation on Crime and Justice,* 2nd ed. (Washington, DC: U.S. Government Printing Office, 1988), p. 90.
91. Matthew R. Durose and Patrick A. Langan, *Felony Sentences in State Courts, 2004* (Washington, DC: Bureau of Justice Statistics, 2007). Data for 1990 come from Matthew R. Durose, David J. Levin, and Patrick A. Langan, *Felony Sentences in State Courts, 1998* (Washington, DC: Bureau of Justice Statistics, 2001).
92. Ibid., p. 2.
93. Sally T. Hillsman, Joyce L. Sichel, and Barry Mahoney, *Fines in Sentencing* (New York: Vera Institute of Justice, 1983).
94. Ibid., p. 2.
95. Ibid., p. 4.
96. Ibid.
97. "Finnish Millionaire Hit with Record Speeding Fine," ABC News Online, February 11, 2004. Web posted at http://www.abc.net.au/news/newsitems/s1042241.htm (accessed May 14, 2004).
98. Douglas C. McDonald, Judith Greene, and Charles Worzella, *Day Fines in American Courts: The Staten Island and Milwaukee Experiments* (Washington, DC: National Institute of Justice, 1992).
99. Ibid., p. 56.
100. Laura A. Winterfield and Sally T. Hillsman, *The Staten Island Day-Fine Project* (Washington, DC: National Institute of Justice, 1993), p. 1.
101. S. Turner and J. Petersilia, *Day Fines in Four U.S. Jurisdictions* (Santa Monica, CA: RAND Corporation, 1996).
102. James S. Tyree and Tony Thornton "Judge Sentences Underwood to Die," *The Oklahoman,* April 3, 2008. Web available at http://newsok.com/article/3224954/1207252268 (accessed May 28, 2008).
103. Capital Punishment Research Project, University of Alabama Law School.
104. Ryan S. King, *The State of Sentencing 2007: Developments in Policy and Practice* (Washington, DC: Sentencing Project, 2008).
105. Richard Willing, "Expansion of Death Penalty to Nonmurders Faces Challenges," *USA Today*, May 14, 1997, p. 6A.
106. *Kennedy* v. *Louisiana*, U.S. Supreme Court, No. 07-343, decided June 25, 2008.
107. Bureau of Justice Statistics, "Capital Punishment Statistics." Web posted at http://www.ojp.usdoj.gov/bjs/cp.htm (accessed September 2, 2008).
108. NAACP Legal Defense and Educational Fund, *Death Row U.S.A.: Winter 2006.* Web posted at http://www.naacpldf.org/content/pdf/pubs/drusa/DRUSA_Winter_2006.pdf (accessed July 22, 2006).
109. In 2004, Utah repealed the use of a firing squad as a method of execution for all persons sentenced to death on or after May 3, 2004 (Utah Code Ann. §77-18-5.5). The law allows for use of a firing squad for those sentenced prior to that date or in the event that lethal injection is found to be unconstitutional.
110. Tracy L. Snell, *Capital Punishment, 2005* (Washington, DC: Bureau of Justice Statistics, 2006), p. 1.
111. Details for this story come from Jenifer Warren and Maura Dolan, "Tookie Williams Is Executed," *Los Angeles Times,* December 13, 2005. Web posted at http://www.latimes.com/news/local/la-me-execution13dec13,0,799154.story?coll=la-home-headlines (accessed May 20, 2006).
112. "Warden: Williams Frustrated at End," CNN.com, December 13, 2005. Web posted at http://www.cnn.com/2005/LAW/12/13/williams.execution (accessed July 2, 2006).
113. "Chief Justice Calls for Limits on Death Row *Habeas* Appeals," *Criminal Justice Newsletter* (February 15, 1989), pp. 6–7.
114. *McCleskey* v. *Zant,* 499 U.S. 467, 493–494 (1991).
115. *Coleman* v. *Thompson,* 501 U.S. 722 (1991).
116. *Schlup* v. *Delo,* 115 S.Ct. 851, 130 L.Ed.2d 808 (1995).
117. Public Law 104-132.
118. *Felker* v. *Turpin,* 117 S.Ct. 30, 135 L.Ed.2d 1123 (1996).
119. *Elledge* v. *Florida,* No. 98-5410 (1998).
120. Michelle Locke, "Victim Forgives," Associated Press wire service, May 19, 1996.
121. Ibid.
122. Arthur Koestler, *Reflections on Hanging* (New York: Macmillan, 1957), p. xii.
123. Death Penalty Information Center, "Innocence: List of Those Freed from Death Row." Web posted at http://www.deathpenaltyinfo.org/ article.php?scid=6&did=110 (accessed July 21, 2008).
124. Edward Connors et al., *Convicted by Juries, Exonerated by Science: Case Studies in the Use of DNA Evidence to Establish Innocence after Trial* (Washington, DC: National Institute of Justice, 1996).
125. Barry Scheck and Peter Neufeld, "DNA and Innocence Scholarship," in Saundra D. Westervelt and John A. Humphrey, eds., *Wrongly Convicted: Perspectives on Failed Justice* (New Brunswick, NJ: Rutgers University Press, 2001), pp. 248–249.
126. Ibid., p. 246.
127. "DNA Test Frees Fla. Inmate after 24 Years," *USA Today,* January 24, 2006, p. 3A (Nationline).
128. The Innocence Project, "Alan Crotzer." Web posted at http://www.innocenceproject.org/case/display_profile.php?id=176 (accessed May 30, 2006).
129. Mitch Stacy, "DNA Exonerates Florida Man after 24 Years in Prison," Associated Press, January 23, 2006. Web posted at http:// www.truthinjustice.org/crotzer.htm (accessed May 30, 2006).
130. James S. Liebman, Jeffrey Fagan, and Simon H. Rifkind, *A Broken System: Error Rates in Capital Cases, 1973–1995* (New York:

Columbia University School of Law, 2000). Web posted at http://justice.policy.net/jpreport/finrep.PDF (accessed March 3, 2004).
131. See, for example, Jim Yardley, "Texas Retooling Criminal Justice in Wake of Furor on Death Penalty," *New York Times*, June 1, 2001.
132. "Jury Finds Former Ill. Gov. Ryan Guilty," *USA Today*, April 17, 2006. Web posted at http://www.usatoday.com/news/nation/2006-04-17-ryan_x.htm (accessed May 10, 2006).
133. Ryan was found guilty of steering state contracts to political insiders while he was Illinois Secretary of State in the 1990s and governor.
134. "New Jersey Suspends Death Penalty Pending a Task Force Review," *Criminal Justice Newsletter* (January 17, 2006), p. 8.
135. Title IV of the Justice for All Act of 2004.
136. At the time the legislation was enacted, Congress estimated that 300,000 rape kits remained unanalyzed in police department evidence lockers across the country.
137. The act also provides funding for the DNA Sexual Assault Justice Act (Title III of the Justice for All Act of 2004) and the Rape Kits and DNA Evidence Backlog Elimination Act of 2000 (42 U.S.C. 14135), authorizing more than $500 million for programs to improve the capacity of crime labs to conduct DNA analysis, reduce non-DNA backlogs, train evidence examiners, support sexual assault forensic examiner programs, and promote the use of DNA to identify missing persons.
138. In those states that accept federal monies under the legislation.
139. Studies include S. Decker and C. Kohfeld, "A Deterrence Study of the Death Penalty in Illinois: 1933–1980," *Journal of Criminal Justice*, Vol. 12, No. 4 (1984), pp. 367–379; and S. Decker and C. Kohfeld, "An Empirical Analysis of the Effect of the Death Penalty in Missouri," *Journal of Crime and Justice*, Vol. 10, No. 1 (1987), pp. 23–46.
140. See, especially, W. C. Bailey, "Deterrence and the Death Penalty for Murders in Utah: A Time Series Analysis," *Journal of Contemporary Law*, Vol. 5, No. 1 (1978), pp. 1–20; and W. C. Bailey, "An Analysis of the Deterrent Effect of the Death Penalty for Murder in California," *Southern California Law Review*, Vol. 52, No. 3 (1979), pp. 743–764.
141. B. E. Forst, "The Deterrent Effect of Capital Punishment: A Cross-State Analysis of the 1960's," *Minnesota Law Review*, Vol. 61, No. 5 (1977), pp. 743–767.
142. Hashem Dezhbakhsh, Paul Rubin, and Joanna Mehlhop Shepherd, "Does Capital Punishment Have a Deterrent Effect? New Evidence from Post-Moratorium Panel Data," Emory University, January 2001. Web posted at http://userwww.service.emory.edu/cozden/Dezhbakhsh_01_01_paper.pdf (accessed November 13, 2006).
143. Ibid., abstract.
144. Ibid., p. 19.
145. "Attorneys Call for Halt to U.S. Executions," Reuters wire service, February 4, 1997.
146. As some of the evidence presented before the Supreme Court in *Furman* v. *Georgia*, 408 U.S. 238 (1972), suggested.
147. *USA Today*, April 27, 1989, p. 12A.
148. Thomas J. Keil and Gennaro F. Vito, "Race and the Death Penalty in Kentucky Murder Trials: 1976–1991," *American Journal of Criminal Justice*, Vol. 20, No. 1 (1995), pp. 17–36 (published December 1996).
149. *McCleskey* v. *Kemp*, 481 U.S. 279, 107 S.Ct. 1756, 95 L.Ed.2d 262 (1987).
150. *The Federal Death Penalty System: Supplementary Data, Analysis and Revised Protocols for Capital Case Review* (Washington, DC: Department of Justice, 2001).
151. David Stout, "Attorney General Says Report Shows No Racial and Ethnic Bias in Federal Death Sentences," *New York Times*, June 7, 2001. Web posted at http://college1.nytimes.com/guests/articles/2001/06/07/850513.xml.
152. "Expanded Study Shows No Bias in Death Penalty, Ashcroft Says," *Criminal Justice Newsletter*, Vol. 31, No. 13 (June 18, 2001), p. 4.
153. Mary P. Gallagher, "Race Found to Have No Effect on Capital Sentencing in New Jersey," *New Jersey Law Journal* (August 21, 2001), p. 1.
154. "Nebraska Death Penalty System Given Mixed Review in a State Study," *Criminal Justice Newsletter*, Vol. 31, No. 16 (August 2001), pp. 4–5.
155. P. Cook, "The Costs of Processing Murder Cases in North Carolina," Duke University (May 1993), as cited in testimony of Richard C. Dieter before the New York State Assembly: Standing Committees on Codes, Judiciary, and Correction, January 25, 2005, p. 6. Web posted at http://www.deathpenaltyinfo.org/NY-RCD-Test.pdf (accessed May 22, 2006).
156. Testimony of Richard C. Dieter before the New York State Assembly: Standing Committees on Codes, Judiciary, and Correction, January 25, 2005, p. 7.
157. Ibid.
158. Mary E. Forsbert, "Money for Nothing? The Financial Cost of New Jersey's Death Penalty," *New Jersey Policy Perspective* (November 2005). Web posted at http://www.njpp.org/rpt_ moneyfornothing.html (accessed May 2, 2006).
159. Details for this story come from Michael Graczyk, "Killer of Pregnant 10-Year-Old Set to Die Tonight," Associated Press, February 10, 2004; and Texas Execution Information Center, "Edward Lagrone." Web posted at http://www.txexeutions.org/reports/318.asp (accessed May 15, 2004).
160. Justice Potter Stewart, as quoted in *USA Today*, April 27, 1989, p. 12A.
161. Koestler, *Reflections on Hanging*, pp. 147–148; and Gennaro F. Vito and Deborah G. Wilson, "Back from the Dead: Tracking the Progress of Kentucky's *Furman*-Commuted Death Row Population," *Justice Quarterly*, Vol. 5, No. 1 (1988), pp. 101–111.
162. *Wilkerson* v. *Utah*, 99 U.S. 130 (1878).
163. *In re Kemmler*, 136 U.S. 436 (1890).
164. Ibid., p. 447.
165. *Louisiana ex rel. Francis* v. *Resweber*, 329 U.S. 459 (1947).
166. *Furman* v. *Georgia*, 408 U.S. 238 (1972).
167. A position first adopted in *Trop* v. *Dulles*, 356 U.S. 86 (1958).
168. "Federal Jury Spares Zacarias Moussaoui a Death Sentence," Court TV Online, May 3, 2006. Web posted at http://www.courttv.com/trials/moussaoui/050306_verdict_ap.html (accessed May 30, 2006).
169. *Gregg* v. *Georgia*, 428 U.S. 153 (1976).
170. Ibid., p. 173.
171. *Coker* v. *Georgia*, 433 U.S. 584 (1977).
172. *Woodson* v. *North Carolina*, 428 U.S. 280 (1976).
173. *Blystone* v. *Pennsylvania*, 494 U.S. 310 (1990).
174. *Boyde* v. *California*, 494 U.S. 370 (1990).
175. *Roper* v. *Simmons*, 543 U.S. 551 (2005).
176. *Deck* v. *Missouri*, 125 S.Ct. 2007 (2005).
177. *Tuilaepa* v. *California*, 114 S.Ct. 2630, 129 L.Ed.2d 750 (1994).
178. *Ring* v. *Arizona*, 536 U.S. 584 (2002).
179. "Dozens of Death Sentences Overturned," Associated Press wire service, June 24, 2002.
180. The ruling could also affect Florida, Alabama, Indiana, and Delaware, where juries recommend sentences in capital cases but judges have the final say.
181. *Summerlin* v. *Stewart*, 341 F.3d 1082 (2003).
182. *Schriro* v. *Summerlin*, 542 U.S. 348 (2004).
183. *Poyner* v. *Murray*, 113 S.Ct. 1573, 123 L.Ed.2d 142 (1993).
184. *Campbell* v. *Wood*, 114 S.Ct. 1337, 127 L.Ed.2d 685 (1994).
185. *Director Gomez, et al.* v. *Fierro and Ruiz*, 117 S.Ct. 285 (1996).
186. The court issued its decision after reviewing two cases: *Dawson* v. *State* and *Moore* v. *State*.
187. Thomas P. Bonczar and Tracy L. Snell, *Capital Punishment, 2004* (Washington, DC: Bureau of Justice Statistics, 2005), p. 4.
188. Adam Liptak, "Judges Set Hurdles for Lethal Injection," *New York Times*, April 12, 2006.
189. "North Carolina, Using Medical Monitoring Device, Executes Killer," Associated Press, April 22, 2006.

190. *Baze* v. *Rees,* U.S. Supreme Court, No. 07-5439 (decided April 16, 2008).
191. *Penry* v. *Johnson,* 532 U.S. 782 (2001).
192. Penry's first death sentence was overturned in *Penry* v. *Lynaugh,* 492 U.S. 302 (1989).
193. Jim Yardley, "Two Groups Help Sway Texas Governor on Veto," *New York Times,* June 19, 2001. Web posted at http://college1.nytimes .com/guests/articles/2001/06/19/852692.xml (accessed November 13, 2006).
194. *Atkins* v. *Virginia,* 122 S.Ct. 2242, 153 L.Ed.2d 355 (2002).
195. Although the term *mental retardation* sometimes carries negative connotations within wider society, it is still used by the courts and the justice system. According to the American Association on Mental Retardation, "Mental retardation is a disability characterized by significant limitations both in intellectual functioning and in adaptive behavior as expressed in conceptual, social, and practical adaptive skills."
196. The justices were citing *Trop* v. *Dulles,* 356 U.S. 86 (1958), in which Chief Justice Earl Warren created a test that continues to govern interpretations of the cruel and unusual clause of the Eighth Amendment to this day.
197. See "Texas Jury Sentences Penry to Death Once Again," Reuters wire service, July 3, 2002.
198. See, for example, "Letters: Ruling on Retarded Convicts Rests on 'Feeble Foundation,'" *USA Today,* June 25, 2002, p. 22A.
199. The European Union president wrote, "The EU strongly believes that the execution of persons suffering from a mental disorder is contrary to widely accepted human rights norms and in contradiction to the minimum standards of human rights set forth in several international human rights instruments." Read the EU letter to the Texas governor at http://www.internationaljustice project.org/pdfs/DEMAR1BPatterson.pdf.
200. Details for this story come from the International Justice Project, "Kelsey Patterson." Web posted at http://www. international justiceproject.org/illnessKPatterson.cfm (accessed July 5, 2005).
201. *Panetti* v. *Quarterman,* U.S. Supreme Court, No. 06-6407 (decided June 28, 2007).
202. *Roper* v. *Simmons,* 543 U.S. 551 (2005).
203. Death Penalty Information Center, "Juvenile Offenders Currently on Death Row, or Executed, by State." Web posted at http://www.deathpenaltyinfo.org/article.php?scid527&did5882 (accessed September 10, 2005).
204. John Ritter, "Calif. Inmate Says He's Too Old, Ill to Die," *USA Today,* January 10, 2006, p. 3A.
205. The Gallup Organization, http://www.gallup.com. Report dated May 27, 2003.
206. See Janet L. Conley, "Execution Protests Wane as Opponents Shift Focus," *Fulton County Daily Report,* August 22, 2002. For the latest information on public opinion polls as they relate to capital punishment, visit the Death Penalty Information Center online at http://www.deathpenaltyinfo.org.
207. James D. Unnever and Francis T. Cullen, "Executing the Innocent and Support for Capital Punishment," *Criminology and Public Policy,* Vol. 4, No. 1 (2005), p. 3.
208. Death Penalty Information Center, *Crisis of Confidence: Americans' Doubts about the Death Penalty* (Washington, DC: DPIC, June 9, 2007).
209. "Illinois Commission Calls for Restrictions on Death Penalty," *Criminal Justice Newsletter,* Vol. 32, No. 7 (April 2002), pp. 1–3.
210. "Death Penalty Freeze to Remain in Illinois," *USA Today,* April 25, 2003, p. 3A.

Probation, Parole, and Community Corrections

10

Chapter Outline

- Introduction
- What Is Probation?
- What Is Parole?
- Probation and Parole: The Pluses and Minuses
- The Legal Environment
- The Job of Probation and Parole Officers
- Intermediate Sanctions
- The Future of Probation and Parole

Learning Objectives

After reading this chapter, you should be able to

- Explain the history, nature, and purposes of probation.
- Explain the history, nature, and purposes of parole.
- Describe the advantages and disadvantages of probation and parole.
- Describe the legal environment surrounding the use of probation and parole, and list the names of significant court cases.
- Explain the nature of the job of probation and parole officers.
- Explain what intermediate sanctions are, and list the advantages of intermediate sanctions over more traditional forms of sentencing.
- Describe the likely future of probation and parole.

" There is ample evidence that well-designed reentry programs reduce recidivism. "

—Senate Judiciary Committee Chairman Arlen Specter[1]

" Community corrections is an integral part of the criminal justice system and should be fully implemented and promoted in order to save expensive and scarce jail and prison space for violent and serious offenders. "

—National Association of Counties, Justice and Public Safety Steering Committee[2]

From Chapter 10 of *Criminal Justice: A Brief Introduction*, Eighth Edition. Frank Schmalleger.

Introduction

▶▶▶ Hear the author discuss this chapter at mycrimekit.com.

In 2008, Connecticut state legislators enacted a number of measures meant to overhaul the state's parole system.[3] The changed laws came in response to a grisly triple homicide in the home of physician William Petit, Jr., and his wife, Jennifer, that apparently took place during a burglary gone wrong. According to investigators, the two men who committed the crime—Steven Hayes, age 44, and Joshua Komisarjevsky, age 26—were both out on parole after having been convicted of more than 20 previous burglaries.[4] The men allegedly broke into the Petit home before sunrise on the morning of July 23, 2007, and bound and then severely beat Dr. Pettit with a baseball bat while holding the couple's 18- and 11-year-old daughters hostage. Then they forced Mrs. Pettit to go to a bank and withdraw cash. Returning to the home, they raped and strangled Mrs. Petit and sexually assaulted her younger daughter. They then tied the two girls to their beds, poured gasoline around them, and set the house on fire. The Petits' two daughters suffocated during the fire, while Dr. Petit, who had been left for dead, regained consciousness and escaped to alert authorities. Hayes and Komisarjevsky were caught fleeing the scene when they rammed Dr. Petit's stolen automobile into a police barricade.

▲ Dr. William Petit, Jr., holds his head in his hand as he is consoled during a memorial for his family at Cheshire High School in Cheshire, Connecticut. Dr. Petit's wife, Jennifer Hawke-Petit, and her two daughters, 18-year-old Hayley and 11-year-old Michaela, were murdered during a home invasion robbery in 2007. Why did the crime result in changes to Connecticut's parole laws?
Jamison C. Bazinet/Republican-American

In yet another sad story (this one involving a probationer), 11-year-old Floridian Carlie Brucia was abducted in 2004 as she took a shortcut to her home from a slumber party at a friend's house. Video footage of Carlie's abduction was captured by an unattended car wash security camera, which showed the girl being grabbed by an unidentified man and led away.[5] Carlie's body was discovered days later in a church parking lot a few miles from her home. Shortly after her abduction, authorities arrested Joseph P. Smith, a 37-year-old auto mechanic and father of three who had a lengthy criminal record. It was soon learned that Smith had been arrested at least 13 times in Florida in the 11 years before Carlie's abduction and had previously been charged with kidnapping and false imprisonment. Only a month before Carlie's murder, a probation officer had asked a Florida judge to declare Smith a probation violator because of unpaid fines and court costs that he had been ordered to pay. The probation officer's request had been denied, and Smith remained free. Smith was convicted of first-degree murder and rape by a Florida jury in 2005, and he was sentenced to death by Florida Judge Andrew Owens in March 2006.[6]

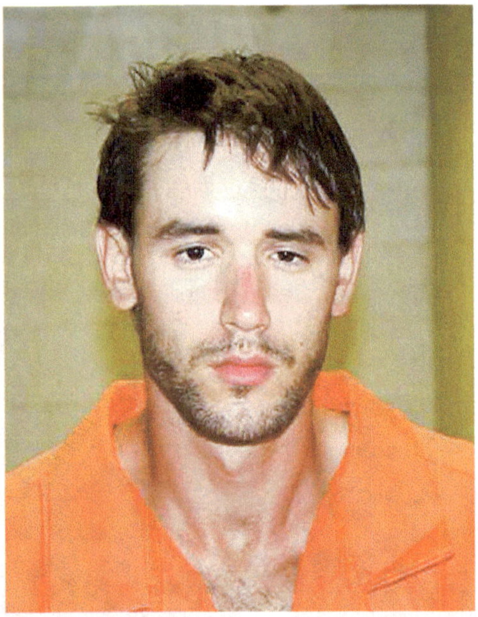

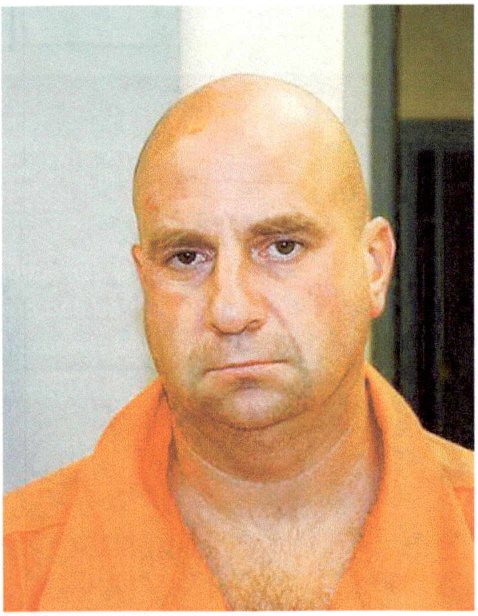

▶ Joshua Komisarjevsky, age 26 (left), and Steven Hayes, age 44, were both charged with murder, burglary, arson, and sexual assault in the 2007 home invasion robbery of the Petit home. Komisarjevsky and Hayes were on parole at the time of the crimes. Might better parole supervision have made a difference?
Connecticut State Police/AP Wide World Photos

Stories with victims like the Petits and Brucia appear all too frequently in the media and cast a harsh light on the early release and poor supervision of criminal offenders. This chapter takes a close look at the realities behind the practice of what we call **community corrections** (also termed *community-based corrections*), which is a sentencing style that depends less on traditional confinement options and more on correctional resources available in the community. Community corrections includes a wide variety of sentencing options, such as probation, parole, home confinement, the electronic monitoring of offenders, and other new and developing programs—all of which are covered in this chapter. Learn more about community corrections by visiting the International Community Corrections Association via Web Extra 10–1 at mycrimekit.com.

community corrections
The use of a variety of officially ordered program-based sanctions that permit convicted offenders to remain in the community under conditional supervision as an alternative to an active prison sentence.

Web EXTRA

What Is Probation?

Probation, one aspect of community corrections, is "a sentence served while under supervision in the community."[7] Like other sentencing options, probation is a court-ordered sanction, and its goal is to retain some control over criminal offenders while using community programs to help rehabilitate them. Most of the alternative sanctions discussed later in this chapter are, in fact, predicated on probationary sentences in which the offender is ordered to abide by certain conditions—such as participation in a specified program—while remaining free in the community. Although the court in many jurisdictions can impose probation directly, most probationers are sentenced first to confinement but then immediately have their sentences suspended and are remanded into the custody of an officer of the court—the probation officer.

probation
A sentence of imprisonment that is suspended. Also, the conditional freedom granted by a judicial officer to a convicted offender, as long as the person meets certain conditions of behavior.

The Extent of Probation

Today, probation is the most common form of criminal sentencing in the United States. Between 20% and 60% of those found guilty of crimes are sentenced to some form of probation. Figure 1 shows that 58% of all offenders under correctional supervision in the United States as of January 1, 2007, were on probation. Not shown is that the number of offenders supervised yearly on probation has increased from slightly more than 1 million in 1980 to more than 4.2 million today—a 300% increase.[8]

Even violent offenders stand about a one in five chance of receiving a probationary term. A Bureau of Justice Statistics study of felony sentences found that 5% of people convicted of homicide were placed on probation, as were 21% of convicted sex offenders[9]; 12% of convicted robbers and 30% of those committing aggravated assault were similarly sentenced to probation rather than active prison time. In one example, 47-year-old Carrie Mote of Vernon, Connecticut, was sentenced to probation for shooting her fiancé in the chest with a .38-caliber handgun after he called off their wedding.[10] Mote, who faced a maximum of 20 years in prison, claimed to be suffering from diminished psychological capacity at the time of the shooting because of

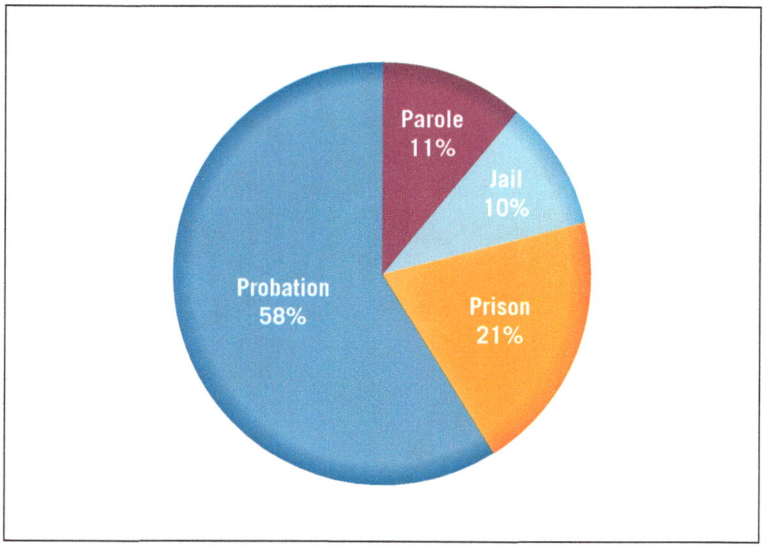

FIGURE 1
Offenders under Correctional Supervision in the United States, by Type of Supervision.
Source: Bureau of Justice Statistics, Correctional Surveys.

the emotional stress brought on by the canceled wedding. In 2007, the *Dallas Morning News* reported on 56 cases in which murderers received probation in exchange for guilty pleas in the Dallas area between 2000 and 2006; the paper said that prosecutors often offered probation in exchange for guilty pleas in cases with shaky evidence.[11]

At the beginning of 2007, a total of 4,237,023 adults were on probation throughout the nation.[12] Individual states, however, make greater or lesser use of probation. North Dakota authorities, with the smallest probationary population, supervise only 4,085 people, while Texas reports 430,301 offenders on probation. On a per capita basis, New Hampshire has the lowest rate of probation (450 for every 100,000 residents), while Massachusetts has the highest (3,396 for every 100,000 residents). The national average is 1,868 for every 100,000 residents. More than half of the 2 million adults discharged from probation in 2006 had successfully met the conditions of their supervision. Approximately 18% of those discharged from supervision, however, were incarcerated because of a rule violation or because they committed a new offense; another 4% absconded, and 12% had their probation sentence revoked without being ordered to serve time.[13] See more statistics describing community corrections at Library Extra 10–1 at mycrimekit.com.

Library EXTRA

Probation Conditions

probation revocation
A court order taking away a convicted offender's probationary status and usually withdrawing the conditional freedom associated with that status in response to a violation of the conditions of probation.

Those sentenced to probation must agree to abide by court-mandated conditions of probation, with a violation of conditions possibly leading to **probation revocation**. Conditions are of two types: general and specific. General conditions apply to all probationers in a given jurisdiction and usually require that the probationer obey all laws, maintain employment, remain within the jurisdiction of the court, possess no firearms, allow the probation officer to visit at home or at work, and so forth. As a general condition of probation, many probationers are also required to pay a fine to the court, usually in a series of installments, that is designed to reimburse victims for damages and to pay lawyers' fees and other court costs.

Special conditions may be mandated by a judge who feels that the probationer is in need of particular guidance or control. Depending on the nature of the offense, a judge may require that

▶ Hotel heiress Paris Hilton arriving for a birthday party for namesake celebrity gossip blogger Perez Hilton in West Hollywood, California, on March 23, 2007. Only two months earlier, Paris had pleaded no contest to an alcohol-related reckless driving offense in Los Angeles and was sentenced to three years' probation. She was also fined $1,500 plus court costs and ordered to participate in an alcohol-education program. Stopped for driving with her lights out not long afterward, she was ordered to spend time in jail—a sentence completed in June 2007. Why wasn't probation enough to deter Paris? What do you think that she learned from her experience?
Francis Specker/Landov Media

Multiculturalism and Diversity

Culturally Skilled Probation Officers

A recent article by Robert Shearer and Patricia Ann King in the journal *Federal Probation* describes the characteristics of "good therapeutic relationships" in probation work and says that "one of the major impediments to building an effective relationship may be found in cross-cultural barriers."

According to the article, probation officers who work with immigrants, or with those whose cultures differ substantially from that of mainstream America, must realize that a client's culture has to be taken into consideration. Doing so can make officers far more effective as both counselors and supervisors.

That's because differences in culture can lead to difficulties in developing the rapport that is necessary to build a helping relationship between an offender and a probation officer. Consequently, effective probation officers work to understand the values, norms, lifestyles, roles, and methods of communicating that characterize their clients.

Culturally skilled probation officers, says the article, are aware of and sensitive to their own cultural heritage, and they value and respect differences as long as they do not lead to continued law violation. Culturally skilled officers are also aware of their own preconceived notions, biases, prejudicial attitudes, feelings, and beliefs. They avoid stereotyping and labeling. Skilled officers are comfortable with the cultural differences that exist between themselves and their clients, and they are comfortable referring clients to someone who may be better qualified to help.

Developing multicultural awareness is the first step to becoming culturally skilled, says the article. Developing awareness is an ongoing process—one that culminates in the ability to understand a client's worldview, or *cultural empathy*.

According to the article, developing cultural empathy involves six steps, as follows:

1. The counselor must understand and accept the context of family and community for clients from different cultural backgrounds (especially important in working with Hispanic clients where relationships within the extended family are highly valued).
2. Counselors should incorporate indigenous healing practices from the client's culture whenever they can (as might be possible when working with Native Americans).
3. Counselors must become knowledgeable about the historical and sociopolitical backgrounds of clients (especially when clients have fled from repressive regimes in their home countries and might still fear authority figures).
4. They must become knowledgeable of the psychosocial adjustment that must be made by clients who have moved from one environment to another (including the sense of loneliness and separation that some immigrants feel on arrival in their adopted country).
5. They must be sensitive to the oppression, discrimination, and racism encountered by many people (for example, Kurdish people who suffered discrimination and experienced genocide under Saddam Hussein).
6. Counselors must facilitate empowerment for those clients who feel underprivileged and devalued (for example, immigrants who may feel forced to accept menial jobs even though they worked in prestigious occupations in their native countries).

Shearer and King conclude that developing cultural awareness provides the probation officer with an effective approach that actively draws the probationer into the therapeutic relationship and that increases the likelihood of a successful outcome.

Reference: Robert A. Shearer and Patricia Ann King, "Multicultural Competencies in Probation: Issues and Challenges," *Federal Probation*, Vol. 68, No. 1 (June 2004), pp. 3–9.

the offender surrender his or her driver's license; submit at reasonable times to warrantless and unannounced searches by a probation officer; supply breath, urine, or blood samples as needed for drug or alcohol testing; complete a specified number of hours of community service; or pass the general equivalency diploma (GED) test within a specified time. The judge may also dictate special conditions tailored to the probationer's situation. Such individualized conditions may prohibit the offender from associating with named others (a codefendant, for example), they may require that the probationer be at home after dark, or they may demand that the offender complete a particular treatment program within a set time.

Texas has one of the toughest parole policies in the country, with the most violent offenders serving 50% of their sentences in actual time and capital offenders sentenced to life serving 40 years of actual time before parole consideration.

—Tony Fabelo
Executive Director of the Texas Criminal Justice Policy Council

The Federal Probation System

The federal probation system, known as the United States Probation and Pretrial Services System, is approximately 80 years old.[14] In 1916 in the *Killets* case,[15] the U.S. Supreme Court ruled that federal judges did not have the authority to suspend sentences and to order probation. After a vigorous campaign by the National Probation Association, Congress passed the National Probation Act in 1925, authorizing the use of probation in federal courts. The bill came just in time to save a burgeoning federal prison system from serious overcrowding. The prostitution-fighting Mann Act,

▲ Angel Coronado, age 20, rushing through the door of the Huntsville (Texas) Prison Unit after being released due to overcrowding. Coronado, who has been in trouble nearly half his life, had spent almost two years in a 6- by 10-foot cell by himself. The U.S. Supreme Court has held that "an inmate who has been released under a program to relieve prison crowding cannot be reincarcerated without getting a chance to show at a hearing that he has met the conditions [of his release] and is entitled to remain free." How likely are people like Coronado to commit new crimes?
Todd Bigelow Photography

Prohibition legislation, and the growth of organized crime all led to increased arrests and a dramatic growth in the number of federal probationers in the early years of the system.

Although the 1925 act authorized one probation officer per federal judge, it allocated only $25,000 for officers' salaries. As a consequence, only eight officers were hired to serve 132 judges, and the system came to rely heavily on voluntary probation officers. Some sources indicate that as many as 40,000 probationers were under the supervision of volunteers at the peak of the system.[16] By 1930, however, Congress had provided adequate funding, and a corps of salaried professionals began to provide probation services to the U.S. courts. Today, approximately 7,750 federal probation officers (also known as *community corrections officers*), whose services are administered through the Administrative Office of the United States Courts, serve the 94 federal judicial districts in more than 500 locations across the country.[17] At any given time they supervise approximately 151,000 offenders—a number that has increased annually throughout the past decade.

Federal probation and pretrial services officers are federal law enforcement officers who have statutory authority to arrest or detain individuals suspected or convicted of federal offenses and to arrest probationers for violations of the conditions of probation. Under existing policy, however, they are encouraged to obtain an arrest warrant from a court, and the warrant is to be executed by the U.S. Marshals Service. Most federal probation officers may carry a firearm for defensive purposes while on duty. Before doing so, however, they must complete rigorous training and certification requirements, provide objective justification for doing so, and be approved to do so on an individual basis. Some federal districts do not allow any probation officers to carry firearms in the performance of their official duties; these include the eastern and western districts of Wisconsin, eastern Virginia, eastern Virgin Islands, central Tennessee, Massachusetts, Connecticut, and central California.[18]

What Is Parole?

Parole is the supervised early release of inmates from correctional confinement. It is a strategy of **prisoner reentry** into the community from prison that differs from probation in both purpose and implementation. Whereas probationers generally avoid serving time in prison, parolees have already been incarcerated. Whereas probation is a sentencing option available to a judge who determines the form probation will take, parole results from an administrative decision by a legally designated paroling authority. Probation is a sentencing strategy; parole is a correctional strategy whose primary purpose is to return offenders gradually to productive lives. By making early release possible, parole can also act as a stimulus for positive behavioral change.

States differ as to the type of parole decision-making mechanism they use, as well as the level at which it operates. Two major models prevail: (1) **Parole boards** (state paroling authorities) grant parole based on the board members' judgment and assessment, and their release decisions are termed *discretionary parole*. (2) Statutory decrees produce mandatory release, with release dates usually set near the completion of the inmate's prison sentence, minus time off for good behavior and other special considerations. Fifteen states have entirely abolished **discretionary release** from prison by a parole board for all offenders; another five states have abolished discretionary release for certain violent offenses or other crimes against a person. Some states, like Alabama, have abandoned traditional parole but continue to make use of parole boards with the authority to revoke the postrelease supervision status of offenders who violate release conditions and to order them returned to custody. As a result of the movement away from release by parole boards, statutory release, usually involving a brief mandatory period of postrelease supervision, has become the most common method of release from prison.[19]

States that do not utilize discretionary parole can still have substantial reentry populations, and everyone who is released from prison faces the challenges of reentering society. California, for example, is one of the states that no longer use parole boards for release decisions, and it

parole
The status of a convicted offender who has been conditionally released from prison by a paroling authority before the expiration of his or her sentence, is placed under the supervision of a parole agency, and is required to observe the conditions of parole.

prisoner reentry
The managed return to the community of individuals released from prison. Also called *reentry*.

parole board
A state paroling authority. Most states have parole boards that decide when an incarcerated offender is ready for conditional release. Some boards also function as revocation hearing panels.

discretionary release
The release of an inmate from prison to supervision that is decided by a parole board or other authority.

has the largest reentry population in the country.[20] (Although it does not have a parole board, California does have a Board of Prison Terms, which determines when the state's most serious offenders are ready for release from prison. These offenders, however, make up only a very small percentage of the state's prison population.)

The Extent of Parole

Parolees make up one of the smallest of the correctional categories shown in Figure 1. The growing reluctance to use parole today seems to be due to the realization that correctional routines have generally been ineffective at producing any substantial reformation among many offenders before their release back into the community. The abandonment of the rehabilitation goal, combined with a return to determinate sentencing in many jurisdictions—including the federal judicial system—has substantially reduced the amount of time the average correctional client spends on supervised parole.

Although discretionary parole releases are far less common than they used to be, about 25% of inmates who are freed from prison are still paroled by a paroling authority such as a parole board.[21] States operating under determinate sentencing guidelines, however, often require that inmates serve a short period of time, such as 90 days, on *reentry parole*—a form of supervised **mandatory release**. Mandatory parole releases have increased 91% since 1990,[22] even though they typically involve either a very small amount of time on parole or no time under supervision. As a result, determinate sentencing schemes have changed the face of parole in America, resulting in a dramatic reduction in the average time spent under postprison supervision. They have, however, had little or no impact on the actual number of persons released from prison.

At the beginning of 2007, 798,202 people were under parole supervision throughout the United States.[23] As they do with probation, states vary considerably in the use they make of parole, influenced as they are by the legislative requirements of sentencing schemes. For example, on January 1, 2007, Maine (a state that is phasing out parole) reported only 34 people under parole supervision (the lowest of all the states), North Dakota had only 302, while California (the highest of all) had a parole population in excess of 111,700, and Texas officials were busy supervising more than 101,916 parolees. The per capita rate at which parole is used varies as well: Only three out of every 100,000 Maine residents are on parole, whereas 1,158 out of every 100,000 District of Columbia residents are on parole; the national average is 352 per 100,000.[24]

Nationwide, approximately 44% of parolees successfully complete parole, about 26% are returned to prison for **parole violations** (failure to meet parole conditions), another 11% go back to prison for new offenses during their parole period, and others may be transferred to new jurisdictions, abscond and not be caught, or die—bringing the total to 100%.[25] (Those on probation who do not meet probation conditions commit **probation violations**.) Learn more about trends in parole via Library Extra 10–2 at mycrimekit.com.

mandatory release
The release of an inmate from prison that is determined by statute or sentencing guidelines and is not decided by a parole board or other authority.[ii]

parole (probation) violation
An act or a failure to act by a parolee (or probationer) that does not conform to the conditions of his or her parole (or probation).

conditions of parole (probation)
The general and special limits imposed on an offender who is released on parole (or probation). General conditions tend to be fixed by state statute, whereas special conditions are mandated by the sentencing authority (court or board) and take into consideration the background of the offender and the circumstances of the offense.

Library EXTRA

Parole Conditions

In those jurisdictions that retain discretionary parole, the **conditions of parole** remain very similar to the **conditions of probation** and usually include agreement not to leave the state as well as to obey extradition requests from other jurisdictions. Parolees must also periodically report to parole officers, and parole officers may visit parolees at their homes and places of business, often arriving unannounced.

The successful continued employment of parolees is one of the major concerns of parole boards and their officers, and studies have found that successful employment is a major factor in reducing the likelihood of repeat offenses.[26] Hence the importance of continued employment is typically stressed on parole agreement forms, with the condition that failure to find employment within 30 days may result in **parole revocation** (loss of parole status and usually a return to prison). As with probationers, parolees who are working can be ordered to pay fines and penalties. A provision for making payments of **restitution** in the form of money or services to the victim or to the community is also frequently included as a condition of parole.

As with probation, special parole conditions may be added by the judge and might require the parolee to pay a "parole supervisory fee" (often around $15 to $20 per month). A relatively new innovation, the parole supervisory fee shifts some of the expense of community corrections to the offender.

parole revocation
The administrative action of a paroling authority removing a person from parole status in response to a violation of lawfully required conditions of parole, including the prohibition against committing a new offense, and usually resulting in a return to prison.

restitution
A court requirement that an alleged or convicted offender pay money or provide services to the victim of the crime or provide services to the community.

CJ News

Upon Release from Prison, Some Can Feel Lost

Walking out of prison in January, 26 years after the gates had closed behind him, Bruce Glover knew he was mostly on his own.

"My mother passed while I was gone," says Glover, 56, who returned to his hometown of Detroit after being released from a state prison. He'd been serving time for running a call-girl ring. "I lost it all."

Glover got help with temporary housing and transportation from a statewide program that pools community resources to help those coming back from prison. "It's very important," he says of such efforts, "because I was like the guy lost in another dimension, a stranger in town, not knowing which way to go."

Throughout the USA, inmates released from prison have traditionally been given little more than a few dollars and a ride to the bus station. Often, they don't even have valid state identification cards, further hindering them when they try to find work.

At least 95% of all state prison inmates will eventually be freed, according to the Bureau of Justice Statistics, prompting communities to reconsider how they deal with hundreds of thousands of inmates released every year from correctional facilities.

"They don't parachute into prison from outer space," says Barry Krisberg, president of the National Council on Crime and Delinquency, a criminal justice research group. "They come from real communities and go back to real communities. Most of what they need to succeed is really not a function of state policies so much as what's available. . . . Is there a place for you to live? Is there someone willing to give you a job? Is there a faith-based group willing to talk to you when you get stressed?"

Those who commit new crimes or violate parole and are sent back to prison or jail add to the escalating costs that have made corrections among the most expensive services states provide.

▲ Bruce Glover, who served 26 years in prison for a crime he didn't commit, working for Shoe Redo in his hometown of Detroit, Michigan. How can people like Glover be helped?
© Santa Fabio

A WIDESPREAD IMPACT

The failure of many ex-inmates to make it on the outside has a far more visceral impact than simply straining budgets, because most return to specific cities and neighborhoods, often overburdening social services, disrupting families and jeopardizing public safety, politicians and crime experts say.

A demonstration project launching next month in New Jersey will provide intensive assistance to a group of ex-inmates and parolees returning to Camden, Trenton and Newark, cities that receive roughly 20% of the state's returning adult ex-inmates, says Ken Zimmerman, chief counsel to Gov. Jon Corzine.

EX-CONS GET HELP: CRIME RATES, PRISON COSTS SPUR PROGRAMS

At least 1,500 adult former inmates return to Newark each year, Mayor Cory Booker says. To help them, the city has given temporary jobs to about 65 ex-inmates and offers tax breaks to developers who agree to hire them. Newark also created a legal services program to help those who risk being sent back to prison for minor parole violations such as failing to pay an old parking ticket.

"I think everybody understands there's an absurdity spending more and more money arresting and re-arresting the same people, and if this money was better used, in halfway houses or ex-inmate programs, [then] you reduce recidivism at a cheaper cost," Booker says.

In addition to lacking valid identification cards, newly freed inmates often "don't have transportation, a résumé," says Russ Marlan, spokesman for the Michigan State Department of Corrections. "It doesn't take a genius to figure out what they're going to do. So we just realized that we can set up a system that can give them a better chance to succeed."

Michigan has increased funding for its Prisoner Re-Entry Initiative to $33 million, enabling it to expand from 15 major metropolitan areas to the entire state by September. In the program's two years, 14% of the 8,000 released inmates who have received help have gone back to prison, a far lower rate than the 48% of former inmates who return to state prison within four years, Marlan says.

Non-profit groups that work with former inmates are glad to see new programs.

"The more the merrier, so long as they're well trained," says Cindy Sneed, chief clinical officer for The Next Door, a Nashville-based organization that has helped more than 380 women, most of whom have been incarcerated, find counseling, housing and job training. "People who are coming out of incarceration need a lot of support or they're going to reoffend."

Mary Lou Leary, executive director of the National Center for Victims of Crime, says victims' advocates have only recently been invited to participate in planning for re-entry programs. "Victims play only a secondary role in the criminal justice system, and I think it's unfortunate," she says.

Marlan says officials worried that some residents would believe the state was coddling prisoners by focusing on their re-integration into society. "It's just a simple philosophy," he says. "They're coming home, coming back to where we all live. Helping them is helping us."

JOB SKILLS ESSENTIAL

One thing is clear to former inmate Albert Sanchez. Without the program that taught him carpentry, he'd probably be back in prison.

When he was released from a California prison in May after serving a two-year sentence for possession of methamphetamine, Sanchez, 38, left with a tool belt and his union dues paid for a year thanks to a carpentry program that teaches skills to inmates and helps them land apprenticeships once they are released. "Pursuing carpentry, I think, was one of the best things to happen to me," Sanchez says. "It keeps you away from everything that you were doing before."

In Detroit, Glover runs two shoeshine booths. "He's been punctual, [and] he's been consistent," says Sammy Mitchell, the booths' owner. "I gave him an opportunity, and he made the most of it."

An opportunity, Glover says, is all he needed. "I stay to myself," he says, "and go to work."

For the latest in crime and justice news, visit the Talk Justice news feed at http://www.crimenews.info.

Source: Charisse Jones, "Upon Release from Prison, Some Can Feel Lost," *USA Today*, December 13, 2007. From USA Today, a division of Garnett Co., Inc. Reprinted with permission. www.usatoday.com.

Certain types of offenders can be subject to unique conditions. In 2007, for example, New Jersey's state parole board imposed a supervision condition on 4,400 sex offenders under parole board supervision that prohibits them from using the Internet to socialize.[27] The parole board imposed the restriction after law enforcement officials reported that data received under subpoena from several social networking websites revealed that sex offenders under parole supervision had created profiles on such sites that could potentially be used to lure new victims.

Federal Parole

Federal parole decisions are made by the U.S. Parole Commission, which uses hearing examiners to visit federal prisons. Examiners typically ask inmates to describe why, in their opinion, they are ready for parole. The inmate's job readiness, home plans, past record, accomplishments while in prison, good behavior, and previous experiences on probation or parole form the basis for the examiners' report to the commission. The 1984 Comprehensive Crime Control Act, which mandated federal fixed sentencing and abolished parole for offenses committed after November 1, 1978, began a planned phaseout of the U.S. Parole Commission. Under the act, the commission was to be abolished by 1992, but various pieces of federal legislation have since extended the life of the commission. Visit the commission's website via Web Extra 10–2 at mycrimekit.com. Read a detailed history of the federal parole system at Library Extra 10–3.

Web EXTRA

Library EXTRA

Probation and Parole: The Pluses and Minuses

Probation is used to meet the needs of offenders who require some correctional supervision short of imprisonment while providing a reasonable degree of security to the community. Parole fulfills a similar purpose for offenders released from prison.

Advantages of Probation and Parole

Both probation and parole provide a number of advantages over imprisonment:

- *Lower cost.* Imprisonment is expensive. Incarcerating a single offender in Georgia, for example, costs approximately $39,501 per year, while the cost of intensive probation is as little as $1,321 per probationer.[28] The expense of imprisonment in some other states may be more than three times as high as it is in Georgia.
- *Increased employment.* Few people in prison have the opportunity for productive employment. Work-release programs, correctional industries, and inmate labor programs operate in most states, but they usually provide only low-paying jobs and require few

skills. At best, such programs include only a small portion of the inmates in any given facility. Probation and parole, on the other hand, make it possible for offenders under correctional supervision to work full-time at jobs in the "free" economy. Offenders can contribute to their own and their families' support, stimulate the local economy by spending their wages, and support the government through the taxes they pay.

- *Restitution.* Offenders who are able to work are candidates for court-ordered restitution. Society's interest in restitution may be better served by a probationary sentence or parole than by imprisonment. Restitution payments to victims may help restore the victims' standard of living and personal confidence while teaching the offenders responsibility.
- *Community support.* The decision to sentence a convicted offender to probation is often partially based on considerations of family and other social ties. Such decisions are made in the belief that offenders will be more subject to control in the community if they participate in a web of positive social relationships. An advantage of both probation and parole is that they allow the offender to continue personal and social relationships. Probation avoids splitting up families, while parole may reunite family members separated from each other by a prison sentence.
- *Reduced risk of criminal socialization.* Criminal values permeate prisons—prison has been called a "school in crime." Probation insulates adjudicated offenders, at least to some degree, from these kinds of values; parole, by virtue of the fact that it follows time served in prison, is less successful than probation in reducing the risk of criminal socialization.
- *Increased use of community services.* Probationers and parolees can take advantage of services offered through the community, including psychological therapy, substance abuse counseling, financial services, support groups, church outreach programs, and social services. While a few similar opportunities may be available in prison, the community environment itself can enhance the effectiveness of treatment programs by reducing the stigmatization of the offender and by allowing the offender to participate in a more "normal" environment.
- *Increased opportunity for rehabilitation.* Probation and parole can both be useful behavioral management tools: They reward cooperative offenders with freedom and allow for the opportunity to shape the behavior of offenders who may be difficult to reach through other programs.

Disadvantages of Probation and Parole

Any honest appraisal of probation and parole must recognize that they share a number of strategic drawbacks:

- *Relative lack of punishment.* The just deserts model of criminal sentencing insists that punishment should be a central theme of the justice process. While rehabilitation and treatment are recognized as worthwhile goals, the model suggests that punishment serves both society's need for protection and victims' need for revenge. Many view probation, however, as practically no punishment at all, and it is coming under increasing criticism as a sentencing strategy. Parole is likewise accused of unhinging the scales of justice because (1) it releases some offenders early, even when they have been convicted of serious crimes while some relatively minor offenders remain in prison, and (2) it is dishonest because it does not require completion of the offender's entire sentence behind bars.
- *Increased risk to the community.* Probation and parole are strategies designed to deal with convicted criminal offenders. The release into the community of such offenders increases the risk that they will commit additional offenses. Community supervision can never be so complete as to eliminate such a possibility, and evaluations of parole have pointed out that an accurate assessment of offender dangerousness is beyond our present capability.[29]
- *Increased social costs.* Some offenders placed on probation and parole will effectively and responsibly discharge their obligations; others, however, will become social liabilities. In addition to the increased risk of new crimes, probation and parole increase the chance that added expenses will accrue to the community in the form of child support, welfare costs, housing expenses, legal aid, indigent health care, and the like.

Freedom or Safety? You Decide.

Should DNA Links to Unsolved Cases Be Used to Deny Parole?

DNA testing has been called the "new fingerprinting in criminal investigations." It is a powerful tool that, when used correctly, leaves little doubt about the personal identity of a criminal suspect. The federal government has a huge DNA database, consisting of millions of records gathered from convicted offenders, members of the military, and federal employees in sensitive positions. Starting in 1990, states and the federal government began sharing access to their DNA records through the nation's Combined DNA Index System, known as CODIS.

While most of the records in CODIS are those of convicted criminals, a number of states (including California, Kansas, Louisiana, Minnesota, New Mexico, Texas, and Virginia) and the federal government recently enacted legislation to allow the collection of DNA samples from all people who are arrested and charged with felonies—and at least six other states (including Illinois, Michigan, New Jersey, New York, and Tennessee) are moving in the same direction.[1] In addition, federal authorities are contemplating adding the genetic records of terrorism suspects arrested overseas and of anyone detained for immigration law violations, including those caught illegally crossing the nation's borders (and often quickly returned to their country of origin). If advocates of preconviction genetic testing have their way, the number of records available through CODIS will soar.

Recently, the American Civil Liberties Union (ACLU) filed suit in federal court in San Francisco, challenging California's law that permits the genetic testing of unconvicted arrestees, saying that such testing amounts to an unconstitutional search. Complicating the picture is the fact that some parole authorities have begun hunting for DNA matches in CODIS for inmates who become eligible for early release and then using such matches to hold suspects longer. In Utah, for example, parole-eligible robber Rudy Romero had his release date pushed back 25 years after DNA linked him to five unsolved rapes—even though he has not been charged with any of them.[2] Authorities now think that Romero is the man who came to be known as the "Parkway Rapist" after an unsolved series of brutal attacks and rapes of 10 teenage girls and three women near Salt Lake City's Jordan River Parkway between 1990 and 1993.

Although advocates of preconvicting testing say that it helps secure justice, some of the matches that turn up involve crimes for which the statute of limitations has expired and that can never be prosecuted. Those opposed to the use of genetic testing to determine parole eligibility say that it is unfair because inmates seeking release do not have the opportunity to defend themselves and that the rules at parole hearings are not like those in criminal trials where defendants are allowed to be represented by attorneys.

YOU DECIDE

1. Should states inventory the DNA of all suspects who have been arrested for felonies? Of those convicted of felonies? Of those arrested for or convicted of misdemeanors?
2. Should parole authorities be allowed to use apparent DNA links to unsolved crimes in denying the release of parole-eligible inmates?

[1]Although most state laws require the DNA records of anyone found not guilty to be expunged from their databases and for their DNA samples to be destroyed, records may still be available for a long time because there are delays in the justice process and because it takes time for the administrative process to conclude.
[2]It is unlikely that rape charges will ever be brought against Romero because Utah has a four-year statute of limitations that bars prosecution.

References: Kevin Johnson and Richard Willing, "New DNA Links Used to Deny Parole," *USA Today*, February 8–10, 2008, p. 1A; Richard Willing, "Many DNA Matches Aren't Acted On," *USA Today*, November 21, 2006, p. 1A; Richard Willing, "Officials Increase DNA Profiles," *USA Today*, May 1, 2006, p. 1A; Richard Willing, "Detainee DNA May Be Put in Database," *USA Today*, January 19–21, 2007, p. 1A; Jennifer Dobner, "DNA May ID 1990s Rapist," *Desert Morning News* (Salt Lake City), September 3, 2004.

The Legal Environment

Eleven especially significant U.S. Supreme Court decisions provide the legal framework for probation and parole supervision. Among those cases, that of ***Griffin* v. *Wisconsin*** (1987)[30] may be the most significant. In *Griffin*, the Supreme Court ruled that probation officers may conduct searches of a probationer's residence without either a search warrant or probable cause. According to the Court, "A probationer's home, like anyone else's, is protected by the Fourth Amendment's requirement that searches be 'reasonable.'" However, "[a] State's operation of a probation system . . . presents 'special needs' beyond normal law enforcement that may justify departures from the usual warrant and probable cause requirements." Probation, the Court concluded, is similar to imprisonment because it is a "form of criminal sanction imposed upon an offender after a determination of guilt."

Similarly, in the 1998 case of ***Pennsylvania Board of Probation and Parole* v. *Scott***,[31] the Court declined to extend the exclusionary rule to apply to searches by parole officers, even where such searches yield evidence of parole violations. The Court stated that "the Court has repeatedly declined to extend the [exclusionary] rule to proceedings other than criminal trials. . . . The social costs of allowing convicted criminals who violate their parole to remain at large are particularly high . . . and are compounded by the fact that parolees . . . are more likely to commit future crimes than are average citizens."

In 2001, the case of ***U.S.* v. *Knights***[32] expanded the search authority normally reserved for probation and parole officers to police officers under certain circumstances. Mark James Knights was a California probationer who had signed a standard state probation form agreeing to waive his constitutional protection against warrantless searches as a condition of his probation. The form did not limit such searches to probation officers but instead required that Knights submit to a search at any time, with or without a search or arrest warrant or reasonable cause, by any probation or law enforcement officer. When Knights came under suspicion of setting a fire that caused $1.5 million in damages, police officers searched his home without a warrant, and the search uncovered evidence that implicated Knights in the arson. A federal district court granted a motion by Knights's attorneys to suppress the evidence because the search was for police investigatory purposes rather than for probationary purposes. The Ninth Circuit Court affirmed the lower court's decision. The U.S. Supreme Court disagreed, however, and held that the warrantless search of Knights's residence, "supported by reasonable suspicion and authorized by a probation condition, satisfied the Fourth Amendment . . . as nothing in Knights' probation condition limits searches to those with a 'probationary purpose.'"

Similarly, in 2006, the U.S. Supreme Court found that the Fourth Amendment does not prohibit police officers from conducting a warrantless search of a person who is subject to a parole search condition, even when there is no suspicion of criminal wrongdoing and the sole reason for the search is because the person is on parole. The case, ***Samson* v. *California***,[33] involved a parolee who was searched by a San Bruno (California) police officer who later admitted that he stopped and searched Samson only because he knew him to be on parole. The search yielded methamphetamine, and Sampson was convicted of drug possession. Relevant to the case, the California legislature had adopted a provision in 1996 requiring that every prisoner eligible for release on state parole "shall agree in writing to be subject to search or seizure by a parole officer or other peace officer at any time of the day or night, with or without a search warrant and with or without cause."[34] Sampson claimed that the California legislative requirement conferred "unfettered discretion on law enforcement officers to conduct searches of parolees" and unjustly diminished the Fourth Amendment's guarantee of personal privacy—an argument that the Court rejected.

revocation hearing

A hearing held before a legally constituted hearing body (such as a parole board) to determine whether a parolee or probationer has violated the conditions and requirements of his or her parole or probation.

conditional release

The release of an inmate from prison to community supervision with a set of conditions for remaining on parole. If a condition is violated, the individual can be returned to prison or face another sanction in the community.[iii]

Other court cases focus on the conduct of probation or parole **revocation hearings**, which may result in an order that a probationer's suspended sentence be made "active" or that a parolee be returned to prison to complete his or her sentence in confinement. Revocation is a common procedure. Annually, about 25% of those on probation and 26% of adults on parole throughout the United States have their **conditional release** (release into the community based on certain conditions) revoked.[35] The supervising officer may request that probation or parole be revoked if a client has violated the conditions of community release or has committed a new crime. The most frequent violations for which revocation occurs are (1) failure to report as required to a probation or parole officer, (2) failure to participate in a stipulated treatment program, and (3) alcohol or drug abuse while under supervision.[36] In a 1935 decision (***Escoe* v. *Zerbst***[37]) that has since been greatly modified, the U.S. Supreme Court held that probation "comes as an act of grace to one convicted of a crime" and that the revocation of probation without hearing or notice to the probationer is acceptable practice. In 1967, however, in the case of ***Mempa* v. *Rhay***,[38] the Warren Court changed direction and declared that both notice and a hearing were required; the Court also held that the probationer should have the opportunity for representation by counsel before a deferred prison sentence could be imposed.[39]

Two of the most widely cited cases affecting probationers and parolees are ***Morrissey* v. *Brewer*** (1972)[40] and ***Gagnon* v. *Scarpelli*** (1973).[41] In *Morrissey*, the Court declared a need for procedural safeguards in revocation hearings involving parolees. After *Morrissey*, revocation proceedings would require that (1) the parolee be given written notice specifying the alleged violation; (2) evidence of the violation be disclosed; (3) a neutral and detached body constitute the hearing authority; (4) the parolee have the chance to appear and offer a defense, including testimony, documents, and witnesses; (5) the parolee have the right to cross-examine witnesses; and (6) a written statement be provided to the parolee at the conclusion of the hearing that includes the hearing body's decision, the testimony considered, and reasons for revoking parole, if such occurs.[42]

In 1973, the Court extended the procedural safeguards of *Morrissey* to probationers in *Gagnon* v. *Scarpelli*. Citing its own decision a year earlier in *Morrissey* v. *Brewer*, the Supreme Court ruled that probationers, because they face a substantial loss of liberty, were entitled to two hearings: (1) a preliminary hearing to determine whether there is "probable cause to believe that he has committed a violation of his parole" and (2) "a somewhat more comprehensive hearing prior to the making of the final revocation decision." The Court also ruled that probation revocation hearings were to be held "under the conditions specified in *Morrissey* v. *Brewer*."

In *Gagnon* and later cases, however, the Court reasserted that probation and parole revocation hearings were not a stage in the criminal prosecution process but were a simple adjunct to it, even though they might result in substantial loss of liberty. The difference is a crucial one, for it permits hearing boards and judicial review officers to function, at least to some degree, outside of the adversarial context of the trial court and with lessened attention to the rights of the criminally accused guaranteed by the Bill of Rights.

In 1997, the U.S. Supreme Court extended the rationale found in *Morrissey* and *Gagnon* to inmates set free from prison under early-release programs. In a unanimous decision, the Court held that "an inmate who has been released under a program to relieve prison crowding cannot be reincarcerated without getting a chance to show at a hearing that he has met the conditions of the program and is entitled to remain free."[43]

In 1979, the case of ***Greenholtz* v. *Nebraska Penal Inmates***[44] established that parole boards do not have to specify the evidence used in deciding to deny parole. The *Greenholtz* case focused on a Nebraska statute that required that inmates denied parole be provided with reasons for the denial. The Court held that reasons for parole denial might be provided in the interest of helping inmates prepare themselves for future review but that to require the disclosure of evidence used in the review hearing would turn the process into an adversarial proceeding.

The 1983 Supreme Court case of ***Bearden* v. *Georgia***[45] established that probation could not be revoked for failure to pay a fine and make restitution if it could not be shown that the defendant was responsible for the failure. The Court also held that alternative forms of punishment must be considered by the hearing authority and must be shown to be inadequate before the defendant can be incarcerated. The Supreme Court decision stated, "If the State determines a fine or restitution to be the appropriate and adequate penalty for the crime, it may not thereafter imprison a person solely because he lacked the resources to pay it."[46] The Court held that if a defendant lacks the capacity to pay a fine or make restitution, then the hearing authority must consider any viable alternatives to incarceration before imposing a prison sentence.

▲ Georgia probation officers preparing to excavate a site at the Tri-State Crematory in Noble, Georgia, in 2002. A probation officer's job can involve a wide variety of duties. Officials found the remains of hundreds of corpses on the crematory's 16-acre grounds. The crematory's operator, Ray Brent Marsh, was charged with 787 felony counts including theft by deception, abuse of a corpse, and burial service fraud. He was also charged with 47 counts of making false statements to authorities. Convicted on many of the charges, he was sentenced to 12 years in prison in 2005. What are some other aspects of a probation officer's job?
Mark Humphrey/AP Wide World Photos

Finally, a probationer's incriminating statements to a probation officer may be used as evidence if the probationer does not specifically claim a right against self-incrimination, according to ***Minnesota* v. *Murphy*** (1984).[47] According to the Court, the burden of invoking the Fifth Amendment privilege against self-incrimination lies with the probationer.

An important legal issue today surrounds the potential liability of probation officers and parole boards for the criminal actions of offenders they supervise or whom they have released. Some courts have held that officers are generally immune from suit because they are performing a judicial function on behalf of the state.[48] Other courts, however, have indicated that parole board members who do not carefully consider mandated criteria for judging parole eligibility could be liable for injurious actions committed by parolees.[49] In general, however, most experts agree that parole board members cannot be successfully sued unless release decisions are made in a grossly negligent or wantonly reckless manner.[50] Discretionary decisions made by individual probation and parole officers that result in harm to members of the public, however, may be more actionable under civil law, especially where their decisions were not reviewed by judicial authority.[51]

The Job of Probation and Parole Officers

Job Descriptions

The tasks performed by probation and parole officers are often quite similar, and some jurisdictions combine the roles of both into one job. This section describes the duties of probation and parole officers, whether separate or performed by the same individuals. Probation or parole work consists primarily of four functions: (1) presentence investigations, (2) intake procedures, (3) diagnosis and needs assessment, and (4) client supervision.

Where probation is a possibility, intake procedures may include a presentence investigation, which examines the offender's background to provide the sentencing judge with facts needed to make an informed sentencing decision. Intake procedures may also involve a dispute-settlement process during which the probation officer works with the defendant and the victim to resolve the complaint before sentencing. Intake duties tend to be more common for juvenile offenders than they are for adults, but all officers may eventually have to recommend to the judge the best sentencing alternative for a particular case.

Diagnosis, the psychological inventorying of the probation or parole client, may be done either formally with written tests administered by certified psychologists or through informal arrangements, which typically depend on the observational skills of the officer. Needs assessment, another area of officer responsibility, extends beyond the psychological needs of the client to a cataloging of the services necessary for a successful experience on probation or parole. Supervision of sentenced probationers or released parolees is the most active stage of the probation or parole process, involving months (and sometimes years) of periodic meetings between the officer and the client and an ongoing assessment of the success of the probation or parole endeavor in each case.

Probation and parole have essentially shifted from legitimate correctional options in their own right to temporary diversionary strategies that we are using while we are trying to figure out how to get tough on crime, [pay] no new taxes, and not pay for any prisons at all, or to pay as little as we can, or pass it off to another generation.

—*Dr. Charles M. Friel*
Sam Houston State University

All probation and parole officers must keep confidential the details of the presentence investigation, including psychological tests, needs assessment, and conversations between their clients and themselves. On the other hand, courts have generally held that communications between the officer and the client are not privileged, as they might be between a doctor and a patient or between a social worker and his or her client.[52] Hence officers can share with the appropriate authorities any incriminating evidence that a client relates.

The Challenges of the Job

One of the biggest challenges that probation and parole officers face is the need to balance two conflicting sets of duties: to provide quasi–social work services and to handle custodial responsibilities. In effect, two inconsistent models of the officer's role coexist. The social work model stresses an officer's service role and views probationers and parolees as clients; in this model, officers are caregivers whose goals are to accurately assess the needs of their clients and to match clients with community resources such as job placement, indigent medical care, family therapy, and psychological and substance abuse counseling. The social work model depicts probation or parole as a "helping profession" wherein officers assist their clients in meeting the conditions imposed on them by their sentence. The other model for officers is correctional; in this model, probation and parole clients are "wards" whom officers are expected to control. This model emphasizes community protection, which officers are supposed to achieve through careful and close supervision. Custodial supervision means that officers will periodically visit their charges at work and at home, often arriving unannounced, and also means that they must be willing to report clients for new offenses and for violations of the conditions of their release.

Most officers, by virtue of their personalities and experiences, probably identify more with one model than with the other. They think of themselves primarily either as caregivers or as correctional officers. Regardless of the emphasis that appeals more to individual officers, however, the demands of the job are bound to generate role conflict at one time or another.

caseload
The number of probation or parole clients assigned to one probation or parole officer for supervision.

A second challenge of probation and parole work is large **caseloads** (number of clients assigned to probation or parole officers). Back in 1973, the President's Commission on Law Enforcement and Administration of Justice recommended that probation and parole caseloads average around 35 clients per officer.[53] However, caseloads of 250 clients are common in some jurisdictions today. Large caseloads, combined with limited training and the time constraints imposed by administrative demands, culminate in stopgap supervisory measures. "Postcard

CJ Careers

U.S. Probation Officer

PERSONAL PROFILE

Name: Jesse J. Gomes
Position: U.S. Probation Officer
City: Boston, Massachusetts
College Attended: Northeastern University
Year Hired: 2000

"I chose a career in probation because it puts me in a position to address issues from both law enforcement and human service perspectives. To work in probation is to quite literally "serve and protect" by serving a population that requires positive intervention while protecting the public from those individuals who choose not to comply.

Working for U.S. Probation was the culmination of seven years of case management and offender supervision experience. I started my career as a case manager at a prerelease and intermediate sanctions program in Boston and was then hired as a probation officer for the state of Massachusetts. Federal probation was the next logical step in my career path.

U.S. probation officers must remain informed and flexible because the nature of the work is ever changing. In general, officers must have strong written and oral skills, be tied into a comprehensive network of treatment and service providers, be able to communicate effectively with a wide array of people, and have a working understanding of applicable laws. Because treatment methodologies, crime, and the laws themselves are all fluid to some extent, officers must be willing and able to implement these changes or anticipate their effects on probationers.

When you do your job well, people's lives are actually improved. That may mean helping an addict establish sobriety, obtaining housing for a homeless person, or ensuring that a dangerous offender is adequately supervised or, if necessary, removed from the community. Much is said about improving people's lives, but in reality that's rarer and more difficult than we would like it to be. But when actual change does occur, it makes up for the many disappointments."

TYPICAL POSITIONS

A U.S. probation officer has a wide range of duties and responsibilities, including supervising offenders, conducting presentence investigations, and preparing presentence reports. Tasks involve interviewing offenders and their families, investigating offenses, determining prior record and financial status of offenders, and contacting law enforcement agencies, attorneys, and victims of crimes.

EMPLOYMENT REQUIREMENTS

To qualify for the position of probation officer at the GS-5 level, an applicant must possess a bachelor's degree from an accredited college or university and must have a minimum of two years of general work experience. General experience must have been acquired after obtaining the bachelor's degree and cannot include experience as a police, custodial, or security officer unless the work involved criminal investigative experience. In lieu of general experience, a bachelor's degree from an accredited college or university in an accepted field of study (including criminology, criminal justice, penology, correctional administration, social work, sociology, public administration, or psychology) will qualify an applicant for immediate employment at the GS-5 level, provided that at least 32 semester hours or 48 quarter hours were taken in one or more of the accepted fields of study. One year of graduate study qualifies applicants for appointment at the GS-7 level, while a master's degree in an appropriate field or a law degree may qualify the applicant for advanced placement.

OTHER REQUIREMENTS

Applicants must be younger than 37 years of age at the time of hiring and must be in excellent physical health. A full field background investigation by the Federal Bureau of Investigation (FBI) and preemployment drug testing are also required.

SALARY

Appointees are typically hired at federal pay grade GS-5 or GS-7, depending on education and prior work history.

BENEFITS

U.S. probation and pretrial services officers are included in the federal hazardous-duty law enforcement classification and are covered by liberal federal health and life insurance programs. A comprehensive retirement program is available to all federal employees.

DIRECT INQUIRIES TO:

Administrative Office of the U.S. Courts
Personnel Office
Washington, D.C. 20544
Phone: (202) 273-1297
Website: http://www.uscourts.gov

For more information on the rapidly expanding criminal justice careers area, read *Where the Jobs Are: Mission Critical Opportunities for America*, available on the Web at http://www.justicestudies.com/jobs.htm.

Note: The views expressed in this profile do not necessarily represent the views of the U.S. Department of Justice, the federal Administrative Office of the United States Courts, or the United States.

probation," in which clients mail in a letter or card once a month to report on their whereabouts and circumstances, is an example of one stopgap measure that harried agencies with large caseloads use to keep track of their wards.

Another difficulty with probation and parole work is the frequent lack of opportunity for career mobility within the profession. Probation and parole officers are generally assigned to small agencies serving limited geographic areas, under the leadership of one or two chief probation officers, so unless retirement or death claims a supervisor, there is little chance for other officers to advance.

A 2005 report by the National Institute of Justice (NIJ) found that probation and parole officers (as well as law enforcement officers) experienced a lot of stress.[54] The major sources of stress for probation and parole officers were found to be high caseloads, excess paperwork, and pressures associated with deadlines. Stress levels have also increased in recent years because offenders who are sentenced to probation and released on parole today have committed more serious crimes than in the past, and more offenders have serious drug abuse histories and show less hesitation in using violence.[55] The NIJ study found that officers typically cope by requesting transfers, retiring early, or taking "mental health days" off from work. The report says, however, that "physical exercise is the method of choice for coping with the stress."[56]

Web EXTRA

Learn more about working as a probation or parole officer at the American Probation and Parole Association (APPA) website via **Web Extra 10–3** at mycrimekit.com.

Intermediate Sanctions

intermediate sanctions
The use of split sentencing, shock probation or parole, shock incarceration, mixed sentencing, community service, intensive probation supervision, or home confinement in lieu of other, more traditional sanctions, such as imprisonment and fines.

Significant new alternative sentencing options have become available to judges during the past few decades, and these options are called **intermediate sanctions** because they employ sentencing alternatives that fall somewhere between outright imprisonment and simple probationary release back into the community (they are also sometimes termed *alternative sentencing strategies*). Michael J. Russell, former director of the NIJ, states:

> [I]ntermediate punishments are intended to provide prosecutors, judges, and corrections officials with sentencing options that permit them to apply appropriate punishments to convicted offenders while not being constrained by the traditional choice between prison and probation. Rather than substituting for prison or probation, however, these sanctions—which include intensive supervision, house arrest with electronic monitoring (also referred to as *remote location monitoring*), and shock incarceration (programs that stress a highly structured and regimented routine, considerable physical work and exercise, and at times intensive substance abuse treatment)—bridge the gap between those options and provide innovative ways to ensure swift and certain punishment.[57]

A number of citizen groups and special-interest organizations are working to widen the use of sentencing alternatives. One organization of special note is the Sentencing Project. The Sentencing Project, based in Washington, D.C., is dedicated to promoting a greater use of alternatives to incarceration and provides technical assistance to public defenders, court officials, and other community organizations.

The Sentencing Project and other groups like it have contributed to the development of more than 100 locally based alternative sentencing services programs. Most alternative sentencing services work in conjunction with defense attorneys to develop written sentencing plans. Such plans are basically well-considered citizen suggestions as to appropriate sentencing in a given instance; they are often quite detailed and may include letters of support from employers, family members, the defendant, and even victims. Sentencing plans may be used in plea bargaining sessions or may be presented to judges following trial and conviction. More than a decade ago, for example, lawyers for country western singer Willie Nelson successfully proposed an alternative option to tax court officials that allowed the singer to pay huge past tax liabilities by performing in concerts for that purpose. Lacking such an alternative, the tax court might have seized Nelson's property or even ordered the singer to be confined to a federal facility. More recently, NBA player DeShawn Stevenson was sentenced to two years of probation in 2002 and ordered to perform 100 hours of community service for the statutory rape of a 14-year-old girl whom he had plied with brandy.[58] Stevenson, who played for the Utah Jazz at the time of the offense, fulfilled the terms of his sentence by delivering motivational speeches at Boys Clubs in California and New York.

The basic philosophy behind intermediate sanctions is this: When judges are offered well-planned alternatives to imprisonment for offenders who appear to represent little or no continuing threat to the community, the likelihood of a prison sentence is reduced. An analysis of alternative sentencing plans like those sponsored by the Sentencing Project shows that judges accept them in up to 80% of the cases in which they are recommended and that as many as two-thirds of offenders who receive intermediate sentences successfully complete them.[59]

Intermediate sanctions have three distinct advantages: (1) They are less expensive to operate per offender than imprisonment; (2) they are socially cost-effective because they keep the offender in the community, thus avoiding both the breakup of the family and the stigmatization of imprisonment; and (3) they provide flexibility in terms of resources, time of involvement, and place of service.[60] Some of these new sentencing options are described in the paragraphs that follow.

▲ A New Mexico boot camp staff member conducting a push-up drill with young offenders. Boot camps use military-style discipline in an attempt to reduce the chance for recidivism among young first-time offenders. Are boot camps likely to reduce recidivism?
*Vladimir Chaloupka/*Las Cruces Sun-News*/AP Wide World Photos*

Split Sentencing

In jurisdictions where **split sentences** are an option, judges may impose a combination of a brief period of imprisonment and probation. Defendants who are given split sentences are often ordered to serve time in a local jail rather than in a long-term confinement facility. Ninety days in jail, together with two years of supervised probation, is a typical split sentence. Split sentences are frequently given to minor drug offenders and serve notice that continued law violations may result in imprisonment for much longer periods.

Shock Probation and Shock Parole

Shock probation strongly resembles split sentencing because the offender serves a relatively short period of time in custody (usually in a prison rather than a jail) and is released on probation by court order, but the difference is that shock probation clients must *apply* for probationary release from confinement and cannot be certain of the judge's decision. In shock probation, the court in effect makes a resentencing decision. Probation is only a statutory possibility and often little more than a vague hope for the offender as imprisonment begins. If probationary release is ordered, it may well come as a "shock" to the offender, who, facing a sudden reprieve, may forswear future criminal involvement. Shock probation was begun in Ohio in 1965[61]; it is used today in about half of the states.[62] Shock probation lowers the cost of confinement, maintains community and family ties, and may be an effective rehabilitative tool.

Similar to shock probation is shock parole. Whereas shock probation is ordered by judicial authority, shock parole is an administrative decision made by a paroling authority. Parole boards or their representatives may order an inmate's early release, hoping that the brief exposure to prison has reoriented the offender's life in a positive direction.

Shock Incarceration

Shock incarceration, which became quite popular during the 1990s, utilizes military-style "boot camp" prison settings to provide highly regimented environments involving strict discipline, physical training, and hard labor.[63] Shock incarceration programs are designed primarily for young first offenders and are of short duration, generally lasting for only 90 to 180 days. Offenders who successfully complete these programs are typically returned to the community under some form of supervision. Program "failures" may be moved into the general prison population for longer terms of confinement.

split sentence
A sentence explicitly requiring the convicted offender to serve a period of confinement in a local, state, or federal facility, followed by a period of probation.

shock probation
The practice of sentencing offenders to prison, allowing them to apply for probationary release, and enacting such release in surprise fashion. Offenders who receive shock probation may not be aware that they will be released on probation and may expect to spend a much longer time behind bars.

shock incarceration
A sentencing option that makes use of "boot camp"–type prisons to impress on convicted offenders the realities of prison life.

▲ Supermodel Naomi Campbell showing off a safety vest and boots at the Manhattan Sanitation Depot after being ordered by a judge to perform community service following an assault on a domestic worker at her residence. Campbell pleaded guilty to hitting her housekeeper on the head with a cell phone after she couldn't find a pair of Campbell's jeans. Was Campbell's sentence appropriate? *Kevin Mazur/Getty Images–WireImage.com*

Georgia established the first shock incarceration program in 1983[64]; following Georgia's lead, more than 30 other states began their own programs.[65] The federal government and some Canadian provinces also operate shock incarceration programs. About half of the states provide for voluntary entry into the program, and a few states allow inmates to decide when and whether they want to quit. Although most states allow judges to place offenders into these programs, some delegate that authority to corrections officials. Two states, Louisiana and Texas, give judges and corrections personnel joint authority in the decision-making process.[66] Some states, including Massachusetts, accept female inmates into boot camp settings; the Massachusetts program, which first accepted women in 1993, requires inmates to spend nearly four months undergoing the rigors of training.

One of the most comprehensive studies to date of boot camp prison programs focused on eight states: Florida, Georgia, Illinois, Louisiana, New York, Oklahoma, South Carolina, and Texas. The report found that boot camp programs have been popular because "they are . . . perceived as being tough on crime" and "have been enthusiastically embraced as a viable correctional option," but "the impact of boot camp programs on offender recidivism is at best negligible."[67] More limited studies, such as one that focused on shock incarceration in New York State, have found that boot camp programs can be effective money savers. The research indicates that such programs save money in two ways: "first by reducing expenditures for care and custody" (since the intense programs reduce time spent in custody, and participation in them is the only way New York inmates can be released from prison before their minimum parole eligibility dates), and "second, by avoiding capital costs for new prison construction."[68] A 1995 study of Oregon's Summit boot camp program reached a similar conclusion. Although they did not study **recidivism** (repetition of criminal behavior), the Oregon researchers found that "the Summit boot camp program is a cost-effective means of reducing prison overcrowding by treating and releasing specially selected inmates earlier than their court-determined minimum period of incarceration."[69]

Mixed Sentencing and Community Service

Some **mixed sentences** require that offenders serve weekends in jail and receive probation supervision during the week. Other types of mixed sentencing require offenders to participate in treatment programs or **community service** (work administered by a community agency) while on probation. Community service programs began in Minnesota in 1972 with the Minnesota Restitution Program, which gave property offenders the opportunity to work and turn over part of their pay as restitution to their victims.[70] Courts throughout the nation quickly adopted the idea and began to build restitution orders into suspended-sentence agreements.

Community service is more an adjunct to rather than a type of correctional sentence and is compatible with most other forms of innovation in probation and parole. Even with home confinement (discussed below), offenders can be sentenced to community service activities that are performed in the home or at a job site during the hours they are permitted to be away from their homes. Washing police cars, cleaning school buses, refurbishing public facilities, and assisting in local government offices are typical forms of community service. Some authors have linked the development of community service sentences to the notion that work and service to others are good for the spirit.[71] Community service participants are usually minor criminals, drunk drivers, and youthful offenders.

One problem with community service sentences is that authorities rarely agree on what they are supposed to accomplish. Most people admit that offenders who work in the community are able to reduce the costs of their own supervision, but there is little agreement on whether such sentences reduce recidivism, act as a deterrent, or serve to rehabilitate offenders.

recidivism
The repetition of criminal behavior. In statistical practice, a recidivism rate may be any of a number of possible counts or instances of arrest, conviction, correctional commitment, or correctional status change related to repetitions of these events within a given period of time.

mixed sentence
A sentence that requires that a convicted offender serve weekends (or other specified periods of time) in a confinement facility (usually a jail) while undergoing probationary supervision in the community.

community service
A sentencing alternative that requires offenders to spend at least part of their time working for a community agency.

Ethics and Professionalism

American Probation and Parole Association Code of Ethics

- I will render professional service to the justice system and the community at large in effecting the social adjustment of the offender.
- I will uphold the law with dignity, displaying an awareness of my responsibility to offenders while recognizing the right of the public to be safeguarded from criminal activity.
- I will strive to be objective in the performance of my duties, recognizing the inalienable right of all persons, appreciating the inherent worth of the individual, and respecting those confidences which can be reposed in me.
- I will conduct my personal life with decorum, neither accepting nor granting favors in connection with my office.
- I will cooperate with my coworkers and related agencies and will continually strive to improve my professional competence through the seeking and sharing of knowledge and understanding.
- I will distinguish clearly, in public, between my statements and actions as an individual and as a representative of my profession.
- I will encourage policy, procedures, and personnel practices, which will enable others to conduct themselves in accordance with the values, goals, and objectives of the American Probation and Parole Association.
- I recognize my office as a symbol of public faith and I accept it as a public trust to be held as long as I am true to the ethics of the American Probation and Parole Association.
- I will constantly strive to achieve these objectives and ideals, dedicating myself to my chosen profession.

THINKING ABOUT ETHICS

1. Which of the ethical principles enumerated here might also apply to correctional officers working in prisons and jails?
2. Which might apply to law enforcement officers?
3. Which might apply to prosecutors and criminal defense attorneys?

Source: American Probation and Parole Association. Reprinted with permission.

Intensive Probation Supervision

Intensive probation supervision (IPS)—described as the "strictest form of probation for adults in the United States"[72]—is designed to achieve control in a community setting over offenders who would otherwise go to prison. Some states have extended a type of IPS to parolees, allowing the early release of some who would otherwise serve longer prison terms.

intensive probation supervision (IPS)
A form of probation supervision involving frequent face-to-face contact between the probationer and the probation officer.

Georgia was the first state to implement IPS, beginning its program in 1982. The Georgia program involves a minimum of five face-to-face contacts between the probationer and the supervising officer per week, mandatory curfew, required employment, weekly check of local arrest records, routine and unannounced alcohol and drug testing, 132 hours of community service, and automatic notification of probation officers via the State Crime Information Network when an IPS client is arrested.[73] The caseloads of probation officers involved in IPS are much lower than the national average. Georgia officers work as a team, with one probation officer and two surveillance officers supervising about 40 probationers.[74]

A study published in 2000 shows that IPS programs can be effective at reducing recidivism, especially if the programs are well planned and fully implemented.[75] The study, which examined programs in California's Contra Costa and Ventura Counties, found that the programs worked because, among other things, they used team approaches in their supervision activities and had clear missions and goals.

home confinement
House arrest. Individuals ordered confined to their homes are sometimes monitored electronically to ensure they do not leave during the hours of confinement. Absence from the home during working hours is often permitted.

Home Confinement and Remote Location Monitoring

Home confinement, also referred to as *house arrest,* can be defined as "a sentence imposed by the court in which offenders are legally ordered to remain confined in their own residences."[76] Home confinement usually makes use of a system of **remote location monitoring**, which is typically performed via a computerized system of electronic bracelets. Participants wear a waterproof, shock-resistant transmitting device around the ankle 24 hours a day. The transmitter continuously emits a radio-frequency signal that is detected by a receiving unit connected to the home telephone. Older systems use random telephone calls that require the offender to insert a computer chip worn in a wristband into a specially installed modem in the home, verifying his or her presence. Some use voice recognition

remote location monitoring
A supervision strategy that uses electronic technology to track offenders who are sentenced to house arrest or those who have been ordered to limit their movements while completing a sentence involving probation or parole.

Probation and parole services are characteristically poorly staffed and often poorly administered.

—President's Commission on Law Enforcement and Administration of Justice

technology and require the offender to verify his or her presence in the home by answering computerized calls. Modern electronic monitoring systems alert the officer when a participant leaves a specific location or tampers with the electronic monitoring equipment, and some systems even make it possible to record the time a supervised person enters or leaves the home.

Much of the electronic monitoring equipment in use today only indicates when participants enter or leave the equipment's range, not where they have gone or how far they have traveled. Newer satellite-supported systems, however, are capable of continuously monitoring an offender's location and tracking him or her as he or she moves from place to place (Figure 2). Satellite-based systems can alert the officer when participants venture into geographically excluded locations or when they fail to present themselves at required locations at specific times.[77]

Most remotely monitored offenders on home confinement may leave home only to go to their jobs, attend to medical emergencies, or buy household essentials. Because of the strict limits it imposes on offender movements, house arrest has been cited as offering a valuable alternative to prison for offenders with special needs. Pregnant women, geriatric convicts, offenders with special handicaps, seriously or terminally ill offenders, and mentally retarded persons may all be better supervised through home confinement than traditional incarceration.

One of the best-known people to recently be placed under house arrest using a remote location monitoring system was 63-year-old Martha Stewart, former CEO of Martha Stewart Living Omnimedia, Inc. Stewart served five months in prison for insider stock transactions and was ordered to serve an additional five months under house arrest at her Bedford, New York,

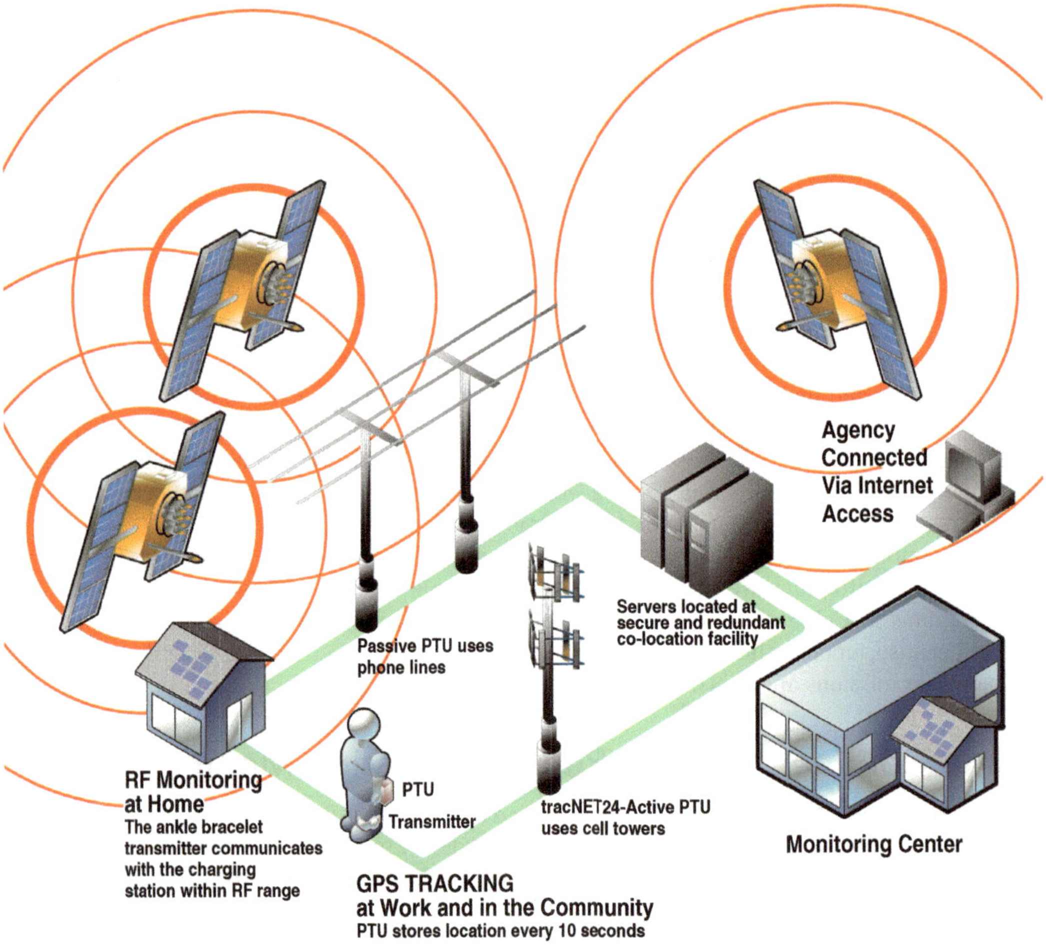

FIGURE 2
Remote Location Monitoring—How It Works.
Source: iSECUREtrac Corporation, 5022 South 114th Street, Omaha, NE 68137; phone: (866)537-0022. Copyright © 2006 iSECUREtrac Corporation. All rights reserved. Used with permission.

estate.[78] She was allowed daily commutes totaling 48 hours weekly to her office in New York City, 40 miles away.[79]

The Community Justice Assistance Division of the Texas Department of Criminal Justice runs one of the most ambitious home confinement programs in the country. In 1997, 89,095 adults (3.5% of the state's probationers) were being electronically monitored on probation.[80] By 2006, parole offices throughout the state had adopted electronic monitoring, and 1,056 electronic monitoring units were available for use with parolees.[81]

The overarching goal of reentry, in my view, is to have returned to our midst an individual who has discharged his legal obligation to society by serving his sentence and has demonstrated an ability to live by society's rules.
—*Jeremy Travis*
President, John Jay College of Criminal Justice

The electronic monitoring of offenders has steadily increased nationwide. A survey by the NIJ in 1987, as the use of electronic monitoring was just beginning, showed only 826 offenders being monitored electronically nationwide.[82] By 2000, however, more than 16,000 defendants and offenders under the supervision of U.S. probation and pretrial services officers were on home confinement, most under electronic monitoring programs.[83] A 2005 estimate put the number of persons in the United States under electronic monitoring at up to 75,000.[84]

In 1999, South Carolina's Probation and Parole Department began using satellites to track felons recently paroled from state prisons. The satellite-tracking plan, which makes use of 21 satellites in the Global Positioning System (GPS), allows the agency's officers to track every move made by convicts wearing electronic bracelets.[85] The system, which also notifies law enforcement officers when a bracelet-wearing offender leaves his or her assigned area, can electronically alert anyone holding a restraint order whenever the offender comes within two miles of him or her.

The home confinement program in the federal court system has three components, or levels of restriction.[86] *Curfew* requires program participants to remain at home every day during certain times, usually in the evening. With *home detention*, the participant remains at home at all times except for preapproved and scheduled absences, such as for work, school, treatment, church, attorney's appointments, court appearances, and other court-ordered obligations. *Home incarceration*, the highest level of restriction, calls for 24-hour-a-day "lockdown" at home, except for medical appointments, court appearances, and other activities that the court specifically approves.

Many states and the federal government view house arrest as a cost-effective response to the high cost of imprisonment. Georgia, for example, estimates that home confinement costs approximately $1,130 per year per supervised probationer and $2,190 per supervised parolee.[87] Incarceration costs are much higher, running around $18,100 per year per Georgia inmate, with another $43,756 needed to build each cell.[88] Advocates of house arrest argue that it is also socially cost-effective because it substantially decreases the opportunity for the kinds of negative socialization that occur in prison.[89] Opponents, however, have pointed out that house arrest may endanger the public and that it may provide little or no actual punishment. Critics of Martha Stewart's home confinement, for example, complained that the sentence was more of a reward than a punishment. Stewart's home, a 153-acre multimillion-dollar mansion with guest quarters, lacks few amenities, and the conditions imposed on Stewart allowed her to entertain colleagues, neighbors, friends, and relatives—as long as they didn't have criminal records.

The Future of Probation and Parole

Parole was widely criticized during the 1980s and 1990s by citizen groups who claimed that it unfairly reduces prison sentences imposed on serious offenders, and official attacks on parole came from some powerful corners. Senator Edward Kennedy called for the abolition of parole, as did former Attorney General Griffin Bell and former U.S. Bureau of Prisons Director Norman Carlson.[90] Academics chimed in, alleging that parole programs can provide no assurance that criminals will not commit further crimes. The media joined the fray, condemning parole for its inability to curb recidivism and highlighting the so-called revolving prison door as representative of the failure of parole.

The abolition of parole has been tried and has failed on a spectacular scale. . . . The absence of parole means that offenders simply walk out the door of prison at the end of a predetermined period of time, no questions asked.
—*American Probation and Parole Association and the Association of Paroling Authorities International*

These criticisms are not without warrant. In 2003, for example, more than 625,000 former prisoners—about 1,700 per day—were released from state and federal prisons and returned to society, most of them on some form of supervised release.[91] If past trends continue, just over half of them will be reincarcerated within three years (although some of them will have suc-

CJ News

More Sex Offenders Tracked by Satellite

Hundreds of convicted sex offenders will have to wear a two-piece electronic tracking device for the rest of their lives under a new Wisconsin law.

Ankle bracelets and a pager-sized unit, often attached to a belt, will use Global Positioning System (GPS) technology to follow their every step. If they enter restricted areas, such as schools, officials will be alerted.

GPS programs will track 285 offenders the first year, beginning July 2007, and up to 400 by the second year, says Dan Leistikow, spokesman for Wisconsin Gov. Jim Doyle.

In May 2006, Wisconsin joined a rapidly rising number of states using GPS to monitor convicted sex offenders. At least 23 states are doing so, according to a survey in February by the Pennsylvania Board of Probation and Parole. Others have since begun or expanded GPS programs.

"In the last several months, it's been exponential growth," says Steve Chapin, president of Pro-Tech, a Florida-based firm that provides GPS services to 27 statewide agencies. He says his business has doubled in the past three months.

As of January 2006, 13 states had laws requiring or allowing GPS tracking, says the National Conference of State Legislatures.

Aside from Wisconsin, governors in at least six states (Arkansas, Georgia, Kansas, Virginia, Washington and Michigan) have signed such bills this year [2006]. New Hampshire Gov. John Lynch plans to do so soon. Similar bills are pending elsewhere.

"It's the law you can't vote against," says Chapin.

Several of the laws are named after Jessica Lunsford, a 9-year-old Florida girl who was kidnapped, raped and killed in February 2005. The man charged with killing her was a convicted sex offender who hadn't reported that he lived across the street from her family. After he fled, it took almost a month to find him.

Even states without specific GPS laws, including Minnesota and Texas, are testing the technology and expanding its use.

Congress may accelerate such efforts. The House and Senate have each passed sex offender bills this year that approve funding for GPS tracking. They need to craft a final bill.

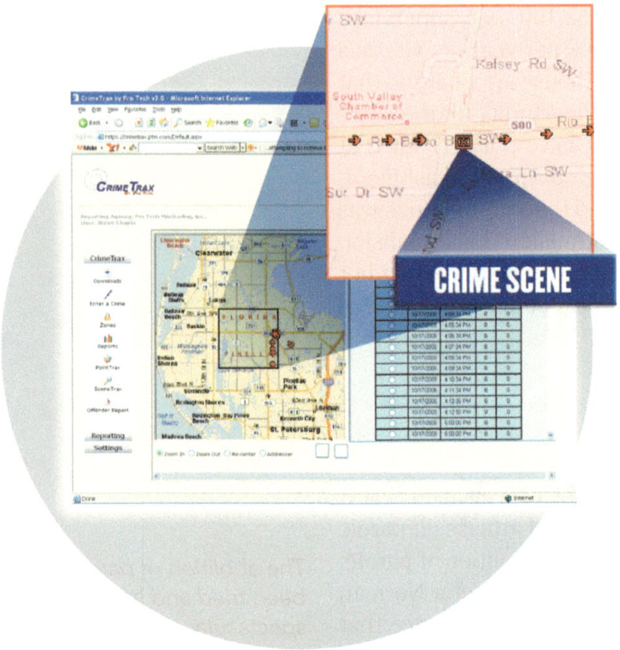

▲ A computer screen image demonstrating how Global Positioning Systems allow parole officers to track the movements of supervised offenders. What do you see as the advantages and disadvantages of this technology? How would individual-rights and public-safety advocates see this technology?
Courtesy of Pro Tech Monitoring

MORE ACCURATE TECHNOLOGY

The surge in GPS use coincides with the technology's dramatic advancements. The devices have become smaller and more accurate, often pinpointing a person's position within 30 feet. They are more precise than older devices that use radio frequencies and detect only when the wearer leaves a certain area, such as home if under house arrest.

GPS units can be programmed to have "exclusion zones" where offenders are not allowed and "inclusion zones" where they should be.

States are spending $5 to $10 daily to track each sex offender. Some require offenders, unless indigent, to pay the tab. They can choose the costlier "active" tracking, which gives real-time reports, or "passive" monitoring, which sends one report daily that lists where the offender went that day.

States have tried both:

- California uses GPS to track 430 sex offenders and has funds to follow 2,500 offenders by 2009, says Elaine Jennings of the California Department of Corrections and Rehabilitation.

  Since the program began in July 2005, 45 offenders have been arrested for violating parole and no new crimes have been committed, she says.

  "It's an excellent supervision tool" but doesn't supplant human supervision, says Jennings.
- Massachusetts has issued eight arrest warrants for violations by the 192 high-risk offenders it has tracked since its "active" GPS program began in May 2005, says Paul Lucci, one of the state's deputy probation commissioners. The state has officers who constantly watch a computer screen recording offenders' whereabouts and who can respond immediately.
- Michigan finished three pilot programs in 2003 and plans this summer [2006] to begin tracking up to 1,000 sex offenders, says Steve Bock of the Michigan Department of Corrections Electronic Monitoring Center.

  Bock says the state will use "passive" monitoring, because "active" GPS is too labor-intensive. He says real-time tracking generates "a ton of messages" that necessitate a 24/7 response team. He says it's problematic if offenders are barred from many areas, because GPS allows only a certain number of exclusion zones. "It can become a nightmare to enforce," Bock says.

OPPOSITION TO GPS TRACKING

Jake Goldenflame, 68, a convicted sex offender released 15 years ago, opposes lifetime GPS tracking. "If a man is so dangerous he needs it, he shouldn't be released," he says. Goldenflame says such monitoring may provide a "false sense of security," because it tells where the offender is, not what he's doing.

"It is not an effective way to prevent sexual assaults," says Richard Wright, a professor of criminal justice at Bridgewater State College. He says many serious sex offenders evade police by failing to register and others may re-offend regardless of tracking. He says no definitive study proves GPS deters crime.

Chapin says GPS reduces recidivism because offenders can't get away as easily. He says a December 2004 analysis by the Florida Department of Corrections found 3.8% of offenders tracked with GPS committed a new felony within two years compared to 7.7% of those supervised without it.

Offenders tracked by GPS were 90% less likely to abscond or re-offend than those not electronically monitored, says a February [2006] study by Florida State University of 75,661 offenders placed on home confinement. GPS did about as well as radio frequency, which costs four times less. "It's not a cost-free device," says Mark Carey, president of the American Probation and Parole Association. "It's an augmentation of what we do. It's not a replacement."

For the latest in crime and justice news, visit the Talk Justice news feed at http://www.crimenews.info.

Source: Wendy Koch, "More Sex Offenders Tracked by Satellite," *USA Today*, June 6, 2006. From USA TODAY, a division of Garnett Co., Inc. Reprinted by permission. www.usatoday.com.

cessfully completed parole prior to their return to prison).[92] Parole violators account for more than half of prison admissions in California (67%), Utah (55%), and Montana and Louisiana (both 53%). Seventy percent of parole violators in prison were arrested or were convicted of a new offense while on parole.[93] Many of these offenses involve drugs. Critics say that numbers like that are indicative of poor reintegration of prisoners into the community and are associated with wide-ranging social costs, including decreased public safety and weakened family and community ties.[94]

Even prisoners have challenged the fairness of parole, saying it is sometimes arbitrarily granted and creates an undue amount of uncertainty and frustration in the lives of inmates. Parolees have complained about the unpredictable nature of the parole experience, citing their powerlessness in the parole contract.

Against the pressure of attacks like these, parole advocates struggled to clarify and communicate the value of supervised release in the correctional process. As more and more states moved toward the elimination of parole, advocates called for moderation. A 1995 report by the APPA, for example, concluded that states that have eliminated parole "have jeopardized public safety and wasted tax dollars." The researchers wrote, "Getting rid of parole dismantles an accountable system of releasing prisoners back into the community and replaces it with a system that bases release decisions solely on whether a prison term has been completed."[95]

I understand that people want violent criminals locked up. We all do. But not every inmate is violent. We must look to supervised probation, to education. We must overcome the fear and think this out.

—Edwin Edwards
Former Louisiana Governor

Changes in Reentry Policies

By the close of the twentieth century, criticisms of parole had begun to wane, and a number of recent reports have been supportive of well-considered offender reentry and postrelease supervision programs. In 2005, for example, the Re-Entry Policy Council, a bipartisan assembly of almost 100 leading elected officials, policy makers, correctional leaders, and practitioners from community-based organizations around the country, released a report on offender reentry titled *Charting the Safe and Successful Return of Prisoners to the Community*. The 500-page report pointed out that virtually every person incarcerated in a jail in this country, as well as 97% of those incarcerated in prisons, will eventually be released back into society. This, said the report, results in nearly 650,000 people being released from prisons, and more than 7 million different individuals being released from jails throughout the United States each year—many of them without any form of postrelease supervision.[96]

As the report pointed out, almost two out of every three people released from prison are re-arrested within three years of their release.[97] Report authors noted that while the number of people reentering society has increased fourfold in the past 20 years and spending on corrections has increased nearly sevenfold in the past two decades, the likelihood of a former prisoner succeeding in the community upon release has not improved.

A host of complex issues create barriers to successful reentry. Three-quarters of those released from prison and jail, for example, have a history of substance abuse, two-thirds have no high school diploma, nearly half of those leaving jail earned less than $600 per month immediately prior to their incarceration, and they leave jail with significantly diminished opportunities for employment. Moreover, said the report, more than a third of jail inmates are saddled with a physical or mental disability, and the rate of serious mental illness among released inmates is at least three times higher than the rate of mental illness among the general population.[98]

The report states that "the multi-faceted—and costly—needs of people returning to their families and communities require a re-inventing of reentry akin to the reinvention of welfare in the 90s."[99] It requires, the report continued, "a multi-system, collaborative approach that takes into account all aspects of [the] problem." In other words, "the problems faced by reentering adults are not merely the problems of corrections or community corrections, but also of public health workers, housing providers, state legislators, workforce development staff, and others."

Library EXTRA

To guide states and local jurisdictions in the creation of successful offender reentry programs, the report provides 35 policy statements, each of which is supported by a series of research highlights. The report can be read in its entirety at mycrimekit.com as Library Extra 10–4. A 24-page summary is available as Library Extra 10–5.

In 2003, the U.S. Department of Justice, in conjunction with other federal agencies, initiated funding for 89 reentry sites across the country under the Serious Violent Offender Reentry Initiative (SVORI).[100] SVORI programs are geared toward serious and violent offenders, particularly adults released from prison, and juveniles released from correctional facilities.[101] The goal of the SVORI initiative is to reduce the likelihood of reincarceration by providing tailored supervision and services to improve the odds for a successful transition to the community. SVORI services include employment assistance, education and skills training, substance abuse counseling, and help with postrelease housing. SVORI programs also try to reduce criminality by closely monitoring participant noncompliance, reoffending, rearrest, reconviction, and reincarceration.[102] The initiative's priorities include providing services both to those adults and juveniles who are most likely to pose a risk to the community upon release and to those who face multiple challenges upon returning to the community. SVORI funding supports the creation of a three-phase continuum of services that begins in prison, moves to a structured reentry phase before and during the early months of release, and continues for several years as released prisoners take on increasingly productive roles in the community. These phases (see Figure 3) have been described in SVORI-related publications as follows[103]:

A critical assessment of probation must begin by placing its ailments within the more encompassing and deeper crisis of legitimacy affecting the entire system of justice.
—*Reinventing Probation Council*

- *Phase 1—Protect and Prepare: Institution-Based Programs.* These programs are designed to prepare offenders to reenter society. Services provided in this phase include education, mental health and substance abuse treatment, job training, mentoring, and full diagnostic and risk assessment.

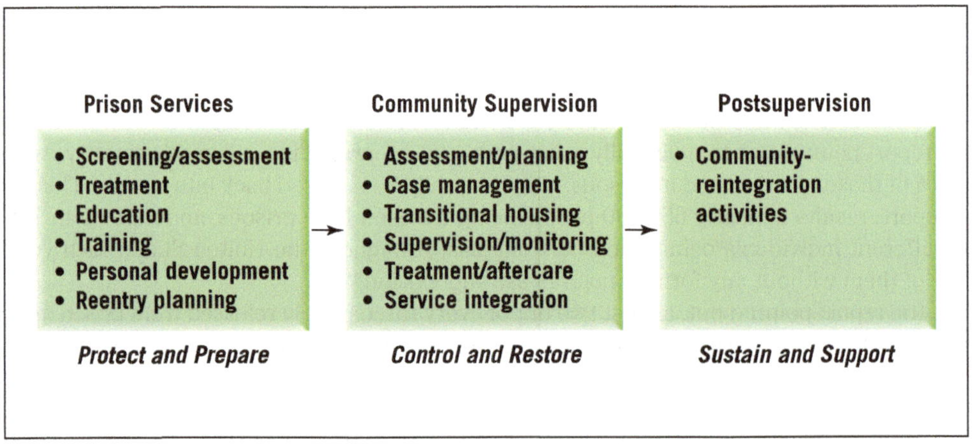

FIGURE 3
The SVORI Program Model.
Source: Laura Winterfield and Susan Brumbaugh, *The Multi-Site Evaluation of the Serious and Violent Offender Reentry Initiative* (RTI International and the Urban Institute, 2006). Reprinted with permission.

- *Phase 2—Control and Restore: Community-Based Transition Programs.* These programs work with offenders prior to and immediately following their release from correctional institutions. Services provided in this phase include, as appropriate, education, monitoring, mentoring, life skills training, assessment, job skills development, and mental health and substance abuse treatment.
- *Phase 3—Sustain and Support: Community-Based Long-Term Support Programs.* These programs connect individuals who have left the supervision of the justice system with a network of social services agencies and community-based organizations to provide ongoing services and mentoring relationships.

Probation will change when those who run probation departments are held accountable for achieving—or failing to achieve—specific outcomes.
—*Reinventing Probation Council*

Although evaluation of SVORI programs is ongoing, a recent review identified several reentry strategies that appear to work. In particular, vocational and work-release programs were found to improve job skills and to reduce recidivism, and some prerelease SVORI-sponsored drug-treatment programs were found to be successful. SVORI evaluators also found that program participants who stayed in halfway houses committed less severe and fewer crimes than those who lived elsewhere, and a number of educational programs were found to be capable of increasing achievement scores among reentry program participants.

One innovative approach to managing former prisoners who are returning to their communities is the use of reentry courts. Reentry courts are based on the drug-court model, begun in Miami in 1989, which functions to rapidly place drug-affected defendants into appropriate treatment programs with close supervision by a single judge familiar with both treatment and the offenders.[104] Similarly, under the reentry court concept, reentry court judges oversee an offender's supervised release into the community.[105] The Indiana Department of Corrections, for example, operates a contemporary SVORI-funded reentry court program.[106] Under the program, when released, participants are brought to Allen County Community Corrections (ACCC) in Fort Wayne, Indiana, and given in-depth risk assessments. A remote location monitoring system keeps track of each offender after release. On the first Friday after release, offenders appear before the reentry court judge for their first reentry court hearing; at the hearing they learn about the program and its goals and are told what's expected of them. Two weeks later, offenders meet with the judge individually, and a reintegration plan is imposed by the court. Successful adherence to the plan is a condition for continued freedom. Participants continue to appear before the court every two to five weeks to review progress and to assess any problems that have arisen. The reentry court offers an array of reintegration services to which participants can be referred and provides continual oversight using a preestablished set of graduated sanctions and rewards. The court also has a strong relationship with the faith-based community, and local pastors attend court hearings and offer mentoring services. Throughout the program, ACCC provides ongoing offender supervision for up to two years, and a reentry case management team makes continual recommendations to the judge.

Faith-based organizations in the SVORI program generally provide services such as emergency aid (such as clothing and food banks), mentoring, pastoral counseling, employment, transportation, and housing; conduct prerelease and postrelease needs assessments for program participants; coordinate family and community support for individual offenders; provide guidance to the program through participation in the program's steering committee or advisory board; and serve as community advocates for the SVORI program. Learn more about the SVORI initiative and the individual programs that comprise it at Library Extra 10–6 at mycrimekit.com. Reports about ongoing SVORI-related research can be read online at Web Extra 10–4.

Library EXTRA

Web EXTRA

In March 2008, in an effort to help the nearly 700,000 people leaving prison each year, the U.S. Congress passed the Second Chance Act.[107] The bill was signed into law by President George W. Bush shortly afterward. The act authorizes the expenditure of approximately $400 million in federal funds between 2008 and 2012 to "break the cycle of criminal recidivism [by assisting] offenders reentering the community from incarceration to establish a self-sustaining and law-abiding life."[108] The legislation funds prison-to-community transition services and programs through grants to nonprofit organizations. Such services and programs include the following:

- Education and job training while in prison
- Mentoring programs for adults and juveniles leaving confinement

- Drug treatment (including family-based treatment) for incarcerated parents during and after incarceration
- Alternatives to incarceration for parents convicted of nonviolent drug offenses
- Supportive programming for children of incarcerated parents
- Early release for certain elderly prisoners convicted of nonviolent offenses
- Reentry research through research awards to study parole and postsupervision revocation and related community safety issues

The legislation also allocates funding for federal Bureau of Prisons–specific programs that do the following:

1. Provide prisoners nearing the completion of their sentences with information concerning health care, nutrition, employment opportunities, money management, and availability of government assistance.
2. Allow certain nonviolent prisoners over 60 years of age to be placed in home detention for the duration of their sentences.
3. Educate juvenile offenders on the consequences of drug use and criminal activity.

The legislation also slightly increases the percentage of federal sentences that can be served in home confinement.

Reinventing of Probation

Although probation has generally fared better than parole, it too has its critics. The primary purpose of probation has always been rehabilitation, and probation is a powerful rehabilitative tool because, at least in theory, it allows the resources of a community to be focused on the offender. Unfortunately for advocates of probation, however, the rehabilitative ideal is far less popular today than it has been in the past. The contemporary demand for "just deserts" appears to have reduced society's tolerance for even relatively minor offenders. Also, because it has been too frequently and inappropriately used with repeat or relatively serious offenders, the image of probation has been tarnished. Probation advocates have been forced to admit that it is not a very powerful deterrent because it is far less punishing than a term of imprisonment.

In a series of reports issued in 1999 and 2000, the Reinventing Probation Council, a project of New York's Manhattan Institute, called for the "reinvention of probation."[109] Probation is cur-

▶ David Duke, the former Ku Klux Klan leader whose case raised eyebrows when he was released on federal parole in 2004. Duke, who served a year in federal prison on fraud charges, was released to a halfway house in Baton Rouge, Louisiana, and met the work requirements of his release by performing duties for the "white civil rights group" that he heads. Might a more suitable placement have been found?
Burt Steel/AP Wide World Photos

rently in the midst of a crisis, said the council, because probationers are not being held to even simple standards of behavior and because the field of probation lacks leadership. The council goes on to say that "probation will be reinvented when the probation profession places public safety first and works with and in the community." Read the council's full reports at Library Extras 10–7 and 10–8 at mycrimekit.com.

Library EXTRA

In an intriguing American Society of Criminology task force report on community corrections, Joan Petersilia notes that the "get tough on criminals" attitude that swept the nation during the 1990s resulted in increased funding for prisons but left in its wake stagnating budgetary allotments for probation and parole services.[110] This result has been especially unfortunate, Petersilia says, because "it has been continually shown that there is a 'highly significant statistical relationship between the extent to which probationers received needed services and the success of probation.' . . . As services have dwindled," she says, "recidivism rates have climbed." Some jurisdictions spend only a few hundred dollars per year on each probation or parole client, even though successful treatment in therapeutic settings is generally acknowledged to cost nearly $15,000 per person per year. The investment of such sums in the treatment of correctional clients, argues Petersilia, is potentially worthwhile because diverting probationers and parolees from lives of continued crime will save society even more money in terms of the costs of crime and the expenses associated with eventual imprisonment. The solution to the crisis that now exists in community corrections, says Petersilia, is to "first regain the public's trust that probation and parole can be meaningful, credible sanctions." She concludes, "Once we have that in place, we need to create a public climate to support a reinvestment in community corrections. Good community corrections cost money, and we should be honest about that."[111]

Summary

- Probation, simply put, is a sentence of imprisonment that is suspended. Its goal is to retain some control over criminal offenders while using community programs to help rehabilitate them. Probation, a court-ordered sanction, is one form of community corrections (also termed *community-based corrections*), that is, a sentencing style that depends less on traditional confinement options and more on correctional resources available in the community. John Augustus, a Boston shoemaker, is generally recognized as the world's first probation officer. By 1925, all 48 states had adopted probation legislation. In that same year, the federal government enacted legislation enabling federal district court judges to appoint paid probation officers and to impose probationary terms.
- Parole, the conditional early release of a convicted offender from prison, is a corrections strategy whose primary purpose is to return offenders gradually to productive lives. Parole differs from probation in that parolees, unlike probationers, have been incarcerated. Parole supported the concept of indeterminate sentencing, which held that a prisoner could earn early release through good behavior and self-improvement.
- Both probation and parole provide opportunities for the reintegration of offenders into the community through the use of resources not readily available in institutional settings. They are far less expensive than imprisonment, lead to increased employment among program participants, make possible restitution payments, and increase opportunities for rehabilitation. Unfortunately, however, increased freedom for criminal offenders also means some degree of increased risk for other members of society and increased social costs. Until and unless we solve the problems of inaccurate risk assessment, increased recidivism, and inadequate supervision, probation and parole will continue to be viewed with suspicion by a public that has become intolerant of crime and criminal offenders.
- Ten especially significant U.S. Supreme Court decisions, each of which was discussed in this chapter, provide the legal framework for probation and parole supervision. The 1987 case of *Griffin* v. *Wisconsin* may be the most significant. In *Griffin*, the Supreme Court ruled that probation officers may conduct searches of a probationer's residence without either a search warrant or probable cause. Other important court decisions include the 1998 case of *Pennsylvania Board of Probation and Parole* v. *Scott*, in which the Court declined to

extend the exclusionary rule to apply to searches by parole officers, and the 2001 case of *U.S.* v. *Knights*, which expanded the search authority normally reserved for probation and parole officers to police officers under certain circumstances.

- Probation or parole work consists primarily of four functions: (1) presentence investigations, (2) other intake procedures, (3) diagnosis and needs assessment, and (4) client supervision. The tasks performed by probation and parole officers are often quite similar, and some jurisdictions combine the roles of both into one job.
- Intermediate sanctions, which are sometimes termed *alternative sentencing strategies*, employ sentencing alternatives that fall somewhere between outright imprisonment and simple probationary release back into the community. These sanctions include shock incarceration, intensive probation supervision, and home confinement with electronic monitoring (also referred to as *remote location monitoring*). Intermediate sanctions have three distinct advantages: (1) They are less expensive than imprisonment, (2) they are socially cost-effective because they keep the offender in the community, and (3) they provide flexibility in terms of resources, time of involvement, and place of service.
- In recent years, parole and sometimes probation have been criticized for increasing the risk of community victimization by known offenders. In response, many states have eliminated or significantly curtailed parole opportunities. The future of parole may lie in an emerging concept of reentry that envisions successfully transitioning released inmates into the community using a variety of resources, including institutional and community programs. The federal Second Chance Act, signed into law by President George W. Bush in 2008, provides an example of new initiatives being undertaken in the reentry arena.

Key Concepts

Terms

caseload
community corrections
community service
conditional release
conditions of parole (probation)
discretionary release
home confinement
intensive probation supervision (IPS)
intermediate sanctions
mandatory release
mixed sentence
parole
parole board
parole (probation) violation
parole revocation
prisoner reentry
probation
probation revocation
recidivism
remote location monitoring
restitution
revocation hearing
shock incarceration
shock probation
split sentence

Cases

Bearden v. *Georgia*
Escoe v. *Zerbst*
Gagnon v. *Scarpelli*
Greenholtz v. *Nebraska Penal Inmates*
Griffin v. *Wisconsin*
Mempa v. *Rhay*
Minnesota v. *Murphy*
Morrissey v. *Brewer*
Pennsylvania Board of Probation and Parole v. *Scott*
Samson v. *California*
U.S. v. *Knights*

Questions for Review

1. What is probation? How did it develop? What purpose does it serve?
2. What is parole? How did it develop? How do probation and parole differ? How are they alike?
3. List and explain the advantages and disadvantages of probation and parole.
4. Name and describe significant court cases that have had an impact on the practices of probation and parole.
5. What do probation and parole officers do? What role do probation officers play in the sentencing of convicted offenders?
6. What are intermediate sanctions? How do they differ from more traditional forms of sentencing? What advantages do they offer?
7. How are probation and parole changing? What does the future hold for each?

To participate in an online discussion of these topics and others, join the CJ Brief e-mail discussion list at mycrimekit.com.

Web Quest

Use the Cybrary (http://www.cybrary.info) to search the World Wide Web to learn as much as you can about the future of probation and parole. In particular, you might want to focus on the use of satellite technology to monitor offenders placed on probation, use of home confinement, or public and media attitudes toward probation and parole; also gather studies on the future of probation and parole. Group your findings under headings (for example, "Innovative Options," "Alternative Sanctions," "Probation in My Home State," and "The Future of Probation and Parole").

Also visit the American Probation and Parole Association (APPA) at http://www.appa-net.org. (The organization is listed in the Cybrary.) What is the mission of the APPA? What are its goals and objectives? What organizations are affiliated with it? How many of them have websites? Submit your findings to your instructor if asked to do so.

To complete this Web Quest online, go to the Web Quest module in Chapter 10 of the *Criminal Justice: A Brief Introduction* Companion Website at mycrimekit.com.

Notes

i. From the "Director's Message" in Dora Schriro, "Correcting Corrections: Missouri's Parallel Universe," *Sentencing and Corrections Issues for the 21st Century: Papers from the Executive Session on Sentencing and Corrections,* No. 8 (Washington, DC: National Institute of Justice, 2000).

ii. Jeremy Travis and Sarah Lawrence, *Beyond the Prison Gates: The State of Parole in America* (Washington, DC: Urban Institute Press, 2002), p. 3.

iii. Ibid.

---

1. Quoted in *Criminal Justice Newsletter,* January 3, 2006, p. 1.
2. Quoted in *Criminal Justice Newsletter,* January 19, 1993, p. 1.
3. "Triple Homicide in Connecticut Prompts Package of Crime Laws," *Criminal Justice Newsletter,* February 1, 2008, p. 5.
4. David Byers, "Men Accused of Triple Killing Were on Parole," Times Online. Web available at http://www.timesonline.co.uk/tol/news/world/us_and_americas/article2140204.ece (accessed July 5, 2008).
5. Details for this story come from "Records: Smith Told His Brother," *The Herald Tribune,* June 3, 2004. Web posted at http://www.accessmylibrary.com/coms2/summary_0286-21538486_ITM (accessed September 2, 2008).
6. "Smith Sentenced to Death for Killing Carlie Brucia," *USA Today,* March 15, 2005. Web posted at http://www.usatoday.com/news/nation/2006-03-15-brucia_x.htm (accessed May 29, 2006).
7. James M. Byrne, *Probation,* National Institute of Justice Crime File Series Study Guide (Washington, DC: U.S. Department of Justice, 1988), p. 1.
8. Lauren E. Glaze and Thomas P. Bonczar, *Probation and Parole in the United States, 2006* (Washington, DC: Bureau of Justice Statistics, December 2007).
9. Jodi M. Brown and Patrick A. Langan, *Felony Sentences in the United States, 1996* (Washington, DC: Bureau of Justice Statistics, 1999).
10. "Woman Gets Probation for Shooting Fiancé," Associated Press wire service, April 16, 1992.
11. "On Deadline: Getting Away with Murder in Dallas," *USA Today,* November 14, 2007, p. 3A.
12. Glaze and Bonczar, *Probation and Parole in the United States, 2006,* p. 2.
13. Ibid.
14. This section owes much to Sanford Bates, "The Establishment and Early Years of the Federal Probation System," *Federal Probation* (June 1987), pp. 4–9.
15. *Ex parte United States,* 242 U.S. 27 (1916).
16. Bates, "The Establishment and Early Years of the Federal Probation System," p. 6.
17. U.S. Probation and Pretrial Services System, *Year-in-Review Report: Fiscal Year 2004* (Washington, DC: U.S. Probation and Pretrial Services System, 2005).
18. See Brian A. Reaves and Timothy C. Hart, *Federal Law Enforcement Officers, 2000* (Washington, DC: Bureau of Justice Statistics, 2002), p. 4, from which some of the wording in this paragraph has been adapted.
19. Adapted from Timothy A. Hughes, Doris James Wilson, and Allen J. Beck, *Trends in State Parole, 1990–2000* (Washington, DC: Bureau of Justice Statistics, 2001), p. 1.
20. Ibid.
21. Ibid.
22. Ibid.
23. Glaze and Bonczar, *Probation and Parole in the United States, 2006,* p. 2.
24. Ibid., p. 5.
25. Ibid., p. 7.
26. "The Effectiveness of Felony Probation: Results from an Eastern State," *Justice Quarterly* (December 1991), pp. 525–543.
27. State of New Jersey, State Parole Board, Media Release, "Parole Board Votes Unanimously to Restrict Sex Offender Internet Socializing," November 29, 2007.
28. State of Georgia, Board of Pardons and Paroles, "Adult Offender Sanction Costs for Fiscal Year 2001." Web posted at http://www.pap.state.ga.us/otisweb/corrcost.html (accessed March 11, 2007).
29. See Andrew von Hirsch and Kathleen J. Hanrahan, *Abolish Parole?* (Washington, DC: Law Enforcement Assistance Administration, 1978).
30. *Griffin* v. *Wisconsin,* 483 U.S. 868, 107 S.Ct. 3164 (1987).
31. *Pennsylvania Board of Probation and Parole* v. *Scott,* 524 U.S. 357 (1998).
32. *U.S.* v. *Knights,* 534 U.S. 112 (2001).
33. *Samson* v. *California,* U.S. Supreme Court, 547 U.S. 843 (2006).
34. California Penal Code 5, Section 3067.
35. Glaze and Bonczar, *Probation and Parole in the United States, 2005.*
36. Robyn. L. Cohen, *Probation and Parole Violators in State Prison, 1991* (Washington, DC: Bureau of Justice Statistics, 1995).
37. *Escoe* v. *Zerbst,* 295 U.S. 490 (1935).
38. *Mempa* v. *Rhay,* 389 U.S. 128 (1967).
39. A deferred sentence involves postponement of the sentencing decision, which may be made at a later time, following an automatic review of the defendant's behavior in the interim. A suspended sentence requires no review unless the probationer violates the law or the conditions of probation. Both may result in imprisonment.
40. *Morrissey* v. *Brewer,* 408 U.S. 471 (1972).
41. *Gagnon* v. *Scarpelli,* 411 U.S. 778 (1973).
42. Alexander B. Smith and Louis Berlin, *Introduction to Probation and Parole* (St. Paul, MN: West, 1976), p. 143.

43. See Linda Greenhouse, *New York Times* wire service, March 18, 1997 (no headline). The case is *Young* v. *Harper*, 520 U.S. 143 (1997).
44. *Greenholtz* v. *Nebraska Penal Inmates*, 442 U.S. 1 (1979).
45. *Bearden* v. *Georgia*, 461 U.S. 660, 103 S.Ct. 2064, 76 L.Ed.2d 221 (1983).
46. Ibid.
47. *Minnesota* v. *Murphy*, 465 U.S. 420 (1984).
48. *Harlow* v. *Clatterbuick*, 30 CrL. 2364 (Va. S.Ct. 1986); *Santangelo* v. *State*, 426 N.Y.S.2d 931 (1980); *Welch* v. *State*, 424 N.Y.S.2d 774 (1980); and *Thompson* v. *County of Alameda*, 614 P.2d 728 (1980).
49. *Tarter* v. *State of New York*, 38 CrL. 2364 (N.Y. Sup. Ct. 1986); *Grimm* v. *Arizona Board of Pardons and Paroles*, 115 Arizona 260, 564 P.2d 1227 (1977); and *Payton* v. *U.S.*, 636 F.2d 132 (5th Cir. 1981).
50. *Rolando* v. *del Carmen: Potential Liabilities of Probation and Parole Officers* (Cincinnati, OH: Anderson, 1986), p. 89.
51. See, for example, *Semler* v. *Psychiatric Institute*, 538 F.2d 121 (4th Cir. 1976).
52. *Minnesota* v. *Murphy* (1984).
53. National Advisory Commission on Criminal Justice Standards and Goals, *Task Force Report: Corrections* (Washington, DC: U.S. Government Printing Office, 1973).
54. National Institute of Justice, *Stress among Probation and Parole Officers and What Can Be Done about It* (Washington, DC: NIJ, 2005).
55. Ibid., p. 1.
56. Ibid., p. ii.
57. From the introduction to James Austin, Michael Jones, and Melissa Bolyard, *The Growing Use of Jail Boot Camps: The Current State of the Art* (Washington, DC: National Institute of Justice, 1993), p. 1.
58. Michael McCarthy and Jodi Upton, "Athletes Lightly Punished after Their Day in Court," *USA Today*, May 4, 2006, p. 1A.
59. Sentencing Project, *Changing the Terms of Sentencing: Defense Counsel and Alternative Sentencing Services* (Washington, DC: Sentencing Project, no date).
60. Joan Petersilia, *Expanding Options for Criminal Sentencing* (Santa Monica, CA: RAND Corporation, 1987).
61. Ohio Revised Code, Section 2946.06.1 (July 1965).
62. Lawrence Greenfield, *Probation and Parole, 1984* (Washington, DC: U.S. Government Printing Office, 1986).
63. For a good overview of such programs, especially as they apply to juvenile corrections, see Doris Layton MacKenzie et al., *A National Study Comparing the Environments of Boot Camps with Traditional Facilities for Juvenile Offenders* (Washington, DC: National Institute of Justice, 2001).
64. Doris Layton MacKenzie and Deanna Bellew Ballow, "Shock Incarceration Programs in State Correctional Jurisdictions—An Update," *NIJ Reports* (May/June 1989), pp. 9–10.
65. "Shock Incarceration Marks a Decade of Expansion," *Corrections Compendium* (September 1996), pp. 10–28.
66. MacKenzie and Ballow, "Shock Incarceration Programs in State Correctional Jurisdictions."
67. National Institute of Justice, *Multisite Evaluation of Shock Incarceration* (Washington, DC: NIJ, 1995).
68. Cherie L. Clark, David W. Aziz, and Doris L. MacKenzie, *Shock Incarceration in New York: Focus on Treatment* (Washington, DC: National Institute of Justice, 1994), p. 8.
69. "Oregon Boot Camp Is Saving the State Money, Study Finds," *Criminal Justice Newsletter*, May 1, 1995, pp. 5–6.
70. Douglas C. McDonald, *Restitution and Community Service*, National Institute of Justice Crime File Series Study Guide (Washington, DC: U.S. Department of Justice, 1988).
71. Richard J. Maher and Henry E. Dufour, "Experimenting with Community Service: A Punitive Alternative to Imprisonment," *Federal Probation* (September 1987), pp. 22–27.
72. James P. Levine, Michael C. Musheno, and Dennis J. Palumbo, *Criminal Justice in America: Law in Action* (New York: John Wiley, 1986), p. 549.
73. Billie S. Erwin and Lawrence A. Bennett, "New Dimensions in Probation: Georgia's Experience with Intensive Probation Supervision," *Research in Brief* (Washington, DC: National Institute of Justice, 1987).
74. Probation Division, State of Georgia, "Intensive and Specialized Probation Supervision." Web posted at http://www.dcor.state.ga.us/ProbationDivision/html/ProbationDivision.html (accessed March 2, 2008).
75. Crystal A. Garcia, "Using Palmer's Global Approach to Evaluate Intensive Supervision Programs: Implications for Practice," *Corrections Management Quarterly*, Vol. 4, No. 4 (2000), pp. 60–69.
76. Joan Petersilia, *House Arrest*, National Institute of Justice Crime File Series Study Guide (Washington, DC: U.S. Department of Justice, 1988).
77. Darren Gowen, "Remote Location Monitoring: A Supervision Strategy to Enhance Risk Control," *Federal Probation*, Vol. 65, No. 2 (2001), p. 39.
78. An additional year and seven months of supervised confinement was to follow.
79. See "Martha Stewart Starts Home Confinement," Associated Press, March 3, 2005. Web posted at http://moneycentral.msn.com/content/invest/extra/P111258.asp (accessed April 26, 2005).
80. *Electronic Monitoring*, TDCJ-CJAD Agency Brief (Austin: Texas Department of Criminal Justice, March 1999).
81. Texas Department of Criminal Justice, Parole Division, *Contract Information: Electronic Monitoring.* Web posted at http://www.tdcj.state.tx.us/parole/parole-contracts/parolecont-em.htm (accessed September 28, 2008).
82. Marc Renzema and David T. Skelton, *The Use of Electronic Monitoring by Criminal Justice Agencies, 1989* (Washington, DC: National Institute of Justice, 1990).
83. U.S. Probation and Pretrial Services, *Court and Community* (Washington, DC: Administrative Office of the U.S. Courts, 2000).
84. *Sourcebook of Criminal Justice Statistics Online* (2005). "Persons under Jail Supervision" (Table 6.14, year 2003). Web posted at http://www.albany.edu/sourcebook/wk1/t614.wk1.
85. "Satellites Tracking People on Parole," Associated Press wire service, April 13, 1999.
86. U.S. Probation and Pretrial Services, "Home Confinement." Web posted at http://www.uscourts.gov/misc/cchome.pdf (accessed March 22, 2008).
87. State of Georgia Board of Pardons and Paroles, "Adult Offender Sanction Costs for Fiscal Year 2001." Web posted at http://www.pap.state.ga.us/otisweb/corrcost.html (accessed September 20, 2005).
88. Construction costs are for cells classified as "medium security."
89. *BI Home Escort: Electronic Monitoring System*, advertising brochure (Boulder, CO: BI Inc., no date).
90. James A. Inciardi, *Criminal Justice*, 2nd ed. (New York: Harcourt Brace Jovanovich, 1987), p. 664.
91. Neely Tucker, "Study Warns of Rising Tide of Released Inmates," *Washington Post*, May 21, 2003, p. A1.
92. Patrick A. Langan and David J. Levin, *National Recidivism Study of Released Prisoners: Recidivism of Prisoners Released in 1994* (Washington, DC: Bureau of Justice Statistics, 2002).
93. "Forty-Two Percent of State Parole Discharges Were Successful," Bureau of Justice Statistics press release, October 3, 2001.
94. Urban Institute and RTI International, *National Portrait of SVORI* (Washington, DC: Urban Institute Press, 2004),
95. American Probation and Parole Association and the Association of Paroling Authorities International, *Abolishing Parole: Why the Emperor Has No Clothes* (Lexington, KY: APPA, 1995).
96. Much of this information is taken from Re-Entry Policy Council, *Report of the Re-Entry Policy Council: Charting the Safe and Successful Return of Prisoners to the Community—Executive Summary* (New York: Council of State Governments, 2005). Web

posted at http://www.reentrypolicy.org/executive-summary.html (accessed July 10, 2005).

97. Patrick A. Langan and David J. Levin, *National Recidivism Study of Released Prisoners: Recidivism of Prisoners Released in 1994* (Washington, DC: Bureau of Justice Statistics, 2002); and *Does Parole Work? Analyzing the Impact of Postprison Supervision on Rearrest Outcomes* (Washington, DC: Urban Institute Press, 2005).
98. Esther Griswold, Jessica Pearson, and Lanae Davis, *Testing a Modification Process for Incarcerated Parents* (Denver: Center for Policy Research), pp. 11–12.
99. Ibid.
100. See Pamela K. Lattimore, "Reentry, Reintegration, Rehabilitation, Recidivism, and Redemption," *The Criminologist,* Vol. 31, No. 3 (May/June 2006), pp. 1, 3–6.
101. Urban Institute and RTI International, *National Portrait of SVORI,* from which some of the wording in this section is taken.
102. See Laura Winterfield and Susan Brumbaugh, *The Multi-Site Evaluation of the Serious and Violent Offender Reentry Initiative* (Washington, DC: Urban Institute Press, 2005).
103. U.S. Department of Justice, Office of Justice Programs, "Learn about Reentry." Web posted at http://www.reentry.gov/learn.html (accessed May 29, 2008).
104. Lane County (Oregon) Circuit Court, "Drug Court." Web posted at http://www.ojd.state.or.us/lan/drugcrt/index.htm (accessed May 29, 2006).
105. See, for example, Jeremy Travis, *But They All Come Back: Facing the Challenges of Prisoner Reentry* (Washington, DC: Urban Institute Press, 2005).
106. Urban Institute and RTI International, *National Portrait of SVORI,* pp. 21, 23.
107. Public Law No. 110-199.
108. Congressional Budget Office, "Cost Estimate: S. 1060, Second Chance Act of 2007," p. 4. Web available at http://www.cbo.gov/ftpdocs/86xx/doc8620/s1060.pdf (accessed August 28, 2008).
109. Reinventing Probation Council, *"Broken Windows" Probation: The Next Step in Fighting Crime* (New York: Manhattan Institute, 1999); and Reinventing Probation Council, *Transforming Probation through Leadership: The "Broken Windows" Model* (New York: Center for Civic Innovation at the Manhattan Institute, 2000), from which some of the quoted material in these paragraphs comes.
110. Joan Petersilia, "A Crime Control Rationale for Reinvesting in Community Corrections," in *Critical Criminal Justice Issues: Task Force Reports from the American Society of Criminology* (Washington, DC: National Institute of Justice, 1997), pp. 104–119.
111. For more about the future of probation and parole, see Joan Petersilia, *Reforming Probation and Parole in the Twenty-First Century* (Lanham, MD: American Correctional Association, 2002).

Prisons and Jails

11

Chapter Outline

- Introduction
- Prisons
- Jails
- Private Prisons

Learning Objectives

After reading this chapter, you should be able to

- Discuss the major characteristics and purposes of today's prisons.
- Explain the role that jails play in American corrections, and discuss the issues that jail administrators currently face.
- Describe the role of private prisons today, and assess their future.

"After a 700-percent increase in the U.S. prison population between 1970 and 2005, you'd think the nation would finally have run out of lawbreakers to put behind bars. But. . . state and federal prisons will swell by more than 192,000 inmates over the next five years. This 13-percent jump triples the projected growth of the general U.S. population and will raise the prison census to a total of more than 1.7 million people."

—Public Safety Performance Project of the Pew Charitable Trusts (2007)[1]

Introduction

▶▶▶ Hear the author discuss this chapter at mycrimekit.com.

On August 27, 2007, the town of Berlin (in northern New Hampshire) held a job fair for people seeking employment in the new medium-security federal correctional institution being built near the town in Coos County. When it opens in two years, the $230 million prison will house around 1,280 federal prisoners. About 350 people showed up for the job fair, looking for construction jobs as the planned 37-month building project was about to get under way. Before federal funds started flowing to the Berlin area, the town's largest employer was a pulp mill, but the company, which had employed generations of townsfolk, closed its doors for good in 2006, leaving hundreds without jobs. Berlin Mayor Bob Danderson thanked U.S. Senator Judd Gregg (R–NH) for his help in bringing the new prison to his town. "The sooner this project starts, the better it will be for the citizens of the North Country," Danderson said. "Senator Gregg has clearly been instrumental in obtaining the necessary funding for this project," he added, "which many people in the North Country will be thankful for because of the jobs and economic stimulus it will create." Construction of the new federal prison is expected to be the second largest public works project ever undertaken in New Hampshire, behind only the Seabrook nuclear power plant. Once completed, the facility is expected to employ around 300 correctional officers and support staff. Learn more about how prisons and prison construction impact local economies at Library Extras 11–1 at mycrimekit.com.

Library EXTRA

Prisons

prison
A state or federal confinement facility that has custodial authority over adults sentenced to confinement.

While new prisons may provide economic windfalls for struggling communities, this chapter considers the wider impact of imprisonment on American society and describes the characteristics of **prisons** (state and federal confinement facilities for incarcerated adults) and prison populations today. There are approximately 1,325 state prisons and 84 federal prisons in operation across the country today.[2] More are being built as both the states and the federal government continue to fund and construct new facilities. America's prison population has more than quadrupled since 1980, although the growth rate has been slowing recently. On January 1, 2007, the nation's state and federal prisons held 1,570,861 sentenced inmates.[3] Slightly more than 7% (or 112,498) of those imprisoned were women.[4] Figure 1 shows the rise in the U.S. prison population during the past 45 years and includes a short-term future projection. A special report released by the Public Safety Performance Project of the Pew Charitable Trusts in 2007 predicts that the nation's prison population will rise to more than 1.72 million by 2011.[5] From a

▶ People lining up at a job fair in Berlin, New Hampshire, hoping for jobs as the construction of a new federal prison in the area begins. How might prison construction help local communities? How might it hurt?
Lorna Colquhou

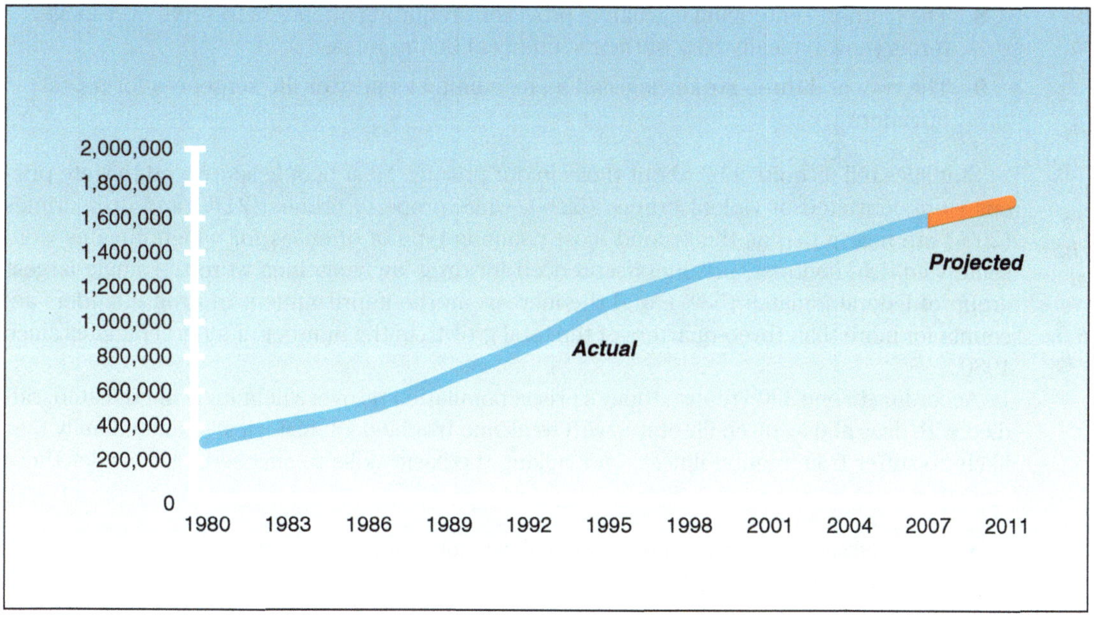

FIGURE 1
U.S. Prison Population, Actual and Projected, 1960–2011.
Source: Bureau of Justice Statistics and the Pew Charitable Trusts.

comparative perspective, the number of people behind bars in the United States is striking, and an even more recent report from Pew notes that "the United States incarcerates more people than any country in the world, including the far more populous nation of China."[6]

The incarceration rate for state and federal prisoners sentenced to more than a year has reached a record 501 prisoners for every 100,000 U.S. residents. This rate means that about 1 in every 200 U.S. residents was serving a prison term of more than one year in early 2007.[7] If incarceration rates remain unchanged, 6.6% of U.S. residents born in 2001 will go to prison sometime during their lifetime.[8]

High incarceration rates persist in the United States today even in the face of declining crime rates. Between 1991 and 2007, the official rate of crime in the United States dropped from 5,897 to 3,730 offenses per every 100,000 residents—a level that had not been seen since 1975.[9] Hence, a 37% *decrease* in the national crime rate over a ten-year period was accompanied by a 62% *increase* in the rate of imprisonment. Crime-control advocates, of course, would argue that increased rates of incarceration are at least partially responsible for reduced crime rates, since incarceration removes those who are likely to reoffend from the community.

Today's high rate of imprisonment can be attributed to a number of historical factors[10]:

1. A staunch "get tough on crime" philosophy that swept America during the mid- to late-twentieth century (and that is still largely with us today)
2. The nation's war on drugs as well as a zero-tolerance policy toward illicit drugs, drug users, and drug sellers
3. The increased use of punishments, including mandated prison terms for drug-related felonies
4. A growing reluctance to release parolees in the face of fears about their likelihood of continued crime commission
5. The new mandates in many jurisdictions requiring probation officers to report technical violations of the conditions of probation committed by those in their charge
6. The elimination of good-time prison credits, resulting in longer prison stays for most offenders
7. The abandonment of discretionary (and therefore often early) parole release decisions and the concomitant elimination of parole boards in many states

Prisons are no longer a response to increasing crime, and crime does not respond to increasing prisons. The prison system just grows like a weed in the yard.

—*Vincent Schiraldi*
Executive Director, Justice Policy Institute

While we certainly want to be smart about who we put into prisons, it would be a mistake to think that we can release any significant number of prisoners without increasing crime rates. One out of every 100 adults is behind bars because one out of every 100 adults has committed a serious criminal offense.

—Paul Cassell, University of Utah law professor and former federal judge[i]

8. The truth-in-sentencing legislative provisions requiring offenders to serve ever-longer terms (now typically 85% of their sentences) before release

9. The two- and three-strikes legislation, mandating lengthy or life sentences for repeat offenders

Statistics tell us quite a bit about those in our prisons. Most people sentenced to state prisons were convicted of violent crimes (52%), while property crimes (21%) and drug crimes (20%) are nearly tied as the second most common type of offenses for which inmates were sentenced.[11] In contrast, prisoners sentenced for drug-law violations were the single largest group of federal inmates (53%), and the increase in the imprisonment of drug offenders accounts for more than three-quarters of the total growth in the number of federal inmates since 1980.[12]

According to one 2008 report, today's prison population "is overwhelmingly uneducated, riddled with drug abuse, often illiterate, with weak and troubled job histories, strained family ties, likely to suffer from mental illness, and lacking the basic skills to succeed."[13] Consider these statistics:

- About 68% of state prisoners lack a high school diploma.
- Roughly half are functionally illiterate.
- About 53% of state prisoners are dependent on drugs.
- The work histories and skills of prisoners are well below those of the general population, and only one in five prisoners has a job lined up at the time of release.
- Roughly 700,000 state and federal prisoners are parents to more than 1.5 million children under the age of 18.
- About 56% of state prisoners and 45% of federal prisoners have a mental health problem.[14]
- One-third of state prisoners have "major depression or mania symptoms," and another one-eighth have psychotic disorders.[15]

An examination of imprisonment statistics by race highlights the huge disparity between African-Americans and Caucasians in prison. While only an estimated 486 Caucasian men are imprisoned in the United States for every 100,000 Caucasian men in the population, the latest figures show an incarceration rate of 3,042 African-American men for every 100,000 African-American men. Worse, nearly 8% of black men ages 30 to 34 were incarcerated as sentenced prisoners under state or federal jurisdiction at the start of 2007—seven times greater than the figure for Caucasians.[16] The imprisonment rate of African-Americans has increased dramatically during the past ten years, while the rate of Caucasian imprisonment grew much more slowly. Almost 17% of adult African-American men in the United States have served time in prison—a rate over twice as high as that for adult Hispanic males (7.7%) and over six times as high as that for adult Caucasian males (2.6%).[17] According to the Bureau of Justice Statistics (BJS), an African-American male living in America today has a 32.3% lifetime chance of going to prison, and an African-American female has a 5.6% lifetime chance of imprisonment, figures that contrast sharply with the lifetime chances of imprisonment for Caucasian males (5.9%) and Caucasian females (0.9%).[18]

The use of imprisonment varies considerably between states. While the average rate of imprisonment in the United States at the start of 2007 was 501 per every 100,000 people in the population,[19] some state rates were nearly double that figure.[20] Louisiana, for example, was holding 846 out of every 100,000 of its citizens in prison on January 1, 2007, while Mississippi was close behind with an incarceration rate of 658. Texas, a state with traditionally high rates of imprisonment, held 683 prisoners per every 100,000 people. Maine had the lowest rate of imprisonment of all the states (151), while other states with low rates were Rhode Island (202), New Hampshire (207), and North Dakota (214). More statistics are available via Library Extra 11–2 at mycrimekit.com.

Library EXTRA

A recent study by David F. Greenberg and Valerie West identified factors that contribute to variation in incarceration rates among states.[21] Greenberg and West found that a state's violent crime rate was a significant determinant of its incarceration rate but was not the only factor involved. Also important were the political leanings of the state's population (more politically

Inmates making collect phone calls at the Davidson County Prison in Tennessee. There are approximately 1,325 state prisons and 84 federal prisons in operation across the country today. Together, they hold more than 1.57 million inmates. The prison shown here is run by the Corrections Corporation of America. Why is the number of inmates growing while the crime rate continues to fall?
A. Ramey/PhotoEdit Inc.

conservative states made greater use of imprisonment), the amount of money available to build and maintain prisons (more money led to more imprisonment), the employment rate (unemployment contributed to higher rates of imprisonment), the percentage of African-American men in the state's population (the higher the percentage, the higher the rate of imprisonment was), and the level of welfare support available to the poor (higher welfare payments meant less imprisonment). The authors also found that income inequality was *not* a predictor of imprisonment rates and that the degree of urbanization in a state had no effect on imprisonment.

Prison and jail populations have skyrocketed during the past two decades, spurring new construction and often generating crowded conditions in our institutions and facilities. Substance abuse is directly and indirectly responsible for a large portion of this population increase.

—James A. Gondles, Jr. Executive Director, the American Correctional Association[ii]

The size of prison facilities varies greatly. One out of every four state institutions is a large maximum-security prison, with a population approaching 1,000 inmates. A few exceed that figure, but the typical state prison is small, with an inmate population of less than 500; community-based facilities average around 50 residents. The typical prison system in relatively populous states consists of the following[22]:

- One high-security prison for long-term, high-risk offenders
- One or more medium-security institutions for non-high-risk offenders
- One institution for adult women
- One or two institutions for young adults (generally under age 25)
- One or two specialized mental hospital–type security prisons for mentally ill prisoners
- One or more open-type institutions for low-risk, nonviolent inmates

Incarceration costs average around $62 per inmate per day at both the state and federal levels when all types of adult correctional facilities are averaged together.[23] Prison systems across the nation face spiraling costs as the number of inmates grows and as the age of the inmate population increases. The cost of running the nation's correctional programs approached $64 billion in 2003, of which more than half, or $39 billion, went to run state prisons.[24]

The Philosophy of Imprisonment

Prisons in this country were originally built for the purpose of rehabilitation and as an alternative to the corporal punishments of earlier times.[25] Although many of today's correctional administrators continue to avow a philosophy of rehabilitation and although American corrections continues to serve a variety of purposes, the central policy that influences the course of our nation's prisons today is retribution. Today's overcrowded prisons with their depressing

justice model
A contemporary model of imprisonment based on the principle of just deserts.

conditions are largely the result of "get tough on crime" attitudes that have swept the nation for the past few decades. These attitudes are based on a perspective that is sometimes referred to as the **justice model** or the *just deserts model*. This model, which emphasizes individual responsibility and the punishment of offenders, has become the operative principle underlying many of today's correctional initiatives. The philosophy is grounded squarely on a just deserts theme, in which imprisonment is seen as a *fully deserved* consequence of criminal behavior.

While many would probably agree that "get tough" philosophies come and go, the current wave of such feelings is far from exhausted. During the 1990s, in recognition of such national sentiments, state legislatures everywhere scrambled to place limits on inmate privileges and to increase the pains of imprisonment. In 1995, for example, Alabama became the first state in modern times to reinstitute the prison chain gang.[26] Under the Alabama system, shotgun-armed guards oversaw prisoners who were chained together by the ankles while they worked the state's roadsides picking up trash, clearing brush, and filling ditches. The system, intended primarily for parole violators who must reenter prison, was tough and unforgiving. Inmates served up to 90 days on chain gangs, during which they worked 12-hour shifts and remained chained even while using portable toilets. Following Alabama's lead, in 1995 Arizona became the second state to field prison chain gangs, followed shortly thereafter by Florida.[27] Alabama chain gangs, which had expanded to include female prisoners, were discontinued in 1996 following a lawsuit against the state.

The Florida Department of Corrections continues to use restricted labor squads (its name for chain gangs) at seven correctional institutions. Florida chain gang inmates are shackled at the ankles but are not connected to each other in any way.[28]

Nationally, chain gang proponents, though dwindling in number, continue to be adamant about the purpose this punishment serves. "If a person knows they're going to be out on the highway in chains, they are going to think twice about committing a crime," says former Georgia Prison Commissioner Ron Jones.[29] Opponents of the chain gang, however, like American Civil Liberties Union (ACLU) National Prison Project spokeswoman Jenni Gainsborough, call it "a giant step backward" and "a return to the dark ages."[30]

In another example of the move toward greater punishments indicative of the just deserts era, Virginia abolished parole on January 1, 1995; increased sentences for certain violent crimes by as much as 700%; and announced that it would build a dozen new prisons.[31] Changes in state law, initiated by the administration of Governor George Allen, were intended to move the state further in the direction of truth in sentencing and to appease the state's voters, who—reflecting what appears to have been a groundswell of public opinion nationwide—demanded a "get tough" stance toward criminals. William P. Barr, former U.S. attorney general under President George Bush and cochair of the Virginia commission that developed the state's plan, explained why no provisions for rehabilitation and crime prevention had been included: "The most effective method of prevention," he said, "is to take the rapist off the street for 12 years instead of four."[32]

"Get tough" initiatives can be seen in the "three strikes and you're out" laws that swept through state legislatures everywhere in the late 1990s.[33] Three-strikes legislation mandates lengthy prison terms for criminal offenders convicted of a third violent crime or felony. While three-strikes laws either have been enacted or are being considered in more than 30 states and by the federal government (which requires life imprisonment for federal criminals convicted of three violent felonies or drug offenses), critics of such laws say that they will not prevent crime.[34] Jerome Skolnick of the University of California at Berkeley, for example, criticizes three-strikes legislation because although it may satisfy society's desire for retribution to "lock 'em up and throw away the key," such a practice will almost certainly not reduce the risk of victimization—especially the risk of becoming a victim of random violence.[35] That is so, says Skolnick, because most violent crimes are committed by young men between the ages of 13 and 23. "It follows," according to Skolnick, "that if we jail them for life after their third conviction, we will get them in the twilight of their careers, and other young offenders will take their place." Three-strikes programs, says Skolnick, will lead to the creation of "the most expensive, taxpayer-supported middle-age and old-age entitlement program in the history of the world," which will provide housing and medical care to older, burned-out law violators. Another author puts it this way: "The question ... is whether it makes sense to continue to incarcerate aged prisoners beyond the time they would have served under ordinary sentences. This is unnecessary from the standpoint of public safety, and it is expensive."[36]

The central aim of a true prison system is the protection of society against crime, not the punishment of criminals.
—Zebulon R. Brockway[iii]

Alan Schuman, past president of the American Probation and Parole Association, feels much the same way. While building more prisons may be a popular quick fix to crime, says Schuman, such a strategy will cost millions of dollars without making streets safer. "The draconian single-level approach of merely building new institutions will cause us problems for decades," Schuman said.[37]

Criticisms like these, however, fail to appreciate the sentiments underlying the current correctional era. Proponents of "get tough" policies, while no doubt interested in personal safety, lower crime rates, and balanced state and federal budgets, are keenly focused on retribution. And where retribution fuels a correctional policy, deterrence, reformation, and economic considerations play only secondary roles. The real issue for those advocating retribution-based correctional policies is not whether they deter crime or lower crime rates but rather the overriding conviction that criminals deserve punishment. As more and more states enacted three-strikes and other "get tough" legislation, prison populations across the nation continued to swell. The just deserts philosophy, however, now provides what has become for many an acceptable rationale for continued prison expansion.

Many now claim that the prevailing retribution-based "lock 'em up" philosophy bodes ill for the future of American corrections. "I am worried there is going to be a disaster in our prisons," says J. Michael Quinlan, director of the Federal Bureau of Prisons (BOP) under Presidents Ronald Reagan and George Bush.[38] The combination of burgeoning prison populations and restrictions on inmate privileges could have a catastrophic and disastrous effect—leading to riots, more prison violence, work stoppages, increased numbers of inmate suicides, and other forms of prison disorder—says Quinlan.[39]

If you don't like the place, don't come here.

—*Joe Arpaio*
Maricopa County (Arizona) Sheriff, offering advice to inmates housed in his desert tent city[iv]

Overcrowding

The Dimensions of Overcrowding

The just deserts philosophy led to substantial and continued increases in the American prison population even as crime rates were dropping. In 1990, for example, the U.S. rate of imprisonment stood at 292 prisoners per every 100,000 residents. By 1995, it had reached 399, and on January 1, 2007, it was 501. While the rate of growth has been slowing, it is still inching higher.[40]

Even though many new prisons have been built throughout the nation during the past 20 years to accommodate the growing number of inmates, prison overcrowding is still very much a reality in many jurisdictions (Figure 2). Some of the most crowded prisons are those in the

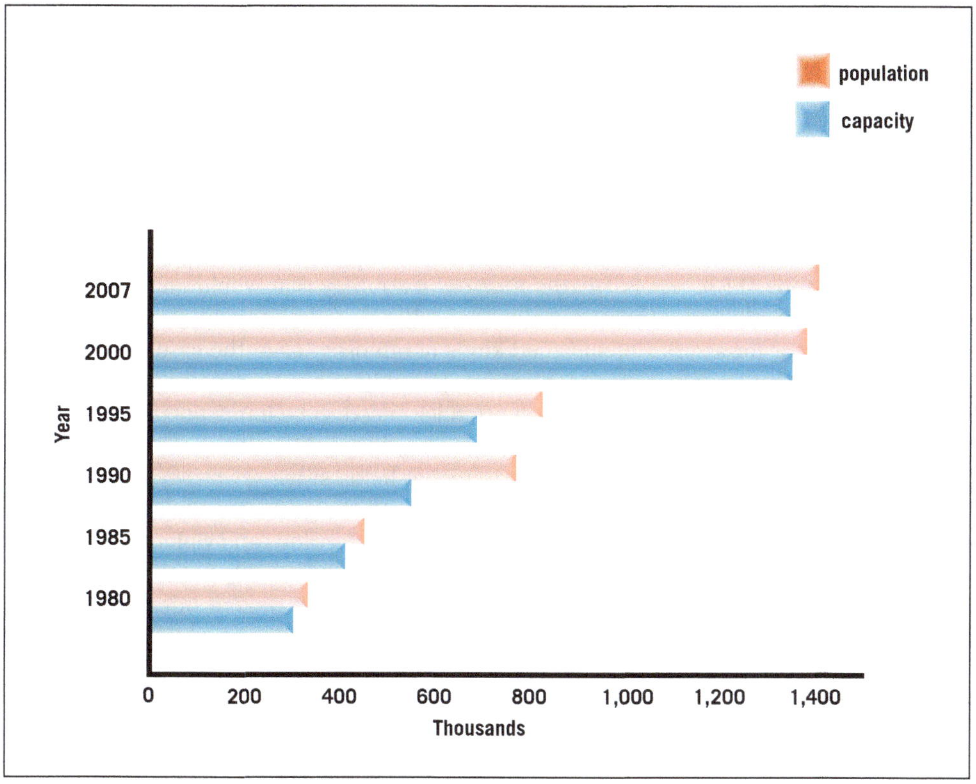

FIGURE 2
State Prison Populations, Inmates versus Capacity, 1980–2007.
Source: Bureau of Justice Statistics, *Correctional Populations in the United States* (Washington, DC: BJS, various years).

Today, with an unprecedented number of people behind bars, we are no safer than before. We are, however, much less free.

—American Civil Liberties Union website

federal system: The crowding rate in federal prisons (which are not included in Figure 2) recently stood at 34% over capacity, while crowding at federal medium-security prisons stood at 62%.[41] Prison overcrowding can be measured along a number of dimensions:

- Space available per inmate (such as square feet of floor space)
- Length of confinement of inmates in cells or housing units (versus time spent on recreation and other activities)
- Living arrangements (for example, single versus double bunks)
- Type of housing (use of segregation facilities, tents, and so on in place of general housing)

prison capacity
The size of the correctional population an institution can effectively hold.[v] There are three types of prison capacity: rated, operational, and design.

rated capacity
The number of inmates a prison can handle according to the judgment of experts.

operational capacity
The number of inmates a prison can effectively accommodate based on management considerations.

design capacity
The number of inmates a prison was intended to hold when it was built or modified.

Further complicating the picture is the fact that prison officials have developed three definitions of **prison capacity** (the size of a prison population that a facility can hold)[42]:

1. **Rated capacity** refers to the size of the inmate population that a facility can handle according to the judgment of experts.
2. **Operational capacity** is the number of inmates that a facility can effectively accommodate based on an appraisal of the institution's staff, programs, and services.
3. **Design capacity** refers to the inmate population that the institution was originally built to handle.

Rated capacity estimates usually yield the largest inmate capacities, while design capacity (on which observations in this chapter are based) typically shows the highest amount of overcrowding.

Overcrowding by itself is not cruel and unusual punishment, according to the U.S. Supreme Court in *Rhodes* v. *Chapman* (1981),[43] which considered the issue of double bunking along with other alleged forms of "deprivation" at the Southern Ohio Correctional Facility. The Court, reasoning that overcrowding is not necessarily dangerous if other prison services are adequate, held that prison housing conditions may be "restrictive and even harsh," for they are part of the penalty that offenders pay for their crimes.

However, overcrowding combined with other negative conditions may lead to a finding against the prison system. The American Correctional Association (ACA) believes that such a totality-of-conditions approach requires courts to assess the overall quality of prison life while viewing overcrowded conditions in combination with other issues:

- The meeting of basic human needs
- The adequacy of the facility's staff
- The program opportunities available to inmates
- The quality and strength of the prison management

Selective Incapacitation: A Strategy to Reduce Prison Populations

Some authors have identified the central issue of imprisonment as one of selective versus collective incapacitation.[44] *Collective incapacitation*, a strategy that would imprison almost all serious offenders, is still found today in states that rely on predetermined, or fixed, sentences for given offenses or for a series of specified kinds of offenses (as in the case of three-strikes legislation). Collective incapacitation is, however, prohibitively expensive as well as unnecessary, in the opinion of many experts. Not all offenders need to be imprisoned because not all represent a continuing threat to society, but those who do are difficult to identify.[45]

In most jurisdictions where the just deserts model holds sway, *selective incapacitation*, which seeks to identify the most dangerous criminals with the goal of removing them from society, has become the rule. Repeat offenders with records of serious and violent crimes are the most likely candidates for incapacitation—as are those who will probably commit violent crimes in the future, even though they have no records. But potentially violent offenders cannot be readily identified, and those thought likely to commit crimes cannot be sentenced to lengthy prison terms for things they have not yet done.

We are the prisoners of the prisoners we have taken.

—J. Clegg

In support of selective incapacitation, many states have enacted career offender statutes that attempt to identify potentially dangerous offenders out of known criminal populations. Selective incapacitation efforts, however, have been criticized for yielding a rate of "false positives" of over 60%,[46] and some authors have called selective incapacitation a "strategy of failure."[47] Nevertheless, in an analysis of recidivism studies, Canadians Paul Gendreau, Tracy Little, and Claire Goggin found that criminal history, a history of preadult antisocial behavior, and "criminogenic needs"—which were defined as measurable antisocial thoughts, values, and behaviors—were all dependable predictors of recidivism.[48]

Some state programs designed to reduce prison overcrowding, however, have run afoul of selective incarceration principles. In 1997, for example, the U.S. Supreme Court ordered Florida to release as many as 2,500 inmates—many of whom had been convicted of violent crimes—under a "gain time" program set up by the state in 1983.[49] Provisions of the program allowed inmates to earn as much as two months off their sentences for every month served. Although the program was originally intended to relieve overcrowding, a change in public sentiment led Florida Attorney General Bob Butterworth to revoke gain time that had already been earned. In ordering the inmates' release, however, the U.S. Supreme Court unanimously ruled that Florida had violated constitutional guarantees against using laws ***ex post facto*** (Latin for "after the fact") and required officials to be bound by the program's original conditions. The release of hundreds of murderers, rapists, robbers, and other felons caused a statewide uproar and media furor.

ex post facto
Latin for "after the fact." The Constitution prohibits the enactment of *ex post facto* laws, which make acts committed before the laws in question were passed punishable as crimes.

Recently, the just deserts philosophy has run headlong into funding realities caused by economic contraction and state budget shortfalls. As a consequence, a number of jurisdictions have begun releasing nonviolent offenders sentenced to short terms of confinement in record numbers, hoping to save the money needed to keep more hard-core offenders behind bars. Los Angeles County jail officials, for example, report releasing around 600 minor offenders each day (47,000 per year) before their sentences have been served in a money-saving effort. Los Angeles County Sheriff Lee Baca says he had hoped the practice would be short term but now sees no end in sight. "For misdemeanor offenders our system has come to a grinding halt," says the sheriff. "With thousands being freed after having paid less than 10 percent of their sentence, there simply is no sense of deterrence whatever. This is no way to run a criminal-justice system."[50] Sharp drops in tax income and resulting budget cuts have seriously impacted prisons and jails across the nation. Budget cuts in California over the past three years, for example, have totaled close to $200 million—equal to about 12 percent of the sheriff's department budget.

In 2008, California Governor Arnold Schwarzenegger released his planned state budget, which called for deep cuts in many state services to address an $18 billion tax shortfall. The plan included the release of "low-risk" California state inmates with less than 20 months remaining on their sentences. Only prisoners serving sentences for nonviolent, non–sex offender types of crimes are eligible for early release. Officials said that the number of inmates released under the cost-savings measure is expected to total around 22,000.[51]

Security Levels

Maximum-custody prisons tend to be massive old buildings with large inmate populations. However, some—like Central Prison in Raleigh, North Carolina—are much newer and incorporate advances in prison architecture to provide tight security without sacrificing building aesthetics. Such institutions provide a high level of security characterized by high fences, thick walls, secure cells, gun towers, and armed prison guards. Maximum-custody prisons tend to locate cells and other inmate living facilities at the center of the institution and place a variety of barriers between the living area and the institution's outer perimeter. Technological innovations, such as electric perimeters, laser motion detectors, electronic and pneumatic locking systems, metal detectors, X-ray machines, television surveillance, radio communications, and computer information systems, are frequently used today to reinforce the more traditional maximum-security strategies. These technologies have helped to lower the cost of new prison construction. However, some people argue that prisons may rely too heavily on electronic detection devices that have not yet been adequately tested.[52] Death-row inmates are all maximum-security prisoners, although the level of security on death row exceeds even that experienced by most prisoners held in maximum custody. Prisoners on death row must spend much of the day in single cells and are often permitted a brief shower only once a week under close supervision.

Incarceration is a crash course in extortion and criminal behavior.
—*Vincent Schiraldi*
Executive Director, Justice Policy Institute

Most states today have one large, centrally located maximum-security institution. Some of these prisons combine more than one custody level and may be both maximum- and medium-security facilities. Medium security is a custody level that in many ways resembles maximum

CJ News

New Way to Cut Budget: Release Prisoners

Lawmakers from California to Kentucky are trying to save money with a drastic and potentially dangerous budget-cutting proposal: releasing tens of thousands of convicts from prison, including drug addicts, thieves and even violent criminals.

Officials acknowledge that the idea carries risks, but they say they have no choice because of huge budget gaps brought on by the slumping economy.

"If we don't find a way to better manage the population at the state prison, we will be forced to spend money to expand the state's prison system—money we don't have," said Jeff Neal, a spokesman for Rhode Island Gov. Don Carcieri.

At least eight states are considering freeing inmates or sending some convicts to rehabilitation programs instead of prison, according to an Associated Press analysis of legislative proposals. If adopted, the early release programs could save an estimated $450 million in California and Kentucky alone.

A Rhode Island proposal would allow inmates to deduct up to 12 days from their sentence for every month they follow rules and work in prison. Even some violent offenders would be eligible but not those serving life sentences.

A plan in Mississippi would offer early parole for people convicted of selling marijuana or prescription drugs. New Jersey, South Carolina and Vermont are considering funneling drug-addicted inmates into treatment, which is cheaper than prison.

▲ Police officer Tori-Lynn Heaton at her home in West Greenwich, R.I., in 2008. Lawmakers across the country are debating plans to grant early release to criminals as a way for cash-strapped states to try to close budget gaps. Heaton, whose ex-husband previously spent time in prison for beating her but who would have been eligible for early release under Rhode Island's current proposal, opposes early-release programs in order to protect the safety of crime victims.
Steven Senne/AP Wide World Photos

The prospect of financial savings offers little comfort to Tori-Lynn Heaton, a police officer in a suburb of Providence whose ex-husband went to prison for beating her. He has already finished his prison term but would have been eligible for early release under the current proposal.

"You're talking about victim safety. You're talking about community member safety," she said. "You can't balance the budget on the backs of victims of crimes."

But prisons "are one of the most expensive parts of the criminal-justice system," said Alison Lawrence, who studies corrections policy for the National Conference of State Legislatures. "That's where they look to first to cut down some of those costs."

Rhode Island Corrections Director A.T. Wall was not sure how many prisoners could be freed early. The payoff for doing so may be relatively small: less than $1 million for the first fiscal year, although that figure would increase over time.

In California, where lawmakers have taken steps to cut a $16 billion budget deficit in half by summer, Gov. Arnold Schwarzenegger proposed saving $400 million by releasing more than 22,000 inmates who had less than 20 months remaining on their sentences. Violent and sex offenders would not be eligible.

Laying off prison guards and making it more difficult to send parole violators back to state prison would account for part of the savings.

Law enforcement officials and Republican lawmakers immediately criticized Schwarzenegger's proposal, which would apply to car thieves, forgers, drunken drivers and some drug dealers. Some would never serve prison time because the standard sentence for those crimes is 20 months or less.

"To open the prison door and release prisoners back into communities is merely placing a state burden onto local governments and will ultimately jeopardize safety in communities," said Fresno Police Chief Jerry Dyer, who could see 1,800 inmates released in his area.

In Kentucky, which faces a $1.3 billion deficit, lawmakers approved legislation Wednesday to grant early release to some prisoners. Initial estimates were that the plan could affect as many as 2,000 inmates and save nearly $50 million.

If the governor signs the bill, the exact number of prisoners would be determined by prison officials. Violent convicts and sexual offenders would be exempt.

Gov. Steve Beshear has said Kentucky must review its policies after the state's inmate population jumped 12 percent last year—the largest increase in the nation.

Kentucky spends more than $18,600 to house one inmate for a year, or roughly $51 a day. In California, each inmate costs an average of $46,104 to incarcerate.

The prison budget in Mississippi has nearly tripled since stricter sentencing laws took effect in 1994.

To curb spending, lawmakers have offered a bill to make about 7,000 drug offenders in prison eligible for parole. A second proposal would allow the parole board to release inmates convicted of selling marijuana and prescription drugs after serving just a quarter of their sentences. Currently, they must serve 85 percent of their terms before release.

Michigan is trying to speed up the parole process for about 3,500 inmates who were convicted of nonviolent, nonsexual offenses, or who are seriously ill.

Barbara Sampson, chairwoman of the Michigan Parole Board, said early release often makes sense, especially for low-risk offenders who get help rebuilding their lives.

"Getting that prisoner back to the community so that he can stay connected to his family, getting him back into the work force . . . that's a positive thing," she said.

But not everyone is sold on the idea.

"Economics cannot be the engine that drives the train of public safety," said Terrence Jungel, executive director of the Michigan Sheriffs' Association. "Government has no greater responsibility than the protection of its citizens."

For the latest in crime and justice news, visit the Talk Justice news feed at http://www.crimenews.info.

Source: Associated Press, "New Way to Cut Budget: Release Prisoners," April 3, 2008.

security; medium-security prisoners, however, are generally permitted more freedom to associate with one another and can go to the prison yard, exercise room, library, and shower and bathroom facilities under less intense supervision than their maximum-security counterparts. An important security tool in medium-security prisons is the count, which is literally a head count of inmates taken at regular intervals. Counts may be taken four times a day and usually require inmates to report to designated areas to be counted. Until the count has been "cleared," all other inmate activity must cease. Medium-security prisons tend to be smaller than maximum-security institutions and often have barbed-wire-topped chain-link fences instead of the more secure stone or concrete block walls found in many of the older maximum-security facilities. Cells and living quarters tend to have more windows and are often located closer to the perimeter of the institution than is the case in maximum-security facilities. Dormitory-style housing, where prisoners live together in ward-like arrangements, may be employed in medium-security facilities, and there are generally more opportunities for inmates to participate in recreational and other prison programs than in maximum-custody facilities.

In minimum-security institutions, inmates are generally housed in dormitory-like settings and are free to walk the yard and to visit most of the prison facilities. Some newer prisons provide minimum-security inmates with private rooms, which they can decorate (within limits) according to their tastes. Inmates usually have free access to a canteen that sells items such as cigarettes, toothpaste, and candy bars. Minimum-security inmates often wear uniforms of a different color from those of inmates in higher custody levels, and in some institutions they may wear civilian clothes. They work under only general supervision and usually have access to recreational, educational, and skills-training programs on the prison grounds. Guards are unarmed, gun towers do not exist, and fences (if they are present at all) are usually low and sometimes even unlocked. Many minimum-security prisoners participate in some sort of work- or study-release program, and some have extensive visitation and furlough privileges. Counts may be taken, although most minimum-security institutions keep track of inmates through daily administrative work schedules. The primary "force" holding inmates in minimum-security institutions is their own restraint. Inmates live with the knowledge that minimum-security institutions are one step removed from close correctional supervision; if they fail to meet the expectations of administrators, they will be transferred into more secure institutions, which will probably delay their release. Inmates returning from assignments in the community may be frisked for contraband, but body-cavity searches are rare in minimum custody, being reserved primarily for inmates suspected of smuggling.

The typical American prison today is medium or minimum custody. Some states have as many as 80 or 90 small institutions, which may originally have been located in every county to serve the needs of public works and highway maintenance. Medium- and minimum-security institutions house the bulk of the country's prison population and offer a number of programs and services designed to assist with the rehabilitation of offenders and to create the conditions necessary for a successful reentry of the inmates into society. Most prisons offer psychiatric services, academic education, vocational education, substance abuse treatment, health care, counseling, recreation, library services, religious programs, and industrial and agricultural

▲ Inmates flashing gang signs for the camera. If you were a warden, what changes might you make to improve the management of a prison like this one?
Damian Dovarganes/AP Wide World Photos

Web EXTRA

training.[53] To learn more about all aspects of contemporary prisons, visit the Corrections Connection via Web Extra 11–1 at mycrimekit.com.

Prison Classification Systems

classification system
A system used by prison administrators to assign inmates to custody levels based on offense history, assessed dangerousness, perceived risk of escape, and other factors.

Most states use a **classification system** to assign new prisoners to initial custody levels based on their type of offense, perceived dangerousness, and escape risk. A prisoner might be assigned to a minimum-, medium-, or maximum-custody institution. Inmates move through custody levels according to the progress they are judged to have made in self-control and demonstrated responsibility. Serious violent criminals who begin their prison careers with lengthy sentences in maximum custody have the opportunity in most states to work their way up to minimum security, although the process usually takes a number of years. Those prisoners who represent continual disciplinary problems are returned to closer custody levels. Minimum-security prisons, as a result, house inmates convicted of all types of criminal offenses.

Once an inmate has been assigned to a custody level, he or she may be reassessed for living and work assignments within the institution. Just as initial (or external) custody classification systems determine security levels, internal classification systems are designed to help determine appropriate housing plans and program interventions within a particular facility for inmates who share a common custody level. In short, initial classification determines the institution in which an inmate is placed, and internal classification determines placement and program assignment within that institution.[54] Learn more about internal prison classification systems at Library Extra 11–3 at mycrimekit.com.

Library EXTRA

Objective prison classification systems were adopted by many states in the 1980s, but it wasn't until the late 1990s that such systems were refined and validated. Fueled by litigation and overcrowding, classification systems are now viewed as the principal management tool for allocating scarce prison resources efficiently and for minimizing the potential for violence or escape. Classification systems are also expected to provide greater accountability and to forecast future prison bed-space needs. A properly functioning classification system is the "brain" of prison management, governing and influencing many important decisions, including such fiscal matters as staffing levels, bed space, and programming.[55]

One of the best-known internal classification systems in use today is the adult internal management system (AIMS). AIMS was developed more than 20 years ago to reduce institutional predatory behavior by identifying potential predators and separating them from vulnerable inmates. AIMS assesses an inmate's predatory potential by quantifying aspects of his or her (1) record of misconduct, (2) ability to follow staff directions, and (3) level of aggression toward other inmates.

Before concluding this discussion of classification, it is important to recognize that the criteria used to classify prisoners must be relevant to the legitimate security needs of the institution. In 2005, for example, the U.S. Supreme Court, in the case of *Johnson* v. *California*,[56] invalidated the California Department of Corrections and Rehabilitation's (CDCR) unwritten policy of racially segregating prisoners in double cells for up to 60 days each time they entered a new correctional facility. The policy had been based on a claim that it prevented violence caused by racial gangs. The Court, however, held that the California policy was "immediately suspect" as an "express racial classification" and found that the CDCR was unable to demonstrate that the practice served a compelling state interest.

We spend $60,000 building a prison cell, another $35,000 a year to keep that inmate. They have central heating and air conditioning. At the same time we spend less than $4,000 on each school student. And many of them don't have air-conditioned or centrally heated schools. Let's put the money in education. That's the only answer to crime.

—*Cleo Fields*
Louisiana Congressman

The Federal Prison System

The federal prison system consists of 103 institutions, six regional offices, the Central Office (headquarters), two staff-training centers, and 28 community corrections offices. The regional offices and the Central Office provide administrative oversight and support to the institutions and to the community corrections offices, which oversee community corrections centers and home-confinement programs. The federal correctional workforce is one of the fastest growing in the country, and at mid-2008, the BOP employed 35,880 persons.[57]

The BOP classifies its institutions according to five security levels: (1) administrative maximum (**ADMAX**), (2) high security, (3) medium security, (4) low security, and (5) minimum security. High-security facilities are called *U.S. penitentiaries* (USPs), medium- and low-security institutions are both called *federal correctional institutions* (FCIs), and minimum-security prisons are termed *federal prison camps* (FPCs).[58] Minimum-security facilities (like Eglin Air Force Base in Florida and Maxwell Air Force Base in Alabama) are essentially honor-type camps with barracks-type housing and no fencing. Low-security facilities in the federal prison system are surrounded by double chain-link fencing and employ vehicle patrols around their perimeters to enhance security. Medium-security facilities (like those in Terminal Island, California; Lompoc, California; and Seagoville, Texas) make use of similar fencing and patrols but supplement

ADMAX
An acronym for administrative maximum. This term is used by the federal government to denote ultra-high-security prisons.

The Federal Bureau of Prisons ADMAX facility in Florence, Colorado, which opened in 1995. It is the only ultra-high-security institution in the federal system. What kinds of inmates are sent there?
Bob Daemmrich/Agence France Presse/Getty Images

With the huge expansion of prisons starting in the 1980s, most prison systems gave up believing they had any responsibility for changing offenders or [for] what happened after offenders were released. The objective became that prisons should be just for punishment, and politicians competed to see who could make prisons more unpleasant.

—Todd Clear
John Jay College of Criminal Justice

them with electronic monitoring of the grounds and perimeter areas. High-security facilities (USPs like those in Atlanta, Georgia; Lewisburg, Pennsylvania; Terre Haute, Indiana; and Leavenworth, Kansas) are architecturally designed to prevent escapes and to contain disturbances, and they also make use of armed patrols and intense electronic surveillance.

A separate federal prison category is that of administrative facilities, consisting of institutions with special missions that are designed to house all types of inmates. Most administrative facilities are metropolitan detention centers (MDCs). MDCs, which are generally located in large cities close to federal courthouses, are the jails of the federal correctional system and hold defendants awaiting trial in federal court. Another five administrative facilities, medical centers for federal prisoners (MCFPs), function as hospitals.

Federal correctional facilities exist either as single institutions or as federal correctional complexes, that is, sites consisting of more than one type of correctional institution (Figure 3). The federal correctional complex at Allenwood, Pennsylvania, for example, consists of a U.S. penitentiary, a federal prison camp, and two federal correctional institutions (one low and one medium security), each with its own warden. Federal institutions can be classified by type as follows: 55 are FPCs (holding 35% of all federal prisoners), 17 are low-security facilities (28%), 26 are medium-security facilities (23%), eight are high-security prisons (13%), and one is an ADMAX facility (1%).

The federal system's only ADMAX unit, the $60 million ultra-high-security prison at Florence, Colorado, is a relatively recent addition to the federal system. Dubbed "the Alcatraz of the Rockies," the 575-bed facility was designed to be the most secure prison ever built by the government.[59] Opened in 1995, it holds mob bosses, spies, terrorists, murderers, and escape artists. Dangerous inmates are confined to their cells 23 hours per day and are not allowed to see or associate with other inmates. Electronically controlled doors throughout the institution channel inmates to individual exercise sessions, and educational courses, religious services, and administrative matters are conducted via closed-circuit television piped directly into the prisoners' cells. Remote-controlled heavy steel doors within the prison allow corrections staff to section off the institution in the event of rioting, and the system can be controlled from outside if the entire prison is compromised.

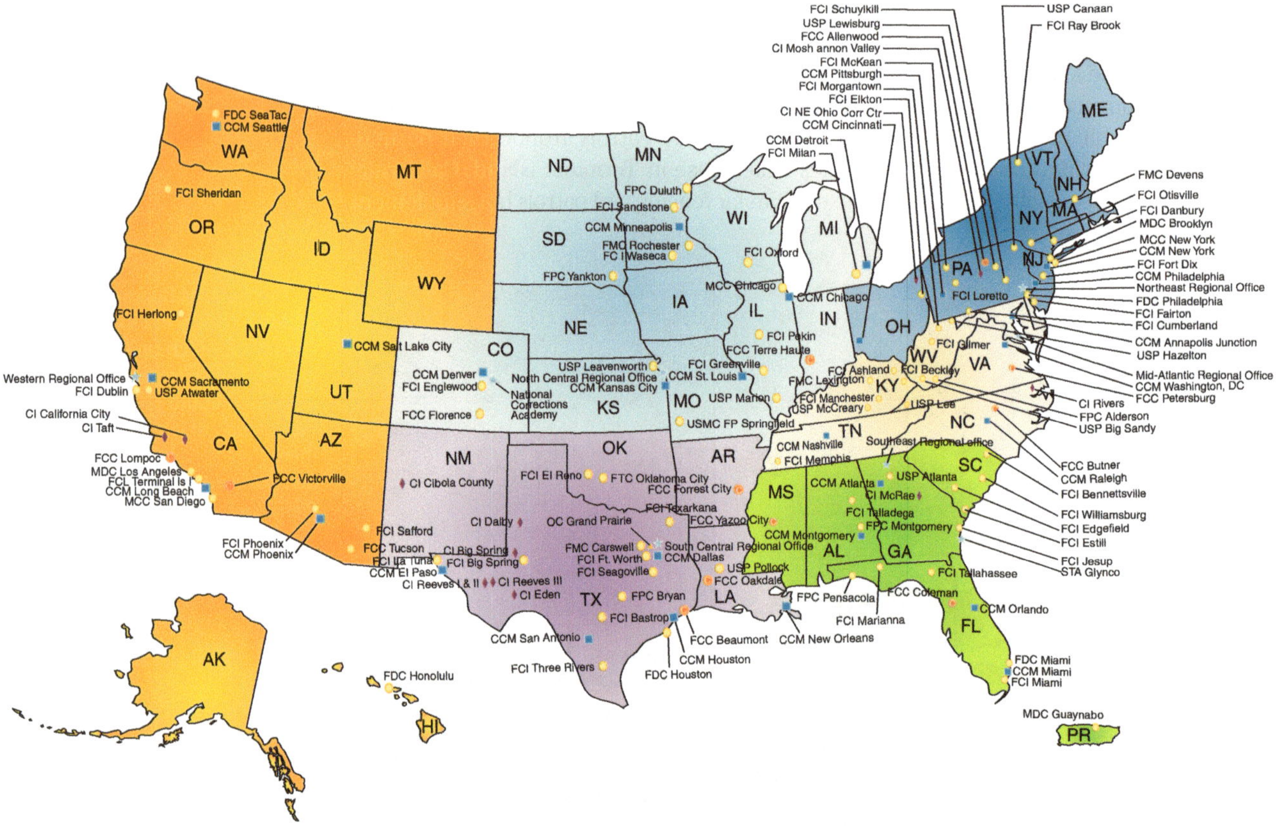

FIGURE 3
Federal Bureau of Prisons Facilities by Region, 2009.
Source: Federal Bureau of Prisons.

In an effort to combat rising expenses associated with a rapidly growing federal prison population, the U.S. Congress passed legislation in 1992 that imposes a "user fee" on federal inmates who are able to pay the costs associated with their incarceration.[60] Under the law, inmates may be assessed a dollar amount up to the cost of a year's incarceration—currently around $22,600.[61] The statute, which was designed so as not to impose hardships on poor offenders or their dependents, directs that collected funds (estimated to total $48 million per year) are to be used to improve alcohol- and drug-abuse programs within federal prisons. To learn more about the BOP, visit Web Extra 11–2 and read Library Extras 11–4 and 11–5 mycrimekit.com.

Web EXTRA

Library EXTRA

Recent Improvements

In the midst of frequent lawsuits, court-ordered changes in prison administration, and overcrowded conditions, outstanding prison facilities are being recognized through the ACA accreditation program. The ACA Commission on Accreditation has developed a set of standards that correctional institutions can use for conducting self-evaluations. Institutions that meet the standards can apply for accreditation under the program.

Another avenue toward improvement of the nation's prisons can be found in the National Academy of Corrections, the training arm of the National Institute of Corrections. The academy, located in Boulder, Colorado, offers seminars, videoconferencing, and training sessions for state and local corrections managers, trainers, personnel directors, sheriffs, and state legislators.[62] Issues covered include strategies to control overcrowding, community corrections program management, prison programs, gangs and disturbances, security, and public and media relations.[63]

Jails

Jails are locally operated short-term confinement facilities originally built to hold suspects following arrest and pending trial. Today's jails also serve other purposes[64]:

jail
A confinement facility administered by an agency of local government, typically a law enforcement agency, intended for adults but sometimes also containing juveniles, which holds people detained pending adjudication or committed after adjudication, usually those sentenced to a year or less.

- Receiving individuals pending their arraignment, and holding them for their trial, conviction, or sentencing
- Readmitting probation, parole, and bail-bond violators and absconders
- Detaining juveniles, the mentally ill, and others temporarily, pending their transfer to appropriate facilities
- Holding individuals for the military, for protective custody, for contempt of court, and for the courts as witnesses
- Releasing convicted inmates to the community upon completion of their sentences
- Transferring inmates to federal, state, or other authorities
- Housing inmates for federal, state, or other authorities because of overcrowding in their facilities
- Operating community-based programs with day reporting, home detention, electronic monitoring, or other types of supervision
- Holding inmates sentenced to short terms (generally under one year)

A 2008 report by the BJS found that the nation's jails held 780,581 inmates, 13% of whom were women.[65] Juveniles held in local jails numbered 6,837. About 62% of jail inmates are pretrial detainees or are defendants involved in some stage of the trial process. Jail authorities also supervised an additional 68,245 men and women in the community under programs that included the following: electronic monitoring (13,121), home detention without electronic monitoring (512), day reporting (6,163), community service (15,327), and weekender programs (10,473).[66]

A total of 3,360 jails operate throughout the United States today, staffed by approximately 207,600 jail employees—the equivalent of about one employee for every three jail inmates.[67] Overall, the nation's jail budget is huge, and facilities are overflowing. State and local governments spend $10 billion every year to operate the nation's jails,[68] with more than $1 billion in additional monies earmarked for new jail construction and for renovation; on average, the housing of one jail inmate costs more than $14,500.[69]

Approximately 20 million people are admitted (or readmitted) to the nation's jails each year. Some jail inmates stay for as little as one day, while others serve extended periods of time.

CJ Careers

Federal Bureau of Prisons (BOP)

PERSONAL PROFILE

Name: Don Drennon Gala, Ph.D.
Position: Correctional Treatment Specialist (Senior Case Manager)/ Federal Officer (Retired)
City: Atlanta, Georgia
Colleges Attended: University of Rochester, University of Central Oklahoma, Rochester Institute of Technology, Monroe Community College
Year Hired: 1983

"The more education I attained, the more open I became to other positions within the law enforcement field. The field of law enforcement is continually evolving as a profession. This is true in federal corrections as well. Today, many federal correctional officers have at least a bachelor's degree and many hold a master's degree. The professionalism of BOP staff is viewed as improving on a daily basis, with all professional personnel holding college or university degrees. Through Unit Management, of which I am a part, a team of professionals provide services that have an impact on inmates' lives following release and on the general public. This work is anything but boring; it demands professionalism and constant attention."

TYPICAL POSITIONS

The basic goals of the BOP include "protecting public safety by ensuring that federal offenders serve their sentences of imprisonment in facilities that are safe, humane, cost-efficient, and appropriately secure."[1] Case managers engage in multiple tasks within and outside the institution. They perform correctional casework and interview inmates for multiple agency needs, such as detecting violations of regulations or law and determining inmate needs in terms of safety and possible central inmate monitoring assignments. They prepare reports for the special investigative agent, addressing violations of regulations, laws, and possible gang activity. They also develop, evaluate, and analyze program needs and other data about inmates (assessment of inmate needs); evaluate progress of individual offenders in the institution; prepare progress reports periodically for transfers, special programs, or release; coordinate and integrate inmate training programs; develop social histories and then prepare written reports; evaluate positive and negative aspects in each case as part of the assessment process; advise new inmates about various available programs; conduct program reviews; conduct individual and group counseling of inmates about their previous lifestyle and problem-solving skills; provide case reports to the U.S. Parole Commission and U.S. Probation; work with inmates, their families, and interested persons in developing parole and release plans; work with the U.S. Probation Office and other agencies in developing and implementing release plans or programs for inmates; coordinate and set up release of inmates to halfway houses, supervised release through U.S. Probation, and any other court-ordered action to be taken; and enforce criminal statutes and judicial sanctions, including investigative, arrest, and detention authority. A case manager also screens new inmates, prepares written reports of information obtained, and conducts physical and electronic surveillance of inmates and visitors utilizing a variety of audio, video, and photographic equipment within a correctional setting

EMPLOYMENT REQUIREMENTS

General employment requirements include (1) an age between 23 and 37; (2) excellent physical health; (3) good vision, 20/20 corrected; (4) good hearing; (5) U.S. citizenship; (6) valid driver's license; (7) successful completion of a comprehensive field background investigation; (8) passing a urinalysis; (9) formal interview; and (10) successful completion of the academy at the Federal Law Enforcement Training Center at Glynco, Georgia.

OTHER REQUIREMENTS

Positions as a psychologist and attorney require the appropriate professional degrees and licenses. The case manager position requires a bachelor's degree from an accredited college or university, including 24 semester hours in the social sciences. Entry-level positions in information technology require a bachelor's degree in computer science or a closely related field. The BOP values education and emphasizes college or university degrees when hiring personnel for most positions above the entry-level correctional officer positions.

SALARY

Correctional officers enter the BOP at the GS-5 or GS-6 level with a bachelor's degree or one year of pertinent experience. Case managers' entry level is at GS-9, and after successfully completing one year in this position, they are eligible to be promoted to GS-11. Throughout one's career, a person can possibly advance to GS-12 as a first-line supervisor and to GS-14 as a middle manager. Positions are available at the GS-15 level and senior executive service.

BENEFITS

Benefits include (1) 13 days of sick leave per fiscal year, (2) two and one-half to five weeks of paid vacation each fiscal year based on time in service, (3) ten paid federal holidays, (4) federal health and life insurance, and (5) participation in the Federal Employees' Retirement System.

DIRECT INQUIRIES TO:

Human Resource Management Division—Staffing
U.S. Department of Justice
Federal Bureau of Prisons
320 First Street, N.W.
Room 700
Washington, DC 20534
(202) 307-3177 or (972) 352-4200
Website: http://www.bop.gov, or visit http://www.usajobs.gov

[1]Retrieved from http://www.bop.gov/about/index.jsp.

Note: The views expressed in this profile do not necessarily represent the views of the U.S. Department of Justice, the Federal Bureau of Prisons, or the United States.

Significantly, one of the fastest-growing sectors of today's jail population consists of sentenced offenders serving time in local jails because overcrowded prisons cannot accept them.

Most people processed through the country's jails are members of minority groups (61%), with 40.1% of jail inmates classifying themselves as African-American, 18.5% as Hispanic, and 2.4% as other minorities; 3% report being of more than one race, and 36% of jail inmates classify themselves as Caucasian.[70] Slightly more than 88% are male, and 7.8% are noncitizens.[71] The typical jail inmate is an unmarried African-American male between 25 and 34 years of age who reports having had some high school education. Typical charges include drug trafficking (12.1%), assault (11.7%), drug possession (10.8%), and larceny (7%).[72]

According to the BJS, about 6% of jail facilities house more than half of all jail inmates in the nation.[73] So although most jails are small—many were built to house 50 or fewer inmates—most people who spend time in jail do so in larger institutions. Across the country, a handful of "megajails" house thousands of inmates each, with the largest such facilities in Los Angeles; New York City; Cook County, Illinois; Harris County, Texas; and Maricopa County, Arizona. Los Angeles County's 4,000-bed Twin Towers Correctional Facility cost $373 million to build and opened in 1997.[74] The largest employer among these huge jails is Cook County Jail, with more than 1,200 personnel on its payroll.[75] In 2007, four states—California, Florida, Georgia, and Texas—incarcerated more than a third of the nation's total jail inmates.[76] The two jurisdictions with the most jail inmates, Los Angeles County and New York City, together held approximately 33,300 inmates, or 5% of the national total. More jail statistics are available via Library Extra 11–6 at mycrimekit.com.

Library EXTRA

Women and Jail

Although women comprise only 13% of the country's jail population, they are the largest growth group in jails nationwide.[77] Jailed women face a number of special problems. Only 25.7% of the nation's jails report having a classification system specifically designed to evaluate female inmates,[78] and although many jurisdictions have plans "to build facilities geared to the female offender,"[79] not all jurisdictions today even provide separate housing areas for women. Educational levels are very low among jailed women, with fewer than half being high school graduates.[80] Drug abuse is another significant source of difficulty for jailed women: Over 30%

▲ Los Angeles County's Men's Central Jail. The $373 million jail, officially known as the Twin Towers Correctional Facility, opened in 1997 and is one of the world's largest jails. What are the differences between a prison and a jail?
A. Ramey/PhotoEdit Inc.

The first two decades of the [twenty-first] century, at least, will see a major growth in prison populations. We have an opportunity now to start doing a better job of handling the responsibilities of the criminal justice system as well as of society. I hope we take both more seriously in the future than we do currently.

—Dr. Alfred Blumstein
Dean of the School of Urban and Public Affairs, Carnegie-Mellon University

of women who are admitted to jail have a substance abuse problem at the time of admission, and in some parts of the country, that figure may be as high as 70%.[81]

Pregnancy is another problem. Nationally, 4% of female inmates are pregnant when they enter jail,[82] but in urban areas, as many as 10% of the female jail population are reported to be pregnant on any given day.[83] As a consequence, a few hundred children are born in jails each year; however, substantive medical programs for female inmates, such as obstetrics and gynecological care, are often lacking. Regarding future medical services for female inmates, some writers have advised jail administrators to expect to see an increasingly common kind of inmate: "an opiate-addicted female who is pregnant with no prior prenatal care having one or more sexually transmitted diseases, and fitting a high-risk category for AIDS (prostitution, IV drug use)."[84]

Not only are jailed mothers separated from their children, but they may have to pay for their support. About 12% of all jails in one study reported requiring employed female inmates to contribute to the support of their dependent children.

When we consider women and jails, female inmates are only half the story, and women who work in corrections are the other half. In one study, Linda Zupan, a member of a new generation of outstanding jail scholars, found that women made up 22% of the correctional officer force in jails across the nation.[85] The deployment of female personnel, however, was disproportionately skewed toward jobs in the lower ranks: Although 60% of all support staff (secretaries, cooks, and janitors) were women, only one in every ten chief administrators was female. Zupan explains this pattern by pointing to the "token status" of female staff members in some of the nation's jails.[86] Even so, Zupan did find that female corrections employees were significantly committed to their careers and that the attitudes of male workers toward female coworkers in jails were generally positive. Zupan's study uncovered 626 jails in which over 50% of the correctional officer force consisted of women, but on the opposite side of the coin, 954 of the nation's 3,316 jails operating at the time of the study had no female officers.[87] Zupan noted that "an obvious problem associated with the lack of female officers in jails housing females concerns the potential for abuse and exploitation of women inmates by male staff."[88]

Jails that do hire women generally accord them equal footing with male staffers. Although cross-gender privacy is a potential area of legal liability, few jails limit the supervisory areas that female officers working in male facilities may visit. In three-quarters of the jails studied by Zupan, female officers were assigned to supervise male housing areas, and only one in four jails that employed women restricted their access to unscreened shower and toilet facilities used by men or to other areas, such as sexual offender units.

The Growth of Jails

Jails have been called the "shame of the criminal justice system." Many are old, poorly funded, scantily staffed by underpaid and poorly trained employees, and given low priority in local budgets. By the end of the 1980s, many of our nation's jails had become seriously overcrowded, and court-ordered caps were sometimes placed on jail populations. One of the first such caps was imposed on the Harris County Jail in Houston (Texas) in 1990. In that year, the jail was forced to release 250 inmates after missing a deadline for reducing its resident population of 6,100 people.[89] A nationwide survey by the BJS, undertaken around the same time, found that 46% of all jails had been built more than 25 years earlier, and of that percentage, over half were more than 50 years old.[90]

A 1983 national census revealed that jails were operating at 85% of their rated capacity (Table 1).[91] In 1990, however, the nation's jails were running at 104% of capacity, and new jails

TABLE 1 Jail Facts

	1983	1988	1993	2000	2005	2007
Number of jails	3,338	3,316	3,304	3,365	3,360	3,365
Number of jail inmates	223,551	343,569	459,804	621,149	747,529	780,581
Rated capacity of jails	261,556	339,949	475,224	677,787	789,001	813,502
Percentage of capacity occupied	85%	101%	97%	92%	95%	96%

Source: William J. Sabol and Todd D. Minton, *Jail Inmates at Midyear 2007* (Washington, DC: Bureau of Justice Statistics, 2008).

could be found on drawing boards and under construction across the country. By 2005, jail capacity had increased substantially, and overall jail occupancy was reported at 95% of rated capacity. Some individual facilities, however, were still desperately overcrowded.[92]

Although jail overcrowding is not the issue it was a decade ago, it is still a problem. Overcrowded prisons have taken a toll on jails, with thousands of inmates being held in local jails because of overcrowding in state and federal prisons. Also, the practice of giving jail sentences to offenders who are unable or unwilling to make restitution, alimony, or child-support payments has added to jail occupancy and has made the local lockup at least partially a debtors' prison. Symptomatic of problems brought on by huge jail populations, the BJS reported 314 suicides in jails across the nation during a recent year.[93] Jail deaths from all causes total about 980 annually.

Other factors conspire to keep jail populations high[94]:

- Inability of jail inmates to make bond due to institutionalized bail-bond practices, and lack of funding sources for indigent defendants
- Unnecessary delays between arrest and final case disposition
- Unnecessarily limited access to vital information about defendants that could be useful in facilitating court-ordered pretrial release
- Limited ability of the criminal justice system to handle cases expeditiously due to a lack of needed resources (judges, assistant prosecuting attorneys, and so on)
- Inappropriate attorney delays in moving cases through court
- Unproductive statutes requiring that specified nonviolent offenders be jailed (including mandatory pretrial jailing of those caught driving while intoxicated, minor drug offenders, second-offense shoplifters, and so on)

Some innovative jurisdictions have successfully contained the growth of jail populations by diverting arrestees to community-based programs. San Diego, California, for example, uses a privately operated detoxification reception program to divert many inebriates from the "drunk tank."[95] Officials in Galveston County, Texas, routinely divert mentally ill arrestees directly to a mental health facility.[96] Other areas use pretrial services and magistrates' offices, which are open 24 hours a day, for setting bail, making release possible. Learn more about jail overcrowding by reading Library Extra 11–7 at mycrimekit.com.

Library EXTRA

Direct-Supervision Jails

Some suggest that the problems found in many jails stem from "mismanagement, lack of fiscal support, heterogeneous inmate populations, overuse and misuse of detention, overemphasis on custodial goals, and political and public apathy."[97] Others propose that environmental and

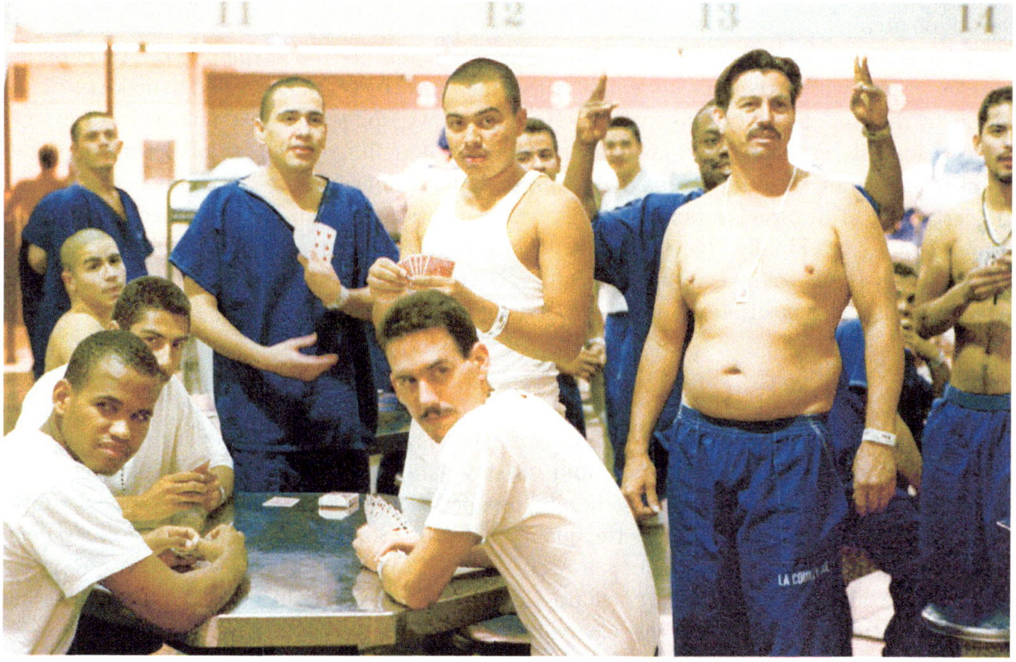

Inmates playing cards at the Los Angeles North County Correctional Facility in Saugus, California. The Los Angeles County jail system is the largest in the world, housing more than 20,000 inmates on a given day. What kinds of inmates do jails hold?
Damian Dovarganes/AP Wide World Photos

organizational aspects of traditional jail architecture and staffing have led to many difficulties.[98] Traditional jails, say these observers, were built on the assumption that inmates are inherently violent and potentially destructive and were constructed to give staff maximum control over inmates through the use of thick walls, bars, and other architectural barriers to the free movement of inmates. Such institutions, however, also limit the corrections staff's visibility and their access to confinement areas. As a consequence, they tend to encourage just the kinds of inmate behavior that jails were meant to control. Today, efficient hallway patrols and expensive video technology help in overcoming the limits that old jail architecture places on supervision.

direct-supervision jail
A temporary confinement facility that eliminates many of the traditional barriers between inmates and corrections staff. Physical barriers in direct-supervision jails are far less common than in traditional jails, allowing staff members the opportunity for greater interaction with, and control over, residents.

In an effort to solve many of the problems that dogged jails in the past, a new jail management strategy emerged during the 1970s. Called the **direct-supervision jail**, or *podular–direct supervision (PDS) jail*, this approach joined "podular/unit architecture with a participative, proactive management philosophy."[99] Often built in a system of pods, or modular self-contained housing areas linked to one another, direct-supervision jails helped eliminate the old physical barriers that separated staff and inmates. Gone were the bars and the isolated, secure observation areas for officers, and they were replaced by an open environment in which inmates and corrections personnel could mingle with relative freedom. In a number of such "new-generation" jails, large reinforced Plexiglas panels supplanted walls and served to separate activity areas, such as classrooms and dining halls, from one another. Soft furniture is the rule throughout such institutions, and individual rooms take the place of cells, allowing inmates at least a modicum of personal privacy. In today's direct-supervision jails, 16 to 46 inmates typically live in one pod, with corrections staffers present among the inmate population around the clock.

Direct-supervision jails have been touted for their tendency to reduce inmate dissatisfaction and for their ability to deter rape and violence among the inmate population. By eliminating architectural barriers to staff–inmate interaction, direct-supervision facilities are said to place officers back in control of institutions. A number of studies have demonstrated the success of such jails at reducing the likelihood of inmate victimization. One such study, published in 1994, also found that staff morale in direct-supervision jails was far higher than in traditional institutions, that inmates reported reduced stress levels, and that fewer inmate-on-inmate and inmate-on-staff assaults occurred.[100] Similarly, sexual assault, jail rape, suicide, and escape have all been found to occur far less frequently in direct-supervision facilities than in traditional institutions.[101] Significantly, new-generation jails appear to be substantially less susceptible to lawsuits brought by inmates and to adverse court-ordered judgments against jail administrators.

While the number of direct-supervision jails has grown rapidly, such facilities are not without their problems. In 1993, for example, the 238-bed Rensselaer County PDS jail in Troy, New York, experienced a disturbance that resulted in "a total loss of control," the removal of officers from the pods, and the escape of two inmates.[102] Somewhat later, the 700-bed San Joaquin County Jail in Stockton, California, experienced numerous problems, including the escape of seven inmates.

Some authors have recognized that new-generation jails are too frequently run by old-style managers and that corrections personnel sometimes lack the training needed to make the transition to the direct style of supervision[103]; others have suggested that managers of direct-supervision jails, especially mid-level managers, could benefit from clearer job descriptions and additional training.[104] In the words of one direct-supervision advocate, "Training becomes particularly critical in direct-supervision jails where relationships are more immediate and are more complex."[105] Finally, those tasked with hiring have recommended psychological screening and intensive use of preemployment interviews to determine the suitability of applicants for correctional officer positions in direct-supervision jails.[106]

Jails and the Future

In contrast to more visible issues confronting the justice system, such as the death penalty, gun control, the war on drugs, terrorism, and big-city gangs, jails have received relatively little attention from the media and have generally escaped close public scrutiny.[107] National efforts are under way, however, to improve the quality of jail life. Some changes involve adding crucial programs for inmates. An American Jail Association (AJA) study of drug-treatment programs in jails, for example, found that "a small fraction (perhaps fewer than 10%) of inmates needing drug treatment actually receive these services."[108]

Ethics and Professionalism

American Jail Association Code of Ethics for Jail Officers

As an officer employed in a detention/correctional capacity, I swear (or affirm) to be a good citizen and a credit to my community, state, and nation at all times. I will abstain from all questionable behavior which might bring disrepute to the agency for which I work, my family, my community, and my associates. My lifestyle will be above and beyond reproach and I will constantly strive to set an example of a professional who performs his/her duties according to the laws of our country, state, and community and the policies, procedures, written and verbal orders, and regulations of the agency for which I work.

On the job I promise to:

Keep the institution secure so as to safeguard my community and the lives of the staff, inmates, and visitors on the premises.

Work with each individual firmly and fairly without regard to rank, status, or condition.

Maintain a positive demeanor when confronted with stressful situations of scorn, ridicule, danger, and/or chaos.

Report either in writing or by word of mouth to the proper authorities those things which should be reported, and keep silent about matters which are to remain confidential according to the laws and rules of the agency and government.

Manage and supervise the inmates in an evenhanded and courteous manner.

Refrain at all times from becoming personally involved in the lives of the inmates and their families.

Treat all visitors to the jail with politeness and respect and do my utmost to ensure that they observe the jail regulations.

Take advantage of all education and training opportunities designed to assist me to become a more competent officer.

Communicate with people in or outside of the jail, whether by phone, written word, or word of mouth, in such a way so as not to reflect in a negative manner upon my agency.

Contribute to a jail environment which will keep the inmate involved in activities designed to improve his/her attitude and character.

Support all activities of a professional nature through membership and participation that will continue to elevate the status of those who operate our nation's jails.

Do my best through word and deed to present an image to the public at large of a jail professional, committed to progress for an improved and enlightened criminal justice system.

THINKING ABOUT ETHICS

1. Why does the AJA Code of Ethics require jail officers to "Take advantage of all education and training opportunities designed to assist me to become a more competent officer"? What does education have to do with ethics?
2. Are there any features or elements that you might add to this code? Are there any that you might delete?

Source: American Jail Association, *Code of Ethics for Jail Officers*, adopted January 10, 1991. Revised May 19, 1993. Reprinted with permission.

Jail industries are another growing programmatic area. The best of them serve the community while training inmates in marketable skills.[109] In an exemplary effort to humanize its megajails, for example, the Los Angeles County Sheriff's Department opened an inmate telephone-answering service.[110] Many callers contact the sheriff's department daily, requesting information about the county's 22,000 jail inmates. These requests for information were becoming increasingly difficult to handle due to the growing fiscal constraints facing local government, so to handle the huge number of calls effectively without tying up sworn law enforcement personnel, the department began using inmates specially trained to handle incoming calls; 80 inmates were assigned to the project, with groups of different sizes covering shifts throughout the day. Each inmate staffer went through a training program to learn how to use proper telephone procedures and how to run computer terminals containing routine data on the department's inmates. The new system now handles 4,000 telephone inquiries a day, and the time needed to answer a call and to provide information has dropped from 30 minutes under the old system to a remarkable ten seconds today.

Jail "boot camps," like the one run by the Harris County (Texas) Probation Department, are also popular. Jail boot camps give offenders who are sentenced to probationary terms a taste of both confinement and the rigors of life behind bars. The Harris County Courts Regimented Intensive Probation Program (CRIPP) facility began operation in 1991 and is located in Humble, Texas. Separate CRIPPs are run for about 400 male and 50 female probationers.[111] The most recent comprehensive study of jail boot camps found only ten such jail-based programs in the country,[112] but current numbers are probably higher.

regional jail
A jail that is built and run using the combined resources of a variety of local jurisdictions.

Capturing much recent attention are **regional jails**, that is, jails that are built and run using the combined resources of a variety of local jurisdictions. Regional jails have begun to replace smaller and often antiquated local jails in at least a few locations. One example of a regional jail is the Western Tidewater Regional Jail, serving the cities of Suffolk and Franklin and the county of Isle of Wright in Virginia.[113] Regional jails, which are just beginning to come into their own, may develop quickly in Virginia, where the state, recognizing the economies of consolidation, offers to reimburse localities up to 50% of the cost of building regional jails.

One final element in the unfolding saga of jail development should be mentioned: the emergence of state jail standards. Of the 50 states, 32 have set standards for municipal and county jails,[114] and in 25 states, those standards are mandatory. The purpose of jail standards is to identify basic minimum conditions necessary for inmate health and safety. On the national level, the Commission on Accreditation for Corrections, operated jointly by the ACA and the federal government, has developed its own set of jail standards,[115] as has the National Sheriff's Association. Both sets of standards are designed to ensure a minimal level of comfort and safety in local lockups. Increased standards, though, are costly. Local jurisdictions, already hard-pressed to meet other budgetary demands, will probably be slow to upgrade their jails to meet such external guidelines unless forced to do so. In a study of 61 jails that was designed to test compliance with National Sheriff's Association guidelines, Ken Kerle discovered that in many standards areas—especially those of tool control, armory planning, community resources, release preparation, and riot planning—the majority of jails were badly out of compliance.[116] Lack of a written plan was the most commonly cited reason for failing to meet the standards. Learn more about jails by visiting the AJA via Web Extra 11–3 at mycrimekit.com.

Web EXTRA

Private Prisons

privatization
The movement toward the wider use of private prisons.

private prison
A correctional institution operated by a private firm on behalf of a local or state government.

State-run prison systems have always contracted with private industries for food, psychological testing, training, and recreational and other services, and it is estimated that more than three dozen states today rely on private businesses to serve a variety of correctional needs. It follows, then, that states have now turned to private industry for the provision of prison space. The movement toward **privatization** (use of privately run rather than government-run prisons), which began in the early 1980s, was slow to catch on, but it has since grown at a rapid pace. In 1986, only 2,620 prisoners could be found in privately run confinement facilities,[117] but by 2007, privately operated correctional facilities serving as prisons and jails held over 113,790 state and federal prisoners across 33 states and the District of Columbia.[118] **Private prisons** (prisons operated by private companies) held 6.2% of all state prisoners and 14.4% of federal prisoners at the start of 2007. One source says that the growth rate of the private prison industry has been around 35% annually,[119] which is comparable to the highest growth rates anywhere in the corporate sector.

Privately run prisons are operated by Cornell Corrections, Corrections Corporation of America (CCA), Correctional Services Corporation (CSC), Wackenhut Corrections Corporation, and numerous other smaller companies. Most states that use private firms to supplement their prison resources contract with such companies to provide a full range of custodial and other correctional services. State corrections administrators use private companies to reduce overcrowding, lower operating expenses, and avoid lawsuits targeted at state officials and employees.[120] But some studies have shown that private prisons may not bring the kinds of cost savings that had been anticipated.[121] One 1996 study was done by the U.S. General Accounting Office.[122] It found, for example, "neither cost savings nor substantial differences in the quality of services" between private and publicly run prisons.[123] Similar findings emerged in a 2001 report by the Bureau of Justice Assistance; that report, titled *Emerging Issues on Privatized Prisons*, found that "private prisons offer only modest cost savings, which are basically a result of moderate reductions in staffing patterns, fringe benefits, and other labor-related costs."[124]

Many hurdles remain before the privatization movement can effectively provide large-scale custodial supervision. Among the most significant barriers to privatization are old state laws that prohibit private involvement in correctional management. Other practical hurdles exist as well. States that do contract with private firms may face the specter of strikes by correctional officers, who do not come under state laws restricting the ability of public employees to strike. Moreover, since responsibility for the protection of inmate rights still lies with the states, their liability will not transfer to private corrections.[125] In today's legal climate, it is unclear whether

CJ Exhibit 1

Arguments for and against the Privatization of Prisons

REASONS TO PRIVATIZE

1. Private operators can provide construction financing options that allow the government to pay only for capacity as needed in lieu of assuming long-term debt.
2. Private companies offer state-of-the-art correctional facility designs that are efficient to operate and that are based on cost–benefit considerations.
3. Private operators typically design and construct a new correctional facility in half the time it takes to build a comparable government project.
4. Private companies provide government with the convenience and accountability of one entity for all compliance issues.
5. Private companies can mobilize rapidly and specialize in unique facility missions.
6. Private companies provide economic development opportunities by hiring and purchasing locally.
7. Government can reduce or share its liability exposure by contracting with private corrections companies.
8. Government can retain flexibility by limiting the contract's duration and by specifying the facility's mission.
9. The addition of alternative service providers injects competition among both public and private organizations.

REASONS NOT TO PRIVATIZE

1. There are certain responsibilities that only the government should meet, such as public safety. The government has legal, political, and moral obligations to provide incarceration. Constitutional issues underlie both public and private corrections and involve deprivation of liberty, discipline, and preservation of the rights of inmates. Related issues include use of force, equitable hiring practices, and segregation.
2. Few private companies are available from which to choose.
3. Private operators may be inexperienced with key corrections issues.
4. A private operator may become a monopoly through political ingratiation, favoritism, and so on.
5. Government may, over time, lose the capability to perform the corrections function.
6. The profit motive will inhibit the proper performance of corrections duties. Private companies have financial incentives to cut corners.
7. The procurement process is slow, inefficient, and open to risks.
8. Creating a good, clear contract is a daunting task.
9. The lack of enforcement remedies in contracts leaves only termination or lawsuits as recourse.

Source: Dennis Cunningham, "Public Strategies for Private Prisons," paper presented at the Private Prison Workshop, Institute on Criminal Justice, University of Minnesota Law School, January 29–30, 1999.

a state can shield itself or its employees through private prison contracting, but it appears that the courts are unlikely to recognize such shielding. To limit their own liability, states will probably have to oversee private operations as well as set standards for training and custody. In 1997, in the case of *Richardson* v. *McKnight*,[126] the U.S. Supreme Court made it clear that correctional officers employed by a private firm are not entitled to qualified immunity from suits by prisoners charging a violation of Section 1983 of Title 42 of the U.S. Code. In 2001, however, in the case of *Correctional Services Corporation* v. *Malesko*,[127] the Court found that private corporations acting under color of federal law cannot be held responsible in a *Bivens* action because the purpose of *Bivens* "is to deter individual federal officers from committing Constitutional violations."[128]

Perhaps the most serious legal issues confront states that contract to hold inmates outside of their own jurisdiction. In 1996, for example, two inmates escaped from a 240-man sex-offender unit run by Corrections CCA under contract with the state of Oregon. Problems immediately arose because the CCA unit was located near Houston, Texas—not in Oregon, where the men had originally been sentenced to confinement. Following the escape, Texas officials were unsure whether they even had arrest power over the former prisoners because the escapees had not committed any crimes in Texas. While prison escape is a crime under Texas law, the law only applies to state-run facilities, not to private facilities where corrections personnel are not employed by the state or empowered in any official capacity by state law. Harris County (Texas) Prosecutor John Holmes explained the situation this way: "They have not committed the offense of escape under Texas law … and the only reason at all that they're subject to being arrested and were arrested was because during their leaving the facility, they assaulted a guard and took his motor vehicle. That we can charge them with and have."[129]

The 2,300-bed California City Correctional Center in the Mojave Desert town of California City. The facility, which opened in December 1999, was built by Corrections Corporation of America (CCA) to provide medium-security correctional services under a contract with the Federal Bureau of Prisons. Nashville-based CCA says that it can run prisons as efficiently as the government, and its supporters claim that private prisons are the way of the future. Do you agree?
Reed Saxon/AP Wide World Photos

Library EXTRA

Web EXTRA

Opponents of the movement toward privatization cite many issues (see CJ Exhibit 1). They claim that, aside from legal concerns, cost reductions via the use of private facilities can only be achieved by lowering standards, and they fear a return to the inhumane conditions of early jails as private firms seek to turn prisons into profit-making operations. For states that do choose to contract with private firms, the National Institute of Justice (NIJ) recommends a "regular and systematic sampling" of former inmates to appraise prison conditions, as well as annual on-site inspections of each privately run institution. State personnel serving as monitors should be stationed in large facilities, says NIJ, and a "meticulous review" of all services should be conducted before the contract renewal date.[130] You can learn more about prison privatization at Library Extra 11–8 and via Web Extra 11–4 at mycrimekit.com.

Summary

- Today's prisons are classified according to security level, such as maximum, medium, and minimum security. Most contemporary American correctional facilities are medium and minimum security. Although the goals of recidivism and deterrence are still important in the minds of corrections administrators, today's prisons tend to warehouse inmates awaiting release. Public disappointment with high rates of recidivism has produced a prison system today that is focused on the concept of just deserts and that is only beginning to emerge from the strong influence of the nothing-works doctrine discussed in this chapter. Overcrowded facilities are still the norm in many jurisdictions, although a prison building boom over the last decade has alleviated some of the extremely overcrowded conditions that had previously existed.
- In contrast to prisons, which are long-term confinement facilities designed to hold those who have been sentenced to serve time for committing crime, jails are short-term confinement facilities whose traditional purpose has been to hold those awaiting trial or sentencing. Inmates who have been tried and sentenced may also be held at jails until their transfer to a prison facility, and today's jails sometimes hold inmates serving short sentences of confinement. Recently, the emergence of direct-supervision jails, in which traditional barriers between inmates and staff have been mostly eliminated, seems to have reduced the incidence of jail violence and can be credited with improving the conditions of jailed inmates in jurisdictions where such facilities operate.

- Privately run correctional facilities, or private prisons, have grown in number over the past few decades as the movement toward the privatization of correctional facilities has gained steam. Private prisons, operated by for-profit corporations, hold inmates on behalf of state governments or the federal government and provide for inmates' care and security. A number of questions remain as to the role such facilities will play in the future, including whether they can be cost-effective and whether they can somehow reduce the legal liability of state governments and government employees that is often associated with confinement.

Key Concepts

Terms

ADMAX
classification system
design capacity
direct-supervision jail
ex post facto
jail
justice model
operational capacity
prison
prison capacity
private prison
privatization
rated capacit
regional jail

Questions for Review

1. What are today's prisons like? What purpose do they serve?
2. What role do jails play in American corrections? What are some of the issues that jail administrators currently face?
3. What is the role of private prisons today? What will be the state of private prisons two or three decades from now?

To participate in an online discussion of these topics and others, join the CJ Brief e-mail discussion list at mycrimekit.com.

Web Quest

Visit the Corrections Connection on the World Wide Web (http://www.corrections.com). What are some of the many features available at this site?

Explore the Legal Issues bulletin board at the Corrections Connection to learn about the latest legal issues of concern to corrections professionals. What are some of those issues?

Participate in one of the Corrections Connections chat rooms. (The "Corrections Lobby" is often a good place to find an ongoing chat.) What topics are being discussed? If no one is in the chat room when you enter, visit the Message Boards and list the most recent topics being discussed. Submit this information to your instructor if asked to do so.

To complete this Web Quest online, go to the Web Quest module in Chapter 11 of the *Criminal Justice: A Brief Introduction* Companion Website at mycrimekit.com.

Notes

i. Adam Liptak, "U.S. Imprisons One in 100 Adults, Report Finds," *New York Times,* february 29, 2008. Web posted at http://select.nytimes.com/mem/tnt.html?emc=tnt&tntget=2008/02/29/us/29prison.html.

ii. James A. Gondles, Jr., "Who Should Be behind Bars?" *Corrections Today* (August 2002). Web posted at http://www.aca.org/admin/pix/ctmagarticles/200208_whoshouldbebehindbars.pdf (accessed September 12, 2005).

iii. Zebulon R. Brockway, *The Ideal of a True Prison System for a State* (1865). Reprinted in *Journal of Correctional Education,* Volume 46, Issue 2 (June 1995), pp. 68–74.

iv. Don Myers, "Crime: What Will It Take to Reclaim Our Country?" *USA Today,* May 26, 1995.

v. Paige M. Harrison and Allen J. Beck, *Prisoners in 2005* (Washington, DC: Bureau of Justice Statistics, 2006), p. 7.

1. Public Safety Performance Project of the Pew Charitable Trusts, *Public Safety, Public Spending: Forecasting America's Prison Population, 2007–2011* (Philadelphia: Pew, February 2007), p. 1.
2. James J. Stephan and Jennifer C. Karberg, *Census of State and Federal Correctional Facilities, 2000* (Washington, DC: Bureau of Justice Statistics, 2003).
3. William J. Sabol, Heather Couture, and Paige M. Harrison, *Prisoners in 2006* (Washington, DC: Bureau of Justice Statistics, 2007). It includes state and federal inmates held in local jails.
4. Ibid.
5. Public Safety Performance Project of the Pew Charitable Trusts, *Public Safety, Public Spending.*
6. Public Safety Performance Project of the Pew Charitable Trusts, *One in 100: Behind Bars in America 2008* (Philadelphia: Pew, 2008), p. 5.
7. Sabol, Couture, and Harrison, *Prisoners in 2006.*
8. Thomas P. Bonczar, *Prevalence of Imprisonment in the U.S. Population, 1974–2001* (Washington, DC: Bureau of Justice Statistics, 2003), p. 1.

9. Federal Bureau of Investigation, *Uniform Crime Reports: Crime in the United States, 2005* (Washington, DC: U.S. Government Printing Office, 2006), and other years.
10. Some of the ideas in this paragraph are taken from Public Safety Performance Project of the Pew Charitable Trusts, *One in 100.*
11. Sabol, Couture, and Harrison, *Prisoners in 2006.*
12. Bureau of Justice Statistics, *National Corrections Reporting Program, 1998* (Ann Arbor, MI: Interuniversity Consortium for Political and Social Research, 2001); and Sabol, Couture, and Harrison, *Prisoners in 2006.*
13. Jim Kessler, Rachel Laser, Michael Earls, and Nikki Yamashiro, *The Impending Crime Wave: Four Dangerous New Trends and How to Stop Them* (Washington, DC: The Third Way Foundation, February 2008).
14. "Study Finds More Than Half of All Prison and Jail Inmates Have Mental Health Problems," U.S. Department of Justice, Office of Justice Programs, press release, September 6, 2006.
15. Most of the items in this list and some of the wording are taken from Kessler, Laser, Earls, and Yamashiro, *The Impending Crime Wave,* p. 7.
16. Sabol, Couture, and Harrison, *Prisoners in 2006.*
17. Bonczar, *Prevalence of Imprisonment in the U.S. Population, 1974–2001,* p. 1.
18. Ibid., p. 8.
19. The number includes both state and federal prisoners.
20. Information in this paragraph comes from Harrison and Beck, *Prisoners in 2007.*
21. David F. Greenberg and Valerie West, "State Prison Populations and Their Growth, 1971–1991," *Criminology,* Vol. 39, No. 3 (2001), p. 615.
22. Robert M. Carter, Richard A. McGee, and E. Kim Nelson, *Corrections in America* (Philadelphia: J. B. Lippincott, 1975), pp. 122–123.
23. James J. Stephan, *State Prison Expenditures, 2001* (Washington, DC: Bureau of Justice Statistics, 2004); and e-mail correspondence with Susan Allison, Federal Bureau of Prisons, October 29, 2001.
24. Kristen A. Hughes, *Justice Expenditure and Employment in the United States, 2003* (Washington, DC: Bureau of Justice Statistics, 2006); and Stephan, *State Prison Expenditures, 2001,* p. 3.
25. See, for example, Harry Elmer Barnes and Negley K. Teeters, *New Horizons in Criminology,* 3rd ed. (Englewood Cliffs, NJ: Prentice Hall, 1959).
26. Although many other states require inmates to work on road maintenance and although the inmates are typically supervised by armed guards, Alabama became the first state in modern times to shackle prisoners.
27. See "Back on the Chain Gang: Florida Becomes Third State to Resurrect Forced Labor," Associated Press wire service, November 22, 1995.
28. Florida Department of Corrections, *Corrections in Florida: 1998 Opinion Survey.* Web posted at http://www.dc.state.fl.us/pub/survey/index.html (accessed January 24, 2006).
29. Lori Sharn and Shannon Tangonan, "Chain Gangs Back in Alabama," *USA Today,* May 4, 1995, p. 3A.
30. Ibid.
31. See Debra L. Dailey, *Summary of the 1998 Annual Conference of the National Association of Sentencing Commissions.* Web posted at http://www.ussc.gov/states/dailefsr.pdf (accessed October 30, 2005).
32. Peter Baker, "Allen Crime Plan Ends Parole; Expensive Va. Proposal Would Strain Budget, Require More Prisons," *Washington Post* wire service, August 17, 1994.
33. The state of Washington is generally credited with having been the first state to pass a three-strikes law by voter initiative (in 1993).
34. For a good overview of the topic, see David Shichor and Dale K. Sechrest, *Three Strikes and You're Out: Vengeance as Public Policy* (Thousand Oaks, CA: Sage, 1996).
35. David S. Broder, "When Tough Isn't Smart," *Washington Post* wire service, March 24, 1994.
36. "The Klaas Case and the Crime Bill," *Washington Post* wire service, February 21, 1994.
37. Bruce Smith, "Crime Solutions," Associated Press wire service, January 11, 1995.
38. Quinlan is now senior vice president at Corrections Corporation of America.
39. Quoted in David Lawsky, "Prison Wardens Decry Overcrowding, Survey Says," Reuters wire service, December 21, 1994.
40. Harrison and Beck, *Prisoners in 2007.*
41. Federal Bureau of Prisons, *State of the Bureau 2004* (Washington, DC: BOP, 2005), p. 7.
42. Adapted from Bureau of Justice Statistics, *Report to the Nation on Crime and Justice,* 2nd ed. (Washington, DC: U.S. Government Printing Office, 1988), p. 108.
43. *Rhodes* v. *Chapman,* 452 U.S. 337 (1981).
44. D. Greenberg, "The Incapacitative Effect of Imprisonment, Some Estimates," *Law and Society Review,* Vol. 9 (1975), pp. 541–580. See also Jacqueline Cohen, "Incapacitating Criminals: Recent Research Findings," National Institute of Justice *Research in Brief* (December 1983).
45. For information on identifying dangerous repeat offenders, see M. Chaiken and J. Chaiken, *Selecting Career Criminals for Priority Prosecution,* final report (Cambridge, MA: Abt Associates, 1987).
46. J. Monahan, *Predicting Violent Behavior: An Assessment of Clinical Techniques* (Beverly Hills, CA: Sage, 1981).
47. S. Van Dine, J. P. Conrad, and S. Dinitz, *Restraining the Wicked: The Incapacitation of the Dangerous Offender* (Lexington, MA: Lexington Books, 1979).
48. Paul Gendreau, Tracy Little, and Claire Goggin, "A Meta-Analysis of the Predictors of Adult Offender Recidivism: What Works!" *Criminology,* Vol. 34, No. 4 (November 1996), pp. 575–607.
49. *Lynce* v. *Mathis,* 519 U.S. 443 (1997).
50. Daniel B. Wood, "Budget Cuts Are Setting Convicts Free," *The Christian Science Monitor,* April 21, 2004.
51. NBC11, "Schwarzenegger to Release 22,000 Prisoners to Make Budget," January 10, 2008. Web available at http://www.nbc11.com/news/15021720/detail.html (accessed May 20, 2008).
52. George Camp and Camille Camp, "Stopping Escapes: Perimeter Security," *Prison Construction Bulletin* (Washington, DC: National Institute of Justice, 1987).
53. Adapted from G. A. Grizzle and A. D. Witte, "Efficiency in Collections Agencies," in Gordon P. Whitaker and Charles D. Phillips, *Evaluating the Performance of Criminal Justice Agencies* (Washington, DC: NIJ, 1983).
54. Patricia L. Hardyman et al., *Internal Prison Classification Systems: Case Studies in Their Development and Implementation* (Washington, DC: National Institutions of Corrections, 2002), from which some of the wording in this section is taken.
55. Ibid.
56. *Johnson* v. *California,* 543 U.S. 499 (2005).
57. Federal Bureau of Prisons, *Staff Breakdown.* Web available at http:/ /www.bop.gov/about/facts.jsp#5 (accessed May 19, 2008).
58. Most of the information in this section comes from telephone conversations with and faxed information from the Federal Bureau of Prisons, August 25, 1995.
59. For additional information, see Dennis Cauchon, "The Alcatraz of the Rockies," *USA Today,* November 16, 1994, p. 6A.
60. "Congress OKs Inmate Fees to Offset Costs of Prison," *Criminal Justice Newsletter,* October 15, 1992, p. 6.
61. Stephan, *State Prison Expenditures, 2001,* p. 3.
62. National Institute of Corrections website, http://www.nicic.org (accessed March 2, 2006).
63. Ibid.
64. James J. Stephan, *Census of Jails, 1999* (Washington, DC: Bureau of Justice Statistics, 2001), p. 2.
65. Much of the information in this paragraph comes from William J. Sabol and Todd D. Minton, *Jail Inmates at Midyear 2007* (Washington, DC: Bureau of Justice Statistics, 2008).

66. Ibid., p. 10.
67. Stephan, *Census of Jails, 1999.*
68. Ibid.
69. Ibid.
70. Three percent of jail inmates report being of more than one race.
71. Doris J. James, *Profile of Jail Inmates, 2002* (Washington, DC: Bureau of Justice Statistics), p. 2.
72. Ibid.
73. Stephan, *Census of Jails, 1999.*
74. See Gale Holland, "L.A. Jail Makes Delayed Debut," *USA Today,* January 27, 1997, p. 3A.
75. See Dale Stockton, "Cook County Illinois Sheriff's Office," *Police* (October 1996), pp. 40–43. The Cook County Department of Correction operates ten separate jails, which house approximately 9,000 inmates. The department employs more than 2,800 correctional officers.
76. Sabol and Minton, *Jail Inmates at Midyear 2007,* p. 4.
77. William Reginald Mills and Heather Barrett, "Meeting the Special Challenge of Providing Health Care to Women Inmates in the '90's," *American Jails,* Vol. 4, No. 3 (September/October 1990), p. 55.
78. Ibid.
79. Ibid., p. 21.
80. Ibid.
81. Ibid., p. 55.
82. American Correctional Association, *Vital Statistics in Corrections* (Laurel, MD: ACA, 2000).
83. Mills and Barrett, "Meeting the Special Challenge," p. 55.
84. Ibid.
85. Linda L. Zupan, "Women Corrections Officers in the Nation's Largest Jails," *American Jails* (January/February 1991), pp. 59–62.
86. Ibid., p. 11.
87. Linda L. Zupan, "Women Corrections Officers in Local Jails," paper presented at the annual meeting of the Academy of Criminal Justice Sciences, Nashville, TN, March 1991.
88. Ibid., p. 6.
89. "Jail Overcrowding in Houston Results in Release of Inmates," *Criminal Justice Newsletter,* October 15, 1990, p. 5.
90. Bureau of Justice Statistics, *Census of Local Jails, 1988* (Washington, DC: BJS, 1991), p. 31.
91. Kathleen Maguire and Ann L. Pastore, *Sourcebook of Criminal Justice Statistics, 1994* (Washington, DC: U.S. Government Printing Office, 1995).
92. Harrison and Beck, *Prisoners in 2007.*
93. Christopher J. Mumola, *Suicide and Homicide in State Prisons and Local Jails* (Washington, DC: Bureau of Justice Statistics, 2005), p. 1.
94. George P. Wilson and Harvey L. McMurray, "System Assessment of Jail Overcrowding Assumptions," paper presented at the annual meeting of the Academy of Criminal Justice Sciences, Nashville, TN, March 1991.
95. Andy Hall, *Systemwide Strategies to Alleviate Jail Crowding* (Washington, DC: National Institute of Justice, 1987).
96. Ibid.
97. Linda L. Zupan and Ben A. Menke, "The New Generation Jail: An Overview," in Joel A. Thompson and G. Larry Mays, eds., *American Jails: Public Policy Issues* (Chicago: Nelson-Hall, 1991), p. 180.
98. Ibid.
99. Herbert R. Sigurdson, Billy Wayson, and Gail Funke, "Empowering Middle Managers of Direct Supervision Jails," *American Jails* (winter 1990), p. 52.
100. Byron Johnson, "Exploring Direct Supervision: A Research Note," *American Jails* (March/April 1994), pp. 63–64.
101. H. Sigurdson, *The Manhattan House of Detention: A Study of Podular Direct Supervision* (Washington, DC: National Institute of Corrections, 1985). For similar conclusions, see Robert Conroy, Wantland J. Smith, and Linda L. Zupan, "Officer Stress in the Direct Supervision Jail: A Preliminary Case Study," *American Jails* (November/December 1991), p. 36.
102. W. Raymond Nelson and Russell M. Davis, "Podular Direct Supervision: The First Twenty Years," *American Jails* (July/August 1995), p. 17.
103. Jerry W. Fuqua, "New Generation Jails: Old Generation Management," *American Jails* (March/April 1991), pp. 80–83.
104. Sigurdson, Wayson, and Funke, "Empowering Middle Managers."
105. Duncan J. McCulloch and Time Stiles, "Technology and the Direct Supervision Jail," *American Jails* (winter 1990), pp. 97–102.
106. Susan W. McCampbell, "Direct Supervision: Looking for the Right People," *American Jails* (November/December 1990), pp. 68–69.
107. For a good overview of the future of American jails, see Ron Carroll, "Jails and the Criminal Justice System in the Twenty-First Century," *American Jails* (March/April 1997), pp. 26–31.
108. Robert L. May II, Roger H. Peters, and William D. Kearns, "The Extent of Drug Treatment Programs in Jails: A Summary Report," *American Jails* (September/October 1990), pp. 32–34.
109. See, for example, John W. Dietler, "Jail Industries: The Best Thing That Can Happen to a Sheriff," *American Jails* (July/August 1990), pp. 80–83.
110. Robert Osborne, "Los Angeles County Sheriff Opens New Inmate Answering Service," *American Jails* (July/August 1990), pp. 61–62.
111. Robert J. Hunter, "A Locally Operated Boot Camp," *American Jails* (July/August 1994), pp. 13–15.
112. James Austin, Michael Jones, and Melissa Bolyard, *The Growing Use of Jail Boot Camps: The Current State of the Art* (Washington, DC: National Institute of Justice, 1993).
113. See J. R. Dewan, "Regional Jail—The New Kid on the Block," *American Jails* (May/June 1995), pp. 70–72.
114. Tom Rosazza, "Jail Standards: Focus on Change," *American Jails* (November/December 1990), pp. 84–87.
115. American Correctional Association, *Manual of Standards for Adult Local Detention Facilities,* 3rd ed. (College Park, MD: ACA, 1991).
116. Ken Kerle, "National Sheriff's Association Jail Audit Review," *American Jails* (spring 1987), pp. 13–21.
117. Allen J. Beck and Paige M. Harrison, *Prisoners in 2000* (Washington, DC: Bureau of Justice Statistics), p. 7.
118. Sabol, Couture, and Harrison, *Prisoners in 2006,* p. 18, from which much of the information in this section is taken.
119. Eric Bates, "Private Prisons: Over the Next Five Years Analysts Expect the Private Share of the Prison 'Market' to More Than Double," *The Nation,* Vol. 266, No. 1 (1998), pp. 11–18.
120. Gary Fields, "Privatized Prisons Pose Problems," *USA Today,* November 11, 1996, p. 3A.
121. Dale K. Sechrest and David Shichor, "Private Jails: Locking Down the Issues," *American Jails* (March/April 1997), pp. 9–18.
122. U.S. General Accounting Office, *Private and Public Prisons: Studies Comparing Operational Costs and/or Quality of Service* (Washington, DC: U.S. Government Printing Office, 1996).
123. Sechrest and Shichor, "Private Jails," p. 10.
124. James Austin and Garry Coventry, *Emerging Issues on Privatized Prisons* (Washington, DC: Bureau of Justice Statistics, 2001), p. ix.
125. For a more detailed discussion of this issue, see Austin and Coventry, *Emerging Issues on Privatized Prisons.*
126. *Richardson* v. *McKnight,* 117 S.Ct. 2100, 138 L.Ed.2d 540 (1997).
127. *Correctional Services Corporation* v. *Malesko,* 122 S.Ct. 515 (2001).
128. Ibid.
129. Quoted in Bates, "Private Prisons."
130. Judith C. Hackett et al., "Contracting for the Operation of Prisons and Jails," National Institute of Justice *Research in Brief* (June 1987), p. 6.

Prison Life

12

Chapter Outline

- Introduction
- The Male Inmate's World
- The Female Inmate's World
- The Staff World
- Prison Riots
- Prisoners' Rights
- Issues Facing Prisons Today

Learning Objectives

After reading this chapter, you should be able to

- Describe the realities of prison life and prison subculture from the inmate's point of view.
- Illustrate the significant differences between men's prisons and women's prisons.
- Describe the realities of prison life from the correctional officer's point of view.
- Describe the causes of prison riots, and list the stages through which most riots progress.
- Discuss the legal aspects of prisoners' rights, and explain the consequences of precedent-setting U.S. Supreme Court cases in the area of prisoners' rights.
- Describe the major problems and issues that prisons face today.

> *"What happens inside jails and prisons does not stay inside jails and prisons. It comes home with prisoners after they are released and with corrections officers at the end of each day's shift. We must create safe and productive conditions of confinement not only because it is the right thing to do, but because it influences the safety, health, and prosperity of us all."*
>
> *Commission on Safety and Abuse in America's Prisons*[1]

Introduction

Prison Life and the Media

▸▸▸ Hear the author discuss this chapter at mycrimekit.com.

On the FOX TV show *Prison Break*, Wentworth Miller plays the role of an engineer named Michael Scofield who holds up a bank so that he can join his brother in the fictional Fox River State Penitentiary. Scofield's brother, Lincoln (Dominic Purcell), has been convicted of a sensational murder and is housed on the prison's death row. The show, which centers around Michael's elaborate plan to break Lincoln out and to prove that he's innocent, draws a large weekly audience and demonstrates the fascination that the American public has with prison life.

For many years, prisons and prison life could be described by the phrase "out of sight, out of mind." Very few citizens cared about prison conditions, and those unfortunate enough to be locked away were regarded as lost to the world. By the mid-twentieth century, however, this attitude started to change. Concerned citizens began to offer their services to prison administrations, neighborhoods began accepting work-release prisoners and halfway houses, and social scientists initiated a serious study of prison life. Today, as shows like *Prison Break* make clear, prisons and prison life have entered the American mainstream. Part of the reason for this is that prisons today hold more people than ever before, and incarceration impacts not only those imprisoned but family members, friends, and victims on the outside.

This chapter describes the realities of prison life, including prisoner lifestyles, prison subcultures, sexuality in prison, prison violence, and prisoners' rights and grievance procedures. We discuss both the inmate world and the staff world. A separate section on women in prison details the social structure of women's prisons, daily life in those facilities, and the various types of female inmates. We begin with a brief overview of early research on prison life.

Research on Prison Life: Total Institutions

In 1935, Hans Reimer, who was then chairman of the Department of Sociology at Indiana University, set the tone for studies of prison life when he voluntarily served three months in prison as an incognito participant-observer.[2] Reimer reported the results of his studies to the American Prison Association, stimulating many other, albeit less spectacular, efforts to examine prison life. Other early studies include Donald Clemmer's *The Prison Community* (1940),[3] Gresham M. Sykes's *The Society of Captives: A Study of a Maximum Security Prison*

▸ Dominic Purcell (left) and Wentworth Miller, stars of the FOX TV show *Prison Break*. The popularity of the show, which is filmed at a former prison that once held serial killer John Wayne Gacy, illustrates a growing awareness of prisons and prison life in American culture today. What do Americans think of prisons and prisoners?
John Zich/CORBIS/Bettmann

A notice posted on a prison wall. Custody and security remain the primary concerns of prison staffers throughout the country—a fact reinforced by this notice. Is the emphasis on custody and security justified?
Mike Fiala/Agence Francis Press/Getty Images

(1958),[4] Richard A. Cloward and Donald R. Cressey's *Theoretical Studies in Social Organization of the Prison* (1960),[5] and Cressey's edited volume, *The Prison: Studies in Institutional Organization and Change* (1961).[6]

These studies and others focused primarily on maximum-security prisons for men. They treated correctional institutions as formal or complex organizations and employed the analytic techniques of organizational sociology, industrial psychology, and administrative science.[7] As modern writers on prisons have observed, "The prison was compared to a primitive society, isolated from the outside world, functionally integrated by a delicate system of mechanisms, which kept it precariously balanced between anarchy and accommodation."[8]

Another approach to the study of prison life was developed by Erving Goffman, who coined the term **total institutions** in a 1961 study of prisons and mental hospitals.[9] Goffman described total institutions as places where the same people work, recreate, worship, eat, and sleep together daily. Such places include prisons, concentration camps, mental hospitals, seminaries, and other facilities in which residents are cut off from the larger society either forcibly or willingly. Total institutions are small societies; they evolve their own distinctive values and styles of life and pressure residents to fulfill rigidly prescribed behavioral roles.

total institution
An enclosed facility separated from society both socially and physically, where the inhabitants share all aspects of their daily lives.

Generally speaking, the work of prison researchers built on findings of other social scientists who discovered that any group with similar characteristics, confined in the same place at the same time, develops its own subculture with specific components that govern hierarchy, behavioral patterns, values, and so on. Prison subcultures, described in the next section, also provide the medium through which prison values are communicated and expectations are made known. Learn more about prison research via Library Extra 12–1 at mycrimekit.com.

Library EXTRA

The Male Inmate's World

Two social realities coexist in prison settings. One is the official structure of rules and procedures put in place by the wider society and enforced by prison staff, and the other is the more informal but decidedly more powerful inmate world.[10] The inmate world, best described by how closely it touches the lives of inmates, is controlled by **prison subculture**, consisting of inmate values and behaviors. The realities of prison life—including a large and often densely packed inmate population that must look to the prison environment for all its needs—mean that prison subculture develops independently of the plans of prison administrators and is not easily subjected to the control of prison authorities.

prison subculture
The values and behavioral patterns characteristic of prison inmates. Prison subculture has been found to be surprisingly consistent across the country.

Inmates entering prison discover a whole new social world in which they must participate or face consequences ranging from dangerous ostracism to physical violence and homicide.[11] The socialization of new inmates into the prison subculture has been described as a process of

prisonization
The process whereby newly institutionalized offenders come to accept prison lifestyles and criminal values. Although many inmates begin their prison experience with only a few values that support criminal behavior, the socialization experience they undergo while incarcerated leads to a much wider acceptance of such values.

prisonization[12]—the new prisoner learning the convict values, attitudes, roles, and even language. By the time this process is complete, new inmates have become "cons." Gresham Sykes and Sheldon Messinger recognized five elements of the prison code in 1960[13]:

1. Don't interfere with the interests of other inmates. Never rat on a con.
2. Don't lose your head. Play it cool and do your own time.
3. Don't exploit inmates. Don't steal. Don't break your word. Be right.
4. Don't whine. Be a man.
5. Don't be a sucker. Don't trust the guards or staff.

Some criminologists have suggested that the prison code is simply a reflection of general criminal values; if so, these values are brought to the institution rather than created there. Either way, the power and pervasiveness of the prison code require convicts to conform to the worldview held by the majority of prisoners.

Stanton Wheeler, Ford Foundation Professor of Law and Social Sciences at the University of Washington, closely examined the concept of prisonization in an early study of the Washington State Reformatory.[14] Wheeler found that the degree of prisonization experienced by inmates tends to vary over time and described changing levels of inmate commitment to prison norms and values by way of a U-shaped curve. When an inmate first enters prison, Wheeler said, the conventional values of outside society are of paramount importance, but as time passes, inmates adopt the lifestyle of the prison. However, within the half year prior to release, most inmates begin to demonstrate a renewed appreciation for conventional values. Learn more about both the positive and negative impacts of imprisonment at Library Extra 12–2 at mycrimekit.com.

Library EXTRA

Different prisons share aspects of a common inmate culture[15]; prison-wise inmates who enter a new facility far from their home will already know the ropes. **Prison argot**, or language, provides one example of how widespread prison subculture can be. The terms used to describe inmate roles in one institution are generally understood in others. The word *rat,* for example, is prison slang for an informer; popularized by crime movies of the 1950s, the term is also understood today by members of the wider society. Other words common to prison argot are shown in CJ Exhibit 1. View an online prisoner's dictionary via Web Extra 12–1 at mycrimekit.com.

prison argot
The slang characteristic of prison subculture and prison life.

Web EXTRA

The Evolution of Prison Subcultures

Prison subcultures change constantly. Like any other American subculture, they evolve to reflect the concerns and experiences of the wider culture, reacting to new crime-control strategies and embracing novel opportunities for crime. The AIDS epidemic of the 1970s and 1980s, for example, brought about changes in prison sexual behavior, at least for a segment of the inmate population, and the emergence of a high-tech criminal group has further differentiated convict types. Because of such changes, John Irwin, as he was completing his classic study titled *The Felon* (1970), expressed worry that his book was already obsolete.[16] *The Felon*, for all its insights into prison subcultures, follows in the descriptive tradition of works by Clemmer and Reimer. Irwin recognized that by 1970, prison subcultures had begun to reflect the cultural changes sweeping America. A decade later, other investigators of prison subcultures were able to write, "It was no longer meaningful to speak of a single inmate culture or even subculture. By the time we began our field research . . . it was clear that the unified, oppositional convict culture, found in the sociological literature on prisons, no longer existed."[17]

The Functions of Prison Subcultures

To protect the public safety, to ensure the safety of Department personnel, and to provide proper care and supervision of all offenders under our jurisdiction while assisting, as appropriate, their reentry into society.
—*Florida Department of Corrections*

How do social scientists and criminologists explain the existence of prison subcultures? Although people around the world live in groups and create their own cultures, in few cases does the intensity of human interaction approach the level found in prisons. Many of today's prisons are densely crowded places where inmates can find no retreat from the constant demands of staff and the pressures of fellow prisoners. Prison subcultures, according to some authors, are fundamentally an adaptation to deprivation and confinement and are a way of addressing the psychological, social, physical, and sexual needs of prisoners living within a highly controlled and regimented institutional setting.

CJ Exhibit 1

Prison Argot: The Language of Confinement

Writers who have studied prison life often comment on prisoners'use of a special language or slang called *prison argot*. This language generally describes the roles assigned by prison culture to types of inmates as well as to prison activities. This box lists a few of the many words and phrases identified in studies by different authors. The first group of words is characteristic of men's prisons; the last few words have been used in women's prisons.

MEN'S PRISON SLANG

Ace duce: Best friend
Badge (bull, hack, the man, or screw): Correctional officer
Banger (burner, shank, or sticker): Knife
Billy: White man
Boneyard: Conjugal visiting area
Cat-J (J-cat): Prisoner in need of psychological or psychiatric therapy or medication
Cellie: Cellmate
Chester: Child molester
Dog: Homeboy or friend
Fag: Male inmate who is believed to be a "natural" or "born" homosexual
Featherwood: White prisoner's woman
Fish: Newly arrived inmate
Gorilla: Inmate who uses force to take what he wants from others
Homeboy: Prisoner from one's hometown or neighborhood
Ink: Tattoos
Lemon squeezer: Inmate who masturbates frequently
Man walking: Phrase used to signal that a guard is coming
Merchant (peddler): One who sells when he should give
Peckerwood (or wood): White prisoner
Punk: Male inmate who is forced into a submissive role during homosexual relations
Rat (snitch): Inmate who squeals (provides information about other inmates to the prison administration)
Schooled: Knowledgeable in the ways of prison life
Shakedown: Search of a cell or of a work area
Tree jumper: Rapist
Turn out: To rape or make into a punk
Wolf: Male inmate who assumes the dominant role during homosexual relations

WOMEN'S PRISON SLANG

Cherry (cherrie): Female inmate who has not yet been introduced to lesbian activities
Fay broad: White female inmate
Femme (mommy): Female inmate who plays the female role during lesbian relations
Safe: Vagina (especially when used for hiding contraband)
Stud broad (daddy): Female inmate who assumes the male role during lesbian relations

---

References: Gresham Sykes, *The Society of Captives* (Princeton, NJ: Princeton University Press, 1958); Rose Giallombardo, *Society of Women: A Study of a Woman's Prison* (New York: John Wiley, 1966); and Richard A. Cloward et al., *Theoretical Studies in Social Organization of the Prison* (New York: Social Science Research Council, 1960). For a more contemporary listing of prison slang terms, see Reinhold Aman, *Hillary Cinton's Pen Pal: A Guide to Life and Lingo in Federal Prison* (Santa Rosa, CA: Maledicta Press, 1996); Jerome Washington, *Iron House: Stories from the Yard* (Ann Arbor, MI: QED Press, 1994); Morrie Camhi, *The Prison Experience* (Boston: Charles Tuttle, 1989); and Harold Long, *Survival in Prison* (Port Townsend, WA: Loompanics, 1990).

What are some of the deprivations that prisoners experience? In *The Society of Captives*, Sykes called felt deprivations the "pains of imprisonment."[18] The pains of imprisonment—the frustrations induced by the rigors of confinement—form the nexus of a *deprivation model* of prison subculture. Sykes said that prisoners are deprived of (1) liberty, (2) goods and services, (3) heterosexual relationships, (4) autonomy, and (5) personal security; Sykes also stated that these deprivations lead to the development of subcultures intended to ameliorate the personal pains that accompany deprivation.

In contrast to the deprivation model, the *importation model* of prison subculture suggests that inmates bring with them values, roles, and behavior patterns from the outside world. Such external values (second nature to career offenders) depend substantially on the criminal worldview. When offenders are confined, these external elements shape the social world of inmates.

It is better to prevent crimes than to punish them.
—*Cesare Bonesana Marchese di Beccaria*

The social structure of the prison, a concept that refers to accepted and relatively permanent social arrangements, is another element that shapes prison subculture. Clemmer's early prison study recognized nine structural dimensions of inmate society[19]:

1. Prisoner–staff dichotomy
2. Three general classes of prisoners
3. Work gangs and cell-house groups

4. Racial groups
5. Type of offense
6. Power of inmate "politicians"
7. Degree of sexual abnormality
8. Record of repeat offenses
9. Personality differences due to preprison socialization

Clemmer's nine structural dimensions are probably still descriptive of prison life today. When applied to individuals, they designate an inmate's position in the prison "pecking order" and create expectations of the appropriate role for that person. Prison roles serve to satisfy the needs of inmates for power, sexual performance, material possessions, individuality, and personal pleasure and to define the status of one prisoner relative to another. For example, inmate leaders, sometimes referred to as "real men" or "toughs" by prisoners in early studies, offer protection to those who live by the rules. They also provide for a redistribution of wealth inside prison and see to it that the rules of the complex prison-derived economic system—based on barter, gambling, and sexual favors—are observed. For an intimate multimedia portrait of life behind bars, visit **Web Extra 12–2** at mycrimekit.com.

Web EXTRA

Prison Lifestyles and Inmate Types

Prison society is strict and often unforgiving. Even so, inmates are able to express some individuality through the choice of a prison lifestyle. John Irwin viewed these lifestyles (like the subcultures of which they are a part) as adaptations to the prison environment.[20] Other writers have since elaborated on these coping mechanisms. Listed in the paragraphs that follow are some of the types of prisoners that researchers have described:

- *The mean dude.* Some inmates adjust to prison by being violent, and other inmates know that these prisoners are best left alone. The mean dude is frequently written up and spends much time in solitary confinement. This role is most common in male institutions and in maximum-security prisons. For some prisoners, the role of mean dude in prison is similar to the role they played in their life prior to being incarcerated. Certain personality types, such as the psychopath, may feel a natural attraction to this role. Plus, prison culture supports violence in two ways: (1) by the expectation that inmates should be tough and (2) through the prevalence of the idea that only the strong survive inside prison.
- *The hedonist.* Some inmates build their lives around the limited pleasures available within the confines of prison. The smuggling of contraband, homosexuality, gambling, drug running, and other officially condemned activities provide the center of interest for prison hedonists. Hedonists generally have an abbreviated view of the future, living only for the "now."
- *The opportunist.* The opportunist takes advantage of the positive experiences prison has to offer. Schooling, trade training, counseling, and other self-improvement activities are the focal points of the opportunist's life in prison. Opportunists are generally well liked by prison staff, but other prisoners shun and mistrust them because they come closest to accepting the role that the staff defines as "model prisoner."
- *The retreatist.* Prison life is rigorous and demanding. Badgering by the staff and actual or feared assaults by other inmates may cause some prisoners to attempt psychological retreat from the realities of imprisonment. Such inmates may experience neurotic or psychotic episodes, become heavily involved in drug and alcohol abuse through the illicit prison economy, or even attempt suicide. Depression and mental illness are the hallmarks of the retreatist personality in prison.
- *The legalist.* The legalist is the "jailhouse lawyer." Convicts facing long sentences, with little possibility for early release through the corrections system, are most likely to turn to the courts in their battle against confinement.
- *The radical.* Radical inmates view themselves as political prisoners. They see society and the successful conformists who populate it as oppressors who have forced criminal-

ity on many "good people" through the creation of a system that distributes wealth and power inequitably. The inmate who takes on the radical role is unlikely to receive much sympathy from prison staff.

- *The colonizer.* Some inmates think of prison as their home and don't look forward to leaving. They "know the ropes," have many "friends" inside, and may feel more comfortable institutionalized than on the streets, and they typically hold positions with power or respect among the inmate population. Once released, some colonizers commit new crimes to return to prison.
- *The religious.* Some prisoners profess a strong religious faith. They may be "born-again" Christians, committed Muslims, or even Satanists or witches. Religious inmates frequently attend services, may form prayer groups, and sometimes ask the prison administration to allocate meeting facilities or to create special diets to accommodate their claimed spiritual needs. While it is certainly true that some inmates have a strong religious faith, staff members are apt to be suspicious of the overly religious prisoner.
- *The gangbanger.* Gangbangers are affiliated with prison gangs and depend upon the gang for defense and protection. They display gang signs, sport gang-related tattoos, and use their gang membership as a channel for the procurement of desired goods and services both inside and outside prison.
- *The realist.* The realist is a prisoner who sees confinement as a natural consequence of criminal activity, and time spent in prison is an unfortunate cost of doing business. This stoic attitude toward incarceration generally leads the realist to "pull his (or her) own time" and to make the best of it. Realists tend to know the inmate code, are able to avoid trouble, and continue in lives of crime once released.

Whilst we have prisons it matters little which of us occupies the cells.

—*George Bernard Shaw (1856–1950)*

Homosexuality and Sexual Victimization in Prison

Sexual behavior inside prisons is both constrained and encouraged by prison subculture. One Houston woman, whose son is serving time in a Texas prison, described the sexual victimization of her son this way: "Within a matter of days, if not hours, an unofficial prison welcome

▲ A male inmate dresses as a female in the protective custody wing of the Ferguson Unit in Midway, Texas. Homosexuality is common in both men's and women's prisons. How does it differ between the two?
Andrew Lichtenstein

wagon sorts new arrivals into those who will fight, those who will pay extortion cash of up to $60 every two weeks, and those who will be servants or slaves." She went on to say, "You're jumped on by two or three prisoners to see if you'll fight. If you don't fight, you become someone's girl, until they're tired of you and they sell you to someone else."[21]

Sykes's early study of prison argot found many words describing sexual activity, and quite a few of them related to homosexuality. Included here are the terms *wolf, punk*, and *fag*: Wolves are aggressive men who assume the masculine role in homosexual relations, punks are forced into submitting to the female role, and fag describes a special category of men who have a natural proclivity toward homosexual activity and effeminate mannerisms. While both wolves and punks are fiercely committed to their heterosexual identity and participate in homosexuality only because of prison conditions, fags generally engage in homosexual lifestyles before their entry into prison and continue to emulate feminine mannerisms and styles of dress once incarcerated.

Prison homosexuality depends to a considerable degree on the naïveté of young inmates experiencing prison for the first time. Even when newly arrived inmates are protected from fights, older prisoners looking for homosexual liaisons may ingratiate themselves by offering cigarettes, money, drugs, food, or protection. At some future time, these "loans" will be called in, with payoffs demanded in sexual favors. Because the inmate code requires the repayment of favors, the "fish" who tries to resist may quickly find himself face-to-face with the brute force of inmate society.

The sexual coercion experiences (episodes involving "persuasion" and other techniques to gain victims' unwilling compliance) of inmates were recently studied by Cindy Struckman-Johnson and David Struckman-Johnson, who obtained survey data from 1,788 male and 263 female inmates in 10 midwestern prisons.[22] Survey results, which were published in 2006, showed that 21% of the men and 19% of the women reported having experienced one or more incidents of pressured or coerced sexual contact during their present incarceration. Most perpetrators of sexual coercion were men (91% of the male victims, but only 51% of the female victims reported a male perpetrator), and men were more likely than women (72% versus 47%) to be coerced by other inmates, while women were far more likely to be coerced into sexual relations by prison staff (41% of women inmates versus 8% of male inmates). More than half of all incidents of sexual coercion, however, involved multiple perpetrators.

Prison rape, which is generally considered to involve physical assault, represents a special category of sexual victimization behind bars. In 2003, Congress created the National Prison Rape Elimination Commission and mandated the collection of statistics on prison rape as part of the Prison Rape Elimination Act (PREA).[23] The purposes of the PREA are as follows[24]:

- Establish a zero-tolerance standard for prison rape.
- Make prison rape prevention a top priority in correctional facilities and systems.
- Develop and implement national standards for the detection, prevention, reduction, and punishment of prison rape.
- Increase the availability of information on the incidence and prevalence of prison rape.
- Increase the accountability of corrections officials with regard to the issue of sexual violence in our nation's prisons.

The PREA requires the Bureau of Justice Statistics (BJS), under the direction of the National Prison Rape Elimination Commission, to collect sexual victimization data in federal and state prisons, county and city jails, and juvenile institutions; the U.S. Census Bureau acts as the official repository for collected data. A recent BJS report, the National Inmate Survey (NIS), involves data gathered between April and August of 2007 and covers 146 state and federal prisons. NIS data show that 4.5% of the inmates who participated in the PREA-mandated survey reported an incident of sexual victimization, either inmate-on-inmate or staff-on-inmate, in the previous 12 months.[25] In response, the National Prison Rape Elimination Commission noted that "given a current U.S. prison population of 1,570,861, that statistic suggests that more than 70,000 prisoners were victims of sexual violence in one year alone."[26] Details from the 2007 BJS survey reveal that inmates in ten facilities reported victimization rates of 9.3% or greater, while inmates in six units covered by the survey reported no sexual victimization. The highest victimization levels were reported at the Estelle Unit in Texas (15.7%) and the Clements Unit, also in Texas (13.9%). Three facilities had prevalence rates of staff-on-inmate sexual misconduct that exceeded 10%. The highest rate of staff sexual misconduct (12.2% of inmates) was reported at the Tecumseh State Correctional Institution in Nebraska, followed by the Clements Unit in Texas (11.6%) and the Charlotte Correctional Institution in Florida (11.4%). Surprisingly, the BJS survey found that the greatest number of reported incidents involved sexual misconduct by staff members (38,600 incidents) and not inmate-on-inmate sexual contact (27,500 incidents).

The 2007 BJS survey included only inmates in state and federal prisons and did not take into account the many other settings in which sexual violence occurs, including jails, community corrections, immigration facilities, and youth detention facilities. In 2008, however, the National Prison Rape Elimination Commission, in conjunction with BJS, published a report on sexual victimization in local jails.[27] The report identified common characteristics of victims and perpetrators of rape in county jails, and the characteristics of U.S. jails with the highest and lowest incidence of rape. That report, *Sexual Victimization in Local Jails Reported by Inmates*, is available at mycrimekit.com at Library Extra 12–3.

Library EXTRA

PREA surveys are only a first step in understanding and eliminating rape. As BJS notes, "Due to fear of reprisal from perpetrators, a code of silence among inmates, personal embarrassment, and lack of trust in staff, victims are often reluctant to report incidents to corrections authorities."[28] Provisions of PREA were extended by congressional action in 2008.[29] Learn more about PREA and read new survey results as they become available at Web Extra 12–3 at mycrimekit.com.

Web EXTRA

An earlier but comprehensive review of rape inside male prisons was published in 2001 by Human Rights Watch. Titled *No Escape: Male Rape in U.S. Prisons*,[30] the 378-page report examined three years of research and interviews with more than 200 prisoners in 34 states. Perpetrators of prison rape were found to be young (generally 20 to 30 years old), larger or stronger than their victims, and "generally more assertive, physically aggressive, and more at home in the prison environment" than their victims. Rapists were also found to be "street smart" and were frequently gang members who were well established in the inmate hierarchy and who had been convicted of violent crimes. A large proportion of sexual aggressors are characterized by low education and poverty, having grown up in a broken home headed by the mother and having a record of violent offenses.[31] Lee H. Bowker, summarizing studies of sexual violence in prison, provides the following observations[32]:

- Most sexual aggressors do not consider themselves homosexuals.
- Sexual release is not the primary motivation for sexual attack.
- Many aggressors must continue to participate in gang rapes to avoid becoming victims themselves.
- The aggressors have themselves suffered much damage to their masculinity in the past.

As in cases of heterosexual rape, sexual assaults in prison are likely to leave psychological scars on the victims long after the physical event is over.[33] Victims of prison rape live in fear, may feel constantly threatened, and can turn to self-destructive activities.[34] Many victims question their masculinity and undergo a personal devaluation; some victims of prison sexual assault become violent, attacking and sometimes killing the person who raped them. The Human Rights Watch researchers found that prisoners "fitting any part of the following description" are more likely to become rape victims: "young, small in size, physically weak, white, gay, first offender, possessing 'feminine' characteristics such as long hair or a high voice; being unassertive, unaggressive, shy, intellectual, not street-smart, or 'passive'; or having been convicted of a sexual offense against a minor." The researchers also noted that "prisoners with several overlapping characteristics are much more likely than other prisoners to be targeted for abuse." The report concluded that to reduce the incidence of prison rape, "prison officials should take considerably more care in matching cell mates, and that, as a general rule, double-celling should be avoided." Learn more about male rape in U.S. prisons at Library Extra 12–4 at mycrimekit.com.

Library EXTRA

The Female Inmate's World

More than 112,000 women were imprisoned in state and federal correctional institutions throughout the United States at the start of 2007, accounting for slightly more than 7% of all prison inmates.[35] Texas had the largest number of female prisoners (13,799), exceeding even the federal government.[36] Figure 1 provides a breakdown of the total American prison population by gender and ethnicity. While there are still far more men imprisoned across the nation than women (approximately 15 men for every woman), the number of female inmates is rising.[37] In 1981, women made up only 4% of the nation's overall prison population, but the number of female inmates nearly tripled during the 1980s and is continuing to grow at a rate greater than that of male inmates.

In 2003, the National Institute of Corrections (NIC) published the results of its three-year project on women offenders in adult correctional settings.[38] Findings from the study produced a national profile of incarcerated women that is shown in Table 1. NIC says that "women involved in the criminal justice system represent a population marginalized by race, class, and gender."[39] African-American women, for example, are overrepresented in correctional populations: While they constitute only 13% of women in the United States, nearly 50% of women in prison are African-American, and African-American women are eight times more likely than white women to be incarcerated.

Study authors found that most women offenders are nonviolent and that their crimes are typically less threatening to community safety than those of male offenders. Female offenders, according to the study, are disproportionately low-income women of color who are undereducated and unskilled, with sporadic employment histories. They are less likely than men to have committed violent offenses and more likely to have been convicted of crimes involving drugs or property. Often, their property offenses are economically driven, motivated by poverty and by the abuse of alcohol and other drugs. The majority of offenses committed by women who are in prisons and jails are nonviolent drug and property crimes.

According to NIC, women face life circumstances that tend to be specific to their gender, such as sexual abuse, sexual assault, and domestic violence as well as the responsibility of being the primary caregiver for dependent children. Research shows that women offenders differ significantly from their male counterparts regarding personal histories and pathways to crime.[40] A female offender, for example, is more likely than a male offender to have been the primary caregiver of young children at the time of her arrest, more likely to have experienced physical and/or sexual abuse, and more likely to have distinctive physical and mental health needs.

Women's most common pathways to crime, said NIC, involve survival strategies that result from physical and sexual abuse, poverty, and substance abuse. Consequently, the first life circumstance that the NIC study examined closely was physical and sexual abuse. "Not

FIGURE 1
Prison Inmates by Gender and Ethnicity in State and Federal Prisons, 2007.
Source: William J. Sabol, Heather Couture, and Paige M. Harrison, *Prisoners in 2006* (Washington, DC: Bureau of Justice Statistics, 2007).

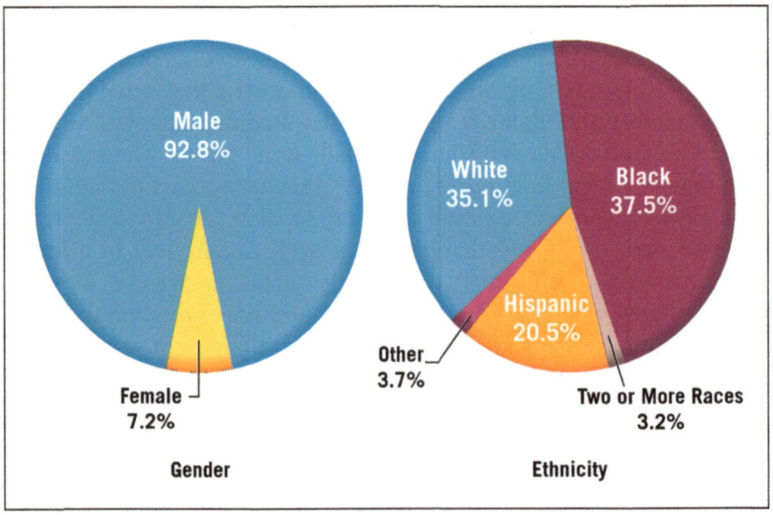

TABLE 1 National Profile of Women Offenders

A profile based on national data for women offenders reveals the following characteristics:

- Disproportionately women of color
- In their early to middle 30s
- Most likely to have been convicted of a drug-related offense
- From fragmented families that include other family members who also have been involved with the criminal justice system
- Survivors of physical and/or sexual abuse as children and adults
- Individuals with significant substance abuse problems
- Individuals with multiple physical and mental health problems
- Unmarried mothers of minor children
- Individuals with a high school or general equivalency diploma (GED) but limited vocational training and sporadic work histories

Source: Barbara Bloom, Barbara Owen, and Stephanie Covington, *Gender-Responsive Strategies: Research, Practice, and Guiding Principles for Women Offenders* (Washington, DC: National Institute of Corrections, 2003).

all women who suffer abuse commit crimes, but one of the things most women in prison share is a background of victimization," says Harvard researcher Angel Browne. Supporting data come from BJS findings showing that about half (48%) of women in jail (but only 13% of men) and half (48%) of women in state and federal prisons (but only 12% of men) had been physically or sexually abused before incarceration.[41] Women in prison are three times more likely to have a history of abuse than men in prison.[42] Approximately 37% of women in state prison, 23% of women in federal prison, 37% of women in jail, and 28% of women on probation reported physical or sexual abuse before the age of 18.[43]

Other studies show a much higher rate of abuse than the BJS data. One study, for example, found that 80% of a sample of incarcerated women in California had been physically and/or sexually abused prior to incarceration.[44] A later study found that more than 80% of the women incarcerated in North Carolina's state prisons had been physically and/or sexually abused.[45] In interviews with women at a New York maximum-security prison, Browne found that 70% of incarcerated women reported physical violence, and nearly 60% reported sexual abuse.[46]

▲ A female inmate being housed in the segregation unit of a Rhode Island correctional facility because of disciplinary problems. The number of women in prison is growing steadily. Why?
Richard Falco/Black Star

The link between female criminality and substance abuse is very strong, and it was the second life circumstance that the NIC study examined. Research shows that women are more likely to be involved in crime if they are drug users.[47] Approximately 80% of women in state prisons have substance abuse problems.[48] About half of women offenders in state prisons had been using alcohol, drugs, or both at the time of their offense, and nearly one in three women serving time in state prisons reported committing the offense to obtain money to support a drug habit; about half described themselves as daily users.[49] To put these statistics into perspective, it is helpful to compare them to statistics on substance abuse among women in the general population. The Substance Abuse and Mental Health Services Administration reports that 2.1% of females in the United States ages 12 and older had engaged in heavy alcohol use

We must remember always that the doors of prisons swing both ways.

—Mary Belle Harris
First federal female warden

within the 30 days preceding the survey, 4.1% had used an illicit drug, and 1.2% had used a psychotherapeutic drug for a nonmedical purpose.[50] By contrast, the National Center on Addiction and Substance Abuse found that 54% of women offenders in state prisons had used an illicit drug during the month before they committed their crimes, and 48% were under the influence of either alcohol or another drug when they committed their crimes.[51] Among women offenders in federal prisons, 27% had used an illicit drug in the month before they committed their crimes, and 20% were under the influence when they committed their crimes.

Some complain that many women are being unfairly sent to prison by current federal drug policies for playing only minor roles in drug-related offenses. "We've gone from being a nation of latchkey kids to a nation of locked-up moms, where women are the invisible prisoners of drug laws, serving hard time for someone else's crime,"[52] says Lenora Lapidus, coauthor of the 2005 report *Caught in the Net: The Impact of Drug Policies on Women and Families*.[53] "Even when they have minimal or no involvement whatsoever in the drug trade," the report claims, "women are increasingly caught in the ever-widening net cast by current drug laws." *Caught in the Net* is available at mycrimekit.com as Library Extra 12–5.

Library EXTRA

The third life circumstance that the NIC study examined was physical health. Women inmates face health issues, including pregnancy, that differ from those of men. Women frequently enter jails and prisons in poor health, and they experience more serious health problems than do their male counterparts. Their poor health is often due to poverty, poor nutrition, inadequate health care, and substance abuse.[54] It is estimated that 20% to 35% of women attend prison sick call daily compared with 7% to 10% of men. Women also have more medical problems related to their reproductive systems than do men. About 5% of women enter prison while pregnant; most of these pregnancies are considered high risk due to a history of inadequate medical care, abuse, and substance abuse.

Sexually transmitted diseases are also a problem among women offenders. Approximately 3.5% of women in prison are HIV-positive, and women prisoners are 50% more likely than male prisoners to be HIV-positive. The number of women infected with HIV has increased 69% since 1991, whereas the number of infected male offenders has decreased by 22%.[55] Women offenders are also at greater risk for breast, lung, and cervical cancer. One study, for example, found that incarcerated women who reported sexual abuse before the age of 17 were six times more likely than those who did not experience this abuse to exhibit precancerous cervical lesions.[56]

Women in prison have a higher incidence of mental disorders than do women in the community, and mental health was the fourth focus of the NIC study. One-quarter of women in state prisons have been identified as suffering from mental illness.[57] The major diagnoses of mental illness are depression, post-traumatic stress disorder (PTSD), and substance abuse. Women offenders have histories of abuse that are associated with psychological trauma, and PTSD is a psychiatric condition often seen in women who have experienced sexual abuse and other trauma. Symptoms of PTSD include depression, low self-esteem, insomnia, panic, nightmares, and flashbacks. Approximately 75% of women who have serious mental illness also suffer from substance abuse disorders, and about one in four of all women in state prisons is receiving medication for psychological disorders. A total of 22.3% of women in jail have been diagnosed with PTSD, 13.7% have been diagnosed with a current episode of depression, and about 17% are receiving medication for psychological disorders.[58] Women with serious mental illness and co-occurring disorders experience significant difficulties in jail and prison settings, and the lack of both appropriate assessment of and treatment for women with mental health issues is an ongoing problem in correctional settings.[59]

Children and marital status were identified as a fifth important life circumstance by the NIC study—80% of women entering prison are mothers, and 85% of those women had custody of their children at the time of admission. Approximately 70% of all women under correctional supervision have at least one child younger than age 18. Two-thirds of incarcerated women have minor children; about two-thirds of women in state prisons and half of women in federal prisons had lived with their young children before entering prison. One out of four women entering prison either has recently given birth or is pregnant; pregnant inmates, many of whom are drug users, malnourished, or sick, often receive little prenatal care, a situation that risks additional complications.

It is estimated that 1.3 million minor children have a mother who is under correctional supervision, and more than 250,000 minor children have mothers in jail or prison.[60] Separation from their children is a significant deprivation for many women. Although husbands or boyfriends may assume responsibility for the children of their imprisoned partners, this situation is the exception rather than the rule. Eventually, many children of imprisoned mothers are placed into foster care or are put up for adoption.

Some states offer parenting classes for female inmates with children. In a national survey of prisons for women, 36 states responded that they provide parenting programs that deal with caretaking, reduction of violence toward children, visitation problems, and related issues.[61] Some offer play areas furnished with toys, while others attempt to alleviate difficulties attending mother–child visits. The typical program studied meets for two hours per week and lasts from four to nine weeks.

Of children whose fathers are incarcerated, approximately 90% live with their mothers; only 25% of the children of women offenders live with their fathers. Grandparents are most likely to be the caregivers of the children of female offenders. Approximately 10% of these children are in foster care or group homes. More than half of the children of women prisoners never visit their mothers during the period of incarceration.[62] The lack of visits is due primarily to the remote location of prisons, a lack of transportation, and the inability of caregivers to arrange visitation.

Women under criminal justice supervision are more likely than the general population never to have been married. In one survey, nearly half of the women in jail and prison reported that they had never been married[63]; 42% of women on probation reported that they had never been married, and about 31% of women in prison reported that they were either separated or divorced.

Education and employment were the final life circumstances that the NIC study examined. An estimated 55% of women in local jails, 56% of women in state prisons, and 73% of women in federal prisons have a high school diploma.[64] Approximately 40% of the women in state prisons report that they were employed full-time at the time of their arrest, compared with almost 60% of males.[65] About 37% of women and 28% of men had incomes of less than $600 per month prior to arrest. Most of the jobs held by women were low-skill entry-level jobs with low pay (two-thirds of the women reported they had never held a job that paid more than $6.50 per hour). Women are less likely than men to have engaged in vocational training before incarceration, and those who have received vocational training in the community have tended to focus on traditional women's jobs, such as cosmetology, clerical work, and food service.

Gender Responsiveness

Critics have long charged that female inmates face a prison system designed for male inmates and run by men. Consequently, meaningful prison programs for women are often lacking, because the ones that are in place were originally based on models adapted from men's prisons or because they are based on traditional views of female roles that leave little room for employment opportunities in the contemporary world. Many trade-training programs still emphasize low-paying jobs, such as cook, beautician, or laundry machine operator, and classes in homemaking are not uncommon.

A central purpose of the NIC report on the female offender was to identify effective gender-responsive approaches for managing women prisoners. The study defined gender responsiveness as "creating an environment . . . that reflects an understanding of the realities of women's lives and addresses the issues of women."[66] The NIC report concluded with a call for recognition of the behavioral and social differences between female and male offenders—especially those that have specific implications for gender-responsive policies and practices. Among the report's recommendations are the following:

- The creation of an effective system for female offenders that is structured differently from a system for male offenders
- The development of gender-responsive policies and practices targeting women's pathways to criminality in order to provide effective interventions that address the intersecting issues of substance abuse, trauma, mental health, and economic marginality

- The modification of criminal justice sanctions and interventions to recognize the low risk to public safety represented by the typical female offender
- The consideration of women's relationships, especially those with their children, and women's roles in the community in deciding appropriate correctional sanctions

Library EXTRA

The NIC study concluded that gender-responsive correctional practices can improve outcomes for women offenders by considering their histories, behaviors, and life circumstances. It also suggested that investments in gender-responsive policies and procedures will likely produce long-term dividends for the criminal justice system and the community as well as for women offenders and their families. Read the entire NIC report at Library Extra 12–6 at mycrimekit.com.

Institutions for Women

Most female inmates are housed in centralized state facilities known as women's prisons, which are dedicated exclusively to incarcerating female felons. Although there is not a typical prison for women, the American Correctional Association (ACA) 1990 report by the Task Force on the Female Offender found that the institutions that house female inmates could be generally described as follows[67]:

- Most prisons for women are located in towns with fewer than 25,000 inhabitants.
- A significant number of facilities were not designed to house female inmates.
- Some facilities that house female inmates also house men.
- Few facilities for women have programs especially designed for female offenders.
- Few major disturbances or escapes are reported among female inmates.
- Substance abuse among female inmates is very high.
- Few work assignments are available to female inmates.

Social Structure in Women's Prisons

"Aside from sharing the experience of being incarcerated," says Professor Marsha Clowers of the John Jay College of Criminal Justice, "female prisoners have much in common. They are likely to be black or Hispanic, poor, uneducated, abuse survivors, single parents, and in poor health."[68] Shared social characteristics may lead to similar values and behaviors. One type of behavior identified by early prison researchers as characteristic of a fair number of incarcerated women concerns the way in which female inmates construct organized pseudofamilies. Typical of such studies are D. Ward and G. Kassebaum's *Women's Prison: Sex and Social Structure* (1966),[69] Esther Heffernan's *Making It in Prison: The Square, the Cool, and the Life* (1972),[70] and Rose Giallombardo's *Society of Women: A Study of Women's Prisons* (1966).[71]

Giallombardo, for example, examined the Federal Reformatory for Women at Alderson, West Virginia, spending a year gathering data in the early 1960s. Focusing closely on the social formation of families among female inmates, she titled one of her chapters "The Homosexual Alliance as a Marriage Unit." In it, she described in great detail the sexual identities assumed by women at Alderson and the symbols they chose to communicate those roles. Hairstyle, dress, language, and mannerisms were all used to signify "maleness" or "femaleness." Giallombardo detailed "the anatomy of the marriage relationship from courtship to 'fall out,' that is, from inception to the parting of the ways, or divorce."[72] Romantic love at Alderson was of central importance to any relationship between inmates, and all homosexual relationships were described as voluntary. Through marriage, the "stud broad" became the husband and the "femme" the wife.

Studies attempting to document the extent of inmate involvement in prison "families" have produced varying results. Some have found as many as 71% of female prisoners involved in the phenomenon, while others have found none.[73] The kinship systems described by Giallombardo and others, however, extend beyond simple "family" ties to the formation of large, intricately related groups involving a large number of nonsexual relationships. In these groups, the roles of "children," "in-laws," "grandparents," and so on may be explicitly recognized. Even "birth order" within a family can become an issue for kinship groups.[74] Kinship groups sometimes occupy a common household, usually a prison cottage or a dormitory area. The descriptions of women's

Female inmates in Sheriff Joe Arpaio's "equal opportunity jail" in Maricopa County, Arizona, being inspected by a correctional officer before leaving for chain-gang duty. Not all states make use of chain gangs, and only a few use female inmates on chain gangs. Should jail chain gangs be more widely used?
Jack Kurtz/The Image Works

prisons provided by authors like Giallombardo show a closed society in which social interactions—including expectations, normative forms of behavior, and emotional ties—are regulated by an inventive system of artificial relationships that mirror those of the outside world.

Many studies of women's prisoners show that incarcerated women suffer intensely from the loss of affectional relationships once they enter prison and that they form homosexual liaisons to compensate for such losses.[75] Those liaisons then become the foundation of prison social organization.

Barbara Owen, Professor of Criminology at California State University, Fresno, conducted a study of women inmates at the Central California Women's Facility (the largest prison for women in the world). Her book, "*In the Mix*": *Struggle and Survival in a Women's Prison*,[76] describes the daily life of the female inmates, with an emphasis on prison social structure. Owen found that prison culture for women is tied directly to the roles that women normally assume in free society as well as to other factors shaped by the conditions of women's lives in prison and in the free world. Like Heffernan's work, "*In the Mix*" describes the lives of women before prison and suggests that those lifestyles shape women's adaptation to prison culture. Owen found that preexisting economic marginalization, self-destructive behaviors, and personal histories of physical, sexual, and substance abuse may be important defining features of inmates' lives before they enter prison.[77] She also discovered that the sentences that women have to serve, along with their work and housing assignments, effectively pattern their daily lives and relationships. Owen described "the mix" as that aspect of prison culture that supports the rule-breaking behavior that propels women into crime and causes them to enter prison. Owen concluded that prison subcultures for women are very different from the violent and predatory structure of contemporary male prisons.[78] Like men, women experience "pains of imprisonment," but their prison culture offers them other ways to survive and adapt to these deprivations.

The person of a prisoner sentenced to imprisonment in the State prison is under the protection of the law, and any injury to his person, not authorized by law, is punishable in the same manner as if he were not convicted or sentenced.
—*Section 2650 of the California Penal Code*

A 2001 study of a women's correctional facility in the southeastern United States found that female inmates who were asked about their preincarceration sexual orientation gave answers that were quite different than when they were asked about their sexual orientation while incarcerated.[79] In general, 64% of inmates interviewed reported being exclusively heterosexual, 28% said they were bisexual, and 8% said that they were lesbians before being incarcerated. In contrast, these same women reported sexual orientations while incarcerated of 55% heterosexual, 31% bisexual, and 13% lesbian. Researchers found that same-sex sexual behavior within the institution was more likely to occur in the lives of young inmates who had had such experiences before entering prison. The study also found that female inmates tended to become more involved in lesbian behavior the longer they were incarcerated.

Finally, a significant aspect of sexual activity far more commonly found in women's prisons than in prisons for men involves sexual misconduct between staff and inmates. While a fair amount of such behavior is attributed to the exploitation of female inmates by male correctional officers acting from positions of power, some studies suggest that female inmates may sometimes attempt to manipulate unsuspecting male officers into illicit relationships in order to gain favors.[80]

Types of Female Inmates

As in institutions for men, the subculture of women's prisons is multidimensional. Esther Heffernan, for example, found that three terms used by the female prisoners she studied—the *square*, the *cool*, and the *life*—were indicative of three styles of adaptation to prison life.[81] Square inmates had few early experiences with criminal lifestyles and tended to sympathize with the values and attitudes of conventional society. Cool prisoners were more likely to be career offenders; they tended to keep to themselves and generally supported inmate values. Women who participated in the life subculture were quite familiar with lives of crime, and many had been arrested repeatedly for prostitution, drug use, theft, and so on. They were full participants in the economic, social, and familial arrangements of the prison. Heffernan believed that the life option offered an alternative lifestyle to women who had experienced early and constant rejection by conventional society. With the life characteristics, women could establish relationships, achieve status, and find meaning in their lives. The square, the cool, and the life represented subcultures to Heffernan because individuals with similar adaptive choices tended to relate closely to one another and to support the lifestyle characteristic of that type.

Recently, the social structure of women's prisons has been altered by the arrival of "crack kids," as they are called in prison argot. Crack kids, whose existence highlights generational differences among female offenders, are streetwise young women with little respect for traditional prison values, for their elders, or even for their own children. Known for frequent fights and for their lack of even simple domestic skills, many older inmates quickly separate themselves from these young women, some of whom call the younger inmates "animalescents."

Violence in Women's Prisons

Some authors have suggested that violence in women's prisons is less frequent than it is in institutions for men. Lee Bowker observes that "except for the behavior of a few 'guerrillas,' it appears that violence is only used in women's prisons to settle questions of dominance and subordination when other manipulative strategies fail to achieve the desired effect."[82] It appears that few homosexual liaisons are forced, perhaps representing a general aversion among women to such victimization in wider society. At least one study, however, has shown the use of sexual violence in women's prisons as a form of revenge against inmates who are overly vocal in their condemnation of lesbian practices among other prisoners.[83]

Not all abuse occurs at the hands of inmates. In 1992, 14 correctional officers (ten men and four women) were indicted for the alleged abuse of female inmates at the 900-bed Women's Correctional Institute in Hardwick, Georgia. The charges resulted from affidavits filed by 90 female inmates alleging "rape, sexual abuse, prostitution, coerced abortions, sex for favors, and retaliation for refusal to participate" in such activities.[84] One inmate who was forced to have an abortion after becoming pregnant by a male staff member said, "As an inmate, I simply felt powerless to avoid the sexual advances of staff and to refuse to have an abortion."[85]

To address the problems of imprisoned women, including violence, the Task Force on the Female Offender recommended a number of changes in the administration of prisons for women[86]:

- Substance abuse programs should be available to female inmates.
- Female inmates need to acquire greater literacy skills, and literacy programs should form the basis on which other programs are built.
- Female offenders should be housed in buildings without male inmates.
- Institutions for women should develop programs for keeping children in the facility in order to "fortify the bond between mother and child."
- To ensure equal access to assistance, institutions should be built to accommodate programs for female offenders.

Library EXTRA

Learn more about women in prison and their special needs via Library Extras 12–7 and 12–8 at mycrimekit.com.

The Staff World

Facts and Figures

The flip side of inmate society can be found in the world of the prison staff, which includes many people working in various professions. Staff roles encompass those of warden, psychologist, counselor, area supervisor, program director, instructor, correctional officer, and—in some large prisons—physician and therapist.

According to the federal government, approximately 748,000 people are employed in corrections,[87] with the majority performing direct custodial tasks in state institutions: 62% of corrections employees work for state governments, followed by 33% at the local level and 5% at the federal level.[88] On a per capita basis, the District of Columbia has the most state and local corrections employees (53.3 per every 10,000 residents), followed by Texas (43.8).[89] Across the nation, 70% of correctional officers are Caucasian, 22% are African-American, and slightly over 5% are Hispanic.[90] Women account for 20% of all correctional officers, with the proportion of female officers increasing at around 19% per year, and the ACA encourages correctional agencies to "ensure that recruitment, selection, and promotion opportunities are open to women."[91]

Correctional officers, generally considered to be at the bottom of the staff hierarchy, may be divided into cell-block guards and tower guards; others are assigned to administrative offices, where they perform clerical tasks. The ratio averages around four inmates for each correctional officer in state prisons.[92]

Like prisoners, correctional officers undergo a socialization process that helps them function by the official and unofficial rules of staff society. In a now-classic study, Lucien X. Lombardo described the process by which officers are socialized into the prison work world.[93] Lombardo interviewed 359 corrections personnel at New York's Auburn Prison and found that rookie officers quickly had to abandon preconceptions of both inmates and other staff members. According to Lombardo, new officers learn that inmates are not the "monsters" much of the public makes them out to be; on the other hand, rookies may be seriously disappointed in their experienced

Tom Hanks playing the role of a correctional officer in the movie *The Green Mile*. The job of a correctional officer centers largely on the custody and control of inmates, but growing professionalism is enhancing both personal opportunities and job satisfaction among officers. Why is professionalism important to job satisfaction?
Photofest

CJ Exhibit 2

The Commission on Safety and Abuse in America's Prisons

On June 8, 2006, the Commission on Safety and Abuse in America's Prisons released its long-awaited final report.[1] The commission had been formed over a year earlier, with support from the Vera Institute of Justice following the widely publicized scandals at Abu Ghraib prison in Iraq. The commission's avowed purpose was to explore the most serious problems inside U.S. correctional facilities and to assess their impact on the incarcerated, corrections personnel, and society at large.[2] "As President Bush was calling the abuse at Abu Ghraib 'un-American,'" said the commission's website, "many Americans raised questions about the treatment of prisoners here at home."

The commission's 21-member nonpartisan panel was co-chaired by former U.S. Attorney General Nicholas Katzenbach and the Honorable John J. Gibbons, former chief judge of the U.S. Third Circuit Court of Appeals.

During much of 2005 and into 2006, the commission held public hearings across the country and interviewed corrections professionals, legislators, and interested parties to explore the most serious problems facing correctional facilities today, including violence, sexual abuse, the degradation of prisoners, overcrowding, treatment for the mentally ill, and the working conditions of correctional officers. Interim reports were released following each hearing.

"How we treat correctional officers and inmates is an issue that goes beyond the walls of our prisons, impacting the families and communities of both correctional officers and inmates," said Senator Patrick Leahy (D–Vt.), the ranking member of the Senate Judiciary Committee in commenting on the commission's work.[3]

The commission's final report was built around practical recommendations intended to be useful to local, state, and federal policy makers seeking to improve conditions in prisons and jails in their jurisdictions. Recommendations were made in the areas of violence reduction, health care, high-security segregation, corrections leadership and professionalism, oversight and accountability, and development, collection, and use of standardized data helpful in the creation of public policy about prison and jails.

A summary of the commission's recommendations in the area of corrections leadership follows:

1. *Promote a culture of mutual respect.* Create a positive culture in jails and prisons grounded in an ethic of respectful behavior and interpersonal communication that benefits prisoners and staff.
2. *Recruit and retain a qualified corps of officers.* Enact changes at the state and local levels to advance the recruitment and retention of a diverse high-quality workforce and otherwise further the professionalism of the workforce.
3. *Support today's leaders and cultivate the next generation.* Governors and local executives must hire the most qualified leaders and support them politically and professionally, and corrections administrators must, in turn, use their positions to promote healthy and safe prisons and jails. Equally important, the skills and capacities of middle-level managers, who play a large role in running safe facilities and are poised to become the next generation of senior leaders, must be developed.

For more information about the commission and to read the commission's final report, visit www.prisoncommission.org.

[1]Commission on Safety and Abuse in America's Prisons, *Confronting Confinement: A Report of the Commission on Safety and Abuse in America's Prisons* (New York: Vera Institute of Justice, 2006).
[2]Vera Institute of Justice, "National Commission to Examine U.S. Prison Conditions: Post–Abu Ghraib, Panel to Study U.S. Prisons and Their Impact on Prisoners, Corrections Officers and Society at Large," press release, March 1, 2005.
[3]Commission on Safety and Abuse in America's Prisons, "Federal Policy Makers Support Commission," press release, March 2, 2005.

colleagues when they realize that the ideals of professionalism, often emphasized during early training, rarely translate into reality. The pressures of the institutional work environment, however, soon force most corrections personnel to adopt a united front when relating to inmates.

One of the leading formative influences on staff culture is the potential threat that inmates pose. Inmates far outnumber corrections personnel in every institution, and the hostility they feel for guards is only barely hidden even at the best of times. Corrections personnel know that however friendly inmates may appear, a sudden change in institutional climate—as can happen with anything from simple disturbances in the yard to full-blown riots—can quickly and violently unmask deep-rooted feelings of mistrust and hatred.

As in years past, prison staffers are still most concerned with custody and control. Society, especially under the just deserts philosophy of criminal sentencing, expects corrections staff to keep inmates in custody—the basic prerequisite of successful job performance. Custody is necessary before any other correctional activities, such as instruction or counseling, can be undertaken. Control, the other major staff concern, ensures order, and an orderly prison is thought to be safe and secure. In routine daily activities, control over almost all aspects of inmate behavior becomes paramount in the minds of most correctional officers. It is the twin interests of custody and control that lead to institutionalized procedures for ensuring security in most facilities. The enforcement of strict rules; body and cell searches; counts; unannounced shake-

Freedom or Safety? You Decide.

Dress Codes and Public Safety

Jasjit Jaggi directing traffic headed toward the Brooklyn Bridge in New York City in 2004. Jaggi, a devout Sikh, quit the NYPD in 2002 because his supervisors would not allow him to wear a turban. His reinstatement by the New York City Commission on Human Rights highlights the clash of cultures for all justice system workers, including correctional officers. What limits (if any) should corrections administrators set on faith-based personal displays? How might such limits relate to the security needs of correctional facilities?
Todd Maisel/New York Daily News

On July 1, 2004, the New York City Commission on Human Rights ordered reinstatement of a New York Police Department (NYPD) officer who had quit the force in 2002 because supervisors would not allow him to wear a turban while working. Jasjit Jaggi is a Sikh, whose religion mandates the wearing of turbans and beards by adult males as a sign of their faith. The order, compelling the police department to grant a Sikh employee a religious accommodation, was the first such ruling in the nation issued to a law enforcement agency.

Although turbaned correctional officers are a rarity, some observers have pointed to the possibility of similar lawsuits in the corrections arena. One way for agencies and businesses to avoid legal action comes from the resolution of a religious bias claim brought against United Airlines by a turban-wearing Sikh employee in 2001. Although airline regulations banned the wearing of headgear by employees while indoors, company officials were able to avoid civil liability by offering the man six alternative jobs where he could wear a turban.

YOU DECIDE

How might dress codes relate to public safety? Should agencies have the authority to enforce dress codes without fear of civil liability if those codes enhance public safety? What if they merely enforce uniformity of appearance? How do these ideas apply to correctional agencies?

References: New York City Commission on Human Rights, "Sikh Traffic Enforcement Agent Returns to Work in Landmark Case," *Newsletter* (summer/fall 2004), p. 1; Sikh Coalition, Office of Community Relations, "Petition to Mayor Bloomberg: Allow Turbaned Sikhs to Serve as Officers in the NYPD." Web posted at http://www.petitiononline.com/SikhNYPD/petition.html; and Bureau of National Affairs, Inc., "Religious Bias, Indoor Head-Gear Ban, Offering Six Other Jobs to Turban-Wearing Sikh Sufficient Accommodation," *Employment Discrimination Report*, Vol. 18, p. 469. Web posted at http://www.bna.com/current/edr/topa.htm.

downs; the control of dangerous items, materials, and contraband; and the extensive use of bars, locks, fencing, cameras, and alarms all support the staff's vigilance in maintaining security. See CJ Exhibit 2 for a commission's report on safety in prisons.

The Professionalization of Correctional Officers

Correctional officers have generally been accorded low occupational status. Historically, the role of prison guard required minimal formal education and held few opportunities for professional growth and career advancement, and the job was typically low paying, frustrating, and often boring. Growing problems in our nation's prisons, including emerging issues of legal liability, however, increasingly require a well-trained and adequately equipped force of professionals. As corrections personnel have become better trained and more proficient, the old

Ethics and Professionalism

American Correctional Association Code of Ethics

PREAMBLE

The American Correctional Association expects of its members unfailing honesty, respect for the dignity and individuality of human beings and a commitment to professional and compassionate service. To this end, we subscribe to the following principles:

- Members shall respect and protect the civil and legal rights of all individuals.
- Members shall treat every professional situation with concern for the welfare of the individuals involved and with no intent [of] personal gain.
- Members shall maintain relationships with colleagues to promote mutual respect within the profession and improve the quality of service.
- Members shall make public criticisms of their colleagues or their agencies only when warranted, verifiable, and constructive.
- Members shall respect the importance of all disciplines within the criminal justice system and work to improve cooperation with each segment.
- Members shall honor the public's right to information and share information with the public to the extent permitted by law subject to individuals' right to privacy.
- Members shall respect and protect the right of the public to be safeguarded from criminal activity.
- Members shall refrain from using their positions to secure personal privileges or advantages.
- Members shall refrain from allowing personal interest to impair objectivity in the performance of duty while acting in an official capacity.
- Members shall refrain from entering into any formal or informal activity or agreement which presents a conflict of interest or is inconsistent with the conscientious performance of duties.
- Members shall refrain from accepting any gift, service, or favor that is or appears to be improper or implies an obligation inconsistent with the free and objective exercise of professional duties.
- Members shall clearly differentiate between personal views/statements and views/statements/positions made on behalf of the agency or association.
- Members shall report to appropriate authorities any corrupt or unethical behaviors in which there is sufficient evidence to justify review.
- Members shall refrain from discriminating against any individual because of race, gender, creed, national origin, religious affiliation, age, disability, or any other type of prohibited discrimination.
- Members shall preserve the integrity of private information; they shall refrain from seeking information on individuals beyond that which is necessary to implement responsibilities and perform their duties; members shall refrain from revealing nonpublic information unless expressly authorized to do so.
- Members shall make all appointments, promotions, and dismissals in accordance with established civil service rules, applicable contract agreements, and individual merit, and not in furtherance of partisan interests.
- Members shall respect, promote, and contribute to a workplace that is safe, healthy, and free of harassment in any form.

THINKING ABOUT ETHICS

1. How does the ACA's Code of Ethics differ from the American Jail Association's Code of Ethics? How is it similar?
2. Do you think that one code of ethics should cover correctional officers working in both jails and prisons? Why or why not?

Adopted August 1975 at the 105th Congress of Correction. Revised August 1990 at the 120th Congress of Correction. Revised August 1994 at the 124th Congress of Correction.
Source: Reprinted with permission of the American Correctional Association, Alexandria, Virginia. Visit the American Correctional Association at http://www.corrections.com/aca.

concept of guard has been supplanted by that of correctional officer. The ACA has published a code of ethics for correctional officers that is reproduced in the Ethics and Professionalism box in this chapter.

Many states and a growing number of large-city correctional systems try to eliminate individuals with potentially harmful personality characteristics from correctional officer applicant pools. New Jersey, New York, Ohio, Pennsylvania, and Rhode Island, for example, all use some form of psychological screening when assessing candidates for prison jobs.[94]

Although only a few states utilize psychological screening, all make use of training programs intended to prepare successful applicants for prison work. New York, for example, requires trainees to complete six weeks of classroom-based instruction, 40 hours of rifle range practice, and six weeks of on-the-job training. Training days begin around 5 A.M. with a mile run and conclude after dark with study halls for students who need extra help. To keep pace with rising inmate populations, the state has often had to run a number of simultaneous training academies.[95]

Prison Riots

In 2004, a disturbance took place at the medium- to high-security Arizona State Prison Complex at Lewis. Two correctional officers and a staff member were injured in a ruckus that broke out during breakfast preparations, and two other officers were captured and held hostage for 15 days in a watchtower. The episode, covered by the major news services, may have begun as an escape attempt. Officials were able to keep disorder from spreading to the rest of the facility, and the incident ended when inmates released the officers and surrendered. "It could have been a lot worse," said Joe Masella, president of the Arizona Correctional Peace Officers' Association. "Once these inmates get a taste of blood, so to speak, there's no telling what they can do."[96]

Although today's prisons are relatively calm, the ten years between 1970 and 1980 were called the "explosive decade" of prison riots.[97] The decade began with a massive uprising at Attica Prison in New York State in September 1971, which resulted in 43 deaths and more than 80 wounded men. The "explosive decade" ended in 1980 at Santa Fe, New Mexico. There, in a riot at the New Mexico Penitentiary, 33 inmates died, the victims of vengeful prisoners out to eliminate rats and informants; many of the deaths involved mutilation and torture, more than 200 other inmates were beaten and sexually assaulted, and the prison was virtually destroyed.

While the number of prison riots decreased after the 1970s, they did continue. For 11 days in 1987, the Atlanta (Georgia) Federal Penitentiary was under the control of inmates. The institution was heavily damaged, and inmates had to be temporarily relocated while it was rebuilt. The Atlanta riot followed on the heels of a similar (but less intense) disturbance at the federal detention center at Oakdale, Louisiana. Both outbreaks were attributed to the dissatisfaction of Cuban inmates, most of whom had arrived in the mass exodus known as the Mariel boat lift.[98]

Easter Sunday 1993 marked the beginning of an 11-day rebellion at the 1,800-inmate Southern Ohio Correctional Facility in Lucasville, one of the country's toughest maximum-security prisons. When the riot ended, nine inmates and one correctional officer were dead (the officer had been hung). The close of the riot—involving a parade of 450 inmates—was televised as prisoners had demanded. Among other demands were (1) no retaliation by officials, (2) review of medical staffing and care, (3) review of mail and visitation rules, (4) review of commissary prices, and (5) better enforcement against what the inmates called "inappropriate supervision."[99]

Riots related to inmate grievances over perceived disparities in federal drug-sentencing policies and the possible loss of weight-lifting equipment occurred throughout the federal prison system in October 1995. Within a few days, the unrest led to a nationwide lockdown of 73 federal prisons. Although fires were set and a number of inmates and guards were injured, no deaths resulted. In February 2000, a riot between 200 black and Hispanic prisoners in California's

◄ The Arizona State Prison Complex at Lewis, where two inmates held two correctional officers hostage in a watchtower in 2004. One officer, a female, was raped. On April 30, 2004, inmate Steven Coy was sentenced to seven consecutive life sentences for his part in the hostage crisis. How can the safety of corrections workers be improved?
Tom Hood/AP Wide World Photos

infamous Pelican Bay State Prison led to the death of one inmate and injuries to 15 other inmates. In November 2000, 32 inmates took a dozen correctional officers hostage at the privately run Torrance County Detention Facility in Estancia, New Mexico; two of the guards were stabbed and seriously injured, while another eight were beaten. The riot was finally quelled after an emergency response team threw tear-gas canisters into the area where the prisoners had barricaded themselves.[100]

In 2005, 42 inmates were injured when a fight broke out during breakfast between Hispanic and Caucasian prisoners at California's San Quentin State Prison. The riot occurred in a section of the prison housing about 900 inmates who were under lockdown because of previous fighting between the groups.[101] Also, in 2008, the Federal Correctional Institution in Three Rivers, Texas, was locked down following two gang-related fights that killed one inmate and injured 22. The altercations were broken up by correctional officers with the help of plumbers, electricians, secretaries, and others who were working at the facility at the time the fights broke out.[102]

Causes of Riots

Researchers have suggested a variety of causes for prison riots[103]:

- *Insensitive prison administration and neglected inmates' demands.* Calls for fairness in disciplinary hearings, better food, more recreational opportunities, and the like may lead to riots when they are ignored.
- *Previous lifestyles of most inmates.* It should be no surprise that prisoners use organized violence when many of them were violent people when they were out on the streets.
- *Dehumanizing prison conditions.* Overcrowded facilities, lack of opportunity for individual expression, and other aspects of total institutions culminate in explosive situations of which riots are but one form.
- *Regulation of inmate society and redistribution of power balances among inmate groups.* Riots provide the opportunity to "cleanse" the prison population of informers and rats and to resolve struggles among power brokers and ethnic groups within the institution.
- *Power vacuums.* Changes in prison administration, the transfer of influential inmates, and court-ordered injunctions significantly alter the power structure and informal social-control mechanisms of the institution.

security threat group (STG)
An inmate group, gang, or organization whose members act together to pose a threat to the safety of corrections staff or the public, who prey on other inmates, or who threaten the secure and orderly operation of a correctional institution.

Although riots are difficult to predict in specific institutions, some state prison systems appear ripe for disorder. The Texas prison system, for example, is home to a number of gangs, referred to by corrections personnel as **security threat groups (STGs)**, among whom turf violations can easily lead to widespread disorder. Gang membership among inmates in the Texas prison system, practically nonexistent in 1983, was estimated at more than 1,200 in 1992.[104] The Texas Syndicate, the Aryan Brotherhood of Texas, and the Mexican Mafia (sometimes known as *La Eme*, Spanish for the letter *M*) are probably the largest gangs functioning in the Texas prison system, and each has around 300 members.[105] Other gangs known to operate in some Texas prisons include the Aryan Warriors, Black Gangster Disciples (mostly in midwestern Texas), Black Guerrilla Family, Confederate Knights of America, and Nuestra Familia (an organization of Hispanic prisoners).

Gangs in Texas grew rapidly in part because of the power vacuum created when a court ruling ended the "building tender" system.[106] Building tenders were tough inmates who were given almost free rein by prison administrators to keep other inmates in line, especially in many of the state's worst prisons. The end of the building tender system dramatically increased demands on the Texas Department of Criminal Justice for increased abilities and professionalism among its guards and other prison staff.

The real reasons for any riot are probably specific to the institution and may not allow for easy generalization. However, it is no simple coincidence that the explosive decade of prison riots coincided with the growth of a revolutionary prisoner subculture. As the old convict code began to give way to an emerging perception of social victimization among inmates, it was probably only a matter of time until those perceptions turned to militancy.

Stages in Riots and Riot Control

Most riots are unplanned and tend to occur spontaneously, the result of some relatively minor precipitating event. Once the stage has been set, prison riots tend to evolve through five phases: (1) explosion, (2) organization into inmate-led groups, (3) confrontation with authority, (4) termination through negotiation or physical confrontation, and (5) reaction and explanation, usually by investigative commissions.[107] Donald R. Cressey points out that the early explosive stages of a riot tend to involve "binges" during which inmates exult in their newfound freedom with virtual orgies of alcohol and drug use or sexual activity.[108] Buildings are burned, facilities are wrecked, and old grudges between individual inmates and inmate groups are settled, often through violence. After this initial explosive stage, leadership changes tend to occur and new leaders emerge, who (at least for a time) may effectively organize inmates into a force that can confront and resist officials' attempts to regain control of the institution. Bargaining strategies then develop, and the process of negotiation begins.

In the past, many correctional facilities depended on informal procedures to quell disturbances, often drawing on the expertise of seasoned correctional officers who were veterans of past skirmishes and riots. Given the large size of many of today's institutions, the changing composition of inmate and staff populations, and increasing tensions caused by overcrowding and reduced inmate privileges, the "old guard" system can no longer be depended on to quell disturbances. Hence most modern facilities have incident-management procedures and systems in place in case a disturbance occurs. Such systems remove the burden of riot control from the individual officer, depending instead on a systematic and deliberate approach developed to deal with a wide variety of correctional incidents.

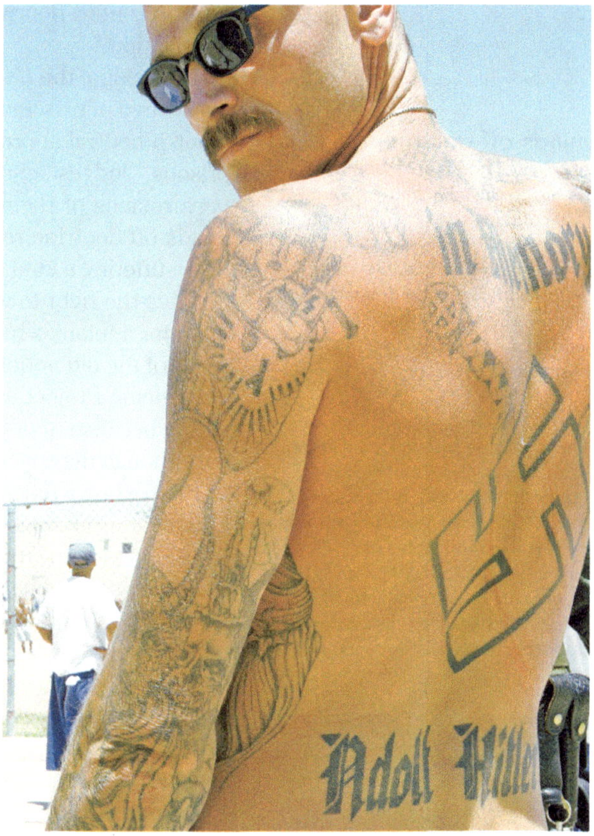

▲ A California inmate with Aryan Brotherhood ties showing off his tattoos in a sensitive-needs housing facility at Calipatria State Prison. What are security threat groups? Can you name some?
© Mark Allen Johnson/ZUMA Press

Prisoners' Rights

In May 1995, Limestone Prison inmate Larry Hope was handcuffed to a hitching post after arguing with another inmate while working on a chain gang near an interstate highway in Alabama.[109] Hope was released two hours later, after a supervising officer determined that Hope had not instigated the altercation. During the two hours that he was coupled to the post, Hope was periodically offered drinking water and bathroom breaks, and his responses to those offers were recorded on an activity log. Because of the height of the hitching post, however, his arms grew tired, and it was later determined that whenever he tried moving his arms to improve his circulation, the handcuffs cut into his wrists, causing pain.

One month later, Hope was punished more severely after he had taken a nap during the morning bus ride to the chain gang's work site. When the bus arrived, he was slow in responding to an order to exit the vehicle. A shouting match soon led to a scuffle with an officer, and four other guards intervened and subdued Hope, handcuffing him and placing him in leg irons for transportation back to the prison. When he arrived at the facility, officers made him take off his shirt and again put him on the hitching post. He stood in the sun for approximately seven hours, sustaining a sunburn; Hope was given water only once or twice during that time and was provided with no bathroom breaks. At one point, an officer taunted him about his thirst. According to Hope: "[The guard] first gave water to some dogs, then brought the water cooler closer to me, removed its lid, and kicked the cooler over, spilling the water onto the ground."

Eventually Hope filed a civil suit against three officers, claiming that he experienced "unnecessary pain" and that the "wanton infliction of pain . . . constitutes cruel and unusual punishment forbidden by the Eighth Amendment." His case eventually reached the U.S. Supreme Court, and on June 27, 2002, the Court found that Hope's treatment was "totally without penological justification" and constituted an Eighth Amendment violation. The Court ruled, "Despite the clear lack of emergency, respondents knowingly subjected [Hope] to a substantial risk of physical harm, unnecessary pain, unnecessary exposure to the sun, prolonged thirst and

The Privilege of the Writ of Habeas Corpus shall not be suspended, unless when in Cases of Rebellion or Invasion the public Safety may require it.
—Article I, Section 9, Clause 2, of the U.S. Constitution

taunting, and a deprivation of bathroom breaks that created a risk of particular discomfort and humiliation."

In deciding the *Hope* case, the Court built on almost 40 years of precedent-setting decisions in the area of prisoners' rights. It may be surprising, but before the 1960s, American courts had taken a neutral approach—commonly called the **hands-off doctrine**—toward the running of prisons. Judges assumed that prison administrators were sufficiently professional in the performance of their duties to balance institutional needs with humane considerations. The hands-off doctrine rested on the belief that defendants lost most of their rights upon conviction, suffering a kind of **civil death**, which many states defined through legislation that denied inmates the right to vote, to hold public office, and even to marry; some states made incarceration for a felony a basis for uncontested divorce at the request of the noncriminal spouse. Aspects of the old notion of civil death are still a reality in a number of jurisdictions today, and the Sentencing Project says that 3.9 million American citizens across the nation are barred from voting because of previous felony convictions.[110]

hands-off doctrine
A policy of nonintervention with regard to prison management that U.S. courts tended to follow until the late 1960s. For 30 years, the doctrine languished as judicial intervention in prison administration dramatically increased, although there is now evidence that a new hands-off era is beginning.

civil death
The legal status of prisoners in some jurisdictions who are denied the opportunity to vote, hold public office, marry, or enter into contracts by virtue of their status as incarcerated felons. While civil death is primarily of historical interest, some jurisdictions still limit the contractual opportunities available to inmates.

Although the concept of civil death has not entirely disappeared, the hands-off doctrine ended in 1970, when a federal court declared the entire Arkansas prison system to be unconstitutional after hearing arguments that it constituted a form of cruel and unusual punishment.[111] The court's decision resulted from what it judged to be pervasive overcrowding and primitive living conditions. Longtime inmates claimed that a number of other inmates had been beaten or shot to death by guards and buried over the years in unmarked graves on prison property. An investigation did unearth some skeletons in old graves, but their origin was never determined.

Detailed media coverage of the Arkansas prison system gave rise to suspicions about correctional institutions everywhere. Within a few years, federal courts intervened in the running of prisons in Florida, Louisiana, Mississippi, New York City, and Virginia.[112] In 1975, in a precedent-setting decision, U.S. District Court Judge Frank M. Johnson issued an order banning the Alabama Board of Corrections from accepting any more inmates. Citing a population that was more than double the capacity of the state's system, Judge Johnson enumerated 44 standards to be met before additional inmates could be admitted to prison; included in the requirements were specific guidelines on living space, staff-to-inmate ratios, visiting privileges, racial makeup of staff, and food service modifications.

The Legal Basis of Prisoners' Rights

In 1974, the U.S. Supreme Court case of ***Pell* v. *Procunier***[113] established a "balancing test" that, although originally addressing only First Amendment rights, eventually served as a general guideline for all prison operations. In *Pell*, the Court ruled that the "prison inmate retains those First Amendment rights that are not inconsistent with his status as a prisoner or with the legitimate penological objectives of the corrections system."[114] In other words, inmates have rights, much the same as people who are not incarcerated, provided that the legitimate needs of the prison for security, custody, and safety are not compromised. Other courts have declared that order maintenance, security, and rehabilitation are all legitimate concerns of prison administration but that financial exigency and convenience are not. As the **balancing test** makes clear, we see reflected in prisoners' rights a microcosm of the individual-rights versus public-order dilemma found in wider society.

balancing test
A principle, developed by the courts and applied to the corrections arena by *Pell* v. *Procunier* (1974), that attempts to weigh the rights of an individual, as guaranteed by the Constitution, against the authority of states to make laws or to otherwise restrict a person's freedom in order to protect the state's interests and its citizens.

Further enforcing the legal rights of prisoners is the Civil Rights of Institutionalized Persons Act (CRIPA) of 1980.[115] The law, which has been amended over time, applies to all adult and juvenile state and local jails, detention centers, prisons, mental hospitals, and other care facilities (such as those operated by a state, county, or city for inmates who are physically challenged or chronically ill). Section 1997a of the act, titled "Initiation of Civil Actions," reads as follows:

> Whenever the Attorney General has reasonable cause to believe that any State, political subdivision of a State, official, employee, or agent thereof, or other person acting on behalf of a State or political subdivision of a State is subjecting persons residing in or confined to an institution . . . to egregious or flagrant conditions which deprive such persons of any rights, privileges, or immunities secured or protected by the Constitution or laws of the United States . . . and that such deprivation is pursuant to a pattern or practice of resistance to the full enjoyment of such rights, privileges, or immunities, the Attorney General, for or in the name of the United States, may institute a civil action in any appropriate United States district court against such party for such equitable relief as may be appropriate.

Freedom or Safety? You Decide.

Censoring Prison Communications

On February 28, 2005, NBC News announced that it had learned that Arab terrorists in federal maximum-security prisons had been sending letters to extremists on the outside exhorting them to attack Western interests. The terrorists included Mohammed Salameh, a follower of radical sheik Omar Abdel-Rahman. Salameh had been sentenced to more than 100 years in prison for his part in the 1993 bombing attack on New York's World Trade Center. That attack, which killed six and injured more than 1,000, blew a huge hole in the basement parking garage of one of the towers but failed to topple the buildings.

The men are being held in the federal ADMAX facility in Florence, Colorado, which is the country's most secure federal prison. While there, NBC News revealed, they sent at least 14 letters to a Spanish terror cell, praised Osama bin Laden in Arabic newspapers, and advocated additional terror attacks. In July 2002, Salameh, a Palestinian with a degree in Islamic law from a Jordanian university, sent a letter to the *Al-Quds* Arabic daily newspaper proclaiming that "Osama Bin Laden is my hero of this generation."

Andy McCarthy, a former federal prosecutor who worked to send the terrorists to prison, said that Salameh's letters were "exhorting acts of terrorism and helping recruit would-be terrorists for the *Jihad*." Michael Macko, who lost his father in the Trade Center bombing, posed this question: "If they are encouraging acts of terrorism internationally, how do we know they're not encouraging acts of terrorism right here on U.S. soil?"

Prison officials told reporters that communications involving the imprisoned bombers had not been closely censored because the men hadn't been considered very dangerous. The letters didn't contain any plans for attacks, nor did they name any specific targets. One Justice Department official said that Salameh was "a low level guy" who was not under any special restrictions and that his letters were seen as "generic stuff" and "no cause for concern."

Rights advocates suggested that inmates should have the right to free speech—even those imprisoned for acts of terrorism—and that advocating terrorism is not the same thing as planning it or carrying it out. After all, they said, calls for a holy war, however repugnant they may be in the current international context, are merely political statements—and politics is not against the law.

YOU DECIDE

What kinds of prison communications should be monitored or restricted (letters, telephone calls, e-mail)? Do you believe that communications containing statements like those described here should be confiscated? What kinds of political statements (if any) should be permitted?

References: Lisa Myers, "Imprisoned Terrorists Still Advocating Terror," NBC Nightly News, February 28, 2005. Web posted at http://www.msnbc.msn.com/id/7046691 (accessed August 28, 2005); Lisa Myers, "Bureau of Prisons under Fire for Jihad Letters," March 1, 2005. Web posted at http://www.msnbc.msn.com/id/7053165 (accessed August 28, 2005).

Significantly, the most recent version of CRIPA also states[116]:

> No action shall be brought with respect to prison conditions under section 1983 of this title, or any other Federal law, by a prisoner confined in any jail, prison, or other correctional facility until such administrative remedies as are available are exhausted.

Prisoners' rights, because they are constrained by the legitimate needs of imprisonment, can be thought of as conditional rights rather than absolute rights. The Second Amendment to the U.S. Constitution, for example, grants citizens the right to bear arms. The right to arms is, however, necessarily compromised by the need for order and security in prison, and we would not expect a court to rule that inmates have a right to weapons. Prisoners' rights must be balanced against the security, order-maintenance, and treatment needs of correctional institutions.

Conditional rights, because they are subject to the exigencies of imprisonment, bear a strong resemblance to privileges, which should not be surprising since privileges were all that inmates officially had until the modern era. The practical difference between privileges and conditional rights is that privileges exist only at the convenience of granting institutions and can be revoked at any time for any reason, whereas the rights of prisoners have a basis in the Constitution and in law external to the institution, so the institution may restrict such rights for legitimate correctional reasons, but those rights may not be infringed without good cause that can be demonstrated in a court of law—mere institutional convenience does not provide a sufficient legal basis for the denial of rights.

The past few decades have seen many lawsuits brought by prisoners challenging the constitutionality of some aspect of confinement. Suits filed by prisoners with the courts are generally called writs of *habeas corpus* and formally request that the person detaining a prisoner bring him or her before a judicial officer to determine the lawfulness of the imprisonment. The ACA says that most prisoner lawsuits are based on "[1] the Eighth Amendment prohibition

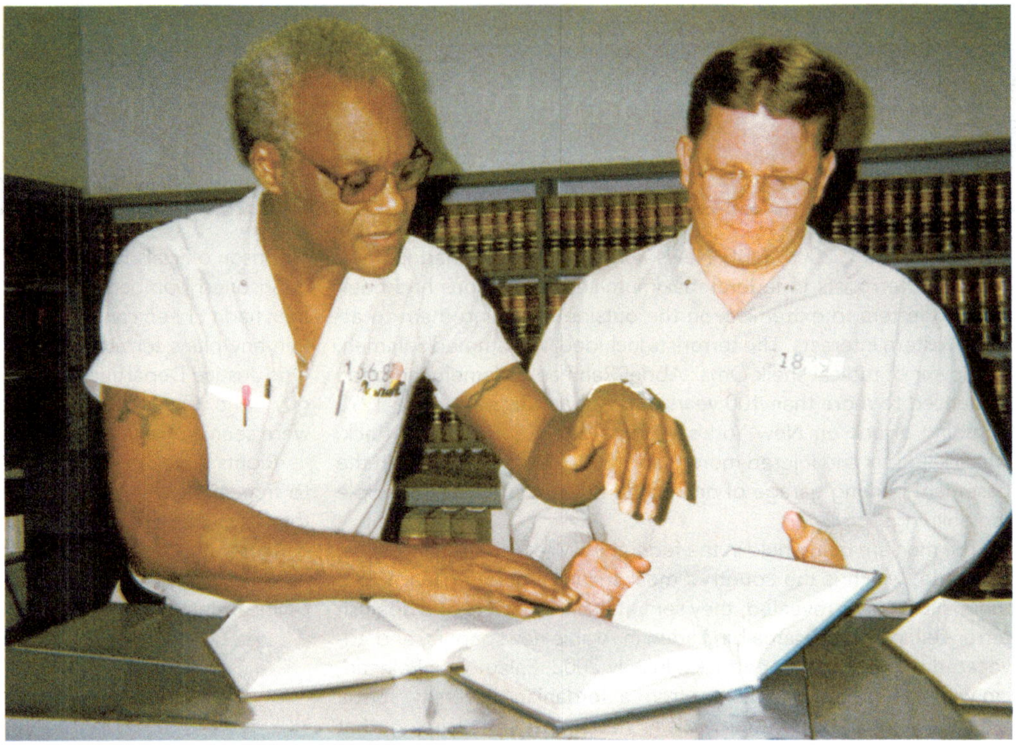

▶ West Virginia inmates Thomas Casey (left) and Robert McCabe reviewing statutes in the Huttonsville Correctional Center's law library. Casey and McCabe are known to others in the institution as jailhouse lawyers. What role do jailhouse lawyers play in today's prisons?
Courtesy Huttonsville Correctional Center

against cruel and unusual punishment; [2] the Fourteenth Amendment prohibition against the taking of life, liberty, or property without due process of law; and [3] the Fourteenth Amendment provision requiring equal protection of the laws."[117] Aside from appeals by inmates that question the propriety of their convictions and sentences, such constitutional challenges represent the bulk of legal action initiated by those who are imprisoned. However, state statutes and federal legislation, including Section 1983 of the Civil Rights Act of 1871, provide other bases for challenges to the legality of specific prison conditions and procedures.

Precedents in Prisoners' Rights

The U.S. Supreme Court has not yet spoken with finality on a number of prisoners' rights questions. Nonetheless, high court decisions of the last few decades and a number of lower court findings can be interpreted to identify the existing conditional rights of prisoners, as shown in Table 2. A number of especially significant Supreme Court decisions are discussed in the pages that follow.

Communications and Visitation

First Amendment guarantees of freedom of speech are applicable to prisoners' rights in three important areas: (1) the receipt of mail, (2) communications with others (especially those on the outside), and (3) visitation.

Courts have generally *not* allowed restrictions on the receipt of published mail, especially magazines and newspapers that do not threaten prison security. In 2006, in the case of *Beard* v. *Banks*,[118] however, the U.S. Supreme Court held that prison officials in Pennsylvania could prohibit the state's most violent inmates from receiving magazines, photographs, and newspapers sent to them in the mail. Pennsylvania Department of Corrections (DOC) rules prohibit all inmates classified as disruptive and problematic and who are housed at the Long Term Segregation Unit (LTSU) in LaBelle, Pennsylvania, from receiving newspapers or magazines from all sources, including publishers and the prison library. LTSU inmates are kept alone in their cells for 23 hours a day and are not permitted access to television or radio, although they are allowed to have and read religious literature. Visits from friends and family members are limited to one per month. Prison officials argued that the restrictions on print materials placed on LTSU

TABLE 2 The Conditional Rights of Inmates[1]

Communications and Visitation

A right to receive publications directly from the publisher
A right to meet with members of the press[2]
A right to communicate with nonprisoners

Religious Freedom

A right of assembly for religious services and groups
A right to attend services of other religious groups
A right to receive visits from ministers
A right to correspond with religious leaders
A right to observe religious dietary laws
A right to wear religious insignia

Access to the Courts and Legal Assistance

A right to have access to the courts[3]
A right to visits from attorneys
A right to have mail communications with lawyers[4]
A right to communicate with legal assistance organizations
A right to consult jailhouse lawyers[5]
A right to assistance in filing legal papers, which should include one of the following:

- Access to an adequate law library
- Paid attorneys
- Paralegal personnel or law students

Medical Care

A right to sanitary and healthy conditions
A right to medical attention for serious physical problems
A right to required medications
A right to treatment in accordance with "doctor's orders"

Protection from Harm

A right to food, water, and shelter
A right to protection from foreseeable attack
A right to protection from predictable sexual abuse
A right to protection against suicide

Institutional Punishment and Discipline

An absolute right against corporal punishments (unless sentenced to such punishments)
A limited right to due process before punishment, including the following:

- A notice of charges
- A fair and impartial hearing
- An opportunity for defense
- A right to present witnesses
- A written decision

[1]All "rights" listed are provisional in that they may be constrained by the legitimate needs of imprisonment.
[2]But this right does not go beyond the opportunities afforded for inmates to meet with members of the general public.
[3]This right is subject to the restrictions in the Prison Litigation Reform Act of 1996.
[4]Mail communications are generally designated as privileged or nonprivileged. Privileged communications include those between inmates and their lawyers or court officials and cannot legitimately be read by prison officials. Nonprivileged communications include most other written communications.
[5]Jailhouse lawyers are inmates with experience in the law, usually gained from filing legal briefs on their own behalf or on the behalf of others. Consultation with jailhouse lawyers was ruled permissible in the Supreme Court case of *Johnson* v. *Avery*, 393 U.S. 483 (1968), unless inmates are provided with paid legal assistance.

inmates served legitimate penological interests by controlling materials that could be used to start fires and by providing incentives for improved inmate behavior. The Court agreed, holding that "prison officials have imposed the deprivation only upon those with serious prison-behavior problems; and those officials, relying on their professional judgment, reached an experience-based conclusion that the policies help to further legitimate prison objectives."

In the case of *Procunier* v. *Martinez* (1974),[119] the Supreme Court ruled that a prisoner's incoming and outgoing mail may be censored if necessary for security purposes. In *McNamara* v. *Moody* (1979),[120] however, a federal court upheld the right of an inmate to write vulgar letters to his girlfriend in which he made disparaging comments about the prison staff. The court reasoned that the letters may have been embarrassing to prison officials but that they did not affect the security or order of the institution. However, libelous materials have generally not been accorded First Amendment protection in or out of institutional contexts.

Concerning publications produced by inmates, legal precedent holds that prisoners have no inherent right to publish newspapers or newsletters for use by other prisoners, although many institutions do permit and finance such periodicals.[121] Publications originating from outside of prison, such as newspapers, magazines, and special-interest tracts, are generally protected when mailed directly from the publisher, although magazines that depict deviant sexual behavior can be banned, according to *Mallery* v. *Lewis* (1983)[122] and other precedents. Nudity by itself is not necessarily obscene, and federal courts have held that prisons cannot ban nude pictures of inmates' wives or girlfriends.[123]

Visitation and access to the news media are other areas that have come under court scrutiny. Maximum-security institutions rarely permit "contact" visits, and some have on occasion suspended all visitation privileges. In the case of ***Block* v. *Rutherford*** (1984),[124] the U.S. Supreme Court upheld the policy of the Los Angeles County Central Jail, which prohibited all visits from friends and relatives; the Court agreed that the large jail population and the conditions under which visits might take place could combine to threaten the security of the jail.

In the 2003 case of ***Overton* v. *Bazzetta***,[125] the Court held that new visitation restrictions imposed by the Michigan DOC in an effort to counter prison security problems caused by an increasing number of visitors and by substance abuse among inmates were acceptable. The regulations allow routine visits for most inmates but state that prisoners who commit two substance abuse violations while incarcerated may receive visits only from clergy and from attorneys. Family members are prohibited from visiting, although substance-abusing inmates can apply for reinstatement of visitation privileges after two years. In upholding the Michigan DOC's visitation regulations, the Court found that "the fact that the regulations bear a rational relation to legitimate penological interests suffices to sustain them."

In *Pell* v. *Procunier* (1974),[126] discussed earlier in regard to the balancing test, the Court found in favor of a California law that denied prisoners the opportunity to hold special meetings with members of the press. The Court reasoned that media interviews could be conducted through regular visitation arrangements and that most of the information desired by the media could be conveyed through correspondence. In *Pell*, the Court also held that any reasonable policy of media access was acceptable as long as it was administered fairly and without bias.

In a later case, the Court ruled that news personnel cannot be denied correspondence with inmates but also ruled that they have no constitutional right to interview inmates or to inspect correctional facilities beyond the visitation opportunities available to the public.[127] This equal-access policy was set forth in ***Houchins* v. *KQED, Inc.*** (1978) by Justice Potter Stewart, who wrote, "The Constitution does no more than assure the public and the press equal access once government has opened its doors."[128]

Religious Freedom

The First and Fourteenth Amendments provide the basis for prisoners' rights claims in the area of religious freedoms. The U.S. Supreme Court case of ***Cruz* v. *Beto*** (1972)[129] established that inmates must be given a "reasonable opportunity" to pursue their faith, even if it differs from traditional forms of worship. Meeting facilities must be provided for religious use when those same facilities are made available to other groups of prisoners for other purposes,[130] but no group can claim exclusive use of a prison area for religious reasons.[131] The right to assemble for religious purposes, however, can be denied to inmates who use such meetings to plan escapes

▲ Inmate Antonio Ferreria participating in a Catholic worship service at Florida's Everglades Correctional Institution. Florida has established what are called "faith-based" programs at nine of its correctional facilities. Faith-based programs are sponsored by religious organizations and supplement government-sponsored training and rehabilitation programs. What special roles might such programs play?
© *Deborah Coleman*/Palm Beach Post

or who take the opportunity to dispense contraband. Similarly, prisoners in segregation can be denied the opportunity to attend group religious services.[132]

Although prisoners cannot be made to attend religious services,[133] records of religious activity can be maintained to administratively determine dietary needs and eligibility for passes to religious services outside of the institution.[134] In *Dettmer* v. *Landon* (1985),[135] a federal district court held that an inmate who claimed to practice witchcraft must be provided with the artifacts necessary for his worship services; included were items such as sea salt, sulfur, a quartz clock, incense, candles, and a white robe without a hood. The district court's opinion was later partially overturned by the U.S. Court of Appeals for the Fourth Circuit. The appellate court recognized the Church of Wicca as a valid religion but held that concerns over prison security could preclude inmates' possession of dangerous items of worship.[136]

Drugs and dangerous substances have not been considered permissible even when inmates claimed they were a necessary part of their religious services.[137] Prison regulations prohibiting the wearing of beards, even those grown for religious reasons, were held acceptable for security reasons in the 1985 federal court case of *Hill* v. *Blackwell*.[138]

A federal law passed in 2000, the Religious Land Use and Institutionalized Persons Act (RLUIPA), has particular relevance to prison programs and activities that are at least partially supported with federal monies. RLUIPA states:

> No government shall impose a substantial burden on the religious exercise of a person residing in or confined to an institution even if the burden results from a rule of general applicability, unless the government demonstrates that imposition of the burden on that person (1) is in furtherance of a compelling governmental interest; and (2) is the least restrictive means of furthering that compelling governmental interest.

In 2005, in the case of *Benning* v. *State*,[139] the Eleventh Circuit U.S. Court of Appeals found in favor of a Georgia inmate who claimed that RLUIPA supported his right as a "Torah observant Jew" to eat only kosher food and wear a yarmulke at all times.

Also in 2005, in the case of *Cutter* v. *Wilkinson*,[140] the U.S. Supreme Court found in favor of past and present inmates of Ohio's correctional system who claimed that the system failed to accommodate their nonmainstream religious practices. Perhaps the most important aspect of the *Cutter* ruling, however, was the Court's finding that RLUIPA does *not* improperly advance religion in violation of the constitutional requirement of separation of church and state.

Access to the Courts and to Legal Assistance

Access to the courts[141] and to legal assistance is a well-established right of prisoners. The right of prisoners to petition the court was recognized in ***Bounds* v. *Smith*** (1977),[142] which at the time was a far-reaching Supreme Court decision. While attempting to define "access," the Court in *Bounds* imposed on the states the duty of assisting inmates in the preparation and filing of legal papers; assistance could be provided through trained personnel knowledgeable in the law or via law libraries in each institution, which all states have since built. In 1996, however, in the case of *Lewis* v. *Casey*,[143] the U.S. Supreme Court repudiated part of the *Bounds* decision, saying that "statements in *Bounds* suggesting that prison authorities must also enable the prisoner to discover grievances, and to litigate effectively once in court . . . have no antecedent in this Court's pre-*Bounds* cases, and are now disclaimed." In *Lewis*, the Court overturned earlier decisions by a federal district court and by the Ninth Circuit Court of Appeals; both lower courts had found in favor of Arizona inmates who had complained that state prison law libraries provided inadequate legal research facilities, thereby depriving them of their right of legal access to the courts, as established by *Bounds*. In turning back portions of *Bounds*, the majority in *Lewis* wrote that inmates raising such claims need to demonstrate "widespread actual injury" to their ability to access the courts, not merely "isolated instances of actual injury." "Moreover," wrote the justices, "*Bounds* does not guarantee inmates the wherewithal to file any and every type of legal claim, but requires only that they be provided with the tools to attack their sentences . . . and to challenge the conditions of their confinement."

In an earlier case, ***Johnson* v. *Avery*** (1968),[144] the Court had ruled that prisoners under correctional supervision have a right to consult "jailhouse lawyers" for advice when assistance from trained professionals is not available. Other court decisions have established that inmates have a right to correspond with their attorneys[145] and with legal assistance organizations, but such letters can be opened and inspected for contraband[146] (but not read) by prison authorities in the presence of the inmates. The right to meet with hired counsel for reasonable lengths of time has also been upheld.[147] Indigent defendants must be provided with stamps for the purpose of legal correspondence,[148] and inmates cannot be disciplined for communicating with lawyers or for requesting legal help. Conversations between inmates and their lawyers can be monitored, although any evidence thus obtained cannot be used in court.[149] Inmates do not, however, have the right to an appointed lawyer, even when indigent, if no judicial proceedings have been initiated against them.[150]

Medical Care

deliberate indifference
A wanton disregard by corrections personnel for the well-being of inmates. Deliberate indifference requires both actual knowledge that a harm is occurring and disregard of the risk of harm that is occurring. A prison official may be held liable under the Eighth Amendment for acting with deliberate indifference to inmate health or safety only if he or she knows that inmates face a substantial risk of serious harm and disregards that risk by failing to take reasonable measures to abate it.

The historic Supreme Court case of ***Estelle* v. *Gamble*** (1976)[151] specified prison officials' duty to provide for inmates' medical care. In *Estelle*, the Court concerned itself with **deliberate indifference** (a wanton disregard for the health of inmates) on the part of the staff toward a prisoner's need for serious medical attention. Although poor treatment, misdiagnosis, and the like may constitute medical malpractice, they do not necessarily constitute deliberate indifference.[152] In 1992, in *Hudson* v. *McMillan*,[153] the Court clarified the concept of "deliberate indifference" by holding that it requires both actual knowledge and disregard of risk of harm.

Two other cases, ***Ruiz* v. *Estelle*** (1980)[154] and *Newman* v. *Alabama* (1972),[155] have had a substantial impact on the rights of prisoners to medical attention. In *Ruiz*, the Texas Department of Criminal Justice was found lacking in its correctional medical treatment programs, and the court ordered an improvement in record keeping, physical facilities, and general medical care while it continued to monitor the progress of the department (see CJ Exhibit 3). In *Newman*, Alabama's prison medical services were found to be so inadequate as to be "shocking to the conscience."

Part of the issue of medical treatment is the question of whether inmates can be forced to take medication. A 1984 state court held that inmates could be medicated against their will in an emergency,[156] but the court did recognize that unwanted medications designed to produce only psychological effects, such as tranquilizers, might be refused more readily than life-sustaining drugs.[157] In the 1984 federal court case of *Bee* v. *Greaves*,[158] the Tenth Circuit Court of Appeals ruled that "less restrictive alternatives" should be considered before the administration of antipsychotic drugs to in-custody pretrial detainees. In 1990, in the case of *Washington* v. *Harper*,[159] the U.S. Supreme Court held that prisoners can refuse the involuntary administration of antipsychotic drugs unless government officials can demonstrate an "overriding justifi-

CJ Exhibit 3

Federal Oversight of the Texas Prison System: A Time Line

1972. Inmate David Ruiz and several other prisoners file a civil rights suit against the Texas Department of Corrections (now called the Texas Department of Criminal Justice), alleging constitutional violations.
October 2, 1978–September 20, 1979. The *Ruiz* case is tried in Houston.
December 10, 1980. U.S. District Court Judge William Wayne Justice finds that confinement in the Texas prison system constitutes cruel and unusual punishment. He cites overcrowding, understaffing, brutality by guards and inmate-guards known as *building tenders,* substandard medical care, and uncontrolled physical abuse among inmates.
January 12, 1981. The judge orders improvements to be made to the system and sets deadlines.
April 19, 1981. Judge Justice appoints a special master to supervise compliance with his order.
April 1982. The state agrees to halt the building tender system and to hire additional correctional officers.
January–June 1983. The Texas legislature passes laws intended to reduce the prison population.
November 1987. Texas voters authorize $500 million in bonds for prison construction.
March 31, 1990. The special master's office is closed.
November 1990. Texas voters approve $672 million in bonds to build 25,300 prison beds and 12,000 drug and alcohol treatment beds.
February 1992. Inmates' attorneys and the Texas Board of Criminal Justice reach an agreement. Texas Attorney General Dan Morales rejects it.
May 1, 1992. Morales offers a settlement proposal.
July 14, 1992. Inmates' attorneys accept the proposal.
December 11, 1992. Judge Justice signs the settlement.
January 21, 1999. Judge Justice begins a hearing to determine whether Texas prisons should be freed of federal court oversight.
March 1, 1999. Judge Justice decides to maintain oversight of the prison system.
March 20, 2001. The Fifth U.S. Circuit Court of Appeals reverses Judge Justice's ruling, ending oversight but giving him 90 days to review the matter.
June 18, 2001. Judge Justice says that the Texas prison system has improved but that oversight is still needed in the areas of "conditions of confinement in administrative segregation, the failure to provide reasonable safety to inmates against assault and abuse, and the excessive use of force by correctional officers." Judge Justice discontinues federal oversight of other aspects of the prison system, including health services and staffing.
June 17, 2002. Judge Justice orders an end to federal judicial oversight. The National Institute of Corrections, an arm of the U.S. Department of Justice, was to provide further recommendations to the Texas Department of Criminal Justice for a period of two years.

Source: Adapted from Ed Timms, "Judge to Lessen Oversight of Texas Prisons," *Dallas Morning News*, June 19, 2001. Web posted at http://www.dallasnews.com/archive (accessed March 12, 2002). Reprinted with permission.

cation" as to why administration of the drugs is necessary. Under *Washington*, an inmate in a correctional institution "may be treated involuntarily with antipsychotic drugs where there is a determination that the inmate is dangerous to himself or others and the treatment is in the inmate's medical interest."

In 1998, in the case of ***Pennsylvania Department of Corrections* v. *Yeskey***,[160] the Supreme Court held that the Americans with Disabilities Act (ADA) of 1990[161] applies to prisons and to prison inmates. In May 1994, Ronald Yeskey was sentenced to serve 18 to 36 months in a Pennsylvania correctional facility, and the sentencing court recommended that he be placed in Pennsylvania's Motivational Boot Camp for first-time offenders, the successful completion of which would have led to his release on parole in just six months. When Yeskey was refused admission because of his medical history of hypertension, he sued the Pennsylvania Department of Corrections and several state officials, alleging that his exclusion violated Title II of the ADA, which prohibits a "public entity" from discriminating against a "qualified individual with a disability" on account of that disability. Lawyers for the state of Pennsylvania argued that state prisoners are not covered by the ADA. The Supreme Court ruled, however, that "state prisons fall squarely within Title II's statutory definition of 'public entity,' which includes 'any . . . instrumentality of a State . . . or local government.' "

Similarly, in the 2006 case of *U.S.* v. *Georgia*,[162] the U.S. Supreme Court ruled in favor of a wheelchair-bound Georgia inmate named Tony Goodman, holding that state's claims of sovereign immunity could not bar suits brought under the ADA. Goodman, a paraplegic who filed a Section 1983 suit, was able to show that his constitutional rights were violated by prison

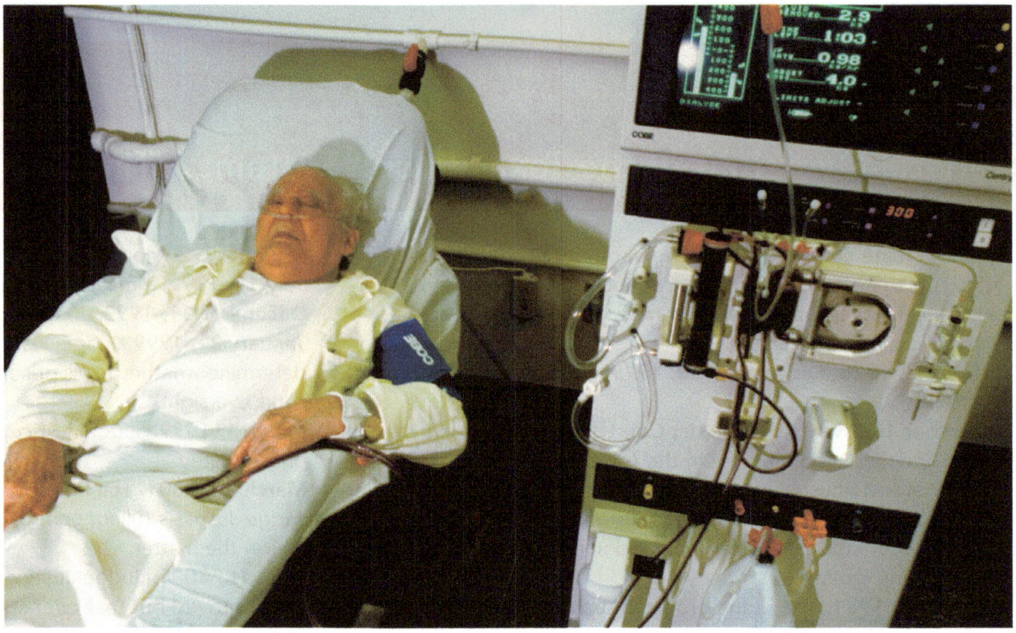

▲ Inmate Santos Pagon undergoing kidney dialysis at Laurel Highlands Prison in Pennsylvania. Court decisions over the years have established a firm set of inmate rights. Among them is the right to necessary health care. What other rights do inmates have?
Mark Peterson/Corbis/SABA Press Photos, Inc.

officials who failed to accommodate his disability. Goodman had been confined for more than 23 hours per day in a cell too narrow for him to turn his wheelchair, making it impossible for him to reach the toilet.

Protection from Harm

Claims that inmates have a right to expect prisons to meet their fundamental human needs for food, water, shelter, and reasonable protection from physical and other harm (including potential harm from corrections personnel, other inmates, and oneself) are largely based on Eighth Amendment protection against cruel and unusual punishment. One well-known court decision in this area is the federal district court case of *Holt* v. *Sarver* (1970),[163] in which conditions at two Arkansas state prison farms were found to constitute punishment disproportionate to any offense. Among other things, the court found that inmates have "the right to be fed, housed, and clothed so as not to be subjected to loss of health or life, . . . the right to be free from the abuses of fellow prisoners in all aspects of daily life," and "the right to be free from the brutality of being guarded by fellow inmates." In *Holt*, the Arkansas prison system was ordered to correct defects in the conditions of confinement throughout its prisons.

In the case of *Farmer* v. *Brennan* (1994),[164] the U.S. Supreme Court provided substantial protections to prison administration and staff when it found that even when a prisoner is harmed and prison officials knew that a risk of harm existed, they cannot be held liable for that harm if they took appropriate steps to mitigate the risk of its happening. The case involved Dee Farmer, a preoperative transsexual with obvious feminine characteristics who had been incarcerated with other males in the federal prison system. While mixing with other inmates, Farmer was beaten and raped by a fellow prisoner. Subsequently, he sued corrections officials, claiming that they had acted with deliberate indifference to his safety because they knew that the penitentiary had a violent environment as well as a history of inmate assaults and because they should have known that Farmer would be particularly vulnerable to sexual attack. Although both a federal district court and the U.S. Court of Appeals for the Seventh Circuit agreed with Farmer, the U.S. Supreme Court sent Farmer's case back to a lower court for rehearing after clarifying what it said was necessary to establish deliberate indifference:

> Prison officials have a duty under the Eighth Amendment to provide humane conditions of confinement. They must ensure that inmates receive adequate food, clothing, shelter, and medical care and must protect prisoners from violence at the hands of other prisoners. How-

> ever, a constitutional violation occurs only where . . . the official has acted with "deliberate indifference" to inmate health or safety. . . . A prison official may be held liable under the Eighth Amendment for acting with "deliberate indifference" to inmate health or safety only if he knows that inmates face a substantial risk of serious harm and disregards that risk by failing to take reasonable measures to abate it.[165]

In 1993, the U.S. Supreme Court indicated that environmental conditions of prison life that pose a threat to inmate health may have to be corrected. In ***Helling v. McKinney***,[166] Nevada inmate William McKinney claimed that exposure to secondary cigarette smoke circulating in his cell was threatening his health, in violation of the Eighth Amendment's prohibition against cruel and unusual punishment. The Court, in ordering that a federal district court provide McKinney with the opportunity to prove his allegations, held that "an injunction cannot be denied to inmates who plainly prove an unsafe, life-threatening condition on the ground that nothing yet has happened to them." In effect, the *Helling* case gave notice to prison officials that they are responsible not only for "inmates' current serious health problems" but also for maintenance of environmental conditions under which health problems might be prevented from developing.

Privacy

The Fourth Amendment to the U.S. Constitution guarantees free citizens the right against unreasonable searches and seizures. Courts, however, have not extended this right to prisoners. Many court decisions, including the Tenth Circuit case of *U.S.* v. *Ready* (1978)[167] and the U.S. Supreme Court decisions of ***Katz v. U.S.*** (1967)[168] and ***Hudson v. Palmer*** (1984),[169] have held that inmates cannot have a reasonable expectation to privacy while incarcerated. Palmer, an inmate in Virginia, claimed that Hudson, a prison guard, had unreasonably destroyed some of his personal (noncontraband) property following a cell search; Palmer's complaint centered on the lack of due process that accompanied the destruction. The Court disagreed, saying that the need for prison officials to conduct thorough and unannounced searches precludes inmate privacy in personal possessions. In *Block* v. *Rutherford* (1984),[170] the Court established that prisoners do not have a right to be present during a search of their cells.

Some lower courts, however, have begun to indicate that body-cavity searches may be unreasonable unless based on a demonstrable suspicion or conducted after prior warning has been given to the inmate.[171] They have also indicated that searches conducted simply to "harass or humiliate" inmates are illegitimate.[172] These cases may be an indication that the Supreme Court will eventually recognize a limited degree of privacy in cell searches, especially those that uncover and remove legal documents and personal papers prepared by the prisoner or documents prepared in his or her behalf.

Institutional Punishment and Discipline

A major area of inmate concern is the hearing of grievances. Complaints may arise in areas as diverse as food service (quality of food or special diets for religious purposes or health regimens), interpersonal relations between inmates and staff, denial of privileges, and alleged misconduct levied against an inmate or a correctional officer.

In 1972, the National Council on Crime and Delinquency developed a Model Act for the Protection of Rights of Prisoners, which included the opportunity for grievances to be heard, and the 1973 National Advisory Commission on Criminal Justice Standards and Goals called for the establishment of responsible practices for the hearing of inmate grievances. In 1977, in the case of ***Jones v. North Carolina Prisoners' Labor Union***,[173] the U.S. Supreme Court held that prisons must establish some formal opportunity for the airing of inmate grievances. Soon, formal grievance plans were established in prisons in an attempt to divert inmate grievances away from the courts.

Today, all sizable prisons have established **grievance procedures**—which range from the use of a hearing board composed of staff members and inmates to a single staff appointee charged with the resolution of complaints—whereby an inmate files a complaint with local authorities and receives a mandated response. Inmates who are dissatisfied with the handling of their grievances can generally appeal beyond the local prison.

grievance procedure
A formalized arrangement, usually involving a neutral hearing board, whereby institutionalized individuals have the opportunity to register complaints about the conditions of their confinement.

Disciplinary actions by prison authorities may also require a formalized hearing process, especially when staff members bring charges of rule violations against inmates that might result in some form of punishment being imposed on them. In a precedent-setting decision in the case of ***Wolff* v. *McDonnell*** (1974),[174] the Supreme Court decided that sanctions could not be levied against inmates without appropriate due process. The *Wolff* case involved an inmate who had been deprived of previously earned good-time credits because of misbehavior. The Court established that good-time credits were a form of "state-created right(s)," which, once created, could not be "arbitrarily abrogated."[175] *Wolff* was especially significant because it began an era of court scrutiny of what came to be called *state-created liberty interests*, which were said to be based on the language used in published prison regulations and were held, in effect, to confer due process guarantees on prisoners. Hence if a prison regulation said that a disciplinary hearing should be held before a prisoner could be sent to solitary confinement and that the hearing should permit a discussion of the evidence for and against the prisoner, courts interpreted that regulation to mean that the prisoner had a state-created right to a hearing and that sending him or her to solitary confinement in violation of the regulation was a violation of a state-created liberty interest. In later court decisions, state-created rights and privileges were called *protected liberties* and were interpreted to include any significant change in a prisoner's status.

In the interest of due process, and especially where written prison regulations governing the hearing process exist, courts have generally held that inmates going before disciplinary hearing boards are entitled to (1) a notice of the charges brought against them, (2) the chance to organize a defense, (3) an impartial hearing, and (4) the opportunity to present witnesses and evidence in their behalf. A written statement of the hearing board's conclusions should be provided to the inmate.[176] In the case of *Ponte* v. *Real* (1985),[177] the Supreme Court held that prison officials must provide an explanation to inmates who are denied the opportunity to have a desired witness at their hearing. The case of *Vitek* v. *Jones* (1980)[178] extended the requirement of due process to inmates about to be transferred from prisons to mental hospitals.

So that inmates will know what is expected of them as they enter prison, the ACA recommends that "a rulebook that contains all chargeable offenses, ranges of penalties and disciplinary procedures [be] posted in a conspicuous and accessible area; [and] a copy . . . given to each inmate and staff member."[179]

A Return to the Hands-Off Doctrine?

Many state-created rights and protected liberties may soon be a thing of the past. In June 1991, an increasingly conservative U.S. Supreme Court signaled the beginning of what appears to be at least a partial return to the hands-off doctrine of earlier times. The case, *Wilson* v. *Seiter*,[180] involved a Section 1983 suit brought against Richard P. Seiter, then-director of the Ohio Department of Rehabilitation and Correction, and Carl Humphreys, warden of the Hocking Correctional Facility (HCF) in Nelsonville, Ohio. In the suit, Pearly L. Wilson, a felon incarcerated at HCF, alleged that a number of the conditions of his confinement constituted cruel and unusual punishment in violation of the Eighth and Fourteenth Amendments to the U.S. Constitution. Specifically, Wilson cited overcrowding, excessive noise, insufficient locker storage space, inadequate heating and cooling, improper ventilation, unclean and inadequate restrooms, unsanitary dining facilities and food preparation, and housing with mentally and physically ill inmates. Wilson asked for a change in prison conditions and sought $900,000 from prison officials in compensatory and punitive damages.

Both the federal district court in which Wilson first filed affidavits and the Sixth Circuit Court of Appeals held that no constitutional violations existed because the conditions cited by Wilson were not the result of malicious intent on the part of officials. The U.S. Supreme Court agreed, noting that the deliberate indifference standard applied in *Estelle* v. *Gamble* (1976)[181] to claims involving medical care is similarly applicable to other cases in which prisoners challenge the conditions of their confinement. In effect, the Court created a standard that effectively means that all future challenges to prison conditions by inmates, which are brought under the Eighth Amendment, must show deliberate indifference by the officials responsible for the existence of those conditions before the Court will hear the complaint.

The written opinion of the Court in *Wilson* v. *Seiter* is telling. Writing for the majority, Justice Antonin Scalia observed that "if a prison boiler malfunctions accidentally during a cold winter, an inmate would have no basis for an Eighth Amendment claim, even if he suffers objectively significant harm. If a guard accidentally stepped on a prisoner's toe and broke it, this

Freedom or Safety? You Decide.

Should Prison Libraries Limit Access to Potentially Inflammatory Literature?

In mid-2007 the Federal Bureau of Prisons (BOP) authorities ordered chaplains at BOP facilities nationwide to remove potentially inflammatory literature from the shelves of chapel libraries. The move came in response to a report by the U.S. Justice Department's Office of the Inspector General, which recommended that prisons should take steps to avoid becoming recruiting grounds for militant Islamists and other radical groups.

Thousands of books were soon removed under what the BOP called the Standardized Chapel Library Project (SCLP), which it admitted was an effort to bar inmate access to literature that the BOP felt could "discriminate, disparage, advocate violence or radicalize." In identifying materials for removal, the BOP relied on the advice of experts who were asked to identify up to 150 book titles and 150 multimedia resources for each of 20 religious categories ranging from Bahaism to Yoruba. Prayer books were explicitly excluded from the list of materials targeted for removal.

Soon after the project was made public, however, members of Congress and a number of religious leaders urged the BOP to reverse its stance and return the books to chapel shelves.

In the fall of 2007, the Republican Study Committee, a group of conservative Republicans in the House of Representatives, sent a letter to BOP Director Harley G. Lappin, saying, "We must ensure that in America the federal government is not the undue arbiter of what may or may not be read by our citizens."

Representative Jeb Hensarling (R–Tex.), who heads the Republican Study Committee, explained that "anything that impinges upon the religious liberties of American citizens, be they incarcerated or not, is something that's going to cause . . . great concern." For its part, the BOP countered that it has a legitimate interest in screening out and removing items from inside of its facilities that could incite violence.

The controversy appeared to have been partially resolved when, on September 26, 2007, a BOP spokesperson announced that "in response to concerns expressed by members of several religious communities, the Bureau of Prisons has decided to alter its planned course of action with respect to the Chapel Library Project [and] the bureau will begin immediately to return to chapel libraries materials that were removed . . . with the exception of any publications that have been found to be inappropriate, such as materials that could be radicalizing or incite violence."

The controversy appears to have ended in 2008 with passage of the Second Chance Act (Public Law No 110-199), federal legislation which funded a number of reentry initiatives for people leaving prison and which required the director of the BOP "to discontinue the Standardized Chapel Library project or any other project that limits prisoner access to reading and other educational material."

YOU DECIDE

1. Should prison libraries be permitted to limit access to library literature that might incite violence or endanger the safety of inmates and staff? Would it matter if that literature is religious in nature?
2. How might the Bureau of Prisons meet the concerns of the Republican Study Committee, religious leaders, and authors of the Second Chance Act while still accomplishing its objective of removing literature that it believes might incite violence?

References: Laurie Goodstein, "Prisons Purging Books on Faith from Libraries," *New York Times*, September 10, 2007; Laurie Goodstein, "Critics Right and Left Protest Book Removals," *New York Times*, September 21, 2007; and Neela Banerjee, "Prisons to Restore Purged Religious Books," *New York Times*, September 27, 2007.

would not be punishment in anything remotely like the accepted meaning of the word." At the time that the *Wilson* decision was handed down, critics voiced concerns that the decision could effectively excuse prison authorities from the need to improve living conditions within institutions on the basis of simple budgetary constraints.

In the 1995 case of ***Sandin v. Conner***,[182] the U.S. Supreme Court took a much more definitive stance in favor of a new type of hands-off doctrine and voted 5 to 4 to reject the argument that any state action taken for a punitive reason encroaches on a prisoner's constitutional due process right to be free from the deprivation of liberty. In *Sandin*, Demont Conner, an inmate at the Halawa Correctional Facility in Hawaii, was serving an indeterminate sentence of 30 years to life for numerous crimes, including murder, kidnapping, robbery, and burglary. In a lawsuit in federal court, Conner alleged that prison officials had deprived him of procedural due process when a hearing committee refused to allow him to present witnesses during a disciplinary hearing and then sentenced him to segregation for alleged misconduct. An appellate court agreed with Conner, concluding that an existing prison regulation that instructed the hearing committee to find guilt in cases where a misconduct charge is supported by substantial evidence meant that the committee could not impose segregation if it did not look at all the evidence available to it.

The Supreme Court, however, reversed the decision of the appellate court, holding that while "such a conclusion may be entirely sensible in the ordinary task of construing a statute defining rights and remedies available to the general public, [i]t is a good deal less sensible in the case of a prison regulation primarily designed to guide corrections officials in the administration of a prison." The Court concluded that "such regulations [are] not designed to confer rights on inmates" but are meant only to provide guidelines to prison staff members.

In *Sandin*, the Court effectively set aside substantial portions of earlier decisions, such as *Wolff* v. *McDonnell* (1974)[183] and *Hewitt* v. *Helms* (1983),[184] which, wrote the justices, focused more on procedural issues than on those of "real substance." As a consequence, the majority opinion held, past cases like these have "impermissibly shifted the focus" away from the nature of a due process deprivation to one based on the language of a particular state or prison regulation. "The *Hewitt* approach," wrote the majority in *Sandin*, "has run counter to the view expressed in several of our cases that federal courts ought to afford appropriate deference and flexibility to state officials trying to manage a volatile environment. The time has come," said the Court, "to return to those due process principles that were correctly established and applied" in earlier times. In short, *Sandin* made it much more difficult for inmates to effectively challenge the administrative regulations and procedures imposed on them by prison officials, even when stated procedures are not explicitly followed.

A more recent case whose findings support the action of federal correctional officers is that of *Ali* v. *Federal Bureau of Prisons.* The case, decided by the U.S. Supreme Court in 2008,[185] involved a federal prisoner named Abdus-Shahid M. S. Ali, who claimed that some of his personal belongings disappeared when he was transferred from one federal prison to another. The missing items, which were to have been shipped in two duffle bags belonging to Ali, included copies of the Koran, a prayer rug, and a number of religious magazines. Ali filed suit against the BOP under the Federal Tort Claims Act (FTCA),[186] which authorizes "claims against the United States for money damages . . . for injury or loss of property . . . caused by the negligent or wrongful act or omission of any employee in the government while acting within the scope of his office or employment." In denying Ali's claim, the Court found that the law specifically provides immunity for federal law enforcement officers and determined that federal corrections personnel are "law enforcement officers" within the meaning of the law.

The Prison Litigation Reform Act of 1996

Only about 2,000 petitions per year concerning inmate problems were filed with the courts in 1961, but by 1975 the number of filings had increased to around 17,000, and in 1996 prisoners filed 68,235 civil rights lawsuits in federal courts nationwide.[187] Some inmate-originated suits seemed patently ludicrous and became the subject of much media coverage in the mid-1990s.[188] One such suit involved Robert Procup, a Florida State Prison inmate serving time for the murder of his business partner. Procup repeatedly sued Florida prison officials—once because he got only one roll with his dinner, again because he didn't get a luncheon salad, a third time because prison-provided TV dinners didn't come with a drink, and a fourth time because his cell had no television. Two other well-publicized cases involved an inmate who went to court asking to be allowed to exercise religious freedom by attending prison chapel services in the nude and an inmate who, thinking he could become pregnant via homosexual relations, sued prison doctors who wouldn't provide him with birth-control pills. An infamous example of seemingly frivolous inmate lawsuits was one brought by inmates claiming religious freedom and demanding that members of the Church of the New Song, or CONS, be provided steak and Harvey's Bristol Cream every Friday in order to celebrate communion. The CONS suit stayed in various courts for ten years before finally being thrown out.[189]

The huge number of inmate-originated lawsuits in the mid-1990s created a backlog of cases in many federal courts and was targeted by the media and by some citizens' groups as an unnecessary waste of taxpayers' money. The National Association of Attorneys General, which supports efforts to restrict frivolous inmate lawsuits, estimated that lawsuits filed by prisoners cost states more than $81 million a year in legal fees alone.[190]

In 1996, the federal Prison Litigation Reform Act (PLRA) became law.[191] The PLRA is a clear legislative effort to restrict inmate filings to worthwhile cases and to reduce the number of suits brought by state prisoners in federal courts by the following means:

- Requiring inmates to exhaust any available administrative remedies (generally, their prison's grievance procedures) before filing a federal lawsuit challenging prison conditions

- Requiring judges to screen all inmate complaints against the federal government and to immediately dismiss those deemed frivolous or without merit
- Prohibiting prisoners from filing a lawsuit for mental or emotional injury unless they can also show there has been physical injury
- Requiring inmates to pay court filing fees (prisoners who don't have the needed funds can pay the filing fee over a period of time through deductions to their prison commissary accounts)
- Limiting the award of attorneys' fees in successful lawsuits brought by inmates
- Revoking the credits earned by federal prisoners toward early release if they file a malicious lawsuit
- Mandating that court orders affecting prison administration cannot go any further than necessary to correct a violation of a particular inmate's civil rights
- Making it possible for state officials to have court orders lifted after two years unless there is a new finding of a continuing violation of federally guaranteed civil rights
- Mandating that any court order requiring the release of prisoners due to overcrowding be approved by a three-member court before it can become effective

To return to society discharged prisoners unreformed is to poison it with the worst elements possible.

—*Zebulon R. Brockway*[i]

The U.S. Supreme Court has upheld provisions of the PLRA on a number of occasions. In 1997, for example, in the case of *Edwards* v. *Balisok*,[192] the Supreme Court made it harder to successfully challenge prison disciplinary convictions, holding that, under the PLRA, prisoners cannot sue for damages under 42 U.S.C. Section 1983 for loss of good time until they sue in state court and get their disciplinary conviction set aside.[193] In *Booth* v. *Churner* (2001),[194] the U.S. Supreme Court held that, under the PLRA, "an inmate seeking only [monetary] damages must complete any prison administrative process capable of addressing the inmate's complaint and providing some form of relief [before filing his or her grievance with a federal court], even if the process does not make specific provision for monetary relief." The case involved Timothy Booth, a Pennsylvania inmate who had filed a Section 1983 action in federal district court seeking financial compensation from the state based on the claim that correctional officers had violated his Eighth Amendment right to be free from cruel and unusual punishment by assaulting him, using excessive force against him, and denying him medical attention to treat his injuries. Similarly, in the case of *Porter* v. *Nussle* (2002),[195] the U.S. Supreme Court held that a Connecticut inmate had inappropriately brought a Section 1983 complaint directly to federal district court without first having filed an inmate grievance as required by Connecticut Department of Correction procedures. In *Porter*, the Court held that the PLRA's exhaustion requirement applies to all inmate suits about prison life, whether they involve general circumstances or particular episodes and whether they allege excessive force or some other wrong.

Finally, in the 2006 case of *Woodford* v. *Ngo*,[196] the Supreme Court found that the PLRA requires proper exhaustion of administrative remedies before a prisoner can use the federal courts to challenge conditions of his or her imprisonment. Proper exhaustion, the Court said, "means using all steps that the agency holds out, and doing so properly." The *Woodford* case involved an inmate seeking to file a federal suit after prison grievance procedures were no longer available to him because he had failed to follow the administrative steps outlined by the prison within the time allotted for such steps to be taken.

According to a 2002 BJS study, the PLRA has been effective in reducing the number of frivolous lawsuits filed by inmates alleging unconstitutional prison conditions.[197] The study found that the filing rate of inmates' civil rights petitions in federal courts had been cut in half four years after passage of the act.

Opponents of the PLRA fear that it might stifle the filing of meritorious suits by inmates facing real deprivations. According to the American Civil Liberties Union (ACLU), for example, "The Prison Litigation Reform Act . . . attempts to slam the courthouse door on society's most vulnerable members. It seeks to strip the federal courts of much of their power to correct even the most egregious prison conditions by altering the basic rules which have always governed prison reform litigation. The PLRA also makes it difficult to settle prison cases by consent decree, and [it] limits the life span of any court judgment."[198] The ACLU is leading a nationwide effort to have many provisions of the PLRA overturned, but so far, the effort has borne little fruit.

CJ Careers

U.S. Customs and Border Protection (CBP)

PERSONAL PROFILE

Name: Jeffrey D. Adami
Position: Customs and Border Protection Inspector
City: Jamaica, New York
College Attended: State University of New York at Brockport
Year Hired: 1999

"Customs and Border Protection has given me an excellent working knowledge of the federal justice system along with endless opportunities for advancement."

TYPICAL POSITIONS

Border patrol agent, immigration inspector, immigration officer, immigration agent, deportation officer, detention enforcement officer, and criminal investigator. The primary mission of U.S. Customs and Border Protection is to detect and prevent the smuggling and unlawful entry of undocumented aliens into the United States. It also acts as the primary drug-interdicting agency along U.S. land borders. Entry-level border patrol agents are stationed in Arizona, California, New Mexico, and Texas along the U.S.–Mexico border. Immigration inspector and criminal investigator positions are available nationwide.

EMPLOYMENT REQUIREMENTS

Applicants for the position of border patrol agent must meet the general requirements for a federal law enforcement officer and must (1) be a U.S. citizen, (2) pass a background investigation, (3) pass a drug-screening test and a medical exam, (4) hold a valid driver's license, (5) be under age 37 at time of appointment, (6) have one year of qualifying experience or a bachelor's degree, and (7) pass the U.S. Customs and Border Protection entrance exam.

OTHER REQUIREMENTS

Border patrol agents must demonstrate proficiency in the Spanish language.

SALARY

New agents are hired at the GS-5 or GS-7 level, depending on education and experience, and are paid at the special salary rate for federal law enforcement personnel.

BENEFITS

Benefits include paid annual vacation, sick leave, life and health insurance, and a liberal retirement plan.

DIRECT INQUIRIES TO:

U.S. Customs and Border Protection
Twin Cities Hiring Center
One Federal Drive, Room 400
Fort Snelling, MN 55111-4055
Website: http://www.cbp.gov

Note: The views expressed in this profile do not necessarily represent the views of the U.S. Department of Justice, the U.S. Customs and Border Protection, or the United States.

Issues Facing Prisons Today

Prisons are society's answer to a number of social problems because they house outcasts, misfits, and some highly dangerous people. Although prisons provide a part of the answer to the question of crime control, they also face problems of their own. A few of those special problems are described here.

AIDS

In 2008, the Justice Department reported finding that 20,450 state and federal inmates were infected with the HIV (human immunodeficiency) virus.[199] At the time of the survey, 2.4% of all female state prison inmates tested positive for HIV infection, as did 1.6% of male prisoners. Some states have especially high rates of HIV infection among their prisoners; almost 6% of New York prison inmates, for example, are HIV-positive.

The incidence of HIV infection among the general population stands at 140 cases per 100,000, according to a recent report by the Centers for Disease Control and Prevention. Among inmates, however, best estimates place the reported HIV infection rate at 510 cases per 100,000[200]—more than three times as great. A few years ago, AIDS was the leading cause of death among prison inmates.[201] Today, however, the number of inmates who die from AIDS (or, more precisely, from

CJ News

Inmates Go to Court for Right to Use the Internet

When a friend sent Georgia inmate Danny Williams some legal research that had been downloaded from the Internet . . . , state prison guards confiscated the package.

Prison officials said the material was prohibited under a 5-year-old regulation that, according to state Department of Corrections Commissioner James Donald, bars inmates from receiving any printed material downloaded from the Internet. The policy is designed to prevent inmates from gaining access to material on the Internet that could compromise security—bomb-making instructions, for example.

Now, Williams is challenging the policy in federal court, the latest in a series of cases in which inmates are seeking changes in prison regulations or state law to try to use the Internet to do research or communicate with the outside world.

State and federal inmates do not have direct access to computers. However, some have used written correspondence with friends or family members to set up and maintain websites and email accounts to air grievances, solicit legal assistance, and express political views. Legal challenges such as Williams'—along with recent reports that several death-row inmates in Texas have posted personal profiles on the social networking site MySpace.com—have ignited a national debate over speech rights and how much contact prisoners should be allowed with the public in the Internet age.

John Boston, a prisoners' rights advocate in New York, says inmates' use of the Internet—albeit indirectly—represents a matter of simple free speech that should be protected.

However, Andy Kahan, director of Houston's crime victims office, says some of that speech, potentially viewable around the world, could reinjure victims.

"It's like getting (harmed) all over again," Kahan says.

In some states, crime victims and prison officials have launched legal and informal campaigns to block all access to the Internet by inmates. Those strategies, however, have been largely unsuccessful:

- In a case similar to Williams' challenge in Georgia, a federal appeals court in California two years ago sided with an inmate who was barred under state prison regulations from receiving printed copies of Internet-generated documents through regular mail. Prison authorities feared that the materials could contain coded messages.
- In Arizona, prisoners' rights groups successfully challenged a state law that once banned inmates from exchanging written mail with Internet service providers or establishing profiles on websites through outside contacts.

The Arizona law, overturned in 2003, called for additional disciplinary sanctions against inmates if they were found to have corresponded with Internet providers or requested that "any person access a provider's website."

The Arizona Department of Corrections, according to court documents, had imposed sanctions against at least five inmates "because their names appeared on Internet websites."

A similar issue surfaced this month in Texas, when Kahan discovered that 30 death-row inmates had profiles on MySpace.com.

"Is it (MySpace's) policy to give killers a platform for all the world to see?" Kahan says. "I'm asking MySpace to take a stand. Do they want convicted killers to infiltrate a system geared to young people?"

Among the most notorious inmates featured on the site is Randy Halprin, 29. He was a member of the "Texas 7," a group of inmates who escaped from the state prison system in 2000 and went on a murderous rampage.

The group was involved in the fatal shooting of a police officer during a botched robbery near Dallas. Halprin was sentenced to death for his role in the slaying.

On MySpace, Halprin established a profile, which included a gallery of photographs chronicling his life from childhood to a current photo of a smiling Halprin on death row. The page is no longer accessible to the public.

Texas Department of Criminal Justice spokeswoman Michelle Lyons says that for years, death row inmates have been using relatives and others to post information on their behalves. "We cannot police the Internet for what outsiders are posting," she says.

MySpace spokesman Jeff Berman says the site is reviewing profiles posted on behalf of inmates and says it will "remove any that violate our terms of service, such as hate speech, advocating violence and threatening conduct.

"Unless you violate the terms of service or break the law, we don't step in the middle of free expression," Berman says. "There's a lot on our site we don't approve of in terms of taste or ideas, but it's not our role to be censors."

Jayne Hawkins says she believes MySpace should do more to discourage inmate profiles. Her son, Aubrey Hawkins, was the police officer killed in the robbery that involved Halprin.

"Websites that allow criminals are helping them turn into romantic figures; that is so detrimental to our children," Hawkins says.

"This kind of thing dishonors Aubrey. What should happen on death row is that these people should sit behind a locked door, and we should be allowed to forget about them."

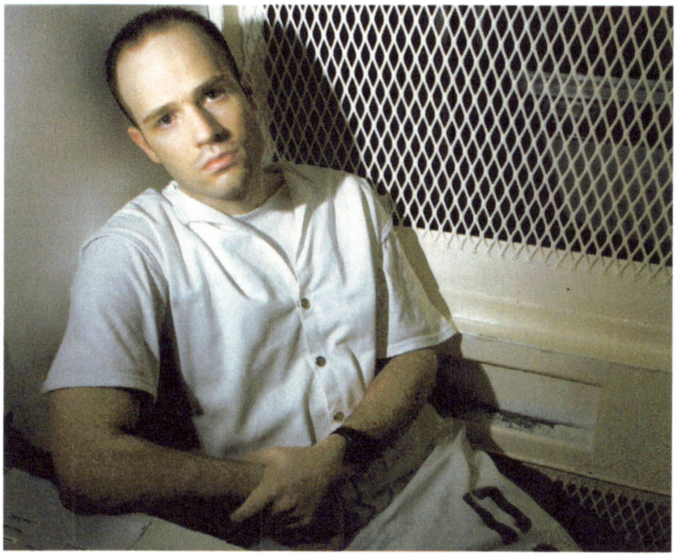

▲ Texas death-row inmate Randy Halprin, who was convicted of the murder of a law enforcement officer in a Dallas suburb. Halprin has a personal profile on MySpace.com featuring photos and a personal diary. Should inmates be allowed Internet access? If so, what limits, if any, should be set?
Brett Coomer/AP Wide World Photos

For the latest in crime and justice news, visit the Talk Justice news feed at http://www.crimenews.info.

Source: Kevin Johnson, "Inmates Go to Court to Seek Right to Use the Internet," *USA Today*, November 24, 2006, p. 5A. From USA Today, a division of Garnett Co., Inc. Reprinted with permission. www.usatoday.com.

AIDS-related complications such as pneumonia or Kaposi's sarcoma) is much lower than it has been in the past. The introduction of drugs such as protease inhibitors and the useful combinations of antiretroviral therapies have reduced inmate deaths from AIDS by 73% since 1995.[202]

Most infected inmates brought the HIV virus into prison with them, and one study found that fewer than 10% of HIV-positive inmates acquired the virus while in prison.[203] Nonetheless, the virus can be spread behind bars through homosexual activity (including rape), intravenous drug use, and the sharing of tainted tattoo and hypodermic needles. Inmates who were infected before entering prison are likely to have had histories of high-risk behavior, especially intravenous drug use.

A report by the National Institute of Justice (NIJ) suggests that corrections administrators can use two types of strategies to reduce the transmission of AIDS.[204] One strategy relies on medical technology to identify seropositive inmates and to segregate them from the rest of the prison population. Mass screening and inmate segregation, however, may be prohibitively expensive, and such actions may also be illegal—some states specifically prohibit HIV testing without the informed consent of the person tested.[205] The related issue of confidentiality may be difficult to manage, especially when the purpose of testing is to segregate infected inmates from others. In addition, civil liability may result if inmates are falsely labeled as infected or if inmates known to be infected are not prevented from spreading the disease. Only Alabama and South Carolina still segregate all known HIV-infected inmates,[206] but more limited forms of separation are practiced elsewhere. Many state prison systems have denied HIV-positive inmates jobs, educational opportunities, visitation privileges, conjugal visits, and home furloughs, causing some researchers to conclude that "inmates with HIV and AIDS are routinely discriminated against and denied equal treatment in ways that have no accepted medical basis."[207] In 1994, for example, a federal appeals court upheld a California prison policy that bars inmates who are HIV-positive from working in food-service jobs.[208] In contrast, in 2001, the Mississippi Department of Correction ended its policy of segregating HIV-positive prisoners from other inmates in educational and vocational programs.

The second strategy is one of prevention through education. Educational programs teach both inmates and staff members about the dangers of high-risk behavior and suggest ways to avoid HIV infection. An NIJ model program recommends the use of simple, straightforward messages presented by knowledgeable and approachable trainers.[209] Alarmism, says NIJ, should be avoided. One survey found that 98% of state and federal prisons provide some form of AIDS/HIV education and that 90% of jails do as well—although most such training is oriented toward corrections staff rather than inmates.[210] Learn more about HIV in prisons and jails via Library Extra 12–9 at mycrimekit.com. Inmate medical problems in general are discussed in Library Extra 12–10.

Library EXTRA

Geriatric Offenders

In 2003, Eugene Guevara of El Monte, California, allegedly shot a physician at Kaiser Permanente's Baldwin Park Medical Center.[211] Surveillance cameras filmed Guevara, who is in his late 70s, fleeing the scene with the aid of a walker. Crimes committed by the elderly, especially violent crimes, have recently been on the decline. Nonetheless, the significant expansion of America's retiree population has led to an increase in the number of elderly people who are behind bars. In fact, crimes of violence are what bring most older people into the correctional system. According to one early study, 52% of inmates who were over the age of 50 when they entered prison had committed violent crimes, compared with 41% of younger inmates.[212] On January 1, 2007, a total of 76,500 inmates ages 55 or older were housed in state and federal prisons, and the number of prisoners older than age 55 increased more than 450% between 1990 and 2007.[213] Similarly, the per capita rate of incarceration for inmates age 55 and over now stands at 258 per 100,000 residents of like age and continues to increase.

Not all of today's elderly inmates were old when they entered prison. Because of harsh sentencing laws passed throughout the country in the 1990s, a small but growing number of inmates (10%) will serve 20 years or more in prison, and 5% will never be released.[214] This means that many inmates who enter prison when they are young will grow old behind bars. Hence the "graying" of America's prison population has a number of causes[215]:

1. The general aging of the American population, which is reflected inside prisons
2. Some new sentencing policies such as "three strikes," "truth in sentencing" and "mandatory minimum" laws that send more criminals to prison for longer stretches

▲ Elderly inmates inside the geriatric unit of Texas's Estelle Prison. Geriatric inmates are becoming an increasingly large part of the inmate population. Why is the proportion of geriatric inmates increasing?
Andrew Lichtenstein/The Image Works

3. A massive prison building boom that took place in the 1980s and 1990s and [that] has provided space for more inmates, reducing the need to release prisoners to alleviate overcrowding
4. Significant changes in parole philosophies and practices

The last point means that state and federal authorities are phasing out or canceling parole programs, thereby forcing jailers to hold inmates with life sentences until they die.

Long-termers and geriatric inmates have special needs: They tend to suffer from handicaps, physical impairments, and illnesses not generally encountered among their more youthful counterparts. Unfortunately, few prisons are equipped to deal adequately with the medical needs of aging offenders. Some large facilities have begun to set aside special sections to care for elderly inmates with "typical" disorders, such as Alzheimer's disease, cancer, or heart disease. Unfortunately, such efforts have barely kept pace with the problems that geriatric offenders present. The number of inmates requiring around-the-clock care is expected to increase dramatically during the next two decades.[216]

The idea of rehabilitation takes on a new meaning where geriatric offenders are concerned. What kinds of programs are most useful in providing the older inmate with the tools needed for success on the outside? Which counseling strategies hold the greatest promise for introducing socially acceptable behavior patterns into the long-established lifestyles of elderly offenders about to be released? There are few answers to these questions. Learn about some of the oldest prisoners in America via **Web Extra 12–4** at mycrimekit.com.

Web EXTRA

Mentally Ill and Mentally Deficient Inmates

Mentally ill inmates make up another group with special needs. Some mentally ill inmates are neurotic or have personality problems, which increase tension in prison; others have serious psychological disorders that may have escaped diagnosis at trial or that did not provide a legal basis for the reduction of criminal responsibility. A fair number of offenders develop psychiatric symptoms while in prison.

Inmates suffering from significant mental illnesses account for a substantial number of those imprisoned. A 2002 lawsuit brought by a New York advocacy group on behalf of mentally ill prisoners in New York's penal institutions put the number of inmates suffering from psychiatric illnesses at 16,000 (out of a total state prison population of 67,000). The suit alleges that problem inmates with psychiatric illnesses are often isolated, exacerbating their condition and resulting in a "cycle of torment" for inmates unable to conform to prison regimens.[217]

In contrast to the allegations made by the lawsuit, a 2000 BJS survey of public and private state-level adult correctional facilities (excluding jails) found that 51% of such institutions provide 24-hour mental health care, while 71% provide therapy and counseling by trained mental health professionals as needed.[218] A large majority of prisons distribute psychotropic medications (when such medications are ordered by a physician), and 66% have programs to help released inmates obtain community mental health services. According to the BJS, 13% of state prisoners were receiving some type of mental health therapy at the time of the survey, and 10% were receiving psychotropic medications (including antidepressants, stimulants, sedatives, and tranquilizers).

Unfortunately, few state-run correctional institutions have any substantial capacity for the in-depth psychiatric treatment of inmates who have serious mental illnesses. A number of states, however, do operate facilities that specialize in psychiatric confinement of convicted criminals. The BJS reports that state governments throughout the nation operate 12 facilities devoted exclusively to the care of mentally ill inmates and that another 143 prisons report psychiatric confinement as one specialty among other functions that they perform.

As mentioned previously, the U.S. Supreme Court has ruled that mentally ill inmates can be required to take antipsychotic drugs, even against their wishes.[219] One BJS study found that the nation's prisons and jails hold an estimated 283,800 mentally ill inmates (16% of those confined) and that 547,800 such offenders are on probation.[220] The government study also found that 40% of mentally ill inmates receive no treatment at all. For more details about the report, visit **Web Extra 12–5** at mycrimekit.com.

Web EXTRA

Mentally deficient inmates constitute still another group with special needs. Some studies estimate the proportion of mentally deficient inmates at about 10%.[221] Inmates with low IQs are less likely than other inmates to complete training and rehabilitative programs successfully, and they also evidence difficulty in adjusting to the routines of prison life. As a consequence, they are likely to exceed the averages in proportion of sentence served.[222] Only seven states report special facilities or programs for the mentally retarded inmate.[223] Other state systems "mainstream" such inmates, making them participate in regular activities with other inmates.

Texas, one state that does provide special services for retarded inmates, began the Mentally Retarded Offender Program in 1984. Inmates in Texas are given a battery of tests that measure intellectual and social adaptability skills, and prisoners who are identified as having mental retardation are housed in special satellite correctional units. The Texas program provides individual and group counseling, along with training in adult life skills.

Terrorism

Today's antiterrorism efforts have brought to light the important role that corrections personnel can play in preventing future attacks on American society and in averting crises that could arise in correctional institutions as a result of terrorist action. In 2005, former New York City Police Commissioner Bernard B. Kerik told participants at the ACA's winter conference that correctional officers can help in the fight against terrorism through effective intelligence gathering and intelligence sharing. "Intelligence—that's the key to the success of this battle," Kerik said.[224] "You have to be part of that, because when we take the people off the streets in this country that go to jail, they communicate and they talk, they work with other criminals, organized gangs, organized units. You've got to collect that information, [and] you have to get it back to the authorities that need it."

Jess Maghan, director of the Forum for Comparative Corrections and professor of criminal justice at the University of Illinois at Chicago, points to the critical role that intelligence gathering and analysis by corrections agencies can play in providing critical information to prevent terrorist attacks. Maghan states that "the interaction of all people in a prison (staff, officers, and inmates) can become important intelligence sources."[225] Moreover, says Maghan, the flow of information between inmates and the outside world must be monitored to detect attack plans, especially when prisons house known terrorist leaders or group members. Vital intelligence, according to Maghan, can be passed through legal visits (where people conveying information may have no idea of its significance), sub-rosa communications networks in prisons that can support communications between inmates and the outside world, and prison transportation systems.

The security problems presented by potential information leaks were demonstrated in 2003 at the U.S. Navy's Guantánamo Bay Naval Station prison in Cuba when a translator working with

Arab internees was accused of having unlawful possession of classified information, including diagrams of the prison layout and names of the prisoners. Prison administrators responsible for the incarceration of suspected al-Qaeda and Taliban members, like those at Guantánamo, face especially delicate situations as opponents of the government's policies challenge the propriety of using military assets in what they argue is a "law enforcement" role.

Prison administrators must also be concerned about the potential impact of outside terrorist activity on their facility's inmate and staff populations. Of particular concern to today's prison administrators is the possibility of bioterrorism because a concentrated population like that of a prison or jail is highly susceptible to the rapid transmission of biological agents.[226]

The threat of a terrorist act being undertaken by inmates within a prison or jail can be an important consideration in facility planning and management, especially because inmates may be particularly vulnerable to recruitment by terrorist organizations. According to Chip Ellis, research and program coordinator for the National Memorial Institute for the Prevention of Terrorism, "Prisoners are a captive audience, and they usually have a diminished sense of self or a need for identity and protection. They're usually a disenchanted or disenfranchised group of people, [and] terrorists can sometimes capitalize on that situation."[227] Inmates can be radicalized in many ways, including exposure to other radical inmates, the distribution of extremist literature, and anti-U.S. sermons heard during religious services.

Officials of the Federal Bureau of Investigation (FBI) say al-Qaeda continues to actively recruit members in U.S. prisons and looks especially to the 9,600 Muslims held in the federal prison system. "These terrorists seek to exploit our freedom to exercise religion to their advantage by using radical forms of Islam to recruit operatives," says FBI Counterterrorism Chief John Pistole. "Unfortunately, U.S. correctional institutions are a viable venue for such radicalization and recruitment."[228] In 2005, the Institute for the Study of Violent Groups, located at Sam Houston State University, charged that the most radical form of Islam, or Wahhabism, was being spread in American prisons by clerics approved by the Islamic Society of North America (ISNA), one of two organizations chosen by the BOP to select prison chaplains.[229] "Proselytizing in prisons," said an institute spokesperson, "can produce new recruits with American citizenship." An example might be Jose Padilla, aka Abdullah al-Mujahir, a Chicago thug who converted to Islam after being exposed to radical Islam while serving time in a Florida jail. According to authorities, Padilla, who was arrested in Chicago, intended to contaminate a U.S. city with a radiological dirty bomb. Likewise, British citizen Richard Reid, convicted for attempting to blow up an American Airlines flight from Paris to Miami with explosives in his shoes, had converted to radical Islam in an English prison.[230]

In 2004 the Office of the Inspector General of the U.S. Department of Justice released its review of the BOP's practices in selecting Muslim clergy to minister to inmates in BOP facilities. The report concluded that the primary threat of radicalization comes from inmates, not chaplains, contractors, or volunteers. The report goes on to say that "inmates from foreign countries politicize Islam and radicalize inmates, who in turn radicalize more inmates when they transfer to other prisons."[231] The report also identified a form of Islam unique to the prison environment called "prison Islam."[232] Prison Islam, the report said, is a form of Islam that adapts itself to prison values and is used by gangs and radical inmates to further unlawful goals; it was found to be especially common in institutions where religious services are led by lay *mullahs* (spiritual leaders)—a practice made necessary by a lack of Muslim chaplains. The report concluded with a number of recommendations, including one that the BOP should provide staff training on Islam so that correctional officers can recognize radical Islamist messages. The report also recommended that "the BOP can and should improve its process for selecting, screening, and supervising Muslim religious services providers. We recommend [that] the BOP take steps to examine all chaplains', religious contractors', and religious volunteers' doctrinal beliefs to screen out anyone who poses a threat to security."

In response, the FBI implemented a number of new practices, and today it coordinates with other federal agencies to share intelligence information about suspected or known terrorists in its inmate population. The FBI closely tracks inmates with known or suspected terrorist ties and monitors their correspondence and other communications. The bureau also trains staff members to recognize terrorist-related activity and to effectively manage convicted terrorists within a correctional environment. A BOP program to counter radicalization efforts among inmates has been in place for the past few years.[233]

CJ News

Feds Target Terrorist Recruiting in Prisons

The federal government is working with prisons in dozens of states to improve intelligence gathering and monitoring of inmates in a stepped-up campaign to curb homegrown terrorism behind bars.

The FBI and Homeland Security Department are urging prison officials to do more extensive background checks on workers and volunteers who meet with inmates. And members of Congress are looking at possible reforms in prison security as a way to combat the spread of extremist Islamic beliefs.

Chief among the concerns is that radical Muslim clerics could have access to prisoners and coerce them with terrorist literature.

"It's a concern because we know that violent extremist groups will target people in prisons," said Donald Van Duyn, the FBI's counterterrorism director. "We're working to improve monitoring, improve training and increase awareness."

The intensified surveillance follows the recent arrests of people alleged to be homegrown terrorism suspects in London and Canada, which have raised concerns that the United States may be vulnerable to terrorism at the hands of its own citizens. British authorities said in August [2006] that they broke up a conspiracy to blow up U.S.-bound airliners with liquid bombs, and Canadian officials charged 17 people in June [2006] with an al-Qaeda-inspired plot to possess 3 tons of bomb-making materials.

Homeland Security officials, who are sending investigators to prisons around the country to gather intelligence on inmate radicalization, are worried that similar plots could be hatched in U.S. prisons. "Prisons can be a breeding ground," says Charles Allen, Homeland Security's top intelligence officer.

Among the steps that the FBI and Homeland Security are urging prisons to take:

- Develop more informants and set up more intelligence units in state prison systems. The FBI is encouraging prison systems to set up their own intelligence units and to work with local agents to share information. The bureau won't say whether it has undercover agents in the nation's prisons.
- Train more prison staff to recognize signs that prisoners are turning to extremist propaganda, sharing radical views, and attempting to convert other inmates.
- Conduct background checks on volunteers and workers to ensure extremist Muslim clerics don't have access to prisoners.

"Our concern is not with prison inmates converting to Islam," says Sen. Susan Collins, R–Maine, chairwoman of the Senate Homeland Security Committee. "For many converts, this religion brings the direction and purpose their lives previously lacked."

A case in California shows how some U.S. prisons have spawned converts to radical forms of Islam.

Members of an extremist group robbed a dozen Los Angeles gas stations in 2005 to raise money to finance terrorist attacks on the United States.

The group's founder, Kevin James, is alleged by the FBI to have recruited members from prison. Four members of the group are awaiting trial on charges including conspiracy to levy war against the U.S. government.

"We have to wonder how many other such conspiracies are taking shape under the radar in other prisons," Collins says.

▲ Muslim inmate Christopher McCullon, with his prayer rug draped over his shoulder, talking with Muslim correctional officer Umar Abddullah after weekly worship in a room used as a mosque at Rikers Island Correctional Institution, located in New York City. How might correctional officers help in the nation's fight against terrorism?
Stephan Savoia/AP Wide World Photos

For the latest in crime and justice news, visit the Talk Justice news feed at http://www.crimenews.info.

Source: Mimi Hall, "Feds Target Terrorist Recruiting in Prisons," *USA Today*, November 7, 2006, p. 1A. From USA TODAY, a division of Garnett Co., Inc. Reprinted with permission.www.usatoday.com

The incarceration of convicted terrorists presents new challenges for corrections administrators at both the state and federal levels. Sheik Omar Abdel-Rahman, a blind Muslim cleric and spiritual leader for many Islamic terrorists (including Osama bin Laden), is currently serving a life sentence in a U.S. federal penitentiary for conspiring to assassinate Egyptian President Hosni Mubarak and to blow up five New York City landmarks in the 1990s. Speculation that the sheik continues to motivate terrorist acts against the United States gained credibility when his attorney and three others were indicted in April 2002 for allegedly passing illegal communications between Abdel-Rahman and an Egyptian-based terrorist organization known as the Islamic Group.[234]

The current world situation, and the environment in which corrections agencies operate, is likely to ensure that the issues identified here will take on ever-increasing significance for prison administrators of the future. Learn more about prison issues of all kinds from the Prison Policy Initiative at **Web Extra 12–6** at mycrimekit.com. Read about concerns about Muslim religious services in correctional institutions at **Library Extra 12–11** at mycrimekit.com.

Web EXTRA

Library EXTRA

Summary

- Prisons are small self-contained societies that are sometimes described as total institutions. Studies of prison life have detailed the existence of prison subcultures, or inmate worlds, replete with inmate values, social roles, and lifestyles. New inmates who are socialized into prison subculture are said to undergo the process of prisonization; prison subcultures are very influential, and both inmates and staff must reckon with them. Today's prisons are miniature societies, reflecting the problems and challenges that exist in the larger society of which they are a part.
- Female inmates represent a small but growing proportion of the nation's prison population. Many female inmates have histories of physical and sexual abuse. Although they are likely to have dependent children, their parenting skills may be limited. Most female inmates are housed in centralized state facilities known as women's prisons, which are dedicated exclusively to incarcerating female felons. Some states, however, particularly those with small populations, continue to keep female prisoners in special wings of what are otherwise institutions for men. Few facilities for women have programs especially designed for female offenders.
- Like prisoners, correctional officers undergo a socialization process that helps them function by the official and unofficial rules of staff society. Prison staffers are most concerned with custody and control. The enforcement of strict rules; body and cell searches; counts; unannounced shakedowns; the control of dangerous items, materials, and contraband; and the extensive use of bars, locks, fencing, cameras, and alarms all support the staff's vigilance in maintaining security. Although concerns with security still command center stage, professionalism is playing an increasing role in corrections today, and today's corrections personnel are better trained and more proficient than ever before.
- As this chapter discusses, the causes of prison riots are diverse. They include (1) unmet inmate needs, (2) violent tendencies of some inmates, (3) dehumanizing conditions of imprisonment, (4) desires to regulate inmate society and redistribute power, and (5) power vacuums created by changes in prison administration, the transfer of influential inmates, or court-ordered injunctions. Riots, when they do occur, typically pass through five phases: (1) explosion, (2) organization into inmate-led groups, (3) confrontation with authority, (4) termination through negotiation or physical confrontation, and (5) reaction and explanation, usually by investigative commissions.
- For many years, courts throughout the nation assumed a hands-off approach to prisons, rarely intervening in the day-to-day administration of prison facilities. That changed in the late 1960s when the U.S. Supreme Court began to identify inmates' rights mandated by the Constitution. Rights identified by the Court include the right to physical integrity, an absolute right to be free from unwarranted corporal punishments, certain religious rights, and procedural rights, such as those involving access to attorneys and to the courts. The conditional rights of prisoners, which have repeatedly been supported by the Court, mandate professionalism among prison administrators and require vigilance in the provision of correctional services. High court decisions have generally established that prison inmates retain those constitutional rights that are not inconsistent with their status as prisoners or with the legitimate penological objectives of the correctional system; in other words, inmates have rights, much the same as people who are not incarcerated, provided that the legitimate needs of the prison for security, custody, and safety are not compromised. The era of prisoners' rights was sharply curtailed in 1996 with the passage of the Prison Litigation Reform Act, spurred on by a growing recognition of the legal morass resulting from unregulated access to federal courts by inmates across the nation.

- The major problems and issues facing prisons today include (1) the threat from infectious diseases (including AIDS), (2) the need to deal with a growing geriatric offender population (the result of longer sentences and the aging of the American population), (3) a sizable number of mentally ill and mentally deficient inmates, and (4) a concern over inmates with terrorist leanings and those incarcerated for terrorism-related crimes.

Key Concepts

Terms

balancing test
civil death
deliberate indifference
grievance procedure
hands-off doctrine
prison argot
prison subculture
prisonization
security threat group (STG)
total institution

Cases

Block v. *Rutherford*
Bounds v. *Smith*
Cruz v. *Beto*
Estelle v. *Gamble*
Helling v. *McKinney*
Houchins v. *KQED, Inc.*
Hudson v. *Palmer*
Johnson v. *Avery*
Jones v. *North Carolina Prisoners' Labor Union*
Katz v. *U.S.*
Overton v. *Bazzetta*
Pell v. *Procunier*
Pennsylvania Department of Corrections v. *Yeskey*
Ruiz v. *Estelle*
Sandin v. *Conner*
Wolff v. *McDonnell*

Questions for Review

1. What are prison subcultures, and how do they influence prison life? How do they develop, and what purpose do they serve?
2. How do women's prisons differ from men's? Why have women's prisons been studied less often than institutions for men?
3. What are the primary concerns of prison staff? What other goals do staff members focus on?
4. What causes prison riots? Through what stages do most riots progress? How might riots be prevented?
5. What are the commonly accepted rights of prisoners in the United States today? Where do these rights come from? What U.S. Supreme Court cases are especially significant in the area of prisoners' rights?
6. What are some of the major issues that prisons face today? What new issues might the future bring?

To participate in an online discussion of these topics and others, join the CJ Brief e-mail discussion list at mycrimekit.com.

Web Quest

Visit the Cybrary, and search for "jobs," "careers," and "employment." What criminal justice–related employment sites can you find? Explore some of the sites you find, and consider the possibility of a career in corrections. Document the sources you used, and list the URLs and the date you accessed each. Then answer these questions[235]:

What is the difference between a job and a career?

What career opportunities are available in corrections?

Why is career planning important? How can you develop an effective career plan?

What is the difference between education and training?

Why are education and training important to building a career in corrections?

What role might professionalism play in building your career?

What traits must you have to achieve your goals and to be successful in a career in corrections?

Submit your answers to your instructor if asked to do so.

To complete this Web Quest online, go to the Web Quest module in Chapter 12 of the *Criminal Justice: A Brief Introduction* Companion Website at mycrimekit.com.

Notes

i. Zebulon R. Brockway, *The Ideal of a True Prison System for a State* (1865). Reprinted in the *Journal of Correctional Education,* Vol. 46, No. 2 (1995), pp. 68–74.

1. Commission on Safety and Abuse in America's Prisons, *Confronting Confinement: A Report of the Commission on Safety and Abuse in America's Prisons* (New York: Vera Institute of Justice, 2006).
2. Hans Reimer, "Socialization in the Prison Community," *Proceedings of the American Prison Association, 1937* (New York: American Prison Association, 1937), pp. 151–155.
3. Donald Clemmer, *The Prison Community* (Boston: Holt, Rinehart and Winston, 1940).
4. Gresham M. Sykes, *The Society of Captives: A Study of a Maximum Security Prison* (Princeton, NJ: Princeton University Press, 1958).
5. Richard A. Cloward et al., *Theoretical Studies in Social Organization of the Prison* (New York: Social Science Research Council, 1960).
6. Donald R. Cressey, ed., *The Prison: Studies in Institutional Organization and Change* (New York: Holt, Rinehart and Winston, 1961).
7. Lawrence Hazelrigg, ed., *Prison within Society: A Reader in Penology* (Garden City, NY: Anchor, 1969), preface.
8. Charles Stastny and Gabrielle Tyrnauer, *Who Rules the Joint? The Changing Political Culture of Maximum-Security Prisons in America* (Lexington, MA: Lexington Books, 1982), p. 131.
9. Erving Goffman, *Asylums: Essays on the Social Situation of Mental Patients and Other Inmates* (Garden City, NY: Anchor, 1961).
10. For a firsthand account of the prison experience, see Victor Hassine, *Life without Parole: Living in Prison Today* (Los Angeles: Roxbury, 1996); and W. Rideau and R. Wikberg, *Life Sentences: Rage and Survival behind Prison Bars* (New York: Times Books, 1992).
11. Gresham M. Sykes and Sheldon L. Messinger, "The Inmate Social System," in Richard A. Cloward et al., eds., *Theoretical Studies in Social Organization of the Prison* (New York: Social Science Research Council, 1960), pp. 5–19.
12. The concept of prisonization is generally attributed to Clemmer, *The Prison Community,* although Quaker penologists of the late eighteenth century were actively concerned with preventing "contamination" (the spread of criminal values) among prisoners.
13. Sykes and Messinger, "The Inmate Social System," p. 5.
14. Stanton Wheeler, "Socialization in Correctional Communities," *American Sociological Review,* Vol. 26 (October 1961), pp. 697–712.
15. Sykes, *The Society of Captives,* p. xiii.
16. As cited in Stastny and Tyrnauer, *Who Rules the Joint?* p. 135.
17. Ibid.
18. Sykes, *The Society of Captives.*
19. Clemmer, *The Prison Community,* pp. 294–296.
20. John Irwin, *The Felon* (Englewood Cliffs, NJ: Prentice Hall, 1970).
21. Joseph L. Galloway, "Into the Heart of Darkness," *U.S. News* online, March 8, 1999. Web posted at http://www.usnews.com/usnews/issue/990308/8pris.htm (accessed March 20, 2005).
22. Cindy Struckman-Johnson and David Struckman-Johnson, "A Comparison of Sexual Coercion Experiences Reported by Men and Women in Prison," *Journal of Interpersonal Violence,* Vol. 21, No. 12 (December 2006), pp. 1591–1615.
23. Public Law 108-79.
24. Dee Halley, "The Prison Rape Elimination Act of 2003: Addressing Sexual Assault in Correctional Settings," *Corrections Today* (June 2005), pp. 30, 100.
25. Allen J. Beck and Paige M. Harrison, *Sexual Victimization in State and Federal Prisons Reported by Inmates, 2007* (Washington, DC: Bureau of Justice Statistics, December, 2007; revised March 19, 2008).
26. "Statement of National Prison Rape Elimination Commission on Bureau of Justice Statistics Report on Sexual Victimization in Prisons," National Prison Rape Elimination Commission press release, December 16, 2007.
27. Bureau of Justice Statistics, *Sexual Victimization in Local Jails Reported by Inmates, 2007* (Washington, DC: BJS, 2008).
28. Halley, "The Prison Rape Elimination Act of 2003," p. 2.
29. Section 261 of the 2008 Second Chance Act (Public Law No. 110-199) amended the Prison Rape Elimination Act of 2003 to extend the date for the report of the National Prison Rape Elimination Commission on the impact of prison rape, thus extending the commission's termination date.
30. Joanne Mariner, *No Escape: Male Rape in U.S. Prisons* (New York: Human Rights Watch, 2001). Web posted at http://www.hrw.org/reports/2001/prison/report.html (accessed September 23, 2005).
31. Lee H. Bowker, *Prison Victimization* (New York: Elsevier, 1980).
32. Ibid., p. 42
33. Ibid., p. 1.
34. Hans Toch, *Living in Prison: The Ecology of Survival* (New York: Free Press, 1977), p. 151.
35. William J. Sabol, Heather Couture, and Paige M. Harrison, *Prisoners in 2006* (Washington, DC: Bureau of Justice Statistics, 2007), p. 3.
36. Ibid.
37. Some of the information in this section comes from the American Correctional Association, Task Force on the Female Offender, *The Female Offender: What Does the Future Hold?* (Washington, DC: St. Mary's Press, 1990); and "The View from behind Bars," *Time* (fall 1990, special issue), pp. 20–22.
38. Much of the information and some of the wording in this section come from Barbara Bloom, Barbara Owen, and Stephanie Covington, *Gender-Responsive Strategies: Research, Practice, and Guiding Principles for Women Offenders* (Washington, DC: National Institute of Corrections, 2003).
39. Barbara Bloom, "Triple Jeopardy: Race, Class and Gender as Factors in Women's Imprisonment," paper presented at the annual meeting of the American Society of Criminology, 1997.
40. Joanne Belknap, *The Invisible Woman: Gender, Crime, and Justice* (Belmont, CA: Wadsworth, 2001).
41. C. W. Harlow, *Prior Abuse Reported by Inmates and Probationers* (Washington, DC: Bureau of Justice Statistics, 1999).
42. Ibid.
43. Ibid.
44. B. Owen and B. Bloom, "Profiling Women Prisoners: Findings from National Survey and California Sample," *The Prison Journal,* Vol. 75, No. 2 (1995), pp. 165–185.
45. B. K. Jordan et al., "Prevalence of Psychiatric Disorders among Incarcerated Women," *Archives of General Psychiatry,* Vol. 53, No. 6 (1996), pp. 513–519.
46. A. Browne, B. Miller, and E. Maguin, "Prevalence and Severity of Lifetime Physical and Sexual Victimization among Incarcerated Women," *International Journal of Law and Psychiatry,* Vol. 22, Nos. 3–4 (1999), pp. 301–322.
47. A. Merlo and J. Pollock, *Women, Law, and Social Control* (Boston: Allyn and Bacon, 1995).
48. Center for Substance Abuse Treatment, *Substance Abuse Treatment for Incarcerated Offenders: Guide to Promising Practices* (Rockville, MD: U.S. Department of Health and Human Services, 1997).
49. Lawrence A. Greenfeld and Tracy L. Snell, *Women Offenders* (Washington, DC: Bureau of Justice Statistics, 1999).
50. Substance Abuse and Mental Health Services Administration, *National Household Survey on Drug Abuse: Population*

Estimates 1992 (Rockville, MD: U.S. Department of Health and Human Services, 1993).

51. National Center on Addiction and Substance Abuse, *Behind Bars: Substance Abuse and America's Prison Population* (New York: Columbia University Press, 1998).
52. Quoted in "Report Cites Unfair Treatment of Female Drug Offenders," *Corrections Journal* (March 22, 2005), p. 4.
53. Lenora Lapidus et al., *Caught in the Net: The Impact of Drug Policies on Women and Families* (New York: American Civil Liberties Union, 2005).
54. L. Acoca, "Defusing the Time Bomb: Understanding and Meeting the Growing Health Care Needs of Incarcerated Women in America," *Crime and Delinquency,* Vol. 44, No. 1 (1998), pp. 49–70; and D. S. Young, "Contributing Factors to Poor Health among Incarcerated Women: A Conceptual Model," *Affilia,* Vol. 11, No. 4 (1996), pp. 440–461.
55. Acoca, "Defusing the Time Bomb."
56. A. L. Coker et al., "Childhood Forced Sex and Cervical Dysplasia among Women Prison Inmates," *Violence against Women,* Vol. 4, No. 5 (1998), pp. 595–608.
57. Allen J. Beck and Laura M. Maruschak, *Mental Health Treatment in State Prisons, 2000* (Washington, DC: Bureau of Justice Statistics, 2001).
58. L. A. Teplin et al., "Prevalence of Psychiatric Disorders among Incarcerated Women," *Archives of General Psychiatry,* Vol. 53, No. 6 (1996), pp. 505–512.
59. B. M. Veysey, *Specific Needs of Women Diagnosed with Mental Illnesses in U.S. Jails* (Delmar, NY: National GAINS Center, 1997); and M. Singer et al., "The Psychosocial Issues of Women Serving Time in Jail," *Social Work,* Vol. 40, No. 1 (1995), pp. 103–113.
60. Greenfeld and Snell, *Women Offenders*; and Mary K. Shilton, *Resources for Mother–Child Community Corrections* (Washington, DC: Bureau of Justice Assistance, 2001), p. 3.
61. Mary Jeanette Clement, "National Survey of Programs for Incarcerated Women," paper presented at the annual meeting of the Academy of Criminal Justice Sciences, Nashville, TN, March 1991, pp. 8–9.
62. B. Bloom and D. Steinhart, *Why Punish the Children? A Reappraisal of the Children of Incarcerated Mothers in America* (San Francisco: National Council on Crime and Delinquency, 1993).
63. Greenfeld and Snell, *Women Offenders.*
64. Ibid.
65. Ibid.
66. Barbara Bloom and Stephanie Covington, "Gendered Justice: Programming for Women in Correctional Settings," paper presented at the annual meeting of the American Society of Criminology, San Francisco, November 2000, p. 11.
67. ACA, *The Female Offender.*
68. Marsha Clowers, "Dykes, Gangs, and Danger: Debunking Popular Myths about Maximum Security Life," *Journal of Criminal Justice and Popular Culture,* Vol. 9, No. 1 (2001), pp. 22–30.
69. D. Ward and G. Kassebaum, *Women's Prison: Sex and Social Structure* (London: Weidenfeld and Nicolson, 1966).
70. Esther Heffernan, *Making It in Prison: The Square, the Cool, and the Life* (London: Wiley-Interscience, 1972).
71. Rose Giallombardo, *Society of Women: A Study of Women's Prisons* (New York: John Wiley, 1966).
72. Ibid., p. 136.
73. For a summary of such studies (including some previously unpublished), see Lee H. Bowker, *Prisoner Subcultures* (Lexington, MA: Lexington Books, 1977) p. 86.
74. Giallombardo, *Society of Women,* p. 162.
75. David Ward and Gene Kassebaum, *Women's Prison: Sex and Social Structure* (Piscataway, NJ: Aldine Transaction, 2008).
76. Barbara Owen, *"In the Mix": Struggle and Survival in a Women's Prison* (Albany: State University of New York Press, 1998).
77. Barbara Owen, "Prisons: Prisons for Women—Prison Subcultures," available online at http://law.jrank.org/pages/1802/Prisons-Prisons-Women-Prison-subcultures.html.
78. See Joanne Belknap, Book Review of Barbara Owen, " 'In the Mix': Struggle and Survival in a Women's Prison," in *Western Criminology Review* (1999). Web available at http://wcr.sonoma.edu/v1n2/belknap.html (accessed April 11, 2008).
79. Mary Koscheski and Christopher Hensley, "Inmate Homosexual Behavior in a Southern Female Correctional Facility," *American Journal of Criminal Justice,* Vol. 25, No. 2 (2001), pp. 269–277.
80. See, for example, Margie J. Phelps, "Sexual Misconduct between Staff and Inmates," *Corrections Technology and Management,* Vol. 12 (1999).
81. Heffernan, *Making It in Prison.*
82. Bowker, *Prison Victimization,* p. 53.
83. Giallombardo, *Society of Women.*
84. "Georgia Indictments Charge Abuse of Female Inmates," *USA Today,* November 16, 1992, p. 3A.
85. Ibid.
86. ACA, *The Female Offender,* p. 39.
87. Kristen A. Hughes, *Justice Expenditure and Employment in the United States, 2003* (Washington, DC: Bureau of Justice Statistics, 2006), p. 7.
88. Ibid., p. 6.
89. Kristen A. Hughes, *Justice Expenditure and Employment in the United States, 2003* (Washington, DC: Bureau of Justice Statistics, 2006); data table 5: "Justice System Employment and Percent Distribution of Full-Time Equivalent Employment, by State and Types of Government."
90. American Correctional Association, "Correctional Officers in Adult Systems," in *Vital Statistics in Corrections* (Laurel, MD: ACA, 2000). "Other" minorities round out the percentages to a total of 100%.
91. Ibid.
92. ACA, "Correctional Officers in Adult Systems."
93. Lucien X. Lombardo, *Guards Imprisoned: Correctional Officers at Work* (New York: Elsevier, 1981), pp. 22–36.
94. Leonard Morgenbesser, "NY State Law Prescribes Psychological Screening for CO Job Applicants," *Correctional Training* (winter 1983), p. 1.
95. "A Sophisticated Approach to Training Prison Guards," *Newsday,* August 12, 1982.
96. "Two Guards Taken Hostage by Inmates at Arizona Prison," *USA Today,* January 18, 2004. Web posted at http://www.usatoday.com/news/nation/2004-01-18-prison-hostage_x.htm (accessed July 12, 2004).
97. Stastny and Tyrnauer, *Who Rules the Joint?* p. 1.
98. See Frederick Talbott, "Reporting from behind the Walls: Do It before the Siren Wails," *The Quill* (February 1988), pp. 16–21.
99. "Ohio Prison Rebellion Is Ended," *USA Today,* April 22, 1993, p. 2A.
100. "Guards Hurt in Prison Riot," Associated Press wire service, November 11, 2000.
101. "San Quentin Prison Riot Leaves 42 Injured," *USA Today,* August 9, 2005, p. 3A.
102. Ralph Blumenthal, "Gang Fights in Prison Injure 22 and Kill One," *New York Times,* March, 29, 2008.
103. See, for example, American Correctional Association, *Riots and Disturbances in Correctional Institutions* (College Park, MD: ACA, 1981); Michael Braswell et al., *Prison Violence in America* (Cincinnati, OH: Anderson, 1985); and R. Conant, "Rioting, Insurrectional and Civil Disorderliness," *American Scholar,* Vol. 37 (summer 1968), pp. 420–433.
104. Robert S. Fong, Ronald E. Vogel, and S. Buentello, "Prison Gang Dynamics: A Look inside the Texas Department of Corrections," in A. V. Merlo and P. Menekos, eds., *Dilemmas and Directions in Corrections* (Cincinnati, OH: Anderson, 1992).

105. Ibid.
106. *Ruiz* v. *Estelle,* 503 F. Supp. 1265 (S.D. Texas, 1980).
107. Vernon Fox, "Prison Riots in a Democratic Society," *Police,* Vol. 26, No. 12 (December 1982), pp. 35–41.
108. Donald R. Cressey, "Adult Felons in Prison," in Lloyd E. Ohlin, ed., *Prisoners in America* (Englewood Cliffs, NJ: Prentice Hall, 1972), pp. 117–150.
109. The facts in this story are taken from *Hope* v. *Pelzer,* 536 U.S. 730 (2002).
110. "Convictions Bar 3.9 Million from Voting," Associated Press wire service, September 22, 2000.
111. *Holt* v. *Sarver,* 309 F. Supp. 362 (E.D. Ark. 1970).
112. Vergil L. Williams, *Dictionary of American Penology: An Introduction* (Westport, CT: Greenwood Press, 1979), pp. 6–7.
113. *Pell* v. *Procunier,* 417 U.S. 817, 822 (1974).
114. Ibid.
115. Title 42 U.S.C.A. 1997, Public Law 104-150.
116. Section 1997e.
117. American Correctional Association, *Legal Responsibility and Authority of Correctional Officers: A Handbook on Courts, Judicial Decisions and Constitutional Requirements* (College Park, MD: ACA, 1987), p. 8.
118. *Beard* v. *Banks,* 548 U.S. 521 (2006).
119. *Procunier* v. *Martinez,* 416 U.S. 396 (1974).
120. *McNamara* v. *Moody,* 606 F.2d 621 (5th Cir. 1979).
121. *Luparar* v. *Stoneman,* 382 F. Supp. 495 (D. Vt. 1974).
122. *Mallery* v. *Lewis,* 106 Idaho 227 (1983).
123. See, for example, *Pepperling* v. *Crist,* 678 F.2d 787 (9th Cir. 1981).
124. *Block* v. *Rutherford,* 486 U.S. 576 (1984).
125. *Overton* v. *Bazzetta,* 539 U.S. 126 (2003).
126. *Pell* v. *Procunier.*
127. *Houchins* v. *KQED, Inc.,* 438 U.S. 11 (1978).
128. Ibid.
129. *Cruz* v. *Beto,* 405 U.S. 319 (1972).
130. *Aziz* v. *LeFevre,* 642 F.2d 1109 (2d Cir. 1981).
131. *Glasshofer* v. *Thornburg,* 514 F. Supp. 1242 (E.D. Pa. 1981).
132. See, for example, *Smith* v. *Coughlin,* 748 F.2d 783 (2d Cir. 1984).
133. *Campbell* v. *Cauthron,* 623 F.2d 503 (8th Cir. 1980).
134. *Smith* v. *Blackledge,* 451 F.2d 1201 (4th Cir. 1971).
135. *Dettmer* v. *Landon,* 617 F. Supp. 592, 594 (D.C. Va. 1985).
136. *Dettmer* v. *Landon,* 799 F.2d 929 (4th Cir. 1986).
137. *Lewellyn (L'Aquarius)* v. *State,* 592 P.2d 538 (Okla. Crim. App. 1979).
138. *Hill* v. *Blackwell,* 774 F.2d 338, 347 (8th Cir. 1985).
139. *Benning* v. *State,* No. 04-10979 (11th Cir. 2005).
140. *Cutter* v. *Wilkinson,* 544 U.S. 709 (2005).
141. For a Supreme Court review of the First Amendment right to petition the courts, see *McDonald* v. *Smith,* 105 S.Ct. 2787 (1985).
142. *Bounds* v. *Smith,* 430 U.S. 817, 821 (1977).
143. *Lewis* v. *Casey,* 516 U.S. 804 (1996).
144. *Johnson* v. *Avery,* 393 U.S. 483 (1968).
145. *Bounds* v. *Smith.*
146. *Taylor* v. *Sterrett,* 532 F.2d 462 (5th Cir. 1976).
147. *In re Harrell,* 87 Cal. Rptr. 504, 470 P.2d 640 (1970).
148. *Guajardo* v. *Estelle,* 432 F. Supp. 1373 (S.D. Texas, 1977).
149. *O'Brien* v. *U.S.,* 386 U.S. 345 (1967); and *Weatherford* v. *Bursey,* 429 U.S. 545 (1977).
150. *U.S.* v. *Gouveia,* 104 S.Ct. 2292, 81 L.Ed.2d 146 (1984).
151. *Estelle* v. *Gamble,* 429 U.S. 97 (1976).
152. Ibid., pp. 105–106.
153. *Hudson* v. *McMillan,* 503 U.S. 1 (1992).
154. *Ruiz* v. *Estelle,* 503 F. Supp. 1265 (S.D. Tex. 1980); *aff'd in part, rev'd in part,* 679 F.2d 1115 (5th Cir. 1982); *amended in part, vacated in part,* 688 F.2d 266 (5th Cir. 1982); *cert. denied,* 460 U.S. 1042 (1983).
155. *Newman* v. *Alabama,* 349 F. Supp. 278 (M.D. Ala. 1972).
156. *In re Caulk,* 35 CrL. 2532 (New Hampshire S. Ct. 1984).
157. Ibid.
158. *Bee* v. *Greaves,* 744 F.2d 1387 (10th Cir. 1984).
159. *Washington* v. *Harper,* 494 U.S. 210 (1990).
160. *Pennsylvania Department of Corrections* v. *Yeskey,* 524 U.S. 206, 209 (1998).
161. 42 U.S.C. Section 12132.
162. *U.S.* v. *Georgia,* 546 U.S. 151 (2006); and *Goodman* v. *Georgia,* 546 U.S. 151 (2006).
163. *Holt* v. *Sarver,* 309 F. Supp. 362 (E.D. Ark. 1970).
164. *Farmer* v. *Brennan,* 114 S.Ct. 1970, 128 L.Ed.2d 811 (1994).
165. Ibid.
166. *Helling* v. *McKinney,* 113 S.Ct. 2475, 125 L.Ed.2d 22 (1993).
167. *U.S.* v. *Ready,* 574 F.2d 1009 (10th Cir. 1978).
168. *Katz* v. *U.S.,* 389 U.S. 347, 88 S.Ct. 507, 19 L.Ed.2d 576 (1967).
169. *Hudson* v. *Palmer,* 468 U.S. 517 (1984).
170. *Block* v. *Rutherford,* 104 S.Ct. 3227, 3234–35 (1984).
171. *U.S.* v. *Lilly,* 576 F.2d 1240 (5th Cir. 1978).
172. *Palmer* v. *Hudson,* 697 F.2d 1220 (4th Cir. 1983).
173. *Jones* v. *North Carolina Prisoners' Labor Union,* 433 U.S. 119, 53 L.Ed.2d 629, 641 (1977).
174. *Wolff* v. *McDonnell,* 94 S.Ct. 2963 (1974).
175. Ibid.
176. Ibid.
177. *Ponte* v. *Real,* 471 U.S. 491, 105 S.Ct. 2192, 85 L.Ed.2d 553 (1985).
178. *Vitek* v. *Jones,* 445 U.S. 480 (1980).
179. American Correctional Association, Standard 2-4346. See ACA, *Legal Responsibility and Authority of Correctional Officers,* p. 49.
180. *Wilson* v. *Seiter,* 501 U.S. 294 (1991).
181. *Estelle* v. *Gamble,* 429 U.S. 97, 106 (1976).
182. *Sandin* v. *Conner,* 63 U.S.L.W. 4601 (1995).
183. *Wolff* v. *McDonnell,* 94 S.Ct. 2963 (1974).
184. *Hewitt* v. *Helms,* 459 U.S. 460 (1983).
185. *Ali* v. *Federal Bureau of Prisons,* U.S. Supreme Court, No. 06-9130 (decided January 22, 2008).
186. 28 U.S.C. Section 1346(b)(1).
187. Laurie Asseo, "Inmate Lawsuits," Associated Press wire service, May 24, 1996; and Bureau of Justice Statistics, "State and Federal Prisoners Filed 68,235 Petitions in U.S. Courts in 1996," press release, October 29, 1997.
188. See, for example, "The Great Prison Pastime," *20/20,* ABC News, September 24, 1993, which is part of the video library available to instructors using this textbook.
189. Ibid.
190. Asseo, "Inmate Lawsuits."
191. 42 U.S.C. Section 1997e(a). Public Law 104-134. Although the PLRA was signed into law on April 26, 1996, and is frequently referred to as the Prison Litigation Reform Act of 1996, the official name of the act is the Prison Litigation Reform Act of 1995.
192. *Edwards* v. *Balisok,* 520 U.S. 641 (1997).
193. American Civil Liberties Union, *Prisoners' Rights—An ACLU Position Paper,* Fall 1999. Web posted at http://www.aclu.org/library/PrisonerRights.pdf (accessed March 5, 2002).
194. *Booth* v. *Churner,* 532 U.S. 731 (2001).
195. *Porter* v. *Nussle,* 534 U.S. 516 (2002).
196. *Woodford* v. *Ngo,* 548 U.S. 81 (2006).
197. John Scalia, *Prisoner Petitions Filed in U.S. District Courts, 2000, with Trends 1980–2000* (Washington, DC: Bureau of Justice Statistics, 2002).
198. American Civil Liberties Union, *Prisoners' Rights.*
199. Laura M. Maruschak, *HIV in Prisons, 2006* (Washington, DC: Bureau of Justice Statistics, 2008).
200. Ibid., p. 1.
201. Dennis Cauchon, "AIDS in Prison: Locked Up and Locked Out," *USA Today,* March 31, 1995, p. 6A.
202. Maruschak, *HIV in Prisons, 2003,* p. 1.
203. Centers for Disease Control and Prevention, "HIV Transmission among Male Inmates in a State Prison System: Georgia, 1992–2005," *Morbidity and Mortality Weekly Report,* Vol. 55, No. 15 (April 21, 2006), pp. 421–426.

204. Theodore M. Hammett, *AIDS in Correctional Facilities: Issues and Options,* 3rd ed. (Washington, DC: National Institute of Justice, 1988), p. 37.
205. At the time of this writing, California, Massachusetts, New York, Wisconsin, and the District of Columbia were among those jurisdictions.
206. "Mississippi Eases Policy of Separating Inmates with HIV," *Corrections Journal,* Vol. 5, No. 6 (2001), p. 5.
207. Cauchon, "AIDS in Prison."
208. See "Court Allows Restriction on HIV-Positive Inmates," *Criminal Justice Newsletter,* Vol. 25, No. 23 (December 1, 1994), pp. 2–3.
209. Ibid.
210. Darrell Bryan, "Inmates, HIV, and the Constitutional Right to Privacy: AIDS in Prison Facilities," *Corrections Compendium,* Vol. 19, No. 9 (September 1994), pp. 1–3.
211. Alexandria Sage, "Doctor Shot at Los Angeles–Area Hospital," Associated Press wire service, September 20, 2003.
212. Lincoln J. Fry, "The Older Prison Inmate: A Profile," *Justice Professional,* Vol. 2, No. 1 (spring 1987), pp. 1–12.
213. Sabol, Couture, and Harrison, *Prisoners in 2006.*
214. "The Nation's Prison Population Grew by 60,000 Inmates Last Year," Bureau of Justice Statistics press release, August 15, 1999.
215. Jim Krane, "Demographic Revolution Rocks U.S. Prisons," APB Online, April 12, 1999. Web posted at http://www.apbonline.com/safestreets/oldprisoners/mainpris0412.html (accessed January 5, 2006).
216. Ronald Wikbert and Burk Foster, "The Longtermers: Louisiana's Longest Serving Inmates and Why They've Stayed So Long," paper presented at the annual meeting of the Academy of Criminal Justice Sciences, Washington, DC, 1989, p. 51.
217. *Disability Advocates, Inc.* v. *New York State Office of Mental Health,* filed in Federal District Court (NY 2002).
218. Allen J. Beck and Laura M. Maruschak, *Mental Health Treatment in State Prisons, 2000,* BJS Special Report (Washington, DC: Bureau of Justice Statistics, 2001), p. 1, from which most of the information in this paragraph and the next is derived.
219. *Washington* v. *Harper,* 494 U.S. 210 (1990).
220. Paula M. Ditton, *Mental Health and Treatment of Inmates and Probationers* (Washington, DC: Bureau of Justice Statistics, 1999).
221. Robert O. Lampert, "The Mentally Retarded Offender in Prison," *Justice Professional,* Vol. 2, No. 1 (spring 1987), p. 61.
222. Ibid., p. 64.
223. George C. Denkowski and Kathryn M. Denkowski, "The Mentally Retarded Offender in the State Prison System: Identification, Prevalence, Adjustment, and Rehabilitation," *Criminal Justice and Behavior,* Vol. 12 (1985), pp. 55–75.
224. "Opening Session: Kerik Emphasizes the Importance of Corrections' Protective Role for the Country." Web posted at http://www.aca.org/conferences/Winter05/updates05.asp (accessed July 20, 2006).
225. Jess Maghan, "Intelligence-Led Penology: Management of Crime Information Obtained from Incarcerated Persons," paper presented at the Investigation of Crime World Conference, 2001, p. 6.
226. Keith Martin, *Corrections Prepares for Terrorism,* Corrections Connection News Network, January 21, 2002. Web posted at http://www.corrections.com (accessed June 15, 2006).
227. Quoted in Meghan Mandeville, "Information Sharing Becomes Crucial to Battling Terrorism behind Bars," Corrections.com, December 8, 2003. Web posted at http://database.corrections.com/news/results2.asp?ID_8988 (accessed July 11, 2006).
228. "FBI: Al-Qaida Recruiting in U.S. Prisons," United Press International wire service, January 7, 2004. Web posted at http://database.corrections.com/news/results2.asp?ID_9148 (accessed July 1, 2006).
229. Institute for the Study of Violent Groups, "Land of Wahhabism," *Crime and Justice International* (March/April 2005), p. 43.
230. Office of the Inspector General, *A Review of the Federal Bureau of Prisons' Selection of Muslim Religious Services Providers* (Washington, DC: U.S. Department of Justice, 2004).
231. Ibid., p. 8.
232. Ibid.
233. Federal Bureau of Prisons, *State of the Bureau 2004* (Washington, DC: BOP, 2005).
234. Associated Press, "Attorney, Three Others Indicted for Alleged 'Support of Terrorism,'" *Dallas Morning News,* April 9, 2002. Web posted at http://www.dallasnews.com/latestnews/stories/040902dnnatterrorindictment.66910.html (accessed July 25, 2003).
235. The questions in this Web Quest were adapted from "Building Your Career in Corrections," *Keeper's Voice,* Vol. 18, No. 1. Web posted at http://www.oict.org/public/toc.efm?series-KV (accessed February 20, 2002).

Juvenile Justice

13

Chapter Outline

- Introduction
- Juvenile Justice throughout History
- The Legal Environment
- The Juvenile Justice Process Today
- The Post–Juvenile Court Era

Learning Objectives

After reading this chapter, you should be able to

- Describe the history and evolution of the juvenile justice system in the Western world.
- Name the important U.S. Supreme Court decisions of relevance to juvenile justice, and describe their impact on the handling of juveniles by the system.
- Explain the similarities and differences between the juvenile and adult systems of justice.
- Identify possible future directions in juvenile justice.

"We worry about what a child will become tomorrow. Yet we forget that he is someone today."

—Stacia Tauscher[1]

"Our society's fearful of our kids. I think we don't know how to set limits on them. They begin to behave in severely outrageous ways, and nobody stops them."

—David York
Cofounder of Tough Love International[2]

Introduction

▶▶▶ Hear the author discuss this chapter at mycrimekit.com.

A few years ago, 13-year-old Tavaris Knight was convicted by a criminal court jury in Tampa, Florida, of kidnapping and raping a 43-year-old woman. Prosecutors proved that Knight, who was 12 years old at the time of the offense, had used a silver toy gun to force the woman away from her four young children at a playground and into the surrounding woods. Knight raped the woman twice and beat her with the gun.[3] His fingerprints were found on the toy gun to which the victim led police. Knight's case had been transferred to adult criminal court because of the serious nature of his crimes. In closing arguments, prosecutor Michael Sinacore pointed to Knight, saying, "That young man is not a child. He stopped being a child when he forced [his victim] into the woods and raped her."[4] Following conviction, Knight was sentenced to 15 years in prison by Florida Circuit Judge Jack Espinosa, Jr. Knight will likely be held at a youth facility for sexual offenders until he is 21 years old, at which time he could be transferred to another youth offender facility until the age of 25, followed by adult prison.[5]

Crimes committed by preteens are not that unusual. In 2005, for example, a nine-year-old girl, identified only as Shanice K., admitted that she fatally stabbed her 11-year-old Brooklyn, New York, playmate in the heart with a steak knife during an argument over a rubber ball.[6] The killing occurred in the midst of a Memorial Day barbecue that was being held at Shanice's home. In another example, two 12-year-old St. Lucie County, Florida, girls were charged in 2001 with trying to drown a classmate in a lake near her home; the victim, 12-year-old Nicole Maines, had refused to surrender her swimming mask and flippers, causing the other girls to jump into the water, grab her gear, and beat her.[7] When the attackers shoved Maines's head underwater, a bystander, 16-year-old Hosea Rivers, jumped into the lake and pulled the girls apart. A police report showed that Maines suffered cuts and bruises all over her body.

A key finding of the Study Group on Serious and Violent Juvenile Offenders, Office of Juvenile Justice and Delinquency Prevention (OJJDP), is that most chronic juvenile offenders begin their delinquency careers before age 12, and some start as early as age ten.[8] The most recent national data show that in 2007 police arrested about 107,000 children ages 12 and younger.[9] These very young offenders (known as *child delinquents*) represent almost 10% of the total number of **juveniles** (those up to age 18) who are arrested.

juvenile
A youth at or below the upper age of juvenile court jurisdiction in a particular state.

Although states vary as to the age at which a person legally enters adulthood, statistics on crime make it clear that young people are disproportionately involved in certain offenses. A recent report, for example, found that nearly 16% of all violent crimes and 26% of all property crimes are committed by people younger than age 18, while this age group makes up 26% of the population of the United States.[10] On average, about 15% of all arrests in any year are of juveniles,[11] and people younger than age 18 have a higher likelihood of being arrested for robbery and other property crimes than do people in any other age group. Figure 1 shows Uniform Crime Report (UCR)/National Incident-Based Reporting System (NIBRS) statistics on juvenile arrests for selected offense categories.

FIGURE 1
Juvenile Involvement in Crime versus System Totals, 2007.
Note: The term *juvenile* refers to people younger than 18 years of age.
Source: Federal Bureau of Investigation: *Crime in the United States, 2007* (Washington, DC: U.S. Government Printing Office, 2008).

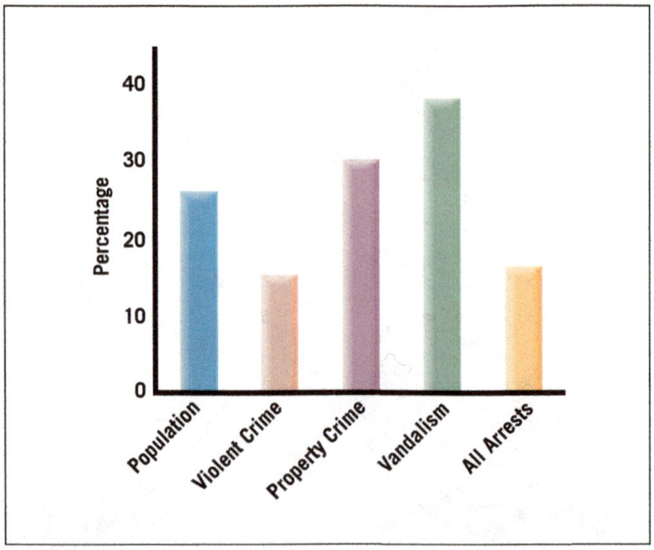

There was nothing to do.
—Terrance Wade, age 15 (on why he and his friends allegedly raped, stomped, stabbed, and ultimately murdered a Boston woman)

The OJJDP is a primary source of information on juvenile justice in the United States. A sweeping OJJDP overview of juvenile crime and the juvenile justice system in America reveals the following[12]:

- About 1.6 million juveniles (under age 18) are arrested annually in America.
- Violent crime by juveniles is decreasing.
- Younger juveniles account for a substantial proportion of juvenile arrests and the juvenile court caseload.
- Female delinquency has grown substantially, increasing 76% in the last ten years.
- The number of juveniles held in public facilities has increased sharply.
- Minority juveniles are greatly overrepresented in the custody population.
- Crowding is a serious problem in juvenile facilities.

Web EXTRA

Learn more about OJJDP via Web Extra 13–1 at mycrimekit.com.

This chapter has four purposes. First, we will briefly look at the history of the **juvenile justice system**, comprising government agencies involved with youth who are offenders or subjects of court oversight. The juvenile justice system has its roots in the adult system, but in the juvenile system, we find a more uniform philosophical base and a relatively clear agreement about the system's purpose. These differences may be due to the fact that the system is relatively new and that society generally agrees that young people who have gone wrong are worth salvaging. However, the philosophy that underlies the juvenile justice system in America is increasingly being questioned by "get tough" advocates of law and order, many of whom are fed up with violent juvenile crime.

juvenile justice system
The government agencies that function to investigate, supervise, adjudicate, care for, or confine youthful offenders and other children subject to the jurisdiction of the juvenile court.

Our second purpose is to compare the juvenile and adult systems as they currently operate. The reasoning behind the juvenile justice system has led to administrative and other procedures that, in many jurisdictions, are not found in the adult system. The juvenile justice process, for example, is frequently not as open as the adult system: Hearings may be held in secret, names of offenders are not published, and records of juvenile proceedings may later be destroyed.[13]

Our third purpose is to describe the agencies, processes, and problems of the juvenile justice system itself. Although each state may have variations, a common system structure is shared by all.

Near the end of this chapter, we will turn to our fourth focus and will consider some of the issues raised by critics of the current system. Although conservative attitudes began to bring changes in the adult criminal justice system during the last few decades, the juvenile justice system has remained relatively unchanged. Based on premises quite different from those of the adult system, juvenile justice has long been a separate decision-making arena in which the best interests of the child have been accorded great importance. As we will see, substantial changes are now afoot.

Juvenile Justice Throughout History

Earliest Times

Before the modern era, children who committed crimes in the Western world received no preferential treatment because of their youth. They were adjudicated and punished alongside adults, and a number of recorded cases have come down through history of children as young as age six being hung or burned at the stake. Children were also imprisoned alongside adults; no segregated juvenile facilities existed. Neither the development of gaols (an old English word for "jails") in the thirteenth century nor the early English prisons provided any leniency on the basis of age.[14] In like fashion, little distinction was made between criminality and **delinquency** (misbehavior or conduct of juveniles in violation of the law) or other kinds of undesirable behavior. Problems such as epilepsy, insanity, retardation, and poverty were seen in the same light as crime,[15] and people suffering from these conditions were shut away in facilities shared by juvenile and adult offenders.

delinquency
In the broadest usage, juvenile actions or conduct in violation of criminal law, juvenile status offenses, and other juvenile misbehavior.

Court philosophy in dealing with juveniles derived from an early Roman principle called *patria postestas*. Under Roman law (circa 753 B.C.), children were members of their family,

parens patriae
A common law principle that allows the state to assume a parental role and to take custody of a child when he or she becomes delinquent, is abandoned, or is in need of care that the natural parents are unable or unwilling to provide.

but the father had absolute control over children, and they in turn had an absolute responsibility to obey his wishes. Roman understanding of the social role of children strongly influenced English culture and eventually led to the development of the legal principle of ***parens patriae***, which allowed the king (or the English state) to take the place of parents in dealing with children who broke the law. *Parens patriae* held that the king was father of the country and thus had parental rights over all his citizens.

By the Middle Ages, social conceptions of children had become strongly influenced by Christian churches, whose doctrine held that children under the age of seven had not yet reached the age of reason and could not be held liable for spiritual transgressions. In adopting the perspective of the Church, English law of the period exempted children under the age of seven from criminal responsibility. Juveniles ages seven to 14 were accorded a special status, being tried as adults only if it could be demonstrated that they fully understood the nature of their criminal acts.[16] Adulthood was considered to begin at age 14, when marriage was also allowed.[17]

Early English institutions placed a large burden of responsibility on the family, and especially the father, who (as head of the household) was held accountable for the behavior of all family members, even his wife. When the father failed in his responsibility to control family members, the king, through the concept of *parens patriae*, could intervene.

The inexorable power of the king, often marked by his personal and unpredictable whims, combined with a widespread fear of the dismal conditions in English institutions made many families hide their problem kin. Those who were retarded, insane, or epileptic were kept in attics or basements, sometimes for their entire lives. Delinquent children were either confined to the home or sent overseas (if their families were wealthy enough) to escape the conditions of asylums and gaols.

Juveniles in Early America

Early American solutions to the problems of delinquency were much like those of the English. Puritan influence in the colonies, with its heavy emphasis on obedience and discipline, led to frequent use of jails and prisons for both juveniles and adults. Legislation reflected the Ten Commandments and often provided harsh punishments for transgressors of almost any age. For example, one seventeenth-century Massachusetts law stipulated the following:

> [I]f a man have a stubborn or rebellious son of sufficient years of understanding, viz. sixteen, which will not obey the voice of his father or the voice of his mother, and that when they have chastened him will not harken to them, then shall his father and mother, being his natural parents, lay hold on him and bring him to the magistrates assembled in Court, and testify to them by sufficient evidence that this their son is stubborn and rebellious and will not obey their voice and chastisement, but lives in sundry notorious crime. Such a son shall be put to death.[18]

Severe punishment was consistent with the Puritan belief that unacknowledged social evils might bring the wrath of God down upon the entire colony. In short, disobedient children had no place in a social group committed to a spiritual salvation understood as strict obedience to the wishes of the Divine.

By the end of the eighteenth century, social conditions in Europe and America began to change. The Enlightenment, a highly significant intellectual and social movement, focused on human potential. It was accompanied by the growth of an industrialized economy, with a corresponding move away from farming. English poor laws (which preceded welfare legislation), lower infant death rates, and social innovations born of the Enlightenment led to a reassessment of the place of children in society. In this new age, children were recognized as the only true heirs to the future, and society became increasingly concerned about their well-being.

The Institutional Era

The nineteenth century was a time of rapid social change in the United States: The population was growing dramatically, cities were burgeoning, and the industrial era was in full swing. Industrial tycoons, the new rich, and frontier-bound settlers lived elbow to elbow with immigrants eking out a living in the sweatshops of the new mercantile centers. In this environment, children took on new value as a source of cheap labor; they fueled assembly lines and proved

▲ Columbine (Colorado) High School shooters Eric Harris (left) and Dylan Klebold examining a sawed-off shotgun in a still image taken from a videotape made at a makeshift shooting range in 1999. About six weeks after the video was made, Harris (age 18) and Klebold (age 17) shot and killed 15 people and injured 20 more at the school. How might such disasters be averted in the future?
Getty News/Getty Images, Inc.

invaluable to shop owners who could not or would not pay fair wages, and parents were gratified by the income-producing opportunities available to their offspring. On the frontier, settlers and farm families put their children to work clearing land and seeding crops.

Unfortunately, economic opportunities and the luck of the draw were not equally favorable to all. Some immigrant families became victims of the cities that drew them, settling in squalor in hastily formed ghettos. Many families, seeing only the economic opportunities represented by their children, neglected to provide them with anything but a rudimentary education, and children who did work labored for long hours and had little time for family closeness. Other children, abandoned by families unable to support them, were forced into lives on the streets, where they formed tattered gangs, surviving off the refuse of the glittering cities.

The House of Refuge

An 1823 report by the Society for the Prevention of Pauperism in the city of New York called for the development of "houses of refuge" to save children from lives of crime and poverty. The society also cited the problems caused by locking up children with mature criminals. Houses of refuge were to be places of care and education, where children could learn positive attitudes about work.

In 1824, the first house of refuge opened in New York City.[19] The New York House of Refuge was intended only for those children who could still be "rescued," and it sheltered mostly young thieves, vagrants, and runaways. Other children, especially those with more severe delinquency problems, were placed in adult prisons and jails. Houses of refuge became popular in New York, and other cities quickly copied them. It was not long, however, before overcrowding developed and living conditions deteriorated.

The 1838 case of *Ex parte Crouse*[20] clarified the power that states had in committing children to institutions. The case involved Mary Ann Crouse, who had been committed to the Philadelphia House of Refuge by a lower court over the objections of her father. The commitment was based on allegations made by the girl's mother that she was incorrigible, that is, beyond the control of her parents. Mary Ann's father petitioned the court to release his daughter on the grounds that she had been denied the right to trial by jury.

The current [juvenile justice] system, a relic from a more innocent time, teaches youthful offenders that crime pays and that they are totally immune and insulated from responsibility.
—National Policy Forum

The decision by the appeals court upheld the legality of Mary Ann's commitment; it pointed to the state's interest in assisting children and denied that punishment or retribution played any part in her treatment. The court also focused on parental responsibilities in general and stressed the need for state intervention to provide for the moral development of children whose parents had failed them. Most important of all, the court built its decision around the doctrine of *parens patriae*, taking what had previously been an English judicial concept and applying it to the American scene.[21]

The Chicago Reform School

Around the middle of the nineteenth century, the child-savers movement began. Child savers espoused a philosophy of productivity and eschewed idleness and unprincipled behavior. Anthony Platt, a modern writer who recognizes the significance of the child-savers movement, suggests that the mid-nineteenth century provided an ideological framework that combined Christian principles with a strong emphasis on the worth of the individual.[22] It was a social perspective that held that children were to be guided and protected.

One product of the child-savers movement was the reform school—a place for delinquent juveniles that embodied the atmosphere of a Christian home. By the middle of the nineteenth century, the reform school approach to handling juveniles was well under way. The Chicago Reform School, which opened in the 1860s, provided an early model for the reform school movement, which focused primarily on predelinquent youth who showed tendencies toward more serious criminal involvement. Reform schools attempted to emulate wholesome family environments to provide the security and affection thought necessary in building moral character.

The reform school movement also emphasized traditional values and the worth of hard work, idealizing country living. Some early reform schools were built in rural settings, and many were farms. A few programs even tried to relocate problem children to the vast open expanses of the western states.

The reform school movement was not without its critics. As Platt writes, "If institutions sought to replicate families, would it not have been better to place the predelinquents directly in real families?"[23] As with houses of refuge, reform schools soon became overcrowded. What began as a meaningful attempt to help children ended in routinized institutional procedures devoid of the reformers' original zeal.

In the 1870s, the Illinois Supreme Court handed down a decision that practically ended the reform school movement. The case of *People ex rel. O'Connell* v. *Turner*[24] centered on Daniel O'Connell, who had been committed to the Chicago Reform School under an Illinois law that permitted confinement for "misfortune." Youngsters classified as "misfortunate" had not necessarily committed any offense but were ordered to reform school either because their families were unable to care for them or because they were seen as social misfits. Because O'Connell had not been convicted of a crime, the Illinois Supreme Court ordered him released. The court reasoned that the power of the state under *parens patriae* could not exceed the power of the natural parents except in punishing crime. The *O'Connell* case is remembered today for the lasting distinction it made between criminal and noncriminal acts committed by juveniles.

The Juvenile Court Era

In 1870, an expanding recognition of children's needs led the state of Massachusetts to enact legislation that required separate hearings for juveniles.[25] New York followed with a similar law in 1877,[26] which also prohibited contact between juvenile and adult offenders. Rhode Island enacted juvenile court legislation in 1898, and in 1899 the Colorado School Law became the first comprehensive legislation designed to adjudicate problem children.[27] It was, however, the 1899 codification of Illinois juvenile law that became the model for juvenile court statutes throughout the nation.

juvenile court
Any court that has jurisdiction over matters involving juveniles.

The Illinois Juvenile Court Act created a **juvenile court**, separate in form and function from adult criminal courts. To avoid the lasting stigma of criminality, the law applied the term *delinquent* rather than *criminal* to young adjudicated offenders. The act specified that juvenile court judges were to use the best interests of the child as a guide for decision making in their deliberations; in effect, judges were to serve as advocates for juveniles, guiding their development, and determining guilt or innocence took second place to the betterment of the child. The law abandoned a strict adherence to the due process requirements of adult prosecutions, allowing informal procedures designed to scrutinize the child's situation. By sheltering the juvenile from the punishment philosophy of the adult system, the Illinois Juvenile Court emphasized reformation in place of retribution.[28]

In 1938, the federal government passed the Juvenile Court Act, which embodied many of the features of the Illinois statute. By 1945, every state had enacted special legislation focusing on the handling of juveniles, and the juvenile court movement became well established.[29]

The juvenile court movement was based on five philosophical principles that can be summarized as follows[30]:

1. The state is the "higher or ultimate parent" of all the children within its borders.
2. Children are worth saving, and nonpunitive procedures should be used to save them.
3. Children should be nurtured, and while the nurturing process is under way, they should be protected from the stigmatizing impact of formal adjudicatory procedures.
4. To accomplish the goal of reformation, justice needs to be individualized, that is, each child is different, and the needs, aspirations, living conditions, and so on of each child must be known in their individual particulars if the court is to be helpful.
5. Noncriminal procedures are necessary to give primary consideration to the needs of the child, so the denial of due process can be justified in the face of constitutional challenges because the court acts not to punish, but to help.

Learn more about the history of juvenile justice and the juvenile court via Library Extra 13–1 at mycrimekit.com.

Library EXTRA

Categories of Children in the Juvenile Justice System

By the time of the Great Depression, most states had expanded juvenile statutes to include the following six categories of children (and these categories are still used today in most jurisdictions to describe the variety of children subject to juvenile court jurisdiction):

1. *Delinquent child.* A **delinquent child** is one who violates the criminal law. If the delinquent child were an adult, the word *criminal* would be applied to the child.
2. *Undisciplined child.* An **undisciplined child** is said to be beyond parental control, as evidenced by his or her refusal to obey legitimate authorities, such as school officials and teachers. Such a child needs state protection.

delinquent child
A child who has engaged in activity that would be considered a crime if the child were an adult. The term *delinquent* is used to avoid the stigma associated with the term *criminal.*

undisciplined child
A child who is beyond parental control, as evidenced by his or her refusal to obey legitimate authorities, such as school officials and teachers.

◄ American juveniles have many opportunities but also face numerous challenges. What are the six categories of children that state juvenile justice statutes usually describe as subject to juvenile court jurisdiction?
Michael Newman/PhotoEdit Inc.

CJ News

Teen Gets Prison Time for Communicating Threats

On July 21, 2005, a teenager accused of plotting a massacre at his suburban Detroit high school was sentenced to at least 4 1/2 years in prison for threatening terrorism and amassing an arsenal in his home.

"Though he has to pay the piper, we want to give him as much a chance for salvation as we can," Circuit Court Judge Matthew Switalski said in sentencing Andrew Osantowski. "You still have a future."

Osantowski, 18, wept while the judge spoke.

"I look back and realize how lost I was," he told the court before he was sentenced. "I am truly sorry for the things I have done. My family never raised me like this."

The case appears to be among the first in the nation in which anti-terrorism laws were applied to school violence, according to law enforcement officials.

Osantowski was found guilty a month earlier of threatening an act of terrorism and using a computer to threaten terrorism after authorities found Internet chat room messages in which he wrote that he might kill students at Chippewa Valley High.

Each charge was punishable by up to 20 years in prison.

Osantowski also was convicted of receiving and concealing guns and possessing a firearm while commiting a felony.

Osantowski was arrested in September, 2004, after a girl he had written to in the chat room shared the messages with her father, a police officer. In some of the messages, Osantowski said he was bullied at school and at home and wanted to take revenge.

"I can't imagine going through life without killing a few people," he wrote.

A search of Osantowski's home yielded weapons, ammunition, bomb-making paraphernalia, videotapes showing the teen in possession of assault weapons, a Nazi flag, and printed materials about Adolf Hitler and white supremacy.

His lawyer argued the jury never should have been allowed to see the weapons.

▲ Andrew Osantowski, age 18, cries while being sentenced to a minimum of four and a half years in prison in Macomb County Circuit Court in Mount Clemens, Michigan, on July 21, 2005, for threatening terrorism. Osantowski was convicted in a jury trial after investigators found Internet chat room messages in which he threatened a massacre at the local Chippewa Valley High School where he was a student. An arsenal of weapons was discovered at his home. Should he have received a longer sentence? A shorter one?
Paul Sancya/AP Wide World Photos

For the latest in crime and justice news, visit the Talk Justice news feed at http://crimenews.info.

Source: Adrienne Schwisow, "Michigan Teen Gets Prison Time for Threats," Associated Press, July 22, 2005. Reprinted with permission.

dependent child
A child who has no parents or whose parents are not available or are unable to care for him or her.

neglected child
A child who is not receiving the proper level of physical or psychological care from his or her parents or guardians or who has been placed up for adoption in violation of the law.

abused child
A child who has been physically, emotionally, or sexually abused. Most states also consider a child who is forced into delinquent activity by a parent or guardian to be abused.

3. *Dependent child.* A **dependent child** typically has no parents or guardians to care for him or her. The child's parents are deceased, the child was placed up for adoption, or the child was abandoned in violation of the law.
4. *Neglected child.* A **neglected child** is one who does not receive proper care from parents or guardians. Such a child may suffer from malnutrition or may not be provided with adequate shelter.
5. *Abused child.* An **abused child** is one who suffers physical abuse at the hands of his or her custodians. This category was later expanded to include emotional and sexual abuse.
6. *Status offender.* The term **status offender** is a special category that embraces children who violate laws written only for them. In some states, status offenders are referred to as persons in need of supervision (PINS).

Status offenses include behavior such as truancy, vagrancy, running away from home, and incorrigibility, and the youthful status of juveniles is a necessary element in such offenses. Adults, for example, may "run away from home" and not violate any law; runaway children, however, are subject to apprehension and juvenile court processing because state laws require that they be subject to parental control.

Status offenses were a natural outgrowth of juvenile court philosophy. As a consequence, however, juveniles in need of help often faced procedural dispositions that treated them as though they were delinquent. Rather than lowering the rate of juvenile incarceration, the juvenile court movement led to its increase. Critics of the juvenile court movement quickly focused on the abandonment of due process rights, especially in the case of status offenders, as a major source of problems. Detention and incarceration, they argued, were inappropriate options for situations in which children had not committed crimes.

status offender
A child who commits an act that is contrary to the law by virtue of the offender's status as a child. Purchasing cigarettes, buying alcohol, and being truant are examples of such behavior.

status offense
An act or conduct that is declared by statute to be an offense, but only when committed by or engaged in by a juvenile, and that can be adjudicated only by a juvenile court.

The Legal Environment

Throughout the first half of the twentieth century, the U.S. Supreme Court followed a hands-off approach to juvenile justice, much like its early approach to prisons (see Chapter 12). The adjudication and further processing of juveniles by the system were left mostly to specialized juvenile courts or to local appeals courts. Although one or two early Supreme Court decisions[31] dealt with issues of juvenile justice, it was not until the 1960s that the Court began close legal scrutiny of the principles underlying the system itself. In the pages that follow, we will discuss some of the most important U.S. Supreme Court cases relating to juvenile justice (Figure 2).

Kent v. *U.S.* (1966)

The U.S. Supreme Court case that ended the hands-off era in juvenile justice was ***Kent* v. *U.S.***,[32] decided in 1966. The *Kent* case, which focused on the long-accepted concept of *parens patriae*, signaled the beginning of the Court's systematic review of all lower-court practices involving delinquency hearings.

Morris Kent, Jr., age 14, was apprehended in the District of Columbia in 1959 and was charged with several house burglaries and an attempted purse snatching. Kent was placed on juvenile probation and was released into the custody of his mother. In 1961, an intruder entered a woman's apartment, took her wallet, and raped her; at the scene, police found fingerprints that matched those on file belonging to Morris Kent. At the time, Kent was 16 years old and, according to the laws of the District of Columbia, was still under the exclusive jurisdiction of the juvenile court.

Kent was taken into custody and interrogated. He volunteered information about the crime and spoke about other offenses involving burglary, robbery, and rape. Following interrogation, his mother retained counsel on his behalf. Kent was kept in custody for another week, during which time psychological and psychiatric evaluations were conducted. The professionals conducting the evaluations concluded that Kent was a "victim of severe psychopathology." Without conferring with Kent, his parents, or his lawyers, the juvenile court judge ruled that Kent should be remanded to the authority of the adult court system, and he was eventually tried in U.S. District Court for the District of Columbia; the judge gave no reasons for assigning Kent to the adult court.

Kent was indicted in criminal court on eight counts of burglary, robbery, and rape. Citing the psychological evaluations performed earlier, Kent's lawyers argued that his behavior was the product of mental disease or defect, but their defense proved fruitless, and Kent was found guilty on six counts of burglary and robbery. He was sentenced to five to 15 years in prison on each count. Kent's lawyers ultimately appealed to the U.S. Supreme Court, where they argued that Kent should have been entitled to an adequate hearing at the level of the juvenile court and that, lacking such a hearing, his transfer to adult jurisdiction was unfair.

The Supreme Court, reflecting the Warren Court ideologies of the times, agreed with Kent's attorneys, reversed the decision of the district court, and ordered adequate hearings for juveniles being considered for transfer to adult court. At these hearings, the Court ruled, juveniles are entitled to representation by attorneys who must have access to their records.

Although it focused only on a narrow issue, the *Kent* decision was especially important because for the first time it recognized the need for at least minimal due process in juvenile court hearings. The *Kent* decision set the stage for what was to come, but it was the *Gault* decision, which we look at next, that turned the juvenile justice system upside down.

Established in the 1960s, status offender systems were created to help parents, schools, and communities get disobedient, but not delinquent, children back on track by providing treatment, counseling, and supervision. Yet despite their good intentions, many status offender systems across the country have had the opposite effect.

—The Vera Institute of Justice[i]

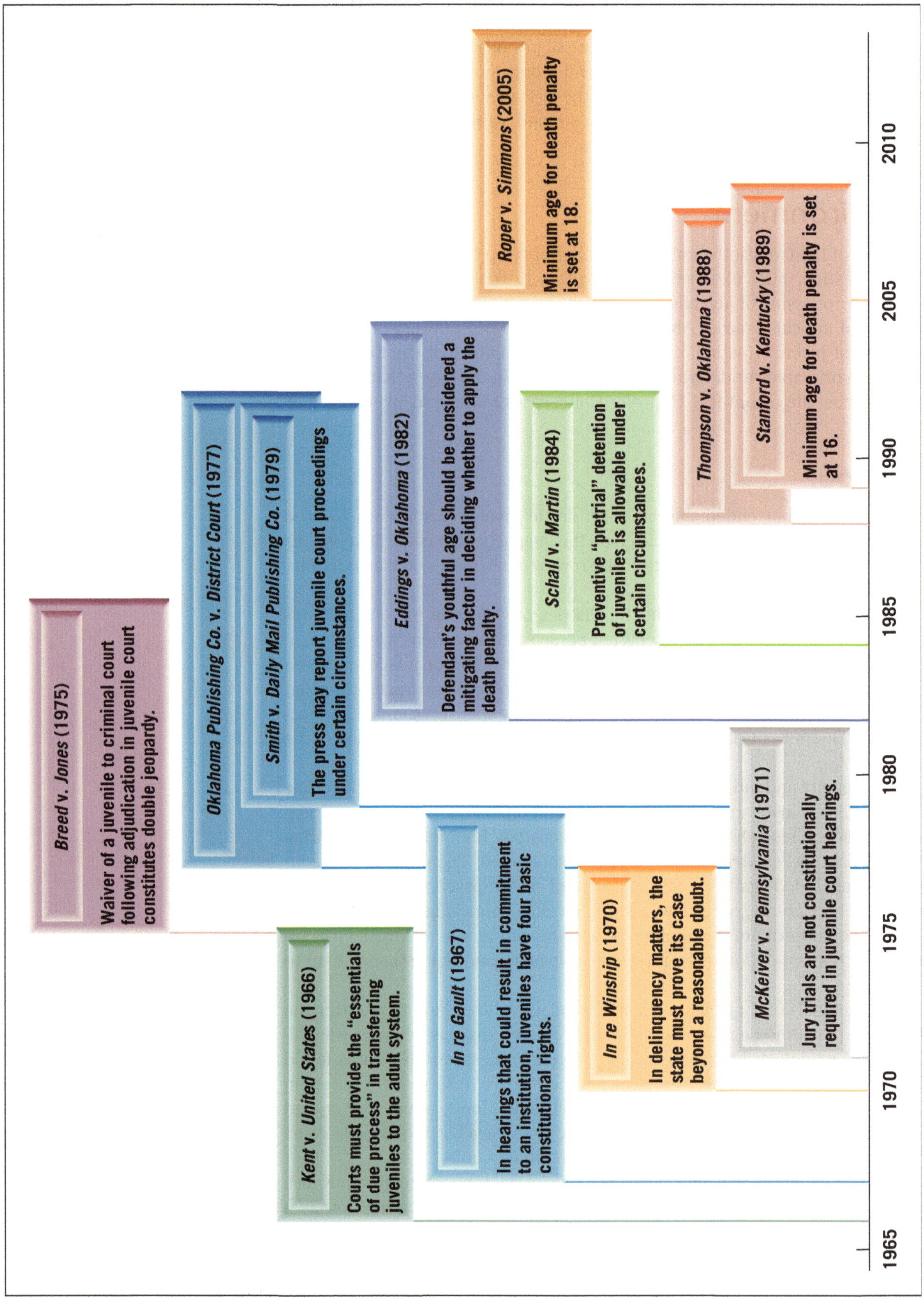

FIGURE 2
U.S. Supreme Court Decisions of Special Relevance to Juvenile Justice.
Source: Adapted from Office of Juvenile Justice and Delinquency Prevention, *Juvenile Offenders and Victims: 2006 National Report* (Washington, DC: OJJDP, 2006), p. 101.

In re Gault (1967)

In 1964, Gerald Gault and a friend, Ronald Lewis, were taken into custody by the sheriff of Gila County, Arizona, on the basis of a neighbor's complaint that the boys had telephoned her and made lewd remarks. At the time, Gault was on probation for having been in the company of another boy who had stolen a wallet.

When Gault was apprehended, his parents were both at work. No notice was posted at their house to indicate that their son had been taken into custody, a fact that they later learned from Lewis's parents. The authorities gave Gault's parents little information. Although they were notified when their son's initial hearing would be held, the Gaults were not told the nature of the complaint against him or the identity of the complainant, who was not present at the hearing.

At the hearing, the only evidence presented was statements made by young Gault and testimony given by the juvenile officer as to what the complainant had alleged. Gault was not represented by counsel. He admitted to having made the phone call but stated that after dialing the number, he had turned the phone over to his friend, Lewis. After hearing the testimony, Judge McGhee ordered a second hearing, to be held a week later. At the second hearing, Mrs. Gault requested that the complainant be present so that she could identify the voice of the person making the lewd call, but Judge McGhee ruled against her request. Finally, young Gault was adjudicated delinquent and remanded to the State Industrial School until his twenty-first birthday. On appeal, eventually to the U.S. Supreme Court, Gault's attorney argued that his constitutional rights were violated because he had been denied due process. The appeal focused specifically on six areas:

1. *Notice of charges.* Gault was not given enough notice to prepare a reasonable defense to the charges against him.
2. *Right to counsel.* Gault was not notified of his right to an attorney or allowed to have one at his hearing.
3. *Right to confront and to cross-examine witnesses.* The court did not require the complainant to appear at the hearing.
4. *Protection against self-incrimination.* Gault was never advised that he had the right to remain silent, nor was he informed that his testimony could be used against him.
5. *Right to a transcript.* In preparing for the appeal, Gault's attorney was not provided a transcript of the adjudicatory hearing.
6. *Right to appeal.* At the time, the state of Arizona did not give juveniles the right to appeal.

The Supreme Court ruled in Gault's favor on four of the six issues raised by his attorneys. The majority opinion of ***In re Gault*** read, in part, as follows:

> In *Kent* v. *United States*, we stated that the Juvenile Court Judge's exercise of the power of the state as *parens patriae* was not unlimited. . . . Notice, to comply with due process requirements, must be given sufficiently in advance of scheduled court proceedings so that reasonable opportunity to prepare will be afforded. . . . The probation officer cannot act as counsel for the child. His role in the adjudicatory hearing, by statute and in fact, is as arresting officer and witness against the child. There is no material difference in this respect between adult and juvenile proceedings of the sort here involved. . . . A proceeding where the issue is whether the child will be found to be "delinquent" and subjected to the loss of his liberty for years is comparable in seriousness to a felony prosecution. The juvenile needs the assistance of counsel to cope with the problems of law, to make skilled inquiry into the facts, to insist upon regularity of the proceedings, and to ascertain whether he has a defense and to prepare and submit it.[33]

The Court did not agree with the contention of Gault's lawyers relative to appeal or with their arguments in favor of transcripts. Right to appeal, where it exists, is usually granted by statute or by state constitution, not by the Constitution of the United States. Similarly, the Court did not require a transcript because (1) there is no constitutional right to a transcript, and (2) no transcripts are produced in the trials of most adult misdemeanants.

There are no illegitimate children—only illegitimate parents.

—U.S. District Court Judge Leon R. Yankwich in Zipkin v. Mozon (1928)

Today, the impact of *Gault* is widely felt in the juvenile justice system, where juveniles are now guaranteed many of the same procedural rights as adults. Most precedent-setting Supreme

Court decisions that followed *Gault* further clarified the rights of juveniles, focusing primarily on those few issues of due process that it had not explicitly addressed.

In re Winship (1970)

At the close of the 1960s, a New York Family Court judge found a 12-year-old boy named Samuel Winship delinquent on the basis of a petition that alleged that he had illegally entered a locker and stolen $112 from a pocketbook. The judge acknowledged to those present at the hearing that the evidence in the case might not be sufficient to establish Winship's guilt beyond a reasonable doubt; statutory authority, however, in the form of the New York Family Court Act required a determination of facts based only on a preponderance of the evidence—the same standard required in civil suits. Winship was sent to a training school for 18 months, subject to extensions until his eighteenth birthday.

Winship's appeal to the U.S. Supreme Court (***In re Winship***) centered on the lower court's standard of evidence. His attorney argued that Winship's guilt should have been proved beyond a reasonable doubt—the evidentiary standard of adult criminal trials. The Court agreed in its ruling:

> [T]he constitutional safeguard of proof beyond a reasonable doubt is as much required during the adjudicatory stage of a delinquency proceeding as are those constitutional guards applied in *Gault*. . . . We therefore hold . . . that where a 12 year old child is charged with an act of stealing which renders him liable to confinement for as long as six years, then, as a matter of due process . . . the case against him must be proved beyond a reasonable doubt.[34]

As a consequence of *Winship*, allegations of delinquency today must be established beyond a reasonable doubt. The Court allowed, however, the continued use of the lower evidentiary standard in adjudicating juveniles charged with status offenses. Even though both standards continue to exist, most jurisdictions have chosen to use the stricter burden-of-proof requirement for all delinquency proceedings.

McKeiver v. *Pennsylvania* (1971)

Cases like *Gault* and *Winship* have not extended all adult procedural rights to juveniles charged with delinquency. For example, juveniles do not have the constitutional right to a trial by a jury of their peers. The case of ***McKeiver* v. *Pennsylvania*** (1971)[35] reiterated what earlier decisions had established and legitimized some generally accepted practices of juvenile courts.

Joseph McKeiver, age 16, was charged with robbery, larceny, and receiving stolen property, all felonies in Pennsylvania. McKeiver had been involved with 20 to 30 other juveniles who chased three teenage boys and took 25 cents from them. He had no previous arrests and was able to demonstrate a record of gainful employment. McKeiver's attorney requested that his client be allowed a jury trial, but the request was denied. McKeiver was adjudicated delinquent and committed to a youth development center. McKeiver's attorney pursued a series of appeals and was finally granted a hearing before the U.S. Supreme Court, where he argued that his client, even though a juvenile, should have been allowed a jury trial as guaranteed by the Sixth and Fourteenth Amendments to the Constitution.

The Court, although recognizing existing problems in the administration of juvenile justice, held to the belief that the Constitution did not mandate jury trials for juveniles. Here is the opinion of the Court:

> [T]he imposition of the jury trial on the juvenile court system would not strengthen greatly, if at all, the fact-finding function, and would contrarily provide an attrition of the juvenile court's assumed ability to function in a unique manner. It would not remedy the defects of the system. . . . If the jury trial were to be injected into the juvenile court system as a matter of right, it would bring with it into that system the traditional delay, the formality, and the clamor of the adversary system and, possibly, the public trial. . . . If the formalities of the criminal adjudicative process are to be superimposed upon the juvenile court system, there is little need for its separate existence.[36]

McKeiver v. *Pennsylvania* did not set any new standards; rather, it reinforced the long-accepted practice of conducting juvenile adjudicatory hearings in the absence of certain due process considerations, particularly those pertaining to trial by jury. It is important to note, however, that the *McKeiver* decision did not specifically prohibit jury trials for juveniles. As a consequence, approximately 12 states today allow the option of jury trials for juveniles.

Breed v. *Jones* (1975)

In 1971, a delinquency complaint was filed against Jones, age 17, alleging that he committed robbery while armed with a deadly weapon. At the adjudicatory hearing, Jones was declared delinquent. A later dispositional hearing determined that Jones was "unfit for treatment as a juvenile," and he was transferred to superior court for trial as an adult. The superior court found Jones guilty of robbery in the first degree and committed him to the custody of the California Division of Juvenile Justice (which at the time was known as the California Youth Authority).

In an appeal eventually heard by the U.S. Supreme Court (***Breed* v. *Jones***), Jones alleged that his transfer to adult court, and the trial that ensued, placed him in double jeopardy because he had already been adjudicated in juvenile court (double jeopardy is prohibited by the Fifth and Fourteenth Amendments to the Constitution). The state of California argued that the superior court trial was only a natural continuation of the juvenile justice process and, as a consequence, did not fall under the rubric of double jeopardy. The state further suggested that double jeopardy existed only where an individual ran the risk of being punished more than once; in the case of Jones, no punishment had been imposed by the juvenile court.

The U.S. Supreme Court did not agree that the possibility of only one punishment negated double jeopardy.[37] The Court pointed to the fact that the double jeopardy clause speaks in terms of "potential risk of trial and conviction—not punishment" and concluded that two separate adjudicatory processes were sufficient to warrant a finding of double jeopardy. Jones's conviction was vacated, clearing the way for him to be returned to juvenile court. However, by the time the litigation had been completed, Jones was beyond the age of juvenile court jurisdiction, and he was released from custody.

The *Jones* case severely restricted the conditions under which transfers from juvenile to adult courts may occur. In effect, the high court mandated that such transfers as do occur must be made before an adjudicatory hearing in juvenile court.

Schall v. *Martin* (1984)

Gregory Martin, age 14, was arrested in New York City, charged with robbery and weapons possession, and detained in a secure detention facility for more than two weeks until his hearing. The detention order drew its authority from a New York preventive detention law that allowed for the jailing of juveniles thought to represent a high risk of continued delinquency.

Martin was adjudicated delinquent. His case, ***Schall* v. *Martin***, eventually reached the U.S. Supreme Court, where his lawyer argued that the New York detention law had effectively denied Martin's freedom before conviction and that it was therefore in violation of the Fourteenth Amendment to the U.S. Constitution.

The Supreme Court, however, upheld the constitutionality of the New York statute, ruling that pretrial detention of juveniles based on "serious risk" does not violate the principle of fundamental fairness required by due process.[38] In so holding, the Court recognized that states have a legitimate interest in preventing future delinquency by juveniles thought to be dangerous. Preventive detention, the Court reasoned, is nonpunitive in its intent and is therefore not a "punishment."

Although the *Schall* decision upheld the practice of preventive detention, it seized on the opportunity provided by the case to impose procedural requirements on the detaining authority. Consequently, preventive detention today cannot be imposed without (1) prior notice, (2) an equitable detention hearing, and (3) a statement by the judge setting forth the reason(s) for detention.

Roper v. *Simmons* (2005)

In 1988, in the case of *Thompson* v. *Oklahoma*,[39] thc U.S. Supreme Court determined that national standards of decency did not permit the execution of any offender who was under age 16 at the time of the crime. The next year, in *Stanford* v. *Kentucky*,[40] the Court considered whether the imposition of capital punishment on offenders ages 16 to 18 violates evolving standards of decency and decided that it does not. In its ruling, the Court said that it looked "not to its own subjective conceptions, but, rather, to the conceptions of modern American society as reflected by objective evidence." The most useful and reliable evidence of a national consensus, said the justices, was "the pattern of federal and state laws," which, at the time, found that 22 of 37 death penalty states permitted capital punishment for those age 16 and older, and 25 states permitted it for 17-year-olds. "This does not," said the Court, "establish the degree of national agreement this Court has previously thought sufficient to label a punishment cruel and unusual."[41] Consequently, the Court ruled that the decision of whether to subject 16- or 17-year-olds to capital punishment must be made by the states and could not be categorically denounced as cruel and unusual punishment.

In 2005, however, in the case of ***Roper* v. *Simmons***,[42] the Court set a new standard when it ruled that age *is* a bar to execution when the offender commits a capital crime when he is younger than age 18. The *Roper* case involved Christopher Simmons, a 17-year-old high school junior, who planned and committed a callous capital murder of a woman whom he bound with duct tape and electrical wire, terrorized, and threw off a bridge. About nine months later, after he had turned 18 years old, he was tried and sentenced to death. Regardless of the heinous nature of Simmons's crime, the justices reasoned that "juveniles' susceptibility to immature and irresponsible behavior means their irresponsible conduct is not as morally reprehensible as that of an adult . . . [and] their own vulnerability and comparative lack of control over their immediate surroundings mean juveniles have a greater claim than adults to be forgiven for failing to escape negative influences in their whole environment." The Court stated, "[The fact] that juveniles still struggle to define their identity means it is less supportable to conclude that even a heinous crime committed by a juvenile is evidence of irretrievably depraved character." The *Roper* ruling invalidated the capital sentences of 72 death-row inmates in 12 states. Among the 962 people put to death between January 1976 and January 2004, 22 had committed their crimes as juveniles.[43]

Legislation Concerning Children and Justice

In response to the rapidly increasing crime rates of the late 1960s, Congress passed the Omnibus Crime Control and Safe Streets Act of 1968, which provided money and technical assistance for states and municipalities seeking to modernize their justice systems. The Safe Streets Act also provided funding for youth services bureaus, which had been recommended by the 1967 presidential commission report *The Challenge of Crime in a Free Society*.[44] These bureaus were available to police, juvenile courts, and probation departments and acted as a centralized community resource for handling delinquents and status offenders. Youth services bureaus also handled juveniles referred by schools and young people who referred themselves. Unfortunately, within a decade after their establishment, most youth services bureaus succumbed to a lack of continued federal funding.

In 1974, recognizing the special needs of juveniles, Congress passed the Juvenile Justice and Delinquency Prevention (JJDP) Act. Employing much the same strategy as the 1968 bill, the JJDP act provided federal grants to states and cities seeking to improve their handling and disposition of delinquents and status offenders. Nearly all the states chose to accept federal funds through the JJDP act. Participating states had to meet two conditions within five years:

1. They had to agree to a "sight and sound separation mandate," under which juveniles would not be held in institutions where they might come into regular contact with adult prisoners.
2. Status offenders had to be deinstitutionalized, with most being released into the community or placed in foster homes.

Within a few years, institutional populations were cut by more than half, and community alternatives to juvenile institutionalization were rapidly being developed. Jailed juveniles were housed in separate wings of adult facilities or were removed from adult jails entirely.

When the JJDP act was reauthorized for funding in 1980, the separation mandate was expanded to require that separate juvenile jails be constructed by the states. Studies supporting reauthorization of the JJDP act in 1984 and 1988, however, found that nearly half the states had failed to come into "substantial compliance" with the new jail and lockup removal mandate; as a consequence, Congress modified the requirements of the act, continuing funding for states making "meaningful progress" toward removing juveniles from adult jails.[45] The 1988 reauthorizing legislation added a "disproportionate minority confinement" (DMC) requirement under which states seeking federal monies in support of their juvenile justice systems had to agree to ameliorate conditions leading to the disproportionate confinement of minority juveniles.[46]

Today we are living with a juvenile justice system that was created around the time of the silent film.

—*Former Attorney General John Ashcroft*

In 1996, in the face of pressures toward punishment and away from treatment for violent juvenile offenders, the OJJDP proposed new rules for jailing juveniles. The new rules allow an adjudicated delinquent to be detained for up to 12 hours in an adult jail before a court appearance and make it easier for states to house juveniles in separate wings of adult jails.[47] The most recent JJDP reauthorization occurred in 2002.[48] It expanded the DMC concept to include all stages of the juvenile justice process. Consequently, DMC has come to mean "disproportionate minority contact" under today's law.[49] By 2005, 56 of 57 eligible states and U.S. territories had agreed to all of the act's requirements and were receiving federal funding under the legislation.[50]

In 2003, Congress passed child-protection legislation in what is commonly called the "AMBER Alert" law. Officially known as the PROTECT Act of 2003 (Prosecutorial Remedies and Other Tools to End the Exploitation of Children Today), the law provides federal funding to the states to ensure creation of a national AMBER (America's Missing: Broadcast Emergency Response) network to facilitate rapid law enforcement and community response to kidnapped or abducted children. The law also established the position of federal AMBER Alert coordinator and set uniform standards for the use of AMBER Alerts across our country. Another provision of the law provides for the prosecution of anyone engaged in pandering of child pornography, and it contains an extraterritorial clause that makes possible the federal prosecution of U.S. citizens who travel outside of the country to engage in child sex tourism.[51] The federal government's AMBER Alert website can be accessed via **Web Extra 13–2** at mycrimekit.com.

Web EXTRA

The Legal Rights of Juveniles

Most jurisdictions today have statutes designed to extend the *Miranda* provisions to juveniles, and many police officers routinely offer *Miranda* warnings to juveniles in their custody before questioning them. It is unclear, however, whether juveniles can legally waive their *Miranda* rights. A 1979 U.S. Supreme Court ruling held that juveniles should be accorded the opportunity for a knowing waiver when they are old enough and sufficiently educated to understand the consequences of a waiver.[52] A later high court ruling upheld the murder conviction of a juvenile who had been advised of his rights and waived them in the presence of his mother.[53]

One important area of juvenile rights centers on investigative procedures. In 1985, for example, the U.S. Supreme Court ruled in *New Jersey* v. *T.L.O.*[54] that schoolchildren have a reasonable expectation of privacy in their personal property. The case involved a 14-year-old girl who was accused of violating school rules by smoking in a high school bathroom. A vice principal searched the girl's purse and found evidence of marijuana use. Juvenile officers were called, and the girl was eventually adjudicated in juvenile court and found delinquent.

On appeal to the New Jersey Supreme Court, the girl's lawyers were successful in having her conviction reversed on the grounds that the search of her purse, as an item of personal property, had been unreasonable. The state's appeal to the U.S. Supreme Court resulted in a ruling that prohibited school officials from engaging in unreasonable searches of students or their property. A reading of the Court's decision leads to the conclusion that a search could be considered reasonable if it (1) is based on a logical suspicion of rule-breaking actions; (2) is required to maintain order, discipline, and safety among students; and (3) does not exceed the scope of the original suspicion.

The Juvenile Justice Process Today

Juvenile court jurisdiction rests on the offender's age and conduct. The majority of states today define a child subject to juvenile court jurisdiction as a person who has not yet turned 18 years of age; a few states set the age at 16, and several use age 17. Figure 3 shows the upper ages of children subject to juvenile court jurisdiction in delinquency matters, by state. When they reach their eighteenth birthday, children in most states become subject to the jurisdiction of adult criminal courts.

FIGURE 3
Limit of Juvenile Court Jurisdiction over Young Offenders, by State.
Source: Office of Juvenile Justice and Delinquency Prevention, Washington, D.C.

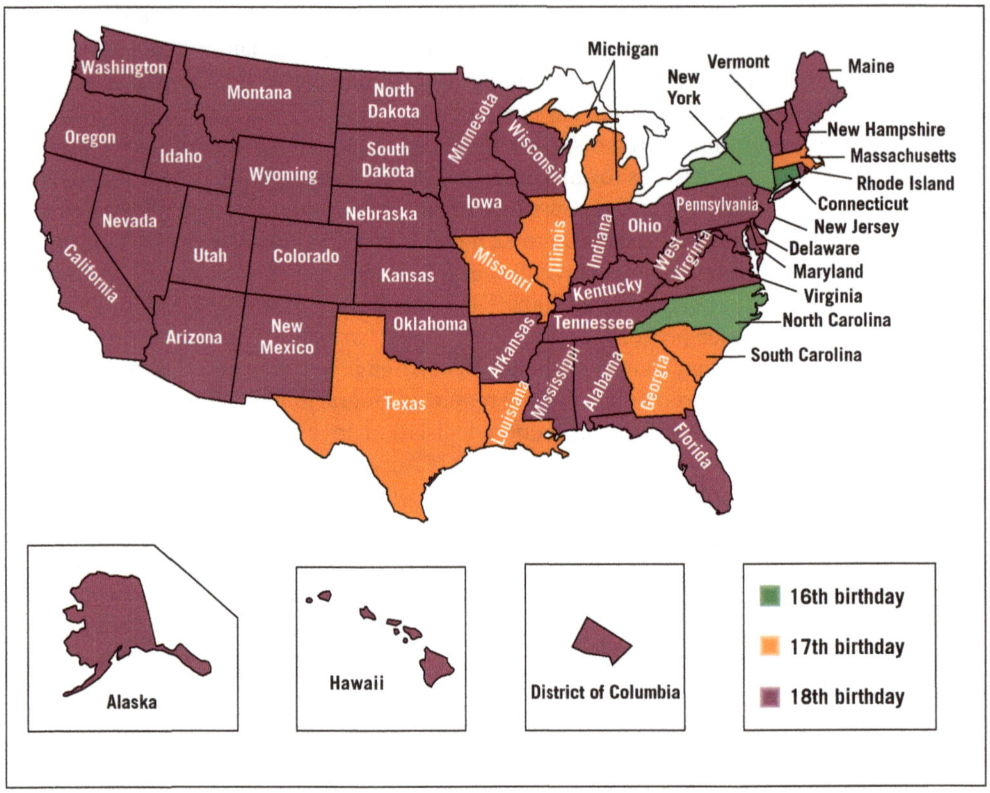

In 2007, OJJDP reported that U.S. courts with juvenile jurisdiction annually handle slightly more than 1.66 million delinquency cases.[55] Depending on the laws of the state and the behavior involved, the jurisdiction of the juvenile court may be exclusive. Exclusive jurisdiction applies when the juvenile court is the only court that has statutory authority to deal with children for specified infractions; for example, status offenses such as truancy normally fall within the exclusive jurisdiction of juvenile courts. Delinquency, which involves violation of the criminal law, however, is often not within the juvenile court's exclusive jurisdiction: All 50 states, the District of Columbia, and the federal government have provisions that allow juveniles who commit serious crimes to be bound over to criminal court; 46 states give juvenile court judges the power to waive jurisdiction over cases involving juveniles so that they can be transferred to criminal court[56]; and 15 states have "direct file" provisions that authorize the prosecutor to decide where to file certain kinds of serious cases, in either juvenile or criminal court.

Juveniles who commit violent crimes or who have prior records are among the most likely to be transferred to adult courts.[57] In a case that made national headlines a few years ago, for example, Lionel Tate, who was 12 years old when he killed a six-year-old playmate while imitating wrestling moves he had seen on TV, was tried as an adult in Fort Lauderdale, Florida. Tate was found guilty of first-degree murder and sentenced to life in prison without the possibility of parole (at the time he was touted as the youngest person in modern American history to be sentenced to life in prison). In 2004, after intense public debate, Tate was released from prison and ordered to serve 11 years on probation and to receive counseling and perform 1,000 hours of community service. At the time of his release, Tate had spent three years behind bars. In 2005, however, 18-year-old Tate was again arrested and charged with pulling a gun on a pizza delivery man at a friend's apartment and beating up the friend.[58] When he was arrested, a knife was found in his pocket. On March 1, 2006, Tate pleaded guilty to armed robbery in a plea arrangement that was to spare him a life sentence for violating probation.[59] A few days later, however, he attempted to withdraw his plea over the objections of his attorney, who then resigned. Broward County Circuit Judge Joel T. Lazarus allowed Tate to withdraw the armed robbery plea but sentenced him in May 2006 to 30 years in prison for violating probation. In the courtroom, the judge told Tate, whose mother is a Florida Highway Patrol trooper,[60] that he had shown "disdain and disrespect" for the law and had "run out of second chances."[61]

CJ Exhibit 1

Adult Criminal Case Processing versus the Juvenile Justice System

CRIMINAL PROCEEDINGS	JUVENILE PROCEEDINGS
Focus on criminality	Focus on delinquency and a special category of "status offenses"
Comprehensive rights against unreasonable searches of person, home, and possessions	Limited rights against unreasonable searches
Assumption of innocence until proven guilty	Right against self-incrimination (waivers are questionable)
	Guilt and innocence not the primary issues (the system focuses on the interests of the child)
Adversarial setting	Helping context
Most arrests based on arrest warrants	Apprehension based on petitions or complaints
Right to an attorney	Right to an attorney
Public trial	Closed hearing; no right to a jury trial
System goals of punishment and reformation	System goals of protection and treatment
No right to treatment	Specific right to treatment
Possibility of bail or release on recognizance	Release into parental custody
Public record of trial and judgment	Sealed records (records may sometimes be destroyed by specified age of offender)
Possible incarceration in adult correctional facility	Separate facilities at all levels

Where juvenile court authority is not exclusive, the jurisdiction of the court may be original or concurrent. *Original jurisdiction* means that a particular offense must originate (begin) with juvenile court authorities, and juvenile courts have original jurisdiction over most delinquency petitions and all status offenses. *Concurrent jurisdiction* exists where other courts have equal statutory authority to originate proceedings. For example, if a juvenile has committed a homicide, rape, or another serious crime, an arrest warrant may be issued by the adult court.

Some states specify that juvenile courts have no jurisdiction over certain excluded offenses. Delaware, Louisiana, and Nevada, for example, allow no juvenile court jurisdiction over children charged with first-degree murder. Another 29 states have statutes that exclude certain serious, violent, and/or repeat offenders from the juvenile court's jurisdiction.

Adult and Juvenile Justice Compared

The court cases of relevance to the juvenile justice system that we have discussed in this chapter have two common characteristics: They all turn on due process guarantees specified by the Bill of Rights, and they all make the claim that adult due process should serve as a model for juvenile proceedings. Due process guarantees, as interpreted by the U.S. Supreme Court, are clearly designed to ensure that juvenile proceedings are fair and that the interests of juveniles are protected. However, the Court's interpretations do not offer any pretense of providing juveniles with the same kinds of protections guaranteed to adult defendants. While the high court has tended to agree that juveniles are entitled to due process protection, it has refrained from declaring that juveniles have a right to all aspects of due process afforded adult defendants. See CJ Exhibit 1 for a comparison of adult criminal proceedings and juvenile proceedings.

Juvenile court philosophy brings with it other differences from the adult system. Among them are (1) reduced concern with legal issues of guilt or innocence and an emphasis on the child's best interests; (2) emphasis on treatment rather than punishment; (3) privacy and protection from public scrutiny through the use of sealed records, laws against publishing the names of juvenile offenders, and so forth; (4) use of the techniques of social science in dispositional decision making rather than sentences determined by a perceived need for punishment; (5) no long-term confinement, with most juveniles being released from institutions by their twenty-first birthday, regardless of offense; (6) separate facilities for juveniles; and (7) broad

Under our Constitution, the condition of being a boy does not justify a kangaroo court.
—In re Gault, *387 U.S. 1 (1967)*

discretionary alternatives at all points in the process.[62] This combination of court philosophy and due process requirements has created a unique justice system for juveniles that takes into consideration the special needs of young people while attempting to offer reasonable protection to society. The juvenile justice process is diagrammed in Figure 4.

The Way the System Works

The juvenile justice system can be viewed as a process that, when carried to completion, moves through four stages: intake, adjudication, disposition, and postadjudicatory review. Though organizationally similar to the adult criminal justice process, the juvenile system is far more likely to maximize the use of discretion and to employ diversion from further formal processing at every point in the process. Each stage is discussed in the pages that follow.

Intake

juvenile petition
A document filed in juvenile court alleging that a juvenile is a delinquent, a status offender, or a dependent and asking that the court assume jurisdiction over the juvenile or that an alleged delinquent be transferred to a criminal court for prosecution as an adult.

Delinquent juveniles may come to the attention of the police or juvenile court authorities either through arrest or through the filing of a **juvenile petition** by an aggrieved party (a juvenile petition is much like a criminal complaint in that it alleges illegal behavior). Juvenile petitions are most often filed by teachers, school administrators, neighbors, store managers, or others who have frequent contact with juveniles; parents who are unable to control the behavior of their teenage children are the source of many other petitions. Crimes in progress bring other juveniles to the attention of the police, with three-quarters of all referrals to juvenile court coming directly from law enforcement authorities.[63]

Many police departments have juvenile officers who are specially trained in dealing with juveniles. Because of the emphasis on rehabilitation that characterizes the juvenile justice process, juvenile officers can usually choose from a number of discretionary alternatives in the form of special programs, especially in the handling of nonviolent offenders. In Delaware County, Pennsylvania, for example, police departments participate in "youth aid panels." These panels are composed of private citizens who volunteer their services to provide an alternative to the formal juvenile court process. Youngsters who are referred to a panel and agree to abide by the decision of the group are diverted from the juvenile court.

Real Justice Conferencing (RJC) is another example of a diversionary program. Started in Bethlehem, Pennsylvania, in 1995, RJC is said to be a cost-effective approach to juvenile crime, school misconduct, and violence prevention and has served as a model for programs in other cities. It makes use of family group conferences (sometimes called *community conferences*) in lieu of school disciplinary or judicial processes or as a supplement to them. The family group conference, built around a restorative justice model, allows young offenders to tell what they did, to hear from those they affected, and to help decide how to repair the harm their actions caused. Successful RJC participants avoid the more formal mechanisms of the juvenile justice process.

However, even youth who are eventually diverted from the system may spend some time in custody. One juvenile case in five involves detention before adjudication.[64] Unlike the adult system, where jail is seen as the primary custodial alternative for people awaiting a first appearance, secure detention for juveniles is acceptable only as a last resort. Detention hearings investigate whether candidates for confinement represent a "clear and immediate danger to themselves and/or to others," a judgment normally rendered within 24 hours of apprehension. Runaways, because they are often not dangerous, are especially difficult to confine. Juveniles who are not detained are generally released into the custody of their parents or guardians or into a supervised temporary shelter, like a group home.

intake
The first step in decision making regarding a juvenile whose behavior or alleged behavior is in violation of the law or could otherwise cause a juvenile court to assume jurisdiction.

Detention Hearing Detention hearings regarding **intake** of a juvenile are conducted by the juvenile court judge or by an officer of the court, such as a juvenile probation officer, who has been given the authority to make this decision based on the (alleged) behavior that violates the law. Intake officers, like their police counterparts, have substantial discretion: Along with detention, they can choose diversion or outright dismissal of some or all of the charges against the juvenile; diverted juveniles may be sent to job-training programs, mental health facilities, drug-treatment programs, educational counseling, or other community services agencies; and when caring parents are present who can afford private counseling or therapy, intake officers may release the juvenile into their custody with the understanding that they will provide for

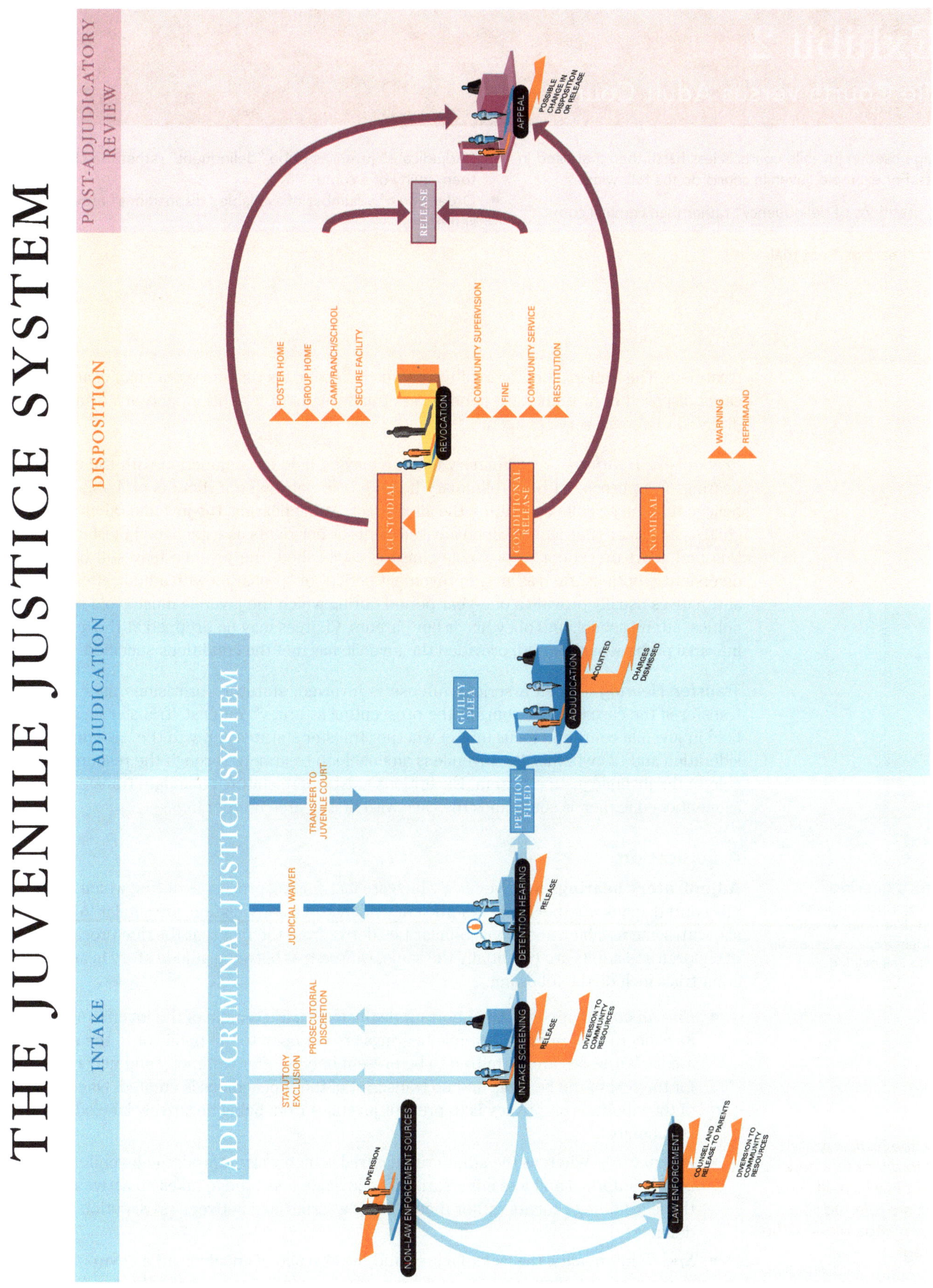

FIGURE 4
The Juvenile Justice System.

CJ Exhibit 2

Juvenile Courts versus Adult Courts

The language used in juvenile courts is less harsh than that used in adult courts. For example, juvenile courts do the following:

- Accept "petitions of delinquency" rather than criminal complaints
- Conduct "hearings," not trials
- "Adjudicate" juveniles to be "delinquent" rather than find them guilty of a crime
- Order one of a number of available "dispositions" rather than sentences

treatment. The National Center for Juvenile Justice estimates that more than half of all juvenile cases disposed of at intake are handled informally, without a petition, and are dismissed or diverted to a social services agency.[65]

Preliminary Hearing A preliminary hearing may be held in conjunction with the detention hearing. The purpose of the preliminary hearing is to determine if there is probable cause to believe that the juvenile committed the alleged act. At the hearing, the juvenile (along with the child's parents or guardians) will be advised of his or her rights as established by state legislation and court precedent. If probable cause is established, the juvenile may still be offered diversionary options, such as an "improvement period" or "probation with adjudication." These alternatives usually provide a one-year period during which the juvenile must avoid legal difficulties, attend school, and obey his or her parents. Charges may be dropped at the end of this informal probationary period, provided the juvenile has met the conditions specified.

Transfer Hearing When a serious offense is involved, statutory provisions may allow for transfer of the case to adult court at the prosecuting attorney's request. Transfer hearings are held in juvenile court and focus on (1) whether transfer statutes apply to the case under consideration and (2) whether the juvenile is amenable to treatment through the resources available to the juvenile justice system. Exceptions exist where statutes mandate transfer (which, as mentioned earlier, is sometimes the case with first-degree murder).

Adjudication

adjudicatory hearing
The fact-finding process wherein the juvenile court determines whether there is sufficient evidence to sustain the allegations in a petition.

Adjudicatory hearings for juveniles, which are fact-finding processes during which the juvenile court decides whether there is sufficient evidence of a law violation, are similar to adult trials, with some notable exceptions. Similarities derive from the fact that the due process rights of children and adults are essentially the same. Differences between adjudicatory hearings and adult trials include the following:

- *Emphasis on privacy.* An important distinctive characteristic of the juvenile system is its concern with privacy. Juvenile hearings are not open to the public or to the mass media. Witnesses are permitted to be present only to offer testimony and may not stay for the rest of the hearing, and no transcript of the proceedings is created. One purpose of the emphasis on privacy is to prevent juveniles from being negatively labeled by the community.
- *Informality.* Whereas the adult criminal trial is highly structured, the juvenile hearing is more informal and less adversarial. The juvenile court judge takes an active role in the fact-finding process rather than serving as arbitrator between prosecution and defense.
- *Speed.* Informality, the lack of a jury, and the absence of an adversarial environment promote speed. While the adult trial may run into weeks or even months, the juvenile hearing is normally completed in a matter of hours or days.

Eventually, the justice system may need to adapt to a new environment in which all criminal matters are referred to a single system, regardless of the offender's age.

—Jeffrey Butts and Ojmarrh Mitchell, Urban Institute[ii]

- *Evidentiary standard.* On completion of the hearing, the juvenile court judge must weigh the evidence. If the charge involves a status offense, the judge may adjudicate the juvenile as a status offender upon finding that a preponderance of the evidence supports this finding (a preponderance of the evidence exists when evidence of an offense is more convincing than evidence offered to the contrary). If the charge involves a criminal-type offense, the evidentiary standard rises to the level of reasonable doubt.
- *Philosophy of the court.* Even in the face of strong evidence pointing to the offender's guilt, the judge may decide that it is not in the child's best interests to be adjudicated delinquent. The judge also has the power, even after the evidence is presented, to divert the juvenile from the system. Juvenile court statistics indicate that only about 57% of all cases disposed of by juvenile courts are processed formally.[66] Formal processing involves the filing of a petition requesting an adjudicatory or transfer hearing; informal cases, on the other hand, are handled without a petition. Among informally handled (nonpetitioned) delinquency cases, almost half were dismissed by the court, whereas 67% of petitioned cases resulted in the child being adjudicated delinquent.
- *No right to trial by jury.* As we discussed in our review of the U.S. Supreme Court decision in *McKeiver* v. *Pennsylvania*,[67] juveniles do not have a constitutional right to trial by jury, and most states do not provide juveniles with a statutory opportunity for a jury trial.[68]

See Exhibit 2 for a comparison of the language used in juvenile and adult courts.

Some jurisdictions, however, allow juveniles to be tried by their peers in **teen courts**. The juvenile court in Columbus County, Georgia, for example, began experimenting with teen courts and peer juries in 1980.[69] In Georgia, peer juries are composed of youth under the age of 17 who receive special training by the court. Jurors are required to be successful in school and may not be under the supervision of the court or have juvenile petitions pending against them. Training consists of classroom exposure to the philosophy of the juvenile court system, Georgia's juvenile code, and Supreme Court decisions affecting juvenile justice.[70] The county's

teen court
An alternative approach to juvenile justice in which alleged offenders are judged and/or sentenced by a jury of their peers.

▲ Juvenile court in action. Juvenile courts are expected to act in the best interests of the children who come before them. Should that rule apply to all juveniles who come before the court, regardless of what their offense might be?
Billy Barnes/Stock Boston

youthful jurors are used only in the dispositional (or sentencing) stage of the court process and only when adjudicated youth volunteer to go before the jury.

Today, hundreds of teen court programs are in operation across the country. OJJDP notes that teen courts are "an effective intervention in many jurisdictions where enforcement of misdemeanor charges is sometimes given low priority because of heavy caseloads and the need to focus on more serious offenders."[71] Teen courts, says OJJDP, "present communities with opportunities to teach young people valuable life and coping skills and promote positive peer influence for youth who are defendants and for volunteer youth who play a variety of roles in the teen court process." Learn more about teen courts via Web Extra 13–3 at mycrimekit.com.

Web EXTRA

Disposition

dispositional hearing
The final stage in the processing of adjudicated juveniles in which a decision is made on the form of treatment or penalty that should be imposed on the child.

Once a juvenile has been found delinquent, the judge will set a **dispositional hearing**, which is similar to an adult sentencing hearing and is used to decide what action the court should take relative to the child. As in adult courts, the judge may order a presentence investigation before making a dispositional decision. This type of investigation is conducted by special court personnel, sometimes called *juvenile court counselors*, who are, in effect, juvenile probation officers. Attorneys on both sides of the issue will also have the opportunity to make recommendations concerning dispositional alternatives.

juvenile disposition
The decision of a juvenile court, concluding a dispositional hearing, that an adjudicated juvenile be committed to a juvenile correctional facility; be placed in a juvenile residence, shelter, or care or treatment program; be required to meet certain standards of conduct; or be released.

The juvenile justice system typically gives the judge a much wider range of sentencing alternatives than does the adult system. Two major classes of **juvenile disposition** exist: to confine or not to confine. Because rehabilitation is still the primary objective of the juvenile court, the judge is likely to select the least restrictive alternative that meets the needs of the juvenile while recognizing the legitimate concerns of society for protection.

Most judges decide not to confine juveniles. Statistics indicate that in 2004 (the latest year for which statistics are available), the court ordered out-of-home placement in 22% of all cases adjudicated delinquent, down from 32% in 1985. Probation was the most restrictive disposition used in 63% (393,100) of the cases adjudicated delinquent in 2004, and it remains the most likely sanction to be imposed by juvenile courts.[72]

Probationary disposition usually means that juveniles will be released into the custody of a parent or guardian and ordered to undergo some form of training, education, or counseling. As in the adult system, juveniles placed on probation may be ordered to pay fines or to make restitution. In 11% of adjudicated delinquency cases, courts order juveniles to pay restitution or a fine, to participate in some form of community service, or to enter a treatment or counseling program—all dispositions that require minimal continuing supervision by probation staff.[73] Because juveniles rarely have financial resources or jobs, most economic sanctions take the form of court-ordered work programs, such as refurbishing schools or cleaning school buses.

The Lehigh County (Pennsylvania) Juvenile Probation Office runs an innovative probation program that places juvenile probation officers in public schools. The officers function much like school counselors, paying special attention to the needs of their charges in areas like tutoring, attendance, and grades. In-school probation officers work at addressing problems as diverse as getting students to school on time (by developing personal schedules), raising grades (through improving study skills, tutoring, and sitting in on classes), and promoting successful involvement in extracurricular activities. The program, which began more than a decade ago, has since been expanded through a federal grant to 29 other Pennsylvania counties.[74]

Of course, not all juveniles who are adjudicated delinquent receive probation. Nearly one-quarter (24%) of adjudicated cases in 1999 resulted in the youth being placed outside the home in a residential facility. In a relatively small number of cases (4%), the juvenile was adjudicated delinquent, but the case was then dismissed or the youth was otherwise released.[75]

Secure Institutions for Juveniles Juveniles who demonstrate the potential for serious new offenses may be ordered to participate in rehabilitative programs within a secure environment, such as a youth center or a training school. As of late 2006, approximately 92,850 young people were being held under custodial supervision in the United States.[76] Of these, 33% were being held for personal crimes like murder, rape, or robbery; 25% were being held for property crimes; 9% were locked up for drug offenses; 11% were being held for public-order offenses (including weapons offenses); and 4% were being held for status offenses. Probation and parole violations accounted for another 16% of those confined.[77]

Most confined juveniles are held in semisecure facilities designed to look less like prisons and more like residential high school campuses. Most states, however, operate at least one secure facility for juveniles that is intended as a home for the most recalcitrant youthful offenders. Halfway houses, "boot camps,"[78] ranches, forestry camps, wilderness programs, group homes, and state-hired private facilities also hold some of the juveniles reported to be under confinement. Children placed in group homes continue to attend school and live in a family-like environment in the company of other adjudicated children, shepherded by "house parents." Learn more about the juvenile justice systems of each state from the National Center for Juvenile Justice's State Juvenile Justice Profiles at Web Extra 13–4.

Web EXTRA

The operative philosophy of custodial programs for juveniles focuses squarely on the rehabilitative ideal. Juveniles are usually committed to secure facilities for indeterminate periods of time, with the typical stay being less than one year. Release is often timed to coincide with the beginning or the end of the school year.

Most juvenile facilities are small, with 80% designed to hold 40 residents or fewer[79]; many institutionalized juveniles are held in the thousand or so homelike facilities across the nation that are limited to ten residents or fewer.[80] At the other end of the scale are the nation's 70 large juvenile institutions, each designed to hold more than 200 hard-core delinquents.[81] Residential facilities for juveniles are intensively staffed. One study found that staff members outnumber residents ten to nine on average in state-run institutions and by an even greater ratio in privately run facilities.[82]

Jurisdictions vary widely in their use of secure detention for juveniles. In 2004, juvenile custody populations ranged from a low of 54 in Vermont to a high of 15,057 in California.[83] This variance reflects population differences as well as economic realities and philosophical beliefs. Some jurisdictions, like California, expect rehabilitative costs to be borne by the state rather than by families or local government agencies. Hence, California shows a higher rate of institutionalization than many other states. Similarly, some states have more firmly embraced the reformation ideal and are more likely to use diversionary options for juveniles.

Characteristics of Juveniles in Confinement Institutionalized juveniles are a small but special category of young people with serious problems. A recent report on institutionalized youth by the Bureau of Justice Statistics found five striking characteristics[84]:

1. The majority (85.5%) were male.
2. In terms of ethnicity, 39.4% were Caucasian, 38.9% were African-American, and 17.3% were Hispanic.
3. About 6.5% were institutionalized for having committed a status offense, such as being truant, running away, or violating curfew.
4. Less than half (42.4%) were in residential facilities for a serious personal or property offense.
5. Only 1% were charged with homicide.

Overcrowding in Juvenile Facilities As in adult prisons, overcrowding exists in many juvenile institutions. In one survey, half of all states reported overcrowding in juvenile facilities, and 22 states were operating facilities at more than 50% over capacity.[85]

A national study of the conditions of confinement in juvenile detention facilities conducted by OJJDP found that "there are several areas in which problems in juvenile facilities are substantial and widespread—most notably living space, health care, security, and control of suicidal behavior."[86] Using a variety of evaluative criteria, the study found that 47% of juveniles were confined in facilities whose populations exceeded their reported design capacity and that 33% of residents had to sleep "in rooms that were smaller than required by nationally recognized standards." To address the problem, the authors of the study recommended the use of alternative placement options so that only juveniles judged to be the most dangerous to their communities would be confined in secure facilities. Similarly, because it found that injuries to residents were most likely to occur within large dormitory-like settings, the OJJDP study recommended that "large dormitories be eliminated from juvenile facilities." Finally, the study recommended that "all juveniles be screened for risk of suicidal behavior immediately upon their admission to confinement" and that initial health screenings be "carried out promptly at admission." Other

Three decades of reform have largely dissolved the traditional juvenile court, and the system that remains is rapidly losing political viability. Policy makers may soon need to devise an entirely new process for handling young offenders.
—*Jeffrey Butts and Adele Harrell, Urban Institute*[iii]

problems that OJJDP found "still important enough to warrant attention" included education and treatment services. Further study of both areas is needed, OJJDP said.

A number of states use private facilities. A survey found that 13 states contract with 328 private facilities—most of which were classified as halfway houses—for the custody of adjudicated juveniles.[87] In the past few years, admissions to private facilities (comprising primarily halfway houses, group homes, shelters, and ranches, camps, or farms) have increased by more than 100%, compared with an increase of only about 10% for public facilities (mostly detention centers and training schools).[88] The fastest-growing category of detained juveniles comprises drug and alcohol offenders. Approximately 12% of all juvenile detainees are being held because of alcohol- and drug-related offenses.[89] Reflecting widespread socioeconomic disparities, an OJJDP report found that "a juvenile held in a public facility . . . was most likely to be black, male, between 14 and 17 years of age, and held for a delinquent offense such as a property crime or a crime against a person. On the other hand, a juvenile held in custody in a private facility . . . was most likely to be white, male, 14 to 17 years of age, and held for a nondelinquent offense such as running away, truancy, or incorrigibility"[90]; the report also noted that "juvenile corrections has become increasingly privatized."

Postadjudicatory Review

The detrimental effects of institutionalization on young offenders may make the opportunity for appellate review more critical for juveniles than it is for adults. However, federal court precedents have yet to establish a clear right to appeal from juvenile court, although most states do have statutory provisions that make such appeals possible.[91]

From a practical point of view, however, juvenile appeals may not be as consequential as are appeals of adult criminal convictions. Most juvenile complaints are handled informally, and only a relatively small proportion of adjudicated delinquents are placed outside the family. Moreover, because sentence lengths are short for most confined juveniles, appellate courts hardly have time to complete the review process before a juvenile is released.

The Post–Juvenile Court Era

In August 2005, Mitchell Johnson was released from a federal facility for youthful offenders.[92] Mitchell, whose release was mandated by law on his twenty-first birthday, was 13 years old in 1998 when he and an 11-year-old friend, Andrew Golden, murdered four children and a teacher

▸ Recent arrivals at a California "boot camp" for juvenile offenders listening to what will be expected of them. Although institutionalized juveniles are housed separately from adult offenders, juvenile institutions share many of the problems of adult facilities. What changes have recently occurred in the handling of juvenile offenders?
Tony Savino/JB Pictures, Ltd./The Image Works

at Westside Middle School in Jonesboro, Arkansas, with hunting rifles they had taken from Golden's grandfather. At the time of the killings, laws in Arkansas and many other states allowed children to be confined only until they reached their eighteenth birthdays—no matter how serious their offense. It was only Johnson's conviction on federal gun charges that kept him locked up for an additional three years.

Cases like Johnson's, combined with extensive media coverage of violent juvenile crime across the United States, fueled public perceptions that violence committed by teenagers had reached epidemic proportions and that no community was immune to random acts of youth violence. At the same time, the apparent "professionalization" of delinquency, the hallmark of which is the repeated and often violent criminal involvement of juveniles in drug-related gang activity, came to be viewed as a major challenge to the idealism of the juvenile justice system. Consequently, by the turn of the twenty-first century, the issue of youth violence was at or near the top of nearly every state legislature's and governor's agenda. Most states took some form of legislative or executive action to stem what was seen as an escalating level of dangerous crime by juveniles. As OJJDP observed, "This level of [legislative and political] activity has occurred only three other times in our nation's history: at the outset of the juvenile court movement at the turn of the [twentieth] century; following the U.S. Supreme Court's *Gault* decision in 1967; and with the enactment of the Juvenile Justice and Delinquency Prevention Act in 1974."[93] OJJDP has identified five significant developments that have taken place in many states during the past decade[94]:

1. *Transfer provisions.* New transfer provisions made it easier to move juvenile offenders from the juvenile justice system to the criminal justice system.
2. *Sentencing authority.* New laws on sentencing have given criminal and juvenile courts the authority to use expanded sentencing options such as the **blended sentence** (the combination of a juvenile disposition followed by a suspended adult sentence if the former is carried out successfully) in cases involving juveniles.
3. *Confidentiality changes.* Modifications were made to laws containing court confidentiality provisions in order to make juvenile records and proceedings more open.
4. *Victims' rights.* Laws were passed that increased the role of victims of juvenile crime in the juvenile justice process.
5. *Correctional programming.* New correctional programs in adult and juvenile facilities were developed to handle juveniles sentenced as adults or as violent juvenile offenders.

blended sentence
A juvenile court disposition that imposes both a juvenile sanction and an adult criminal sentence on an adjudicated delinquent. The adult sentence is suspended on the condition that the juvenile offender successfully completes the term of the juvenile disposition and refrains from committing any new offense.[iv]

Jeffrey Butts and Ojmarrh Mitchell (members of the Program on Law and Behavior at the Urban Institute in Washington, D.C., and experts on juvenile justice) say that "[current] policymakers throughout the United States have greatly dissolved the border between juvenile and criminal justice. Young people who violate the law are no longer guaranteed special consideration from the legal system. Some form of juvenile court still exists in every state, but the purposes and procedures of juvenile courts are becoming indistinguishable from those of criminal courts."[95] Butts and Mitchell also claim that "changes in juvenile law and juvenile court procedure are slowly dismantling the jurisdictional border between juvenile and criminal justice."[96] As evidence, Butts and Mitchell note that juvenile courts across the United States are becoming increasingly similar to criminal courts in the methods they use to reach conclusions and to process cases, as well as in the general atmosphere that characterizes them.

As a result of ongoing changes, some say that many states have substantially "criminalized" juvenile courts. In March 2000, for example, California voters endorsed sweeping changes in the state's juvenile justice system by passing Proposition 21, the Gang Violence and Juvenile Crime Prevention Act. The law reduces confidentiality in the juvenile court, limits the use of probation for young offenders, and increases the power of prosecutors to send juveniles to adult court and to put them in adult prisons. Public support for the measure was undiminished by projections that it would increase operational costs in the California juvenile justice system by $500 million annually.[97] Because laws like California's Proposition 21 are being passed at a growing rate throughout the country, a leading expert on juvenile justice notes that "the similarities of juvenile and adult courts are becoming greater than the differences between them."[98]

Cindy Lederman, presiding judge of the Miami-Dade Juvenile Court, refers to the changes as the "adultification" of the juvenile justice system.[99] The juvenile court, says Lederman, has undergone significant change since it was created. In the early twentieth century, the juvenile court focused on social welfare and was primarily concerned with acting in a child's best

Children are the living messages we send to a time we will not see.
—*John W. Whitehead*[v]

interest, but by the mid-twentieth century, it had seized on the issue of children's due process rights as an important guiding principle; the court today, says Lederman, has turned its focus to accountability and punishment.

Proposals for further change abound. In 2001, the Task Force on Juvenile Justice Reform (TFJJR) of the American Academy of Child and Adolescent Psychiatry issued a report on juvenile justice reform.[100] The report covered many areas, including competence to stand trial, forensic evaluations of children and adolescents, recommended standards for juvenile detention and confinement facilities, health care in the juvenile justice system, females in the juvenile justice system, disproportionate minority confinement, educational needs of youth in juvenile justice facilities, and transfers of juvenile cases to criminal court. Read the entire report at Library Extra 13–2 at mycrimekit.com.

Library EXTRA

The Department of Justice Authorization Act for fiscal year 2003[101] set dramatic new accountability standards for federally funded programs for juveniles who violate the law.[102] The law built on the premise that young people who violate criminal laws should be held accountable for their offenses through the swift and consistent application of sanctions that are proportionate to the offense.[103] Lawmakers made it clear that it was their belief that enhanced accountability and swift sanctions were both a matter of basic justice and a way to combat delinquency and improve the quality of life in our nation's communities.

The Washington, D.C.–based Sentencing Project stated that "the treatment of juveniles, especially those nearing adulthood, is a contentious issue in many states."[104] The decision to prosecute children as adults, say Sentencing Project authors, "has lasting ramifications on their experience within the criminal justice system and their prospects for rehabilitation." True to this understanding, legislators nationwide have worked to distinguish between serious and habitual juvenile offenders and those whose law-breaking behavior is relatively minor and likely to be transitory.

In 2007, for example, California's Senate Bill (SB) 81, passed by state legislators with bipartisan support and quickly enacted into law, mandated that juveniles charged with all but the most serious felonies be adjudicated and supervised within their counties of residence.[105] Touted as a landmark reform to California's juvenile justice system, SB 81 is expected to reduce the population of the state's juvenile detention facilities by half by the year 2011. To address the needs of juveniles who are diverted from state facilities, SB 81 provides money for the development of county-based rehabilitative programs, and it awards counties an average of $130,000 per supervised youth annually. SB 81 shifts nonviolent juvenile offenders out of secure facilities operated by the state Division of Juvenile Justice (DJJ) (formerly, the California Youth Authority) and into county facilities and programs.

Bill highlights include:

- By banning future commitments of nonviolent juvenile offenders to state facilities, SB 81 will cut the population from 2,500 to about 1,500 incarcerated juvenile offenders within two years.
- Counties will now be responsible for the custody and care of juvenile offenders who can no longer be sent to state institutions.
- SB 81 provides counties with block grant funds to pay for local alternatives to state commitment, at an average of $130,000 per ward.
- The bill authorizes up to $100 million statewide in construction bonds for the design and construction of new or renovated county facilities for youthful offenders.
- The bill requires the state Juvenile Justice Commission, a 12-member statewide commission of stakeholders, to produce a Juvenile Operations Master Plan, including standardized risk–needs assessments, standard data-collection elements, and recommended evidence-based programs, for youthful offenders by January 2009.

Summary

- Under today's laws, children occupy a special status that is tied closely to cultural advances that occurred in the Western world during the past 200 years. Before the modern era, children who committed crimes received no preferential treatment and were adjudicated, punished, and imprisoned alongside adults. Beginning a few hundred years ago, England (from which we derive many of our legal traditions) adapted the principle of *parens patriae*. That principle allowed the government to take the place of parents in dealing with children who broke the law. Around the middle of the nineteenth century, the child-savers movement began in the United States; it espoused a philosophy of productivity and eschewed idleness and unprincipled behavior. Not long afterward, the 1899 codification of Illinois juvenile law became the model for juvenile court statutes throughout the United States. It created a juvenile court separate in form and function from adult criminal courts and based on the principle of *parens patriae*. To avoid the lasting stigma of criminality, the term *delinquent* (rather than *criminal*) began to be applied to young adjudicated offenders. Soon, juvenile courts across the country focused primarily on the best interests of the child as a guide in their deliberations.
- Important U.S. Supreme Court decisions of special relevance to the handling of juveniles by the justice system include (1) *Kent* v. *U.S.* (1966), which established minimal due process standards for juvenile hearings; (2) *In re Gault* (1967), in which the Court found that a child has many of the same due process rights as an adult; (3) *In re Winship* (1970), which held that the constitutional safeguard of proof beyond a reasonable doubt is required during the adjudicatory stage of a delinquency proceeding; (4) *McKeiver* v. *Pennsylvania* (1971), which held that jury trials were not required in delinquency cases; (5) *Breed* v. *Jones* (1975), which restricted the conditions under which transfers from juvenile to adult court may occur; (6) *Schall* v. *Martin* (1984), in which the Court held that pretrial detention of juveniles based on "serious risk" does not violate due process, although prior notice, an equitable detention hearing, and a statement by the juvenile court judge explaining the reasons for detention are required; and (7) *Roper* v. *Simmons* (2005), which held that age *is* a bar to capital punishment when the offender commits a capital crime when he or she is younger than age 18.
- The juvenile justice system of today is infused with due process guarantees designed to ensure that juvenile proceedings are fair and that the interests of juveniles are protected. Although the U.S. Supreme Court has established that juveniles are entitled to fundamental due process protections, it has refrained from declaring that juveniles have a right to all aspects of due process afforded adult defendants. The juvenile justice system differs from the adult system in a number of ways: (1) It is less concerned with legal issues of guilt or innocence and focuses on the child's best interests; (2) it emphasizes treatment rather than punishment; (3) it ensures privacy and protection from public scrutiny through the use of sealed records and laws against publishing the names of juvenile offenders; (4) it uses the techniques of social science in dispositional decision making rather than sentences determined by a perceived need for punishment; (5) it does not order long-term confinement, with most juveniles being released from institutions by their twenty-first birthday; (6) it has separate facilities for juveniles; and (7) it allows broad discretionary alternatives at all points in the process.
- The juvenile justice system's commitment to a philosophy of protection and restoration, expressed in the juvenile court movement of the late nineteenth and early twentieth centuries, has begun to dissipate. The present juvenile system, for the most part, still differs substantially from the adult system in the multitude of opportunities it provides for diversion and in the emphasis it places on rehabilitation rather than punishment. However, the "professionalization" of delinquency, the hallmark of which is the repeated and often violent criminal involvement of juveniles in drug-related gang activity, represents a major challenge to the idealism of the juvenile justice system. Efforts to address that challenge are starting to result in what some have called the "adultification" of the juvenile justice system.

Key Concepts

Terms

abused child
adjudicatory hearing
blended sentence
delinquency
delinquent child
dependent child
dispositional hearing
intake
juvenile
juvenile court
juvenile disposition
juvenile justice system
juvenile petition
neglected child
parens patriae
status offender
status offense
teen court
undisciplined child

Cases

Breed v. *Jones*
In re Gault
In re Winship
Kent v. *U.S.*
McKeiver v. *Pennsylvania*
Roper v. *Simmons*
Schall v. *Martin*

Questions for Review

1. Describe the history and evolution of the juvenile justice system in the Western world, and list the six categories of children recognized by the laws of most states.
2. Name the important U.S. Supreme Court decisions of relevance to juvenile justice. What was the impact of each of these decisions on juvenile justice in America?
3. What are the major similarities and differences between the juvenile and adult justice systems?
4. In your opinion, should juveniles continue to receive what many regard as preferential treatment from the courts? Why or why not?

To participate in an online discussion of these topics and others, join the CJ Brief e-mail discussion list at mycrimekit.com.

Web Quest

Visit the National Council on Crime and Delinquency (NCCD) at www.nccd-crc.org. What are some of the areas in which NCCD is working to prevent and understand delinquency? What other areas do you think it should be exploring?

Use the Cybrary to identify other juvenile justice research and delinquency prevention sites on the Web. Which sites contain information about school shootings? What, if anything, do they suggest can be done to reduce the incidence of these crimes? Submit your findings to your instructor if asked to do so.

To complete this Web Quest online, go to the Web Quest module in Chapter 13 of the *Criminal Justice: A Brief Introduction* Companion Website at mycrimekit.com.

Notes

i. Tina Chiu and Sara Mogulescu, *Changing the Status Quo for Status Offenders: New York State's Efforts to Support Troubled Teens* (New York: Vera Institute of Justice, 2005).
ii. Jeffrey A. Butts and Ojmarrh Mitchell, "Brick by Brick: Dismantling the Border between Juvenile and Adult Justice," in Phyllis McDonald and Janice Munsterman, eds., *Criminal Justice 2000, Vol. 2: Boundary Changes in Criminal Justice Organizations* (Washington, DC: National Institute of Justice, 2000), pp. 167–213.
iii. Jeffrey A. Butts and Adele V. Harrell, *Delinquents or Criminals: Policy Options for Young Criminals* (Washington, DC: Urban Institute Press, 1998).
iv. Howard N. Snyder and Melissa Sickmund, *Juvenile Offenders and Victims: 2006 National Report* (Washington, DC: Office of Juvenile Justice and Delinquency Prevention, 2006).
v. John W. Whitehead, *The Stealing of America* (Wheaton, IL: Crossway Books, 1983).

1. National Center for Juvenile Justice, *Annual Report 2003* (Pittsburgh, PA: NCJJ), p. 4.
2. Elliot Grossman, "Toughlove Parents Scared," *Allentown (Pa.) Morning Call*, March 7, 1995, p. B1.
3. Many of the details for this story come from David Karp, "Boy, 13, Found Guilty of Rape," *St. Petersburg (Fla.) Times*, September 8, 2001. Web posted at http://www.sptimes.com/News/090801/TampaBay/Boy_13_found_guilty.shtml (accessed August 31, 2008).
4. Ibid.
5. "Judge Sentences 13-Year-Old to 15 Years for Daytime Park Rape," Associated Press wire service, November 9, 2001.
6. "9-Year-Old Pleads Guilty to Manslaughter," Associated Press, October 8, 2005. Web posted at http://www.msnbc.com/id/9626361 (accessed May 20, 2006).
7. "Florida Girls Charged with Attempting to Drown Classmate," Associated Press wire service, March 14, 2001.
8. Office of Juvenile Justice and Delinquency Prevention, *OJJDP Research, 2000* (Washington, DC: OJJDP, 2001).
9. Federal Bureau of Investigation, *Crime in the United States, 2007* (Washington, DC: U.S. Government Printing Office, 2008).
10. Ibid.; and U.S. Census Bureau, *Age, 2000: A Census 2000 Brief* (Washington, DC: U.S. Census Bureau, 2001). Web posted at http:/

/www.census.gov/prod/2001pubs/c2kbr01-12.pdf (accessed January 2, 2008).
11. The term *juvenile* refers to people under 18 years of age.
12. H. Snyder, C. Puzzanchera, and W. Kang, *Easy Access to FBI Arrest Statistics 1994–2002* (Washington, DC: Office of Juvenile Justice and Delinquency Prevention, 2005). Web posted at http://ojjdp.ncjrs.org/ojstatbb/ezaucr (accessed November 11, 2008).
13. A reform movement, now under way, may soon lead to changes in the way juvenile records are handled.
14. For an excellent review of the handling of juveniles throughout history, see Wiley B. Sanders, ed., *Juvenile Offenders for a Thousand Years* (Chapel Hill: University of North Carolina Press, 1970).
15. Robert M. Mennel, *Thorns and Thistles: Juvenile Delinquents in the United States, 1925–1940* (Hanover, NH: University Press of New England, 1973).
16. Thomas A. Johnson, *Introduction to the Juvenile Justice System* (St. Paul, MN: West, 1975), p. 1.
17. Charles E. Springer, *Justice for Juveniles,* 2nd ed. (Washington, DC: Office of Juvenile Justice and Delinquency Prevention, 1987), p. 18.
18. Ibid., p. 50.
19. See Sanford Fox, "Juvenile Justice Reform: An Historical Perspective," in Sanford Fox, ed., *Modern Juvenile Justice: Cases and Materials* (St. Paul, MN: West, 1972), pp. 15–48.
20. *Ex parte Crouse,* 4 Whart. 9 (Pa. 1838).
21. Fox, "Juvenile Justice Reform," p. 27.
22. Anthony Platt, *The Child Savers: The Invention of Delinquency,* 2nd ed. (Chicago: University of Chicago Press, 1977).
23. Ibid., p. 29.
24. *People ex rel. O'Connell* v. *Turner,* 55 Ill. 280, 8 Am. Rep. 645 (1870).
25. Johnson, *Introduction to the Juvenile Justice System,* p. 3.
26. Ibid.
27. Ibid.
28. Fox, "Juvenile Justice Reform," p. 47.
29. Ibid., p. 5.
30. Principles adapted from Robert G. Caldwell, "The Juvenile Court: Its Development and Some Major Problems," in Rose Giallombardo, ed., *Juvenile Delinquency: A Book of Readings* (New York: John Wiley, 1966), p. 358.
31. See, for example, *Haley* v. *Ohio,* 332 U.S. 596 (1948).
32. *Kent* v. *U.S.,* 383 U.S. 541 (1966).
33. *In re Gault,* 387 U.S. 1 (1967).
34. *In re Winship,* 397 U.S. 358 (1970).
35. *McKeiver* v. *Pennsylvania,* 403 U.S. 528 (1971).
36. Ibid.
37. *Breed* v. *Jones,* 421 U.S. 519 (1975).
38. *Schall* v. *Martin,* 467 U.S. 253 (1984).
39. *Thompson* v. *Oklahoma,* 487 U.S. 815, 818–838 (1988).
40. *Stanford* v. *Kentucky,* 492 U.S. 361 (1989).
41. Ibid., pp. 370–371.
42. *Roper* v. *Simmons,* 543 U.S. 551(2005).
43. Death Penalty Information Center, "Juvenile Offenders Currently on Death Row, or Executed, by State." Web posted at http://www.deathpenaltyinfo.org/article.php?scid527&did5882 (accessed September 10, 2007).
44. President's Commission on Law Enforcement and Administration of Justice, *The Challenge of Crime in a Free Society* (Washington, DC: U.S. Government Printing Office, 1967).
45. "Drug Bill Includes Extension of OJJDP, with Many Changes," *Criminal Justice Newsletter,* Vol. 19, No. 22 (November 15, 1988), p. 4.
46. The Formula Grants Program supports state and local delinquency prevention and intervention efforts and juvenile justice system improvements. Through this program, OJJDP provides funds directly to states, territories, and the District of Columbia to help them implement comprehensive state juvenile justice plans based on detailed studies of needs in their jurisdictions. The Formula Grants Program is authorized under the JJDP Act of 2002 (42 U.S.C. 5601 *et seq.*).
47. See "OJJDP Eases Rules on Juvenile Confinement," *Corrections Compendium* (November 1996), p. 25.
48. The Juvenile Justice and Delinquency Prevention Act of 2002 (Public Law 107-273).
49. Howard N. Snyder and Melissa Sickmund, *Juvenile Offenders and Victims: 2006 National Report* (Washington, DC: Office of Juvenile Justice and Delinquency Prevention, 2006).
50. Ibid., p. 97.
51. See, for example, *United States* v. *Williams,* U.S. Supreme Court, 2008 (No. 06-694), which upheld the law's provision criminalizing the possession and distribution of material pandered as child pornography; and U.S. Department of State, *Trafficking in Persons Report* (Washington, DC: U.S. Department of State, June 2007), p.72.
52. *Fare* v. *Michael C.,* 442 U.S. 707 (1979).
53. *California* v. *Prysock,* 453 U.S. 355 (1981).
54. *New Jersey* v. *T.L.O.,* 105 S.Ct. 733 (1985).
55. Anne L. Stahl et al., *Juvenile Court Statistics, 2003–2004* (Washington, DC: Office of Juvenile Justice and Delinquency Prevention, 2007), p. 6.
56. National Center for Juvenile Justice, *State Juvenile Justice Profiles.* Web posted at http://www.ncjj.org/stateprofiles (accessed August 10, 2008).
57. Charles M. Puzzanchera, *Delinquency Cases Waived to Criminal Court, 1990–1999* (Washington, DC: Office of Juvenile Justice and Delinquency Prevention, 2003).
58. "Young Killer Lionel Tate Held in Pizza Delivery Robbery," Associated Press, May 24, 2005.
59. Terry Aguayo, "Youth Who Killed at 12 Will Return to Prison, But Not for Life," *New York Times,* March 2, 2006. Web posted at http://www.nytimes.com/2006/03/02/national/02tate.html (accessed May 20, 2008).
60. "Lionel Tate's FHP Mother Reprimanded for Gun Lapse," CBS4.com (Ft. Lauderdale), March 28, 2006. Web posted at http://lionel-tate-news.newslib.com/story/201-3137189 (accessed May 20, 2007).
61. Brian Skoloff, "Lionel Tate Sentenced to 30 Years," *The Ledger* online, May 18, 2006. Web posted at http://www.theledger.com/apps/pbcs.dll/article?AID=/20060518/BREAKING/60518010 (accessed May 22, 2008).
62. Adapted from Peter Greenwood, *Juvenile Offenders: A Crime File Study Guide* (Washington, DC: National Institute of Justice, no date).
63. Bureau of Justice Statistics, *Report to the Nation on Crime and Justice,* 2nd ed. (Washington, DC: U.S. Government Printing Office, 1988), p. 78.
64. Ibid.
65. Ibid.
66. Stahl et al., *Juvenile Court Statistics, 2003–2004,* various pages.
67. *McKeiver* v. *Pennsylvania.*
68. Some states, like West Virginia, do provide juveniles with a statutory right to trial.
69. Other early peer juries in juvenile courts began operating in Denver, Colorado; Duluth, Minnesota; Deerfield, Illinois; Thompkins County, New York; and Spanish Fork City, Utah, at about the same time. See Philip Reichel and Carole Seyfrit, "A Peer Jury in the Juvenile Court," *Crime and Delinquency,* Vol. 30, No. 3 (July 1984), pp. 423–438.
70. Ibid.
71. Tracy M. Godwin, *A Guide for Implementing Teen Court Programs* (Washington, DC: Office of Juvenile Justice and Delinquency Prevention, 1996).
72. Ibid.
73. Stahl et al., *Juvenile Court Statistics, 2003–2004,* p. 56.
74. Bethany Gardner, "Successful Pennsylvania School-Based Probation Expands," *Corrections Compendium,* Vol. 19, No. 8 (August 1994), pp. 1–3.

75. Charles M. Puzzanchera, *Juvenile Delinquency Probation Caseload, 1990–1999* (Washington, DC: Office of Juvenile Justice and Delinquency Prevention, 2003), p. 1.
76. Melissa Sickmund, T. J. Sladky, and Wei Kang, *Census of Juveniles in Residential Placement Databook.* Web posted at http://www.ojjdp.ncjrs.gov/ojstatbb/cjrp (accessed May 24, 2008).
77. Ibid. Figures may not total 100% due to rounding.
78. See, for example, Blair B. Bourque et al., "Boot Camps for Juvenile Offenders: An Implementation Evaluation of Three Demonstration Programs," *NIJ Research in Brief* (Washington, DC: National Institute of Justice, 1996).
79. Melissa Sickmund, *Juvenile Offenders in Residential Placement, 1997* (Washington, DC: Office of Juvenile Justice and Delinquency Prevention, 2002), p. 110.
80. Ibid.
81. Ibid.
82. Ibid.
83. Sickmund, Sladky, and Kang, *Census of Juveniles in Residential Placement Databook.*
84. Ibid.
85. "Juvenile Offenders in Residential Placement, 1997," in *Office of Juvenile Justice and Delinquency Prevention Fact Sheet* (Washington, DC: OJJDP, 1999).
86. Dale G. Parent et al., *Conditions of Confinement: Juvenile Detention and Corrections Facilities* (Washington, DC: Office of Juvenile Justice and Delinquency Prevention, 1994).
87. *Corrections Compendium* (December 1993), p. 14.
88. Ibid.
89. Ibid., p. 22.
90. Office of Juvenile Justice and Delinquency Prevention, *National Juvenile Custody Trends, 1978–1989* (Washington, DC: U.S. Department of Justice, 1992), p. 2.
91. Section 59 of the Uniform Juvenile Court Act recommends the granting of a right to appeal for juveniles (National Conference of Commissioners on Uniform State Laws, Uniform Juvenile Court Act, 1968).
92. Mark Memmott, "Release of Ark. School Killer Raises Questions of Justice," *USA Today,* August 12, 2005, p. 1A.
93. Patricia Torbet et al., *State Responses to Serious and Violent Juvenile Crime* (Washington, DC: Office of Juvenile Justice and Delinquency Prevention, 1996).
94. Snyder and Sickmund, *Juvenile Offenders and Victims,* pp. 96–97.
95. Jeffrey A. Butts and Ojmarrh Mitchell, "Brick by Brick: Dismantling the Border between Juvenile and Adult Justice," in Phyllis McDonald and Janice Munsterman, eds., *Criminal Justice 2000, Vol. 2: Boundary Changes in Criminal Justice Organizations* (Washington, DC: National Institute of Justice, 2000), p. 207.
96. Ibid., p. 167.
97. Ibid., pp. 167–213.
98. Barry C. Feld, "Abolish the Juvenile Court: Youthfulness, Criminal Responsibility, and Sentencing Policy," *Journal of Criminal Law and Criminology* (winter 1998), pp. 68–136.
99. Cindy S. Lederman, "The Juvenile Court: Putting Research to Work for Prevention," *Juvenile Justice,* Vol. 6, No. 2 (Washington, DC: Office of Juvenile Justice and Delinquency Prevention, 1999), p. 23.
100. American Academy of Child and Adolescent Psychiatry Task Force on Juvenile Justice Reform, *Recommendations for Juvenile Justice Reform* (Washington, DC: AACAP, 2001).
101. Public Law 107-273.
102. Activities funded under the legislation fall under the Juvenile Accountability Block Grants (JABG) program.
103. See Cheryl Andrews and Lynn Marble, "Changes to OJJDP's Juvenile Accountability Program," *Juvenile Justice Bulletin* (Washington, DC: OJJDP, 2003).
104. Ryan S. King, *The State of Sentencing 2007: Developments in Policy and Practice* (Washington, DC: Sentencing Project, 2008), p. 19.
105. Much of the information and some of the wording in this paragraph are taken from Ryan S. King, *The State of Sentencing 2007: Developments in Policy and Practice* (Washington, DC: Sentencing Project, 2008), p. 21.

Appendix:

Bill of Rights

The first ten amendments to the U.S. Constitution are known as the *Bill of Rights*. These amendments, ratified in 1791, have special relevance to criminal justice and are reproduced here. The entire U.S. Constitution can be found online at mycrimekit.com. You can save it to your desktop or print it.

Amendment I

Congress shall make no law respecting an establishment of religion, or prohibiting the free exercise thereof; or abridging the freedom of speech, or of the press; or the right of the people peaceably to assemble, and to petition the Government for a redress of grievances.

Amendment II

A well regulated Militia, being necessary to the security of a free State, the right of the people to keep and bear Arms, shall not be infringed.

Amendment III

No Soldier shall, in time of peace be quartered in any house, without the consent of the Owner, nor in time of war, but in a manner to be prescribed by law.

Amendment IV

The right of the people to be secure in their persons, houses, papers, and effects, against unreasonable searches and seizures, shall not be violated, and no Warrants shall issue, but upon probable cause, supported by Oath or affirmation, and particularly describing the place to be searched, and the persons or things to be seized.

Amendment V

No person shall be held to answer for a capital, or otherwise infamous crime, unless on a presentment or indictment of a Grand Jury, except in cases arising in the land or naval forces, or in the Militia, when in actual service in time of War or public danger; nor shall any person be subject for the same offence to be twice put in jeopardy of life or limb; nor shall be compelled in any criminal case to be a witness against himself, nor be deprived of life, liberty, or property, without due process of law; nor shall private property be taken for public use, without just compensation.

Amendment VI

In all criminal prosecutions, the accused shall enjoy the right to a speedy and public trial, by an impartial jury of the State and district wherein the crime shall have been committed, which district shall have been previously ascertained by law, and to be informed of the nature and cause of the accusation; to be confronted with the witnesses against him; to have compulsory process for obtaining witnesses in his favor, and to have the Assistance of Counsel for his defence.

Amendment VII

In suits at common law, where the value in controversy shall exceed twenty dollars, the right of trial by jury shall be preserved, and no fact tried by a jury, shall be otherwise reexamined in any Court of the United States, than according to the rules of the common law.

Amendment VIII

Excessive bail shall not be required, nor excessive fines imposed, nor cruel and unusual punishments inflicted.

Amendment IX

The enumeration in the Constitution, of certain rights, shall not be construed to deny or disparage others retained by the people.

Amendment X

The powers not delegated to the United States by the Constitution, nor prohibited by it to the States, are reserved to the States respectively, or to the people.

Appendix:

List of Acronyms

ABA	American Bar Association
ACA	American Correctional Association
ACJS	Academy of Criminal Justice Sciences
ACLU	American Civil Liberties Union
ADAM	Arrestee Drug Abuse Monitoring
ADMAX	administrative maximum
AEDPA	Antiterrorism and Effective Death Penalty Act (1996)
AFDA	Association of Federal Defense Attorneys
AFIS	automated fingerprint identification system
AIDS	acquired immunodeficiency syndrome
AJA	American Jail Association
ALI	American Law Institute
AMBER	America's Missing Broadcast Emergency Response
AOUSC	Administrative Office of the United States Courts
APIS	Advanced Passenger Information System
APPA	American Probation and Parole Association
ASC	American Society of Criminology
ASIS	American Society for Industrial Security
ASLET	American Society for Law Enforcement Training
ATF	Bureau of Alcohol, Tobacco, Firearms and Explosives
BJA	Bureau of Justice Assistance
BJS	Bureau of Justice Statistics
BOP	Bureau of Prisons
CALEA	Commission on Accreditation for Law Enforcement Agencies
CAPS	Chicago's Alternative Policing Strategy
CAT	computer-aided transcription
CCA	Corrections Corporation of America
CCJJDP	Coordinating Council on Juvenile Justice and Delinquency Prevention
CDA	Communications Decency Act (1996)
CFAA	Computer Fraud and Abuse Act (1986)
CIA	Central Intelligence Agency
CID	Criminal Investigative Division
CJIS	Criminal Justice Information Services (FBI)
CLET	Certified Law Enforcement Trainer
CODIS	Combined DNA Index System (FBI)
COPE	Citizen Oriented Police Enforcement (Baltimore)
COPS	Community Oriented Policing Services
CPOP	Community Police Officer Program (New York City)
CPTED	crime prevention through environmental design
CRIPA	Civil Rights of Institutionalized Persons Act (1980)
CRIPP	Courts Regimented Intensive Probation Program
CSA	Controlled Substances Act (1970)
CSC	Correctional Services Corporation
DARE	Drug Abuse Resistance Education
DAWN	Drug Abuse Warning Network
DCA	district court of appeals
DEA	Drug Enforcement Administration
DHS	Department of Homeland Security
DNA	deoxyribonucleic acid
DOJ	U.S. Department of Justice
DPIC	Death Penalty Information Center
DUF	Drug Use Forecasting
DUI	driving under the influence (of alcohol or drugs)
DWI	driving while intoxicated
ECPA	Electronic Communications Privacy Act (1986)
EUROPOL	European Police Office
FBI	Federal Bureau of Investigation
FCC	federal correctional complex
FCI	federal correctional institution
FLETC	Federal Law Enforcement Training Center
FLIR	forward-looking infrared
FOP	Fraternal Order of Police
FPC	federal prison camp
FTCA	Federal Tort Claims Act (1946)
GBMI	guilty but mentally ill
HIV	human immunodeficiency virus
IACP	International Association of Chiefs of Police
IAFIS	Integrated Automated Fingerprint Identification System (FBI)
ICC	International Criminal Court
ICE	Bureau of Immigration and Customs Enforcement
IDRA	Insanity Defense Reform Act (1984)
ILC	International Law Commission (United Nations)
ILEA	International Law Enforcement Academy (FBI)
INTERPOL	International Criminal Police Organization
IPS	intensive probation supervision
JJDP	Juvenile Justice and Delinquency Prevention Act (1974)
JTTF	Joint Terrorism Task Force
LAPD	Los Angeles Police Department
LEAA	Law Enforcement Assistance Administration

LEEP	Law Enforcement Education Program
LEMAS	Law Enforcement Management and Administrative Statistics
MCFP	medical center for federal prisoners
MDC	metropolitan detention center
MPC	Model Penal Code
NAACP	National Association for the Advancement of Colored People
NACDL	National Association of Criminal Defense Lawyers
NCAVC	National Center for the Analysis of Violent Crime
NCCD	National Council on Crime and Delinquency
NCCS	National Computer Crime Squad (FBI)
NCIC	National Crime Information Center (FBI)
NCISP	National Criminal Intelligence Sharing Plan
NCJRS	National Criminal Justice Reference Service
NCPC	National Crime Prevention Council
NCSC	National Center for State Courts
NCVS	National Crime Victimization Survey
NCWP	National Center for Women and Policing
NDAA	National District Attorneys Association
NDIS	National DNA Index System (FBI)
NIBRS	National Incident-Based Reporting System (FBI)
NIJ	National Institute of Justice
NJC	National Judicial College
NLADA	National Legal Aid and Defender Association
NOBLE	National Organization of Black Law Enforcement Executives
NVAWS	National Violence Against Women Survey
NVC	National Victims Center
NVCAN	National Victims' Constitutional Amendment Network
NWCCC	National White Collar Crime Center
NYGC	National Youth Gang Center
NYPD	New York Police Department
OJJDP	Office of Juvenile Justice and Delinquency Prevention
OJP	Office of Justice Programs
ONDCP	Office of National Drug Control Policy
PCR	police–community relations
PDS	podular/direct supervision
PERF	Police Executive Research Forum
PINS	persons in need of supervision
PLRA	Prison Litigation Reform Act (1996)
POST	Peace Officer Standards and Training
PROTECT Act	Prosecutorial Remedies and Other Tools to End the Exploitation of Children Today Act (2003)
RICO	Racketeer Influenced and Corrupt Organizations (statute)
RISE	Reintegrative Shaming Experiments (Australian Institute of Criminology)
RJC	Real Justice Conferencing (Pennsylvania)
ROR	release on recognizance
RTTF	Regional Terrorism Task Force
SAMHSA	Substance Abuse and Mental Health Services Administration
SBI	State Bureau of Investigation
SCU	Street Crimes Unit (New York City)
SEARCH	National Consortium for Justice Information and Statistics
SIIA	Software Industry & Information Association
STG	security threat group
SVORI	Serious Violent Offender Reentry Initiative
SWAT	special weapons and tactics
TFJJR	Task Force on Juvenile Justice Reform
TIPS	Terrorist Information and Prevention System
TWGCSI	Technical Working Group on Crime Scene Investigation (DOJ)
TWGEDE	Technical Working Group for the Examination of Digital Evidence
UCR	Uniform Crime Reports (FBI)
USA PATRIOT Act	Uniting and Strengthening America by Providing Appropriate Tools Required to Intercept and Obstruct Terrorism Act (2001)
USBP	United States Border Patrol
U.S.C.	United States Code
USIA	United States Information Agency
USP	United States Penitentiary
USSC	United States Sentencing Commission
VAWA	Violence against Women Act (1994)
VCAN	Victims' Constitutional Amendment Network
VICAP	Violent Criminal Apprehension Program (FBI)
VOCA	Victims of Crime Act (1984)
VWPA	Victim and Witness Protection Act (1982)

Index

D

T